Krugman's

Economics for the AP® Course

Fourth Edition

David Anderson
Centre College

Margaret Ray
Texas A&M University

bedford, freeman & worth publishers
BOSTON | NEW YORK

Krugman's Economics for the AP® Course
Fourth Edition

Executive Vice President, General Manager: Charles Linsmeier
Vice President, Social Sciences and High School: Shani Fisher
Executive Program Director, High School: Ann Heath
Development Editor: Andrew Sylvester
Editorial Assistant: Sophie Dora Tulchin
Director of High School Marketing: Janie Pierce-Bratcher
Assistant Marketing Manager: Tiffani Tang
Marketing Assistant: Nicollette Brady
Senior Media Editor: Justin Perry
Lead Media Project Manager: Jodi Isman
Senior Director, Content Management Enhancement: Tracey Kuehn
Senior Managing Editor: Lisa Kinne
Lead Content Project Manager: Won McIntosh
Senior Workflow Project Manager: Paul Rohloff
Executive Permissions Editor: Cecilia Varas
Photo Researcher: Krystyna Borgen, Lumina Datamatics, Inc.
Director of Design, Content Management: Diana Blume
Senior Design Services Manager: Natasha A. S. Wolfe
Interior Design: Tamara Newnam
Senior Cover Design Manager: John Callahan
Art Manager: Matthew McAdams
Illustration Coordinator: Janice Donnola
Illustrations: Network Graphics
Composition: Lumina Datamatics, Inc.
Printing and Binding: Transcontinental

Library of Congress Control Number: 2022943722
ISBN-13: 978-1-319-40932-6
ISBN-10: 1-319-40932-6
Printed in Canada
1 2 3 4 5 6 27 26 25 24 23 22

BFW Publishers, 120 Broadway, New York, NY 10271
bfwpub.com/catalog

To beginning students everywhere,
which we all were at one time.

About the Authors

Courtesy Margaret Ray

MARGARET RAY teaches economics at both the university and high school levels. She is an AP® Economics instructor for Johns Hopkins University's Center for Talented Youth and is a member of the economics department faculty at Texas A&M University in College Station, Texas. She received her BS in economics from Oklahoma State University and her PhD in economics from the University of Tennessee. In 2012, she received her MEd in curriculum and instruction and became certified to teach K–12 social studies. She has taught AP® Economics at several high schools in Virginia and has received the Council on Economic Education's Excellence in Teaching Economics award. She has been involved in the AP® Economics program since 1992, serving as a reader and question leader, writing test items, overseeing the AP® course audit, writing College Board® "Special Focus" articles, and editing the Council on Economic Education's AP® Macroeconomics resource. She has been a College Board® Endorsed Consultant for economics since 2001, and she conducts several professional development workshops and institutes each year. Her favorite hobby is showing hunter-jumper horses adopted from racehorse rescue organizations. She lives on a small farm in central Texas.

Courtesy David Anderson

DAVID ANDERSON is the Paul G. Blazer Professor of Economics at Centre College. He received his BA in economics from the University of Michigan and his MA and PhD in economics from Duke University. Anderson has been involved in the AP® Economics program since 1994. For five years, he led the grading of one or both of the AP® Economics exams, and he speaks regularly at AP® conferences and workshops. He has authored dozens of scholarly articles and 15 books, including *Survey of Economics, Explorations in Economics, Cracking the AP® Economics Exam, Economics by Example, Favorite Ways to Learn Economics*, and *Environmental Economics and Natural Resource Management*. His research is primarily on economic education, environmental economics, law and economics, and labor economics. Anderson loves teaching introductory economics and has won awards for excellence and innovation in the classroom. His favorite hobby is running, and he competes in marathons and triathlons. His family resides in Danville, Kentucky.

PAUL KRUGMAN, recipient of the 2008 Nobel Memorial Prize in Economic Sciences, is a faculty member of the Graduate Center of the City University of New York, associated with the Luxembourg Income Study, which tracks and analyzes income inequality around the world. Prior to that, he taught at Princeton University for 14 years. He received his BA from Yale and his PhD from MIT. Before Princeton, he taught at Yale, Stanford, and MIT. He also spent a year on the staff of the Council of Economic Advisers in 1982–1983. His research has included pathbreaking work on international trade, economic geography, and currency crises. In 1991, Krugman received the American Economic Association's John Bates Clark medal.

ROBIN WELLS was a lecturer and researcher in economics at Princeton University. She received her BA from the University of Chicago and her PhD from the University of California at Berkeley; she then did postdoctoral work at MIT. She has taught at the University of Michigan, the University of Southampton (United Kingdom), Stanford, and MIT.

Key Contributors and Advisors

We would like to thank the following individuals, and other anonymous contributors, for helping us to improve the quality and usability of the fourth edition. We are grateful for their thoughtful reviews, accuracy checks, and contributions to developing stronger AP® style questions and answers. We are also grateful for their contributions to the supporting resources.

S. Regan Borucke, Student, University of Virginia
Julia Frankland, Malone University, Ohio
Mike Fullington, Port Charlotte High School, Florida
Mary Hansen, American University, Washington, D.C.
Ashley Ledford, Lenoir County Public Schools, North Carolina
Julie Meek, West Plano High School, Texas
Sally Meek, West Plano High School, Texas
Matt Pedlow, Chelsea High School, Michigan
Ravi Radhakrishnan, Centre College, Kentucky
Gabriel Sanchez, Bonita High School, California
Shaun Waldron, Niles West High School, Illinois

We also wish the thank the following survey participants whose advice helped to guide the fourth edition.

Tonya Aitken, Hampshire Regional High School, MA
Kevin Attaway, East High School, WI
Jessica Bowen, Advanced Math & Science Academy, MA
Sarah Boy, Cartersville High School, GA
Kenneth Broda, Columbus High School, GA
Craig Brownson, Travis High School, TX
Rick Campbell, Oakmont High School, CA
Marie Curry, Ranney School, NJ
Joshua Fix, Charleston Catholic High School, WV
Taylor Fremming, Grand Prairie Fine Arts Academy, TX
Tom Fugate, Homestead High School, WI
Timothy Gardner, Southaven High School, MS
Melinda Goodwin, The Weber School, GA
Mart Grams, Shawano High School, WI
Caroline Gray, Tate High School, FL
Jeff Hackman, Dock Mennonite Academy, PA
Randall Haney, Kingwood High School, TX
Dina Heffner, Fleetwood Area High School, PA
Arik Heim, Wheat Ridge High School, CO
Rachel Henricks, The Potter's School, VA
Luke Jansen, Glenbard East High School, IL
Sarah Keller, Fort Collins High School, CO
Michael Kraft, Cherry Creek High School, CO
Jean Legere, Marina High School, CA
Megan Malone, Townview Talented and Gifted High School, TX
Alisha Martini, Bishop England High School, SC
Michael McCaffity, Woodrow Wilson High School, TX
Lena McKim, Coatesville Area Senior High School, PA
Thomas Metro-Zapata, Hamilton High School, CA
Dave Michaelson, Dickinson High School, ND
Ruth Narvaiz, James Bowie High School, TX
Patrick Nugent, West Catholic High School, MI
Lindsey Pahs, Chaparral High School, CO
Kim Patterson, West Allegheny High School, PA
Dawn Patterson, Ardrey Kell High School, NC
Kristen Peterson, St. Joseph Catholic Academy, WI
Steve Prescott, William Mason High School, OH
Amanda Propst, Lake Brantley High School, FL
Christopher Reid, Stafford High School, TX
Matt Romano, Marist School, GA
Doug Schoemer, Flint Hill School, VA
Melissa Schram, Millard West High School, NE
Francis Seery, Cordova High School, TN
Birthe Seferian, The Wheatley School, NY
Glenn Tracey, Greely High School, ME
Paul Trevizo, Townview Magnet High School, TX
Christina Tsuei, Hill Country Christian School of Austin, TX
Melinda Unger, Wilmot Union High School, WI
Daniel VanOver, Taft High School, IL
Shaun Waldron, Niles West High School, IL

Brief Contents

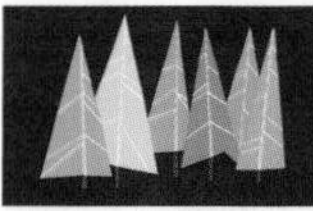

Macroeconomics

Microeconomics

Contents

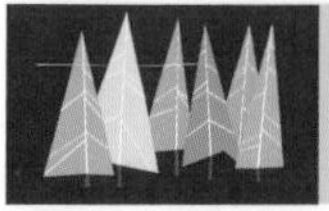

Macroeconomics

How to Get the Most from This Program

The AP® Economics course represents a wonderful opportunity for high school students to be challenged by the rigor of a college-level course while learning life-relevant concepts from the discipline of economics. We understand the unique challenges of teaching and learning AP® Macroeconomics and AP® Microeconomics and have designed this book and its support program to be the most effective possible resources to help you succeed.

This fourth edition has been reorganized to match College Board's AP® Macroeconomics and AP® Microeconomics Course and Exam Descriptions perfectly. The Table of Contents mirrors that of the AP® Course Framework and emphasis is placed throughout on the relevant skills. Each Module adheres to a topic in the AP® Course Framework to ensure that students master the concepts and skills and integrated "Tackle the Test" problems offer daily practice. The result is an easy-to-read and use program that prepares students for the AP® exam from day one while achieving an enduring understanding of the fundamental ideas of economics.

Take a look at the pages that follow for an introduction to the features that will help you realize success in the course and on the AP® Economics exams.

To learn about the digital and other resources that support this textbook, visit:

bfwpub.com/krugmanAP4e

READ THE TEXT and use the features to help GRASP THE BIG IDEAS

Using your text effectively will help you learn the concepts and skills to realize success on the AP® exam. Mastering the AP® Economics content may seem like climbing a mountain, but by taking it step by step you will build confidence and reach the summit.

The Units in this book mirror those found in each AP® Economics Course Framework, so it is easy for you to stay on track when you use AP® Classroom and other useful tools.

Each Unit is divided into short **Modules** that match the topics outlined in the AP® Course.

The AP® Economics Skills emphasized in this Unit are highlighted on the opening page and revisited throughout the Unit.

Read the **Opening Story**. Each Unit opens with a compelling story that often extends through the Modules. These opening stories, drawn from news headlines and world events, are designed to pique your interest and build your intuition as you prepare to learn about the economics concepts that follow.

UNIT 1
MACRO

Basic Economic Concepts

AP® Economics Skills

1. Principles and Models (1.A, 1.C)
4. Graphing and Visuals (4.A, 4.C)

Economics: What's It All About?

Did you know that economics is about far more than money? Consider your breakfast this morning. Did you take the time to assemble a balanced meal of fruits, grains, and protein, or did you grab a quick snack before heading out the door? Did you eat cereal purchased in bulk days before, or did you buy a breakfast sandwich at an eatery on the way to school? Were you in such a hurry that you skipped breakfast altogether, or did you arrive at school early to take advantage of their breakfast offerings? Each of these options comes with its own costs in terms of time, money, and resources. Similar considerations attend decisions related to sports, food, the environment, families, health, tourism, and many elements of your daily life. Economics can help ... rade-offs ... tudy of ... se is the ... under- ... onomy. ... omy is ... focus of ... n econ- ... nd how individual choices make up the economy as a whole. In our global economy, even the simplest decisions—say, what to have for breakfast—shape, and are shaped by, the decisions of thousands of other people, from the farmer in Costa Rica who decided to grow bananas rather than beets, to the landowner in Iowa who decided to use their land as a dairy farm instead of a housing development. The economy as a whole is the sum of all of the economy-wide interactions of individual decision makers. Understanding the effects of these interactions allows us to understand, and even to change, the state of the economy.

pp1/Shutterstock

Put simply: *Microeconomics* helps us understand many important economic interactions by looking at individual choice and the markets for individual goods—for example, the market for bananas. *Macroeconomics* is our window into economy-wide interactions that shows us how they lead to the ups and downs in the economy as a whole.

In this Unit, we discuss the implications of scarcity to the study of economics. We present the *production possibilities curve* model and use it to understand opportunity cost and the gains from ... basic suppl... serves as t... what we c... graphical ... study of ec... ture heavily on the AP® Exam, they are emphasized throughout this course. For further review, an appendix on the use of graphs is available at the end of this book.

Macro • Unit 1 Basic Economic Concepts 3

. . . and the important concepts and skills—TOPIC by TOPIC.

MODULE 1.1 Scarcity and Choice

In this Module, you will learn to:
- Explain how scarcity and choice are central to the study of economics
- Define each category of resources
- Explain the importance of opportunity cost to decision making
- Distinguish between the two main branches of economics

The Modules follow the numbering and pacing of the AP® Course Framework. They present the core concepts and skills in manageable chunks to help you learn and practice—one topic at a time.

Scan the **Learning Objectives** for an overview of the critical concepts you will be learning in the Module. Focus on mastering this **essential knowledge** and the **economics skills**.

Scarcity and Choice: The Core of Economics

Economics is the study of scarcity and choice. To be scarce, something must be desired in quantities beyond the available supply. Can you think of goods or services that are available to everyone in unlimited supplies? Air, perhaps, although pollution and air-borne diseases have limited the availability of clean air. We can appreciate the breadth of economics by considering how few things *are not* scarce.

Everything, from art museums to zippers, are limited in supply—that is, they are scarce. So the principles of economics apply to most things. Let's take a closer look at the causes and implications of scarcity.

Resources Are Scarce

You can't always get what you want. You might like to have a beautiful bike, the best smartphone, the finest shoes, and the latest equipment for your hobbies. But not many people can afford all of that. So each individual faces trade-offs. You make a **trade-off**

ics is the study of and choice.

ke a **trade-off** when up something to get ng else.

rce or **factor of** tion is anything that can to produce something

fers to all resources e from nature, such as wind, and petroleum.

Labor is the effort of workers.

Capital refers to manufactured goods used to make other goods and services.

Entrepreneurship describes the efforts of entrepreneurs in organizing resources for production, taking risks to create new enterprises, and innovating to develop new products and production processes.

A **scarce** resource is not available in sufficient quantities to satisfy all the various ways a society wants to use it.

acro • Unit 1 Basic Economic Co

An individual has a **comparative advantage** in producing a good or service if that person's opportunity cost is the lowest among the people who could produce that good or service.

An individual has an **absolute advantage** in producing a good or service if they can make more of it with a given amount of time and resources.

AP® ECON TIP

Having an *absolute* advantage is not the same thing as having a *comparative* advantage. For example, it is quite possible to be able to make more of something than other producers (that is, to have an absolute advantage) but to have a higher opportunity cost than other producers (that is, to have a comparative *dis*advantage).

MODULE 1.2 Opportunity Cost and the Production Possibilities Curve Model

In this Module, you will learn to:
- Summarize the crucial role of models as simplified representations of economic realities
- Explain how the production possibilities curve graph illustrates trade-offs
- Use the production possibilities curve model to illustrate scarcity, efficiency, and opportunity cost
- Explain how changes in technology and the availability of resources influence economic growth and the production possibilities curve

Economic models help us navigate complex situations, just as this mapping app lets us navigate a city.

A **model** is a simplified representation used to better

A good economic model, like a good street map app, can be a tremendous aid to navigating complex situations. In this Module, we look at one such model, the *production possibilities curve*, a model that helps economists think about the trade-offs necessary in every economy. The production possibilities curve helps us understand three important aspects of the real economy: efficiency, opportunity cost, and economic growth.

The Use of Models in Economics

In 1901, one year after their first glider flights at Kitty Hawk, the Wright brothers built something else that would change the world—a wind tunnel. This apparatus let them experiment with many different designs for wings and control surfaces. These experiments gave them knowledge that would make heavier-than-air flight possible. Needless to say, testing an airplane design in a wind tunnel is cheaper and safer than building a full-scale version and hoping it will fly. Today, pilots train with flight simulators and cockpit models that allow them to practice maneuvers without ever leaving the ground. Likewise, models play a crucial role in almost all scientific research—economics included.

A **model** is any simplified version of reality used to better understand a real-life situation. But how do we create a simplified representation of an economic situation? One possibility—an economist's equivalent of a wind tunnel—is to find or create a real but simplified economy. For example, economists interested in the role of money have studied the system of exchange that developed in World War II prison camps, in which cigarettes became a universally accepted form of payment, even among prisoners who didn't smoke.

Another modeling option is to simulate the workings of the economy on a computer. For example, when changes in tax law are proposed, government officials use *tax models*—large mathematical computer programs—to assess how the proposed changes would affect different groups of people.

Models are important because their simplicity allows economists to focus on the influence of only one change at a time. That is, they allow us to hold everything else ... outcome. So when

To succeed in AP® Economics, you must learn a lot of new vocabulary. Watch for the green **Key Term** boxes, which define terms at point of use. The terms are repeated in the Unit Review and in the Glossary/Glosario at the end of the book.

Watch for **AP® ECON TIPS** that provide advice on what to read closely and how **AP® Skills** are applied in practice.

STUDY THE GRAPHS and figures. To succeed, you must be able to draw and interpret graphs correctly.

FIGURE 1.2-2 Increasing Opportunity Cost

The concave (bowed-out) shape of the production possibilities curve reflects increasing opportunity cost. In this example, to produce the first 20 fish, Alexis must give up 5 coconuts. But to produce an additional 20 fish, she must give up 25 more coconuts. The opportunity cost of fish increases because as Alexis catches more fish, she must make increasing use of resources specialized for coconut production.

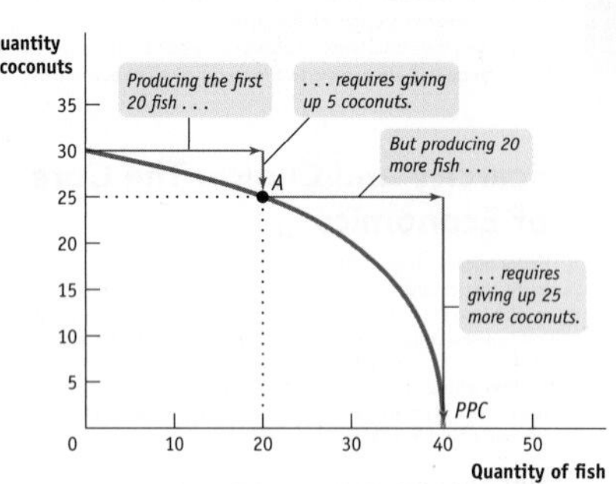

AP® ECON TIP

The use of specialized resources makes the production possibilities curve *concave to the origin*, meaning that it is bowed out as shown in Figure 1.2-2. When there is *no* specialization of resources for the production of the goods, there can be *no* increase in the opportunity cost of making more of either good, and *no* change in the slope of the production possibilities curve—it is a straight line.

Although it's often useful to work with the simple assumption that the production possibilities curve is a straight line, in reality, opportunity costs are typically increasing. When only a small amount of a good is produced, the opportunity cost of producing that good is relatively low because the economy needs to use only those resources that are especially well suited for its production. For instance, if an economy grows only a small amount of corn, that corn can be grown in places where the soil and climate are perfect for growing corn but less suitable for growing another crop, such as wheat. So growing that corn involves giving up only a small amount of wheat production. Once the economy grows a lot of corn, however, land that is well suited for wheat but isn't so great for corn must be used to produce corn anyway. As a result, increases in corn produ... as mo... specia... the pr... In... are eq...

14 Macro • Unit 1 Basic Economic C...

Figures and **graphs** hold volumes of information. Study them carefully, read the captions, and pay attention to any related **AP® ECON TIPs.** Mastering the creation and interpretation of economic models is important to realizing success on the AP® exam.

FIGURE 3.5-1 The *AD–AS* Model

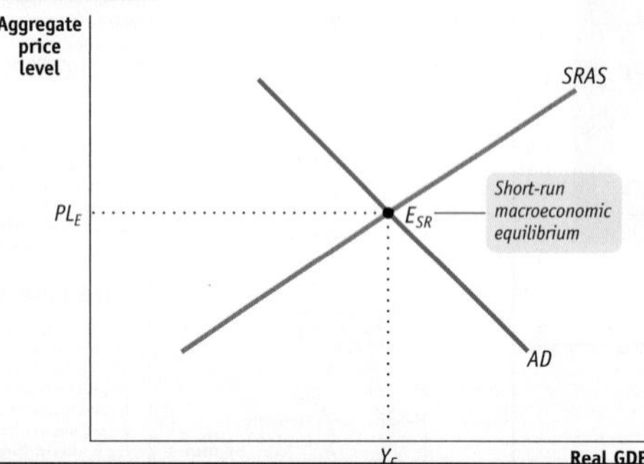

The *AD–AS* model combines the aggregate demand curve and the short-run aggregate supply curve. Their point of intersection, E_{SR}, is the point of short-run macroeconomic equilibrium where the quantity of aggregate output demanded is equal to the quantity of aggregate output supplied. PL_E is the short-run equilibrium aggregate price level, and Y_E is the short-run equilibrium level of aggregate output.

All graphs are carefully labeled and color is used consistently throughout the book to distinguish between demand (blue) and supply (red) curves.

AP® Economics Skills Appendix

Graphs In Economics

In this Appendix, you will learn to:
- Recognize the importance of graphs in studying economics
- Describe the basic components of a graph
- Explain how graphs illustrate the relationship between variables
- Explain how to calculate the slope of a curve and discuss what the slope value
- ...graphs

For review and extra help on Graphing, consult the **AP® Economics Skills Appendix: Graphs in Economics** at the end of the book, and watch the short videos for a quick review of important graphing skills.

Get ready to TACKLE THE AP® TEST by practicing what you've learned with integrated AP®-style questions.

Answer the **Check Your Understanding** questions at the end of each Module to make sure you grasp the content. If you struggle to answer these questions, go back and re-read the Module.

Module 1.2 Review

Adventures in AP® Economics
Watch the video: *Production Possibilities Curve*

Check Your Understanding

1. True or false? Explain your answer.
   a. An increase in the amount of resources available to Alexis for use in producing coconuts and fish does not change her production possibilities curve.
   b. A technological change that allows Alexis to catch more fish relative to any amount of coconuts gathered results in a change in her production possibilities curve.
   c. Points inside a production possibilities curve are efficient, and points outside a production possibilities curve are inefficient.

Tackle the AP® Test: Multiple-Choice Questions

Feeling confident? Test yourself by answering each of the AP®-style Module-ending **multiple-choice questions**. These practice questions help you become comfortable with the language and format you'll see in the multiple-choice section of the AP® exam. Many of the questions ask you to demonstrate your understanding by analyzing data and interpreting tables and graphs.

Refer to the graph to answer Questions 1–5.

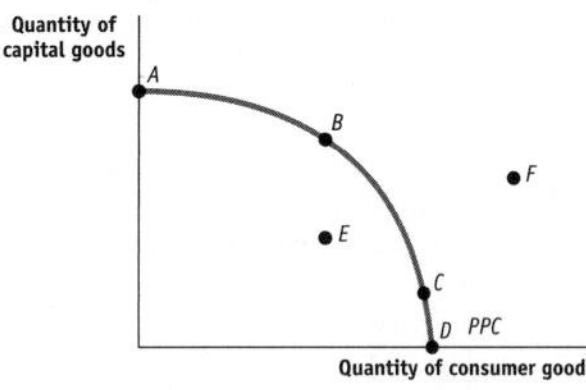

1. Which point(s) on the graph represent efficiency in production?
   a. *B* and *C*
   b. *A* and *D*
   c. *A*, *B*, *C*, and *D*
   d. *A*, *B*, *C*, *D*, and *E*
   e. *A*, *B*, *C*, *D*, *E*, and *F*
2. For this economy, an increase in the quantity of capital goods (such as hammers) without a corresponding decrease in the quantity of consumer goods (such as shirts)
   a. cannot happen because there is always an opportunity cost.
   b. is represented by a movement from point *E* to point *A*.
   c. is represented by a movement from point *C* to point *B*.
   d. is represented by a movement from point *E* to point *B*.
   e. is possible only with an increase in resources or ...

...resented by a

4. Which of the following might allow economic growth and a movement from point *B* to point *F*?
   a. more workers
   b. discovery of new resources
   c. building new factories
   d. technological advances
   e. all of the above
5. This production possibilities curve shows the trade-off between consumer goods and capital goods. Since capital goods are a resource, an increase in the production of capital goods today will increase the economy's production possibilities in the future. Therefore, all other things equal (*ceteris paribus*), producing at which point today will result in the largest outward shift of the *PPC* in the future?
   a. *A*
   b. *B*
   c. *C*
   d. *D*
   e. *E*
6. The production possibilities curve will certainly be straight if
   a. making more of one good means that less of the other good can be made.
   b. the opportunity cost of making each good increases as more is made.
   c. no resources are specialized for the production of either good.
   d. the opportunity cost of making the first unit of each good is the same.
   e. the economy experiences decreasing opportunity costs for the production of both goods.

Module 1.2 Review 17

Tackle the AP® Test: Free-Response Questions

1. Refer to the graph. Assume that the country is producing at point *C*.

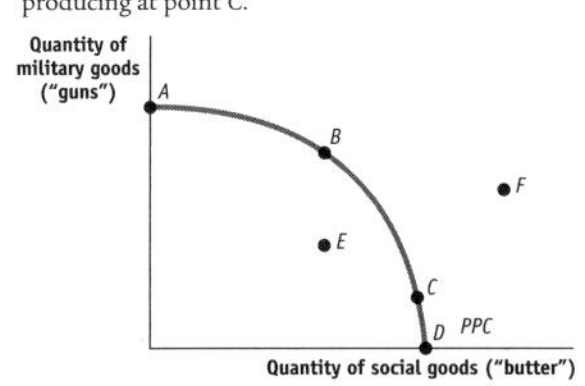

   a. Does this country's production possibilities curve exhibit increasing opportunity costs? Explain.
   b. Suppose point *C* initially represents the best allocation of resources for this country, but then the country goes to war. Before any of the country's resources are lost in the fighting, which point is the most likely to represent an efficient allocation of resources for the country when it is at war? Explain.
   c. If the economy experiences a major hurricane that severely disrupts production, the country would move from point *C* to which point? Explain.

Rubric for FRQ 1 (5 points)

1 point: Yes. The *PPC* is concave (bowed outward), so with each additional unit of butter produced, the opportunity cost in terms of gun production (indicated by the slope of the line) increases. Likewise, as more guns are produced, the opportunity cost in terms of butter increases.

1 point: *B*

1 point: The country would choose an efficient point with more (but not all) military goods with which to fight the war. Point *A* would be an unlikely choice, because at that point there is no production of any social goods, some of which are needed to maintain a minimal standard of living.

1 point: *E*

1 point: A recession, which causes unemployment, is represented by a point below t...

2. Assume that an economy can choose between producing food and producing shelter at a constant opportunity cost. Draw a correctly labeled production possibilities curve for the economy. On your graph:
   a. Use the letter *E* to label one of the points at which production is efficient.
   b. Use the letter *U* to label one of the points at which there might be unemployment.
   c. Use the letter *I* to label one of the points that is not feasible. **(5 points)**

Several mini AP®-style **free-response questions** are also provided at the end of each Module. The FRQs on the AP® exam are much more complex, but these practice FRQs train you to read questions carefully, analyze graphs and data, and address each component of the questions that are asked. A sample grading rubric is given for the first FRQ to show you how answers are scored and to help you learn to write thoughtful and complete answers. The second problem asks you to practice answering an FRQ without help from the rubric.

WATCH THE VIDEOS and work the AP® Exam Practice Questions at the end of each Unit.

UNIT 1

Review

Adventures in AP® Economics Videos

Mod 1.1 Graphing Tricks & Tips
Mod 1.2 Production Possibilities Curve
Mod 1.3 Comparative Advantage and Absolute Advantage
Mod 1.4 Demand
Mod 1.5 Supply
Mod 1.6 Market Equilibrium

economics by example
The Coffee Market's Hot; Why Are Bean Prices Not?

UNIT 1 Review Video

Module 1.1

1. Everyone has to make choices about what to do and what *not* to do. Choice is the basis of **economics**—if it doesn't involve choice, it isn't economics.
2. The reason choices must be made is that **resources**—anything that can be used to produce something else—are **scarce**. The four categories of resources, also called **factors of production**, are **land**, **labor**, **capital**, and **entrepreneurship**. Individuals are limited in their choices by money and time; economies are limited by their supplies of resources.
3. Because you must choose among limited alternatives, the true cost of anything is what you must give up to get it—all costs are **opportunity costs**.
4. **Microeconomics** is the branch of economics that focuses on how choices are made by individuals, **households**, and **firms**. **Macroeconomics** is concerned with the overall ups and downs of the economy and focuses on economic aggregates, such as the unemployment rate and gross domestic product, that summarize data across many different markets.
5. Economists use economic models for positive economics, which describes how the economy works, and for normative economics, which prescribes how the economy *should* work. Positive economics often involves making forecasts. Economics can determine correct answers for positive questions, but typically not for normative questions, which involve value judgments. Exceptions occur when policies designed to achieve a certain prescription can be clearly ranked in terms of prefe

Module 1.2

6. Almost all economics is based on **models**, "thought

Start your review of each Unit by watching the **Unit Review Video**, which reviews the key skills and models an FRQ solution. Then watch or re-watch any of the **Adventures in Economics videos** that address content you find difficult.

For an easy- to-read applied overview of the Unit contents, read the online **economics by example** case study.

assumption, p. 11	Change in demand, p. 30	Complements in production, p. 41
Production possibilities curve, p. 11	Movement along the demand curve, p. 30	Equilibrium, p. 46
Efficient, p. 12	Substitutes, p. 33	Equilibrium price, p. 46
Economic growth, p. 15	Complements, p. 33	Equilibrium quantity, p. 46
Technology, p. 16	Normal good, p. 34	Disequilibrium, p. 48
Trade, p. 19	Inferior good, p. 34	Surplus, p. 49
Specialization, p. 19	Quantity supplied, p. 37	Shortage, p. 49
Comparative advantage, p. 21		

Read the **Unit Review** and study the **Key Terms** at the end of each Unit. Understanding the language of economics is critical to being successful on the AP® exam.

AP® Exam Practice Questions

Multiple-Choice Questions

1. Which of the following pairs indicates a category of resources and an example of that resource?

Category	*Example*
a. money	investment
b. capital	money
c. capital	minerals
d. land	factory
e. land	timber

2. You can either go to a movie or study for an exam. Which of the following is an opportunity cost of studying for the exam?
   a. a higher grade on the exam
   b. the price of a movie ticket
   c. the cost of paper, pens, books, and other study materials
   d. the enjoyment from seeing the movie
   e. the sense of achievement from learning
3. Which of the follow

   d. the national rate of inflation
   e. government efforts to end a recession

Refer to the following table and information for Questions 5–8.

Suppose that Atlantis is a small, isolated island in the South Atlantic. The inhabitants grow potatoes and catch fish. The following table shows the maximum annual output combinations of potatoes and fish that can be produced.

Maximum annual output options	Quantity of potatoes (pounds)	Quantity of fish (pounds)
A	1,000	0
B	800	300
C	600	500
D	400	600
E	200	650
F	0	675

5. Atlantis can produce which of the following

Free-Response Questions

1. Suppose the country of Lunchland produces only peanut butter and jelly using resources that are not equally useful for producing both goods.
   a. Draw a correctly labeled production possibilities curve graph for Lunchland and label the following:
      i. point *A*, indicating an inefficient use of resources.
      ii. point *B*, indicating quantities of peanut butter and jelly that are currently not possible.
   b. Identify two things that could happen to enable Lunchland to produce or consume the quantities identified in part a (ii). **(5 points)**

Test yourself at the end of each Unit by tackling the **AP® Exam Practice Questions**, which include 25 **multiple-choice questions** and an additional 3 **FRQs**. These questions draw from concepts and skills covered across multiple Modules and give you confidence that you've mastered the Economics content *and* the style and structure of the questions you'll see on the AP® exam!

Reaching the summit . . . Putting It All Together and comprehensive AP® Practice Tests!

MACRO APPENDIX

Putting It All Together

In this Appendix, you will learn to:
- Use macroeconomic models to conduct policy analysis
- Improve your approach to free-response macroeconomics questions

Having completed our study of basic macroeconomic models, we can use them to analyze scenarios and evaluate policy recommendations. In this Appendix, we develop a step-by-step approach to macroeconomic analysis. You can adapt this approach to problems involving any macroeconomic model, including models of aggregate demand and supply, production possibilities, money markets, and the Phillips curve. By the end of this Appendix, you will be able to combine mastery of the principles of macroeconomics with problem-solving skills to analyze a new scenario on your own.

alexsl/Getty Images

A Structure for Macroeconomic Analysis

In our study of macroeconomics, we have seen questions about the macroeconomy take many different forms. No matter what the specific question, most macroeconomic problems have the following components:

1. *A starting point.* To analyze any situation, you have to know where to start.
2. *A pivotal event.* This might be a change in the economy or a policy response initial situation.
3. *Initial effects of the event.* An event will generally have some initial, short-run eff
4. *Secondary and long-run effects of the event.* After the short-run effects run their c there are typic

Macro Appendix: Putting It All Together—A structure for macroeconomic analysis. This special Module in macroeconomics teaches you how to use what you have learned to answer comprehensive, "real-world" questions about the macroeconomy and to employ the skills you've learned to answer the long FRQ on the AP® exam.

AP® Macroeconomics Exam Practice Test

Multiple-Choice Questions

Refer to the figure below to answer Question 1.

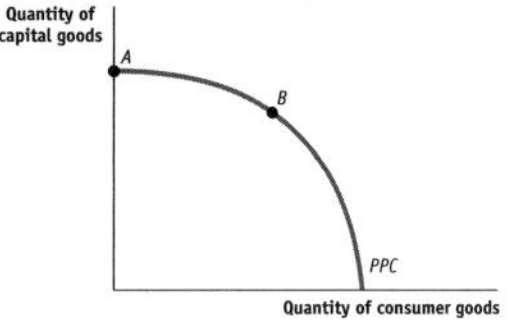

1. A movement from point *B* to point *A* illustrates which of the following?
   a. a choice to produce only capital goods
   b. an advance in technology
   c. a decrease in available resources used to produce consumer goods
   price of capital goods
   iciency

answer Question 2.

3. According to the concept of comparative advantage, which of the following is true when countries specialize and trade?
   a. Each country obtains an absolute advantage.
   b. Total world output increases.
   c. The production possibilities curve for both countries shifts outward.
   d. Prices fall in both countries.
   e. Deadweight loss is created.

Refer to the figure below to answer Question 4.

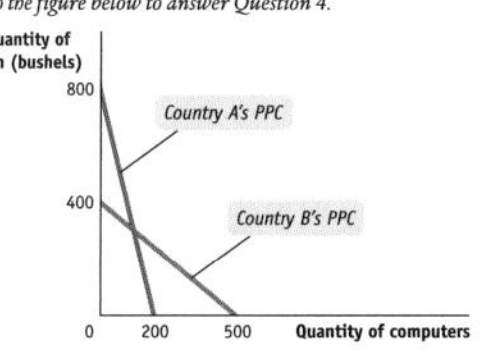

4. Using equal amounts of labor hours, two countries, Country A and Country B, can produce corn and computers as shown. Based on the information provided, which of the following is true?
   a. Country A has an absolute advantage in the

Test your knowledge and readiness for the AP® exam by taking the concluding **AP®-style Practice Exam** for Macro or Micro. Each exam, includes 60 multiple-choice questions and three FRQs per exam, just like the official tests. Time yourself to simulate the actual exam environment.

Free-Response Questions

1. Assume the country of Boland is currently in long-run equilibrium.
   a. Draw a correctly labeled production possibilities curve if Boland produces only corn and textiles. On your graph, label point *X*, a point that illustrates a productively efficient output combination for Boland.
   b. Draw a correctly labeled aggregate supply and aggregate demand graph for Boland. Show each of the following:
      i. equilibrium output, labeled Y_1
      ii. equilibrium price level, labeled PL_1
   c. Assume the government of Boland has a balanced budget and decides to raise government spending.
      i. What effect will the increase in spending have on Boland's budget?
      ii. Show the short-run effect of the increase in spending on your graph from part b, labeling the new equilibrium output and price level Y_2 and PL_2, respectively.

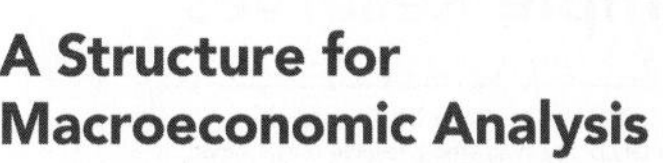

Learning about Economics doesn't stop after you take the exam.

EM A

Recession and Recovery During the Pandemic

In this Module, you will learn to:
- Describe the changes in U.S. macroeconomic measures during the Pandemic Recession
- Discuss the differential effects of the Pandemic Recession on different demographic groups in the United States

The Pandemic and the Economy

In January 2020, the United States declared a public health emergency in response to the spread of the COVID-19 virus. February 2020 marked the beginning of the pandemic in the United States, and it also marked the end of the longest period of economic expansion in U.S. history. On March 13, 2020, President Trump declared a national emergency. In response, local governments advised people to shelter in place

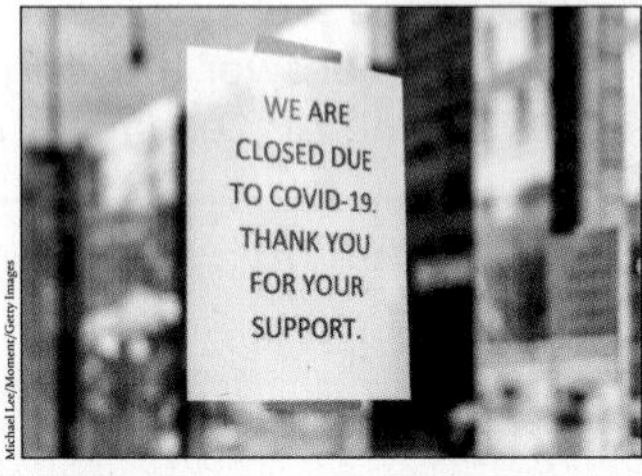
WE ARE
CLOSED DUE
TO COVID-19.
THANK YOU
FOR YOUR
SUPPORT.
Michael Lee/Moment/Getty Images

Continue your study of Economics with **Enrichment Modules** and the **Financial Literacy Handbook** to help round out the course and to prepare you for further Economics study in college and beyond.

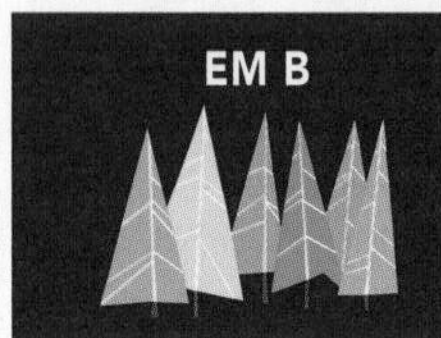
EM B

Federal Reserve Monetary Policy with Ample Reserves

In this Module, you will learn to:
- Describe the implementation of monetary policy in an ample-reserves environment
- Use a graph of the market for reserves to show how the federal funds rate is set by the Federal Reserve

In Units 4 and 5, we discuss how central bank monetary policy can be used to shift aggregate demand in order to move the economy to full employment (thereby addressing recessions and inflation). Unit 4 presents the transmission mechanism that translates the change of a monetary policy tool into a change in aggregate demand to stabilize the economy with both **limited reserves** and **ample reserves**.

In January 2019, the United States Federal Reserve announced its plans to remain in an ample-reserve regime and conduct monetary policy using administered rates. In this Enrichment Module, we describe the Fed's transition to an ample-reserves monetary policy regime over the decade since the Great Recession of 2007–2008. We also expand upon our discussion from Unit 4 on how the Federal Reserve uses administered rates, including the interest paid on reserves and the repurchase agreement rate, to conduct monetary policy in the United States. To begin, we'll reconsider monetary policy with limited reserves. Then we will go on to describe how the Federal Reserve conducts monetary policy when there are ample reserves in the economy.

In an economy with **limited reserves**, in which reserves are scarce, relatively small changes in the supply of reserves will change the nominal interest rate.

In an economy with **ample reserves**, in which reserves are plentiful, changes in the supply of reserves do not affect the nominal interest rate. The Fed instead uses administered rates to set the target federal funds rate.

Monetary Policy with Limited Reserves

Prior to the Great Recession of 2007–2008, open market operations (OMOs) were the Fed's most frequently used monetary policy tool. With limited reserves in the banking system, the daily use of … within a target r… small changes i… could be used to…

FLH Financial Literacy Handbook

Part 1 Take It to the Bank
Part 2 Get Interested in Money Math
Part 3 Learn to Earn
Part 4 Save and Invest Money
Part 5 Give Yourself Some Credit
Part 6 Borrow Without Sorrow
Part 7 Manage Your Money
Part 8 Protect Yourself from Risk

Three addition Microeconomics Enrichment Modules are included in the full text and digital platform:

- Module C Behavioral Economics
- Module D The Economics of Information
- Module E Indifference Curves and Consumer Choice

READ, STUDY, AND PRACTICE
when and where you want.
Resources for Additional Practice and Exam Preparation.

Created and supported by educators, our robust **Digital Platform with Homework and e-book** includes all of the resources you need in one convenient place. The interactive, mobile ready e-book allows you to read and reference the text when you are working online or to download it to read when an internet connection is not available.

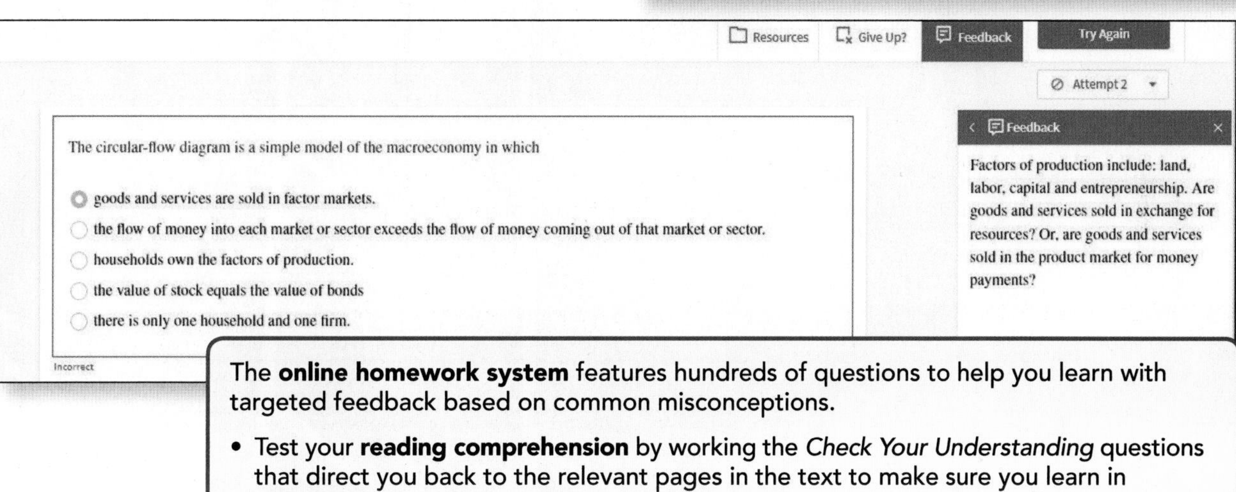

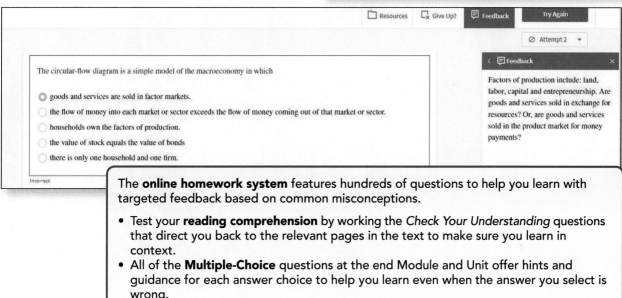

The **online homework system** features hundreds of questions to help you learn with targeted feedback based on common misconceptions.

- Test your **reading comprehension** by working the *Check Your Understanding* questions that direct you back to the relevant pages in the text to make sure you learn in context.
- All of the **Multiple-Choice** questions at the end Module and Unit offer hints and guidance for each answer choice to help you learn even when the answer you select is wrong.
- End of Module and Unit **Free Response Questions** are offered in an essay format that lets you a practice writing complete answers and drawing graphs, just like on the AP® Exam.

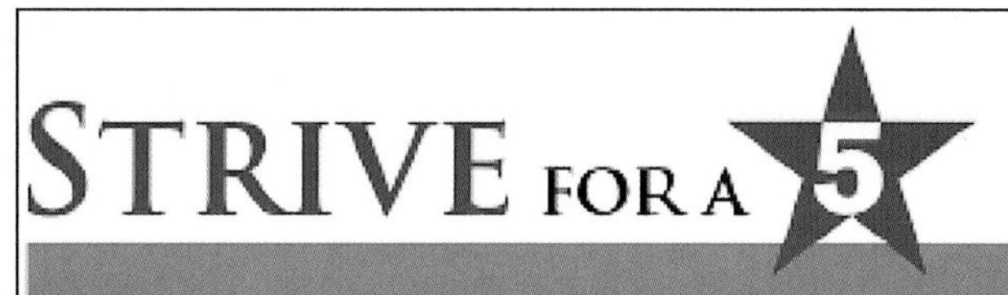

Use the **Strive for a 5 Guide** companions to the Macro and/or Micro portion of this text. Each Guide was written to work hand-in-glove with the text and includes a study guide followed by tips and advice on taking the exam and two more full AP® Practice Exams per guide.

MACROECONOMICS

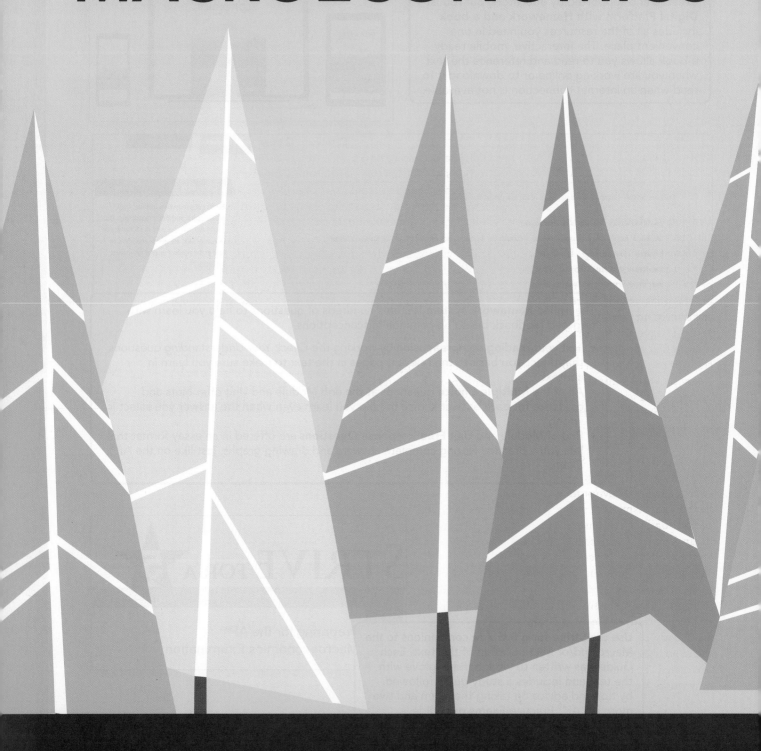

UNIT 1
MACRO

Basic Economic Concepts

AP® Economics Skills

1. Principles and Models (1.A, 1.C)
4. Graphing and Visuals (4.A, 4.C)

Economics: What's It All About?

Did you know that economics is about far more than money? Consider your breakfast this morning. Did you take the time to assemble a balanced meal of fruits, grains, and protein, or did you grab a quick snack before heading out the door? Did you eat cereal purchased in bulk days before, or did you buy a breakfast sandwich at an eatery on the way to school? Were you in such a hurry that you skipped breakfast altogether, or did you arrive at school early to take advantage of their breakfast offerings? Each of these options comes with its own costs in terms of time, money, and resources. Similar considerations attend decisions related to sports, food, the environment, families, health, tourism, and many elements of your daily life. Economics can help us understand the necessary trade-offs and make better choices. The study of individual decisions such as these is the focus of *microeconomics*.

Economics can also help us understand the health of the overall economy. The study of the overall economy is called *macroeconomics* and is the focus of this course. To understand how an economy works, we need to understand how individual choices make up the economy as a whole. In our global economy, even the simplest decisions – say, what to have for breakfast – shape, and are shaped by, the decisions of thousands of other people, from the farmer in Costa Rica who decided to grow bananas rather than beets, to the landowner in Iowa who decided to use their land as a dairy farm instead of a housing development. The economy as a whole is the sum of all of the economy-wide interactions of individual decision makers. Understanding the effects of these interactions allows us to understand, and even to change, the state of the economy.

pp1/Shutterstock

Put simply: *Microeconomics* helps us understand many important economic interactions by looking at individual choice and the markets for individual goods – for example, the market for bananas. *Macroeconomics* is our window into economy-wide interactions that shows us how they lead to the ups and downs in the economy as a whole.

In this Unit, we discuss the implications of scarcity to the study of economics. We present the *production possibilities curve* model and use it to understand opportunity cost and the gains from trade. Finally, we look at the basic supply and demand model, which serves as the foundation for much of what we cover in later units. Because graphical models are central to the study of economics and therefore feature heavily on the AP® Exam, they are emphasized throughout this course. For further review, an appendix on the use of graphs is available at the end of this book.

MODULE 1.1

Scarcity and Choice

In this Module, you will learn to:

- Explain how scarcity and choice are central to the study of economics
- Define each category of resources
- Explain the importance of opportunity cost to decision making
- Distinguish between the two main branches of economics

Economics is the study of scarcity and choice.

You make a **trade-off** when you give up something to get something else.

A **resource** or **factor of production** is anything that can be used to produce something else.

Land refers to all resources that come from nature, such as timber, wind, and petroleum.

Labor is the effort of workers.

Capital refers to manufactured goods used to make other goods and services.

Entrepreneurship describes the efforts of entrepreneurs in organizing resources for production, taking risks to create new enterprises, and innovating to develop new products and production processes.

A **scarce** resource is not available in sufficient quantities to satisfy all the various ways a society wants to use it.

Scarcity and Choice: The Core of Economics

Economics is the study of scarcity and choice. To be scarce, something must be desired in quantities beyond the available supply. Can you think of goods or services that are available to everyone in unlimited supplies? Air, perhaps, although pollution and airborne diseases have limited the availability of clean air. We can appreciate the breadth of economics by considering how few things *are not* scarce.

Everything, from art museums to zippers, are limited in supply—that is, they are scarce. So the principles of economics apply to most things. Let's take a closer look at the causes and implications of scarcity.

Resources Are Scarce

You can't always get what you want. You might like to have a beautiful bike, the best smartphone, the finest shoes, and the latest equipment for your hobbies. But not many people can afford all of that. So each individual faces trade-offs. You make a **trade-off** whenever you give up something in order to have something else. Perhaps you can buy a bike this year if you don't upgrade your phone, or you can buy a new pair of shoes if you don't buy a new fishing pole.

Limited income isn't the only barrier to people having everything they want. Time is also in limited supply: there are only 24 hours in a day. And because the time we have is limited, choosing to spend time on one activity also means choosing not to spend time on a different activity—spending time studying for an exam means forgoing watching a movie. Indeed, many people feel so limited by the number of hours in the day that they are willing to trade money for time. For example, convenience stores usually charge higher prices than larger supermarkets. The closer, smaller convenience stores often appeal to customers who would rather pay more than spend extra time traveling to a supermarket where they might also have to wait in longer lines.

Eric Raptosh Photography/Getty Images

Every economic issue involves individual choice—decisions by individuals about what to do and what *not* to do. Why do individuals have to make choices? The ultimate reason is that, with few exceptions, *resources are scarce*. A **resource** is anything that can be used to produce something else. The economy's resources, also called **factors of production**, can be classified into four categories: **land** (all resources that come directly from nature, including plants, water, and minerals), **labor** (the effort of workers), **capital** (manufactured goods used to make other goods and services, such as machinery, buildings, and tools), and **entrepreneurship** (risk taking, innovation, and the organization of resources for production). A resource is **scarce** when there is not enough of it available to satisfy all of the various ways a society wants to use it. For example, there are limited supplies of oil and coal, which currently provide most of the energy used to produce and deliver everything we buy.

Just as individuals must make choices, the scarcity of resources means that society as a whole must make choices. One way for a society to make choices is simply to allow them to emerge out of many individual choices. For example, there are only 168 hours in a week, and Americans must decide how to spend their time. How many hours will they spend going to supermarkets to get lower prices rather than saving time by shopping at convenience stores? The answer is the sum of individual decisions: society's choice about where to shop is simply the sum of the choices made by the millions of individuals in the economy.

> **AP® ECON TIP**
>
> Economists have special meanings for many words. For example, economists use the term *land* in reference to all sorts of natural resources and raw materials such as silicon, cotton, and even water. Economists generally use the term *capital* to refer to the category of factors of production made up of manufactured goods used to make other goods and services. Don't confuse this type of capital with *financial capital* such as money, stocks, and bonds.

Opportunity Cost: The Real Cost of Something Is What You Must Give Up to Get It

Suppose it is your last year of high school and you are deciding which college to attend. You have narrowed your choices to a small college near home or a large state university several hours away. If you decide to attend the small local college, what is the cost of that decision? Of course, you will have to pay for tuition, textbooks, and housing no matter which college you choose. Added to the cost of choosing the local college is the forgone opportunity to attend the large state university, your next best alternative. The value of going to the state university may be small or large, depending on your interests and preferences. Economists call the value of the next best alternative that you must give up when you make a particular choice an **opportunity cost**.

The real cost of an item is its **opportunity cost**: the value of the next best alternative that you must give up in order to get the item.

Opportunity costs are crucial to choices because, in the end, all costs are opportunity costs. That's because with every choice, an alternative is forgone—money or time spent on one thing can't be spent on another. If you spend $10 on a pizza, you forgo the opportunity to spend that $10 on a hamburger. If you spend Saturday afternoon at the park, you can't spend Saturday afternoon doing homework. And if you attend one school, you can't attend another.

The park and school examples show that economists are concerned with more than just costs paid in dollars and cents. The forgone opportunity to do homework has no direct monetary cost, but it is an opportunity cost nonetheless. And if the local college and the state university have the same tuition and fees, the cost of choosing one school over the other has nothing to do with payments and everything to do with forgone opportunities.

Now, suppose tuition and fees at the state university are $5,000 less than at the local college. In that case, what you give up to attend the local college is the ability to attend the state university *plus* the benefit you could have gained from spending $5,000 on other things. So the opportunity cost of a choice includes all the costs—whether or not they are monetary costs—of making that choice.

The choice to go to college *at all* provides another important example of opportunity costs. High school graduates can either go to college or seek immediate employment. Even with a full scholarship that would make college "free" in terms of monetary costs, going to college would still be an expensive proposition because the time spent on schoolwork can't be spent earning money. By going to college, students forgo the income they could have earned if they had gone straight to work instead. Therefore, the opportunity cost of attending college is the value of all necessary monetary payments for tuition and fees *plus* the forgone income from the best available job that could take the place of going to college.

The opportunity cost of going to college is high for people who could earn a lot during what would otherwise be their college years. Soccer standout Mallory Pugh withdrew from her first year in college because the opportunity cost of continuing would have included her salary and Nike endorsement deal as a professional soccer player. Facebook co-founder Mark Zuckerberg, Dropbox co-founder Arash Ferdowsi, and singer Taylor Swift are among the high achievers who decided that the opportunity cost of completing college was prohibitive. Despite these notable exceptions, however, for most people the value of a college degree far exceeds the value of alternative earnings.

Cory Knowlton/ZUMA Press, Inc./Alamy

Mallory Pugh understood the concept of opportunity cost.

Microeconomics is the study of how individuals, households, and firms make decisions and how those decisions interact.

A **household** is a person or group of people who share their income.

A **firm** is any organization that produces goods or services for sale.

Macroeconomics is concerned with the overall ups and downs of the economy.

Microeconomics Versus Macroeconomics

We have presented economics as the study of scarcity and choice and described how, at its most basic level, economics is about individual choice. The branch of economics concerned with how individuals make decisions and how those decisions interact is called **microeconomics**. Microeconomics focuses on choices made by individuals, households, or firms – the smaller parts that make up the economy as a whole. A **household** is a person or group of people who share their income. If you have a parent or guardian who provides your food and housing, the two of you are members of the same household. A **firm** is any organization that produces goods or services for sale, such as a hair salon, bank, software company, grocery store, or carrot farm.

Macroeconomics, in contrast, focuses on the bigger picture – the overall ups and downs of the economy. Consider this analogy: If microeconomics is the study of individual trees, macroeconomics is the study of the entire forest. When you study macroeconomics, you learn how economists explain these fluctuations and how governments can use economic policy to minimize the resulting damage. Macroeconomics focuses on *economic aggregates* – economic measures such as the unemployment rate, the inflation rate, and gross domestic product – that summarize data across many different markets.

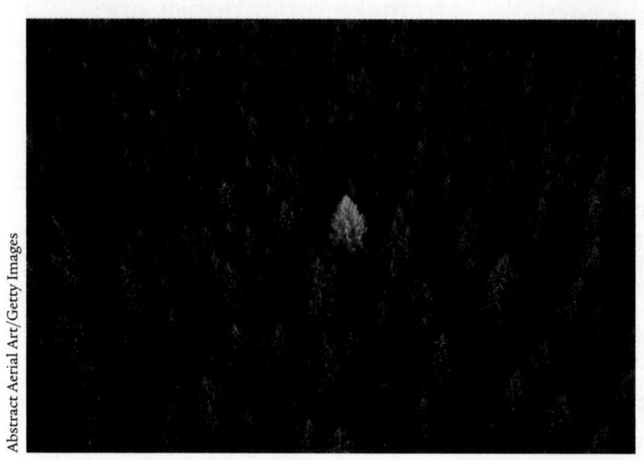

Abstract Aerial Art/Getty Images

Table 1.1-1 lists some typical questions that involve economics. A microeconomic version of the question appears on the left, paired with a similar macroeconomic question on the right. By comparing the questions, you can begin to get a sense of the difference between microeconomics and macroeconomics.

Table 1.1-1 Microeconomic Versus Macroeconomic Questions

Microeconomic Questions	Macroeconomic Questions
How many years of education should I receive before I start my career?	How many people are employed in the economy as a whole this year?
What determines the salary that Citibank offers to a new college graduate?	What determines the average salary paid to workers in the economy?
What is the cost to a high school of offering a new course?	What is the overall level of prices in the economy as a whole?
What government policies would encourage more students to choose to attend college?	What government policies would promote employment and growth in the economy as a whole?
What determines the number of iPhones exported to France?	What determines the overall trade in goods, services, and financial assets between the United States and the rest of the world?

As these questions illustrate, microeconomics focuses on how individuals and firms make decisions, and the consequences of those decisions. For example, a school will use microeconomics to determine how much it would cost to offer a new course, which includes the instructor's salary, the cost of class materials, and so on. By weighing the costs and benefits, the school can then decide whether or not to offer the course. Macroeconomics, in contrast, examines the *overall* behavior of the economy – how the actions of all of the individuals and firms in the economy interact to produce a particular economy-wide level of economic performance. For example, macroeconomics is concerned with the general level of prices in the economy and how high or low they are relative to prices last year, rather than with the price of a particular good or service.

Positive Versus Normative Economics

Economic analysis draws on a set of basic economic principles. How these principles are applied depends on the purpose of the analysis. Economic analysis that is used to answer questions about the way the economy works — questions that have definite right and wrong answers — is known as *positive economics*. In contrast, economic analysis that involves saying how the economy *should* work is known as *normative economics*.

Imagine you are an economic adviser to the governor of a state, and the governor is considering an increase in the toll that drivers are charged when driving on state highways. Below are three questions the governor might ask you.

1. How much revenue will the tolls yield next year without an increase?
2. How much higher would that revenue be if the toll were raised from $2.00 to $3.00?
3. Should the toll be raised, bearing in mind that a toll increase would lower the volume of traffic and air pollution in the area but impose a financial hardship on frequent commuters?

There is a notable difference between the first two questions and the third one. The first two are questions about facts. Your forecast of next year's toll revenue without any increase will be proved right or wrong when the numbers actually come in. Your estimate of the impact of a change in the toll is a little harder to check — the increase in revenue depends on other factors besides the toll, and it may be hard to disentangle the causes of any change in revenue. Still, in principle there is only one right answer.

But the question of whether or not tolls should be raised may not have a "right" answer — two people who agree on the effects of a higher toll could still disagree about whether raising the toll is a good idea. For example, someone who lives near the turnpike but doesn't commute on it will care a lot about noise and air pollution but not so much about commuting costs. A regular commuter who doesn't live near the turnpike will have the opposite priorities.

This example highlights a key distinction between the two roles of economic analysis and presents another way to think about the distinction between positive and normative analysis: positive economics is about description, and normative economics is about prescription. Positive economics occupies most of the time and effort of economists.

Looking back at the three questions the governor might ask, it is worth noting a subtle but important difference between questions 1 and 2. Question 1 asks for a simple prediction about next year's revenue — a forecast. Question 2 is a "what if" question, asking how revenue would change if the toll were to increase. Economists are often called upon to answer both types of questions. Economic *models*, which provide simplified representations of reality using, for example, graphs or equations, are especially useful for answering "what if" questions.

The answers to such questions often serve as a guide to policy, but they are still predictions, not prescriptions. That is, they attempt to tell you what will happen if a policy is changed, but they don't tell you whether or not that result is good. Suppose that your economic model tells you that the governor's proposed increase in highway tolls will likely raise property values in communities near the road but will tax or inconvenience people who currently use the turnpike to get to work. Does that information make this proposed toll increase a good idea or a bad one? It depends on whom you ask. As we've just seen, someone who is very concerned with the communities near the road will support the increase, but someone who is very concerned with the welfare of drivers will feel differently. That's a value judgment — it's not a question of positive economic analysis.

Should the toll be raised?

Mira/Alamy Stock Photo

Still, economists often do engage in normative economics and give policy advice. How can they do this when there may be no "right" answer? One reason is that economists are also citizens, and they have their own opinions. But economic analysis can often be used to show that some policies are clearly better than others, regardless of individual opinions.

Suppose that policies A and B achieve the same goal, but everyone will be better off with policy A than with policy B—or at least policy A makes some people better off without making other people worse off, while policy B does the opposite. Then A is clearly more beneficial than B. That's not a value judgment: we're talking about how best to achieve a goal, not about the goal itself.

The study of economics can provide clarity on both the way the economy works and the best decisions going forward.

Module 1.1 Review

Watch the video:
Graphing Tricks & Tips

Check Your Understanding

1. What is it about most resources that forces everyone to make choices?
2. Under which category does each of the following resources fall?
   - **a.** time spent making pizzas at a restaurant
   - **b.** a bulldozer
   - **c.** a river
3. You make $45,000 per year at your current job with MCJ Consultants. You are considering a job offer from Analysis, Inc., which would pay you $50,000 per year, and you must consider the trade-offs. Is each of the following elements an opportunity cost of accepting the new job at Analysis, Inc.? Answer yes or no, and explain your answer.
   - **a.** the increased time spent commuting to your new job
   - **b.** the $45,000 salary from your old job
   - **c.** the more spacious office at your new job

Tackle the AP® Test: Multiple-Choice Questions

1. Which of the following is an example of capital?
   - **a.** a cheeseburger dinner
   - **b.** a construction worker
   - **c.** petroleum
   - **d.** a factory
   - **e.** an acre of farmland
2. Which of the following is not an example of resource scarcity?
   - **a.** There is a finite amount of petroleum in the world.
   - **b.** Farming communities are experiencing droughts.
   - **c.** There are not enough physicians to satisfy all desires for health care in the United States.
   - **d.** Cassette tapes are no longer being produced.
   - **e.** Teachers would like to have more instructional technology in their classrooms.
3. Suppose that you prefer reading a book you already own to watching videos and that you prefer watching videos to listening to music. If these are your only three choices, what is the opportunity cost of reading?
   - **a.** watching videos and listening to music
   - **b.** watching videos
   - **c.** listening to music
   - **d.** sleeping
   - **e.** the price of the book
4. Which of the following statements is normative?
   - **a.** The price of gasoline is rising.
   - **b.** The price of gasoline is too high.
   - **c.** Gas prices are expected to fall in the near future.
   - **d.** Cars can run on gasoline, electricity, or diesel fuel.
   - **e.** When the price of gasoline rises, drivers buy less gasoline.

5. Which of the following questions is studied in microeconomics?
   a. Should I go to college or get a job after I graduate?
   b. What government policies should be adopted to promote employment in the economy?
   c. How many people are employed in the economy this year?
   d. Has the overall level of prices in the economy increased or decreased this year?
   e. What determines the overall salary levels paid to workers in a given year?

6. A study of the unemployment rate in Brazil is part of which branch of economics?
   a. macroeconomics
   b. microeconomics
   c. international
   d. normative
   e. positive

7. All opportunity costs are
   a. nonmonetary.
   b. forgone monetary payments.
   c. losses of time.
   d. values of alternatives that must be given up.
   e. related to educational opportunities.

Tackle the AP® Test: Free-Response Questions

1. Define the term *economics* and explain why that definition encompasses much more than money. Define the term *resources* and list the four categories of resources.

Rubric for FRQ 1 (7 points)

1 point: Economics is the study of scarcity and choice.

1 point: Almost everything is scarce, so economics can apply to almost everything.

1 point: Resources are anything that can be used to produce something else.

1 point each: The four categories of the economy's resources are land, labor, capital, and entrepreneurship.

2. In what type of economic analysis do questions have a "right" or "wrong" answer? In what type of economic analysis do questions not necessarily have a "right" answer? What type of economics focuses on the big picture in the economy? What type of economics focuses on individuals, households, and firms? **(4 points)**

MODULE 1.2

Opportunity Cost and the Production Possibilities Curve Model

In this Module, you will learn to:
- Summarize the crucial role of models as simplified representations of economic realities
- Explain how the production possibilities curve graph illustrates trade-offs
- Use the production possibilities curve model to illustrate scarcity, efficiency, and opportunity cost
- Explain how changes in technology and the availability of resources influence economic growth and the production possibilities curve

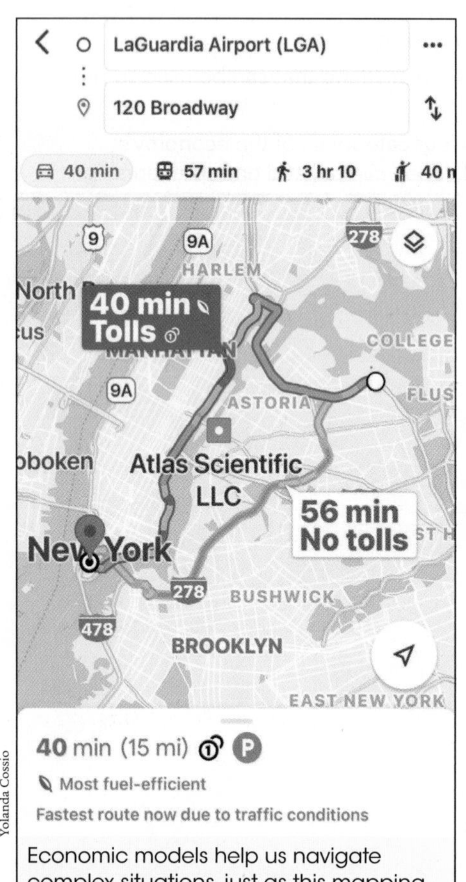

Yolanda Cossio

Economic models help us navigate complex situations, just as this mapping app lets us navigate a city.

A **model** is a simplified representation used to better understand a real-life situation.

A good economic model, like a good street map app, can be a tremendous aid to navigating complex situations. In this Module, we look at one such model, the *production possibilities curve*, a model that helps economists think about the trade-offs necessary in every economy. The production possibilities curve helps us understand three important aspects of the real economy: efficiency, opportunity cost, and economic growth.

The Use of Models in Economics

In 1901, one year after their first glider flights at Kitty Hawk, the Wright brothers built something else that would change the world – a wind tunnel. This apparatus let them experiment with many different designs for wings and control surfaces. These experiments gave them knowledge that would make heavier-than-air flight possible. Needless to say, testing an airplane design in a wind tunnel is cheaper and safer than building a full-scale version and hoping it will fly. Today, pilots train with flight simulators and cockpit models that allow them to practice maneuvers without ever leaving the ground. Likewise, models play a crucial role in almost all scientific research – economics included.

A **model** is any simplified version of reality used to better understand a real-life situation. But how do we create a simplified representation of an economic situation? One possibility – an economist's equivalent of a wind tunnel – is to find or create a real but simplified economy. For example, economists interested in the role of money have studied the system of exchange that developed in World War II prison camps, in which cigarettes became a universally accepted form of payment, even among prisoners who didn't smoke.

Another modeling option is to simulate the workings of the economy on a computer. For example, when changes in tax law are proposed, government officials use *tax models* – large mathematical computer programs – to assess how the proposed changes would affect different groups of people.

Models are important because their simplicity allows economists to focus on the influence of only one change at a time. That is, they allow us to hold everything else constant and study how one change affects the overall economic outcome. So when building economic models, it is important to make the **other things equal assumption**, which means that all other relevant factors remain unchanged. Sometimes the Latin phrase *ceteris paribus*, which means "other things equal," is used.

The **other things equal assumption** means that all other relevant factors remain unchanged. This is also known as the *ceteris paribus* assumption.

It isn't always possible to find or create a small-scale version of the whole economy, and a computer program is only as good as the data it uses. (Programmers have a saying: garbage in, garbage out.) For many purposes, the most effective form of economic modeling is the construction of "thought experiments": simplified, hypothetical versions of real-life situations.

Models can also be depicted by graphs and equations. In this Module, you will see how graphical models illustrate the relationships between variables and reveal the effects of changes in the economy. One such graph is the *production possibilities curve*, a model that helps economists think about the choices to be made in every economy.

Trade-offs: The Production Possibilities Curve

The true story of Alexander Selkirk may have inspired Daniel Defoe's 1719 novel about shipwrecked hero Robinson Crusoe. In 1704, Selkirk was a crew member on a ship that he correctly feared was not seaworthy. Before the ship met its fate at the bottom of the sea, Selkirk quarreled with the captain about the need for repairs, and then abandoned the ship during a stop at a deserted island near Chile. As in the story of Robinson Crusoe, Selkirk was alone and had limited resources: the natural resources of the island, a few items he brought from the ship, and, of course, his own time and effort. With that, he had to make a life for four and a half years. In effect, he became a one-man economy.

SJ Travel Photo and Video/Shutterstock

One of the important principles of economics we introduced in Module 1 was that resources are scarce. As a result, participants in any economy — whether it contains one person or millions of people — face trade-offs. For example, if castaways on a tropical island devote more resources to catching fish, they benefit by catching more fish, but they cannot use those same resources to gather coconuts, so the trade-off is that they have fewer coconuts.

To think about the trade-offs necessary in any economy, economists often use the **production possibilities curve** model. The idea behind this model is to improve our understanding of trade-offs by considering a simplified economy that produces only two goods. This simplification enables us to show the trade-offs graphically.

The **production possibilities curve** illustrates the necessary trade-offs in an economy that produces only two goods. It shows the maximum quantity of one good that can be produced for each possible quantity of the other good produced.

Figure 1.2-1 shows a hypothetical production possibilities curve for Alexis, a castaway alone on an island, who must make a trade-off between fish production and coconut production. The curve shows the maximum quantity of fish Alexis can catch during a week *given* the quantity of coconuts she gathers, and vice versa. That is, it answers questions of the form, "What is the maximum quantity of fish Alexis can catch if she also gathers 9 (or 15, or 30) coconuts?"

There is a crucial distinction between points *inside* or *on* the production possibilities curve (the shaded area in Figure 1.2-1) and points *outside* the curve. If a production point lies inside or on the curve — like point *C*, at which Alexis catches 20 fish and gathers 9 coconuts — it is feasible. After all, the curve tells us that if Alexis catches 20 fish, she could also gather a maximum of 15 coconuts, so she could certainly gather 9 coconuts. Production inside the curve indicates that resources are underutilized, which can mean that land or capital lies idle or that workers are unemployed. A production point outside the curve — such as point *D*, which would have Alexis catching 40 fish and

FIGURE 1.2-1 The Production Possibilities Curve

The production possibilities curve illustrates the trade-offs facing an economy that produces two goods. It shows the maximum quantity of one good that can be produced, given the quantity of the other good produced. Here, the maximum quantity of coconuts that Alexis can gather depends on the quantity of fish she catches, and vice versa. Her feasible production is shown by the area *inside* or *on* the curve. Production at point *D* is not feasible. Production at point *C* is feasible but not efficient and indicates underutilized resources. Points *A* and *B* are feasible and *productively efficient,* meaning resources are fully utilized and the only way to make more of one good is to make less of the other good.

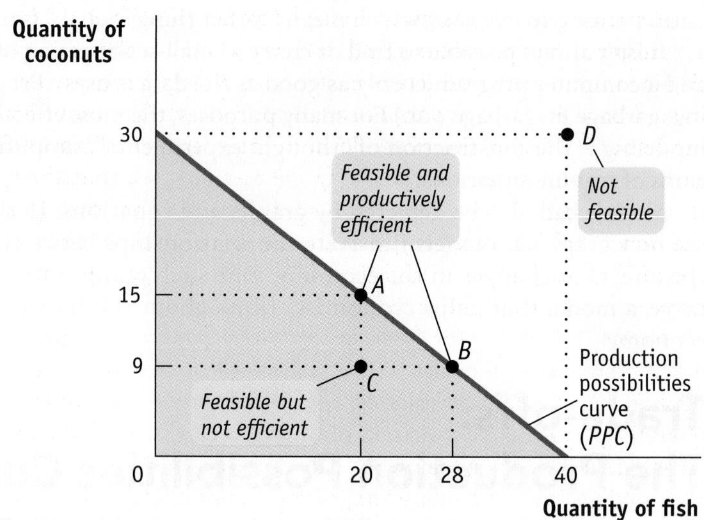

gathering 30 coconuts—isn't feasible because the economy's resources and technology are not sufficient to reach that point.

In Figure 1.2-1, the production possibilities curve intersects the horizontal axis at 40 fish. This means that if Alexis devoted all her resources to catching fish, she would catch 40 fish per week but would have no resources left over to gather coconuts. The production possibilities curve intersects the vertical axis at 30 coconuts. This means that if Alexis devoted all her resources to gathering coconuts, she could gather 30 coconuts per week but would have no resources left over to catch fish. Thus, if Alexis wants 30 coconuts, the trade-off is that she can't have any fish.

The curve also shows less extreme trade-offs. For example, if Alexis decides to catch 20 fish, she would be able to gather at most 15 coconuts; this production choice is illustrated by point *A*. If Alexis decides to catch 28 fish, she could gather at most 9 coconuts, as shown by point *B*.

Thinking in terms of a production possibilities curve simplifies the complexities of reality. The real-world economy produces millions of different goods. Even a castaway on an island would produce more than two different items (for example, Alexis would need clothing and housing as well as food). But in this model we imagine an economy that produces only two goods, because in a model with many goods, it would be much harder to study trade-offs, efficiency, and economic growth.

Efficiency

An economy is **efficient** if there is no way to make anyone better off without making at least one person worse off.

The production possibilities curve is useful for illustrating the general economic concept of efficiency. An economy is **efficient** if there are no missed opportunities—meaning that there is no way to make some people better off without making other people worse off. For example, suppose a course you are taking meets in a classroom that is too small for the number of students—some may be forced to sit on the floor or stand—while a larger classroom nearby sits empty. Economists would say that this is an *inefficient* use of resources because there is a way to make some people better off without making anyone worse off—after all, the larger classroom is empty. The school is not using its resources efficiently. When an economy is using all of its resources efficiently, the only way to make one person better off is to change the use of resources in a way that makes someone else worse off. So in our classroom example, if all larger classrooms were already fully occupied, we could say that the school was run in an efficient way; your classmates could be made better off only by making people in the larger classroom worse off—by moving them to the room that is too small.

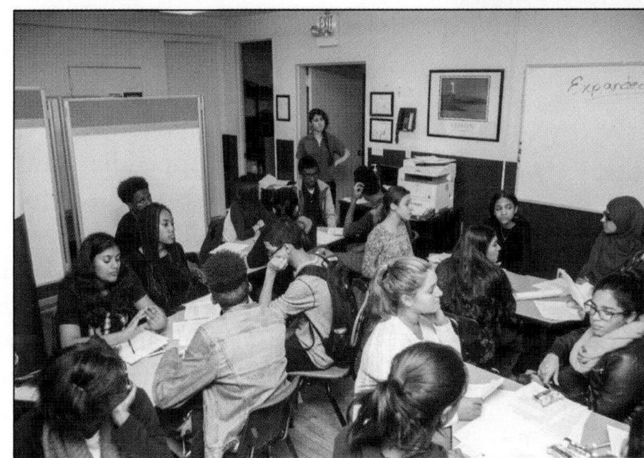

David Grossman/Alamy

A crowded classroom reflects inefficiency if switching to a larger classroom would make some students better off without making anyone worse off.

Returning to our castaway example, as long as Alexis produces a combination of coconuts and fish that is on the production possibilities curve, her production is efficient. No resources are being wasted, so there is no way to make more of one good without making less of the other. For example, at point *A*, the 15 coconuts she gathers are the maximum quantity she can get *given* that she has chosen to catch 20 fish. At point *B*, the 9 coconuts she gathers are the maximum she can get *given* her choice to catch 28 fish. The economy is producing efficiently if it is producing at any point on its production possibilities curve.

Now suppose that for some reason Alexis is at point *C*, producing 20 fish and 9 coconuts. Then this one-person economy is producing inefficiently: it is missing the opportunity to produce more of either or both goods with no trade-off. Likewise, production at any other point inside (below) the production possibilities curve is also inefficient. By moving from point *C* to point *A*, the economy could produce more coconuts without giving up any fish. By moving from point *C* to point *B*, the economy could produce more fish with no loss of coconuts. Or by moving to any point between point *A* and point *B*, the economy could make both more coconuts and more fish.

Another example of inefficiency in production occurs when people in an economy are involuntarily unemployed: they want to work but are unable to find jobs. When that happens, the economy is not efficient because it could produce more output if those people were employed. The production possibilities curve shows all the combinations of two goods that could be produced if all resources were fully employed. Changes in unemployment move the economy closer to, or further away from, the production possibilities curve (*PPC*). But the curve itself is determined by what would be possible if there were no unemployment in the economy. Greater unemployment is represented by points farther below the *PPC*—the economy is not reaching its possibilities if it is not using all of its resources. Lower unemployment is represented by points closer to the *PPC*—as unemployment decreases, the economy moves closer to reaching its possibilities.

Opportunity Cost

AP® ECON TIP

Opportunity Cost = Opportunity Lost (the financial or nonfinancial cost of a choice not taken)

The production possibilities curve reminds us that the true cost of any good is not only its price, but also everything else in addition to money that must be given up in order to get that good—the *opportunity cost*. If, for example, Alexis decides to go from point *A* to point *B*, she will produce 8 more fish but 6 fewer coconuts. So the opportunity cost of those 8 fish is the 6 coconuts not gathered. Since 8 extra fish have an opportunity cost of 6 coconuts, 1 fish has an opportunity cost of $6/8 = 3/4$ of a coconut.

Is the opportunity cost of an extra fish in terms of coconuts always the same, no matter how many fish Alexis catches? In the example illustrated by Figure 1.2-1, the answer is yes. If Alexis increases her catch from 28 to 40 fish, an increase of 12, the number of coconuts she gathers falls from 9 to zero. So her opportunity cost per additional fish is $9/12 = 3/4$ of a coconut, the same as it was when her catch went from 20 fish to 28. However, the unchanging opportunity cost of an additional fish in this example is a result of an assumption we've made, an assumption that's reflected in the way Figure 1.2-1 is drawn. Specifically, whenever we assume that the opportunity cost of an additional unit of a good doesn't change regardless of the output mix, the production possibilities curve is a straight line.

Creativ Studio Heinemann/Getty Images

Moreover, as you might have already guessed, the slope of a straight-line production possibilities curve is equal to the opportunity cost—specifically, the opportunity cost for the good measured on the horizontal axis in terms of the good measured on the vertical axis. In Figure 1.2-1, the production possibilities curve has a *constant slope* of $-\frac{3}{4}$, implying that Alexis faces a *constant opportunity cost* per fish equal to $\frac{3}{4}$ of a coconut. (A review of how to calculate the slope of a straight line is found in the Appendix.) This is the simplest case, but the production possibilities curve model can also be used to examine situations in which opportunity costs change as the mix of output changes.

Figure 1.2-2 illustrates a different assumption, a case in which Alexis faces *increasing opportunity cost*. Here, the more fish she catches, the more coconuts she has to give up, and vice versa. For example, to go from producing zero fish to producing 20 fish, she has to give up 5 coconuts. So the opportunity cost of those 20 fish is 5 coconuts. But to increase her fish production from 20 to 40 – that is, to produce an additional 20 fish – she must give up 25 more coconuts, a much higher opportunity cost. As you can see in Figure 1.2-2, when opportunity costs are increasing rather than constant, the production possibilities curve is a concave-shaped (bowed-out) curve rather than a straight line.

FIGURE 1.2-2 Increasing Opportunity Cost

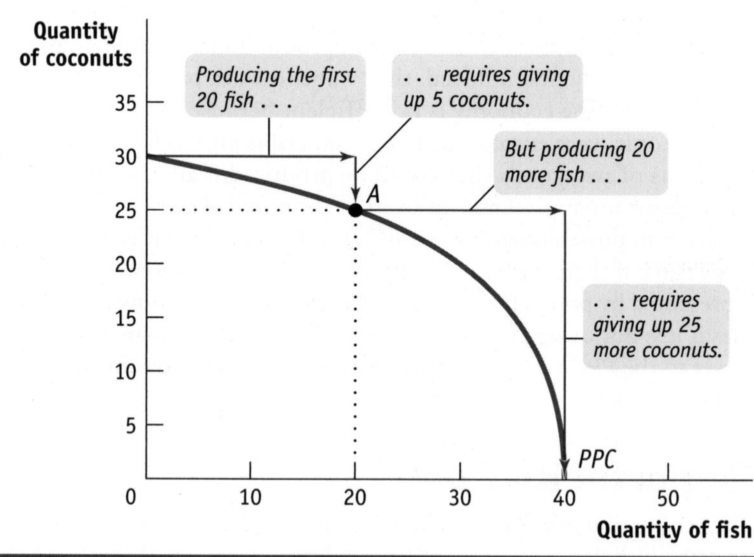

The concave (bowed-out) shape of the production possibilities curve reflects increasing opportunity cost. In this example, to produce the first 20 fish, Alexis must give up 5 coconuts. But to produce an additional 20 fish, she must give up 25 more coconuts. The opportunity cost of fish increases because as Alexis catches more fish, she must make increasing use of resources specialized for coconut production.

AP® ECON TIP

The use of specialized resources makes the production possibilities curve *concave to the origin*, meaning that it is bowed out as shown in Figure 1.2-2. When there is *no* specialization of resources for the production of the goods, there can be *no* increase in the opportunity cost of making more of either good, and *no* change in the slope of the production possibilities curve—it is a straight line.

Although it's often useful to work with the simple assumption that the production possibilities curve is a straight line, in reality, opportunity costs are typically increasing. When only a small amount of a good is produced, the opportunity cost of producing that good is relatively low because the economy needs to use only those resources that are especially well suited for its production. For instance, if an economy grows only a small amount of corn, that corn can be grown in places where the soil and climate are perfect for growing corn but less suitable for growing another crop, such as wheat. So growing that corn involves giving up only a small amount of wheat production. Once the economy grows a lot of corn, however, land that is well suited for wheat but isn't so great for corn must be used to produce corn anyway. As a result, increases in corn production involve sacrificing more and more wheat per unit of corn. In other words, as more of a good is produced, its opportunity cost typically rises because resources specialized for the production of that good are used up and resources specialized for the production of the other good must be used instead.

In some cases, there is no specialization of resources, meaning that all resources are equally suitable for the production of each good. That might be the case when the two goods are leather belts and leather hats, pizzas and calzones, or cappuccinos and lattes. When there is no specialization of resources, the opportunity cost of each unit remains the same as more of a good is made. For example, assuming that two leather belts could be made with the labor, leather, and other resources needed to make one leather hat, the opportunity cost of *each* leather hat is two belts. When no resources are specialized for the production of either good, the production possibilities curve is a straight, downward-sloping line like the one in Figure 1.2-1.

Economic Growth

Finally, the production possibilities curve helps us understand what it means to talk about **economic growth**, which is an increase in the maximum possible output of an economy. When are we justified in saying that an economy has grown over time? After all, although the U.S. economy today produces more of many things than it did a century ago, it produces less of other things, such as horse-drawn carriages. In other words, production of many goods is actually down. So how can we say for sure that the economy as a whole has grown?

Economic growth is an increase in the maximum amount of goods and services an economy can produce.

The answer, illustrated in **Figure 1.2-3**, is that economic growth means an *expansion of the economy's production possibilities*: the economy *can* produce more of everything. For example, if Alexis's production is initially at point *A* (20 fish and 25 coconuts), with economic growth she could move to point *E* (25 fish and 30 coconuts). Point *E* lies outside the original curve, so in the production possibilities curve model, growth is shown as an outward shift of the curve. Unless the *PPC* shifts outward, the points beyond the *PPC* are unattainable because they are beyond the economy's production possibilities.

FIGURE 1.2-3 Economic Growth

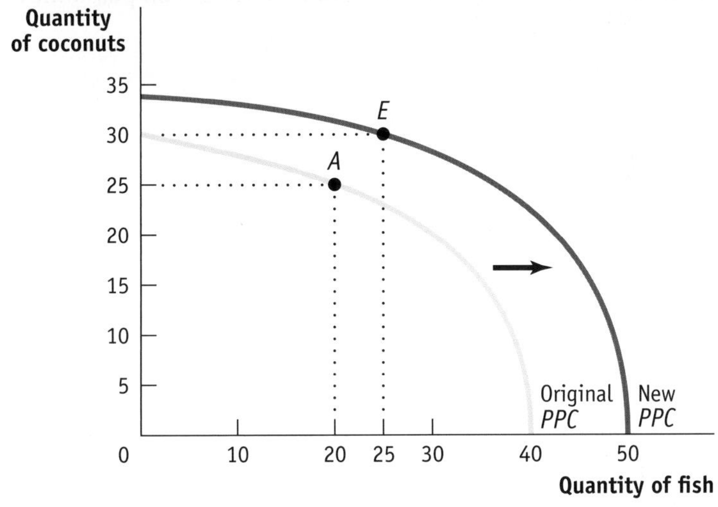

Economic growth results in an *outward shift* of the production possibilities curve because production possibilities are expanded. The economy can now produce more of everything. For example, if production is initially at point *A* (20 fish and 25 coconuts), with sufficient economic growth it could move to point *E* (25 fish and 30 coconuts).

What can cause the production possibilities curve to shift outward? There are two general sources of economic growth. One is an increase in the availability of resources (also called *factors of production*) used to produce goods and services: labor, land, capital, and entrepreneurship. To see how adding to an economy's resources leads to economic growth, suppose that fish become more abundant in the waters around Alexis's island. She can then catch more fish in the course of a day spent fishing. The number of additional fish Alexis catches depends on how much time she decides to spend fishing now that there are more fish in her part of the sea. But because the increased fish population makes her fishing more productive, she can catch more fish without reducing the number of coconuts she gathers, or she can gather more coconuts without reducing her fish catch. So her production possibilities curve shifts outward.

Technology is the technical means for producing goods and services.

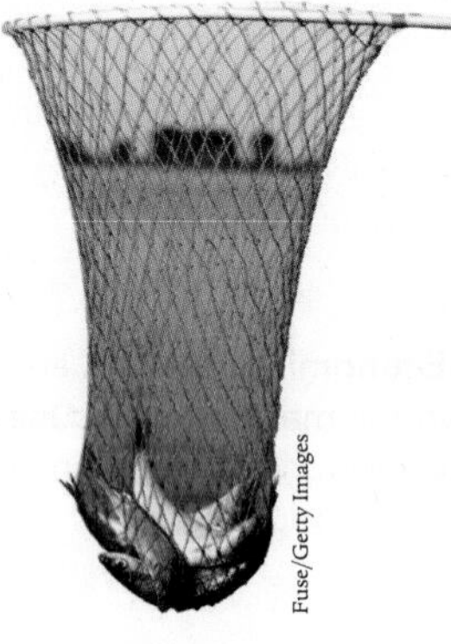
Fuse/Getty Images

The other source of economic growth is improved **technology**, the technical means for the production of goods and services. Suppose Alexis figures out a better way either to catch fish or to gather coconuts—say, by inventing a fishing net or a wagon for transporting coconuts. Either invention would shift her production possibilities curve outward. However, the shift would not be a simple outward expansion of every point along the *PPC*. Technology specific to the production of only one good has no effect if all resources are devoted to the other good: a fishing net will be of no use if Alexis produces nothing but coconuts. So the point on the *PPC* that represents the number of coconuts that can be produced if there is no fishing will not change. In real-world economies, innovations in the techniques we use to produce goods and services have been a crucial force behind economic growth.

Remember, economic growth means an increase in what the economy *can* produce. What the economy actually produces depends on the choices people make. After her production possibilities expand, Alexis might not choose to produce both more fish and more coconuts; she might choose to increase production of only one good, or she might even choose to produce less of one good. For example, if she gets better at catching fish, she might decide to go on an all-fish diet and skip the coconuts, just as the introduction of motor vehicles led most people to give up horse-drawn carriages. But even if, for some reason, she chooses to produce either fewer coconuts or fewer fish than before, we would still say that her economy has grown, because she *could* have produced more of everything.

If an economy's production possibilities curve shifts inward, the economy become smaller. This could happen if the economy loses resources or technology, as could result from war or natural disaster. **Figure 1.2-4** shows what could happen if a hurricane destroyed some of the trees and fishing nets on the island. If Alexis's production is initially at point *A* (20 fish and 25 coconuts), the storm could drive production down to point *F* (15 fish and 20 coconuts). Point *F* lies inside the original curve, so the shrinkage of the economy is shown as an inward shift of the production possibilities curve.

FIGURE 1.2-4 **A Shrinking Economy**

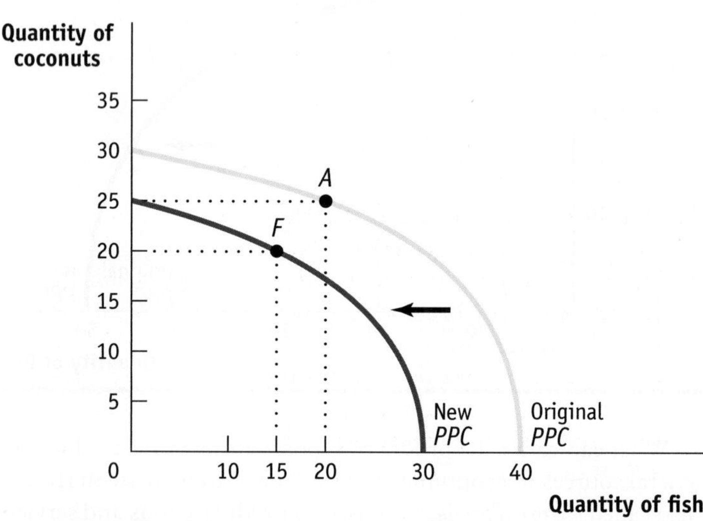

A shrinking economy results in an *inward shift* of the production possibilities curve because production possibilities have diminished. The economy cannot produce as much of either good as it could before. For example, if production starts at point *A* (20 fish and 25 coconuts), after the shrinkage production could move to point *F* (15 fish and 20 coconuts).

The production possibilities curve is a very simplified model of an economy, yet it teaches us important lessons about real-life economies. It gives us our first clear sense of what constitutes economic efficiency, it illustrates the concept of opportunity cost, and it shows what economic growth is all about.

Module 1.2 Review

Adventures in AP® Economics
Watch the video:
Production Possibilities Curve

Check Your Understanding

1. True or false? Explain your answer.
   a. An increase in the amount of resources available to Alexis for use in producing coconuts and fish does not change her production possibilities curve.
   b. A technological change that allows Alexis to catch more fish relative to any amount of coconuts gathered results in a change in her production possibilities curve.
   c. Points inside a production possibilities curve are efficient, and points outside a production possibilities curve are inefficient.

Tackle the AP® Test: Multiple-Choice Questions

Refer to the graph to answer Questions 1–5.

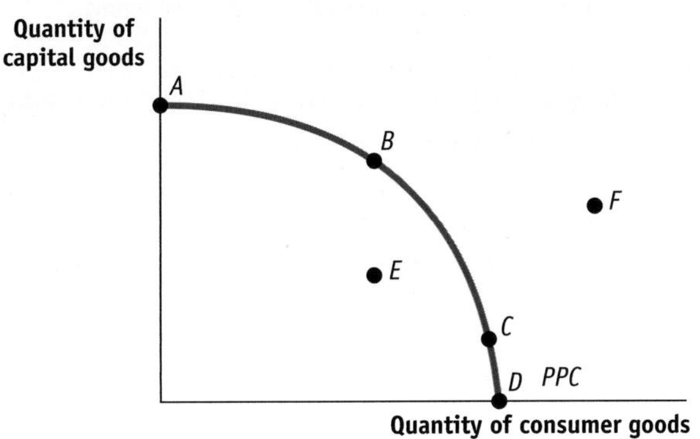

1. Which point(s) on the graph represent efficiency in production?
   a. *B* and *C*
   b. *A* and *D*
   c. *A*, *B*, *C*, and *D*
   d. *A*, *B*, *C*, *D*, and *E*
   e. *A*, *B*, *C*, *D*, *E*, and *F*
2. For this economy, an increase in the quantity of capital goods (such as hammers) without a corresponding decrease in the quantity of consumer goods (such as shirts)
   a. cannot happen because there is always an opportunity cost.
   b. is represented by a movement from point *E* to point *A*.
   c. is represented by a movement from point *C* to point *B*.
   d. is represented by a movement from point *E* to point *B*.
   e. is possible only with an increase in resources or technology.
3. An increase in unemployment could be represented by a movement from point
   a. *D* to point *C*.
   b. *B* to point *A*.
   c. *C* to point *F*.
   d. *B* to point *E*.
   e. *E* to point *B*.
4. Which of the following might allow economic growth and a movement from point *B* to point *F*?
   a. more workers
   b. discovery of new resources
   c. building new factories
   d. technological advances
   e. all of the above
5. This production possibilities curve shows the trade-off between consumer goods and capital goods. Since capital goods are a resource, an increase in the production of capital goods today will increase the economy's production possibilities in the future. Therefore, all other things equal (*ceteris paribus*), producing at which point today will result in the largest outward shift of the *PPC* in the future?
   a. *A*
   b. *B*
   c. *C*
   d. *D*
   e. *E*
6. The production possibilities curve will certainly be straight if
   a. making more of one good means that less of the other good can be made.
   b. the opportunity cost of making each good increases as more is made.
   c. no resources are specialized for the production of either good.
   d. the opportunity cost of making the first unit of each good is the same.
   e. the economy experiences decreasing opportunity costs for the production of both goods.

7. The allocation of resources in the economy is inefficient
   a. at every point along a production possibilities curve.
   b. at every point above a production possibilities curve.
   c. at every point below a production possibilities curve.
   d. at the points on a production possibilities curve that intersect the axes.
   e. at points along a production possibilities curve that make consumers as well off as possible.

Tackle the AP® Test: Free-Response Questions

1. Refer to the graph. Assume that the country is producing at point *C*.

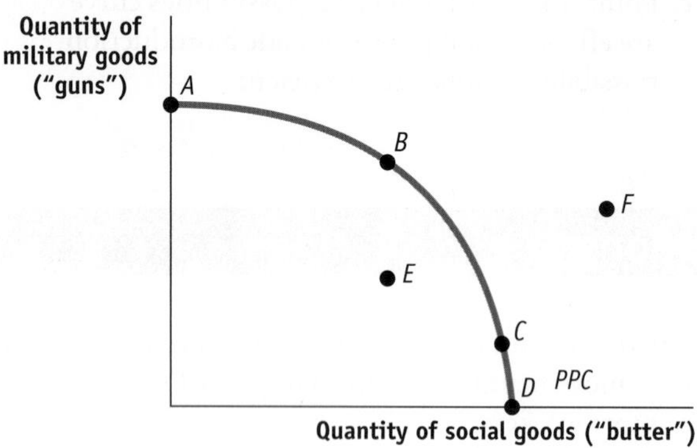

   a. Does this country's production possibilities curve exhibit increasing opportunity costs? Explain.
   b. Suppose point *C* initially represents the best allocation of resources for this country, but then the country goes to war. Before any of the country's resources are lost in the fighting, which point is the most likely to represent an efficient allocation of resources for the country when it is at war? Explain.
   c. If the economy experiences a major hurricane that severely disrupts production, the country would move from point *C* to which point? Explain.

Rubric for FRQ 1 (5 points)

1 point: Yes. The *PPC* is concave (bowed outward), so with each additional unit of butter produced, the opportunity cost in terms of gun production (indicated by the slope of the line) increases. Likewise, as more guns are produced, the opportunity cost in terms of butter increases.

1 point: *B*

1 point: The country would choose an efficient point with more (but not all) military goods with which to fight the war. Point *A* would be an unlikely choice, because at that point there is no production of any social goods, some of which are needed to maintain a minimal standard of living.

1 point: *E*

1 point: A recession, which causes unemployment, is represented by a point below the *PPC*.

2. Assume that an economy can choose between producing food and producing shelter at a constant opportunity cost. Draw a correctly labeled production possibilities curve for the economy. On your graph:
   a. Use the letter *E* to label one of the points at which production is efficient.
   b. Use the letter *U* to label one of the points at which there might be unemployment.
   c. Use the letter *I* to label one of the points that is not feasible. **(5 points)**

Comparative Advantage and Gains from Trade

In this Module, you will learn to:

- Explain how trade leads to gains for individuals and economies
- Define absolute advantage and comparative advantage
- Use production possibilities curves to determine absolute and comparative advantages
- Describe how comparative advantage determines how trading partners should specialize
- Calculate mutually beneficial terms of trade

Gains from Trade

A family could try to take care of all its own needs – growing its own food, sewing its own clothing, providing itself with entertainment, and writing its own economics textbooks. But trying to live that way would be hard. A much higher standard of living can be attained for everyone by dividing tasks such that each person provides one or more goods or services in return for different desired goods and services. This system describes **trade.**

In a market economy, individuals engage in **trade**: they provide goods and services to others and receive goods and services in return.

The reason we have an economy, rather than many self-sufficient individuals, is to take advantage of the gains from trade: by dividing tasks and trading, two people (or 7 billion people) can each get more of what they want than they could get by being self-sufficient. The division of tasks that allows gains from trade is known as **specialization**, which allows each person to engage in a task that they are particularly good at performing.

The gains from trade come from **specialization**: each person specializes in the task that they are good at performing.

The advantages of specialization, and the resulting gains from trade, were the starting point for Adam Smith's 1776 book *The Wealth of Nations*, which many regard as the beginning of economics as a discipline. Smith's book begins with a description of an eighteenth-century pin factory where, rather than each of the 10 workers making a pin from start to finish, each worker specialized in one of the many steps in pin-making:

> One man draws out the wire, another straights it, a third cuts it, a fourth points it, a fifth grinds it at the top for receiving the head; to make the head requires two or three distinct operations; to put it on, is a particular business, to whiten the pins is another; it is even a trade by itself to put them into the paper; and the important business of making a pin is, in this manner, divided into about eighteen distinct operations. . . . Those ten persons, therefore, could make among them upwards of forty-eight thousand pins in a day. But if they had all wrought separately and independently, and without any of them having been educated to this particular business, they certainly could not each of them have made twenty, perhaps not one pin a day. . . .

Ryan Pyle/Getty Images

The concept of specialization allows for the mass production of most of the devices and appliances that we use today.

The same principle applies when we look at how people divide tasks among themselves and trade in an economy. The economy as a whole can produce more when each person *specializes* in a task and *trades* with others.

The benefits of specialization are the reason a person typically focuses on the production of only one type of good or service. It takes many years of study and experience to become a doctor; it also takes many years of study and experience to become a commercial airline pilot. Many doctors might have the potential to become excellent pilots, and vice versa, but it is very unlikely that anyone who decided to pursue both careers would be as good a pilot or as good a doctor as someone who specialized in only one of those professions. So it is to everyone's advantage when individuals specialize in their career choices.

Markets are what allow a doctor and a pilot to specialize in their respective fields. Because markets for commercial flights and for doctors' services exist, a doctor is assured to find a flight and a pilot is assured to find a doctor. As long as individuals know they can find the goods and services they want in the market, they are willing to forgo self-sufficiency and specialize instead.

Roderick Chen/Getty Images

Comparative Advantage and Gains from Trade

The production possibilities curve model is particularly useful for illustrating gains from trade—trade based on *comparative advantage*. Let's stick with Alexis being stranded on her island, but now we'll suppose that a second castaway, Jacob, has washed ashore. Can Alexis and Jacob benefit from trading with each other?

It's obvious that there will be potential gains from trade if the two castaways do different things particularly well. For example, if Alexis is a skilled fisher and Jacob is very good at climbing trees, clearly it makes sense for Alexis to catch fish and Jacob to gather coconuts—and for both castaways to trade the products of their efforts.

But one of the most important insights in all of economics is that there are gains from trade even if one of the trading parties isn't especially good at anything. Suppose, for example, that Jacob is less well suited to primitive life than Alexis; he's not nearly as good at catching fish, and compared to Alexis, even his coconut gathering leaves something to be desired. Nonetheless, what we'll see is that both Alexis and Jacob can live better by trading with each other than either could alone.

For the purposes of this example, let's go back to the simple case of straight-line production possibilities curves. Alexis's production possibilities are represented by the production possibilities curve in panel (a) of **Figure 1.3-1**, which is the same as

FIGURE 1.3-1 Production Possibilities for Two Castaways

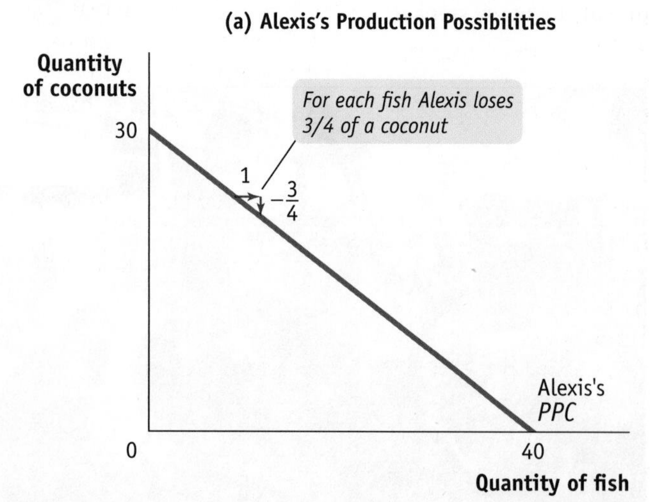

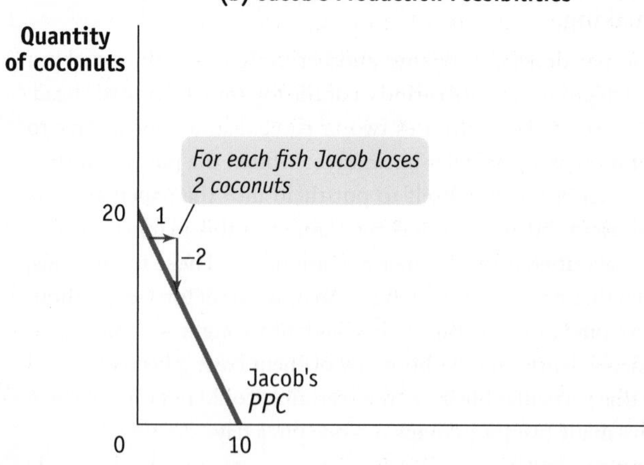

Here, each of the two castaways has a constant opportunity cost of fish, and therefore a straight-line production possibilities curve. In Alexis's case, each fish has an opportunity cost of ¾ of a coconut. In Jacob's case, each fish has an opportunity cost of 2 coconuts.

the production possibilities curve in Figure 1.2-1. According to this *PPC*, Alexis could catch 40 fish, but only if she gathered no coconuts, and she could gather 30 coconuts, but only if she caught no fish. Recall that this means the slope of her production possibilities curve is $-3/4$: her opportunity cost of 1 fish is $3/4$ of a coconut.

Panel (b) of Figure 1.3-1 shows Jacob's production possibilities. Like that of Alexis, Jacob's production possibilities curve is a straight line, implying a constant opportunity cost of fish in terms of coconuts. His production possibilities curve has a constant slope of -2. Jacob is less productive all around: at most he can produce 10 fish or 20 coconuts. But he is particularly bad at fishing: whereas Alexis sacrifices $3/4$ of a coconut per fish caught, for Jacob, the opportunity cost of a fish is 2 whole coconuts. **Table 1.3-1** summarizes the two castaways' opportunity costs of fish and coconuts.

Table 1.3-1 Alexis's and Jacob's Opportunity Costs of Fish and Coconuts

	Alexis's Opportunity Cost	Jacob's Opportunity Cost
One fish	$3/4$ coconut	2 coconuts
One coconut	$4/3$ fish	$1/2$ fish

With information on opportunity costs we can determine who has the *comparative advantage* in producing each good. An individual has a **comparative advantage** in producing something if they have the lowest opportunity cost among the producers. In other words, Jacob has a comparative advantage over Alexis in producing a particular good or service if Jacob's opportunity cost of producing that good or service is lower than Alexis's opportunity cost. In this case, Jacob has a comparative advantage in gathering coconuts because his opportunity cost of $1/2$ fish is lower than Alexis's opportunity cost of $4/3$ fish, and Alexis has a comparative advantage in catching fish because her opportunity cost of $3/4$ coconut is lower than Jacob's opportunity cost of 2 coconuts.

An individual has a **comparative advantage** in producing a good or service if that person's opportunity cost is the lowest among the people who could produce that good or service.

An individual has an **absolute advantage** in producing a good or service if they can make more of it with a given amount of time and resources.

Notice that Alexis is better than Jacob at producing both goods: If both castaways devoted their efforts to catching fish, Alexis would catch 40 fish per week while Jacob caught 10, and if they devoted their efforts to gathering coconuts, Alexis would gather 30 coconuts per week while Jacob gathered 20. Information on possible output levels allows us to determine absolute advantages. An individual has an **absolute advantage** in producing something if that person can produce more of it with a given amount of time and resources. Since Alexis can make more of either good than Jacob, Alexis has an absolute advantage in both activities.

AP® ECON TIP

Having an *absolute* advantage is not the same thing as having a *comparative* advantage. For example, it is quite possible to be able to make more of something than other producers (that is, to have an absolute advantage) but to have a higher opportunity cost than other producers (that is, to have a comparative *dis*advantage).

To examine the gains from trade, our point of comparison will be the alternative to trade: Alexis and Jacob could go their separate ways, each living on their own side of the island, catching their own fish and gathering their own coconuts. Let's suppose they start out that way and make the consumption choices shown in **Figure 1.3-2**: in the absence of trade, Alexis consumes 28 fish and 9 coconuts per week, while Jacob consumes 6 fish and 8 coconuts.

Is this the best they can do? No, it isn't. Given that the two castaways have different opportunity costs, each has a comparative advantage in one good or the other. They can specialize on the basis of their comparative advantages and strike a trade deal that makes both of them better off. **Table 1.3-2** shows how such a deal can work: Alexis specializes in the production of fish, catching 40 per week, and gives 10 to Jacob. Meanwhile, Jacob specializes in the production of coconuts, gathering 20 per week, and gives 10 to Alexis. The result is shown by the points above the PPCs in Figure 1.3-2. Alexis now consumes more of both goods than before: instead of 28 fish and 9 coconuts, she consumes 30 fish and 10 coconuts. Jacob also consumes more, going from 6 fish and 8 coconuts to 10 fish and 10 coconuts. As Table 1.3-2 also shows, both Alexis and Jacob experience gains from trade: Alexis's consumption of fish increases by two, and her consumption of coconuts increases by one. Jacob's consumption of fish increases by four, and his consumption of coconuts increases by two.

FIGURE 1.3-2 Comparative Advantage and Gains from Trade

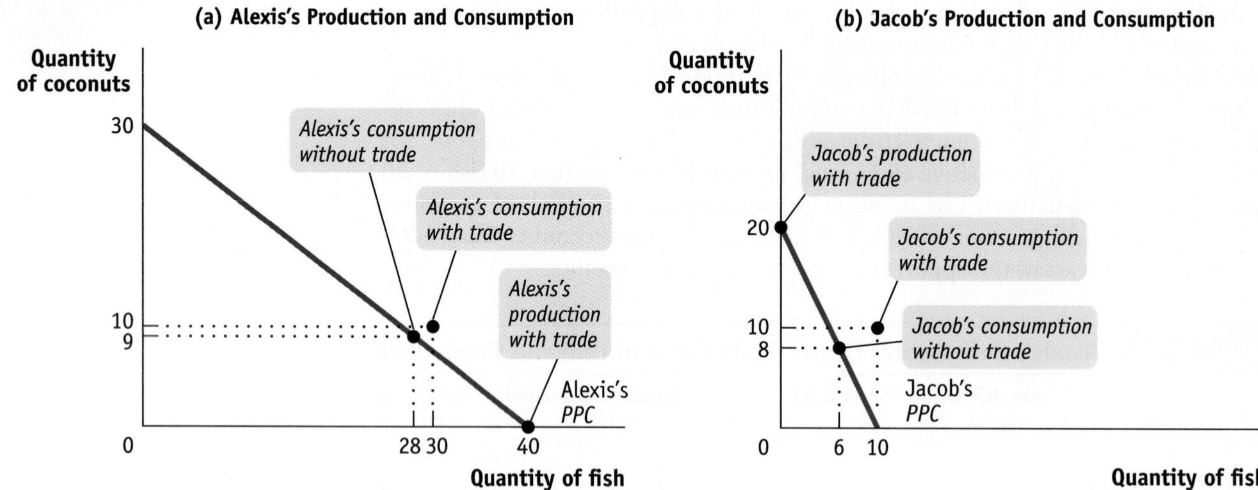

By specializing and trading, the two castaways can produce and consume more of both goods. Alexis specializes in catching fish, her comparative advantage, and Jacob—who has an *absolute* disadvantage in both goods but a *comparative* advantage in coconuts—specializes in gathering coconuts. The result is that each castaway can consume more of both goods than either could without trade.

Table 1.3-2 How the Castaways Gain from Trade

		Without Trade		With Trade		Gains from Trade
		Production	Consumption	Production	Consumption	
Alexis	Fish	28	28	40	30	+2
	Coconuts	9	9	0	10	+1
Jacob	Fish	6	6	0	10	+4
	Coconuts	8	8	20	10	+2

So both castaways are better off when they each specialize in what they are good at and trade with each other. It's a good idea for Alexis to catch the fish for both of them, because her opportunity cost of catching a fish is relatively low and she therefore has a comparative advantage in catching fish. Correspondingly, it's a good idea for Jacob to gather coconuts for both of them.

Or we could describe the situation in a different way. Because Alexis is so good at catching fish, her opportunity cost of gathering coconuts is relatively high, which gives her a comparative disadvantage in gathering coconuts. Because Jacob is relatively bad at fishing, his opportunity cost of gathering coconuts is much lower, giving him a comparative advantage in gathering coconuts.

It might seem as though Alexis has nothing to gain from trading with less competent Jacob. But we've just seen that Alexis can indeed benefit from a deal with Jacob because *comparative*, not *absolute*, advantage is the basis for mutual gain. It doesn't matter that it takes Jacob more time to gather a coconut; what matters is that for him, the opportunity cost of that coconut in terms of fish is lower. So, despite his absolute disadvantage in both activities, Jacob's comparative advantage in coconut gathering makes mutually beneficial trade possible.

Mutually Beneficial Terms of Trade

The **terms of trade** indicate the rate at which one good can be exchanged for another. In our story, Alexis and Jacob traded 10 coconuts for 10 fish, so each coconut traded for 1 fish. Why not some other terms of trade, such as ¾ fish per coconut? Indeed, there are many terms of trade that would make both Alexis and Jacob better off than if they didn't trade. There are also terms that Alexis or Jacob would certainly reject. For example, Alexis would not trade 2 fish per coconut, because she only gives up 4⁄3 fish per coconut without trade.

The **terms of trade** indicate the rate at which one good can be exchanged for another.

To find the range of mutually beneficial terms of trade for a coconut, look at each person's opportunity cost of producing a coconut. *Any price per coconut between the opportunity cost of the coconut producer and the opportunity cost of the coconut buyer will make both sides better off than in the absence of trade.* We know that Jacob will produce coconuts because he has a comparative advantage in gathering coconuts. Jacob's opportunity cost is ½ fish per coconut. Alexis, the buyer of coconuts, has an opportunity cost of 4⁄3 fish per coconut. So any terms of trade between ½ fish per coconut and 4⁄3 fish per coconut would benefit both Alexis and Jacob.

To understand why, consider the opportunity costs summarized in Table 1.3-1 When Jacob doesn't trade with Alexis, Jacob can gain ½ fish by giving up a coconut, because his opportunity cost of each coconut is ½ fish. Jacob will clearly reject any deal with Alexis that provides him with less than ½ fish per coconut—he's better off not trading at all and getting ½ fish per coconut. But Jacob benefits from trade if he receives more than ½ fish per coconut. So the terms of 1 fish per coconut, as in our story, are acceptable to Jacob.

It also makes sense from Alexis's perspective. When Alexis doesn't trade with Jacob, Alexis gives up 4⁄3 fish to get a coconut—her opportunity cost of a coconut is 4⁄3 fish. Alexis will reject any deal that requires her to pay more than 4⁄3 fish per coconut. But Alexis benefits from trade if she pays less than 4⁄3 fish per coconut. The terms of 1 fish per coconut are thus acceptable to Alexis as well. Both islanders would also be made better off by terms of ¾ fish per coconut or 5⁄4 fish per coconut or any other price between ½ fish and 4⁄3 fish per coconut. Their negotiation skills determine where the terms of trade fall within that range.

AP® ECON TIP

The mutually beneficial terms of trade for a good fall between the producer's opportunity cost for the good and the buyer's opportunity cost for the good.

So remember, Alexis and Jacob will engage in trade only if the "price" of the good each person obtains from trade is less than their own opportunity cost of producing the good. The same is true for international trade. Whenever two parties trade voluntarily, the terms of trade for each good are found between the opportunity cost of the producer and the opportunity cost of the buyer.

The story of Alexis and Jacob clearly simplifies reality. Yet it teaches us some very important lessons that also apply to the real economy. First, the story illustrates the gains from trade. By agreeing to specialize and trade, Alexis and Jacob can each consume more of both goods than if each tried to be self-sufficient. Second, the story demonstrates a key point that is often overlooked in real-world arguments: as long as potential trading partners have different opportunity costs, *each has a comparative advantage in something and each has a comparative disadvantage in something else, so each can benefit from trade.*

The idea of comparative advantage applies to many activities in the economy. Perhaps its most important application is in trade—not between individuals, but between countries. So let's look briefly at how the model of comparative advantage helps us understand both the causes and the effects of international trade.

AP® ECON TIP

The producer with the *absolute advantage* can produce the largest quantity of the good. However, it is the producer with the *comparative advantage*, and not necessarily the one with the absolute advantage, who should specialize in the production of that good to achieve mutual gains from trade.

Comparative Advantage and International Trade

International trade provides much of what we buy. Look at the label on most manufactured goods sold in the United States, and you will probably find it was produced in some other country—in China, Japan, or even Canada. On the other hand, many U.S. industries sell a large portion of their output overseas. This is particularly true for the agriculture, high technology, and entertainment industries.

Steve Russell/Getty Images

Canada has a comparative advantage in this jacket.

Should we celebrate this international exchange of goods and services, or should it cause us concern? Politicians and the public sometimes question the desirability of international trade, arguing that the nation should produce goods for itself rather than buy them from other countries. Industries around the world demand protection from foreign competition: Japanese farmers want to keep out American rice, and American steelworkers want to keep out European steel. These demands are often supported by public opinion.

Economists, however, have a very positive view of international trade. Why? Because they view it in terms of comparative advantage. **Figure 1.3-3** shows how international trade can be interpreted in terms of comparative advantage. Although the example is hypothetical, it is based on an actual pattern of international trade: American exports of pork to Canada and Canadian exports of aircraft to the United States. Panels (a) and (b) illustrate hypothetical production possibilities curves for the United States and Canada, with pork measured on the horizontal axis and aircraft measured on the vertical axis. The U.S. production possibilities curve is flatter than the Canadian production possibilities curve, implying that producing one more ton of pork costs fewer aircraft in the United States than it does in Canada. This means that the United States has a comparative advantage in pork, and Canada has a comparative advantage in aircraft.

FIGURE 1.3-3 Comparative Advantage and International Trade

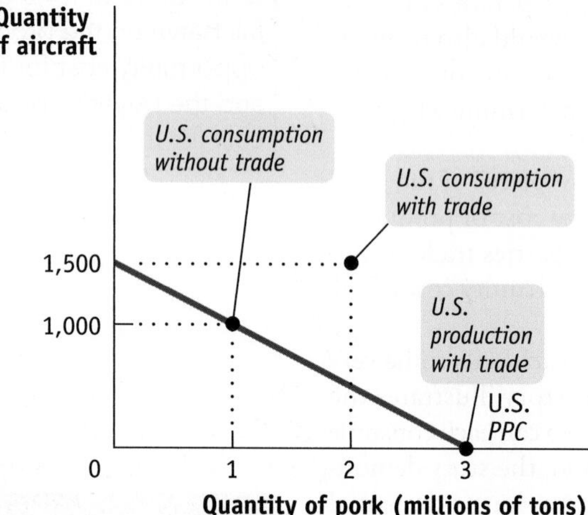

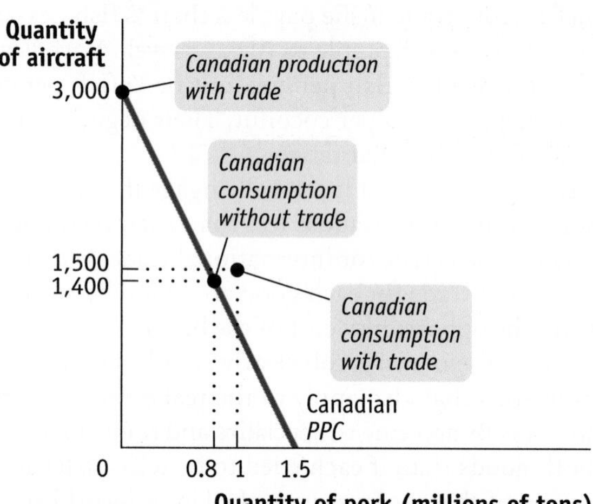

In this hypothetical example, Canada and the United States produce only two goods: pork and aircraft. Aircraft are measured on the vertical axis and pork on the horizontal axis. Panel (a) shows the U.S. production possibilities curve. It is relatively flat, implying that the United States has a comparative advantage in pork production. Panel (b) shows the Canadian production possibilities curve. It is relatively steep, implying that Canada has a comparative advantage in aircraft production. Just like two individuals, both countries gain from specialization and trade.

Although the consumption points in Figure 1.3-3 are hypothetical, they illustrate a general principle: as in the example of Alexis and Jacob, the United States and Canada can both achieve mutual gains from trade. If the United States concentrates on producing pork and sells some of its output to Canada, while Canada concentrates on aircraft and sells some of its output to the United States, both countries can consume more than if they insisted on being self-sufficient. For example, the United States could trade 1 million tons of pork for 1,500 aircraft from Canada. This would allow both countries to consume at a point outside of their production possibilities curves.

Moreover, these mutual gains don't depend on each country's being better at producing one kind of good. Even if, say, one country has remarkably productive workers who give it an absolute advantage in both industries, there are still mutual gains from trade.

Adventures in AP® Economics

Watch the video: ***Comparative Advantage and Absolute Advantage***

Module 1.3 Review

Check Your Understanding

1. In the country of Imsmall, an automobile can be produced by 8 workers in one day and a washing machine by 3 workers in one day. In the country of Sosmall, an automobile can be produced by 6 workers in one day, and a washing machine by 2 workers in one day. Suppose each country has 24 workers.
   a. How many automobiles could each country make if it made nothing else?
   b. How many washing machines could each country make if it made nothing else?
   c. Which country has an absolute advantage in the production of automobiles? in washing machines?
   d. Which country has a comparative advantage in the production of washing machines? in automobiles?
   e. What type of specialization results in the greatest gains from trade between the two countries?
2. Refer to the story of Alexis and Jacob illustrated by Figure 1.3-1 in the text. Explain why Alexis and Jacob are willing to engage in a trade of 1 fish for 1½ coconuts.

Tackle the AP® Test: Multiple-Choice Questions

Refer to the graph below to answer questions 1–6.

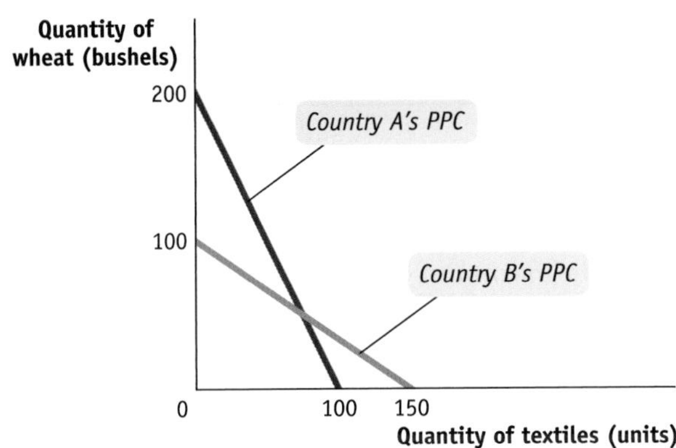

1. Use the graph to determine which country has an absolute advantage in producing each good.

Absolute advantage in wheat production	*Absolute advantage in textile production*
a. Country A	Country B
b. Country A	Country A
c. Country B	Country A
d. Country B	Country B
e. Country A	Neither country

2. For Country A, the opportunity cost of a bushel of wheat is
   a. ½ unit of textiles.
   b. ⅔ unit of textiles.
   c. 1⅓ units of textiles.
   d. 1½ units of textiles.
   e. 2 units of textiles.

3. Use the graph to determine which country has a comparative advantage in producing each good.

Comparative advantage in wheat production	*Comparative advantage in textile production*
a. Country A	Country B
b. Country A	Country A
c. Country B	Country A
d. Country B	Country B
e. Country A	Neither country

4. If the two countries specialize and trade, which of the choices below describes the countries' imports?

Import wheat	*Import textiles*
a. Country A	Country A
b. Country A	Country B
c. Country B	Country B
d. Country B	Country A
e. Neither country	Country B

5. What is the highest price Country B is willing to pay to buy wheat from Country A?
   a. ½ unit of textiles
   b. ⅔ unit of textiles
   c. 1 unit of textiles
   d. 1½ units of textiles
   e. 2 units of textiles

6. What are the mutually beneficial terms of trade, measured in units of wheat from Country A per unit of textiles from Country B?
   a. between 1 and 2
   b. between ⅔ and 2
   c. between ½ and 1½
   d. between ⅔ and 1½
   e. between ½ and 2

7. There are opportunities for mutually beneficial trade between two countries whenever
   a. one can produce more of everything than the other.
   b. the production possibilities curves of the two countries are identical.
   c. each country has a comparative advantage in making something.
   d. the countries are similar in size.
   e. no country has an absolute advantage in producing both goods.

Tackle the AP® Test: Free-Response Questions

1. Refer to the graph below to answer the following questions.

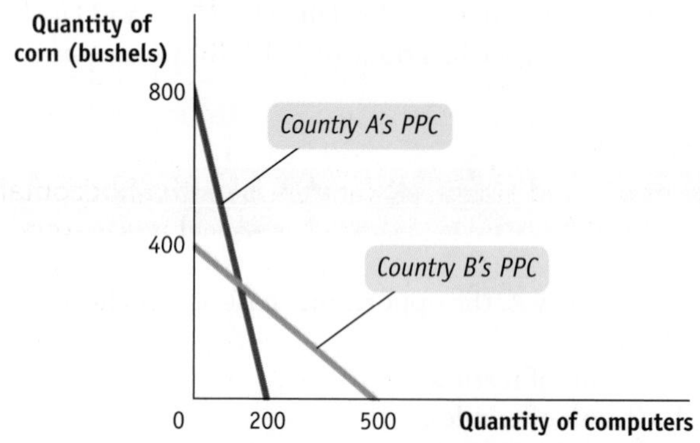

   a. What is the opportunity cost of a bushel of corn in each country?
   b. Which country has an absolute advantage in computer production? Explain.
   c. Which country has a comparative advantage in corn production? Explain.
   d. If each country specializes, what good will Country B import? Explain.
   e. What is the minimum price Country A will accept to export corn to Country B? Explain.
   f. What is the maximum price Country B will pay to import corn from Country A?

Rubric for FRQ 1 (10 points)

1 point: Country A, ¼ computer; Country B, 1¼ computers

1 point: Country B

1 point: Because Country B can produce more computers than Country A (500 versus 200).

1 point: Country A

1 point: Because Country A can produce corn at a lower opportunity cost (¼ computer versus 1¼ computers).

1 point: Corn

1 point: Country B has a comparative advantage in the production of computers, so it will produce computers and import corn (Country A has a comparative advantage in corn production, so it will specialize in corn and import computers from Country B).

1 point: ¼ computer

1 point: Country A's opportunity cost of producing corn is ¼ computer, so that is the lowest price it will accept to sell corn to Country B.

1 point: 1¼ computers

2. Refer to the table below to answer the following questions. These two countries are producing textiles and wheat using equal amounts of resources. The table indicates the maximum weekly output for workers who produce wheat or textiles.

	Weekly output per worker	
	Country A	Country B
Bushels of wheat	15	10
Units of textiles	60	60

   a. What is the opportunity cost of producing a bushel of wheat for each country?
   b. Which country has the absolute advantage in wheat production?
   c. Which country has the comparative advantage in textile production? Explain. **(5 points)**

Demand

In this Module, you will learn to:

- Draw a demand curve and interpret its meaning
- Define the law of demand and explain the relationship between the price of a good or service and the quantity demanded
- Explain the difference between movements along a demand curve and changes in demand
- Explain the determinants of demand

The most well-known economic model is the *supply and demand model,* and it can be used to understand how markets determine the price and quantity sold of a good or service. Markets are made up of buyers, who demand goods and services, and sellers, who produce them. The behavior of many different markets are well described by the **supply and demand model**, which is made up of six key elements:

- The *demand curve*
- The set of factors that cause the demand curve to shift
- The *supply curve*
- The set of factors that cause the supply curve to shift
- The *market equilibrium,* which includes the *equilibrium price* and *equilibrium quantity*
- The way the market equilibrium changes when the supply curve or demand curve shifts

To explain the supply and demand model, we will examine each of these elements in turn. In this Module, we begin with the demand curve and then discuss the factors that cause the demand curve to shift.

The **supply and demand model** is a model of how competitive markets work.

AP® ECON TIP

In several common economics graphs, including the graph of supply and demand, the dependent variable is on the vertical axis and the independent variable is on the horizontal axis. You may have learned the opposite convention in math and science classes, but don't let that confuse you—economists go their own way.

The Demand Curve

To illustrate the demand curve, consider the worldwide market for lumber in which lumber is measured in board feet. How many board feet of lumber do consumers around the world want to buy in a given year? The answer depends on the price of lumber. For decades, the price of lumber remained relatively steady. When the price of lumber rises – as it did in from 2018 to 2021 in response to a pine beetle infestation that killed trees, and then to labor shortages due to the COVID-19 pandemic – some people will respond to the higher price of lumber either by forgoing the purchase of a new home, or by having their home built with wood substitutes, such as plastic composites or steel. In general, the quantity of lumber, or of any good or service that people *want* to buy (taking "want" to mean they are willing and able to buy it), depends on the price. The higher the price, the less of the good or service people want to purchase; alternatively, the lower the price, the more they want to purchase.

So the answer to the question "How many board feet of lumber do consumers want to buy?" depends on the price of lumber. If you don't yet know what the price will be, you can start by making a table of how much lumber people would want to buy at a number of different prices. Such a table is known as a *demand schedule.* This demand schedule, in turn, can be used to draw a *demand curve,* which is one of the key elements of the supply and demand model.

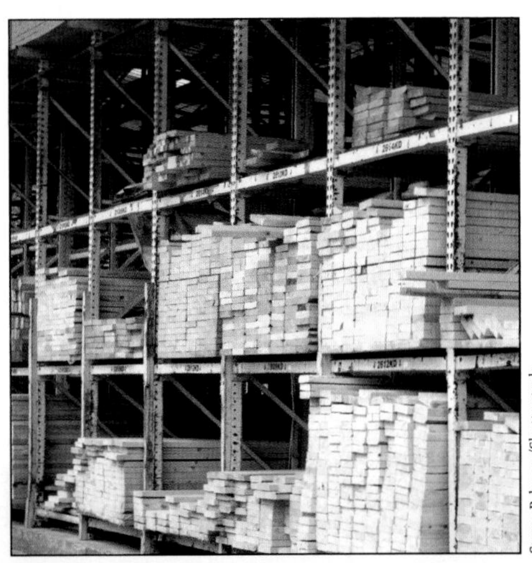

Steven Belanger/Shutterstock

The Demand Schedule and the Demand Curve

A **demand schedule** is a table that shows how much of a good or service consumers will be willing and able to buy at different prices.

A **demand schedule** is a table that shows how much of a good or service consumers will want to buy at different prices. On the right side of **Figure 1.4-1**, we show a hypothetical demand schedule for lumber. It's hypothetical in that it doesn't use actual data on the world demand for lumber. The demand schedule assumes that all lumber is standardized, although in reality there are various grades and sizes.

FIGURE 1.4-1 The Demand Schedule and the Demand Curve

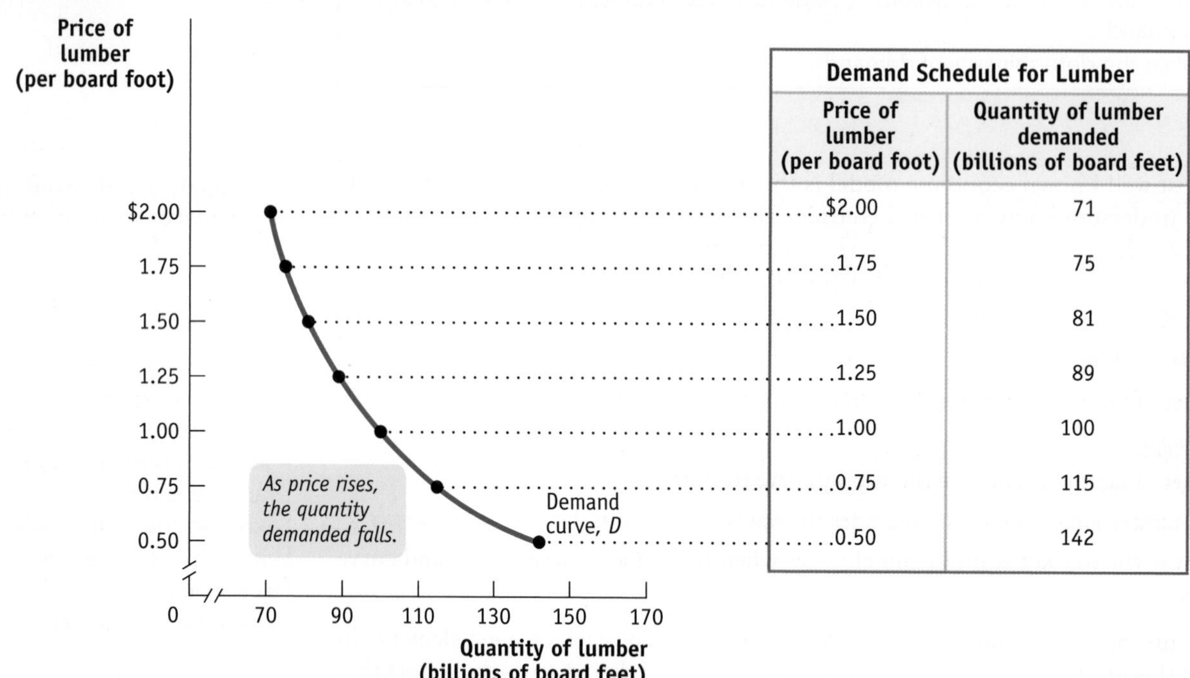

Demand Schedule for Lumber	
Price of lumber (per board foot)	Quantity of lumber demanded (billions of board feet)
$2.00	71
1.75	75
1.50	81
1.25	89
1.00	100
0.75	115
0.50	142

The demand schedule for lumber yields the corresponding demand curve, which shows how much of a good or service consumers want to buy at any given price. The demand curve and the demand schedule reflect the law of demand: As price rises, the quantity demanded falls. Similarly, a decrease in price raises the quantity demanded. As a result, the demand curve is downward-sloping.

According to the table, if lumber costs $1.00 per board foot, consumers around the world will want to purchase 100 billion board feet of lumber over the course of a year. If the price is $1.25 a board foot, they will want to buy only 89 billion board feet; if the price is only $0.75 a board foot, they will want to buy 115 billion board feet; and so on. So the higher the price, the fewer board feet of lumber consumers will want to purchase. In other words, as the price rises, the **quantity demanded** of lumber—the actual amount consumers are willing and able to buy at a specific price—falls.

The **quantity demanded** is the actual amount of a good or service consumers are willing and able to buy at some specific price. It is shown as a single point in a demand schedule or along a demand curve.

A **demand curve** is a graphical representation of the demand schedule. It shows the relationship between quantity demanded and price.

The graph in Figure 1.4-1 is a visual representation of the demand schedule. The vertical axis shows the price of a board foot of lumber, and the horizontal axis shows the quantity of lumber in board feet. Each point on the graph corresponds to one of the entries in the table. The curve that connects these points is a **demand curve**, which is another way of showing the relationship between the quantity demanded and the price.

Note that the demand curve shown in Figure 1.4-1 slopes downward. This reflects the general proposition that a higher price reduces the quantity demanded. For example, construction companies know they will sell fewer homes when their price is higher, reflecting a $2.00 price per board foot of lumber, compared to the number they will sell when the price is lower, reflecting a price of only $1.00 per board foot of lumber. When home prices are relatively high, some people will decide not to build a new home, delay the construction of their home, build a smaller home, or use less wood in their home.

In the real world, demand curves almost always slope downward. It is so likely that, all other things being equal, a higher price for a good will lead people to demand a smaller quantity of it, that economists are willing to call it a "law"—the **law of demand**.

The **law of demand** says that a higher price for a good or service, all other things being equal, leads people to demand a smaller quantity of that good or service.

Changes in factors other than price will decrease (or increase) the demand for a good or service. Next, we discuss the *determinants of demand*—the factors that can cause a change in demand.

AP® ECON TIP

A price change causes a change in the quantity demanded, shown by a movement along the demand curve. When something other than price causes demand to change, it is shown as a shift of the demand curve. It is correct to say that an increase in the price of apples decreases the *quantity of apples demanded*; it is incorrect to say that an increase in the price of apples decreases the *demand for* apples.

Shifts of the Demand Curve

Even though lumber prices were higher in 2021 than they had been in 2020, the total consumption of lumber was also higher in 2021 than in 2020. How can we reconcile this fact with the law of demand, which says that a higher price reduces the quantity demanded, all other things being equal?

The answer lies in the crucial phrase *all other things being equal*. In this case, all other things weren't equal: there were changes between 2020 and 2021 that increased the quantity of lumber demanded at any given price. For example, the COVID-19 pandemic changed consumers' tastes for single-family homes, as some workers could work remotely and therefore didn't need to live in cities. This change in taste led to an increase in the quantity of lumber demanded at any given price. **Figure 1.4-2** illustrates this phenomenon using the demand schedule and demand curve for lumber. (As before, the numbers in Figure 1.4-2 are hypothetical.)

FIGURE 1.4-2 An Increase in Demand

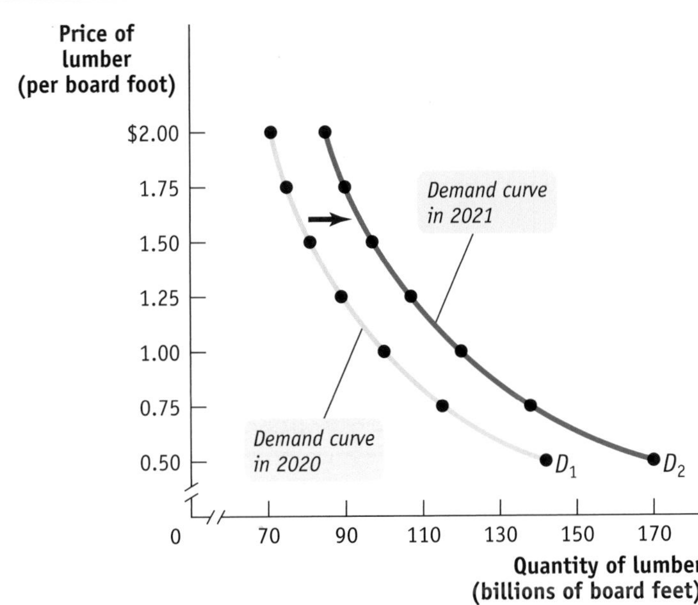

Demand Schedules for Lumber		
Price of lumber (per board foot)	Quantity of lumber demanded (billions of board feet)	
	in 2020	in 2021
$2.00	71	85
1.75	75	90
1.50	81	97
1.25	89	107
1.00	100	120
0.75	115	138
0.50	142	170

Changes in tastes and increases in income, among other changes, generate an increase in demand—a rise in the quantity demanded at any given price. This is represented by the two demand schedules—one showing demand in 2020 (D_1), and the other showing demand in 2021 (D_2), after the rise in population and income—and their corresponding demand curves. The increase in demand shifts the demand curve to the right.

The table in Figure 1.4-2 shows two demand schedules. The first is a demand schedule for 2020, the same one shown in Figure 1.4-1. The second is a demand schedule for 2021. That demand schedule differs from the 2020 demand schedule due to factors such as changing tastes for new homes and higher incomes, factors that led to an increase in the quantity of lumber demanded at any given price. So at each price, the 2021 schedule shows a larger quantity demanded than the 2020 schedule. For example, the quantity of lumber consumers wanted to buy at a price of $1 per board foot increased from 100 billion to 120 billion board feet per year, the quantity demanded at $1.25 per board foot went from 89 billion to 107 billion board feet, and so on.

A **change in demand** is a shift of the demand curve, which changes the quantity demanded at any given price.

A **movement along the demand curve** is a change in the quantity demanded of a good that is the result of a change in that good's price.

What is clear from this example is that the changes that occurred between 2020 and 2021 generated a *new* demand schedule, one in which the quantity demanded was greater at any given price than in the original demand schedule. The two curves in Figure 1.4-2 show the same information graphically. As you can see, the demand schedule for 2021 corresponds to a new demand curve, D_2, that is to the right of the demand curve for 2020, D_1. This **change in demand** shows the increase in the quantity demanded at any given price, represented by the shift in position of the original demand curve, D_1, to its new location at D_2.

It's crucial to make the distinction between such changes in demand and **movements along the demand curve**, which are changes in the quantity demanded of a good that result from a change in that good's price. **Figure 1.4-3** illustrates the difference.

FIGURE 1.4-3 A Movement Along the Demand Curve Versus a Shift of the Demand Curve

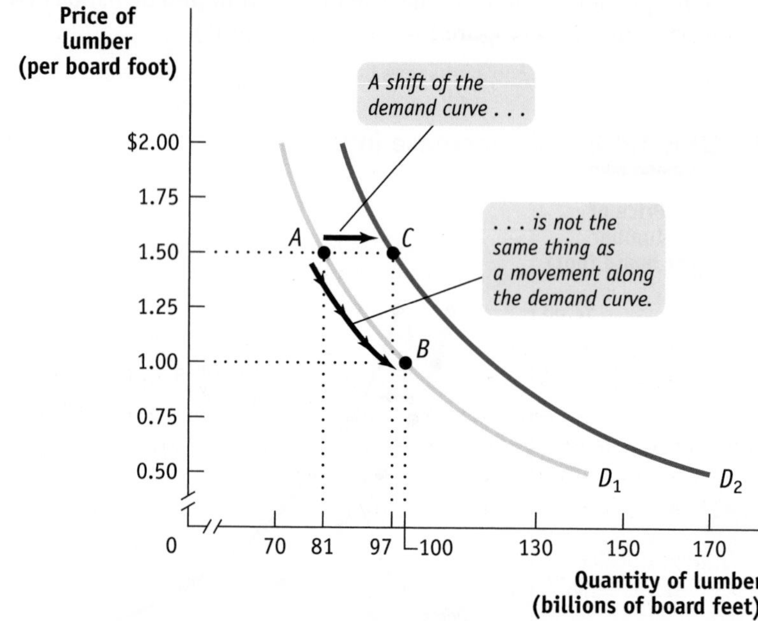

The rise in the quantity demanded when going from point *A* to point *B* reflects a movement along the demand curve: it is the result of a fall in the price of the good. The rise in the quantity demanded when going from point *A* to point *C* reflects a change in demand: this shift to the right, from D_1 to D_2, is the result of a rise in the quantity demanded at any given price.

The movement from point *A* to point *B* is a movement along the demand curve: the quantity demanded rises due to a fall in price as you move down D_1. Here, a fall in the price of lumber from $1.50 to $1 per board foot generates a rise in the quantity demanded from 81 billion to 100 billion board feet per year. But the quantity demanded can also rise when the price is unchanged if there is an *increase in demand*—a rightward shift of the demand curve. This is illustrated in Figure 1.4-3 by the shift of the demand curve from D_1 to D_2. Holding the price constant at $1.50 per board foot, the quantity demanded rises from 81 billion board feet at point *A* on D_1 to 97 billion board feet at point *C* on D_2.

When economists talk about a "change in demand," saying "the demand for *X* increased" or "the demand for *Y* decreased," they mean that the demand curve for *X* or *Y* shifted—*not* that the quantity demanded rose or fell because of a change in the price.

> **AP® ECON TIP**
>
> When shifting curves, a decrease is shown as a movement to the left, and an increase is shown as a movement to the right. Quantity is measured on the horizontal axis and is lower to the left and higher to the right. Remember, *left is less and right is more.*

Understanding Shifts of the Demand Curve

Figure 1.4-4 illustrates the two basic ways in which demand curves can shift. When economists talk about an "increase in demand," they mean a *rightward* shift of the demand curve: at any given price, consumers demand a larger quantity of the good or service than before. This is shown in our figure by the rightward shift of the original demand curve D_1 to D_2. And when economists talk about a "decrease in demand," they mean a *leftward* shift of the demand curve: at any given price, consumers demand a smaller quantity of the good or service than before. This is shown by the leftward shift of the original demand curve D_1 to D_3.

FIGURE 1.4-4 Shifts of the Demand Curve

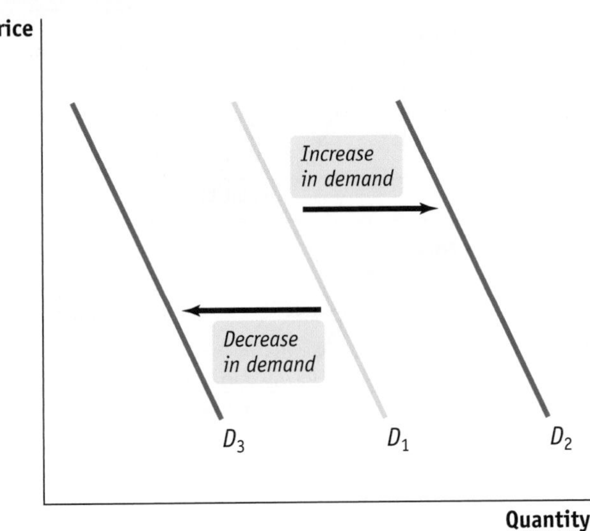

Any event that increases demand shifts the demand curve to the right, reflecting a rise in the quantity demanded at any given price. Any event that decreases demand shifts the demand curve to the left, reflecting a fall in the quantity demanded at any given price.

What caused the demand curve for lumber to shift? We have already mentioned reasons that include changes in tastes and income. If you think about it, you can come up with other things that would be likely to shift the demand curve for lumber. For example, suppose the price of house rentals rises. This will induce some people who were previously content renting to buy a new home instead, increasing the demand for lumber.

There are five principal factors that shift the demand curve for a good or service:

- Changes in tastes
- Changes in the prices of related goods or services
- Changes in income
- Changes in the number of consumers (buyers)
- Changes in expectations

Although this is not an exhaustive list, it contains the five most important factors that can shift demand curves. Changes in demand can generally be viewed as a change in one of these factors. When we say that the quantity of a good or service demanded falls as its price rises, *all other things being equal*, we are in fact stating that the factors that shift demand are remaining unchanged.

Table 1.4-1 gives an overview of the ways that these five factors can shift demand. Next, we explore in detail *how* these factors shift the demand curve.

> **AP® ECON TIP**
>
> The mnemonic *TRIBE* can help you remember the factors that shift demand. Demand is shifted by changes in . . . **T**astes, prices of **R**elated goods, **I**ncome, the number of **B**uyers, and **E**xpectations.

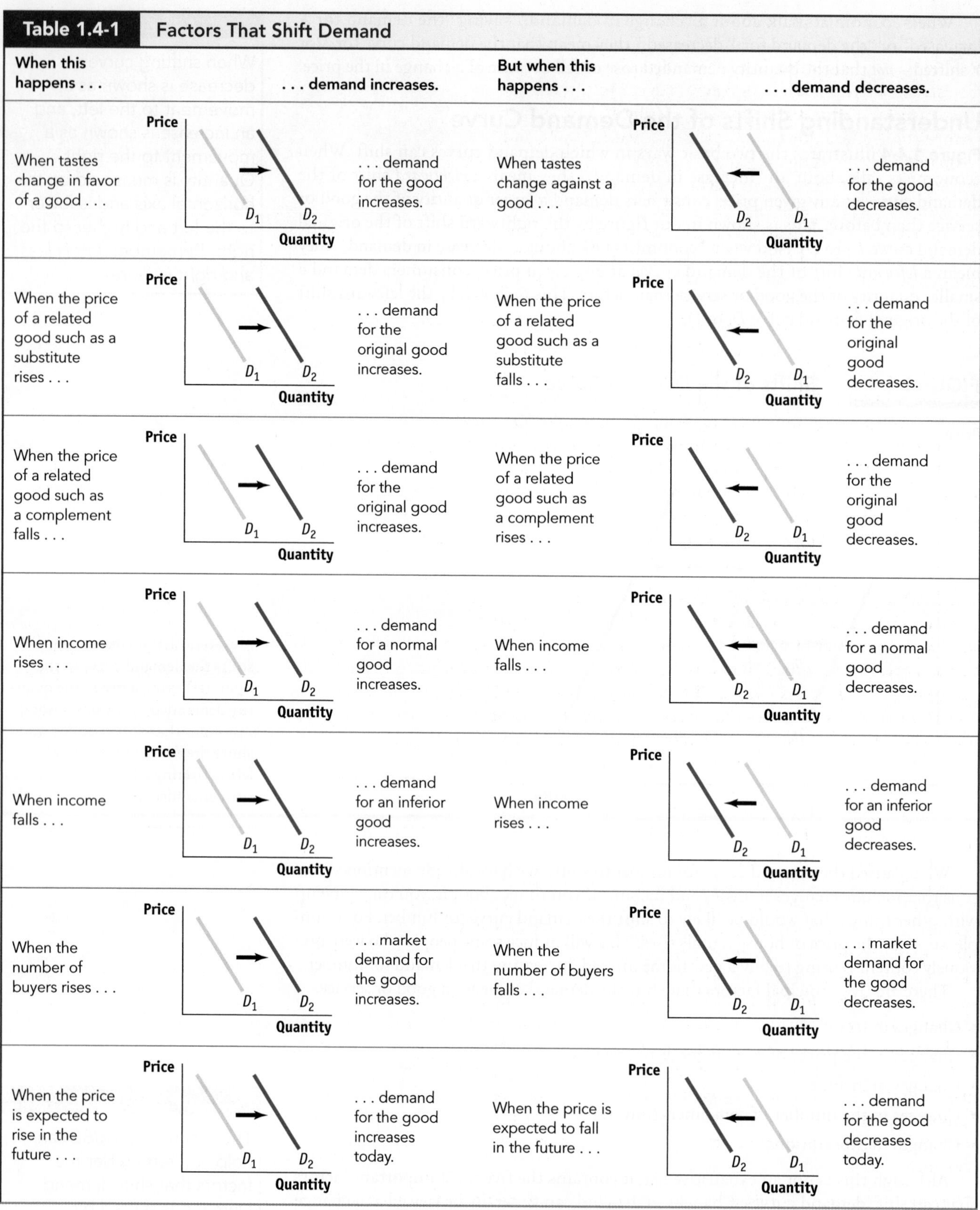

Table 1.4-1 Factors That Shift Demand

When this happens . . .	. . . demand increases.	But when this happens . . .	. . . demand decreases.
When tastes change in favor of a good . . .	. . . demand for the good increases.	When tastes change against a good . . .	. . . demand for the good decreases.
When the price of a related good such as a substitute rises . . .	. . . demand for the original good increases.	When the price of a related good such as a substitute falls . . .	. . . demand for the original good decreases.
When the price of a related good such as a complement falls . . .	. . . demand for the original good increases.	When the price of a related good such as a complement rises . . .	. . . demand for the original good decreases.
When income rises . . .	. . . demand for a normal good increases.	When income falls . . .	. . . demand for a normal good decreases.
When income falls . . .	. . . demand for an inferior good increases.	When income rises . . .	. . . demand for an inferior good decreases.
When the number of buyers rises . . .	. . . market demand for the good increases.	When the number of buyers falls . . .	. . . market demand for the good decreases.
When the price is expected to rise in the future . . .	. . . demand for the good increases today.	When the price is expected to fall in the future . . .	. . . demand for the good decreases today.

Changes in Tastes Why do people want what they want? Fortunately, we don't need to answer that question—we just need to acknowledge that people have certain preferences, or tastes, that determine what they choose to consume and that these tastes can change. Economists usually lump together changes in demand due to fads, beliefs, cultural shifts, and so on under the heading of changes in *tastes*.

Kar-Tr/Getty Images

Consider this recent example: In a press release in July 2020, the Centers for Disease Control and Prevention (CDC) recommended that Americans wear masks to prevent the spread of the COVID-19 virus. As a result, many people who did not previously own masks began purchasing and wearing them. Requirements that masks be worn in certain situations—for example, on airplanes and federal properties—followed. The result of the CDC recommendation and the mask requirements was a change in tastes and preferences that affected the demand for masks: Many people preferred to wear masks after the CDC announced that they could prevent the transmission of the COVID-19 virus and after they were required for important activities like travel and work.

Economists have little to say about the forces that influence consumers' tastes. (Marketers and advertisers, however, have plenty to say about them!) However, a *change* in tastes has a predictable impact on demand. When tastes change in favor of a good, more people want to buy it at any given price, so the demand curve shifts to the right. When tastes change against a good, fewer people want to buy it at any given price, so the demand curve shifts to the left.

Changes in the Prices of Related Goods or Services While there's nothing quite like a comfortable pair of all-cotton blue jeans, for some purposes khakis—typically made from polyester blends—aren't a bad alternative. Khakis are what economists call a *substitute* for jeans. A pair of goods are **substitutes** if a rise in the price of one good (jeans) makes consumers more willing to buy the other good (polyester-blend khakis). Substitutes are usually goods that in some way serve a similar function: coffee and tea, muffins and doughnuts, train rides and airplane rides, lumber and plastic composites. A rise in the price of the alternative good provides an incentive for some consumers to purchase the original good *instead* of the alternative good, shifting demand for the original good to the right. Likewise, when the price of the alternative good falls, some consumers switch from the original good to the alternative, shifting the demand curve for the original good to the left.

Two goods are **substitutes** if a rise in the price of one of the goods leads to an increase in the demand for the other good.

Two goods are **complements** if a rise in the price of one of the goods leads to a decrease in the demand for the other good.

But sometimes a fall in the price of one good makes consumers *more* willing to buy another good. Such pairs of goods are known as **complements**. Complements are goods that in some sense are consumed together: smartphones and apps, cookies and milk, cars and gasoline. Because consumers like to consume a good and its complement together, a change in the price of one of the goods will affect the demand for its complement. In particular, when the price of one good rises, the demand for its complement decreases, shifting the demand curve for the complement to the left. So a rise in the price of cookies is likely to cause a leftward shift in the demand curve for milk, as people consume fewer snacks of cookies and milk. Likewise, when the price of one good falls, the demand for its complement increases, shifting the demand curve for the complement to the right. This means that if, for some reason, the price of cookies falls, we should see a rightward shift in the demand curve for milk, as people consume more cookies *and* more milk.

Felix Choo/Alamy

Changes in Income Limited income is a constraint on consumers' purchasing decisions. When individuals have more income, they are normally more likely to purchase a good or service at any given price. For example, if a family's income rises, it is more likely to take that summer trip to Disney World—and therefore also more likely to buy plane tickets. So a rise in consumer incomes will cause the demand curves for most goods to shift to the right.

When a rise in income increases the demand for a good—the normal case—it is a **normal good**. When a rise in income decreases the demand for a good, it is an **inferior good**.

Why do we say "most goods," rather than "all goods"? Most goods are **normal goods** – the demand for them increases when consumer incomes rise. However, the demand for some goods decreases when incomes rise – these goods are known as **inferior goods**. Usually an inferior good is one that is considered less desirable than more expensive alternatives – such as a bus ride versus a taxi ride. When they can afford to, people stop buying an inferior good and switch their consumption to the preferred, more expensive alternative. So when a good is inferior, a rise in income shifts the demand curve to the left. And, not surprisingly, a fall in income shifts the demand curve to the right.

Consider the difference between so-called casual-dining restaurants such as Applebee's and Olive Garden and fast-food chains such as McDonald's and KFC. When their incomes rise, Americans tend to eat out more at casual-dining restaurants. However, some of this increased dining out comes at the expense of fast-food venues – to some extent, people visit McDonald's less once they can afford to move upscale. So casual dining is a normal good, while fast food appears to be an inferior good.

Changes in the Number of Consumers (Buyers) A growing world population increases the demand for most things, including fast food, clothing, and lumber. With more people needing housing and furniture, the overall demand for lumber rises and the lumber demand curve shifts to the right, even if each individual's demand for lumber remains unchanged. How the number of consumers affects the market demand curve is described in detail shortly.

Changes in Expectations When consumers have some choice about when to make a purchase, current demand for a good or service is often affected by expectations about its future price. For example, savvy shoppers often wait for seasonal sales – say, buying next year's holiday gifts during the post-holiday markdowns. In this case, expectations of a future drop in price lead to a decrease in demand today. Alternatively, expectations of a future rise in price are likely to cause an increase in demand today. For example, if you heard that the price of jeans would increase next year, you might go out and buy an extra pair now.

Changes in expectations about future income can also lead to changes in demand. If you learned today that you would inherit a large sum of money sometime in the future, you might borrow some money today and increase your demand for certain goods. Maybe you would buy more electronics, jewelry, or sports equipment. On the other hand, if you learned that you would earn less in the future than you thought, you might reduce your demand for those goods and save more money today. *Consumption smoothing* of this type shifts your demand curves for those goods to the right when your expected future income increases, and to the left when your expected future income decreases. Your own demand curves for goods and services are known as *individual demand curves*, which we'll explore next.

Individual Versus Market Demand Curves

We have discussed both the demand of individuals and the market demand for various goods. Now let's distinguish between an *individual demand curve*, which shows the relationship between quantity demanded and price for an individual consumer, and a market demand curve, which shows the combined demand by all consumers. Suppose that Darla is a consumer of blue jeans. Also suppose that all blue jeans are the same, so they sell for the same price. Panel (a) of **Figure 1.4-5** shows how many pairs of jeans she will buy per year at any given price per pair. Then D_{Darla} is Darla's individual demand curve.

The *market demand curve* shows how the combined quantity demanded by all consumers depends on the market price of that good. (Most of the time, when economists refer to the demand curve, they mean the market demand curve.) The market demand curve is the *horizontal sum* of the individual demand curves of all consumers in that market. To see what we mean by the term *horizontal sum*, assume for a moment that there are only two consumers of blue jeans, Darla and Dino. Dino's individual

FIGURE 1.4-5 Individual Demand Curves and the Market Demand Curve

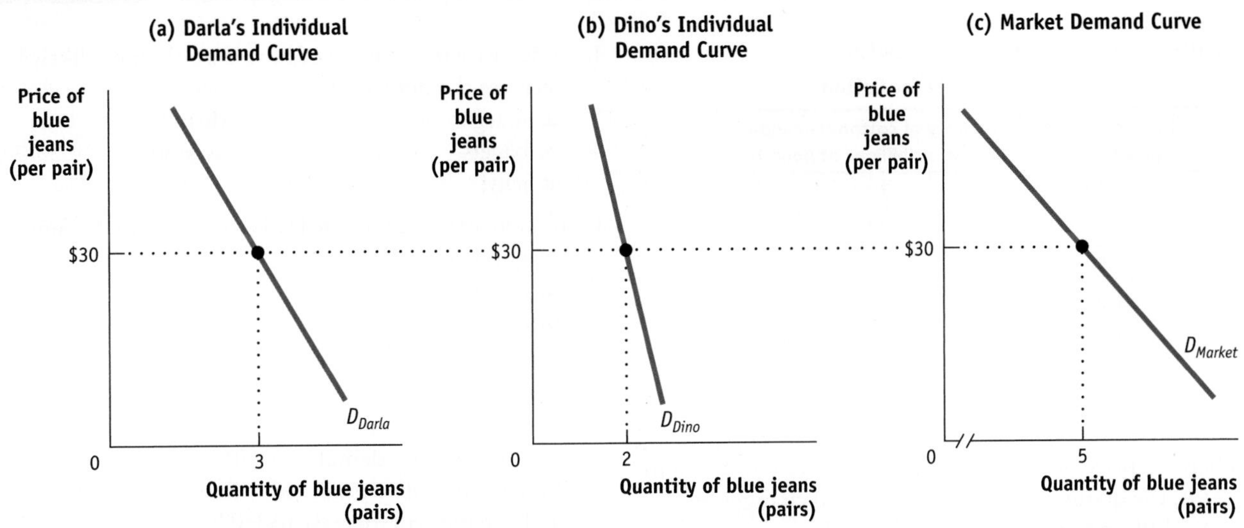

Darla and Dino are the only two consumers of blue jeans in the market. Panel (a) shows Darla's individual demand curve: the number of pairs of jeans she will buy per year at any given price. Panel (b) shows Dino's individual demand curve. Given that Darla and Dino are the only two consumers, the *market demand curve*, which shows the quantity of blue jeans demanded by all consumers at any given price, is shown in panel (c). The market demand curve is the *horizontal sum* of the individual demand curves of all consumers. In this case, at any given price, the quantity demanded by the market is the sum of the quantities demanded by Darla and Dino.

demand curve, D_{Dino}, is shown in panel (b). Panel (c) shows the market demand curve. At any given price, the quantity demanded by the market is the sum of the quantities demanded by Darla and Dino. For example, at a price of $30 per pair, Darla demands three pairs of jeans per year and Dino demands two pairs per year. So the quantity demanded by the market is five pairs per year.

Clearly, the quantity demanded by the market at any given price is larger with Dino present than it would be if Darla were the only consumer. The quantity demanded at any given price would be even larger if we added a third consumer, then a fourth, and so on. So an increase in the number of consumers leads to an increase in demand.

Adventures in AP® Economics
Watch the video:
Demand

Module 1.4 Review

Check Your Understanding

1. Explain whether each of the following events represents (i) a *change in* demand (a *shift* of the demand curve) or (ii) a *movement along* the demand curve (a *change in the quantity demanded*).
   a. A store owner finds that customers are willing to pay more for umbrellas on rainy days.
   b. When XYZ Mobile, a cellular plan provider, offered reduced rates on data charges, its volume data usage by users increased sharply.
   c. People buy more long-stem roses the week of Valentine's Day, even though the prices are higher than at other times during the year.
   d. A sharp rise in the price of gasoline leads many commuters to join carpools in order to reduce their gasoline purchases.

Tackle the AP® Test: Multiple-Choice Questions

Refer to the table to answer Questions 1 and 2.

Demand Schedule for Cotton

Price of cotton (per pound)	Quantity of cotton demanded in Year A (billions of pounds)
$2.00	7.1
1.75	7.5
1.50	8.1
1.25	8.9
1.00	10.0
0.75	11.5
0.50	14.2

1. When the price of cotton changes from $1.50 to $1.25 in Year A, the quantity of cotton demanded changes by
   a. 9.7 billion pounds.
   b. 8.1 billion pounds.
   c. 1.1 billion pounds.
   d. 1 billion pounds.
   e. 0.8 billion pounds.

2. The data provided in the table show that the relationship between price and the quantity demanded is
   a. positive.
   b. negative.
   c. direct.
   d. unclear.
   e. weak.

3. An increase in demand for a normal good would result from a decrease in
   a. price.
   b. income.
   c. the price of a substitute.
   d. consumer taste for a good.
   e. the price of a complement.

4. A decrease in the price of butter would most likely decrease the demand for
   a. margarine.
   b. bagels.
   c. jelly.
   d. milk.
   e. syrup.

5. If an increase in income leads to a decrease in demand, the good is
   a. a complement.
   b. a substitute.
   c. inferior.
   d. abnormal.
   e. normal.

6. Which of the following will occur if consumers expect the price of a good to fall in the coming months?
   a. The quantity demanded will rise today.
   b. The quantity demanded will remain the same today.
   c. Demand will increase today.
   d. Demand will decrease today.
   e. No change will occur today.

7. Which of the following will increase the demand for disposable diapers?
   a. a new "baby boom"
   b. concern over the environmental effect of landfills
   c. a decrease in the price of cloth diapers
   d. a move toward earlier potty training of children
   e. a decrease in the price of disposable diapers

Tackle the AP® Test: Free-Response Questions

1. Create a table with two hypothetical prices for a good and two corresponding quantities demanded. Choose the prices and quantities so that they illustrate the law of demand. Using your data, draw a correctly labeled graph showing the demand curve for the good. Using the same graph, illustrate an increase in demand for the good.

Rubric for FRQ 1 (5 points)

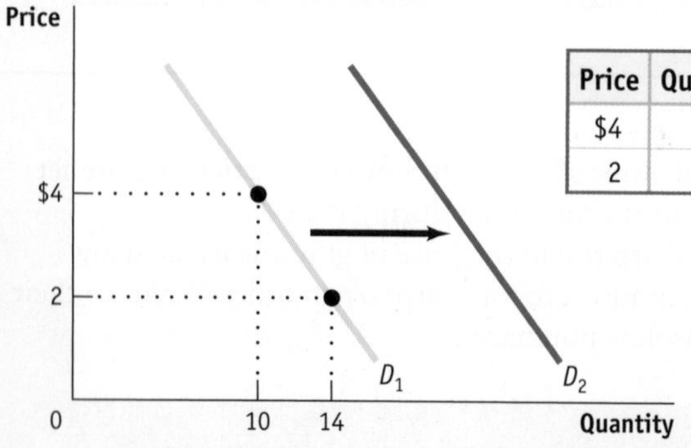

Price	Quantity
$4	10
2	14

1 point: Table with data labeled "Price" (or "P") and "Quantity" (or "Q")

1 point: Values in the table show a negative relationship between P and Q

1 point: Graph with "Price" on the vertical axis and "Quantity" on the horizontal axis and negatively sloped curve labeled "Demand" or "D"

1 point: Demand curve correctly plots the data from the table

1 point: A second demand curve (with a label such as D_2) shown to the right of the original demand curve

2. Draw a correctly labeled graph showing the demand for apples. On your graph, illustrate what happens to the demand for apples if
   i. a new report from the Surgeon General finds that an apple a day really *does* keep the doctor away.
   ii. The price of oranges, a substitute for apples, increases. Explain. **(5 points)**

Supply

In this Module, you will learn to:

- Draw a supply curve and interpret its meaning
- Define the law of supply and explain the relationship between the price of a good or service and the quantity supplied
- Contrast the difference between movements along the supply curve with changes in supply
- Explain the determinants of supply

The Supply Curve

Some parts of the world are especially well suited to growing hardwood trees for lumber production, and the United States is among them. But even in the United States, some land is better suited to growing hardwood trees than other land. Whether American tree farmers restrict their tree growing to only the most ideal locations or expand it to less suitable land depends on the price they expect to get for their logs, which depends on the price sawmills can get for their lumber. Moreover, there are many other areas in the world where hardwood trees could be grown – such as China, Canada, and Germany. The number of hardwood trees actually grown and harvested in those places depends, again, on the price.

Blink Photo/Alamy Stock Photo

So just as the quantity of lumber that consumers want to buy depends on the price they have to pay, the quantity that producers are willing to produce and sell – the **quantity supplied** – depends on the price they are offered.

The Supply Schedule and the Supply Curve

The table in **Figure 1.5-1** shows how the quantity of lumber made available varies with the price – that is, it shows a hypothetical **supply schedule** for lumber.

A supply schedule works the same way as the demand schedule. In the case presented in Figure 1.5-1, the table shows the number of board feet of lumber sawmills are willing to sell at different prices. At a price of $0.50 per board foot, sawmills are willing to sell only 80 billion board feet of lumber per year. At $0.75 per board foot, they're willing to sell 91 billion board feet. At $1, they're willing to sell 100 billion board feet, and so on.

In the same way that a demand schedule can be represented graphically by a demand curve, a supply schedule can be represented by a **supply curve**, as shown in Figure 1.5-1. Each point on the curve represents an entry from the table.

Suppose that the price of lumber rises from $1 to $1.25; we can see that the quantity of lumber sawmills are willing to sell rises from 100 billion to 107 billion board feet. This is the normal situation for a supply curve: a higher price leads to a higher quantity supplied. Some economists refer to this positive relationship as the **law of supply**. So just as demand curves normally slope downward, supply curves normally slope upward: the higher the price being offered, the more of any good or service producers will be willing to sell.

As we found in Module 1.4, there is a distinction between *demand* and *quantity demanded*, such that it would be correct to say that an increase in the price of lumber

The **quantity supplied** is the actual amount of a good or service people are willing to sell at some specific price.

A **supply schedule** shows how much of a good or service producers would supply at different prices.

A **supply curve** shows the relationship between the quantity supplied and the price.

The **law of supply** says that, other things being equal, the price and quantity supplied of a good are positively related.

FIGURE 1.5-1 The Supply Schedule and the Supply Curve

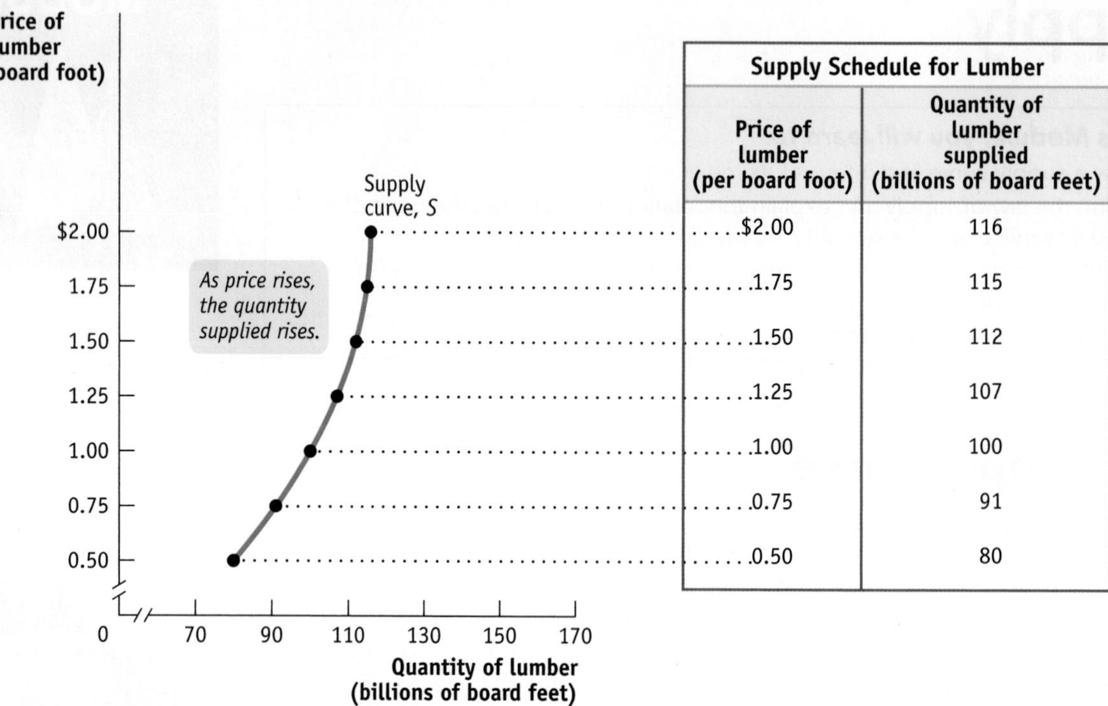

Supply Schedule for Lumber	
Price of lumber (per board foot)	Quantity of lumber supplied (billions of board feet)
$2.00	116
1.75	115
1.50	112
1.25	107
1.00	100
0.75	91
0.50	80

The supply schedule for lumber is plotted to yield the corresponding supply curve, which shows how much lumber producers are willing to sell at any given price. The supply curve and the supply schedule reflect the fact that supply curves are usually upward-sloping: the quantity supplied rises when the price rises.

decreases the *quantity of lumber demanded*, but it would be incorrect to say that an increase in the price of lumber decreases the *demand for lumber*. Similarly, a price change causes a change in the quantity supplied, shown by a movement along the supply curve. However, when something other than price causes supply to change, it is shown as a shift of the supply curve. Changes in factors other than price decrease (or increase) the supply of lumber.

Also note that a change in demand does not affect supply (either the supply schedule or the supply curve). And a change in supply does not affect demand (either the demand schedule or the demand curve). However, if a change in demand causes a change in price, it will affect the quantity supplied by causing a movement along the supply curve. And if a change in supply causes a change in price, it will affect the quantity demanded by causing a movement along the demand curve.

Sviatlana Lazarenka/Getty Images

Lumber production isn't what it used to be. Advancements in sawmill technology helped to keep lumber prices low for decades.

Shifts of the Supply Curve

For many decades following World War II, lumber remained relatively cheap. One reason is that the number of trees harvested for lumber production increased. Another factor accounting for lumber's relative cheapness was advances in sawmill technology, including the advent of the portable chainsaw

FIGURE 1.5-2 An Increase in Supply

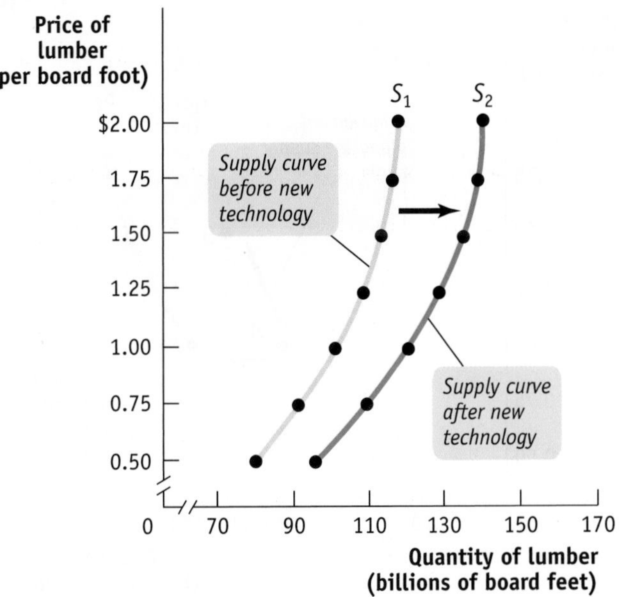

Supply Schedules for Lumber		
Price of lumber (per board foot)	Quantity of lumber supplied (billions of board feet)	
	Before new technology	After new technology
$2.00	116	139
1.75	115	138
1.50	112	134
1.25	107	128
1.00	100	120
0.75	91	109
0.50	80	96

The adoption of improved sawmill technology generated an increase in supply—a rise in the quantity supplied at any given price. This event is represented by the two supply schedules—one showing supply before the new technology was adopted (S_1), the other showing supply after the new technology was adopted (S_2)—and their corresponding supply curves. The increase in supply shifts the supply curve to the right.

and the automation of many formerly difficult and dangerous sawing processes. **Figure 1.5-2** illustrates how these events affected the supply schedule and the supply curve for lumber.

The table in Figure 1.5-2 shows two supply schedules. The schedule for before improved sawmill technology was adopted is the same one as in Figure 1.5-1. The second schedule shows the supply of lumber *after* the improved technology was adopted. When technology or anything else changes the quantity supplied at each price, this change in the supply schedule constitutes a **change in supply** and is illustrated by a shift in the supply curve. Figure 1.5-2 shows the shift of the supply curve from S_1, its position before the adoption of new sawmill technology, to S_2, its position after the adoption of new sawmill technology. Notice that S_2 lies to the right of S_1, reflecting the fact that the quantity supplied rises at any given price.

As in the analysis of demand, it's crucial to draw a distinction between such changes in supply and **movements along the supply curve**—changes in the quantity supplied arising from a change in price. We can see this difference in **Figure 1.5-3**. The movement from point *A* to point *B* is a movement along the supply curve: the quantity supplied rises along S_1 due to a rise in price. Here, a rise in price from $1 to $1.50 leads to a rise in the quantity supplied from 100 billion to 110.2 billion board feet of lumber. But the quantity supplied can also rise when the price is unchanged if there is an increase in supply—a rightward shift of the supply curve. This is shown by the rightward shift of the supply curve from S_1 to S_2. Holding the price constant at $1, the quantity supplied rises from 100 billion board feet at point *A* on S_1 to 120 billion board feet at point *C* on S_2.

Next, we discuss the determinants of supply—the factors that can cause a change in supply.

AP® ECON TIP

A change in supply is shown by a shift of the curve, indicating a change in the quantity supplied at every price. Remember, *left is less and right is more.* But looks can be deceiving. When supply decreases, the supply curve shifts to the left—which is up, not down. When supply increases, the supply curve shifts to the right—which is down, not up. Always think "right" and "left" (not "up" and "down") when shifting supply and demand curves.

A **change in supply** is a shift of the supply curve, which indicates a change in the quantity supplied at any given price.

A **movement along the supply curve** is a change in the quantity supplied of a good arising from a change in the good's price.

FIGURE 1.5-3 A Movement Along the Supply Curve Versus a Shift of the Supply Curve

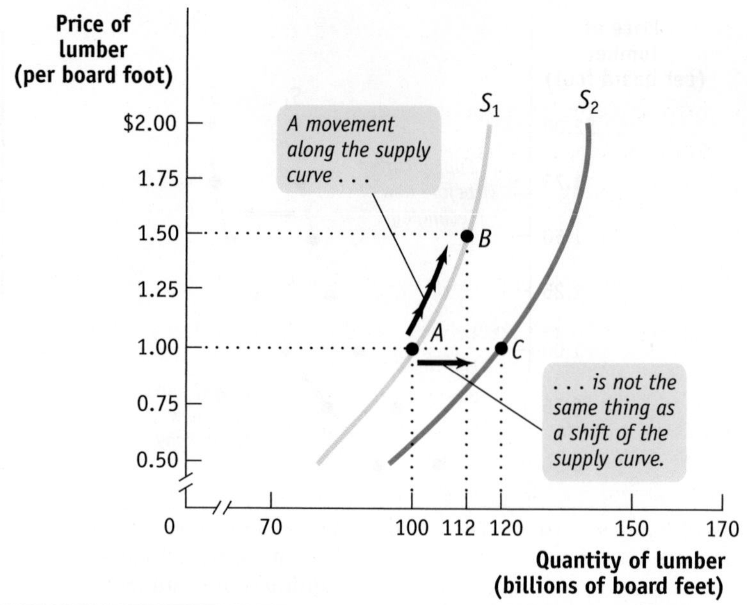

The increase in quantity supplied when going from point *A* to point *B* reflects a movement along the supply curve: it is the result of a rise in the price of the good. The increase in quantity supplied when going from point *A* to point *C* reflects a shift of the supply curve from S_1 to S_2: it is the result of an increase in the quantity supplied at any given price.

Understanding Shifts of the Supply Curve

Figure 1.5-4 illustrates the two basic ways in which supply curves can shift. When economists talk about an "increase in supply," they mean a *rightward* shift of the supply curve: at any given price, producers supply a larger quantity of the good than before. This is shown in Figure 1.5-4 by the rightward shift of the original supply curve S_1 to S_2. And when economists talk about a "decrease in supply," they mean a *leftward* shift of the supply curve: at any given price, producers supply a smaller quantity of the good than before. This is represented by the leftward shift of S_1 to S_3.

FIGURE 1.5-4 Shifts of the Supply Curve

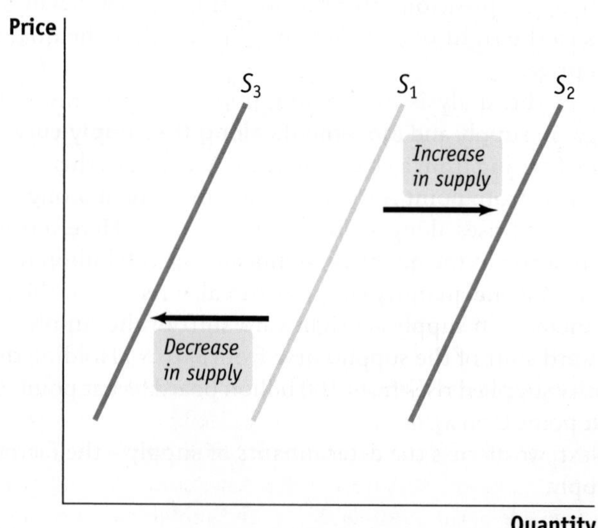

Any event that increases supply shifts the supply curve to the right, reflecting a rise in the quantity supplied at any given price. Any event that decreases supply shifts the supply curve to the left, reflecting a fall in the quantity supplied at any given price.

Shifts of the supply curve for a good or service are typically the result of a change in one of five determinants of supply (though, as in the case of demand, there are other possible causes):

- input prices
- the prices of related goods or services
- producer expectations
- the number of producers
- technology

Table 1.5-1 provides an overview of the factors that shift supply.

Changes in Input Prices To produce output, you need *inputs*. An **input** is any good or service used to produce another good or service. For example, to make vanilla ice cream, you need vanilla beans, cream, sugar, and so on. Inputs, like outputs, have prices. And an increase in the price of an input makes the production of the final good more costly for those who produce and sell it. So producers are less willing to supply the final good at any given price, and the supply curve shifts to the left. For example, when lumber prices surged in 2021, construction companies began cutting back on new projects. Similarly, a fall in the price of an input makes the production of the final good less costly for sellers. They are more willing to supply the good at any given price, and the supply curve shifts to the right.

Changes in the Prices of Related Goods or Services A single producer often produces a mix of goods rather than a single product. For example, an oil refinery produces gasoline from crude oil, but it also produces heating oil and other products from the same raw material. When a producer sells several products, the quantity of any one good it is willing to supply at any given price depends on the prices of its other co-produced goods.

How a price change for one of the goods affects the supply of a related good depends on the relationship between the goods. When a producer can use the same inputs to make either one good or the other, the two goods are **substitutes in production**. For such goods, an increase in the price of one good creates an incentive for the producer to use more inputs to produce the good whose price has risen and to supply less of the other good. For example, when the price of heating oil rises, an oil refiner will use more crude oil to make heating oil and supply less gasoline at any given price, shifting the supply curve for gasoline to the left. When the price of heating oil falls, the oil refiner will supply more gasoline at any given price, shifting the supply curve for gasoline to the right.

When two goods are jointly produced, meaning that increased production of either of the goods creates more of the other good, the two goods are **complements in production**. For example, producers of crude oil – oil-well drillers – find that oil wells often produce natural gas as a by-product of oil extraction. The higher the price of natural gas, the more oil wells it will drill to produce natural gas along with oil, so the more oil it will supply at any given price for oil. As a result, natural gas is a complement in production for crude oil.

Changes in Producer Expectations Just as changes in consumer expectations can shift the demand curve, they can also shift the supply curve. When suppliers have some choice about when they put their good up for sale, changes in the expected future price of the good can lead a supplier to supply less or more of the good today.

For example, gasoline and other oil products are often stored for significant periods of time at oil refineries before being sold to consumers. In fact, storage is normally part of producers' business strategy. Knowing that the demand for gasoline peaks in the summer, oil refiners normally reserve some of their gasoline produced during the spring for sale in the summer. Similarly, knowing that the demand for heating oil peaks in the winter, they normally reserve some of their heating oil produced during the fall

AP® ECON TIP

A price change causes a change in the quantity supplied, shown by a movement along the supply curve. When a nonprice determinant of supply changes, this changes supply and therefore shifts the supply curve. It is correct to say that an increase in the price of lumber increases the *quantity of lumber supplied*; it is incorrect to say that an increase in the price of lumber increases the *supply of lumber*.

An **input** is a good or service that is used to produce another good or service.

Two goods are **substitutes in production** if producers can use the same inputs to make either one good or the other.

Two goods are **complements in production** if increased production of either good creates more of the other.

AP® ECON TIP

The mnemonic *I-RENT* can help you remember the factors that shift supply. Supply is shifted by changes in . . . **I**nput (resource) prices, prices of **R**elated goods and services, producer **E**xpectations, the **N**umber of producers, and **T**echnology.

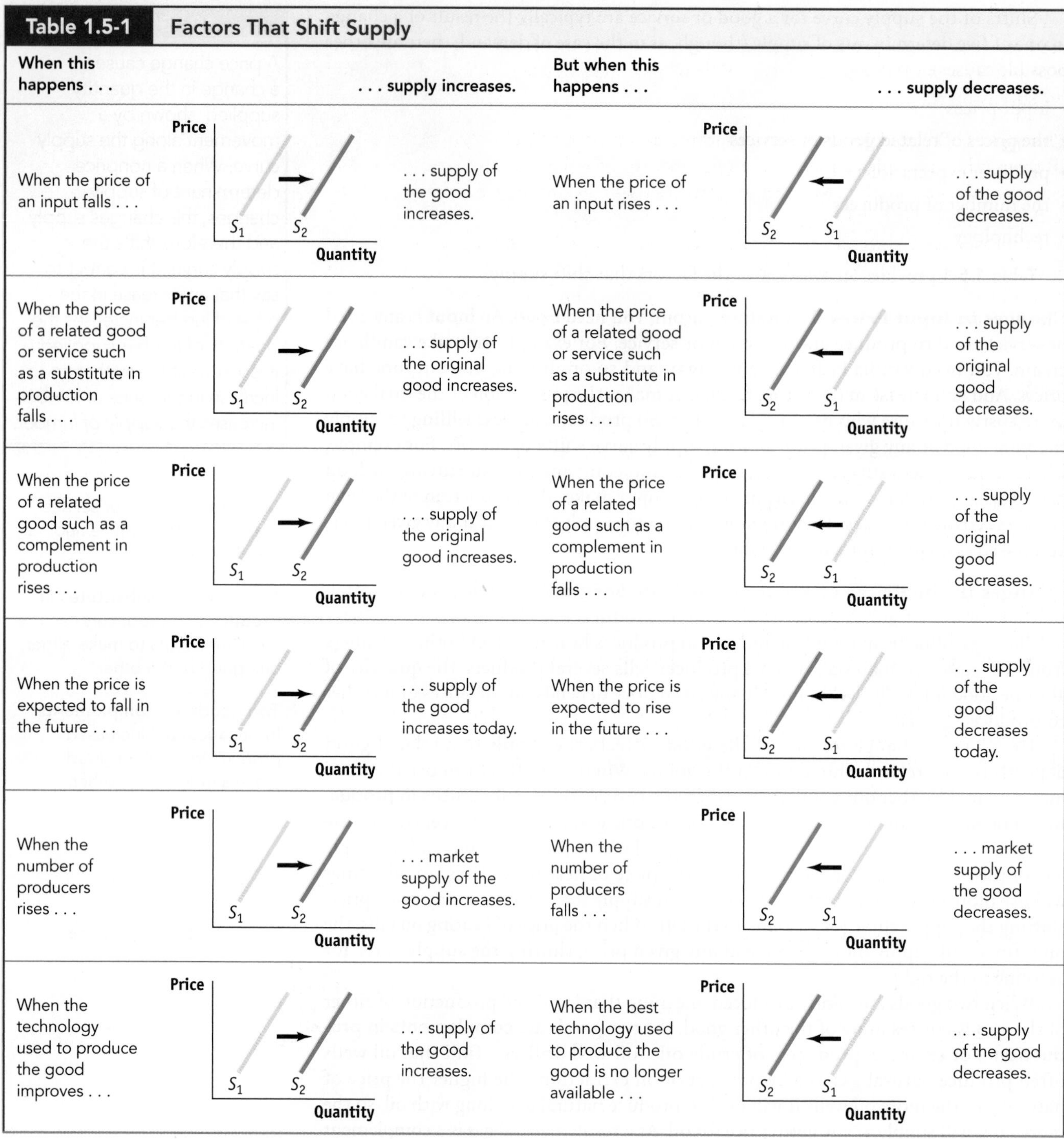

Table 1.5-1 Factors That Shift Supply

When this happens . . .	. . . supply increases.	But when this happens . . .	. . . supply decreases.
When the price of an input falls . . .	. . . supply of the good increases.	When the price of an input rises . . .	. . . supply of the good decreases.
When the price of a related good or service such as a substitute in production falls . . .	. . . supply of the original good increases.	When the price of a related good or service such as a substitute in production rises . . .	. . . supply of the original good decreases.
When the price of a related good such as a complement in production rises . . .	. . . supply of the original good increases.	When the price of a related good such as a complement in production falls . . .	. . . supply of the original good decreases.
When the price is expected to fall in the future . . .	. . . supply of the good increases today.	When the price is expected to rise in the future . . .	. . . supply of the good decreases today.
When the number of producers rises . . .	. . . market supply of the good increases.	When the number of producers falls . . .	. . . market supply of the good decreases.
When the technology used to produce the good improves . . .	. . . supply of the good increases.	When the best technology used to produce the good is no longer available . . .	. . . supply of the good decreases.

for sale in the winter. In each case, producers make a decision of when to sell a given product based on a comparison of the current price versus the expected future price. This example illustrates how changes in expectations can alter supply: an increase in the anticipated future price of a good or service reduces supply today, a leftward shift of the supply curve. Similarly, a fall in the anticipated future price increases supply today, a rightward shift of the supply curve.

Changes in the Number of Producers Just as a change in the number of consumers affects the demand curve, a change in the number of producers affects the supply curve. A market with many producers will supply a larger quantity of a good than a market with a single producer, all other things equal. For example, when the patent runs out on a profitable pharmaceutical drug, new suppliers can enter the market and the supply increases.

Changes in Technology When economists talk about "technology," they mean all the methods people can use to turn inputs into useful goods and services. In that sense, the whole complex sequence of activities that turn lumber from harvested and milled in Canada into the shelves in your closet is technology.

Improvements in technology enable producers to spend less on inputs yet still produce the same output. When a better technology becomes available, reducing the cost of production, supply increases, and the supply curve shifts to the right. As we have already mentioned, improved technology enabled sawmills to keep lumber prices low for decades, even as worldwide demand grew.

Individual Versus Market Supply Curves

Now that we have introduced the market supply curve, let's examine how it relates to a producer's *individual supply curve*. Look at panel (a) in **Figure 1.5-5**. The individual supply curve shows the relationship between quantity supplied and price for an individual producer. For example, suppose that Mr. Silva owns a sawmill in Brazil and that panel (a) of Figure 1.5-5 shows how many board feet of lumber he will supply per year at any given price. Then S_{Silva} is his individual supply curve.

The *market supply curve* shows how the combined total quantity supplied by all individual producers in the market depends on the market price of that good. Just as the market demand curve is the horizontal sum of the individual demand curves of all consumers, the market supply curve is the horizontal sum of the individual supply curves of all producers. Assume for a moment that there are only two producers of lumber, Mr. Silva and Ms. Liu, who operates a sawmill in China. Ms. Liu's individual supply curve is shown in panel (b). Panel (c) shows the market supply curve. At any given price, the quantity supplied to the market is the sum of the quantities supplied

FIGURE 1.5-5 Individual Supply Curves and the Market Supply Curve

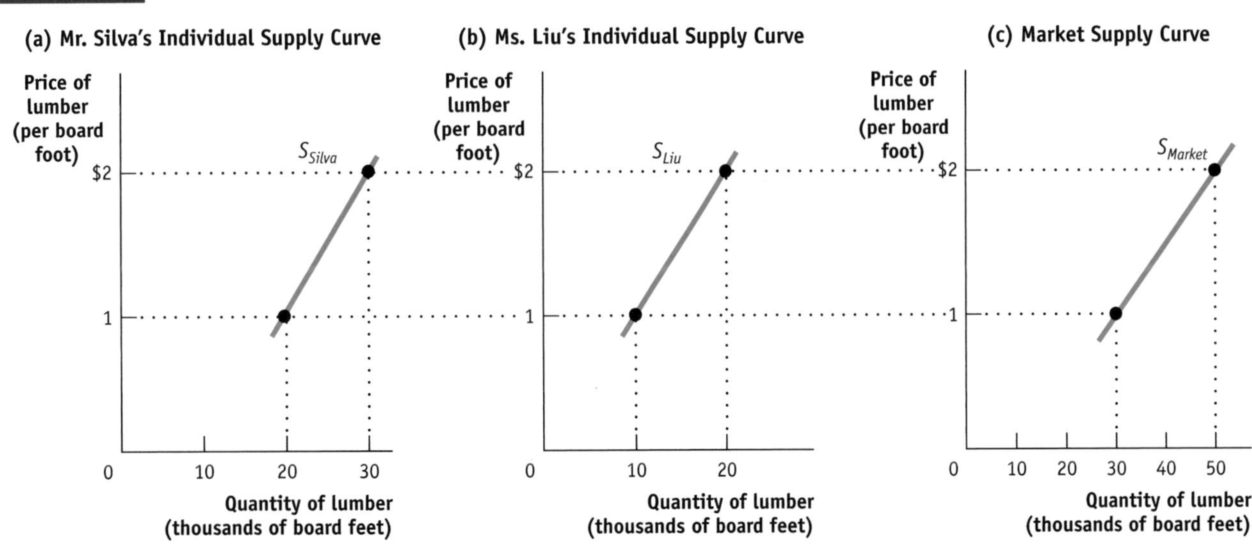

Panel (a) shows the individual supply curve for Mr. Silva, S_{Silva}, which indicates the quantity of lumber he will sell at any given price. Panel (b) shows the individual supply curve for Ms. Liu, S_{Liu}. The *market supply curve*, which shows the quantity of lumber supplied by all producers at any given price, is in panel (c). The market supply curve is the *horizontal sum* of the individual supply curves of all producers.

by Mr. Silva and Ms. Liu. For example, at a price of $2 per board foot, Mr. Silva supplies 30,000 board feet of lumber per year and Ms. Liu supplies 20,000 board feet per year, making the quantity supplied to the market 50,000 board feet.

Clearly, the quantity supplied to the market at any given price is larger with Ms. Liu present than it would be if Mr. Silva were the only supplier. The quantity supplied at a given price would be even larger if we added a third producer, then a fourth, and so on. So an increase in the number of producers leads to an increase in supply and a rightward shift of the supply curve.

Watch the video: ***Supply***

Module 1.5 Review

Check Your Understanding

1. Explain whether each of the following events represents (i) a *change in* supply (a *shift* in the supply curve) or (ii) a *movement along* the supply curve (a *change in the quantity supplied*).
   a. During a real estate boom that causes home prices to rise, more homeowners put their homes up for sale.
   b. Many strawberry farmers open temporary roadside stands during harvest season, even though prices are usually low at that time.
   c. Immediately after the school year begins, fewer young people are available to work. Fast-food chains must raise wages, which represent the price of labor, to attract workers.
   d. Many construction workers temporarily move to areas that have suffered hurricane damage, lured by higher wages.
   e. Since new technologies have made it possible to build larger cruise ships (which are cheaper to run per passenger), Caribbean cruise lines have offered more cabins, at lower prices, than before.
2. After each of the following events, will the supply curve for the good that is mentioned shift to the left, shift to the right, or remain unchanged?
   a. The coffee berry borer beetle destroys large quantities of coffee berries.
   b. Consumers demand more bike helmets than ever.
   c. The number of tea producers increases.
   d. The price of leather, an input in wallet production, increases.

Tackle the AP® Test: Multiple-Choice Questions

1. The law of supply states that the relationship between price and quantity supplied is
   a. positive.
   b. negative.
   c. indirect.
   d. unclear.
   e. weak.
2. Because the market supply curve is the sum of individual producers' supply curves, an increase in the number of producers will cause which of the following?
   a. the supply curve to shift to the left
   b. the supply curve to shift to the right
   c. a movement to the right along the supply curve
   d. a movement to the left along the supply curve
   e. the supply to decrease
3. Which of the following will decrease the supply of rice?
   a. There is a technological advance that affects the production of *all* goods.
   b. The price of rice falls.
   c. The price of corn (which consumers regard as a substitute for rice) decreases.
   d. The wages of workers producing rice increase.
   e. The demand for rice decreases.
4. An increase in the demand for steak, which increases the price of steak, will lead to an increase in which of the following?
   a. the supply of steak
   b. the supply of hamburger (a substitute in production)
   c. the supply of chicken (a substitute in consumption)
   d. the supply of leather (a complement in production)
   e. the demand for leather

5. A technological advance in textbook production will lead to which of the following?
   a. a decrease in textbook supply
   b. an increase in textbook demand
   c. an increase in textbook supply
   d. a movement along the supply curve for textbooks
   e. an increase in textbook prices

6. Expectations among hiking-boot makers that boot prices will rise significantly in the future will lead to which of the following now?
   a. an increase in boot supply
   b. no change in boot supply
   c. a decrease in boot supply
   d. a movement to the left along the boot supply curve
   e. a movement to the right along the boot supply curve

7. Starch from the stalks of potato plants is used to make packing peanuts, a complement in production. A decrease in potato demand that lowers potato prices will cause which of the following in the packing-peanut market?
   a. an increase in supply and no change in demand
   b. an increase in supply and a decrease in demand
   c. a decrease in both demand and supply
   d. a decrease in supply and no change in demand
   e. a decrease in supply and an increase in demand

Tackle the AP® Test: Free-Response Questions

1. Tesla Motors makes sports cars powered by lithium batteries.
   a. Draw a correctly labeled graph showing a hypothetical supply curve for Tesla sports cars.
   b. On the same graph, show the effect of a major new discovery of lithium that lowers the price of lithium. Explain.
   c. Suppose Tesla Motors expects to be able to sell its cars for a higher price next month. Explain the effect that will have on the supply of Tesla cars this month.

Rubric for FRQ 1 (5 points)

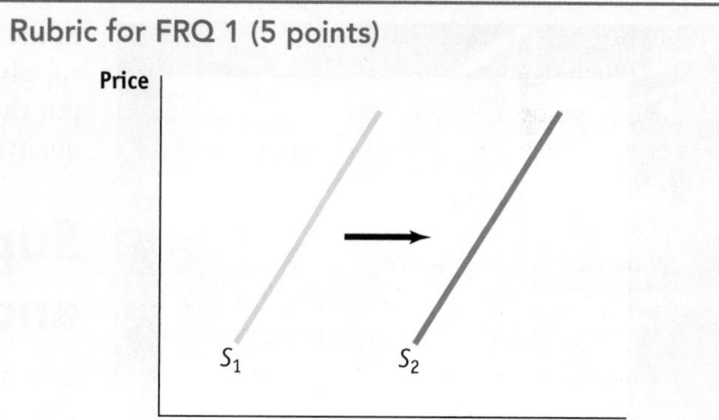

1 point: Graph with "Price" or "*P*" on the vertical axis and "Quantity" or "*Q*" on the horizontal axis

1 point: A positively sloped curve labeled "Supply" or "*S*"

1 point: A second supply curve shown to the right of the original supply curve with a label such as S_2, indicating that it is the new supply curve

1 point: Lithium is an input into the production of Tesla cars. A decrease in the price of lithium will increase the supply of Tesla cars.

1 point: Correct explanation that the expectation of higher prices next month would lead to a decrease in the supply of Tesla cars this month because the company will want to sell more of its cars when the price is higher

2. Suppose AP® Economics students at your school offer tutoring services to students in regular economics courses.
   a. Draw a correctly labeled graph showing the supply curve for tutoring services measured in hours. Label the supply curve "S_1."
   b. Suppose the wage paid for babysitting, an alternative activity for AP® Economics students, increases. Explain how the wage increase affects the supply of tutoring. Show the effect of this wage increase on the graph you drew for part a. Label the new supply curve "S_2."
   c. Suppose instead that the number of AP® Economics students increases. Explain how the change in the number of AP® Economics students affects the supply of tutoring. Show the effect of this increase in AP® Economics students on the same graph you drew for parts a and b. Label the new supply curve "S_3." **(5 points)**

MODULE 1.6

Market Equilibrium, Disequilibrium, and Changes in Equilibrium

In this Module, you will learn to:
- Define market equilibrium and identify it on a supply and demand graph
- Explain how the equilibrium price and quantity are determined
- Define and calculate a market surplus and a market shortage
- Explain how prices adjust to restore equilibrium
- Explain how changes in demand or supply affect equilibrium price and equilibrium quantity

Roberto Machado Noa/Getty Images

Over time, competitive markets, like grocery lines, settle into equilibrium.

In the previous two Modules, we learned about the demand curve, the supply curve, and the set of factors that shift each curve. We can now put these elements together to show how they determine the price and quantity sold in the market for a good or service.

Supply, Demand, and Equilibrium

In competitive markets, the forces of supply and demand tend to move price and quantity toward what economists call *equilibrium*. An economic situation is in **equilibrium** when no individual would be better off doing something different. Imagine a busy afternoon at your local supermarket; there are long lines at the checkout counters. Then one of the previously closed registers opens. The first thing that happens is a rush to the newly opened register. But soon enough, things settle down and shoppers have rearranged themselves so that the line at the newly opened register is about as long as all the others. When all the checkout lines are the same length, and none of the shoppers can be better off by doing something different, this situation is in equilibrium.

An economic situation is in **equilibrium** when no individual would be better off doing something different. Equilibrium in a competitive market occurs where the supply and demand curves intersect.

A competitive market is in equilibrium when the price has moved to a level at which the quantity demanded of a good equals the quantity supplied of that good. The price at which this takes place is the **equilibrium price**, also referred to as the *market-clearing price*. The quantity of the good bought and sold at that price is the **equilibrium quantity**.

The concept of equilibrium helps us understand the price at which a good or service is bought and sold as well as the quantity of the good or service bought and sold. A competitive market is in equilibrium when the price has moved to a level at which the quantity of a good demanded equals the quantity supplied. At that price, no seller would gain by offering to sell more or less of the good, and no buyer would gain by offering to buy more or less of the good. Recall the shoppers at the supermarket who cannot make themselves better off (cannot save time) by changing lines. Similarly, at the market equilibrium, the price has moved to a level that exactly matches the quantity demanded by consumers to the quantity supplied by sellers.

The price that matches the quantity supplied and the quantity demanded is the **equilibrium price**; the quantity bought and sold at that price is the **equilibrium quantity**. The equilibrium price is also known as the *market-clearing price*: it is the price that "clears the market" by ensuring that every buyer willing to pay that price finds a seller willing to sell at that price, and vice versa. So how do we find the equilibrium price and quantity?

Finding the Equilibrium Price and Quantity

The easiest way to determine the equilibrium price and quantity in a market is by putting the supply curve and the demand curve on the same diagram. Since the supply curve shows the quantity supplied at any given price and the demand curve shows the quantity demanded at any given price, the price at which the two curves cross is the equilibrium price: the price at which quantity supplied equals quantity demanded.

Figure 1.6-1 shows supply and demand curves for a hypothetical lumber market. The supply and demand curves *intersect* at point *E*, which is the equilibrium of this market; $1 is the equilibrium price, and 100 billion board feet is the equilibrium quantity. Let's confirm that point *E* fits our definition of equilibrium. At a price of $1 per board foot, farmers are willing to sell 100 billion board feet of lumber, and lumber consumers want to buy 100 billion board feet. So at the price of $1 per board foot, the quantity of lumber supplied equals the quantity demanded. Notice that at any other price, the market would not clear: some willing buyers would not be able to find a willing seller, or vice versa. More specifically, if the price were more than $1, the quantity supplied would exceed the quantity demanded; if the price were less than $1, the quantity demanded would exceed the quantity supplied.

AP® ECON TIP

Equilibrium price and quantity are found where the supply and demand curves intersect on the graph, but the values for price and quantity must be shown on the axes. Points labeled inside the graph do not show equilibrium price and quantity.

FIGURE 1.6-1 Market Equilibrium

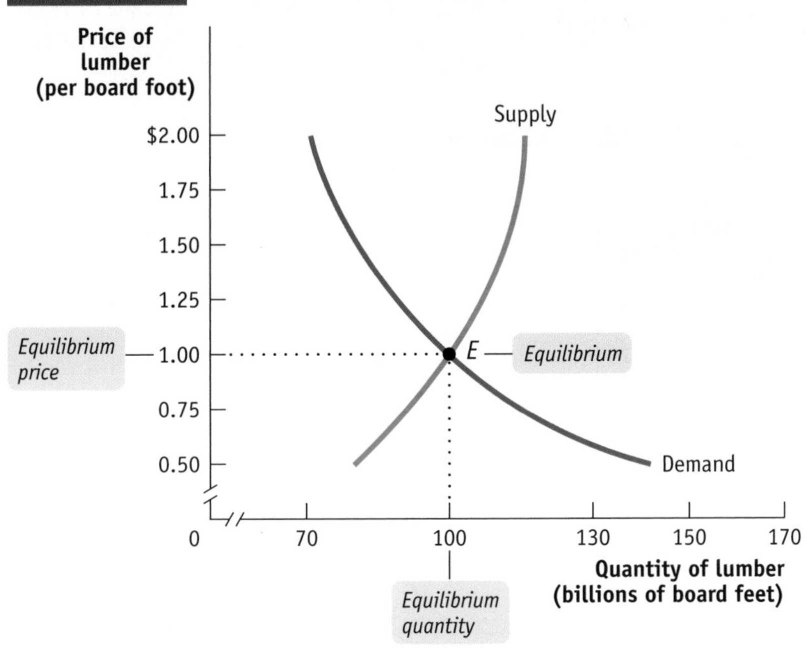

Market equilibrium occurs at point *E*, where the supply curve and the demand curve intersect. In equilibrium, the quantity demanded is equal to the quantity supplied. In this market, $1 is the equilibrium price, and 100 billion board feet is the equilibrium quantity.

The model of supply and demand, then, predicts that given the demand and supply curves shown in Figure 1.6-1, 100 billion board feet of lumber would change hands at a price of $1 per board foot. But how can we be sure that the market will arrive at the equilibrium price?

Why Do All Sales and Purchases in a Market Take Place at the Same Price?

There are some markets where the same good can sell for many different prices, depending on who is selling or who is buying. For example, have you ever bought a souvenir in a popular tourist destination and then seen the same item on sale somewhere else (perhaps even in the shop next door) for a lower price? Because tourists

Katharine Andriotis/Alamy

Prices in a tourist market fluctuate widely because buyers can't comparison shop, like they would in a well-established market where prices tend to converge.

don't know which shops offer the best deals and don't have time for comparison shopping, sellers in tourist areas can charge different prices for the same good.

But in any market in which the buyers and sellers have both been around for some time, sales and purchases tend to converge at a generally uniform price, so we can safely talk about *the* market price. It's easy to see why. Suppose a seller offered a potential buyer a price noticeably above what the buyer knew other people were paying. The buyer would clearly be better off shopping elsewhere—unless the seller were prepared to offer a better deal. Conversely, a seller would not be willing to sell for significantly less than the amount she knew most buyers were paying; she would be better off waiting to get a more reasonable customer. So in any well-established, ongoing market, all sellers receive, and all buyers pay, approximately the same price. This is what we call the *market price*.

Why Does the Market Price Fall If It Is Above the Equilibrium Price?

A market is in **disequilibrium** when the market price is above or below the price that equates the quantity demanded with the quantity supplied.

Figure 1.6-2 illustrates the lumber market in **disequilibrium,** meaning that the market price differs from the price that would equate the quantity demanded with the quantity supplied. In this example, the market price of $1.50 is above the equilibrium price of $1. Why can't the price stay there?

FIGURE 1.6-2 Price Above Its Equilibrium Level Creates a Surplus

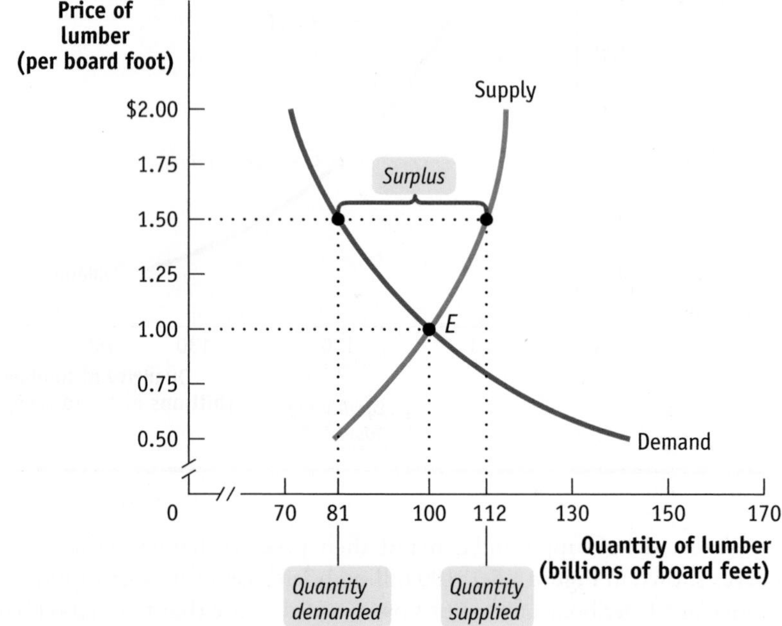

The market price of $1.50 is above the equilibrium price of $1. This places the market in disequilibrium and creates a surplus: at a price of $1.50, producers would like to sell 112 billion board feet but consumers want to buy only 81 billion board feet, so there is a surplus of 31 billion board feet. This surplus will push the price down until it reaches the equilibrium price of $1.

As the figure shows, at a price of $1.50, there would be more board feet of lumber available than consumers wanted to buy: 11.2 billion board feet would be demanded and 8.1 billion board feet would be supplied. When the quantity supplied exceeds the quantity demanded, the difference between the quantity supplied and the quantity demanded is described as the **surplus**—also known as the *excess supply*. The difference of 3.1 billion board feet is the surplus of lumber at a price of $1.50. This surplus of the quantity supplied over the quantity demanded that exists when the market is in disequilibrium should not to be confused with consumer surplus or producer surplus. Consumer surplus and producer surplus constitute net gains from buying or selling a good, and both can exist whether the market is in equilibrium or disequilibrium.

This surplus means that some lumber producers are frustrated: at the current price, they cannot find consumers who want to buy their lumber. The surplus offers an incentive for those frustrated would-be sellers to offer a lower price in order to poach business from other producers and entice more consumers to buy. The result of this price cutting will be to push the prevailing price down until it reaches the equilibrium price. So the price of a good will fall whenever there is a surplus—that is, whenever the market price is above its equilibrium level.

AP® ECON TIP

Consider what you would do if you were selling something for a price that didn't attract enough buyers to purchase the quantity you chose to supply. If you would lower the price, you exemplify the behavior that brings market prices to equilibrium.

There is a **surplus** of a good or service when the quantity supplied exceeds the quantity demanded. Surpluses occur when the price is above its equilibrium level.

Why Does the Market Price Rise If It Is Below the Equilibrium Price?

Now suppose the price is below its equilibrium level—say, at $0.75 per board foot, as shown in **Figure 1.6-3**. In this case, the quantity demanded, 115 billion board feet, exceeds the quantity supplied, 91 billion board feet, implying that there are would-be buyers who cannot find lumber: there is a **shortage**, also known as an *excess demand*, of 24 billion board feet.

There is a **shortage** of a good or service when the quantity demanded exceeds the quantity supplied. Shortages occur when the price is below its equilibrium level.

FIGURE 1.6-3 Price Below Its Equilibrium Level Creates a Shortage

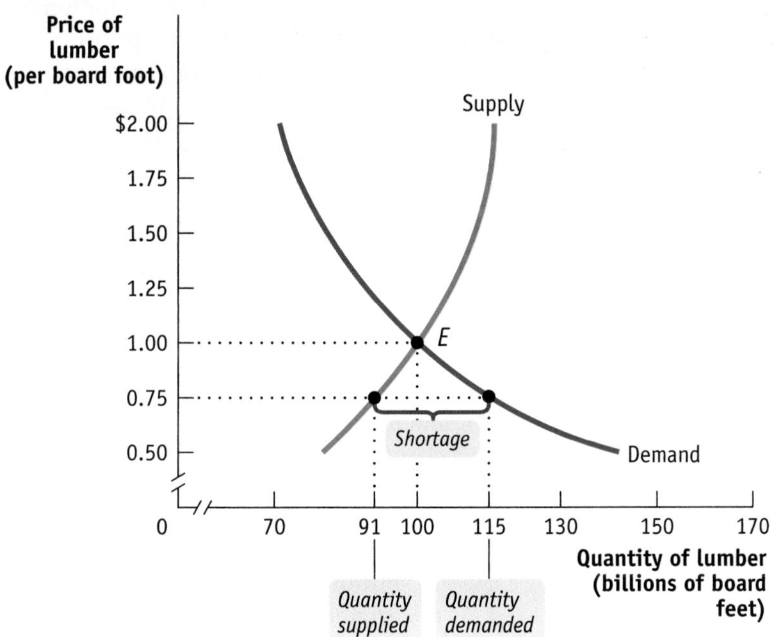

The market price of $0.75 is below the equilibrium price of $1. This creates a shortage: consumers want to buy 115 billion board feet, but only 91 billion board feet are for sale, so there is a shortage of 24 billion board feet. This shortage will push the price up until it reaches the equilibrium price of $1.

When there is a shortage, there are frustrated would-be buyers—people who want to purchase lumber but cannot find willing sellers at the current price. In this situation, either buyers will offer more than the prevailing price, or sellers will realize that they can charge higher prices. Either way, the result is to drive up the prevailing price. This bidding up of prices happens whenever there are shortages—and there will be shortages whenever the price is below its equilibrium level. So the market price will rise if it is below the equilibrium level.

Using Equilibrium to Describe Markets

We have now seen that a market tends to have a single price, the *equilibrium price*. If the market price is above the equilibrium level, the ensuing surplus leads buyers and sellers to take actions that lower the price. And if the market price is below the equilibrium level, the ensuing shortage leads buyers and sellers to take actions that raise the price. So the market price always *moves toward* the equilibrium price, the price at which there is neither a surplus nor a shortage.

Changes in Supply and Demand

The devastation of forests by the pine beetle in recent years came as a surprise, but the subsequent increase in the price of lumber was no surprise at all. Suddenly, there was a decrease in supply: the quantity of lumber available at any given price fell. Predictably, a decrease in supply raises the equilibrium price.

A beetle infestation is an example of an event that can shift the supply curve for a good without having much effect on the demand curve. There are many such events. There are also events that can shift the demand curve without shifting the supply curve. For example, a medical report that chocolate is good for you increases the demand for chocolate but does not affect the supply. Events generally shift either the supply curve or the demand curve, but not both; it is therefore useful to ask what happens in each case.

What Happens When the Demand Curve Shifts

Wood composites made from plastic and wood fibers are a substitute for lumber. If the price of composites rises, the demand for lumber will increase as more consumers use lumber rather than composites. If the price of composites falls, the demand for lumber will decrease as more consumers are drawn away from lumber by the lower price of composites. But how does the price of composites affect the *market equilibrium* for lumber?

Figure 1.6-4 shows the effect of changes in the price of wood composites on the market for lumber. The rise in the price of composites increases the demand for lumber, and a decrease in the price of composites decreases the demand for lumber. Point E_1 shows the equilibrium corresponding to the original demand curve, with P_1 the equilibrium price and Q_1 the equilibrium quantity bought and sold.

An increase in demand is indicated by a *rightward* shift of the demand curve from D_1 to D_2, as shown in panel (a). At the original market price P_1, this market is no longer in equilibrium: a shortage occurs because the quantity demanded exceeds the quantity supplied. So the price of lumber rises and generates an increase in the quantity supplied, an upward *movement along the supply curve.* A new equilibrium is established at point E_2, with a higher equilibrium price, P_2, and higher equilibrium quantity, Q_2.

This sequence of events resulting from a change in demand reflect a general principle: *When demand for a good or service increases, the equilibrium price and the equilibrium quantity of the good or service both rise.*

What would happen in the reverse case of a fall in the price of wood composites? A decrease in demand is indicated by a *leftward* shift of the demand curve from D_1 to D_2, as shown in panel (b) of Figure 1.6-4. At the original market price P_1, this market is no longer in equilibrium: a surplus occurs because the quantity supplied exceeds the quantity demanded. So the price of lumber falls and generates a decrease in the quantity supplied, a downward *movement along the supply curve.* A new equilibrium is established at point E_2, with a lower equilibrium price, P_2, and lower equilibrium quantity, Q_2.

A fall in the price of composites reduces the demand for lumber, shifting the demand curve to the *left*. At the original price, a surplus occurs as quantity supplied exceeds quantity demanded. The price falls and leads to a decrease in the quantity supplied, resulting in a lower equilibrium price and a lower equilibrium quantity. This illustrates another general principle: *When demand for a good or service decreases, the equilibrium price and the equilibrium quantity of the good or service both fall.*

AP® ECON TIP

The term *equilibrium* is used in a variety of situations to indicate *balance* or *no tendency for change*. In the supply and demand model, when a market is in equilibrium, $Q_s = Q_d$ and there is no shortage or surplus, so there is no tendency for the price to change.

FIGURE 1.6-4 Equilibrium and Shifts of the Demand Curve

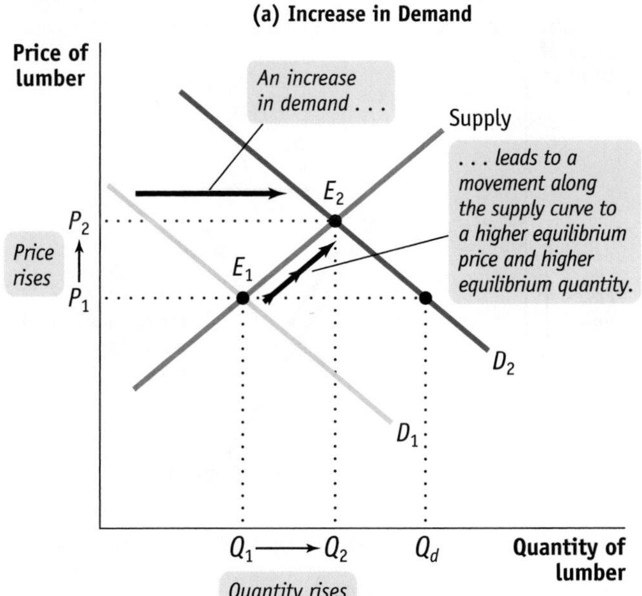

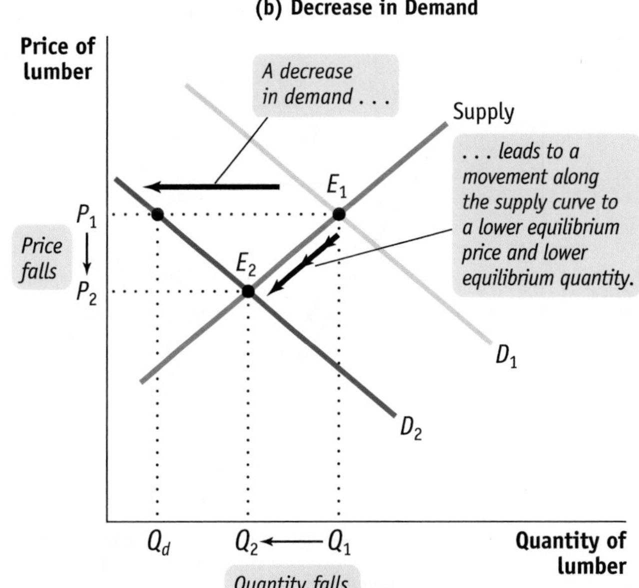

(a) The original equilibrium in the market for lumber is at E_1. A *rise* in the price of wood composites, a lumber substitute, shifts the demand curve D_1 *rightward* to D_2. A *shortage* equal to $(Q_d - Q_1)$ exists at the original price, P_1, causing both the price and quantity supplied to rise, a movement along the supply curve. A new equilibrium is reached at E_2, where quantity demanded is again equal to quantity supplied with a higher equilibrium price, P_2, and a higher equilibrium quantity, Q_2. (b) A *fall* in the price of wood composites shifts the demand curve D_1 *leftward* to D_2. A *surplus* equal to $(Q_1 - Q_d)$ exists at the original price, P_1, causing both the price and quantity supplied to fall, a movement along the supply curve. A new equilibrium is reached at E_2, where quantity demanded is again equal to quantity supplied with a lower equilibrium price, P_2, and a lower equilibrium quantity, Q_2.

To summarize how a market responds to a change in demand: *An increase in demand leads to a rise in both the equilibrium price and the equilibrium quantity. A decrease in demand leads to a fall in both the equilibrium price and the equilibrium quantity.* That is, a change in demand causes equilibrium price and quantity to move in the same direction.

What Happens When the Supply Curve Shifts

In the real world, it is a bit easier to predict changes in supply than changes in demand. Physical factors that affect supply, such as weather or the availability of inputs, are easier to get a handle on than the fickle tastes that affect demand. Still, with supply as with demand, what we can best predict are the *effects* of shifts of the supply curve.

As we mentioned earlier, forest devastation by pine beetles sharply reduced the supply of lumber in recent years. Conversely, advances in technology have increased the supply of lumber. **Figure 1.6-5** shows how such shifts affect the market equilibrium. The original equilibrium is at E_1, the point of intersection of the original supply curve, S_1, and the demand curve, with an equilibrium price P_1 and equilibrium quantity Q_1. As a result of insect damage, supply decreases and S_1 shifts *leftward* to S_2, as shown in panel (a). At the original price P_1, a shortage of lumber now exists, and the market is no longer in equilibrium. The shortage causes a rise in price and a fall in quantity demanded, an upward movement along the demand curve. The new equilibrium is at E_2, with an equilibrium price P_2 and an equilibrium quantity Q_2. In the new equilibrium, E_2, the price is higher and the equilibrium quantity is lower than before. This can be stated as a general principle: *When supply of a good or service decreases, the equilibrium price of the good or service rises, and the equilibrium quantity of the good or service falls.*

AP® ECON TIP

The graph never lies! To see what happens to price and quantity when supply or demand shifts, draw the graph of a market in equilibrium and then shift the appropriate curve to show the new equilibrium price and quantity. Compare the price and quantity at the old and new equilibriums to find your answer! A quick drawing can even help you answer supply and demand questions.

FIGURE 1.6-5 Equilibrium and Shifts of the Supply Curve

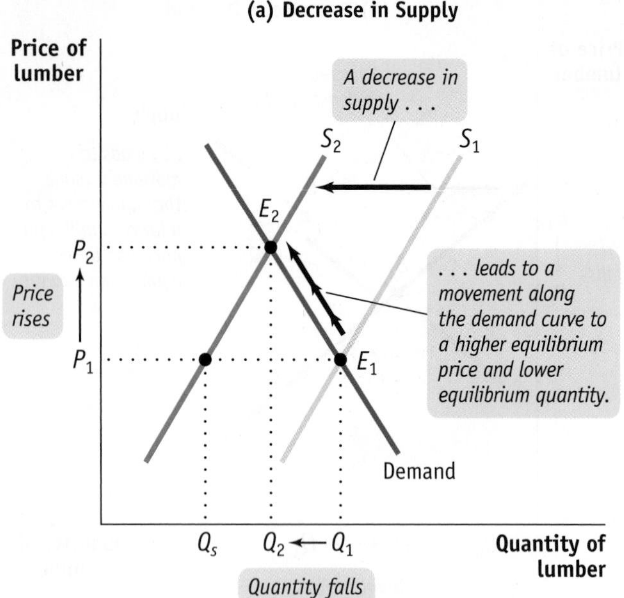

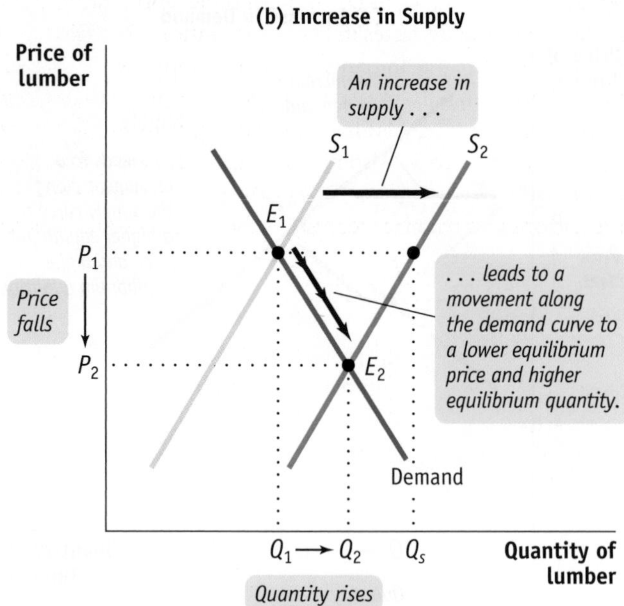

(a) Insect infestation in lumber-growing areas shifts the supply curve *leftward* from S_1 to S_2, creating a *shortage* equal to $(Q_1 - Q_s)$ at the original price, causing an increase in price and a decrease in quantity supplied and a movement along the demand curve. A new equilibrium is established at E_2, where quantity demanded equals quantity supplied with a higher equilibrium price, P_2, and a lower equilibrium quantity, Q_2. (b) The advance in sawmill technology shifts the supply curve *rightward* from S_1 to S_2, creating a *surplus* equal to $(Q_s - Q_1)$ at the original price, causing a decrease in price and an increase in quantity supplied and a movement along the demand curve. A new equilibrium is established at E_2, where quantity demanded again equals quantity supplied with a lower equilibrium price, P_2, and a higher equilibrium quantity, Q_2.

What happens to the market when supply increases? An increase in supply leads to a *rightward* shift of the supply curve, as shown in panel (b) of Figure 1.6-5. The original equilibrium is at E_1, the point of intersection of the original supply curve, S_1, and the demand curve, with an equilibrium price P_1 and equilibrium quantity Q_1. As a result of an advance in technology, supply increases and S_1 shifts *rightward* to S_2. At the original price, P_1, a surplus of lumber now exists and the market is no longer in equilibrium. The surplus causes a fall in price and an increase in quantity demanded, represented by a downward movement along the demand curve. The new equilibrium is at E_2, with an equilibrium price P_2 and an equilibrium quantity Q_2. In the new equilibrium, E_2, the price is lower and the equilibrium quantity is higher than before. This can be stated as a general principle: *When supply of a good or service increases, the equilibrium price of the good or service falls, and the equilibrium quantity of the good or service rises.*

Note that a shift of the supply curve does not cause a shift of the demand curve. A change in the equilibrium price causes a movement *along* the demand curve.

To summarize how a market responds to a change in supply: *A decrease in supply leads to a rise in the equilibrium price and a fall in the equilibrium quantity. An increase in supply leads to a fall in the equilibrium price and a rise in the equilibrium quantity.* That is, a change in supply causes equilibrium price and quantity to move in opposite directions.

AP® ECON TIP

A shift of the demand curve does not cause a shift of the supply curve, and a shift of the supply curve does not cause a shift of the demand curve. A change in the equilibrium price causes a movement *along* the curve that didn't shift.

Simultaneous Shifts of Supply and Demand Curves

It sometimes happens that simultaneous events shift *both* the demand and supply curves at the same time. This is not unusual; in real life, supply curves and demand curves for many goods and services shift quite often because the economic environment continually changes.

Figure 1.6-6 illustrates two examples of simultaneous shifts of the supply and demand curves. In both panels there is an increase in demand—that is, a rightward shift of the demand curve, from D_1 to D_2—for example, representing an increase in the demand for lumber due to changing tastes in home renovations. Notice that the rightward shift in panel (a) is larger than the one in panel (b): we can suppose that panel (a) represents a year in which many more people than usual choose to improve their homes and panel (b) represents a normal year. Both panels also show a decrease in supply—that is, a leftward shift of the supply curve from S_1 to S_2. Also notice that the leftward shift in panel (b) is larger than the one in panel (a): we can suppose that panel (b) represents the effect of particularly severe beetle infestations and panel (a) represents the effect of much less severe insect damage.

FIGURE 1.6-6 Simultaneous Shifts of the Demand and Supply Curves

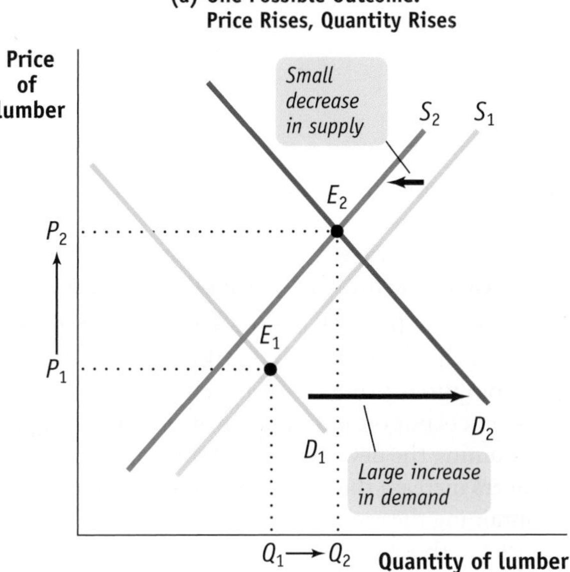

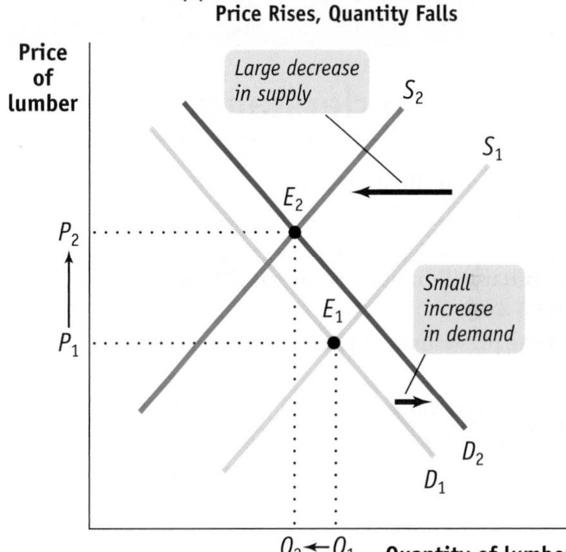

In panel (a) there is a simultaneous rightward shift of the demand curve and leftward shift of the supply curve. Here the increase in demand is sufficiently large relative to the decrease in supply to cause both the equilibrium price and the equilibrium quantity to rise. In panel (b) there is also a simultaneous rightward shift of the demand curve and leftward shift of the supply curve. Here the decrease in supply is large enough relative to the increase in demand to cause the equilibrium price to fall while the equilibrium price rises.

In both cases, the equilibrium price rises from P_1 to P_2 as the equilibrium moves from E_1 to E_2. But what happens to the equilibrium quantity, the quantity of lumber bought and sold? In panel (a) the increase in demand is large enough relative to the decrease in supply so that the equilibrium quantity rises as a result. In panel (b), the decrease in supply is sufficiently large relative to the increase in demand to cause the equilibrium quantity to fall as a result. That is, when demand increases and supply decreases, the actual quantity bought and sold can go either way, depending on the *relative sizes* of the shifts in demand and supply.

In general, when supply and demand shift in opposite directions, we can't predict the ultimate effect on the quantity bought and sold. Without information on the relative sizes of the shifts, we can only make the following prediction about the outcome:

- When demand increases and supply decreases, the equilibrium price rises, but the change in the equilibrium quantity is ambiguous.
- When demand decreases and supply increases, the equilibrium price falls, but the change in the equilibrium quantity is ambiguous.

Now suppose that the demand and supply curves shift in the same direction. Can we safely make any predictions about the changes in price and quantity? In this

AP® ECON TIP

To clarify what you know and what you don't know about the effect of simultaneous shifts, treat each shift individually and identify the effect on equilibrium price and quantity. Both shifts will have the same effect on either price or quantity, so you know how that has changed. The shifts will have opposite effects on either price or quantity, so unless you know the relative sizes of the shifts, that result is ambiguous.

situation, the change in quantity bought and sold can be predicted, but the change in price is ambiguous. The two possible outcomes when the supply and demand curves shift in the same direction (which you should check for yourself) are as follows:

- When both demand and supply increase, the equilibrium quantity rises, but the change in the equilibrium price is ambiguous.
- When both demand and supply decrease, the equilibrium quantity falls, but the change in the equilibrium price is ambiguous.

Adventures in AP® Economics
Watch the video:
Market Equilibrium

Module 1.6 Review

Check Your Understanding

1. In the following three situations, the market is initially in equilibrium. After each event described below, does a surplus or shortage exist at the original equilibrium price? What will happen to the equilibrium price as a result?
   a. In the previous year there was a bumper crop of grapes.
   b. After a hurricane, Florida hoteliers often find that many people cancel their upcoming vacations, leaving them with empty hotel rooms.
   c. After a heavy snowfall, many people want to buy second-hand snowblowers at the local tool shop.
2. For each of the following examples, explain how the indicated change affects supply or demand for the good in question and how the shift you describe affects the equilibrium price and quantity.
   a. As the price of gasoline increases, more people buy electric cars.
   b. A technological innovation has lowered the cost of paper production.
   c. When a movie-streaming service lowers its price, local movie theaters have more unfilled seats.
3. A computer-chip maker introduces a new chip that is faster than the previous one. In response, demand for computers using the earlier chip decreases as customers put off purchases in anticipation of machines containing the new chip. Simultaneously, computer makers increase their production of computers containing the earlier chip in order to clear out their stocks of those chips.

   Draw two diagrams of the market for computers containing the earlier chip: (a) one in which the equilibrium quantity falls in response to these events, and (b) one in which the equilibrium quantity rises. What happens to the equilibrium price in each diagram?

Tackle the AP® Test: Multiple-Choice Questions

1. Which of the following describes equilibrium in the supply and demand model?
   a. Supply equals demand.
   b. There is no tendency for price to change.
   c. The market has either a surplus or a shortage.
   d. Price is equal to quantity.
   e. The number of buyers and sellers is balanced.
2. Price will tend to fall when
   a. there is a shortage.
   b. quantity demanded is greater than quantity supplied.
   c. quantity supplied is less than quantity demanded.
   d. price is above equilibrium.
   e. price is below equilibrium.
3. Which of the following describes what will happen in the market for tomatoes if a salmonella outbreak is attributed to tainted tomatoes?
   a. Supply will decrease and price will increase.
   b. Supply will decrease and price will decrease.
   c. Demand will decrease and price will increase.
   d. Demand will decrease and price will decrease.
   e. Supply and demand will both decrease.

4. Which of the following will lead to an increase in the equilibrium price of product X?
   a. an increase in consumer incomes if product X is an inferior good
   b. an increase in the price of machinery used to produce product X
   c. a technological advance in the production of good X
   d. a decrease in the price of good Y (a substitute for good X)
   e. an expectation by consumers that the price of good X is going to fall

5. The equilibrium price will rise, but the equilibrium quantity may increase, decrease, or stay the same if
   a. demand increases and supply decreases.
   b. demand increases and supply increases.
   c. demand decreases and supply increases.
   d. demand decreases and supply decreases.
   e. demand increases and supply does not change.

6. An increase in the number of buyers and a technological advance will cause
   a. demand to increase and supply to increase.
   b. demand to increase and supply to decrease.
   c. demand to decrease and supply to increase.
   d. demand to decrease and supply to decrease.
   e. no change in demand and an increase in supply.

7. Which of the following is certainly true if demand and supply increase at the same time?
   a. The equilibrium price will increase.
   b. The equilibrium price will decrease.
   c. The equilibrium quantity will increase.
   d. The equilibrium quantity will decrease.
   e. The equilibrium quantity may increase, decrease, or stay the same.

Tackle the AP® Test: Free-Response Questions

1. Draw a correctly labeled graph showing the market for tomatoes in equilibrium. Label the equilibrium price "P_E" and the equilibrium quantity "Q_E." On your graph, draw a horizontal line indicating a price, labeled "P_C," that would lead to a shortage of tomatoes. Label the size of the shortage on your graph.

Rubric for FRQ 1 (5 points)

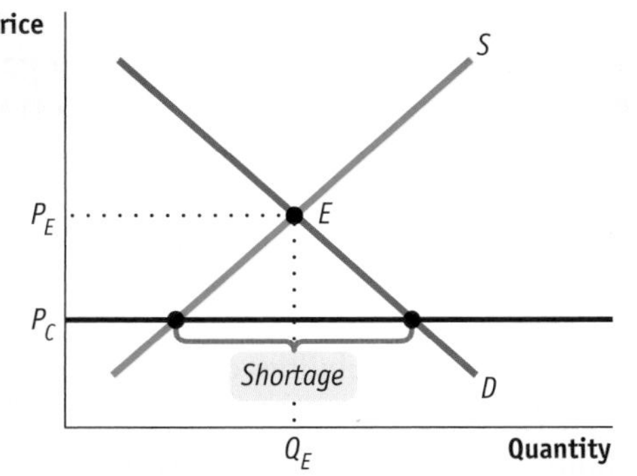

1 point: Graph with the vertical axis labeled "Price" or "P" and the horizontal axis labeled "Quantity" or "Q"

1 point: Downward-sloping demand curve labeled "Demand" or "D" and upward-sloping supply curve labeled "Supply" or "S"

1 point: Equilibrium price "P_E" labeled on the vertical axis and quantity "Q_E" labeled on the horizontal axis at the intersection of the supply and demand curves

1 point: Price line at a price "P_C" below the equilibrium price

1 point: Correct indication of the shortage, which is the horizontal distance between the quantity demanded and the quantity supplied at the height of P_C

2. Draw a correctly labeled graph showing the market for cups of coffee in equilibrium. Label the equilibrium price P_1 and the equilibrium quantity Q_1.
   a. On your graph, show the effect of a decrease in the price of coffee beans on the equilibrium price and the equilibrium quantity in the market for cups of coffee. Label the new equilibrium price and quantity P_2 and Q_2, respectively.
   b. Explain how a simultaneous decrease in the price of coffee beans and increase in the demand for cups of coffee will affect each of the following;
      i. The equilibrium price of a cup of coffee
      ii. The equilibrium quantity of cups of coffee

   (5 points)

UNIT 1 Review

Adventures in AP® Economics Videos

Mod 1.1 Graphing Tricks & Tips
Mod 1.2 Production Possibilities Curve
Mod 1.3 Comparative Advantage and Absolute Advantage
Mod 1.4 Demand
Mod 1.5 Supply
Mod 1.6 Market Equilibrium

economics by example
The Coffee Market's Hot; Why Are Bean Prices Not?

UNIT 1 Review Video

Module 1.1

1. Everyone has to make choices about what to do and what *not* to do. Choice is the basis of **economics**—if it doesn't involve choice, it isn't economics.
2. The reason choices must be made is that **resources**—anything that can be used to produce something else—are **scarce**. The four categories of resources, also called **factors of production**, are **land**, **labor**, **capital**, and **entrepreneurship**. Individuals are limited in their choices by money and time; economies are limited by their supplies of resources.
3. Because you must choose among limited alternatives, the true cost of anything is what you must give up to get it—all costs are **opportunity costs**.
4. **Microeconomics** is the branch of economics that focuses on how choices are made by individuals, **households**, and **firms**. **Macroeconomics** is concerned with the overall ups and downs of the economy and focuses on economic aggregates, such as the unemployment rate and gross domestic product, that summarize data across many different markets.
5. Economists use economic models for positive economics, which describes how the economy works, and for normative economics, which prescribes how the economy *should* work. Positive economics often involves making forecasts. Economics can determine correct answers for positive questions, but typically not for normative questions, which involve value judgments. Exceptions occur when policies designed to achieve a certain prescription can be clearly ranked in terms of preference.

Module 1.2

6. Almost all economics is based on **models**, "thought experiments" or simplified versions of reality, many of which use analytical tools such as mathematics and graphs. An important assumption in economic models is the **other things equal (*ceteris paribus*) assumption**, which allows analysis of the effect of change in one factor by holding all other relevant factors unchanged.
7. One important economic model is the **production possibilities curve**, which illustrates the **trade-offs** facing an economy that produces only two goods. The production possibilities curve illustrates three elements: opportunity cost (showing how much less of one good must be produced if more of the other good is produced), **efficiency** (an economy produces efficiently if it produces on the production possibilities curve and it allocates resources efficiently if it produces the mix of goods and services that people most want to consume), and **economic growth** (an increase in the economy's maximum possible output shown by an outward shift of the production possibilities curve).
8. There are two basic sources of growth in the production possibilities curve model: an increase in resources and improved **technology**.

Module 1.3

9. There are **gains from trade**: by engaging in the **trade** of goods and services with one another, the members of an economy can all be made better off. Underlying gains from trade are the advantages of **specialization**, of having individuals specialize in the tasks they are comparatively good at.
10. The existence of **comparative advantages** explains the source of gains from trade between individuals and countries. Having a comparative advantage means that you can make a good or service at a lower opportunity cost than everyone else. This is often confused with an **absolute advantage**, which is an ability to produce more of a particular good or service or to use fewer resources to produce a particular good or service than anyone else. This confusion leads some to erroneously conclude that there are no gains from trade between people or countries.

11. As long as a comparative advantage exists between two parties, there are opportunities for mutually beneficial trade. The **terms of trade** indicate the rate at which one good can be exchanged for another. The range of mutually beneficial terms of trade for a good are found between the producer's opportunity cost of making the good and the buyer's opportunity cost of making the same good.

Module 1.4

12. The **supply and demand model** illustrates how markets work. The **demand schedule** shows the **quantity demanded** at each price and is represented graphically by a **demand curve**. The **law of demand** says that demand curves slope downward, meaning that as price decreases, the quantity demanded increases.
13. A **movement along the demand curve** occurs when the price changes and causes a change in the quantity demanded. When economists talk of **changes in demand**, they mean shifts of the demand curve—a change in the quantity demanded at any given price. An increase in demand causes a rightward shift of the demand curve. A decrease in demand causes a leftward shift.
14. There are five main factors that shift the demand curve:
    - a change in tastes
    - a change in the prices of related goods, such as **substitutes** or **complements**
    - a change in income: when income rises, the demand for **normal goods** increases and the demand for **inferior goods** decreases
    - a change in the number of consumers (buyers)
    - a change in expectations

Module 1.5

15. The **supply schedule** shows the **quantity supplied** at each price and is represented graphically by a **supply curve**. According to the **law of supply**, supply curves slope upward, meaning that as price increases, the quantity demanded increases.
16. A **movement along the supply curve** occurs when the price changes and causes a change in the quantity supplied. When economists talk of **changes in supply**, they mean shifts of the supply curve—a change in the quantity supplied at any given price. An increase in supply causes a rightward shift of the supply curve. A decrease in supply causes a leftward shift.
17. There are five main factors that shift the supply curve:
    - a change in **input** prices
    - a change in the prices of related goods and services
    - a change in expectations
    - a change in the number of producers
    - a change in technology
18. Two related goods can be **substitutes in production**, meaning that the same inputs used to make one of the goods could instead be used to produce the other, or **complements in production**, which means the two goods are produced together using the same inputs.

Module 1.6

19. An economic situation is in **equilibrium** when no individual would be better off doing something different. The supply and demand model is based on the principle that the price in a market moves to its **equilibrium price**, or market-clearing price, the price at which the quantity demanded is equal to the quantity supplied. This quantity is the **equilibrium quantity**.
20. When the price is above its market-clearing level, there is a **surplus** that pushes the price down. When the price is below its market-clearing level, there is a **shortage** that pushes the price up.
21. An increase in demand increases both the equilibrium price and the equilibrium quantity; a decrease in demand has the opposite effect. An increase in supply reduces the equilibrium price and increases the equilibrium quantity; a decrease in supply has the opposite effect.
22. Shifts of the demand curve and the supply curve can happen simultaneously. When they shift in opposite directions, the change in price is predictable, but the change in quantity is not. When they shift in the same direction, the change in quantity is predictable, but the change in price is not. In general, the curve that shifts the greater distance has a greater effect on the changes in price and quantity.

Key Terms

Economics, p. 4
Trade-off, p. 4
Resource, p. 4
Factor of production, p. 4
Land, p. 4
Labor, p. 4
Capital, p. 4
Entrepreneurship, p. 4
Scarce, p. 4

Opportunity cost, p. 5
Microeconomics, p. 6
Household, p. 6
Firm, p. 6
Macroeconomics, p. 6
Model, p. 10
"Other things equal" (*ceteris paribus*) assumption, p. 11
Production possibilities curve, p. 11
Efficient, p. 12
Economic growth, p. 15
Technology, p. 16
Trade, p. 19
Specialization, p. 19
Comparative advantage, p. 21
Absolute advantage, p. 21
Terms of trade, p. 23
Supply and demand model, p. 27
Demand schedule, p. 28
Quantity demanded, p. 28
Demand curve, p. 28
Law of demand, p. 29
Change in demand, p. 30
Movement along the demand curve, p. 30
Substitutes, p. 33
Complements, p. 33
Normal good, p. 34
Inferior good, p. 34
Quantity supplied, p. 37
Supply schedule, p. 37
Supply curve, p. 37
Law of supply, p. 37
Change in supply, p. 39
Movement along the supply curve, p. 39
Input, p. 41
Substitutes in production, p. 41
Complements in production, p. 41
Equilibrium, p. 46
Equilibrium price, p. 46
Equilibrium quantity, p. 46
Disequilibrium, p. 48
Surplus, p. 49
Shortage, p. 49

AP® Exam Practice Questions

Multiple-Choice Questions

1. Which of the following pairs indicates a category of resources and an example of that resource?

Category	*Example*
a. money	investment
b. capital	money
c. capital	minerals
d. land	factory
e. land	timber

2. You can either go to a movie or study for an exam. Which of the following is an opportunity cost of studying for the exam?
a. a higher grade on the exam
b. the price of a movie ticket
c. the cost of paper, pens, books, and other study materials
d. the enjoyment from seeing the movie
e. the sense of achievement from learning

3. Which of the following situations is explained by increasing opportunity costs?
a. More people go to college when the job market is good.
b. More people do their own home repairs when hourly wages fall.
c. There are more parks in crowded cities than in suburban areas.
d. Convenience stores cater to busy people.
e. People with higher wages are more likely to mow their own lawns.

4. Which of the following is a microeconomic issue?
a. the unemployment rate in your country
b. the gross domestic product for France
c. the wage rate for employees at your school
d. the national rate of inflation
e. government efforts to end a recession

Refer to the following table and information for Questions 5–8.

Suppose that Atlantis is a small, isolated island in the South Atlantic. The inhabitants grow potatoes and catch fish. The following table shows the maximum annual output combinations of potatoes and fish that can be produced.

Maximum annual output options	Quantity of potatoes (pounds)	Quantity of fish (pounds)
A	1,000	0
B	800	300
C	600	500
D	400	600
E	200	650
F	0	675

5. Atlantis can produce which of the following combinations of output?

Pounds of potatoes	*Pounds of fish*
a. 1,000	675
b. 600	600
c. 400	600
d. 300	800
e. 200	675

6. If Atlantis is efficient in production, what is the opportunity cost of increasing the annual output of potatoes from 600 to 800 pounds?
a. 200 pounds of fish
b. 300 pounds of fish
c. 500 pounds of fish
d. 675 pounds of fish
e. 800 pounds of fish

7. As Atlantis produces more potatoes, what is true about the opportunity cost of producing potatoes?

a. It stays the same.
b. It continually increases.
c. It continually decreases.
d. It increases and then decreases.
e. It decreases and then increases.

8. Which of the following combinations of output is efficient?

Pounds of potatoes	*Pounds of fish*
a. 1,000	0
b. 600	600
c. 400	500
d. 300	400
e. 0	0

Refer to the following information for Questions 9–10.

In the ancient country of Roma, only two goods—spaghetti and meatballs—are produced. There are two tribes in Roma, the Tivoli and the Frivoli. By themselves, in a given month, the Tivoli can produce 30 pounds of spaghetti and no meatballs, 50 pounds of meatballs and no spaghetti, or any combination in between. In the same month, the Frivoli can produce 40 pounds of spaghetti and no meatballs, 30 pounds of meatballs and no spaghetti, or any combination in between.

9. Which tribe has a comparative advantage in meatball and spaghetti production?

Meatballs	*Spaghetti*
a. Tivoli	Tivoli
b. Frivoli	Frivoli
c. Tivoli	Frivoli
d. Frivoli	Tivoli
e. Neither	both

10. In CE 100, the Frivoli discovered a new technique for making meatballs and doubled the quantity of meatballs they could produce each month. After the discovery of this new technique in Frivoli only, which tribe had an absolute advantage in meatball production, and which had a comparative advantage in meatball production?

Absolute advantage	*Comparative advantage*
a. Tivoli	Tivoli
b. Frivoli	Frivoli
c. Tivoli	Frivoli
d. Frivoli	Tivoli
e. Frivoli	both

11. Which of the following is a basic source of economic growth in the production possibilities model?

a. specialization
b. efficiency
c. opportunity cost
d. trade-offs
e. improved technology

12. Comparative advantage explains which of the following?

a. a country's ability to produce more of a particular good or service
b. when production is considered efficient
c. why the production possibilities curve is bowed outward
d. the source of gains from trade
e. why the production possibilities curve shifts outward

13. If there is no specialization of resources in the production of milk and cream, the production possibilities curve for an economy that produces these two goods is

a. bowed out and downward-sloping.
b. straight and downward-sloping.
c. bowed in and downward-sloping.
d. horizontal.
e. vertical.

14. Suppose that in a day Nobu can make three placemats or one gallon of maple syrup, and Pauline can make two placemats or two gallons of maple syrup. Which of the following terms of trade would be mutually beneficial for Nobu and Pauline?

a. Nobu trades one placemat for ½ gallon of maple syrup from Pauline.
b. Pauline trades one placemat for ½ gallon of maple syrup from Nobu.
c. Nobu trades one placemat for two gallons of maple syrup from Pauline.
d. Pauline trades one placemat for two gallons of maple syrup from Nobu.
e. Nobu trades one placemat for ¼ gallon of maple syrup from Pauline.

15. Economic growth is defined as an increase in

a. the output of an economy.
b. the employment level in an economy.
c. the spending level in an economy.
d. the quality of life in an economy.
e. the maximum possible output of an economy.

16. Which of the following changes will most likely result in an increase in the demand for hamburgers in your hometown?

a. The price of hot dogs decreases.
b. The price of drinks sold at hamburger restaurants increases.
c. Income in your town decreases and hamburgers are a normal good.
d. The local newspaper publishes a story on health problems caused by red meat.
e. The number of vegetarians in your town decreases and the population size remains the same.

17. Which of the following changes will most likely result in a decrease in the supply of guitars?
  a. The popularity of guitar music increases.
  b. Consumer incomes decrease.
  c. A new firm enters the guitar industry.
  d. The guitar-making process is reengineered to be more efficient.
  e. The wages of guitar makers increase.

18. Which of the following will most likely result in a decrease in the quantity of lemons demanded?
  a. an increase in the price of lemons
  b. an increase in the price of limes
  c. an increase in the price of lemonade
  d. an increase in the number of lemonade stands
  e. a decrease in consumer income

19. Which of the following will occur if consumer incomes increase?
  a. The demand for inferior goods will increase.
  b. The demand for normal goods will increase.
  c. The demand for all goods will increase.
  d. The demand for normal goods will decrease.
  e. The demand for all goods will decrease.

20. If two goods are complements, an increase in the price of one good will cause which of the following?
  a. a decrease in the demand for the other
  b. a decrease in the quantity demanded of the other
  c. an increase in the demand for the other
  d. an increase in the quantity demanded of the other
  e. no change in the demand for the other

21. An increase in the wages of workers producing a good will most likely lead to which of the following?
  a. a decrease in the quantity of the good supplied
  b. a decrease in the supply of the good
  c. an increase in the quantity of the good supplied
  d. an increase in the supply of the good
  e. no change in the supply of the good

22. Which of the following is true at the equilibrium price in a market?
  a. Consumers who purchase the good may be better off buying something else instead.
  b. The market has not yet cleared.
  c. There is a tendency for the price to decrease over time.
  d. There may be either a surplus or a shortage of the good.
  e. The quantity demanded of the good equals the quantity supplied.

23. A survey indicated that chocolate is America's favorite ice cream flavor. Which of the following will lead to a decrease in the price of chocolate ice cream?
  a. A drought in the Midwest causes farmers to reduce the number of dairy cows they raise.
  b. A new report from the American Medical Association concludes that chocolate has significant health benefits.
  c. The price of vanilla ice cream increases.
  d. New freezer technology lowers the cost of producing ice cream.
  e. The price of ice cream toppings decreases.

24. Which of the following events will increase both the price and the quantity of pizza?
  a. The price of mozzarella cheese increases.
  b. New health hazards of eating pizza are widely publicized.
  c. The price of pizza ovens rises.
  d. Consumers expect the price of pizza to fall next week.
  e. Consumer income falls and pizza is an inferior good.

Use the following situation and diagram to answer Question 25.

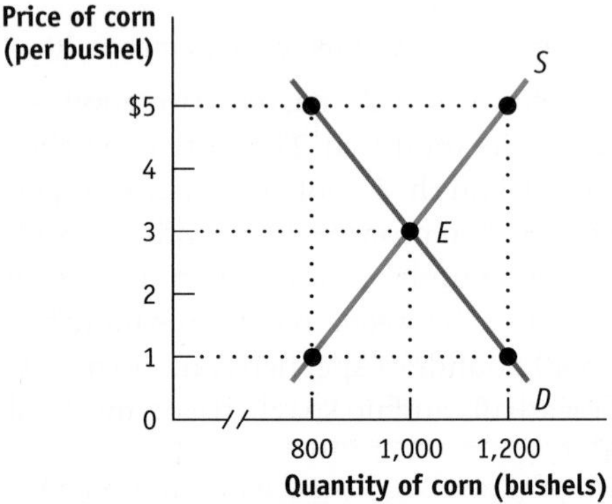

25. What are the equilibrium price and quantity in the market for corn?

	Price	*Quantity*
a.	$1	800
b.	$1	1,200
c.	$3	1,000
d.	$5	800
e.	$5	1,200

Free-Response Questions

1. Suppose the country of Lunchland produces only peanut butter and jelly using resources that are not equally useful for producing both goods.
  a. Draw a correctly labeled production possibilities curve graph for Lunchland and label the following:
    i. point *A*, indicating an inefficient use of resources.
    ii. point *B*, indicating quantities of peanut butter and jelly that are currently not possible.
  b. Identify two things that could happen to enable Lunchland to produce or consume the quantities identified in part a (ii). **(5 points)**

2. Fruity Farm and Peachy Farm have identical resources and produce oranges and/or peaches at a constant opportunity cost. The table below shows the maximum quantity of oranges and peaches each farm could produce if it devoted all of its resources to that fruit.

	Output (bushels per day)	
	Oranges	**Peaches**
Fruity Farm	80	40
Peachy Farm	60	20

a. On a correctly labeled graph, and using the numbers in the table, draw the production possibilities curve for Peachy Farm.

b. What is Fruity Farm's opportunity cost of producing one bushel of peaches?

c. Suppose each farm agrees to specialize in one good and trade for the other good.

i. Which farm should specialize in peaches? Explain.

ii. If the farms specialize as indicated in part c (i), would the terms of trade of four oranges in exchange for one peach be acceptable to both farms? Explain.

d. Now suppose Peachy Farm obtains new technology used only for the production of peaches. Show the effect of this change on the graph drawn for part a. **(5 points)**

3. Assume the market for sandals is competitive.

a. Draw a correctly labeled graph of the market for sandals showing each of the following:

i. the supply of sandals and the demand for sandals

ii. the equilibrium price and quantity in the market for sandals, labeled P_1 and Q_1

b. On your graph from part a, illustrate the effect on the equilibrium price and quantity of sandals if consumer income increases and sandals are a normal good. Label the new equilibrium price and quantity P_2 and Q_2.

c. Does the market for sandals adjust to a new equilibrium in part b as a result of a surplus or a shortage? Indicate the amount of the surplus or shortage that occurs at P_1 on your graph from part a.

d. If the wages of workers producing sandals decrease at the same time consumer income increases, will the equilibrium quantity of sandals increase, decrease, or remain the same compared to Q_1 and P_1? Explain. **(10 points)**

UNIT 2
MACRO

Economic Indicators and the Business Cycle

AP® Economic Skills

1. Principle and Models (1.A, 1.B, 1.C, 1.D)
2. Interpretation (2.C)
3. Manipulation (3.A)

What Does It Mean to Be #1?

By some measures China, as a whole, has the world's largest economy. Other measures show that the U.S. economy is the largest, as it has been for the past 100 years. But what does it mean to have the largest economy in the world? If you compare China with the United States, you find that they do quite different things. China, for example, produces much of the world's clothing, while the U.S. clothing manufacturing industry has largely disappeared. On the other hand, America produces around half of the world's passenger jets, while China is just getting into the aircraft industry. So you might think that trying to compare the sizes of the two economies would be a matter of comparing apples and oranges—well, pajamas and airplanes, but you get the idea.

Economists routinely compare the sizes of economies—for example, they compare the size of the U.S. economy with that of China, and they also compare the size of the U.S. economy today with its size in the past. They do this using a measure known as *gross domestic product*, or *GDP*, the total value of goods and services produced in a country, and a closely related measure, *real GDP*, which corrects GDP for price changes. When economists say that one country's economy has overtaken the other's, they mean that China's real GDP has surpassed that of the United States (or that the United States' real GDP has surpassed that of China).

GDP and real GDP are two of the most important measures used to track the macroeconomy—that is, to quantify movements in the overall level of output and prices. In this Unit, we explain how macroeconomists measure three key aspects of the economy: gross domestic product, unemployment, and inflation.

Eric Yang/Getty Images

MODULE 2.1

The Circular Flow and Gross Domestic Product

In this Module, you will learn to:

- Explain how an economy's performance can be measured by economic indicators
- Draw a circular-flow diagram of the economy showing the flow of income and expenditure
- Define and calculate nominal gross domestic product (GDP) using each of the three approaches; expenditures, income, and value-added
- Use the circular flow diagram to explain the components of GDP and how GDP is measured

B Christopher/Alamy

National income and product accounts, or **national accounts**, keep track of the flows of money among different sectors of the economy.

The National Accounts

Almost all countries calculate a set of numbers known as the *national income and product accounts*. The **national income and product accounts**, often referred to simply as the **national accounts**, keep track of the spending of consumers, sales of producers, business investment spending, government purchases, and a variety of other flows of money among different sectors of the economy. In the United States, these numbers are calculated by the Bureau of Economic Analysis, a division of the U.S. government's Department of Commerce. Let's see how national accounts work.

The Circular-Flow Diagram

To understand the principles behind the national accounts, it helps to look at a graphic called the *circular-flow diagram*. This diagram is a simplified representation of the macroeconomy. It shows the flows of money, goods and services, and factors of production through the economy and allows us to visualize the key concepts behind the national accounts. The underlying principle of the circular-flow diagram is that the flow of money into each market or sector is equal to the flow of money coming out of that market or sector.

AP® ECON TIP

Draw the simple circular-flow diagram with two markets (product markets and factor markets) and two sectors (firms and households). Add the government sector as shown in Figure 2.1-2. Correctly label the markets and sectors and the flows between them. Add the financial and international sectors to your diagram to help you understand the expanded model we will build throughout later Modules.

The Simple Circular-Flow Diagram

The U.S. economy is a vastly complex entity, with over 150 million workers employed by millions of companies, producing millions of different goods and services. Yet you can learn some very important things about the economy by considering a simple diagram, shown in **Figure 2.1-1**. This simple model of the macroeconomy represents the transactions that take place in the economy by two kinds of flows: physical things such as goods, services, labor, or raw materials flow in one direction, and payments for these things flow in the opposite direction. In this figure, the physical flows are shown in yellow, and the money flows are shown in green.

The simplest circular-flow diagram illustrates an economy that contains only two groups: households and firms. In Figure 2.1-1, households are shown on the top and firms are shown on the bottom. Figure 2.1-1 also shows the two kinds of markets in the simple economy. To the right are **product markets** in which households buy the products (goods and services) they want from firms. Household

Product markets are where goods and services are bought and sold.

FIGURE 2.1-1 The Circular-Flow Diagram

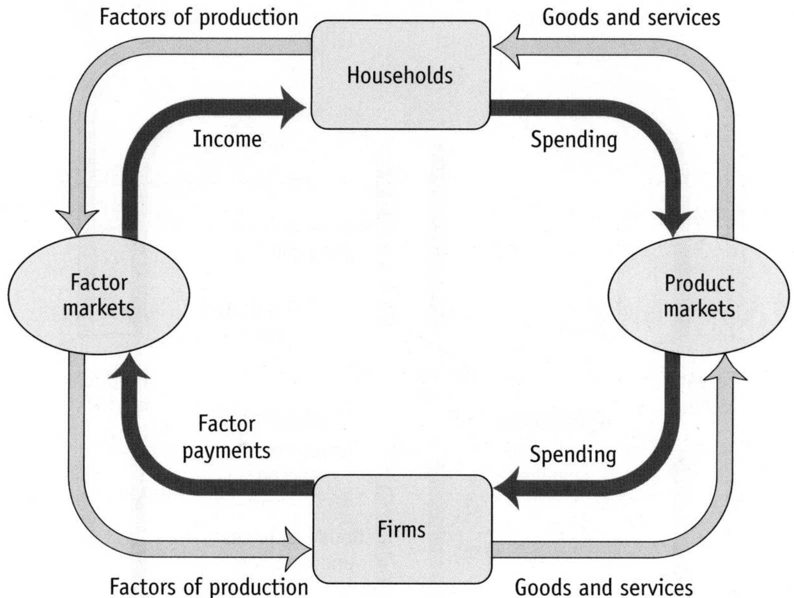

The circular flow diagram shows the flows of money, factors of production, and goods and services in the economy. In product markets, households receive goods and services from firms, generating a flow of money to the firm. Factors of production (resources) are provided to firms by households in return for payments for those factors.

payments for goods and services are called **consumer spending**. Consumer spending produces a flow of goods and services to the households and a return flow of money to the firms.

To the left are **factor markets** in which firms buy the factors of production (also known as resources) needed to produce goods and services from households. Households ultimately own, and receive income from, all of the factors of production: labor, land, capital, and entrepreneurship. The best-known factor market is the *labor market.* While most households derive the bulk of their income from wages earned by selling their labor, households also receive income in the form of rent, interest, and profit as well as wages.

This simple circular-flow diagram omits a number of real-world complications. However, the diagram is a useful aid to thinking about the economy—and we can use it as the starting point for developing a more realistic (and therefore more complicated) circular-flow model.

Consumer spending is household spending on goods and services.

Factor markets are where resources, especially capital and labor, are bought and sold.

AP® ECON TIP

Know that resources can be divided into four categories. You should become so familiar with the four categories of factors of production (labor, land, capital, and entrepreneurship) and the payments to those factors (wages, rent, interest, and profit) that you can remember and recite them from memory.

The Expanded Circular-Flow Diagram

Figure 2.1-2 is an expanded circular-flow diagram that shows how the government is involved in flows between the households and firms in the economy.

In Figure 2.1-2, the flows between households and firms remain, but flows to and from the government are added. The government injects funds into the circular flow through government spending, and funds leak out of the circular flow through taxing. **Government spending** is the total of purchases made by federal, state, and local governments, including everything from national military spending on ammunition to your local public school's spending on chalk, erasers, and teacher salaries. The government uses tax payments received from households and firms to finance much of its spending. **Taxes** are payments that firms and households are required to make to the government, and **tax revenue** refers to the funds the government receives from taxes.

Firms must pay taxes on the consumer and government spending they receive through the product markets. The funds remaining after taxes are then allocated to pay wages, rent, interest, and profit to households through the factor markets.

Government spending is total expenditures on goods and services by federal, state, and local governments.

Taxes are required payments to the government.

Tax revenue is the total amount of funds the government receives from taxes.

FIGURE 2.1-2 An Expanded Circular-Flow Diagram: How Money Flows Through the Economy

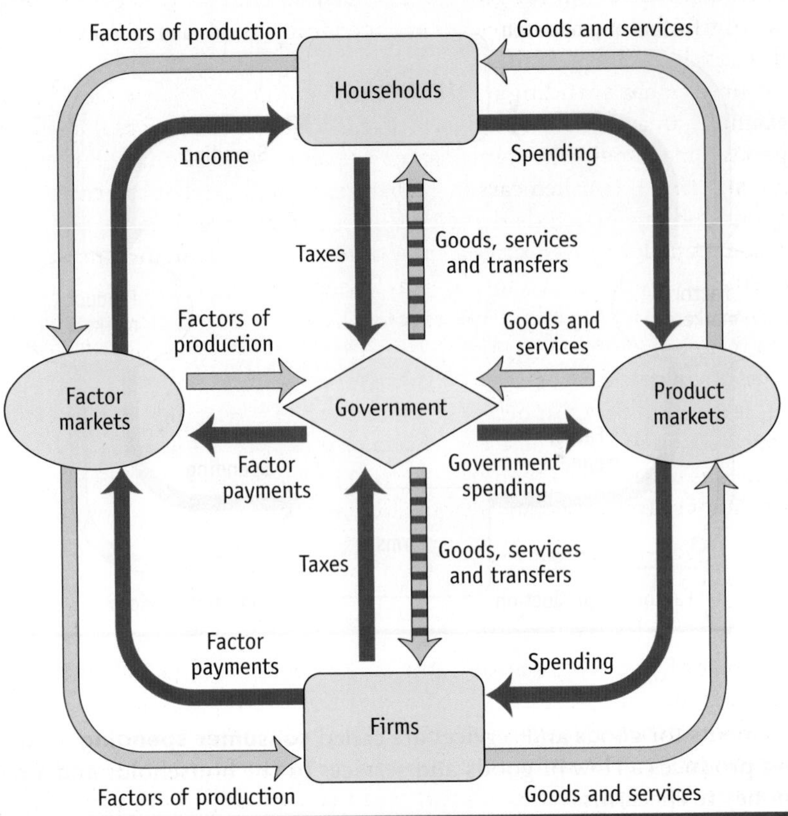

In the expanded diagram, a circular flow of funds connects the three sectors of the economy—households, firms, and government. Taxes flow to the government from both firms and households. *Government spending* on goods and services flows to the product market. Goods and services flow from the product market to the government and then on from the government to both households and firms.

Disposable income, equal to income plus government transfers minus taxes, is the total amount of household income available to spend on consumption.

Government transfers are payments that the government makes to individuals without expecting a good or service in return.

Private savings, equal to disposable income minus consumer spending, is a household's disposable income that is not spent on consumption.

Financial markets channel private savings into investment spending and government borrowing.

Households must also pay taxes to the government. After paying taxes, households allocate their remaining income—*disposable income*—to consumer spending. **Disposable income** is the total amount of household income available to spend on consumption.

In addition to collecting taxes from households and firms, the government makes payments to households and firms. **Government transfers** are payments that the government makes to households or firms without expecting a good or service in return. So in addition to receiving income from selling factors of production, some households receive income in the form of government transfers. Unemployment insurance payments are one example of a government transfer. Finally, the government uses part of its spending to provide goods and services to households and firms.

Adding Financial Markets to the Circular Flow

Some households do not spend all of their disposable income on goods and services. But that unspent income does not disappear from the circular flow. Rather, this unspent income can be represented in the diagram as a flow into and out of *financial markets.* The addition of financial markets would make our circular flow diagram very complicated, but we can use the idea of flows between markets and sections to understand how financial markets are involved in the flow of money in the economy.

Household income that is not spent on consumption becomes the household's savings. Since household savings is not spent, it leaks out of the circular flow. This **private savings** is frequently held by financial institutions (such as banks) that inject it back into the circular flow in the form of loans. **Financial markets** channel private savings into **government borrowing** and **investment spending**. The government borrows funds to pay for government spending not covered by tax revenue and firms borrow funds to finance investment spending. The financial sector of the economy is discussed in detail in Unit 4.

Government borrowing is the amount of funds borrowed by the government in the financial markets.

Investment spending includes firms' spending on new productive capital. For example, an automobile company that is building a new factory will buy investment goods – machinery like stamping presses and welding robots. Firms also accumulate an *inventory* of finished cars in preparation for shipment to dealers. **Inventories** are goods and raw materials that firms hold to facilitate their operations. The national accounts include inventories as part of investment spending. Increases in inventories of finished goods are counted as investment spending because, like machinery, they influence the ability of a firm to make future sales. Spending on additional inventory is a form of investment spending by a firm. Conversely, decreasing inventories reduces investment spending because it leads to lower future sales.

Investment spending is spending by firms on new productive physical capital, such as machinery and structures, and on changes in inventories.

Inventories are stocks of goods and raw materials held to facilitate business operations.

It's important to understand that investment spending includes spending on the construction of any structure, including a new house. Why include the construction of homes as investment spending? Because, like a factory, a new house produces a future stream of output – housing services for its occupants.

Adding the Rest of the World to the Circular Flow

The rest of the world participates in the U.S. economy in three ways. First, some of the goods and services produced in the United States are sold to residents of other countries. For example, more than half of America's annual wheat and cotton crops are sold abroad. Goods and services sold to other countries are known as **exports**. Payments for exports lead to an injection of funds from the rest of the world into the United States' circular flow. Second, some of the goods and services purchased by residents of the United States are produced abroad. For example, many consumer goods are made in China. Goods and services purchased from other countries are known as **imports**. Import purchases lead to a leakage of funds out of the United States' circular flow. Third, foreigners can participate in U.S. financial markets. Foreign lending – lending by foreigners to borrowers in the United States – generates a flow of funds into the United States from the rest of the world. Conversely, foreign borrowing – borrowing by foreigners from U.S. lenders – leads to a flow of funds out of the United States to the rest of the world. The international sector of the economy is discussed in detail in Unit 6.

Exports are goods and services sold to other countries.

Imports are goods and services purchased from other countries.

Gross domestic product or **GDP** is the total value of all final goods and services produced in the economy during a given year.

The underlying principle of this expanded circular flow is still that the inflow of money into each market or sector must equal the outflow of money coming from that market or sector. And we can use the monetary flows within the circular-flow model to measure the size of an economy. Calculating the dollar value of all the final goods and services produced in an economy, shown in the circular flow, gives us the economy's gross domestic product, one of the most important measures used to track the macroeconomy.

Michael Wolf/laif/Redux

The United States is a net importer of goods and services, such as these toys made on a production line in China.

Gross Domestic Product

Gross domestic product, or **GDP**, is a measure of the final output of an economy. It is equal to the total value of all *final goods and services* produced in an economy during a given period, usually a year. The calculated value of GDP is also known as *nominal* GDP, which will be distinguished from *real* GDP (nominal GDP

The **expenditure approach** to calculating GDP adds up **aggregate spending** on domestically produced final goods and services in the economy—the sum of consumer spending, investment spending, government purchases of goods and services, and exports minus imports.

The **income approach** to calculating GDP adds up the total factor income earned by households from firms in the economy, including rent, wages, interest, and profit.

The **value-added approach** to calculating GDP surveys firms and adds up their contributions to the value of final goods and services.

adjusted for changes in prices) in Module 2.6. In 2020, the GDP of the United States was $20,937 billion, or about $63,544 per person. The calculation of a country's GDP can be explained using our circular-flow model.

There are three ways to measure GDP. The **expenditure approach** adds up **aggregate spending** on domestically produced final goods and services in the economy—shown in the right half of Figure 2.1-2. The **income approach** adds up the total factor income earned by households from firms in the economy, including rent, wages, interest, and profit—shown in the left half of Figure 2.1-2. Recall from the discussion on circular flow that inflows must equal outflows, so these approaches will yield the same result. The **value-added approach**, the third and most complex approach to calculating GDP, surveys firms and adds up their individual contributions to the value of each final good and service.

Government statisticians use all three approaches to calculate GDP. To illustrate how they work, we will consider a hypothetical economy, shown in **Figure 2.1-3**. This economy consists of three firms—American Motors, Inc., which produces one car per year; American Steel, Inc., which produces the steel that goes into the car; and American Ore, Inc., which mines the iron ore that goes into the steel. GDP in this economy is $21,500, the value of the one car per year the economy produces. Let's look at how the three different methods of calculating GDP yield the same result.

FIGURE 2.1-3 Calculating GDP

Expenditures approach: Aggregate spending on domestically produced final goods and services = $21,500

	American Ore, Inc.	American Steel, Inc.	American Motors, Inc.	Total factor income
Value of sales	$4,200 (ore)	$9,000 (steel)	$21,500 (car)	
Intermediate goods	0	4,200 (iron ore)	9,000 (steel)	
Wages	2,000	3,700	10,000	$15,700
Interest payments	1,000	600	1,000	2,600
Rent	200	300	500	1,000
Profit	1,000	200	1,000	2,200
Total expenditure by firm	4,200	9,000	21,500	
Value added per firm = Value of sales − cost of intermediate goods	4,200	4,800	12,500	

Income approach: Total payments to factors = $21,500

Value-added approach: Sum of value added = $21,500

In this hypothetical economy consisting of three firms, GDP can be calculated in three different ways: measuring GDP as aggregate spending on domestically produced final goods and services, measuring GDP as factor income earned by households from firms in the economy, and summing the value added by each firm.

The Expenditure Approach

Final goods and services are goods and services sold to the final, or end, user.

The most common way to calculate GDP is by adding up aggregate spending on domestically produced final goods and services. That is, GDP can be measured by the flow of funds into firms, but it is important that this measurement be carried out in a way that avoids *double-counting.* A consumer's purchase of a new car from a dealership is one example of a sale of **final goods and services**: goods and services sold to the final, or end, user. In contrast, an automobile manufacturer's purchase of steel from a steel foundry or glass from a glassmaker is an example of a sale of **intermediate goods and services**: goods and services that are inputs into the production of final goods and services. In the case of intermediate goods and services, the purchaser—another firm—is *not* the final user.

Intermediate goods and services are goods and services bought from one firm by another firm to be used as inputs into the production of final goods and services.

In terms of our steel and auto example, we don't want to count both consumer spending on a car (represented in Figure 2.1-3 by the sales price of the car) and the auto producer's spending on steel (represented in Figure 2.1-3 by the price of a car's worth of steel). If we counted both expenditures, we would be counting the steel embodied in the car twice. We solve this problem by counting only the value of sales to *final buyers*, such as consumers, firms that purchase investment goods, the government, or foreign buyers. In other words, in order to avoid the double-counting of spending, we omit sales of intermediate goods and services from one business to another when estimating GDP using spending data. You can see from Figure 2.1-3 that aggregate spending on final goods and services—the finished car—is $21,500.

Photodisc/Getty Images

Steel is an intermediate good because it is sold to other product manufacturers, such as automakers or refrigerator makers, and rarely to the final consumer.

As we've already pointed out, the national accounts *do* include investment spending by firms as a part of final spending. That is, an auto company's purchase of steel to make a car isn't considered a part of final spending, but the company's purchase of new machinery for its factory *is* considered a part of final spending. What's the difference? Steel is an input that is used up in production; machinery will last for a number of years. Since purchases of capital goods that will last for a considerable time aren't closely tied to current production, the national accounts consider such purchases a form of final sales.

There are four groups that purchase goods and services in an economy: households, firms, the government, and people in foreign countries. The expenditure approach to calculating GDP adds up the spending by these four sources of aggregate spending. The largest category of spending is consumer spending by households, which we will denote with the symbol *C*. The three other components of spending are investment spending by firms, which we will denote by *I*; government purchases of goods and services, which we will denote by *G*; and spending by foreigners on domestically produced goods and services—that is, exports—which we will denote by *X*.

In reality, not all of this final spending goes toward domestically produced goods and services. Some of the consumption, investment, and government spending is for goods and services produced in other countries—imports. We must take account of spending on imports, which we will denote by *M*. Income spent on imports is income not spent on domestic goods and services—it is income that has "leaked" across national borders. So to calculate domestic production using spending data, we must subtract spending on imports. Putting this all together gives us the following equation, which breaks GDP down by the four sources of aggregate spending:

$$\textbf{(2.1-1)} \quad GDP = C + I + G + (X - M)$$

Note that the value of $(X - M)$—the difference between the value of exports and the value of imports—is known as **net exports**. We'll be seeing a lot of Equation 2.1-1 in later Modules!

AP® ECON TIP

Exports represent the flow of goods and services out of the economy into another country, with payment for the exports flowing back in. Imports represent the flow of goods and services into the economy from another country, with payment for the imports flowing back out. Because of this constant exchange of goods and services and payments, we focus on *net exports* $(X - M)$.

The Income Approach

Another way to calculate GDP is to add up all the income earned by factors of production in the economy—the wages earned by labor; the interest earned by those who

Net exports are the difference between the value of exports and the value of imports, denoted as $(X - M)$.

> **AP® ECON TIP**
> If $X > M$, then net exports will be positive, indicating a net outflow of goods and services and a net inflow of payments. If $M > X$, then net exports will be negative, indicating a net inflow of goods and services and a net outflow of payments.

lend their savings to firms and the government; the rent earned by those who lease their land or structures to firms; and the profits (money not paid to wages, interest, or rent) earned by the owners of the firms' physical capital. This income approach is a valid measure because the money that firms earn by selling goods and services must go somewhere.

Figure 2.1-3 shows how this calculation works for our simplified economy. The shaded column at the far right shows the total wages, interest, and rent paid by all these firms, as well as their total profit. Adding up all of these yields a total factor income of $21,500—again, equal to GDP.

We won't emphasize the income approach as much as the expenditure approach to calculating GDP. It's important to keep in mind, however, that all the money spent on domestically produced goods and services generates factor income to households—that is, there really is a circular flow.

> **AP® ECON TIP**
> The expenditure approach is the basis for the model of the macroeconomy presented in this course. You should be familiar with all three methods of calculating GDP (and the fact that the circular flow means you will get the same result with all three), but a solid understanding of the expenditure approach is crucial. Remember the mantra: $GDP = C + I + G + (X - M)$

The Value-Added Approach

The third way to calculate GDP is to add up the contribution of each firm along the way to the total value of the final good or service. For example, in Figure 2.1-3, the total value of the sale of all goods, intermediate and final, is $34,700: $21,500 from the sale of the car, plus $9,000 from the sale of the steel, plus $4,200 from the sale of the iron ore. Yet we know that GDP—the total value of all final goods and services in a given year—is only $21,500. Another way to avoid double-counting is to count only the **value added** by each producer in the calculation of GDP: the difference between the value of its sales and the value of the inputs it purchases from other businesses. That is, at each stage of the production process, we subtract the cost of inputs—the intermediate goods—at that stage. In this case, the value added by the auto producer is the dollar value of the cars it manufactures *minus* the cost of the steel it buys, or $12,500. The value added by the steel producer is the dollar value of the steel it produces *minus* the cost of the ore it buys, or $4,800. Only the ore producer, who we have assumed doesn't buy any inputs, has value added equal to its total sales, $4,200. The sum of the value added by all three producers is $12,500 + $4,800 + $4,200 = $21,500, equal to GDP.

> The **value added** by a producer is the value of its sales minus the value of its purchases of inputs.

Watch the video: ***The Circular Flow***

Module 2.1 Review

Check Your Understanding

1. Explain why the three methods of calculating GDP produce the same estimate of GDP.
2. Identify each of the sectors to which firms make sales. What are the various ways in which households are linked with other sectors of the economy?
3. Consider Figure 2.1-3. Explain why it would be incorrect to calculate total value added as $30,500, the sum of the sales price of a car and a car's worth of steel.

Tackle the AP® Test: Multiple-Choice Questions

1. Which of the following is not a flow represented in the circular flow diagram?
   a. prices and employment
   b. taxes and government spending
   c. income and expenditures
   d. factors of production and factor payments
   e. saving and lending
2. Which of the following leaks out of the circular flow in the expanded circular-flow model?
   a. investment spending
   b. government transfers
   c. private savings
   d. the value of exports
   e. government spending

3. Which of the following is injected into the circular flow in the expanded circular-flow model?
   a. the value of imports
   b. government transfer payments
   c. taxes
   d. private savings
   e. factor payments

4. GDP is equal to
   a. the total value of all final goods and services produced in an economy during a given period.
   b. $C + I + G + M$.
   c. the total value of intermediate goods plus final goods.
   d. the total income received by producers of final goods and services.
   e. the total of all goods and services sold during a year.

5. To calculate GDP using the income approach requires summing which of the following?
   a. wages, rent, interest, and profit
   b. C, I, G, and $(X - M)$
   c. the value of all intermediate goods
   d. all injections into the circular flow
   e. disposable income of all households

6. The value-added approach to calculating GDP involves adding up
   a. the total income spent on all final goods and services.
   b. the contributions of each firm to the total value of each final good or service.
   c. the combined earnings of each factor of production.
   d. the total cost of producing each final good and service.
   e. the income and expenditure flows in the circular flow of the economy.

7. Which of the following components makes up the largest percentage of GDP measured by aggregate spending?
   a. consumer spending
   b. investment spending
   c. government purchases of goods and services
   d. exports
   e. imports

Tackle the AP® Test: Free-Response Questions

1. The table below shows data for the country of Boland from the most recent full calendar year.

Wages	700
Consumption	600
Investment	250
Rent	100
Government Spending	100
Tax Revenue	75
Exports	100
Imports	50
Profit	100

   a. The type of data provided in the table could be used to calculate GDP using which two approaches?
   b. There is sufficient data provided in the table to calculate GDP using which method?
   c. What additional data would be required to calculate GDP using the other method you identified in part a?
   d. Calculate GDP for the country of Boland for this year. Show your work.

Rubric for FRQ 1 (5 points)

1 point: For stating that this type of data is used for the expenditures approach

1 point: For stating that this type of data can be used for the income approach

1 point: There is sufficient data to use the expenditures approach

1 point: Interest would be needed to calculate GDP using the income approach

1 point: 600 + 250 + 100 + (100 – 50) = 1000

2. a. Draw a correctly labeled circular-flow diagram showing the flows between the markets for goods and services and the factor markets.
   b. Add the government to your diagram from part a, and show how money leaks out of the economy to the government and how money is injected back into the economy by the government. **(5 points)**

MODULE 2.2

Limitations of Gross Domestic Product

In this Module, you will learn to:

- Explain why GDP can be a useful indicator of economic performance
- Identify the limitations of GDP as an indicator of economic performance

Creating the National Accounts

The national accounts owe their creation to the Great Depression. As the economy plunged, government officials found their ability to respond crippled by the lack of adequate information. They could only guess at what was happening to the economy as a whole. In response to this perceived lack of information, the Department of Commerce commissioned Simon Kuznets, a young Russian-born economist, to develop a set of national income accounts. (Kuznets later won the Nobel Prize in economics for his work.)

During World War II, policy makers felt the urgent need for a more comprehensive measure of the economy's performance than the original national accounts provided. The federal government began issuing estimates of gross domestic product and gross national product in 1942. Almost 60 years later, in its publication *Survey of Current Business*, the Department of Commerce ran an article titled "GDP: One of the Great Inventions of the 20th Century." This may seem a bit over the top, but national income accounting, invented in the United States, has since become a tool of economic analysis and policy making around the world.

Universal History Archive/Getty Images

National accounts were an important tool for policy makers to measure economic performance during World War II.

The "invention" of GDP helped economists and policy makers plan the war effort during World War II, and GDP has remained an important measure of economic performance used for economic analysis ever since. But keep in mind that the inventors of GDP had to first define what they were trying to measure to support war planning and then identify the values that were available to measure it. There was necessarily an emphasis on production and the capacity of the economy to produce output to support the war. In addition, there was an emphasis on market production, which could more easily provide information about the value of production. So, while GDP provides important information about production in the economy, it has some limitations as a more general measure of economic performance. It is important to understand exactly what is and is not included in GDP.

GDP in Practice

In Module 2.1, we learned how GDP is calculated in principle. Here, we will focus on calculating GDP in practice. **Figure 2.2-1** shows the breakdown of GDP according to the four components of aggregate spending.

The bar in Figure 2.2-1 corresponds to the expenditure approach to calculating GDP and shows the breakdown by the four types of aggregate spending. Consumer spending (*C*), which was 68.9% of GDP, dominated. Investment spending (*I*) constituted 17.3% of GDP, while government purchases of goods and services (*G*) constituted 17.6% of GDP. But some of that spending was on foreign-produced goods and services. In 2021, the value of net exports, the difference between the value of exports and the value of imports

FIGURE 2.2-1 U.S. GDP and Its Components

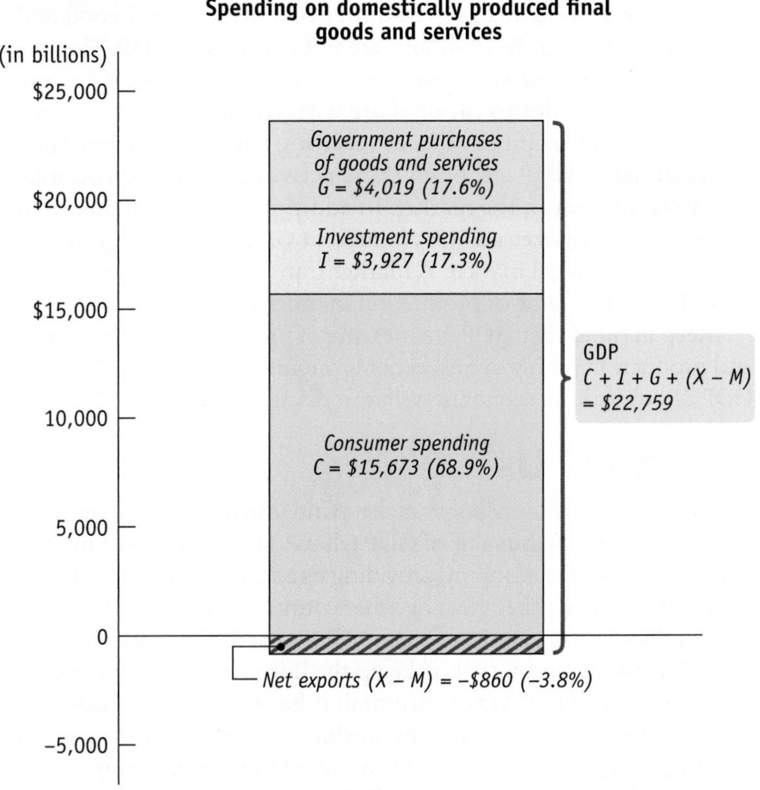

The bar in this figure, which represents U.S. GDP in the second quarter (Q2) of 2021, shows the breakdown of GDP according to the four types of aggregate spending: *C*, *I*, *G*, and $(X - M)$. It has a total height of \$22,759 billion = \$15,673 billion + \$3,927 billion + \$4,019 billion − \$860 billion. The \$860 billion shown as the purple area extending below the horizontal axis is the value of net exports, which was negative in Q2 of 2021.
Data Source: Bureau of Economic Analysis.

$(X - M$, in Equation 2.1-1), was negative \$860 billion, or −3.8% of GDP, indicating that the United States was a net importer of foreign goods and services. Thus, a portion of the bar extends below the horizontal axis to represent the negative value for net exports.

What Is (and Isn't) Included in GDP

Let's pause here to emphasize some things that are included in GDP. Recall that GDP is the total value of all *final goods and services* produced in an economy during a given year. GDP *includes* investment by firms in new capital goods, new construction of structures, and inventories.

Intermediate goods, used goods, financial assets (like stocks and bonds), transfer payments, and goods and services produced in other countries (imports) are not included in GDP. Including these items would lead to an overestimate of production in the economy by including some production twice and including other values that do not represent domestic production. Recall from the previous Module that including intermediate goods in GDP leads to double-counting, so only final goods are included. Used goods are not included in GDP for a similar reason. Used goods were already counted in the year that they were produced, and to include them again would be to double-count them. Financial assets such as stocks and bonds are not included in GDP because they don't represent either the production or the sale of final goods and services. A *bond* represents a promise to repay with interest, and a *stock* represents ownership of a firm. Recall that transfer payments represent a transfer of funds that is *not* in exchange for a good or service. And obviously, foreign-produced goods and services are not included in calculations of gross *domestic* product because they were not produced domestically.

Nonmarket production is also not included in GDP. Excluding these types of production leads to an *underestimate* of production in the economy. Examples of **nonmarket transactions** include bartered goods and services, home production (activities such as home maintenance and family care carried out by the household),

AP® ECON TIP

Understand what is and is not included as part of investment spending (*I*). Investment spending is spending on capital, the construction of structures (residential as well as commercial), and changes to inventories. Spending on inputs is not considered part of investment spending. Inputs, such as steel, are used up in production, but capital, like a metal stamp machine, is not.

Nonmarket transactions involve goods and services that are not bought and sold in a legal market.

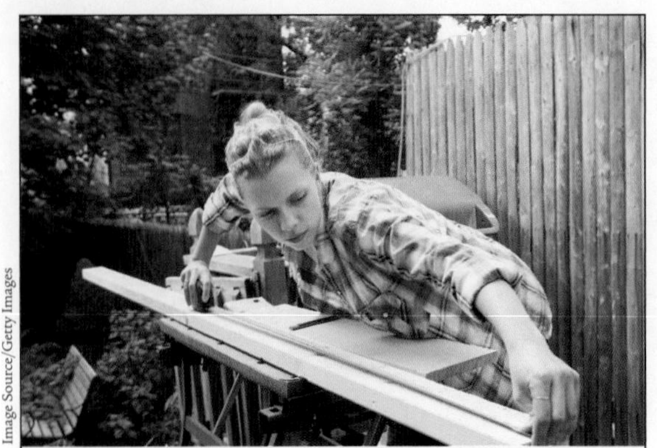
Image Source/Getty Images

Nonmarket transactions are not included in GDP, leading to an underestimate of production.

and transactions in the underground economy. If I build a fence for my neighbor and in exchange my neighbor does my taxes, the value of the fence and the tax preparation, which were a final good and a service produced in the economy, are not counted in GDP. They were produced, but no *market transaction* took place. Similarly, if you grow your own vegetables to eat or share with friends, or if you provide care for a family member without receiving payment, the services are not counted in GDP – though these activities would be counted if they were paid for in the market. In addition, the production of illegal goods and services are not counted in GDP because they were not exchanged in a legal market. A market transaction is required to reliably identify the value of production in order to include it in GDP.

Keep in mind that GDP is a measure of production in the economy, and production is only one aspect of economic performance. The use of GDP as a measure of economic welfare is discussed further in Module 2.6.

What GDP Can Tell Us

Why did Depression and World War II-era policy makers find it so important to create the national accounts? What exactly *can* the value of GDP tell us? The most important use of GDP is as a measure of the size of the economy, providing us a scale against which to compare the economic performance of other years or other countries. For example, in 2020, U.S. GDP was $20,937 billion. By comparison, Japan's GDP that year was $4,975 billion, and the combined GDP of the countries that make up the European Union was $15,276 billion. This comparison tells us that Japan, although it has the world's third-largest national economy, has a significantly smaller economy than the United States. And when taken in aggregate, Europe's economy is comparable in size to the U.S. economy.

Still, one must be careful when drawing conclusions using GDP numbers, especially when making comparisons over time or comparisons between different-sized countries. In part, the increase in the value of GDP over time represents increases in the *prices* of goods and services rather than an increase solely in output. Prices must be held constant to make comparisons in production over time. And when comparing countries with different population sizes – such as the United States and Japan – it is important to adjust for the number of people sharing the output produced in the economy. Adjusting GDP to account for changes in prices over time and for differences in population is presented in Module 2.6.

Gross domestic product is an important measure of economic performance, but it is not the only measure economists use. In the next Module, we introduce unemployment and the unemployment rate as another important measure of economic performance.

AP® ECON TIP

Know what is and is not included in GDP. *Included*: domestically produced final goods and services, capital goods, new construction of structures, and changes to inventories. *Not included*: nonmarket transactions, intermediate goods and services, inputs, used goods, financial assets such as stocks and bonds, and foreign-produced goods and services.

Module 2.2 Review

Check Your Understanding

1. Identify four types of transactions that are not included in GDP because they would overestimate the level of production.
2. Identify three types of transactions that cause GDP to be underestimated because they are not included.
3. Explain why an adjustment to GDP should be made when measuring production in an economy over time or comparing production between countries with different population sizes.

Tackle the AP® Test: Multiple-Choice Questions

1. When and why was GDP "invented"?
   a. in the 1960s in response to the environmental revolution
   b. in the 1860s in response to the Civil War
   c. in the late 1700s in response to the founding of the United States
   d. in the 1940s in response to World War II
   e. in the 1950s in response to the Cold War
2. Which of the following is included in GDP?
   a. changes to inventories
   b. intermediate goods
   c. used goods
   d. financial assets (stocks and bonds)
   e. foreign-produced goods
3. Which of the following is *not* included in GDP?
   a. capital goods such as machinery
   b. imports
   c. the value of domestically produced services
   d. government purchases of goods and services
   e. the construction of structures
4. Including which of the following in GDP would overestimate production?
   a. household production
   b. bartered goods
   c. used goods
   d. illegal goods
   e. nonmarket production
5. Not including which of the following in calculations of GDP causes it to underestimate production?
   a. intermediate goods
   b. used goods
   c. household production
   d. financial assets
   e. foreign-produced goods
6. GDP measures changes in which of the following over time?
   a. leisure time
   b. environmental quality
   c. distribution of goods
   d. harmful effects of production and consumption
   e. increases in output and prices
7. In order to measure only increases in an economy's output over time, changes in GDP must be adjusted to account for changes in which of the following?
   a. production
   b. prices
   c. population
   d. tastes
   e. technology

Tackle the AP® Test: Free-Response Questions

1. Are each of the following transactions included in calculations of GDP for the United States? Explain why or why not.
   a. Coca-Cola builds a new bottling plant in the United States.
   b. Delta Air Lines sells one of its existing airplanes to Korean Air.
   c. Ms. Moneybags buys an existing share of Walt Disney Company stock.
   d. A California farm produces almonds and sells them to a customer in Montreal, Canada.
   e. An American buys a bottle of French perfume in their hometown.
   f. A book publisher produces too many copies of a new book; the books don't sell this year, so the publisher adds the surplus books to its inventories.

Rubric for FRQ 1 (6 points)

1 point: Yes. New structures built in the United States are included in U.S. GDP.

1 point: No. The airplane is used, and sales of used goods are not included in GDP.

1 point: No. This is a transfer of ownership—not new production.

1 point: Yes. This is an export.

1 point: No. This is an import—it was not produced in the United States.

1 point: Yes. Additions to inventories are considered investments.

2. Identify three examples of nonmarket transactions and explain how nonmarket transactions lead GDP to be underestimated. **(5 points)**

MODULE 2.3 Unemployment

In this Module, you will learn to:

- Define the labor force and explain how unemployment is measured
- Define and calculate the labor force participation rate and the unemployment rate
- Explain how changes in employment and the labor market affect the unemployment rate and the labor force participation rate
- Define the three types of unemployment and the natural rate of unemployment
- Describe the limitations of the unemployment rate, including discouraged and part-time workers

damircudic/Getty Images

The unemployment rate rose during the COVID-19 pandemic, as schools and businesses closed and working parents were needed to care for children at home.

The Unemployment Rate

The unemployment rate is an important measure of an economy's performance, and it fluctuates widely over time. For example, there was concern when the unemployment rate in the United States reached 14.7% in April 2020 amid the COVID-19 pandemic. That was the highest unemployment rate reported for the United States since the 1930s, when it peaked at 24.9% during the Great Depression. On the other hand, the unemployment rate fell to as low as 1.2% in 1944, during World War II, and has frequently hovered below 5% and been of little concern.

Figure 2.3-1 shows the U.S. unemployment rate from 1948 through 2020. As you can see, the unemployment rate has fluctuated widely over the past 70 years. What does the unemployment rate mean, and when and why does it become a major concern? To make sense of the

FIGURE 2.3-1 The U.S. Unemployment Rate, 1948–2020

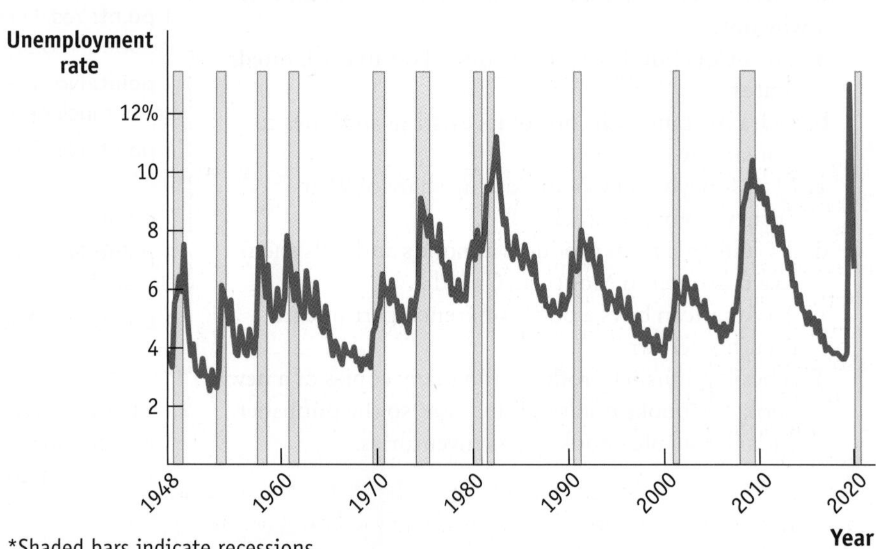

The unemployment rate fluctuates widely over time. It always rises during *recessions* (periods of economic downturn), which are shown by the shaded bars. It usually, but not always, falls during periods of economic expansion.
Data Source: Bureau of Labor Statistics; National Bureau of Economic Research.

importance of employment and unemployment as measures of economic performance, we need to first understand how they are defined and calculated.

Defining and Measuring Labor Force Participation and Unemployment

It's easy to define employment: you are **employed** if and only if you have a job. Unemployment, however, is a more subtle concept. Just because a person isn't working doesn't mean that we consider that person *unemployed*. For example, in April 2020, over 46 million retired workers in the United States received Social Security checks. Most of them were probably happy that they were no longer working, so we wouldn't consider someone who has settled into a comfortable retirement to be unemployed. There were also approximately 10 million disabled U.S. workers receiving benefits because they were unable to work. Again, although they weren't working, we wouldn't normally consider them to be unemployed.

Employed people are currently holding a job in the economy, either full time or part time.

The U.S. Census Bureau, the federal agency that collects data on unemployment, considers the *unemployed* to be those individuals who are "jobless, looking for jobs, and available for work." Retired people don't count as unemployed because they aren't looking for jobs; those who are unable to work don't count as unemployed because they aren't available for work. More specifically, an individual is considered unemployed if they don't currently have a job and have been actively seeking a job during the past four weeks. So the **unemployed** are people who are actively looking for work but aren't currently employed.

A country's **labor force** is the sum of the employed and the unemployed—that is, the people who are currently working and the people who are currently looking for work. The labor force includes all people willing and able to work. The percentage of the working age population that is willing and able to work is the **labor force participation rate.** The labor force participation rate is defined as the share of the working-age population that is in the labor force, and it is calculated as follows:

Unemployed people are actively looking for work but aren't currently employed.

The **labor force** is equal to the sum of the employed and the unemployed.

The **labor force participation rate** is the percentage of the working age population (those aged 16 or older in the United States) that is in the labor force.

The **unemployment rate** is the percentage of the total number of people in the labor force who are unemployed.

$$\textbf{(2.3-1)} \quad \text{Labor force participation rate} = \frac{\text{Labor force}}{\text{Population age 16 and older}} \times 100$$

The **unemployment rate**, defined as the percentage of the total number of people in the labor force who are unemployed, is calculated as follows:

$$\textbf{(2.3-2)} \quad \text{Unemployment rate} = \frac{\text{Number of unemployed workers}}{\text{Labor force}} \times 100$$

To estimate the numbers that go into calculating the unemployment rate, the U.S. Census Bureau carries out a monthly survey called the Current Population Survey, which involves interviewing a random sample of 60,000 American families. People are asked whether they are currently employed. If they are not employed, they are asked whether they have been looking for a job during the past four weeks. The results are then scaled up, using estimates of the total population, to estimate the total number of employed and unemployed Americans.

In general, the unemployment rate is a good indicator of how easy or difficult it is to find a job given the current state of the economy. When the unemployment rate is low, for example when it was 3.5% in February 2020 just prior to the onset of the pandemic, nearly everyone who wants a job can find one—available workers are so scarce that employers often joke that if the worker is breathing, they will be hired! By contrast, in the midst of a *recession* (an economic downturn), it is much harder to

AP® ECON TIP

You will need to calculate the size of the labor force, the labor force participation rate, and the unemployment rate. Remember: an unemployed person must be willing and able to work and be actively seeking employment. The labor force is made up of both employed and unemployed people. The labor force participation rate is the percentage of the working-age *population* in the labor force, and the unemployment rate is the percentage of the *labor force* that is unemployed.

Michael Siluk/UCG/Getty Images

Discouraged workers are nonworking people who are capable of working but have given up looking for a job due to the state of the job market.

The **underemployed** are workers who would like to work more hours or who are overqualified for their jobs.

find a job. For example, during the Great Recession in 2009, the unemployment rate in 17 states rose to over 10% (close to 15% in Michigan), with many highly qualified workers having lost their jobs and having a hard time finding new ones. (We'll learn more about recessions and depressions when we turn to business cycles in Module 2.7.)

Although the unemployment rate is a good indicator of current labor market conditions, it is not a perfect measure, as we will see next.

Limitations of the Unemployment Rate

Not everyone who would like to work but isn't working will be counted as unemployed. In particular, an individual who has given up looking for a job for the time being because there are no jobs available isn't counted as unemployed because they have not been searching for a job during the previous four weeks. Individuals who want to work but aren't currently searching because they see little prospect of finding a job given the state of the job market are known as **discouraged workers**. Because it does not count discouraged workers, the measured unemployment rate may *understate* the percentage of people who want to work but are unable to find jobs.

Another category of available workers who aren't counted as unemployed are the **underemployed**: workers who are currently employed but would like to work more hours or are overqualified for their jobs. For example, some part-time workers would like to work full time, and some college graduates work as fast-food clerks despite being overqualified. Again, these workers are not counted in the unemployment rate. Because discouraged, part-time, and underemployed workers are not counted as unemployed, the unemployment rate *understates* the level of joblessness in the economy.

The Bureau of Labor Statistics (BLS) is the federal agency that calculates the official unemployment rate. It also calculates broader "measures of labor underutilization" – for example, unemployment plus discouraged workers. **Figure 2.3-2** shows what happens to the measured unemployment rate once discouraged workers are counted.

The BLS's broadest measure of unemployment and underemployment, known as *U6*, is the sum of all undercounted workers plus the unemployed; this rate is substantially higher than the unemployment rate usually quoted by the news media. But U6 and the unemployment rate move very much in parallel, so changes in the unemployment rate remain a useful guide to what's happening in the overall labor market.

On the other hand, the unemployment rate may indicate a larger issue with unemployment than actually exists in the economy. People searching for work frequently take at least a few weeks to find a suitable job. Yet a worker who is quite confident of finding a job, but who has not yet accepted a position, is counted as unemployed. As a consequence, the unemployment rate never falls to zero, even in boom times when jobs are plentiful. In addition, people may indicate that they are willing and able to work and are actively seeking employment when they are not. For example, often people must indicate that they have looked for work in order to receive unemployment benefits. If someone indicates that they have looked for work to qualify for benefits, when in reality they are not seeking a job, the unemployment rate will be *overstated*.

Finally, it's important to realize that the unemployment rate varies greatly among demographic groups. Other things equal, jobs are generally easier to find for more experienced workers and for workers during their "prime" working years, from ages 25 to 54. For younger workers, as well as workers nearing retirement age, jobs are typically harder to find. Unemployment rates also differ by gender. **Figure 2.3-3** shows the unemployment rates for different ethnic and racial groups in 2021, when the U.S. unemployment rate reached 14.7%. As you can see, the unemployment rate for African-American workers was much higher than the national average (8.4% versus 5.2%); the unemployment

FIGURE 2.3-2 Alternative Measure of Unemployment, 1994–2020

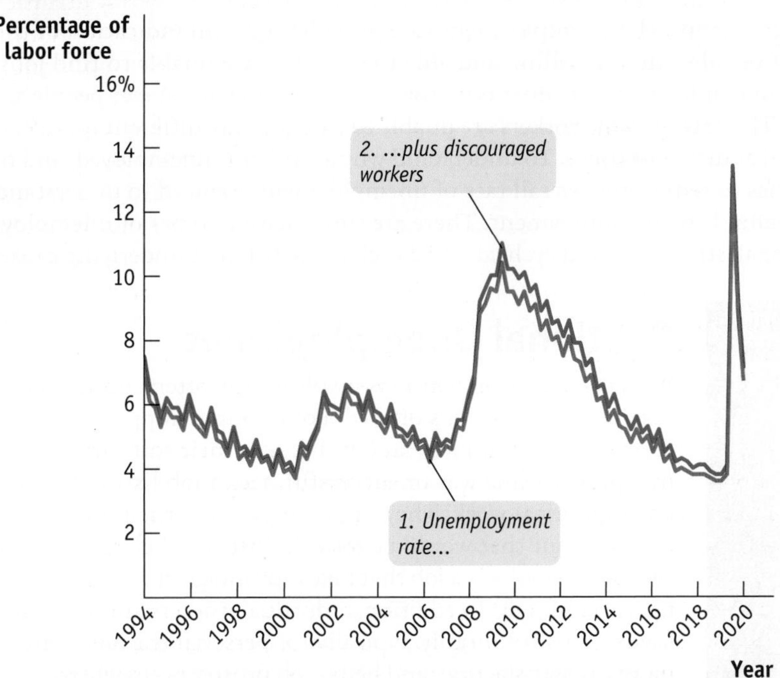

The unemployment number usually quoted in the news media counts people as unemployed only if they have been looking for work during the past four weeks. A broader measure also counts discouraged workers. The broader measure shows a higher unemployment rate—but moves closely in parallel with the narrower rate. *Data Source:* Bureau of Labor Statistics.

rate for White teenagers (ages 16–19) was 9.6% compared to the national average of 5.2%; and the unemployment rate for Black or African American teenagers, at 15.9%, was over three times the national average. (Bear in mind that a teenager isn't considered unemployed, even if they aren't working, unless that teenager is looking for work but can't find it.) So even at a time when the overall unemployment rate is relatively low, jobs are harder to find for some groups.

Although the unemployment rate is not an exact measure of the percentage of people unable to find jobs, it is a good indicator of overall labor market conditions. The ups and downs of the unemployment rate closely reflect economic changes that have a significant impact on people's lives.

AP® ECON TIP

GDP and unemployment move in opposite directions because more production means more workers must be hired, and less production means fewer workers are hired.

FIGURE 2.3-3 Unemployment Rates of Different Groups, 2021

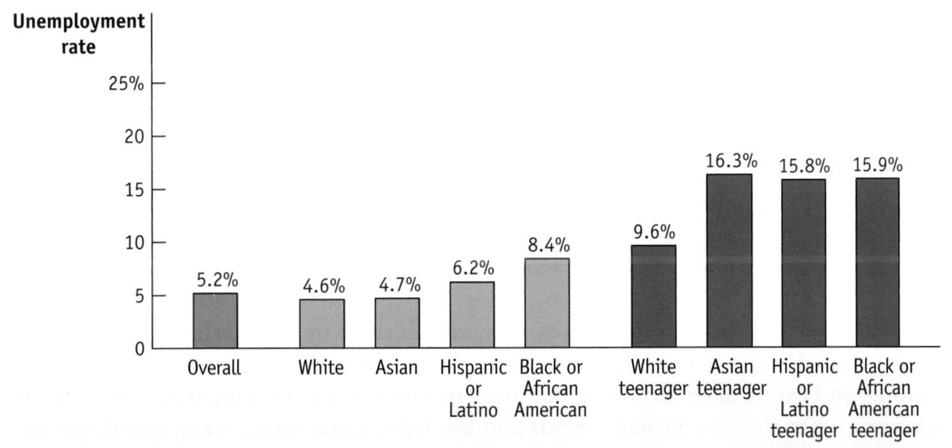

Unemployment rates vary greatly among different demographic groups. For example, although the overall unemployment rate in the third quarter of 2021 was 5.2%, the unemployment rate among Asian teenagers was 16.3%. As a result, even during periods of low overall unemployment, unemployment remains a serious problem for some groups. *Data Source:* Bureau of Labor Statistics.

AP® ECON TIP

Know how to identify the type of unemployment—frictional, structural, or cyclical—given a specific scenario.

Types of Unemployment

Despite its limitations, the unemployment rate provides a useful indication of the percentage of people who are willing and able to work but are unable to find jobs. However, the unemployment rate does not provide information about *why* people are unemployed. The reasons why workers are unable to find jobs are different for different people and at different times. To understand why a worker is unemployed, and to identify policies to reduce the overall rate of unemployment, we need to understand the reasons behind the unemployment. There are three distinct types of unemployment – frictional, structural, and cyclical – and each has a different underlying cause.

Bill Varie/Getty Images

Frictional Unemployment

Workers who lose their jobs involuntarily often choose not to take the first new jobs offered. For example, suppose a skilled computer programmer, laid off because their software company's product line was unsuccessful, sees a job listing for low-paying clerical work. They might respond to the post and get the job – but that would be foolish. Instead, they should take the time to look for a job that takes advantage of their skills and pays accordingly. In addition, individual workers are constantly leaving jobs voluntarily, typically for personal reasons – family moves, dissatisfaction, and better job prospects elsewhere.

Economists say that workers who spend time looking for employment are engaged in job search. If all workers and all jobs were alike, job search wouldn't be necessary; if information about jobs and workers were perfect, job search would be very quick. In practice, however, it's normal for a worker who leaves or loses a job, or a young worker seeking a first job, to spend at least a few weeks searching.

Frictional unemployment is unemployment due to the time workers spend in job search.

Frictional unemployment is unemployment due to the time workers spend in job search. A certain amount of frictional unemployment is inevitable, for two reasons. One is the constant process of job creation and job destruction. The second reason is the fact that new workers are always entering the labor market.

A limited amount of frictional unemployment is relatively harmless and may even be a good thing. The economy is more productive if workers take the time to find jobs that are well matched to their skills, and workers who are unemployed for a brief period while searching for the right job don't experience great hardship. In fact, when there is a low unemployment rate, periods of unemployment tend to be quite short, suggesting that much of the unemployment is frictional. **Figure 2.3-4** shows the composition of unemployment in 2019, when the unemployment rate was only 3.5%: 34.8% of the unemployed had been unemployed for less than 5 weeks, and only 35.4% had been unemployed for 15 or more weeks. Just 21.1% were considered to be "long-term unemployed" – unemployed for 27 or more weeks. The picture looked very different in 2010, after unemployment had been high for an extended period of time.

In periods of higher unemployment, workers tend to be jobless for longer periods of time, suggesting that a smaller share of unemployment is frictional. By early 2010, when unemployment had been high for several months, for instance, the fraction of unemployed workers considered "long-term unemployed" had jumped to 41%.

AP® ECON TIP

Frictional unemployment always exists in an economy because there will always be people looking for jobs —either their first job or a better job. When describing this concept, remember that frictional unemployment does not necessarily indicate a problem for the economy, and a limited amount of it is even a good thing if people are finding jobs that match their skills and preferences.

Public policy designed to help workers who lose their jobs can lead to frictional unemployment as an unintended side effect. Most economically advanced countries provide benefits to laid-off workers as a way to tide them over until they find a new job. In the United States, these benefits typically replace only a small fraction of a worker's income and expire after 26 weeks, in most cases. In other countries, particularly some in Europe, benefits are more generous and last longer. However, unemployment benefits in the United States were expanded in 2020 in response to the dramatic increase in

FIGURE 2.3-4 Distribution of the Unemployed by Duration of Unemployment, 2010 and 2019

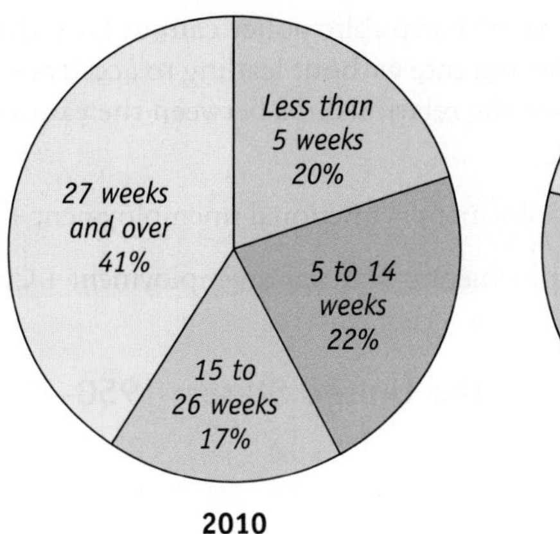

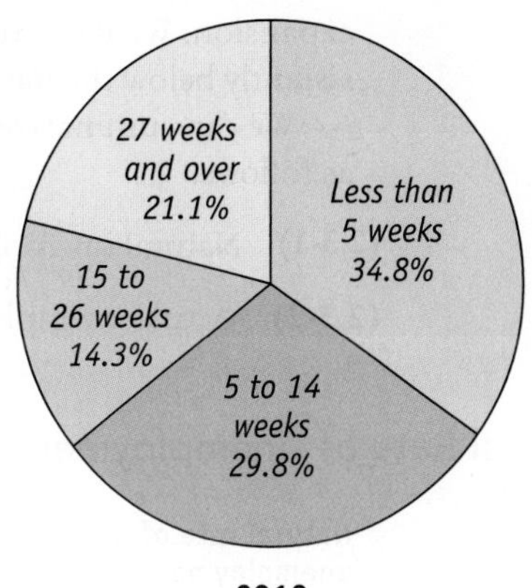

In years when the unemployment rate is low, most unemployed workers are unemployed for only a short period. In 2019, a year of low unemployment, 34.8% of the unemployed had been unemployed for less than 5 weeks and 64.6% for less than 15 weeks. The short duration of unemployment for most workers suggests that most unemployment in 2019 was frictional. In early 2010, by contrast, only 20% of the unemployed had been unemployed for less than 5 weeks, but 41% had been unemployed for 27 or more weeks, indicating that during periods of high unemployment, a smaller share of unemployment is frictional.
Data Source: Bureau of Labor Statistics.

the unemployment rate at the start of the COVID-19 pandemic. The federal government expanded unemployment benefits through the Families First Coronavirus Response Act (FFCRA) and the Coronavirus Aid, Relief, and Economic Security (CARES) Act. These laws provided additional flexibility and funding for state unemployment insurance agencies to provide unemployment insurance for many workers impacted by the pandemic (including for workers who are not ordinarily eligible for unemployment benefits) and to extend the duration of unemployment benefit payments. The drawback to generous unemployment benefits is that they reduce the incentive to quickly find a new job. By keeping more people searching for longer, the benefits increase frictional unemployment.

> **AP® ECON TIP**
>
> Make sure you can recognize examples of structural unemployment. Its causes include a mismatch between workers' skills and job requirements, technological change, and automation. Job training is a way to address structural unemployment.

Structural Unemployment

Structural unemployment is unemployment that results from a mismatch between the characteristics of job seekers and the types of jobs available in the economy—workers either lack the skills required for the available jobs or there are more people seeking jobs in a labor market than there are jobs available at the current wage rate. In other words, structural unemployment indicates a mismatch between supply and demand in labor markets.

Structural unemployment is unemployment that results when workers lack the skills required for the available jobs, or there are more people seeking jobs in a labor market than there are jobs available at the current wage rate.

Cyclical Unemployment and the Natural Rate of Unemployment

Because some frictional unemployment is inevitable and because many economies also suffer from structural unemployment, a certain amount of unemployment is normal, or "natural." Actual unemployment fluctuates around this normal level. The **natural rate of unemployment** is the rate of unemployment that arises from the effects of frictional plus structural unemployment. It is the normal, or *minimum feasible*, unemployment rate around which the actual unemployment rate fluctuates.

There is no specific value for the natural rate of unemployment, but **Figure 2.3-5** provides estimates of the natural rates of unemployment in the United States between 1950 and 2020. The graph shows that the natural unemployment rate has changed very slowly and stayed within a 1.7% range over this time period. **Cyclical unemployment** is the deviation of the actual rate of unemployment from the natural rate; that is, it is the difference between the actual and natural rates of unemployment. As the name

The **natural rate of unemployment** is the unemployment rate that arises from the effects of frictional plus structural unemployment.

Cyclical unemployment is the deviation of the actual rate of unemployment from the natural rate.

suggests, cyclical unemployment is the share of unemployment that arises from the business cycle. Jobs lost due to a recession will return after the economy moves into expansion. We'll see later that public policy cannot keep the unemployment rate persistently below the natural rate without leading to accelerating inflation.

We can summarize the relationships between the various types of unemployment as follows:

(2.3-1) Natural unemployment = Frictional unemployment + Structural unemployment

(2.3-2) Actual unemployment = Natural unemployment + Cyclical unemployment

FIGURE 2.3-5 **Natural Rate of Unemployment in the United States, 1950–2020**

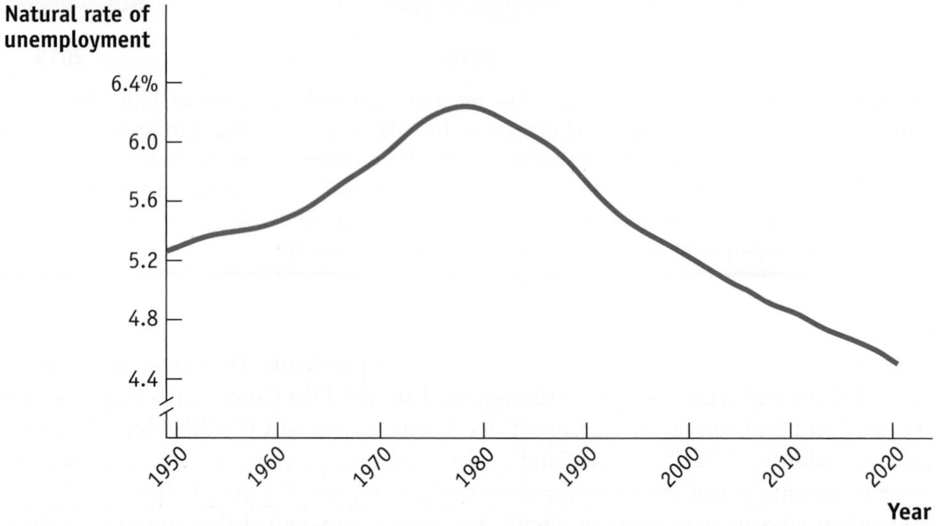

The Federal Reserve now reports its estimate of the natural rate of unemployment under the title "Noncyclical Rate of Unemployment" – the previous title was the Natural Rate of Unemployment (Long Term). This is the rate of unemployment arising from all sources except cyclical unemployment. Over time, the natural rate of unemployment in the United States has remained between 4.5% and 6.2%.
Data Source: FRED.

AP® ECON TIP

The natural rate of unemployment is never zero because frictional employment always exists. Think of the natural rate as the lowest feasible level of unemployment that can be reached—a level that will be identified in the models of the macroeconomy presented later in the course. Numerical estimates of the natural rate differ based on when, where, and why they are estimated, but the concept of the natural unemployment rate is always the same.

Perhaps because of its name, people often imagine that the natural rate of unemployment is a constant that doesn't change over time and can't be affected by policy. Neither proposition is true. Let's take a moment to stress two facts: the natural rate of unemployment changes over time, and it can be affected by economic policies.

Changes in the Natural Rate of Unemployment

Private-sector economists and government agencies need estimates of the natural rate of unemployment both to make forecasts and to conduct policy analyses. Almost all these estimates show that the U.S. natural rate rises and falls over time. For example, the data from the Federal Reserve Bank of St. Louis shown in Figure 2.3-5 indicates that the U.S. natural rate of unemployment was 5.28% in 1950, rose to 6.27% by the end of the 1970s, and then fell to a low of 4.5% in 2020. European countries have experienced even larger swings in their natural rates of unemployment.

What causes the natural rate of unemployment to change? The most important factors are changes in the characteristics of the labor force, changes in labor market institutions, and changes in government policies. Let's look briefly at each factor.

Changes in Labor Force Characteristics

In July 2021, the overall rate of unemployment in the United States was 5.4%. Young workers, however, had much higher unemployment rates: 9.2% for workers aged 16 to 24. Workers aged 25 to 54 had an unemployment rate of only 5.1%.

In general, unemployment rates tend to be lower for experienced workers than for inexperienced workers. Because experienced workers tend to stay in a given job longer than do inexperienced ones, they have lower frictional unemployment. Also, because older workers are more likely than young workers to be family breadwinners, they have a stronger incentive to find and keep jobs.

One reason the natural rate of unemployment rose during the 1970s was a large rise in the number of new workers—children of the post-World War II baby boom entered the labor force, as did a rising percentage of married women. As **Figure 2.3-6** shows, both the percentage of the labor force less than 25 years old and the percentage of women in the labor force surged in the 1970s. By the end of the 1990s, however, the share of women in the labor force had leveled off and the percentage of workers under 25 had fallen sharply. As a result, the labor force as a whole is more experienced today than it was in the 1970s, one likely reason that the natural rate of unemployment is lower today than in the 1970s.

FIGURE 2.3-6 **The Changing Makeup of the U.S. Labor Force, 1948–2020**

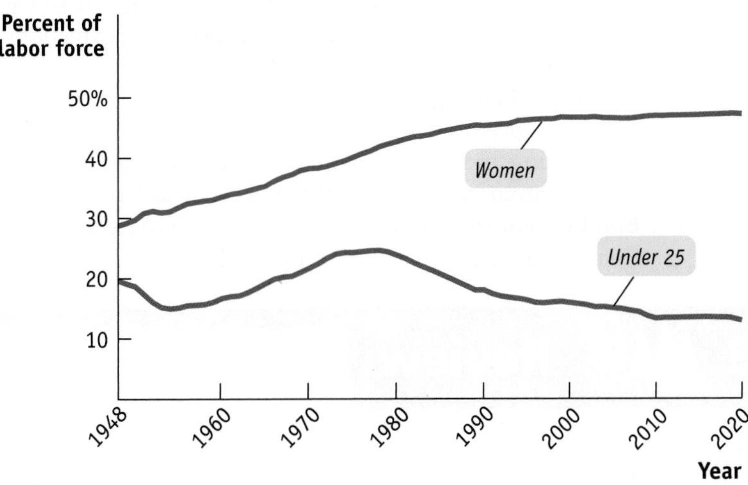

In the 1970s the percentage of the labor force consisting of women rose rapidly, as did the percentage under age 25. These changes reflected the entry of large numbers of women into the paid labor force for the first time and the fact that baby boomers were reaching working age. The natural rate of unemployment may have risen because many of these workers were relatively inexperienced. Today, the labor force is much more experienced, which is one possible reason the natural rate has fallen since the 1970s.
Data Source: Bureau of Labor Statistics.

Changes in Labor Market Institutions

The natural rate of unemployment can change as a result of changes in *labor market institutions*, which refer to the policy interventions and organizations within labor markets. Changes in several important labor market institutions have affected the natural rate of unemployment in the United States and other countries.

For example, labor unions are associations of workers that protect worker rights and interests, including bargaining for higher wages. Labor unions that negotiate wages above the equilibrium level can be a source of structural unemployment. Some economists believe that strong labor unions are one of the reasons for the high natural rate of unemployment in some European countries. In the United States, a sharp fall in union membership after 1980 may have been one reason the natural rate of unemployment fell between the 1970s and the 1990s.

Other institutional changes may also have been at work. For example, some labor economists believe that temporary employment agencies reduce frictional unemployment by matching workers to jobs. Furthermore, networking and job search sites and social media have reduced frictional unemployment by making information about job openings and job-seekers more widely available, thereby helping workers avoid a prolonged job search.

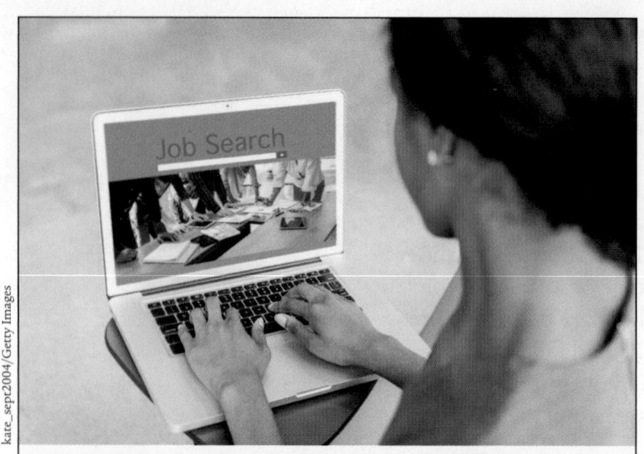

kate_sept2004/Getty Images

Online job search engines have reduced frictional unemployment by helping to match employers with job-seekers.

Technological change, coupled with labor market institutions, can also affect the natural rate of unemployment. Technological change leads to an increase in the demand for skilled workers who are familiar with the relevant technology and a reduction in the demand for unskilled workers, who are not. Economic theory predicts that wages should increase for skilled workers and decrease for unskilled workers. But if wages for unskilled workers cannot go down – say, due to laws or contracts – increased structural unemployment, and therefore a higher natural rate of unemployment, will result.

Changes in Government Policies

A high minimum wage can cause structural unemployment if the quantity of workers supplied at the wage exceeds the quantity demanded. Generous unemployment benefits, like those provided in 2020 in response to the COVID-19 pandemic, can increase frictional unemployment by reducing the cost of unemployment. So government policies intended to help workers can have the undesirable side effect of raising the natural rate of unemployment.

Some government policies, however, may reduce the natural rate. Two examples are job training and employment subsidies. Job-training programs are supposed to provide unemployed workers with skills that widen the range of jobs they can perform. Employment subsidies are payments either to workers or to employers that provide a financial incentive to accept or offer jobs.

Module 2.3 Review

Check Your Understanding

1. Suppose that innovative employment websites are more quickly able to match job-seekers with suitable jobs. What effect will this have on the unemployment rate over time? Also suppose that these websites encourage job-seekers who had given up their searches to begin looking again. What effect will this have on the unemployment rate?
2. For each of the following examples, is the person identified counted as unemployed? Explain.
   - **a.** Rosa, an older worker, has been laid off and gave up looking for work months ago.
   - **b.** Anthony, a schoolteacher, has chosen not to work during his three-month summer break.
   - **c.** Grace, an investment banker, has been laid off and is currently searching for another position.
   - **d.** Sergio, a classically trained musician, can only find work playing for local parties.
   - **e.** Natasha, a graduate student, went back to school because jobs were scarce.
3. Explain the following statements.
   - **a.** Frictional unemployment always exists.
   - **b.** Frictional unemployment accounts for a larger share of total unemployment when the unemployment rate is low.

Tackle the AP® Test: Multiple-Choice Questions

1. To be considered unemployed, a person must
   - **a.** collect unemployment insurance.
   - **b.** work more than 30 hours per week.
   - **c.** have been laid off from a job that was held for one year or longer.
   - **d.** not be working but want to have a job.
   - **e.** not be working but be available for and actively seeking a job.
2. The unemployment problem in an economy may be understated by the unemployment rate due to
   - **a.** people lying about seeking a job.
   - **b.** discouraged workers.
   - **c.** job candidates with one offer but waiting for more.
   - **d.** overemployed workers.
   - **e.** none of the above.

Use the information for a hypothetical economy presented in the following table to answer Questions 3–4.

Population age 16 and older = 200,000
Labor force = 100,000
Number of people working part time = 20,000
Number of people working full time = 70,000

3. What is the labor force participation rate?
a. 70%
b. 50%
c. 20%
d. 10%
e. 5%

4. What is the unemployment rate?
a. 70%
b. 50%
c. 20%
d. 10%
e. 5%

5. If real GDP is falling, which of the following is true?
a. The economy is in an expansion.
b. Unemployment is rising.
c. The number of discouraged workers is decreasing.
d. Underemployment is falling.
e. None of the above are true.

6. What type of unemployment is created by a recession?
a. frictional
b. structural
c. cyclical
d. natural
e. full

7. A person who is unemployed because of a mismatch between the quantity of labor supplied and the quantity of labor demanded is experiencing what type of unemployment?
a. frictional
b. structural
c. cyclical
d. natural
e. full

8. Which of the following is true of the natural rate of unemployment?
a. It includes frictional unemployment.
b. It includes cyclical unemployment.
c. It includes all types of unemployment.
d. It is equal to 0%.
e. All of the above are true.

9. Which of the following is an example of structural unemployment?
a. an assembly line worker laid off during a recession
b. a college graduate looking for their first job
c. a cable TV installer laid off because people aren't using cable
d. a worker who quit their job to find another that is closer to family
e. all of the above

10. Actual unemployment is equal to natural unemployment
a. minus structural unemployment.
b. plus cyclical unemployment.
c. plus frictional unemployment.
d. minus cyclical unemployment.
e. minus frictional unemployment.

Tackle the AP® Test: Free-Response Questions

1. Use the data provided in the following table to calculate each of the following. Show how you calculate each.
a. the size of the labor force
b. the labor force participation rate
c. the unemployment rate

Population age 16 and older = 12 million
Employment = 5 million
Unemployment = 1 million

Rubric for FRQ 1 (6 points)

1 point: 6 million

1 point: employment + unemployment = 5 million + 1 million = 6 million

1 point: 50%

1 point: (labor force/population) × 100
= ((5 million + 1 million)/12 million) × 100
= (6 million/12 million) × 100 = 50%

1 point: 16.67%

1 point: (unemployment / labor force) × 100
= (1 million/(5 million + 1 million)) × 100
= (1 million/6 million) × 100 = 16.67%

2. **a.** The natural rate of unemployment is made up of which types of unemployment?
b. Explain how cyclical unemployment relates to the natural rate of unemployment.
c. List three factors that can lead to a change in the natural rate of unemployment. **(5 points)**

MODULE 2.4

Price Indices and Inflation

In this Module, you will learn to:

- Define the Consumer Price Index (CPI), inflation, deflation, and disinflation
- Explain how price indices can be used to calculate the inflation rate and to compare nominal values over time
- Identify shortcomings of the CPI as a measure of inflation, including substitution bias
- Differentiate between nominal and real values of income and wages
- Use the CPI to calculate changes in real values

Inflation, Deflation, and Price Stability

In the United States in 1970, the average worker was paid $3.40 an hour. As of February 2021, the average hourly earnings for such a worker had risen to $30.54. Three cheers for economic progress!

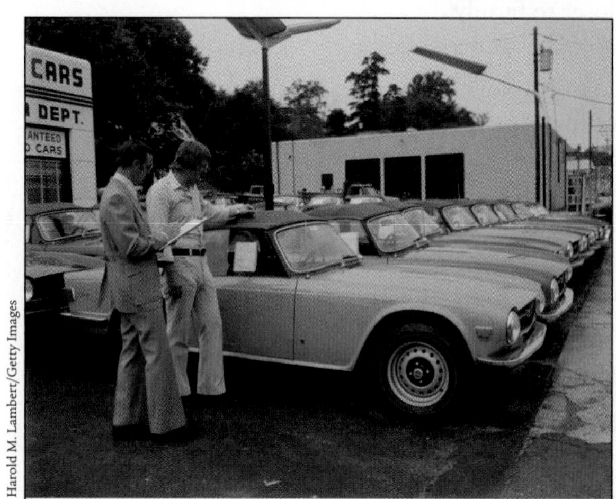

Harold M. Lambert/Getty Images

In 1970, the average price of goods and services, such as a new car, was much lower than it is today.

But wait—American workers may have been paid much more in 2021, but they also faced a much higher cost of living. In 1970, a new car cost only about $3,500; in 2021, the average new car cost was around $36,000. The price of a loaf of white bread went from about $0.20 to $2.54. And the price of a pound of tomatoes rose from just $0.19 to $1.89. If we compare the percentage increase in earnings between 1970 and 2021 with the increase in the overall price level (the price level for all goods and services), we see that the average worker's paycheck goes only slightly farther today than it did 50 years ago. In other words, the increase in the cost of living wiped out many of the wage gains of the typical worker from 1970 to 2021. What caused this situation?

Between 1970 and 2021, the economy experienced substantial **inflation**, a rise in the overall level of prices. The opposite of inflation is **deflation**, a fall in the overall level of prices. Bringing down the rate of increase in the price level is known as *disinflation*—which is different from a decrease in the price level and is discussed further in Module 2.5. A change in the prices of a few goods changes the opportunity cost of purchasing those goods but does not constitute inflation or deflation. These terms are reserved for more general changes in the prices of goods and services throughout the economy.

A rising overall price level is **inflation**. A falling overall price level is **deflation**.

Both inflation and deflation can pose problems for the economy. Inflation discourages people from holding on to cash, because if the price level is rising, cash loses value. That is, if the price level rises, a dollar will buy less than it would have before the rise. As we will see in our more detailed discussion of inflation later in this Module, in periods of rapidly rising prices, people stop holding cash altogether and instead trade goods for goods.

Deflation can cause the opposite problem. That is, if the overall price level falls, a dollar will buy more than it would have before. In this situation, it can be more attractive for people to hold on to the cash they currently have rather than to invest it in new factories and other productive assets. This tendency can deepen a recession.

The economy has **price stability** when the overall price level is changing only slowly if at all.

In Module 2.5, we will look at other costs of inflation and deflation. For now, note that economists have a general goal of **price stability**—meaning that the overall price level is changing only slowly if at all—because it avoids uncertainty about prices and helps to keep the economy stable.

Inflation and Deflation

As we'll see shortly, inflation can be measured as a percentage change in price level over a year. Between 1990 and 2020, the rate of inflation in the United States fluctuated between −.04% and 4.2%. During 2021, monthly inflation rates rose to more than 5.4% amid growing concern over the increasing price level. And in March 2022, inflation hit 8.5%, the highest it had been in over 40 years. While an inflation rate of 8.5% is far from *hyperinflation* – very high and accelerating rates of inflation – it does represent an increase beyond the range of inflation rates seen in the United States over the previous 30 years. For comparison, with the worst hyperinflation, some countries saw their inflation rates increase by 100% *every day*.

Why is high inflation a problem in an economy? Why are policy makers so concerned about hyperinflation that they get anxious when they see the inflation rate moving upward even slightly? Before we answer that question, we first need to understand how inflation is calculated.

The Level of Prices Doesn't Matter . . .

The most common misconception about inflation is that an increase in the price level makes everyone poorer – after all, a given amount of money buys less. But inflation does *not* make everyone poorer. To see why, it's helpful to imagine what would happen if a country replaced its currency with a new currency.

filmfoto/Alamy Stock Photo

An example of this kind of currency conversion happened in 2002, when France, like many other European countries, replaced its national currency, the franc, with the euro. People turned in their franc coins and notes, and received euro coins and notes in exchange, at a rate of 6.55957 francs per euro. At the same time, all contracts were restated in euros at the same rate of exchange. For example, if a French citizen had a home mortgage debt of 500,000 francs, this became a debt of 500,000/6.55957 = 76,224.51 euros. If a worker's contract specified that they should be paid 100 francs per hour, it became a contract specifying a wage of 100/6.55957 = 15.2449 euros per hour, and so on.

You could imagine doing the same thing in the United States, replacing the dollar with a "new dollar" at a rate of exchange of, say, 7 to 1. If you owed $140,000 on your home, that would become a debt of 20,000 new dollars. If you had a wage rate of $14 an hour, it would become 2 new dollars an hour, and so on. This would bring the overall U.S. price level back to about what it was when John F. Kennedy was president.

So would everyone be richer as a result because prices would be only one-seventh as high? Of course not. Prices would be lower, but so would wages and incomes. The *nominal* wages and incomes that people receive (that is, the wages and incomes unadjusted for inflation) would decrease, but their *real* wages and incomes (wages and incomes adjusted for inflation) would stay the same. If you cut a worker's wage to one-seventh of its previous value, but also cut all prices to one-seventh of their previous level, the worker's **real wage** – the wage rate divided by the price level to adjust for the effects of inflation or deflation – doesn't change. In fact, bringing the overall price level back to what it was during the Kennedy administration would have no effect on overall purchasing power, because doing so would reduce income exactly as much as it reduced prices. Conversely, the rise in prices that has actually taken place since the early 1960s hasn't made America poorer, because it has also raised incomes by the same amount: **real income** – income divided by the price level to adjust for the effects of inflation or deflation – hasn't been affected by the rise in overall prices.

The moral of this story is that the *level* of prices doesn't matter: the United States would be no richer than it is now if the overall level of prices was still as low as it was in 1970; conversely, the rise in prices over the past 50 years hasn't made us poorer.

AP® ECON TIP

"Real" values (including real wages, real income, real interest rates, and real GDP) have been adjusted for changes in the price level—whether through inflation or deflation—while nominal values have not. You can remember the difference between real and nominal by thinking, "Nominal now!"

The **real wage** is the wage rate divided by the price level to adjust for the effects of inflation or deflation.

Real income is income divided by the price level to adjust for the effects of inflation or deflation.

. . . But the Rate of Change of Prices Does

The **inflation rate** is the percentage increase in the overall level of prices per year.

The conclusion that the level of prices doesn't matter might seem to imply that the inflation rate doesn't matter either. But that's not true. To see why, it's crucial to distinguish between the *level of prices* and the *inflation rate*. For now, let's look at the **inflation rate**, the percentage increase in the overall level of prices per year. The inflation rate is calculated as follows:

$$\text{Inflation rate} = \frac{\text{Price level in year 2} - \text{Price level in year 1}}{\text{Price level in year 1}} \times 100$$

Figure 2.4-1 highlights the difference between the price level and the inflation rate in the United States since 1969, with the price level measured along the left vertical axis and the inflation rate measured along the right vertical axis. In the 2000s, the overall level of prices in the United States was much higher than it was in 1969—but that, as we've learned, didn't matter. The inflation rate in the 2000s, however, was much lower than in the 1970s—and that almost certainly made the economy richer than it would have been if high inflation had continued. We will look in more detail at the causes of inflation in Unit 5.

FIGURE 2.4-1 The Price Level Versus the Inflation Rate, 1969–2020

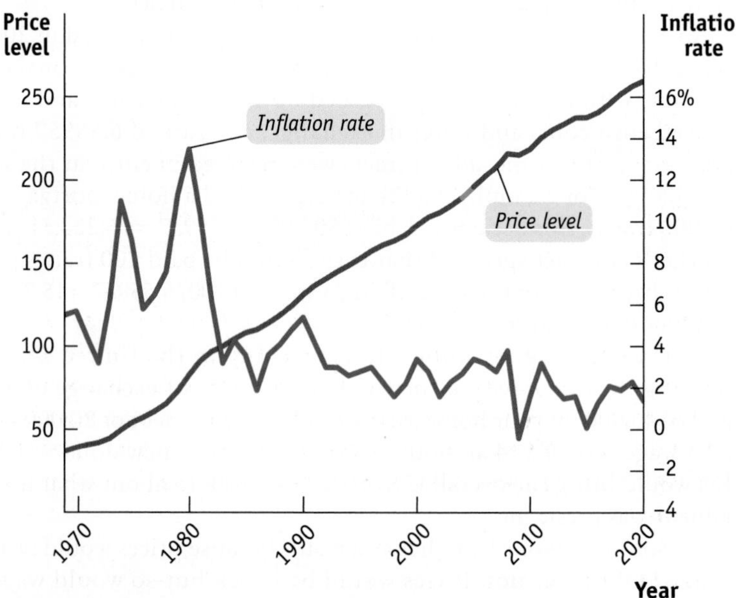

Over the past half century, the price level has continuously gone up. But the *inflation rate*—the rate at which consumer prices are rising—has had both ups and downs.
Data Source: Bureau of Labor Statistics.

Price Indices and the Aggregate Price Level

The **aggregate price level** is a measure of the overall level of prices in the economy.

Just as macroeconomists find it useful to have a single number, GDP, to represent the overall level of output, they also find it useful to have a single number to represent the overall level of prices: the **aggregate price level**. Yet a huge variety of goods and services are produced and consumed in the economy. How can we summarize the prices of all these goods and services with a single number? The answer lies in the concept of a *price index*—a concept best introduced with an example.

Suppose that a frost in Florida destroys most of the citrus harvest. As a result, the price of oranges rises from $0.20 each to $0.40 each, the price of grapefruit rises from

$0.60 to $1.00, and the price of lemons rises from $0.25 to $0.45. How much has the price of citrus fruit increased?

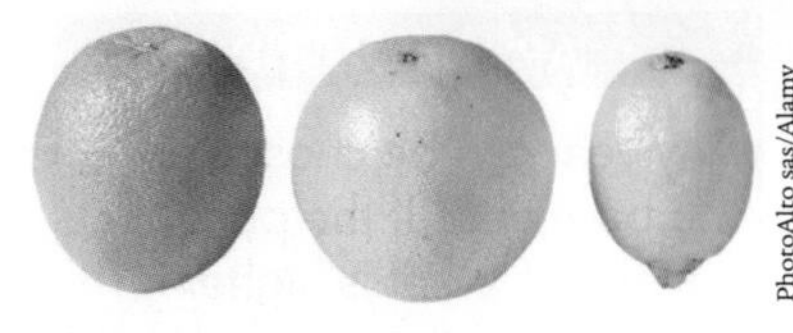
PhotoAlto sas/Alamy

One way to answer that question is to state three numbers—the changes in prices for oranges, grapefruit, and lemons. But this is a very cumbersome method. Rather than having to recite three numbers in an effort to track changes in the prices of citrus fruit, economists prefer to have some kind of overall measure of the *average* price change.

To measure average price changes for consumer goods and services, economists track changes in the cost of a typical consumer's *consumption bundle*—a typical group of goods and services purchased. A hypothetical consumption bundle, used to measure changes in the overall price level, is known as a **market basket**. For our market basket in this example, we will suppose that, before the frost, a typical consumer bought 200 oranges, 50 grapefruit, and 100 lemons over the course of a year.

A **market basket** is a hypothetical set of consumer purchases of goods and services.

Table 2.4-1 shows the pre-frost and post-frost costs of this market basket. Before the frost, it cost $95; after the frost, the same basket of goods cost $175. Since $175/$95 = 1.842, the post-frost basket costs 1.842 times the cost of the pre-frost basket, a cost increase of 84.2%. In this example, the average price of citrus fruit has increased 84.2% since the base year as a result of the frost, where the base year is the initial year used in the measurement of the price change.

Table 2.4-1 Calculating the Cost of a Market Basket

	Pre-frost	Post-frost
Price of orange	$0.20	$0.40
Price of grapefruit	0.60	1.00
Price of lemon	0.25	0.45
Cost of market basket (200 oranges, 50 grapefruit, 100 lemons)	(200 × $0.20) + (50 × $0.60) + (100 × $0.25) = $95.00	(200 × $0.40) + (50 × $1.00) + (100 × $0.45) = $175.00

Economists use the same method to measure changes in the overall price level: they track changes in the cost of buying a given market basket. The changes are calculated relative to a **base year**, the year chosen as the one to use for comparison. Using a market basket and a base year, we obtain what is known as a **price index**, a measure of the overall price level compared to the prices in the base year. A price index is calculated for a specific year using a specified base year. A price index can be calculated using the following formula:

AP® ECON TIP

The term *market basket* refers to a group of goods and services that represents what consumers buy. On the AP® exam, market baskets usually consist of three or four goods, a simplification of the market basket used to compute the Consumer Price Index, or CPI, the most commonly used price index.

$$\textbf{(2.4-1)} \quad \text{Price index in a given year} = \frac{\text{Cost of market basket in a given year}}{\text{Cost of market basket in base year}} \times 100$$

In our example, the citrus fruit market basket cost $95 in the base year, the year before the frost. So by applying Equation 2.4-1, we define the price index for citrus fruit as (cost of market basket in the current year/$95) × 100, yielding an index of 100 for the period before the frost and 184.2 after the frost. You should note that applying Equation 2.4-1 to calculate the price index *for the base year* always results in a price index of (cost of market in base year/cost of market basket in base year) × 100 = 100.

The **base year** is the year arbitrarily chosen for comparison when calculating a price index. The price level compares the price of the market basket of goods in a given year to its price in the base year.

The price index makes it clear that the average price of citrus has risen 84.2% as a consequence of the frost. Because of its simplicity and intuitive appeal, the method we've just described is used to calculate a variety of price indices to track average price changes among a variety of different groups of goods and services. Examples include the *consumer price index* and the *producer price index*, which we'll discuss shortly.

A **price index** measures the cost of purchasing a given market basket in a given year. The index value is always equal to 100 in the selected base year.

AP® ECON TIP

Any year can be chosen as the base year. If the price of a market basket is higher in a given year than in the base year, the price index will be greater than 100; if it is lower, the price index will be lower than 100. Remember: the price index in the base year is always equal to 100 because prices in the base year are always 100% of what they are in the base year!

Price indices are also the basis for measuring inflation. The inflation rate from year 1 to year 2 is thus calculated using the following formula, with year 1 and year 2 being consecutive years.

$$\textbf{(2.4-2)}\quad \text{Inflation rate} = \frac{\text{Price index in year 2} - \text{Price index in year 1}}{\text{Price index in year 1}} \times 100$$

Though different price indices can be used to measure inflation, typically a news report that cites "the inflation rate" is referring to the annual percentage change in the consumer price index.

The Consumer Price Index

The most widely used measure of the overall price level in the United States is the **consumer price index** (often referred to simply as the **CPI**), which is intended to show how the cost of all purchases by a typical urban family has changed over time. It is calculated by surveying market prices for a market basket that is constructed to represent the consumption of a typical family of four living in a typical American city. Rather than having a single base year, the CPI currently has a base period of 1982–1984.

The **consumer price index**, or **CPI,** measures the cost of the market basket of a typical urban American family.

The market basket used to calculate the CPI is far more complex than the three-fruit market basket we described above. In fact, to calculate the CPI, the Bureau of Labor Statistics sends its employees out to survey supermarkets, gas stations, hardware stores, hospitals, and so on—some 23,000 retail outlets in 87 cities. Every month it tabulates about 80,000 prices, on everything from romaine lettuce to a medical checkup. For the most part, the items used to calculate the CPI stay the same each year, with only occasional additions or deletions.

Dave and Les Jacobs/Lloyd Dobbie/AGE Fotostock

Figure 2.4-2 shows the weight of major categories in the consumer price index as of December 2019. **Figure 2.4-3** shows how the CPI has changed since measurement began in 1913. Since 1940, the CPI has risen steadily, although its annual percentage increases in recent years have been much smaller than those of the 1970s and early 1980s. A logarithmic scale is used so that equal percentage changes in the CPI appear the same.

FIGURE 2.4-2 **The Makeup of the Consumer Price Index in 2019**

Education 2.3%
Other goods and services 17.9%
Food and beverages 13.9%
Recreation 4.9%
Housing 32.8%
Medical care 8.2%
Transportation 17%*
Apparel 3%

*Excludes motor fuel.

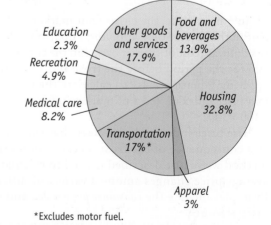

This chart shows the percentage shares of major types of spending in the CPI as of December 2019. *Data Source:* Bureau of Labor Statistics.

FIGURE 2.4-3 The CPI, 1913–2020

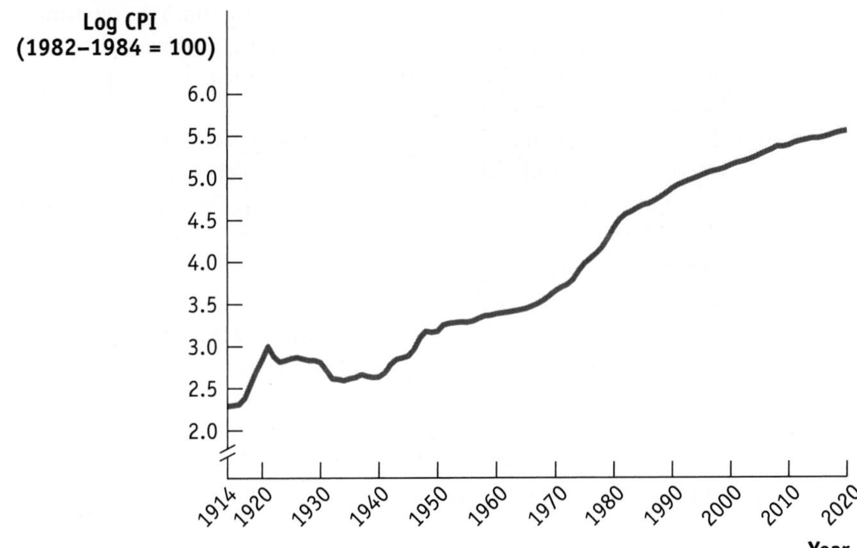

Since 1940, the CPI has risen steadily. But the annual percentage increases in recent years have been much smaller than those of the 1970s and early 1980s. (The vertical axis is measured on a logarithmic scale so that equal percentage changes in the CPI appear the same.)
Data Source: Bureau of Labor Statistics.

The CPI has a direct and immediate impact on millions of Americans. Many payments are tied, or "indexed," to the CPI, and the amount paid for goods and services rises or falls when the CPI rises or falls. For example, over 69 million people today receive checks from Social Security, a national program that accounts for almost a quarter of current total federal spending. The amount of an individual's check is determined by a formula that reflects that individual's previous payments into the system, as well as other factors. In addition, all Social Security payments are adjusted each year to offset any increase in consumer prices over the previous year. The CPI is used to calculate the official estimate of the inflation rate used to adjust these payments annually. So every percentage point added to the official estimate of the rate of inflation adds 1% to the checks received by tens of millions of individuals.

A small change in the CPI has large consequences for those who depend on Social Security payments.

David Forbert/SuperStock

Other government payments are also indexed to the CPI, as are income tax brackets — the bands of income levels that determine a taxpayer's income tax rate. In the private sector, many private contracts, including some wage settlements, contain cost-of-living allowances (called COLAs) that adjust payments in proportion to changes in the CPI.

Because the CPI plays such an important and direct role in people's lives, it is a politically sensitive number. The Bureau of Labor Statistics, which calculates the CPI, takes great care in collecting and interpreting price and consumption data. It uses a complex method in which households are surveyed to determine what they buy and where they shop, and a carefully selected sample of stores are surveyed to get representative prices. However, there is still controversy about whether the CPI accurately measures inflation.

Shortcomings of the CPI as a Measure of Inflation

Some economists believe that the consumer price index systematically overstates the actual rate of inflation. Why? Suppose the price of everything in the market basket used to calculate the CPI increased by 10% over the past year. The typical consumer

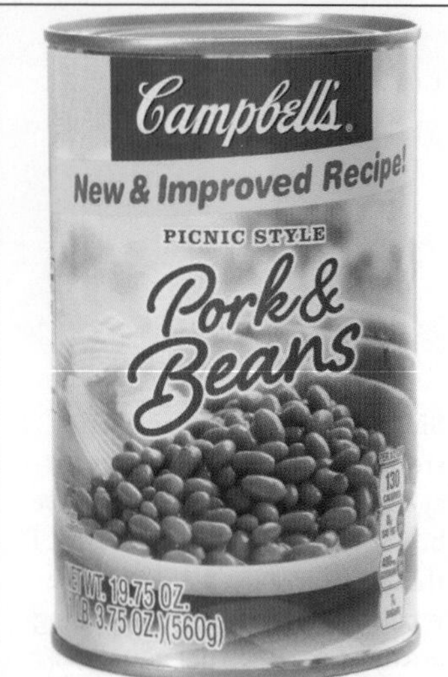

Product improvements can lead to overestimates of the CPI. On the other hand, sometimes the only thing that has been improved is the packaging.

might not need to spend 10% more this year to be as well off as last year, for three reasons.

First, each item remains in the studied market basket for four years. Yet consumers frequently alter the mix of goods and services they buy, reducing purchases of products that have become relatively more expensive and increasing purchases of products that have become relatively cheaper. For example, suppose that the price of hamburgers suddenly doubled. Americans currently eat a lot of hamburgers, but in the face of such a price rise, many of them would switch to chicken sandwiches, pizza, or other substitutes whose prices hadn't increased as much. As a result, a price index based on a market basket with a lot of hamburgers in it would overstate the true rise in the cost of living. This is called **substitution bias**.

Substitution bias occurs in the CPI because, over time, items with prices that have risen most receive too much weight (because households substitute away from them), while items with prices that have risen least are given too little weight (because households shift their spending toward them).

The second reason arises from product improvements. It's likely that over the years your favorite toothpaste, laundry detergent, and snack foods have both increased in price and come out in "new and improved" versions. If what you're getting is really better than before, you aren't paying more for the same product. Rather, you're paying more and getting more. The Bureau of Labor Statistics does its best to make adjustments for changes in product quality, but it is hard to measure the extent to which consumers are getting more as opposed to simply paying more.

The third reason that inflation rate estimates may be misleading is innovation. Every new year brings new items, such as new electronic gadgets, new smartphone apps, new health care solutions, and new clothing options. By widening the range of consumer choice, innovation makes a given amount of money worth more. That is, innovation creates benefits similar to those of a fall in consumer prices.

For all of these reasons, changes in the CPI may overstate changes in the cost of maintaining a particular standard of living. However, with more frequent updates of the market basket, among other tweaks in its methods, the Bureau of Labor Statistics has improved the accuracy of the CPI in recent years. And, despite some remaining controversy, the CPI remains the basis for most estimates of inflation.

AP® ECON TIP

Explain the shortcomings of the CPI as a measure of inflation, especially how substitution bias causes the CPI to overstate the true inflation rate.

The United States is not the only country that calculates a consumer price index. In fact, nearly every country calculates one. As you might expect, the market baskets that make up these indices differ quite a lot from country to country. In poor countries, where people must spend a high proportion of their income just to feed themselves, food makes up a large share of the price index. Among high-income countries, differences in consumption patterns lead to differences in the price indices: the Japanese price index puts a larger weight on raw fish and a smaller weight on beef than ours does, and the French price index puts a larger weight on wine.

Other Price Indices

The **producer price index,** or **PPI,** measures the prices of goods and services purchased by producers.

Two other price measures are also widely used to track economy-wide price changes. One is the **producer price index (PPI).** As its name suggests, the producer price index measures the cost of a typical basket of goods and services – containing raw commodities such as steel, electricity, coal, and so on – purchased by producers. Because commodity producers are relatively quick to raise prices when they perceive a change in overall demand for their goods, the PPI often responds to inflationary or deflationary pressures more quickly than the CPI. As a result, the PPI is often regarded as an "early warning signal" of changes in the inflation rate.

AP® ECON TIP

You should know the producer price index (PPI) and understand how it differs from the CPI, but calculating the PPI is beyond the scope of the course.

The other widely used price measure is the *GDP deflator*. The GDP deflator is used to adjust GDP to account for changes in the price level and will be discussed in detail in Module 2.6.

Module 2.4 Review

Check Your Understanding

1. Refer back to Table 2.4-1, but suppose that the market basket is composed of 100 oranges, 50 grapefruit, and 200 lemons. How does this change in quantity affect the pre-frost and post-frost consumer price indices? Explain. Generalize your answer to explain how the construction of the new market basket affects the CPI.
2. For each of the following events, explain how the use of a 10-year-old market basket would bias measurements of price changes over the past decade.
   - **a.** A typical family today owns more cars than it would have a decade ago. Over that time, the average price of a car has increased more than the average prices of other goods.
   - **b.** Virtually no households had tablet PCs a decade ago. Now many households have them, and their prices have been falling.
3. If the consumer price index increased from 214.537 in year 1 to 218.056 in year 2, what was the inflation rate between year 1 and year 2?

Tackle the AP® Test: Multiple-Choice Questions

1. Which of the following is true regarding the price level in an economy?
   - **a.** An increase in the price level is called inflation.
   - **b.** The price level only increases over time.
   - **c.** A decrease in the price level is called disinflation.
   - **d.** The price level decreases during a recession.
   - **e.** All of the above are true.
2. If the cost of a market basket of goods increases from $100 in year 1 to $108 in year 2, what does the consumer price index in year 2 equal if year 1 is the base year?
   - **a.** 8
   - **b.** 10
   - **c.** 100
   - **d.** 108
   - **e.** 110
3. If the consumer price index increases from 80 to 120 from one year to the next, the inflation rate over that time period was
   - **a.** 20%.
   - **b.** 40%.
   - **c.** 50%.
   - **d.** 80%.
   - **e.** 120%.
4. Which of the following is true of the CPI?
   - **a.** It is the most common measure of the price level.
   - **b.** It measures the price of a typical market basket of goods.
   - **c.** It is used to index Social Security payments.
   - **d.** It is calculated for a particular base year or period.
   - **e.** All of the above are true.
5. The value of a price index in the base year is
   - **a.** 0.
   - **b.** 100.
   - **c.** 200.
   - **d.** the same as the inflation rate.
   - **e.** equal to the average cost of a market basket of goods.
6. A market basket is
   - **a.** made up of all goods and services purchased by a typical urban family.
   - **b.** a hypothetical consumption bundle.
   - **c.** a set of goods and services typically purchased by producers.
   - **d.** an arbitrary set of goods and services purchased by an individual.
   - **e.** a fixed set of goods and services identified in 1982.
7. Use Table 2.4-1 (shown here) to answer the following question. What is the value of the price index in the pre-frost and post-frost year if the post-frost year is the base year?

	Pre-frost	Post-frost
Price of orange	$0.20	$0.40
Price of grapefruit	0.60	1.00
Price of lemon	0.25	0.45
Cost of market basket (200 oranges, 50 grapefruit, 100 lemons)	(200 × $0.20) + (50 × $0.60) + (100 × $0.25) = $95.00	(200 × $0.40) + (50 × $1.00) + (100 × $0.45) = $175.00

	Pre-frost	*Post-frost*
a.	54	100
b.	100	54
c.	184	100
d.	100	184
e.	54	184

Tackle the AP® Test: Free-Response Questions

1. Suppose the year 2010 is the base year for a price index. Between 2010 and 2030 prices double, and at the same time your nominal income increases from $40,000 to $80,000.
   a. What is the value of the price index in 2010?
   b. What is the value of the price index in 2030?
   c. What is the percentage increase in your nominal income between 2010 and 2030?
   d. What has happened to your real income between 2010 and 2030? Explain.

Rubric for FRQ 1 (5 points)

1 point: 100

1 point: 200

1 point: 100%

1 point: It stayed the same.

1 point: Real income is a measure of the purchasing power of my income, and because my income and the price level both doubled, the purchasing power of my income has not been affected: $40,000/100 = $80,000/200.

2. The accompanying table contains the values of the CPI for year 1 and year 2.
   a. What does the CPI measure?
   b. Calculate the inflation rate from year 1 to year 2.

Year	CPI
1	229.6
2	233.0

(2 points)

Costs of Inflation

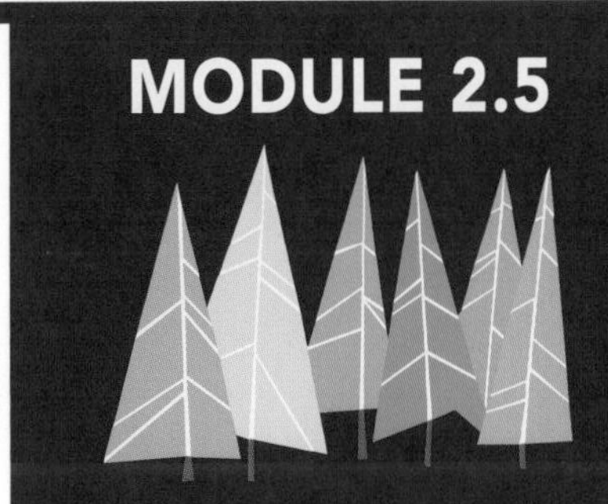

In this Module, you will learn to:

- Explain the costs that unexpected inflation or deflation imposes on the economy
- Explain the relationship between inflation and the arbitrary redistribution of wealth
- Identify the individuals and groups in the economy that gain and lose from unexpected inflation

The Expected Costs of Inflation

Economists believe that high rates of inflation can impose significant economic costs. Some of these costs are created from inflation, whether it is expected or not. Other costs are imposed only when inflation is unexpected. Let's begin with the costs of inflation, expected or unexpected. The most important of these costs are *shoe-leather costs, menu costs,* and *unit-of-account costs.* We'll discuss each in turn.

Shoe-Leather Costs

People hold money—cash in their wallets and bank deposits from which they can withdraw funds—for convenience in making transactions. As we learned in Module 2.4, however, a high inflation rate discourages people from holding money, because the purchasing power of the cash in their wallets and the funds in their bank accounts steadily erodes as the overall level of prices rises. This leads people to search for ways to reduce the amount of money they hold, often at considerable economic cost.

Vaidas Bucys/EyeEm/Getty Images

Inflation imposes a number of costs on the economy, including shoe-leather costs, as people run around trying to spend their money before it becomes worthless.

During the most famous of all inflations, the German *hyperinflation* of 1921–1923, merchants employed runners, workers who would take their cash to the bank many times a day to convert it into something that would hold its value, such as a stable foreign currency. In an effort to avoid having the purchasing power of their money eroded, people used up valuable resources—the time and labor of the runners—that could have been used productively elsewhere. During the German hyperinflation, so many banking transactions were taking place that the number of employees at German banks nearly quadrupled—from around 100,000 in 1913 to 375,000 in 1923. Brazil experienced hyperinflation during the early 1990s; during that episode, the Brazilian banking sector grew so large that it accounted for 15% of GDP, more than twice the size of the financial sector in the United States measured as a share of GDP. The large increase in the Brazilian banking sector that was needed to cope with the consequences of inflation represented a loss of real resources to its society.

Increased costs of transactions caused by inflation are known as *shoe-leather costs*, an allusion to the wear and tear caused by the extra running around that takes place when people are trying to avoid holding money. Shoe-leather costs are substantial in economies with very high inflation rates, as anyone who has lived in such an economy—say, one suffering inflation of 100% or more per year—can attest. Most estimates suggest, however, that the shoe-leather costs of inflation at the rates seen in the United States—which in peacetime has never had inflation above 15%—are quite small.

Menu Costs

In a modern economy, most of the things people buy have a listed price. There's a price listed under each item on a supermarket shelf or on a website, a price placed in advertisements, and a price listed for each dish on a restaurant's menu. Changing a listed

Bettmann/Getty Images

During the German hyperinflation of the early 1920s, people burned worthless paper money in their stoves.

price has a real cost, called a *menu cost.* For example, to change a price in a supermarket may require a clerk to change the price listed under the item on the shelf and an office worker to change the price associated with the item's UPC code in the store's computer. Even for items sold online, a change in price requires those changes to be reflected in databases and on sales reports, in addition to changes in any advertising materials. In the face of inflation, of course, firms are forced to change prices more often than they would if the price level was more or less stable. Given the enormous number of prices in the economy, this means higher costs for the economy as a whole.

In times of very high inflation rates, menu costs can be substantial. During the Brazilian inflation of the early 1990s, for instance, supermarket workers reportedly spent half of their time replacing old price stickers with new ones. When the inflation rate is high, merchants may decide to stop listing prices in terms of the local currency and use either an artificial unit—in effect, measuring prices relative to one another—or a more stable currency, such as the U.S. dollar. This is exactly what the Israeli real estate market began doing in the mid-1980s: prices were quoted in U.S. dollars, even though payment was made in Israeli shekels. This is also what happened in Zimbabwe when, in May 2008, official estimates of the inflation rate reached 1,694,000%.

Menu costs are also present in low-inflation economies, but they are not severe. In low-inflation economies, businesses might update their prices only sporadically—not daily or even more frequently, as is the case in high-inflation or hyperinflation economies. And technological advances have made menu costs less and less important, since prices can be changed electronically and fewer merchants attach price stickers to merchandise. But it still takes some type of effort to determine and implement any price change.

Unit-of-Account Costs

In the Middle Ages in Europe, contracts were often specified "in kind": for example, a tenant might be obliged to provide his landlord with a certain number of cattle each year (the phrase *in kind* may come from an ancient word for cattle, *kine*). This may have made sense at the time, but it would be an awkward way to conduct modern business. Instead, we state contracts in monetary terms: a renter owes a certain number of dollars per month, a company that issues a bond promises to pay the bondholder the dollar value of the bond when it comes due, and so on. We also tend to make our economic calculations in dollars: a family planning its budget, or a small business owner trying to figure out how well the business is doing, makes estimates of the amount of money coming in and going out.

This role of the dollar as a basis for contracts and calculation is called the *unit-of-account* role of money. It's an important aspect of the modern economy. Yet it's a role that can be degraded by inflation, which causes the purchasing power of a dollar to change over time—a dollar next year is worth less than a dollar this year. The effect, many economists argue, is to reduce the quality of economic decisions: the economy as a whole makes less efficient use of its resources because of the uncertainty caused by changes in the unit of account, the dollar. The *unit-of-account costs* of inflation are the costs arising from the way inflation makes money a less reliable unit of measurement.

Unit-of-account costs may be particularly important in the tax system, because inflation can distort the measures of income on which taxes are collected. Here's an example: assume that the inflation rate is 10%, so that the overall level of prices rises 10% each year. Suppose that a business buys an asset, such as a piece of land, for $100,000 and then resells it a year later at a price of $110,000. In a fundamental sense, the business didn't make a profit on the deal: in real terms, it got no more for the land than it paid for it, because the $110,000 would purchase no more goods than the $100,000 would have a year earlier. But U.S. tax law would say that the business made a capital gain of $10,000, and it would have to pay taxes on that phantom gain.

During the 1970s, when the United States had a relatively high inflation rate, the distorting effects of inflation on the tax system were a serious problem. Some businesses were discouraged from productive investment spending because they found themselves paying taxes on phantom gains. Meanwhile, some unproductive investments became attractive because they led to phantom losses that reduced tax bills. When the inflation rate fell in the 1980s—and tax rates were reduced—these problems became much less important.

Tetra Images/Alamy

Winners and Losers from Unexpected Inflation

As we've just learned, a high inflation rate imposes overall costs on the economy. In addition, *unexpected* inflation can produce winners and losers within the economy. The main reason inflation sometimes helps some people while hurting others is that economic transactions, such as loans, often involve contracts that extend over a period of time, and these contracts are normally specified in *nominal*—that is, in dollar—terms. In the case of a loan, the borrower receives a certain amount of funds at the beginning, and the loan contract specifies how much the borrower must repay at some future date. But what that dollar repayment is worth in *real* terms—that is, in terms of purchasing power—depends greatly on the rate of inflation over the intervening years of the loan.

The *interest rate* on a loan is the percentage of the loan amount that the borrower must pay to the lender, typically on an annual basis, in addition to the repayment of the loan amount itself. Economists summarize the effect of inflation on borrowers and lenders by distinguishing between *nominal* interest rates and *real* interest rates. The **nominal interest rate** is the interest rate that is actually paid for a loan, unadjusted for the effects of inflation. For example, the interest rates advertised on student loans and every interest rate you see listed by a bank is a nominal rate. The **real interest rate** is the nominal interest rate adjusted for inflation. This adjustment is achieved by simply subtracting the inflation rate from the nominal interest rate. For example, if a loan carries a nominal interest rate of 8%, but the inflation rate is 5%, the real interest rate is 8% – 5% = 3%.

The **nominal interest rate** is the interest rate actually paid for a loan.

The **real interest rate** is the nominal interest rate minus the rate of inflation.

When a borrower and a lender enter into a loan contract, the contract normally specifies a nominal interest rate. But each party has an expectation about the future rate of inflation and therefore an expectation about the real interest rate on the loan. If the actual inflation rate is *higher* than expected, borrowers gain at the expense of lenders: borrowers will repay their loans with funds that have a lower real value than had been expected—since the funds can purchase fewer goods and services than expected due to the surprisingly high inflation rate. Conversely, if the inflation rate is *lower* than expected, lenders will gain at the expense of borrowers: borrowers must repay their loans with funds that have a higher real value than had been expected.

Historically, the fact that inflation creates winners and losers has sometimes been a major source of political controversy. In 1896, William Jennings Bryan electrified the Democratic presidential convention with a speech in which he declared, "You shall not crucify mankind on a cross of gold." What he was actually demanding was an inflationary policy. At the time, the U.S. dollar had a fixed value in terms of gold. Bryan wanted the U.S. government to abandon the gold standard and print more money, which would have raised the level of prices and, he believed, helped the nation's farmers who were deeply in debt.

AP® ECON TIP

In general, borrowers are helped by inflation because it decreases the real value of what they must repay. Lenders, savers, and people with fixed incomes are hurt by inflation because it decreases the real value of the money available to them in the future.

Home mortgages (loans for the purchase of homes) are the most important source of gains and losses from inflation. Americans who took out mortgages in the early 1970s quickly found their real payments reduced by the higher-than-expected inflation experienced later that decade: by 1983, the purchasing power of a dollar was only 45% of what it had been in 1973. Borrowers paid back their mortgage loans with dollars that could buy less than expected when the loan was made. In contrast, the homeowners who took out mortgages in the early 1990s were not so lucky, because the inflation rate fell to lower-than-expected levels during the 1990s: in 2003 the purchasing power of a dollar was 78% of what it had been in 1993. Borrowers paid back their mortgage loans with dollars that would buy more than expected when the loan was made.

Because gains for some and losses for others result from inflation that is either higher or lower than expected, yet another problem arises: uncertainty about the future inflation rate discourages people from entering into any form of long-term contract. This is an additional cost of high inflation, because high rates of inflation are usually unpredictable, too. In countries with high and uncertain inflation, long-term loans are rare. This, in turn, makes it difficult for people to commit to long-term investments.

One last point: unexpected deflation – a surprise fall in the price level – creates winners and losers, too. Between 1929 and 1933, as the U.S. economy plunged into the Great Depression, the price level fell by 35%. This meant that debtors, including many farmers and homeowners, saw a sharp rise in the real value of their debts, which led to widespread bankruptcy and helped create a banking crisis, as lenders found their customers unable to pay back their loans.

Inflation Is Easy; Disinflation Is Hard

Disinflation is the process of bringing the inflation rate down.

There is not much evidence that a rise in the inflation rate from, say, 2% to 5% would do a great deal of harm to the economy. Still, policy makers generally move forcefully to bring inflation back down when it creeps above 2% or 3%. Why? Because experience shows that bringing the inflation rate down – a process called **disinflation** – is very difficult and costly once a higher rate of inflation has become well established in the economy.

Figure 2.5-1 shows the inflation rate and the unemployment rate in the United States over a crucial decade, from 1978 to 1988. The decade began with an alarming rise in the inflation rate, but by the end of the period inflation averaged only about 4%. This was considered a major economic achievement – but it came at a high cost. Much of the fall in inflation probably resulted from the very severe recession of 1981–1982, which drove the unemployment rate to 10.8% – its highest level since the Great Depression.

FIGURE 2.5-1 The Cost of Disinflation

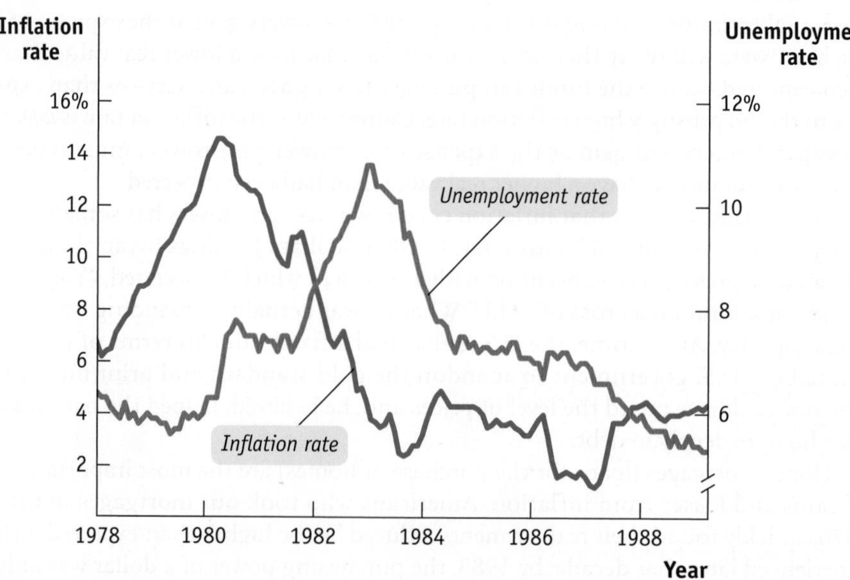

The U.S. inflation rate peaked in 1980 and then fell sharply. Progress against inflation, however, was accompanied by a temporary but very large increase in the unemployment rate, demonstrating the high cost of disinflation.
Data Source: Bureau of Labor Statistics.

Many economists believe that this period of high unemployment was necessary, because they believe that the only way to reduce inflation that has become deeply embedded in the economy is through policies that temporarily depress the economy. The best way to avoid having to put the economy through a wringer to reduce inflation, however, is to avoid having a serious inflation problem in the first place. So, policy makers respond forcefully to signs that inflation may be accelerating as a form of preventive medicine for the economy.

Watch the video: *Real and Nominal Values*

Module 2.5 Review

Check Your Understanding

1. The widespread use of technology has revolutionized the banking industry, making it much easier for customers to access and manage their money. Does this mean that the shoe-leather costs of inflation are higher or lower than they used to be? Explain.
2. Most people in the United States have grown accustomed to a modest inflation rate of around 2 to 3%. Who would gain and who would lose if inflation came to a complete stop for several years? Explain.

Tackle the AP® Test: Multiple-Choice Questions

1. If inflation causes people to frequently convert their dollars into other assets, the economy experiences what type of cost?
   a. price level
   b. shoe-leather
   c. menu
   d. unit-of-account
   e. none of the above
2. Because dollars are used as the basis for contracts, inflation leads to which type of cost?
   a. price level
   b. shoe-leather
   c. menu
   d. unit-of-account
   e. none of the above
3. Changing the listed price when inflation leads to a price increase is an example of which type of cost?
   a. price level
   b. shoe-leather
   c. menu
   d. unit-of-account
   e. none of the above
4. Which of the following groups is helped by unexpected inflation?
   a. borrowers
   b. lenders
   c. savers
   d. people on fixed incomes
   e. people receiving Social Security
5. If a bank makes a loan at an interest rate of 5% and expects no inflation, which of the following would be true?
   a. The bank will gain if there is inflation.
   b. Deflation will decrease the bank's real interest rate.
   c. The bank's real interest rate is equal to its nominal interest rate if inflation is zero.
   d. Inflation will increase the bank's real interest rate.
   e. The bank expects a real interest rate above 5%.
6. Which of the following individuals is most likely hurt by unexpected inflation?
   a. a mortgage holder
   b. a student with college loans
   c. a Social Security recipient
   d. a saver
   e. an investor
7. If a loan has a nominal interest rate of 3% and the inflation rate is 2%, the real interest rate is which of the following?
   a. 1%
   b. 2%
   c. 3%
   d. 5%
   e. 6%

Tackle the AP® Test: Free-Response Questions

1. For the following examples: (i) indicate whether inflation imposes a cost on the economy; (ii) explain your answer; and (iii) identify the type of net cost involved, if there is one.
   a. When inflation is expected to be high, workers get paid more frequently and make more trips to the bank.
   b. Lanwei is reimburased by her company for her work-related travel expenses. Sometimes, however, the company takes a long time to reimburse her. So when inflation is high, she is less willing to travel for her job.
   c. Hector Homeowner has a mortgage loan that he took out five years ago with a fixed 6% nominal interest rate. Over the years, the inflation rate has crept up unexpectedly to its present level of 7%.
   d. In response to unexpectedly high inflation, the manager of Cozy Cottages of Cape Cod must reprint and resend expensive color brochures correcting the price of rentals this season.

Rubric for FRQ 1 (11 points)

1 point: There is a cost to the economy.

1 point: There is an increase in the cost of financial transactions imposed by inflation.

1 point: This type of cost is called a shoe-leather cost.

1 point: There is a cost to the economy.

1 point: Lanwei's forgone output is a cost to the economy.

1 point: This type of cost is called a unit-of-account cost.

1 point: No cost to the economy can be defined.

1 point: Hector gains and the bank loses because the money Hector pays back is worth less than expected.

1 point: There is a cost to the economy.

1 point: Cozy Cottages must reprint and resend expensive brochures when inflation causes rental prices to rise.

1 point: This type of cost is called a menu cost.

2. You borrow $1,000 for one year at 5% interest to buy a couch. Although you did not anticipate any inflation, there is unexpected inflation of 5% over the life of your loan.
   a. What was the real interest rate on your loan?
   b. Explain how you gained from the inflation.
   c. Who lost as a result of the situation described? Explain. **(4 points)**

Real Versus Nominal Gross Domestic Product

In this Module, you will learn to:

- Define and differentiate between nominal and real GDP
- Evaluate variables using both current and constant prices
- Use the GDP deflator to convert between nominal GDP and real GDP
- Explain the use of real GDP per capita as a measure of living standards

Real GDP: A Measure of Aggregate Output

At the beginning of this Unit, we described how today, by some measures, China has the world's largest economy. When economists compare the sizes of different economies, they use GDP and a closely related measure, *real GDP*, which corrects GDP for price changes. Generally, when economists say that one country's economy has overtaken the other's, they are comparing real GDP. GDP can grow because the economy grows, but it can also grow simply because of inflation. Even if an economy's output doesn't change, GDP will go up if the prices of the goods and services the economy produces increase. Likewise, GDP can fall either because the economy is producing less or because prices have fallen.

To measure the economy's growth with accuracy, we need a measure of **aggregate output**: the total quantity of final goods and services the economy produces. The measure that is used for this purpose is *real GDP*. By tracking real GDP over time, we avoid the problem of changes in prices distorting the value of changes in production over time. Let's look first at how real GDP is calculated and then at what it means.

Aggregate output is the total quantity of final goods and services produced within an economy.

Calculating Real GDP

U.S. GDP was \$8,578 billion in 1997 and had more than doubled to \$20,937 billion by 2020. But U.S. production didn't more than double over that period; part of the increase in GDP was due to an increase in the price of goods and services. To measure actual changes in aggregate output, we need to use a modified version of GDP that is adjusted for price changes—*real GDP*.

To understand how real GDP is calculated, imagine an economy in which only two goods, apples and oranges, are produced and in which both goods are sold only to final consumers. The outputs and prices of the two fruits for two consecutive years are shown in **Table 2.6-1**.

The first thing we can say about these data is that the value of sales increased from year 1 to year 2. In the first year, the total value of sales was (2,000 billion × \$0.25) + (1,000 billion × \$0.50) = \$1,000 billion; in the second, it was (2,200 billion × (\$0.30) + (1,200 billion × \$0.70) = \$1,500 billion, which is 50% larger. But it is also clear from the table that this increase in the dollar value of GDP overstates the real growth in the economy. Although the quantities of both apples and oranges increased, the prices of

Paul Maguire/Alamy

Table 2.6-1 Calculating GDP and Real GDP in a Simple Economy		
	Year 1	Year 2
Quantity of apples (billions)	2,000	2,200
Price of an apple	$0.25	$0.30
Quantity of oranges (billions)	1,000	1,200
Price of an orange	$0.50	$0.70
GDP (billions of dollars)	$1,000	$1,500
Real GDP (billions of year 1 dollars)	$1,000	$1,150

both apples and oranges also rose. So part of the 50% increase in the dollar value of GDP simply reflects higher prices, not increased production.

To estimate the true increase in aggregate output produced, we have to ask the following question: How much would GDP have gone up if prices had *not* changed? To answer this question, we need to find the value of output in year 2 expressed in year 1 prices. In year 1, the price of apples was $0.25 each and the price of oranges $0.50 each. So year 2 output *at year 1 prices* is (2,200 billion × $0.25) + (1,200 billion × $0.50) = $1,150 billion. Since output in year 1 at year 1 prices was $1,000 billion, GDP measured in year 1 prices rose 15%—from $1,000 billion to $1,150 billion.

Real GDP is the total value of all final goods and services produced in the economy during a given year, calculated using the prices of a selected base year in order to remove the effects of price changes.

Nominal GDP is the total value of all final goods and services produced in the economy during a given year, calculated with the prices current in the year in which the output is produced.

Now we can define **real GDP**: it is the total value of all final goods and services produced in the economy during a year, calculated as if prices had stayed constant at the level of some given base year in order to remove the effects of price changes. A real GDP number always comes with information about what the base year is. A GDP number that has not been adjusted for changes in prices is calculated using the prices in the year in which the output is produced. Economists call this measure **nominal GDP**, or GDP at current prices. Our first calculation above used nominal GDP to measure the change in output from year 1 to year 2, which is why we overstated the true growth in output: we claimed it to be 50%, when in fact it was only 15%. By comparing output in the two years using a common set of prices—the year 1 prices in this example—we are able to focus solely on changes in the quantity of output by eliminating the influence of changes in prices.

Table 2.6-2 shows a real-life version of our apples-and-oranges example. The second column shows nominal GDP in 2000, 2009, and 2017. The third column shows real GDP for each year in 2009 dollars (that is, using the value of the dollar in the year 2009). For 2009, the nominal GDP and the real GDP are the same. But real GDP in 2000 expressed in 2009 dollars was higher than nominal GDP in 2000, reflecting the fact that prices were in general higher in 2009 than in 2000. Real GDP in 2017 expressed in 2009 dollars, however, was less than nominal GDP in 2017 because prices in 2009 were lower than in 2017.

Table 2.6-2 Nominal Versus Real GDP in 2000, 2009, and 2017		
	Nominal GDP (billions of current dollars)	Real GDP (billions of 2009 dollars)
2000	$10,285	$12,560
2009	14,419	14,419
2017	19,386	17,092

Data Source: Bureau of Economic Analysis.

You might have noticed that there is an alternative way to calculate real GDP using the data in Table 2.6-1. Why not measure it using the prices of year 2 rather than year 1 as the base-year prices? This procedure seems equally valid. According to that calculation, real GDP in year 1 at year 2 prices is

Lim Yong Hian/Shutterstock

(2,000 billion × \$0.30) + (1,000 billion × \$0.70) = \$1,300 billion; real GDP in year 2 at year 2 prices is \$1,500 billion, the same as nominal GDP in year 2. So using year 2 prices as the base year, the growth rate of real GDP is equal to (\$1,500 billion − \$1,300 billion)/\$1,300 billion = 0.154, or 15.4%. This is slightly higher than the figure we got from the previous calculation, in which year 1 prices were the base-year prices. In that calculation, we found that real GDP increased by 15.0%.

Neither answer, 15.4% versus 15.0%, is more "correct" than the other. In reality, the government economists who put together the U.S. national accounts have adopted a method to measure the change in real GDP known as chain-linking, which uses the average between the GDP growth rate calculated using an early base year and the GDP growth rate calculated using a late base year. As a result, U.S. statistics on real GDP are always expressed in *chained dollars*, which splits the difference between using early and late base years.

Recall from Module 2.4 that price indices, like the CPI, can be used to measure and adjust for changes in the price level over time. We can use a tool known as the **GDP deflator** for a similar purpose; measuring and adjusting nominal GDP for changes in the price level over time. While the GDP deflator isn't exactly a price index, it serves the same purpose. The GDP deflator for a given year is 100 times the ratio of nominal GDP to real GDP in that year. Since the Bureau of Economic Analysis – the source of the GDP deflator – calculates real GDP using a base year of 2009, the nominal GDP and the real GDP for 2009 are the same. This makes the GDP deflator for 2009 equal to 100. For this reason, later in this book you will see measures of the aggregate price level with the designation "GDP Deflator, 2009 = 100." And in many cases, you will see real GDP measured in 2009 dollars. Inflation raises nominal GDP but not real GDP, causing the GDP deflator to rise. If nominal GDP doubles but real GDP does not change, the GDP deflator indicates that the aggregate price level has doubled.

The **GDP deflator** for a given year is 100 times the ratio of nominal GDP to real GDP in that year.

Here is the equation for the GDP deflator:

$$\textbf{(2.6-1)} \quad \text{GDP deflator} = (\text{nominal GDP}/\text{real GDP}) \times 100$$

AP® ECON TIP

To distinguish between "real" and "nominal" values for a variety of variables, such as income, wages, and interest rates, remember that real values have been adjusted for price changes (for example, inflation), and nominal values, which use current year prices, have not.

Real GDP per Capita

GDP is a measure of a country's aggregate output. Other things equal, a country with a larger population will have higher GDP simply because there are more people working. If we want to compare GDP across countries, but we want to eliminate the effect of differences in population size, we use the measure **GDP per capita** – GDP divided by the size of the population, equivalent to the average GDP per person. Correspondingly, real GDP per capita is the average real GDP per person.

GDP per capita is GDP divided by the size of the population; it is equivalent to the average GDP per person.

What Real GDP Doesn't Measure

Real GDP per capita can be a useful measure in some circumstances, such as in a comparison of labor productivity between two countries. However, despite the fact that it is a rough measure of the average real output per person, real GDP per capita has well-known limitations as a measure of a country's living standards. Every once in a while, economists are accused of believing that growth in real GDP per capita is the only thing that matters – that is, thinking that increasing real GDP per capita is a goal in itself. In fact, most economists rarely make that mistake. Let's take a moment to be clear about why a country's real GDP per capita is not a sufficient measure of human welfare in that country and why growth in real GDP per capita is not an appropriate policy goal in itself.

AP® ECON TIP

In addition to defining and calculating real GDP, make sure you understand the limitations of GDP for measuring economic welfare.

Real GDP does not include many of the things that contribute to happiness, such as leisure time, volunteerism, housework, and natural beauty. And real GDP increases as spending increases on things that make people unhappy, including disease, divorce, crime, and natural disasters.

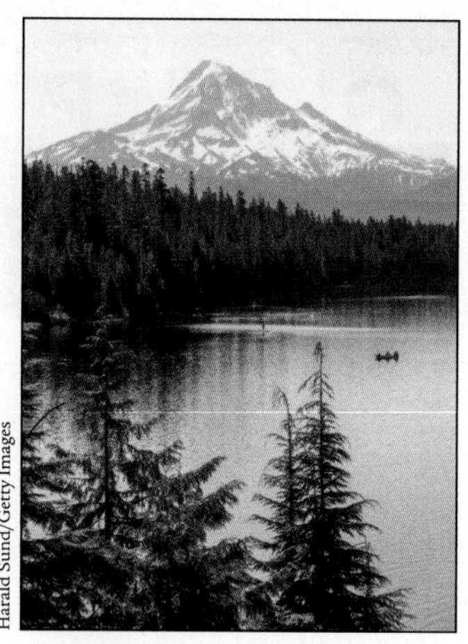
Harald Sund/Getty Images

Real GDP per capita is a measure of an economy's average aggregate output per person—an indication of the economy's potential for certain achievements. Having studied the income approach to calculating GDP in Module 2.1, you know that the value of output corresponds to the value of income. A country with a relatively high GDP per capita can afford relatively high expenditures on health, education, and other goods and services that contribute to a high quality of life. But how output is actually used is another matter. To put it differently, your income might be higher this year than last year, but whether you use that higher income to actually improve your quality of life is up to you. There is not a one-to-one match between real GDP and the quality of life. The real GDP per capita measure does not indicate how income is distributed. It doesn't include some sources of well-being, and it does include some things that are detriments to well-being.

Module 2.6 Review

Check Your Understanding

1. Assume there are only two goods in the economy, french fries and onion rings. In year 1, 1,000,000 servings of french fries were sold for $0.40 each and 800,000 servings of onion rings were sold for $0.60 each. From year 1 to year 2, the price of french fries rose to $0.50 and the servings sold fell to 900,000; the price of onion rings fell to $0.51 and the servings sold rose to 840,000.
   a. Calculate nominal GDP in year 1 and year 2. Calculate real GDP in year 2 using year 1 prices.
   b. Why would an assessment of growth using nominal GDP be misguided?

2. Indicate the effect of each of the following on real GDP:
   a. Chevrolet increases its production of Corvettes.
   b. Consumer expenditures increase as a result of inflation.
   c. A total of $50 billion is spent on hurricane cleanup.
   d. Citizens spend 10,000 hours as neighborhood watch volunteers.

Tackle the AP® Test: Multiple-Choice Questions

1. The real interest rate is the nominal interest rate
   a. plus the rate of inflation.
   b. minus the rate of inflation.
   c. multiplied by the rate of inflation.
   d. divided by the rate of inflation.
   e. charged by banks during inflationary periods.

2. If your real wage decreases while your nominal wage stays the same, the economy must have experienced
   a. inflation.
   b. deflation.
   c. disinflation.
   d. zero inflation.
   e. unemployment.

3. Which of the following is true of real GDP?
   a. It is adjusted for changes in prices.
   b. It is always equal to nominal GDP.
   c. It decreases whenever aggregate output increases.
   d. It is equal to nominal GDP minus the inflation rate.
   e. All of the above are true.

4. The best measure for comparing a country's standard of living over time is
   a. nominal GDP.
   b. real GDP.
   c. nominal GDP per capita.
   d. real GDP per capita.
   e. average GDP per capita.

5. Use the information provided in the table below for an economy that produces only apples and oranges. Assume year 1 is the base year.

	Year 1	Year 2
Quantity of apples	3,000	4,000
Price of an apple	$0.20	$0.30
Quantity of oranges	2,000	3,000
Price of an orange	$0.40	$0.50

What was the value of real GDP in each year?

	Year 1	*Year 2*
a.	$1,400	$2,700
b.	$1,900	$2,700
c.	$1,400	$2,000
d.	$1,900	$2,000
e.	$1,400	$1,900

6. Which of the following would cause real GDP to exceed nominal GDP?
   a. a large increase in aggregate output
   b. a large decease in aggregate output
   c. a significant decrease in prices
   d. an increase in population
   e. using the value-added approach to calculate GDP

7. Which of the following would lead to an increase in real GDP per capita, all other things equal?
   a. a decrease in population
   b. an increase in population
   c. an increase in prices
   d. a decrease in aggregate output
   e. the use of chain-linking

Tackle the AP® Test: Free-Response Questions

1. The economy of Britannica produces three goods: computers, T-shirts, and sunglasses. The accompanying table shows the prices and output of the three goods for year 1 and year 2.

	Computers		T-shirts		Sunglasses	
Year	**Price**	**Quantity**	**Price**	**Quantity**	**Price**	**Quantity**
Year 1	$900	10	$10	100	$15	2
Year 2	$1,050	12	$14	110	$17	3

   a. Calculate the nominal GDP in Britannica for year 1.
   b. Calculate the real GDP in Britannica for year 1 using year 1 as the base year.
   c. Calculate the real GDP in Britannica for year 2 using year 1 as the base year.

Rubric for FRQ 1 (3 points)

1 point: $(\$900 \times 10) + (\$10 \times 100) + (\$15 \times 2) = \$9,000 + \$1,000 + \$30 = \$10,030$

1 point: Real GDP equals nominal GDP in the base year, so this answer is the same as in part a.

1 point: $(\$900 \times 12) + (\$10 \times 110) + (\$15 \times 3) = \$10,800 + \$1,100 + \$45 = \$11,945$

2. The country of Hungry produces only pizzas and the country of Thirsty produces only smoothies. Use the information in the table to answer the following questions:
   a. Calculate the number of pizzas made in Hungry and the number of smoothies made in Thirsty in each year.
   b. Calculate the real GDP in each country in year 2 using year 1 prices.
   c. In which country did real GDP increase the most between year 1 and year 2?
   d. In which country did real GDP per capita decrease the most between year 1 and year 2? Show your work.

	Nominal GDP	Price	Population
Hungry			
Year 1	$10,000	$10	5
Year 2	$20,000	$10	16
Thirsty			
Year 1	$10,000	$10	5
Year 2	$30,000	$20	10

(6 points)

MODULE 2.7

Business Cycles

In this Module, you will learn to:

- Correlate fluctuations in aggregate output and employment to business cycles
- Identify the four phases of a business cycle; recession, expansion, peak, and trough
- Define and explain the phases of a business cycle using data and graphs
- Identify potential output as the full-employment level of output where unemployment is equal to the natural rate of unemployment
- Identify the difference between actual output and potential output as the output gap

Macroeconomics and the Business Cycle

Today everyone can enjoy walking, biking, and horseback riding through New York's beautiful Central Park. But in 1932, many people lived there in squalor. At that time, Central Park contained one of many "Hoovervilles" – the shantytowns that had sprung up across America as a result of a catastrophic economic slump that had started in 1929. Millions of people were out of work and unable to feed, clothe, and house themselves and their families.

Central Park today looks quite different from how it looked in the early 1930s, at the height of the Great Depression.

Why the name "Hooverville"? These shantytowns were named after President Herbert Hoover, who had been elected in 1928. When the Depression struck, many people blamed the president: neither he nor his economic advisers seemed to understand what had happened or how to improve the situation. At that time, the field of macroeconomics was still in its infancy. It was only after the economy was plunged into catastrophe that economists began to closely examine how the economy works and to develop policies that might prevent such disasters in the future. Today, efforts to understand economic slumps and find ways to prevent them remains at the core of macroeconomics.

In this Module, we explore business cycles and how unemployment, employment, and aggregate output can change as the economy moves up and down over time.

The Business Cycle

The alternation between economic downturns and upturns in the macroeconomy is known as the **business cycle**. In the previous Modules, we've read about recessions and depressions in the context of specific measures of an economy. Here, we'll define these terms in the context of the overall fluctuations in the economy. The economy experiences occasional economic downturns known as **recessions**, periods in which output and employment are falling. The lowest point of a recession, just before output and employment start to turn up again, is called the **trough** of a business cycle. The trough is followed by an economic upturn – a period in which output and employment are rising – known as an **expansion**, or initially as a *recovery*. The highest point of an expansion, just before the economy turns down again, is called the **peak** of a business cycle. A **depression** is a very deep and prolonged downturn; fortunately, the United States hasn't had one since the Great Depression of the 1930s.

The **business cycle** is the alternation between economic downturns, known as *recessions*, and economic upturns, known as *expansions*.

How do we know whether the economy is in a recession or an expansion, or at a peak or trough? The National Bureau of Economic Research (NBER) is responsible for deciding the official dates when the U.S. economy passes through each phase of the business cycle. The NBER's Business Cycle Dating Committee identifies the dates of peaks and troughs and recessions and expansions. For example, according to the NBER, February and April 2020 were the business cycle peak and trough, respectively, during the COVID-19 pandemic.

Recessions are periods of economic downturns when output and employment are falling. The **trough** of a business cycle is the lowest point of a recession, before the economy starts to expand. **Expansions,** or recoveries, are periods of economic upturns when output and employment are rising. The **peak** of a business cycle is the highest point of an expansion before the economy goes into a recession. A **depression** is a very deep and prolonged downturn.

The NBER generally identifies a recession based on a decline in economic activity that is spread across the economy and lasts more than a few months. Because a recession must influence the economy broadly and not be confined to one sector, the NBER emphasizes economy-wide measures of economic activity. The determination of the month of a peak or a trough is based on a variety of measures of aggregate real economic activity, including data on income, employment, consumption expenditures, sales, and industrial production. There is no fixed rule about what measures are used or how they are weighted. In recent decades, NBER has put the most weight on income and employment measures. Real GDP is also an important measure used by the NBER to determine business cycle peaks and troughs.

The NBER waits until sufficient data are available, and therefore it tends to identify peaks and troughs several months after they have actually occurred. So we are never certain what phase of the business cycle we are currently in—we only know what phase we *were* in after the NBER has enough data to look back and be certain.

Let's consider a general graph of a business cycle showing ups and downs in aggregate economic activity over time. The NBER dates business cycles using data for a variety of aggregate measures of the economy, but we can look at a representative business cycle using the two aggregate measures we have developed earlier in this Unit: real GDP and the unemployment rate.

Figure 2.7-1 illustrates the four phases of a business cycle. The graph shows a hypothetical business cycle measured by real GDP. When GDP is falling, the economy is in a recession. When real GDP reaches a minimum, this is the business cycle trough. The increase in real GDP that follows is an expansion, and when real GDP

FIGURE 2.7-1 Phases of a Business Cycle

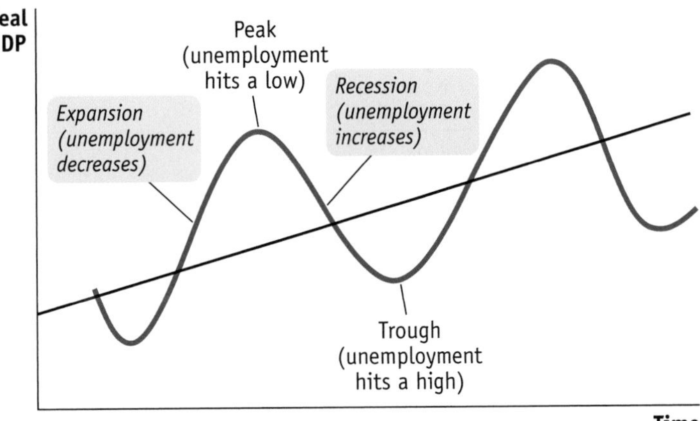

Over time, the macroeconomy alternates between downturns and upturns. When the economy completes an upturn and a downturn, it is known as a business cycle. There are four phases of a business cycle; recession, trough, expansion, and peak. The four phases can be illustrated using data for real GDP. Because production and employment are positively related, employment over the business cycle moves with real GDP. Production and employment both rise during expansions and fall during recessions. However, as you may recall from previous Modules, unemployment and production are inversely related. Unemployment rises when production falls and falls when production rises, so unemployment over the business cycle increases during recession, hitting its maximum at the trough, and decreases during expansion, hitting its minimum at the peak.

reaches a maximum, it is the business cycle peak. The unemployment rate moves in the opposite direction of the GDP. The unemployment rate falls during an economic expansion and is at its lowest point at the peak of the business cycle. Conversely, the unemployment rate rises during a recession, reaching its highest point at the trough of the business cycle.

Measuring Business Cycles

When does a downturn officially become a recession? Economists in many countries mark the beginning of a recession after two consecutive quarters (a quarter is three months) of falling output in the economy. In the United States, the NBER considers a variety of economic indicators to determine the beginning and end of recessions.

Key dates from the most recent eight business cycles are shown in **Table 2.7-1.** Notice the difference in the length of the two most recent business cycles: The Great Recession lasted 18 months (from December 2007 to June 2009), while the recession associated with the COVID-19 pandemic lasted only 2 months in 2020.

Table 2.7-1 U.S. Business Cycles Since 1969

Business Cycle Reference Dates		Contraction	Expansions	Cycle	
Peak (Quarter)	Trough (Quarter)	Peak to Trough (Months)	Previous Trough to this Peak (Months)	Trough from Previous Trough (Months)	Peak from Previous Peak (Months)
December 1969 (4)	November 1970 (4)	11	106	117	116
November 1973 (4)	March 1975 (1)	16	36	52	47
January 1980 (1)	July 1980 (3)	6	58	64	74
July 1981 (3)	November 1982 (4)	16	12	28	18
July 1990 (3)	March 1991 (1)	8	92	100	108
March 2001 (1)	November 2001 (4)	8	120	128	128
December 2007 (4)	June 2009 (2)	18	73	91	81
February 2020 (2019, 4)	April 2020 (2)	2	128	130	146

Data from NBER, US Business Cycle Expansions and Contractions.

AP® ECON TIP

Be prepared to identify the different phases of the business cycle so you can relate each phase to changes in employment, output, and unemployment.

Business cycles vary greatly in their length and depth. According to the NBER, there have been 12 recessions in the United States since World War II. During that period, the average recession lasted 11 months, and the average expansion lasted 58 months. The average length of a business cycle, from the beginning of one recession to the beginning of the next recession (peak to peak, in Table 2.7-1), has been 5 years and 8 months.

Figure 2.7-2 shows the history of the U.S. unemployment rate since 1989 and the timing of business cycles. Recessions are indicated in the figure by shaded areas.

FIGURE 2.7-2 The U.S. Unemployment Rate and the Timing of Business Cycles, 1989–2021

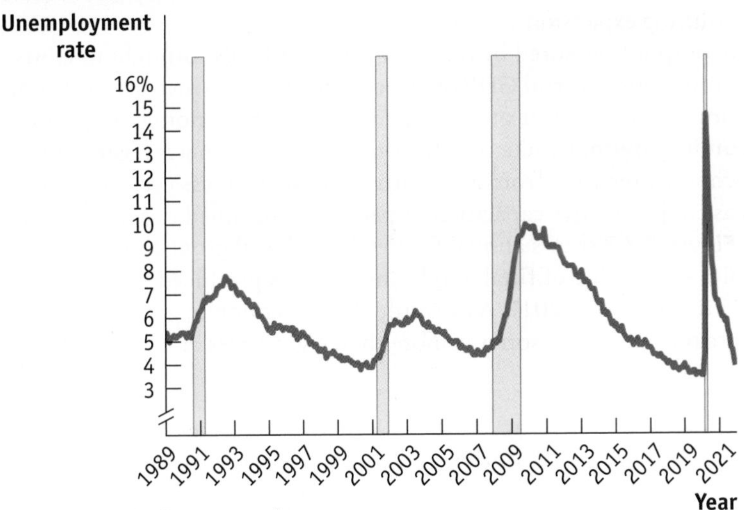

*Shaded bars indicate recessions.

The unemployment rate, a measure of joblessness, rises sharply during recessions (indicated by shaded areas) and usually falls during expansions.
Data Source: Bureau of Labor Statistics.

The business cycle is an enduring feature of the economy. But even though ups and downs seem to be inevitable, most people believe that macroeconomic analysis has guided policies that help smooth out the business cycle and stabilize the economy. What happens during a business cycle, and how can macroeconomic policies address the downturns? Let's take a closer look at unemployment/employment and aggregate output during business cycles.

Employment, Unemployment, and the Business Cycle

Although not as severe as a depression, a recession is clearly an undesirable event. Like a depression, a recession leads to joblessness, reduced production, reduced incomes, and lower living standards.

As we learned in Module 2.4, the unemployment rate – the percentage of the labor force that is unemployed – is usually a good indicator of what conditions are like in the job market. A high unemployment rate signals a poor job market in which jobs are hard to find; a low unemployment rate indicates a good job market in which jobs are relatively easy to find. In general, during recessions the unemployment rate is rising, and during expansions it is falling. Look again at Figure 2.7-2, which shows the unemployment rate from 1989 through early 2020. The graph shows significant changes in the unemployment rate. Note that even in the most prosperous times, there is some unemployment. A booming economy, like that of the late 1990s, can push the unemployment rate down to 4% or even lower. But a severe recession, like the one that began in 2007, can push the unemployment rate into double digits.

Economic growth has made the luxuries of the 1950s commonplace today.

Aggregate Output and the Business Cycle

Rising unemployment is the most painful consequence of a recession, and falling unemployment is the most urgently desired feature of an expansion. But the business cycle isn't just about jobs – it's also about output: the quantity of goods and services produced. During the business cycle, the economy's level of output and its unemployment rate move in opposite directions. At lower levels of output, fewer workers are needed, and the unemployment rate is relatively high. Growth in output requires the efforts of more workers, which lowers the unemployment rate. To measure the rise and fall of an economy's output, we look at real GDP. Real GDP normally falls during recessions and rises during expansions.

While aggregate output (measured by real GDP) rises and falls throughout a business cycle, the maximum possible real GDP of an economy tends to increase over time. An increase in the maximum amount of goods and services an economy can produce is known as **economic growth**. Unlike the short-term increases in aggregate output that occur as an economy recovers from a downturn in the business cycle, economic growth is an increase in productive capacity that permits a sustained rise in aggregate output over time. **Figure 2.7-3** shows annual figures for U.S. real gross domestic product (GDP) per capita – the value of final goods and services produced in the United States per person – from 1900 to 2017. As a result of this economic growth, the U.S. economy's aggregate output per person was more than eight times as large in 2017 as it was in 1900.

Economic growth is an increase in the maximum amount of goods and services an economy can produce.

FIGURE 2.7-3 Growth, the Long View

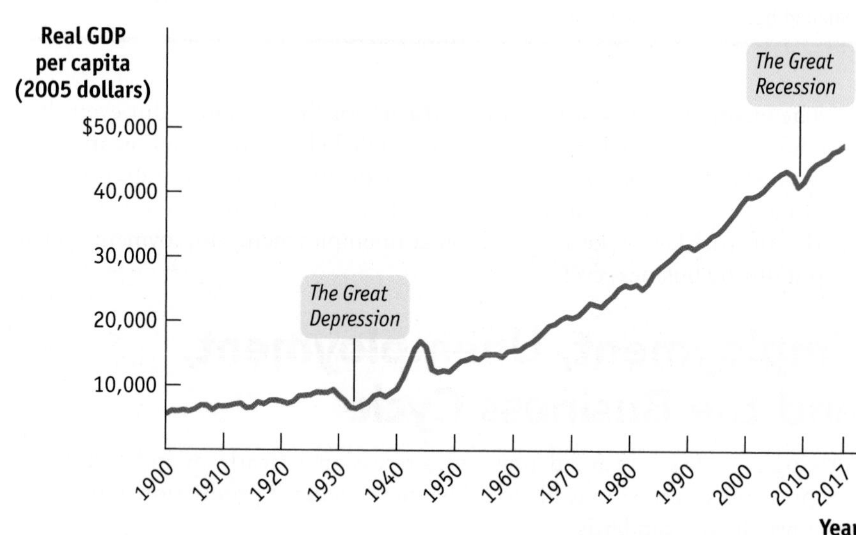

Over the long run, growth in real GDP per capita has dwarfed the ups and downs of the business cycle. Except for the Great Recession from 2007 to 2009 and the recession that began the Great Depression in 1929, recessions are almost invisible.
Data Sources: Angus Maddison, "Statistics on World Population, GDP and Per Capita GDP, 1-2006 AD," http://www.ggdc.net/maddison/; Jutta Bolt and Jan Luiten van Zanden, "The First Update of the Maddison Project; Re-estimating Growth Before 1820"; and Bureau of Economic Analysis.

Economic growth is fundamental to a nation's prosperity. A sustained rise in output per person allows for higher wages and a rising standard of living. The need for economic growth is urgent in poorer, less developed countries, where a lack of basic necessities makes growth a central concern of economic policy. As you will see when studying macroeconomics, the goal of economic growth can be in conflict with the goal of hastening recovery from an economic downturn. What is good for economic growth can be bad for short-run stabilization of the business cycle, and vice versa.

Actual Output Versus Potential Output

In Module 2.3, we saw that the unemployment rate will never equal zero – there is a *natural rate of unemployment* for the economy that includes frictional and structural unemployment. The natural rate of unemployment corresponds to the **full-employment level of output** – the level of real GDP the economy can produce when all resources are fully employed. The full-employment level of output represents an economy's **potential output**, the maximum level of output that could be produced using all available resources. Unlike actual GDP, potential GDP can't be calculated; it can only be estimated.

Full-employment level of output is the level of real GDP the economy can produce when all resources are fully employed. **Potential output** is what an economy can produce when operating at maximum sustainable employment (that is, at the natural rate of unemployment). The **output gap** is the difference between actual output and potential output.

During a recession, unemployment rises to a level above the natural rate of unemployment. Recall that *cyclical unemployment* is the deviation of the actual rate of unemployment from the natural rate; that is, it is the difference between the actual and natural rates of unemployment. As the name suggests, cyclical unemployment is the share of unemployment that arises from the business cycle. As a result of cyclical unemployment, during a recession the actual level of output falls below potential output because some resources are not being used for production. The difference between actual and potential output is called the **output gap**. In Unit 3 we will look more closely at output gaps, as well as policies that can be used to help close output gaps and move the economy toward full employment.

> **AP® ECON TIP**
>
> For the AP® exam you should know that some increases in output do not represent economic growth. Economic growth is an increase in the economy's potential output. Temporary fluctuations in economic conditions often alter real GDP (output) when there has been no change in the economy's potential output.

Module 2.7 Review

Check Your Understanding

1. Sketch a graph showing fluctuations in either employment, unemployment, or real GDP over time. On your graph, identify the four phases of the business cycle.
2. If actual GDP is less than potential GDP, is the output gap greater than, less than, or equal to zero? What phase of the business cycle is the economy experiencing if actual GDP is less than potential GDP?
3. When the unemployment rate is equal to the natural rate, is the output level in the economy greater than, less than, or equal to the full-employment output level? Explain.

Tackle the AP® Test: Multiple-Choice Questions

1. During the recession phase of a business cycle, which of the following is likely to increase?
   a. the unemployment rate
   b. the price level
   c. economic growth rate
   d. the labor force
   e. wages
2. Which of the following provides a long-term increase in the productive capacity of an economy?
   a. an expansion
   b. a recovery
   c. a recession
   d. a depression
   e. economic growth
3. In the United States, a recession officially begins after
   a. the NBER makes a judgment call that it has.
   b. the business cycle stops rising.
   c. two consecutive quarters of falling aggregate output.
   d. six weeks or rising unemployment.
   e. a depression has worsened for two consecutive months.
4. The lowest unemployment rate during a business cycle occurs
   a. during the expansion phase.
   b. during the recession phase.
   c. during the peak.
   d. during the trough.
   e. when aggregate output is lowest.
5. The full-employment level of output occurs when the unemployment rate is equal to
   a. the potential rate.
   b. zero.
   c. the cyclical rate.
   d. the natural rate.
   e. 4%.
6. At the trough of a business cycle, which of the following is at its highest?
   a. unemployment
   b. employment
   c. potential output
   d. actual output
   e. inflation

7. An output gap exists when potential output
   a. exceeds actual output.
   b. exceeds full-employment output.
   c. is less than full-employment output.
   d. is equal to full-employment output.
   e. is less than natural output.

Tackle the AP® Test: Free-Response Questions

1. a. Define *expansion* and *economic growth* and explain the difference between these two concepts.
   b. What happens to each of the following during an economic expansion?
      i. unemployment
      ii. employment
      iii. aggregate output

Rubric for FRQ 1 (6 points)

1 point: An expansion is the period of recovery after an economic downturn.

1 point: Economic growth is an increase in the productive capacity of the economy.

1 point: An expansion can occur regardless of any increase in the economy's long-term potential for production, and it only lasts until the next downturn, while economic growth increases the economy's ability to produce more goods and services over the long term.

1 point: unemployment decreases

1 point: employment increases

1 point: aggregate output increases

2. When the economy is experiencing cyclical unemployment, what is true of each of the following?
   a. The actual unemployment rate compared to the natural unemployment rate
   b. Actual output compared to potential output
   c. Potential output compared to full-employment output **(3 points)**

UNIT 2 Review

Adventures in AP® Economics Videos

Mod 2.1: The Circular Flow
Mod 2.5: Real and Nominal Values

UNIT 2 Review Video

economics by example
How Can GDP Be Up When We're Feeling Down?

Module 2.1

1. Economists keep track of the flows of money between sectors with the **national income and product accounts**, or **national accounts**. The flow of income and expenditure in the economy can be illustrated using a circular flow diagram. Households earn income via the **factor markets** from wages, interest on bonds, profit accruing to owners of stocks, and rent on land. In addition, they receive **government transfers**. **Disposable income**, total household income minus taxes plus government transfers, is allocated to **consumer spending** (C) in the **product markets** and **private savings**. Via the **financial markets**, private savings and foreign lending are channeled to **investment spending** (I), government borrowing, and foreign borrowing. Government purchases of goods and services (G) are paid for by **tax revenues** and **government borrowing**. **Exports** (X) generate an inflow of funds into the country from the rest of the world, but **imports** (M) lead to an outflow of funds to the rest of the world. Foreigners can also buy stocks and bonds in the U.S. financial markets.
2. **Gross domestic product**, or **GDP**, measures the value of all **final goods and services** produced in the economy. It does not include the value of **intermediate goods and services**, but it does include inventories and **net exports** ($X - M$). There are three approaches to calculating GDP: the **value-added approach** of adding up the **value added** by all producers; the **expenditure approach** of adding up all spending on domestically produced final goods and services, leading to the equation $GDP = C + I + G + X - M$, also known as **aggregate spending**; and the **income approach** of adding up all the income paid by domestic firms to factors of production. These three methods are equivalent because in the economy as a whole, total income paid by domestic firms to factors of production must equal total spending on domestically produced final goods and services.

Module 2.2

3. The national accounts and the calculation of GDP were created during the Great Depression and implemented as a result of World War II. GDP is a useful indicator of a nation's economic performance. GDP includes new capital goods, new construction, and inventories, but it does not include intermediate goods, financial assets (such as stocks or bonds), transfer payments, used goods, nonmarket transactions, or imports.

Module 2.3

4. **Employed** people currently hold a part-time or full-time job; **unemployed** people do not hold a job but are actively looking for work. Their sum is equal to the **labor force**; the **labor force participation rate** is the percentage of the population age 16 or older that is in the labor force.
5. The **unemployment rate**, the percentage of the labor force that is unemployed and actively looking for work, can overstate or understate the true level of unemployment. It can overstate because it counts as unemployed those who are continuing to search for a job despite having been offered one. It can understate because it ignores frustrated workers, such as **discouraged workers**, and the **underemployed**. In addition, the unemployment rate varies greatly among different groups in the population; it is typically higher for younger workers and for workers near retirement age than for workers in their prime working years.
6. There are three categories of unemployment; frictional, structural, and cyclical. **Frictional unemployment** results from workers' job search. **Structural unemployment** results when workers lack the skills required for the available jobs. The **natural rate of unemployment**, the sum of frictional and structural unemployment, is well above zero, even when jobs are plentiful. The natural rate of unemployment changes

over time, largely in response to changes in labor force characteristics, labor market institutions, and government policies. **Cyclical unemployment** is the share of unemployment that depends on fluctuations in the business cycle.

Module 2.4

7. An overall increase in the level of prices in the economy is called **inflation**. The opposite, an overall decrease in the level of prices in the economy, is called **deflation**. **Disinflation** refers to a decrease in the rate of inflation.
8. To measure the **aggregate price level**, economists calculate the cost of purchasing a **market basket**. A price index is the ratio of the current cost of that market basket to the cost in a selected **base year**, multiplied by 100.
9. The inflation rate is calculated as the annual percentage change in a price index, typically based on the **consumer price index**, or **CPI,** the most common measure of the aggregate price level. The CPI is frequently used for indexing payments, but CPI may overstate the rise in price levels because of factors like **substitution bias**, product improvements, and innovation. A similar index for goods and services purchased by firms is the **producer price index**.
10. Price indices are used to adjust nominal values of GDP, income, or wages for changes in the price level (for example, inflation or deflation). Values adjusted for price changes are known as real values, for example **real GDP**, real income, and real wages.

Module 2.5

11. Inflation does not, as many assume, make everyone poorer by raising the level of prices. That's because if wages and incomes are adjusted to take into account a rising price level, **real wages** and **real income** remain unchanged. However, a high **inflation rate** imposes overall costs on the economy: shoe-leather costs, menu costs, and unit-of-account costs.
12. Inflation can produce winners and losers within the economy, because long-term contracts are generally written in dollar terms. Loans typically specify a **nominal interest rate**, which differs from the **real interest rate** due to inflation. A higher-than-expected inflation rate is good for borrowers and bad for lenders. A lower-than-expected inflation rate is good for lenders and bad for borrowers.

Module 2.6

13. **Real GDP** is the value of the final goods and services produced, calculated using the prices of a selected base year. Except in the base year, real GDP is not the same as **nominal GDP**, the value of **aggregate output** calculated using current prices. Nominal GDP can be converted to real GDP using the **GDP deflator**.
14. Analysis of the growth rate of aggregate output must use real GDP because doing so eliminates any change in the value of aggregate output due solely to price changes. Real **GDP per capita** is a measure of average aggregate output per person but is not in itself an appropriate policy goal. U.S. statistics on real GDP are always expressed in "chained dollars," which means they are calculated with the chain-linking method of averaging the GDP growth rate found using an early base year and the GDP growth rate found using a late base year.

Module 2.7

15. The **business cycle** refers to the ups and downs of the economy as measured by aggregate data, for example real GDP, unemployment, income, and production. There are two phases of the business cycle: **recession** and **expansion**. The turning points where the economy turns from recession to expansion and expansion to recession are called the **trough** and **peak** of the business cycle. A **depression** is an extended period of recession. The phases and turning points of a business cycle can be illustrated on a graph using measures of the aggregate economy.
16. The unemployment rate is affected by the business cycle. The unemployment rate generally falls when the growth rate of real GDP is above average and generally rises when the growth rate of real GDP is below average. An increase over time in the maximum amount of goods and services an economy can produce is known as **economic growth**.
17. The difference between actual output and potential output is the **output gap**. **Potential output** is also called **full-employment output**. It is the level of GDP where unemployment is equal to the natural rate of unemployment.

Key Terms

National income and product accounts (national accounts), p. 64
Product markets, p. 64
Consumer spending, p. 65
Factor markets, p. 65
Government spending, p. 65
Taxes, p. 65
Tax revenue, p. 65
Disposable income, p. 66
Government transfers, p. 66
Private savings, p. 66
Financial markets, p. 66
Government borrowing, p. 67
Investment spending, p. 67
Inventories, p. 67
Exports, p. 67
Imports, p. 67
Gross domestic product (GDP), p. 67
Expenditure approach, p. 68
Aggregate spending, p. 68
Income approach, p. 68
Value-added approach, p. 68
Final goods and services, p. 68
Intermediate goods and services, p. 69
Net exports, p. 69
Value added, p. 70
Nonmarket transactions, p. 73
Employed, p. 77
Unemployed, p. 77
Labor force, p. 77
Labor force participation rate, p. 77
Unemployment rate, p. 77
Discouraged workers, p. 78
Underemployed, p. 78
Frictional unemployment, p. 80
Structural unemployment, p. 81
Natural rate of unemployment, p. 81
Cyclical unemployment, p. 81
Inflation, p. 86
Deflation, p. 86
Price stability, p. 86
Real wage, p. 87
Real income, p. 87
Inflation rate, p. 88
Aggregate price level, p. 88
Market basket, p. 89
Base year, p. 89
Price index, p. 89
Consumer price index (CPI), p. 90
Substitution bias, p. 92
Producer price index (PPI), p. 92
Nominal interest rate, p. 97
Real interest rate, p. 97
Disinflation, p. 98
Aggregate output, p. 101
Real GDP, p. 102
Nominal GDP, p. 102
GDP deflator, p. 103
GDP per capita, p. 103
Business cycle, p. 106
Recession, p. 106
Trough, p. 106
Expansion, p. 106
Peak, p. 106
Depression, p. 106
Economic growth, p. 110
Full-employment level of output, p. 110
Potential output, p. 110
Output gap, p. 111

AP® Exam Practice Questions

Multiple-Choice Questions

Refer to the following diagram for Questions 1–3.

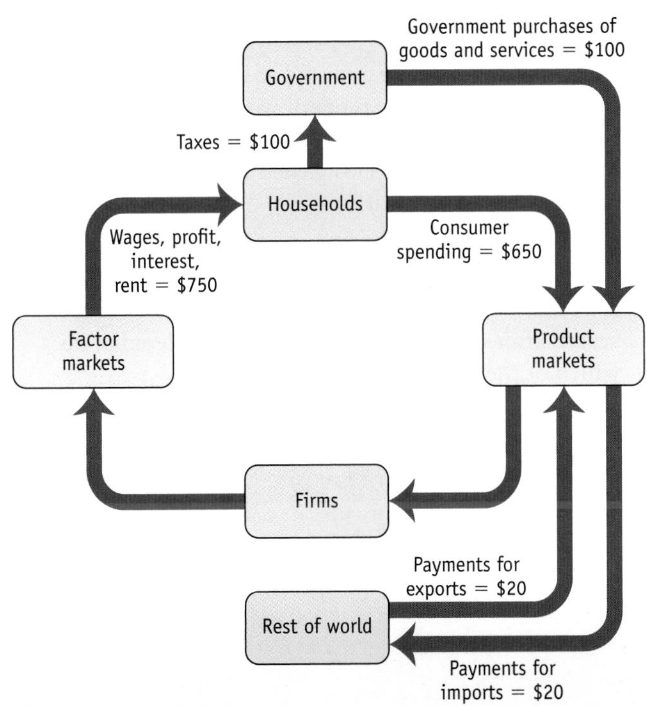

1. What is the value of GDP?
   a. $550
   b. $650
   c. $750
   d. $770
   e. $790

2. What is the value of disposable income?
   a. $750
   b. $650
   c. $550
   d. $530
   e. $510

3. The $750 of wages, profit, interest, and rent shown by the arrow pointing into the factor markets box illustrates the calculation of GDP using which approach?
   a. value-added
   b. aggregate spending
   c. expenditure
   d. income
   e. resource

Refer to the following table for Questions 4–5.

Category	Components of GDP (billions of dollars)
Consumer spending	
Durable goods	$1,000
Nondurable goods	$2,000
Services	$7,000
Private Investment Spending	
Fixed investment spending	$1,700
Nonresidential	$1,400
Structures	$500
Equipment and software	$900
Residential	$300
Change in private inventories	–$100
Net exports	
Exports	$1,500
Imports	$2,000
Government purchases of goods and services and government investment spending	
Federal	$1,400
State and local	$1,600

4. What is the value of GDP?
a. $10,000
b. $11,600
c. $14,100
d. $15,100
e. $18,100

5. What is the value of net exports?
a. $3,500
b. $2,000
c. $1,500
d. $500
e. –$500

6. Which of the following refers to a loan in the form of an IOU that pays interest?
a. stock
b. bond
c. disposable income
d. government transfer
e. investment

7. Investment spending includes spending on which of the following?
a. stocks
b. physical capital
c. inputs
d. services
e. reductions in inventories

8. Which of the following is included in the calculation of GDP?
a. intermediate goods and services
b. used goods
c. stocks and bonds
d. foreign-produced goods and services
e. domestically produced capital goods

9. Which of the following is true for the current year if real GDP is greater than nominal GDP?
a. The price level has decreased since the base year.
b. The consumer price index has increased since the base year.
c. The economy is experiencing inflation.
d. There has been economic growth.
e. Net exports are positive.

10. A country's labor force is equal to which of the following?
a. the number of people aged 16 and above
b. the number of people employed plus the number retired
c. the number of people employed plus the number unemployed
d. the number of people working for pay
e. the number of people employed for pay plus the number who have given up looking for work

11. The number of people who are considered unemployed is equal to the number of people who are not working and
a. are receiving unemployment compensation.
b. have given up seeking work.
c. plan to look for work in the future.
d. have looked for work in the recent past.
e. are actively seeking work.

12. The unemployment rate is the number of people unemployed divided by the number
a. employed.
b. employed plus the number discouraged.
c. in the labor force.
d. in the population aged 16 and above.
e. in the population.

13. The number of people counted as unemployed includes which of the following types of workers?
a. discouraged workers
b. aspiring workers seeking their first job
c. underemployed workers
d. retired workers
e. part-time workers

14. A worker who is not working while engaged in a job search after moving to a new city is considered to be which of the following?
a. frictionally unemployed
b. structurally unemployed
c. cyclically unemployed
d. underemployed
e. a discouraged worker

15. A worker who is not working because that worker's skills are no longer demanded in the labor market is considered to be which of the following?
  a. frictionally unemployed
  b. structurally unemployed
  c. cyclically unemployed
  d. underemployed
  e. a discouraged worker

16. The normal unemployment rate around which the actual unemployment rate fluctuates is known as which of the following?
  a. frictional unemployment rate
  b. structural unemployment rate
  c. cyclical unemployment rate
  d. natural rate of unemployment
  e. maximum unemployment rate

17. Which of the following is true if the real wage rate is equal to the nominal wage rate?
  a. Real income is constant.
  b. The price level for the current year is the same as the price level in the base year.
  c. The CPI is increasing.
  d. The demand for labor is increasing.
  e. The economy is experiencing deflation.

18. A worker who is unemployed due to fluctuations in the business cycle is considered to be which of the following?
  a. frictionally unemployed
  b. structurally unemployed
  c. cyclically unemployed
  d. underemployed
  e. a discouraged worker

19. When inflation makes money a less reliable unit of measurement, the economy is experiencing which of the following costs of inflation?
  a. unit-of-account
  b. shoe-leather
  c. menu
  d. measurement
  e. monetary

20. Bringing down the inflation rate is known as
  a. negative inflation.
  b. deflation.
  c. bubble popping.
  d. disinflation.
  e. contraction.

21. The real interest rate is equal to the nominal interest rate
  a. minus the inflation rate.
  b. plus the inflation rate.
  c. divided by the inflation rate.
  d. times the inflation rate.
  e. plus the real interest rate divided by the inflation rate.

22. Who loses from unanticipated inflation?
  a. borrowers
  b. the government
  c. investors
  d. mortgage owners
  e. people on fixed incomes

23. Assume a country has a population of 1,000. If 400 people are employed and 100 people are unemployed, what is the country's unemployment rate?
  a. 50%
  b. 40%
  c. 25%
  d. 20%
  e. 10%

24. Which of the following changes will result in an increase in the natural rate of unemployment?
  a. More teenagers focus on their studies and do not look for jobs until after college.
  b. The government increases the time during which an unemployed worker can receive benefits.
  c. Greater access to the internet makes it easier for job-seekers to find a job.
  d. Union membership declines.
  e. Opportunities for job training improve.

25. If the consumer price index rises from 120 to 132, what is the inflation rate?
  a. 8%
  b. 10%
  c. 12%
  d. 20%
  e. 32%

26. Which of the following leaks out of the circular flow in the expanded circular-flow model?
  a. investment spending
  b. government transfers
  c. private borrowing
  d. the value of imports
  e. the value of exports

27. An increase in government spending will have which of the following effects on an economy's circular flow?
  a. leakages will exceed injections
  b. the international sector will increase
  c. the circular flow will expand
  d. flows into the product market will decrease
  e. flows into the factor market will decrease

Refer to the graph showing a hypothetical business cycle to answer questions 28–30.

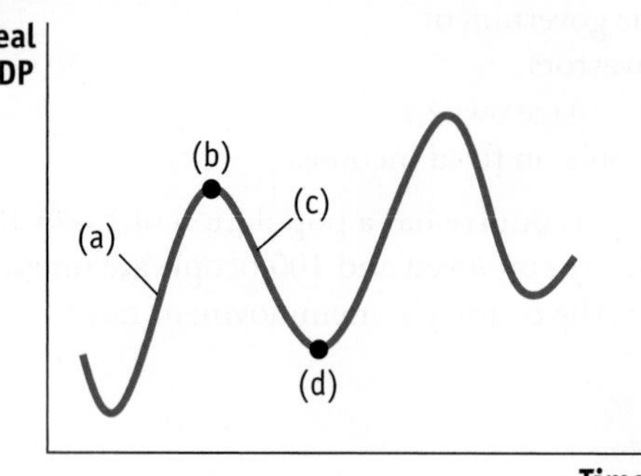

28. What is true of real GDP at point (d)?

a. It is decreasing.
b. It is increasing.
c. It is at its highest for the business cycle.
d. It is at its lowest for the business cycle.
e. It is equal to the natural rate of unemployment.

29. At what point on the graph will the cyclical unemployment rate be highest?

a. (a)
b. (b)
c. (c)
d. (d)
e. This can't be determined.

30. At point (c), actual real GDP is less than which of the following?

a. the natural rate of unemployment
b. the full employment level of unemployment
c. nominal GDP
d. potential output
e. real GDP at the trough of the business cycle

Free-Response Questions

1. Draw a correctly labeled simple circular-flow diagram.

a. On your diagram, illustrate each of the following:
  i. Households and firms
  ii. The factor and product markets
b. Add the government to your diagram to illustrate how taxes, government spending, and goods and services enter and exit the circular flow.
c. Explain how the international sector creates a leakage from and an injection into the circular flow. **(10 points)**

2. Assume the country of Technologia invests in an online application that efficiently matches job-seekers with employers and significantly reduces the time required for job searches.

a. Which type of unemployment will Technologia's investment affect?
b. Will unemployment increase or decrease?
c. Given the change in unemployment from part b, what will happen to the natural rate of unemployment in Technologia? Explain.
d. Given your answer to part b, what will happen to real GDP in Technologia? Explain. **(5 points)**

3. Use the price level information in the table below to answer the following questions. Assume year 2 is the base year.

	Price level
Year 1	$400
Year 2	$800
Year 3	$1,000
Year 4	$800

a. Calculate the price index for year 1 and 2. Show your work.
b. Calculate the inflation rate between year 1 and year 2. Show your work.
c. The economy experienced deflation between which two years? Explain.
d. The economy experienced disinflation between which two years? Explain. **(5 points)**

UNIT 3
MACRO

National Income and Price Determination

AP® Economic Skills

1. Principle and Models (1.A, 1.B, 1.D)
2. Interpretation (2.A)
3. Manipulation (3.C)
4. Graphing and Visuals (4.A, 4.C)

Recession and Recovery During the Pandemic

From 2007 to 2021, the U.S. economy experienced two significant contractions and expansions. The Great Recession of 2007–2009 was an 18-month contraction that represented the worst economic downturn since the 1929–1933 Great Depression. This downturn was immediately followed by the longest period of economic expansion in U.S. history, which lasted 128 months, during which the annual average real GDP grew by 2.3%. This business cycle's peak was in February 2020, when real GDP grew by 3.5%. But just the month prior, in January 2020, the global spread of a particularly aggressive and deadly strain of the coronavirus began to reach the United States. In March 2020, President Trump declared a national emergency in response to the COVID-19 pandemic. As a result of the pandemic, U.S. real GDP fell by 31.2% in the second quarter of 2020 and the unemployment rate rose to 14.8%, the highest since data collection started in 1948 and reminiscent of estimates those values regularly hit during the Great Depression.

How did the COVID-19 pandemic bring an end to the 2009–2020 expansion? In response to the national emergency declaration, people in the United States were encouraged to shelter in place. Schools were shut down and nonessential businesses were closed in efforts to keep people from spreading the virus and overwhelming hospitals. The entertainment, retail, and hospitality industries were hit the hardest; U.S. retail sales fell 16.4% and restaurant and bar sales dropped 29.5% in one month. The government-ordered shut-downs slowed both the spread of the outbreak and economic activity, as incomes and consumer spending were reduced.

The extreme economic decline ended in April 2020, making it a short (two-month) recession. Between the second quarter of 2020 and the first quarter of 2021, real GDP grew by 14.1%! And the unemployment rate fell to 4.2% by November 2021. This turnaround is largely attributed to government stimulus efforts that replaced much of the loss of income and spending resulting from the decrease in economic activity caused by the pandemic shut-down. In March 2020, the U.S. Congress passed several acts to provide financial aid to families and businesses. The Coronavirus Preparedness and Response Supplemental Appropriations Act provided $8.3 billion to federal agencies to respond to the pandemic. The Families First Coronavirus Response Act provided $3.5 billion in paid sick leave, insurance coverage of coronavirus testing, and unemployment benefits. And the Coronavirus Aid, Relief, and Economic Security Act, aka the CARES Act, provided $2 trillion in aid for households, businesses, and local governments.

timnewman/Getty Images

Why did the sharp economic contraction brought on by the pandemic last for only two months, and what enabled the rapid expansion that followed? Changes in income and consumer spending contributed to both the steep decline and relatively sudden recovery. The dramatic changes in consumer spending were magnified – or multiplied – to create the dramatic effects on the economy as a whole.

In this Unit, we will study how this multiplier process works to magnify the effects of changes in consumer spending (as well as business and government spending) on the aggregate economy. As a first step, we will look at the role of consumer spending and investment as components of aggregate demand. Changes in aggregate demand are central to the multiplier process that helps us understand the business cycle. We will then explore how aggregate demand and aggregate supply determine the level of prices and real output. Finally, we will consider how the federal government can use fiscal policy to influence prices and output in the economy to reduce the length and depth of recessions.

MODULE 3.1

Aggregate Demand

In this Module, you will learn to:

- Identify and define the components of aggregate demand: consumption (C), investment (I), government spending (G), and net exports ($X - M$)
- Describe the three effects that explain why the aggregate demand curve has a negative slope: the real wealth effect, the interest rate effect, and the exchange rate effect
- Identify the determinants of aggregate demand that cause the *AD* curve to shift

The Components of Aggregate Demand

In Unit 2, we defined real GDP as the dollar value of all final goods and services produced in the economy. We also defined the aggregate price level and considered how it changes as a result of inflation or deflation. In this Unit, we develop the *aggregate demand and aggregate supply model* (*AD–AS model*), which allows us to determine the level of real GDP and the aggregate price level in the economy.

To begin our development of the aggregate demand and aggregate supply model, let's look more closely at aggregate demand. You were introduced to the components of aggregate demand in the discussion of GDP in Module 2.1: consumer spending (C) is the largest component of aggregate demand, accounting for roughly 60%. In the United States, government spending (G) is a distant second, at 23%, and investment (I) accounts for 15%. Net exports ($X - M$) account for a mere 1% of U.S. aggregate demand.

Don Mason/The Image Bank/Getty Images

Let's look more closely at the two most important components of aggregate demand: consumption and investment. Consumption is important because it makes up the largest component of aggregate demand. And though investment makes up a much smaller portion of aggregate demand than consumption, slumps in investment are frequently cited by economists as the cause of economic downturns. We will look more closely at government spending later in this Unit and at net exports in our discussion of international trade in Unit 6.

Consumption

Should you splurge on a restaurant meal or save money by eating at home? Should you buy a new car and, if so, how much should you spend? Households are constantly confronted with spending choices—not just about what to buy but also about how much to spend in total. These choices, in turn, have a powerful effect on the economy, since consumer spending normally accounts for two-thirds of total spending on final goods and services. But what determines how much consumers spend?

The most important factor affecting a household's consumer spending is its current disposable income—income after taxes are paid and government transfers are received. It's obvious from daily life that people with high disposable incomes on average drive more expensive cars, live in more expensive houses, and spend more on meals, clothing, and entertainment than people with lower disposable incomes. And the relationship between current disposable income and spending is reflected in the data.

Factors other than current disposable income can also cause households to consume more or less at every level of income. There are two principal causes of changes in consumption other than disposable income: changes in expected future disposable income, and changes in aggregate wealth.

Suppose you land a well-paying job upon graduating from college—but the job, and the paychecks, won't start for several months. So, your disposable income hasn't risen yet. Even so, it's likely that you will start spending more on final goods and services before your first paycheck arrives—for example, you may buy an expensive outfit for work—because you know that higher income is coming. Conversely, suppose you have a good job but learn that the company is planning to downsize your division, raising the possibility that you may lose your job and have to take a lower-paying one somewhere else. Even though your disposable income hasn't gone down yet, you might well cut back on spending even while still employed, to save money for a rainy day. Both of these examples show how changes in *expected future disposable income* can either increase or decrease consumer spending at all levels of disposable income.

Changes in **wealth** can also cause consumption to increase or decrease. Wealth refers to an individual's or household's accumulated savings. Imagine two individuals, Maria and Mark, both of whom expect to earn $30,000 this year. Suppose, however, that they have different employment histories. Maria has been working steadily for the past 10 years, owns her own home, and has $200,000 in the bank. Mark is the same age as Maria, but he has been in and out of work, has never owned a home, and has very little in savings. In this case, Maria has something that Mark doesn't have: wealth. Even though they have the same disposable income, other things equal, you would expect Maria to spend more on consumption than Mark. That is, wealth has an effect on consumer spending.

Wealth is the value of a household's accumulated savings.

Most people try to *smooth* their consumption over their lifetimes—they save some of their current disposable income during their years of peak earnings (typically occurring during a worker's 40s and 50s) and live off the wealth they accumulated while working during their retirement.

Because wealth affects household consumer spending, changes in wealth across the economy can change consumption. A rise in aggregate wealth—say, because of a booming stock market—increases aggregate consumption at all levels of disposable income in the same way as does an expected increase in future disposable income. A decline in aggregate wealth—say, because of a fall in housing prices, as occurred in 2008—reduces aggregate consumption at all levels of disposable income.

Rubberball/Mike Kemp/Getty Images

Investment Spending

Although consumer spending is much greater than investment spending, booms and busts in investment spending tend to drive the business cycle. In fact, most recessions originate as a fall in investment spending. **Figure 3.1-1** illustrates this point; it shows the annual percentage change of investment spending and consumer spending in the United States, both measured in 2005 dollars, during seven recessions from 1973 to 2020. As you can see, swings in investment spending are much more dramatic than those in consumer spending. Economists believe that declines in consumer spending are often the result of slumps in investment spending.

FIGURE 3.1-1 Fluctuations in Investment Spending and Consumer Spending

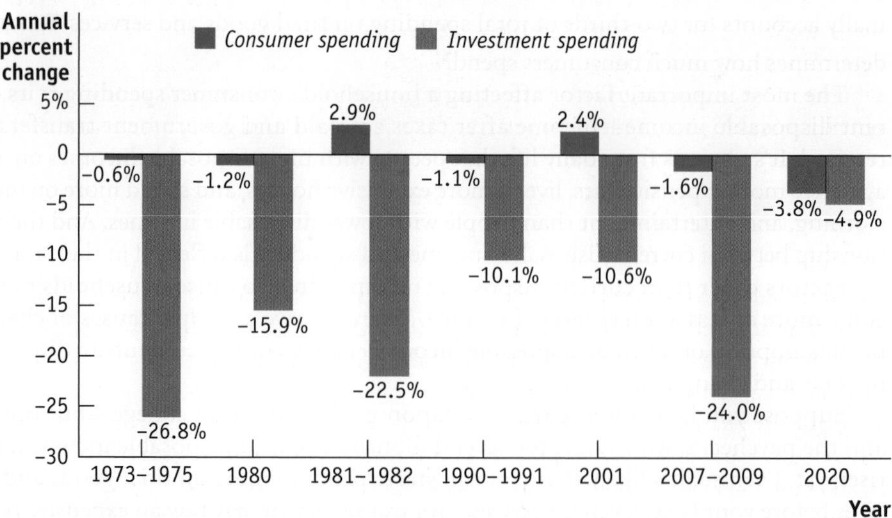

The bars illustrate the annual percentage change in investment spending and consumer spending during seven recent recessions. As the heights of the bars show, swings in investment spending were much larger in percentage terms than those in consumer spending. The pattern has led economists to believe that, unlike the 2020 recession described in the Unit opener, recessions typically originate as a slump in investment spending.

Planned investment spending is the investment spending that businesses intend to undertake during a given period.

What factors determine investment spending? **Planned investment spending** is the investment spending that firms *intend* to undertake during a given period. For reasons explained shortly, the level of investment spending that businesses *actually* carry out is sometimes not the same level as was planned. Planned investment spending depends on three principal factors: the interest rate, the expected future level of real GDP, and the current level of production capacity.

The Interest Rate and Investment Spending

Interest rates have their clearest effect on one particular form of investment spending: spending on residential construction — that is, on the construction of homes. The reason is straightforward: home-builders build only houses they think they can sell, and houses are more affordable — and therefore more likely to sell — when the interest rate is low. As we learned in Module 2.5, lower interest rates are better for borrowers. Consider a potential home-buying family that needs to borrow $150,000 to buy a house. At an interest rate of 7.5%, a 30-year home mortgage will mean payments of $1,048 per month. At an interest rate of 5.5%, those payments would be only $851 per month, making houses significantly more affordable.

Interest rates also affect other forms of investment spending. Firms will go ahead with a project that requires investment spending only if they expect a rate of return higher than the cost of the funds they would have to borrow to finance that project. If the interest rate rises, the cost of borrowing also rises, and fewer projects will pass that test — as a result, investment spending will be lower.

You might think that a firm faces a different trade-off if it can fund its investment project with its past profits rather than through borrowing. Past profits used to finance investment spending are called *retained earnings*. But even if a firm pays for investment spending out of retained earnings, the trade-off it must make in deciding whether or not to fund a project remains the same because the firm must take into account the opportunity cost of its funds. For example, instead of purchasing new equipment, the firm could lend out the funds and earn interest. The forgone interest earned is the opportunity cost of using retained earnings to fund an investment project.

Interest rates have a direct impact on whether or not construction companies decide to invest in the construction of new homes.

Either way, a rise in the market interest rate makes any given investment project less profitable. Conversely, a fall in the interest rate makes some investment projects that were unprofitable before profitable at the new lower interest rate. So planned investment spending – spending on investment projects that firms voluntarily decide whether or not to undertake – is negatively related to the interest rate. Other things equal, a higher interest rate leads to a lower level of planned investment spending.

Expected Future Real GDP, Production Capacity, and Investment Spending

Suppose a firm has enough capacity to continue to produce the amount of goods it is currently selling, but doesn't expect its sales to grow in the future. In this case, the firm will engage in investment spending only to replace existing equipment and structures that wear out or are rendered obsolete by new technologies. But if, instead, the firm expects its sales to grow rapidly in the future, it will find its existing production capacity insufficient for its future production needs. So the firm will undertake investment spending to meet those needs. This pattern implies that, other things equal, firms will undertake more investment spending when there is *growth in expected future sales*.

Suppose that a firm has considerably more capacity than necessary to meet its current production needs. Even if it expects sales to grow, it won't have to undertake investment spending for a while – not until the growth in sales catches up with its excess capacity. This pattern illustrates the fact that, other things equal, the *current level of productive capacity* has a negative effect on investment spending: in other words, other things equal, the higher the current capacity, the lower the investment spending.

If we consider the effects on investment spending of (1) growth in expected future sales and (2) the size of current production capacity, we can predict one situation in which firms will most likely undertake high levels of investment spending: when the firm expects sales to grow rapidly. In these cases, even if a firm has excess production capacity, that excess will soon be used up, leading the firm to resume investment spending.

What is an indicator of high expected growth in future sales? The answer is a high expected future growth rate of real GDP. A *higher expected future growth rate of real GDP* results in a higher level of planned investment spending. Conversely, a lower expected future growth rate of real GDP leads to lower planned investment spending.

But not all investments by a firm are planned. How does a firm make an *unplanned* investment? Most firms maintain inventories, stocks of goods held to satisfy future sales. Firms hold inventories so they can quickly satisfy buyers – a consumer can purchase an item off the shelf rather than waiting for it to be manufactured. In addition, businesses often hold inventories of their inputs to be sure they have a steady supply of necessary materials and spare parts.

At the beginning of 2021, the overall value of inventories in the U.S. economy was estimated at approximately $2 trillion, roughly 10% of GDP. Suppose that the U.S. auto industry produces 800,000 cars per month, but it sells only 700,000. The remaining 100,000 cars are added to the inventory at auto company warehouses or car dealerships, ready to be sold in the future.

Inventory investment is the value of the change in total inventories held in the economy during a given period. Unlike other forms of investment spending, inventory investment can actually be negative. If, for example, the auto industry reduces its inventory over the course of a month, we say that it has engaged in negative inventory investment.

Inventory investment is the value of the change in inventories held in the economy during a given period.

Inventory investment is unplanned when a difference between *actual sales* and *expected sales* leads to the change in inventories. *Actual inventory investment* is the sum of planned and unplanned inventory investment. In any given period, *actual investment spending* is equal to planned investment spending plus unplanned inventory investment.

The Aggregate Demand Curve

The majority of economists agree that the 2020 recession was the result of a sudden negative demand shock. What does that mean? When economists talk about a fall in the demand for a particular good or service, they're referring to a leftward shift of the demand curve. Similarly, when economists talk about a negative demand shock to the economy as a whole, they are referring to a leftward shift of the **aggregate demand curve**, a curve that shows the relationship between the aggregate price level and the quantity of aggregate output demanded by households, firms, the government, and the rest of the world.

The **aggregate demand curve** shows the relationship between the aggregate price level and the quantity of aggregate output demanded by households, businesses, the government, and the rest of the world.

Figure 3.1-2 shows what the aggregate demand curve may have looked like in 1933, at the end of the 1929–1933 recession. The horizontal axis shows the total quantity of domestic goods and services demanded, measured in 2005 dollars. Real GDP is used to measure aggregate output, and we will use the two terms interchangeably. The vertical axis shows the aggregate price level, measured by the GDP deflator. With these variables on the axes, we can draw a curve, *AD*, that shows how much aggregate output would have been demanded at any given aggregate price level. Since *AD* is meant to illustrate aggregate demand in 1933, one point on the curve corresponds to actual data for 1933, when the aggregate price level was 7.9 and the total quantity of domestic final goods and services purchased was $716 billion in 2005 dollars.

FIGURE 3.1-2 The Aggregate Demand Curve

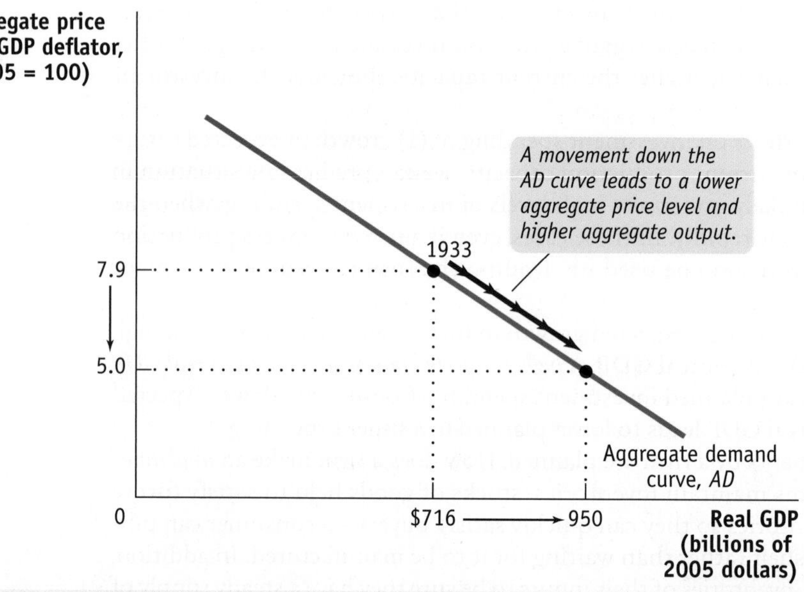

The aggregate demand curve shows the relationship between the aggregate price level and the quantity of aggregate output demanded. Corresponding to the actual 1933 data, here the total quantity of goods and services demanded at an aggregate price level of 7.9 is $716 billion in 2005 dollars. According to our hypothetical curve, however, if the aggregate price level had been only 5.0, the quantity of aggregate output demanded would have risen to $950 billion.

As drawn in Figure 3.1-2, the aggregate demand curve is downward-sloping, indicating a negative relationship between the aggregate price level and the quantity of aggregate output demanded. A higher aggregate price level, other things equal, reduces the quantity of aggregate output demanded; a lower aggregate price level, other things equal, increases the quantity of aggregate output demanded. According to Figure 3.1-2, if the price level in 1933 had been 5.0 instead of 7.9, the total quantity of domestic final goods and services demanded would have been $950 billion in 2005 dollars instead of $716 billion.

The first key question about the aggregate demand curve involves its negative slope.

Why Is the Aggregate Demand Curve Downward-Sloping?

In Figure 3.1-2, the curve *AD* slopes downward. Why? Recall the basic equation of national income accounting from Module 2.1:

$$\textbf{(3.1-1)} \quad GDP = C + I + G + (X - M)$$

where *C* is consumer spending, *I* is investment spending, *G* is government purchases of goods and services, *X* is exports to other countries, and *M* is imports. If we measure these variables in constant dollars – that is, in prices of a base year – then $C + I + G + (X - M)$ represents the quantity of domestically produced final goods and services demanded during a given period. *G* is decided by the government, but the other variables are private-sector decisions. To understand why the aggregate demand curve slopes downward, we need to understand why a rise in the aggregate price level reduces *C*, *I*, and $(X - M)$.

AP® ECON TIP

Aggregate demand is the demand for all goods and services in all markets rather than the demand for one good or service in one market, so make sure to use correct labels when you graph *AD*. *P* and *Q* were the correct labels for an individual market, but the price level (*PL*) and real GDP are the correct labels for a graph of the entire economy.

You might think that the downward slope of the aggregate demand curve is a natural consequence of the *law of demand*. That is, since the demand curve for any one good is downward-sloping, isn't it natural that the demand curve for aggregate output is also downward-sloping? This turns out, however, to be a misleading parallel. The demand curve for any individual good shows how the quantity demanded depends on the price of that good, *holding the prices of other goods and services constant*. The main reason the quantity of a good demanded falls when the price of that good rises – that is, the quantity of a good demanded falls as we move up the demand curve – is that people switch their consumption to other goods and services that have become relatively less expensive. But aggregate demand includes *all* goods and services, so the idea of switching consumption to other goods and services can't apply – there are no other goods and services to substitute at a lower relative price!

When we consider movements up or down the aggregate demand curve, we're considering *a simultaneous change in the prices of all final goods and services*. Furthermore, changes in the composition of goods and services in consumer spending aren't relevant to the aggregate demand curve: if consumers decide to buy fewer clothes but more cars, this doesn't necessarily change the total quantity of final goods and services they demand.

Why, then, does a rise in the aggregate price level lead to a fall in the quantity of all domestically produced final goods and services demanded? There are three reasons: the *real wealth effect*, the *interest rate effect*, and the *exchange rate effect* of a change in the aggregate price level.

Karl Gehring/Getty Images

When the aggregate price level falls, the purchasing power of consumers' assets rises, leading shoppers to place more items in their carts.

The Real Wealth Effect

An increase in the aggregate price level, other things equal, reduces the purchasing power of many assets. Consider, for example, someone who has \$5,000 in a bank account. If the aggregate price level were to rise by 25%, that \$5,000 would buy only as much as \$4,000 would have bought previously. With the loss in purchasing power, the owner of that bank account would probably scale back their consumption plans. Millions of other people would respond the same way, leading to a fall in spending on final goods and services, because a rise in the aggregate price level reduces the purchasing power of everyone's bank account.

Correspondingly, a fall in the aggregate price level increases the purchasing power of consumers' assets and leads to more consumer demand. The **real wealth effect** of a change in the aggregate price level is the change in consumer spending caused by the altered purchasing power of consumers' assets. Because of the real wealth effect, consumer spending, *C*, falls when the aggregate price level rises, leading to a downward-sloping aggregate demand curve.

The **real wealth effect** of a change in the aggregate price level is the change in consumer spending caused by the altered purchasing power of consumers' assets.

The Interest Rate Effect

Economists use the term *money* in its narrowest sense to refer to cash and bank deposits on which people can withdraw funds. People and firms hold money because it reduces the cost and inconvenience of making transactions. An increase in the aggregate price level, other things equal, reduces the purchasing power of a given amount of money holdings. To purchase the same basket of goods and services as before, people and firms now need to hold more money. So, in response to an increase in the aggregate price level, the public tries to increase its money holdings, either by borrowing more or by selling assets such as bonds. This activity reduces the funds available for lending to other borrowers and drives interest rates up. A rise in the interest rate reduces investment spending because it makes the cost of borrowing higher. It also reduces consumer spending because households save more of their disposable income. So a rise in the aggregate price level depresses investment spending, *I*, and consumer spending, *C*, through its effect on the purchasing power of money holdings, an effect known as the **interest rate effect** of a change in the aggregate price level. This effect also leads to a downward-sloping aggregate demand curve.

The **interest rate effect** of a change in the aggregate price level is the change in investment and consumer spending caused by altered interest rates that result from changes in the demand for money.

The Exchange Rate Effect

Net exports ($X - M$) are the fourth component of the basic equation of national income accounting. A change in the aggregate price level will also have an effect on net exports for two reasons that can help to explain why the aggregate demand curve slopes downward. First, there is the direct effect on net exports. As the domestic aggregate price level changes, a country's goods and services become more or less expensive relative to the goods and services in other countries. For example, as the domestic aggregate price level increases relative to the aggregate price level in another country, exports become more expensive for foreign buyers, and imports become less expensive. This increase in the price level results in a decrease in net exports and real GDP, so the *AD* curve has a negative slope.

AP® ECON TIP

Identify and describe the three effects (real wealth, interest rate, and exchange rate) that explain why the aggregate demand curve slopes downward. You should know how to explain why *AD* is downward-sloping—and these three effects are the answer!

Second, a change in aggregate price level produces an indirect effect on net exports through the foreign exchange market where currencies are exchanged. As the domestic aggregate price level changes, it causes a change in domestic interest rates, which affects financial investment flows between countries. For example, as the domestic aggregate price level and interest rates decrease relative to other countries, domestic financial investors invest more in other countries, where the return on their investment is higher. The resulting increase in the flow of domestic currency to other countries causes a decrease in the value of that currency in the foreign exchange market (known as the *exchange rate*– discussed in detail in Unit 6). The decrease in the value of the domestic currency increases net exports because domestic goods and services become relatively cheaper for foreign buyers with now-higher-valued currency. This is called the **exchange rate effect** of a change in the aggregate price level. The decrease in the price level results in an increase in real GDP, so the *AD* curve has a negative slope.

The **exchange rate effect** of a change in the aggregate price level is the change in net exports caused by a change in the value of the domestic currency, which leads to change in the relative price of domestic and foreign goods and services.

Shifts of the Aggregate Demand Curve

When we introduced the analysis of supply and demand in the market for an individual good in Modules 1.4 and 1.5, we stressed the importance of the distinction between *movements along* the demand curve and *shifts of* the demand curve. The same distinction applies to the aggregate demand curve. Figure 3.1-2 shows a *movement along* the aggregate demand curve, a change in the aggregate quantity of goods and services demanded as the aggregate price level changes. But there can also be *shifts of* the aggregate demand curve, changes in the quantity of goods and services demanded at any given price level, as shown in **Figure 3.1-3**. When we talk about an increase in aggregate demand, we mean a shift of the aggregate demand curve to the right, as shown in panel (a) by the shift from AD_1 to AD_2. A rightward shift occurs when the quantity of aggregate output demanded increases at any given aggregate price level. A decrease in aggregate demand means that the *AD* curve shifts to the

FIGURE 3.1-3 Shifts of the Aggregate Demand Curve

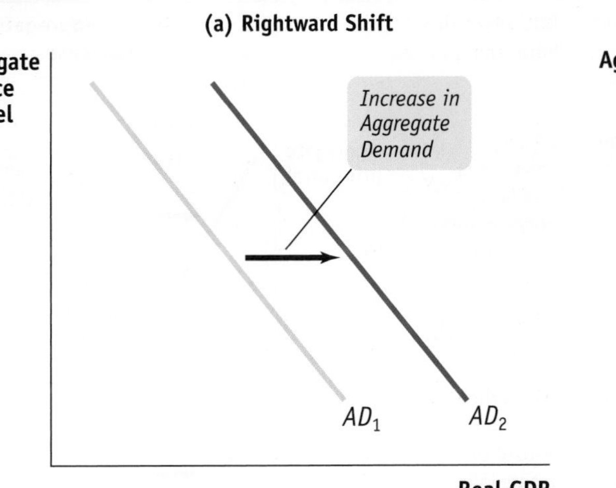

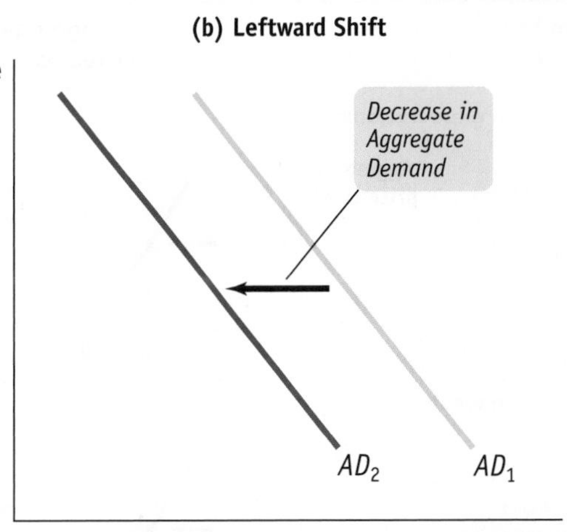

Panel (a) shows the effect of events that increase the quantity of aggregate output demanded at any given aggregate price level, such as a rise in consumer optimism about future income or a rise in government spending. Such changes shift the aggregate demand curve to the right, from AD_1 to AD_2. Panel (b) shows the effect of events that decrease the quantity of aggregate output demanded at any given aggregate price level, such as a fall in wealth caused by a stock market decline. This shifts the aggregate demand curve leftward from AD_1 to AD_2.

left, as in panel (b). A leftward shift implies that the quantity of aggregate output demanded falls at any given aggregate price level. Since aggregate demand is comprised of C, I, G, and $(X - M)$, changes that affect any of these values will cause real GDP to be higher or lower at any given price level.

A number of factors can shift the aggregate demand curve. Among the most important factors are changes in expectations, changes in wealth, and the size of the existing stock of physical capital. In addition, both fiscal and monetary policy can shift the aggregate demand curve. All five factors set the *expenditure multiplier* process in motion—this process, through which a change in spending leads to a multiplied effect on real GDP, is detailed in the next Module. By causing an initial rise or fall in real GDP, these factors change disposable income, which leads to additional changes in aggregate spending, which lead to further changes in real GDP, and so on. The factors that shift the aggregate demand curve are shown in **Table 3.1-1**. Each of these factors has an effect on one or more of the components of aggregate demand; C, I, G, or $(X - M)$.

Changes in Expectations

As we learned at the beginning of this Module, both consumer spending and planned investment spending depend in part on people's expectations about the future. Consumers base their spending not only on the income they have now but also on the income they expect to have in the future. Firms base their planned investment spending not only on current conditions but also on the sales they expect to make in the future. As a result, changes in expectations can push consumer spending and planned investment spending up or down. If consumers and firms become more optimistic, aggregate spending rises; if they become more pessimistic, aggregate spending falls. In fact, short-run economic forecasters pay careful attention to surveys of consumer and business sentiment. In particular, forecasters watch the Consumer Confidence Index, a monthly measure calculated by the Conference Board, and the Michigan Consumer Sentiment Index, a similar measure calculated by the University of Michigan.

Changes in Wealth

Consumer spending depends in part on the value of household assets. When the real value of these assets rises, the purchasing power they embody also rises, leading to an

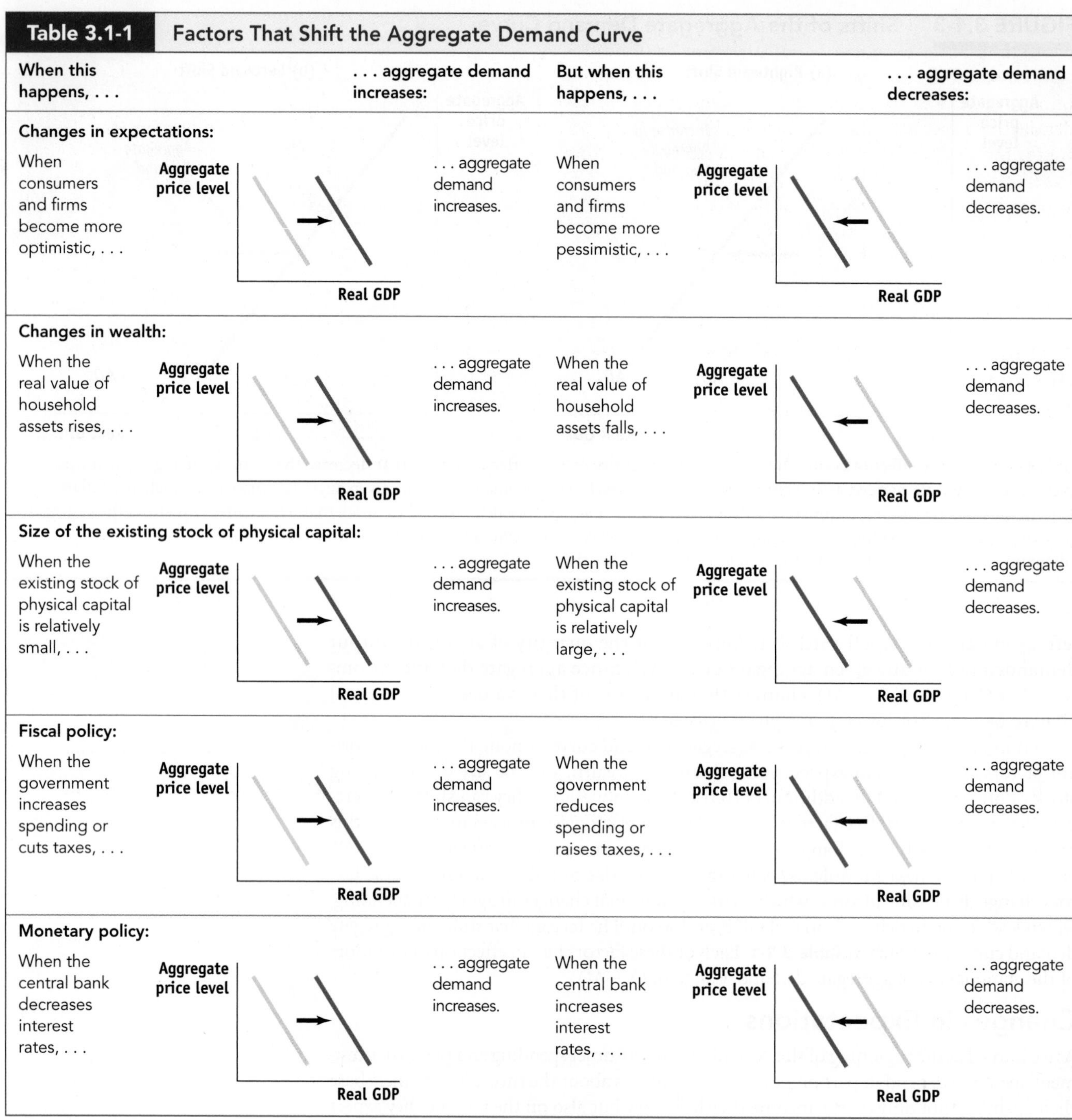

Table 3.1-1 Factors That Shift the Aggregate Demand Curve

When this happens, . . .		. . . aggregate demand increases:	But when this happens, . . .		. . . aggregate demand decreases:
Changes in expectations:					
When consumers and firms become more optimistic, . . .	Aggregate price level / Real GDP	. . . aggregate demand increases.	When consumers and firms become more pessimistic, . . .	Aggregate price level / Real GDP	. . . aggregate demand decreases.
Changes in wealth:					
When the real value of household assets rises, . . .	Aggregate price level / Real GDP	. . . aggregate demand increases.	When the real value of household assets falls, . . .	Aggregate price level / Real GDP	. . . aggregate demand decreases.
Size of the existing stock of physical capital:					
When the existing stock of physical capital is relatively small, . . .	Aggregate price level / Real GDP	. . . aggregate demand increases.	When the existing stock of physical capital is relatively large, . . .	Aggregate price level / Real GDP	. . . aggregate demand decreases.
Fiscal policy:					
When the government increases spending or cuts taxes, . . .	Aggregate price level / Real GDP	. . . aggregate demand increases.	When the government reduces spending or raises taxes, . . .	Aggregate price level / Real GDP	. . . aggregate demand decreases.
Monetary policy:					
When the central bank decreases interest rates, . . .	Aggregate price level / Real GDP	. . . aggregate demand increases.	When the central bank increases interest rates, . . .	Aggregate price level / Real GDP	. . . aggregate demand decreases.

increase in aggregate spending. For example, in the 1990s, there was a significant rise in the stock market that increased aggregate demand. And when the real value of household assets falls—for example, because of a stock market crash—the purchasing power they embody is reduced, and aggregate demand also falls. The stock market crash of 1929 was a significant factor leading to the Great Depression. Similarly, a sharp decline in real estate values was a major factor depressing consumer spending in 2008.

The Existing Stock of Physical Capital

As we also learned earlier, firms engage in planned investment spending to add to their stock of physical capital. Their incentive to spend depends in part on how much physical capital they already have: the more they have, the less they will feel a need to add more, other things equal. The same applies to other types of investment spending—for example, if a large number of houses have been built in recent years, this will depress the demand for new houses and, as a result, will also tend to reduce residential investment spending. In fact, that's part of the reason for the deep slump in residential investment spending that began in 2006. The housing boom of the previous few years had created an oversupply of houses: by spring 2008, the inventory of unsold houses on the market was equal to more than 11 months of sales, and prices had fallen more than 20% from their peak. This gave the construction industry little incentive to build even more homes.

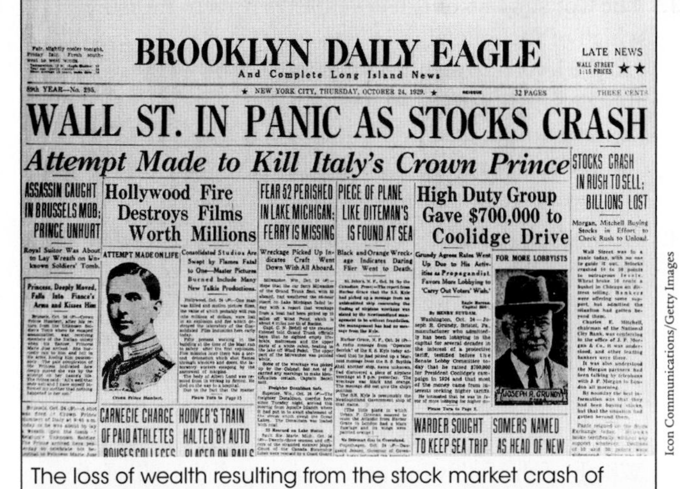
BROOKLYN DAILY EAGLE
And Complete Long Island News
LATE NEWS WALL STREET 1:15 PRICES ★★
NEW YORK CITY, THURSDAY, OCTOBER 24, 1929
32 PAGES
THREE CENTS

WALL ST. IN PANIC AS STOCKS CRASH

Attempt Made to Kill Italy's Crown Prince

STOCKS CRASH IN RUSH TO SELL; BILLIONS LOST

ASSASSIN CAUGHT IN BRUSSELS MOB; PRINCE UNHURT

Hollywood Fire Destroys Films Worth Millions

FEAR 52 PERISHED IN LAKE MICHIGAN; FERRY IS MISSING

PIECE OF PLANE LIKE DITEMAN'S IS FOUND AT SEA

High Duty Group Gave $700,000 to Coolidge Drive

CARNEGIE CHARGE OF PAID ATHLETES

HOOVER'S TRAIN HALTED BY AUTO

WARDER SOUGHT TO KEEP SEA TRIP

SOMERS NAMED AS HEAD OF NEW

The loss of wealth resulting from the stock market crash of 1929 was a significant factor leading to the Great Depression.

Icon Communications/Getty Images

Government Policies and Aggregate Demand

One of the key insights of macroeconomics is that the government can have a powerful influence on aggregate demand and that, in some circumstances, this influence can be used to improve economic performance. The two main ways the government can influence the aggregate demand curve are through *fiscal policy* and *monetary policy*. We'll discuss the influence of fiscal policy on aggregate demand in Module 3.8; monetary policy will be discussed in Unit 4.

Module 3.1  Review

Check Your Understanding

1. Explain why a decline in investment spending caused by a change in business expectations leads to a fall in consumer spending.
2. Determine the effect on aggregate demand of each of the following events. Explain whether it represents a movement along the aggregate demand curve (up or down) or a shift of the curve (leftward or rightward).
   - **a.** a rise in the interest rate caused by a change in monetary policy
   - **b.** a fall in the real value of money in the economy due to a higher aggregate price level
   - **c.** news of a worse-than-expected job market next year
   - **d.** a fall in tax rates
   - **e.** a rise in the real value of assets in the economy due to a lower aggregate price level
   - **f.** a rise in the real value of assets in the economy due to a surge in real estate values

Tackle the AP® Test: Multiple-Choice Questions

1. Which of the following does NOT explain the slope of the aggregate demand curve?
   - **a.** the real wealth effect of a change in the aggregate price level
   - **b.** the interest rate effect of a change in the aggregate price level
   - **c.** the product-substitution effect of a change in the aggregate price level
   - **d.** the exchange rate effect of a change in the aggregate price level
   - **e.** a change in interest-sensitive consumer spending resulting from a change in interest rates
2. Which of the following will shift the aggregate demand curve to the right?
   - **a.** an increase in wealth
   - **b.** pessimistic consumer expectations
   - **c.** an increase in the existing stock of capital
   - **d.** contractionary fiscal policy
   - **e.** an increase in the interest rate

3. The Consumer Confidence Index is used to measure which of the following?
   a. the level of consumer spending
   b. the rate of return on investments
   c. consumer expectations
   d. planned investment spending
   e. the level of current disposable income

4. Declines in the stock market decrease aggregate demand by decreasing which of the following?
   a. consumer wealth
   b. the price level
   c. the stock of existing physical capital
   d. interest rates
   e. tax revenues

5. Which of the following government policies will shift the aggregate demand curve to the left?
   a. an increase in government purchases of goods and services
   b. a decrease in government purchases of goods and services
   c. a decrease in taxes
   d. a decrease in interest rates
   e. an increase in government transfers

6. A change in consumer spending that results from a change in consumers' purchasing power is known as the ____________ effect of a change in the aggregate price level.
   a. interest rate
   b. exchange rate
   c. real wealth
   d. price
   e. income

7. A change in real GDP that results when the domestic price level increases relative to a foreign price level is the ____________ effect of a change in the price level.
   a. foreign
   b. exchange rate
   c. real wealth
   d. price
   e. income

Tackle the AP® Test: Free-Response Questions

1. **a.** Draw a correctly labeled graph showing aggregate demand.
   b. On your graph from part a, illustrate an increase in aggregate demand.
   c. List the four factors that shift aggregate demand.
   d. Describe a change in each determinant of aggregate demand that would lead to the shift you illustrated in part b.

Rubric for FRQ 1 (10 points)

1 point: Vertical axis labeled "Aggregate price level" (or "Price level") and horizontal axis labeled "Real GDP"

1 point: Downward-sloping curve labeled "*AD*" and a second curve labeled "*AD*" that is shifted to the right

1 point: Expectations

1 point: Wealth

1 point: Size of existing stock of physical capital

1 point: Government policies

1 point: An increase in the confidence of consumers/producers

1 point: An increase in wealth

1 point: A reduction in existing stock of physical capital

1 point: An increase in government spending or a decrease in the interest rate

2. Identify the three effects that cause the aggregate demand curve to have a downward slope. Explain each. **(6 points)**

Multipliers

In this Module, you will learn to:

- Define the marginal propensity to consume (*MPC*), the marginal propensity to save (*MPS*), the expenditure multiplier, and the tax multiplier
- Explain why the sum of the *MPC* and the *MPS* is equal to one
- Explain how the expenditure multiplier and the tax multiplier depend on the *MPC*
- Explain how changes in any of the components of aggregate demand lead to changes in real GDP
- Explain how changes in taxes lead to the changes in real GDP
- Use the expenditure multiplier to calculate the size of the change in aggregate demand resulting from a change in spending
- Use the tax multiplier to calculate the size of the change in aggregate demand resulting from a change in taxes

The Multiplier Process

The previous Module described the factors that shift the aggregate demand curve. In this Module, we look more closely at the multiplier effect of an initial change in one of those factors. The *multiplier effect* is a magnified effect on the macroeconomy that results from an initial change in spending. To explain the multiplier effect, we will start by measuring how a change in income leads to an initial—and then a multiplied—change in consumption spending. Later, we will see how the multiplier effect also results from a change in taxes.

The Marginal Propensity to Consume and the Marginal Propensity to Save

As a household's income rises, its consumption can increase. A household will choose how much to increase consumption in response to an increase in income. It can choose to spend all of the additional income it receives, none of it, or some amount in between. To understand how much additional consumption results from an increase in disposable income, we can measure how much consumers spend out of each additional dollar of income they receive. That figure gives us the additional consumption *per dollar* of additional income received. The increase in consumer spending out of each $1 increase in disposable income is called the **marginal propensity to consume**, or ***MPC***. When consumer spending changes because of a rise or fall in disposable income, the *MPC* is the change in consumer spending divided by the change in disposable income:

The **marginal propensity to consume**, or ***MPC***, is the increase in consumer spending when disposable income rises by $1.

$$\textbf{(3.2-1)}\quad MPC = \frac{\Delta \text{ Consumer spending}}{\Delta \text{ Disposable income}}$$

Because consumers normally spend only a portion of an additional dollar of disposable income, *MPC* is a number between 0 and 1. An *MPC* of 0 means that consumers spend none of an additional dollar they receive; an *MPC* of 1 means that they spend it all. If consumers spend half of an additional dollar of income, the *MPC* is 0.5. The additional disposable income that consumers don't spend is saved. The **marginal propensity to save**, or ***MPS***, is the fraction of an additional $1 of disposable income that is saved. Because consumers must either spend or save an

The marginal propensity to save, or ***MPS***, is the increase in household savings when disposable income rises by $1.

AP® ECON TIP

The *MPC* is central to the multiplier process. To understand the meaning of the *MPC*, consider the literal meaning of the term. The *MPC* is the marginal (additional) propensity (tendency) to consume. In other words, the *MPC* is the tendency for a consumer to spend any additional income received.

additional dollar, the *MPC* plus the *MPS* will equal 1; therefore, the $MPC = 1 - MPS$ and the $MPS = 1 - MPC$.

But when a consumer spends from additional income received, the process doesn't stop there. Let's say that an increase in income causes a consumer to spend to purchase new clothes. The spending for the clothes becomes income for the clothing store. This generates a rise in disposable income for the store owner, which leads to another increase in consumer spending, and so on. In other words, the initial increase in consumer spending results in multiple rounds of increases in aggregate output.

Now let's consider what happens if there is a change in a different component of aggregate demand, investment spending. Imagine that for some reason home-builders decide to spend an extra \$100 billion on home construction over the next year. The direct effect of this increase in investment spending will be to increase income and the value of aggregate output by the same amount. That happens because each dollar spent on home construction translates into a dollar's worth of income for construction workers, suppliers of building materials, electricians, and so on. If the process stopped there, the increase of \$100 billion in residential investment spending would raise overall income by exactly \$100 billion.

YOORAN PARK/Alamy

Many businesses, such as those that support home improvement and interior design, benefit during housing booms.

But again, the process doesn't stop there. Many businesses, such as those that support home improvement and interior design, benefit during housing booms. The increase in aggregate output leads to an increase in disposable income that flows to households in the form of profits and wages. The increase in households' disposable income leads to a rise in consumer spending, which, in turn, induces firms to increase output yet again. This generates another rise in disposable income, which leads to another round of consumer spending increases, and so on. In other words, the initial increase in investment spending results in multiple rounds of increases in aggregate output.

How large is the total effect on aggregate output if we sum the effect from all the rounds of spending increases associated with an initial change in consumption or investment? Each \$1 increase in spending raises both real GDP and disposable income by \$1. So the \$100 billion increase in investment spending initially raises real GDP by \$100 billion. The corresponding \$100 billion increase in disposable income leads to a second-round increase in consumer spending, which raises real GDP by a further $MPC \times \$100$ billion. This second-round increase in real GDP is followed by a third-round increase in consumer spending of $MPC \times MPC \times \$100$ billion, and so on. After an infinite number of rounds, the total effect on real GDP is

$$\begin{aligned}
&\text{Increase in investment spending} &&= \$100 \text{ billion}\\
&+ \text{Second-round increase in consumer spending} &&= MPC \times \$100 \text{ billion}\\
&+ \text{Third-round increase in consumer spending} &&= MPC^2 \times \$100 \text{ billion}\\
&+ \text{Fourth-round increase in consumer spending} &&= MPC^3 \times \$100 \text{ billion}\\
&\qquad\vdots &&\qquad\vdots\\
\hline
&\text{Total increase in real GDP} = (1 + MPC + MPC^2 + MPC^3 + \cdots) \times \$100 \text{ billion}
\end{aligned}$$

The \$100 billion increase in investment spending sets off a chain reaction in the economy, and the net result is a change in real GDP that is a multiple of the size of that initial change in spending.

How large is this multiple? Clearly, the size of the *MPC* is integral to determining how much spending is passed on each round.[1] The *MPC* is used to calculate the *expenditure multiplier*, which is used to calculate the total change in real GDP resulting

[1]To determine the exact amount of the multiple, we can use the mathematical fact that an infinite series of the form $1 + x + x^2 + x^3 + \cdots$, where x is between 0 and 1, is equal to $1/(1 - x)$.

from an initial change in spending. The expenditure multiplier, discussed in detail below, is equal to $1/(1 - MPC)$, which shows that the *MPC* and the multiplier are directly related; as the *MPC* increases, more spending is passed on in each round and the multiplier effect increases. A lower *MPC* means that less spending is passed on in each round and the multiplier effect is smaller. So the total effect of a $100 billion increase in investment spending, *I*, taking into account all the subsequent increases in consumer spending (and assuming no taxes and no international trade), is found as shown:

$$\text{Total increase in real GDP} = \frac{1}{(1 - MPC)} \times \$100 \text{ billion}$$

Therefore,

$$\textbf{(3.2-2)}\ \text{Total change in real GDP} = \frac{1}{(1 - MPC)} \times \text{initial change in investment spending}$$

Let's consider a numerical example in which $MPC = 0.6$; in other words, each $1 in additional disposable income causes a $0.60 rise in consumer spending. A $100 billion increase in investment spending raises real GDP by $100 billion in the first round. The second-round increase in consumer spending raises real GDP by an additional $0.6 \times \$100$ billion, or $60 billion. The third-round increase in consumer spending raises real GDP by $0.6 \times \$60$ billion, or $36 billion. This process continues until the amount of spending in the next round would be virtually zero. If you continued the process of passing on 0.6 times the amount in each round and then added up the spending created in each round, you will find that the total increase in real GDP from an initial $100 billion rise in investment spending equals $250 billion. But an easier way to calculate the total increase is to use the expenditure multiplier:

$$\frac{1}{(1 - 0.6)} \times \$100 \text{ billion} = 2.5 \times \$100 \text{ billion} = \$250 \text{ billion}$$

Notice that even though there can be a nearly endless number of rounds of expansion of real GDP, the total rise in real GDP is limited to $250 billion. The reason is that at each stage, some of the rise in disposable income "leaks out" because it is saved, leaving less to be spent in the next round. How much of each additional dollar of disposable income is saved depends on *MPS*, the marginal propensity to save.

We've described the effects of a change in investment spending, but the same analysis can be applied to any other change in spending. The important thing is to distinguish between the initial change in aggregate spending, before real GDP rises, and the additional change in aggregate spending caused by the change in real GDP as the chain reaction unfolds. For example, suppose that a boom in housing prices makes consumers feel richer and that, as a result, they are willing to spend more at any given level of disposable income. This will lead to an initial rise in consumer spending, before real GDP rises. But it will also lead to subsequent rounds of higher consumer spending as real GDP and disposable income rise.

A Formal Introduction to the Expenditure Multiplier

An initial rise or fall in aggregate spending at a given level of real GDP is called an *autonomous change*. It is autonomous—which means "self-governing"—because it is the cause, not the result, of the chain reaction just described. Formally, the **expenditure multiplier** is the ratio of the total change in real GDP caused by an autonomous change in aggregate spending to the size of that autonomous change. If we let ΔAAS stand for the autonomous change in aggregate spending and ΔY stand for the total change in real GDP, then the expenditure multiplier is equal to $\Delta Y/\Delta AAS$.

The **expenditure multiplier** is equal to $1/(1 - MPC)$ or $1/MPS$. It is the ratio of the total change in real GDP caused by an autonomous change in aggregate spending to the size of that autonomous change. It indicates the total rise in real GDP that results from each $1 of an initial rise in spending.

Equation 3.2-2 shows us the value of the expenditure multiplier. Assuming no taxes and no trade, the total change in real GDP caused by an autonomous change in aggregate spending is

> **AP® ECON TIP**
>
> Calculate the expenditure multiplier and use it to determine the effect of an autonomous change on real GDP. To calculate the multiplier, you need to know the *MPC*. The *MPC* can also be found using the *MPS*, since the *MPC* is equal to 1 – *MPS*. The expenditure multiplier is equal to 1/(1 – *MPC*), or 1/*MPS*. Remember: *MPC* + *MPS* = 1!

$$\textbf{(3.2-3)} \quad \Delta Y = \frac{1}{(1 - MPC)} \times \Delta AAS$$

So the expenditure multiplier is

$$\textbf{(3.2-4)} \quad \frac{\Delta Y}{\Delta AAS} = \frac{1}{(1 - MPC)}$$

The expenditure multiplier is also expressed as the ratio of the total change in real GDP caused by an autonomous change in aggregate spending to the size of that autonomous change. It indicates the total rise in real GDP that results from each $1 of an initial rise in spending.

Notice that the size of the expenditure multiplier depends on *MPC*. If the marginal propensity to consume is high, so is the expenditure multiplier. This is true because the size of *MPC* determines how large each round of expansion is compared with the previous round. To put it another way, the higher *MPC* is, the less disposable income "leaks out" into savings at each round of expansion.

The Tax Multiplier

Table 3.2-1 shows a comparison of two hypothetical situations that demonstrate the effect of the expenditure multiplier on real GDP: one in which the government directly purchases $100 billion in goods and services and one in which the government decreases taxes by $100 billion instead. Both scenarios assume an *MPC* equal to 0.75 and an expenditure multiplier equal to 1/(1 – 0.75) or 4. Note that *increasing* spending and *decreasing* taxes will both increase real GDP. The effect of taxes on real GDP is the opposite of the effect of changes in the components of aggregate demand. Increasing taxes reduces disposable income and spending; decreasing taxes raises disposable income and spending. In each case, there is a first-round effect on real GDP, either from purchases by the government or from purchases by the consumers who receive an increase in disposable income due to the decrease in taxes. This first round is followed by a series of additional rounds as rising real GDP raises income, which in turn raises consumption.

Table 3.2-1 Hypothetical Effects of a Change in Spending or Taxes with an Expenditure Multiplier of 4

Effect on real GDP	$100 billion rise in government spending	$100 billion decrease in taxes
First round	$100 billion	$75 billion
Second round	$75 billion	$56.25 billion
Third round	$56.25 billion	$42.19 billion
•	•	•
•	•	•
•	•	•
Eventual effect	$400 billion	$300 billion

However, the first-round effect of the tax decrease is smaller than the first-round effect of increased government spending; because we have assumed that the *MPC* is 0.75, only $75 billion of the $100 billion is spent, with the other $25 billion saved. As a result, all the further rounds are smaller, too. In the end, the decrease in taxes increases real GDP by only $300 billion. In comparison, a $100 billion increase in government purchases produces a $400 billion increase in real GDP.

A tax decrease increases disposable income, leading to a series of increases in consumer spending. But the overall effect is smaller than that of an equal-sized increase in government purchases of goods and services: the autonomous increase in aggregate spending is smaller because households save part of the amount of the tax cut. They save a fraction of the tax cut equal to their *MPS* (which equals $1 - MPC$). So, for each $1 decrease in taxes, spending increases only by the portion of the dollar that is not saved: the *MPC*. A tax increase has the opposite effect. For each $1 of additional taxes collected, savings decrease by the *MPS* and spending decreases by the *MPC*.

The **tax multiplier** is the factor by which we multiply a change in tax collections to find the total change in real GDP. Recall that the expenditure multiplier is $1/(1 - MPC)$. The tax multiplier has "*MPC*" in place of "1" in the numerator to reflect the initial spending decrease of $*MPC*, rather than $1 for each $1 of taxes collected. And the tax multiplier is negative because spending decreases when taxes increase, and spending increases when taxes decrease. Therefore, the tax multiplier is equal to:

$$-MPC / (1 - MPC)$$

For example, if the *MPC* is 0.75, then the tax multiplier is $-0.75/(1 - 0.75) = -3$. So the $100 billion increase in taxes would cause a change in spending of $-3 \times \$100$ billion $= -\$300$ billion.

The expenditure and tax multipliers allow us to calculate the ultimate size of the effect of an initial change in any autonomous change in aggregate spending. In later Modules, we'll use expenditure and tax multipliers to analyze the effects of fiscal policies on the economy.

AP® ECON TIP

The *MPC* values on the AP® exam are likely to be round numbers that make multiplier values easy to calculate, as shown in the table below. Recognize these common *MPC*/multiplier combinations.

MPC	Expenditure Multiplier	Tax Multiplier
0.9	10	–9
0.8	5	–4
0.75	4	–3
0.6	2.5	–1.5
0.5	2	1

The **tax multiplier**, which is equal to $-MPC/(1 - MPC)$, is the factor by which a change in tax collections changes real GDP.

Module 3.2 Review

Check Your Understanding

1. What are the expenditure multiplier and tax multiplier if the marginal propensity to consume is 0.8?
2. Explain why the tax multiplier is negative and smaller than the expenditure multiplier.

Tackle the AP® Test: Multiple-Choice Questions

1. If the *MPS* is equal to 0.1, what is the value of the expenditure multiplier?
   - **a.** 0.1
   - **b.** 0.9
   - **c.** 1.11
   - **d.** 9
   - **e.** 10
2. An autonomous increase in aggregate spending of $100 million would lead to a total increase in real GDP of how much if the *MPC* is equal to 0.8?
   - **a.** $80 million
   - **b.** $100 million
   - **c.** $125 million
   - **d.** $500 million
   - **e.** $800 million
3. The marginal propensity to consume
   - **a.** has a negative relationship to the expenditure multiplier.
   - **b.** is always equal to 1.
   - **c.** represents the proportion of a consumer's income that is spent.
   - **d.** is equal to $1/MPS$.
   - **e.** is the increase in consumption when disposable income increases by $1.

4. The maximum effect on real GDP of a $100 million increase in government purchases of goods and services will be
   a. an increase of $100 million.
   b. an increase of more than $100 million.
   c. an increase of less than $100 million.
   d. an increase of either more than or less than $100 million, depending on the *MPC*.
   e. a decrease of $100 million.
5. As the *MPC* increases, the
   a. expenditure multiplier will increase.
   b. expenditure multiplier will not change.
   c. tax multiplier will decrease.
   d. tax multiplier will not change.
   e. expenditure multiplier AND the tax multiplier will decrease.
6. The maximum effect on real GDP of a $100 million increase in taxes will be
   a. an increase of $100 million.
   b. a decrease of more than $100 million.
   c. a decrease of less than $100 million.
   d. an increase of more than $100 million.
   e. an increase of either more than or less than $100 million, depending on the *MPC*.
7. If the *MPC* is 0.75 and government spending and taxes are both increased by $10 million, which of the following is true?
   a. The expenditure multiplier is 5.
   b. The tax multiplier is equal to 4.
   c. The budget deficit will increase.
   d. Real GDP will decrease by $10 million.
   e. Real GDP will increase by $10 million.

Tackle the AP® Test: Free-Response Questions

1. Assume the *MPC* in an economy is 0.8 and the government increases government purchases of goods and services by $60 million. Also assume the absence of taxes, international trade, and changes in the aggregate price level.
   a. What is the value of the expenditure multiplier?
   b. By how much will real GDP change as a result of the increase in government purchases?
   c. What would happen to the size of the effect on real GDP if the *MPC* fell? Explain.
   d. Suppose the government collects $60 million in taxes to balance its $60 million in expenditures. By how much would real GDP change as a result of this increase in both government spending and taxes?

Rubric for FRQ 1 (5 points)

1 point: Expenditure multiplier = 1/(1 – *MPC*) = 1/(1 – 0.8) = 1/0.2 = 5

1 point: $60 million × 5 = $300 million

1 point: It would decrease.

1 point: The expenditure multiplier is 1/(1 – *MPC*). A fall in *MPC* increases the denominator, (1 – *MPC*), and therefore decreases the expenditure multiplier.

1 point: $60 million

2. A change in government purchases of goods and services results in a change in real GDP equal to $200 million.
   a. Suppose that the *MPC* is equal to 0.75. What was the size of the change in government purchases of goods and services that resulted in the increase in real GDP of $200 million?
   b. Now suppose that the change in government purchases of goods and services was $20 million. What value of the expenditure multiplier would result in an increase in real GDP of $200 million?
   c. Given the value of the expenditure multiplier you calculated in part b, what marginal propensity to save would have led to that value of the expenditure multiplier? **(3 points)**

Short-Run Aggregate Supply

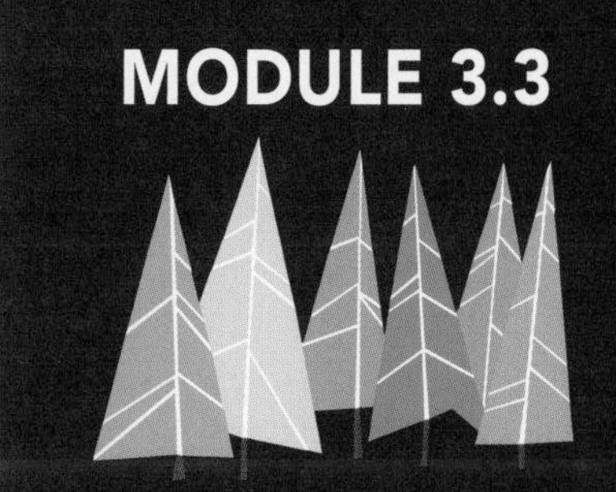

In this Module, you will learn to:

- Define short-run aggregate supply
- Use the short-run aggregate supply curve to illustrate the relationship between the aggregate price level and the quantity of aggregate output supplied in the economy
- Explain the upward slope of the short-run aggregate supply curve as a result of sticky wages and prices
- Identify the factors that cause production costs to change and shift the short-run aggregate supply curve
- Explain how inflationary expectations cause the short-run aggregate supply curve to shift
- Use a movement along the short-run aggregate supply curve to explain the short-run trade-off between inflation and unemployment

Aggregate Supply

Between 1929 and 1933, there was a sharp fall in aggregate demand—a reduction in the quantity of goods and services demanded at any given price level. One consequence of the economy-wide decline in demand was a fall in the prices of most goods and services. By 1933, the GDP deflator (one of the price indices) was 26% below its 1929 level, and other indices were down by similar amounts. A second consequence was a decline in the output of most goods and services: by 1933, real GDP was 27% below its 1929 level. A third consequence, closely tied to the fall in real GDP, was a surge in the unemployment rate from 3% to 25%.

Photo 12/Alamy

The association between the plunge in real GDP and the plunge in prices wasn't an accident. Between 1929 and 1933, the U.S. economy was moving down its **aggregate supply curve**, which shows the relationship between the economy's aggregate price level (the overall price level of final goods and services in the economy) and aggregate output (the total quantity of final goods and services) producers are willing to supply. More specifically, between 1929 and 1933, the U.S. economy moved down its *short-run* aggregate supply curve.

The **aggregate supply curve** shows the relationship between the aggregate price level and the quantity of aggregate output supplied in the economy.

The Short-Run Aggregate Supply Curve

The period from 1929 to 1933 demonstrated that there is a positive relationship in the short run between the aggregate price level and the quantity of aggregate output supplied. That is, a rise in the aggregate price level is associated with a rise in the quantity of aggregate output supplied, other things equal; a fall in the aggregate price level is associated with a fall in the quantity of aggregate output supplied, other things equal. To understand why this positive relationship exists, consider the most basic question facing a producer: is producing a unit of output profitable or not? Let's define profit per unit of output:

(3.3-1) Profit per unit = Price per unit – Production cost per unit

Thus, the answer to the question depends on whether the price the producer receives for a unit of output is greater or less than the cost of producing that unit of output. At any given point in time, many of the costs producers face are fixed per unit of output and can't be changed for an extended period of time. Typically, the largest source of inflexible production cost is the wages paid to workers. *Wages* here refers to all forms of worker compensation, including employer-paid health care and retirement benefits in addition to earnings.

Wages are typically an inflexible production cost because the dollar amount of any given wage paid, called the **nominal wage**, is often determined by contracts that were signed in the past. And even when there are no formal contracts, there are often informal agreements between management and workers, making companies reluctant to change wages in response to economic conditions. For example, companies are not quick to reduce wages during poor economic times—unless the downturn has been particularly long and severe—for fear of generating worker resentment. Correspondingly, companies typically won't raise wages during better economic times—until they are at risk of losing workers to competitors—because they don't want to encourage workers to routinely demand higher wages. As a result of both formal and informal agreements, then, the economy is characterized by **sticky wages**: nominal wages that are slow to fall even in the face of high unemployment and slow to rise even in the face of labor shortages. It's important to note, however, that nominal wages cannot be sticky forever: ultimately, formal contracts and informal agreements will be renegotiated to take into account changed economic circumstances. How long it takes for nominal wages to become flexible is an integral component of what distinguishes the short run from the long run.

The **nominal wage** is the dollar amount of the wage paid.

Sticky wages are nominal wages that are slow to fall even in the face of high unemployment and slow to rise even in the face of labor shortages.

The **short-run aggregate supply curve** shows the positive relationship between the aggregate price level and the quantity of aggregate output supplied that exists in the short run, the time period when many production costs can be taken as fixed.

When the price level increases and wages are sticky, nominal wages do not immediately adjust and therefore the firm's profit per unit will increase as *real wages* (nominal wages divided by the price level) decrease. Until nominal wages adjust to the change in the price level, firms will earn a higher profit per unit which will cause them to produce more. So the increase in the price level is associated with an increase in aggregate output in the short run. Conversely, when the price level decreases, nominal wages do not increase while wages are sticky, and therefore real wages increase. Until nominal wages adjust to the change in the price level, firms will earn less profit per unit, which will cause them to produce less. So the decrease in the price level is associated with a decrease in aggregate output in the short run.

The **short-run aggregate supply curve** illustrates the positive relationship between the aggregate price level and the quantity of aggregate output producers are willing to supply during the time period when many production costs (particularly nominal wages) can be taken as fixed. The positive relationship between the aggregate price level and aggregate output in the short run gives the short-run aggregate supply curve its upward slope. **Figure 3.3-1** shows a hypothetical short-run aggregate supply curve, *SRAS*, that matches actual U.S. data for 1929 and 1933. On the horizontal axis is aggregate output (real GDP)—the total quantity of final goods and services supplied in the economy—measured in 2005 dollars. On the vertical axis is the aggregate price level as measured by the GDP deflator, with the value for the year 2005 equal to 100. In 1929, the aggregate price level was 10.6, and real GDP was $977 billion. In 1933, the aggregate price level was 7.9, and real GDP was only $716 billion. The movement down the *SRAS* curve corresponds to the deflation and fall in aggregate output experienced over those years.

AP® ECON TIP

Draw the short-run aggregate supply curve as upward-sloping. The upward slope of the short-run aggregate supply curve is explained by sticky wages. Sticky wages mean that nominal wages are slow to rise and fall in response to unemployment levels because of set wage contracts and agreements. In the long run, these agreements expire and wages become flexible.

The Short-Run Trade-Off Between Inflation and Unemployment

The upward slope of the *SRAS* curve illustrates the positive relationship between the price level and aggregate output. Since the level of unemployment is inversely related to aggregate output—more workers are hired when production increases, and fewer workers are hired when production decreases—we can also use the *SRAS* curve to infer the

FIGURE 3.3-1 The Short-Run Aggregate Supply Curve

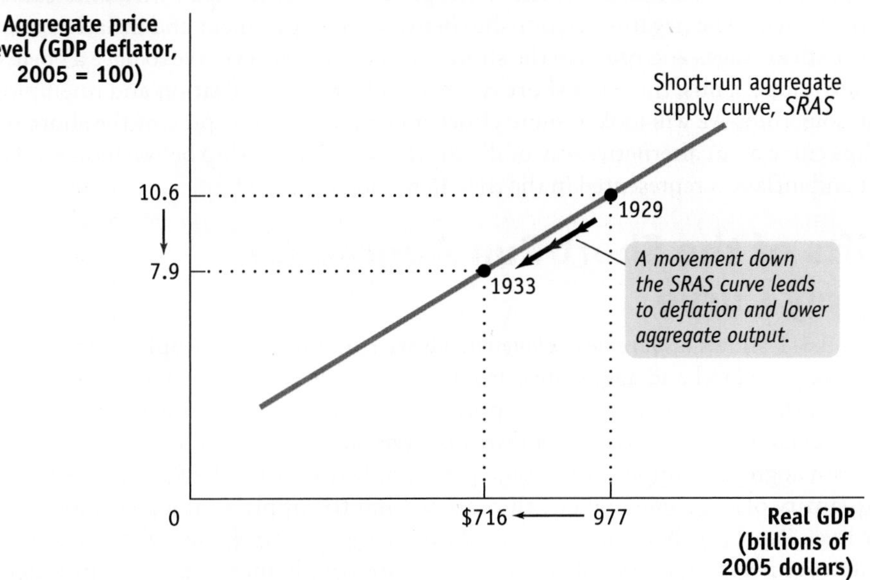

The short-run aggregate supply curve shows the relationship between the aggregate price level and the quantity of aggregate output supplied in the short run, the period in which many production costs such as nominal wages are fixed. Here we show numbers corresponding to the Great Depression, from 1929 and 1933: when deflation occurred and the aggregate price level fell from 10.6 (in 1929) to 7.9 (in 1933), firms responded by reducing the quantity of aggregate output supplied from $977 billion to $716 billion measured in 2005 dollars.

relationship between the price level and unemployment. Panel (a) in **Figure 3.3-2** compares the relationship between the price level and employment on a *SRAS* curve; panel (b) shows the short-run relationship between inflation and unemployment. Moving along the *SRAS* curve to the right in panel (a), an increase in the price level is associated with an increase in aggregate output, which means employment must be rising to produce the increased output. All other things equal, rising employment means falling unemployment—so an increase in the price level is associated with a decrease in unemployment.

FIGURE 3.3-2 The Short-Run Trade-Off Between Inflation and Unemployment

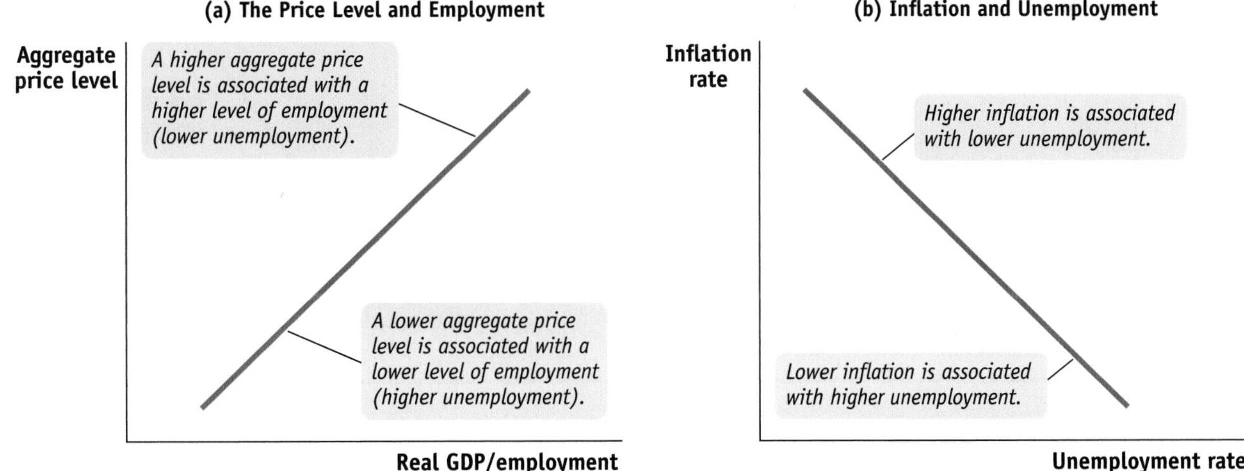

In the short run, the aggregate supply curve shows a positive relationship between the aggregate price level and real GDP shown in panel (a). An increase in the price level will increase aggregate output, and therefore employment, while a decrease in the price level will decrease aggregate output and employment. All other things equal, employment and unemployment are inversely related—an increase in employment means a decrease in unemployment, and vice versa. An increase in the price level indicates inflation in the economy, so panel (b) shows the relationship between the price level and real GDP shown with the short-run aggregate supply curve, translated as the short-run relationship between inflation and unemployment.

Conversely, in panel (b) showing the short-run relationship between inflation and unemployment, we see that a decrease in the price level is associated with an increase in unemployment. The negative relationship between unemployment and inflation exists because sticky wages and prices in the short run cause the *SRAS* curve to have a positive (upward) slope. Thus, there is a short-run trade-off between inflation and unemployment, something we will look at more closely in Unit 5, when we present the short-run Phillips curve as an alternative way of illustrating the relationship between unemployment and inflation represented in the *AD–AS* model.

Shifts of the Short-Run Aggregate Supply Curve

Figure 3.3-1 shows a *movement along* the short-run aggregate supply curve, as the aggregate price level and aggregate output fell from 1929 to 1933. But there can also be *shifts of* the short-run aggregate supply curve, as shown in **Figure 3.3-3**. Panel (a) of Figure 3.3-3 shows a *decrease in short-run aggregate supply*—a leftward shift of the short-run aggregate supply curve. Aggregate supply decreases when producers reduce the quantity of aggregate output they are willing to supply at any given aggregate price level. Panel (b) shows an *increase in short-run aggregate supply*—a rightward shift of the short-run aggregate supply curve. Aggregate supply increases when producers increase the quantity of aggregate output they are willing to supply at any given aggregate price level.

FIGURE 3.3-3 Shifts of the Short-Run Aggregate Supply Curve

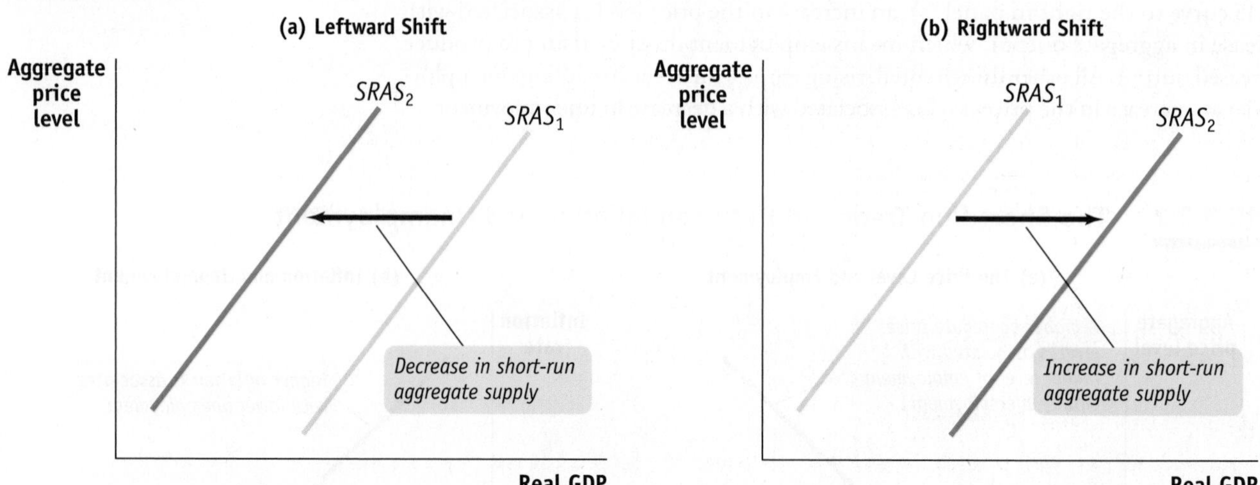

Panel (a) shows a decrease in short-run aggregate supply: the short-run aggregate supply curve shifts leftward from $SRAS_1$ to $SRAS_2$, and the quantity of aggregate output supplied at any given aggregate price level falls. Panel (b) shows an increase in short-run aggregate supply: the short-run aggregate supply curve shifts rightward from $SRAS_1$ to $SRAS_2$, and the quantity of aggregate output supplied at any given aggregate price level rises.

To understand why the short-run aggregate supply curve can shift, it's important to recall that producers make output decisions based on their profit per unit of output. The short-run aggregate supply curve illustrates the relationship between the aggregate price level and aggregate output: because some production costs are fixed in the short run, a change in the aggregate price level leads to a change in producers' profit per unit of output and, in turn, to a change in aggregate output. But other factors besides the aggregate price level can affect profit per unit and, in turn, aggregate output. Changes in these other factors, which we will read about next, will shift the short-run aggregate supply curve.

To develop some intuition, suppose something happens that raises production costs throughout the economy — say, an increase in the price of oil. At any given price of output, a producer now earns a smaller profit per unit of output. As a result, producers reduce the quantity supplied at any given aggregate price level, and the short-run aggregate supply curve shifts to the left. If, by contrast, something happens that lowers production costs — say, a fall in the nominal wage — a producer now earns a higher profit per unit of output at any given price of output. This leads producers to increase the quantity of aggregate output supplied at any given aggregate price level, and the short-run aggregate supply curve shifts to the right.

Now we'll look more closely at the link between important factors that affect producers' profit per unit and shifts in the short-run aggregate supply curve.

AP® ECON TIP

You learned that with supply and demand curves, "left is less and right is more." The same idea applies to aggregate supply and demand curves. Values for real GDP, which is measured on the horizontal axis, are lower to the left and higher to the right.

Changes in Commodity Prices

A surge in the price of oil caused problems for the U.S. economy in the 1970s and in early 2008. Oil is a *commodity*, a standardized input bought and sold in bulk quantities. An increase in the price of a commodity — in this case, oil — raised production costs across the economy and reduced the quantity of aggregate output supplied at any given aggregate price level, shifting the short-run aggregate supply curve to the left. Conversely, a decline in commodity prices reduces production costs, leading to an increase in the quantity supplied at any given aggregate price level and a rightward shift of the short-run aggregate supply curve.

Why isn't the influence of commodity prices already captured by the short-run aggregate supply curve? Because commodities — unlike, say, soft drinks — are not a final good, their prices are not included in the calculation of the aggregate price level. Furthermore, commodities represent a significant cost of production to most suppliers, just like nominal wages do. So changes in commodity prices have large impacts on production costs. And in contrast to noncommodities, the prices of commodities can sometimes change drastically due to industry-specific shocks to supply — such as conflicts in oil-producing regions or rising demand in newly industrialized countries that leaves less oil for the United States.

Signs of the times: high oil prices caused gasoline prices to also rise in 2021.

Al Seib/Getty Images

Changes in Nominal Wages

As we explained, at any given point in time, nominal wages are fixed because they are set by contracts or informal agreements made in the past, but these wages can change once enough time has passed for terms to be renegotiated. Suppose, for example, that there is an economy-wide rise in the cost of health care insurance premiums paid by employers as part of employees' wages. From the employers' perspective, this is equivalent to a rise in nominal wages because it is an increase in employer-paid compensation. So this rise in nominal wages increases production costs and shifts the short-run aggregate supply curve to the left. Conversely, suppose there is an economy-wide fall in the cost of such premiums. This is equivalent to a fall in nominal wages from the point of view of employers; it reduces production costs and shifts the short-run aggregate supply curve to the right.

An important historical fact is that during the 1970s, the surge in the price of oil had the indirect effect of also raising nominal wages. This "knock-on" effect occurred because many wage contracts included *cost-of-living allowances* that automatically raised the nominal wage when consumer prices increased. Through this channel, the surge in the price of oil—which led to an increase in overall consumer prices—ultimately caused a rise in nominal wages. So the economy, in the end, experienced two leftward shifts of the aggregate supply curve: the first generated by the initial surge in the price of oil, and the second generated by the induced increase in nominal wages. The negative effect of rising oil prices on the economy was greatly magnified through the cost-of-living allowances in wage contracts. Today, cost-of-living allowances in wage contracts are rare.

Changes in Productivity

An increase in productivity means that a worker can produce more units of output with the same quantity of inputs. For example, the introduction of bar-code scanners in retail stores greatly increased the ability of a single worker to stock, inventory, and resupply store shelves. As a result, the cost to a store of "producing" a dollar of sales fell and profit rose. And, correspondingly, the quantity supplied increased. (Think of Walmart or Costco and the increase in the number of their stores as an increase in aggregate supply.) So a rise in productivity, whatever the source, increases producers' profits and shifts the short-run aggregate supply curve to the right.

Juanmonino/E+/Getty Images

Additional safety protocols enacted during the pandemic in 2020 led to a fall in productivity, as employees had to shift more of their time to cleaning.

Conversely, a fall in productivity—say, due to new regulations that require workers to spend more time filling out forms—reduces the number of units of output a worker can produce with the same quantity of inputs. Consequently, the cost per unit of output rises, profit falls, and quantity supplied falls. This shifts the short-run aggregate supply curve to the left.

Changes in Expectations About Inflation

If inflation is expected to be higher than previously thought, workers will seek higher nominal wages to keep pace with the higher prices. Suppose you noticed prices rising more rapidly than in the recent past. You might expect a particularly high inflation rate over the coming year. To prevent the expected inflation from eroding your real wages, you and other workers would pressure employers to raise nominal wages. As we've discussed, nominal wages are temporarily inflexible due to wage contracts, but when contracts are renewed and nominal wages rise, the short-run aggregate supply curve shifts to the left. Likewise, if inflation is expected to be lower than previously thought, workers will accept lower nominal wages and the short-run aggregate supply curve will shift to the right.

When the *SRAS* curve shifts to the left or the right, the price level associated with any given level of aggregate output increases or decreases, which means that the price level associated with any given level of employment also increases or decreases. When we develop the Phillips curve model in Unit 5, we will see that a shift in the *SRAS* curve also changes the price level associated with each level of unemployment.

For a summary of the factors that shift the short-run aggregate supply curve, see **Table 3.3-1**. We will return to these factors when we discuss supply shocks later in this Unit.

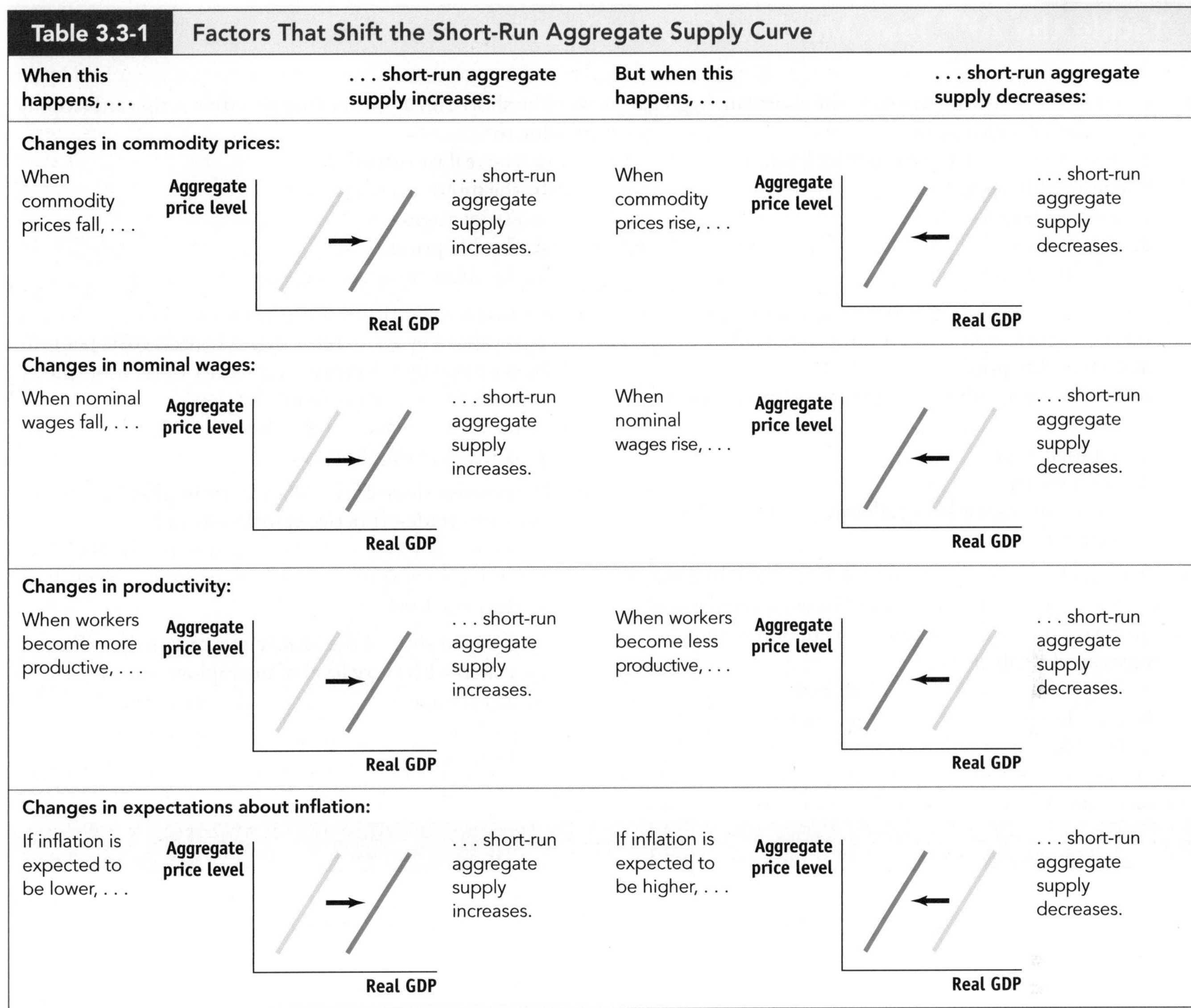

Table 3.3-1 Factors That Shift the Short-Run Aggregate Supply Curve

When this happens, . . .		. . . short-run aggregate supply increases:	But when this happens, . . .		. . . short-run aggregate supply decreases:
Changes in commodity prices:					
When commodity prices fall, . . .	Aggregate price level / Real GDP	. . . short-run aggregate supply increases.	When commodity prices rise, . . .	Aggregate price level / Real GDP	. . . short-run aggregate supply decreases.
Changes in nominal wages:					
When nominal wages fall, . . .	Aggregate price level / Real GDP	. . . short-run aggregate supply increases.	When nominal wages rise, . . .	Aggregate price level / Real GDP	. . . short-run aggregate supply decreases.
Changes in productivity:					
When workers become more productive, . . .	Aggregate price level / Real GDP	. . . short-run aggregate supply increases.	When workers become less productive, . . .	Aggregate price level / Real GDP	. . . short-run aggregate supply decreases.
Changes in expectations about inflation:					
If inflation is expected to be lower, . . .	Aggregate price level / Real GDP	. . . short-run aggregate supply increases.	If inflation is expected to be higher, . . .	Aggregate price level / Real GDP	. . . short-run aggregate supply decreases.

Module 3.3 Review

Check Your Understanding

1. Explain why the short-run aggregate supply curve is upward-sloping.
2. Determine the effect on short-run aggregate supply of each of the following events. Explain whether it represents a movement along the *SRAS* curve or a shift of the *SRAS* curve.
   a. A rise in the consumer price index (CPI) leads producers to increase output.
   b. A fall in the price of oil leads producers to increase output.
   c. A rise in legally mandated retirement benefits paid to workers leads producers to reduce output.

Tackle the AP® Test: Multiple-Choice Questions

1. Which of the following will shift the short-run aggregate supply curve? A change in
   a. profit per unit at any given price level.
   b. commodity prices.
   c. nominal wages.
   d. productivity.
   e. all of the above

2. A decrease in which of the following will cause the short-run aggregate supply curve to shift to the left?
   a. commodity prices
   b. the cost of health care insurance premiums paid by employers
   c. nominal wages
   d. productivity
   e. the use of cost-of-living allowances in labor contracts

3. That employers are reluctant to decrease nominal wages during economic downturns and raise nominal wages during economic expansions is one reason nominal wages are described as
   a. long-run.
   b. unyielding.
   c. flexible.
   d. real.
   e. sticky.

4. The short-run aggregate supply curve is upward-sloping due to
   a. the real wealth effect.
   b. the interest rate effect.
   c. sticky wages.
   d. flexible prices.
   e. the substitution effect.

5. An increase in a firm's profit per unit
   a. is caused by an increase in production costs per unit.
   b. is caused by a decrease in the price of their output.
   c. leads to an increase in production.
   d. leads to a decrease in production.
   e. is sticky in the short run.

6. The positive slope of the *SRAS* curve implies a positive short-run trade-off between inflation and
   a. productivity.
   b. aggregate output.
   c. the price level.
   d. nominal wages.
   e. unemployment.

7. A rightward shift of the *SRAS* curve causes the inflation associated with every level of unemployment to
   a. stay the same.
   b. increase.
   c. decrease.
   d. equal zero.
   e. equal the natural rate.

Tackle the AP® Test: Free-Response Questions

1. Draw a correctly labeled *SRAS* curve and indicate each of the following on your graph:
   a. An increase in the price level.
   b. The change in aggregate output resulting from your increase in the price level.
   c. The direction of change in the employment and unemployment rates associated with the change in aggregate output resulting from your increase in the price level.

Rubric for FRQ 1 (5 points)

1 point: Correctly labeled graph with *PL* on the vertical axis and real GDP on the vertical axis

1 point: Labeled, upward-sloping *SRAS* curve

1 point: Movement to the right between two points along the upward-sloping *SRAS* curve, indicating an increase in aggregate output on the horizontal axis

1 point: Indication of an increase in employment corresponding to the increase in aggregate output

1 point: Indication of a decrease in unemployment corresponding to the increase in aggregate output

2. a. Draw a correctly labeled *SRAS* curve.
   b. On your graph from part a, illustrate a decrease in short-run aggregate supply.
   c. List three types of changes, including the factor that changes and the direction of the change, that could lead to a decrease in short-run aggregate supply.
   (5 points)

Long-Run Aggregate Supply

In this Module, you will learn to:

- Define the short run and the long run
- Use a long-run aggregate supply curve to illustrate an economy's maximum sustainable capacity
- Explain how flexible wages and prices in the long run result in *no* long-run trade-off between inflation and unemployment
- Explain how the long-run aggregate supply curve corresponds to the production possibilities curve
- Explain why the long-run aggregate supply curve is vertical at the full-employment level of output

The Short Versus the Long Run

We've just seen that in the short run, a fall in the aggregate price level leads to a decline in the quantity of aggregate output supplied, and a rise in the aggregate price level leads to a decline in the quantity of aggregate output supplied. This relationship is partially the result of nominal wages that are sticky in **the short run**. But as we noted in the previous Module, contracts and informal agreements are renegotiated in the long run. So in **the long run**, nominal wages – like the aggregate price level – are flexible, not sticky. Wage flexibility greatly alters the long-run relationship between the aggregate price level and aggregate supply. In fact, in the long run, the aggregate price level has *no* effect on the quantity of aggregate output supplied.

The short run is the time period in which many production costs, including nominal wages, are not fully flexible.

The long run is the time period in which all prices, including nominal wages, are fully flexible.

To see why, let's conduct a thought experiment. Imagine that you could wave a magic wand – or maybe a magic bar-code scanner – and cut *all prices* in the economy in half at the same time. By "all prices" we mean the prices of all inputs, including nominal wages, as well as the prices of final goods and services. What would happen to aggregate output, given that the aggregate price level has been halved and all input prices, including nominal wages, have been halved?

The answer is . . . *nothing*. Consider profits per unit as shown in Equation 3.3-1 again: each producer would receive a lower price for its product, but costs would fall by the same proportion. As a result, every unit of output that was profitable to produce before the change in prices would still be profitable to produce after the change in prices. So a halving of *all* prices in the economy has no effect on the economy's aggregate output. In other words, changes in the aggregate price level now have no effect on the quantity of aggregate output supplied.

In reality, of course, no one can change all prices by the same proportion at the same time. But let's consider the *long run*, the period of time over which all prices are fully flexible. In the long run, inflation or deflation has the same effect as someone changing all prices by the same proportion. As a result, changes in the aggregate price level do not change the quantity of aggregate output supplied in the long run. That's because changes in the aggregate price level, in the long run, will be accompanied by equal proportional changes in *all* input prices, including nominal wages.

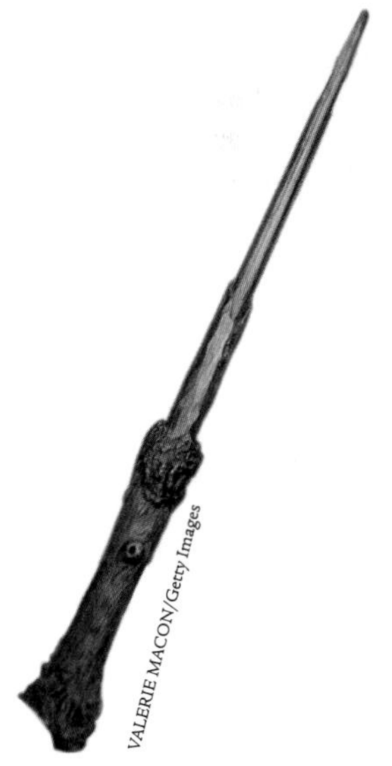

Even with a magic wand, changes in aggregate price have no effect on the quantity of aggregate output in the long run.

The Long-Run Aggregate Supply Curve

The **long-run aggregate supply curve** shows the relationship between the aggregate price level and the quantity of aggregate output supplied that would exist if all prices, including nominal wages, were fully flexible.

The **long-run aggregate supply curve**, illustrated in **Figure 3.4-1** by the curve *LRAS*, shows the relationship between the aggregate price level and the quantity of aggregate output supplied that would exist if all prices, including nominal wages, were fully flexible. The long-run aggregate supply curve is vertical because changes in the aggregate price level have *no* effect on aggregate output in the long run. At an aggregate price level of 15.0, for example, the quantity of aggregate output supplied is $800 billion in 2005 dollars. If the aggregate price level falls by 50% to 7.5, the quantity of aggregate output supplied is unchanged in the long run at $800 billion in 2005 dollars.

FIGURE 3.4-1 The Long-Run Aggregate Supply Curve

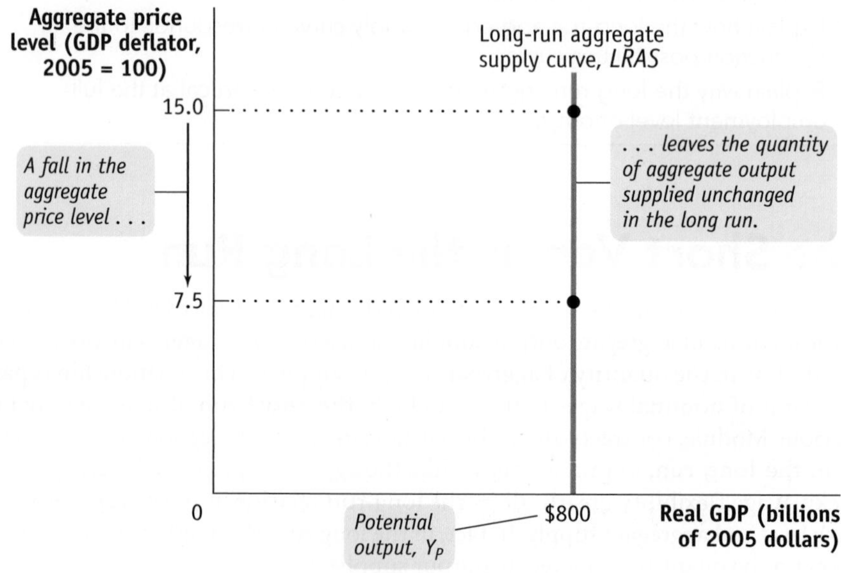

The long-run aggregate supply curve shows the quantity of aggregate output supplied when all prices, including nominal wages, are flexible. It is vertical at potential output, Y_P, because in the long run a change in the aggregate price level has no effect on the quantity of aggregate output supplied.

AP® ECON TIP

The *LRAS* curve should always be drawn as a vertical line with its horizontal intercept at the full-employment level of real GDP.

It's important to understand not only that the *LRAS* curve is vertical, but also that its position along the horizontal axis marks a significant benchmark for output. The horizontal intercept in Figure 3.4-1, where *LRAS* touches the horizontal axis ($800 billion in 2005 dollars), is the economy's **potential output**, Y_P: the level of real GDP the economy would produce if all prices, including nominal wages, were fully flexible. Another way to describe Y_P is the **full-employment output level**, the GDP that the economy can attain with full employment of all of its resources. Recall that the full-employment output level is consistent with the natural rate of unemployment from Unit 2. All of these values represent the economy's *maximum sustainable capacity for production.*

Potential output is the level of real GDP the economy would produce if all prices, including nominal wages, were fully flexible. It represents the economy's maximum sustainable production capacity.

The **full-employment output level** is the level of real GDP the economy can produce if all resources are fully employed.

You may recall from Unit 1 that the production possibilities curve (*PPC*) also illustrates an economy's potential output (and full-employment output level). The *LRAS* curve corresponds to the *PPC* because they both represent an economy's maximum sustainable capacity, the aggregate output that can be produced if all resources are fully employed. An economy can't produce a level of aggregate output that is beyond the *PPC* or to the right of the *LRAS* curve.

In reality, the actual level of real GDP is almost always either above or below potential output. We'll see why in the next Module, when we discuss the *AD–AS* model. Still, an economy's potential output is an important number because it defines the trend around which actual aggregate output fluctuates from year to year.

In the United States, the Congressional Budget Office (CBO) estimates annual potential output for the purpose of federal budget analysis. In **Figure 3.4-2**, the CBO's estimates of U.S. potential output from 1989 to 2020 are represented by the orange line and the actual values of U.S. real GDP over the same period are represented by the blue line. Years shaded purple on the horizontal axis correspond to periods in which actual aggregate output fell short of potential output, while years shaded green correspond to periods in which actual aggregate output exceeded potential output.

FIGURE 3.4-2 Actual and Potential Output from 1989 to 2020

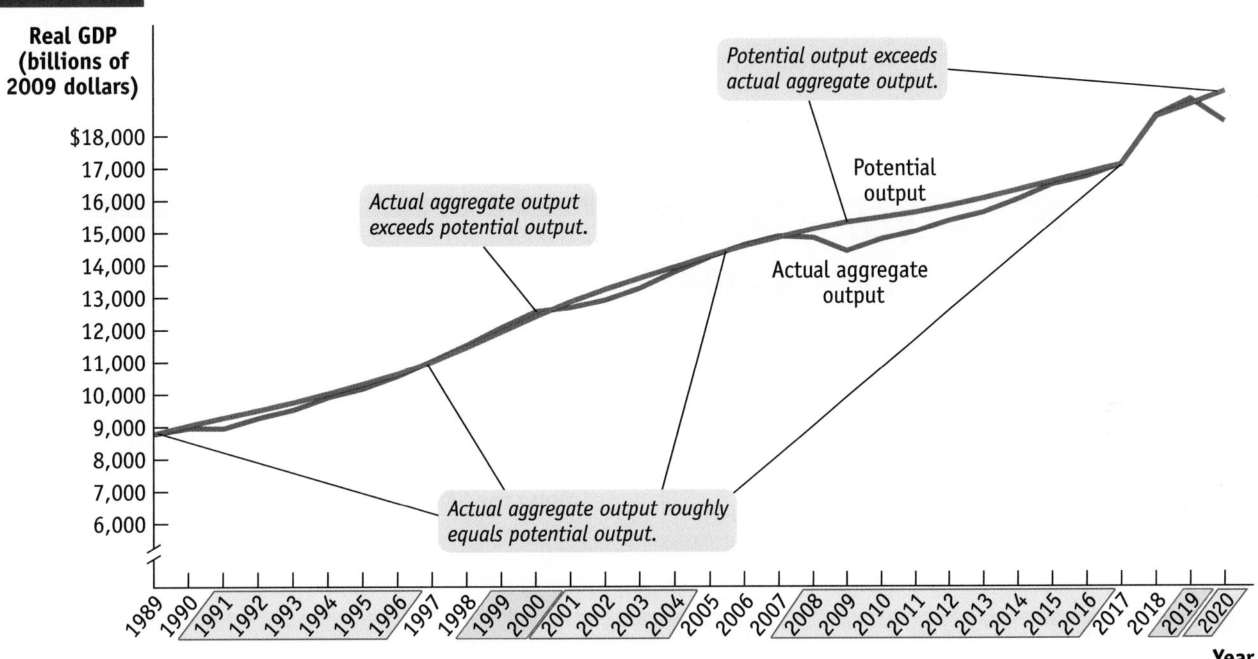

This figure shows the performance of actual and potential output in the United States from 1989 to 2020. The orange line shows estimates, produced by the Congressional Budget Office, of U.S. potential output, and the blue line shows actual aggregate output. The purple-shaded years are periods in which actual aggregate output fell below potential output, while the green-shaded years are periods in which actual aggregate output exceeded potential output. As shown, significant shortfalls occurred in the recessions of the early 1990s and after 2000—particularly during the recession that began in 2007. Actual aggregate output was above potential output in the boom of the late 1990s.
Data Source: Bureau of Economic Research; Congressional Budget Office.

As you can see, U.S. potential output has risen steadily over time—implying a series of rightward shifts of the *LRAS* curve. What has caused these rightward shifts? The answer lies in the factors related to long-run growth—the same factors that caused the *PPC* to shift outward:

- increases in the quantity of resources, including land, labor, capital, and entrepreneurship,
- increases in the quality of resources, such as a better-educated workforce, or
- technological progress.

Over the long run, as the size of the labor force and the productivity of labor both rise, the level of real GDP that the economy is capable of producing also rises. Indeed, one way to think about economic growth is that it is the growth in the economy's potential output. We generally think of the long-run aggregate supply curve as shifting to the right over time as an economy experiences long-run growth.

AP® ECON TIP

The level of an economy's potential output corresponds to its full-employment level of output. Therefore, you might see this point referred to as either potential output or full-employment output on the AP® exam. Both of these levels correspond to the natural rate of unemployment.

AP® ECON TIP

The *LRAS* curve shifts only when there is a change to one of the factors that cause an increase in the maximum sustainable capacity of the economy—an increase in the quantity or quality of resources, like an increase in an economy's capital stock or an advance in technology. These are the same factors that shift the *PPC* to the right.

The Long-Run Trade-Off Between Inflation and Unemployment

In the long run, there is no relationship between changes in the aggregate price level and aggregate output, as illustrated by the vertical *LRAS* curve. This means that there is also no relationship between the aggregate price level and employment or unemployment in the long run. Flexible wages and prices mean that the *LRAS* curve is vertical at the full-employment level of output and, therefore, there is no trade-off between inflation and unemployment in the long-run. In Unit 5, we will see that the in the long run, the unemployment rate will always equal the natural rate of unemployment – the level of unemployment associated with the full-employment level of aggregate output. Thus, we will also see a vertical long-run Phillips curve in the Phillips curve model in Unit 5.

Module 3.4 Review

Check Your Understanding

1. Explain how flexible wages and prices cause the *LRAS* curve to be vertical.
2. Suppose the economy is initially at potential output and the quantity of aggregate output supplied increases. What information would you need to determine whether the increase in aggregate output was due to a movement along the *SRAS* curve or a shift of the *LRAS* curve?

Tackle the AP® Test: Multiple-Choice Questions

1. Because changes in the aggregate price level have no effect on aggregate output in the long run, the long-run aggregate supply curve is
   a. vertical.
   b. horizontal.
   c. fixed.
   d. negatively sloped.
   e. positively sloped.
2. The horizontal intercept of the long-run aggregate supply curve is
   a. at the origin.
   b. negative.
   c. at potential output.
   d. equal to the vertical intercept.
   e. always the same as the horizontal intercept of the short-run aggregate supply curve.
3. The full-employment level of output corresponds to which of the following?
   a. potential output
   b. the horizontal intercept of the long-run aggregate demand curve
   c. short-run equilibrium
   d. the level of real GDP when wages are sticky
   e. all of the above
4. Which of the following can change as you move along a *LRAS* curve?
   a. aggregate output
   b. aggregate price level
   c. unemployment
   d. employment
   e. potential output
5. What does a vertical *LRAS* curve indicate about the trade-off between unemployment and inflation?
   a. It is increasing.
   b. It is decreasing.
   c. It is negative.
   d. It cannot be determined.
   e. It does not exist.
6. An outward shift of the *PPC* is shown on an *AD–AS* graph by a(n)
   a. rightward movement along the *LRAS* curve.
   b. leftward movement along the *LRAS* curve.
   c. rightward shift of the *LRAS* curve.
   d. leftward shift of the *LRAS* curve.
   e. upward slope of the *LRAS* curve.

7. When an economy experiences a recession, the level of real GDP will be
   a. higher along the *LRAS* curve.
   b. lower along the *LRAS* curve.
   c. to the right of the *LRAS* curve.
   d. to the left of the *LRAS* curve.
   e. beyond the *PPC* curve.

Tackle the AP® Test: Free-Response Questions

1. a. Draw a correctly labeled graph illustrating a long-run aggregate supply curve.
   b. On your graph from part a, label potential output.
   c. On your graph from part a, illustrate an increase in long-run aggregate supply.
   d. What could have caused the change you illustrated in part c? List three possible causes.

Rubric for FRQ 1 (8 points)

1 point: Vertical axis labeled "Aggregate price level" (or "Price level")

1 point: Horizontal axis labeled "Real GDP"

1 point: Vertical curve labeled "*LRAS*" (or "$LRAS_1$")

1 point: Potential output labeled Y_P (or Y_{P1}) on the horizontal axis at the intercept of the long-run aggregate supply curve

1 point: Long-run aggregate supply curve shifted to the right

1 point: An increase in the quantity of resources (land, labor, capital, or entrepreneurship)

1 point: An increase in the quality of resources

1 point: Technological progress

2. How would a leftward shift of the *LRAS* curve affect each of the following?
   a. potential output
   b. the natural rate of unemployment
   c. the aggregate price level
   d. the full-employment level of output
   e. the full-employment level of employment
   (5 points)

MODULE 3.5

Equilibrium in the Aggregate Demand–Aggregate Supply Model

In this Module, you will learn to:

- Identify short-run equilibrium in the aggregate demand–aggregate supply model as where the *AD* and *SRAS* curves intersect
- Show the short-run equilibrium aggregate price level and real GDP on the axes of an *AD–AS* graph where the aggregate quantity demanded and aggregate quantity supplied are equal
- Identify long-run equilibrium where the *SRAS* curve and *AD* curve intersect on the *LRAS* curve (i.e., at the full-employment level of output)
- Explain why the short-run equilibrium output can be above or below the full-employment level of output, creating recessionary or inflationary gaps

The *AD–AS* Model

From 1929 to 1933, the U.S. economy moved down the short-run aggregate supply curve as the aggregate price level fell. In contrast, from 1979 to 1980, the U.S. economy moved up the aggregate demand curve as the aggregate price level rose. In each case, the cause of the movement along the curve was a shift of the other curve. In 1929–1933, it was a leftward shift of the aggregate demand curve—a major fall in consumer spending during the Great Depression. In 1979–1980, it was a leftward shift of the short-run aggregate supply curve—a dramatic fall in short-run aggregate supply caused by the oil price shock.

To understand the behavior of the economy, we must put the aggregate supply curve and the aggregate demand curve together. The ***AD–AS* model** is the basic model we use to understand economic fluctuations—changes in real GDP, employment, and the aggregate price level.

In the ***AD–AS* model**, the aggregate supply curve and the aggregate demand curve are used together to analyze fluctuations in the price level and real GDP.

The **short-run macroeconomic equilibrium** occurs where the quantity of aggregate output supplied is equal to the quantity of aggregate output demanded—that is, where the *AD* and *SRAS* curves intersect.

The **short-run equilibrium aggregate price level** is the aggregate price level in the short-run macroeconomic equilibrium. It is identified on the vertical axis of an *AD–AS* graph.

Short-run equilibrium aggregate output is the quantity of aggregate output produced in the short-run macroeconomic equilibrium. It is identified on the horizontal axis of an *AD–AS* graph.

Short-Run Macroeconomic Equilibrium

We'll begin our analysis by focusing on the short run. **Figure 3.5-1** shows the aggregate demand curve and the short-run aggregate supply curve in the same diagram. The point at which the *AD* and *SRAS* curves intersect, E_{SR}, is the **short-run macroeconomic equilibrium**: the point at which the quantity of aggregate output supplied is equal to the quantity demanded by domestic households, businesses, the government, and the rest of the world. The aggregate price level at E_{SR} is the **short-run equilibrium aggregate price level**, PL_E. The level of aggregate output at E_{SR} is the **short-run equilibrium aggregate output**, Y_E.

We have seen that a shortage of any individual good causes its market price to rise and a surplus of the good causes its market price to fall. These forces ensure that an individual market reaches equilibrium. A similar logic applies to short-run macroeconomic equilibrium. If the aggregate price level is above its equilibrium level, the quantity of aggregate output supplied exceeds the quantity of aggregate output demanded. This leads to a fall in the aggregate price level and pushes it toward its equilibrium level. If the aggregate price level is below its equilibrium level, the quantity of aggregate output supplied is less than the quantity of aggregate output demanded. This leads to

FIGURE 3.5-1 The *AD–AS* Model

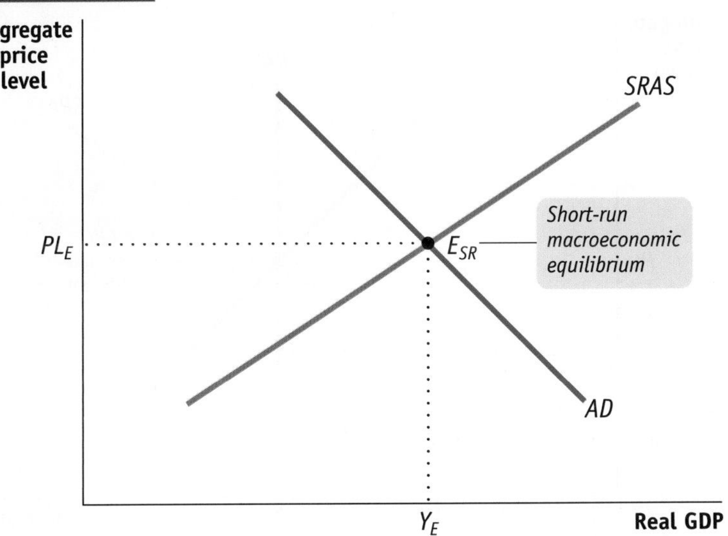

The *AD–AS* model combines the aggregate demand curve and the short-run aggregate supply curve. Their point of intersection, E_{SR}, is the point of short-run macroeconomic equilibrium where the quantity of aggregate output demanded is equal to the quantity of aggregate output supplied. PL_E is the short-run equilibrium aggregate price level, and Y_E is the short-run equilibrium level of aggregate output.

a rise in the aggregate price level, again pushing it toward its equilibrium level. In the discussion that follows, we'll assume that the economy is always in short-run macroeconomic equilibrium.

We'll also make another important simplification based on the observation that, in reality, there is a long-term upward trend in both aggregate output and the aggregate price level. We'll assume that a fall in either variable really means a fall compared to the long-run trend. For example, if the aggregate price level normally rises 4% per year, a year in which the aggregate price level rises only 3% would count, for our purposes, as a 1% decline. In fact, since the Great Depression there have been few years in which the aggregate price level of any major nation actually declined—Japan's period of deflation from 1995 to 2005 is one of the few exceptions. However, there have been many cases in which the aggregate price level fell relative to the long-run trend.

AP® ECON TIP

The *AD–AS* model is central to the AP® Macroeconomics course. You will need to draw correctly labeled *AD–AS* graphs on the exam. Make sure you can illustrate and explain the effects of shifts in aggregate supply and aggregate demand, and (after completing later Modules) the effects of economic policy using the *AD–AS* model.

Long-Run Macroeconomic Equilibrium

Figure 3.5-2 combines the aggregate demand curve with both the short-run and long-run aggregate supply curves. The aggregate demand curve, *AD*, crosses the short-run aggregate supply curve, *SRAS*, at E_{LR}. Here we assume that enough time has elapsed that the economy is also on the long-run aggregate supply curve, *LRAS*. As a result, E_{LR} is at the intersection of all three curves—*SRAS*, *LRAS*, and *AD*. So short-run equilibrium aggregate output is equal to potential output, Y_P. Such a situation, in which the point of short-run macroeconomic equilibrium is on the long-run aggregate supply curve, is known as **long-run macroeconomic equilibrium**.

Long-run macroeconomic equilibrium occurs when a short-run macroeconomic equilibrium is at the full-employment level of output (on the *LRAS* curve).

Short-Run Output Gaps

At times, changes in either the *AD* or the *SRAS* curve can move the short-run equilibrium away from long-run macroeconomic equilibrium, creating an **output gap**. An output gap is the difference between actual aggregate output and potential output. In the long run, the output gap tends toward zero. But in the short run, actual real GDP can be at a short-run equilibrium above or below potential output. Next, we consider two situations that can cause the short-run equilibrium output to fall above or below potential output.

The **output gap** is the difference between actual aggregate output and potential output.

FIGURE 3.5-2 Long-Run Macroeconomic Equilibrium

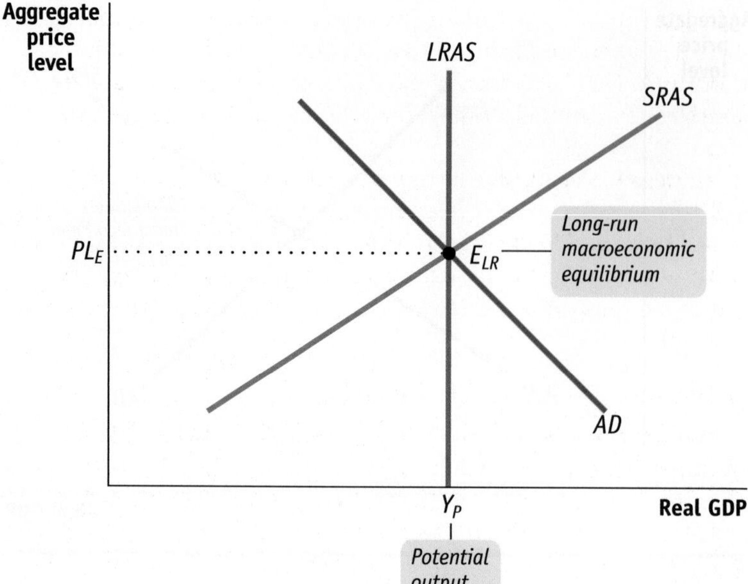

Here short-run macroeconomic equilibrium also lies on the long-run aggregate supply curve, *LRAS*. As a result, short-run equilibrium aggregate output is equal to potential output, Y_P. The economy is in long-run macroeconomic equilibrium at E_{LR}.

Recessionary Output Gaps

Let's assume that in the economy described by **Figure 3.5-3**, the initial aggregate demand curve is AD_1 and the initial short-run aggregate supply curve is $SRAS_1$. So the initial macroeconomic equilibrium is at E_1, which lies on the long-run aggregate supply curve, *LRAS*. The economy, then, starts from a point of short-run and long-run macroeconomic equilibrium, and short-run equilibrium aggregate output equals potential output at Y_1.

FIGURE 3.5-3 Recessionary Gap

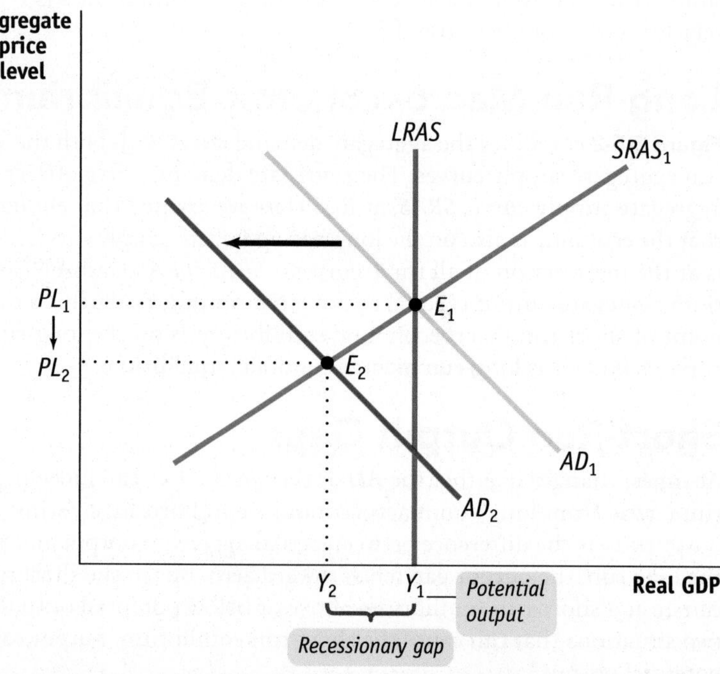

Starting at E_1, a decrease in aggregate demand shifts AD_1 leftward to AD_2. In the short run, the economy moves to E_2 and a recessionary gap arises: the aggregate price level declines from PL_1 to PL_2, aggregate output declines from Y_1 to Y_2, and unemployment rises.

Now suppose that for some reason—such as a sudden worsening of business and consumer expectations—aggregate demand falls and the aggregate demand curve shifts leftward to AD_2. This shift results in a lower equilibrium aggregate price level at PL_2 and a lower equilibrium aggregate output level at Y_2 as the economy settles in the short run at E_2. The short-run effect of such a fall in aggregate demand is what the U.S. economy experienced in 1929–1933: a falling aggregate price level and falling aggregate output.

Aggregate output in this new short-run equilibrium, E_2, is below potential output. When this happens, the economy faces a negative output gap. Because potential output is greater than actual output, actual output minus potential output is negative. A negative output gap is also known as a **recessionary gap**. A recessionary gap inflicts a great deal of pain because it corresponds to a level of unemployment below full employment.

There is a **recessionary gap** when aggregate output is below potential output.

AP® ECON TIP

Know how to draw each of the three possible states of the economy: long-run equilibrium, a recessionary gap, and an inflationary gap. In long-run equilibrium, *AD* and *SRAS* intersect on the *LRAS* curve at potential output. In a recessionary gap, the intersection of *AD* and *SRAS* showing short-run equilibrium should be to the left of *LRAS* and potential output, and in an inflationary gap, this intersection should be to the right.

Inflationary Output Gaps

What if, instead of a decrease in aggregate demand, our hypothetical economy experienced an increase? The results are shown in **Figure 3.5-4**, where we again assume that the initial aggregate demand curve is AD_1 and the initial short-run aggregate supply curve is $SRAS_1$. The initial macroeconomic equilibrium, at E_1, lies on the long-run aggregate supply curve, *LRAS*. Initially, then, the economy is in long-run macroeconomic equilibrium.

FIGURE 3.5-4 Inflationary Gap

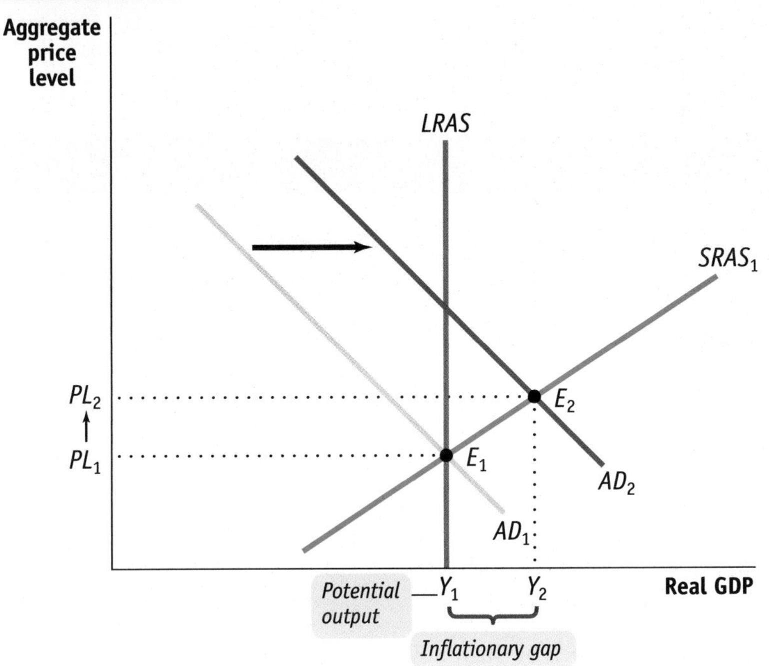

Starting at E_1, an increase in aggregate demand shifts AD_1 rightward to AD_2, and the economy moves to E_2 in the short run. This results in an inflationary gap as aggregate output rises from Y_1 to Y_2, the aggregate price level rises from PL_1 to PL_2, and unemployment falls to a low level.

Now suppose that aggregate demand rises, and the *AD* curve shifts rightward to AD_2. This shift results in a higher aggregate price level, at PL_2, and a higher aggregate output level, at Y_2, as the economy settles in the short run at E_2. Aggregate output in this new short-run equilibrium is above potential output. When this happens, the economy faces a positive output gap. Because potential output is less than actual output, actual output minus potential output is positive. A positive output gap is also known as an **inflationary gap**. An inflationary gap indicates an increase in aggregate demand that is greater than the economy's maximum sustainable capacity.

There is an **inflationary gap** when aggregate output is above potential output.

This creates inflationary pressure in the economy as increasing demand and employment will push prices up over time.

A recessionary gap occurs when there is a negative output gap, and an inflationary gap occurs when there is a positive output gap. Changes in aggregate demand or short-run aggregate supply will create output gaps in the short run, but they will not have the same effect in the long run. As we will see in the next Modules, recessionary and inflationary gaps may result in long run self-adjustment or in fiscal policies meant to restore full-employment output.

Watch the video: *Aggregate Demand and Aggregate Supply*

Module 3.5 Review

Check Your Understanding

1. Draw a correctly labeled graph showing short-run equilibrium in the economy. For each of the following, where will the long-run aggregate supply curve be, relative to the short-run equilibrium real GDP on your graph (to the left, to the right, or equal to)?
   a. a recessionary gap
   b. an inflationary gap
   c. long-run equilibrium

2. What type of gap exists and what is the value of the output (positive or negative) when actual output is above potential output? What if actual output is below potential output?

Tackle the AP® Test: Multiple-Choice Questions

1. In the *AD–AS* model, equilibrium real GDP is labeled
   a. at the point where *SRAS* and *AD* intersect.
   b. on the vertical axis where *SRAS* and *AD* intersect.
   c. on the horizontal axis where *SRAS* and *AD* intersect.
   d. as the difference between potential output and actual output on the horizontal axis.
   e. as the difference between the short-run and long-run equilibrium price level on the vertical axis.

2. If an economy is at full employment, a decrease in aggregate demand would lead to a(n)
   a. positive output gap.
   b. recessionary output gap.
   c. inflationary output gap.
   d. reduction of the existing output gap.
   e. increase in the existing output gap.

3. If an economy is at full employment, an increase in short-run aggregate demand would lead to a(n)
   a. negative output gap.
   b. recessionary output gap.
   c. inflationary output gap.
   d. reduction of the existing output gap.
   e. increase in the existing output gap.

Refer to the graph for Questions 4 and 5.

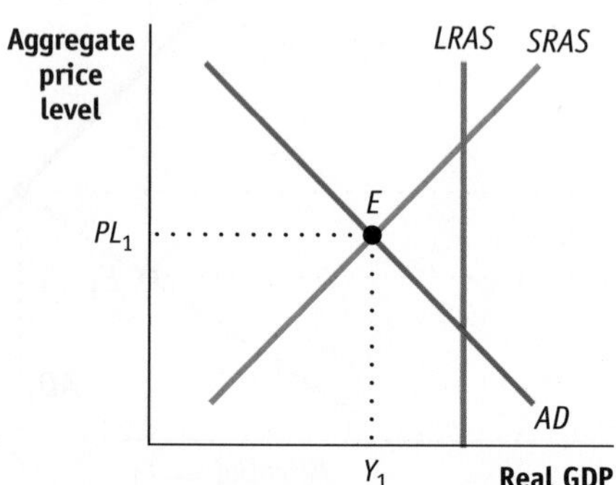

4. Which of the following statements is true if this economy is operating at PL_1 and Y_1?
   a. The level of aggregate output equals potential output.
   b. The economy is in short-run macroeconomic equilibrium.
   c. The economy is in long-run macroeconomic equilibrium.
   d. There is an inflationary gap.
   e. Wages will rise and *SRAS* will shift to the right.

5. The economy depicted in the graph is experiencing a(n)
   a. contractionary gap.
   b. recessionary gap.
   c. inflationary gap.
   d. demand gap.
   e. supply gap.

6. Which of the following is true if real GDP is above potential output?
   a. The economy is experiencing a negative output gap.
   b. The economy is experiencing a recessionary gap.
   c. The economy is experiencing an inflationary gap.
   d. The economy is in long-run equilibrium.
   e. The economy is not in short-run equilibrium.

7. When the economy is in long-run macroeconomic equilibrium, which of the following is true?
   a. There is a positive output gap.
   b. There is a negative output gap.
   c. The output gap equals zero.
   d. There is a recessionary gap.
   e. There is an inflationary gap.

Tackle the AP® Test: Free-Response Questions

1. Refer to the following graph, with the economy operating at PL_1 and Y_1.
   a. Is the economy in short-run macroeconomic equilibrium? Explain.
   b. Is the economy in long-run macroeconomic equilibrium? Explain.
   c. What type of gap exists in this economy?

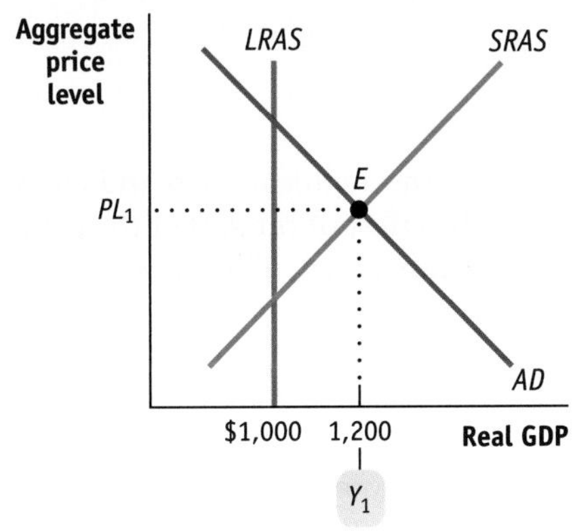

Rubric for FRQ 1 (5 points)

1 point: Yes

1 point: The economy is in short-run equilibrium because it operates at the point where short-run aggregate supply and aggregate demand intersect.

1 point: No

1 point: Short-run equilibrium occurs at a level of aggregate output that is not equal to potential output.

1 point: Inflationary gap

2. Draw a correctly labeled aggregate demand and aggregate supply graph illustrating an economy in long-run macroeconomic equilibrium. **(5 points)**

MODULE 3.6

Short-Run Changes in the Aggregate Demand–Aggregate Supply Model

In this Module, you will learn to:

- Identify a positive or negative shock in aggregate demand and its effect on output, employment, and the price level
- Identify a positive or negative shock in short-run aggregate supply and its effect on output, employment, and the price level
- Distinguish between demand-pull and cost-push inflation

AP® ECON TIP

When asked on the exam to graph the effect of a change, make sure you understand whether the question is asking you to graph the short run or the long run. If short run or long run is not specified, graph the short run.

The short-run equilibrium aggregate output and the short-run equilibrium aggregate price level we identified in the previous Module can change because of shifts of either the aggregate demand curve or the short-run aggregate supply curve. A shift of the *AD* curve is called a *demand shock*, and a shift of the SRAS curve is called a *supply shock*. Let's look at each case in turn.

Demand Shocks

An event that shifts the aggregate demand curve is a **demand shock**.

As we learned in Module 3.1, factors that shift the aggregate demand curve include changes in consumer expectations or wealth, the effect of the size of the existing stock of physical capital, or the use of fiscal or monetary policy. These events are known as **demand shocks**. The Great Depression was caused by a negative demand shock, the collapse of wealth and loss of business and consumer confidence that followed the stock market crash of 1929 and the banking crises of 1930–1931. The Great Depression was ended by a positive demand shock – the huge increase in government purchases during World War II. In March 2020, the U.S. economy experienced another significant negative demand shock as the COVID-19 pandemic led people to remain at home, resulting in a decrease in income and spending. The associated economic recovery and expansion that followed resulted from a positive demand shock created by government spending on stimulus packages. The shocks associated with the coronavirus pandemic are discussed further in Enrichment Module A: Recession and Recovery During the Pandemic. The Great Depression and pandemic recession were both caused by a negative demand shock and ended by a positive demand shock.

Toshi Sasaki/Getty Images

New York's Times Square, previously a hub of commercial activity, sat empty during the pandemic.

Figure 3.6-1 shows the short-run effects of negative and positive demand shocks. A negative demand shock shifts the aggregate demand curve, *AD*, to the left, from AD_1 to AD_2, as shown in panel (a). The economy moves down along the *SRAS* curve from E_1 to E_2, leading to lower short-run equilibrium aggregate output and a lower short-run equilibrium aggregate price level. A positive demand shock shifts the aggregate demand curve, *AD*, to the right, as shown in panel (b). Here, the economy moves up along the *SRAS* curve, from E_1 to E_2. This leads to higher short-run equilibrium aggregate output and a higher short-run equilibrium aggregate price level. Demand shocks cause aggregate output and the aggregate price level to move in the same direction.

FIGURE 3.6-1 Demand Shocks

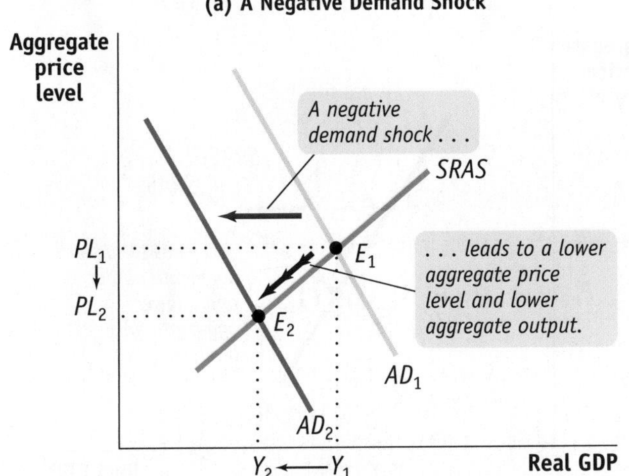

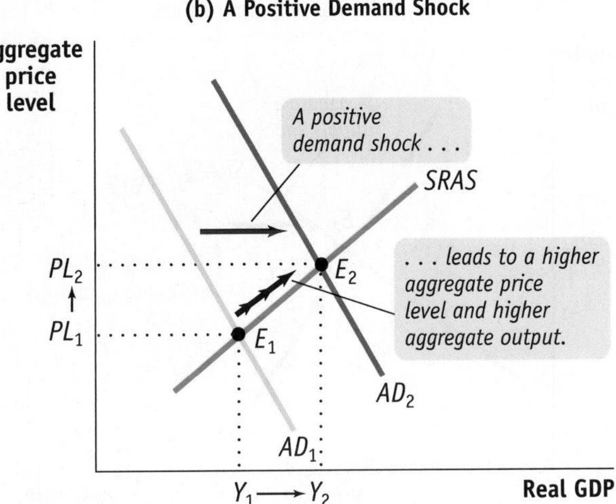

A demand shock shifts the aggregate demand curve, moving the aggregate price level and aggregate output in the same direction. In panel (a), a negative demand shock shifts the aggregate demand curve leftward from AD_1 to AD_2, reducing the aggregate price level from PL_1 to PL_2 and aggregate output from Y_1 to Y_2. In panel (b), a positive demand shock shifts the aggregate demand curve rightward, increasing the aggregate price level from PL_1 to PL_2 and aggregate output from Y_1 to Y_2.

Supply Shocks

As we learned in Module 3.3, factors that shift the short-run aggregate supply curve include changes in commodity prices, inflationary expectations, nominal wages, or productivity. These events are known as **supply shocks**. A *negative* supply shock raises production costs and reduces the quantity producers are willing to supply at any given aggregate price level, leading to a leftward shift of the short-run aggregate supply curve. The U.S. economy experienced severe negative supply shocks following disruptions to world oil supplies in 1973 and 1979. In contrast, a *positive* supply shock reduces production costs and increases the quantity supplied at any given aggregate price level, leading to a rightward shift of the short-run aggregate supply curve. The United States experienced a positive supply shock between 1995 and 2000, when the increasing use of the internet and other information technologies caused productivity growth to increase.

An event that shifts the short-run aggregate supply curve is a **supply shock**.

Gabriela Maj/Bloomberg/Getty Images

The combination of inflation and falling aggregate output shown in panel (a) of **Figure 3.6-2** has a special name: **stagflation**, for "stagnation plus inflation." When an economy experiences stagflation, it gets the "worst of both worlds": falling aggregate output leads to rising unemployment, and people feel that their purchasing power is squeezed by rising prices. Stagflation in the 1970s led to a mood of national pessimism. As we'll see in later Modules, it also poses a dilemma for policy makers.

Stagflation is the combination of inflation and stagnating (or falling) aggregate output.

A positive supply shock, shown in panel (b), has the exact opposite effects. A rightward shift of the *SRAS* curve, from $SRAS_1$ to $SRAS_2$, results in a rise in aggregate output and a fall in the aggregate price level—a downward movement along the *AD* curve, creating "the best of both worlds." The favorable supply shocks of the late 1990s led to a combination of full employment and declining inflation. That is, the aggregate price level fell compared with the long-run trend. For a few years, this combination produced a great wave of national optimism.

The distinctive feature of supply shocks, both negative and positive, is that, unlike demand shocks, they cause the aggregate price level and aggregate output to move in *opposite* directions.

FIGURE 3.6-2 Supply Shocks

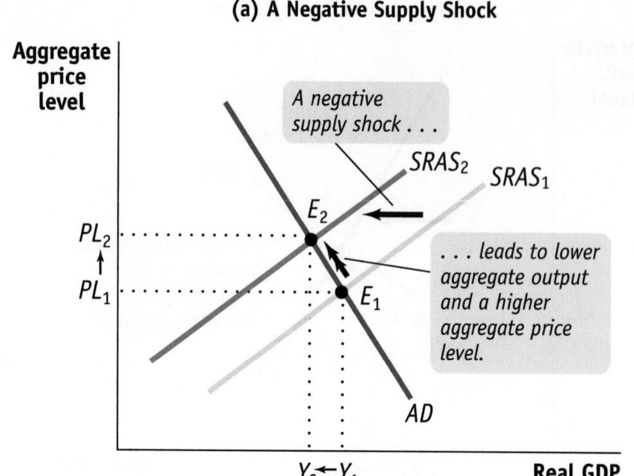

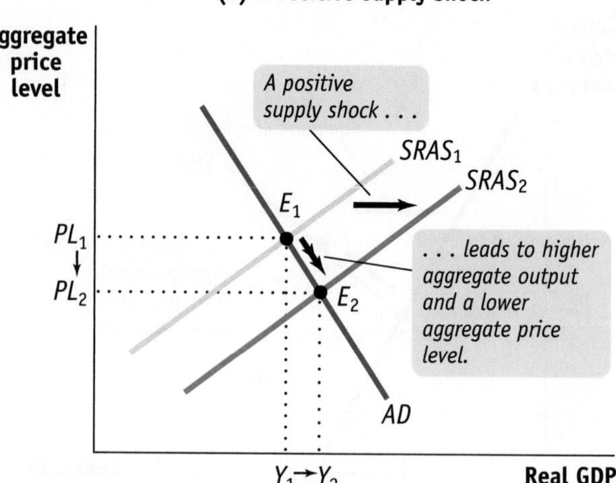

The effects of a negative supply shock are shown in panel (a) of Figure 3.6-2. The initial equilibrium is at E_1, with aggregate price level PL_1 and aggregate output Y_1. The disruption in the oil supply causes the short-run aggregate supply curve to shift to the left, from $SRAS_1$ to $SRAS_2$. As a consequence, aggregate output falls and the aggregate price level rises, an upward movement along the *AD* curve. At the new equilibrium, E_2, the short-run equilibrium aggregate price level, PL_2, is higher, and the short-run equilibrium aggregate output level, Y_2, is lower than before.

Cost-push inflation is inflation that is caused by a significant increase in the price of an input with economy-wide importance.

Demand-pull inflation is inflation that is caused by an increase in aggregate demand.

AP® ECON TIP

Inflation and deflation are shown as changes in price level on the vertical axis of the aggregate supply and demand graph. Inflation caused by a rightward shift of the aggregate demand curve is known as demand-pull inflation. Inflation caused by a leftward shift of the aggregate supply curve is known as cost-push inflation (because the leftward shift is caused by an increase in production costs). Make sure you can graph and explain cost-push inflation and demand-pull inflation!

There's another important contrast between supply shocks and demand shocks. As we will see in later Modules, monetary policy and fiscal policy enable the government to shift the *AD* curve, meaning that governments are in a position to create the kinds of shocks shown in Figure 3.6-1. It's much harder for governments to shift the *AS* curve.

Demand and Supply Shocks and Inflation

So far in this Unit, we have focused on aggregate output and the relationship between potential output and actual output when aggregate demand or short-run aggregate supply change. But what about the changes in the price level that accompany supply and demand shocks?

Using the aggregate demand–aggregate supply (*AD–AS*) model, we can see that there are two possible changes that can lead to an increase in the aggregate price level: a decrease in short-run aggregate supply and an increase in aggregate demand. Inflation that is caused by a significant increase in the price of an input with economy-wide importance that decreases short-run aggregate is called **cost-push inflation**. For example, some economists argue that the oil crisis in the 1970s led to an increase in energy prices in the United States, causing a leftward shift of the aggregate supply curve, which in turn increased the aggregate price level. However, aside from crude oil, it is difficult to think of examples of inputs with economy-wide importance that experience significant price increases.

Inflation that is caused by an increase in aggregate demand is known as **demand-pull inflation**. When a rightward shift of the aggregate demand curve leads to an increase in the aggregate price level, the economy experiences demand-pull inflation. This situation is sometimes described by the phrase "too much money chasing too few goods," which means that the aggregate demand for goods and services is outpacing short-run aggregate supply and driving up the prices of goods. For example, large increases in government spending during World War II led to large increases in income and consumer spending after the war ended. Because production during the war had shifted from consumer goods to military goods to support the war effort, the supply of consumer goods was limited. Demand-pull inflation resulted from the combination of high consumer demand ("too much money") and low supply of consumer goods ("too few goods").

In the short run, policies that produce a booming economy through an increase in aggregate demand also tend to lead to higher inflation, and policies that reduce inflation by decreasing aggregate demand tend to depress the economy. This creates both temptations and dilemmas for governments that we will look at more closely in Module 3.8.

Module 3.6 Review

Check Your Understanding

1. Assume an economy starts in long-run equilibrium. How will each of the following events affect aggregate output, employment, unemployment, and the price level in the short run?
   a. a positive demand shock
   b. a negative demand shock
   c. a positive supply shock
   d. a negative supply shock

2. Identify the primary causes of cost-push inflation and demand-pull inflation.

Tackle the AP® Test: Multiple-Choice Questions

1. Which of the following would cause a negative supply shock?
   a. a technological advance
   b. increasing productivity
   c. an increase in oil prices
   d. a decrease in government spending
   e. a decrease in consumption

2. Which of the following would cause a positive demand shock?
   a. an increase in wealth
   b. pessimistic consumer expectations
   c. a decrease in government spending
   d. an increase in taxes
   e. a relatively high existing stock of capital

3. During stagflation, what happens to the aggregate price level and real GDP?

	Aggregate price level	*Real GDP*
a.	decreases	increases
b.	decreases	decreases
c.	increases	increases
d.	increases	decreases
e.	stays the same	stays the same

4. Which of the following will lead to stagflation in an economy at full-employment aggregate output?
   a. a positive demand shock
   b. a negative demand shock
   c. a positive supply shock
   d. a negative supply shock
   e. a simultaneous negative demand shock and positive supply shock

5. If an economy is in long-run equilibrium, which of the following will increase aggregate output without causing inflation?
   a. a positive demand shock
   b. a positive supply shock
   c. a negative supply shock
   d. an increase in aggregate demand
   e. a decrease in short-run aggregate supply

6. An increase in the price level resulting from an increase in energy prices is an example of
   a. demand-pull inflation.
   b. re-inflation.
   c. cost-push inflation.
   d. input inflation.
   e. hyperinflation.

7. Demand-pull inflation is caused by which of the following?
   a. an increase in wages
   b. "too little money chasing too few goods"
   c. contractionary monetary policy
   d. an increase in aggregate demand
   e. a decrease in aggregate supply

Tackle the AP® Test: Free-Response Questions

1. Use a correctly labeled aggregate demand–aggregate supply graph starting at long-run equilibrium to illustrate cost-push inflation. Give an example of what might cause cost-push inflation in the economy.

Rubric for FRQ 1 (9 points)

1 point: Graph labeled "Aggregate price level" or "*PL*" on the vertical axis and "Real GDP" on the horizontal axis

1 point: *AD* downward-sloping and labeled

1 point: *SRAS* upward-sloping and labeled

1 point: *LRAS* vertical and labeled

1 point: Potential output labeled at horizontal intercept of *LRAS*

1 point: Long-run macroeconomic equilibrium aggregate price level labeled on vertical axis at intersection of *SRAS*, *LRAS*, and *AD*

1 point: Leftward shift of the SRAS curve

1 point: Higher equilibrium aggregate price level at new intersection of *SRAS* and *AD*

1 point: This could be caused by anything that would shift the short-run aggregate supply curve to the left, such as an increase in the price of energy, labor, or another input with economy-wide importance.

2. Describe the short-run effects of each of the following shocks on the aggregate price level and on aggregate output:
   a. The government sharply increases the minimum wage, raising the wages of many workers.
   b. Solar energy firms launch a major program of investment spending.
   c. Congress raises taxes and cuts spending.
   d. Severe weather destroys crops around the world.
   (8 points)

Long-Run Self-Adjustment in the Aggregate Demand–Aggregate Supply Model

MODULE 3.7

In this Module, you will learn to:

- Explain how flexible wages and prices will adjust to restore full employment in the long run
- Use an *AD–AS* graph to show how unemployment will revert to its natural rate following a demand or supply shock
- Show a shift in the long-run aggregate supply curve that changes the full-employment level of output
- Explain how a shift of the long-run aggregate supply curve can be used to illustrate economic growth

From the Short Run to the Long Run

We have just seen how supply and demand shocks can move the economy away from long-run equilibrium. In Modules 3.8 and 3.9, we will see how the government can attempt to move the economy back to long-run equilibrium when shocks to the economy lead to recessions or inflation. But first, we will consider what happens if the economy experiences a shock that moves the economy out of equilibrium and no action is taken by the government. Will the shock cause the economy to remain in a state of disequilibrium until another shock brings it back to full employment? As we will see, in the long run, in the absence of government policy actions, flexible wages and prices will adjust to restore full employment and move unemployment to the natural rate following a demand or supply shock. Let's look at the economy's long-run self-adjustment process.

In Module 3.4, we saw that the economy normally produces more or less than potential output: actual aggregate output was below potential output in the early 1990s, above potential output in the late 1990s, and below potential output for most of the 2000s (see **Figure 3.7-1**). So the economy is normally operating at a point on its short-run aggregate supply curve—but not at a point on its long-run aggregate supply curve. Why, then, is the long-run curve relevant? Does the economy ever move from the short run to the long run? And if so, how?

The first step to answering these questions is to understand that the economy is always in one of only two states with respect to the short-run and long-run aggregate supply curves. It can be on both curves simultaneously by being at a point where the curves cross (as in those few years, not highlighted in Figure 3.7-1, in which actual aggregate output and potential output nearly coincided). Or it can be on the short-run aggregate supply curve but not the long-run aggregate supply curve (as in those years, highlighted in purple or green, in which actual aggregate output and potential output *did not* coincide). But that is not the end of the story. If the economy is on the short-run but not the long-run aggregate supply curve, the short-run aggregate supply curve will shift over time until the economy is at a point where both curves cross—a point where actual aggregate output is equal to potential output.

FIGURE 3.7-1 Actual and Potential Output from 1989 to 2020

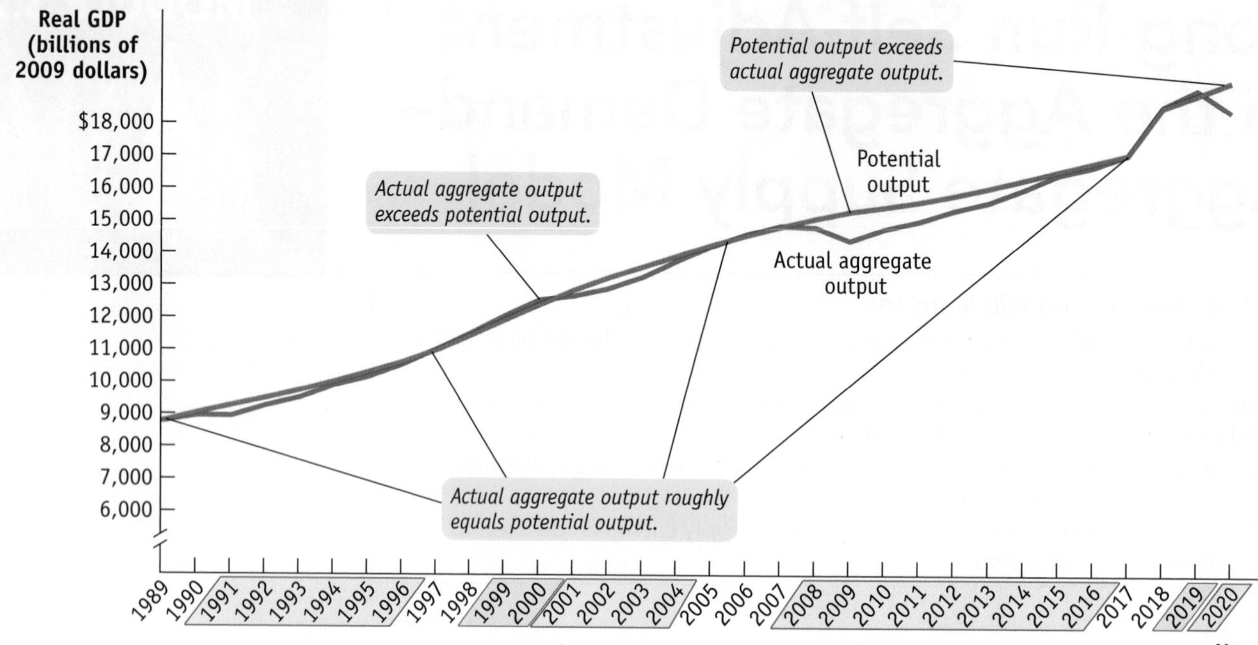

When potential output is equal to actual output, the economy is in long-run equilibrium, represented by the coinciding of the orange and blue curves in this graph. When potential output is above or below actual output, the economy is in short-run, but not long-run, equilibrium. When the economy is not in long-run equilibrium, the *SRAS* curve will shift over time until potential and actual output are equal. The purple-shaded years are periods in which actual output fell below potential output and the green-shaded years are periods in which actual output exceeded potential output.

Figure 3.7-2 illustrates how this process works. In both panels, *LRAS* is the long-run aggregate supply curve, $SRAS_1$ is the initial short-run aggregate supply curve, and the aggregate price level is at PL_1. In panel (a) the economy starts at the initial production point, A_1, which corresponds to a quantity of aggregate output supplied, Y_1, that is higher than potential output, Y_P. Producing an aggregate output level (such as Y_1) that is higher than potential output (Y_P) is possible only because nominal wages have not yet fully adjusted upward. Until this upward adjustment in nominal wages occurs, producers are earning high profits and producing a high level of output. But a level of aggregate output higher than potential output means a low level of unemployment. Because jobs are abundant and workers are scarce, nominal wages will rise over time, gradually shifting the short-run aggregate supply curve leftward. Eventually, it will be in a new position, such as $SRAS_2$.

In panel (b), the initial production point, A_1, corresponds to an aggregate output level, Y_1, that is lower than potential output, Y_P. Producing an aggregate output level (such as Y_1) that is lower than potential output (Y_P) is possible only because nominal wages have not yet fully adjusted downward (because, as we learned in Module 3.3, wages are sticky in the short run). Until this downward adjustment occurs, producers are earning low (or negative) profits and producing a low level of output. An aggregate output level lower than potential output means high unemployment. Because workers are abundant and jobs are scarce, nominal wages will fall over time, shifting the short-run aggregate supply curve gradually to the right. Eventually, it will be in a new position, such as $SRAS_2$.

AP® ECON TIP

Show the long-run adjustment process that brings the economy back to equilibrium after a supply or demand shock if there is no government policy response. In the long run, flexible wages and prices will shift the short-run aggregate supply curve to bring the economy back to long-run equilibrium.

Long-Run Self-Adjustment

Shifts of the short-run aggregate supply curve due to the adjustment of wages and prices will return the economy to potential output in the long run. This self-adjustment assures the economy always moves toward full employment (the natural rate of unemployment) where the economy is producing the potential level of aggregate

FIGURE 3.7-2 From the Short Run to the Long Run

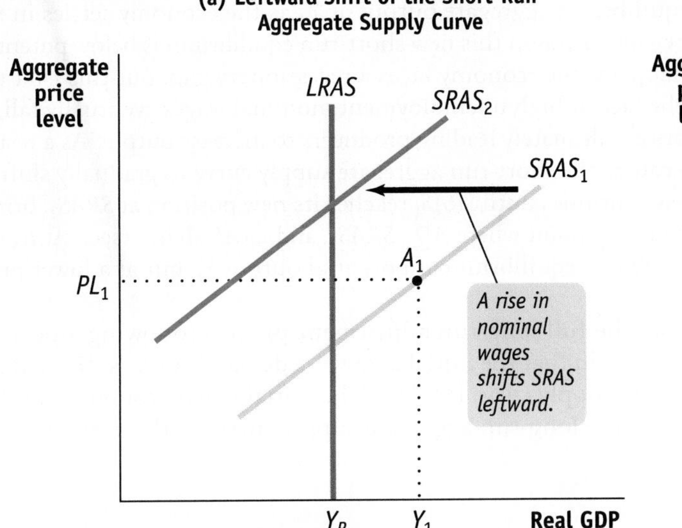

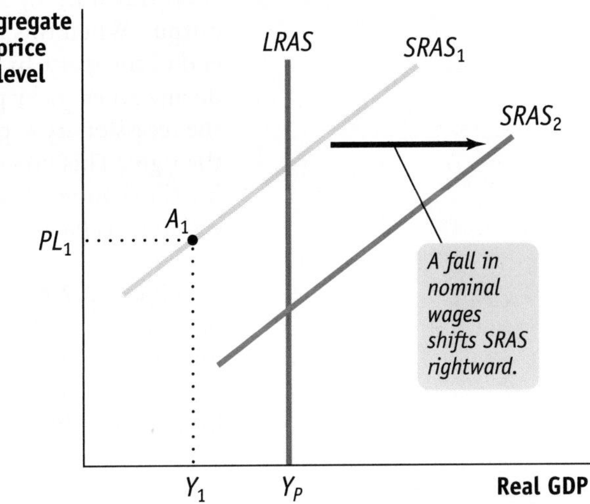

In panel (a), the initial short-run aggregate supply curve is $SRAS_1$. At the aggregate price level, PL_1, the quantity of aggregate output supplied, Y_1, exceeds potential output, Y_P. Eventually, low unemployment will cause nominal wages to rise, leading to a leftward shift of the short-run aggregate supply curve from $SRAS_1$ to $SRAS_2$.

In panel (b), the reverse happens: at the aggregate price level, PL_1, the quantity of aggregate output supplied is less than potential output. High unemployment eventually leads to a fall in nominal wages over time and a rightward shift of the short-run aggregate supply curve.

output. To explain how an economy self-adjusts in the long run, we'll draw on two concepts from Module 3.5: the recessionary gap and the inflationary gap.

Figure 3.7-3 shows the full long-run adjustment of the economy following a negative demand shock. Suppose that for some reason—such as a sudden worsening of

FIGURE 3.7-3 Short-Run Versus Long-Run Effects of a Negative Demand Shock

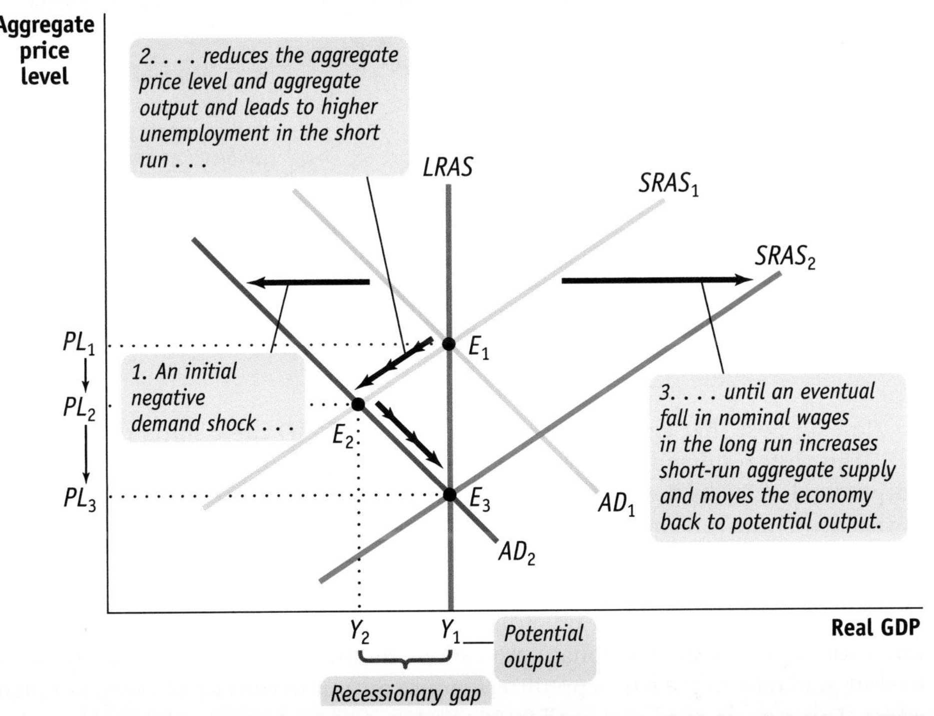

Starting at E_1, a negative demand shock shifts AD_1 leftward to AD_2. In the short run, the economy moves to E_2 and a recessionary gap arises: the aggregate price level declines from PL_1 to PL_2, aggregate output declines from Y_1 to Y_2, and unemployment rises. But in the long run, nominal wages fall in response to high unemployment at Y_2, and $SRAS_1$ shifts rightward to $SRAS_2$. Aggregate output rises from Y_2 to Y_1, and the aggregate price level declines again, from PL_2 to PL_3. Long-run macroeconomic equilibrium is eventually restored at E_3.

business and consumer expectations — aggregate demand falls and the aggregate demand shifts leftward to AD_2. This results in a lower equilibrium aggregate price level at PL_2 and a lower equilibrium aggregate output at Y_2 as the economy settles in the short run at E_2. Aggregate output in this new short-run equilibrium is below potential output. When this happens, the economy faces a recessionary gap. But this isn't the end of the story. In the face of high unemployment, nominal wages eventually fall, as do any other sticky prices, ultimately leading producers to increase output. As a result, the recessionary gap causes the short-run aggregate supply curve to gradually shift to the right. This process continues until $SRAS_1$ reaches its new position at $SRAS_2$, bringing the economy back to the point where AD_2, $SRAS_2$, and $LRAS$ all intersect. At E_3 the economy is back in long-run equilibrium at potential output Y_1, but at a lower price level, PL_3.

Figure 3.7-4 shows the full long-run adjustment process following a positive demand shock. Assume again that the initial aggregate demand curve is AD_1 and the initial sort-run aggregate supply curve is $SRAS_1$. The initial macroeconomic equilibrium is at E_1 and lies on the long-run aggregate supply curve, so the economy is in long-run equilibrium.

FIGURE 3.7-4 **Short-Run Versus Long-Run Effects of a Positive Demand Shock**

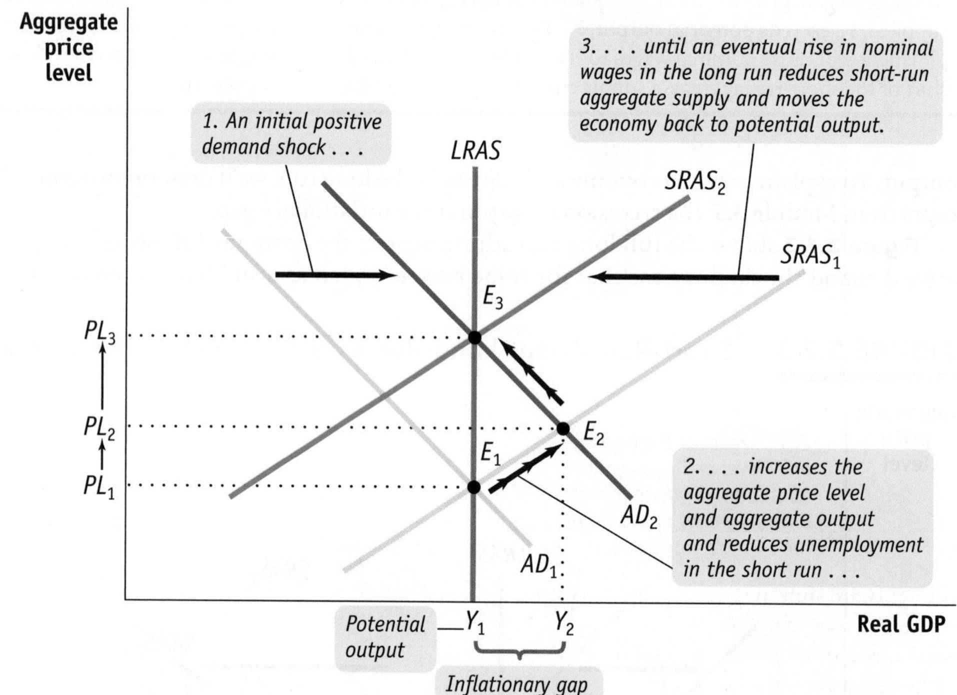

Starting at E_1, a positive demand shock shifts AD_1 rightward to AD_2, and the economy moves to E_2 in the short run. This results in an inflationary gap as aggregate output rises from Y_1 to Y_2, the aggregate price level rises from PL_1 to PL_2, and unemployment falls to a low level. In the long run, $SRAS_1$ shifts leftward to $SRAS_2$ as nominal wages rise in response to low unemployment at Y_2. Aggregate output falls back to Y_1, the aggregate price level rises again to PL_3, and the economy returns to long-run macroeconomic equilibrium at E_3.

Now suppose that aggregate demand rises and the AD curve shifts rightward to AD_2. This shift results in a higher aggregate price level, at P_2, and a higher aggregate output level, at Y_2, as the economy settles, in the short run, at E_2. Aggregate output in this new short-run equilibrium is above potential output, and unemployment is low in order to produce this higher level of aggregate output. When this happens, the economy experiences an inflationary gap. As in the case of a recessionary gap, this isn't the end of the story. In the face of low unemployment, nominal wages will rise, as will other sticky prices. An inflationary gap causes the short-run aggregate supply curve to shift gradually to the left as producers reduce output in the face of rising nominal wages. This process continues until $SRAS_1$ reaches its new position at $SRAS_2$, the point where AD_2, $SRAS_2$, and *LRAS* all intersect. At E_3, the economy is back in long-run macroeconomic equilibrium at potential output Y_1, but at a higher price level, PL_3.

Shifts in the Long-Run Aggregate Supply Curve

The economy always moves toward a long-run equilibrium where aggregate demand and short-run aggregate intersect at a point on the long-run aggregate supply curve. But over time, the long-run aggregate supply curve can also change, as shown in **Figure 3.7-5**. Shifts in the long-run aggregate supply curve indicate a change in the potential level of output. A rightward shift of the long-run aggregate supply curve, shown in panel (a), indicates an increase in the economy's potential output, which means the economy has experienced economic growth. An increase in potential output, shown as a movement to the right along the horizontal axis from Y_P to Y_{P1}, is associated with an increase in the full-employment level of output. The same increase in potential output and the full-employment level of output was shown as an outward shift of the production possibilities curve (*PPC*) in Unit 1. Panel (b) in Figure 3.7-5 shows economic growth as a movement from the original *PPC* to the new *PPC*.

AP® ECON TIP

Distinguish between a short-run fluctuation (recession or inflation) and long-run economic growth. On the *AD-AS* graph, the former is shown by shifts of the *AD* or *SRAS* curve, and the latter is shown by a rightward shift of the *LRAS* curve.

FIGURE 3.7-5 Economic Growth

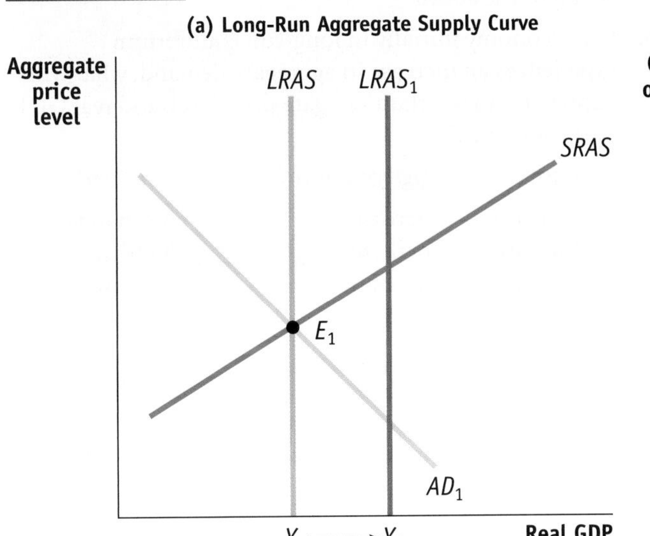

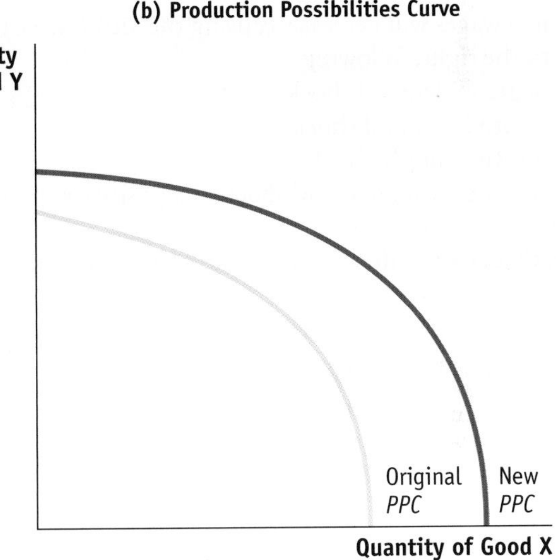

A rightward shift in the *LRAS* curve indicates an increase in the potential level of output, which means the economy has experienced economic growth. A rightward shift of the *PPC* also shows an increase in potential output, illustrating economic growth. In panel (a), the economy is in long-run equilibrium at E_1 and potential output is at Y_P. Economic growth is shown as a shift of the long-run aggregate supply curve to Y_{P1}. The rightward shift of the *LRAS* curve shows a higher level of full employment. Panel (b) illustrates economic growth as a rightward shift of the production possibilities curve (*PPC*).

Economic growth, illustrated by a rightward shift of the *LRAS* curve, can be caused by increases in productivity, human capital, or physical capital (capital stock) in the economy. Economic growth will be discussed in depth in Module 5.6.

Over time, the economy will experience demand and supply shocks. With no government intervention, flexible wages and prices will move the economy back toward long-run equilibrium through a shift of the short-run aggregate supply curve. As the economy self-adjusts to move back to full employment after demand or supply shocks, it can also experience economic growth, shown as a rightward shift of the long-run aggregate supply curve (or a rightward shift of the production possibilities curve). Next, we will consider how the government might step in with fiscal policy to attempt to move the economy more quickly toward equilibrium.

Module 3.7 Review

Check Your Understanding

1. Explain how an adjustment of nominal wages will bring the economy back to long-run equilibrium after a negative demand shock.

2. Explain how an adjustment of nominal wages will bring the economy back to long-run equilibrium after a positive demand shock.

Tackle the AP® Test: Multiple-Choice Questions

1. Long-run self-adjustment of the economy occurs as a result of which of the following?
   a. sticky wages and prices
   b. fiscal policy
   c. monetary policy
   d. flexible wages
   e. technological change

2. Nominal wages will decrease, causing the *SRAS* curve to shift to the right, following
   a. a negative demand shock.
   b. a positive demand shock.
   c. a positive supply shock.
   d. either a positive demand shock or a positive supply shock.
   e. both a positive demand shock and a positive supply shock.

3. Nominal wages will rise in the long run as a result of
   a. a decrease in the price level.
   b. an increase in the price level.
   c. an increase in potential output.
   d. a decrease in potential output.
   e. a recession.

4. An increase in potential output is illustrated by which of the following?
   a. a leftward shift of the *LRAS* curve
   b. a rightward shift of the *LRAS* curve
   c. a rightward shift of the *PPC*
   d. a leftward shift of the *PPC*
   e. either a rightward shift of the *SRAS* curve or the *PPC*

5. Economic growth is shown as a rightward shift of which of the following?
   a. the *LRAS* curve
   b. the *AD* curve
   c. the *SRAS* curve
   d. the Phillips curve
   e. all of the above

6. If an economy initially in long-run equilibrium experiences an increase in aggregate demand, what will happen to wages, the aggregate price level, and real GDP in the long run?

	Wages	*Aggregate price level*	*Real GDP*
a.	increase	increase	no change
b.	increase	increase	increase
c.	increase	no change	increase
d.	decrease	increase	decrease
e.	decrease	decrease	decrease

7. If an economy initially in long-run equilibrium experiences a negative demand shock, what will happen to wages, the aggregate price level, and real GDP in the long run?

	Wages	*Aggregate price level*	*Real GDP*
a.	decrease	decrease	no change
b.	increase	increase	increase
c.	increase	no change	increase
d.	decrease	increase	decrease
e.	decrease	decrease	decrease

Tackle the AP® Test: Free-Response Questions

1. Draw a correctly labeled *AD–AS* graph showing an economy in long-run equilibrium. Label the price level and level of aggregate output as PL_1 and Y_1.
   a. Assume the economy experiences a negative demand shock. Show the effect of the demand shock on your graph. Label the new price level and level of real GDP as PL_2 and Y_2.
   b. If the government takes no action, what will happen to nominal wages? Explain.
   c. Show the effect of the change in nominal wages from part b on your graph. Indicate the new long-run equilibrium price level and real GDP on your graph as PL_3 and Y_3.

Rubric for FRQ 1 (10 points)

1 point: *PL* label on the vertical axis, real GDP label on the horizontal axis, upward-sloping and labeled *AD* curve, downward-sloping and labeled *SRAS* curve

1 point: Vertical *LRAS* curve labeled Y_1 where it intersects the horizontal axis

1 point: Long-run equilibrium price level labeled PL_1 on the vertical axis where *SRAS, AD,* and *LRAS* intersect

1 point: New, labeled *AD* curve shown shifted to the left

1 point: New price level labeled PL_2 on the vertical axis where the original *SRAS* and new *AD* intersect

1 point: New level of real GDP labeled Y_2 on the horizontal axis where the original *SRAS* and new *AD* curve intersect

1 point: The decrease in the price level from the negative demand shock will cause nominal wage to fall.

1 point: New, labeled, *SRAS* shown shifted to the right

1 point: New price level is labeled PL_3 on the vertical axis where *AD, SRAS,* and *LRAS* intersect.

1 point: New real GDP level is labeled Y_3 at the initial (Y_1) level of real GDP.

2. Draw a correctly labeled *AD–AS* graph showing an economy that is experiencing an inflationary gap. Label the price level and real GDP as PL_1 and Y_1.
   a. Label the initial full-employment level of output as Y_f.
   b. On your graph, illustrate how economic growth can move the economy back to long-run equilibrium.
   (5 points)

MODULE 3.8

Fiscal Policy

In this Module, you will learn to:

- Define fiscal policy and identify the tools government uses to implement it
- Explain how changes in government spending affect aggregate demand directly
- Explain how changes in taxes and transfers affect aggregate demand indirectly
- Define expansionary and contractionary fiscal policies and explain when and how they are used to restore full employment
- Use an *AD–AS* graph to demonstrate the short-run effects of fiscal policy
- Explain the difference in the size of the expenditure and tax multipliers and use them to calculate the short-run effects of a fiscal policy
- Explain why there are lags to discretionary fiscal policy

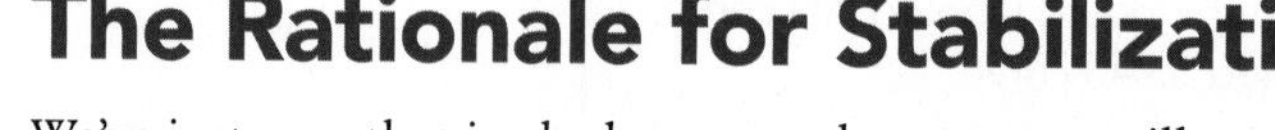

The Rationale for Stabilization

Tim Gidal/Getty Images

"In the long run we are all dead." —John Maynard Keynes (1883–1946)

We've just seen that in the long run, the economy will eventually trend back to potential output. Most macroeconomists believe, however, that the adjustment process typically takes a decade or more. In particular, if aggregate output is below potential output, the economy can suffer an extended period of depressed aggregate output and high unemployment before it returns to long-run equilibrium.

This belief in the tendency for long-run self-correction of the economy to be slow underlies one of the most famous quotations in economics: John Maynard Keynes's declaration, "In the long run we are all dead." Economists usually interpret Keynes's statement as a recommendation that governments should not wait for the economy to correct itself. Instead, it is argued by many economists—but not all—that the government should use fiscal policy to push the economy back to potential output in the aftermath of a shift of the aggregate demand curve. This is the rationale for active *stabilization policy*, which is the use of government policy to reduce the severity of recessions and rein in excessively strong expansions.

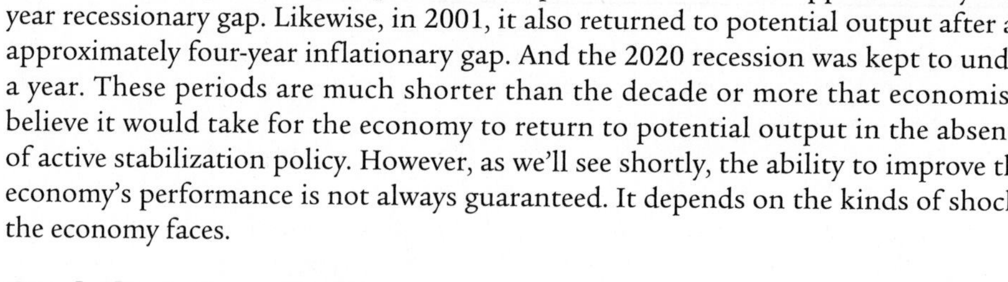

Can stabilization policy improve the economy's performance? As we saw in Figure 3.7-1, the answer certainly appears to be yes. Under active stabilization policy, the U.S. economy returned to potential output in 1996 after an approximately five-year recessionary gap. Likewise, in 2001, it also returned to potential output after an approximately four-year inflationary gap. And the 2020 recession was kept to under a year. These periods are much shorter than the decade or more that economists believe it would take for the economy to return to potential output in the absence of active stabilization policy. However, as we'll see shortly, the ability to improve the economy's performance is not always guaranteed. It depends on the kinds of shocks the economy faces.

Stabilization Policy

Stabilization policy includes the government's use of fiscal policy or monetary policy to prevent recessions and inflation. In this Module, we introduce the use of fiscal policy. We will focus on monetary policy in Unit 4 and look at the *long-run* consequences of stabilization policies—both fiscal and monetary—in Unit 5.

Fiscal policy is the use of government purchases of goods and services, government transfers, or tax policy to stabilize the economy.

Fiscal policy is the use of either government spending—government purchases of final goods and services and government transfers—or tax policy to stabilize the economy. Fiscal policy is used to achieve macroeconomic goals, including full employment and stable prices, through changes in aggregate demand. In practice, governments often respond to recessions by increasing spending, cutting taxes, or both. They often respond to inflation by reducing spending or increasing taxes.

The effect of government purchases of final goods and services, G, on the aggregate demand curve is *direct* because government purchases are themselves a component of aggregate demand. So an increase in government purchases shifts the aggregate demand curve to the right, and a decrease shifts it to the left. History's most dramatic example of how increased government purchases affect aggregate demand was the effect of wartime government spending during World War II. Because of the war, purchases by the U.S. federal government surged by 400%. This increase in purchases is usually credited with ending the Great Depression.

In contrast, changes in either tax rates, *T*, or government transfers, *Tr*, influence the economy *indirectly* through their effect on disposable income. Lower taxes means that consumers get to keep more of what they earn, increasing their disposable income. An increase in government transfers also increases consumers' disposable income. In either case, this increases consumer spending and shifts the aggregate demand curve to the right. Higher taxes or a reduction in transfers reduces the amount of disposable income received by consumers, which reduces consumer spending and shifts the aggregate demand curve to the left.

In 2020, the U.S. government used the pandemic stimulus packages that included increased transfer payments to increase income and consumption in the economy in an effort to increase aggregate demand in the face of stay-at-home behaviors and business shut-downs that sent the economy into recession. Government transfer payments, which totaled $2,418 billion in the pre-pandemic first quarter of 2020, rose to $4,767 billion in the second quarter of 2020, following the passage of the stimulus, and rose further to $5,071 billion in the first quarter of 2021.

Using Fiscal Policy to Stabilize the Economy

To understand how fiscal policy can be used to close output gaps, let's review the basic equation of national income accounting from Module 2.1:

$$\textbf{(3.8-1)}\quad GDP = C + I + G + (X - M)$$

The left-hand side of this equation is GDP, the value of all final goods and services produced in the economy. The right-hand side is aggregate spending, the total spending on final goods and services produced in the economy. Aggregate spending is the sum of consumer spending (*C*), investment spending (*I*), government purchases of goods and services (*G*), and the value of exports (*X*) minus the value of imports (*M*). Aggregate spending includes all the sources of aggregate demand.

The government directly controls one of the variables on the right-hand side of Equation 3.8-1: government purchases of goods and services (*G*). But that's not the only way fiscal policy can affect aggregate spending in the economy. Through changes in taxes and transfers, the government can also influence consumer spending (*C*) and, in some cases, investment spending (*I*).

Because the government itself is one source of spending in the economy, and because taxes and transfers can affect spending by consumers and firms, the government can use changes in taxes, transfers, or government spending to *shift the aggregate demand curve*. Why would the government want to shift the aggregate demand curve? Because it wants to close either a recessionary gap, created when aggregate output falls below potential output, or an inflationary gap, created when aggregate output exceeds potential output.

In early 2020, there was bipartisan agreement that the U.S. government should act to prevent a fall in aggregate demand – that is, to move the aggregate demand curve to the right of where it would otherwise be. The resulting pandemic stimulus payments were classic examples of fiscal policy: the use of taxes, government transfers, or government purchases of goods and services to stabilize the economy by shifting the aggregate demand curve.

Expansionary and Contractionary Fiscal Policy

Recall from Module 3.5 that a recessionary gap exists when short-run equilibrium is below full employment and an inflationary gap exists when it is above full employment. When the economy experiences a recessionary gap, aggregate demand must increase for the economy to move equilibrium aggregate output to equal potential output. **Expansionary fiscal policy** is used to increase aggregate demand to close a recessionary gap. Expansionary fiscal policy can include increasing government spending or transfers, or decreasing taxes. When the economy is experiencing an inflationary gap, aggregate demand must decrease to move equilibrium output to equal potential output and reduce the price level. **Contractionary fiscal policy** is used to decreases aggregate demand to close an inflationary gap. Contractionary fiscal policy can include decreasing government spending or transfers, or increasing taxes.

Expansionary fiscal policy increases aggregate demand to close a recessionary gap; it involves the government increasing spending or transfer payments, or decreasing taxes.

Contractionary fiscal policy decreases aggregate demand to close an inflationary gap; it involves the government decreasing spending or transfer payments, or increasing taxes.

Figure 3.8-1 shows an economy facing a recessionary gap. *SRAS* is the short-run aggregate supply curve, *LRAS* is the long-run aggregate supply curve, and AD_1 is the initial aggregate demand curve. At the initial short-run macroeconomic equilibrium, E_1, aggregate output is Y_1, below potential output Y_P. The government would like to increase aggregate demand, shifting the aggregate demand curve rightward to AD_2. This would increase aggregate output, making it equal to potential output. Expansionary fiscal policy, which increases aggregate demand, normally takes one of three forms:

- an increase in government purchases of goods and services
- an increase in government transfers
- a cut in taxes.

FIGURE 3.8-1 Expansionary Fiscal Policy Can Close a Recessionary Gap

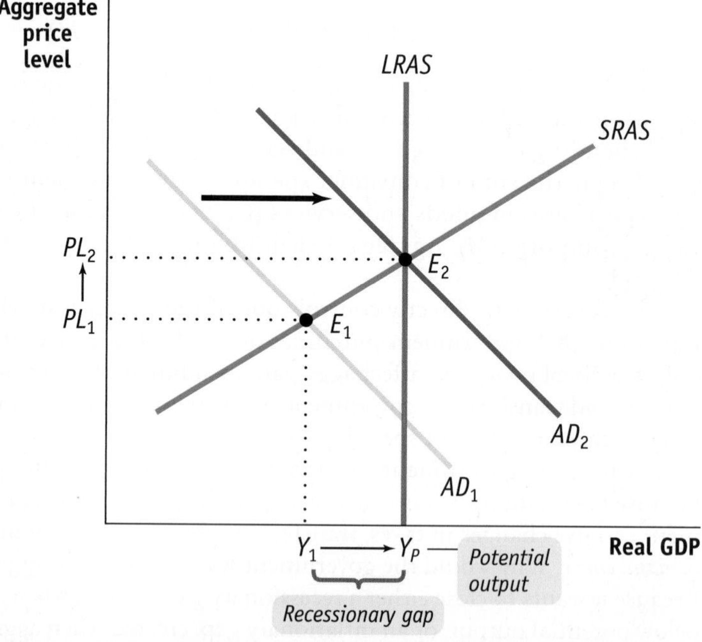

At E_1, the economy is in short-run macroeconomic equilibrium and there is a recessionary gap of $Y_P - Y_1$. Expansionary fiscal policy shifts the aggregate demand curve rightward from AD_1 to AD_2, moving the economy to long-run macroeconomic equilibrium.

Figure 3.8-2 shows the opposite case—an economy facing an inflationary gap. At the initial equilibrium, E_1, aggregate output is Y_1, above potential output, Y_P. Policy makers often try to head off inflation by eliminating inflationary gaps. To eliminate the inflationary gap shown in Figure 3.8-2, fiscal policy must reduce aggregate demand

FIGURE 3.8-2 Contractionary Fiscal Policy Can Close an Inflationary Gap

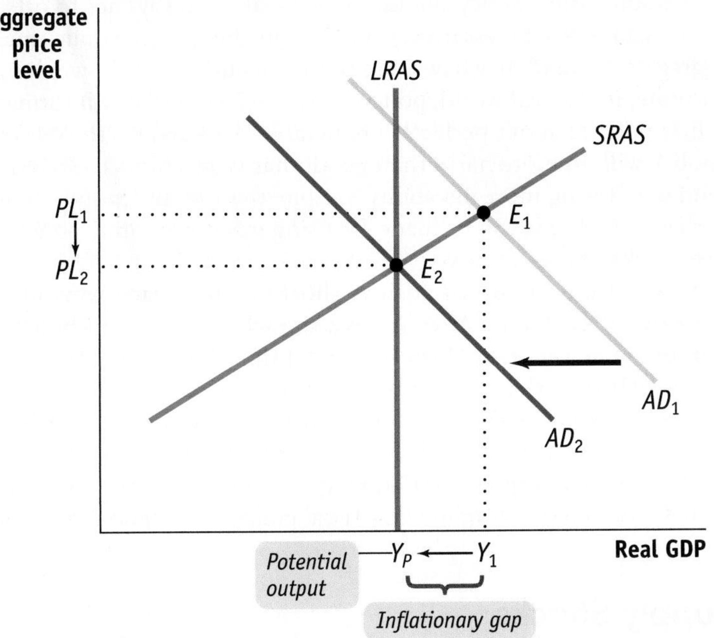

At E_1, the economy is in short-run macroeconomic equilibrium and there is an inflationary gap of $Y_1 - Y_P$. Contractionary fiscal policy shifts the aggregate demand curve leftward from AD_1 to AD_2, moving the economy to long-run macroeconomic equilibrium.

and shift the aggregate demand curve leftward to AD_2. This reduces aggregate output and makes it equal to potential output. Contractionary fiscal policy, which reduces aggregate demand, is implemented by

- a reduction in government purchases of goods and services,
- a reduction in government transfers, and
- an increase in taxes.

A classic example of contractionary fiscal policy occurred in 1968, when U.S. policy makers grew worried about rising inflation. President Lyndon Johnson imposed a temporary 10% surcharge on income taxes—everyone's income taxes were increased by 10%. He also tried to scale back government purchases of goods and services, which had risen dramatically because of the cost of the Vietnam War. To address demand-pull inflation—where too much money was chasing too few goods—contractionary fiscal policy reduced the amount of disposable income ("money") chasing goods in the economy.

AP® ECON TIP

Expansionary fiscal policy is used when there is a recessionary gap, and it involves the government increasing *G* or *Tr*, or decreasing *T*. Contractionary fiscal policy is used when there is an inflationary gap, and it involves the government decreasing *G* or *Tr*, or increasing *T*.

The Role of Fiscal Policy in Offsetting Supply and Demand Shocks

If fiscal policy were able to perfectly anticipate shifts of the aggregate demand curve and counteract them, it could short-circuit the whole long-run adjustment process shown in Figure 3.7-3. Instead of going through a period of low aggregate output and falling prices, the government could manage the economy so that it would stay at E_1.

Why might a policy that short-circuits the adjustment shown in Figure 3.7-3 and maintains the economy at its original equilibrium be desirable? There are two reasons: First, the temporary fall in aggregate output that would happen without policy intervention is a bad thing, particularly because such a decline is associated with high unemployment. Second, *price stability* is generally regarded as a desirable goal. So preventing both inflation and deflation—a fall in the aggregate price level—is a good thing.

Offsetting Demand Shocks

Given the benefits of stabilization policy, should policy makers always act to offset declines in aggregate demand? Not necessarily. As we'll see in Unit 5, some policy measures to increase aggregate demand may have long-term costs in terms of lower long-run growth. Furthermore, in the real world, policy makers aren't perfectly informed, and the effects of their policies aren't perfectly predictable. This creates the danger that stabilization policy will do more harm than good; that is, attempts to stabilize the economy may end up creating more instability. Despite these qualifications, most economists believe that a good case can be made for using macroeconomic policy to offset major negative shocks to the *AD* curve.

Should policy makers also try to offset positive shocks to aggregate demand? It may not seem obvious that they should. After all, even though inflation may be a bad thing, isn't more output and lower unemployment a good thing? Again, not necessarily. Most economists now believe that any short-run gains from an inflationary gap must be paid back later. So policy makers today usually try to offset positive as well as negative demand shocks. For reasons we'll explain later, except in extreme cases, attempts to eliminate recessionary gaps and inflationary gaps usually rely on monetary rather than fiscal policy. For now, let's explore how fiscal policy can respond to supply shocks.

Offsetting Supply Shocks

In panel (a) of Figure 3.6-2, we showed the effects of a negative supply shock: in the short run, such a shock leads to lower aggregate output and a higher aggregate price level. As we've noted, policy makers can respond to a negative *demand* shock by increasing aggregate demand to its original level. But what can or should they do about a negative *supply* shock?

In contrast to the case of a demand shock, there are no easy remedies for a supply shock. That is, there are no government policies that can easily counteract the changes in production costs that shift the short-run aggregate supply curve. So the policy response to a negative supply shock cannot aim to simply push the curve that shifted back to its original position.

To further complicate matters, when an economy is experiencing a supply shock, two bad things are happening simultaneously: a fall in aggregate output leading to a rise in unemployment *and* a rise in the aggregate price level. Any fiscal policy that shifts the aggregate demand curve alleviates one problem only by making the other problem worse. If the government acts to increase aggregate demand and limit the rise in unemployment, it will reduce the decline in output, but it will also cause even more inflation. If it acts to reduce aggregate demand, it will curb inflation, but it will also cause a further rise in unemployment. The advisability of using fiscal policy to address supply shocks in the economy is much less clear than in the case of demand shocks.

Multiplier Effects and Fiscal Policy

Once a government that has decided to pursue fiscal policy to stabilize the economy has identified the type of policy required – expansionary or contractionary – it must then decide whether to change government spending, transfers, or taxes to close the output gap in the economy. In addition, the government must also consider additional calculations. Recall from Module 3.2 that, because of the multiplier process, the government must calculate the initial change in government spending, transfers, or taxes that will move aggregate demand the required amount to close the output gap. The multiplier – either the expenditure or the tax multiplier – is required to calculate the initial change needed to stabilize the economy considering all rounds of spending that result from the initial change.

Multiplier Effects of Changes in Government Purchases

Increases in government spending, such as the American Recovery and Reinvestment Act of 2009 or the CARES Act of 2020, shift the aggregate demand curve to the right. A decrease in government spending addresses inflation by shifting the aggregate demand curve to the left. For policy makers, however, knowing the direction of the shift isn't enough: they also need estimates of *how much* the aggregate demand curve will be shifted by a given policy. To get these estimates, they use multipliers.

Suppose that a government decides to spend $50 billion to build bridges and roads. The government's purchases of goods and services will directly increase total spending on final goods and services by $50 billion. But, as we saw in Module 3.2, there will also be an indirect effect because the government's purchases will start a chain reaction throughout the economy. The firms producing the goods and services purchased by the government will earn revenues that flow to households in the form of wages, profit, interest, and rent. This increase in disposable income will lead to a rise in consumer spending. The rise in consumer spending, in turn, will induce firms to increase output, leading to a further rise in disposable income, which will lead to another round of consumer spending increases, and so on. We can use the expenditure multiplier – the factor by which we multiply the amount of an autonomous change in aggregate spending – to find the resulting change in real GDP. An increase in government purchases of goods and services is an example of an autonomous increase in aggregate spending. The initial change in spending multiplied by the expenditure multiplier gives us the final change in real GDP.

Consider this example: If the marginal propensity to consume is 0.5, the expenditure multiplier is $1/(1 - 0.5) = 1/0.5 = 2$. Given an expenditure multiplier of 2, a $50 billion increase in government purchases of goods and services would increase real GDP by $100 billion. Of that $100 billion, $50 billion is the initial, or autonomous, effect from the increase in G, and the remaining $50 billion is the subsequent effect of more production leading to more income, which leads to more consumer spending, which leads to more production, and so on.

What happens if government purchases of goods and services are reduced instead? The math is exactly the same, except that there's a minus sign in front: if government purchases of goods and services fall by $50 billion and the marginal propensity to consume is 0.5, real GDP falls by $100 billion. This is the result of less production leading to less income, which leads to less consumption, which leads to less production, and so on.

SAUL LOEB/Getty Images

When the government hires Boeing to build military aircraft, Boeing employees spend their earnings on things like cars, and the automakers spend their earnings on things like education, and so on, creating a multiplier effect.

Multiplier Effects of Changes in Taxes or Transfer Payments

The government can also affect aggregate demand in the economy by changing taxes or transfers. Recall that consumer spending depends primarily on disposable income – income that households have left to spend after paying taxes. So, in addition to affecting aggregate demand directly through changes in government spending, the government can affect it indirectly through changes in taxes or transfers. Recall that in general, however, a change in taxes or transfers shifts the aggregate demand curve by *less* than an equal-sized change in government purchases, resulting in a smaller effect on real GDP.

For example, imagine that instead of spending $50 billion to build bridges, the government simply reduces taxes by $50 billion. In this case, there is no direct effect on aggregate demand as there was with government purchases of goods and services. Real GDP and income grow only because households spend some of that $50 billion – and they probably won't spend it all. In fact, they will spend additional income according to the *MPC*. If the *MPC* is 0.5, households will spend only 50 cents of every additional dollar they receive in income, or \$25 billion. Recall that if the marginal propensity to consume is 0.5, the tax multiplier is $-0.5/(1-0.5)=-0.5/0.5=-1$. Given a tax multiplier of -1, a \$50 billion decrease in government purchases of goods and services would increase real GDP by \$50 billion. Of that \$50 billion, \$25 billion is the initial change in spending from the decrease in taxes, and the remaining \$25 billion is the subsequent effect of more production leading to more income, which leads to more consumer spending, which leads to more production, and so on.

The absolute value of the tax multiplier is used to calculate the required change in transfer payments. The numerator of the multiplier is the *MPC* because transfer payments have an indirect effect on aggregate demand, but the sign of the multiplier is positive because increasing transfer payments will increase income (the opposite of an increase in taxes).

Estimating Initial Changes in Government Spending, Taxes, and Transfer Payments

We can use an example to see how the government can use the multiplier to estimate the required initial change in government spending, taxes, or transfer payments to close an output gap and move the economy back to long-run equilibrium at potential output. Refer to panel (a) in **Figure 3.8-3**, which shows an economy experiencing a recessionary gap. To close a recessionary gap, the government would use expansionary fiscal policy. Note that short-run equilibrium output is *below* potential output and the negative output gap is equal to (500 – 300), or 200. So the government can close the negative output gap of 200 by *increasing* government spending (*G*), *increasing* transfer payments (*Tr*), or *decreasing* taxes (*T*).

FIGURE 3.8-3 **Estimating Aggregate Demand Change to Close an Output Gap (*MPC* = 0.8)**

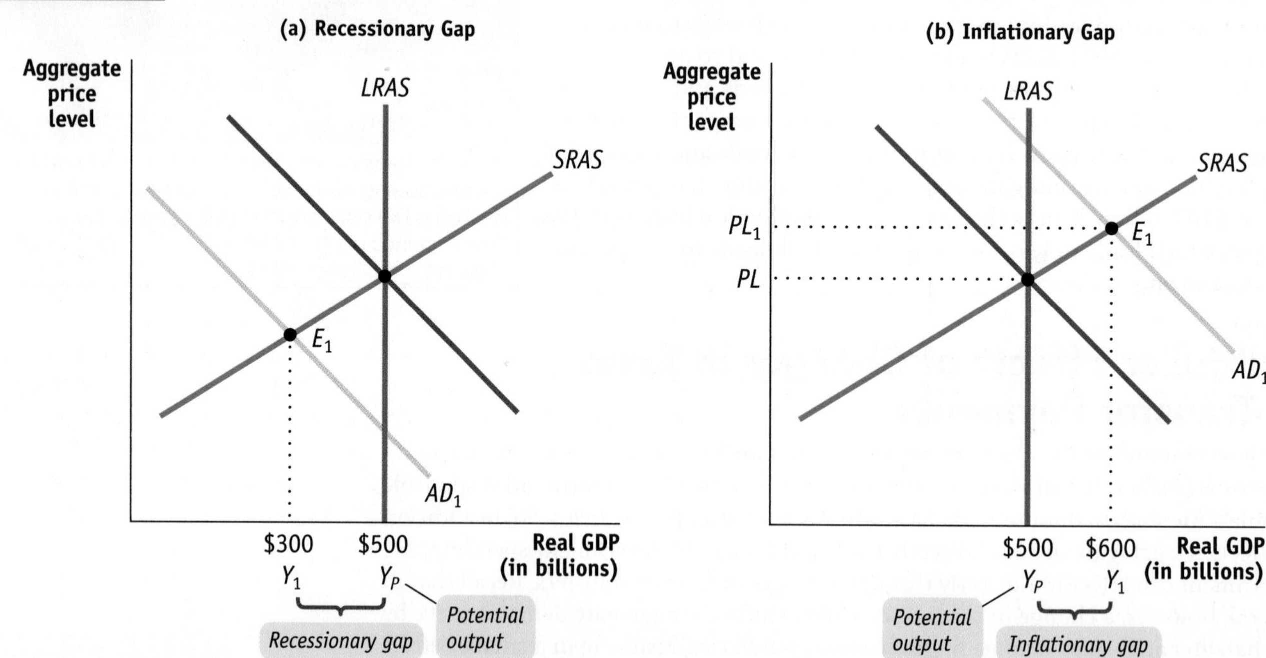

Panel (a) shows an economy experiencing a recessionary gap equal to 200. The government can close the negative output gap of 200 by *increasing* government spending (G), *increasing* transfer payments (*Tr*), or *decreasing* taxes (*T*). Panel (b) shows an economy experiencing an inflationary gap equal to 100. The government can close the positive output gap of 100 by *decreasing* government spending (G), *decreasing* transfer payments (*Tr*), or *increasing* taxes (*T*).

With an *MPC* of 0.8, we can calculate both the expenditure multiplier and the tax multiplier and use them to calculate the required initial change in G, *Tr*, or *T*. (Note: While the government could use a combination of changes in G, *Tr*, and/or *T*, we will only consider changes in each individually.) The expenditure multiplier is equal to $1/(1-0.8)=1/0.2=5$, and the tax multiplier is equal to $-0.8/(1-0.8)=-0.8/0.2=-4$. The absolute value of the tax multiplier is used to calculate the required change in *Tr*. So we can now use these values to calculate the initial changes required to close the negative output gap of 200 as shown below:

$$\Delta G \times \text{expenditure multiplier} = 200$$
$$\Delta G \times 5 = 200$$
$$\Delta G = 200/5 = 40$$

$$\Delta Tr \times \text{tax multiplier} = 200$$
$$\Delta Tr \times 4 = 200$$
$$\Delta Tr = 200/4 = 50$$

$$\Delta T \times \text{tax multiplier} = 200$$
$$\Delta T \times -4 = 200$$
$$\Delta T = 200/-4 = -50$$

Now let's calculate the initial changes required to close an inflationary gap. Panel (b) in Figure 3.8-3 shows an economy experiencing an inflationary gap. Note that short-run equilibrium output is *above* potential output and the positive output gap is equal to (600 – 500), or 100. So the government can close the positive output gap of 100 by *decreasing* government spending (G), *decreasing* transfer payments (*Tr*), or *increasing* taxes (*T*). With the *MPC* of 0.8, we know the expenditure multiplier is equal to 5 and the tax multiplier is equal to –4. So we can now use these values to calculate the initial changes required to close the positive output gap of 100 as shown below:

$$\Delta G \times \text{expenditure multiplier} = -100$$
$$\Delta G \times 5 = -100$$
$$\Delta G = -100/5 = -20$$

$$\Delta Tr \times \text{tax multiplier} = -100$$
$$\Delta Tr \times 4 = -100$$
$$\Delta Tr = -100/4 = -25$$

$$\Delta T \times \text{tax multiplier} = -100$$
$$\Delta T \times -4 = -100$$
$$\Delta T = -100/-4 = 25$$

Because the multipliers are different, the size of the initial changes in G and *T* required to close the gap are different. The expenditure multiplier will always be larger than the tax multiplier because G has a direct effect on aggregate demand, while the effect of *T* (and *Tr*) is indirect. In fact, the absolute difference between the expenditure multiplier and the tax multiplier will always be equal to 1. In our example, 5 – 4 = 1.

The difference between the expenditure and tax multipliers has an important implication for fiscal policy. When a government collects taxes to cover its expenditures, it keeps its budget balanced. Increasing government spending and taxes activates both the expenditure multiplier and the tax multiplier. The expenditure multiplier applies to the government spending, and the tax multiplier applies to the equivalent taxes. We can use the example above to see what happens when government spending and taxes increase by the same amount, keeping the government budget balanced.

An increase in spending of 100 would be multiplied by 5 (the expenditure multiplier), causing a total increase in real GDP of 500. An equivalent increase in taxes of 100 would be multiplied by –4 (the tax multiplier), causing a decrease in real GDP of 400. The budget would be balanced, but the net effect on real GDP is an increase of 500 – 400 = 100. Notice that this figure is the same as the original change in both government spending and taxes! This situation describes what is known as the **balanced budget multiplier**.

AP® ECON TIP

Simplify your calculations! The tax multiplier is always 1 less than the expenditure multiplier and has the opposite sign. When taxes and government spending both increase or decrease by the same amount, the net change in real GDP is simply the change in government spending. That is, the *balanced budget multiplier* is simply 1.

The **balanced budget multiplier** is the factor by which a change in both spending and taxes changes real GDP.

We find the balanced budget multiplier by adding the spending and tax multipliers together: $[1/(1-MPC)]+[(-MPC)/(1-MPC)]=(1-MPC)/(1-MPC)=1$. The balanced budget multiplier shows that the factor by which we multiply a simultaneous change in both spending and taxes to find the resulting total change in real GDP is always equal to 1, as confirmed by our example above. Any equal change in G and T will change real GDP by that amount.

Creative Crop/Getty Images

In practice, economists often argue that it also matters *who* among the population gets tax cuts or increases in government transfers. For example, consider the effects of an increase in unemployment benefits compared to the effects of a cut in taxes on corporate profits. Consumer surveys suggest that the average unemployed person will spend a higher share of any increase in their disposable income than would the average recipient of corporate profits. That is, people who are unemployed tend to have a higher *MPC* and tend to save less of any increase in disposable income. If that's true, a dollar spent on unemployment benefits increases aggregate demand more than a dollar's worth of corporate tax cuts. Such arguments played an important role in debates about the final provisions of the 2008 and 2020 stimulus packages.

A Cautionary Note: Lags in Fiscal Policy

Given our discussion of the use of the *AD–AS* model to close recessionary and inflationary gaps using fiscal policy, it may seem obvious that the government should actively use fiscal policy—that it should always adopt an expansionary fiscal policy when the economy faces a recessionary gap and always adopt a contractionary fiscal policy when the economy faces an inflationary gap. But many economists caution against an extremely active stabilization policy, arguing that a government that tries too hard to stabilize the economy through fiscal policy may end up making the economy less stable.

One key reason for caution when using fiscal policy is that there are important *time lags*. To understand the nature of these lags, think about what has to happen before the government increases spending to fight a recessionary gap. First, the government has to realize that the recessionary gap exists: it takes time for economic data to be collected and analyzed, and recessions are often recognized only months after they have begun. Second, the government has to develop a spending plan, which can itself take months, particularly if politicians take time debating how the money should be spent before passing legislation. Finally, it takes time to actually spend the money. For example, a road construction project begins with relatively inexpensive activities, such as surveying. It may be quite some time before the big spending begins.

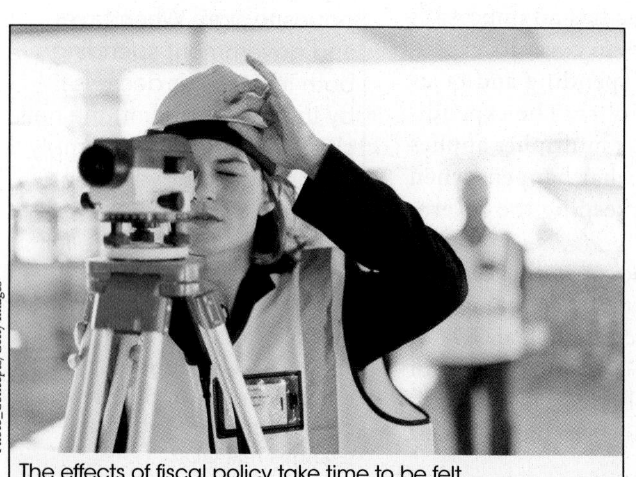
Photo_Concepts/Getty Images

The effects of fiscal policy take time to be felt.

Because of these lags, an attempt to increase spending to fight a recessionary gap may take so long to get going that the economy has already recovered on its own. In fact, the recessionary gap may have turned into an inflationary gap by the time the fiscal policy takes effect. In that case, the fiscal policy will make things worse instead of better.

This doesn't mean that fiscal policy should never be actively used. In early 2008, for example, there was good reason to believe that the U.S. economy had begun a lengthy slowdown caused by turmoil in the financial markets. And in 2020, the economic shut-down in response to the COVID-19 pandemic made it clear that the economy would experience a recession. In each of these cases, a fiscal stimulus designed to arrive quickly would almost surely push aggregate demand in the right direction. But the problem of lags makes the actual use of fiscal policy harder than you might think based on a simple analysis, like the one we have just given.

Adventures in AP® Economics

Watch the video: *Fiscal Policy*

Module 3.8 Review

Check Your Understanding

1. In each of the following cases, determine whether the policy described is an expansionary or contractionary fiscal policy:
   a. Several military bases around the country, which together employ tens of thousands of people, are closed.
   b. The number of weeks an unemployed person is eligible for unemployment benefits is increased.
   c. The federal tax on gasoline is increased.
2. Explain why a $500 million increase in government purchases of goods and services will generate a larger rise in real GDP than a $500 million increase in government transfers. Why is the tax multiplier smaller than the expenditure multiplier for a decrease in government purchases?
3. Explain why federal disaster relief, which quickly disburses funds to victims of natural disasters such as hurricanes, floods, and large-scale crop failures, will stabilize the economy more effectively after a disaster than relief that must be legislated.

Tackle the AP® Test: Multiple-Choice Questions

1. Which of the following contributes to the lag in implementing fiscal policy?
   a. It takes time for policy makers to agree on and pass spending and tax changes.
   b. Current economic data take time to collect and analyze.
   c. It takes time for policy makers to realize an output gap exists.
   d. It takes time for changes in spending and tax policy to take effect.
   e. All of the above contribute.
2. Which of the following is an example of expansionary fiscal policy?
   a. increasing taxes
   b. increasing government spending
   c. decreasing government transfers
   d. decreasing interest rates
   e. increasing the money supply
3. Which of the following is a fiscal policy that is appropriate to combat inflation?
   a. decreasing taxes
   b. decreasing government spending
   c. increasing government transfers
   d. decreasing interest rates
   e. expansionary fiscal policy
4. A cut in income taxes is an example of
   a. an expansionary fiscal policy.
   b. a contractionary fiscal policy.
   c. an expansionary monetary policy.
   d. a contractionary monetary policy.
   e. none of the above
5. Which of the following is an example of a fiscal policy appropriate to combat unemployment?
   a. increasing taxes
   b. decreasing government spending
   c. increasing government transfers
   d. increasing interest rates
   e. contractionary fiscal policy
6. The maximum effect on real GDP of a $10 million increase in government purchases of goods and services will be
   a. an increase of $10 million.
   b. an increase of more than $10 million.
   c. an increase of less than $10 million.
   d. an increase of either more than or less than $10 million, depending on the *MPC*.
   e. a decrease of $10 million.
7. If the *MPC* is 0.8 and government spending and taxes are both increased by $10 million, which of the following is true?
   a. The expenditure multiplier is 5.
   b. The tax multiplier is equal to −4.
   c. The budget deficit will not increase.
   d. Real GDP will increase by $10 million.
   e. All of the above are true.

Tackle the AP® Test: Free-Response Questions

1. Assume the *MPC* in an economy is 0.8 and the government increases government purchases of goods and services by $60 million.
   a. What is the value of the expenditure multiplier?
   b. By how much will real GDP change as a result of the increase in government purchases?
   c. What would happen to the size of the effect on real GDP if the *MPC* fell? Explain.
   d. Suppose the government collects $60 million in taxes to balance its $60 million in expenditures. By how much would real GDP change as a result of this increase in both government spending and taxes?

Rubric for FRQ 1 (5 points)

1 point: Expenditure multiplier = 1/(1 – *MPC*) = 1/(1 – 0.8) = 1/0.2 = 5

1 point: $60 million × 5 = $300 million

1 point: It would decrease.

1 point: The expenditure multiplier is 1/(1 – *MPC*). A fall in *MPC* increases the denominator.

1 point: $60 million × 1 = $60 million

2. A change in government purchases of goods and services results in a change in real GDP equal to $200 million.
   a. Suppose that the *MPC* is equal to 0.75. What was the size of the change in government purchases of goods and services that resulted in the increase in real GDP of $200 million?
   b. Now suppose that the change in government purchases of goods and services was $20 million. What value of the expenditure multiplier would result in an increase in real GDP of $200 million?
   c. Given the value of the expenditure multiplier you calculated in part b, what marginal propensity to save would have led to that value of the expenditure multiplier? **(3 points)**

Automatic Stabilizers

MODULE 3.9

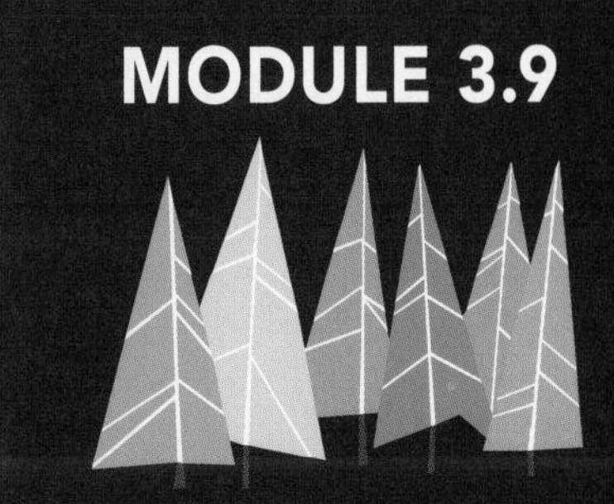

In this Module, you will learn to:

- Define automatic stabilizers and describe how they moderate business cycles
- Explain how automatic stabilizers support the economy during recessions and help prevent inflation during expansionary periods
- Describe how tax revenues and social service programs can act as automatic stabilizers
- Describe and compare alternative ways the economy moves toward full-employment output following a demand shock

A Brief History of Stabilization Policy

In the previous Module, we described the theoretical rationale for stabilization policy as a way of responding to demand shocks. But does stabilization policy actually stabilize the economy? One way we might try to answer this question is to look at the long-term historical record, as shown in **Figure 3.9-1.**

FIGURE 3.9-1 Stabilization Policy, 1890–2019

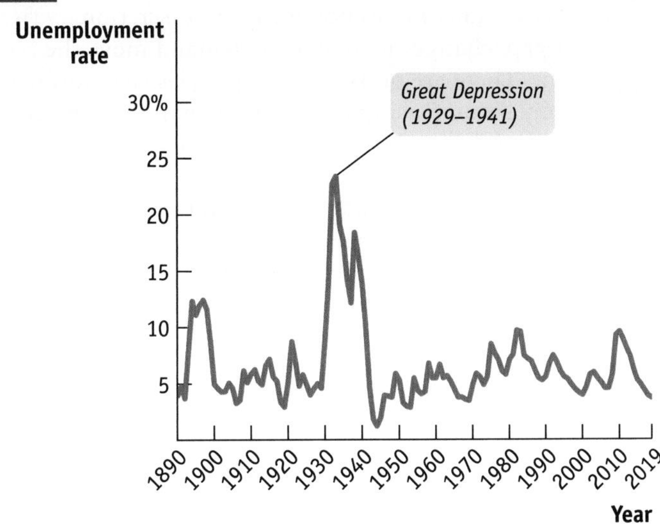

The data show the number of unemployed as a percentage of the nonfarm labor force from 1890 to 2019. The unemployment rate fluctuated significantly before World War II compared to the years after, suggesting that the government's stabilization policies were effective.

Before World War II, the U.S. government didn't really have a stabilization policy, largely because macroeconomics as we know it didn't exist and there was no consensus about what to do in the event of a shock. Since World War II, and especially since 1960, active stabilization policy has become standard practice.

So here's the question: Has the U.S. economy actually become more stable since the government began trying to stabilize it? The answer is a qualified yes. It's qualified because data from the pre–World War II era are less reliable than more modern data. But there still seems to be a clear reduction in the size of economic fluctuations.

Figure 3.9-1 shows the number of unemployed as a percentage of the nonfarm labor force since 1890. (We focus on nonfarm workers sometimes because farmers, though they often suffer economic hardship, are rarely reported as unemployed.) Even ignoring the huge spike in unemployment during the Great Depression, unemployment seems to have varied a lot more before World War II than after. It's also worth noticing that the peaks in postwar unemployment in 1975 and 1982 corresponded to major supply shocks—the kind of shock for which stabilization policy has no good answer.

It's possible that the increased stability of the post–World War II economy reflects good luck rather than policy. But on the face of it, the evidence suggests that stabilization policy is indeed stabilizing. However, stabilization of the economy is not only accomplished by the government taking an action regarding *G*, *T*, or *Tr*. Some stabilizing fiscal policies have been built into the economy. In this Module, we will look at built-in stabilization policies in the economy.

Discretionary Versus Non-Discretionary Fiscal Policy

The fiscal policies discussed in Module 3.8 are examples of **discretionary fiscal policy.** Discretionary fiscal policy is fiscal policy that is the direct result of deliberate actions by policy makers. For example, during a recession, the government may pass legislation that cuts taxes and increases government spending or transfers in order to stimulate the economy. Or, when the economy is experiencing inflation, the government may pass legislation that raises taxes or decreases government spending in order to reduce price-level increases. In general, mainly due to problems with time lags as discussed in the previous Module, economists tend to support the use of discretionary fiscal policy only in special circumstances, such as during an especially severe recession.

But even when the government does not engage in discretionary fiscal policy in response to an output gap, changes in aggregate demand move the economy back toward full employment. There are built-in fiscal policies that automatically work to stabilize the economy by increasing aggregate demand during recessions and reducing aggregate demand during inflation. These *non-discretionary policies* require no legislation or other action—they happen automatically based on established rules created by government. Government spending and taxation rules can cause fiscal policy to be automatically expansionary when the economy contracts and automatically contractionary when the economy expands. These rules, which stabilize the economy without requiring any deliberate action by policy makers, are called **automatic stabilizers**.

Discretionary fiscal policy is fiscal policy that is the result of deliberate actions by policy makers rather than rules.

Automatic stabilizers are government spending and taxation rules that cause fiscal policy to be automatically expansionary when the economy contracts and automatically contractionary when the economy expands.

One example of an automatic stabilizer is the rules that govern tax collection. The increase in government tax revenue when real GDP rises is not the result of a deliberate decision or action by the government. Rather, it is a consequence of the way the tax laws are written, which causes most sources of government revenue to increase *automatically* when real GDP goes up. For example, income tax receipts increase when real GDP rises because the amount each individual owes in taxes depends positively on their income, and households' taxable income rises when real GDP rises. Sales tax receipts increase when real GDP rises because people with more income spend more on goods and services. And corporate profit tax receipts increase when real GDP rises because profits increase when the economy expands.

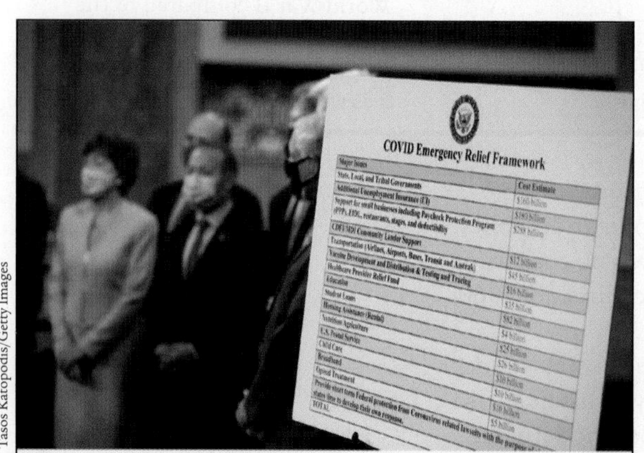

Tasos Karopodis/Getty Images

Discretionary fiscal policy was demonstrated by the government response to the COVID pandemic, including the CARES Act and other legislative proposals to stabilize the economy.

The effect of these automatic increases in tax revenue is to reduce the size of the expenditure and tax multipliers. Remember, the multipliers are the result of a chain reaction in which higher real GDP leads to higher disposable income, which leads to higher consumer spending, which leads to further increases in real GDP. The fact that the government siphons off some of any increase in real GDP means that at each stage of this process, the increase in consumer spending is smaller than it would be if taxes weren't part of the picture. As a result, these multipliers become smaller.

Many macroeconomists believe it's a good thing that taxes reduce the multipliers in real life. Most, though not all, recessions are the result of negative demand shocks. The same mechanism that causes tax revenue to increase when the economy expands causes it to decrease when the economy contracts. Since tax receipts decrease when real GDP falls, the effects of these negative demand shocks are smaller than they would be if there were no taxes. In other words, the decrease in tax revenue reduces the adverse effect of the initial fall in aggregate demand. The automatic decrease in government tax revenue generated by a fall in real GDP – caused by a decrease in the amount of taxes households pay – acts like an automatic expansionary fiscal policy implemented in the face of a recession. Similarly, when the economy expands, the government finds itself automatically pursuing a contractionary fiscal policy – a tax increase.

> **AP® ECON TIP**
>
> Discretionary fiscal policy requires an action by the government. Automatic stabilizers are an example of non-discretionary fiscal policy because no action by the government is required—they stabilize the economy *automatically*.

The rules that govern tax collection aren't the only automatic stabilizers, although they are the most important ones. Some types of government transfers also play a stabilizing role. For example, more people receive unemployment insurance when the economy is in a recession than when it is expanding. The same is true of Medicaid (means-tested health insurance) and SNAP (the Supplemental Nutrition Assistance Program), programs that provide medical and food assistance. As income falls during a recession, more people become eligible for these programs and as the economy recovers, fewer people remain eligible. So transfer payments tend to automatically rise when the economy is contracting and fall when the economy is expanding. Like changes in tax revenue, these automatic changes in transfers tend to reduce the size of the multipliers because the total change in disposable income that results from a given rise or fall in real GDP is smaller.

> **AP® ECON TIP**
>
> Automatic stabilizers include a tax system in which tax revenue is positively related to income and spending on social programs—including unemployment insurance, Medicaid, and the SNAP program—is negatively related to income.

As in the case of government tax revenue, many macroeconomists believe that it's a good thing that government transfers reduce the expenditure and tax multipliers. Expansionary and contractionary fiscal policies that are the result of automatic stabilizers are widely considered helpful to macroeconomic stabilization, because they blunt the extremes of the business cycle.

Alternative Responses to Supply and Demand Shocks

In Modules 3.7 and 3.8, and in this Module, we have seen different ways that an economy can adjust back to a long-run equilibrium following a demand or supply shock. Now we can review and compare these adjustment processes when the economy faces a recessionary or inflationary gap.

Adjustment Following a Negative Demand Shock

We have seen that a negative demand shock can cause the short-run equilibrium aggregate output to fall below potential real GDP. Let's review each of the ways an economy can adjust back to a long-run equilibrium at potential output after experiencing a negative shock.

A negative demand shock decreases the short-run equilibrium real GDP by shifting the aggregate demand curve to the left, creating a recessionary gap. We have seen three different ways that the economy can be moved back toward a long-run equilibrium at full-employment real GDP: long-run self-adjustment, discretionary fiscal policy, and automatic stabilizers. In reality, each of these processes can contribute to recovery from a recession. But here we will consider each adjustment process individually.

Long-Run Self-Adjustment

As we saw in Module 3.7, in the absence of government policy actions, flexible wages and prices will adjust to restore full employment and potential real GDP. That is, the unemployment rate will increase to its natural rate after a negative demand or supply shock through an eventual decrease in nominal wages. With a recessionary gap, high unemployment (a surplus of workers) will drive down nominal wages, which causes the short-run aggregate supply curve to shift to the right, moving the economy back to the higher long-run equilibrium aggregate output.

The long-run adjustment process will occur only after wages and prices become flexible—that is, in the long run. The time it takes for the economy to self-adjust depends on the severity of the recession and the flexibility of wages and prices. During the time it takes the economy to adjust, people experience considerable pain from the reduced income and employment. And as John Maynard Keynes noted, in the long run we're all dead.

Discretionary Fiscal Policy

If the government chooses not to wait for the economy to self-adjust, it can pursue expansionary fiscal policy to close a recessionary gap. In the case of a recession, the government could increase government spending or transfer payments, or it can decrease taxes. The government would need to use the expenditure or tax multiplier to determine the initial change in autonomous spending required to close the recessionary gap and return the economy to full employment. But in reality, the process for discretionary fiscal policy is not so simple, and in some situations it could take longer than the self-adjustment process!

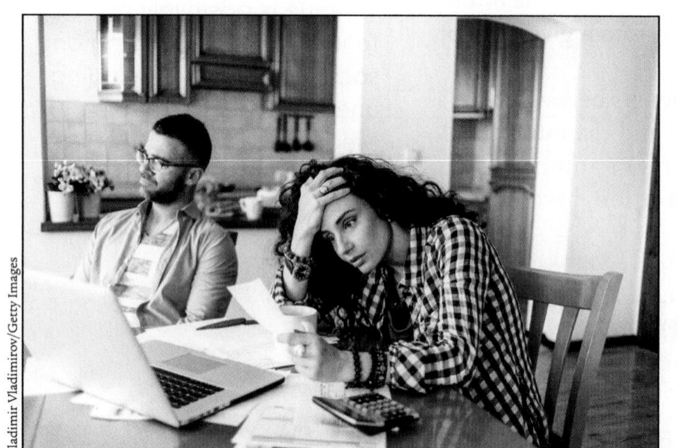
Vladimir Vladimirov/Getty Images

Policy makers rely on leading indicators—such as surveys suggesting consumer pessimism—to tell them that the economy might be in recession.

In order to pursue expansionary fiscal policy to close the recessionary gap, the government would need to first recognize that the economy is experiencing a recession. To identify or predict a recession, policy makers and economists look at *leading indicators*—data that provide an advance warning of an economic downturn. Leading economic indicators include surveys of business and consumer confidence. For example, when people become pessimistic about the economy, consumers will likely begin saving more (for the expected "rainy day") and businesses will delay planned investment (because they expect real GDP, and therefore their sales, to fall). If consumption and investment decrease, pessimism becomes a self-fulfilling prophecy of falling aggregate demand.

As this example illustrates, confidence indices can be leading economic indicators and provide advanced warning of a recession. But forecasts based on these data are not always correct or precise. It takes time for data to be collected and analyzed to confirm there has been a demand or supply shock. These data and recognition lags make it difficult to quickly implement discretionary fiscal policy following an economic shock. It also takes time for policy makers to deliberate and implement a desired discretionary fiscal policy—politics can often make changes in the government budget a long and difficult process. In addition, response lags also result from the time it takes for the increase in government spending, taxes, or transfers to initially change incomes and then for the multiplier process to play out. Finally, changes in taxes can also take time to take effect as a result of tax rules that make some taxes an annual payment.

To sum up: A variety of implementation lags, including *data lags*, *recognition lags*, and *response lags*, add to the time it takes for discretionary fiscal policy to adjust the economy back to long-run equilibrium.

Automatic Stabilizers

During a recession, equilibrium real GDP falls below potential real GDP. The fall in real GDP and corresponding increase in unemployment results in a decrease in people's income. Lower incomes automatically lead to a decrease in taxes, because taxes are often paid as a percentage of income; lower income, lower taxes. The decrease in taxes partially offsets the decrease in income and helps to prevent a larger decline in spending in the economy. Another automatic consequence of reduced income in the economy is that more people become eligible for programs designed to support unemployed and low-income households, such as unemployment insurance, Medicaid, and SNAP programs. Increased transfer payments through these programs partially offset income reductions resulting from the recession. Since these policies are built into the rules for tax and transfer programs, they do not experience all of the lags associated with discretionary fiscal policy. But while automatic stabilizers work automatically and relatively quickly, they only partially offset decreases in income and therefore only partially offset the negative demand shock that led to the recession.

AP® ECON TIP

There are lags to discretionary fiscal policy because of the time it takes to decide on and implement a policy action. It also takes time for the policy to take effect. Lags affecting fiscal policy include data lags, recognition lags, and response lags.

Adjustment Following a Positive Demand Shock

We have seen that a positive demand shock can cause the short-run equilibrium aggregate output to rise above potential real GDP, creating inflationary pressures in the economy. Let's review each of the ways an economy can adjust back to a long-run equilibrium at full-employment output after experiencing inflation resulting from a positive demand shock.

A positive demand shock increases the short-run equilibrium real GDP by shifting the aggregate demand curve to the right, creating an inflationary gap. We have seen three different ways that the economy can adjust back toward a long-run equilibrium at full-employment real GDP: long-run self-adjustment, discretionary fiscal policy, and automatic stabilizers. As with negative demand shocks, each of these processes can contribute to addressing an inflationary gap. We will consider each adjustment process individually.

Long-Run Self-Adjustment

Again, as we saw in Module 3.7, in the absence of government policy actions, flexible wages and prices will adjust to restore long-run equilibrium. That is, the unemployment rate will decrease to below its natural rate in the short run after a positive demand shock, which will eventually increase nominal wages. With an inflationary gap, low unemployment (a shortage of workers) will drive up nominal wages, which causes the short-run aggregate supply curve to shift to the left, moving the economy back to long-run equilibrium at the full-employment level of aggregate output *but at an even higher price level.* While the long-run adjustment process moves the economy to potential output, it leads to further inflation in the economy.

Discretionary Fiscal Policy

If the government chooses not to wait for self-adjustment, it can pursue contractionary fiscal policy to close an inflationary gap. To address inflation, the government could decrease government spending or transfer payments or increase taxes. The government would need to use the expenditure or tax multiplier to determine the initial change in autonomous spending that would close the inflationary gap and return the economy to full employment and reduce the price level. But pursuing contractionary fiscal policy can be as difficult as pursuing expansionary fiscal policy—and perhaps even more difficult because of the unique political difficulties related to cutting government spending and transfer payments or increasing taxes.

Like expansionary fiscal policy, contractionary fiscal policy would still involve data lags, recognition lags, and response lags.

ak_phuong/Getty Images

Delays, including congressional debates over spending and transfers, can impact the implementation of discretionary fiscal policy to close an inflation gap.

Automatic Stabilizers

With an inflationary gap, equilibrium real GDP increases to above the full-employment level. The rise in real GDP and corresponding decrease in unemployment results in an increase in people's income. Higher incomes automatically lead to an increase in government tax revenues, because taxes are positively related to income: higher income, higher taxes. The increase in taxes partially offsets the increase in income and helps to prevent "too much money chasing too few goods" that results in demand-pull inflation in the economy. Another automatic consequence of increased income in the economy is that fewer people become eligible for programs designed to support unemployed and low-income people. Decreased transfer payments through these programs partially offset income increases resulting from unemployment rates below the natural rate. Since these policies are built into the rules for tax and transfer programs, the lags associated with discretionary fiscal policy don't apply. But while automatic stabilizers work automatically and relatively quickly, they only partially offset the positive demand shock that led to the inflation.

Long-run self-adjustment process, discretionary fiscal policy, and automatic stabilizers can all move the economy back toward long-run equilibrium in response to a positive or negative demand shock. In the next Unit, we will consider another alternative for stabilizing the economy—*monetary policy*.

Module 3.9 Review

Check Your Understanding

1. What are the political and economic advantages of automatic stabilizers as compared to discretionary fiscal policy?
2. Why does discretionary fiscal policy take longer to begin addressing an output gap than non-discretionary fiscal policy?

Tackle the AP® Test: Multiple-Choice Questions

1. Which of the following is NOT an automatic stabilizer?
   - **a.** income taxes
   - **b.** unemployment insurance
   - **c.** Medicaid payments
   - **d.** SNAP payments
   - **e.** monetary policy
2. During a recession, automatic stabilizers act to stabilize the economy through which of the following?
   - **a.** actions taken by government to increase spending
   - **b.** the long-run self-adjustment process
   - **c.** actions taken by the government to increase taxes
   - **d.** monetary policy undertaken by the central bank
   - **e.** established rules for taxes and transfer payments
3. Which of the following is an example of a discretionary fiscal policy to close an inflationary gap?
   - **a.** the government increasing government spending
   - **b.** the government increasing the income tax rate
   - **c.** an increase in transfer payments due to increased eligibility
   - **d.** an increase in payments through existing social programs
   - **e.** a decrease in disposable income due to higher annual tax bills
4. Automatic stabilizers will cause which of the following to happen during a recession?
   - **a.** Transfer payments will decrease.
   - **b.** Income tax payments will increase.
   - **c.** Unemployment insurance payments will increase.
   - **d.** The government will increase spending.
   - **e.** all of the above
5. As the economy recovers from a recession, payments to low-income families through government social programs will
   - **a.** increase.
   - **b.** decrease.
   - **c.** end.
   - **d.** not change.
   - **e.** need to be reauthorized by the government.
6. Relative to automatic stabilizers, which of the following is a drawback of using discretionary fiscal policy to close an output gap?
   - **a.** data lag
   - **b.** recognition lag
   - **c.** implementation lags
   - **d.** response lag
   - **e.** all of the above

7. Relative to discretionary fiscal policy, which of the following is a drawback of using automatic stabilizers to close an output gap?
   a. The government must take an action.
   b. They include implementation lags.
   c. They only partially offset changes in aggregate demand.
   d. They more than offset changes in aggregate demand.
   e. They do not change consumer spending.

Tackle the AP® Test: Free-Response Questions

1. Refer to the following graph.

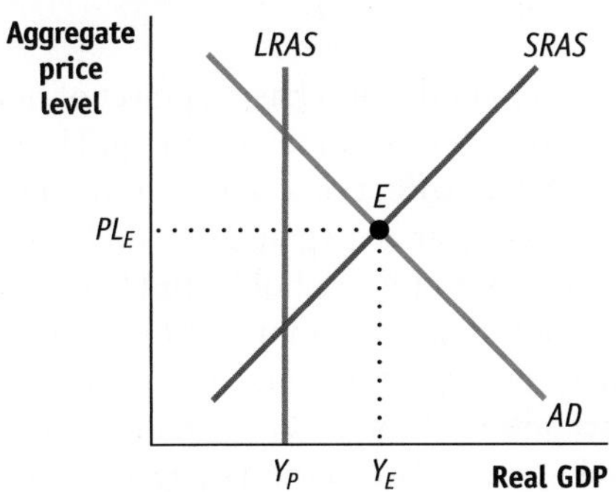

   a. What type of gap exists in this economy and what type of discretionary fiscal policy is appropriate in this situation?
   b. List the three variables the government can change to implement fiscal policy. How would each variable need to be changed to implement this policy?
   c. Assume the government takes no action to address the output gap in the economy. Identify the automatic stabilizers in the economy and explain how they will change income and move the economy back toward potential real GDP.

Rubric for FRQ 1 (10 points)

1 point: Inflationary
1 point: Contractionary
1 point: Taxes
1 point: Government transfers
1 point: Government purchases of goods and services
1 point: Increase taxes
1 point: Decrease government transfers
1 point: Decrease government purchases of goods and services
1 point: Either taxes as a percentage of income or a social program
1 point: An increase in taxes paid/decrease in transfer payments received will decrease disposable income, which will decrease consumer spending and therefore aggregate demand.

2. Draw a correctly labeled *AD–AS* graph showing an economy experiencing a recession. Label full-employment output on your graph as Y_f.
   a. Explain how the economy would self-adjust if the government decides to take no action.
   b. Identify the automatic stabilizers in the economy. If the government decides to take no action, explain how automatic stabilizers will move the economy toward the full-employment level of output. Show the resulting change on your graph.
   c. If the government decides to take an action, what type of discretionary fiscal policy is appropriate and how would the government change *G* and *T* to close the output gap? **(10 points)**

UNIT 3 Review

Adventures in AP® Economics Videos

Module 3.5: Aggregate Demand and Aggregate Supply
Module 3.8: Fiscal Policy

 UNIT 3 Review Video

economics by example
How Much Debt Is Too Much?

Module 3.1

1. The components of aggregate demand are C, I, G, and $(X - M)$. Consumption and investment are important components of aggregate demand discussed in this Module. G and $(X - M)$ are discussed in this Unit and in Unit 6. Consumer spending depends on disposable income and wealth. **Planned investment spending** depends negatively on the interest rate and on existing production capacity; it depends positively on expected future real GDP. **Inventory investment** is positive when firms add to their inventories, negative when they reduce them. Often, however, changes in inventories are not a deliberate decision but the result of mistakes in forecasts about sales.
2. The **aggregate demand curve** shows the relationship between the aggregate price level and the quantity of aggregate output demanded. It is downward-sloping for three reasons. The first is the **real wealth effect** of a change in the aggregate price level—a higher aggregate price level reduces the purchasing power of households' wealth and reduces consumer spending. The second is the **interest rate effect** of a change in the aggregate price level—a higher aggregate price level reduces the purchasing power of households' and firms' money holdings, leading to a rise in interest rates and a fall in investment spending and consumer spending. The third is the **exchange rate effect** of a change in the aggregate price level—an increase in the aggregate price level increases the relative price of exports and decreases the relative price of imports, which decreases net exports.
3. The aggregate demand curve shifts as a result of a change in any of the components of aggregate demand—C, I, G, X, or M—not due to changes in the price level. In particular, aggregate demand can shift because of changes in expectations, changes in wealth, and the effect of the size of the existing stock of physical capital. Policy makers can also influence aggregate demand.

Module 3.2

4. The **marginal propensity to consume, *MPC***, is the fraction of an additional dollar of disposable income spent on consumption. The fraction of an additional dollar of disposable income that is saved is called the **marginal propensity to save, *MPS***. The sum of the *MPC* and the *MPS* is equal to 1.
5. An **autonomous change in aggregate spending** leads to further changes in total expenditures and aggregate output. Initial changes in C, I, or G cause a chain reaction in which the total change in real GDP is equal to the expenditure multiplier times the initial change in aggregate spending. The **expenditure multiplier** quantifies the size of the change in aggregate demand that results from a change in any of the components of aggregate demand. A change in taxes will lead to a change in disposable income that will also have a multiplied effect on aggregate demand. The **tax multiplier** quantifies the size of the change in aggregate demand that results from a change in taxes. The size of the expenditure multiplier, $1/(1 - MPC)$, and the size of the tax multiplier, $-MPC/(1 - MPC)$, depend on the *MPC*. The larger the *MPC*, the larger the multiplier, and the larger the change in real GDP for any given autonomous change in aggregate spending.

Module 3.3

6. The **aggregate supply curve** shows the relationship between the aggregate price level and the quantity of aggregate output supplied.
7. The **short-run aggregate supply curve** is upward-sloping because **nominal wages** are **sticky** in the short run: a higher aggregate price level leads to higher profit per unit of output and increased aggregate output in the short run.
8. Any factor that causes production costs to change, such as a change in inflationary expectations, will cause the short-run aggregate supply curve to shift.
9. If the labor force is held constant, there is a short-run trade-off between inflation and unemployment. Holding the labor force constant, moving along the short-run aggregate supply curve is associated with moving along a graph of the inflation rate and the unemployment rate.

Module 3.4

10. In the long run, all prices, including nominal wages, are flexible and the economy produces at its **potential output**. So there is no *long-run* trade-off between inflation and unemployment. Another way to describe potential output is as the **full-employment output level** – the GDP that the economy can attain with full employment of all of its resources. The **long-run aggregate supply curve** is vertical at potential output.
11. The long-run aggregate supply curve corresponds to the production possibilities curve because they both represent maximum sustainable capacity – the total output an economy can produce if all resources are fully employed.

Module 3.5

12. In the ***AD–AS* model**, the intersection of the short-run aggregate supply curve and the aggregate demand curve is the point of **short-run equilibrium.** This is where the aggregate quantity of output demanded is equal to the aggregate quantity of output supplied. The **short-run aggregate price level** is found on the vertical axis at the equilibrium point, and the level of **short-run equilibrium aggregate output** is found on the horizontal axis at the equilibrium point. **Long-run equilibrium** occurs when short-run equilibrium occurs at the full-employment level of output along the long-run aggregate supply curve. That is, when the *AD*, *SRAS*, and *LRAS* curves all intersect.
13. The short-run equilibrium output can be at the full-employment output, above it, or below it. A **recessionary gap**, also known as a negative output gap, occurs when the equilibrium output is below the full-employment output. An **inflationary gap**, also known as a positive output gap, occurs when equilibrium output is above the full-employment output.

Module 3.6

14. Economic fluctuations occur because of a shift of the aggregate demand curve (a *demand shock*) or the short-run aggregate supply curve (a *supply shock*). A **demand shock** causes the aggregate price level and aggregate output to move in the same direction as the economy moves along the short-run aggregate supply curve. A **supply shock** causes them to move in opposite directions as the economy moves along the aggregate demand curve. A particularly nasty occurrence is **stagflation** – inflation and falling aggregate output – which is caused by a negative supply shock.
15. **Demand-pull inflation** is caused by changes in aggregate demand. And **cost-push inflation** is caused by changes in aggregate supply.

Module 3.7

16. In the long run, in the absence of government policy actions, flexible wages and prices will adjust to move the economy back to long-run equilibrium at the full-employment level of aggregate output after a shock to aggregate demand or short-run aggregate supply. If actual aggregate output exceeds potential output, nominal wages will eventually rise in response to low unemployment and aggregate output will fall. If potential output exceeds actual aggregate output, nominal wages will eventually fall in response to high unemployment, and aggregate output will rise.
17. Shifts in the long-run aggregate supply curve indicate changes in the full-employment level of output and economic growth.

Module 3.8

18. The high cost – in terms of unemployment – of a recessionary gap and the future adverse consequences of an inflationary gap lead many economists to advocate active stabilization policy: using **fiscal policy** to offset demand shocks. The government's fiscal policy tools are government spending, and taxes and transfers.
19. Negative supply shocks pose a policy dilemma: a policy that counteracts the fall in aggregate output by increasing aggregate demand will lead to higher inflation, but a policy that counteracts inflation by reducing aggregate demand will deepen the output slump.
20. Government purchases of goods and services *directly* affect aggregate demand, and changes in taxes and government transfers affect aggregate demand *indirectly* by changing households' disposable income. **Expansionary fiscal policy** is used to restore full employment when the economy is in a negative (recessionary) gap. Expansionary fiscal policy shifts the aggregate demand curve rightward, leading to an increase in real GDP; **contractionary fiscal policy** is used to restore full employment when the economy is in a positive (inflationary) output gap. Contractionary

fiscal policy shifts the aggregate demand curve leftward, leading to a decrease in real GDP.

21. Fiscal policy has a multiplied effect on the economy. Because part of any change in taxes or transfers is absorbed by savings in the first round of spending, changes in government purchases of goods and services have a larger multiplier than taxes and transfers. The **balanced budget multiplier** indicates the total increase in aggregate spending that results from each $1 increase in both government spending and taxes will equal $1.
22. In reality, implementing discretionary fiscal policy involves **lags** between the time a demand shock occurs and the time it takes to decide on and implement a policy action.

Module 3.9

23. Rules governing taxes and some transfers act as **automatic stabilizers**, reducing the size of the expenditure multiplier and automatically reducing the size of output gaps. In contrast, **discretionary fiscal policy** arises from deliberate actions by policy makers rather than from the business cycle.
24. Automatic stabilizers increase income during recessions and decrease income during expansions, to partially offset changes in aggregate demand and reduce output gaps. Tax revenues increase automatically as GDP rises, slowing consumption and preventing the economy from overheating. Tax revenues decrease automatically as GDP falls, preventing consumption and the economy from declining further. Social service transfer programs also act as automatic stabilizers, offsetting increases and decreases in income through corresponding decreases and increases in eligibility for transfer payments.

Key Terms

Wealth, p. 121
Planned investment spending, p. 122
Inventory investment, p. 123
Aggregate demand curve, p. 124
Real wealth effect, p. 125
Interest rate effect, p. 126
Exchange rate effect, p. 126
Marginal propensity to consume (*MPC*), p. 131
Marginal propensity to save (*MPS*), p. 131
Expenditure multiplier, p. 133
Tax multiplier, p. 135
Aggregate supply curve, p. 137
Nominal wage, p. 138
Sticky wages, p. 138
Short-run aggregate supply curve, p. 138
The short run, p. 145
The long run, p. 145
Long-run aggregate supply curve, p. 146
Potential output, p. 146
Full-employment output level, p. 146
AD–AS model, p. 150
Short-run macroeconomic equilibrium, p. 150
Short-run equilibrium aggregate price level, p. 150
Short-run equilibrium aggregate output, p. 150
Long-run macroeconomic equilibrium, p. 151
Output gap, p. 151
Recessionary gap, p. 153
Inflationary gap, p. 153
Demand shock, p. 156
Supply shock, p. 157
Stagflation, p. 157
Cost-push inflation, p. 158
Demand-pull inflation, p. 158
Fiscal policy, p. 168
Expansionary fiscal policy, p. 170
Contractionary fiscal policy, p. 170
Balanced budget multiplier, p. 175
Discretionary fiscal policy, p. 180
Automatic stabilizers, p. 180

AP® Exam Practice Questions

Multiple-Choice Questions

1. Which of the following will occur if the federal government reduces defense spending?
   a. Aggregate demand will increase.
   b. Aggregate demand will decrease.
   c. There will be no change in aggregate demand or supply.
   d. Aggregate supply will increase.
   e. Aggregate supply will decrease.
2. Which of the following will occur if an increase in interest rates leads to a decrease in investment spending?
   a. Aggregate demand will increase.
   b. Aggregate demand will decrease.
   c. There will be no change in aggregate demand or supply.
   d. Aggregate supply will increase.
   e. Aggregate supply will decrease.

3. Which of the following will occur in the short run as a result of an increase in the aggregate price level?
   a. Aggregate demand will increase.
   b. Aggregate demand will decrease.
   c. There will be no change in aggregate demand or supply.
   d. Aggregate supply will increase.
   e. Aggregate supply will decrease.

4. Which of the following will occur if the price of steel decreases as a result of the discovery of new deposits of iron ore used to make steel?
   a. Aggregate demand will increase.
   b. Aggregate demand will decrease.
   c. There will be no change in aggregate demand or supply.
   d. Aggregate supply will increase.
   e. Aggregate supply will decrease.

5. Sticky nominal wages in the short run cause the short-run aggregate supply curve to
   a. shift to the right.
   b. shift to the left.
   c. slope upward.
   d. slope downward.
   e. be vertical.

6. As a result of the real wealth effect, a higher aggregate price level will reduce which of the following?
   a. households' purchasing power
   b. interest rates
   c. investment spending
   d. nominal wages
   e. aggregate demand

7. The interest rate effect of a decrease in the aggregate price level will increase which of the following?
   a. the purchasing power of money holdings
   b. investment spending
   c. interest rates
   d. aggregate supply
   e. aggregate demand

8. Which of the following types of shocks poses a policy dilemma due to the inability to use stabilization policy to address inflation and unemployment at the same time?
   a. negative supply shock
   b. positive supply shock
   c. negative demand shock
   d. positive demand shock
   e. negative budget shock

9. A higher aggregate price level leads to higher profit per unit of output and increased output in the short run because of which of the following?
   a. the real wealth effect
   b. the interest rate effect
   c. sticky nominal wages
   d. productivity gains
   e. stabilization policy

10. If potential output is equal to actual aggregate output, which of the following is true?
    a. The economy is experiencing inflation.
    b. The economy is experiencing cyclical unemployment.
    c. Nominal wages are sticky.
    d. The economy is in long-run equilibrium.
    e. The aggregate price level is rising.

11. Which of the following is true about the long-run aggregate supply curve?
    a. It is horizontal.
    b. It is the result of nominal wages being fully flexible.
    c. It is the result of sticky prices.
    d. It is upward-sloping.
    e. It intersects the horizontal axis at the actual level of real GDP.

12. Short-run equilibrium aggregate output is the quantity of aggregate output produced when
    a. the aggregate demand curve and the short-run aggregate supply curve are identical.
    b. the quantity of aggregate output supplied is equal to the quantity demanded.
    c. the economy reaches its potential output.
    d. the short-run aggregate supply curve is vertical.
    e. all prices, including nominal wages, are fully flexible.

13. The collapse of wealth and of business and consumer confidence that caused the Great Depression is an example of which type of shock?
    a. negative supply shock
    b. positive supply shock
    c. negative demand shock
    d. positive demand shock
    e. negative recessionary shock

14. Which of the following is an example of a positive demand shock?
    a. a large increase in defense spending
    b. the stock market crash of 1929
    c. the discovery of a large, previously unknown oil field
    d. a reduction in the aggregate price level
    e. an increase in nominal wages

15. A positive supply shock will lead to which of the following?
    a. stagflation
    b. an increase in the aggregate price level
    c. a recession
    d. a rightward shift of the short-run aggregate supply curve
    e. an increase in aggregate output along with inflation

16. Which of the following is an example of a negative supply shock?
    a. Production costs decrease.
    b. Information technologies lead to productivity growth.
    c. The stock market collapses.
    d. The government runs a budget deficit.
    e. World oil supplies are disrupted.

17. Which of the following is true when the economy is experiencing a recessionary gap?
   a. Potential output is below aggregate output.
   b. Aggregate demand is below aggregate supply.
   c. There is high unemployment.
   d. The aggregate price level is rising.
   e. The economy has self-corrected.

18. When the economy is experiencing an inflationary gap, the output gap is
   a. positive.
   b. negative.
   c. zero.
   d. decreasing.
   e. increasing.

19. Which of the following leads to self-correction when the economy is experiencing a recessionary gap?
   a. Nominal wages and prices rise.
   b. The short-run aggregate supply curve decreases.
   c. The long-run aggregate supply curve decreases.
   d. The short-run aggregate supply curve shifts to the right.
   e. Unemployment leads to an increase in aggregate demand.

20. Which type of policy can be used to address a decrease in aggregate output to below potential output?
   a. expansionary
   b. contractionary
   c. indiscretionary
   d. recessionary
   e. inflationary

21. If the marginal propensity to consume is equal to 0.80, the expenditure multiplier is
   a. 0.80.
   b. 1.25.
   c. 4.00.
   d. −4.00.
   e. 5.00.

22. If the marginal propensity to consume is 0.75, an initial increase in aggregate spending of $1,000 will lead to a total change in real GDP equal to
   a. $750.
   b. $1,000.
   c. $1,333.
   d. $4,000.
   e. $7,500.

23. If the marginal propensity to consume is 0.9, every $10 billion change in taxes will cause a change in spending equal to
   a. $100 billion.
   b. $90 billion.
   c. $10 billion.
   d. $9 billion.
   e. $0.9 billion.

24. Compared to an increase in taxes, an equal-sized increase in government spending will have what effect on real GDP?
   a. a larger, negative effect
   b. a smaller, negative effect
   c. a larger, positive effect
   d. a smaller, positive effect
   e. an equal, offsetting effect

25. Which of the following is an example of an automatic stabilizer?
   a. the Works Progress Administration established during the Great Depression
   b. lump-sum taxes
   c. a balanced budget requirement for the government
   d. sales taxes
   e. economic stimulus checks from the government

Free-Response Questions

1. Consider an economy operating at full employment.
   a. Draw a correctly labeled aggregate supply–aggregate demand graph for the economy. On your graph, show each of the following:
      i. equilibrium price level, labeled PL_1
      ii. equilibrium output level, labeled Y_1
      iii. potential output, labeled Y_P
   b. Assume the government increases transfer payments to families with dependent children.
      i. Show the effect of the increase in transfer payments on your graph.
      ii. Label the new short-run equilibrium price level PL_2 and the new short-run equilibrium output level Y_2.
   c. Refer to the new short-run equilibrium shown on your graph in response to part b.
      i. The new short-run equilibrium illustrates what type of output gap?
      ii. What type of fiscal policy would be appropriate for an economy facing a persistent gap of the type you identified in part i? **(10 points)**

2. Assume the *MPS* for an economy is 0.1.
   a. What is the value of the expenditure multiplier? Show your work.
   b. What is the value of the tax multiplier? Show your work.
   c. What is the maximum increase in real GDP as a result of an increase in government spending of $200 million? Show your work.
   d. If government spending and taxes are both increased by $200 million, what is the net effect on real GDP? Explain. **(5 points)**

3. The real GDP in Macroland is currently $100 million below potential output.
   a. What type of gap is Macroland experiencing? What type of policy would be used to close this gap?
   b. If the *MPC* in Macroland is 0.8, what is the value of the expenditure multiplier? Show your work.
   c. To return Macroland to long-run equilibrium, by how much should the government change taxes? Show your work.
   d. Would the change in government spending needed to close the gap be greater than, less than, or equal to the change in taxes? **(5 points)**

The Financial Sector

AP® Economics Skills

1. Principle and Models (1.A, 1.B, 1.D)
2. Interpretation (2.A)
3. Manipulation (3.C)
4. Graphing and Visuals (4.A, 4.C)

Money (That's What I Want)

From *The Beatles* to *Rihanna* to *Notorious B.I.G.*, money is the subject of many famous songs, poems, and quotes that speak to the important role it plays in our daily lives. Money has been described as providing us with freedom, security, power, and self-dependence. It has been called a *nonnegotiable, indispensable commodity in every person's life.* But what IS money? Where does it come from, and why does it have value?

When most people think of money, they think of a country's currency. Currency is issued by a country's central bank, which also has the responsibility for maintaining the currency and its value. Maintaining currency can include everything from participating in the design of currency and ensuring that the currency is kept fit for commerce, to helping prevent counterfeiting and assuring an adequate money supply. In addition to providing financial services, central banks like the Federal Reserve (the central bank of the United States) supervise and regulate the banking system, and conduct monetary policy. Even though many people don't know about their country's central bank, it plays a key role in the economy, for example by maintaining price stability and promoting maximum sustainable employment. A change in a central bank's policy is big news — at least for the people who know what it does!

A survey of news headlines from just a single month (for example, September 2021) reveals the actions taken by central banks around the world: "Brazilian Central Bank Raises Rates and Promises Further Hikes"; "Chilean Central Bank Steps Up Policy Targeting"; "China to Improve Monetary Policy Controls, Build Warning System"; Moldova Makes Second Rate Hike in Two Months"; "Bank of England Cuts UK Growth Forecast"; "US Fed Officials Say Tapering Could Still Begin This Year"; "European Central Bank Announces Moderate Cut in Net Assets Purchases"; "Zambia Holds Rates Despite Double-Digit Inflation". These headlines refer to actions like tapering, raising or lowering rates, and targeting. Even though each central bank focuses on the economy of its country, you can see from these headlines that the decisions facing central banks in September 2021, the year following the COVID-19 pandemic, were quite similar.

In this Unit, we will look more closely at the definition and functions of money and other financial assets in the economy. We will also investigate the role of central banks that issue currency, maintain the money supply, and implement monetary policy.

mgkaya/Getty Images

MODULE 4.1

Financial Assets

In this Module, you will learn to:

- Understand that the opportunity cost of holding cash is the interest it could have earned from purchasing interest-bearing assets
- Define liquidity, rate of return, and risk—important characteristics of a financial asset
- Identify the liquidity of various assets, including cash and demand deposits
- Define stocks and bonds and describe their attributes as financial assets
- Explain why the price of previously issued bonds and the interest rate on bonds are negatively related

The Opportunity Cost of Cash

Cash is perhaps the most familiar type of financial asset. Most of us carry some of it with us every day. Individuals and firms find it useful to hold some of their assets as cash because of the convenience that cash provides: it can be used to make purchases directly, while other assets can't. But there is a price to be paid – an opportunity cost – for that convenience: cash held in your wallet earns no *interest.* Interest is the amount paid to borrow money, determined by the **interest rate**. But while cash in your pocket does not earn interest, it is still the most convenient option in some situations.

The **interest rate** is the price, calculated as a percentage of the amount borrowed, charged by lenders to borrowers for the use of their savings.

As an example of how the convenience of holding cash makes it worth incurring some opportunity costs, consider the fact that even today – with the prevalence of credit cards, debit cards, and mobile payment options – people continue to keep some cash in their wallets rather than leave it in an interest-bearing account. They do this because they don't want to have to use their card or phone every time they want to make a small purchase. In other words, the convenience of keeping some cash in your wallet is more valuable than the interest you would earn by keeping that money in the bank.

Radharc Images/Alamy

Cash in your pocket might not earn you any interest, but it is still the most convenient option in some situations, such as when you leave a tip at a restaurant.

Even holding money in a checking account involves a trade-off between convenience and interest payments. That's because you can earn a higher interest rate by putting your money in assets other than a checking account. For example, many banks offer certificates of deposit, or CDs, which may pay a higher interest rate than ordinary bank accounts. But CDs also carry a penalty if you withdraw the funds before a certain amount of time – say, six months – has elapsed. An individual who keeps funds in a checking account is forgoing the higher interest rate those funds would have earned if placed in a CD in return for the convenience of having cash readily available when needed.

People must weigh the convenience of holding cash against its opportunity cost – the interest that could be earned from holding other financial assets. To understand the major types of alternative financial assets and their role in the economy, we first need to understand the financial system.

The Financial System

A household's **wealth** is the value of its accumulated savings.

Financial markets are where households invest their current savings and their accumulated savings, or **wealth**, by purchasing financial assets. In general, an *asset* is something of value.

More specifically, a **financial asset** is a nonphysical asset that entitles the buyer to future income from the seller. For example, when a saver lends funds to a company, the loan is a financial asset sold by the company and purchased by the saver. The loan entitles the saver to future income from the company. A household can also invest its current savings or wealth by purchasing a **physical asset**, a claim on a tangible object, such as a preexisting house or a preexisting piece of equipment. The title to a car, for example, is the claim to ownership of a physical asset (the car). This claim gives the owner the right to dispose of the object as they wish (for example, rent it or sell it).

A **financial asset** is a nonphysical asset that entitles the buyer to future income from the seller.

A **physical asset** is a tangible object that the owner has the right to use or dispose of as they wish.

If you were to go to your local bank and get a loan—say, to buy a new car—you and the bank would be creating a financial asset: your loan. A *loan* is one important kind of financial asset in the real world, one that is owned by the lender—in this case, your local bank. In creating this loan, you and the bank would also be creating a **liability**, a requirement to pay money in the future. So, although your loan is a financial asset from the bank's point of view, it is a liability from your point of view: a requirement that you repay the loan, including any interest.

A **liability** is a requirement to pay money in the future.

In addition to loans, there are three other important kinds of financial assets: stocks, bonds, and bank deposits. Because a financial asset is a claim to future income that someone has to pay, it is also someone else's liability. Shortly, we'll explain in detail who bears the liability for each type of financial asset.

The economy has developed a set of specialized markets for these four types of financial assets—loans, stocks, bonds, and bank deposits. The stock market, the bond market, and specialized institutions, such as banks, facilitate the flow of funds from savers to borrowers. A well-functioning financial system is a critical ingredient in achieving long-run growth because it encourages greater and more efficient savings and investment spending. To understand how this occurs, we first need to know what tasks the financial system needs to accomplish. Then we can see how the job gets done.

Three Tasks of a Financial System

There are three important problems facing borrowers and lenders: transaction costs, financial risk, and the desire for liquidity. The three tasks of a financial system are to reduce these problems in a cost-effective way. Doing so enhances the efficiency of financial markets: it makes it more likely that savers and borrowers will make mutually beneficial trades—trades that make society as a whole richer.

Reducing Transaction Costs

Transaction costs are the expenses of actually putting together and executing a deal. For example, arranging a loan requires spending time and money negotiating the terms of the deal, verifying the borrower's ability to pay, drawing up and executing legal documents, and so on. Suppose a large business decides that it wants to raise $1 billion for investment spending. No individual would be willing to lend that much. And negotiating individual loans from thousands of different people, each willing to lend a modest amount, would impose very large total costs because each individual transaction would incur a cost. Total costs would be so large that the entire deal would probably be unprofitable for the business.

Nikada/iStock Photo

The corner of Wall and Broad Streets is at the center of New York City's financial district.

Fortunately, that's not necessary: when large businesses want to borrow money, they either get a loan from a bank or sell bonds in the bond market. Obtaining a loan from a bank avoids large transaction costs because it involves only a single borrower and a single lender. We'll explain more about how bonds work in the next section. For now, it is enough to know that the principal reason there is a bond market is that it allows companies to borrow large sums of money without incurring large transaction costs.

Reducing Risk

Financial risk is uncertainty about future outcomes that involve financial losses and gains.

A second problem that real-world borrowers and lenders face is **financial risk**, uncertainty about future outcomes that involve financial losses or gains. Financial risk (which from now on we'll simply call "risk") is a problem because the future is uncertain; it holds the potential for losses as well as gains.

Most people are reluctant to take risks, although to differing degrees. A well-functioning financial system helps people reduce their exposure to risk. Suppose the owner of a business expects to make a greater profit if they buy additional capital equipment but they aren't completely sure of this result. The owner could pay for the equipment by using their savings or selling their house. But if the profit is significantly less than expected, they will have lost their savings, or their house, or both. That is, the owner would be exposing themself to a lot of risk due to uncertainty about how well or poorly the business performs. So, being risk-averse, this business owner wants to share the risk of purchasing new capital equipment with someone, even if that requires sharing some of the profit if all goes well. How can the owner do this? By selling shares of their company, known as stocks, to other people and using the money they receive from selling shares, rather than money from the sale of their other assets, to finance the equipment purchase. By selling shares in their company, the owner reduces their personal losses if the profit is less than expected: they won't have lost their other assets. But if things go well, the shareholders earn a share of the profit as a return on their investment.

REB Images/AGE Fotostock

By selling a share of their business, the owner has been able to invest in several things in a way that lowers the total risk. They have maintained their investment in their bank account, a financial asset; in ownership of their house, a physical asset; and in ownership of the unsold portion of their business, also a physical asset. By engaging in *diversification* – investing in several assets with unrelated, or independent, risks – our business owner has lowered the total risk of loss. The desire of individuals to reduce their total risk by engaging in diversification is why we have stocks and a stock market.

Providing Liquidity

The third and final task of the financial system is to provide investors with *liquidity*, which – like risk – becomes relevant because the future is uncertain. Suppose that you want to start a new business at some point. Even if you have no concerns about the risk of the business failing, you probably won't want to invest all of your savings into the business. This is because you might suddenly find yourself in need of cash – say, to pay for a medical emergency. Money invested in a business is not easily converted into cash in the event that it is needed for other purposes. For this reason, savvy investors are reluctant to lock up too much money in businesses among other large purchases.

An asset is **liquid** if it can be quickly converted into cash without much loss of value.

An asset is **illiquid** if it cannot be quickly converted into cash without much loss of value.

An asset is **liquid** if, as with money deposited in a bank, it can be quickly converted into cash without much loss of value. An asset is **illiquid** if, as with a business, car, or home, it cannot. The reluctance to invest heavily in illiquid assets would deter business growth and many major purchases if financial systems offered no remedy. As we'll see, however, the initial sale of stocks and bonds can resolve some liquidity problems by raising money for new and expanding projects. And, by taking deposits and lending them out, banks allow individuals to own liquid assets (their deposits) while financing investments in illiquid assets such as businesses and homes.

To help savers and borrowers make mutually beneficial deals, then, the economy needs ways to reduce transaction costs, to reduce and manage risk through diversification, and to provide liquidity. How does it achieve these tasks? With a variety of financial assets.

Types of Financial Assets

In the modern economy there are four basic types of financial assets: loans, bonds, stocks, and bank deposits. In addition, financial innovation has allowed the creation of a wide range of assets created by pooling individual loans and selling shares in that pool. Each type of asset serves a somewhat different purpose. We'll explain loans, bonds, and stocks first. Then we'll turn to bank deposits, when we explain the role banks play as financial intermediaries.

Loans

A **loan** is a lending agreement between an individual lender and an individual borrower. Most people encounter loans in the form of bank loans to finance the purchase of a car or a house. And small businesses usually use bank loans to buy new equipment.

Loans have a greater benefit when they are tailored to the needs of the borrower. Before a small business can get a loan, it usually has to discuss its business plans, its profits, and so on with the lender. This process results in a loan that meets the borrower's needs and ability to repay.

However, loans require a relatively complex transaction that creates a cost—for example, a loan creates transaction costs associated with identifying qualified buyers. To minimize these costs, large borrowers such as major corporations and governments often take a more streamlined approach: they sell (or issue) bonds.

A **loan** is a lending agreement between an individual lender and an individual borrower.

A **bond** is an interest-bearing asset that represents a loan to a company or government.

PhotoSpin, Inc/Alamy

Bonds

A **bond** is an interest-bearing asset. It can be thought of as an IOU ("I owe you") issued by the borrower. Normally, the seller of the bond promises to pay a fixed sum of interest each year and to repay the *principal*—the value stated on the face of the bond—to the owner of the bond on a particular date. So a bond is a financial asset from its owner's point of view and a liability from its issuer's point of view. A bond issuer sells a number of bonds with a given interest rate and maturity date to whoever is willing to buy them, a process that avoids costly negotiation of the terms of a loan with many individual lenders.

Bond purchasers can acquire information free of charge on the quality of the bond issuer, such as the bond issuer's credit history, from *bond-rating agencies*, rather than having to incur the expense of investigating it themselves. A particular concern for investors is the possibility of default, the risk that the bond issuer might fail to make payments as specified by the bond contract. Once a bond's risk of default has been rated, it can be sold on the bond market as a more or less standardized product—a product with clearly defined terms and quality. In general, bonds with a higher default risk must pay a higher interest rate to attract investors.

Another important advantage of bonds is that they are easy to resell. This provides liquidity to bond purchasers. Indeed, a bond will often pass through many hands before it finally comes due.

The price of a previously issued bond is inversely related to the interest rate in the economy. When the interest rate in the economy increases, preexisting bond prices generally fall. The price of the bond falls because bond buyers could purchase a new bond paying the higher interest rate. They would not buy a preexisting bond unless the price of that bond decreases (to make up for the difference between the interest rates on new and preexisting bonds). When the interest rate in the economy falls, preexisting bond prices generally rise. Because bond buyers can only purchase new bonds paying lower interest rates, bond owners can raise the price of higher interest preexisting bonds.

AP® ECON TIP

The price of previously issued bonds always moves in the opposite direction of the interest rate.

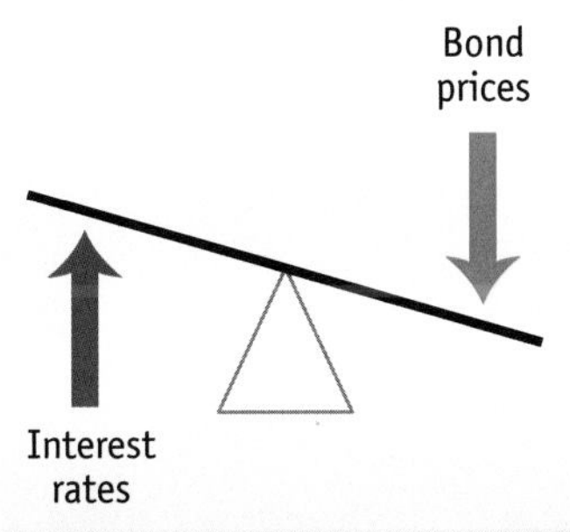

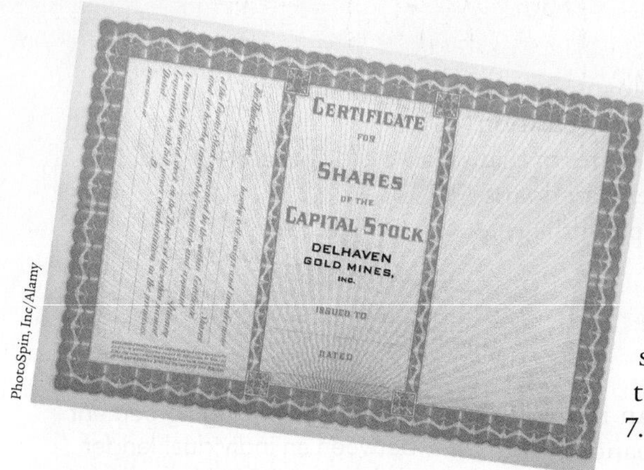

PhotoSpin, Inc/Alamy

Stocks

A **stock** is a share in the ownership of a company. It is a type of *equity* – ownership in the value of an asset or business. A share of stock is a financial asset from its owner's point of view and a liability from the company's point of view. Not all companies sell shares of their stock; "privately held" companies are owned by an individual or a few partners who get to keep all of the company's profit. Most large companies, however, do sell stock. For example, as this book goes to press, Microsoft has almost 7.52 billion shares outstanding; if you buy one of those shares, you are entitled to less than one-eight billionth of the company's profit, as well as 1 of 7.52 billion votes on company decisions.

A **stock** is a type of equity that represents ownership of a company.

Why does Microsoft, historically a very profitable company, allow you to buy a share in its ownership? Why didn't Bill Gates and Paul Allen, the two founders of Microsoft, keep complete ownership for themselves and just sell bonds for their investment spending needs? The reason, as we have just learned, is risk: few individuals are risk-tolerant enough to face the risk involved in being the sole owner of a large company.

Reducing the risk that business owners face, however, is not the only way in which the existence of stocks improves society's welfare: it also improves the welfare of investors who buy stocks (that is, shareholders). Shareholders are able to enjoy a higher *rate of return* over time that stocks generally offer in comparison to bonds. (The rate of return on a financial asset is the net gain or loss expressed as a percentage of the initial amount.) But as investment companies warn you, "Past performance is no guarantee of future performance." And there is a downside: owning the stock of a given company is riskier than owning a bond issued by the same company. Why? Loosely speaking, a bond is a promise, while a stock is a hope: by law, a company must pay what it owes its lenders (bondholders) before it distributes any profit to its shareholders. And if the company should fail (that is, be unable to pay its interest obligations and declare bankruptcy), its physical and financial assets go to its bondholders – its lenders – while its shareholders typically receive nothing. So, although a stock generally provides a higher return to an investor than a bond, it also carries higher risk.

The financial system has devised ways to help investors as well as business owners simultaneously manage risk and enjoy somewhat higher returns. It does that through the services of institutions known as *financial intermediaries.*

Financial Intermediaries

A financial intermediary is an institution that transforms funds gathered from many individuals into financial assets. Two important types of financial intermediaries are *mutual funds* and *banks.* Along with cash, stocks, and bonds, deposits in banks and other financial institutions and shares of mutual funds make up the top five largest categories of financial assets.

Mutual Funds

As we've explained, owning shares of a company entails risk in return for a higher potential reward. But it should come as no surprise that stock investors can lower their total risk by engaging in diversification. By owning a *diversified portfolio* of stocks – a group of stocks in which risks are unrelated to, or offset, one another – rather than concentrating investment in the shares of a single company or a group of related companies, investors can reduce their risk. In addition, financial advisers, aware that most people are risk-averse, almost always advise their clients to diversify not only their stock portfolio but also their entire wealth by holding other assets in addition to stocks – assets such as bonds, real estate, and cash. (And, for good measure, to have plenty of insurance in case of accidental losses!)

However, for individuals who don't have a large amount of money to invest — say, \$1 million or more — building a diversified stock portfolio can incur high transaction costs (particularly fees paid to stockbrokers) because they are buying a few shares of a lot of companies. Fortunately for such investors, mutual funds help solve the problem of achieving diversification without high transaction costs. A *mutual fund* is a financial intermediary that creates a stock portfolio by buying and holding shares in companies and then selling *shares of the stock portfolio* to individual investors. By buying these shares, investors with a relatively small amount of money to invest can indirectly hold a diversified portfolio, achieving a better return for any given level of risk than they could otherwise achieve.

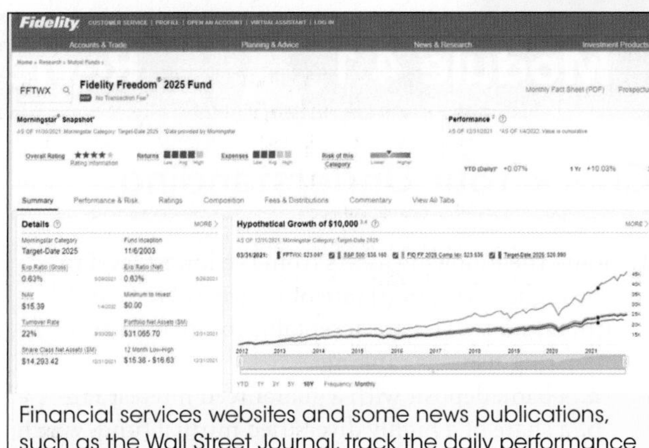

Financial services websites and some news publications, such as the Wall Street Journal, track the daily performance of hundreds of different mutual funds.

Banks

Recall the problem of liquidity: other things equal, people want assets that can be readily converted into cash. Bonds and stocks are much more liquid than physical assets or loans, yet the transaction costs of selling bonds or stocks to meet a sudden expense can be large. Furthermore, for many small and moderate-sized companies, the cost of issuing bonds and stocks is too large, given the modest amount of money they seek to raise. A *bank* is an institution that helps resolve the conflict between lenders' needs for liquidity and the financing needs of borrowers who don't want to use the stock or bond markets.

A bank works by first accepting funds from *depositors*: when you put your money in a bank, you are essentially becoming a lender by lending the bank your money. In return, you receive credit for a **bank deposit** — a claim on the bank, which is obliged to give you your cash. In most cases, a bank is required to give a depositor their cash immediately when they demand it, and the deposit is called a *demand deposit*. A bank deposit is a financial asset owned by the depositor and a liability of the bank that holds it.

A **bank deposit** is a claim on a bank that obliges the bank to give the depositor their cash.

A bank, however, keeps only a fraction of its customers' deposits in the form of ready cash. Most of its deposits are lent out to businesses, buyers of new homes, and other borrowers. These loans come with a long-term commitment by the bank to the borrower: as long as the borrower makes their payments on time, the loan cannot be recalled by the bank and converted into cash. So a bank enables those who wish to borrow for long lengths of time to use the funds of those who wish to lend but simultaneously want to maintain the ability to get their cash back on demand. More formally, a **bank** is a financial intermediary that provides liquid financial assets in the form of deposits to lenders and uses their funds to finance borrowers' investment spending on illiquid assets.

A **bank** is a financial intermediary that provides liquid assets in the form of bank deposits to lenders and uses those funds to finance borrowers' investment spending on illiquid assets.

In essence, a bank is engaging in a kind of mismatch: lending for long periods of time but also subject to the condition that its depositors could demand their funds back at any time. How can it manage that?

The bank counts on the fact that, on average, only a small fraction of its depositors will want their cash at the same time. On any given day, some people will make withdrawals and others will make new deposits; these will roughly cancel each other out. So the bank needs to keep only a limited amount of cash on hand to satisfy its depositors. In addition, if a bank becomes financially incapable of paying its depositors, individual bank deposits are currently guaranteed to depositors up to \$250,000 by the Federal Deposit Insurance Corporation, or FDIC, a federal agency. This reduces the risk to a depositor of holding a bank deposit, in turn reducing the incentive to withdraw funds if concerns about the financial state of the bank should arise. So, under normal conditions, banks need to hold only a fraction of their depositors' cash.

Now that we understand financial markets, we can look more closely at interest rates, the return on many financial assets, and the opportunity cost of holding cash.

Module 4.1 Review

Check Your Understanding

1. Rank the following assets from the lowest level to the highest level of (i) rate of return, (ii) risk, and (iii) liquidity. Ties are acceptable for items that have indistinguishable rankings.
   a. a bank deposit with a guaranteed interest rate
   b. a share of a highly diversified mutual fund, which can be quickly sold
   c. a share of the family business, which can be sold only if you find a buyer and all other family members agree to the sale
2. Explain the relationship between the interest rate in the economy and the price of previously issued bonds.

Tackle The AP® Test: Multiple-Choice Questions

1. Which of the following is a task of the financial system?
   a. decreasing transaction costs
   b. increasing risk
   c. creating illiquidity
   d. increasing inefficiency
   e. creating capital outflow
2. Which of the following is NOT a type of financial asset?
   a. bonds
   b. stocks
   c. bank deposits
   d. loans
   e. houses
3. An asset that can be easily converted into cash is considered
   a. risky.
   b. interest-bearing.
   c. secure.
   d. liquid.
   e. an equity.
4. A financial intermediary that creates a stock portfolio by buying and holding shares in companies and then selling shares of the stock portfolio to individual investors is a
   a. mutual fund.
   b. bank.
   c. corporation.
   d. pension fund.
   e. life insurance company.
5. Stocks
   a. represent ownership of a business.
   b. have a higher historical rate of return than bonds.
   c. are an example of an equity.
   d. are used by business owners to reduce risk.
   e. all of the above
6. When the interest rate increases, the price of previously issued bonds will
   a. increase proportionally.
   b. increase by a smaller amount.
   c. not be affected.
   d. equal zero.
   e. decrease.
7. Bonds are
   a. IOUs issued by a borrower.
   b. a financial asset for the bond owner.
   c. a liability for the bond issuer.
   d. relatively easy to resell.
   e. all of the above

Tackle The AP® Test: Free-Response Questions

1. Identify and describe the three tasks of a well-functioning financial system.

Rubric for FRQ 1 (6 points)

1 point: Decrease transaction costs

1 point: A well-functioning financial system facilitates investment spending by allowing companies to borrow large sums of money without incurring large transaction costs.

1 point: Decrease risk

1 point: A well-functioning financial system helps people reduce their exposure to risk, so that they are more willing to engage in investment spending in the face of uncertainty in the economy.

1 point: Provide liquidity

1 point: A well-functioning financial system allows the fast, low-cost conversion of assets into cash.

2. **a.** Explain how each of the following will affect the rate of return on a financial asset.
   i. higher risk
   ii. increased liquidity
   b. Describe the level of risk and liquidity associated with holding cash as a financial asset. **(5 points)**

Nominal Versus Real Interest Rates

In this Module, you will learn to:

- Define the nominal and real interest rates
- Calculate the nominal interest rate as the sum of expected real interest rates and expected inflation
- Calculate the real interest rate, in hindsight, as the nominal inflation rate minus the inflation rate
- Explain the relationship between changes in the nominal interest rate, expected inflation rate, and real interest rate

Calculating Nominal and Real Interest Rates

The previous Module discussed the interest rate as both the opportunity cost of holding money and the return from holding financial assets. But recall from Unit 2 that people holding fixed-value assets can lose as a result of inflation. Over time, an increase in the price level will erode the purchasing power of any returns received after prices have increased. For example, lenders earn a rate of return on a loan equal to the interest rate. The *interest rate* on a loan is the percentage of the loan amount that the borrower must pay to the lender over time. The effect of inflation on lenders can be measured by the difference between the *nominal* interest rate paid, which is established in the loan contract, and the *real* interest rate received by the lender.

PM Images/Getty Images

Because it is adjusted for inflation, the real interest rate represents the opportunity cost of loaning funds.

Recall from Module 2.5 that the **nominal interest rate** is the interest rate that is actually paid for a loan, unadjusted for the effects of inflation. The nominal interest rate is a monetary value and is not necessarily the actual return on the loan. The **real interest rate** is the nominal interest rate adjusted for inflation. It takes into account the opportunity cost of loaning the funds and the value of what can be purchased after an increase in prices. Only when there is no inflation will the real interest rate equal the nominal interest rate.

The **nominal interest rate** is the interest rate actually paid for a loan.

The **real interest rate** is the nominal interest rate adjusted for inflation.

The adjustment from nominal interest rate to real interest rate is achieved by subtracting the inflation rate from the nominal interest rate. For example, if a loan carries a nominal interest rate of 8%, but the inflation rate is 5%, the real interest rate is 8% – 5% = 3%. The real interest rate can be determined in hindsight, after the actual rate of inflation is known, using Equation 4.2-1.

(4.2-1) Real interest rate = nominal interest rate – inflation rate

Therefore, the nominal interest rate is calculated as

(4.2-2) Nominal interest rate = real interest rate + inflation rate

But since the interest rate on a loan is determined before the loan is made, the actual rate of inflation over the period of the loan will not be known. Since lenders and borrowers do not know with certainty what the inflation rate will be over the period of

> **AP® ECON TIP**
> The way the real interest rate is calculated differs depending on when it is calculated—in advance or after the fact. In advance, the real interest rate is estimated as the nominal interest rate minus the expected inflation rate. In hindsight, when the inflation rate is known, the real interest rate will be equal to the nominal interest rate minus the inflation rate.

a loan, they must set the nominal interest rate to achieve the desired real interest rate based on their expectations for inflation in the future. The *expected* real interest rate can be determined in advance using Equation 4.2-3.

(4.2-3) Expected real interest rate = nominal interest rate - expected inflation rate

Which means that the nominal interest rate is determined as

(4.2-4) Nominal interest rate = expected real interest rate + expected inflation rate

Expected Real Interest Rates and Expected Inflation

When a borrower and a lender enter into a loan contract, the contract normally specifies a nominal interest rate. But each party has an expectation about the future rate of inflation and therefore an expectation about the real interest rate on the loan. If the actual inflation rate is *higher* than expected, borrowers gain at the expense of lenders: borrowers will repay their loans with funds that have a lower real value than had been expected, since the funds can purchase fewer goods and services than expected due to the higher-than-expected inflation rate. Conversely, if the inflation rate is *lower* than expected, lenders will gain at the expense of borrowers: borrowers must repay their loans with funds that have a higher real value than had been expected.

Let's consider an example. A bank has determined that it wants to receive a real interest rate of 4% on its loans in order to cover its expenses and the opportunity cost of alternative uses for the loan amount. The bank expects the inflation rate over the period of the loan to equal 2%. In order to earn the desired real interest rate of 4% on its funds, the bank must charge a nominal interest rate of 6%—the desired 4% real interest rate *plus* the expected 2% inflation. If the actual rate of inflation is 3%, the bank will receive a real interest rate of only 6 – 3 = 3% on the loan, less than the desired 4%. But if the actual rate of inflation is only 1%, the banks' real interest rate on the loan will equal 6 – 1 = 5%, 1% higher than desired.

So, if the bank's expectations for inflation are correct, it will receive its desired real return on the loan. But if their expectations of inflation are higher or lower than actual inflation, the bank's return will be higher or lower than the desired real interest rate.

Borrowers must make the same calculation when considering the interest rate for a loan contract. They may gain as a result of inflation that is higher than they expect (and built into the nominal interest rate for the loan) because the purchasing power of the money that they pay back for the loan after inflation has decreased. But if inflation is lower than they expect, borrowers will pay a higher real interest rate than they intended because inflation did not lower the purchasing power of the money they repay as much as expected (and as was built into the nominal interest rate).

Nominal interest rates are the rates published by financial institutions and written in loan contracts. But since real interest rates aren't known until after the rate of inflation is known, real interest rates must be calculated using either the actual inflation rate (after the fact) or the expected inflation rate (in advance).

Figure 4.2-1 shows real and nominal interest rates for the United States between 1960 and 2020. As discussed above, the difference between the nominal and real interest rates is the rate of inflation. Notice that the lending interest rates were high in the late 1970s and early 1980s, while the real interest rates were much lower, illustrating the high rate of inflation during that time. Also note that the nominal interest rate stays above zero on the graph, while real interest rates fall below zero in 1975—when actual inflation rose above expected inflation before people were able to incorporate the 1974 spike in inflation in to their expectations.

> **AP® ECON TIP**
> In general, holders of fixed-value assets are hurt by inflation because it decreases the real value of the money available to them in the future. Holders of assets with values that are variable—e.g., tied to inflation using a cost-of-living adjustment (COLA)—are not.

FIGURE 4.2-1 Real and Nominal Interest Rates in the United States, 1960–2020

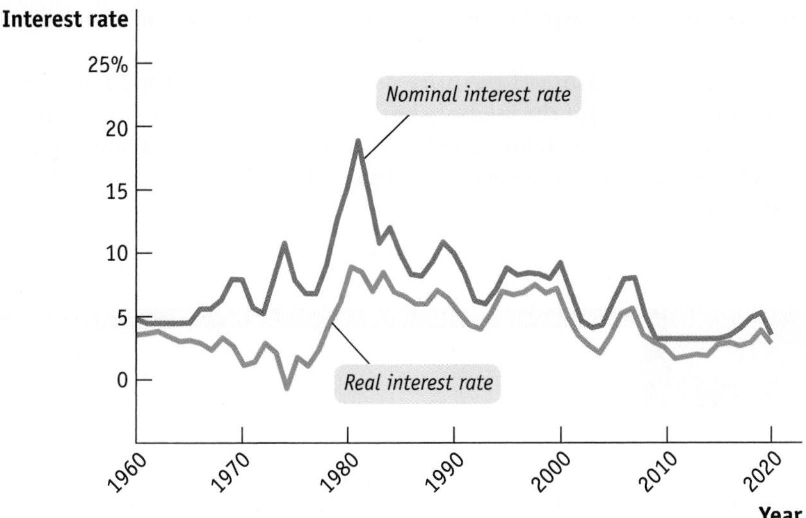

The difference between the nominal interest rate and real interest rate is the rate of inflation. High inflation causes the real interest rate to fall farther below the nominal rate, as shown by the relatively large difference between the real and nominal interest rate during the late 1970s and early 1980s. Low inflation results in a smaller difference between real and nominal interest rates, as shown by the smaller difference between real and nominal interest rates during the 2010s.
Source: The World Bank.

Are Interest Rates Always Positive?

An important difference between nominal and real interest rates is that nominal interest rates charged by lenders don't go below zero, but real interest rates can be negative. Let's consider the logic behind negative interest rates. A negative nominal interest rate would mean that the contract for a loan specifies that the borrower pay back *less* than was borrowed – the amount of the loan *minus* a percentage of that amount. The lender would actually be paying someone to borrow their funds! Since zero is the lowest possible opportunity cost for holding money, lenders would never pay someone to take out a loan. They would simply purchase other assets with a positive nominal interest rate or hold their funds as cash and earn a zero interest. While a central bank might use negative interest rates during a period of deflation (central banks are considered in more detail in the next few Modules), commercial lenders with the goal of maximizing their returns will not.

Refer back to Equation 4.2-2: The nominal interest rate is equal to the real interest rate plus the actual rate of inflation. Lenders will always charge a positive real interest rate, so the nominal interest rate will always be positive. If the inflation rate is equal to zero, the nominal interest rate will equal the (positive) real interest rate. And with inflation, the nominal interest rate will be even higher. In a situation where deflation is expected, lenders can hold their funds as cash and purchase goods at lower prices in the future.

The real interest rate, in contrast, *can* be negative if a lender's expectation about inflation that was used to set the nominal interest rate in a contract is wrong. For example, if a lender wants to receive a real interest rate of 4% and they expect inflation to equal 1%, they will make a loan at a nominal interest rate of 5%. But what if the actual inflation rate ends up being 6%? That would mean that the real interest rate is $5 - 6 = -1\%$. The amount that is paid back for the loan can't purchase what it could before, let alone provide any return.

Using Equation 4.2-3, we can see that the real interest rate can be negative. The expected real interest rate is equal to the nominal interest rate minus the expected rate of inflation. If the actual rate of inflation is greater than the nominal interest rate, the expected real interest rate will be greater than the real interest rate, and the

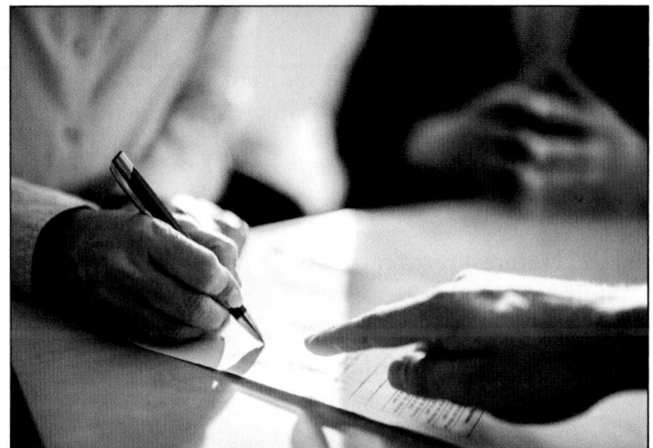
skynesher/Getty Images

Lenders loan funds at a nominal interest rate based on their expectations of what the real interest rate will be.

AP® ECON TIP

While the real interest for a loan can be negative when expected inflation is less than actual inflation, lenders will not set negative nominal interest rates.

real interest rate will be negative. In the example above, the expected real interest rate is 4%, the nominal interest rate is 5%, and the expected rate of inflation is 1%. If the actual rate of inflation turns out to be 6%, the real interest rate, according to Equation 4.2-1, will be $5 - 6 = -1\%$.

Interest rates provide a measure of the price of money that is borrowed or saved. But it is important to understand the relationship between changes in nominal interest rates, expected inflation, and real interest rates in order to understand how interest rates affect the macroeconomy. In the next Module, we take a closer look at the role of money in the economy.

Module 4.2 Review

Check Your Understanding

1. Explain the relationship between the nominal interest rate and the real interest rate. What does it mean to say that the real interest rate is *derived*?

2. If the nominal interest rate is equal to the expected real interest rate, what can be said about the expected rate of inflation? What if the nominal interest rate is greater than the expected real interest rate?

Tackle the AP® Test: Multiple-Choice Questions

1. The interest rate published by a bank in an advertisement is the
   a. real interest rate.
   b. nominal interest rate.
   c. prime interest rate.
   d. expected interest rate.
   e. discount rate.

2. When the expected inflation rate is 2% and lenders want a return of 3% on their loans, the nominal interest rate will be set at
   a. 1%.
   b. 2%.
   c. 3%.
   d. 5%.
   e. 6%.

3. If the actual rate of inflation exceeds the expected rate of inflation, which of the following is true?
   a. Lenders are hurt.
   b. The real interest is lower than expected.
   c. The real interest rate is lower than the nominal interest rate.
   d. Borrowers benefit.
   e. all of the above

4. Real interest rates can be negative when which of the following is true?
   a. Inflation rates are high.
   b. Lenders expect high inflation.
   c. Actual inflation is greater than expected inflation.
   d. Actual inflation is greater than the nominal interest rate.
   e. all of the above

5. The real interest rate will equal the nominal interest rate when inflation is equal to
   a. zero.
   b. the nominal interest rate.
   c. the real interest rate.
   d. expected inflation.
   e. the expected rate of return.

6. When lenders begin to expect inflation, nominal interest rates will
   a. fall.
   b. rise.
   c. equal real interest rates.
   d. equal zero.
   e. be negative.

7. If nominal interest rates equal 3% and real interest rates are 2%, the expected rate of inflation
   a. can't be determined.
   b. is equal to zero.
   c. is 1%.
   d. is 2%.
   e. is 3%.

Tackle the AP® Test: Free-Response Questions

1. Assume that lenders expect the rate of inflation to be 3% over the next year and will only loan money if they receive a return of 4%.
   a. Will lenders make loans at a nominal interest rate of 7%? Explain.
   b. If actual inflation is 4%, what will the real interest rate equal?
   c. Now assume the nominal interest rate is 6%.
      i. What is the expected real interest rate?
      ii. What would the actual inflation rate need to equal for the real interest rate to be negative?

Rubric for FRQ 1 (5 points)

1 point: Yes.

1 point: because the expected real interest rate is 3 + 4 = 7%, which is equal to lenders' required rate of return

1 point: 7 – 4 = 3%

1 point: 6 – 3 = 3%

1 point: greater than 6%

2. As the expected rate of inflation decreases, does each of the following increase, decrease, or not change? Explain.
   a. nominal interest rates
   b. real interest rates
   c. actual inflation rates **(6 points)**

MODULE 4.3A

Definition, Measurement, and Functions of Money

In this Module, you will learn to:

- Define money as any asset accepted as a means of payment
- Explain the three main functions of money: as a medium of exchange, as a store of value, and as a unit of account
- Define monetary aggregates (M1 and M2) as measures of the money supply
- Calculate monetary aggregates and the monetary base (aka M0 or MB)

The Meaning of Money

In everyday conversation, people often use the word *money* to mean "wealth." If you ask, "How much money does Elon Musk have?" most people would answer something like, "Oh, $100 or 200 billion or so, but who's counting?" This number would include the value of the stocks, bonds, real estate, and other assets he owns.

But the economist's definition of money doesn't include all forms of wealth. The dollar bills in your wallet are one form of money; other forms of wealth – such as cars, houses, and stocks – aren't money. Let's examine what, according to economists, distinguishes money from other forms of wealth.

What Is Money?

Money is any asset that can easily be used to purchase goods and services.

Economists define money in terms of what it does: **money** is any asset that can easily be used to purchase goods and services. For ease of use, money must be widely accepted by sellers. It is also desirable for money to be durable, portable, uniform, in limited supply, and divisible into smaller units, as with dollars and cents. In Module 4.1, we defined an asset as *liquid* if it can easily be converted into cash. Money can include cash itself, which is liquid by definition, as well as other assets that are highly liquid.

wavebreakmedia/Shutterstock

Money includes deposits in an account accessed by a debit card or digital payment service.

You can see the distinction between money and other assets by asking yourself how you pay for groceries. The person at the cash register will accept dollar bills in return for milk and frozen pizza – but they won't accept stock certificates or a collection of vintage baseball cards. If you want to convert stock certificates or vintage baseball cards into groceries, you have to sell them – trade them for money – and then use the money to buy groceries.

Of course, many stores allow you to pay for goods with a debit card or mobile payment app linked to your bank account. Does that mean that your bank account is money, even if you haven't converted it into cash? Yes. Currency in circulation – actual cash in the hands of the public – is considered money. So are checkable bank deposits – bank accounts on which people can write checks, debit funds, or make electronic payments. *Checkable deposits* refer to funds in accounts that can be withdrawn using a check, a debit card, or a digital payment service, such as Zelle, Venmo, or PayPal.

The **money supply** is the total value of financial assets in the economy that are considered money.

Are currency and checkable bank deposits the only assets that are considered money? It depends. As we'll see later in this Unit, there are two widely used definitions of the **money supply**, which is the total value of financial assets in the economy that are considered money. The narrower definition considers only the most liquid assets to be money: currency in circulation and checkable bank deposits. The broader definition includes these categories plus other assets that are "almost" checkable, such as savings account deposits that can be transferred into a checking account online with a few clicks. Both definitions of the money supply, however, make a distinction between those assets that can easily be used to purchase goods and services, and those that can't.

Money plays a crucial role in generating *gains from trade* because it makes indirect exchange possible. Think of what happens when a doctor buys a new refrigerator. The doctor has valuable services to offer – namely, providing health care. The owner of the store has valuable goods to offer: refrigerators and other appliances. It would be extremely difficult for both parties if, instead of using money, they had to directly barter the goods and services they sell. In a barter system, a doctor and an appliance store owner could trade only if the store owner happened to need health care *and* the doctor happened to want a new refrigerator. This is known as the problem of finding a "double coincidence of wants": in a barter system, two parties can trade only when each wants what the other has to offer. Money solves this problem: individuals can trade what they have to offer for money and trade money for what they want.

Because the ability to make transactions with money rather than relying on bartering makes it easier to achieve gains from trade, the existence of money increases welfare, even though money does not directly produce anything. As Adam Smith put it, money "may very properly be compared to a highway, which, while it circulates and carries to market all the grass and corn of the country, produces itself not a single pile of either."

Let's take a closer look at the roles money plays in the economy.

Functions of Money

Money has three main functions in a modern economy: it is a *medium of exchange*, a *store of value*, and a *unit of account*.

Medium of Exchange

Our doctor/appliance store owner example illustrates the role of money as a **medium of exchange** – an asset that individuals use to trade for goods and services rather than for consumption. People can't eat dollar bills; rather, they use dollar bills to trade for food among other goods and services.

A **medium of exchange** is an asset that individuals acquire for the purpose of trading for goods and services rather than for their own consumption.

In normal times, the official money of a given country – the dollar in the United States, the peso in Mexico, and so on – is also the medium of exchange in virtually all transactions in that country. During troubled economic times, however, other goods or assets often play that role instead. For example, during economic turmoil, people often turn to other countries' moneys as the medium of exchange: U.S. dollars have played this role in troubled Latin American countries, as have euros in troubled Eastern European countries. In a famous example, cigarettes functioned as the medium of exchange in World War II prisoner-of-war camps, for smokers and nonsmokers alike, because they could be easily traded for other items. During the extreme German inflation of 1923, goods such as eggs and lumps of coal briefly became mediums of exchange.

With permission of the New Zealand Ministry for Culture and Heritage

Gambling at the Stalag 383 prisoner of war camp during World War II was carried out using cigarettes as currency.

Store of Value

In order to act as a medium of exchange, money must also be a **store of value** – a means of holding purchasing power over time. To see why this is necessary, imagine trying to operate an economy in which ice cream cones were the medium of exchange. Such an economy would quickly suffer from, well, monetary meltdown: your medium of exchange would often turn into a sticky puddle before you could use it to buy something else. Of course, money is by no means the only store of value. Any asset that holds its purchasing power over time is a store of value. Examples include farmland and classic cars. So the store-of-value role is a necessary but not a distinctive feature of money.

A **store of value** is a means of holding purchasing power over time.

Unit of Account

A **unit of account** is a measure used to set prices and make economic calculations.

Finally, money normally serves as the **unit of account** — the commonly accepted measure individuals use to set prices and make economic calculations. To understand the importance of this role, consider a historical fact: during the Middle Ages, peasants typically were required to provide landowners with goods and labor rather than money in exchange for a place to live. For example, a peasant might be required to work on the landowner's land one day a week and also hand over one-fifth of their harvest. Today, rents, like other prices, are almost always specified in money terms. That makes things much clearer: imagine how hard it would be to decide which apartment to rent if modern landowners followed medieval practice. Suppose, for example, that Mr. Garcia says he'll let you have a place if you clean his house twice a week and bring him a pound of steak every day, whereas Ms. Williams wants you to clean her house just once a week but wants four pounds of chicken every day. Who's offering the better deal? It's hard to say. If, on the other hand, Mr. Garcia wants $600 a month and Ms. Williams wants $700, the comparison is easy. In other words, without a commonly accepted measure, the terms of a transaction are harder to determine, making it more difficult to make transactions and achieve gains from trade.

Types of Money

Commodity money is a good used as a medium of exchange that has intrinsic value in other uses.

In some form or another, money has been in use for thousands of years. For most of that period, people used **commodity money**: the medium of exchange was a good, normally gold or silver, that had intrinsic value in other uses. These alternative uses gave commodity money value independent of its role as a medium of exchange. For example, the cigarettes that served as money in World War II POW camps were valuable because many prisoners smoked. Gold was valuable because it was used for jewelry and ornamentation, aside from the fact that it was minted into coins.

By 1776, the year in which the United States declared its independence and Adam Smith published *The Wealth of Nations*, there was widespread use of paper money in addition to gold and silver coins. Unlike modern dollar bills, however, this paper money consisted of notes issued by private banks, which promised to exchange their notes for gold or silver coins on demand. So the paper currency that initially replaced commodity money was **commodity-backed money**, a medium of exchange with no intrinsic value, but whose ultimate value was guaranteed by a promise that it could always be converted into valuable goods on demand.

Commodity-backed money is a medium of exchange with no intrinsic value, but whose ultimate value is guaranteed by a promise that it can be converted into valuable goods.

The big advantage of commodity-backed money over simple commodity money, like gold and silver coins, was that it tied up fewer valuable resources. Although a note-issuing bank still had to keep some gold and silver on hand, it had to keep only enough to satisfy demand for redemption of its notes. And it could rely on the fact that only a fraction of its paper notes would be redeemed on a normal day. So the bank needed to keep only a portion of the total value of its notes in circulation in the form of gold and silver in its vaults. It could lend out the remaining gold and silver to those who wished to use it. This allowed society to use the remaining gold and silver for other purposes, all with no loss in the ability to achieve gains from trade.

In a famous passage in *The Wealth of Nations,* Adam Smith described paper money as a "waggon-way through the air." Smith was making an analogy between money and an imaginary highway that did not absorb the valuable land beneath it. An actual highway provides a useful service but at a cost: land that could be used to grow crops is instead paved over. If the highway could be built through the air, it wouldn't destroy useful land. As Smith understood, when banks replaced gold and silver money with paper notes, they accomplished a similar feat: they reduced the amount of real resources used by society to provide the functions of money.

Andrey Nekrasov/imageBROKER/AGE Fotostock

When issued, this commodity-backed one-dollar silver certificate could have been converted into silver.

At this point you may ask, why make any use at all of gold and silver in the monetary system, even to back paper money? In fact, today's monetary system goes even further than the system Smith admired, having eliminated any role for gold and silver. A U.S. dollar bill isn't commodity money, and it isn't even commodity-backed. Rather, its value arises entirely from the fact that it is generally accepted as a means of payment, a role that is ultimately decreed by the U.S. government. Money whose value derives entirely from its official status as a means of exchange is known as **fiat money** because it exists by government *fiat*, a historical term for a policy declared by a ruler.

Fiat money is a medium of exchange whose value derives entirely from its official status as a means of payment.

Fiat money has two major advantages over commodity-backed money. First, it is even more of a "waggon-way through the air" – it doesn't tie up any real resources, except for the paper it's printed on. Second, the money supply can be managed based on the needs of the economy, instead of being determined by the amount of gold and silver prospectors happen to discover.

On the other hand, fiat money poses some risks. One such risk is counterfeiting. Counterfeiters usurp a privilege of the U.S. government, which has the sole legal right to print dollar bills. And the benefit that counterfeiters get by exchanging fake bills for real goods and services comes at the expense of the U.S. federal government, which covers a small but nontrivial part of its own expenses by issuing new currency to meet a growing demand for money.

The larger risk is that government officials who have the authority to print money will be tempted to abuse the privilege by printing so much money that they create inflation.

DON HEUPEL/AP Images

U.S. bills employ a variety of anti-counterfeiting measures including color-shifting ink, watermarks, security threads, raised print, and microprinting.

Measuring the Money Supply

Central banks calculate the size of several **monetary aggregates**, which are the overall measures of money in an economy. These measures differ in how strictly they define money. The first type of monetary aggregate is the **monetary base**. The monetary base, also known as M0 or MB, is the total amount of currency that is in circulation or kept on reserve by commercial banks. This measure of the money supply is the most liquid because it includes only cash. One way to think about the monetary base is that it is the currency in the economy – either in your wallet or in the vault of a bank. In some situations, central banks may conduct monetary policy by increasing or decreasing the monetary base through purchases and sales of government bonds, as discussed in detail in the remaining Modules in this Unit.

A **monetary aggregate** is an overall measure of the money supply.

The **monetary base** (also known as M0 or MB) is the total amount of currency (cash) in circulation or kept on reserve by commercial banks.

Two additional monetary aggregates measure the money supply in the economy are known, not so cryptically, as M1 and M2. (There used to be other aggregates, including one named – you guessed it – M3, but they are no longer measured.) These two monetary aggregates are the most common measures of the money supply. **M1**, the narrower definition, contains the most liquid forms of wealth – currency in circulation, checkable bank deposits, and other liquid deposits (including certain savings deposits and money market deposit accounts). Assets included in M1 carry the opportunity cost of earning zero or very little interest. **M2** starts with M1 and adds several other kinds of assets, often referred to as *near-moneys* – financial assets that aren't directly usable as a medium of exchange but can be readily converted into cash or checkable bank deposits. Examples include certain savings accounts and small-denomination time deposits, which are interest-bearing deposits with a fixed term, such as balances in retail money market funds. These near-moneys pay interest while cash (currency in circulation) does not; in addition, they typically pay higher interest rates than any offered on checkable bank deposits. Because currency and checkable deposits are directly usable as a medium of exchange, however, M1 is more liquid than M2.

The **M1** monetary aggregate includes currency in circulation, checkable bank deposits, and other liquid deposits.

The **M2** monetary aggregate includes M1 plus less liquid "near monies" (financial assets that can be readily converted into cash).

What determines whether a deposit is included in M1? It depends on the rules regarding the number of transactions permitted on the account. Stricter limits on the number of transactions allowed make an account less liquid, and therefore not part of M1. In the United States, savings accounts, which are less liquid than other deposits, have traditionally been included in M2 only, but in April 2020, the Federal Reserve

AP® ECON TIP

References to the money supply usually refer to the M1 measure.

made a rule change on the transaction limits permitted on savings deposit accounts. According to the new rule, if a bank suspends the limits on accounts, it may choose to report the account as a more liquid "transaction account," rather than a savings account, making it part of M1. As explained by the Federal Reserve in a FRED® blog post from January 11, 2021, "it seems that the modification of (the regulation)...has effectively rendered savings accounts almost indistinguishable from checking accounts from the perspective of most depositors and banks. Accordingly, the composition of M2 between M1 and non-M1 components conveys little economic information." Consequently, in April 2020, M1 was only $4774.4 billion, but in May 2020, after the rule change, M1 increased to $16,262.0 billion.

In July 2021, the monetary base in the United States was just over $130 billion. M1 was valued at $19,402 billion, with approximately 11% accounted for by currency in circulation. M1 made up almost 95% of M2, which was valued at $20,535 billion in August 2021. Modules 4.3B and 4.4 consider how money is provided and expanded by the banking system.

Module 4.3A Review

Check Your Understanding

1. Suppose you hold a gift certificate, good for certain products at participating stores. Is this gift certificate money? Why or why not?
2. Although most bank accounts pay some interest, depositors can often get a higher interest rate by buying a certificate of deposit, or CD. The difference between a CD and a checking account is that the depositor pays a penalty for withdrawing the money before the CD comes due—a period of months or even years. Small CDs are counted in M2, but not in M1. Explain why they are not part of M1.

Tackle the AP® Test: Multiple-Choice Questions

1. When you use money to purchase lunch, money is serving which role?
   a. medium of exchange
   b. store of value
   c. unit of account
   d. measure of usefulness
   e. all of the above
2. When you decide you want "$10 worth" of a product, money is serving which role?
   a. medium of exchange
   b. store of value
   c. unit of account
   d. measure of usefulness
   e. all of the above
3. In the United States, the dollar is
   a. backed by silver.
   b. backed by gold and silver.
   c. commodity-backed money.
   d. commodity money.
   e. fiat money.
4. Which of the following is the most liquid measure of the money supply?
   a. M1
   b. M2
   c. M3
   d. near-moneys
   e. dollar bills
5. Which of the following is the best example of using money as a store of value?
   a. A customer pays in advance for $10 worth of gasoline at a gas station.
   b. A babysitter puts her earnings in a dresser drawer while she saves to buy a bicycle.
   c. Travelers buy meals on board an airline flight.
   d. Foreign visitors to the United States convert their currency to dollars at the airport.
   e. You use $1 bills to purchase soda from a vending machine.
6. The monetary base includes which of the following?
   a. bank reserves
   b. savings deposits
   c. checkable deposits
   d. certificates of deposit
   e. near-money

7. In most countries, including the United States, the money supply is
   a. made up of only currency in circulation.
   b. made up of only illiquid assets.
   c. considered commodity-backed.
   d. commonly defined as either M1 or M2.
   e. always defined to include "near moneys."

Tackle the AP® Test: Free-Response Questions

1. a. What does it mean for an asset to be liquid?
   b. Which of the following assets is the most liquid? Explain.
      Currency
      A savings account deposit
      A house
   c. Which of the assets listed in part b is the least liquid? Explain.
   d. In which monetary aggregate(s) is currency included?

Rubric for FRQ 1 (5 points)

1 point: It can easily be converted into cash.

1 point: Currency

1 point: It is already cash.

1 point: A house; it takes time and resources to sell a house.

1 point: M1 and M2

2. a. What "backs" fiat money?
   b. Is the money used in the United States today commodity money or fiat money? Explain.
   c. Give two historical examples of commodity money.
   (5 points)

MODULE 4.3B

Managing Money and Credit: Central Banks and the Federal Reserve

In this Module, you will learn to:

- Define a central bank and explain its purpose
- Explain the role of a central bank in the financial system and economy
- Identify the Federal Reserve System as the central bank of the United States
- Describe the basic the structure and functions of the Federal Reserve System

Central Banks

The introduction to this Unit presented a selection of news headlines related to central banks around the world—you'll find a more comprehensive list in **Table 4.3B-1**. In the previous Module we defined several ways that central banks measure the money supply and explained that central banks control the monetary base when they conduct monetary policy. In this Module, we define the central bank and dig into its functions. In doing so, we'll discuss the Federal Reserve, the central bank of the United States—which has a unique structure different from other central banks around the world.

Table 4.3B-1	Headlines for Central Bank News Articles, September 2021
Australia	Australia's Central Bank Sticks to Tapering
Brazil	Brazilian Central Bank Raises Rates and Promises Further Hikes
Canada	Bank of Canada on Hold as Growth Proves Weaker than Expected
Chile	Chilean Central Bank Steps Up Policy Targeting
China	China to Improve Monetary Policy Controls, Build Warning System
India	Reserve Bank of India Steps Up Work on Climate Change
Kazakhstan	Kazakhstan Hikes Main Rate as Fund Prices Balloon
Moldova	Moldova Makes Second Rate Hike in Two Months
Norway	Norges Bank Becomes First in G-10 to Raise Rates
Paraguay	Paraguay's Central Bank Raises Rates to 1.5%
Peru	Peru's Central Bank Doubles Rates on Higher Inflation
Sweden	Above-Target Inflation May Push Riksbank to Taper
Turkey	Turkey Cuts Rates Despite Rising Inflation
United Kingdom	Bank of England Cuts UK Growth Forecast
United States	US Fed Officials Say Tapering Could Still Begin This Year
Zambia (areas)	Zambia Holds Rates Despite Double-Digit Inflation
Europe	European Central Bank Announces Moderate Cut in Net Asset Purchases
Africa	African Central Banks Reported Setting Policy Less Frequently Than Peers
(general)	Central Banks Still in No Rush to Raise Rates as Inflation Takes Back Seat

Source: Central Banking, https://www.centralbanking.com/topics/monetary-policy, and *The Business Times*, https://www.businesstimes.com.sg/keywords/monetary-policy

Central banks have been around for a long time. Sweden created the Riksbank, the world's first central bank, in 1668. The Bank of England followed in 1694, and many others have followed since. But what is a central bank? A commercial bank, such as the one where you might deposit your savings or paycheck, is a financial institution that serves the public by accepting deposits and making loans in order to earn a profit (the commercial banking system is described in the next Module). In contrast, a **central bank**, sometimes called a reserve bank, is a government institution that issues a country's currency, oversees and regulates the country's banking system, controls its monetary base, and implements monetary policy.

A **central bank** is a government institution that issues currency, oversees and regulates the banking system, controls the monetary base, and implements monetary policy.

Most countries have a central bank, though a handful of very small countries do not. Seventy-five percent of the world's central bank assets are controlled by the central banks of China, the United States, Japan, and countries in the Eurozone (a monetary union of 19 European Union countries). In addition, the European Union has its own central bank – the European Central Bank, or ECB. Working with the central banks of its member countries, the ECB has the same functions as other central banks – it safeguards the value of the Euro, the common currency of European Union countries, and the stability of the European financial system, and it conducts monetary policy. The ECB and many, but not all, central banks act independently of their governments. That is, these central banks are free to pursue monetary policy independently and without political pressure. However, an independent central bank's monetary policy must be guided by its mandate from the government. Central bank mandates are often broad; for example, maintaining price stability and promoting maximum employment or economic growth.

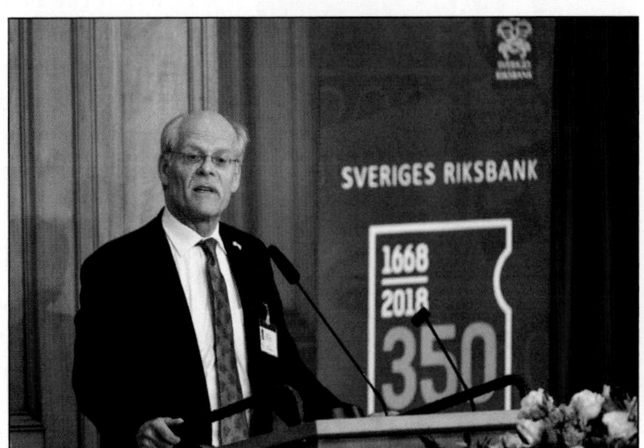

Mikael Sjober/Bloomberg/Getty Images

Governor of the Sveriges Riksbank, Stephan Ingves, speaks at a conference celebrating the 350th anniversary of the Riksbank in Stockholm, Sweden, in May 2018.

Common functions of a central bank are summarized in **Table 4.3B-2**. Central banks issue and maintain a country's currency and coins so that they are acceptable for use in commerce. They provide banking services to the government, similar to the services you can receive from a commercial bank; they hold cash balances, make payments (for example, paying salaries to government workers), transfer funds, and provide loans. Central banks monitor the stability of the financial system and implement regulations to promote stability. As a "banker's bank," a central bank provides for commercial banks the services that commercial banks provide for customers – such as holding deposits, transferring funds, and making loans. Should a financial institution be unable to find another source of funds when faced with a financial difficulty, the central bank can provide a loan as a "lender of last resort." Often central bank officers act as the government's representative to international financial organizations and institutions. In order to serve their various functions, central banks collect and analyze a tremendous amount of data, much of which they provide publicly for people to review and analyze. (In fact, many of the graphs in this book were created using data from the Federal Reserve economic database, or FRED®, maintained by the research department at the Federal Reserve Bank of St. Louis.)

Table 4.3B-2 Common Central Bank Functions
Issue and maintain currency
Provide banking services to the government
Supervise and regulate financial institutions
Act as a "banker's bank"
Serve as a "lender of last resort"
Manage relationships with international financial groups
Collect and publish data
Conduct monetary policy
Maintain exchange rate stability

In addition to these day-to-day activities, central banks implement a country's monetary policy. Monetary policy, which will be discussed in detail in the remaining Modules in this Unit, refers to the actions a central bank can take to promote price stability, maximum employment, and economic growth in its country's economy. Since the exchange rate is directly linked to economic stability, central banks also monitor the foreign exchange market.

Now that we have a general idea about what a central bank is and does, we can look more closely at the Federal Reserve, the central bank of the United States.

The Federal Reserve System

The Morgan Library & Museum/Art Resource, NY

The Panic of 1907 led to an epidemic of bank runs like the one pictured here.

The Federal Reserve, the United States' central bank, was created in 1913 in response to the Panic of 1907, which was the first worldwide financial crisis of the twentieth century. The 1907 Panic was created when depositors, panicked at the possibility that they would not be able to access their deposits, began withdrawing money from their accounts. When many depositors panic and attempt to withdraw their deposits from an individual bank, it is known as a *bank run*. Unlike a run on a single bank that has effects limited to that bank, the panic-related withdrawals in 1907 became a systemic panic that led to a widespread banking crisis. In 1907, the economy did not have institutions designed to bring stability to banking and financial markets. In the aftermath of the crisis, several institutions, including the Federal Reserve, were created to prevent future financial crises.

When the Federal Reserve System, also known as "the Fed," was created, it was given responsibility for issuing currency in order to make the money supply sufficiently responsive to economic conditions around the country. It was also given the authority to compel all deposit-taking institutions to hold adequate reserves to cover depositors' withdrawals and to open their accounts to inspection by regulators. These responsibilities were designed to prevent future financial panics.

AP® ECON TIP

The Federal Reserve is responsible for conducting monetary policy for the United States. Other nations have central banks with different names.

The Structure of the Fed

In the opening discussion of central banks, we noted that many operate independently of their governments. The legal status of the Fed, however, is unusual: it is not exactly part of the U.S. government, but it is not really a private institution either. The Federal Reserve System consists of both a public and a private part: the Board of Governors (part of the federal government) and 12 private regional Federal Reserve Banks.

The Board of Governors, which oversees the entire system from its offices in Washington, D.C., is constituted like a government agency: its seven members are appointed by the U.S. president and must be approved by the Senate. However, they are appointed for 14-year terms, to insulate them from political pressure in their conduct of monetary policy. Although the chair is appointed more frequently—every four years—it is traditional for the chair to be reappointed. Because they first completed the terms of Governors who served less than a full term before beginning their own terms, William McChesney Martin was chair of the Fed from 1951 until 1970, and Alan Greenspan, appointed in 1987, served as the Fed's chair until 2006.

Win McNamee/Getty Images

Alan Greenspan (center), shown here with Vice-Chairman Roger Ferguson Jr. (right), was chair of the Federal Reserve from 1987 to 2006.

The 12 Federal Reserve Banks each serve a region of the country, known as a *Federal Reserve district*. Each regional Federal Reserve Bank is owned by those private commercial banks in their district that are members of the Federal Reserve System and is run by a board of directors chosen from the local banking and business community. The regional Federal Reserve Banks provide various banking and supervisory services to their members. One of their jobs, for example, is to audit the books of private-sector banks to ensure their financial health. The Federal Reserve Bank of New York plays a special role: it carries out *open market operations*, as discussed shortly and in Module 4.6. **Figure 4.3B-1** shows the 12 Federal Reserve districts and the city in which each regional Federal Reserve Bank is located.

Decisions about monetary policy are made by the Federal Open Market Committee (FOMC), which consists of the Board of Governors plus five of the regional bank presidents. The president of the Federal Reserve Bank of New York is always on the FOMC, and the other four seats rotate among the 11 other regional bank presidents. The chair of the Board of Governors normally also serves as the chair of the Federal Open Market Committee.

The effect of this complex structure is to create an institution that is ultimately accountable to the voting public because the Board of Governors is chosen by the president and confirmed by the Senate, all of

FIGURE 4.3B-1 The Federal Reserve System

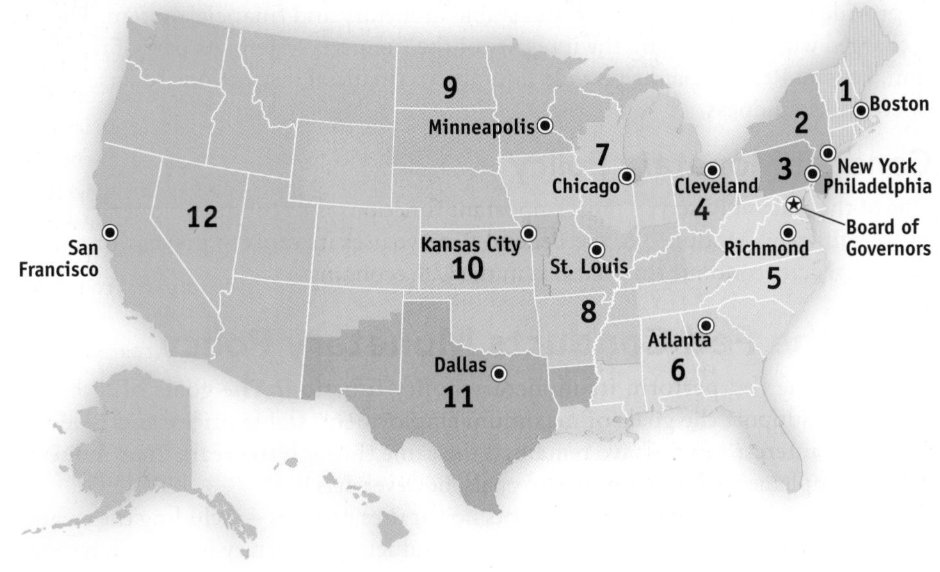

The Federal Reserve System consists of the Board of Governors in Washington, D.C., plus 12 regional Federal Reserve Banks. This map shows each of the 12 Federal Reserve districts.
Data Source: Board of Governors of the Federal Reserve System.

whom are themselves elected officials. But the long terms served by board members, as well as the indirectness of their appointment process, largely insulate them from short-term political pressures.

The Functions of the Federal Reserve System

The functions of the Federal Reserve have evolved since its creation in 1913 and are similar to the functions of other central banks. Today, the Federal Reserve's functions fall into four basic categories: providing financial services to depository institutions, supervising and regulating banks and other financial institutions, maintaining the stability of the financial system, and conducting monetary policy. Let's look at each in turn.

Provide Financial Services

The 12 regional Federal Reserve Banks provide financial services to *depository institutions* such as banks, credit unions, and other large institutions, and the U.S. government. The Federal Reserve is sometimes referred to as the "banker's bank" because it holds reserves, clears checks, provides cash, and transfers funds for commercial banks – all services that banks provide for their customers. The Federal Reserve also acts as the banker and fiscal agent for the federal government. The U.S. Treasury has its checking account with the Federal Reserve, so when the federal government writes a check, it is written on an account at the Fed.

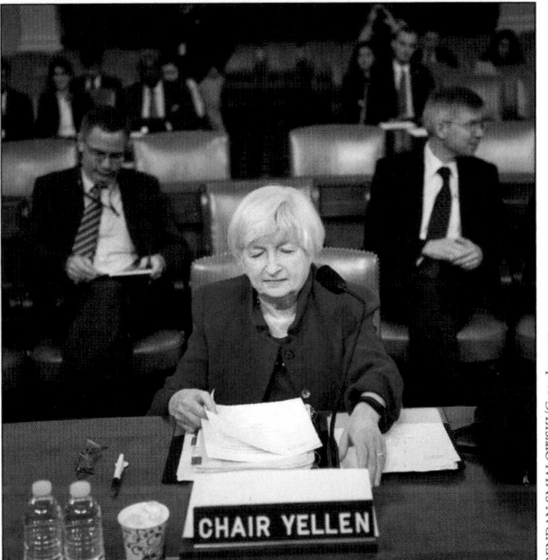

BRENDAN SMIALOWSKI/Getty Images

Economist Janet Yellen was chair of the Fed from 2014 to 2018, the first woman to serve in this role. Yellen was appointed Secretary of the Treasury in 2021.

Supervise and Regulate Banking Institutions

Each regional Federal Reserve Bank examines and regulates member commercial banks in its district. The Board of Governors also engages in regulation and supervision of banks and other financial institutions to evaluate their financial condition and compliance with banking laws and regulations.

Maintain the Stability of the Financial System

As we have seen, one of the major reasons the Federal Reserve System was created was to provide the nation with a safe and stable monetary and financial system. The Fed is charged with maintaining the integrity of the financial system. As part of this function, Federal Reserve Banks provide liquidity to financial institutions to ensure their safety and soundness.

AP® ECON TIP

The interest rate targeted by the Federal Reserve when it conducts monetary policy is the *federal funds rate*.

Conduct Monetary Policy

One of the Federal Reserve's most important functions is to conduct monetary policy. As we will see in Module 4.6, the Federal Reserve uses its tools to prevent or address extreme macroeconomic fluctuations in the U.S. economy.

How the Fed Conducts Monetary Policy

How does the Fed perform its monetary policy function? The goals of monetary policy – to support the goals of maximum employment, stable prices, and moderate long-term interest rates – have remained the same through the years. *How* monetary policy is implemented to pursue these goals, however, has not.

The Federal Reserve adapts how it uses its tools – including the creation of new tools and new methods of conducting monetary policy – in response to changes in the economy. How the Fed implements monetary policy is known as its *implementation regime*. In 2019, the Fed announced that it was moving to an *ample-reserve regime* for implementing monetary policy in the United States. An excerpt from this announcement is provided here. The change to an ample reserve regime moved the focus of monetary policy from controlling the level of bank reserves in the banking system – the traditional approach used by the Fed – to more directly setting interest rates using an expanded set of tools. This approach is discussed in more detail in Module 4.6 and Enrichment Module B.

> The Committee intends to continue to implement monetary policy in a regime in which an ample supply of reserves ensures that control over the level of the federal funds rate and other short-term interest rates is exercised primarily through the setting of the Federal Reserve's administered rates, and in which active management of the supply of reserves is not required.
>
> From the FOMC's *Statement Regarding Monetary Policy Implementation and Balance Sheet Normalization, January 2019*

So, what are bank reserves? In the next Module, we will see that the reserves in the banking system represent the amount of cash that banks are required to keep on hand to meet demand (as well as any additional amount above this requirement that banks may choose to keep). In the past, when bank reserves were scarce, as they were in the years leading up to the 2007–2009 financial crisis, the Federal Reserve had three main policy tools: *reserve requirements*, the *discount rate*, and, historically the most frequently used tool of the three, *open market operations*. However, in the aftermath of the financial crisis, the Fed adapted to the new economic conditions by adding new policy tools. For example, between 2008 and 2014, and again in response to the 2020 pandemic, the Fed used *quantitative easing* – purchasing government bonds or other financial assets to inject money into the economy as a way to keep interest rates low, influence the decisions of banks and firms, and ultimately decrease unemployment. Furthermore, in 2008, the Fed started paying interest on reserves held by banks, and this *interest rate on reserves* has since become an additional tool of monetary policy used by the Fed.

Next, we consider the traditional approach to implementing monetary policy. In Module 4.6, we will look more closely at the implementation of monetary policy in either a traditional (limited reserves) or an ample-reserve environment to achieve the goals of monetary policy.

The Federal Reserve's Balance Sheet

Like the banks it oversees, the Federal Reserve has assets and liabilities. The Fed's assets traditionally consist of its holdings of debt issued by the U.S. government, mainly short-term U.S. government bonds with a maturity of less than one year, known as U.S. Treasury bills. Remember, the Fed and the U.S. government are not one entity; U.S. Treasury bills held by the Fed are a liability of the government but an asset of the Fed.

The Fed's liabilities consist of currency in circulation and bank reserves. **Figure 4.3B-2** summarizes the normal assets and liabilities of the Fed in the form of a *T-account*, which shows what an institution owns (assets) and what it owes (liabilities).

FIGURE 4.3B-2 The Federal Reserve's Assets and Liabilities

Assets	Liabilities
Government debt (Treasury bills)	Monetary base (Currency in circulation + bank reserves)

The Federal Reserve holds its assets mostly in short-term government bonds called U.S. Treasury bills. Its liabilities are the monetary base—currency in circulation plus bank reserves.

In an **open market operation (OMO)**, the Federal Reserve traditionally buys or sells U.S. Treasury bills, normally through a transaction with commercial banks. The Fed never buys U.S. Treasury bills directly from the federal government. (In Module 4.6, we will see that the Fed has developed additional open market operations it uses for implementing monetary policy.)

An **open market operation (OMO)** is a purchase or sale of government debt (bond) by the Fed.

The two panels of **Figure 4.3B-3** show the changes in the financial position of both the Fed and commercial banks that result from open market operations. (We'll explore T-accounts in the context of the commercial banking system in Module 4.4.) When the Fed buys U.S. Treasury bills from a commercial bank, it pays by crediting the bank's reserve account by an amount equal to the value of the Treasury bills. This is illustrated in panel (a): the Fed buys $100 million of U.S. Treasury bills from commercial banks, which increases the monetary base by $100 million because it increases bank reserves by $100 million. When the Fed sells U.S. Treasury bills to commercial banks, it debits the banks' accounts, reducing their reserves. This is shown in panel (b), where the Fed sells $100 million of U.S. Treasury bills. Here, bank reserves and the monetary base decrease.

FIGURE 4.3B-3 Open Market Operations by the Federal Reserve

(a) An Open Market Purchase of $100 Million

	Assets		Liabilities	
Federal Reserve	Treasury bills	+$100 million	Monetary base	+$100 million

	Assets		Liabilities
Commercial banks	Treasury bills	−$100 million	No change
	Reserves	+$100 million	

(b) An Open Market Sale of $100 Million

	Assets		Liabilities	
Federal Reserve	Treasury bills	−$100 million	Monetary base	−$100 million

	Assets		Liabilities
Commercial banks	Treasury bills	+$100 million	No change
	Reserves	−$100 million	

In panel (a), the Federal Reserve increases the monetary base by purchasing assets, traditionally U.S. Treasury bills, from private commercial banks in an open market operation. Here, a $100 million purchase of U.S. Treasury bills by the Federal Reserve is paid for by a $100 million increase in the monetary base. In panel (b), the Federal Reserve reduces the monetary base by selling U.S. Treasury bills to private commercial banks in an open market operation. Here, a $100 million sale of U.S. Treasury bills leads to a $100 million reduction in commercial bank reserves, resulting in a $100 million decrease in the monetary base.

You might wonder where the Fed gets the funds to purchase U.S. Treasury bills from banks. The answer is that it simply creates them with the stroke of the pen – or, these days, the click of the button – that credits the banks' accounts with extra reserves. The Fed issues currency to pay for Treasury bills only when banks want the additional reserves in the form of currency. Remember, the modern dollar is fiat money, which isn't backed by anything. So the Fed can add to the monetary base at its own discretion.

The change in bank reserves caused by an open market operation doesn't directly affect the money supply. Instead, it can start the money multiplier in motion. After the $100 million increase in reserves shown in panel (a), commercial banks would lend out their additional reserves, immediately increasing the money supply by $100 million. Some of those loans would be deposited back into the banking system, increasing reserves again and permitting a further round of loans, and so on, leading to a rise in the money supply. An open market sale can have the reverse effect: bank reserves fall, requiring banks to reduce their loans, leading to a fall in the money supply.

Economists often say, loosely, that the Fed controls the U.S. money supply – checkable deposits plus currency in circulation. In fact, it controls only the monetary base – bank reserves plus currency in circulation. But by increasing or decreasing the monetary base, the Fed can exert influence on the money supply and interest rates. This influence can be part of monetary policy, as discussed in detail in Module 4.6.

Module 4.3B Review

Check Your Understanding

1. What is a central bank, and what is a benefit of having an independent central bank?
2. Why was the Federal Reserve created, and what are its four basic functions?

Tackle the AP® Test: Multiple-Choice Questions

1. Which of the following is true regarding central banks?
   a. They only exist in the United States and Europe.
   b. They oversee and regulate the banking system.
   c. They are structured to be part public and part private.
   d. They include multiple regional reserve banks.
   e. All of the above are true.
2. Which of the following contributed to the creation of the Federal Reserve System?
   a. the bank Panic of 1907
   b. the Great Depression
   c. the savings and loan crisis of the 1980s
   d. the financial crisis of 2008
   e. the aftermath of World War II
3. Which of the following institutions controls the monetary base?
   a. the central bank
   b. the Treasury
   c. Congress
   d. commercial banks
   e. investment banks
4. Which of the following is NOT a role of the Federal Reserve System?
   a. controlling bank reserves
   b. printing currency
   c. carrying out monetary policy
   d. supervising and regulating banks
   e. holding reserves for commercial banks
5. Who oversees the Federal Reserve System?
   a. Congress
   b. the president of the United States
   c. the Federal Open Market Committee
   d. the Board of Governors of the Federal Reserve System
   e. the Reconstruction Finance Corporation
6. The Federal Open Market Committee is made up of which of the following?
   a. members of the Board of Governors
   b. five voting Federal Reserve Bank presidents
   c. the president of the Federal Reserve Bank of New York
   d. eleven Federal Reserve Bank presidents on a rotating basis
   e. all of the above

7. A central bank could do which of the following in order to change the monetary base?
   a. change the reserve requirement
   b. change the discount rate
   c. sell government bonds
   d. change the interest rate on reserves
   e. all of the above

Tackle the AP® Test: Free-Response Questions

1. a. What group determines U.S. monetary policy?
   b. How many members serve in this group?
   c. Who always serves in this group?
   d. Who sometimes serves in this group? Explain.

Rubric for FRQ 1 (5 points)

1 point: The Federal Open Market Committee (FOMC)

1 point: 12

1 point: Members of the Board of Governors and the New York Federal Reserve Bank president

1 point: Four of the other 11 Federal Reserve Bank presidents

1 point: The 11 other Federal Reserve Bank presidents rotate their service on the FOMC.

2. What are the three traditional tools of a central bank, and what would the Federal Reserve do with each to decrease the monetary base? What are two additional tools the Federal Reserve uses to conduct monetary policy? **(5 points)**

MODULE 4.4

Banking and the Expansion of the Money Supply

In this Module, you will learn to:

- Explain how depository institutions, such as commercial banks, organize their assets and liabilities on balance sheets
- Define a fractional reserve banking system
- Define required reserves, excess reserves, and a fractional reserve banking system
- Define the money multiplier as the ratio of the money supply to the monetary base and also as the reciprocal of the reserve requirement
- Explain how the banking system creates and expands the money supply
- Calculate the effects of changes in the banking system
- Explain how excess reserves and the public holding currency can decrease the money multiplier and cause the simple money multiplier to overstate the effect of a change in the banking system

The Monetary Role of Banks

As we learned in Module 4.3, M1, the narrowest definition of the money supply, includes currency in circulation – those bills and coins held by the public. You may already know where U.S. currency comes from: it is printed or minted by the U.S. Treasury. But the rest of M1 consists of demand deposits, and other deposits account for a significant portion of M2, the broader definition of the money supply. By either measure, then, bank deposits are an important part of the money supply. And this fact brings us to our next topic: the monetary role of commercial banks and other depository institutions.

Sonja Pacho/Getty Images

What Banks Do

A bank is a *financial intermediary* operated for profit that uses bank deposits to finance borrowers' investments in illiquid assets such as businesses and homes. Banks can lend depositors' money to investors and thereby create liquidity (and earn a profit) because it isn't necessary for a bank to keep all of its deposits on hand. Except in the case of a *bank run*, all of a bank's depositors won't want to withdraw their funds at the same time. A banking system in which banks do not keep all of their deposits on reserve, but rather loan out some of their deposits, is known as a **fractional reserve banking system**.

However, banks can't lend out *all* the funds placed in their hands by depositors because they have to satisfy any depositor who wants to withdraw their funds. In order to meet these demands, a bank must keep substantial quantities of liquid assets on hand. In modern banking systems, these assets take the form of either currency in the bank's vault or deposits held in the bank's own account at the central bank. As we'll see shortly, the latter can be converted into currency more or less instantly. Currency in bank vaults and bank deposits held by central banks are called **bank reserves**. Because bank reserves are in bank vaults and at the central bank, not held by the public, they are not part of currency in circulation.

In a **fractional reserve banking system**, only a fraction of bank deposits are backed by cash on hand and available for withdrawal.

Bank reserves are the currency that banks hold in their vaults plus their deposits at the central bank.

To understand the role of banks in determining the money supply, we'll use the same simple tool introduced in Module 4.3B for analyzing an institution's financial position: the T-account. A business's T-account summarizes its financial position by showing, in a single table, the business's assets and liabilities, with assets on the left and liabilities on the right. **Figure 4.4-1** shows the T-account, also known as a balance sheet, for a hypothetical business that *isn't* a bank—Samantha's Smoothies. According to Figure 4.4-1, Samantha's Smoothies owns a building worth $30,000 and has $15,000 worth of smoothie-making equipment. These are assets, so they're on the left side of the table. To finance its opening, the business borrowed $20,000 from a local bank. That's a liability, so the loan is on the right side of the table. *Owner's equity* of $25,000 balances the two sides of the T-account. Owner's equity is equal to the amount of assets minus the amount of liabilities and represents the owner's financial investment in the business. By looking at this T-account, you can immediately see what Samantha's Smoothies owns and what it owes. This type of table is called a T-account because the lines in the table make a T-shape.

FIGURE 4.4-1 A T-Account for Samantha's Smoothies

Assets		Liabilities and Owner's Equity	
Building	$30,000	Loan from bank	$20,000
Smoothie-making machines	$15,000	Owner's equity	$25,000

A T-account summarizes a business's financial position. Its assets, in this case consisting of a building and some smoothie-making machinery, are on the left side. Its liabilities—the money it owes to a local bank—are on the right side, along with the owner's equity.

Samantha's Smoothies is an ordinary, nonbank business. Now let's look at the T-account for a hypothetical bank, First Street Bank, which is the repository of $1 million in bank deposits.

Figure 4.4-2 shows First Street's financial position. The loans First Street has made are on the left side because they are assets: they represent funds that those who have borrowed from the bank are expected to repay. The bank's only other assets, in this simplified example, are its reserves, which, as we've learned, can take the form of either cash in the bank's vault or deposits at the central bank. On the right side we show the bank's liabilities, which in this example consist entirely of deposits made by customers at First Street. These are liabilities because they represent funds that must ultimately be repaid to depositors. Notice, by the way, that in this example First Street's assets are larger than its liabilities by the amount of the bank's capital. That's the way it's supposed to be! In fact, banks are required by law to maintain assets larger than their liabilities by a specific percentage.

AP® ECON TIP

A T-account is a simple way to organize and present information. T-accounts are often used to present information about banks and the banking system. For example, they may be used to show the level of currency, deposits, loans, or reserves. These values allow you to determine other values such as M1, excess reserves, or reserve requirements.

FIGURE 4.4-2 Assets and Liabilities of First Street Bank

Assets		Liabilities and Bank's Capital	
Loans	$1,000,000	Deposits	$1,000,000
Reserves	$100,000	Bank's capital	$100,000

First Street Bank's assets consist of $1,000,000 in loans and $100,000 in reserves. Its liabilities consist of $1,000,000 in deposits—money owed to people who have placed funds in First Street's hands; this amount is combined with the bank's capital of $100,000.

In this example, First Street Bank holds reserves equal to 10% of its customers' bank deposits. The fraction of bank deposits that a bank holds as reserves is its **reserve ratio**. In modern banking systems, the central bank—which, among other things,

The **reserve ratio** is the fraction of bank deposits that a bank holds as reserves.

The **required reserve ratio** is the smallest fraction of deposits that the central bank requires banks to hold.

regulates banks – sets a **required reserve ratio**, which is the smallest fraction of bank deposits that a bank must hold. To understand why banks are regulated, let's consider a problem banks can face: *bank runs.*

The Problem of Bank Runs

A bank can lend out most of the funds deposited in its care because in normal times only a small fraction of its depositors want to withdraw their funds on any given day. But what would happen if, for some reason, all or at least a large fraction of its depositors *did* try to withdraw their funds during a short period of time, such as a couple of days?

The answer is that the bank wouldn't be able to raise enough cash to meet those demands. The reason is that banks convert most of their depositors' funds into loans made to borrowers; this is how banks earn revenue – by charging interest on loans. Bank loans, however, are illiquid: they can't easily be converted into cash on short notice. To see why, imagine that First Street Bank has lent $100,000 to Drive-a-Peach Used Cars, a local dealership. To raise cash to meet demands for withdrawals, First Street can sell its Drive-a-Peach loan to someone else – another bank or an individual investor. But if First Street tries to sell the loan quickly, potential buyers will be wary: they will suspect that First Street wants to sell the loan because there is significant risk that the loan might not be repaid. As a result, First Street Bank can sell the loan quickly only by offering it for sale at a deep discount – say, a discount of 50%, or $50,000.

The upshot is that, if a significant number of First Street's depositors suddenly decided to withdraw their funds, the bank's efforts to raise the necessary cash quickly would force it to sell off its assets very cheaply. Inevitably, this would lead to a *bank failure*: the bank would be unable to pay off its depositors in full.

What might lead First Street's depositors to rush to pull their money out? A plausible answer is a spreading rumor that the bank is in financial trouble. Even if depositors aren't sure the rumor is true, they are likely to play it safe and get their money out while they still can. And it gets worse: a depositor who simply thinks that *other* depositors are going to panic and try to get their money out will realize that this could "break the bank." So this depositor joins the rush. In other words, fear about a bank's financial condition can be a self-fulfilling prophecy: depositors who believe that other depositors will rush to the exit will rush to the exit themselves.

A *bank run* is a phenomenon in which many of a bank's depositors try to withdraw their funds due to fears of a bank failure. Moreover, bank runs aren't bad only for the bank in question and its depositors. Historically, they have often proved contagious, with a run on one bank leading to a loss of faith in other banks, causing additional bank runs. A wave of bank runs that swept across the United States at the start of the Great Depression eventually led 40% of banks to fail by the end of 1932. In response to that experience and similar experiences in other countries, the United States and most other modern governments have established a system of bank regulations that protects depositors and prevents most bank runs.

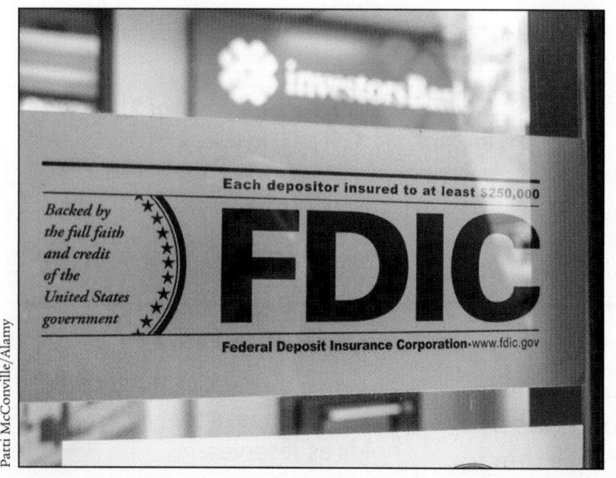

Patti McConville/Alamy

Bank Regulation

Should depositors today worry about losing money in a bank run? After the banking crises of the 1930s, the United States and many other countries put into place a system designed to protect depositors and the economy as a whole against bank runs. In the United States, this system had three main features: *deposit insurance*, *capital requirements*, and *reserve requirements*. In addition, banks have access to the *discount window*, a source of loans from the central bank.

Deposit Insurance

Almost all banks in the United States advertise themselves as a "member of the FDIC" – the Federal Deposit Insurance Corporation. The FDIC provides deposit insurance, a guarantee that depositors will be paid even if the bank can't come up with the funds, up to a maximum amount per account. In 2008, the FDIC increased the maximum amount covered per depositor, per account to $250,000.

It's important to realize that deposit insurance doesn't just protect depositors if a bank actually fails. The insurance also eliminates the main reason for bank runs: since depositors know their funds are safe even if a bank fails, they have no incentive to rush to pull them out because of a rumor that the bank is in trouble.

Capital Requirements

Deposit insurance, although it protects the banking system against bank runs, creates a well-known incentive problem. Because depositors are protected from loss, they have no incentive to monitor their bank's financial health, allowing risky behavior by the bank to go undetected. At the same time, the owners of banks have an incentive to engage in overly risky investment behavior, such as making questionable loans at high interest rates. That's because if all goes well, the owners profit; and if things go badly, the government covers the losses through federal deposit insurance.

To reduce the incentive for excessive risk-taking, regulators require that the owners of banks hold substantially more assets than the value of bank deposits. That way, the bank will have assets larger than its deposits even if some of its loans go bad, and losses will accrue against the bank owners' assets, rather than against the government. The excess of a bank's assets over its bank deposits and other liabilities is called the *bank's capital,* or *equity*. For example, First Street Bank has capital of $100,000, equal to 9% of the total value of its assets. In practice, a bank is required to have capital equal to at least 7% of the value of its assets.

Reserve Requirements

Another regulation that can be used to reduce the risk of bank runs is the **reserve requirement**, the rule set by the central bank that establishes the required reserve ratio for banks. In some cases, the reserve requirement can be set to zero. For example, in 2019 the U. S. Federal Reserve announced its intention to implement monetary policy with ample reserves, and in 2020, it reduced its reserve requirement to zero percent. (These changes are discussed in detail in Enrichment Module B.)

Reserve requirements are rules set by the central bank that determine the required reserve ratio for banks.

The Discount Window

One final protection against bank runs is the fact that the central bank stands ready to lend money to banks through a channel known as the discount window (originally an actual window at the Fed, though this is no longer the case). The ability to borrow money means a bank can avoid being forced to sell its assets at fire-sale prices in order to satisfy the demands of a sudden rush of depositors demanding cash. Instead, it can turn to the central bank and borrow the funds it needs to pay off depositors.

Determining the Money Supply

Without banks, there would be no checkable deposits, and so the quantity of currency in circulation would equal the money supply. In that case, the money supply would be determined solely by whoever controls government minting and printing presses. But banks do exist, and through their creation of checkable bank deposits, they affect the money supply in two ways. First, banks remove some currency from circulation: dollar bills that are sitting in bank vaults, as opposed to sitting in people's wallets, aren't part of the money supply. Second, and much more importantly, banks create money by accepting deposits and making loans – that is, they make the money supply larger than just the value of currency in circulation. Our next topic is how banks create money, and what determines the amount of money they create.

AP® ECON TIP

When we say that banks create money, we mean that they increase the amount recorded in depositors' accounts; they don't print more currency—only the Treasury does that.

How Banks Can Create Money

To see how banks can create money, let's examine what happens when someone decides to deposit currency in a bank. Consider the example of Silas, a miser who keeps a shoebox full of cash under his bed. Suppose Silas realizes that it would be safer, as well as more convenient, to deposit that cash in the bank and to use his debit card when shopping. Assume that he deposits $1,000 into a checkable account at First Street Bank. What effect will Silas's actions have on the money supply?

Panel (a) of **Figure 4.4-3** shows the initial effect of his deposit. First Street Bank credits Silas with $1,000 in his account, so the economy's checkable bank deposits rise by $1,000. Meanwhile, Silas's cash goes into the vault, raising First Street's reserves by $1,000 as well.

FIGURE 4.4-3 Effect on the Money Supply of Turning Cash into a Checkable Deposit at First Street Bank

(a) Initial Effect Before Bank Makes a New Loan

Assets		Liabilities	
Loans	No change	Checkable deposits	+$1,000
Reserves	+$1,000		

(b) Effect When Bank Makes a New Loan

Assets		Liabilities
Loans	+$900	No change
Reserves	−$900	

When Silas deposits $1,000 (which had been stashed under his bed) into a checkable bank account, there is initially no effect on the money supply: currency in circulation falls by $1,000, but checkable bank deposits rise by $1,000. The corresponding entries on the bank's T-account, depicted in panel (a), show deposits initially rising by $1,000 and the bank's reserves initially rising by $1,000. In the second stage, depicted in panel (b), the bank holds 10% of Silas's deposit ($100) as reserves and lends out the rest ($900) to Mariama. As a result, its reserves fall by $900 and its loans increase by $900. Its liabilities, including Silas's $1,000 deposit, are unchanged. The money supply, the sum of checkable bank deposits and currency in circulation, has now increased by $900 – the $900 now held by Mariama.

Jonathan Kitchen/Getty Images

This initial transaction has no effect on the money supply. Currency in circulation, part of the money supply, falls by $1,000; checkable bank deposits, also part of the money supply, rise by the same amount.

But this is not the end of the story, because First Street Bank can now lend out part of Silas's deposit. Assume that it holds 10% of Silas's deposit – $100 – in reserves and lends the rest out in cash to Silas's neighbor, Mariama. The effect of this second stage is shown in panel (b) of Figure 4.4-3. First Street's deposits remain unchanged, and so does the value of its assets. But the composition of its assets changes: by making the loan, it reduces its reserves by $900, so that they are only $100 larger than they were before Silas made his deposit. In the place of the $900 reduction in reserves, the bank has acquired an IOU, its $900 cash loan to Mariama. So by putting $900 of Silas's cash back into circulation by lending it to Mariama, First Street Bank has, in fact, increased the money supply. That is, the sum of currency in circulation and checkable bank deposits has risen by $900 compared to what it had been when Silas's cash was still in a shoebox under his bed. Although Silas is still the owner of $1,000, now in the form of a checkable deposit, Mariama has the use of $900 from her loan.

This may not be the end of the story either. Suppose that Mariama uses her cash to buy a laptop from Acme Computers. What does Aanya Acme, the store's owner, do with the cash? If she holds on to it, the money supply doesn't increase any further. But suppose she deposits the $900 into a checkable bank deposit – say, at Second Street Bank. Second Street Bank, in turn, will keep only part of that deposit in reserves, lending out the rest, creating still more money.

Assume that Second Street Bank, like First Street Bank, keeps 10% of any bank deposit in reserves and lends out the rest. Then it will keep $90 in reserves and lend out $810 of Aanya's deposit to another borrower, further increasing the money supply.

Table 4.4-1 shows the process of money creation we have described so far. At first the money supply consists only of Silas's $1,000. After he deposits that cash into a checkable bank deposit and the bank makes a loan, the money supply rises to $1,900. After the second deposit and the second loan, the money supply rises to $2,710. And the process will, of course, continue from there. (Although we have considered the case in which Silas places his cash in a checkable bank deposit, the results would be the same if he put it into any type of near-money.) This process will also work in reverse. When loans are repaid, money is destroyed.

Table 4.4-1 How Banks Create Money

	Currency in circulation	Checkable bank deposits	Money supply
First stage: Silas keeps his cash under his bed.	$1,000	$0	$1,000
Second stage: Silas deposits cash in First Street Bank, which lends out $900 to Mariama, who then pays it to Aanya Acme.	900	1,000	1,900
Third stage: Aanya Acme deposits $900 in Second Street Bank, which lends out $810 to another borrower.	810	1,900	2,710

This process of money creation and destruction may sound familiar. Recall the *expenditure multiplier process* that we described in Module 3.8: an initial increase in spending leads to a rise in real GDP, which leads to a further rise in spending, which leads to a further rise in real GDP, and so on. What we have here is another kind of multiplier – the *money multiplier*. Next, we'll learn what determines the size of this multiplier.

Reserves, Bank Deposits, and the Money Multiplier

In tracing out the effect of Silas's deposit in Table 4.4-1, we assumed that the funds a bank lends out always end up being deposited either in the same bank or in another bank – so funds disbursed as loans come back to the banking system, even if not to the lending bank itself. In reality, some of these loaned funds may be held by borrowers in their wallets and not deposited in a bank, meaning that some of the loaned amount "leaks" out of the banking system. Such leaks reduce the size of the money multiplier, just as leaks of real income into savings reduce the size of the expenditure multiplier (Bear in mind, however, that the "leak" here comes from the fact that borrowers keep some of their funds in currency, rather than the fact that consumers save some of their income.) But let's set that complication aside for a moment and consider how the money supply is determined in a "checkable-deposits-only" monetary system, in which funds are always deposited in bank accounts and none are held in wallets as currency. That is, in our checkable-deposits-only monetary system, any and all funds borrowed from a bank are immediately deposited into a checkable bank account.

In our scenario, we'll assume that banks are required to satisfy a minimum reserve ratio of 10% and that every bank lends out all of its reserves over and above the amount needed to satisfy the minimum reserve ratio. In a typical banking system, a bank's total reserves are made up of two parts: **required reserves** mandated by the central bank

Required reserves are the reserves that banks must hold, as mandated by the central bank.

Excess reserves are a bank's reserves over and above its required reserves.

and **excess reserves** (any additional reserves a bank chooses to hold). Excess reserves represent the funds available for banks to loan out to borrowers.

Now suppose that for some reason, a bank suddenly finds itself with \$1,000 in excess reserves. What happens? The answer is that the bank will lend out that \$1,000, which will end up as a checkable bank deposit somewhere in the banking system, launching a money multiplier process very similar to the process shown in Table 4.4-1. In the first stage, the bank lends out its excess reserves of \$1,000, which becomes a checkable bank deposit somewhere. The bank that receives the \$1,000 deposit keeps 10%, or \$100, as reserves and lends out the remaining 90%, or \$900, which again becomes a checkable bank deposit somewhere. The bank receiving this \$900 deposit again keeps 10%, which is \$90, as reserves and lends out the remaining \$810. The bank receiving this \$810 keeps \$81 in reserves and lends out the remaining \$729, and so on. As a result of this process, the total increase in checkable bank deposits is equal to a sum that looks like:

$$\$1,000 + \$900 + \$810 + \$729 + \ldots$$

We'll use the symbol *rr* for the reserve ratio. More generally, the total increase in checkable bank deposits that is generated when a bank lends out \$1,000 in excess reserves is:

$$\textbf{(4.4-1)} \quad \$1,000 + \$1,000 \times (1 - rr) + \$1,000 \times (1 - rr)^2 + \$1,000 \times (1 - rr)^3 + \ldots$$

As we saw in Module 3.2, an infinite series of this form can be simplified to $\$1,000/rr$. We will formally define the money multiplier in the next section, but we can now see its usefulness: it is the factor by which we multiply an initial increase in excess reserves to find the total resulting increase in checkable bank deposits:

$$\textbf{(4.4-2)} \quad \text{Money multiplier} = \frac{1}{rr}$$

AP® ECON TIP

The simple money multiplier is $\frac{1}{rr}$, where *rr* is the reserve ratio. The money multiplier is used to explain and calculate money creation.

Given a reserve ratio of 10%, or 0.1, a \$1,000 increase in excess reserves will increase the total value of checkable bank deposits by $\$1,000 \times 1/rr = \$1,000/0.1 = \$10,000$. In fact, in a checkable deposits-only monetary system, the total value of checkable bank deposits will be equal to the value of bank reserves divided by the reserve ratio. Or, to put it a different way, if the reserve ratio is 10%, each \$1 of reserves held by a bank supports $\$1/rr = \$1/0.1 = \$10$ of checkable bank deposits.

Note that the money multiplier as we have discussed it relies on the reserve requirement set by the central bank. However, we have also seen that the central bank can set the reserve requirement to zero, as the U. S. Federal Reserve did in 2020. A reserve requirement of zero means that all reserves become excess reserves. In such a case, we can think of the money multiplier as using the *desired* reserve ratio rather than the required reserve ratio.

The Money Multiplier in Reality

In reality, the determination of the money supply is more complicated than our simple model suggests, because it depends not only on the ratio of reserves to bank deposits but also on the fraction of the money supply that individuals choose to hold in the form of currency. In fact, we already saw this in our example of Silas depositing the cash instead of holding it under his bed: when he chose to hold a checkable bank deposit instead of currency, he set in motion an increase in the money supply.

To define the money multiplier in practice, we need to understand that central banks control the *monetary base*, which, as we learned in the discussion of monetary aggregates in Module 4.3A, is the sum of currency in circulation and the reserves held by banks. A central bank does not determine how that sum is allocated between bank reserves and currency in circulation. Consider Silas and his deposit one more time: by taking the cash from under his bed and depositing it in a bank, he reduced the quantity of currency in circulation but increased bank reserves by an equal amount. So while the allocation of the monetary base changes—the amount in reserves grows and the amount in circulation shrinks—the total of these two, the monetary base, remains unchanged.

The monetary base is different from the money supply in two ways. First, as we noted above, bank reserves, which are part of the monetary base, aren't considered part of the money supply. A $1 bill in someone's wallet is considered part of the money supply because it's available for an individual to spend, but a $1 bill held as bank reserves in a bank vault or deposited at a central bank isn't considered part of the money supply because it's not available for spending. Second, checkable bank deposits, which are part of the money supply because they are available for spending, aren't part of the monetary base.

Figure 4.4-4 shows the two concepts schematically. The circle on the left represents the monetary base, consisting of bank reserves plus currency in circulation. The circle on the right represents the money supply, consisting mainly of currency in circulation plus checkable or near-checkable bank deposits. As the figure indicates, currency in circulation is part of both the monetary base and the money supply. But bank reserves aren't part of the money supply, and checkable or near-checkable bank deposits aren't part of the monetary base. Normally, less than half of the monetary base consists of currency in circulation, which makes up a small part of the money supply.

Steve Hamblin/Alamy

Currency held as bank reserves isn't part of the money supply, but it is part of the monetary base.

FIGURE 4.4-4 **The Monetary Base and the Money Supply**

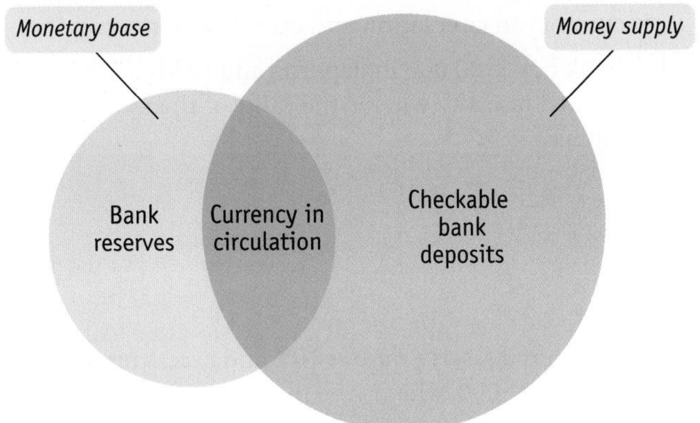

The monetary base is equal to bank reserves plus currency in circulation. It is different from the money supply, which consists mainly of checkable or near-checkable bank deposits plus currency in circulation. Each dollar of bank reserves backs several dollars of bank deposits, making the money supply larger than the monetary base. In the next Module, we develop the money market and look at how changes in the money supply or money demand affect nominal interest rates in the economy.

Now we can formally define the **money multiplier**: it's the ratio of the money supply to the monetary base. This tells us the total number of dollars created in the banking system by each $1 addition to the monetary base. We have seen that in a simple situation in which banks hold no excess reserves and all cash is deposited in banks, the money multiplier is $1/rr$. So if the reserve requirement is 0.1, the money multiplier is $1/0.1 = 10$; if the central bank adds $100 to the monetary base, the money supply will increase by $10 \times \$100 = \$1{,}000$. The actual money multiplier is generally smaller than the simple money multiplier due to the fact that people hold significant amounts of cash. A dollar of currency in circulation, unlike a dollar in reserves, doesn't support multiple dollars of the money supply. In fact, currency in circulation normally accounts for more than 90% of the monetary base.

The **money multiplier** is the ratio of the money supply to the monetary base. It indicates the total number of dollars created in the banking system by each $1 addition to the monetary base.

Module 4.4 Review

> **Adventures in AP® Economics**
> Watch the video:
> ***The Money Multiplier***

Check Your Understanding

1. Assume that total reserves are equal to $200 and total checkable bank deposits are equal to $1,000. Also assume that the public does not hold any currency and banks hold no excess reserves. Now suppose that the required reserve ratio falls from 20% to 10%. Trace out how this leads to an expansion in bank deposits.

2. Take the example of Silas depositing his $1,000 in cash into First Street Bank and assume that the required reserve ratio is 10%. But now assume that each recipient of a bank loan keeps half the loan in cash and deposits the rest. Calculate the resulting expansion in the money supply through at least three stages of deposits.

Tackle the AP® Test: Multiple-Choice Questions

1. Bank reserves include which of the following?
   a. currency in circulation
   b. bank deposits held in accounts at the central bank
   c. customer deposits in bank checking accounts
   d. the monetary base
   e. all of the above

2. Bank deposits *actually* held as reserves are equal to which of the following?
   a. reserved reserves
   b. excess reserves
   c. required and excess reserves
   d. the monetary base
   e. currency in circulation

3. Which of the following helps to prevent bank runs?
   a. deposit insurance
   b. capital requirements
   c. reserve requirements
   d. the discount window
   e. all of the above

4. Which of the following changes would be the most likely to reduce the size of the money multiplier?
   a. a decrease in the required reserve ratio
   b. a decrease in excess reserves
   c. an increase in cash holding by consumers
   d. a decrease in bank runs
   e. an increase in deposit insurance

5. Which of the following is part of both the monetary base and the money supply?
   a. currency in circulation
   b. bank reserves
   c. currency in circulation and bank reserves
   d. currency in circulation and required bank reserves
   e. currency in circulation and excess bank reserves

6. If a bank has $100,000 in deposits and holds $5,000 in required reserves, what is the value of the money multiplier?
   a. 0.05
   b. 0.5
   c. 5
   d. 20
   e. 50

7. If the required reserve ratio is 10% and excess reserves increase by $1,000, what is the maximum possible increase in checkable deposits throughout the banking system?
   a. $0
   b. $100
   c. $1,000
   d. $10,000
   e. $100,000

Tackle the AP® Test: Free-Response Questions

1. How will each of the following affect the money supply through the money multiplier process? Explain.
   a. People hold more cash.
   b. Banks hold more reserves.
   c. The central bank increases the required reserve ratio.

Rubric for FRQ 1 (6 points)

1 point: a: It will decrease.

1 point: Money held as cash does not support multiple dollars in the money supply.

1 point: b: It will decrease.

1 point: Excess reserves are not loaned out and therefore do not expand the money supply.

1 point: c: It will decrease.

1 point: Banks will have to hold more as reserves and therefore loan out less.

2. Suppose the required reserve ratio is 5%.
   a. If a bank has deposits of $100,000 and holds $10,000 as reserves, how much of the $10,000 is excess reserves? Explain.
   b. If a bank holds no excess reserves and it receives a new deposit of $1,000, how much of that $1,000 can the bank lend out, and how much is the bank required to add to its reserves? Explain.
   c. By how much can an increase in excess reserves of $2,000 change the money supply in a checkable deposits-only system? Explain. **(5 points)**

MODULE 4.5

The Money Market

In this Module, you will learn to:

- Define the money market, money demand, and money supply
- Explain the relationship between the nominal interest rate and the quantity of money demanded, and why the money supply is independent of the nominal interest rate
- Use a correctly labeled graph of the money market to show how the nominal interest rate is determined by the money supply and money demand, and to identify equilibrium and disequilibrium in the money market
- Explain how nominal interest rates adjust to restore equilibrium in the money market
- Identify the determinants of demand and supply in the money market
- Use a correctly labeled graph to show how changes in demand or supply affect the equilibrium nominal interest rate

What Is the Money Market?

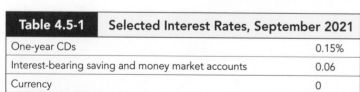

The *money market* is similar to the market for goods and services; the demand for money and the supply of money interact to determine the equilibrium price of money (the interest rate) and the equilibrium quantity of money. In the money market, borrowers and lenders agree to short-term loans. In this Module, we consider the demand for money, the supply of money, and how equilibrium is determined in the money market.

Joshua Minso/Shutterstock

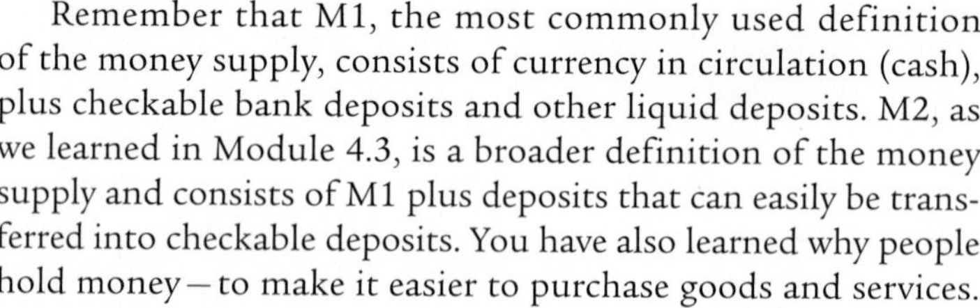

Remember that M1, the most commonly used definition of the money supply, consists of currency in circulation (cash), plus checkable bank deposits and other liquid deposits. M2, as we learned in Module 4.3, is a broader definition of the money supply and consists of M1 plus deposits that can easily be transferred into checkable deposits. You have also learned why people hold money – to make it easier to purchase goods and services. Now we'll go deeper, examining what determines *how much* money individuals and firms want to hold at any given time.

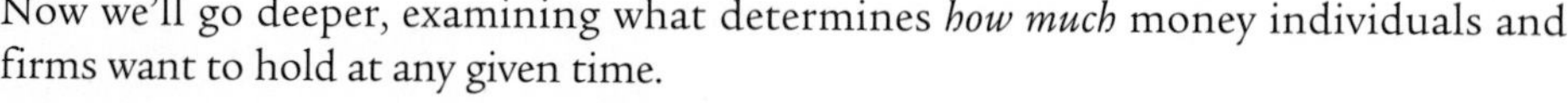

The Demand for Money

Individuals and firms find it useful to hold some of their assets in the form of money because of the convenience money provides: money can be used to make purchases directly, while other assets can't. But there is an opportunity cost for that convenience: money held in your wallet earns no interest.

In January 2022, the interest on savings accounts was around 0.4%, which leads to a very low opportunity cost of holding money. **Table 4.5-1** illustrates the opportunity cost of holding money in a specific month. The first row shows the interest rate on one-year certificates of deposit (CDs) – that is, the interest rate individuals could get if they were willing to tie their funds up for one year. In September 2021, the one-year CDs yielded 0.15%. The second row shows the interest rate on interest-bearing savings and money market accounts. Funds in these accounts were more accessible than those in CDs, but the price of that convenience was a much lower interest rate, only 0.06%. Finally, the last row shows the interest rate on currency – cash in your wallet – which, of course, was zero.

Table 4.5-1	**Selected Interest Rates, September 2021**
One-year CDs	0.15%
Interest-bearing saving and money market accounts	0.06
Currency	0

Source: Bankrate.com.

Table 4.5-1 shows the opportunity cost of holding money at one point in time, but the opportunity cost of holding money changes when there is a change in the overall level of interest rates. Specifically, when the overall level of interest rates falls, the opportunity cost of holding money falls, too.

Because there are many alternatives to holding money in your wallet, each with its own interest payment, there are many different interest rates in the economy. But, with rare exceptions, all short-term interest rates – rates on financial assets that come due, or mature, within a year – tend to move together because no asset will consistently offer a higher-than-average or a lower-than-average interest rate. At any given moment, long-term interest rates – interest rates on financial assets that mature, or come due, a number of years in the future – may be different from short-term interest rates.

In practice, long-term interest rates reflect the average expectation in the market about what's going to happen to short-term rates in the future. When long-term rates are higher than short-term rates, the market is signaling that it expects short-term rates to rise in the future. Moreover, short-term rates, rather than long-term rates, affect money demand because the decision to hold money involves trading off the convenience of holding cash versus the payoff from holding assets that mature in the short term – a year or less.

For our current purposes, however, it's useful to ignore the distinction between short-term and long-term rates and assume that there is only one interest rate.

AP® ECON TIP

We focus on the role of interest rates in the economy by considering a single, representative short-run interest rate, *i* (though we know there are many different interest rates).

The Money Demand Curve

Because the overall level of interest rates affects the opportunity cost of holding money, the quantity of money individuals and firms want to hold, other things equal, is negatively related to the interest rate. In **Figure 4.5-1**, the horizontal axis shows the quantity of money demanded, and the vertical axis shows the nominal interest rate, *i*, which you can think of as a representative short-term interest rate such as the rate on one-month CDs. Why do we place the nominal interest rate and not the real interest rate on the vertical axis? Because, as you'll recall from Module 4.1, the opportunity cost of holding money includes both the real return that could be earned on a bank deposit and the erosion in purchasing power caused by inflation. The nominal interest rate includes both the forgone real return and the expected loss due to inflation. Hence, *i* in Figure 4.5-1 and all subsequent figures is the nominal interest rate.

FIGURE 4.5-1 The Money Demand Curve

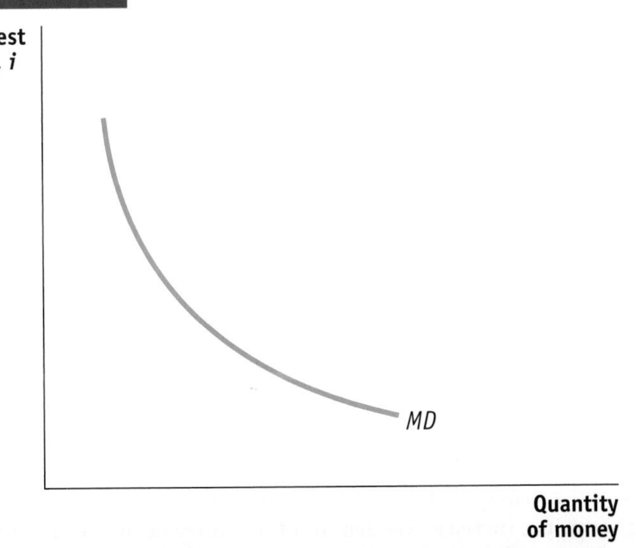

The money demand curve (*MD*) illustrates the relationship between the nominal interest rate and the quantity of money demanded. It slopes downward: a higher interest rate leads to a higher opportunity cost of holding money and reduces the quantity of money demanded.

The **money demand curve** shows the relationship between the quantity of money demanded and the nominal interest rate.

The relationship between the nominal interest rate and the quantity of money demanded by the public is illustrated by the **money demand curve, *MD***, in Figure 4.5-1. The money demand curve slopes downward because, other things equal, a higher interest rate increases the opportunity cost of holding money, leading the public to reduce the quantity of money it demands. For example, if the interest rate is very low—say, 0.15%, the one-year CD rate in September 2021—the interest forgone by holding money is relatively small. As a result, individuals and firms will tend to hold relatively large amounts of money to avoid the cost and nuisance of converting other assets into money when making purchases. By contrast, if the interest rate is relatively high—say, 15%, a level it reached in the United States in the early 1980s—the opportunity cost of holding money is high. People will respond by keeping only small amounts in cash and deposits, converting assets into money only when needed.

Shifts of the Money Demand Curve

Like the demand curve for an ordinary good, the money demand curve can be shifted by a number of factors. As **Figure 4.5-2** shows, an increase in the demand for money corresponds to a rightward shift of the *MD* curve, raising the quantity of money demanded at any given nominal interest rate; a fall in the demand for money corresponds to a leftward shift of the *MD* curve, reducing the quantity of money demanded at any given interest rate. The most important factors causing the money demand curve to shift are changes in the aggregate price level, changes in real GDP, changes in banking technology, and changes in banking regulations.

FIGURE 4.5-2 Increases and Decreases in the Demand for Money

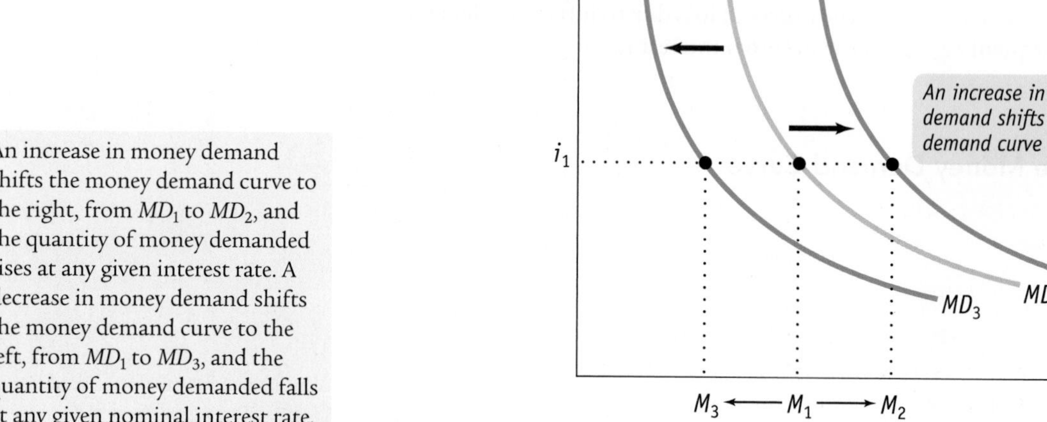

An increase in money demand shifts the money demand curve to the right, from MD_1 to MD_2, and the quantity of money demanded rises at any given interest rate. A decrease in money demand shifts the money demand curve to the left, from MD_1 to MD_3, and the quantity of money demanded falls at any given nominal interest rate.

Changes in the Aggregate Price Level

Americans keep a lot more cash in their wallets and funds in their checking accounts today than they did in the past. One reason is that they have to if they want to be able to buy anything: almost everything costs more now than it did decades ago, when you could get a burger, fries, and a drink at McDonald's for 45 cents and a gallon of gasoline for 29 cents. So higher prices increase the demand for money (a rightward shift of the *MD* curve), and lower prices decrease the demand for money (a leftward shift of the *MD* curve).

We can actually be more specific than this: other things equal, the demand for money is *proportional* to the price level. That is, if the aggregate price level rises by 20%, the quantity of money demanded at any given interest rate, such as i_1 in Figure 4.5-2, also rises by 20% – the movement from M_1 to M_2. Why? Because if the price of everything rises by 20%, it takes 20% more money to buy the same basket of goods and services. And if the aggregate price level falls by 20%, at any given interest rate the quantity of money demanded falls by 20% – shown by the movement from M_1 to M_3 at the interest rate i_1. As we'll see later, the fact that money demand is proportional to the price level has important implications for the long-run effects of monetary policy.

Changes in Real GDP

Households and firms hold money as a way to facilitate purchases of goods and services. The larger the quantity of goods and services they buy, the larger the quantity of money they will want to hold at any given interest rate. So an increase in real GDP – the total quantity of goods and services produced and sold in the economy – shifts the money demand curve rightward. A fall in real GDP shifts the money demand curve leftward.

Changes in Technology

There was a time when withdrawing cash from a bank account required a visit during the bank's hours of operation. Since most people did their banking during their lunch hour, they often found themselves standing in line. As a result, people limited the number of times they needed to withdraw funds by keeping substantial amounts of cash on hand. Not surprisingly, this tendency diminished greatly with the advent of ATMs and debit cards in the 1970s. More recent examples of technology that has reduced the need for cash include digital payment systems, such as PayPal, Venmo, and Zelle, that allow payments to be made using computers, smartphones, and other devices. Changes in technology such as these decrease the demand for money and shift the money demand curve to the left.

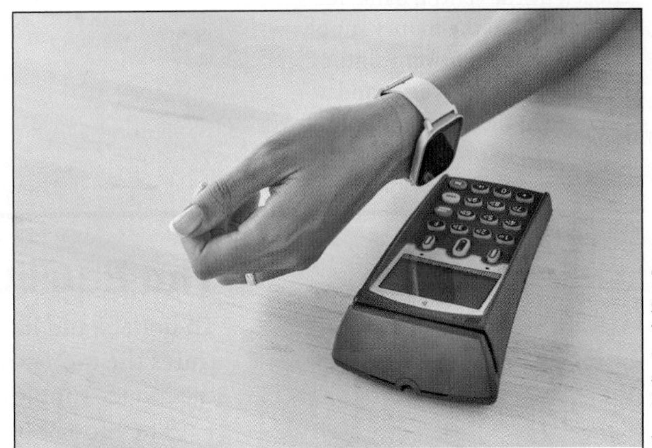

Alvaro Medina Jurado/Getty Images

Recent technologies have made it easy for people to use their smartphones or other devices to make purchases, further decreasing the demand for money.

These events illustrate how changes in technology can affect the demand for money. In general, advances in information technology have tended to reduce the demand for money by making it easier for the public to make purchases without holding significant amounts of cash.

Changes in Regulations

Changes in regulations can increase or decrease the demand for money. For example, until 1980, U.S. banks weren't allowed to offer interest on checking accounts. So the interest you would forgo by holding funds in a checking account instead of an interest-bearing asset made the opportunity cost of holding funds in checking accounts very high. When banking regulations changed, allowing banks to pay interest on checking account funds, the demand for money rose and shifted the money demand curve to the right.

AP® ECON TIP

Changes in the aggregate price level, real GDP, technology, and banking institutions increase or decrease money demand. These changes can be shown on a money market graph as a shift of the money demand curve.

The Supply of Money

The supply of money in the economy is set by the central bank, which determines the money supply, for example, through its control of the country's currency and reserve requirements or through open-market operations and the use of quantitative easing

The **money supply curve** shows the relationship between the quantity of money supplied and the nominal interest rate— the money supply curve is independent of the nominal interest rate.

(purchasing assets and securities such as long-term government bonds). So, for a given monetary base (also determined by the central bank), the money supply is independent of the nominal interest rate.

The central bank can increase or decrease the money supply by shifting the **money supply curve, *MS***, as shown in **Figure 4.5-3**, which shows the relationship between the quantity of money supplied by the central bank and the interest rate.

FIGURE 4.5-3 Increases and Decreases in the Supply of Money

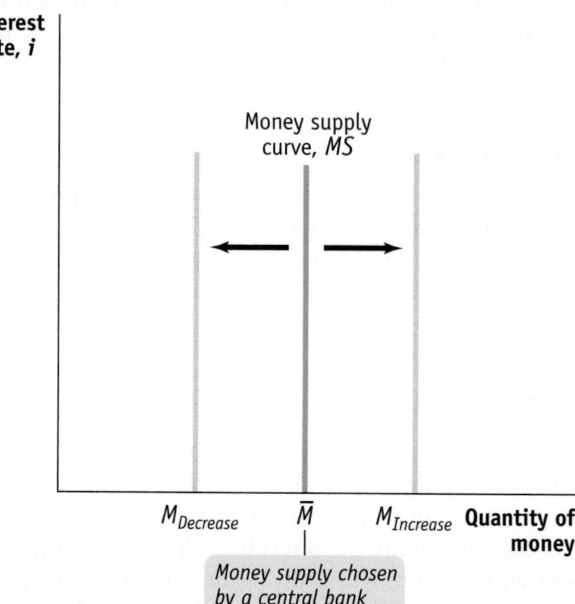

The money supply curve, *MS*, is vertical at the money supply chosen by the central bank, $\overline{M}$. An increase in the money supply is shown as a rightward shift of the money supply curve, and a decrease in the money supply is shown as a leftward shift of the money supply curve.

The Equilibrium Interest Rate

To understand how the interest rate is determined, consider **Figure 4.5-4**, which illustrates the money market. Figure 4.5-4 combines the money demand curve, *MD*, with the money supply curve, *MS*.

The money supply curve is a vertical line, *MS* in Figure 4.5-4, with a horizontal intercept corresponding to the money supply chosen by the Fed, $\overline{M}$. The money market equilibrium is at *E*, where *MS* and *MD* cross. At *E*, the quantity of money demanded equals the money supply, $\overline{M}$, leading to an equilibrium interest rate of i_E.

To understand why i_E is the equilibrium interest rate, consider what happens if the money market is not at equilibrium. When the nominal interest rate is not equal to the equilibrium nominal interest rate, the money market is in *disequilibrium*—for example, at a point like *L*, where the interest rate, i_L, is below i_E. At i_L, the public wants to hold the quantity of money M_L, an amount larger than the actual money supply, $\overline{M}$. This means that at point *L*, the public wants to shift some of its wealth out of interest-bearing assets such as high-denomination CDs (which are nonmoney assets) into money. This change has two implications. One is that the quantity of money demanded is *more* than the quantity of money supplied, creating a *shortage* in the money market. The other is that the quantity of interest-bearing nonmoney assets demanded is *less* than the quantity supplied. So those trying to sell nonmoney assets will find that they have to offer a higher interest rate to attract buyers. As a result, the interest rate will be driven up from i_L until the public wants to hold the quantity of money that is actually available, $\overline{M}$. That is, the interest rate will rise until it is equal to i_E.

Now consider what happens if the money market is at a point such as *H* in Figure 4.5-4, where the interest rate i_H is above the equilibrium rate i_E. In that case the quantity of money demanded, M_H, is less than the quantity of money supplied, creating a *surplus* in the money market. Correspondingly, the quantity of interest-bearing nonmoney

FIGURE 4.5-4 Equilibrium in the Money Market

The money supply curve, MS, is vertical at the money supply chosen by the central bank, $\overline{M}$. The money market is in equilibrium at the interest rate i_E: the quantity of money demanded by the public is equal to $\overline{M}$, the quantity of money supplied. At a point such as L, the interest rate, i_L, is below i_E and the corresponding quantity of money demanded, M_L, exceeds the money supply, $\overline{M}$, causing a shortage. In an attempt to shift their wealth out of nonmoney interest-bearing financial assets and raise their money holdings, investors drive the interest rate up to i_E. At a point such as H, the interest rate i_H is above i_E and the corresponding quantity of money demanded, M_H, is less than the money supply, $\overline{M}$, causing a surplus. In an attempt to shift out of money holdings into nonmoney interest-bearing financial assets, investors drive the interest rate down to i_E.

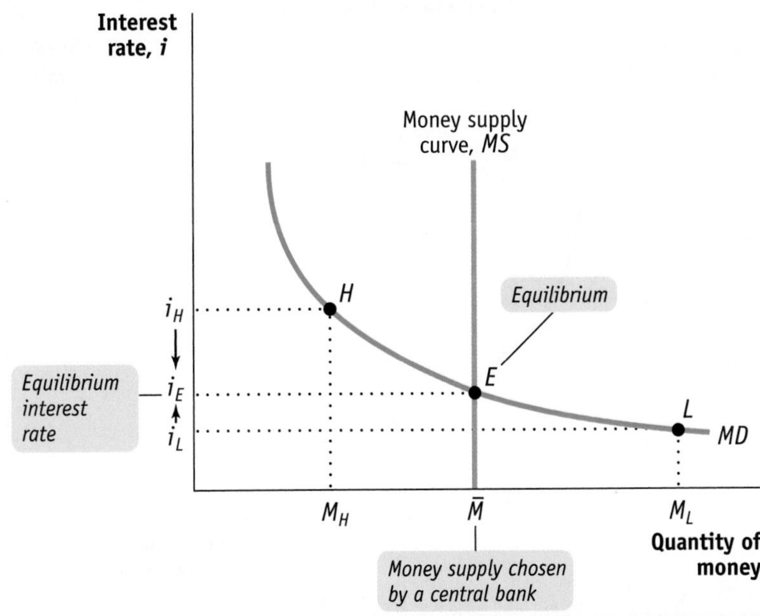

assets demanded is greater than the quantity supplied. Those trying to sell interest-bearing nonmoney assets will find that they can offer a lower interest rate and still find willing buyers. This leads to a fall in the interest rate from i_H. It falls until the public wants to hold the quantity of money that is actually available, $\overline{M}$. Again, the interest rate will end up at i_E.

Changes in the Equilibrium Nominal Interest Rate

Changes in money demand or money supply will result in changes in the equilibrium nominal interest rate. **Figure 4.5-5** shows the changes that lead to an increase in the equilibrium nominal interest rate. As shown in panel (a), the central bank can increase the nominal interest rate by decreasing the money supply—shifting the money supply curve, *MS*, to the left. An increase in the demand for money can be caused by a change in a determinant of the demand for money—for example, an increase in the price level, an increase in real GDP—shifting the money demand curve, *MD*, to the right, as shown in panel (b). Either of these changes will lead to an increase in the nominal interest rate.

Figure 4.5-6 shows the changes that lead to a decrease in the equilibrium nominal interest rate. In panel (a) the central bank increases the money supply—shifting the money supply curve to the right. A decrease in the demand for money can be caused by a change in a determinant of money demand—for example, a decrease in the price level, a decrease in real GDP, or an advance in technology that decreases the need to carry cash—shifting the money demand curve, *MD,* to the left, as shown in panel (b). Either of these changes will lead to a decrease in the nominal interest rate.

The central bank's ability to affect the equilibrium nominal interest rate through its control of the money supply illustrates how monetary policy can be used to affect the macroeconomy—as we discuss in the next Module.

An Alternative Model of the Interest Rate

In this Module we developed the money market model and looked at how changes affect the equilibrium nominal interest rate in the economy. The money market model is different from, but consistent with, another model, known as the *loanable funds model* of the interest rate. In the loanable funds model, the *real* interest rate matches

FIGURE 4.5-5 Increases in the Equilibrium Nominal Interest Rate

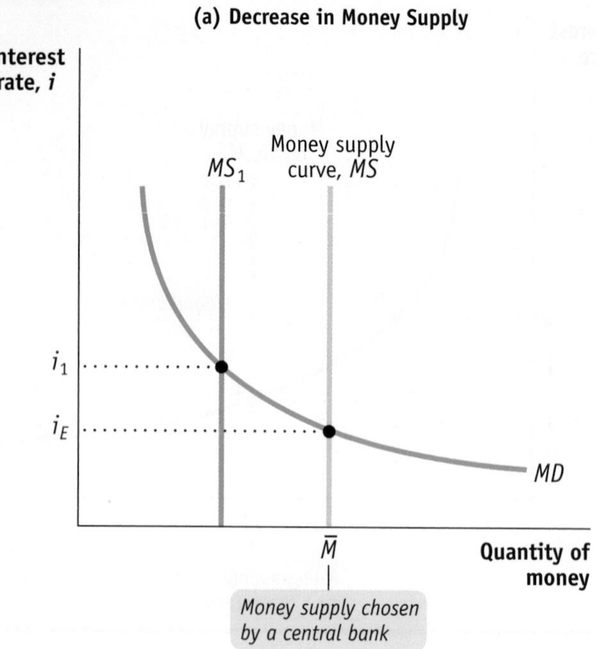

(b) Increase in Money Demand

Interest rate, *i*

Money supply curve, *MS*

i_1

i_E

MD_1

MD

$\overline{M}$

Quantity of money

Money supply chosen by a central bank

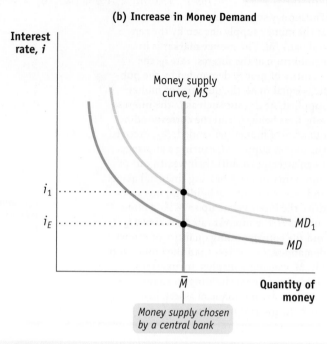

Panel (a) shows an increase in the equilibrium nominal interest rate caused by a leftward shift of the money supply curve (a decrease in the money supply). Panel (b) shows an increase in the equilibrium nominal interest rate caused by a rightward shift of the money demand curve (an increase in the demand for money). In both cases, the nominal interest rate rises from i_E to i_1.

FIGURE 4.5-6 Decreases in the Equilibrium Nominal Interest Rate

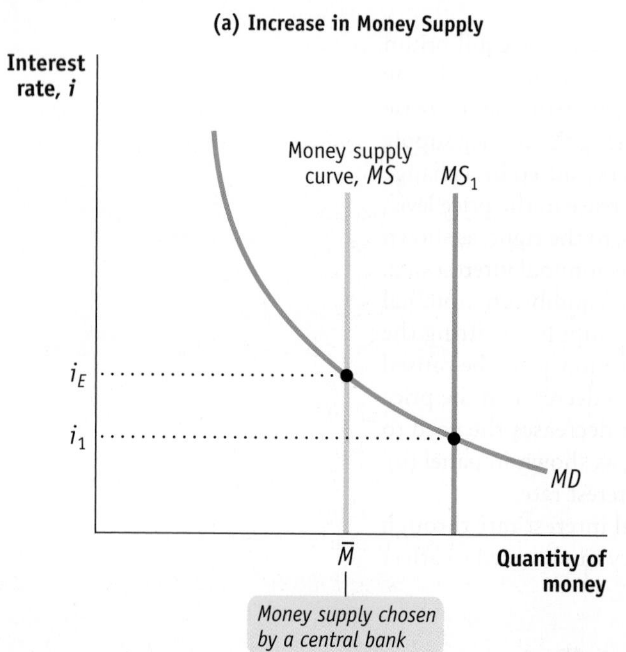

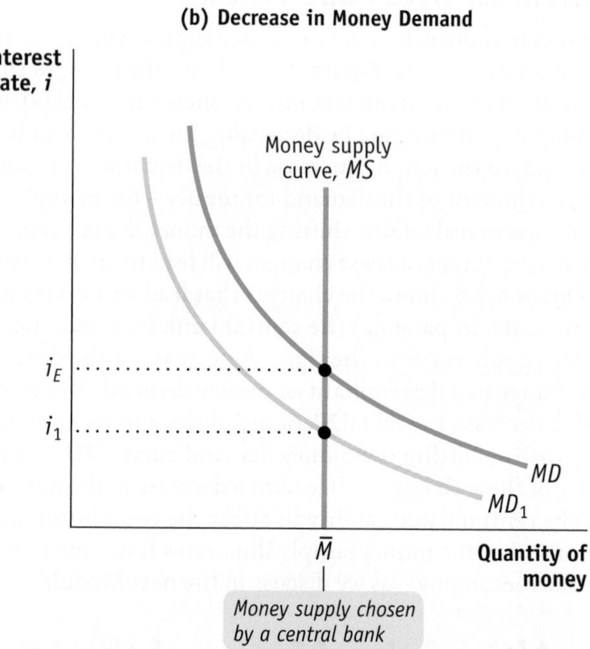

Panel (a) shows a decrease in the equilibrium nominal interest rate caused by a rightward shift of the money supply curve (an increase in the supply of money). Panel (b) shows a decrease in the equilibrium nominal interest rate caused by a leftward shift of the money demand curve (a decrease in the demand for money). In both cases, the nominal interest rate falls from i_E to i_1.

the quantity of loanable funds supplied by savers with the quantity of loanable funds demanded for investment spending. We will develop the loanable funds model in Module 4.7.

Module 4.5 Review

Check Your Understanding

1. Explain how each of the following would affect the quantity of money demanded. Indicate whether each change would cause a movement along the money demand curve or a shift of the money demand curve.
   a. The short-term interest rate rises from 5% to 30%.
   b. All prices fall by 10%.
   c. In order to avoid paying taxes, a vast underground economy develops in which workers are paid their wages in cash rather than with checks.

2. What is the relationship between the quantity of money supplied and the nominal interest rate? How is the supply of money determined?

Tackle the AP® Test: Multiple-Choice Questions

1. A change in which of the following will cause movement along the money demand curve?
   a. the aggregate price level
   b. technology
   c. real GDP
   d. banking regulations
   e. the nominal interest rate

2. Which of the following will decrease the demand for money, shifting the demand curve to the left?
   a. an increase in the interest rate
   b. inflation
   c. an increase in real GDP
   d. an increase in the variety of electronic payments
   e. a change to allow banks to pay interest on checkable account balances

3. What will happen to the money supply and the equilibrium interest rate if a central bank sells government bonds?

Money supply	*Equilibrium interest rate*
a. increase	increase
b. decrease	increase
c. increase	decrease
d. decrease	decrease
e. decrease	no change

4. Which of the following is a way for a central bank to increase the money supply?
   a. increase the currency in circulation
   b. decrease the reserve requirement
   c. buy government bonds
   d. enact quantitative easing
   e. all of the above

5. The quantity of money demanded rises when
   a. the aggregate price level increases.
   b. the aggregate price level falls.
   c. real GDP increases.
   d. new technology makes banking easier.
   e. the nominal interest rate falls.

6. Which of the following will lead to an increase in the nominal interest rate?
   a. an increase in real GDP
   b. a decrease in the aggregate price level
   c. an increase in the money supply
   d. open market bond purchases
   e. a decrease in the federal funds rate

7. Which of the following is true of the money demand curve?
   a. It is set by the central bank.
   b. It is vertical.
   c. It is horizontal.
   d. It illustrates the opportunity cost of holding money.
   e. It shows a positive relationship between the interest rate and the quantity of money held as cash.

Tackle the AP® Test: Free-Response Questions

1. Draw three correctly labeled graphs of the money market to illustrate the effect of each of the following changes.
   a. The aggregate price level increases.
   b. Real GDP falls.
   c. There is a dramatic increase in online banking.

Rubric for FRQ 1 (5 points)

1 point: The vertical axis is labeled "Interest rate" or "*i*" and the horizontal axis is labeled "Quantity of money."

1 point: The money supply curve is vertical and labeled and the money demand curve is negatively sloped and labeled.

1 point: a: The money demand curve shifts right.

1 point: b: The money demand curve shifts left.

1 point: c: The money demand curve shifts left.

2. Draw a correctly labeled graph showing equilibrium in the money market. Label the equilibrium interest rate i_E and label an interest rate below the equilibrium interest rate i_L. Explain what occurs in the market when the interest rate is at i_L and what steps will lead the market to eventually return to equilibrium. **(5 points)**

Monetary Policy

MODULE 4.6

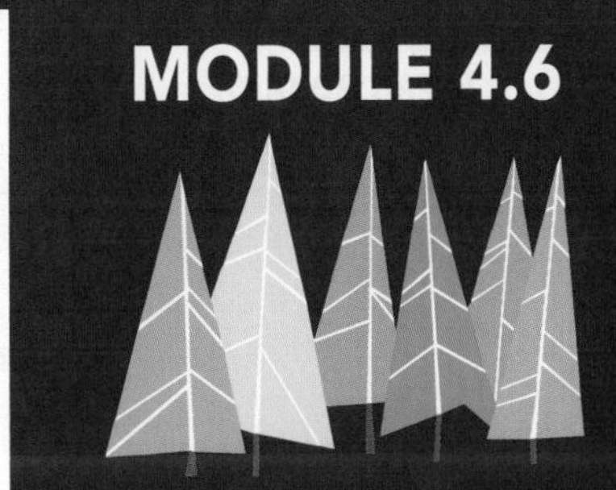

In this Module, you will learn to:

- Define monetary policy and identify the tools of monetary policy
- Explain how central banks influence the nominal interest rate, which in turn affects investment and consumption (two components of aggregate demand), real GDP, and the price level
- Recognize the use of expansionary monetary policy to restore full employment when there is a recessionary (negative) output gap and contractionary monetary policy to restore full employment when there is an inflationary (positive) output gap
- Use correctly labeled money market graphs to explain the short-run effects of a monetary policy action in an economy with limited reserves
- Calculate the effects of a monetary policy action in an economy with limited reserves
- Use correctly labeled reserve market graphs to explain the short-run effects of a monetary policy action in an economy with ample reserves
- Explain why there are lags to monetary policy

Conducting Monetary Policy

Module 3.8 explored how fiscal policy can be used to stabilize the economy by influencing aggregate demand. Now we will see how monetary policy—changes in interest rates—can play the same role.

Central banks conduct monetary policy through their influence on the amount of money and credit in the economy. They change the availability of money and credit in order to increase or decrease interest rates in response to economic conditions. A primary goal of monetary policy is to promote price stability—to prevent deflation or "high" rates of inflation. Many central banks, including the Federal Reserve, have explicit *inflation targets*. These central banks conduct monetary policy in an attempt to hit their target rate of inflation. This method of setting monetary policy is called **inflation targeting**.

Inflation targeting occurs when the central bank sets an explicit target for the inflation rate and adjusts monetary policy in order to hit that target.

Next, we consider how central banks work to achieve their target and pursue other monetary policy goals.

Expansionary and Contractionary Monetary Policy

Whether a central bank has an explicit inflation target or not, it will conduct monetary policy in response to either an inflationary or a recessionary gap in the economy. Monetary policy works by shifting the aggregate demand curve through its effect on the interest rate. **Figure 4.6-1** illustrates the process. If the central bank wants to expand the economy, it will decrease the nominal interest rate. A lower interest rate will lead to more investment spending. It will also increase interest-sensitive consumption—spending on things, such as houses and cars, that people borrow funds to purchase. Increases in investment and interest-sensitive consumption increase aggregate demand, leading to higher real GDP, which will lead to higher consumer spending, and so on through the

Scott Eells/Bloomberg/Getty Images

In 2012, Fed Chair Ben Bernanke announced that the Fed would now have an explicit inflation target.

FIGURE 4.6-1 Expansionary and Contractionary Monetary Policy

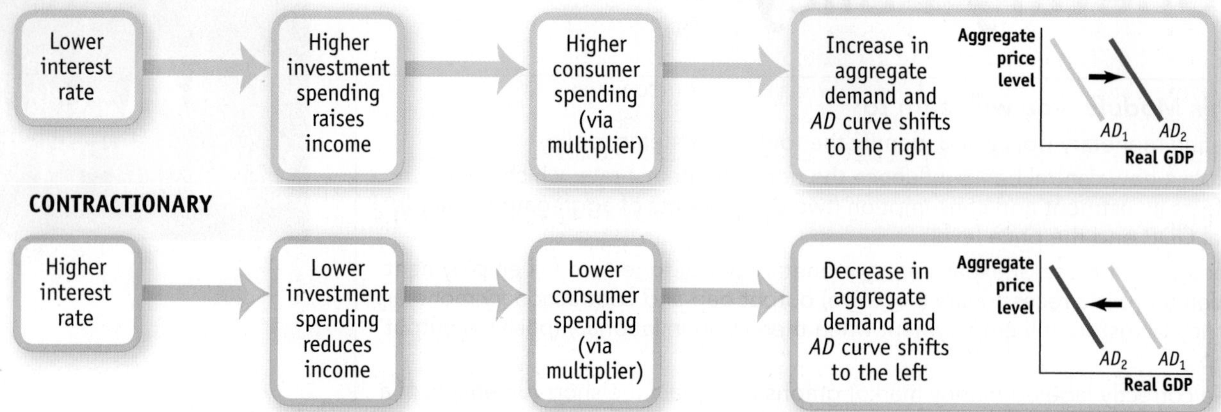

The top portion shows what happens when the central bank adopts an expansionary monetary policy and decreases the nominal interest rate. Interest rates fall, leading to higher investment spending, which raises income, which, in turn, raises consumer spending and shifts the *AD* curve to the right. The bottom portion shows what happens when the central bank adopts a contractionary monetary policy and increases the nominal interest rate. Interest rates rise, leading to lower investment spending and a reduction in income. This change in the interest rate lowers consumer spending and shifts the *AD* curve to the left.

Expansionary monetary policy is monetary policy that increases aggregate demand.

Contractionary monetary policy is monetary policy that reduces aggregate demand.

AP® ECON TIP

The aggregate demand curve shifts to the right when the central bank conducts expansionary monetary policy and to the left when it conducts contractionary monetary policy.

multiplier process. So the total quantity of goods and services demanded at any given aggregate price level rises when the interest rate decreases and the *AD* curve shifts to the right. Monetary policy that shifts the *AD* curve to the right, as illustrated in the top portion of Figure 4.6-1, is known as **expansionary monetary policy**.

Suppose, alternatively, that the central bank increases the nominal interest rate. A higher interest rate leads to lower investment spending (and lower interest-sensitive consumption). Lower investment and interest-sensitive consumption decrease aggregate demand, which leads to lower real GDP, which leads to lower consumer spending, and so on. So the total quantity of goods and services demanded falls when the interest rate is increased, and the *AD* curve shifts to the left. Monetary policy that shifts the *AD* curve to the left, as illustrated in the lower portion of Figure 4.6-1, is called **contractionary monetary policy**.

When the economy is operating below full employment—that is, when it is experiencing a recession—the central bank can use expansionary monetary policy to close the negative output gap and restore full employment. Expansionary monetary policy decreases interest rates, which will increase aggregate demand and therefore real GDP by increasing investment and interest-sensitive consumption. Expansionary monetary policy will also lead to an increase in the equilibrium aggregate price level as the aggregate demand curve shifts to the right.

When the economy is experiencing inflation, the central bank can use contractionary monetary policy to close the positive output gap and restore price stability. Contractionary monetary policy increases interest rates, which will decrease aggregate demand and therefore decrease the equilibrium aggregate price level. Contractionary monetary policy will also lead to a decrease in the equilibrium real GDP as the aggregate demand curve shifts to the left.

The Overnight Interbank Lending Rate

There are many different interest rates in the economy, but because these different interest rates tend to move up or down together, we often talk about "the" interest rate in our basic model. When the central bank sets its *target* interest rate, the rate it targets is the *overnight interbank lending rate,* and it is through this rate that the central bank influences other interest rates in the economy.

The **overnight interbank lending rate**, the interest rate at which funds are borrowed and lent among banks, is the rate most commonly targeted as part of monetary policy. This rate is sometimes referred to as the central bank's **policy rate**. The overnight interbank lending rate in the United States is the **federal funds rate** (or *fed funds rate*) and it is determined in the federal funds market, a financial market that allows banks that need or want additional liquidity to borrow (usually just overnight) from banks that want to lend their excess reserves. The interest rate in this market is determined by supply and demand, but the supply and demand for bank reserves can be strongly affected by central bank actions.

Central banks evaluate the state of the economy periodically and propose a change (or no change) to their policy rate. Central banks often set a target overnight interbank lending rate and use their policy tools to achieve their target. For example, the Federal Open Market Committee usually meets about every 6 weeks. It issues a policy statement after each meeting that summarizes its outlook for the economy and its monetary policy decision. The Fed sets a target federal funds rate, a desired level for the overnight interbank lending rate in the United States.

The **overnight interbank lending rate** is the interest rate that banks charge other banks for overnight loans. The central bank's **policy rate** is its target range for an overnight interbank lending rate.

In the United States, banks make overnight loans to each other in the federal funds market, and the **federal funds rate** is the interest rate in that market.

AP® ECON TIP

The *policy rate* is the central bank's target for the *overnight interbank lending rate,* which for the Fed is known as the *federal funds rate*—the interest rate that U.S. commercial banks charge each other for overnight loans.

Implementing Monetary Policy

How exactly does a central bank implement its chosen policy? That is, how does the central bank cause the interbank overnight interest rate, or policy rate, to increase or decrease? How a central bank implements monetary policy to achieve its target interest rate depends on whether the economy is operating in an economy with **limited reserves** or **ample reserves**.

As explained in previous Modules, the central bank has three traditional policy tools it can use in economies with limited (scarce) reserves, in which minor changes in reserve supply will shift the money supply curve, affecting the interest rate: *reserve requirements*, the *discount rate*, and *open market operations (OMOs)*. In economies with ample reserves, where changes in reserve supply do not significantly affect interest rates, central banks implement monetary policy using additional tools, including quantitative easing, the *interest rate paid on reserve balances* (IORB), and other interest rates administered by the central bank.

Next, we will outline how a central bank can use the traditional policy tools to affect the economy through the money supply during recessions and inflation in an economy with limited reserves. Then, we will look at how a central bank implements monetary policy using its administered interest rates in an economy with ample reserves. As we explore how central banks use these tools, keep in mind that the way that monetary policy is implemented does not affect the goals of monetary policy or the use of interest rates to pursue those goals.

Figure 4.6-2 shows the transmission mechanism for monetary policy—that is, how a change in the target interest rate ultimately achieves the monetary policy goal. The implementation regime used to achieve the target interest rate is represented by the red arrow. As you can see, though there are different implementation regimes that can

In an economy with **limited reserves**, reserves are scarce and therefore relatively small changes in the supply of reserves shifts the money supply curve and changes the interest rate.

In an economy with **ample reserves**, banks hold high levels of excess reserves and therefore changes in the supply of reserves does not change the interest rate significantly.

FIGURE 4.6-2 Monetary Policy Transmission Mechanism

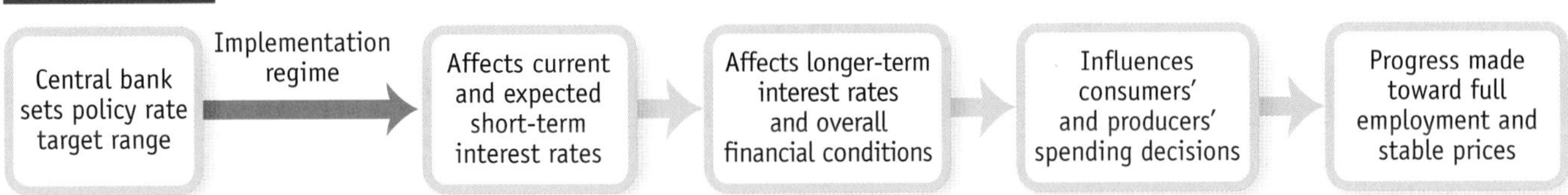

The chain of events that shows how monetary policy ultimately results in a movement of equilibrium toward full employment output is illustrated by the transmission mechanism shown here. The transmission is the same for both traditional and nontraditional monetary policy tools—the only difference is the implementation of the target interest rate.

be used to influence interest rates, the process and outcomes are the same. Next, we consider both traditional limited reserves and more modern ample reserves monetary policy implementation regimes.

Implementing Monetary Policy in an Economy with Limited Reserves

In most economies in the past, and more recently in those economies with limited reserves, central banks implement their chosen monetary policy using traditional tools, most commonly open-market operations. We begin by looking at how reserve requirements and the discount rate are used to implement monetary policy in a limited reserve environment before describing the more common use of open-market operations.

The Reserve Requirement

In our discussion of bank runs in Module 4.4, we noted that a central bank can set a minimum required reserve ratio for demand deposits and banks that fail to maintain at least the required reserve ratio face penalties. What can a bank do if it has insufficient reserves to meet the central bank's reserve requirement? Normally, it borrows additional reserves from other banks in the interbank overnight lending market. An increase in the reserve requirement would lead to more borrowing, increasing demand for reserves and the equilibrium overnight interbank lending rate. When banks must pay a higher interest rate, they are inclined to charge their customers a higher interest rate. A decrease in the reserve requirement would reduce the amount of borrowing, decreasing the demand for reserves and the equilibrium overnight interbank lending rate. Banks are then inclined to reduce the interest rate they charge their customers.

When central banks change the reserve requirement, they affect interest rates in another way as well. When the required reserve ratio is decreased, banks are allowed to lend a larger percentage of their deposits, leading them to supply more loans and increase the money supply via the money multiplier. The increase in the money supply leads to lower interest rates, more investment and interest-sensitive consumption, and higher GDP, as shown in Figure 4.6-2. If the central bank increases the required reserve ratio, banks are forced to reduce their lending, leading to a fall in the money supply via the money multiplier, higher interest rates, and lower GDP.

The People's Bank of China provides a recent example of a central bank using their reserve requirement as a tool of monetary policy. In July 2021, China's central bank cut their reserve requirement by 0.5% to support economic recovery following the COVID-19 pandemic.

However, central banks do not generally rely on the reserve requirement to actively manage interest rates. In fact, in March 2020, the U. S. Federal Reserve decreased its reserve requirement to zero. U.S. banks' excess reserves the following month exceeded $2.95 trillion, indicating that banks held ample reserves despite the zero-percent reserve requirement. Later in this Module, we will look in more detail at how central banks, including the Federal Reserve, implement monetary policy when banks hold excess reserves – a system known as an *ample reserve regime.*

AP® ECON TIP

When answering any question about monetary policy, be careful to note whether the banking system has ample reserves or limited reserves. Quantity-based policies, like OMOs and reserve requirements, are used by central banks to change the nominal interest rate only in economies with limited reserves. In economies with ample reserves, like the United States, the central bank changes the nominal interest rate using administered rates, for example the interest rate paid on reserves.

The Discount Rate

The **discount rate** is the interest rate the central bank charges on loans to banks.

Banks in need of reserves can also borrow from the central bank. The interest rate charged by central banks on those loans is called the **discount rate**. The term "discount rate" originates from the fact that banks went to a teller's window (the *discount window*) at a district reserve bank to borrow funds, as introduced in Module 4.4. The name has remained, even though the loans are no longer made through a literal window. In the United States, discount rates are set by the Federal Reserve. Typically, discount rates in the United States have been set just above the federal funds rate and move with other short-term interest rates. In March 2020, at the start of the pandemic, the Federal Reserve narrowed the spread between the discount rate and the federal funds rate in an effort to promote more bank borrowing through the discount window. In addition, the Fed extended the allowable length of discount window loans to 90 days—also encouraging borrowing from the Fed.

Central banks affect other interest rates when they change the discount rate. If the central bank reduces the discount rate, the cost to banks of borrowing from the central bank falls. Banks respond by increasing their lending, thereby increasing the money supply and reducing the interest rate in the economy. If the discount rate rises, banks borrow less from the central bank and the supply of bank loans decreases, which decreases the money supply and increases the interest rate. However, central banks normally don't use the discount rate to actively manage the money supply.

Open Market Operations

Like the banks it oversees, a central bank has assets and liabilities. The central bank's assets include its holdings of government debt, for example government bonds, and its liabilities include currency in circulation and bank reserves. As described in Module 4.3B and shown in Figure 4.3B-3, in a traditional **open market operation (OMO)**, the central bank buys or sells government bonds in the open market. As we will see later in this Module, there are additional types of open market operations a central bank can use to implement monetary policy in economies with ample reserves.

Central banks conduct open-market purchases or sales of securities, such as government bonds, to affect the level of bank reserves in the economy. For example, the Fed holds government debt mainly in the form of short-term U.S. government bonds called U.S. Treasury bills. Remember, the Federal Reserve and the U.S. government are not one entity, so U.S. Treasury bills held by the Fed are a liability of the government but an asset of the Fed. The Federal Reserve can buy or sell U.S. Treasury bills, normally through a transaction with commercial banks.

Through open-market operations, the central bank controls the monetary base—bank reserves plus currency in circulation. By increasing or decreasing the monetary base, the central bank can influence on the money supply, and therefore interest rates, in an economy with limited reserves.

AP® ECON TIP

Again, in questions about monetary policy, be careful to note whether the monetary environment is one of ample reserves or limited reserves. The money market is used to show how central bank policies, like OMOs, affect nominal interest rates in the economy. The market for reserves is used to show how central bank policies, like changes in the IOR, affect nominal interest rates in the economy.

Open market operations (OMOs) include the purchase or sale of government debt (e.g. a bond) by a central bank.

Open Market Operations and the Interest Rate

Now let's examine how a central bank can buy or sell government bonds in order to affect the interest rate in an economy with limited reserves. **Figure 4.6-3** shows what happens when a central bank buys bonds to increase the money supply from $\overline{M}_1$ to $\overline{M}_2$. The economy is originally in equilibrium at E_1, with the equilibrium interest rate i_1 and the money supply $\overline{M}_1$. When the central bank increases the money supply to $\overline{M}_2$, the money supply curve shifts to the right, from MS_1 to MS_2, and the equilibrium interest rate falls to i_2. Why? Because i_2 is the only interest rate at which the public is willing to hold the quantity of money actually supplied, $\overline{M}_2$. So, as we've seen previously, an increase in the money supply drives the interest rate down. Similarly, a reduction in the money supply drives the interest rate up. By adjusting the money supply up or down, the central bank can set the interest rate.

Figure 4.6-4 shows how interest rate targeting using traditional OMOs works in an economy with limited reserves. In both panels, i_T is the target overnight interbank lending rate. In panel (a), the initial money supply curve is MS_1 with money supply $\overline{M}_1$, and the equilibrium interest rate, i_1, is above the target rate. To lower the interest rate to i_T, the central bank makes an open-market purchase of government bonds, which leads to an

Samuel Corum/Bloomberg/Getty Images

The Fed holds government debt in the form of U.S. Treasury bills, but it never buys T-bills directly from the government. When a central bank buys government debt directly from the government, it is lending directly to the government—in effect, the central bank is issuing money to finance the government's budget deficit—which has historically been a formula for disastrous levels of inflation.

FIGURE 4.6-3 The Effect of an Open Market Purchase in an Economy with Limited Reserves

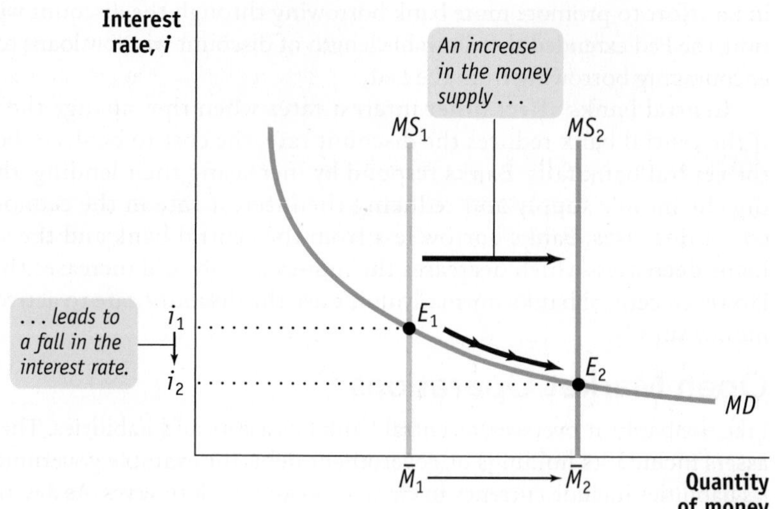

A central bank can lower the interest rate by increasing the money supply. Here, the equilibrium interest rate falls from i_1 to i_2 in response to an increase in the money supply from $\overline{M}_1$ to $\overline{M}_2$.

increase in the money supply via the money multiplier. This is illustrated in panel (a) by the rightward shift of the money supply curve from MS_1 to MS_2 and an increase in the money supply to $\overline{M}_2$. This drives the equilibrium interest rate *down* to the target rate, i_T. Other interest rates in the economy also move in response to the change in the target rate. Panel (b) shows the opposite case. Again, the initial money supply curve is MS_1 with money supply $\overline{M}_1$. But this time the equilibrium interest rate, i_1, is below the target overnight interbank lending rate, i_T. In this case, the central bank will make an open-market sale of government bonds, leading to a fall in the money supply to $\overline{M}_2$, via

FIGURE 4.6-4 Targeting the Overnight Interbank Lending Rate in an Economy with Limited Reserves

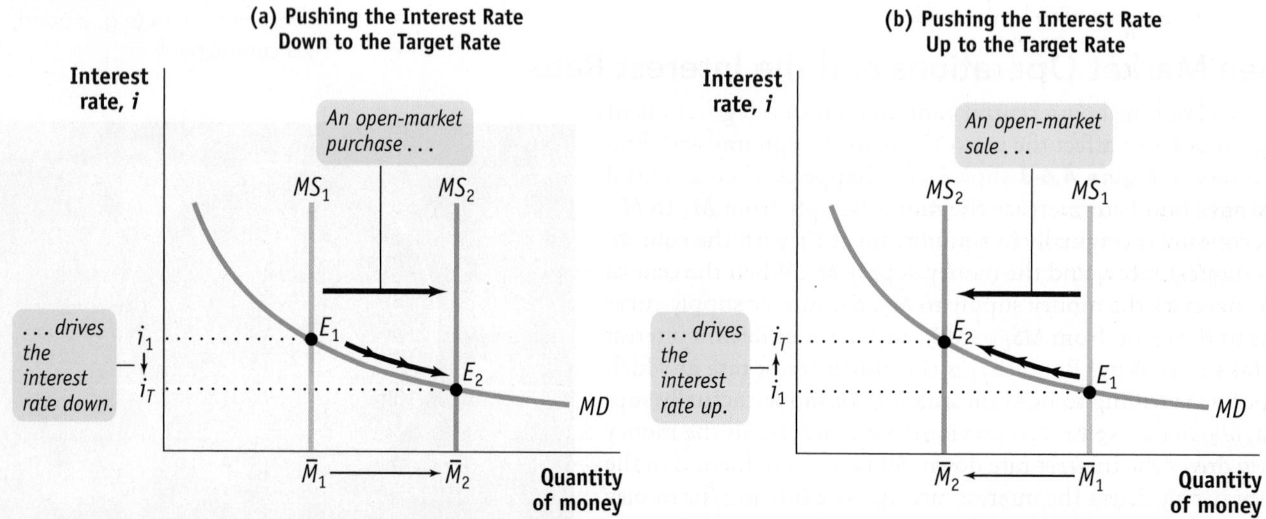

The central bank can set a target for the overnight interbank lending rate and use traditional open-market operations to achieve that target. In both panels, the target rate is i_T. In panel (a) the initial equilibrium interest rate, i_1, is above the target rate. The central bank increases the money supply by making an open-market purchase of government bonds, pushing the money supply curve rightward, from MS_1 to MS_2, and driving the interest rate down to i_T. In panel (b) the initial equilibrium interest rate, i_1, is below the target rate. The central bank reduces the money supply by making an open-market sale of government bonds, pushing the money supply curve leftward, from MS_1 to MS_2, and driving the interest rate up to i_T.

the money multiplier. The money supply curve shifts leftward from MS_1 to MS_2, driving the equilibrium interest rate *up* to the target federal funds rate, i_T, and increasing other interest rates in the economy.

In the United States, open-market operations were once used daily by the Federal Reserve to target the federal funds rate. Today, however, they are only used occasionally by the Fed to help keep ample reserves in the banking system.

Modern Monetary Policy Tools

The 2007–2008 financial crisis required the Federal Reserve to use innovative tools to provide enough liquidity to prevent the Great Recession from becoming worse. During the crisis, the Fed was unable to use traditional monetary policy tools because it had already targeted a federal funds rate of zero, and was therefore up against the **zero-bound** – the inability to lower the federal funds rate below zero. In addition, the way that financial markets had evolved to be more diverse and interconnected made traditional approaches less effective. The Fed had to make substantial and innovative changes to its monetary policy tools, including lending directly to both depository institutions (e.g. banks) and non-depository financial institutions, reducing the stigma associated with borrowing from the Fed's discount window, and increasing transparency with respect to its policy actions.

A central bank is up against the **zero bound** when the short-term interest rate has already been lowered to zero. Further economic stimulus, if needed, requires the central bank to use nontraditional policy tools.

As we will discuss shortly, central banks, including the Federal Reserve, implement monetary policy in an economy with ample reserves using tools adapted or created following the 2008 financial crisis. The goals of monetary policy and the use of interest rates to pursue them haven't changed, but there have been significant changes in the way that central banks achieve their target interest rate when there are ample reserves.

Quantitative Easing The open-market operation known as **quantitative easing (QE)**, which is the large-scale purchase of assets by central banks to stimulate the economy (or combat deflation) by providing liquidity, was an important monetary policy tool during the 2007–2008 financial crisis. Any OMO involves altering reserves in the banking system to help achieve a target interest rate by buying and selling assets on the open market, and that is what QE does. However, QE is different from traditional OMOs: where traditional OMOs involve buying and selling relatively short-term government bonds, QE involves expanding the central bank balance sheet to include various financial assets. Examples of the assets include longer-term government bonds, private corporate bonds, and mortgage-backed securities, which are investments similar to bonds that bundle home loans purchased from the banks that issued them.

Quantitative easing (QE) is an expansionary monetary policy that involves central banks purchasing longer-term government bonds and other private financial assets.

The **interest on reserve balances (IORB)** is the amount the central bank pays in interest to banks for their balances held in reserve.

Interest Rates on Reserve Balances A number of central banks, including the Bank of England and the European Central Bank, use an additional monetary policy tool – paying **interest on reserve balances (IORB)**. In 2006, the Federal Reserve was authorized to begin paying interest on the reserves it holds for banks beginning in 2011. The date was moved up to 2008 when the Emergency Economic Stabilization Act was enacted in response to the 2007–2008 financial crisis.

The *interest on reserves* (IOR) is the rate the central bank pays in interest to banks for their reserve balances. Paying interest on reserves reduces banks' opportunity cost of holding reserves rather than holding other financial assets. It also reduces the incentive for banks to lend at rates below the IOR because banks would earn less from loaning their cash than they would by simply holding it as reserves.

When the central bank raises the interest rate paid on reserve balances, banks respond by holding more cash as excess reserves (rather than making loans with it). Lowering the IOR prompts banks to make more loans because they earn less by keeping cash in reserves.. The IOR acts more as a "carrot" to hold reserves, compared to the "stick" of a reserve requirement. The IOR is another way for central banks to influence other interest rates in the economy.

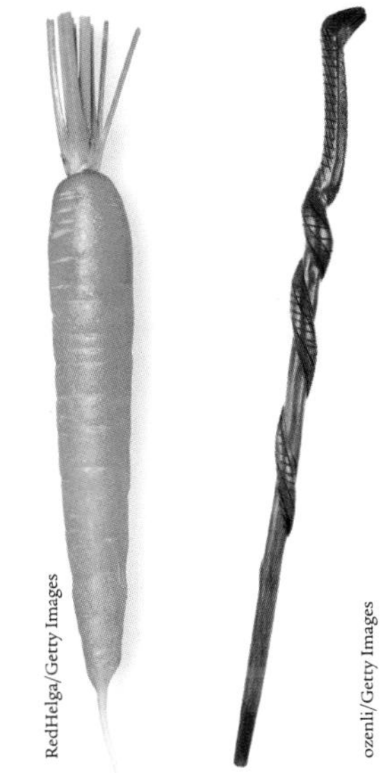
RedHelga/Getty Images
ozenli/Getty Images

The IOR is the carrot and the reserve requirement is the stick.

Administered Interest Rates as a Monetary Policy Tool

In 2019, Jerome Powell, Chair of the FOMC, explained "The Federal Reserve sets two overnight interest rates: the interest rate paid on banks' reserve balances and the rate on our reverse repurchase agreements. We use these two administered rates to keep a market-determined rate, the federal funds rate, within a target range set by the FOMC." With ample reserves, these two rates administered by the Fed are used to create a range for the federal funds rate, making the IORB the primary tool, and reverse repurchase agreements (RRAs) a supplemental tool, for setting the federal funds rate. Repurchase agreements, reverse repurchase agreements, and their role as a supplemental monetary policy tool are discussed in Enrichment Module B.

With ample reserves, the federal funds rate will move with the interest rate the Fed pays on reserves. Eventually, banks reach a level of reserves high enough that the only way to benefit from holding additional reserves is earning interest from the Fed. At that level of reserves, if the federal funds rate were to fall below the interest rate paid on reserves, banks can borrow from the federal funds market at the lower interest rate and hold the borrowed funds as reserves to earn the higher interest rate, making the difference as profits. This is a bank reserves version of "buy low, sell high," known as *arbitrage*. Arbitrage in the federal funds market would increase the federal funds rate and eliminate the interest rate gap. So arbitrage assures that the federal funds rate will not fall much below the interest rate on reserves.

Non-depository financial institutions can't earn interest on reserves, but they can participate in the Fed's overnight reverse repurchase program. Enrichment Module B explains how the rate for RRAs acts as a floor for the fed funds rate.

Monetary Policy in an Economy with Ample Reserves

Now let's consider monetary policy in an economy with ample reserves. In an economy with ample reserves, banks hold high levels of excess reserves and changes in the supply of reserves do not change the policy rate significantly. When there are ample reserves, the central bank instead uses administered rates to set the target rate.

The Federal Reserve issues press releases to provide transparency and to communicate updated information regarding current Fed policies and intentions for future Fed policy. As we explained in Module 4.3B, in a January 2019 press release, the Board of Governors of the Fed described its intent to provide *ample reserves* in the banking system and rely on *administered interest rates* to implement monetary policy. In addition, the Fed provided information on its long-run monetary policy plans, indicating that it was prepared to use quantitative easing should economic conditions require expansionary policy beyond what can be achieved by lowering interest rates. The press release read, in part:

> The Committee intends to continue to implement monetary policy in a regime in which an ample supply of reserves ensures that control over the level of the federal funds rate and other short-term interest rates is exercised primarily through the setting of the Federal Reserve's administered rates, and in which active management of the supply of reserves is not required.
>
> The Committee continues to view changes in the target range for the federal funds rate as its primary means of adjusting the stance of monetary policy. The Committee is prepared to adjust any of the details for completing balance sheet normalization in light of economic and financial developments. Moreover, the Committee would be prepared to use its full range of tools, including altering the size and composition of its balance sheet, if future economic conditions were to warrant a more accommodative monetary policy than can be achieved solely by reducing the federal funds rate.

Next, we will see how a central bank can use administrative rates to achieve its monetary policy goals.

Administered Interest Rates and the Market for Reserves

Let's consider again Chairman Powell's statement from October 2019 explaining that "The Federal Reserve sets two overnight interest rates: the interest rate paid on banks' reserve balances and the rate on our reverse repurchase agreements. We use these two administered rates to keep a market-determined rate, the federal funds rate, within a target range set by the FOMC."

We have already discussed the interest rate paid on bank reserves (IOR). With ample reserves, a central bank can use the IORB as its primary monetary policy tool for setting the policy rate, as shown in the **Figure 4.6-5**.

FIGURE 4.6-5 The Market for Reserves in an Economy with Ample Reserves

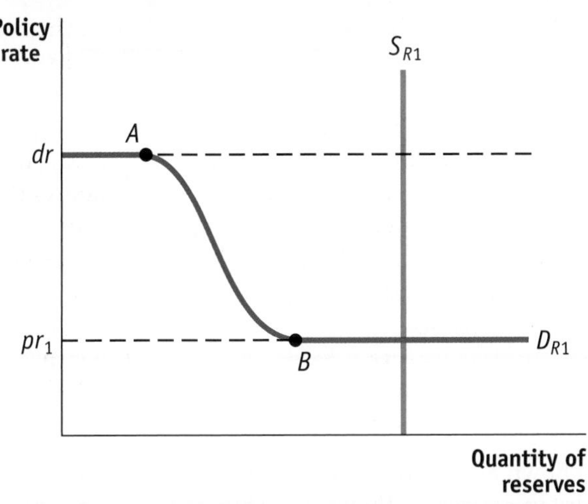

In an environment with ample reserves, the demand curve in the market for reserves (D_{R1}) has three distinct segments: a horizontal section at very low levels of reserves, a downward-sloping section in the middle range showing a negative relationship between the policy rate and the quantity of reserves demanded, and a third section, where reserves are ample, which is horizontal at a policy rate very close to the interest rate on reserves.

Figure 4.6-5 shows the market for reserves under an ample-reserve regime. In the case of ample reserves, the reserves demand curve (D_{R1}) has three sections: it is horizontal at the discount rate (*dr*) from very low levels of reserves up to point *A*, negatively sloped as reserves increase to point *B*, and then horizontal again at the policy rate (pr_1) when reserves are ample. Because banks can borrow from the central bank at the discount rate, they will not demand reserves from the overnight interbank lending market if that rate is above the discount rate. To the right of point *A*, the policy rate and the quantity of reserves demanded are inversely related until the policy rate is equal to the interest rate paid for reserves, at point *B*.

In an ample reserve regime, the central bank maintains the supply of reserves in the horizontal range of the demand curve for reserves—to the right of point *B*, where reserves are "ample." The level of reserves, maintained by the central bank, does not depend on the policy rate, therefore the supply curve for reserves (S_{R1}) is vertical.

As explained above, arbitrage will keep the policy rate close to the IOR paid by the central bank, and the policy rate will be determined by the interest rate paid on reserves.

Demand and Supply Changes in the Market for Reserves

Changes in the administered rates set by the central bank—for example, the IOR—will shift the demand curve for reserves, as shown in **Figure 4.6-6**. An increase in the IOR will shift the lower horizontal section of the demand curve upward, while a decrease will shift it downward as arbitrage assures the policy rate moves with the IOR. Because equilibrium in the market for reserves is in the horizontal section of the demand curve, where reserves are ample, changes in the IOR lead to changes in the policy rate. Increases and decreases in the discount rate will similarly raise and lower the upper horizontal section of the demand curve.

PeopleImages/Getty Images

Central banks have some more creative ways than this to stabilize the economy.

FIGURE 4.6-6 Changes in the Demand for Reserves in an Economy with Ample Reserves

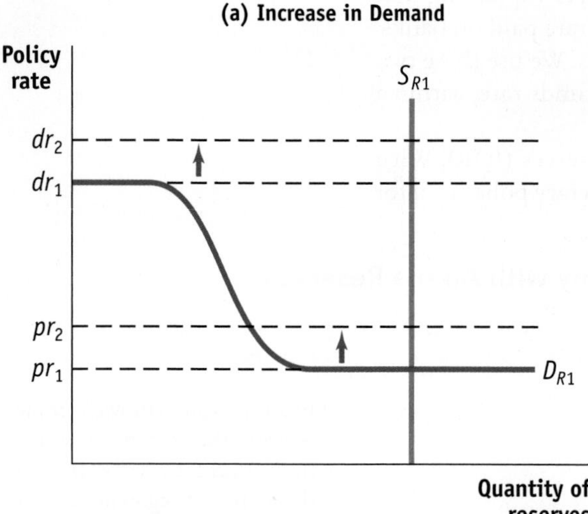

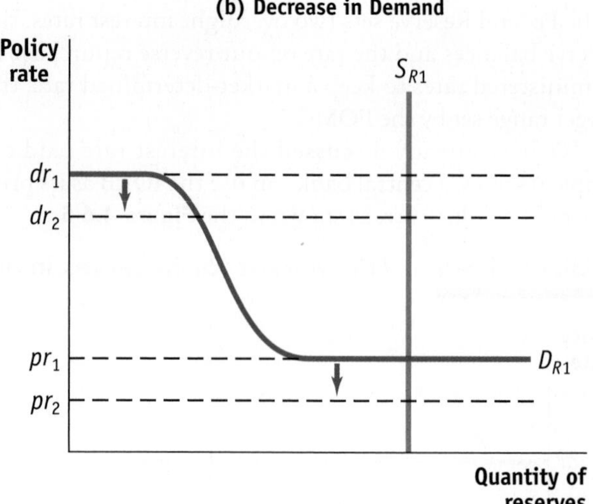

An increase in the IOR will shift the lower horizontal section of the demand curve for reserves upward and a decrease in the IOR will shift it downward. The equilibrium in the market for reserves coincides with the horizontal section of the demand curve for reserves, where reserves are ample, indicating that the policy rate changes with the IOR. Similarly, an increase or decrease in the discount rate will raise or lower the upper horizontal section of the demand curve for reserves.

Adjustments to reserves are shown as a shift of the supply curve for reserves, as shown in **Figure 4.6-7**. An increase in reserves is shown as a shift of the supply curve to the right and a decrease is shown as a shift to the left. So long as the supply and demand for reserves intersect to the right of point *B*, in the horizontal range of the demand curve for reserves (that is, as long as there are ample reserves in the economy), the policy rate will be determined by the rates administered by the central bank. To maintain an environment of ample reserves, the supply of reserves must be to the right of point *B*, where reserves are "ample."

A more detailed explanation of monetary policy using the market for reserves in an economy with ample reserves is included in Enrichment Module B.

FIGURE 4.6-7 Changes in the Supply of Reserves in an Economy with Ample Reserves

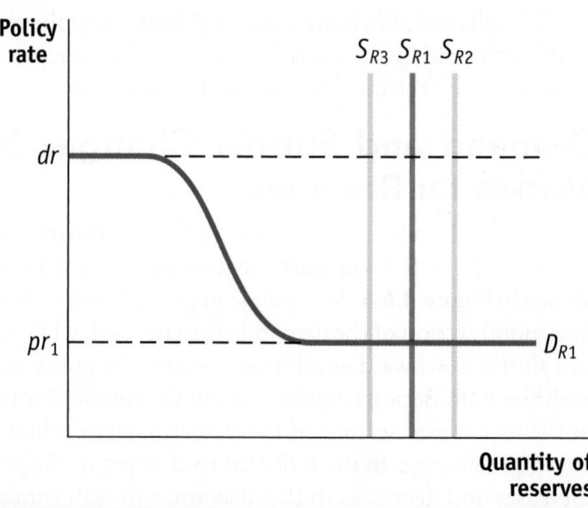

An increase in reserves is shown as a shift of the supply curve for reserves to the right (to S_{R2}) and a decrease is shown as a shift to the left (to S_{R3}). So long as the supply and demand for reserves intersect in the horizontal range of the demand curve for reserves (that is, as long as there are ample reserves in the economy), the policy rate will be determined by the rates administered by the central bank.

Monetary Policy Versus Fiscal Policy

We have learned that policy makers try to fight recessions and to ensure *price stability*, which is characterized by low (though usually not zero) inflation. Actual monetary policy reflects a combination of these goals, and it is monetary policy, rather than fiscal policy, that is more often used as a way to stabilize the economy. Like fiscal policy, monetary policy is subject to lags: it takes time for a central bank to recognize economic problems and time for monetary policy to affect the economy. However, since a central bank can move much more quickly than the government, **monetary policy lags** are shorter than fiscal policy lags, which makes monetary policy the preferred tool.

Monetary policy lags result from the time it takes to recognize a problem in the economy and the time it takes for a monetary policy action to take effect in the economy.

In this Module, we have shown how changes in the interest rate can be used to address recession and inflation in the economy. Though the way that monetary policy is implemented differs depending on whether an economy has limited reserves or ample reserves, in the short run, a decrease in the interest rate leads to an increase in aggregate demand and an increase in the interest rate leads to a decrease in aggregate demand.

The short run effects of monetary policy, however, are not the whole story. The long-run consequences of both monetary and fiscal policy and policies promoting economic growth are the focus of Unit 5, and in Module 5.3 we will describe the limitations of monetary policy in the long run.

Watch the video: ***Monetary Policy and the Federal Reserve System***

Module 4.6 Review

Check Your Understanding

1. Explain when a central bank should use expansionary monetary policy and when it should use contractionary monetary policy.
2. Use symbols and arrows to explain the chain of events that causes an increase in the money supply to close a recessionary gap in an economy with limited reserves.

Tackle the AP® Test: Multiple Choice Questions

1. Which of the following actions can the central bank take to decrease the equilibrium interest rate in an economy with limited reserves?
   - **a.** increase the money supply
   - **b.** increase money demand
   - **c.** decrease the money supply
   - **d.** decrease money demand
   - **e.** both (a) and (d)
2. Contractionary monetary policy attempts to ____________ aggregate demand by ____________ interest rates.

a.	decrease	increasing
b.	increase	decreasing
c.	decrease	decreasing
d.	increase	increasing
e.	increase	maintaining

3. Which of the following is a goal of monetary policy?
   - **a.** zero inflation
   - **b.** deflation
   - **c.** price stability
   - **d.** increased potential output
   - **e.** decreased actual real GDP
4. Which of the following correctly describes how contractionary monetary policy will ultimately affect real GDP?
   - **a.** $\uparrow i \rightarrow \downarrow I \rightarrow \uparrow C \rightarrow \downarrow AD \rightarrow \downarrow$ real GDP
   - **b.** $\uparrow i \rightarrow \downarrow I \rightarrow \downarrow C \rightarrow \downarrow AD \rightarrow \downarrow$ real GDP
   - **c.** $\uparrow i \rightarrow \uparrow I \rightarrow \uparrow C \rightarrow \downarrow AD \rightarrow \downarrow$ real GDP
   - **d.** $\downarrow i \rightarrow \downarrow I \rightarrow \downarrow C \rightarrow \uparrow AD \rightarrow \downarrow$ real GDP
   - **e.** $\downarrow i \rightarrow \downarrow I \rightarrow \downarrow C \rightarrow \downarrow AD \rightarrow \downarrow$ real GDP

5. If the central bank in an economy with ample reserves raises the interest rate on reserves, what happens to bank reserves?
   a. They will increase.
   b. They will decrease.
   c. They will fall to zero.
   d. They will not change.
   e. They will be loaned out.

6. When commercial banks make loans to each other, they charge the
   a. prime rate.
   b. discount rate.
   c. overnight interbank lending rate.
   d. CD rate.
   e. mortgage rate.

7. In an economy with ample reserves, which of the following central bank actions would be used to combat inflation?
   a. quantitative easing
   b. buying bonds
   c. increasing the interest paid on reserves
   d. raising reserve requirements
   e. increasing the discount rate

Tackle the AP® Test: Free-Response Questions

1. Assume an economy with limited reserves is experiencing a recession.
   a. What five tools can a central bank can use to address the recession?
   b. What would the central bank do with each to increase the money supply? Explain.

Rubric for FRQ 1 (10 points)

1 point: Decrease the discount rate

1 point: A lower discount rate makes it cheaper to borrow from the central bank so the money supply increases.

1 point: Decrease the reserve requirement

1 point: A lower reserve requirement allows banks to loan more, increasing the money supply.

1 point: Buy bonds

1 point: When the central bank buys bonds, banks' excess reserves increase. When lent out, these excess reserves increase the money supply with the assistance of the money multiplier.

1 point: Decrease the IOR

1 point: When the IOR is lower, the opportunity cost of lending decreases and banks make more loans, increasing the money supply.

1 point: Implement Quantitative Easing

1 point: Expand the central bank's balance sheet by purchasing long term assets

2. Assume the economy is experiencing an inflationary gap.
   a. What type of monetary policy should the central bank pursue?
   b. Use a correctly labeled graph of the market for reserves to explain how the central bank's use of the monetary policy from part a affects the policy rate and level of reserves in an economy with ample reserves.
   c. Explain how the policy rate change you graphed in part b affects aggregate supply and demand in the short run.
   d. Use a correctly labeled aggregate demand and supply graph to show how the changes from part c affect aggregate output and the price level in the short run.
   (10 points)

The Loanable Funds Market

MODULE 4.7

In this Module, you will learn to:

- Define national savings in both a closed and an open economy
- Define the loanable funds market and describe how it matches savers and investors
- Explain the relationship between the real interest rate and the quantity of loanable funds demanded and supplied
- Identify equilibrium and disequilibrium in the loanable funds market
- Explain how real interest rates adjust to restore equilibrium in the loanable funds market
- Identify the determinants of demand and supply in the loanable funds market
- Use a correctly labeled graph to show how the effect of changes in the supply or demand in the loanable funds affects the real interest rate and quantity of loanable funds

Matching Up Savings and Investment Spending

Recall from the circular-flow model in Module 2.1 that, for the economy as a whole, savings always equals investment spending. In a *closed* economy – an economy with no international sector – savings is equal to national savings. In an *open* economy, savings is equal to national savings plus any capital inflow from the international sector. At any given time, however, savers, the people with funds to lend, are usually not the same as borrowers, the people who want to borrow to finance their investment spending. How are savers and borrowers brought together?

Financial markets are where savers and borrowers can match up.

EyeEm/Alamy

Savers and borrowers are matched up with one another in much the same way producers and consumers are matched up: through markets governed by the forces of supply and demand. In our discussion of the circular-flow diagram, we noted that the *financial markets* channel the savings of households to businesses that want to borrow in order to purchase capital equipment. It's now time to take a look at how those financial markets work.

Two instrumental sources of economic growth are increases in the skills and knowledge of the workforce, known as *human capital*, and increases in capital – goods used to make other goods – which can also be called *physical capital* to distinguish it from human capital. Human capital is largely provided through education. But physical capital, with the exception of infrastructure such as roads and bridges, is mainly created through private investment spending – that is, spending by firms rather than by the government.

Google's private investment spending is used to create physical capital, such as their corporate facilities.

Renaud Rebardy/Alamy

Who pays for private investment spending? In some cases it's the people or corporations who actually do the spending – for example, a family that owns a business might use its own savings to buy new equipment or a new building, or a corporation might reinvest some of its own profits to build a new factory. In the modern economy, however, individuals and firms who create physical capital often do it with other people's money – money that they borrow (or raise by selling stock). If they borrow money to create physical capital, they are charged an interest rate.

To understand how investment spending is financed, we need to look first at how savings and investment spending are related to each other for the economy as a whole.

The Savings–Investment Spending Identity

The most basic point to understand about savings and investment spending is that they are always equal. This is not a theory; it's a fact of accounting called the *savings–investment spending identity.*

To see why the savings–investment spending identity must be true, first imagine a highly simplified economy in which there is no government and no interaction with other countries. The overall income of this simplified economy, by definition, would be equal to total spending in the economy. Why? Because the only way people could earn income would be by selling something to someone else, and every dollar spent in the economy would create income for somebody. So, in this simplified economy,

(4.7-1) Total income = Total spending

So, what can people do with income? They can either spend it on consumption or save it. Then it must be true that

(4.7-2) Total income = Consumer spending + Savings

Meanwhile, spending consists of either consumer spending or investment spending:

(4.7-3) Total spending = Consumer spending + Investment spending

Putting these together, we get:

(4.7-4) Consumer spending + Savings = Consumer spending + Investment spending

Subtract consumer spending from both sides, and we get:

(4.7-5) Savings = Investment spending

As we said, it's a basic accounting fact that savings equals investment spending for the economy as a whole.

So far, however, we've looked only at a simplified economy in which there is no government and no economic interaction with the rest of the world. Bringing these realistic complications back into the story changes things in two ways. First, households are not the only parties that can save in an economy. In any given year, the government can save, too, if it collects more tax revenue than it spends. When this occurs, the difference is called a **budget surplus** and is equivalent to savings by the government. If, alternatively, government spending exceeds tax revenue, there is a **budget deficit** – a negative budget surplus. In this case, we often say that the government is "dissaving": by spending more than its tax revenues, the government is engaged in the opposite of saving. We'll define the term *budget balance* to refer to both cases, with the understanding that the budget balance can be positive (a budget surplus) or negative (a budget deficit). **National savings** is equal to the sum of private savings and the budget balance, whereas private savings is disposable income (income after taxes) minus consumption.

The **budget surplus** is the difference between tax revenue and government spending when tax revenue exceeds government spending.

The **budget deficit** is the difference between tax revenue and government spending when government spending exceeds tax revenue.

National savings, the sum of private savings and the budget balance, is the total amount of savings generated within the economy.

Net capital inflow is equal to the total inflow of foreign funds minus the total outflow of domestic funds to other countries.

Second, the fact that any one country is part of a wider world economy means that savings need not be spent on physical capital located in the same country in which the savings are generated. That's because the savings of people who live in any one country can be used to finance investment spending that takes place in other countries. So any given country can receive *inflows* of funds – foreign savings that finance investment spending in the country. Any given country can also generate *outflows* of funds – domestic savings that finance investment spending in another country.

The net effect of international inflows and outflows of funds on the total savings available for investment spending in any given country is known as the **net capital inflow** into that country, equal to the total inflow of foreign funds minus the total outflow of domestic funds to other countries. Like the budget balance, a net capital inflow can be negative—that is, more capital can flow out of a country than flows into it. In recent years, the United States has experienced a consistent net inflow of capital from foreigners, who view our economy as an attractive place to put their savings. In January 2020, for example, new investments into the United States by foreign direct investors were $120.7 billion.

The application of the savings–investment spending identity to an economy that is open to inflows or outflows of capital means that investment spending is equal to savings, where savings is equal to national savings *plus* net capital inflow. That is, in an economy with a positive capital inflow, some investment spending is funded by the savings of foreigners. And, in an economy with a negative net capital inflow (a net capital outflow), some portion of national savings funds investment spending in other countries.

So for an open economy, investment will be equal to national savings plus net capital inflow,

$$\textbf{(4.7-6)} \quad \text{Investment} = \text{national savings} + \text{net capital inflows}$$

In the United States in 2020, investment spending totaled $3,637.8 billion. Private savings were $1,190.9 billion, offset by a budget deficit of $3,129.2 billion and supplemented by capital inflows. Notice that these numbers don't quite add up; because data collection isn't perfect, there will always be a "statistical discrepancy." But we know that this is an error in the data, not in the theory, because the savings–investment spending identity must hold in reality.

The Equilibrium Interest Rate

There are many different financial markets in the financial system, including the bond market and the stock market. However, economists often work with a simplified model in which they assume that there is just one market that brings together those who want to lend money (savers) and those who want to borrow money (firms with investment spending projects). This hypothetical market is known as the **loanable funds market**. The price that is determined in the loanable funds market is the real interest rate, denoted by r. It is the return a lender receives for allowing borrowers the use of a dollar for one year, calculated as a percentage of the amount borrowed.

The **loanable funds market** is a hypothetical market that brings together those who want to lend money and those who want to borrow money.

Recall that in the money market, the *nominal* interest rate is of central importance and always serves as the "price" measured on the vertical axis in a money market graph. Investors and savers in the loanable funds market care about the *real* interest rate, which tells them the price paid for the use of money aside from the amount paid to keep up with inflation, and they base their decisions on the real interest rate they expect to receive for borrowing and loaning funds.

We should also reiterate at this point that, in reality, there are many different kinds of interest rates because there are many different kinds of loans—short-term loans, long-term loans, loans made to corporate borrowers, loans made to governments, and so on. In the interest of simplicity, we'll ignore those differences and assume that there is only one type of loan.

Figure 4.7-1 illustrates the hypothetical demand for loanable funds. On the horizontal axis we show the quantity of loanable funds demanded. On the vertical axis we show the real interest rate, which is the "price" of borrowing. To see why the demand curve for loanable funds, D_{LF}, slopes downward, imagine that there are many businesses, each of which has one potential investment project. How does a given business decide whether or not to borrow money to finance its project? The decision depends on the interest rate the business faces and the *rate of return* on its project—the profit earned on the project expressed as a percentage of its cost. This can be expressed in a formula as:

$$\textbf{(4.7-7)} \quad \text{Rate of return} = \frac{\text{Revenue from project} - \text{Cost of project}}{\text{Cost of project}} \times 100$$

For example, a project that costs $300,000 and produces revenue of $315,000 provides a rate of return of [($315,000 − $300,000)/$300,000] × 100 = 5%.

FIGURE 4.7-1 The Demand for Loanable Funds

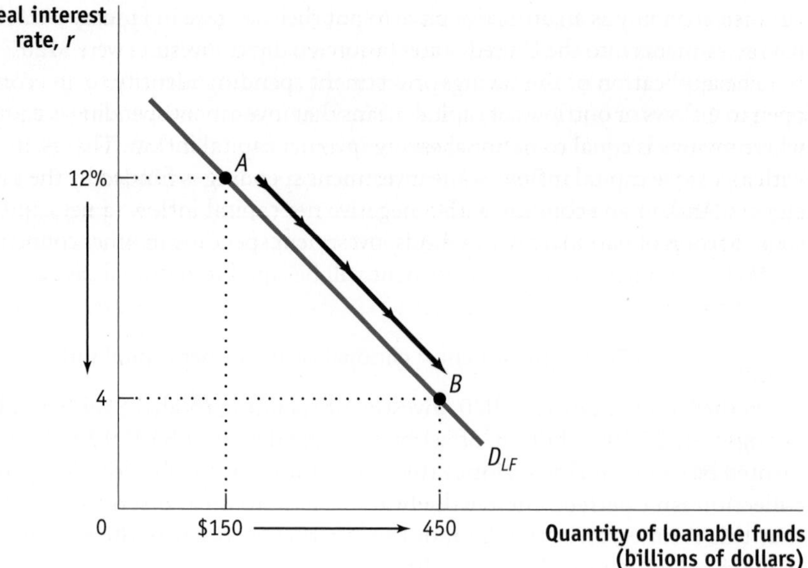

The demand curve for loanable funds (D_{LF}) slopes downward: the lower the interest rate, the greater the quantity of loanable funds demanded. Here, reducing the interest rate from 12% to 4% increases the quantity of loanable funds demanded from $150 billion to $450 billion.

A business will want a loan when the rate of return on its project is greater than or equal to the interest rate. So, for example, at an interest rate of 12%, only businesses with projects that yield a rate of return greater than or equal to 12% will want a loan. A business will not pay 12% interest to fund a project with a 5% rate of return. The demand curve in Figure 4.7-1 shows that if the interest rate is 12%, businesses will want to borrow $150 billion (point *A*); if the interest rate is only 4%, businesses will want to borrow a larger amount, $450 billion (point *B*). That's a consequence of our assumption that the demand curve slopes downward: the lower the interest rate, the larger the total quantity of loanable funds demanded. Why do we make that assumption? Because, in reality, the number of potential investment projects that yield at least 4% is always greater than the number that yield at least 12%.

Figure 4.7-2 shows the hypothetical supply of loanable funds. Again, the interest rate plays the same role that the price plays in ordinary supply and demand

FIGURE 4.7-2 The Supply of Loanable Funds

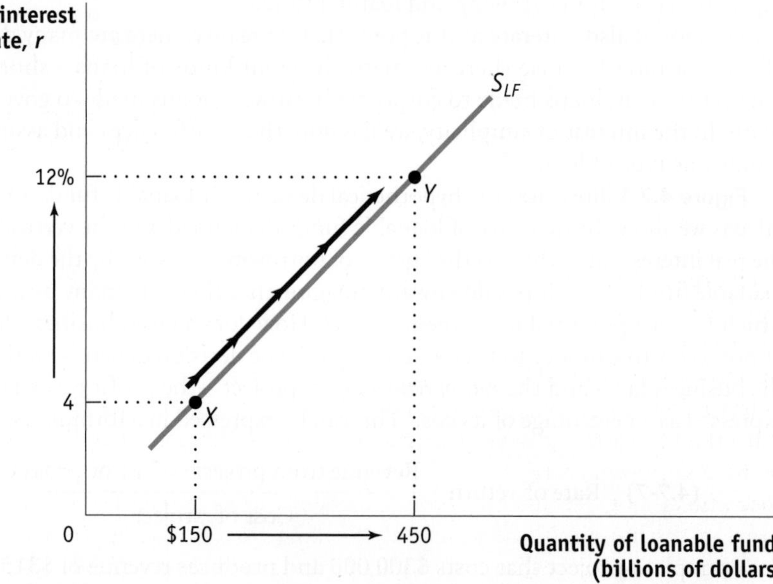

The supply curve for loanable funds (S_{LF}) slopes upward: the higher the interest rate, the greater the quantity of loanable funds supplied. Here, increasing the interest rate from 4% to 12% increases the quantity of loanable funds supplied from $150 billion to $450 billion.

analysis. Savers incur an opportunity cost when they lend to a business; the funds could instead be spent on consumption – say, a vacation. Whether a given individual becomes a lender by making funds available to borrowers depends on the interest rate received in return. By saving your money today and earning interest on it, you are rewarded with higher consumption in the future when your loan is repaid with interest. So it is a good assumption that more people are willing to forgo current consumption and make a loan when the interest rate is higher. As a result, our hypothetical supply curve of loanable funds slopes upward. In Figure 4.7-2, lenders will supply $150 billion to the loanable funds market at an interest rate of 4% (point *X*); if the interest rate rises to 12%, the quantity of loanable funds supplied will rise to $450 billion (point *Y*).

The equilibrium interest rate is the interest rate at which the quantity of loanable funds supplied equals the quantity of loanable funds demanded. As you can see in **Figure 4.7-3**, the equilibrium interest rate, r_E, and the total quantity of lending, Q_E, are determined by the intersection of the supply and demand curves, at point *E*. Here, the equilibrium interest rate is 8%, at which $300 billion is lent and borrowed. Investment spending projects with a rate of return of 8% or more are funded; projects with a rate of return of less than 8% are not. Correspondingly, only lenders who are willing to accept an interest rate of 8% or less will have their offers to lend funds accepted.

AP® ECON TIP

The incentive to lend money is higher when the interest rate is higher, so the supply curve for loanable funds has an upward slope. Make sure you know the differences between the money market and the loanable funds market. The horizontal axis has a different label and the supply curve is vertical in the money market.

FIGURE 4.7-3 Equilibrium in the Loanable Funds Market

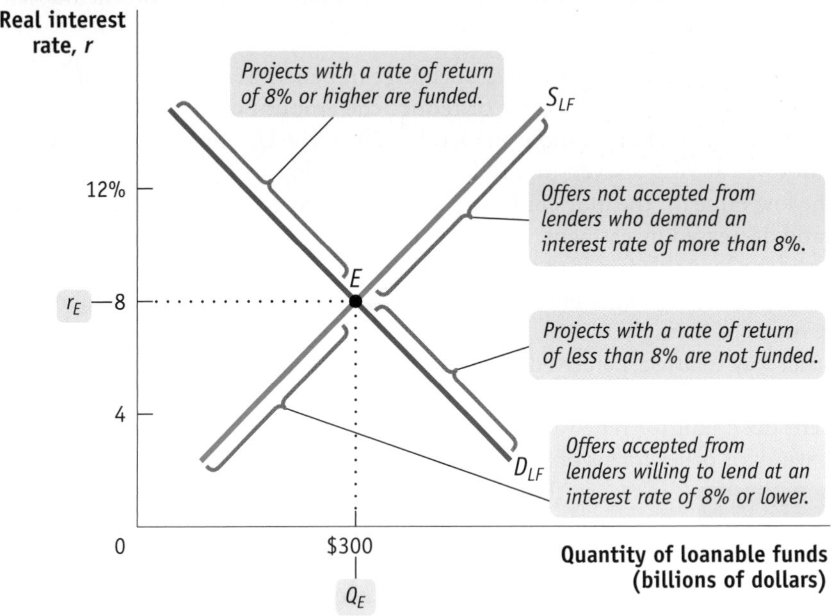

At the equilibrium interest rate, the quantity of loanable funds supplied equals the quantity of loanable funds demanded. Here, the equilibrium interest rate is 8%, with $300 billion of funds lent and borrowed. Investment spending projects with a rate of return of 8% or higher receive funding; those with a lower rate of return do not. Lenders who demand an interest rate of 8% or lower have their offers of loans accepted; those who demand a higher interest rate do not.

Figure 4.7-3 shows how the market for loanable funds matches up desired savings with desired investment spending: in equilibrium, the quantity of funds that savers want to lend is equal to the quantity of funds that firms want to borrow. The figure also shows that this matchup is efficient in two senses. First, the right investments get made: the investment spending projects that are actually financed have higher rates of return than those that do not get financed. Second, the right people do the saving: the potential savers who actually lend funds are willing to lend for lower interest rates than those who do not. The insight that the loanable funds market leads to an efficient use of savings, although drawn from a highly simplified model, has important implications for real life. As we'll see shortly, it is the reason that a well-functioning financial system increases an economy's long-run economic growth rate.

But what if the loanable funds market is not in equilibrium? *Disequilibrium* in the loanable funds market occurs when real interest rates are above or below the equilibrium real interest rate. If the real interest rate were higher than the equilibrium real interest rate — for example, 12% in Figure 4.7-3 — the quantity of loanable funds supplied would be higher (because savers want to save more at the higher interest rate), but the quantity of loanable funds demanded will be lower (because fewer investment projects will have a rate of return greater than 12%). This imbalance leads to a surplus of loanable funds that will drive the real interest rate back down to equilibrium.

With a real interest rate below equilibrium — for example, 4% in Figure 4.7-3 — the quantity of loanable funds supplied will be lower than the quantity of loanable funds demanded, creating a shortage of loanable funds. The shortage in the loanable funds market will drive real interest rates back up to equilibrium.

So real interest rates will increase or decrease in response to surpluses and shortages to move the loanable funds market back to the equilibrium real interest rate. Now let's consider how the market for loanable funds responds to shifts of demand and supply.

Shifts in the Demand for Loanable Funds

The equilibrium interest rate changes when there are shifts of the demand curve for loanable funds, the supply curve for loanable funds, or both. Let's start by looking at the causes and effects of changes in demand.

The factors that can cause the demand curve for loanable funds to shift include the following:

- *Changes in perceived business opportunities.* A change in beliefs about the rate of return on investment spending can increase or reduce the amount of desired spending at any given interest rate. For example, in October 2021, the U.S. Small Business Optimism Index was at 98.2, a seven-month low and well below its high of around 108 in 2018. The low value for the index indicates pessimistic expectations for business conditions and decreased investment. Decreases in investment by small businesses shift the demand for loanable funds to the left. An increase in business optimism, such as what the United States experienced between 2016 and 2018, shifts the demand for loanable funds to the right.

An **investment tax credit** is an amount that firms are allowed by law to deduct from their taxes based on their investment spending.

  Another way to affect perceived business opportunities is through a government **investment tax credit**, which firms can deduct from their taxes. For example, an investment tax credit for renewable energy provides an incentive for firms to invest in solar, wind, or other forms of renewable energy. The investment tax credit would increase the rate of return on these investments, thereby increasing the demand for loanable funds and shifting the demand curve for loanable funds to the right.

Sergio Flores/Bloomberg/Getty Images

Government tax credits can be used as incentives for investment in new opportunities, such as solar energy.

- *Changes in the government's borrowing.* Governments that run budget deficits are major sources of the demand for loanable funds. As a result, changes in the budget deficit can shift the demand curve for loanable funds. For example, between 2000 and 2003, as the U.S. federal government went from a budget surplus to a budget deficit, net federal borrowing went from *minus* \$189 billion — that is, in 2000 the federal government was actually providing loanable funds to the market because it was paying off some of its debt — to *plus* \$377.6 billion because in 2003 the government had to borrow large sums to pay its bills. In 2020, net federal borrowing again increased as the budget deficit rose to an historical high of \$3,131.9 billion. Changes in the federal budget position have the effect, other things equal, of shifting the demand curve for loanable funds. Increases in government borrowing shift the demand for loanable funds to the right, and decreases shift it to the left.

Figure 4.7-4 shows the effects of an increase in the demand for loanable funds. *S* is the supply of loanable funds, and D_{LF1} is the initial demand curve. The initial equilibrium interest rate is r_1. An increase in the demand for loanable funds means that the quantity of funds demanded rises at any given interest rate, so the demand curve shifts rightward to D_{LF2}. As a result, the equilibrium interest rate rises to r_2.

FIGURE 4.7-4 An Increase in the Demand for Loanable Funds

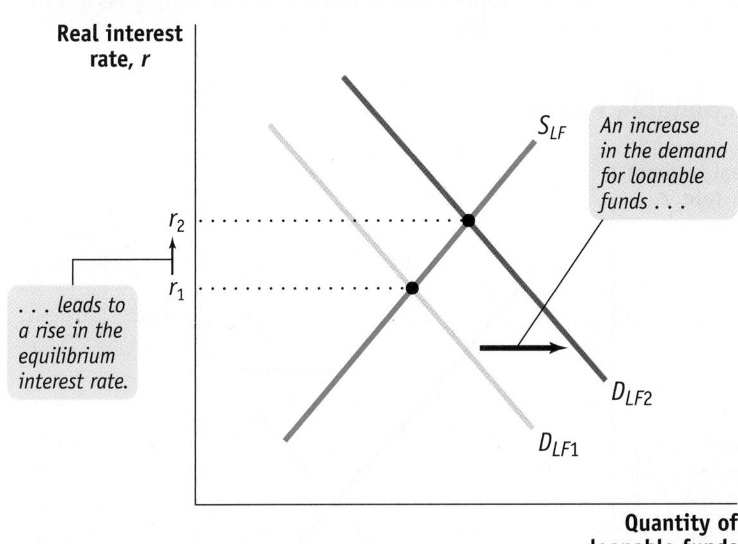

If the quantity of funds demanded by borrowers rises at any given interest rate, the demand for loanable funds shifts rightward from D_{LF1} to D_{LF2}. As a result, the equilibrium interest rate rises from r_1 to r_2.

The fact that, other things equal, an increase in the demand for loanable funds leads to a rise in the real interest rate has one especially important implication: beyond concern about repayment, there are other reasons to be wary of government budget deficits. As we've already seen, an increase in the government's deficit shifts the demand curve for loanable funds to the right, which leads to a higher interest rate. If the interest rate rises, businesses will cut back on their investment spending. So a rise in the government budget deficit tends to reduce overall investment spending. Economists call the negative effect of government budget deficits on investment spending **crowding out**. The threat of crowding out is a key source of concern about persistent budget deficits, which we discuss in detail in Module 5.5.

Crowding out occurs when a government deficit drives up the interest rate and leads to reduced investment spending.

Shifts in the Supply of Loanable Funds

Like the demand for loanable funds, the supply of loanable funds can shift. Among the factors that can cause the supply of loanable funds to shift are the following:

- *Changes in private saving behavior*. A number of factors can cause the level of private savings to change at any given rate of interest. For example, between 2000 and 2006, rising home prices in the United States made many homeowners feel richer, making them willing to spend more and save less. This had the effect of shifting the supply of loanable funds to the left. The drop in home prices between 2006 and 2009 had the opposite effect, shifting the supply of loanable funds to the right.

Capital inflows can lead to an increase in investment spending in areas like residential property.

- *Changes in capital inflows.* Capital flows into a country can change as investors' perceptions of that country change. For example, from 2009 to 2016, Brazil experienced large capital inflows because international investors believed that years of economic reforms made it a safe place to put their funds. Capital flows into the United States averaged \$22,189 million from 1978 to 2019, with much of the capital inflows coming from China. We discuss net capital inflows in more detail in Module 6.6.

Figure 4.7-5 shows the effects of an increase in the supply of loanable funds. D_{LF} is the demand for loanable funds, and S_{LF1} is the initial supply curve. The initial equilibrium interest rate is r_1. An increase in the supply of loanable funds means that the quantity of funds supplied rises at any given interest rate, so the supply curve shifts rightward to S_{LF2}. As a result, the equilibrium interest rate falls to r_2.

FIGURE 4.7-5 An Increase in the Supply of Loanable Funds

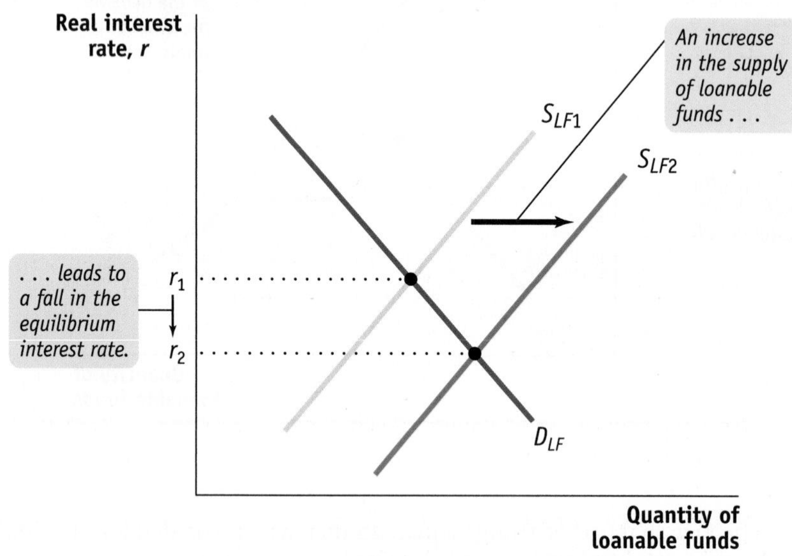

If the quantity of funds supplied by lenders rises at any given interest rate, the supply of loanable funds shifts rightward from S_{LF1} to S_{LF2}. As a result, the equilibrium interest rate falls from r_1 to r_2.

Inflation and Interest Rates

In our loanable funds market graphs, anything that shifts either the supply of loanable funds curve or the demand for loanable funds curve changes the real interest rate. Historically, major changes in interest rates have been driven by many factors, including changes in government policy and technological innovations that created new investment opportunities. However, arguably the most important factor affecting interest rates over time—the reason, for example, why interest rates today are much lower than they were in the late 1970s and early 1980s—is changing expectations about future inflation, which shift both the supply of and the demand for loanable funds.

To understand the effect of expected inflation on interest rates, recall our discussion of nominal versus real interest rates in Module 4.2. We know that economists capture the effect of inflation on borrowers and lenders by distinguishing between the *nominal interest rate* and the *real interest rate*, where the distinction is as follows:

$$\text{Real interest rate} = \text{Nominal interest rate} - \text{Inflation rate}$$

Recall that the true cost of borrowing is the real interest rate, not the nominal interest rate. To see why, suppose a firm borrows \$10,000 for one year at a 10% nominal interest rate. At the end of the year, it must repay $11,000 – the amount borrowed plus the interest. But suppose that over the course of the year the average level of prices increases by 10%, so that the real interest rate is zero. Then the $11,000 repayment has the same purchasing power as the original $10,000 loan. In effect, the borrower has received a zero-interest loan.

Similarly, the true payoff to lending is the real interest rate, not the nominal rate. The bank that makes the one-year $10,000 loan at a 10% nominal interest rate receives an $11,000 repayment at the end of the year. But the 10% increase in the average level of prices means that the purchasing power of the money the bank gets back is no more than that of the money it lent out. In effect, the bank has made a zero-interest loan.

As we learned earlier in this Unit, we can only know the real inflation rate in hindsight, so calculating the real interest rate as the nominal interest rate minus the inflation rate can only be done after the fact. Before the fact, savers and borrowers must determine the expected real interest rate using the *expected* rate of inflation. So expected increases in inflation increase nominal interest rates, and expected decreases in inflation decrease nominal interest rates. And if the expected inflation rate is different from the actual inflation rate – that is, if savers' or borrowers' expectations are wrong – it will lead to the redistribution of wealth from one group to another, as discussed in Module 2.5.

AP® ECON TIP

Even though the real interest rate is equal to the nominal interest rate minus the inflation rate, simply knowing two of the values will not necessarily tell you the effect on the third. For example, an increase in the nominal interest rate and a decrease in the inflation rate will both lead to an increase in the real interest rate. But if both the nominal interest rate and the inflation rate increase at the same time, it is impossible to tell what will happen to the real interest rate unless you know which rate changed by more.

Module 4.7 Review

Check Your Understanding

1. Use a diagram of the loanable funds market to illustrate the effect of the following events on the equilibrium interest rate and quantity of loanable funds.
   a. An economy is opened to international movements of capital, and a capital inflow occurs.
   b. Retired people generally save less than working people at any interest rate. The proportion of retired people in the population goes up.
2. Suppose that expected inflation rises from 3% to 6%.
   a. How will the real interest rate be affected by this change?
   b. How will the nominal interest rate be affected by this change?
   c. What will happen to the equilibrium quantity of loanable funds?

Tackle the AP® Test: Multiple-Choice Questions

1. The federal government is said to be "dissaving" when
   a. there is a budget deficit.
   b. there is a budget surplus.
   c. there is no budget surplus or deficit.
   d. savings does not equal investment spending.
   e. national savings equals private savings.
2. It is a basic accounting fact that the level of investment for a closed economy must equal the level of
   a. capital inflows.
   b. capital outflows.
   c. wealth.
   d. financial assets.
   e. national savings.
3. A business will decide whether or not to borrow money to finance a project based on a comparison of the interest rate with the ___________ from its project.
   a. expected revenue
   b. profit
   c. rate of return
   d. cost generated
   e. demand generated
4. Which of the following will increase the demand for loanable funds?
   a. a federal government budget surplus
   b. an increase in perceived business opportunities
   c. a decrease in the interest rate
   d. positive capital inflows
   e. a decrease in private saving rates

5. Which of the following will increase the supply of loanable funds?
   a. an increase in perceived business opportunities
   b. decreased government borrowing
   c. an increase in private saving rates
   d. an increase in the expected inflation rate
   e. a decrease in capital inflows

6. Both lenders and borrowers base their decisions on
   a. expected real interest rates.
   b. expected nominal interest rates.
   c. real interest rates.
   d. nominal interest rates.
   e. nominal interest rates minus real interest rates.

7. The graph of the loanable funds market is different from that of the money market in which of the following ways?
   a. The demand curve slopes downward.
   b. The demand curve slopes upward.
   c. The supply curve slopes downward.
   d. The supply curve slopes upward.
   e. Price is on the vertical axis.

Tackle the AP® Test: Free-Response Questions

1. Draw a correctly labeled graph showing equilibrium in the loanable funds market. Illustrate crowding out on your graph.

Rubric for FRQ 1 (5 points)

1 point: Vertical axis labeled "Interest rate" or "r," horizontal axis labeled "Quantity of loanable funds"

1 point: Downward-sloping demand curve for loanable funds (labeled)

1 point: Upward-sloping supply curve for loanable funds (labeled)

1 point: Equilibrium quantity of loanable funds shown on horizontal axis below where curves intersect and equilibrium interest rate shown on vertical axis across from where curves intersect

1 point: A new demand curve is shown to the right and the new equilibrium real interest rate is higher

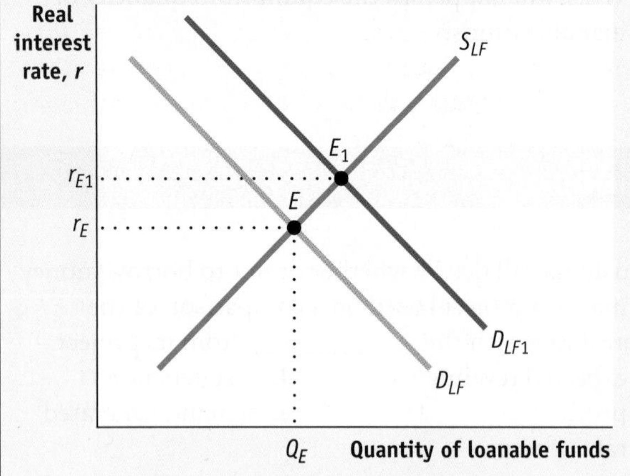

2. Does each of the following affect either the supply or the demand for loanable funds, and if so, does the affected curve increase (shift to the right) or decrease (shift to the left)?
   a. There is an increase in capital inflows into the economy.
   b. Businesses are pessimistic about future business conditions.
   c. The government increases borrowing.
   d. The private saving rate decreases. **(4 points)**

UNIT 4 Review

Adventures in AP® Economics Videos

Module 4.4: The Money Multiplier
Module 4.6: Monetary Policy and the Federal Reserve System

UNIT 4 Review Video

economics by example
How Should We Wield the Tool of Monetary Policy?

Module 4.1

1. A **financial asset** is a nonphysical asset that entitles the buyer to future income from the seller. Cash is the most **liquid** example of a financial asset— there is no cost involved to turn cash into cash. The opportunity cost of holding cash is the interest that could have been earned if an interest-bearing asset were held instead. The rate of return on a financial asset depends on its **liquidity** and **financial risk**, the uncertainty about future outcomes that involve financial losses and gains.
2. Other financial assets include **bonds** and **stocks**. A **bond** is an interest-bearing asset that can be thought of as an IOU issued by the borrower. The price of previously issued bonds and the interest rates are inversely related.

Module 4.2

3. The **nominal interest rate** is the interest rate that is actually paid for a loan, unadjusted for the effects of inflation. The nominal interest rate is a monetary value and is not necessarily the actual return on the loan. The **real interest rate** is the nominal interest rate adjusted for inflation. It takes into account the opportunity cost of loaning the funds and the value of what they can purchase after price changes. The real interest rate is calculated in hindsight as the nominal inflation rate minus the rate of inflation. The expected real interest rate is the nominal interest rate minus the expected rate of inflation.

Module 4.3A

4. **Money** is any asset that can easily be used to purchase goods and services. Currency in circulation and demand deposits are both considered part of the **money supply**. Money plays three roles: it is a **medium of exchange** used for transactions, a **store of value** that holds purchasing power over time, and a **unit of account** in which prices are stated.
5. The central bank calculates two measures of the money supply. M1 is the narrowest **monetary aggregate**; it contains only currency in circulation, demand deposits, and other liquid deposits. M2 includes a wider range of assets called near-moneys, mainly other forms of bank deposits, that can easily be converted into demand deposits. The **monetary base** (M0) includes currency in circulation and bank reserves.

Module 4.3B

6. A **central bank** is a government institution that issues currency, oversees and regulates the banking system, and controls the monetary base and monetary policy. The Federal Reserve, or "the Fed," is the **central bank** of the United States. The three main functions of the Fed are to provide financial services, supervise and regulate banks, and conduct monetary policy. The Fed is made up of the Board of Governors and the 12 regional Federal Reserve Banks. The Federal Open Market Committee (FOMC) conducts U.S. monetary policy.

Module 4.4

7. With **fractional reserve banking**, banks allow depositors immediate access to their funds, but they also lend out most of the funds deposited in their care. To meet demands for cash, they maintain **bank reserves** composed of both currency held in vaults and deposits at a central bank. The **reserve ratio** is the ratio of bank reserves to bank deposits. Bank reserves include **required reserves**, mandated by the central bank and **excess reserves** above that amount. A T-account, also known as a balance sheet, summarizes a bank's financial position, with loans and reserves counted as assets, and deposits counted as liabilities.

8. In an economy with limited reserves, when currency is deposited in a bank, it starts a multiplier process in which banks lend out **excess reserves**, leading to an increase in the money supply—which is how banks create money. If the entire money supply consisted of demand deposits, the money supply would be equal to the value of reserves divided by the reserve ratio. In reality, much of the monetary base consists of currency in circulation, and the **money multiplier** is the ratio of the money supply to the monetary base. The amount of money supply expansion predicted by the simple money multiplier (1/reserve requirement) may be overstated as a result of currency held by the public or excess reserves held by banks.

Module 4.5

9. The **money demand curve** arises from a trade-off between the opportunity cost of holding money and the liquidity that money provides. There is an inverse relationship between the nominal interest rate and the quantity of money demanded. Changes in the aggregate price level, real GDP, technology, and institutions shift the money demand curve.

10. The equilibrium nominal interest rate is determined in the money market by the money demand curve and the **money supply curve**. The money supply curve is independent of the nominal interest rate. Equilibrium in the money market is found where the quantity of money demanded is equal to the quantity of money supplied. In an economy with limited reserves, the central bank can change the interest rate in the short run by shifting the money supply curve.

Module 4.6

11. Many central banks carry out policy to hit a target range for the **overnight interbank lending rate** (the **federal funds rate** in the United States). **Expansionary monetary policy** is used to restore full employment when the economy is in a recessionary gap. **Contractionary monetary policy** is used to restore full employment when there is an inflationary gap. Monetary policy involves a change in the money supply to influence the interest rate and therefore investment. Changes in investment affect aggregate demand, the price level, and real GDP. The money market and aggregate demand and aggregate supply models are used to demonstrate the short-run effects of monetary policy. In reality, there are **monetary policy lags** that delay the effects of monetary policy.

12. Central banks implement monetary policies to achieve macroeconomic goals such as price stability and maximum employment. The traditional tools of monetary policy used in an economy with limited reserves include the **reserve requirement**, the **discount rate**, and **open market operations.** More modern tools used in an economy with ample reserves include **quantitative easing**, **interest on reserves**, and **repurchase agreements** (RAs).

13. **Open market operations** by the central bank are used in an economy with limited reserves to increase or reduce the monetary base and include buying or selling bonds. The effect of an open market purchase or sale of bonds is greater than the effect on the monetary base due to the **money multiplier**.

14. Recent Federal Reserve monetary policy is conducted in an ample reserve environment and focuses on two administered rates—interest rate on reserves and the rate on repurchase agreements—to set the target federal funds rate. The level of reserves and the policy rate are determined in the market for reserves.

Module 4.7

15. **National saving** is the sum of public saving and private saving. Investment is equal to **national savings** plus **net capital inflow**.

16. The **loanable funds market** shows how loans from savers are allocated among borrowers with investment spending projects. In equilibrium, only those projects with a rate of return greater than or equal to the equilibrium interest rate will be funded. So there is an inverse relationship between the real interest rate and the quantity of loanable funds demanded.

17. The supply of loanable funds shows the positive relationship between real interest rates and the quantity of loanable funds supplied. Savers will want to supply more loanable funds as the real interest rate increases because the real interest rate is the opportunity cost of holding cash. The equilibrium real interest rate is found where the quantity of loanable funds demanded is equal to the quantity of loanable funds supplied.

18. Government budget deficits can raise the interest rate and can lead to **crowding out** of investment spending. Changes in perceived business opportunities, including incentives such as **investment tax credits,** and in government borrowing shift the demand curve for loanable funds; changes in private savings and capital inflows shift the supply curve.

Key Terms

Interest rate, p. 192
Wealth, p. 192
Financial asset, p. 193
Physical asset, p. 193
Liability, p. 193
Financial risk, p. 194
Liquid, p. 194
Illiquid, p. 194
Loan, p. 195
Bond, p. 195
Stock, p. 196
Bank deposit, p. 197
Bank, p. 197
Nominal interest rate, p. 199
Real interest rate, p. 199
Money, p. 204
Money supply, p. 204
Medium of exchange, p. 205
Store of value, p. 205
Unit of account, p. 206
Commodity money, p. 206
Commodity-backed money, p. 206
Fiat money, p. 207
Monetary aggregate, p. 207
Monetary base, p. 207
M1, p. 207
M2, p. 207
Central bank, p. 211
Open market operations (OMOs), p. 215
Fractional reserve banking system, p. 218
Bank reserves, p. 218
Reserve ratio, p. 219
Required reserve ratio, p. 220
Reserve requirements, p. 221
Required reserves, p. 223
Excess reserves, p. 224
Money multiplier, p. 225
Money demand curve (*MD*), p. 230
Money supply curve (*MS*), p. 232
inflation targeting, p. 237
expansionary monetary policy, p. 238
contractionary monetary policy, p. 238
overnight interbank lending rate, p. 239
policy rate, p. 239
federal funds rate, p. 239
limited reserves, p. 239
ample reserves, p. 239
discount rate, p. 240
Open market operations (OMOs), p. 241
zero bound, p. 243
Quantitative easing (QE), p. 243
interest on reserve balances (IORB), p. 243
Monetary policy lags, p. 247
Budget surplus, p. 250
Budget deficit, p. 250
National savings, p. 250
Net capital inflow, p. 250
Loanable funds market, p. 251
Investment tax credit, p. 254
Crowding out, p. 255

AP® Exam Practice Questions

Multiple-Choice Questions

1. The interest rate is
- **a.** the opportunity cost of lending money.
- **b.** the price borrowers pay for the use of lenders' savings.
- **c.** a percentage of the amount saved by borrowers.
- **d.** the rate charged by banks to hold savings for one year.
- **e.** the amount earned by using profits to build a new factory.

2. Which of the following correctly shows the chain of events through which an increase in IOR will affect real GDP?
- **a.** $\uparrow i \rightarrow \uparrow I \rightarrow \uparrow AD \rightarrow \uparrow$real GDP
- **b.** $\uparrow i \rightarrow \downarrow I \rightarrow \uparrow AD \rightarrow \downarrow$real GDP
- **c.** $\downarrow i \rightarrow \uparrow I \rightarrow \uparrow AD \rightarrow \uparrow$real GDP
- **d.** $\uparrow i \rightarrow \downarrow I \rightarrow \downarrow AD \rightarrow \downarrow$real GDP
- **e.** savings = investment spending

3. A budget surplus exists when the government does which of the following?
- **a.** saves
- **b.** collects less tax revenue than it spends
- **c.** has a negative budget balance
- **d.** increases the national debt
- **e.** uses expansionary fiscal policy

4. Which of the following is a task of an economy's financial system?
- **a.** maximizing risk
- **b.** increasing transaction costs
- **c.** decreasing diversification
- **d.** eliminating liquidity
- **e.** enhancing the efficiency of financial markets

5. Which of the following tools would a central bank use in response to a recession in an economy with ample reserves?
- **a.** quantitative easing
- **b.** raising the interest paid on bank reserves
- **c.** lowering taxes
- **d.** lowering the rate on repurchase agreements
- **e.** decreasing the money supply

6. Which of the following assets is most liquid?
- **a.** stock
- **b.** bond
- **c.** loan
- **d.** mutual fund
- **e.** cash

7. When money acts as a means of holding purchasing power over time, it is serving which function?
- **a.** medium of exchange
- **b.** source of liquidity
- **c.** store of value
- **d.** unit of account
- **e.** source of wealth

8. Which of the following is an example of using money as a unit of account?
   a. buying a new T-shirt
   b. purchasing $10 worth of candy
   c. keeping the dollar you receive each year for your birthday for 10 years
   d. putting money into your savings account
   e. paying for lunch with your debit card

9. The central bank sets a target for which of the following?
   a. the income tax rate
   b. the overnight interbank lending rate
   c. the money supply
   d. the prime interest rate
   e. the unemployment rate

10. The real interest rate is calculated in hindsight as the nominal interest rate
   a. plus the rate of inflation.
   b. minus the rate of inflation.
   c. minus the expected rate of inflation.
   d. plus the expected rate of inflation.
   e. unadjusted for inflation.

11. Compared to the M1 money supply, the M2 money supply is
   a. smaller.
   b. less liquid.
   c. more narrowly defined.
   d. easier to measure.
   e. All of these

12. If lenders require a real interest rate of 3% and they expect 2% inflation, the nominal interest rate will equal
   a. 1%.
   b. 2%.
   c. 3%.
   d. 5%.
   e. 6%.

13. Which of the following actions could the central bank use to address inflation?
   a. buy government bonds
   b. increase interest rates
   c. pursue quantitative easing
   d. decrease money demand
   e. raise taxes

14. The liquid assets banks keep in their vaults are known as bank
   a. deposits.
   b. savings.
   c. reserves.
   d. money.
   e. returns.

15. The required reserve ratio is
   a. the most cash that banks are allowed to hold in their vault.
   b. set by the central bank.
   c. responsible for most bank runs.
   d. equal to 5% of bank deposits.
   e. the fraction of bank loans held as reserves.

16. If rr is the reserve requirement, the money multiplier is equal to
   a. rr.
   b. $1 - rr$.
   c. $1/rr$.
   d. rr^2.
   e. $1/rr^2$.

17. Which of the following is part of the M1 money supply but not part of the monetary base?
   a. demand deposits
   b. bank reserves
   c. currency in circulation
   d. deposits at the central bank
   e. savings accounts

18. The Federal Reserve is a(n)
   a. single central bank located in New York.
   b. government agency overseen by the Secretary of the Treasury.
   c. system of 10 regional banks.
   d. institution that oversees the banking system.
   e. depository institution that lends to large corporations.

19. A central bank is charged with doing all of the following EXCEPT
   a. providing financial services to commercial banks.
   b. supervising and regulating banks.
   c. maintaining the stability of the financial system.
   d. conducting monetary policy.
   e. insuring bank deposits.

20. Which of the following will increase the demand for money?
   a. a fall in the aggregate price level
   b. an increase in real GDP
   c. technological advances
   d. open market operations by the central bank
   e. a decrease in the interest rate

21. The money supply curve is
   a. upward sloping.
   b. vertical.
   c. horizontal.
   d. downward sloping.
   e. U-shaped.

22. Which of the following will occur if the central bank lowers the interest paid on bank reserves (IOR)?
   a. The opportunity cost of making loans will decrease.
   b. Banks will hold more reserves.
   c. The money supply curve will shift to the left.
   d. Interest rates will rise.
   e. Aggregate demand will decrease.

23. Which of the following will shift the supply curve for loanable funds to the right?
   a. an increase in the rate of return on investment spending
   b. an increase in the government budget deficit
   c. a decrease in the national saving rate
   d. an increase in expected inflation
   e. capital inflows from abroad

24. Crowding out is illustrated by which of the following changes in the loanable funds market?
   a. a decreasing equilibrium interest rate
   b. an increase in the demand for loanable funds
   c. a decrease in the demand for loanable funds
   d. an increase in the supply of loanable funds
   e. a decrease in the supply of loanable funds

25. The supply curve for loanable funds is
   a. upward sloping.
   b. vertical.
   c. horizontal.
   d. downward sloping.
   e. U-shaped.

Free-Response Questions

1. a. Draw a correctly labeled graph of the market for loanable funds. On your graph, indicate each of the following:
      i. the equilibrium interest rate, labeled r_1
      ii. the equilibrium quantity of loanable funds, labeled Q_1
   b. Use your graph from part a to show how an increase in government spending affects the loanable funds market. On the graph, indicate each of the following:
      i. the new equilibrium interest rate, labeled r_2
      ii. the new equilibrium quantity of loanable funds, labeled Q_2
   c. Explain how the new interest rate affects the level of real GDP. **(5 points)**

2. a. Draw a correctly labeled graph of the market for reserves. On your graph, indicate each of the following:
      i. the supply and demand for reserves, labeled D_{R1} and S_{R1}
      ii. the policy rate and level of reserves in the economy, labeled P_{R1} and Q_1
   b. Use your graph from part a to show how expansionary monetary policy in an economy with ample reserve affects the market for reserves. On the graph, indicate each of the following:
      i. the new policy rate, labeled P_{R2}
      ii. the new quantity of reserves, labeled Q_2
   c. Draw an aggregate demand and aggregate supply graph to show how the new interest rate affects *AD*, the price level, and the level of real GDP.
   (10 points)

3. Suppose the economy is experiencing inflation.
   a. What type of monetary policy will the central bank pursue and how will this policy change the policy rate?
   b. Given the change in the policy rate from part a, will investment and interest-sensitive consumption increase or decrease? Explain.
   c. Draw a correctly labeled *AS-AD* graph showing an economy with an inflationary gap. On your graph, show each of the following:
      i. the equilibrium price level, labeled PL_1
      ii. the short-run equilibrium level of real GDP, labeled Y_1
      iii. the new aggregate demand curve after the expansionary monetary policy, labeled AD_1
   (5 points)

Long-Run Consequences of Stabilization Policies

AP® Economic Skills

2. Interpretation (2.A, 2.B)
3. Manipulation (3.A, 3.B)
4. Graphing and Visuals (4.B)

Choices Have Consequences—Both Short-Run AND Long-Run

When the COVID-19 pandemic hit in early 2020, the U.S. economy experienced a dramatic downturn, with unemployment rates increasing to over 14%. In response, the government implemented expansionary fiscal policy while at the same time the Federal Reserve implemented expansionary monetary policy. Congress quickly authorized legislation in response to the pandemic. Around the same time, the Fed met in a special meeting, *before* its regularly scheduled Federal Open Market Committee (FOMC) meeting, to reduce the federal funds rate to near zero and set in motion further actions including emergency lending and the purchase of financial assets. These combined fiscal and monetary policy actions helped to *increase* personal income in the second quarter of 2020, despite the economy having just experienced the largest decline on record in the first quarter.

The combination of expansionary monetary and fiscal policy ended the 2020 recession after only two months. The fast and substantial actions offset much of the economic shock created by the pandemic lockdown. But the fiscal policy actions cost over $3 trillion—the equivalent of about 14.5% of U.S. GDP in Q4 of 2019—and the government had to borrow that money. The monetary policy action left the federal funds rate very near the zero bound. And in November 2021, the inflation rate rose to over 6.8%. The short-run effect of the fast and effective use of fiscal and monetary policy was to quickly end the sharp decline set off by the pandemic shutdown in early 2020, but what about long-term consequences? What effect will over $3 trillion in additional borrowing have on the economy? How will a federal funds rate equal to zero affect markets and monetary policy in the future? And how will the two simultaneous expansionary policies affect inflation and employment in the long run?

In Unit 3, we developed the aggregate demand and supply model and introduced the use of fiscal policy to stabilize the economy. In Unit 4, we introduced money, banking, and monetary policy. In this Unit, we use the models introduced in Units 3 and 4 to further develop our understanding of stabilization policies (both fiscal and monetary), including their long-run effects on the economy. In addition, we introduce the Phillips curve—a short-run trade-off between unexpected inflation and unemployment—and investigate the role of expectations in the economy.

LeoPatrizi/Getty Images

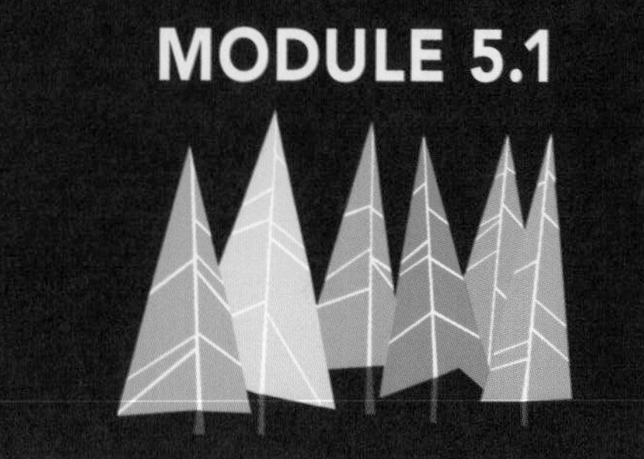

MODULE 5.1

Fiscal and Monetary Policy Actions in the Short Run

In this Module, you will learn to:

- Explain the effects of combined fiscal and monetary policy
- Explain how a combination of expansionary or contractionary fiscal and monetary policies can restore full employment
- Use a correctly labeled *AD–AS* graph to show the effects of expansionary policies addressing a recessionary (negative) economic gap
- Use a correctly labeled *AD–AS* graph to show the effects of contractionary policies addressing an inflationary (positive) economic gap

The Independence of Fiscal and Monetary Policy

Monetary policy refers to the actions of central banks to achieve macroeconomic policy objectives such as price stability, full employment, and economic growth. Fiscal policy refers to the tax and spending policies of the government. Fiscal policy decisions are determined by the government when it determines its budget; central banks generally don't play any role in determining fiscal policy.

In some countries, central banks are made independent. For example, in the United States, Congress gave the Federal Reserve the mandate to pursue maximum employment and price stability, sometimes referred to as a dual mandate. Beyond these broad goals, Congress decided that monetary policy should be free from political influence. As a result, the Federal Reserve is an independent agency. Independent central banks determine monetary policy; governments generally don't play any role in determining monetary policy.

A government may base its determination of the need for fiscal policy in part on its expectations for the central bank's conduct of monetary policy. In this way, monetary policy will be considered when the government implements fiscal policy. For example, if the central bank lowers the overnight interbank lending rate, the government will assess how the expansionary monetary policy will affect employment and prices—and adjust its estimation of the need for fiscal policy. And the central bank will likely consider how current and projected fiscal policy could affect real GDP, employment, and the price level. In this way, fiscal policy will have an indirect effect on monetary policy through its influence on the aggregate economy. For example, if the government passed a large tax cut, the central bank would respond by assessing how that action would affect employment and prices—and make appropriate adjustments to its monetary policy tools. But beyond each policy-making body's awareness of the actions considered or taken by the other, and their likely effect on the economy, there is no formal coordination of fiscal and monetary policy. However, if the government and the central bank each accurately evaluate the state of the economy and choose the policy actions that move the economy back to full employment, both of their policies will be either expansionary or contractionary, depending on the circumstances.

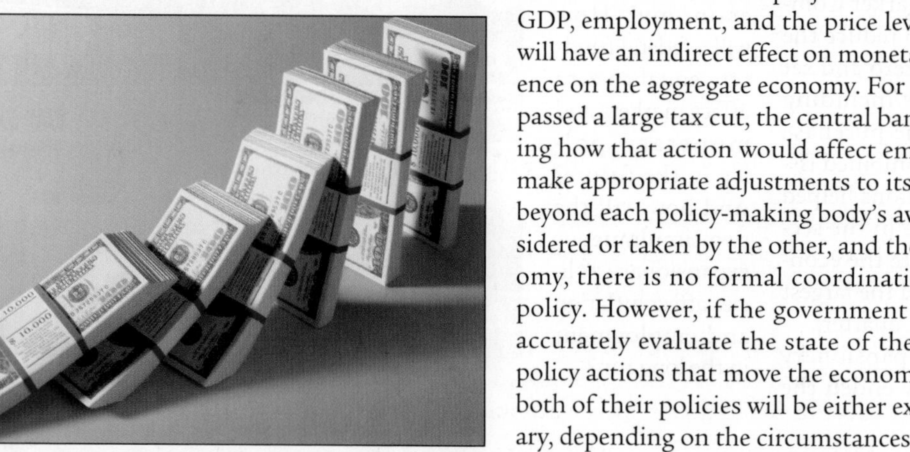

Grafissimo/Getty Images

In this Module, we review the combined short-run effects of fiscal and monetary policy on aggregate demand, real GDP, the price level, and interest rates.

> **AP® ECON TIP**
>
> Fiscal policy is controlled by the government through its budget and monetary policy is controlled by the central bank. While both the central bank and the government will consider the effects of past and potential future monetary and fiscal policy on the economy, the two policies are not connected. Monetary and fiscal policy will be determined independently in our *AD–AS* model.

Using Expansionary Fiscal and Monetary Policy to Close a Negative Output Gap

In Units 3 and 4, we saw how fiscal and monetary policy can have a short-run effect on macroeconomic outcomes. When the economy is experiencing a negative output gap, the government and central bank implement expansionary policy to increase employment and output. During recessions, the government can increase spending (G) and/or decrease taxes (*T*) to increase aggregate demand, while the central bank can increase aggregate demand by decreasing interest rates.

Figure 5.1-1 summarizes how fiscal and monetary policy increase aggregate demand, closing a negative (recessionary) output gap. In the aggregate demand and aggregate supply (*AD–AS*) model, the expansionary policies shift the aggregate demand (*AD*) curve to the right, moving the economy toward long-run equilibrium with a higher real GDP and price level (*PL*), as shown in Figure 5.1-1.

FIGURE 5.1-1 Combining Fiscal and Monetary Policy to Close a Recessionary Gap

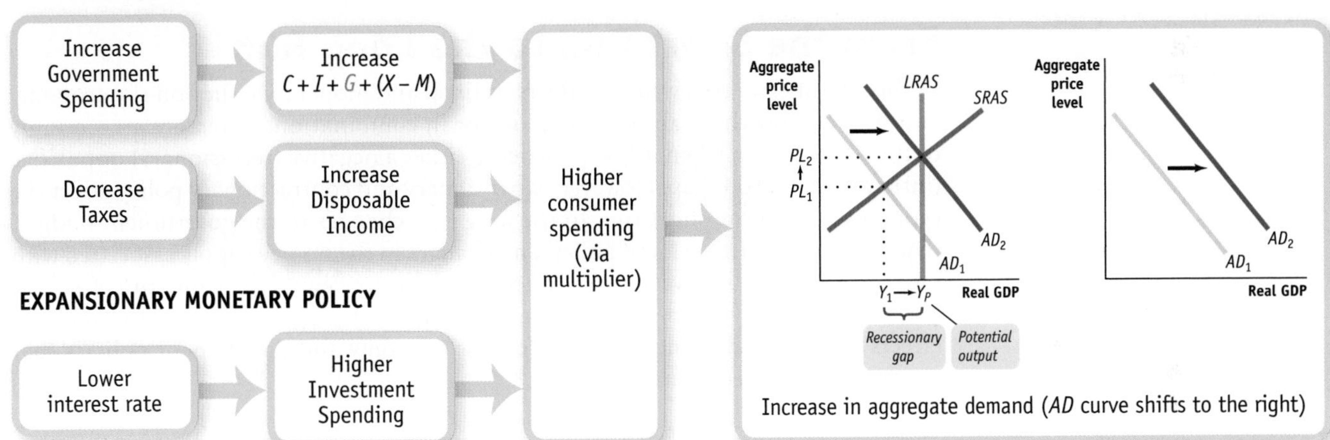

While the tools of fiscal and monetary policy are different, their common goal is to increase aggregate demand to close a negative output gap during a recession. Expansionary fiscal policy includes increasing government spending and lowering taxes to increase income and spending. Expansionary monetary policy focuses on lowering interest rates to increase investment and interest-sensitive consumption.

Using Contractionary Fiscal and Monetary Policy to Close a Positive Output Gap

A combination of fiscal and monetary policy can also be used to address inflationary pressures when the economy is experiencing a positive output gap. With a positive output gap, the government and central bank implement contractionary policy to move the economy toward full employment and stabilize prices. In response to inflationary pressures, the government can decrease spending (G) and/or increase taxes (*T*) to decrease aggregate demand, while the central bank can decrease aggregate demand by increasing interest rates (*i*).

Figure 5.1-2 summarizes how fiscal and monetary policy increase aggregate demand, closing a positive (inflationary) output gap. In the *AD–AS* model, the contractionary policies shift the *AD* curve to the left, moving the economy toward long-run equilibrium with a lower price level (*PL*), as shown in Figure 5.1-2.

FIGURE 5.1-2 Combining Fiscal and Monetary Policy to Close an Inflationary Gap

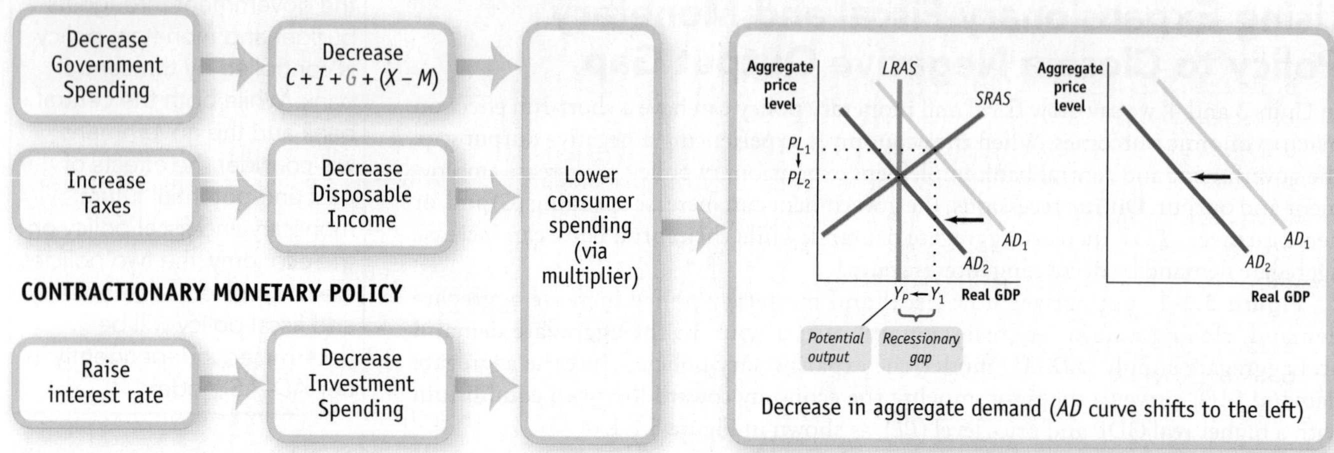

Fiscal and monetary policy can also be used to decrease aggregate demand in order to close a positive output gap to control inflation. Contractionary fiscal policy includes decreasing government spending and raising taxes to decrease income and consumer spending. Contractionary monetary policy focuses on raising interest rates to decrease investment and interest-sensitive consumption.

From the Short Run to the Long Run

In this Module, we reviewed the effects of fiscal and monetary policy on the economy and showed how they can be used, alone or in combination, to restore an economy to full employment when it is experiencing either a negative (recessionary) or positive (inflationary) output gap. However, expansionary and contractionary policy affect the economy only in the short run. In the long run, changes to the government budget, required for conducting fiscal policy, and changes in the money supply associated with monetary policy can have adverse effects. With our review of the short-run effects of fiscal and monetary policy in mind, the remainder of this Unit focuses on the long-run effects of fiscal and monetary policy on the economy and government policies that promote long-run economic growth.

Module 5.1 Review

Check Your Understanding

1. How would the government and the central bank respond to positive and negative output gaps using fiscal and monetary policy?

2. Assume that a government is required to always maintain a balanced budget. How would this requirement affect the use of fiscal and monetary policy by the government and central bank to address output gaps?

Tackle the AP® Test: Multiple-Choice Questions

1. Which of the following best describes how a central bank considers fiscal policy when it implements a country's monetary policy? The central bank
   a. is required by law to consider fiscal policy.
   b. never considers fiscal policy.
   c. considers how fiscal policy might affect real GDP.
   d. is subject to political pressure to consider fiscal policy.
   e. works closely with the government when setting monetary policy.

2. Which of the following correctly describes fiscal and monetary policy when the economy has a recessionary gap?

Fiscal Policy	*Monetary Policy*
a. Raise G	Raise i
b. Raise T	Raise i
c. Lower G	Lower i
d. Lower T	Lower i
e. Raise T	Lower i

3. When the economy is experiencing an inflationary gap, the government will ____________ spending and/or ____________ taxes. The central bank will ____________ short-term interest rates.
   a. lower; raise; raise
   b. lower; lower; lower
   c. raise; lower; lower
   d. raise; raise; lower
   e. raise; raise; raise

4. Expansionary fiscal and monetary policy affect the economy through a ____________ shift of the aggregate ____________ curve.
   a. rightward; demand
   b. leftward; demand
   c. rightward; supply
   d. leftward; supply
   e. leftward; output

5. Contractionary fiscal or monetary policy will ultimately result in a short-term increase in which of the following?
   a. employment
   b. inflation
   c. aggregate demand
   d. unemployment
   e. real GDP

6. Disposable income is affected when which of the following changes?
   a. consumption
   b. investment
   c. government spending
   d. taxes
   e. net exports

7. Fiscal and monetary policies will have
   a. only short-run effects on the economy.
   b. only long-run effects on the economy.
   c. neither short-run nor long-run effects on the economy.
   d. both short-run and long-run effects on the economy.
   e. undetermined effects on the economy.

Tackle the AP® Test: Free-Response Questions

1. Describe the cause-and-effect chain that explains how each of the following affects real GDP and the price level.
   a. Expansionary fiscal policy
   b. Contractionary monetary policy

Rubric for FRQ 1 (10 points)

1 point: $\uparrow G \rightarrow$ and/or $\downarrow T$
1 point: $\uparrow C$
1 point: $\uparrow AD \rightarrow$
1 point: $\uparrow$real GDP
1 point: $\uparrow PL$

1 point: $\uparrow i \rightarrow$
1 point: $\downarrow I$ and/or interest-sensitive $C \rightarrow$
1 point: $\downarrow AD \rightarrow$
1 point: $\downarrow$real GDP
1 point: $\downarrow PL$

2. Draw a correctly labeled *AD–AS* graph showing an economy in long-run equilibrium. On your graph, show the effect of a tax decrease on the price level. **(5 points)**

MODULE 5.2

The Phillips Curve

In this Module, you will learn to:

- Illustrate the short-run trade-off between unemployment and inflation using a short-run Phillips curve
- Illustrate the long-run trade-off between unemployment and inflation using a long-run Phillips curve that is vertical at the natural rate of unemployment
- Identify the factors that cause the long-run Phillips curve to shift
- Use a correctly labeled Phillips curve graph to illustrate short-run and long-run equilibrium
- Show points on a correctly labeled Phillips curve graph corresponding to inflationary and recessionary gaps

The Output Gap and Unemployment

We learned in Module 3.5 that the unemployment rate is composed of natural unemployment and cyclical unemployment – the portion of the unemployment rate affected by the business cycle. So there is a relationship between the unemployment rate and the output gap. This relationship is defined by two rules:

- When actual aggregate output is equal to potential output, the actual unemployment rate is equal to the natural rate of unemployment.
- When the output gap is positive (an inflationary gap), the unemployment rate is *below* the natural rate. When the output gap is negative (a recessionary gap), the unemployment rate is *above* the natural rate.

JohnnyGreig/Getty Images

During times in high inflation, unemployment is below the natural rate; during a recession, it is above the natural rate.

In other words, fluctuations of aggregate output around the long-run trend of potential output correspond to fluctuations of the unemployment rate around the natural rate.

This makes sense. When the economy is producing less than potential output – when the output gap is negative – it is not making full use of its productive resources. Among the resources that are not fully used is labor. So we would expect a negative output gap to be associated with unusually high unemployment. Conversely, when the economy is producing more than potential output, it is temporarily using resources at higher-than-normal rates. With this positive output gap, we would expect to see lower-than-normal unemployment.

In addition to its relationship to the output gap, the unemployment rate is also related to the rate of inflation; next, we consider this relationship using a short-run Phillips curve.

The Short-Run Phillips Curve

There is a short-run trade-off between unemployment and inflation – lower unemployment tends to lead to higher inflation, and higher unemployment tends to lead to lower inflation. This key relationship is shown by the *Phillips curve*. An economy is always operating somewhere along its short-run Phillips curve.

The origins of the Phillips curve lie in a famous 1958 paper by the New Zealand-born economist Alban W. H. Phillips. Looking at historical data for Britain, Phillips found that when the unemployment rate was high, the wage rate tended to fall, and when the unemployment rate was low, the wage rate tended to rise. With high unemployment, many workers are seeking jobs, which means that employers can offer a lower wage. But with low unemployment, few workers are seeking jobs, so employers must offer a higher wage. Using data from Britain, the United States, and elsewhere, other economists soon found a similar apparent relationship between the unemployment rate and the rate of inflation—that is, the rate of change in the aggregate price level. For example, **Figure 5.2-1** shows the U.S. unemployment rate and the rate of consumer price inflation over each subsequent year from 1955 to 1968, with each dot representing one year's data.

FIGURE 5.2-1 Unemployment and Inflation, 1955–1968

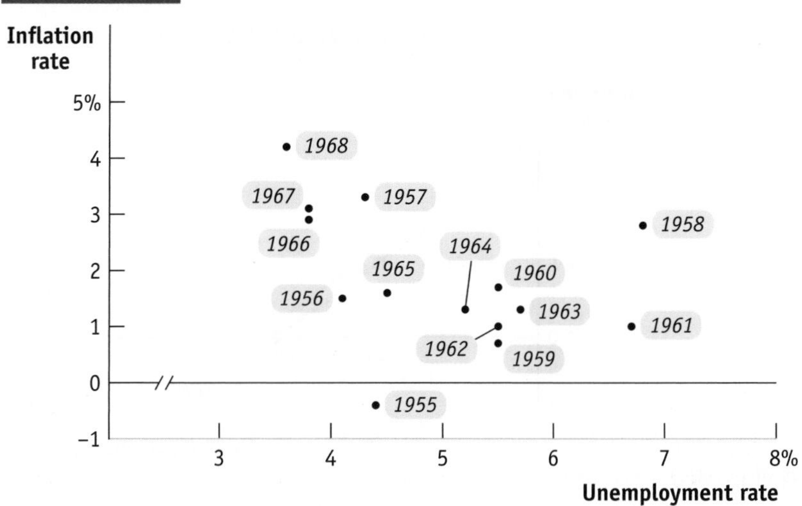

Each dot shows the average U.S. unemployment rate for one year and the percentage increase in the consumer price index over the subsequent year. Data like this lay behind the initial concept of the Phillips curve.
Data Source: Bureau of Labor Statistics.

Figure 5.2-1 shows a negative short-run relationship between the unemployment rate and the inflation rate, represented by the **short-run Phillips curve**, or ***SRPC***. (We'll explain the difference between the short-run and the long-run Phillips curve soon.) **Figure 5.2-2** shows a hypothetical short-run Phillips curve.

The **short-run Phillips curve (*SRPC*)** represents the negative short-run relationship between the unemployment rate and the inflation rate.

FIGURE 5.2-2 The Short-Run Phillips Curve

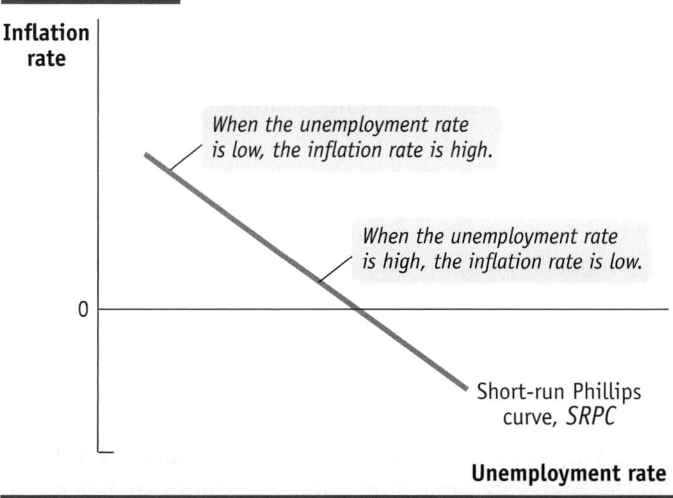

The short-run Phillips curve, *SRPC*, slopes downward because the relationship between the unemployment rate and the inflation rate is negative.

Movements along the *SRPC*

We can better understand the shape of the Phillips curve by examining its ties to the *AD–AS* model. Panel (a) of **Figure 5.2-3** shows how changes in the aggregate price level and the output gap depend on changes in aggregate demand. Assume that in year 1, the aggregate demand curve is AD_1, the long-run aggregate supply curve is *LRAS*, and the short-run aggregate supply curve is *SRAS*. The initial macroeconomic equilibrium is at E_1, where the price level is 100 and real GDP is $10 trillion. Notice that at E_1, real GDP is equal to potential output, so the output gap is zero. Assume as well that the natural rate of unemployment in year 1 is 6%.

FIGURE 5.2-3 The *AD–AS* Model and the Short-Run Phillips Curve: Inflationary Gap

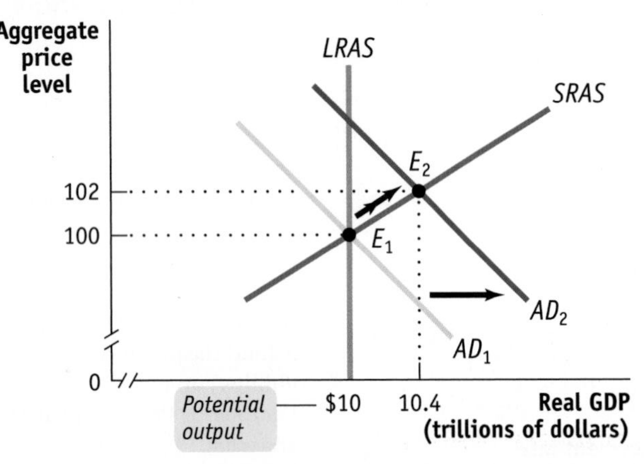

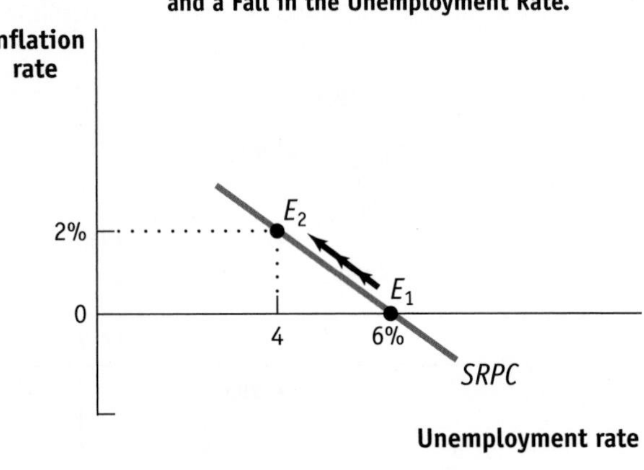

Shifts in aggregate demand lead to movements along the Phillips curve. In panel (a), the economy is initially in equilibrium at E_1. If the aggregate demand curve remains at AD_1, there is an output gap of zero and 0% inflation. If the aggregate demand curve shifts rightward to AD_2, the positive output gap reduces unemployment to 4%, and inflation rises to 2%. Assuming that the natural rate of unemployment is 6%, the implications for unemployment and inflation are shown in panel (b): with aggregate demand at AD_1, 6% unemployment and 0% inflation will result; if aggregate demand increases to AD_2, 4% unemployment and 2% inflation will result.

Now consider what happens if aggregate demand shifts rightward to AD_2 and the economy moves to E_2. At E_2, real GDP is $10.4 trillion, $0.4 trillion more than potential output—forming a 4% positive output gap. Meanwhile, at E_2, the aggregate price level has risen to 102—a 2% increase. So panel (a) indicates that in this example, a zero output gap is associated with zero inflation and a 4% positive output gap is associated with 2% inflation. Remember that in the short run, input prices and inflationary expectations are relatively fixed, so the increase in output above full employment is associated with an increase in inflation.

Panel (b) shows what this shift in aggregate demand implies for the relationship between unemployment and inflation: an increase in aggregate demand leads to a fall in the unemployment rate and an increase in the inflation rate. E_1 and E_2 in panel (a) correspond to E_1 and E_2 in panel (b). At E_1, the unemployment rate is 6% and the inflation rate is 0%. At E_2, the unemployment rate is 4%—because an output gap of 4% reduces the unemployment rate below its natural rate of 6%—and the inflation rate is 2%. This is an example of the negative relationship between unemployment and inflation.

Going in the other direction, a decrease in aggregate demand leads to a rise in the unemployment rate and a fall in the inflation rate, as shown in **Figure 5.2-4**. Panel (a) shows how changes in the aggregate price level and the output gap depend on

FIGURE 5.2-4 The *AD–AS* Model and the Short-Run Phillips Curve: Recessionary Gap

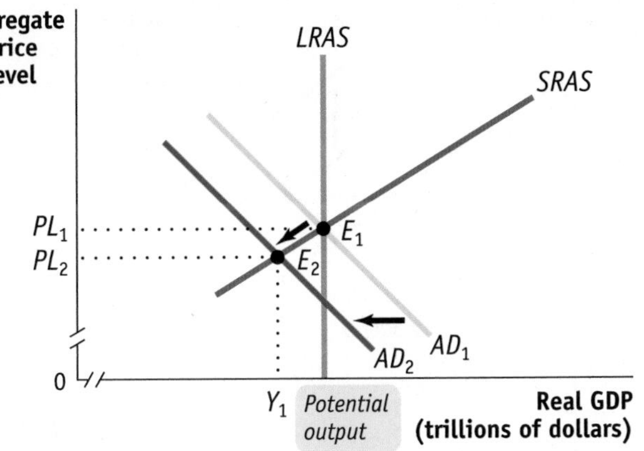

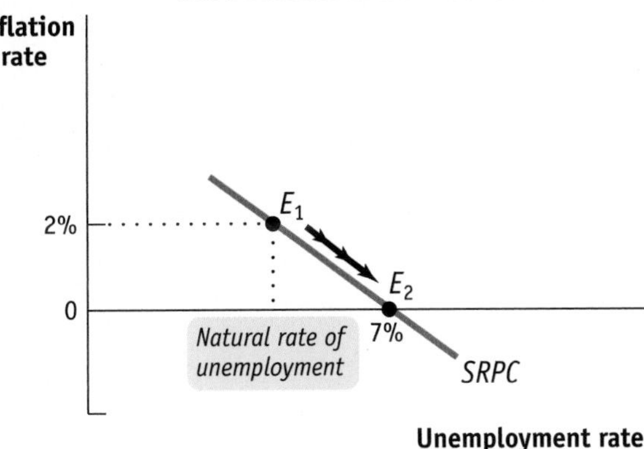

Shifts in aggregate demand lead to movements along the Phillips curve. In panel (a), the economy is initially in equilibrium at E_1. If the aggregate demand curve remains at AD_1, there is an output gap of zero and the economy is at potential output. Assume the inflation rate is at the target rate of 2%. If the aggregate demand curve shifts left to AD_2, the negative output gap increases the unemployment to 7%, and inflation falls to 0%. The implications for unemployment and inflation are shown in panel (b): with aggregate demand at AD_1, the natural rate of unemployment and the target rate of 2% inflation will be the result; if aggregate demand decreases to AD_2, 7% unemployment and 0% inflation will be the result.

changes in aggregate demand. Again, in year 1, the aggregate demand curve is AD_1, the long-run aggregate supply curve is *LRAS*, and the short-run aggregate supply curve is *SRAS*. The initial macroeconomic equilibrium is at E_1, where the price level is at PL_1, the target inflation rate, and real GDP is at potential output, so the output gap is zero.

Now consider what happens if aggregate demand shifts leftward to AD_2 and the economy moves to E_2. At E_2, Real GDP is Y_1, less than potential output—forming a negative output gap and the aggregate price level has fallen. So panel (a) indicates that in this example a zero output gap is associated with 2% inflation and the negative output gap is associated with 0% inflation.

Panel (b) shows what this shift implies for the relationship between unemployment and inflation: a decrease in aggregate demand leads to an increase in the unemployment rate and a decrease in the inflation rate. E_1 and E_2 in panel (a) correspond to E_1 and E_2 in panel (b). At E_1, the unemployment is at the natural rate and the inflation rate is the target rate of 2%. At E_2, the unemployment rate is 7%—because a negative output gap increases the unemployment rate to a level above the natural rate—and the inflation rate falls to 0%. Again, this is an example of the negative relationship between unemployment and inflation.

To summarize; increases and decreases in aggregate demand result in movements to the left and right along the short-run Phillips curve.

Shifts of the *SRPC*

Changes in aggregate supply also affect the short-run Phillips curve. Previously, we discussed the effect of *supply shocks*, such as sudden changes in the price of oil, that shift the short-run aggregate supply (*SRAS*) curve. Such shocks also shift the short-run Phillips curve. In general, a negative supply shock shifts *SRPC* up, as the inflation rate increases for every level of the unemployment rate, and a positive supply shock shifts it down as the inflation rate falls for every level of the unemployment rate. Both outcomes are shown in **Figure 5.2-5.**

AP® ECON TIP

Demand shocks (shifts of the *AD* curve) correspond to a movement along a short-run Phillips curve. Supply shocks (shifts of the *SRAS* curve) correspond to a shift of the short-run Phillips curve.

FIGURE 5.2-5 The Short-Run Phillips Curve and Supply Shocks

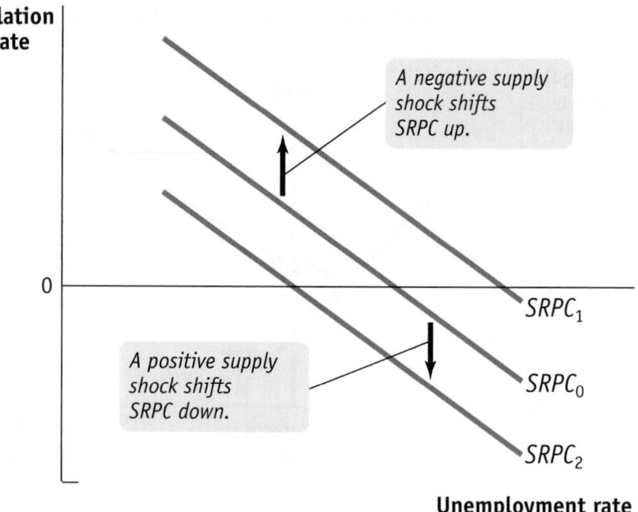

A negative supply shock shifts the *SRPC* up, and a positive supply shock shifts the *SRPC* down.

Inflation Expectations and the Short-Run Phillips Curve

Supply shocks are not the only factors that can shift the Phillips curve. The rate of inflation that employers and workers expect in the near future is also an important factor affecting inflation. The expected rate of inflation is the rate that employers and workers expect in the near future. Why do changes in expected inflation affect the short-run Phillips curve? The wage rate that workers and employers agree to will be higher if everyone expects high inflation (including rising wages) than if everyone expects prices to be stable. The worker will want a wage rate that takes into account future declines in the purchasing power of earnings. And the employer will be more willing to agree to a wage increase now if hiring workers later will be even more expensive. Also, rising prices will make paying a higher wage rate more affordable for the employer because the employer's output will sell for more.

PM Images/Getty Images

Expectations about the inflation rate and future purchasing power affects inflation.

For these reasons, an increase in expected inflation shifts the short-run Phillips curve upward: the actual rate of inflation at any given unemployment rate is higher when the expected inflation rate is higher.

Figure 5.2-6 shows how the expected rate of inflation affects the short-run Phillips curve. First, suppose that the expected rate of inflation is 0%. $SRPC_0$ is the short-run Phillips curve when the public expects 0% inflation. According to $SRPC_0$, the actual inflation rate will be 0% if the unemployment rate is 6%; it will be 2% if the unemployment rate is 4%.

Alternatively, suppose the expected rate of inflation is 2%. In this case, employers and workers will build this expectation into wages and prices: at any given unemployment rate, the actual inflation rate will be 2 percentage points higher than it would be if people expected 0% inflation. $SRPC_2$, which shows the Phillips curve when the expected inflation rate is 2%, is $SRPC_0$ shifted upward by 2 percentage points at every level of unemployment. According to $SRPC_2$, the actual inflation rate will be 2% if the unemployment rate is 6%; it will be 4% if the unemployment rate is 4%.

In general, people base their expectations about inflation on experience. If the inflation rate has hovered around 0% in the last few years, people will expect it to be around 0% in the near future. But if the inflation rate has averaged around 5% lately, people will expect inflation to be around 5% in the near future.

AP® ECON TIP

Changes in inflationary expectations shift the *SRAS* curve and the *SRPC* as a result of their effect on wages. An increase in expected inflation shifts the *SRAS* curve to the left and the *SRPC* to the right. A decrease in expected inflation shifts the *SRAS* curve to the right and the *SRPC* to the left.

FIGURE 5.2-6 Expected Inflation and the Short-Run Phillips Curve

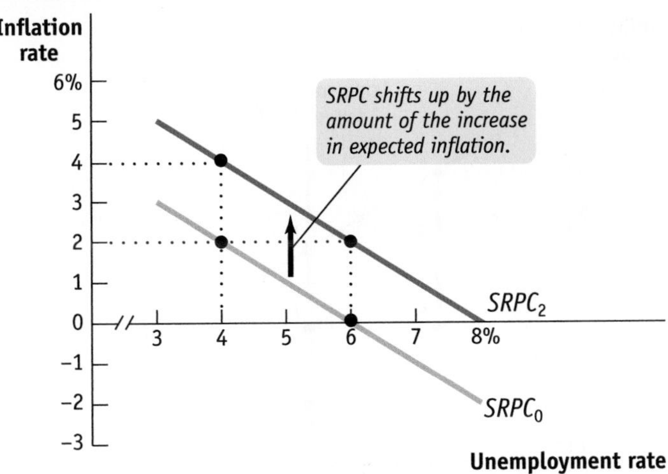

An increase in expected inflation shifts the short-run Phillips curve up. $SRPC_0$ is the initial short-run Phillips curve with an expected inflation rate of 0%; $SRPC_2$ is the short-run Phillips curve with an expected inflation rate of 2%. Each additional percentage point of expected inflation eventually raises the actual inflation rate at any given unemployment rate by 1 percentage point.

Inflation and Unemployment in the Long Run

The short-run Phillips curve suggests that at any given point in time there is a trade-off between unemployment and inflation. According to this tradeoff, policy makers have a choice: they can choose to accept the price of high inflation in order to achieve low unemployment, or they can reject high inflation and pay the price of high unemployment. In fact, during the 1960s many economists believed that this trade-off represented a real choice.

However, this view was altered by the recognition that expected inflation affects the short-run Phillips curve. And in the short run, expectations often diverge from reality. In the long run, however, expectations will adjust to reflect any consistent rate of inflation. If inflation is consistently high, people will come to expect more of the same; if inflation is consistently low, low inflation will become part of expectations. So what does the trade-off between inflation and unemployment look like in the long run, when actual inflation is incorporated into expectations? There is no long-run trade-off. That is, it is not possible to achieve lower unemployment in the long run by accepting higher inflation. To see why, we need to introduce another concept: the *long-run Phillips curve.*

The Long-Run Phillips Curve

Figure 5.2-7 reproduces the two short-run Phillips curves from Figure 5.2-6, $SRPC_0$ and $SRPC_2$. It also adds an additional short-run Phillips curve, $SRPC_4$, representing a 4% expected rate of inflation. In a moment, we'll explain the significance of the vertical long-run Phillips curve, *LRPC.*

Suppose that the economy has had a 0% inflation rate in the past. In that case, the current short-run Phillips curve will be $SRPC_0$, reflecting a 0% expected inflation rate. If the unemployment rate is 6%, the actual inflation rate will be 0%.

Also suppose that policy makers decide to trade off lower unemployment for a higher rate of inflation. They use monetary policy, fiscal policy, or both to drive the unemployment rate down to 4%. This puts the economy at point *A* on $SRPC_0$, leading to an actual inflation rate of 2%.

Over time, the public will come to expect a 2% inflation rate. *This increase in inflationary expectations will shift the short-run Phillips curve upward* to $SRPC_2$. Now, when the unemployment rate is 6%, the actual inflation rate will be 2%. Given this new short-run

FIGURE 5.2-7 The Natural Rate of Unemployment and the Long-Run Phillips Curve

$SRPC_0$ is the short-run Phillips curve when the expected inflation rate is 0%. At a 4% unemployment rate, the economy is at point *A* with an actual inflation rate of 2%. The higher inflation rate will be incorporated into expectations, and the *SRPC* will shift upward to $SRPC_2$. If policy makers act to keep the unemployment rate at 4%, the actual inflation rate will rise to 4% (point *B*). Inflationary expectations will be revised upward again, and *SRPC* will shift to $SRPC_4$. At a 4% unemployment rate, the actual inflation rate will rise to 6% (point *C*). Here, an unemployment rate of 6% is the natural rate of unemployment, or nonaccelerating inflation rate of unemployment. As long as unemployment is at the natural rate of unemployment, the actual inflation rate will match expectations and remain constant. The long-run Phillips curve, *LRPC*, passes through E_0, E_2, and E_4 and is vertical, showing no long-run trade-off between unemployment and inflation.

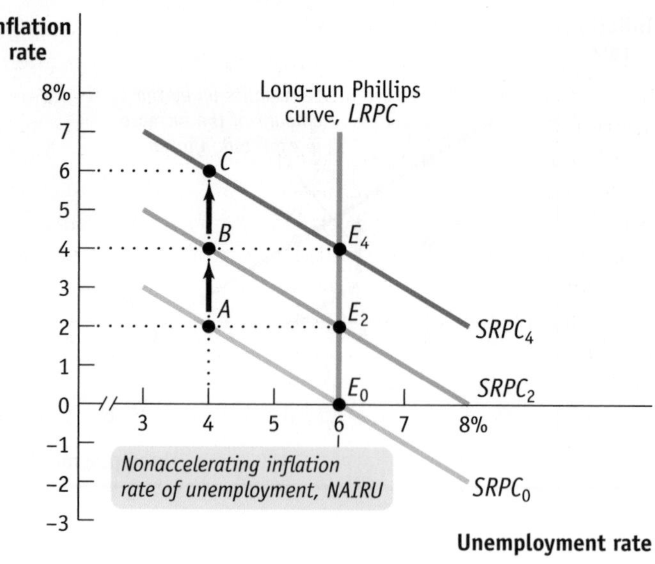

JLGutierrez/Getty Images

Phillips curve, policies adopted to keep the unemployment rate at 4% will lead to a 4% actual inflation rate—point *B* on $SRPC_2$—rather than point *A* with a 2% actual inflation rate.

Eventually, the 4% actual inflation rate gets built into expectations about the future inflation rate, and the short-run Phillips curve shifts upward yet again to $SRPC_4$. To keep the unemployment rate at 4% would now require accepting a 6% actual inflation rate, point *C* on $SRPC_4$, and so on. In short, a persistent attempt to trade off lower unemployment for higher inflation leads to *accelerating* inflation over time.

To avoid accelerating inflation over time, the unemployment rate must be high enough that the actual rate of inflation matches the expected rate of inflation. This is the situation at E_0 on $SRPC_0$: when the expected inflation rate is 0% and the unemployment rate is 6%, the actual inflation rate is 0%. It is also the situation at E_2 on $SRPC_2$: when the expected inflation rate is 2% and the unemployment rate is 6%, the actual inflation rate is 2%. And it is the situation at E_4 on $SRPC_4$: when the expected inflation rate is 4% and the unemployment rate is 6%, the actual inflation rate is 4%.

Keeping the unemployment rate below the natural rate of unemployment leads to ever-accelerating inflation and cannot be maintained. Therefore, there is no long-run trade-off between unemployment and inflation.

The **long-run Phillips curve (*LRPC*)** shows the relationship between unemployment and inflation after expectations of inflation have had time to adjust to experience.

We can now explain the significance of the vertical line in Figure 5.2-7. It is the **long-run Phillips curve (*LRPC*)**, which shows the relationship between unemployment and inflation in the long run, after expectations of inflation have had time to adjust to experience. The *LRPC* is vertical because any unemployment rate below the natural rate of unemployment leads to ever-accelerating inflation. In other words, the long-run Phillips curve shows that there are limits to expansionary policies because an unemployment rate below the natural rate of unemployment cannot be maintained in the long run. Moreover, there is a corresponding point we have not yet emphasized: any unemployment rate above the natural rate of unemployment leads to decelerating inflation.

Long-Run Equilibrium in the Phillips Curve Model

Long-run equilibrium in the Phillips curve model is found where the short-run and the long-run Phillips curves intersect, as shown in **Figure 5.2-8**. The equilibrium inflation rate is found on the vertical axis and the equilibrium unemployment rate is found on the horizontal axis. As explained using the graphs above, movements along the short-run Phillips curve (away from long-run equilibrium) move the economy away from a zero output gap and correspond to positive (inflationary) and negative (recessionary) output gaps. Points to the left of long-run equilibrium in Figure 5.2-8 represent inflationary gaps. For example, at point *B*, the unemployment rate is below the natural rate of unemployment and the inflation rate is higher than in long-run equilibrium – consistent with an inflationary gap. Points to the right of long-run equilibrium in Figure 5.2-8 represent recessionary gaps. For example, at point *A*, the unemployment rate is above the natural rate of unemployment – consistent with a recessionary gap.

FIGURE 5.2-8 Long-Run Equilibrium in the Phillips Curve Model

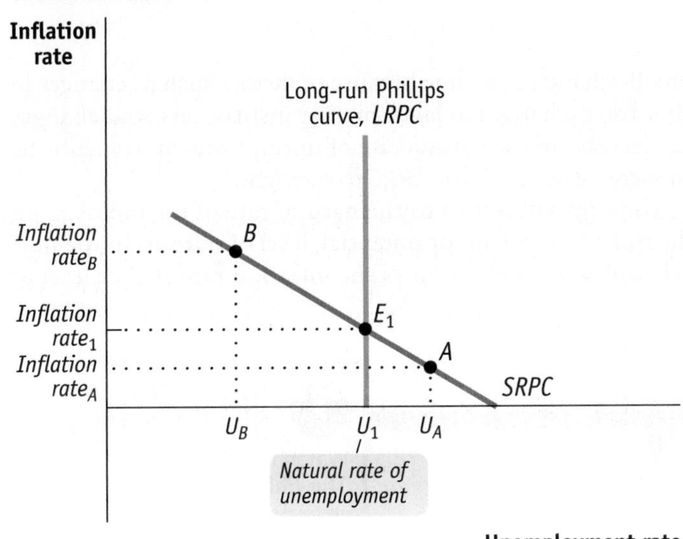

Long-run equilibrium in the Phillips curve model occurs at E_1, where the *SRPC* and *LRPC* intersect. The equilibrium inflation rate is found on the vertical axis, labeled 1, and the equilibrium unemployment rate is at the natural rate of unemployment. Point *A* corresponds to an unemployment rate above the natural rate and a lower inflation rate experienced during a negative (recessionary) output gap. Point *B* corresponds to a higher inflation rate and an unemployment rate below the natural rate experienced during a positive (inflationary) output gap.

If the economy is experiencing a positive or negative output gap, inflationary expectations will eventually adjust to the new level of inflation and shift the short-run Phillips curve to move the economy back to the long-run equilibrium, as shown in **Figure 5.2-9**. The lower inflation rates at point *A* will shift the *SRPC* down to $SPRC_1$ and a new long-run equilibrium at E_A. The higher inflation rates at point *B* will shift the *SRPC* up to $SRPC_2$ and a new long-run equilibrium at E_B.

In the long run, the economy will return to the natural rate of unemployment, with the level of inflation affected by inflationary expectations.

Shifts of the Long-Run Phillips Curve

Over time, the long-run Phillips curve can also shift. Because the *LRPC* is vertical at the natural rate of unemployment, factors that change the natural rate of unemployment will cause the *LRPC* to shift. In Module 2.3, we learned that the natural rate of

FIGURE 5.2-9 Short-Run Adjustments Move the Economy Back to Long-Run Equilibrium

Decreased inflationary expectations that developed when the economy moves along the *SRPC* to point *A* cause the *SRPC* to shift to $SRPC_1$, leading to a new long-run equilibrium point E_A at the natural rate of unemployment and a lower inflation rate. Increased inflationary expectations that developed when the economy moves along the *SRPC* to point *B* cause the *SRPC* to shift to $SRPC_2$, leading to a new long-run equilibrium point at E_B at the natural rate of unemployment and a higher rate of inflation.

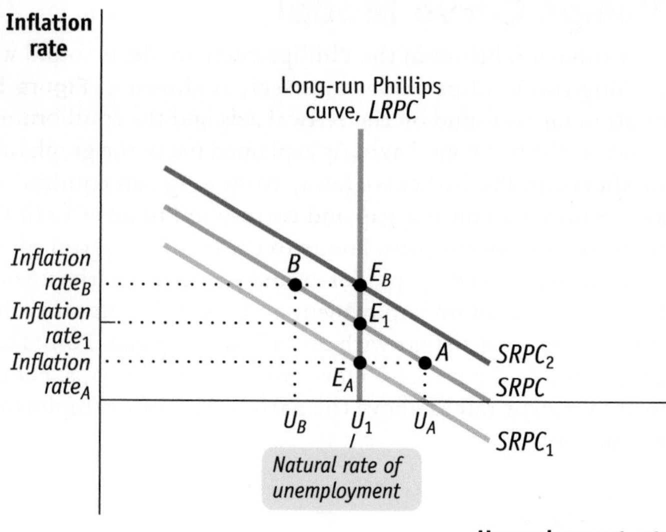

unemployment can gradually change over time because of factors such as changes in characteristics of the labor force, changes in labor market institutions, and changes in government policies. A decrease in the natural rate of unemployment will shift the *LRPC* to the left, while an increase will shift the *LRPC* to the right.

In the long run, the economy will return to the natural rate of unemployment, which corresponds to the full employment, or potential, level of output. In the next Module, we look more closely at what determines the inflation rate at that level of unemployment/output.

Module 5.2 Review

Adventures in AP® Economics
Watch the video:
The Phillips Curve

Check Your Understanding

1. Explain why a decrease in aggregate demand causes a movement along the short-run Phillips curve.
2. Explain how a decrease in short-run aggregate supply affects the short-run Phillips curve.
3. Why is there no long-run trade-off between unemployment and inflation?

Tackle the AP® Test: Multiple-Choice Questions

1. The long-run Phillips curve is
   a. equivalent to the short-run Phillips curve.
   b. equal to the short-run Phillips curve plus expected inflation.
   c. negatively sloped.
   d. horizontal.
   e. none of the above.

2. The short-run Phillips curve shows a ____________ relationship between ____________.
   a. negative; the aggregate price level and aggregate output
   b. positive; the aggregate price level and aggregate output
   c. negative; unemployment and inflation
   d. positive; unemployment and aggregate output
   e. positive; unemployment and the aggregate price level

3. An increase in expected inflation will shift
   a. the short-run Phillips curve downward.
   b. the short-run Phillips curve upward.
   c. the long-run Phillips curve upward.
   d. the long-run Phillips curve downward.
   e. neither the short-run nor the long-run Phillips curve.

4. A point along the *SRPC* to the right of the long-run equilibrium point corresponds to which of the following?
   a. a positive output gap
   b. a recession
   c. inflation
   d. the natural rate of unemployment
   e. an unemployment rate below the natural rate

5. The inflation rate in the economy will increase when there is a(n)
   a. movement to the left along a *SRPC*.
   b. movement to the right along a *SRPC*.
   c. downward shift of the *SRPC*.
   d. increase in the natural rate of unemployment.
   e. decrease in inflationary expectations in the economy.

6. The *LRPC* will shift to the left whenever which of the following occurs?
   a. The *SRPC* shifts upward.
   b. The *SRPC* shifts downward.
   c. There is a recessionary gap.
   d. There is a positive output gap.
   e. The labor force has more experienced workers.

7. Which of the following will cause the short-run Phillips curve to shift upward?
   a. a positive supply shock
   b. a negative demand shock
   c. an increase in inflation expectations
   d. a decrease in oil prices
   e. all of the above

Tackle the AP® Test: Free-Response Questions

1. a. Draw a correctly labeled graph showing a short-run Phillips curve with an expected inflation rate of 0% and the corresponding long-run Phillips curve.
   b. On your graph, label the natural rate of unemployment.
   c. On your graph, show what happens in the long run if the government decides to decrease the unemployment rate below the natural rate of unemployment. Explain.

Rubric for FRQ 1 (8 points)

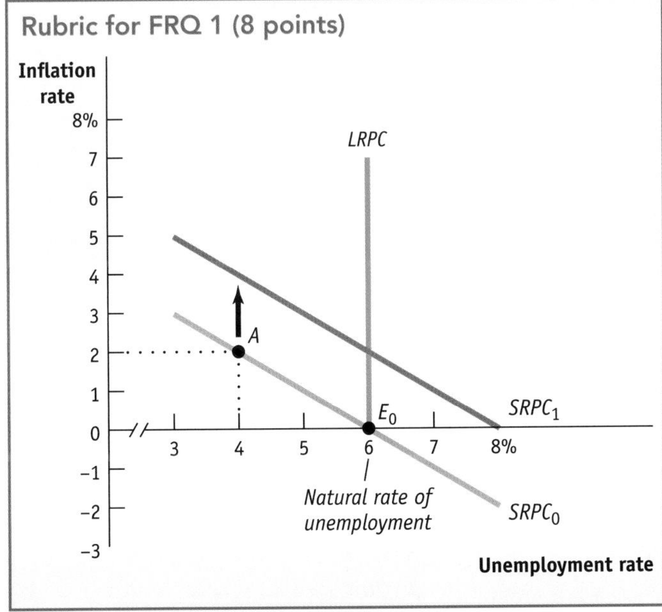

1 point: Vertical axis labeled "Inflation rate"

1 point: Horizontal axis labeled "Unemployment rate"

1 point: Downward-sloping curve labeled "$SRPC_0$"

1 point: Vertical curve labeled "*LRPC*"

1 point: $SRPC_0$ crosses horizontal axis where it crosses *LRPC*

1 point: Natural rate of unemployment is labeled where $SRPC_0$ crosses *LRPC* and horizontal axis

1 point: New *SRPC* is labeled, for example, as "$SRPC_1$" and is shown above the original $SRPC_0$

1 point: When the unemployment rate moves below the natural rate of unemployment, it creates inflation and moves the economy to a point such as *A*. This leads to positive inflationary expectations, which shift the *SRPC* up as shown by $SRPC_1$.

2. The table below shows the inflation rate and the unemployment rate in Country A.

Year	Inflation rate	Unemployment rate
Year 1	3%	7%
Year 2	5%	4%

a. Draw a correctly labeled graph of the short-run Phillips curve, labeled *SRPC*, for Country A. On your graph, show the actual unemployment and inflation rate for Year 1 and Year 2.

b. Assume short-run aggregate supply has decreased.

i. On your graph from part a, show the effect of the decrease in *SRAS*.

ii. Identify one factor that could have caused the decrease in *SRAS*.

c. Assume that the natural rate of unemployment is 6%. Draw a correctly labeled long-run Phillips curve, labeled *LRPC*. **(5 points)**

Money Growth and Inflation

In this Module, you will learn to:

- Explain how inflation can result from increasing the money supply and deflation can result from decreasing the money supply
- Define the Quantity Theory of Money and understand its explanation of the long-run inflation as determined by the growth rate of the money supply
- Calculate the money supply, velocity of money, price level, and real output using the Quantity Theory of Money

Short-Run and Long-Run Effects of an Increase in the Money Supply

Recall our analysis of the long-run effects of an increase in aggregate demand from Module 3.7, shown in **Figure 5.3-1**. The economy begins in equilibrium at potential output Y_1. The initial short-run aggregate supply curve is $SRAS_1$, the long-run aggregate supply curve is *LRAS*, and the initial aggregate demand curve is AD_1. The economy's initial equilibrium is at E_1, a point of both short-run and long-run macroeconomic equilibrium because it is on both the short-run and the long-run aggregate supply curves. Real GDP is at potential output Y_1.

FIGURE 5.3-1 **The Short-Run and Long-Run Effects of an Increase in Aggregate Demand**

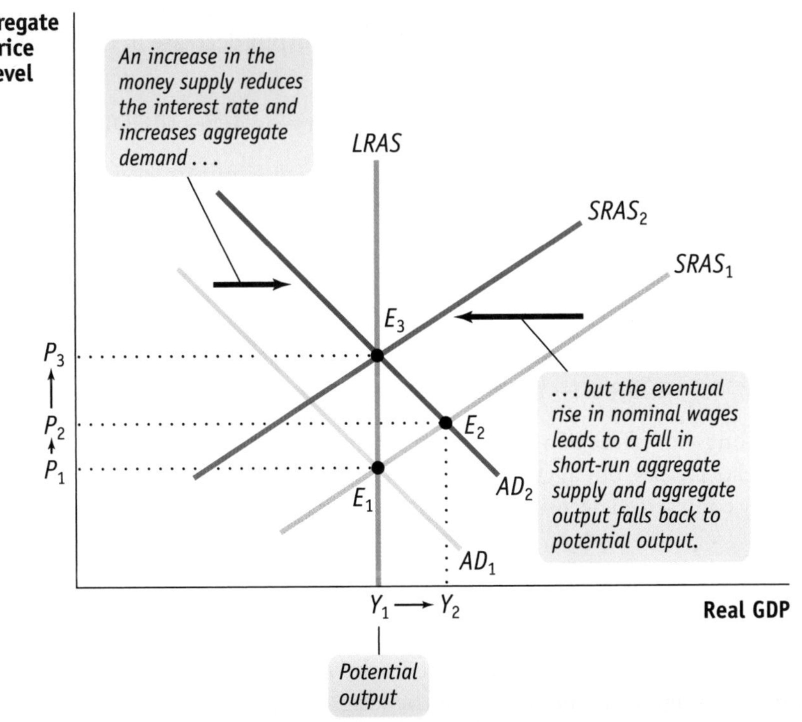

An increase in the money supply generates a positive short-run effect (seen in the shift from E_1 to E_2), but no long-run effect, on real GDP (see the shift back to E_3).

Now suppose there is an increase in the money supply. Other things equal, an increase in the money supply reduces the interest rate, which increases investment spending, which leads to a multiplied rise in consumer spending. So an increase in the money supply increases the demand for goods and services, shifting the *AD* curve rightward to AD_2. In the short run, the economy moves to a new short-run macroeconomic equilibrium at E_2. The price level rises from PL_1 to PL_2, and real GDP rises from Y_1 to Y_2. That is, both the aggregate price level and aggregate output increase in the short run. This chain of events can be represented as follows:

$$\textbf{(5.3-1)}\quad \uparrow MS \rightarrow \downarrow i \rightarrow \uparrow I \rightarrow \uparrow C\text{ (multiplier)} \rightarrow \uparrow AD \rightarrow \uparrow \text{RGDP and } \uparrow PL$$

But the aggregate output level in Figure 5.3-1, Y_2, is above potential output. Production at a level above potential output leads to low unemployment, which brings about a rise in nominal wages (W) over time, causing the short-run aggregate supply curve to shift leftward. This process stops only when the *SRAS* curve ends up at $SRAS_2$ and the economy ends up at point E_3, a point of both short-run and long-run macroeconomic equilibrium. This long-run chain of events can be represented as follows:

$$\textbf{(5.3-2)}\quad \uparrow MS \rightarrow \downarrow i \rightarrow \uparrow I \rightarrow \uparrow C\text{ (multiplier)} \rightarrow \uparrow AD \rightarrow \uparrow \text{RGDP and } \uparrow PL \rightarrow \uparrow W$$
$$\rightarrow \downarrow SRAS \rightarrow \downarrow \text{RGDP (back to full emp.) and } \uparrow PL\text{ (further)}$$

The long-run effect of an increase in the money supply, then, is that the aggregate price level has increased from PL_1 to PL_3. But aggregate output is back at potential output Y_1. In the long run, a monetary expansion raises the aggregate price level but has no effect on real GDP.

If the money supply decreases, the story we have just told plays out in reverse. Other things equal, a decrease in the money supply raises the interest rate, which decreases investment spending, which leads to a further decrease in consumer spending, and so on. So a decrease in the money supply decreases the demand for goods and services at any given aggregate price level, shifting the aggregate demand curve to the left. In the short run, the economy moves to a new short-run macroeconomic equilibrium at a level of real GDP below potential output and a lower aggregate price level. That is, both the aggregate price level and aggregate output decrease in the short run. This chain of events can be represented as follows:

Henrik5000/Getty Images

$$\textbf{(5.3-3)}\quad \downarrow MS \rightarrow \uparrow i \rightarrow \downarrow I \rightarrow \downarrow C\text{ (multiplier)} \rightarrow \downarrow AD \rightarrow \downarrow \text{RGDP and } \downarrow PL$$

But what happens over time? When the aggregate output level is below potential output, nominal wages fall. When this happens, the short-run aggregate supply curve shifts rightward. This process stops only when the *SRAS* curve ends up at a point of both short-run and long-run macroeconomic equilibrium. This long-run chain of events can be represented as follows:

$$\textbf{(5.3-4)}\quad \downarrow MS \rightarrow \uparrow i \rightarrow \downarrow I \rightarrow \downarrow C\text{ (multiplier)} \rightarrow \downarrow AD \rightarrow \downarrow \text{RGDP and } \downarrow PL \rightarrow \downarrow W$$
$$\rightarrow \uparrow SRAS \rightarrow \uparrow \text{RGDP (back to full emp.) and } \downarrow PL\text{ (further)}$$

The long-run effect of a decrease in the money supply, then, is that the aggregate price level decreases, but aggregate output is back at potential output. In the long run, a monetary contraction decreases the aggregate price level but has no effect on real GDP.

Monetary Neutrality

How much does a change in the money supply change the aggregate price level in the long run? The answer is that a change in the money supply leads to a proportional change in the aggregate price level in the long run. For example, if the money supply falls 25%, the aggregate price level falls 25% in the long run; if the money supply rises 50%, the aggregate price level rises 50% in the long run.

How do we know this? Consider the following thought experiment: suppose all prices in the economy—prices of final goods and services and also factor prices, such as nominal wage rates—double. And suppose the money supply doubles at the same time. What difference does this make to the economy in real terms? None. All real variables in the economy—such as real GDP and the real value of the money supply (the amount of goods and services it can buy)—are unchanged. So there is no reason for anyone to behave any differently.

We can state this argument in reverse: if the economy starts out in long-run macroeconomic equilibrium and the money supply changes, restoring long-run macroeconomic equilibrium requires restoring all real values to their original values. This includes restoring the real value of the money supply to its original level. So if the money supply falls 25%, the aggregate price level must fall 25%; if the money supply rises 50%, the price level must rise 50%; and so on.

Money is neutral: If wages rise at the same rate as the cost of goods and services, then there is no real effect on behavior or the economy.

Justin Sullivan/Getty Images

This analysis demonstrates the concept known as *monetary neutrality*, in which changes in the money supply have no real effects on the economy. In the long run, the only effect of an increase in the money supply is to raise the aggregate price level by an equal percentage. For this reason, economists argue that *money is neutral in the long run.*

However, this is a good time to recall the dictum of John Maynard Keynes: "In the long run we are all dead." In the long run, changes in the money supply don't have any effect on real GDP, interest rates, or anything else except the price level. But it would be foolish to conclude from this that the central bank is irrelevant. Monetary policy does have powerful real effects on the economy in the short run, often making the difference between recession and expansion. And that matters a lot for society's welfare.

AP® ECON TIP

Because money is neutral, changes in the money supply will not affect *real* values in the long run. The only long-run effect of monetary policy is to change the aggregate price level.

The Quantity Theory of Money

In their 1963 publication, *A Monetary History of the United States, 1867–1960*, Milton Friedman and Anna Schwartz showed that business cycles had historically been associated with fluctuations in the money supply. Their argument persuaded most economists that monetary policy should play a key role in economic management. The monetary policy was significant because it suggested that the burden of managing the economy could be shifted away from fiscal policy—meaning that economic management could largely be taken out of the hands of politicians. Fiscal policy, which must involve changing tax rates or government spending, necessitates political choices. If the government tries to stimulate the economy by cutting taxes, it must decide whose taxes will be cut. If it tries to stimulate the economy with government spending, it must decide what to spend the money on.

Economists and co-authors Milton Friedman and Anna Schwartz.

Brooks Kraft/Corbis Historical/Getty Images; Chris Kleponis/Bloomberg/Getty Images

Monetary policy, by contrast, does not involve such choices: when the central bank cuts interest rates to fight a recession, it cuts everyone's interest rate at the same time. So a shift from relying on fiscal policy to relying on monetary policy makes macroeconomics a more technical, less political issue. In fact, monetary policy in most major economies is set by an independent central bank that is insulated from the political process.

In response to the lags and other problems associated with activist fiscal policy—as well as the lags associated with monetary policy—Milton Friedman led a movement, called *monetarism*, that sought to eliminate macroeconomic policy activism while maintaining the importance of monetary policy. Monetarism asserts that GDP will grow steadily if the money supply grows steadily. Friedman favored a monetary policy that followed a *monetary policy rule* calling for slow, steady growth of the money supply that leaves little discretion to the central bank. Underlying this view was the *Quantity Theory of Money.*

The **Quantity Theory of Money** emphasizes the positive relationship between the price level and the money supply. It relies on the equation ($M \times V = P \times Y$).

The **velocity of money** is the ratio of nominal GDP to the money supply. It is a measure of the number of times the average dollar bill is spent per year.

The **Quantity Theory of Money** relies on the relationship between the price level and the money supply, as shown in Equation 5.3-5, where M is the money supply, P is the aggregate price level, Y is real GDP, and V stands for the *velocity* of money. P and Y are familiar terms—and $PL \times Y$, the aggregate price level times real GDP, represents nominal GDP (the dollar value of the output produced). The **velocity of money** measures the number of times the average dollar is spent per year. When a dollar is spent, it continues circulating in the economy, being spent multiple times. The number of dollars in the money supply, multiplied by the number of times each is spent, give the total dollar amount of transactions in the economy. The *equation of exchange* shows that the total dollar value of transactions in the economy will equal nominal GDP—the total amount spent will equal the value of output produced.

$$\textbf{(5.3-5)} \quad M \times V = P \times Y$$

$$\textbf{(5.3-6)} \quad \text{dollar value of transactions} = \text{nominal GDP}$$

From the 1960s until 1980, the velocity of money followed a smooth upward trend. According to the Quantity Theory of Money, if the velocity of money (V) is stable, steady growth in the money supply (M) by the central bank would ensure steady growth in spending ($M \times V$), and therefore in GDP. But large increases in the money supply (M) with a stable velocity (V) would lead to large increases in ($M \times V$). When the economy is at full employment, changes in the money supply have no effect on real output (Y). With real GDP constant at potential output in the long run, large increases in the money supply (M) will only lead to large increases in the price level—inflation—in the economy. This relationship is shown in Equation 5.3-7, where the bar over V indicates that velocity is stable and the bar over Y indicates that real GDP is constant at potential output in the long run:

$$\textbf{(5.3-7)} \quad \uparrow M \times \bar{V} = \uparrow P \times \bar{Y}$$

The Quantity Theory of Money in the Long Run

Inflation results from increasing the money supply at too rapid of a rate over a sustained period of time, while deflation results from a sustained decrease in the money supply. In the long run, the growth rate of the money supply determines the growth rate of the price level. The Quantity Theory of Money shows that prices will vary in proportion to changes in the supply of money in the economy; this relationship between the money supply and inflation is why economists refer to inflation as a *monetary phenomenon*. According to the Quantity Theory of Money, in the long run, variable growth of the money supply will result in inflation: this is the same result we saw using aggregate demand and aggregate supply at the beginning of this Module.

In the long run, a change in the *nominal* money supply, M, leads to a change in the aggregate price level, P, that leaves the *real* quantity of money, M/P, at its original level. As a result, there is no long-run effect on aggregate demand or real GDP. For example, when Turkey dropped six zeros from its currency, the Turkish lira, in January 2005, Turkish real GDP did not change. The only thing that changed was the number of zeros in prices: instead of something costing 2,000,000 lira, it cost 2 lira.

Andrew Paterson/Alamy

Ivan Vdovin/Alamy

The Turkish currency is the lira. When Turkey made 1,000,000 "old" lira equivalent to 1 "new" lira, real GDP was unaffected because of the neutrality of money.

But is the velocity of money stable enough for a simple policy rule to work? **Figure 5.3-2** shows the velocity of money in the United States, as measured by the ratio of nominal GDP to M1, from 1960 to 2021. As you can see, until 1980, velocity followed a fairly smooth, seemingly predictable trend. But from 1980 to 2008, the velocity of money began moving erratically. Since 2008, the velocity of money has declined. Although the data show variation in the velocity of money over time, the concern held by monetarists that too much discretionary monetary policy can actually destabilize the economy has become widely accepted.

FIGURE 5.3-2 **The Velocity of Money in the United States 1960–2021**

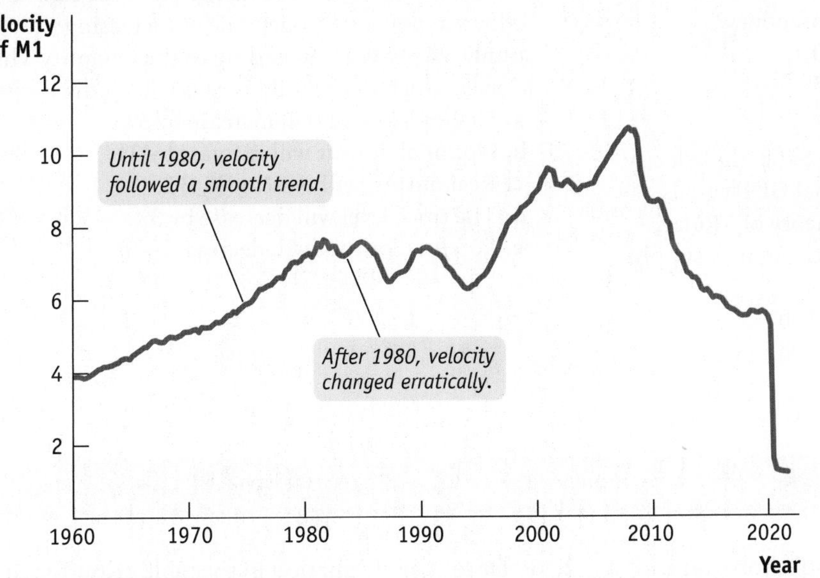

From 1960 to 1980, the velocity of money was stable, leading monetarists to believe that steady growth in the money supply would lead to a stable economy. From 1980 to 2008, however, velocity began moving erratically. Since 2008, the velocity of money has declined.
Data Sources: Bureau of Economic Analysis; Federal Reserve Bank of St. Louis.

In this Module, we considered the long-run consequences of monetary policy and money growth. In the Modules that follow, we turn to the long-run consequences of fiscal policy.

Module 5.3 Review

Check Your Understanding

1. Suppose the economy begins in long-run macroeconomic equilibrium. What is the long-run effect on the aggregate price level of a 5% increase in the money supply? Explain.
2. Suppose the economy begins in long-run macroeconomic equilibrium. What is the long-run effect on the interest rate of a 5% increase in the money supply? Explain.

Tackle the AP® Test: Multiple-Choice Questions

1. In the long run, changes in the quantity of money affect which of the following?
   a. real aggregate output
   b. real interest rates
   c. the aggregate price level
   d. real wages
   e. all of the above
2. An increase in the money supply will lead to which of the following in the short run?
   a. higher interest rates
   b. decreased investment spending
   c. decreased consumer spending
   d. increased aggregate demand
   e. lower real GDP
3. A 10% decrease in the money supply will change the aggregate price level in the long run by
   a. zero.
   b. less than 10%.
   c. 10%.
   d. 20%.
   e. more than 20%.
4. Monetary neutrality means that, in the long run, changes in the money supply
   a. cannot happen.
   b. have no effect on the economy.
   c. have no real effect on the economy.
   d. increase real GDP.
   e. change real interest rates.

5. According to the Quantity Theory of Money, if the money supply is $50m, real output is $100m, and the price level is 1.5, what is the velocity of money?
   a. 5.0
   b. 3.3
   c. 3.0
   d. 2.0
   e. 1.5

6. Assume the money supply is equal to $40b, the velocity of money is constant at 6, and nominal GDP equals $240b. According to the Quantity Theory of Money, by how much will a $10b increase in the money supply change nominal GDP?
   a. $10b
   b. $50b
   c. $60b
   d. $250b
   e. $300b

7. Assume an economy is currently at full employment, the velocity of money is constant, and the central bank follows a monetary policy rule of increasing the money supply 3% per year. According to the Quantity Theory of Money, which of the following is true in the long run?
   a. Unemployment will increase by 3%.
   b. Nominal output will increase by 3%.
   c. Real output will increase by 3%.
   d. The price level will decrease by 3%.
   e. Potential output will decrease by 3%.

Tackle the AP® Test: Free-Response Questions

1. Assume the economy is initially in both short-run and long-run macroeconomic equilibrium when the central bank increases the quantity of money by 25%. Describe the effects, in the short run and in the long run (giving numbers where possible), on the following:
   a. aggregate output
   b. the aggregate price level
   c. the real value of the money supply (its purchasing power for goods and services)
   d. the interest rate

Rubric for FRQ 1 (8 points)

1 point: Aggregate output rises in the short run.

1 point: Aggregate output falls back to potential output in the long run.

1 point: The aggregate price level rises in the short run (by less than 25%).

1 point: The aggregate price level rises by 25% in the long run.

1 point: The real value of the money supply increases in the short run.

1 point: The real value of the money supply does not change (relative to its original value) in the long run.

1 point: The interest rate falls in the short run.

1 point: The interest rate rises back to its original level in the long run.

2. Refer to the information in the table below for an economy operating at long-run equilibrium.

M	$120b
V	constant at 5
Real GDP	$600b

   a. Calculate the value of nominal GDP
   b. Calculate the value of the price index.
   c. Calculate the increase in nominal GDP if the central bank increases the money supply by $1b.
   d. How will the $1b increase in the money supply affect real GDP? Explain.
   e. How will the increase in nominal GDP you calculated in (c) be affected if the velocity of money falls to 4? Explain. **(5 points)**

Government Deficits and the National Debt

MODULE 5.4

In this Module, you will learn to:

- Define government surpluses and deficits, and the national debt, and summarize the relationship between an annual budget deficit or surplus and the national debt
- Explain the significance of government interest payments on the national debt—and the opportunity cost of debt financing
- Explain the issues involved with the burden of the national debt

In Module 3.8, we discussed how discretionary fiscal policy can be used to stabilize the economy in the short run. During a recession, an expansionary fiscal policy – raising government spending, lowering taxes, or both – can be used to shift the aggregate demand curve to the right. And when there are inflationary pressures in the economy, a contractionary fiscal policy – lowering government spending, raising taxes, or both – can be used to shift the aggregate demand curve to the left. But how do these policies affect the economy over a long period of time? In this Module, we will look at some of the long-term effects of fiscal policy, including the budget balance and government debt.

The Government Budget Balance

Headlines about the government's budget tend to focus on just two points: whether the government is running a budget surplus or a budget deficit and, in either case, how big. People usually think of surpluses as good: when the federal government ran a record surplus in 2000, many people regarded it as a cause for celebration. Conversely, people usually think of deficits as bad: when the Congressional Budget Office projected a budget deficit of over $3 trillion in 2021, many people regarded it as a cause for concern.

How do surpluses and deficits fit into the analysis of fiscal policy? Are deficits ever a good thing and surpluses ever a bad thing? To answer those questions, let's look at the causes and consequences of surpluses and deficits.

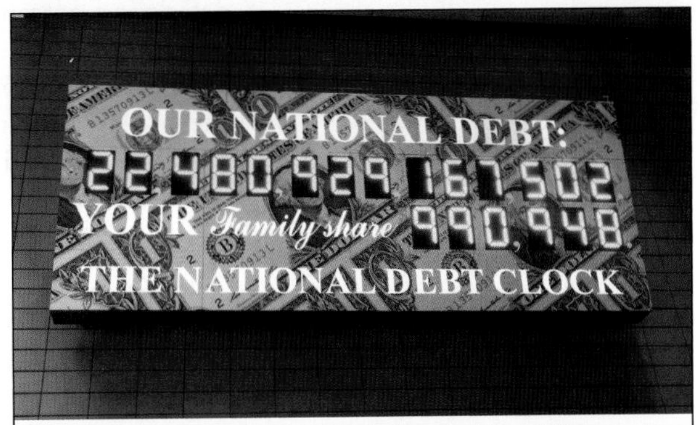

Sipa USA/Alamy Stock Photo

The digital National Debt Clock, located in midtown Manhattan, displays the current gross national debt of the United States. As of April 29, 2020, it exceeded 22 trillion dollars.

The Budget Balance as a Measure of Fiscal Policy

What do we mean by surpluses and deficits? The budget balance is the difference between the government's tax revenue and its spending, both on goods and services and on government transfers, in a given year. That is, the budget balance – savings by government – is defined by Equation 5.4-1:

$$\textbf{(5.4-1)}\quad \text{Budget balance} = T - G - TR$$

where T is the value of tax revenues, G is government purchases of goods and services, and TR is the value of government transfers. A **budget surplus** is a positive budget balance, and a **budget deficit** is a negative budget balance.

A **budget surplus** exists when tax revenues exceed government spending on goods, services, and transfer payments.

A **budget deficit** exists when government spending on goods, services, and transfer payments exceeds tax revenue.

> **AP® ECON TIP**
>
> When transfer payments are included as part of government spending, budget deficits and surpluses can be easily calculated. When $G > T$, the government has a budget deficit equal to $(G - T)$. When $T > G$, the government has a budget surplus equal to $(T - G)$.

Other things equal, expansionary fiscal policies—increased government purchases of goods and services, higher government transfers, or lower taxes—reduce the budget balance for that year. That is, expansionary fiscal policies make a budget surplus smaller or a budget deficit bigger. Conversely, contractionary fiscal policies—reduced government purchases of goods and services, lower government transfers, or higher taxes—increase the budget balance for that year, making a budget surplus larger or a budget deficit smaller.

You might think this means that changes in the budget balance can be used to measure fiscal policy. In fact, economists often do just that: they use changes in the budget balance as a quick way to assess whether current fiscal policy is expansionary or contractionary. But they always keep in mind two reasons this quick approach is sometimes misleading:

- Two different changes in fiscal policy that have equal-sized effects on the budget balance may have quite unequal effects on the economy. As we have already seen when discussing multipliers in Module 3.2, changes in government purchases of goods and services have a larger effect on real GDP than equal-sized changes in taxes and government transfers.
- Often, changes in the budget balance are themselves the result, not the cause, of fluctuations in the economy.

To understand the second point, we need to examine the effects of the business cycle on the budget.

The Business Cycle and the Cyclically Adjusted Budget Balance

Historically, there has been a strong relationship between the federal government's budget balance and the business cycle. The budget tends to move into deficit when the economy experiences a recession, but deficits tend to get smaller or even turn into surpluses when the economy is expanding. **Figure 5.4-1** shows the federal budget deficit as a percentage of GDP from 1970 to 2020. Shaded areas indicate recessions; unshaded areas indicate expansions. As you can see, the federal budget deficit increased around the time of each recession and usually declined during expansions. In fact, in the late stages of the long expansion from 1991 to 2000, the deficit actually became negative—the budget deficit became a budget surplus.

FIGURE 5.4-1 The U.S. Federal Budget Deficit and the Business Cycle

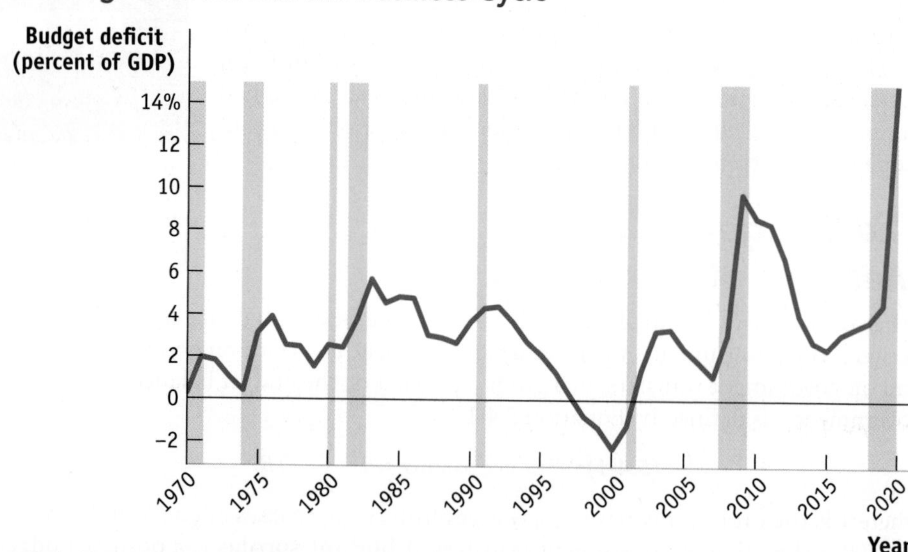

The budget deficit as a percentage of GDP tends to rise during recessions (indicated by shaded areas) and fall during expansions.
Data Source: Bureau of Economic Analysis; National Bureau of Economic Research.

The relationship between the business cycle and the budget balance is even more clear if we compare the budget deficit as a percentage of GDP with the unemployment rate, as we do in **Figure 5.4-2**. The budget deficit almost always rises when the unemployment rate rises and falls when the unemployment rate falls.

FIGURE 5.4-2 **The U.S. Federal Budget Deficit and the Unemployment Rate**

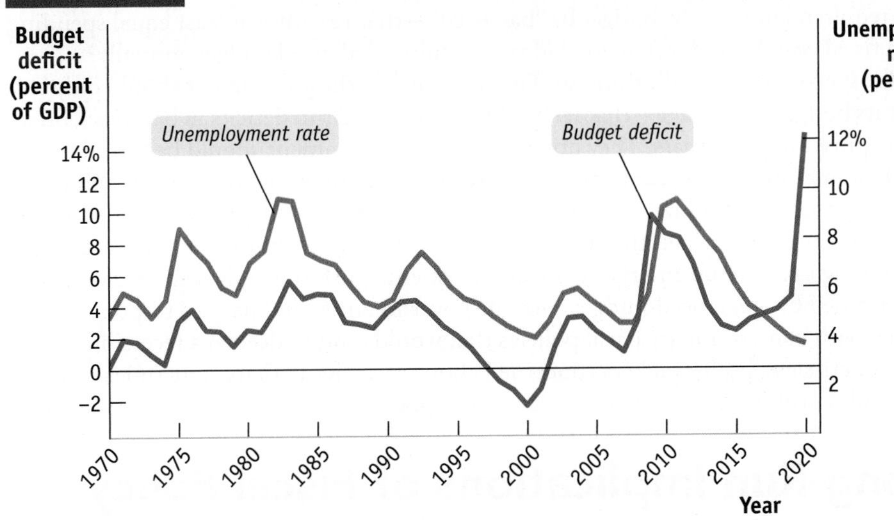

There is a close relationship between the budget balance and the business cycle: a recession moves the budget balance toward deficit, but an expansion moves it toward surplus. Here the budget deficit as a percentage of GDP moves closely in tandem with the unemployment rate.
Data Source: Bureau of Economic Analysis; Bureau of Labor Statistics.

Is this relationship between the business cycle and the budget balance evidence that policy makers engage in discretionary fiscal policy? Not necessarily. It is largely automatic stabilizers that drive the relationship shown in the figures above. As we learned in the discussion of automatic stabilizers in Module 3.9, government tax revenue tends to rise and some government transfers, such as unemployment insurance payments, tend to fall when the economy expands. Conversely, government tax revenue tends to fall and some government transfers tend to rise when the economy contracts. So the budget tends to move toward surplus during expansions and toward deficit during recessions even without any deliberate action on the part of policy makers.

In assessing budget policy, it's often useful to separate movements in the budget balance due to the business cycle from movements due to discretionary fiscal policy changes. The former are affected by automatic stabilizers and the latter by deliberate changes in government purchases, government transfers, or taxes. It's important to realize that business-cycle effects on the budget balance are temporary: both recessionary gaps (in which real GDP is below potential output) and inflationary gaps (in which real GDP is above potential output) tend to be eliminated in the long run. Removing their effects on the budget balance sheds light on whether the government's taxing and spending policies are sustainable in the long run. In other words, do the government's tax policies yield enough revenue to fund its spending? As we'll learn shortly, this is a fundamentally more important question than whether the government runs a budget surplus or deficit in the current year.

To separate the effect of the business cycle from the effects of other factors, many governments produce an estimate of what the budget balance would be if there was neither a recessionary nor an inflationary gap. The *cyclically adjusted budget balance* is an estimate of what the budget balance would be if real GDP were exactly equal to potential output. It takes into account the extra tax revenue the government would collect and the transfers it would save if a recessionary gap were eliminated—or the revenue the government would lose and the extra transfers it would make if an inflationary gap were eliminated.

Should the Budget Be Balanced?

Persistent budget deficits can cause problems for both the government and the economy. Yet politicians are always tempted to run deficits because this allows them to cater to voters by cutting taxes without cutting spending or by increasing spending without increasing taxes. As a result, there are occasional attempts by policy makers to force fiscal discipline by introducing legislation – even a constitutional amendment – forbidding the government from running budget deficits. This is usually stated as a requirement that the budget be "balanced" – that revenues at least equal spending each fiscal year. Would it be a good idea to require a balanced budget annually?

Most economists don't think so. They believe that the government should only balance its budget on average – that it should be allowed to run deficits in bad years, offset by surpluses in good years. They don't believe the government should be forced to run a balanced budget *every year* because this would undermine the role of taxes and transfers as automatic stabilizers. As we learned earlier, the tendency of tax revenue to fall and transfers to rise when the economy contracts helps to limit the size of recessions. But falling tax revenue and rising transfer payments push the budget toward deficit. If constrained by a balanced-budget rule, the government would have to respond to this deficit with contractionary fiscal policies that would tend to deepen a recession.

Nonetheless, policy makers concerned about excessive deficits sometimes feel that rigid rules prohibiting – or at least setting an upper limit on – deficits are necessary.

Long-Run Implications of Fiscal Policy

Government debt is the accumulation of past budget deficits, minus past budget surpluses.

During the 1990s, the Japanese government engaged in massive deficit spending in an effort to increase aggregate demand. That policy was partly successful: although Japan's economy was sluggish during the 1990s, it avoided a severe slump comparable to what happened to many countries in the 1930s. Yet the fact that Japan was running large budget deficits year after year made many observers uneasy, as Japan's **government debt** – the accumulation of past budget deficits, minus past budget surpluses – climbed to alarming levels. Now that we understand how budget deficits and surpluses arise, let's take a closer look at their long-run effects on the economy.

AP® ECON TIP

Government debt, sometimes called the national debt, is equal to the sum of all of the government's past annual deficits and surpluses. A budget deficit or surplus is for a single budget year. The national debt is the accumulated total amount the government currently owes.

Deficits, Surpluses, and Debt

When a family spends more than it earns over the course of a year, it has to raise the extra funds either by selling assets or by borrowing. And if a family borrows year after year, it will eventually end up with a lot of debt.

The same is true for governments. With a few exceptions, governments don't raise large sums by selling assets such as national parkland. Instead, when a government spends more than the tax revenue it receives – when it runs a budget deficit – it almost always borrows the extra funds. And governments that run persistent budget deficits end up with substantial debts.

At the end of fiscal 2020, the budget deficit of the U.S. federal government was $3.1 trillion, or about 14.9% of gross domestic product. U.S. federal government public debt at the end of fiscal 2020 was larger than it was at the end of fiscal 2019 because the federal government ran a budget deficit during fiscal 2020. A government that runs persistent budget deficits will experience a rising level of debt. Why is this a problem?

Prasit photo/Getty Images

Problems Posed by Rising Government Debt

There are two reasons to be concerned when a government runs persistent budget deficits. We described one reason in Module 4.7: when the economy is at potential output and the government borrows funds in the financial markets, it is competing with firms that plan to borrow funds for investment spending. As a result, the government's borrowing may lead to a *crowding out* of private investment and reduction in economic growth.

Government borrowing increases the demand for loanable funds (D_{LF}), which increases the real interest rate (r). A higher real interest rate decreases investment spending (I) and interest-sensitive consumption (interest-sensitive C; consumption financed by borrowing, such as spending on houses and cars), which leads to a decrease in aggregate demand (AD) and, therefore, in real GDP. This chain of events can be illustrated as follows:

$$\uparrow \text{government borrowing} \rightarrow \uparrow D_{LF} \rightarrow \uparrow r \rightarrow \downarrow I/\text{investment-sensitive } C$$
$$\rightarrow \downarrow AD \rightarrow \downarrow \text{real GDP}$$

In the long run, the decrease in investment can lead to a lower rate of capital accumulation and therefore lower economic growth. We will discuss crowding out in detail in the next Module.

The second reason to be concerned about persistent government budget deficits: today's deficits, by increasing the government's debt, place financial pressure on future budgets. The impact of current deficits on future budgets is straightforward. Like individuals, governments must pay their bills, including interest payments on their accumulated debt. When a government is deeply in debt, those interest payments can be substantial. In fiscal 2020, the U.S. federal government paid 1.6% of GDP – $345 billion – in interest on its debt. And although this is a relatively large fraction of GDP, other countries pay even greater fractions of their GDP to service their debt. For example, in 2021, Japan paid interest of about 3.2% of its GDP.

Japanese Prime Minister Fumio Kishida at a press conference to discuss the federal budget.

Anadolu Agency/Getty Images

Other things equal, a government paying large sums in interest must raise more revenue from taxes or spend less than it would otherwise be able to afford – or it must borrow even more to cover the gap. Interest paid on government debt has alternative uses. That is, there is an opportunity cost of spending on interest payments – the foregone alternatives including spending on goods and services or transfer payments, lowering taxes, or paying down the debt. A government that borrows to pay interest on its outstanding debt pushes itself even deeper into debt. This process can eventually push a government to the point at which lenders question its ability to repay. Like consumers who have maxed out their credit cards, the government will find that lenders are unwilling to lend any more funds. The result can be that the government defaults on its debt – it stops paying what it owes. Default is often followed by deep financial and economic turmoil.

The idea of a government defaulting sounds far-fetched, but it is not impossible. In the 1990s, Argentina, a relatively high-income developing country, was widely praised for its economic policies – and it was able to borrow large sums from foreign lenders. By 2001, however, Argentina's interest payments were spiraling out of control, and the country stopped paying the sums that were due. In the end, Argentina reached a settlement with most of its lenders under which it paid less than a third of the amount originally due. Similarly, the government of Greece faced default in 2012, and bond holders agreed to trade their bonds for new ones worth less than half as much. In the same year, concerns about economic frailty forced the governments of Ireland, Portugal, Italy, and Spain to pay high interest rates on their debt to compensate for the risk of default.

Default creates havoc in a country's financial markets and badly shakes public confidence in both the government and the economy. For example, Argentina's debt default was accompanied by a crisis in the country's banking system and a very severe recession. And even if a highly indebted government avoids default, a heavy debt burden typically forces it to slash spending or raise taxes, politically unpopular measures that can also damage the economy.

One question some people ask is: can't a government that has trouble borrowing just print money to pay its bills? Yes, it can, but this leads to another problem: inflation.

In fact, budget problems can be the cause of very severe inflation. Remember from Module 3.6 that demand-pull inflation can be described as "too much money chasing too few goods" – and printing money to pay off large debt adds too much money to the economy. The point for now is that governments do not want to find themselves in the position of choosing between defaulting on their debts or inflating those debts away.

Concerns about the long-run effects of deficits need not rule out the use of fiscal policy to stimulate the economy when it is depressed. However, these concerns do mean that governments should try to offset budget deficits in bad years with budget surpluses in good years. In other words, governments should run a budget that is approximately balanced over time.

Deficits and Debt in Practice

Figure 5.4-3 shows how the U.S. federal government's budget deficit and its debt have evolved since 1940. Panel (a) shows the federal deficit as a percentage of GDP. As you can see, the federal government ran huge deficits during World War II. It briefly ran surpluses after the war, but, with the exception of 1998 to 2001, it has typically run deficits ever since. Since the United States has experienced many business cycles since 1940, this trend seems inconsistent with the advice that governments should offset deficits in bad times with surpluses in good times.

FIGURE 5.4-3 U.S. Federal Deficits and Debt

(a) The U.S. Federal Budget Deficit Since 1940

Budget deficit (percent of GDP)
30%
20
10
0
−10
−20
1940 1950 1960 1970 1980 1990 2000 2010 2020
Year

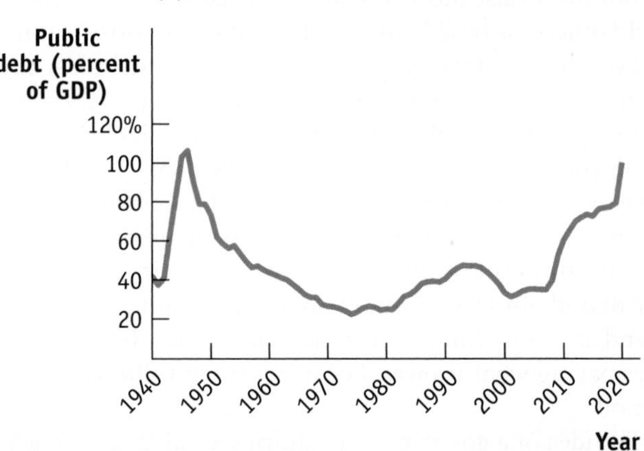

Panel (a) shows the U.S. federal budget deficit as a percentage of GDP since 1940. The U.S. government ran huge deficits during World War II and has run deficits during most years ever since. Panel (b) shows the U.S. debt-GDP ratio. Comparing panels (a) and (b), you can see that in many years the debt-GDP ratio has declined in spite of government deficits. This seeming paradox reflects the fact that the debt-GDP ratio can fall, even when debt is rising, as long as GDP grows faster than debt. The effect of federal deficits in response to the 2008 financial crisis and the COVID-19 pandemic in 2020 are shown as increases in both graphs.

Data Source: Office of Management and Budget.

The **debt–GDP ratio** is the government's debt as a percentage of GDP.

Panel (b) of Figure 5.4-3 shows the effect of persistent budget deficits on the federal debt. To assess the ability of governments to pay their debt, we often use the **debt–GDP ratio**, the government's debt as a percentage of GDP. We use this measure, rather than simply looking at the size of the debt, because GDP, which measures the size of the economy as a whole, is a good indicator of the potential taxes the government can collect. If the government's debt grows more slowly than GDP, the burden of paying that debt is actually falling compared with the government's potential tax revenue. Figure 5.4-3(b) also shows how the federal response to the financial crisis increased public debt as a percentage of GDP after 2010, and again as part of the initial effect of the federal response to the COVID-19 pandemic in 2020.

As you can see from Figure 5.4-3, the government paid for World War II by borrowing on a huge scale. By the war's end, the public debt was more than 100% of GDP, and many people worried about how it could ever be paid off.

The truth is that it never was paid off. In 1946, the public debt was $242 billion; that number dipped slightly in the next few years, as the United States ran postwar budget surpluses, but the government budget went back into deficit in 1950 with the start of the Korean War. By 1962, the public debt was back up to $248 billion.

But by that time nobody was worried about the fiscal health of the U.S. government because the debt–GDP ratio had fallen by more than half. The reason? Vigorous economic growth, plus mild inflation, had led to a rapid rise in GDP. The experience was a clear lesson in the peculiar fact that modern governments can run deficits forever, as long as they aren't too large.

What we see from panel (b) is that, although the federal debt has grown in almost every year, the debt–GDP ratio fell for 30 years after the end of World War II. This shows that the debt–GDP ratio can fall, even when debt is rising, as long as GDP grows faster than debt. Growth and inflation sometimes allow a government that runs persistent budget deficits to have a declining debt–GDP ratio nevertheless.

However, if rising deficits are not offset by economic growth, the debt–GDP ratio will rise as federal debt rises. This was the case following the financial crisis in 2008 and the COVID-19 pandemic in 2020, when large deficits were not offset by economic growth, resulting in rising debt–GDP ratios. During 2008–2010, the federal government's bank bailouts and expansionary spending and tax policies led to large budget deficits during a period of slow economic growth, reflected in the rising debt–GDP ratios during that period in Figure 5.4-3. The federal government also enacted expansionary fiscal policy in response to the COVID-19 pandemic. In 2020, several coronavirus relief bills contributed to a federal budget deficit of $3.1 trillion, more than triple the deficit in 2019. As of 2022, efforts by the federal government in response to the pandemic are projected to increase budget deficits by $2.6 trillion by the year 2030. High deficits combined with slow economic growth explain rising debt–GDP ratios in 2020 and beyond.

Doug Mills-Pool/Getty Images

The response by the federal government, including the passage of the 2021 COVID relief bill shown here being signed into law, are projected to add significantly to the deficit in the future.

Implicit Liabilities

Looking at Figure 5.4-3, you might be tempted to conclude that, until the 2008 economic crisis struck, the U.S. federal budget was in fairly decent shape: the return to budget deficits after 2001 caused the debt–GDP ratio to rise a bit, but that ratio was still low compared with both historical experience and some other wealthy countries. However, experts on long-run budget issues view the situation of the United States (and other countries with high public debt, such as Japan and Greece) with alarm. The reason is the problem of *implicit liabilities*. Implicit liabilities are spending promises made by governments that are effectively a debt despite the fact that they are not included in the usual debt statistics.

The largest implicit liabilities of the U.S. government arise from two transfer programs that principally benefit older Americans: Social Security and Medicare. The third-largest implicit liability, Medicaid, benefits low-income families. In each of these cases, the government has promised to provide transfer payments to future as well as current beneficiaries. So these programs represent a future debt that must be honored, even though the debt does not currently show up in the usual statistics. Together, these three programs accounted for about 34% of federal spending in 2021.

The implicit liabilities created by these transfer programs worry fiscal experts. **Figure 5.4-4** shows why. It shows actual spending on Social Security and on Medicare

FIGURE 5.4-4 Future Demands on the Federal Budget

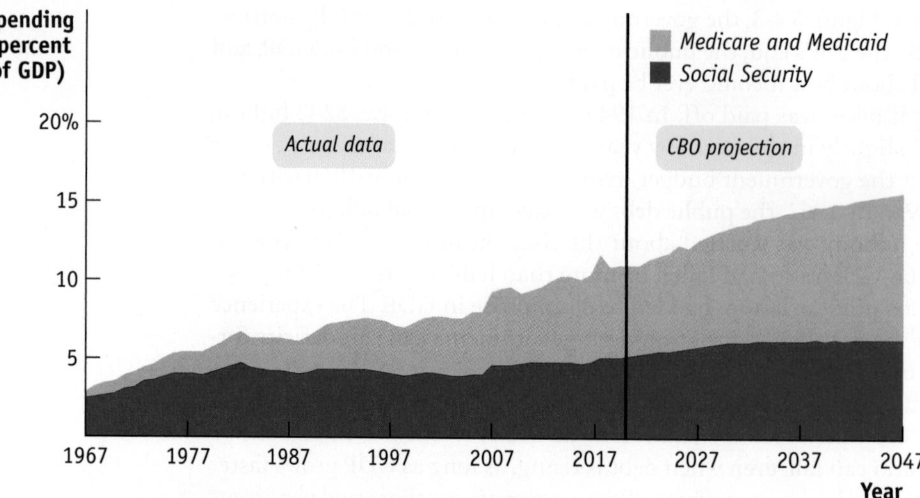

This figure shows actual and projected spending on social insurance programs as a share of GDP. Partly as a result of an aging population, but mainly because of rising health care costs, these programs are expected to become much more expensive over time, posing problems for the federal budget.
Data Source: Congressional Budget Office.

and Medicaid as percentages of GDP from 1980 to 2020, with Congressional Budget Office projections of spending through 2051. According to these projections, spending on Social Security will rise substantially over the next few decades, and spending on the two health care programs will soar.

Changes in government spending and taxes affect a country's budget balance. So the conduct of fiscal policy will have long-run implications for the economy. In the next Module, we look more closely at crowding out, an important potential effect of government borrowing.

Module 5.4 Review

Check Your Understanding

1. Why is the cyclically adjusted budget balance a better measure of the long-run sustainability of government policies than the actual budget balance?
2. Explain why countries required by their constitutions to balance their budgets are likely to experience more severe economic fluctuations than countries that are not held to that requirement.
3. Explain how each of the following events would affect the public debt of the U.S. government, other things equal.
   a. The growth rate of real GDP increases.
   b. Medicare recipients live longer.
   c. Tax revenue decreases.
   d. The government borrows to pay interest on its current public debt.

Tackle the AP® Test: Multiple-Choice Questions

1. If government spending exceeds tax revenues, which of the following is necessarily true? There is a
   a. positive budget balance.
   b. budget deficit.
   c. recession.
   d. government debt.
   e. contractionary fiscal policy.

2. Which of the following fiscal policies is expansionary?

	Taxes	*Government spending*
a.	increase by $100 million	increases by $100 million
b.	decrease by $100 million	decreases by $100 million
c.	increase by $100 million	decreases by $100 million
d.	decrease by $100 million	increases by $100 million
e.	both (a) and (d)	

3. The cyclically adjusted budget deficit is an estimate of what the budget balance would be if real GDP were
   a. greater than potential output.
   b. equal to nominal GDP.
   c. equal to potential output.
   d. falling.
   e. calculated during a recession.

4. During a recession in the United States, what happens automatically to tax revenues and government spending?

	Tax revenues	*Government spending*
a.	increase	increases
b.	decrease	decreases
c.	increase	decreases
d.	decrease	increases
e.	decrease	does not change

5. Which of the following is a reason to be concerned about persistent budget deficits?
   a. crowding out
   b. government default
   c. the opportunity cost of future interest payments
   d. higher interest rates leading to decreased long-run growth
   e. all of the above

6. The opportunity cost of rising government debt is the
   a. higher taxes that must automatically be paid.
   b. lost benefits from automatic cuts in transfer payments.
   c. best alternative use of interest paid on the debt.
   d. inflation resulting from printing money to pay the debt.
   e. all of the above

7. Which of the following is used to assess a government's ability to pay its debt?
   a. debt–GDP ratio
   b. interest owed on the debt
   c. interest owed on the debt as a percentage of GDP
   d. total debt per capita
   e. total tax revenue

Tackle the AP® Test: Free-Response Questions

1. Consider the information provided below for the hypothetical country of Zeta.

Tax revenues = $2,000
Government purchases of goods and services = $1,500
Government transfers = $1,000
Real GDP = $20,000
Potential output = $18,000

   a. Is the budget balance in Zeta positive or negative? What is the amount of the budget balance?
   b. Zeta is currently in what phase of the business cycle? Explain.
   c. Is Zeta implementing the appropriate fiscal policy given the current state of the economy? Explain.
   d. How does Zeta's cyclically adjusted budget deficit compare with its actual budget deficit? Explain.

Rubric for FRQ 1 (8 points)

1 point: Negative
1 point: –$500
1 point: Expansion
1 point: Real GDP > potential output
1 point: No
1 point: Zeta is running a budget deficit during an expansion.
1 point: It is larger.
1 point: If real GDP equaled potential output, then tax revenues would be lower and government transfers would be higher.

2. The government of Colland spends $100b and taxes $100b. Assume Colland is currently in long-run equilibrium.
   a. Does Colland have a budget deficit, surplus, or balanced budget?
   b. Calculate the amount of Colland's budget balance.
   c. Does Colland's budget balance represent expansionary fiscal policy, contractionary fiscal policy, or no fiscal policy. Explain.
   d. What would happen to Colland's budget balance if it uses fiscal policy to respond to an inflationary gap? Explain. **(5 points)**

MODULE 5.5

Crowding Out

In this Module, you will learn to:

- Explain how a government finances its debt and how a government's use of fiscal policy can affect the market for loanable funds
- Define crowding out and explain how it affects the level of private investment
- Use a correctly labeled graph of the loanable funds market to show the effect of government borrowing on the equilibrium real interest rate
- Describe how crowding out can impact the rate of physical capital accumulation and economic growth in the long run

Financing Government Debt

In the previous Module, we discussed the government's budget balance and described some of the issues that arise when a government faces persistent budget deficits. In this Module, we look at how the government finances the debt created by an accumulation of budget deficits over time. A country's national debt is generally financed by the sale of government bonds to the private sector. Government bonds are sold by a designated office of the government and tend to be purchased by financial institutions, but they are also purchased by pension funds and individuals because they pay interest and provide a secure investment. Because the government must pay interest on the bonds it sells, the primary goal of a county's debt management policy is to minimize the cost of financing the debt over the long term.

In the United Kingdom, the government debt is financed through the Debt Management Office, an agency sponsored by HM Treasury, through the sale of government bonds, bills, and gilts (a type of bond). In the United States, the Treasury Department implements a debt management policy, independent of the Federal Reserve's monetary policy, by selling Treasury bills, Treasury notes, Treasury bonds, Treasury Inflation Protected Securities (TIPS), and Floating Rate Notes (FRNs). The following quote from the U.S. Department of the Treasury's debt management policy alludes to the complexity of their goal.

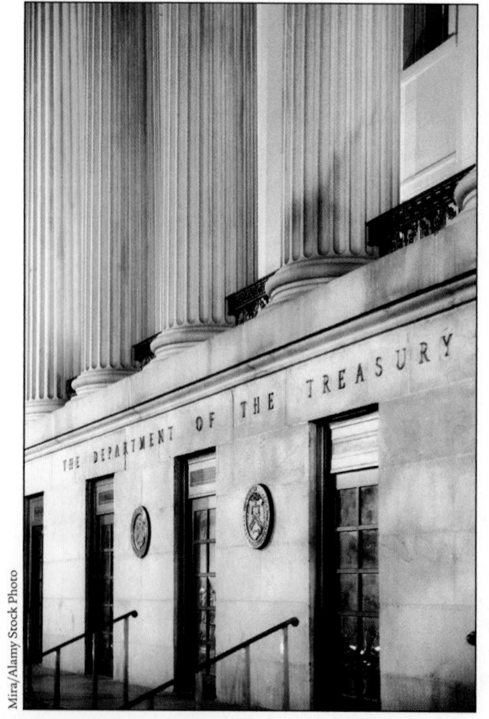

Mira/Alamy Stock Photo

> In creating and executing our financing plans, we must contend with various uncertainties and potential challenges, such as unexpected changes in our borrowing needs, changes in the demand for our securities, and anything that inhibits efficient and timely sales of our securities. To manage these risks, we closely monitor economic conditions, fiscal policy, and market activity, and, where appropriate, respond with appropriate changes in debt issuance based on our analysis and consultation with market participants.

This statement by the U.S. Treasury summarizes the difficulty of financing government debt faced by monetary authorities around the world.

Government debt can also be financed through printing money. However, as we have seen in previous Modules, monetizing government debt this way can lead to inflation, or even hyperinflation, and therefore is not a good option. It has even been prohibited in some countries.

So when governments run budget deficits that result in a national debt, they typically borrow to finance it by selling bonds, requiring interest payments on the debt. In addition to the opportunity cost of spending on interest payments (i.e., the next best alternative for spending that amount), there are potential long-term consequences of a country's deficits and debt. As mentioned in Modules 4.7 and 5.4, persistent budget deficits and rising government debt can lead to higher real interest rates in the market for loanable funds as a result of increased demand for loanable funds caused by increased government borrowing. The increase in the demand for loanable funds causes the equilibrium real interest rate to rise.

A higher real interest rate has one especially important implication (beyond concern about repayment). We know that the real interest rate is an important determinant of investment. A higher real interest rate increases the cost of borrowing and therefore reduces business investment, while a lower real interest rate makes borrowing less expensive and increases business investment. So a rise in the government budget deficit that increases real interest rates tends to reduce overall investment spending. Economists call a negative effect of government budget deficits on investment spending **crowding out**. The threat of crowding out is a key source of concern about persistent budget deficits.

Crowding out occurs when a government deficit drives up the interest rate and leads to reduced investment spending.

The Effect of an Increasing Real Interest Rate

Figure 5.5-1 shows the potential effects of government borrowing on the real interest rate using a graph of the loanable funds market. An increase in government borrowing increases the demand for loanable funds, shifting it to the right from D_{LF1} to D_{LF2}. The new equilibrium is at a higher real interest rate, r_2, and a higher quantity of loanable funds. Because of the higher real interest rate, private investment will decrease. The government's increased "purchase" of loanable funds (that is, sale of government bonds), has crowded out private investment. At higher real interest rates, fewer investment projects have a high enough rate of return to be funded, reducing physical capital accumulation in the economy. The higher real interest rate also crowds out interest-sensitive spending on items that consumers purchase on credit—like houses and cars.

FIGURE 5.5-1 An Increase in the Demand for Loanable Funds

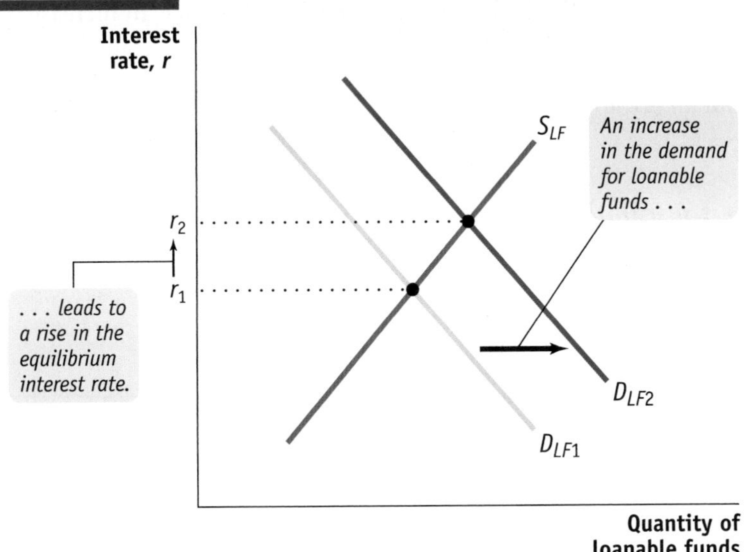

If the quantity of funds demanded by borrowers (including the government) rises at any given interest rate, the demand for loanable funds shifts rightward from D_{LF1} to D_{LF2}. As a result, the equilibrium interest rate rises from r_1 to r_2.

But there must be a sufficient increase in government borrowing in order for it to raise real interest rates and crowd out private investment. **Figure 5.5-2** shows the U.S. federal government deficit or surplus from 1900 to 2020. Notice the first significant budget deficit in the 1940s, when government spending increased during World War II. You can also see the deficits as a result of the recession of the 1980s, followed by the budget surpluses resulting from the economic expansion of the 1990s. But the largest deficits shown are during the financial crisis of 2007–2008, the 2018 tax cuts, and the 2020 pandemic.

FIGURE 5.5-2 U.S. Federal Government Surplus or Deficit 1900–2020

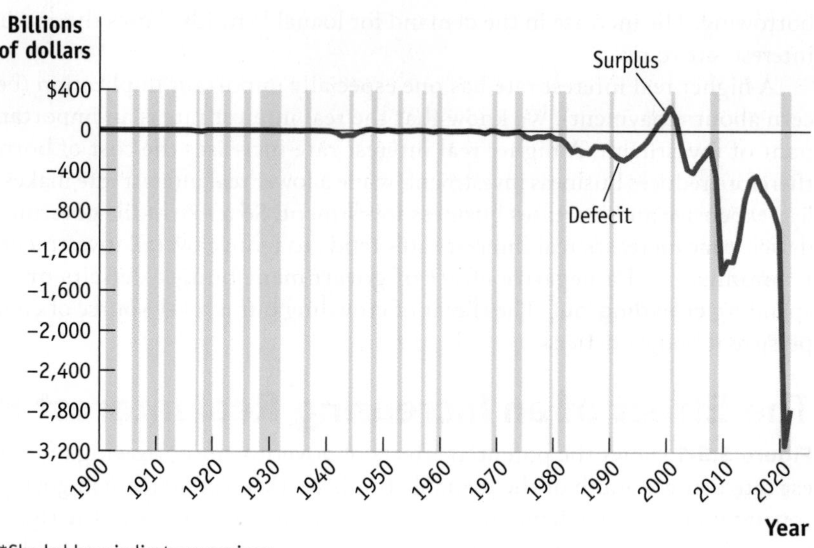

The graph shows the U. S. federal budget deficit or surplus from 1900 to 2020. The first significant deficit in the 1940s was a result of World War II. Deficits occur again during the 1970s recession and continue through the remaining years, with the exception of a period of surplus during the late 1990s and early 2000s. Large increases in the deficit are seen during the 2008 financial crisis and the 2020 pandemic recession.

Have these significant increases in government deficits led to an increase in real interest rates? **Figure 5.5-3** shows average long-term interest rates on inflation-indexed Treasury securities from 2000 to 2021. With the exception of an increase following 2012, the average interest rate shown has generally declined, even during periods of large budget deficits.

So while crowding out is certainly a potential negative long-run consequence of large or persistent budget deficits, the United States has yet to see an increase in interest rates associated with its increased government borrowing in recent decades. But while there is little empirical evidence for extreme crowding out, in which deficit spending crowds out *all* private investment and consumption, few economists believe

FIGURE 5.5-3 Average Annual Interest Rate for Inflation-Indexed Long-Term U.S. Treasury Securities, 2000–2020

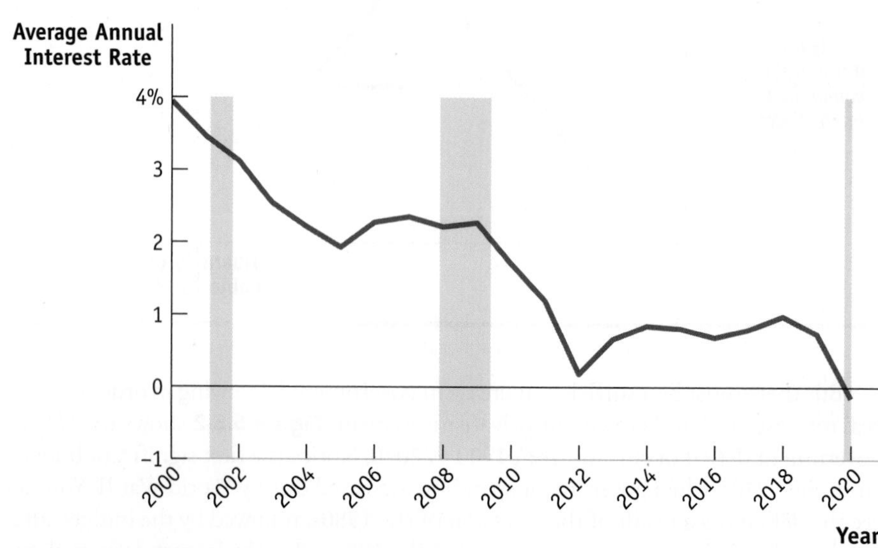

The graph shows average long-term interest rates in the United States from 2000 to 2021. Increases in the average long term interest rates do not correspond to the large budget deficits shown in Figure 5.5-2, indicating that extreme crowding out did not occur during this time period.

that *no* crowding out has occurred as a result of the high levels of government borrowing in recent decades.

Economists tend to agree that expansionary fiscal policy is more likely to be effective in the short run than in the long run. That is, in the long run, the government cannot "get something for nothing." Therefore, most economists concur that the government should not run large, persistent budget deficits.

Crowding out refers to the adverse effect of increased government borrowing on real interest rates and private investment. An important potential long-run impact of crowding out is a lower rate of investment and therefore less physical capital accumulation in the economy. As we will see in the next Module, physical capital is an important determinant of economic growth. So the most important long-run consequence of government borrowing, if it leads to higher real interest rates and a lower rate of physical capital accumulation, is a decrease in long-run economic growth.

Module 5.5 Review

Check Your Understanding

1. Use a correctly labeled graph of the loanable funds market to show and explain how large government deficits can lead to higher real interest rates.

2. Define crowding out and explain the possible effects of crowding out on short-run aggregate output and long-run economic growth.

Tackle the AP® Test: Multiple-Choice Questions

1. What is the most common way for governments to finance their debt?
   a. printing money
   b. selling assets
   c. buying government securities
   d. selling bonds
   e. borrowing from neighboring countries

2. Which of the following is the primary goal of debt management policy?
   a. minimizing the cost of borrowing
   b. selling the most bonds
   c. closing output gaps
   d. stabilizing prices
   e. implementing monetary policy

3. Crowding out occurs when government borrowing causes the demand for loanable funds to ____________ and the real interest rate to ____________.
   a. increase; increase
   b. increase; decrease
   c. decrease; increase
   d. decrease; decrease
   e. stay the same; increase

4. Fiscal policy can lead to crowding out as a result of which of the following?
   a. budget surpluses
   b. increased government spending
   c. decreased taxes
   d. budget deficits
   e. increased taxes

5. Which of the following is an adverse effect of increased government borrowing?
   a. increased interest-sensitive consumption
   b. decreased private investment
   c. higher unemployment
   d. deflation
   e. all of the above

6. Which of the following will decrease the rate of physical capital accumulation in the economy?
   a. an increase in the supply of loanable funds
   b. a decrease in the demand for loanable funds
   c. a decrease in investment spending
   d. a decrease in the real interest rate
   e. none of the above

7. Which of the following best describes the relationship between physical capital accumulation and long-run economic growth?
   a. positive
   b. inverse
   c. negative
   d. parabolic
   e. unrelated

Tackle the AP® Test: Free-Response Questions

1. Assume an economy in long-run equilibrium with a large government debt runs persistent budget surpluses for many years and uses the surplus to pay down its debt.
   a. Draw a correctly labeled graph of the loanable funds market. On your graph label the equilibrium real interest rate, r_1.
   b. Draw a correctly labeled aggregate demand and aggregate supply graph. Label the equilibrium price level and real GDP as PL_1 and Y_1.
   c. Show the effect of the persistent budget surpluses on the demand for loanable funds and the equilibrium real interest rate on your loanable funds market graph. Label the new real interest rate, r_2.
   d. How will the change in the real interest rate from part c affect private investment? Explain.
   e. How will the change in the real interest rate from part c affect investment and therefore physical capital accumulation? Explain.
   f. Show the short-run effect of the change in real interest rate from part c on your aggregate demand and aggregate supply graph. Label the new equilibrium price level and real GDP as PL_2 and Y_2.
   g. How will the change in physical capital accumulation from part e affect the long-run aggregate supply curve? Explain.

Rubric for FRQ 1 (10 points)

1 point: Loanable funds market with *r* on the vertical axis and Q_{LF} on the horizontal axis. Downward-sloping, labeled demand curve and upward-sloping and labeled supply curve.

1 point: Equilibrium real interest rate labeled r_1 on the vertical axis where supply and demand intersect.

1 point: *AD–AS* graph with *PL* on the vertical axis and RGDP on the horizontal axis. Downward-sloping and labeled *AD* curve, upward-sloping and labeled *SRAS* curve.

1 point: Vertical *LRAS* curve intersecting where *AS* and *AD* cross. PL_1 on the vertical axis and Y_1 on the horizontal axis where *AD* and *SRAS* intersect

1 point: Demand for loanable funds shows shifted to the left, r_2 is shown on the vertical axis where the new demand curve and supply curve intersect, below r_1.

1 point: Private investment will increase because the real interest is lower; the real interest rate and private investment are inversely related.

1 point: Physical capital accumulation will increase because investment has increased.

1 point: *AD* is shown shifted to the right.

1 point: The new higher equilibrium price level and real GDP are shown on the axes where the new *AD* curve intersects the *SRAS* curve and are labeled PL_2 and Y_2.

1 point: *LRAS* will shift further to the right with the higher rate of physical capital accumulation associated with the lower rate of physical capital accumulation. Physical capital is positively related to long-run growth illustrated by a rightward shift of the *LRAS* curve.

2. Draw a correctly labeled graph of the market for loanable funds.
   a. On your graph, label equilibrium real interest rate and quantity of loanable funds as r_1 and Q_{LF1}.
   b. On your graph from part a, show the effect of a persistent budget deficit on demand for loanable funds and the equilibrium real interest rate. Explain why a persistent budget deficit has this effect.
   c. Explain the effect of the change in the real interest rate from part b on the rate of physical capital accumulation and long-run economic growth.
   (5 points)

Economic Growth

MODULE 5.6

In this Module, you will learn to:

- Define the measurements of economic growth and explain its determinants
- Calculate per capita GDP and economic growth
- Explain and draw a correctly labeled aggregate production function
- Define and calculate average productivity as output per worker and identify technology, physical capital, and human capital as determinants of productivity
- Explain how economic growth is shown as an outward shift of a production possibilities curve and a rightward shift of the long-run aggregate supply curve

Many economists have argued that long-run economic growth – why it happens and how to achieve it – is the single most important issue in macroeconomics. In this Module, we define the measures and determinants of economic growth and use an aggregate production function to illustrate it graphically. In doing so, we will revisit two models of economic growth developed in previous Units – the production possibilities curve model and the aggregate demand and aggregate supply model.

Real GDP per Capita

The key statistic used to track economic growth is *real GDP per capita*, which is real GDP divided by the population size. Economists focus on *GDP* because, as we have learned, GDP measures the total value of an economy's production of final goods and services as well as the income earned in that economy in a given year. We use *real* GDP because we want to separate changes in the quantity of goods and services from the effects of a rising price level. We focus on real GDP *per capita* because we want to isolate the effect of changes in the population and focus on the amount of real GDP per person. For example, other things equal, an increase in the population lowers the standard of living for the average person – there are now more people to share a given amount of real GDP. An increase in real GDP that only matches an increase in population leaves the real GDP per capita unchanged. To increase a country's standard of living, the level of real GDP must increase so that there is, on average, higher real GDP per person.

Real GDP per capita serves as a very useful summary measure of a country's economic progress over time. **Figure 5.6-1** shows real GDP per capita for the United States, India, and China, measured in 2005 dollars, from 1910 to 2018. The vertical axis is drawn so that equal percentage changes in real GDP per capita across countries are the same size in the graph.

In most countries, the income of the typical family normally grows more or less in proportion to per capita income. For example, a 1% increase in real GDP per capita corresponds, roughly, to a 1% increase in the income of the median or typical family – a family at the center of the income distribution. In 2020, the median American household had a real income of about $67,521. Real GDP per capita in 1910 was the equivalent of an annual income of around $8,916 in today's dollars, representing a standard of living that we would now consider severe poverty. If the average American family today were forced to live as an average family from 1910, they would feel quite deprived.

DNY59/Getty Images

For many decades, Americans dreamed of owning a single-family home in a well-manicured neighborhood.

FIGURE 5.6-1 Economic Growth in the United States, India, and China over the Past Century

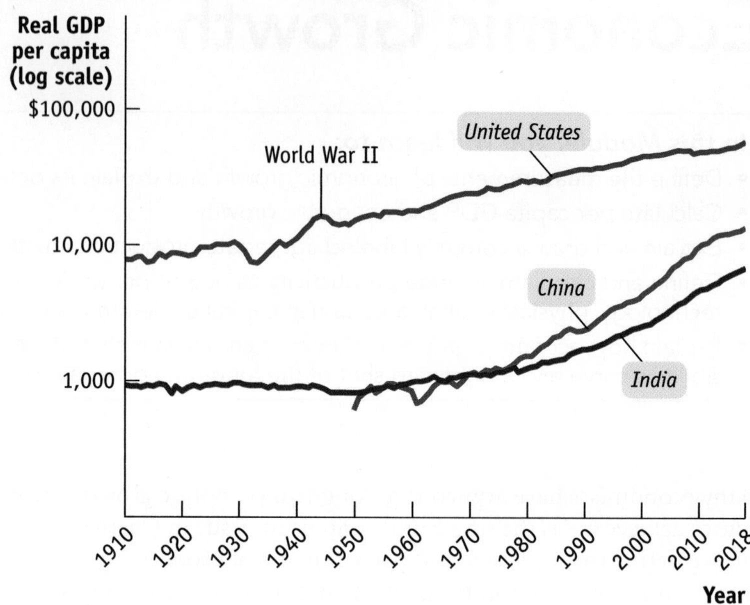

Real GDP per capita from 1910 to 2018, measured in 2005 dollars, is shown for the United States, India, and China (*note:* data for China prior to 1950 is unavailable). Equal percentage changes in real GDP per capita are drawn the same size. India and China currently have a much higher growth rate than the United States. However, China has only recently attained the standard of living achieved in the United States in 1910, while India is still poorer than the United States was in 1910.
Data Source: Maddison Project Database, 2020; Groningen Growth and Development Centre, University of Groningen, https://www.rug.nl/ggdc/historicaldevelopment/maddison/

Yet many people in the world have a standard of living equal to or lower than that of the United States a century ago. That's the message about China and India in Figure 5.6-1: despite dramatic economic growth in China in recent decades and the less dramatic acceleration of economic growth in India, China has only recently attained the standard of living that the United States enjoyed in 1910, while India is still poorer than the United States was in 1910. And much of the world today is poorer than China and India.

Long-Run Growth in the United States

In 2020, the United States was much richer than it was in 1953; in 1953, it was much richer than it had been in 1903. But how did 1853 compare with 1803? Or 1753? How far back does long-run economic growth go?

The answer is that long-run growth is a relatively modern phenomenon. The U.S. economy was already growing steadily by the mid-nineteenth century—think railroads. But if you go back to the period before 1800, you find a world economy that grew extremely slowly by today's standards. Furthermore, the population grew almost as fast as the economy, so there was very little increase in output per person. According to the economic historian Angus Maddison, from the year 1000 to 1800, real aggregate output around the world grew less than 0.2% per year, with population rising at about the same rate. Economic stagnation meant unchanging living standards. However, long-run economic growth has increased significantly since 1800. In the last 60 years or so, real GDP per capita worldwide has grown at a rate of about 2% per year, as can be seen in **Figure 5.6-2**. Let's examine the implications of high and low growth rates.

Growth Rates

How did the United States manage to produce approximately seven times more per person in 2020 than in 1910? A little bit at a time. Long-run economic growth is normally a gradual process in which real GDP per capita grows at most a few percent per year. From 1910 to 2010, real GDP per capita in the United States increased by an average of 2.1% each year.

FIGURE 5.6-2 Worldwide Real GDP, 1960–2020

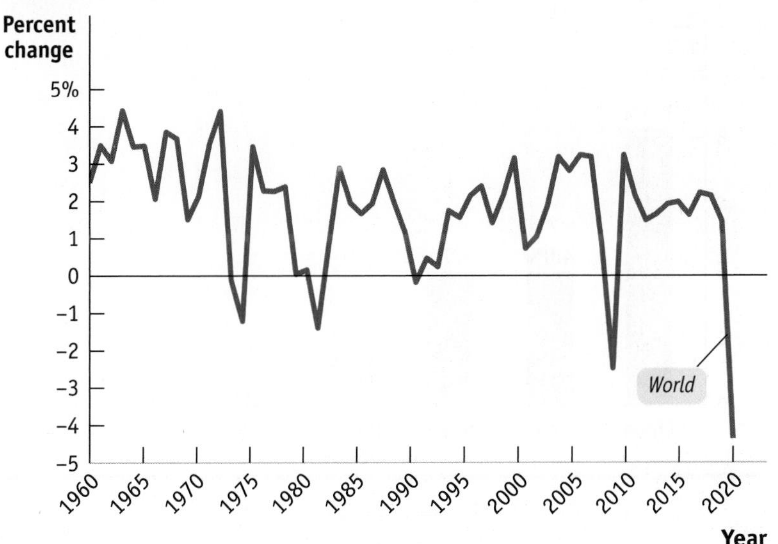

The real GDP per capita worldwide growth rate has fluctuated around 2% per year from 1960 to 2020, as shown in the graph. Two notable exceptions are the large negative growth rates shown during the 2007–2008 financial crisis and the 2020 pandemic recession, both of which were felt worldwide.

To have a sense of the relationship between the annual growth rate of real GDP per capita and the long-run change in real GDP per capita, it's helpful to keep in mind the Rule of 70, a mathematical formula that tells us how long it takes real GDP per capita, or any other variable that grows gradually over time, to double. The approximate answer is:

$$\textbf{(5.6-1)}\quad \text{Number of years for variable to double} = \frac{70}{\text{Annual growth rate of variable}}$$

(Note that the Rule of 70 can only be applied to a positive growth rate.)

The Rule of 70 tells us that the time it takes a variable that grows gradually over time to double is approximately 70 divided by that variable's annual growth rate.

So if real GDP per capita grows at 1% per year, it will take 70 years to double. If it grows at 2% per year, it will take only 35 years to double. Applying the Rule of 70 to the 2.1% average growth rate in the United States implies that it should have taken 33.3 years for real GDP per capita to double; it would have taken 100 years—three periods of 33.3 years each—for U.S. real GDP per capita to double three times. That is, the Rule of 70 implies that over the course of 100 years, U.S. real GDP per capita should have increased by a factor of $2 \times 2 \times 2 = 8$. And this turns out to be a pretty good approximation of reality. Over the century from 1910 to 2010, real GDP per capita rose just about eightfold.

Figure 5.6-3 shows the average annual rate of growth of real GDP per capita for selected countries from 1980 to 2020. Some countries have been notable success stories; we've already mentioned China, which has made spectacular progress. India, although not matching China's performance, has also achieved impressive growth. Some countries, though, have had very disappointing growth. This includes many of the countries in Africa and South America, where growth rates below 1% are not uncommon—note, for example, the growth rates for Argentina and Zimbabwe shown in Figure 5.6-3.

What explains these differences in growth rates? To answer that question, we need to examine the sources of long-run growth.

FIGURE 5.6-3 Comparing Recent Growth Rates, 1980–2020

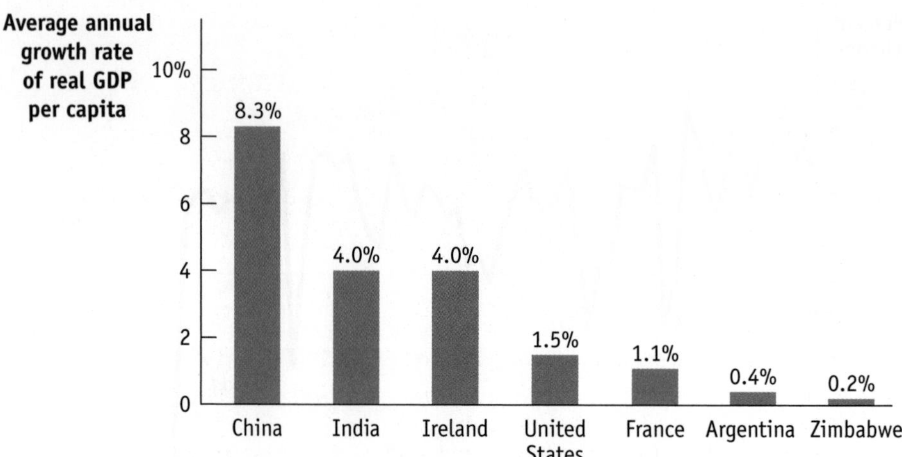

Here the average annual rate of growth of real GDP per capita from 1980 to 2020 is shown for selected countries. China and, to a lesser extent, India and Ireland have achieved impressive growth. The United States and France have had low to moderate growth. Still others, such as Argentina and Zimbabwe, experienced very low growth.
Data Source: World Bank.

The Sources of Long-Run Growth

Long-run economic growth depends almost entirely on one ingredient: rising *productivity*. However, a number of factors affect the growth of productivity. Let's look first at why productivity is the key ingredient. After that, we'll examine what affects it.

The Crucial Importance of Productivity

Labor productivity, often referred to simply as **productivity**, is output per worker.

Sustained growth in real GDP per capita occurs only when the amount of output produced by the average worker increases steadily. The term **labor productivity** (or **productivity**, for short) is generally used to refer to output per worker. For the economy as a whole, productivity—output per worker—is simply real GDP divided by the number of people working.

You might wonder why we say that higher productivity is the only source of long-run growth in real GDP per capita. Can't an economy also increase its real GDP per capita by putting more of the population to work? The answer is, yes, but there is more to it than that. For short periods of time, an economy can experience a burst of growth in output per capita by putting a higher percentage of the population to work. That happened in the United States during World War II, when millions of women who previously worked only in the home entered the paid workforce. The percentage of adult civilians employed outside the home rose from 50% in 1941 to 58% in 1944, resulting in a bump in real GDP per capita during those years.

Over the longer run, however, the rate of employment growth is never very different from the rate of population growth. In general, overall real GDP can grow because of population growth, but any large increase in real GDP *per capita* must be the result of increased output *per worker*. That is, it must be due to higher productivity.

Increased productivity is the key to long-run economic growth. But what leads to higher productivity?

AP® ECON TIP

There is an important distinction between short-run fluctuations in real GDP due to the business cycle and long-run economic growth. Anything that causes a shift in the *SRAS* or *AD* curve causes short-run fluctuations. Economic growth is shown by a rightward shift of the *LRAS* curve (or *PPC*). Increased productivity, caused by advances in technology, improvements in human capital, or increases in an economy's stock of physical capital, leads to economic growth.

Explaining Growth in Productivity

There are three main reasons why the average worker today produces far more than their counterpart a century ago. First, the modern worker has far more *physical capital*, such as tools and office space, to work with. Second, the modern worker is much better educated and so possesses much more *human capital*. Finally, modern firms have the advantage of a century's accumulation of technical advancements, reflecting a great deal of *technological progress*. The accumulated existing capital in an economy is referred to as its stock of capital, or *capital stock*.

Let's look at each of these factors in turn.

AP® ECON TIP

Be careful when describing what leads to an increase in long-run economic growth. "Increased investment in physical capital" leads to long-run economic growth because physical capital accumulation leads to an increase in productivity. "Increased investment" leads to a short-run fluctuation in aggregate demand because investment is a component of aggregate demand.

Physical Capital

Capital – manufactured goods used to produce other goods and services – is often described as physical capital to distinguish it from human capital and financial capital. **Physical capital**, such as buildings and machinery, makes workers more productive. For example, a worker operating a backhoe can dig a lot more feet of trench per day than one equipped with only a shovel.

Human Capital

It's not enough for workers to have good equipment – they must also know what to do with it. **Human capital** refers to the improvement in labor created by the education and knowledge embodied in the workforce.

The human capital of the United States has increased dramatically over the past century. Although most Americans living a century ago were able to read and write, very few had an extensive education. In 1910, only 13.5% of Americans over 25 had graduated from high school and only 3% had four-year college degrees. By 2020, those percentages were 90% and 36%, respectively. It would be impossible to run today's economy with a population as poorly educated as that of a century ago.

Analyses suggest that education – and its effect on productivity – is an even more important determinant of growth than increases in physical capital.

Physical capital consists of human-made goods such as buildings and machines used to produce other goods and services.

Human capital is the improvement in labor created by the education and knowledge of members of the workforce.

Technology is the technical means for the production of goods and services.

Technology

Probably the most important driver of productivity growth is progress in **technology**, which is broadly defined as the technical means for the production of goods and services. We'll see shortly how economists measure the impact of technology on growth.

Workers today are able to produce more than those in the past, even with the same amount of physical and human capital, because technology has advanced over time. It's important to realize that economically important technological progress need not be flashy or rely on cutting-edge science. Historians have noted that past economic growth has been driven not only by major inventions, such as the railroad or the semiconductor chip, but also by thousands of modest innovations. For example, the flat-bottomed paper bag, patented in 1870, made packing groceries and many other goods much easier, and the Post-it note, introduced in 1981, has had surprisingly large benefits for office productivity. Experts attribute much of the productivity surge that took place in the United States late in the twentieth century to new technology adopted by retail companies, such as computerized inventories and bar codes, rather than to high-technology companies. Wireless networks, invented in 1991, and video conferencing, introduced in 2001, are examples of information and communications technologies (ICTs) credited with contributing to high rates of economic growth in the 1990s and 2000s.

SDI Productions/Getty Images

The combination of better education and high-tech tools has allowed the average U.S. worker today to produce far more than workers in the past.

Economic Growth and the Aggregate Production Function

We know that productivity is higher, other things equal, when workers are equipped with more physical capital, more human capital, better technology, or any combination of the three. Economists use an *aggregate production function* to show how aggregate output depends on the quantities of physical and human capital as well as the state of technology. In general, all three factors tend to rise over time, as workers are equipped with more machinery, receive more education, and benefit from technological advances. The **aggregate production function** allows economists to represent the effects of these three factors on overall productivity. In general, the aggregate output in an economy depends on the level of inputs (such as capital and labor). The general production function can be shown as follows:

The **aggregate production function** is a hypothetical function that shows how aggregate output depends on the stock of physical capital and the quantity and quality of labor resources, as well as the state of technology.

$$\textbf{(5.6-1)} \quad \text{aggregate output} = f(\text{inputs})$$

where f is read as "is function of" or "depends on." A more specific aggregate production function can be shown as follows:

$$\textbf{(5.6-2)} \quad \text{real GDP} = f(K, L)$$

where K is the stock of physical capital and L is a measure of the quantity, and quality—human capital—of labor.

But what about land resources? Theoretically, the quantity and quality of land resources can affect aggregate output in an economy. However, in modern economies, land is far less important than the stock of physical capital and the quantity and quality of labor resources. In some less developed economies, land and livestock are important inputs to production, but they are not included in typical measures of capital stock. So in our simplest production function, we consider only physical capital stock and labor resources.

The aggregate production functions above show that the output produced in the economy depends on the economy's capital and labor resources. In addition, the overall efficiency of the economy in transforming inputs into outputs, sometimes called *total factor productivity*, also affects the amount of aggregate output produced from a given level of inputs. Anything that allows the same level of inputs to produce a higher level of aggregate output has increased total factor productivity. Technological advances and innovations affecting production are examples of changes that increase total factor productivity. We will see how changes in total factor productivity affect our production function when we consider a graph of the aggregate production function next.

The Law of Diminishing Returns

An aggregate production function exhibits **diminishing returns to physical capital** when, holding the quantity and quality of labor and the state of technology fixed, each successive increase in the amount of physical capital leads to a smaller increase in productivity.

In analyzing historical economic growth, economists have discovered a crucial fact about estimated aggregate production functions: they exhibit **diminishing returns to physical capital**. That is, when the quantity and quality of labor resources and the state of technology are held fixed, each successive increase in the amount of physical capital leads to a smaller increase in productivity. **Table 5.6-1** gives a hypothetical example of how the level of physical capital might affect the level of real GDP, holding labor resources and technology constant.

As you can see from the table, there is a big payoff from the first $15,000 invested in physical capital: real GDP per worker rises by $30,000. The second $15,000 worth of physical capital also raises productivity, but by not as much: real GDP per worker goes up by only $15,000. The third $15,000 worth of physical capital raises real GDP per worker by only $10,000.

Table 5.6-1 A Hypothetical Example: How Physical Capital Affects Productivity, Holding Labor Resources and Technology Fixed

Physical capital investment per worker	Real GDP per worker
$0	$0
15,000	30,000
30,000	45,000
45,000	55,000

To see why the relationship between physical capital per worker and productivity exhibits diminishing returns, think about how having farm equipment affects the productivity of farm workers. A little bit of equipment makes a big difference: a worker equipped with a tractor can do much more than a worker without one. And, other things equal, a worker using more expensive equipment will be more productive: a worker with a $30,000 tractor will normally be able to cultivate more farmland in a given amount of time than a worker with a $15,000 tractor because the more expensive machine will be more powerful, perform more tasks, or both.

But will a worker with a $30,000 tractor, holding human capital and technology constant, be twice as productive as a worker with a $15,000 tractor? Probably not: there's a huge difference between not having a tractor at all and having even an inexpensive tractor; there's much less difference between having an inexpensive tractor and having a better tractor. A worker with a $150,000 tractor won't be 10 times as productive: a tractor can be improved only so much. Because the same is true of other kinds of equipment, the aggregate production function shows diminishing returns to physical capital.

Christopher May/Alamy

Figure 5.6-4 is a graphical representation of the aggregate production function with diminishing returns to physical capital. As the figure illustrates, more physical capital leads to more output, holding labor and technology constant. But each $30,000 increment in physical capital adds less to productivity. By comparing points *A*, *B*, and *C*, you can also see that, as physical capital rises, output also rises—but at a diminishing rate. Going from point *A* to point *B*, representing a $30,000 increase in physical capital, leads to an increase of $20,000 in real GDP. Going from point *B* to point *C*, a second $30,000 increase in physical capital, leads to an increase of only $10,000 in real GDP.

FIGURE 5.6-4 The Aggregate Production Function

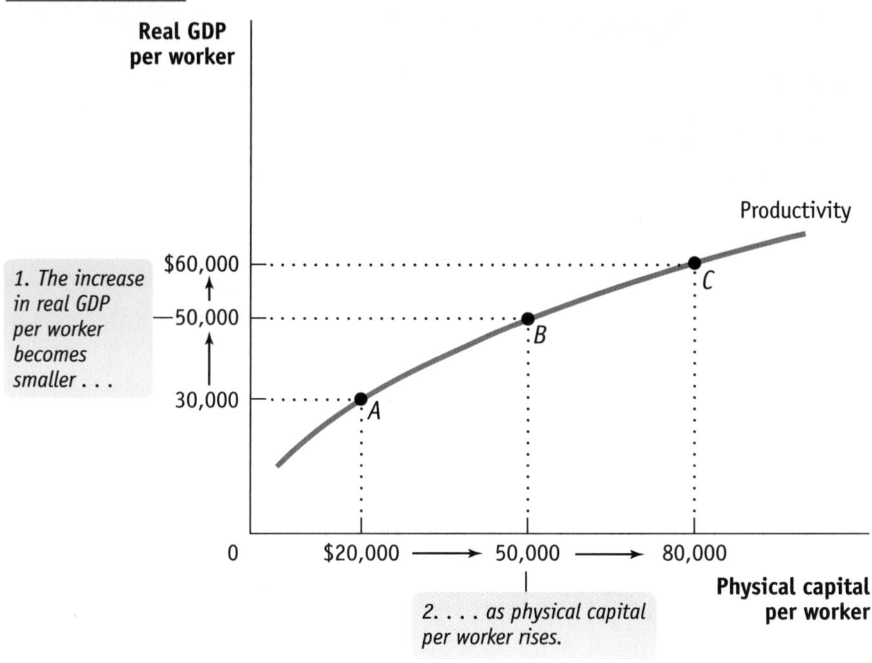

Holding labor resources and technology constant, a greater quantity of physical capital leads to higher real GDP but is subject to diminishing returns: each successive addition to physical capital produces a smaller increase in productivity. Starting at point *A*, with $20,000 in physical capital, a $30,000 increase in physical capital leads to an increase of $20,000 in real GDP. At point *B*, with $50,000 in physical capital, a $30,000 increase in physical capital leads to an increase of only $10,000 in real GDP.

It's important to emphasize that diminishing returns to physical capital is an "other things equal" phenomenon: additional amounts of physical capital are less productive *when the quantity or quality of labor and the technology are held fixed*. Diminishing returns may disappear if we increase the quantity or quality of labor, or improve the technology, or both, when the amount of physical capital is increased. For example, a worker with a $30,000 tractor who has also been trained in the most advanced cultivation techniques may in fact be more than twice as productive as a worker with only a $15,000 tractor and no additional human capital. But diminishing returns to any

AP® ECON TIP

The concept of diminishing returns is applied throughout economics. The general idea is that the more you do anything, the harder it is to keep doing it. Because the activity gets harder to do, the returns from doing it diminish. For example, the longer your study session, the less you learn in each additional hour. This same idea applies to investing in physical capital—each added unit will increase productivity by less and less. The concept of diminishing returns explains the shape of the aggregate production function.

one input—regardless of whether it is physical capital, human capital, or labor—is a pervasive characteristic of production.

We could also use an aggregate production function to show the effect of an increase in labor resources holding physical capital and technology constant. In this case, labor resources would be measured on the horizontal axis and the productivity curve would show the same general shape due to the law of diminishing returns to labor.

In reality, all the factors contributing to higher productivity tend to rise during the course of economic growth: both physical capital and human capital increase, and technology advances as well. But how does a technological advance affect the aggregate production function?

To see how a change in technology is shown using an aggregate production function, let's assume that there is no increase in labor resources so that we can focus on changes in physical capital and in technology. In **Figure 5.6-5**, the lower curve shows the same hypothetical relationship between physical capital and output shown in Figure 5.6-4. Let's assume that this was the relationship given the technology available in 1950. The upper curve also shows a relationship between physical capital and productivity, but this time given the technology available in 2020. (We've chosen a 70-year stretch to allow us to use the Rule of 70.) The 2020 curve is shifted up compared to the 1950 curve because technologies developed over the previous 70 years make it possible to produce more output for a given amount of physical capital than was possible with the technology available in 1950. (Note that the two curves are measured in constant dollars.)

FIGURE 5.6-5 Technological Progress and the Aggregate Production Function

Technological progress shifts the productivity curve upward. Here we hold the quantity and quality of labor fixed. We assume that the lower curve (the same curve as in Figure 5.6-4) reflects technology in 1950 and that the upper curve reflects technology in 2020. Holding technology and labor resources fixed, quadrupling physical capital per worker from \$20,000 to \$80,000 leads to a doubling of real GDP, from \$30,000 to \$60,000. This is shown by the movement from point *A* to point *C*, reflecting an approximately 1% per year rise in real GDP. In reality, technological progress shifted the productivity curve upward, and the actual rise in real GDP is shown by the movement from point *A* to point *D*. Real GDP per worker grew 2% per year, leading to a quadrupling during the period. The extra 1% in growth of real GDP is due to higher total factor productivity.

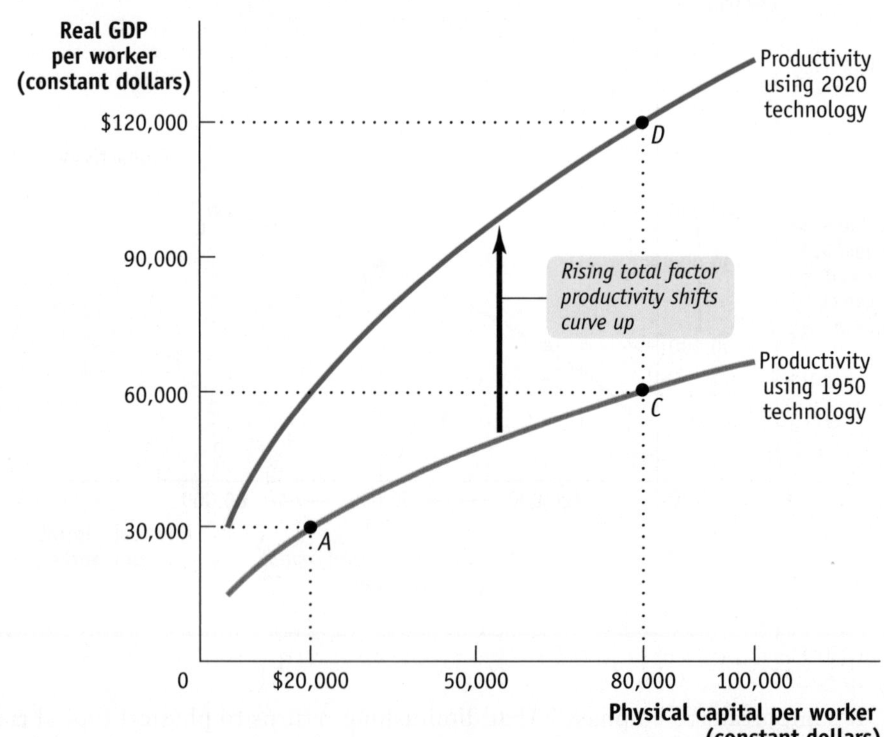

Let's assume that between 1950 and 2020 the amount of physical capital rose from \$20,000 to \$80,000. If this increase in physical capital had taken place without any technological progress, the economy would have moved from *A* to *C*: output per worker would have risen, but only from \$30,000 to \$60,000, or 1% per year (using the

Rule of 70 tells us that a 1% growth rate over 70 years doubles output). In fact, however, the economy moved from *A* to *D*: output rose from $30,000 to $120,000, or 2% per year. There was an increase in both physical capital and technological progress, which shifted the aggregate production function.

In this case, 50% of the annual 2% increase in productivity – that is, 1% in annual productivity growth – is due to higher *total factor productivity*, the amount of output that can be produced with a given amount of factor inputs. So when total factor productivity increases, the economy can produce more output with the same quantity of physical capital, human capital, and labor.

Most estimates find that increases in total factor productivity are central to a country's economic growth. Economists believe that observed increases in total factor productivity in fact measure the economic effects of technological progress, which implies that technological change is crucial to economic growth.

Long-Run Economic Growth and the Production Possibilities Curve

Recall from Unit 1 that we defined the production possibilities curve (*PPC*) as a graph that illustrates the trade-offs facing an economy that produces only two goods. In our example, we developed the production possibilities curve for Alexis, a castaway facing a trade-off between producing fish and coconuts. Looking at **Figure 5.6-6**, we see that economic growth is shown as an outward shift of the production possibilities curve. Now let's return to the production possibilities curve model and use a different example to illustrate how economic growth policies can lead to long-run economic growth.

FIGURE 5.6-6 Economic Growth in the Production Possibilities Curve

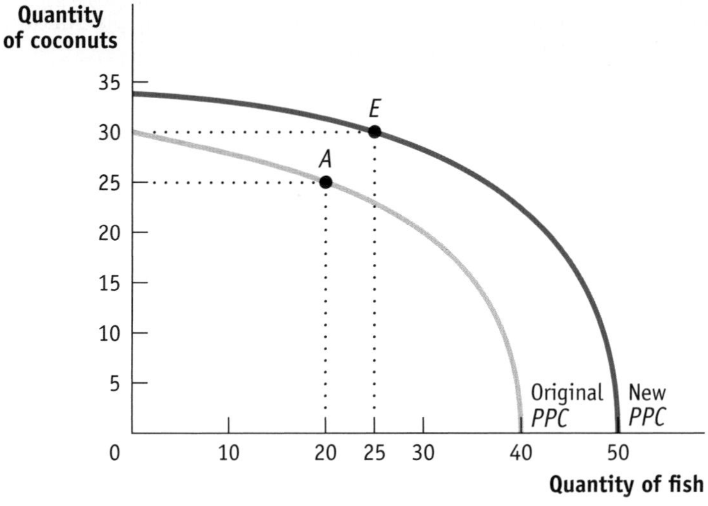

Economic growth results in an *outward shift* of the production possibilities curve because production possibilities are expanded. The economy can now produce more of everything. For example, if production is initially at point *A* (20 fish and 25 coconuts), it could move to point *E* (25 fish and 30 coconuts).

Figure 5.6-7 shows a hypothetical production possibilities curve for the fictional country of Kyland. In our previous production possibilities examples, the trade-off was between producing quantities of two different goods. In this example, our production possibilities curve illustrates Kyland's trade-off between two different *categories* of goods. The production possibilities curve shows the alternative combinations of investment goods and consumer goods that Kyland can produce. The consumer goods category includes everything purchased for consumption by households, such as food, clothing, and sporting goods. Investment goods include all forms of physical capital, that is, goods that are used to produce other goods. Kyland's production possibilities curve shows the trade-off between the production of consumer goods and the

AP® ECON TIP

In the production possibilities model, economic growth is shown as an outward shift of the curve. Long-run growth is distinct from short-run economic fluctuations, which are shown by movements between points on and below the *PPC*.

FIGURE 5.6-7 The Trade-off Between Investment and Consumer Goods

This production possibilities curve illustrates Kyland's trade-off between the production of investment goods and consumer goods. At point *A*, Kyland produces all investment goods and no consumer goods. At point *D*, Kyland produces all consumer goods and no investment goods. Points *B* and *C* represent two of the many possible combinations of investment goods and consumer goods.

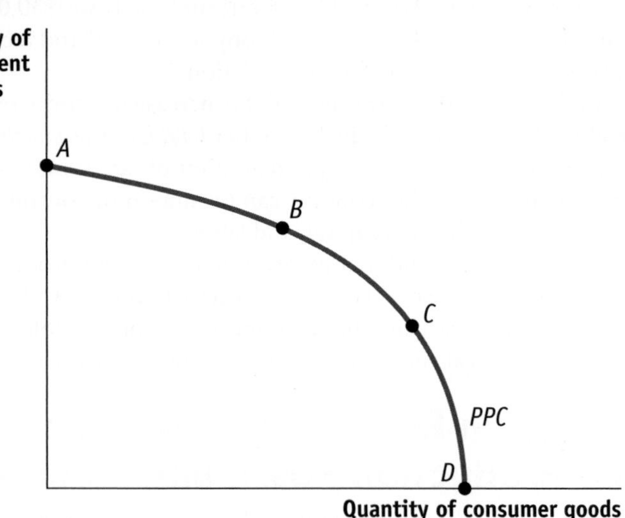

production of investment goods. Recall that the bowed-out shape of the production possibilities curve reflects increasing opportunity cost.

Kyland's production possibilities curve shows all possible combinations of consumer and investment goods that can be produced with full and efficient use of all of Kyland's resources. However, the production possibilities curve model does not tell us which of the possible points Kyland *should* select.

Figure 5.6-7 illustrates four points on Kyland's production possibilities curve. At point *A*, Kyland is producing all investment goods and no consumer goods. Investment in physical capital, one of the economy's factors of production, causes the production possibilities curve to shift outward. Choosing to produce at a point on the production possibilities curve that creates more capital for the economy will result in greater production possibilities in the future. Note that at point *A*, there are no consumer goods being produced, a situation which the economy cannot survive in the long run.

Depreciation occurs when the value of a physical asset is reduced by wear, age, or obsolescence.

At point *D*, Kyland is producing all consumer goods and no investment goods. While this point provides goods and services for consumers in Kyland, it does not include the production of any physical capital. Over time, as an economy produces more goods and services, some of its capital is used up in that production. A loss in the value of physical capital due to wear, age, or obsolescence is called **depreciation**. If Kyland were to produce at point *D* year after year, it would soon find its stock of physical capital depreciating and its production possibilities curve would shift inward over time, indicating a decrease in production possibilities.

Qian Weizhong/VCG/Getty Images

Government investment in infrastructure projects, such as commercial docks, airports, and transit rail systems, can promote long-run growth and encourage private investment spending.

Points *B* and *C* represent a mix of consumer and investment goods for the economy. While we can see that points *A* and *D* would not be acceptable choices over a long period of time, the choice between points *B* and *C* would depend on the values, politics, and other details related to the economy and people of Kyland. What we do know is that the choice made by Kyland each year will affect the position of the production possibilities curve in the future. An emphasis on the production of consumer goods will make consumers better off in the short run but will prevent the production possibilities curve from moving farther out in the future. An emphasis on investment goods will shift the production possibilities curve out farther in the future but will decrease the quantity of consumer goods available in the short run.

So what does the production possibilities curve tell us about economic growth? Since long-run economic growth depends almost entirely on rising productivity, a country's decision regarding investment in physical capital, human capital, and technology affects its long-run economic growth. Governments can promote long-run economic growth, shifting the country's production possibilities curve outward over time, by investing in physical capital such as infrastructure. They can also encourage high rates of private investment in physical capital by promoting a well-functioning financial system, property rights, and political stability.

Long-Run Economic Growth and the Aggregate Demand–Aggregate Supply Model

The aggregate demand and supply model we developed in Unit 3 is another useful tool for understanding long-run economic growth. Recall that in the aggregate demand–aggregate supply model, the long-run aggregate supply (*LRAS*) curve shows the relationship between the aggregate price level and the quantity of aggregate output supplied when all prices, including nominal wages, are flexible. As shown in **Figure 5.6-8**, the long-run aggregate supply curve is vertical at the level of potential output, Y_P^1. While actual real GDP is almost always above or below potential output, reflecting the current phase of the business cycle, potential output is the level of output around which actual aggregate output fluctuates. Potential output in the United States has risen steadily over time. This corresponds to a rightward shift of the long-run aggregate supply curve, as shown in the shift to Y_P^2 and Y_P^3. Thus, the same government policies that promote an outward shift of the production possibilities curve promote a rightward shift of the long-run aggregate supply curve.

AP® ECON TIP

The *LRAS* curve is vertical at the economy's potential output (also known as full employment output), which corresponds to the natural rate of unemployment. Economic growth is illustrated in the *AD–AS* model by a rightward shift of the vertical *LRAS* curve. Long-run growth is distinct from short-run economic fluctuations, which are shown by changes in short-run equilibrium due to changes in *SRAS* or *AD*.

FIGURE 5.6-8 The Long-Run Aggregate Supply Curve

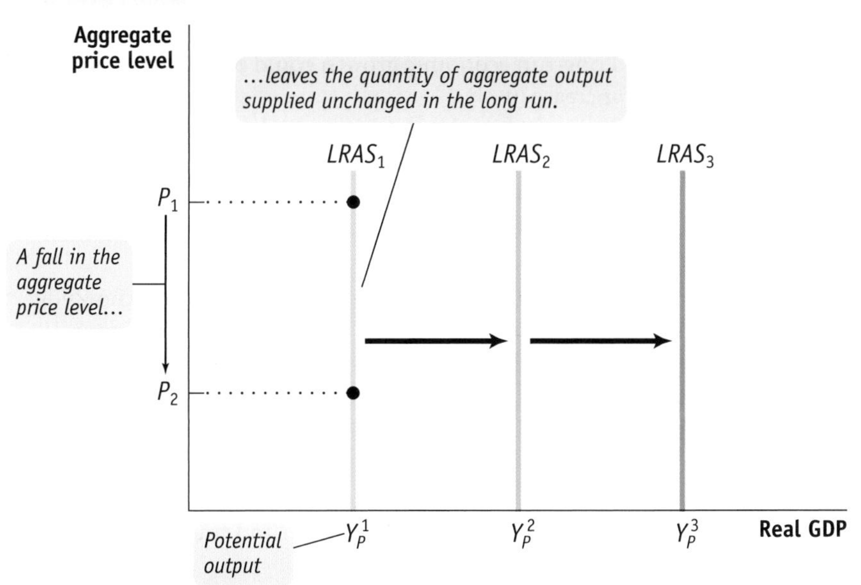

The long-run aggregate supply (*LRAS*) curve shows the quantity of aggregate output supplied when all prices, including nominal wages, are flexible. It is vertical at potential output, Y_P^1, because in the long run, a change in the aggregate price level has no effect on the quantity of aggregate output supplied. The growth in potential output over time can be shown as a rightward shift of the long-run aggregate supply curve.

When considering changes in real GDP, it is important to distinguish long-run growth from short-run fluctuations due to the business cycle. The long-run aggregate supply (*LRAS*) curve shows the quantity of aggregate output supplied when all prices, including nominal wages, are flexible. It is vertical at potential output, because in the long run a change in the aggregate price level has no effect on the quantity of aggregate output supplied. The growth in potential output over time can be shown as a rightward shift of the long-run aggregate supply curve.

In the aggregate demand–aggregate supply model, fluctuations of actual aggregate output around potential output are illustrated by shifts of aggregate demand or short-run aggregate supply that result in a short-run macroeconomic equilibrium above or below potential output. When short-run equilibrium differs from the long-run equilibrium, it is due to the business cycle. Long-run economic growth is represented by a rightward shift of the long-run aggregate supply curve and corresponds to an increase in the economy's level of potential output, as we see in Figure 5.6-8.

Watch the video:
Economic Growth

Module 5.6 Review

Check Your Understanding

1. Why do economists focus on real GDP per capita as a measure of economic progress rather than on some other measure, such as nominal GDP per capita or real GDP?
2. Describe the shift in, or movement along, the aggregate production function caused by each of the following:
   a. The amounts of physical and human capital per worker are unchanged, but there is significant technological progress.
   b. The amount of physical capital per worker grows, but the level of human capital per worker and technology are unchanged.
3. List and briefly describe the three major determinants of productivity.

Tackle the AP® Test: Multiple-Choice Questions

1. Which of the following is the key statistic used to track economic growth?
   a. GDP
   b. real GDP
   c. real GDP per capita
   d. median real GDP
   e. median real GDP per capita
2. A movement from a point below the *PPC* to a point on the *PPC* illustrates which of the following?
   a. increased inefficiency
   b. economic expansion
   c. long-run economic growth
   d. decreased unemployment
   e. economic recession
3. Which of the following will cause the long-run aggregate supply curve to shift to the left?
   a. an increase in aggregate demand
   b. a decrease in aggregate supply
   c. a decrease in an economy's stock of physical capital
   d. investment in infrastructure
   e. all of the above
4. Long-run economic growth depends almost entirely on
   a. technological change.
   b. rising productivity.
   c. increased labor force participation.
   d. rising real GDP per capita.
   e. population growth.
5. Long-run economic growth could be caused by an increase in
   a. capital stock.
   b. investment.
   c. consumption.
   d. aggregate demand.
   e. short-run aggregate supply.
6. Which of the following leads to an increase in human capital?
   a. education
   b. job training
   c. work experience
   d. increased knowledge
   e. all of the above
7. Which of the following is a source of productivity growth?
   a. increased physical capital
   b. increased human capital
   c. increased worker education and training
   d. technological progress
   e. all of the above
8. Which of the following is an example of physical capital?
   a. machinery
   b. health care
   c. education
   d. money
   e. all of the above

9. The aggregate production function shows the relationship between inputs and
   a. output.
   b. technology.
   c. human capital.
   d. the price level.
   e. physical capital.

10. Diminishing returns to physical capital explains why the aggregate production function shows real GDP
   a. increasing at an increasing rate.
   b. increasing at a decreasing rate.
   c. decreasing at a decreasing rate.
   d. decreasing at an increasing rate.
   e. diminishing at a constant rate.

Tackle the AP® Test: Free-Response Questions

1. a. Draw a correctly labeled graph of an aggregate production function that illustrates diminishing returns to physical capital.
   b. Explain what it is about your productivity curve that indicates that there are diminishing returns to physical capital.
   c. On your graph, show the effect of technological progress.
   d. How is the level of human capital addressed on your graph?

Rubric for FRQ 1 (7 points)

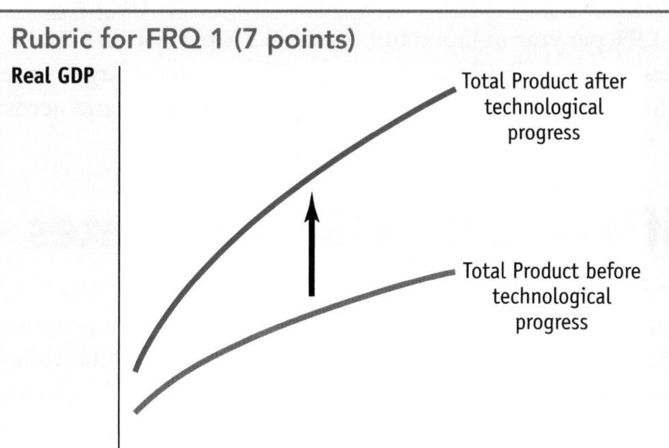

1 point: Vertical axis is labeled "Real GDP."

1 point: Horizontal axis is labeled "Physical capital."

1 point: Upward-sloping curve is labeled "Total product" (or equivalent).

1 point: Curve increases at a decreasing rate (the slope is positive and decreasing).

1 point: Equal increases in physical capital per worker lead to smaller increases in real GDP.

1 point: Upward shift of production function is labeled to indicate technological progress.

1 point: Human capital is held constant.

2. Refer to the graph provided.

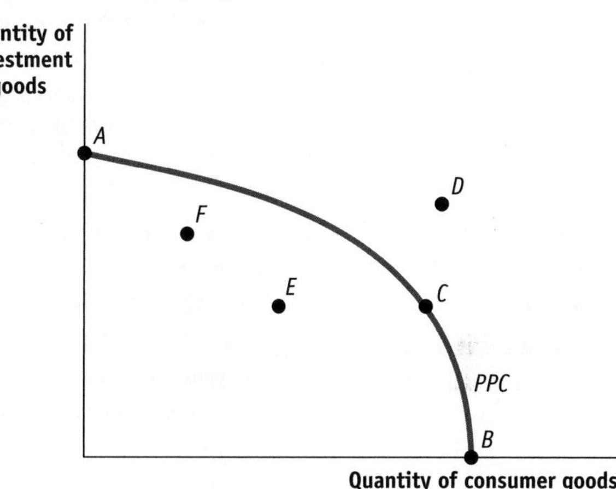

   a. Which point(s) could represent a downturn in the business cycle?
   b. Which point(s) represent efficient production?
   c. Which point(s) are attainable only after long-run economic growth?
   d. How would long-run economic growth be represented on this graph?
   e. Policy that results in an increase in the production of consumer goods without reducing the production of investment goods is represented by a movement between which two points?
   f. Producing at which efficient point this year would lead to the most economic growth next year? **(6 points)**

MODULE 5.7

Public Policy and Economic Growth

In this Module, you will learn to:

- Identify and explain policies that impact a country's productivity, labor force participation, and real GDP per capita
- Explain how investments in technology and infrastructure affect economic growth
- Describe how incentives affect the economic behavior of households and businesses
- Define supply-side fiscal policies and explain how they affect aggregate demand, aggregate supply, and potential output in the short run and long run

In 1820, according to estimates by the economic historian Angus Maddison, Mexico had somewhat higher real GDP per capita than Japan. Today, Japan has higher real GDP per capita than most European nations, and Mexico is considered a low-income country, though by no means among the lowest. The difference? Over the long run, real GDP per capita grew at 1.9% per year in Japan but at only 1.2% per year in Mexico.

As this example illustrates, even small differences in growth rates have large consequences over the long run. So why do growth rates differ across countries and across periods of time?

Explaining Differences in Growth Rates

As one might expect, economies with rapid growth tend to be economies that add physical capital, increase their human capital, or experience rapid technological progress. Striking economic success stories, like Japan in the 1950s and 1960s or China today, tend to be countries that do all three: rapidly add to their physical capital, upgrade their educational level, and make fast technological progress.

Adding to Physical Capital

One reason for differences in growth rates among countries is that some countries are increasing their stock of physical capital much more rapidly than others, through high rates of investment spending. In the 1960s, Japan was the fastest-growing major economy; it also spent a much higher share of its GDP on investment goods than other major economies. Today, China is the fastest-growing major economy, and it similarly spends a very large share of its GDP on investment goods. In 2021, investment spending was approximately 43% of China's GDP, compared with only about 19% in the United States.

Where does the money for high investment spending come from? We have already analyzed how financial markets channel savings into investment spending. The key point is that investment spending must be paid for either out of savings from domestic households or by an inflow of foreign capital—that is, savings from foreign households. Foreign capital has played an important role in the long-run economic growth of some countries, including the United States, which relied heavily on foreign funds during its early industrialization. For the most part, however, countries that invest a large share of their GDP are able to do so because they have high domestic savings. One reason for differences in growth rates, then, is that countries have different rates of savings and investment spending.

Adding to Human Capital

Just as countries differ substantially in the rate at which they add to their physical capital, there have been large differences in the rates at which countries add to their human capital through education.

A case in point is the comparison between Argentina and China. In both countries, the average educational level has risen steadily over time, but it has risen much faster in China. **Figure 5.7-1** shows the average years of education of adults in China, which we have highlighted as a spectacular example of long-run growth, and in Argentina, a country whose growth has been disappointing. Seventy years ago, the population of Argentina was much more educated than that of China, where much of the population was illiterate. Today, the average educational level in China is still slightly below that in Argentina—but that's mainly because there are still many elderly adults in China who never received basic education. In terms of high school and college education, China has outstripped once-rich Argentina.

Li Xin/Xinhua/Alamy Live News

Over the past several decades, China has made significant investments in human capital in the form of education, embodied in these recent graduates from Beijing's Tsinghua University.

FIGURE 5.7-1 China's Students Are Catching Up

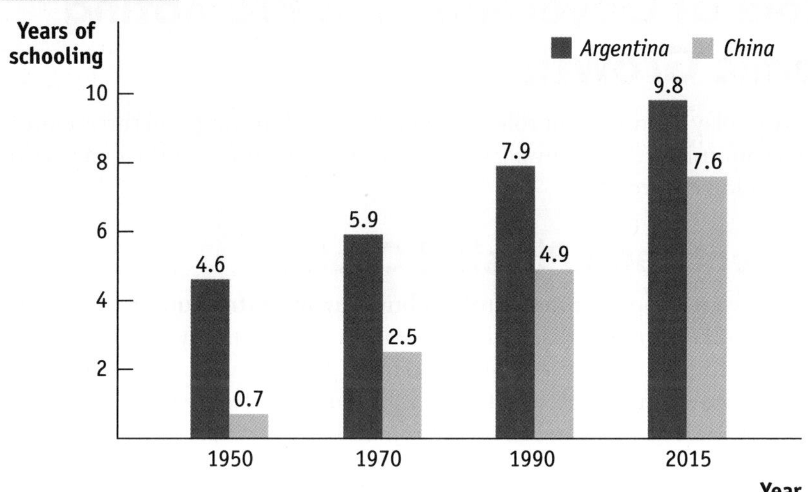

In both China and Argentina, the average educational level—measured by the number of years the average adult aged 25 or older has spent in school—has risen over time. Although China still lags behind Argentina, it is catching up—and China's success at adding human capital is one key to its spectacular long-run growth.
Data Source: Robert Barro and Jong-Wha Lee, "A New Data Set of Educational Attainment in the World, 1950–2010," NBER Working Paper No. 15902 (April 2010).

Technological Progress

The advance of technology is a key force behind economic growth. But what drives advances in technology? Scientific advances make new technologies possible. To take the most spectacular example in today's world, the semiconductor chip—which is the basis for all modern information technology—could not have been developed without the theory of quantum mechanics in physics.

But science alone is not enough: scientific knowledge must be translated into useful products and processes. And that often requires devoting a lot of resources to research and development, or R&D, spending to create new technologies and prepare them for practical use.

Thomas Edison is best known as the inventor of the light bulb and the phonograph. But his biggest invention may surprise you: he invented research and development. Before Edison's time, of course, there had been many inventors. Some of them worked in teams. But in 1875 Edison created something new: his Menlo Park, New Jersey, laboratory. It employed 25 men full time to generate new products and processes for business. In other words, he did not set out to pursue a particular idea and then cash in. He created an organization whose purpose was to create new ideas year after year.

NurPhoto/Getty Images

As with Edison a century before, many modern-day entrepreneurs—such as Elon Musk, shown here discussing his SpaceX program—are using their wealth to fund research and development projects.

Edison's Menlo Park lab is now a museum. "To name a few of the products that were developed in Menlo Park," says the museum's website, "we can list the following: the carbon button mouthpiece for the telephone, the phonograph, the incandescent light bulb and the electrical distribution system, the electric train, ore separation, the Edison effect bulb, early experiments in wireless, the grasshopper telegraph, and improvements in telegraphic transmission."

You could say that before Edison's lab, technology just sort of happened: people came up with ideas, but businesses didn't plan to make continuous technological progress. Now R&D operations, often much bigger than Edison's original team, are standard practice throughout the business world. The R&D conducted by Edison was paid for by the private sector, which still is common today. The United States became the world's leading economy in large part because American businesses were among the first to make systematic research and development a part of their operations. However, some R&D is conducted by governments.

Developing new technology is one thing; applying it is another. There have often been notable differences in the pace at which different countries take advantage of new technologies. America's surge in productivity growth after 1995, as firms learned to make use of information technology, was initially not matched in Europe.

The Role of Government in Promoting Economic Growth

Governments can play an important role in promoting—or blocking—all three sources of long-term economic growth: physical capital, human capital and the quantity of labor, and technological progress.

Governments and Physical Capital

Roads, power lines, ports, information networks, and other underpinnings for economic activity are known as **Infrastructure**.

Governments play an important direct role in building **infrastructure**: roads, power lines, ports, information networks, and other parts of an economy's physical capital that provide a foundation for economic activity. Although some infrastructure is provided by private companies, much of it is either provided by the government or requires a great deal of government regulation and support. Ireland, whose economy really took off in the 1990s, is often cited as an example of the importance of government-provided infrastructure: the government invested in an excellent telecommunications infrastructure in the 1980s, and this helped make Ireland a favored location for high-technology companies.

Poor infrastructure—for example, a power grid that often fails, cutting off electricity to homes and businesses—is a major obstacle to economic growth in some countries. To provide good infrastructure, an economy must be able to afford it, but it must also have the political discipline to maintain it and provide for the future.

Perhaps the most crucial infrastructure is something we rarely think about: basic public health measures in the form of a clean water supply and disease control. Poor health infrastructure is a major obstacle to economic growth in low-income countries, especially those in Africa.

AP® ECON TIP

Increased government spending will not automatically lead to economic growth. Not all government spending is used for research and development, physical capital, and human capital. Also, not all R&D spending leads to useful discoveries and advancement. It is important to be specific about the type of government spending when discussing causes of economic growth.

Governments also play an important indirect role in making high rates of private investment spending possible. Both the amount of savings and the ability of an economy to direct savings into productive investment spending depend on the economy's institutions, notably its financial system. In particular, a well-functioning banking system is very important for economic growth because, in most countries, it is the principal way in which savings are channeled into business investment spending. If a country's citizens trust their banks, they will place their savings in bank deposits, which the banks will then lend to their business customers. But if people don't trust their banks, they will hoard gold or foreign currency, keeping their savings in safe deposit boxes or under their mattresses, where it cannot be turned into productive investment spending. A well-functioning financial system requires appropriate government regulation that assures depositors that their funds are protected.

Large-scale infrastructure projects, such as the Caculo Cabaca Hydropower Station under construction in Angola (construction of which was inaugurated by Angolan president José Eduardo dos Santos in 2017, shown here), are key to increasing economic growth in low-income countries.

Xinhua/Alamy Stock Photo

Governments and Labor Resources

An economy's physical capital is created mainly through investment spending by individuals and private companies. Much of an economy's investment in human capital, by contrast, is the result of government spending on education. In wealthy countries, the government pays for the great bulk of primary and secondary education, although individuals pay a significant share of the costs of higher education.

As a result, differences in the rate at which countries add to their human capital largely reflect government policy. For example, East Asia now has a more educated population than Latin America. This isn't because East Asia is richer than Latin America and so can afford to spend more on education. Until relatively recently, East Asia, on average, was poorer than Latin America. Instead, it reflects the fact that Asian governments made broad education of the population a higher priority.

Labor force participation also has an important effect on an economy's labor resources. In the United States, labor force participation has declined significantly since the early 2000s. The labor force participation rate (LFPR) hit a high of 67.2% in March 2000 and fell to 62.4% in September 2015, mostly due to demographic trends, such as the baby-boom generation entering retirement. These labor force participation rates correspond to a decrease in the annual growth of GDP per capita from 2.2% per year before the Great Recession to 1.6% from 2007 to 2018.

The LFPR in the United States fell again during the pandemic recession, from 63.4% in February 2020 to 60.2% in April 2020, its lowest level since 1973, before climbing back up to 61.9% at the start of 2022. The decline in the LFPR in 2020 was attributed to health concerns and childcare issues as the pandemic spread and schools were closed. The government plays a role in public health and labor policies that can affect labor force participation.

Governments and Technology

As we've discussed, technological progress is largely the result of private initiative. But important R&D is done by government agencies. For example, the agricultural boom that Brazil experienced over the past two decades was made possible by government researchers who discovered that adding crucial nutrients to the soil would allow crops to be grown on previously unusable land. Government researchers also developed new varieties of soybeans and breeds of cattle that flourish in Brazil's tropical climate.

Agriculture is an important industry in Brazil, a country with immense agricultural resources available to it. Its most significant products in this sphere are, in order of importance, coffee, soybeans (pictured here), wheat, rice, corn, sugarcane, cocoa, citrus, and beef.

Paulo Fridman/Bloomberg/Getty Images

Political Stability, Property Rights, and Excessive Government Intervention

There's not much point in investing in a business if rioting mobs are likely to destroy it. And why save your money if someone with political connections can steal it? Political stability and protection of property rights can affect total factor productivity and are crucial ingredients in long-run economic growth.

Long-run economic growth in successful economies has been possible because there are good laws, institutions that enforce those laws, and a stable political system that maintains those institutions.

The law must say that your property is really yours so that someone else can't take it away. The courts and the police must be honest so that they can't be bribed to ignore the law. And the political system must be stable so that the law doesn't change capriciously.

Many Americans take these preconditions for granted, but they are by no means guaranteed. Aside from the disruption caused by war or revolution, many countries find that their economic growth suffers due to corruption among the government officials who should be enforcing the law. And even when governments aren't corrupt, excessive government intervention can be a brake on economic growth. If large parts of the economy are supported by government subsidies, protected from imports, or otherwise insulated from competition, productivity tends to suffer because of a lack of incentives. Excessive government intervention is one often-cited explanation for slow growth in Latin America.

Economic Growth and the Environment

Economic growth, other things equal, tends to increase the human impact on the environment. For example, economic growth brings a spectacular increase in air pollution. It's important to realize, however, that other things aren't necessarily equal: countries can and do take action to protect their environments. In fact, air and water quality in today's advanced countries is generally much better than it was a few decades ago. London's famous "fog" – actually a form of air pollution called smog, which killed 4,000 people during a particularly intense two-week episode in 1952 – is gone, thanks to regulations that virtually eliminated the use of coal heat. The equally famous smog of Los Angeles, although not extinguished, is far less severe than it was in the 1960s and early 1970s, again thanks to pollution regulations.

Despite these past environmental success stories, there is widespread concern today about the environmental impacts of continuing economic growth, reflecting a change in the scale of the problem. Environmental success stories have mainly involved dealing with *local* impacts of economic growth, such as the effect of widespread car ownership on air quality in the Los Angeles basin. Today, however, we are faced with *global* environmental issues – the adverse impacts on the environment of the Earth as a whole by worldwide economic growth. The biggest of these issues involves the impact of fossil-fuel consumption on the world's climate.

The problem of climate change is clearly linked to economic growth. **Figure 5.7-2** shows carbon dioxide emissions from the United States, Europe, and China since 1980.

FIGURE 5.7-2 Climate Change and Growth, 1980–2020

Greenhouse gas emissions are positively related to growth. As shown here by the United States and Europe, wealthy countries have historically been responsible for the great bulk of greenhouse gas emissions because of their richer and faster-growing economies. As China, India, and other emerging economies have grown, they have begun to emit much more carbon dioxide.
Data Source: Global Carbon Atlas, http://globalcarbonatlas.org/en/CO2-emissions.

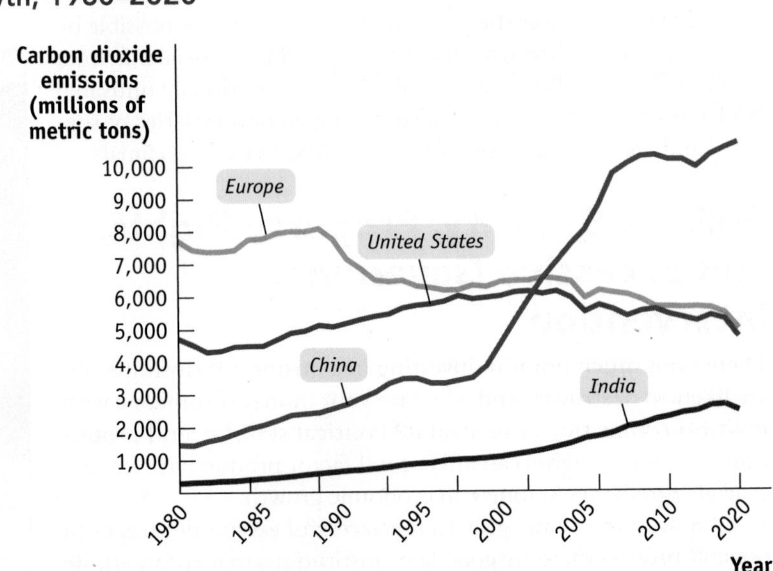

Historically, the wealthy nations have been responsible for the bulk of these emissions because they have consumed far more energy per person than poorer countries. As China and other emerging economies have grown, however, they have begun to consume much more energy and emit much more carbon dioxide.

Howard C/Getty Images

Reduced economic activity in 2020, in response to the COVID-19 pandemic, led to a reduction in carbon emissions, though at a very high cost.

The connection between economic activity and carbon emission was illustrated dramatically in 2020. From cleaner water in Venice to blue skies in Beijing, the COVID-19 pandemic led to a variety of positive environmental benefits. Of course, those benefits came at a high cost.

During the pandemic, governments worldwide mandated lock-down measures. In addition, citizens voluntarily reduced nonessential trips and activities. These measures caused significant alterations in some sectors, especially transportation and power generation. For example, there was a marked decrease in road and air traffic during the pandemic as well as a decrease in energy demand and coal power production. These changes significantly affected emissions of carbon dioxide (CO_2) and other air pollutants—in fact, from January through April 2020, worldwide CO_2 emissions decreased by an estimated 14.3%.

The reduction of economic activity as a result of the pandemic led to a 4.9% decrease in global GDP for the second quarter of 2020. The short but deep worldwide recession reduced production and therefore reduced the associated pollution. Since the United States, the European Union, China, and India represent almost 60% of anthropogenic carbon emissions (emissions caused by human activity), their steep decline in economic activity during 2020 contributed significantly to a decrease in global carbon emissions. But as with other previous crises, as the economy rebounded, production and emissions did also. The pandemic illustrates the positive relationship between production and emissions, but that doesn't mean that decreasing economic growth is the only way to address climate change.

Is it possible to continue long-run economic growth while curbing the emissions of greenhouse gases? The answer, according to most economists who have studied the issue, is yes. It should be possible to reduce greenhouse gas emissions in a wide variety of ways, ranging from the use of non-fossil-fuel energy sources such as wind, solar, and nuclear power; to preventive measures such as carbon sequestration (capturing carbon dioxide and storing it); to simpler things like designing buildings so that they require less energy to keep warm in winter and cool in summer. Such measures would impose costs on the economy, but the best available estimates suggest that a large reduction in greenhouse gas emissions over the next few decades could be accomplished with only modest declines in the long-term rise in real GDP per capita.

So there is a broad consensus among economists that government action is needed to deal with climate change. But the added problem of international burden sharing presents a stumbling block for consensus. As Figure 5.7-2 shows, today's rich countries have historically been responsible for most greenhouse gas emissions, but newly emerging economies like China are responsible for most of the recent growth. Inevitably, rich countries are reluctant to pay the price of reducing emissions only to have their efforts frustrated by rapidly growing emissions from new players. On the other hand, countries like China and India, which still have relatively low incomes, consider it unfair that they should be expected to bear the burden of protecting an environment threatened by the past actions of higher-income countries.

Despite political issues and the need for compromise, the general moral of this story is that it is possible to reconcile long-run economic growth with environmental protection. The main question is how to get political consensus around the necessary policies.

Matthias Tunger/Getty Images

Increased household consumption can help with short-term fluctuations but might slow long-term growth.

Economic Growth in the Short and Long Run

Long-run economic growth is fundamental to solving many of today's most pressing economic problems. It is even more critical in lower-income, less developed countries. But the policies we have studied in earlier Units to address short-run fluctuations and the business cycle may not encourage long-run economic growth. For example, an increase in household consumption can help an economy recover from a recession. However, when households increase consumption, they decrease their savings, which leads to decreased investment spending and slows long-run economic growth. In addition to understanding short-run stabilization policies, we need to understand the factors that influence economic growth and how choices by governments and individuals can promote or retard that growth in the long run.

A theme throughout Modules 5.6 and 5.7 is that long-run economic growth depends almost entirely on rising productivity. Good macroeconomic policy, including the policies discussed in previous Modules and the supply-side fiscal policies presented next, strives to foster increases in productivity, which in turn leads to long-run economic growth.

Supply-Side Fiscal Policies and Economic Growth

Supply-side fiscal policies are government policies that seek to promote economic growth by affecting short-run and long-run aggregate supply.

As we have seen, the government can implement fiscal policies to affect the economy by shifting the aggregate demand curve. It can also affect the economy and promote economic growth by shifting the short- and long-run aggregate supply curves. Policies to promote economic growth by affecting the *SRAS* and *LRAS* curves are called **supply-side fiscal policies**. These policies can affect aggregate demand, aggregate supply, and potential output in the short run and long run, as shown in **Figure 5.7-3**.

FIGURE 5.7-3 The Effects of Supply-Side Policy

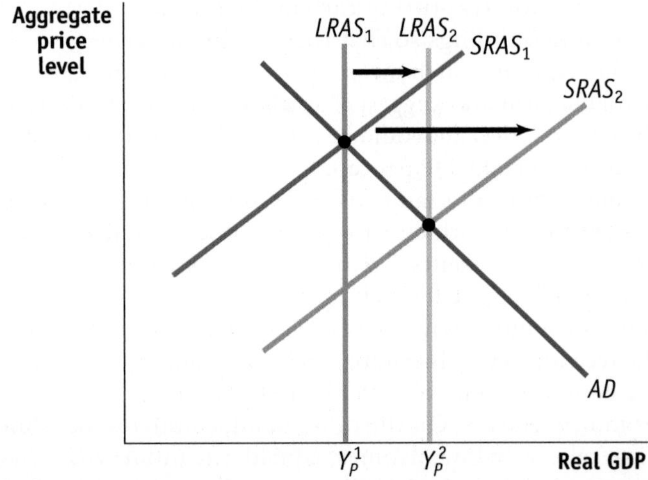

Government policies that incentivize households and firms to save and invest can increase potential output and create economic growth, shifting both the *SRAS* curve and the *LRAS* curve to a new short-run equilibrium to the right.

Supply-side policies can be divided into two categories: policies that promote productivity in private markets and policies that increase public investment in infrastructure that increases productivity. Supply-side policies aimed at private markets include increasing investment in physical capital, for example, through income tax reductions, investment tax credits, and reductions in regulations. These policies create incentives that affect household and business economic behavior resulting in increased private investment, output, and productivity. Examples of public investment in productivity include spending on education, transportation, and communication networks. Spending on education and infrastructure in the economy increases total factor productivity. These two types of policies have in common a goal of shifting the short-run and long-run supply curves to the right by increasing productivity and potential output.

One potential issue faced by governments using supply-side fiscal policies to promote long-run economic growth is the effect these policies could have on their budget. All other things equal, reductions in tax rates and increases in government spending will move the government budget toward deficit. And, as we have learned, larger budget deficits have the potential to create crowding out and decrease economic growth.

Proponents of supply-side economics note that lower tax rates *could* actually lead to higher government revenue if those lower tax rates are applied to sufficiently high levels of income. That is, if all other things *are not* equal, the reduction in tax rates increases **incentives** for households to work and invest more. This idea can be shown using a Laffer curve, a hypothetical relationship between tax rates and total tax revenue that slopes upward at low tax rates (meaning higher taxes bring higher tax revenues) but turns downward when tax rates are very high (meaning at some point, higher taxes bring lower tax revenues). **Figure 5.7-4** illustrates the Laffer curve.

An **incentive** is a reward or punishment that motivates particular choices. Incentives in supply-side policy are motivation for household and business to work, save, and invest.

FIGURE 5.7-4 The Laffer Curve

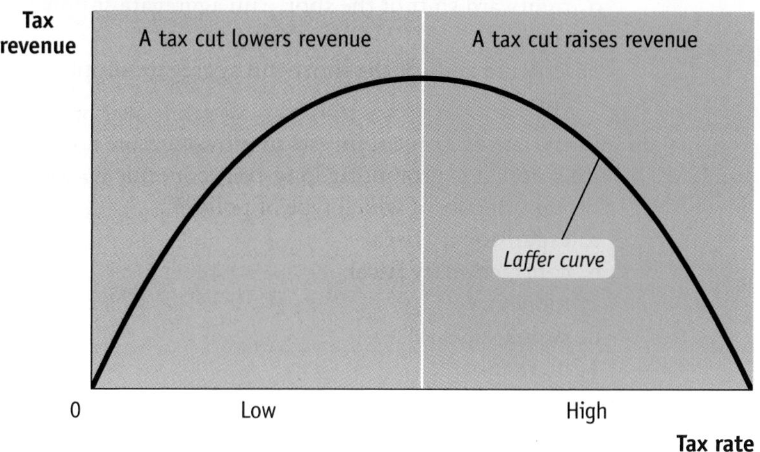

In the pink area on the left, the Laffer curve slopes upward, meaning higher taxes bring higher tax revenues when tax rates are low. In the green area to the right, the Laffer curve turns downward, meaning higher taxes bring lower tax revenues when tax rates are too high. The effect of a decrease in taxes on tax revenues depends on whether the tax rate is to the left or right of the peak of the curve, where the pink and green areas meet.

While almost all economists agree that tax cuts increase the incentives to work, save, and invest, they do not agree that tax cuts will lead to higher tax revenues or sharply higher potential output. That is, it is not clear that tax rates are in the green range of the Laffer curve in most or all countries. What is clear is that supply-side fiscal policies have the potential to shift both the short-run and long-run aggregate supply curves, which would lead to long-run economic growth as illustrated by an increase in potential output in the *AD–AS* model.

Long-run economic growth, as measured by real GDP per capita over time, is a measure of an economy's standard of living. Over time, real GDP per capita tends to increase. However, government policies that invest in infrastructure and technology, increase labor force participation, and provide incentives for households and businesses to work, save, and invest have the effect of promoting long-run growth to increase living standards.

In the next, and final, Unit we will finally consider the international sector in detail and expand our model to allow for an open economy.

Module 5.7 Review

Adventures in AP® Economics

Watch the video:
Economic Growth

Check Your Understanding

1. Explain how governments can promote long-run economic growth through policies that effect physical capital, labor resources, technology, and a country's political climate.

2. What are supply-side policies, and how do they promote long-run economic growth?

Tackle the AP® Test: Multiple-Choice Questions

1. Economies experience more rapid economic growth when they do which of the following?
   - **a.** invest in infrastructure
   - **b.** limit human capital
   - **c.** increase government spending
   - **d.** eliminate public health programs
   - **e.** raise taxes

2. Which of the following can lead to increases in physical capital in an economy?
   - **a.** increased investment spending
   - **b.** increased savings by domestic households
   - **c.** increased savings from foreign households
   - **d.** an inflow of foreign capital
   - **e.** all of the above

3. Which of the following is an example of a government infrastructure investment?
   - **a.** roads
   - **b.** power lines
   - **c.** ports
   - **d.** information networks
   - **e.** all of the above

4. Which of the following will shift the production possibilities curve outward?
   - **a.** technological progress
   - **b.** an increase in the production of consumer goods
   - **c.** a decrease in available labor resources
   - **d.** depreciation of capital
   - **e.** all of the above

5. In the aggregate demand–aggregate supply model, long-run economic growth is shown by a
   - **a.** leftward shift of the aggregate demand curve.
   - **b.** rightward shift of the aggregate demand curve.
   - **c.** rightward shift of the long-run aggregate supply curve.
   - **d.** rightward shift of the short-run aggregate supply curve.
   - **e.** leftward shift of the short-run aggregate supply curve.

6. When the government invests in infrastructure and education, it is promoting long-run economic growth through the use of which type of policy?
   - **a.** expansionary fiscal
   - **b.** contractionary fiscal
   - **c.** monetary
   - **d.** supply-side
   - **e.** market-based

7. Supply-side policies include which of the following?
   - **a.** investment tax credits
   - **b.** decreased income taxes
   - **c.** deregulation
   - **d.** promotion of political stability
   - **e.** all of the above

Tackle the AP® Test: Free-Response Questions

1. List and explain five different actions the government can take to promote long-run economic growth.

Rubric for FRQ 1 (10 points)

A maximum of 10 points can be earned for any five of the possible actions/descriptions.

1 point: Build infrastructure

1 point: The government can provide roads, power lines, ports, rail lines, and related systems to support economic activity.

1 point: Invest in human capital

1 point: The government can improve access to quality education.

1 point: Invest in research and development

1 point: The government can promote technological progress by having government agencies support and participate in R&D.

1 point: Provide political stability

1 point: The government can create and maintain institutions that make and enforce laws that promote stability.

1 point: Establish and protect property rights

1 point: Growth is promoted by laws that define what property belongs to whom and by institutions that defend those property rights.

1 point: Minimize government intervention

1 point: The government can limit its intervention in the economy and promote competition.

1 point: Use supply-side policies

1 point: e.g. implement tax credits, tax decreases, or deregulation to increase incentives to work, save, and invest, in order to shift the *LRAS*

2. Long-run economic growth over time contributes to an increase in a country's standard of living.
   a. How is long-run economic growth measured?
   b. Draw a separate, correctly labeled aggregate demand and supply graph to show each of the following situations. On each of your graphs, include the relevant short-run aggregate supply curve(s), long-run aggregate supply curve(s), and aggregate demand curve(s).
      i. Expansionary fiscal policy moves the economy out of a recession.
      ii. Investment in infrastructure by the government leads to long-run economic growth.
      iii. Investment tax credits lead to an increase in the stock of physical capital

   (10 points)

Review

Adventures in AP® Economics Videos

Mod 5.2: The Phillips Curve
Mods 5.6 and 5.7: Economic Growth

UNIT 5 Review Video

economics by example
Will Technology Put Everyone Out of Work?

Module 5.1

1. Combinations of monetary and fiscal policies may be used to restore full employment in the economy in the event of recessionary and inflationary gaps. Long-run consequences of monetary and fiscal policy result from changes in the government budget and money supply. In the long run, changes in the money supply affect the aggregate price level but not real GDP or the interest rate. Data show that the concept of *monetary neutrality* holds: changes in the money supply have no real effect on the economy in the long run.

Module 5.2

2. At a given point in time, there is a negative relationship between unemployment and inflation known as the **short-run Phillips curve**. The economy moves along the *SRPC* when the economy moves away from full employment. The *SRPC* curve is shifted by supply shocks and changes in the expected rate of inflation. The **long-run Phillips curve**, which shows the relationship between unemployment and inflation once expectations have had time to adjust, is vertical at the natural rate of unemployment. Equilibrium is found where the long-run Phillips curve and the short-run Phillips curve intersect.

Module 5.3

3. Increasing the money supply too rapidly for a sustained period of time results in inflation and decreasing it results in deflation. In the long-run, changes in the money supply have no effect on real output—money is neutral.
4. The **Quantity Theory of Money** says that $MV = PY$, where M is the money supply, V is the **velocity of money**, and PY is nominal GDP. Changes in the money supply affect the price level and inflation in the economy.

Module 5.4

5. Annual **budget deficits**, minus **budget surpluses**, accumulate into **government debt**. The government must pay interest on its accumulated debt. Persistent budget deficits have long-run consequences because they lead to an increase in public debt. This can be a problem for two reasons. Public debt may cause *crowding out* of investment spending, which may lead to a decrease in long-run economic growth. And in extreme cases, rising debt may lead to government default, resulting in economic and financial turmoil.

Module 5.5

6. When a government runs a budget deficit, it generally borrows to finance its spending. A government's debt must be managed by a government agency. Government debt financing can crowd out private investment. **Crowding out** occurs when government borrowing leads to an increase in the demand for loanable funds that increases real interest rates. Higher interest rates lead to decreased levels of interest-sensitive private spending (consumption or investment) in the short run. Crowding out can lead to lower rates of physical capital accumulation and less economic growth in the long run.

Module 5.6

7. Economic growth is a sustained increase in the productive capacity of an economy and can be measured as changes in real GDP per capita. This measurement eliminates the effects of changes in both the price level and population size. Growth rates of real GDP per capita vary widely. According to the *Rule of 70*, the number of years it takes for real GDP per capita to double is equal to 70 divided by the annual growth rate of real GDP per capita.
8. The key to long-run economic growth is rising **labor productivity**, also referred to as simply **productivity**, which is output per worker. Increases in productivity arise from increases in **physical capital** per worker and **human capital** per worker as well as advances in **technology**.
9. The **aggregate production function** shows how real GDP per worker depends on physical capital per worker, human capital per worker, and technology. Other things equal, there are **diminishing returns to physical capital**: holding human capital per worker and technology fixed, each successive addition to physical capital per worker yields a smaller increase in productivity than the one before. Similarly, there are diminishing returns to human capital among other inputs.
10. Economic growth is shown as an outward shift of a country's *PPC* or a rightward shift of its *LRAS* curve.

Module 5.7

11. The large differences in countries' growth rates are largely due to differences in their rates of accumulation of physical and human capital, as well as differences in technological progress. Government actions that contribute to growth include investment in **infrastructure**, particularly for transportation and public health; the creation and regulation of a well-functioning banking system that channels savings into investment spending; and the financing of both education and R&D. Government actions that slow growth are corruption, political instability, excessive government intervention, and the neglect or violation of property rights.
12. **Supply-side fiscal policy**, which seeks to incentivize investment and saving and spur economic growth, has the potential to create long-run economic growth by shifting the *SRAS* and *LRAS* curves. Supply-side public policies affect household and business behavior, for example through tax incentives. The *Laffer curve* illustrates the effect of tax decreases on tax revenues.

Key Terms

Short-run Phillips curve (*SRPC*), p. 271
Long-run Phillips curve (*LRPC*), p. 276
Quantity Theory of Money, p. 284
Velocity of money, p. 284
Budget surplus, p. 287
Budget deficit, p. 287
Government debt, p. 290
Debt–GDP ratio, p. 292
Crowding out, p. 297
Labor productivity (productivity), p. 304
Physical capital, p. 305
Human capital, p. 305
Technology, p. 305
Aggregate production function, p. 306
Diminishing returns to physical capital, p. 306
Depreciation, p. 310
Infrastructure, p. 316
Supply-side fiscal policies, p. 320
Incentive, p. 321

AP® Exam Practice Questions

Multiple-Choice Questions

1. The cyclically adjusted budget deficit adjusts the actual budget deficit for the effect of
   - **a.** discretionary fiscal policy.
   - **b.** discretionary monetary policy.
   - **c.** inflation.
   - **d.** transfer payments.
   - **e.** the business cycle.
2. The public debt increases when
   - **a.** the government collects more in taxes than it spends.
   - **b.** the government runs a budget deficit.
   - **c.** taxes exceed transfer payments.
   - **d.** the budget balance is positive.
   - **e.** individuals borrow for goods like houses and cars.

3. Which of the following is a potential problem with persistent increases in government debt?
   a. Government borrowing may crowd out private investment.
   b. Government debt is caused by budget deficits, which are always bad for the economy.
   c. It will always lead the government to default.
   d. It creates inflation because the government has to print money to pay it off.
   e. It causes automatic stabilizers to raise taxes in the future.

4. An increase in the money supply will generate which of the following?
   a. a negative short-run effect on real GDP
   b. an increase in real GDP in the long run
   c. a decrease in real GDP in the long run
   d. a decrease in the aggregate price level in the long run
   e. an increase in the aggregate price level in the short run and the long run

5. According to the concept of monetary neutrality, changes in the money supply will affect which of the following in the long run?
   a. only real values
   b. the aggregate price level
   c. employment
   d. aggregate output
   e. aggregate demand

6. The short-run Phillips curve shows the relationship between the inflation rate and the
   a. GDP growth rate.
   b. unemployment rate.
   c. employment rate.
   d. real interest rate.
   e. nominal interest rate.

7. An increase in expected inflation has what effect on the short-run Phillips curve?
   a. a movement up and to the left along the curve
   b. a movement down and to the right along the curve
   c. an upward shift of the curve
   d. a downward shift of the curve
   e. an increase in the slope of the curve

8. The long-run Phillips curve is
   a. horizontal.
   b. vertical.
   c. upward-sloping.
   d. downward-sloping.
   e. U-shaped.

9. The long-run Phillips curve illustrates which of the following?
   a. a positive relationship between unemployment and inflation
   b. a negative relationship between unemployment and inflation
   c. that unemployment will always return to the natural rate
   d. that unemployment will adjust so that the economy experiences 2% inflation
   e. that output will adjust so that there is no unemployment or inflation in the long run

10. According to the Quantity Theory of Money,
   a. the money supply times velocity is equal to nominal GDP.
   b. velocity varies significantly with the business cycle.
   c. changes in the money supply have no long-run effect on the economy.
   d. activist monetary policy is necessary to promote economic growth.
   e. monetary policy rules promote business-cycle fluctuations.

11. Which of the following measures the number of times the average dollar bill is spent per year?
   a. the natural rate of unemployment
   b. the inflation tax
   c. the unit of account
   d. the velocity of money
   e. $(M + P)/Y$

12. Which of the following equations represents the Quantity Theory of Money?
   a. $M \times V = P \times Y$
   b. $M \times V =$ real GDP
   c. $M \times V =$ full employment GDP
   d. $M \times P = V \times Y$
   e. $Y/M = V$

13. What is the most important determinant of long-run economic growth?
   a. increased labor productivity
   b. increased population
   c. low price level
   d. expansionary monetary and fiscal policies
   e. deficit spending

14. Which of the following is a major reason for productivity growth?
   a. financial investment
   b. an increase in aggregate demand
   c. a decrease in the amount of capital available
   d. an increase in the price of capital
   e. technological progress

Refer to the following figure for Questions 15 and 16.

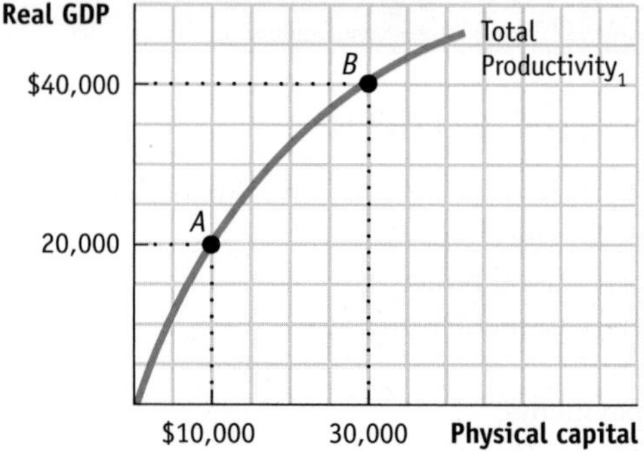

15. Assuming diminishing returns to physical capital, if physical capital per worker is $50,000, real GDP per worker will most likely equal which of the following?
- **a.** more than $60,000
- **b.** $60,000
- **c.** less than $60,000 but greater than $40,000
- **d.** $40,000
- **e.** $0

16. An upward shift of the curve could be caused by which of the following?
- **a.** an increase in real GDP per worker
- **b.** investment in physical capital
- **c.** diminishing returns to physical capital
- **d.** increases in population
- **e.** rising total factor productivity

17. When the government spends money to create and implement new technologies, it has invested in
- **a.** human capital.
- **b.** physical capital.
- **c.** infrastructure.
- **d.** research and development.
- **e.** political stability.

18. An outward shift of the production possibilities curve indicates which of the following?
- **a.** a decrease in cyclical unemployment
- **b.** long-run economic growth
- **c.** a reduction in productive resources
- **d.** a decrease in opportunity cost
- **e.** a decrease in potential output and the natural rate of unemployment

19. In the aggregate demand and supply model, a rightward shift of the *LRAS* curve indicates which of the following?
- **a.** long-run economic growth
- **b.** an increase in unemployment
- **c.** a decrease in real GDP
- **d.** an increase in the aggregate price level
- **e.** an economic recovery

20. Which of the following will lead to long-run economic growth?
- **a.** a decrease in nominal wages
- **b.** a decrease in the aggregate price level
- **c.** an increase in the production of consumer goods
- **d.** an increase in total factor productivity
- **e.** actual output that exceeds potential output

21. The government can promote long-run economic growth by
- **a.** increasing education subsidies.
- **b.** increasing Social Security funding.
- **c.** decreasing unemployment compensation.
- **d.** increasing military spending.
- **e.** cutting taxes.

Use the following graph to answer Question 22.

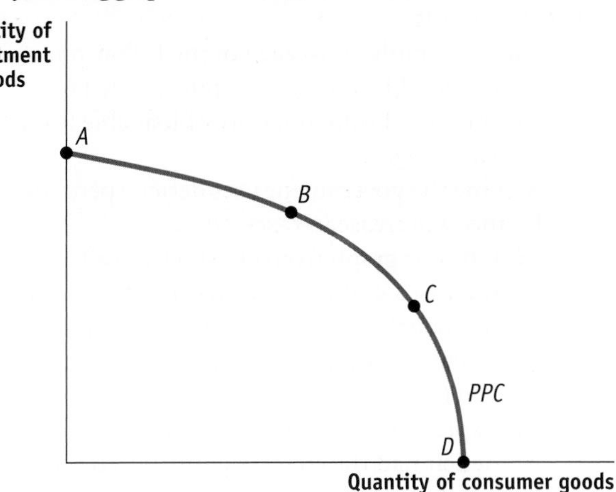

22. Which point on the graph will result in the least long-run growth?
- **a.** *A*
- **b.** *B*
- **c.** *C*
- **d.** *D*
- **e.** cannot be determined

23. Crowding out leads to which of the following?
- **a.** increased demand for loanable funds
- **b.** increased real interest rates
- **c.** decreased interest-sensitive spending
- **d.** lower rates of physical capital accumulation
- **e.** all of the above

24. Which of the following is a supply-side policy?
- **a.** decreasing incentives for saving and investing
- **b.** increasing tax rates
- **c.** reducing infrastructure investment
- **d.** providing investment tax credits
- **e.** all of the above

25. Supply-side fiscal policies have which of the following effects?
- **a.** decreasing *SRAS*
- **b.** shifting the *LRAS* to the right
- **c.** decreasing potential output
- **d.** decreasing aggregate demand
- **e.** increasing the money supply

Free-Response Questions

1. Draw a correctly labeled graph showing a short-run Phillips curve.
- **a.** On your graph, show a long-run Phillips curve and label each of the following
  - **i.** the natural rate of unemployment
  - **ii.** the equilibrium inflation rate
- **b.** On your graph, show the effect of an increase in the expected inflation rate. **(5 points)**

2. Draw a correctly labeled graph of the market for loanable funds.
   a. On your graph, show each of the following:
      i. the equilibrium interest rate, labeled r_1
      ii. the equilibrium quantity of loanable funds, labeled Q_1
   b. Assume the government uses deficit spending to finance a decrease in taxes.
      i. On your graph from (a), show the effect of the increased government deficit in the market for loanable funds. Label the new equilibrium interest rate and quantity of loanable funds r_2 and Q_2.
      ii. Explain why the increase in the government deficit had the effect you illustrated on your graph.

   (5 points)

3. Draw a correctly labeled aggregate supply and demand graph showing an economy in long-run equilibrium.
   a. Label each of the following on your graph:
      i. equilibrium price level, *PL*
      ii. equilibrium output level, *Y*
      iii. *LRAS*
   b. Assume the government invests in infrastructure and implements new investment tax credits.
      i. Explain how these policies will affect business and household behavior.
      ii. Show the short-run effect of these policies on your graph.
   c. Assume the government policies lead to long-run economic growth. Show a new long-run equilibrium on your graph from part a. **(10 points)**

UNIT 6
MACRO

International Trade and Finance

AP® Economic Skills

1. Principles and Models (1.A, 1.C)
3. Manipulation (3.A, 3.B)
4. Graphing and Visuals (4.A, 4.C)

How Much for Two All-Beef Patties, Special Sauce, Lettuce, Cheese, and So On. . .?

If you were in China in 2021, you could buy a Big Mac for approximately 22.40 yuan (¥). In Britain, a Big Mac would have cost an average of 3.49 pounds (£). In the United States you would pay around 5.65 dollars ($) for a Big Mac. But if you were in Beijing or London with only U.S. dollars, how much would you need in order to purchase one of the iconic burgers? You can figure this out using the theory of *purchasing power parity*—the idea that long-run exchange rates between their currencies will equalize the price of identical goods in two countries. Using the price of a Big Mac, the implied exchange rate between British pounds and U.S. dollars is 0.62 (3.49/5.65) pounds per dollar. You would need to exchange $5.65 for British pounds, yielding 5.65 × 0.62 = £3.50—enough to buy your burger in London. A Chinese visitor in London with a hankering for a Big Mac could join you by exchanging ¥22.40 for £3.58 at the implied exchange rate of £0.16 per ¥1 (22.40 × 0.16 = £3.58).

But at any point in time, the implied exchange rate can differ from the actual exchange rate. Actual exchange rates are determined in foreign exchange markets, not by purchasing power parity between two goods. The Big Mac index, an index that uses the price of Big Macs to calculate implied exchange rates, was created by *The Economist* magazine in 1986 as a "lighthearted guide to whether currencies are at their 'correct' level" with the goal of making exchange-rates "more digestible."

urbanbuzz/Alamy Stock Photo

In this final Macroeconomics Unit, we incorporate the international sector into our aggregate demand and aggregate supply model, allowing for an open economy. In this process, we will take a closer look at net exports, foreign exchange markets, and international capital flows.

MODULE 6.1

Balance of Payments Accounts

In this Module, you will learn to:

- Define the balance of trade, current account, capital and financial accounts, and balance of payments
- Explain how changes in the current account and capital and financial accounts effect a country's balance of payments
- Explain what it means when the current account (CA) or the capital and financial account (CFA) is not balanced—that is, when the CA or CFA is at a surplus or deficit
- Identify transactions that cause money flows into a country as credits to its balance of payments, and transactions that cause money flows out of a country as debits to its balance of payments
- Calculate a country's current account, capital and financial account, and balance of payments

Capital Flows and the Balance of Payments

In 2020, people living in the United States sold about $2.1 trillion worth of stuff to people living in other countries and bought about $2.8 trillion worth of stuff from other countries. What kind of stuff? All kinds. Residents of the United States sold airplanes, bonds, wheat, and many other items to residents of other countries. Residents of the United States bought cars, stocks, oil, and many other items from residents of other countries.

How can we keep track of these transactions? Earlier we learned that economists keep track of the domestic economy using the national income and product accounts. Economists keep track of international transactions using a different but related set of numbers, the *balance of payments accounts*.

Balance of Payments Accounts

Balance of payments (BOP) accounts are a summary of a country's transactions with other countries.

A country's **balance of payments (BOP) accounts** are a summary of the country's transactions with other countries.

To understand the basic idea behind the balance of payments accounts, let's consider a small-scale example: not a country, but a family farm. Let's say that we know the following about how last year went financially for the Costas, who own a small artichoke farm in California:

Andia/Alamy

- They made $100,000 by selling artichokes.
- They spent $70,000 on running the farm, including purchases of new farm machinery, and another $40,000 buying food, paying utility bills for their home, and replacing their worn-out car.
- They received $500 in interest on their bank account but paid $10,000 in interest on their mortgage.
- They took out a new $25,000 loan to help pay for farm improvements but didn't use all the money immediately. So they put the extra in the bank.

How could we summarize the Costas' year? One way would be with a table like **Table 6.1-1**, which shows sources of cash coming in and money going out, characterized under a few broad headings. Row 1 of Table 6.1-1 shows sales and purchases of goods and services: sales of artichokes; purchases of farm machinery, groceries, heating oil, a new car, and so on. Row 2 shows interest payments: the interest the Costas received from their bank account and the interest they paid on their mortgage. Row 3 shows cash coming in from new borrowing versus money deposited in the bank.

Table 6.1-1 The Costas' Financial Year

	Sources of cash	Uses of cash	Net
1. Sales and purchases of goods and services	Artichoke sales: $100,000	Farm operation and living expenses: $110,000	–$10,000
2. Interest payments	Interest received on bank account: $500	Interest paid on mortgage: $10,000	–$9,500
3. Loans and deposits	Funds received from new loan: $25,000	Funds deposited in bank: $5,500	+$19,500
Total	**$125,500**	**$125,500**	**$0**

In each row we show the net inflow of cash from that type of transaction. So the net in Row 1 is –$10,000 because the Costas spent $10,000 more than they earned. The net in Row 2 is –$9,500, the difference between the interest the Costas received on their bank account and the interest they paid on the mortgage. The net in Row 3 is $19,500: the Costas brought in $25,000 with their new loan but put only $5,500 of that sum in the bank.

The last row shows the sum of cash coming in from all sources and the sum of all cash used. These sums are equal, by definition: every dollar has a source, and every dollar received gets used somewhere. (What if the Costas hid money under the mattress? Then that would be counted as another "use" of cash.)

A country's balance of payments accounts summarize its transactions with the rest of the world using a table similar to the one we just used to summarize the Costas' financial year.

Table 6.1-2 shows a simplified version of the U.S. balance of payments accounts for 2020. Where the Costa family's accounts show sources and uses of cash, the balance of payments accounts show payments from foreigners – in effect, sources of cash for the United States as a whole – and payments to foreigners.

Table 6.1-2 The U.S. Balance of Payments in 2020 (billions of dollars)

	Payments from foreigners	Payments to foreigners	Net
1. Sales and purchases of goods and services	$2,134	$2,811	–$677
2. Factor income	957	769	188
3. Transfers	166	294	–128
Current account (1 + 2 + 3)			**–617**
4. Net increase in assets/Financial capital inflow	1,457	–	1,457
5. Net increase in liabilities/Financial capital outflow	–	809	809
Financial account (4 – 5)			**648**
Total (statistical discrepancy)	**–**	**–**	**–31**

Source: Bureau of Economic Analysis.

Marc Piasecki/Getty Images

Profits from Disneyland Paris count as Payments from Foreigners in the U.S. factor income accounting.

Row 1 of Table 6.1-2 shows payments that arise from sales and purchases of goods and services. For example, the value of U.S. wheat exports and the fees foreigners pay to U.S. consulting companies appear in the Payments from Foreigners column of row 1; the value of U.S. oil imports and the fees American companies pay to Indian call centers – the people who often answer your toll-free calls – appear in the Payments to Foreigners column of row 1.

Row 2 shows *factor income* – payments for the use of factors of production owned by residents of other countries. Mostly this means investment income: interest paid on loans from overseas, the profits of foreign-owned corporations, and so on. For example, the profits earned by Disneyland Paris, which is owned by the U.S.-based Walt Disney Company, appear in the Payments from Foreigners column of row 2; the profits earned by the U.S. operations of Japanese auto companies appear in the Payments to Foreigners column. Factor income also includes labor income. For example, the wages of an American engineer who works temporarily on a construction site in Dubai are counted in the Payments from Foreigners column of row 2.

AP® ECON TIP

The current account includes the balance of payments on goods and services and cash transfers. Make sure you can distinguish transactions counted in a country's current account from transactions counted in its capital and financial account.

Row 3 shows *international transfers* – funds sent by residents of one country to residents of another. The main element here is the remittances that immigrants, such as the millions of foreign-born workers employed in the United States, send to their families in their country of origin.

The next two rows of Table 6.1-2 show financial inflows from other countries into the United States and financial outflows from the United States into other countries. Because more capital flowed into the United States in 2020 than flowed out to other countries, the value for this category is positive.

In laying out Table 6.1-2, we have separated rows 1, 2, and 3 into one group (*current accounts*) and rows 4 and 5 into another (*financial accounts*). This separation reflects a fundamental difference in how these two groups of transactions affect the economy.

A country's *balance of payments on the current account*, or, **current account (CA)**, is its balance of payments on goods and services plus net international transfer payments and factor income.

A country's **balance of payments on goods and services** is the difference between the value of its exports and the value of its imports during a given period.

The **trade balance** is the difference between the value of a country's exports and imports; also referred to as a country's *net exports.*

A country's **financial account** is the difference between its sales of assets to foreigners and its purchases of assets from foreigners during a given period. A country's **capital account** measures transfers of assets not included in the financial account. The **capital and financial account (CFA)** includes both the financial and capital accounts and measures the status of a country as a net debtor or creditor to the rest of the world.

When a U.S. resident sells a good, such as wheat, to a foreigner, that's the end of the transaction. But a financial asset, such as a bond, is different. Remember, a bond is a promise to pay interest and principal in the future. So when a U.S. resident sells a bond to a foreigner, that sale creates a liability: the U.S. resident will have to pay interest and repay principal in the future. The balance of payments accounts distinguish between those transactions that don't create liabilities and those that do.

Transactions that don't create liabilities are considered part of the *balance of payments on the current account*, often referred to simply as the **current account**: the balance of payments on goods and services plus factor income and net international transfer payments. The balance of row 1 of Table 6.1-2, –$677 billion, corresponds to the most important part of the current account: the **balance of payments on goods and services**, the difference between the value of exports and the value of imports during a given period.

By the way, if you read news reports on the economy, you may see references to another measure, the **trade balance**. This is the difference between the value of a country's exports and imports. A country's *balance of trade* is also referred to as its *net exports.*

The current account, as we've just learned, consists of international transactions that don't create liabilities. Transactions that involve the sale or purchase of assets, and therefore do create future liabilities, are considered part of the *balance of payments on the financial account*, also referred to as simply the **financial account**. The financial account measures increases or decreases in international ownership of assets such as real estate, stocks, and bonds. A country's **capital account** records international capital transfers. The capital account measures transfers of assets not included in the financial account – for example, migrant payments, debt forgiveness, and the purchase or sale of natural resources. A positive **capital and financial account (CFA)** indicates that a country has more debits than credits, making it a net debtor to the world. Negative accounts make the country a net creditor.

So how does it all add up? The shaded rows of Table 6.1-2 show the bottom lines: the overall U.S. current account and financial account for the year. As you can see, in 2020, the United States ran a current account deficit: the amount it paid to foreigners for goods, services, factors, and transfers was greater than the amount it received. Simultaneously, it ran a financial account surplus: the value of the assets it sold to foreigners was greater than the value of the assets it bought from foreigners. A country can run either a deficit or a surplus in its current account. For example, in 2020 China ran a current account surplus equal to over 2 trillion yuan (about $310 billion) while simultaneously running a financial account deficit.

In the official data, the U.S. current account deficit and financial account surplus almost, but not quite, offset each other. But that's just due to statistical error reflecting the imperfection of official data. In fact, it's a basic rule of balance of payments accounting that the current account and the capital and financial account *must* sum to zero:

$$\textbf{(6.1-1)} \quad \text{Current account } (CA) + \text{Capital and Financial Account } (CFA) = 0$$

or

$$CA = -CFA$$

Why must Equation 6.1-1 be true? We already saw the fundamental explanation in Table 6.1-1, which showed the accounts of the Costas family: in total, the sources of cash must equal the uses of cash. The same applies to balance of payments accounts. **Figure 6.1-1**, a variant on the circular-flow diagram — first introduced in Module 2.1, and which we have found useful in discussing domestic macroeconomics — may help you visualize how this adding up works.

AP® ECON TIP

In other models, *capital* has always referred to goods that are used to produce other goods. When discussing the balance of payments, we use the term *financial capital* (investment funds). Keep in mind that *capital inflows* and *capital outflows* refer to *financial capital*, not physical capital.

AP® ECON TIP

Remember that the financial account tracks assets such as real estate, stocks, and bonds. You may be asked to identify transactions that affect a country's financial account on the AP® exam.

FIGURE 6.1-1 The Balance of Payments

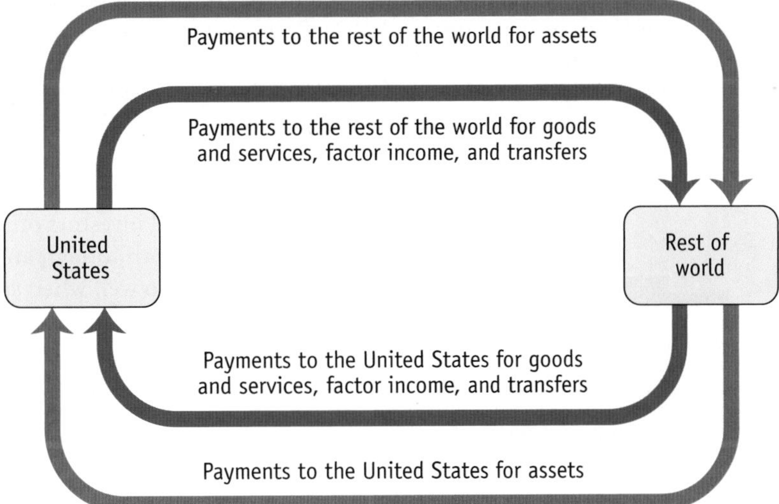

The green arrows represent payments that are counted in the current account. The red arrows represent payments that are counted in the capital and financial account. Because the total flow into the United States must equal the total flow out of the United States, the sum of the current account plus the capital and financial account is zero.

Instead of showing the flow of money *within* a national economy, Figure 6.1-1 shows the flow of money *between* national economies. Money flows into the United States from the rest of the world as payment for U.S. exports of goods and services, as payment for the use of U.S.-owned factors of production, and as transfer payments.

These flows (indicated by the lower green arrow) are the positive components of the U.S. current account. Money also flows into the United States from foreigners who purchase U.S. assets (as shown by the lower red arrow) – the positive component of the U.S. capital and financial account.

At the same time, money flows from the United States to the rest of the world as payment for U.S. imports of goods and services, as payment for the use of foreign-owned factors of production, and as transfer payments. These flows, indicated by the upper green arrow, are the negative components of the U.S. current account. Money also flows from the United States to purchase foreign assets, as shown by the upper red arrow – the negative component of the U.S. capital and financial account. As in all circular-flow diagrams, the flow into a box and the flow out of a box are equal. This means that the sum of the red and green arrows going into the United States is equal to the sum of the red and green arrows going out of the United States. In other words, the current account and the capital and financial account balance.

AP® ECON TIP

The current and capital and financial accounts must always balance. If there is a surplus in one account, there is a deficit in the other.

But what determines the current account and the capital and financial account?

Modeling the Capital and Financial Account

A country's capital and financial account measures its net sales of assets, such as currencies, securities, and factories, to foreigners. Those assets are exchanged for a type of capital called *financial capital*, which is funds from savings that are available for investment spending. So we can think of the capital and financial account as a measure of *capital inflows* in the form of foreign savings that become available to finance domestic investment spending. At the end of the third quarter of 2021, the difference between U.S. residents' foreign financial assets and liabilities was –$16.07 trillion.

In Module 6.6, we will use the loanable funds model, introduced in Module 4.7, to show how real interest rates determine the direction of *net* capital flows – the excess of inflows into a country over outflows, or vice versa. As we saw in Table 6.1-2, however, *gross* flows take place in both directions: for example, the United States both sells assets to foreigners and buys assets from foreigners. Why does capital move in both directions? One reason for international capital flows is that investors seek a higher rate of interest for their funds than can be found domestically, as will be discussed in Module 6.6. Another reason might be that individual investors often seek to diversify against risk by buying both foreign and domestic stocks. Stocks in Europe may do well when stocks in the United States do badly, or vice versa, so investors in Europe try to reduce their risk by buying some U.S. stocks, even as investors in the United States try to reduce their risk by buying some European stocks. The result is capital flows in both directions. Meanwhile, corporations often engage in international investment as part of their business strategy – for example, auto companies may find that they can compete better in a national market if they assemble some of their cars locally. Such business investments can also lead to two-way capital flows, as, say, European carmakers build plants in the United States even as U.S. computer companies open facilities in Europe.

REUTERS/Alamy Stock Photo

Ford Motor Company, like many other companies, has opened plants in South Africa – including this recently expanded assembly plant in Silverton, Pretoria – to take advantage of low labor costs and to gain better access to African and other international markets.

Finally, some countries, including the United States, are international banking centers: people from all over the world put money in U.S. financial institutions, which then invest many of those funds overseas.

Module 6.1 Review

Check Your Understanding

1. Explain why a country's current account balance plus its capital and financial account balance must equal zero.

2. Will financial capital flow into or out of a country that has higher interest rates? Explain.

Tackle the AP® Test: Multiple-Choice Questions

1. The current account includes which of the following?
   a. payments for goods and services, gross international transfer payments, and factor income
   b. payments for goods and services, net international transfer payments, and factor income
   c. sales of assets to foreigners minus purchases of assets from foreigners
   d. sales of assets to foreigners plus purchases of assets from foreigners
   e. payments for goods and services, net international transfers payments, and sales of assets to foreigners

2. The balance of payments on the current account plus the balance of payments on the capital and financial account is equal to
   a. zero.
   b. one.
   c. the trade balance.
   d. net capital flows.
   e. the size of the trade deficit.

3. Which of the following is true of the capital and financial account?
   a. It must equal zero.
   b. It measures net financial flows.
   c. It includes the value of imports and exports.
   d. Capital inflows are recorded as a debit.
   e. Capital outflows are recorded as a credit.

4. The trade balance includes which of the following?
   a. capital inflows
   b. capital outflows
   c. net capital flows
   d. imports minus exports
   e. exports minus imports

5. A transaction that causes money to flow into a country is considered a balance of payments
   a. credit.
   b. debit.
   c. asset.
   d. liability.
   e. surplus.

6. The financial account records which of the following?
   a. net income from abroad
   b. net exports
   c. net unilateral transfers
   d. purchase and sales of assets
   e. a country's balance of trade

7. If a country has a current account deficit, its capital and financial account will
   a. equal zero.
   b. also be in deficit.
   c. be in surplus.
   d. be negative.
   e. decrease.

Tackle the AP® Test: Free-Response Questions

1. **a.** How would a decrease in real income in the United States affect the U.S. current account balance? Explain.
   b. Explain how a country can have net capital inflows of $2 trillion and gross capital outflows of $4 trillion at the same time. What would the country's gross capital inflows equal in this case?

Rubric for FRQ 1 (4 points)

1 point: The current account balance would increase (or move toward a surplus).

1 point: The decrease in income would cause imports to decrease.

1 point: Net capital inflows are equal to gross capital inflows minus gross capital outflows. If gross capital inflows exceed gross capital outflows, the country will have positive net capital inflows.

1 point: Gross capital inflows would equal $6 trillion (6 – 4 = 2).

2. Explain which of the balance of payments accounts each of the following events affects.
   a. Boeing, a U.S.-based company, sells a newly built airplane to China.
   b. Chinese investors buy stock in Boeing from Americans.
   c. A Chinese company buys a used airplane from American Airlines and ships it to China.
   d. A Chinese investor who owns property in the United States buys a corporate jet, which he will keep in the United States so he can travel around America.
   (8 points)

MODULE 6.2

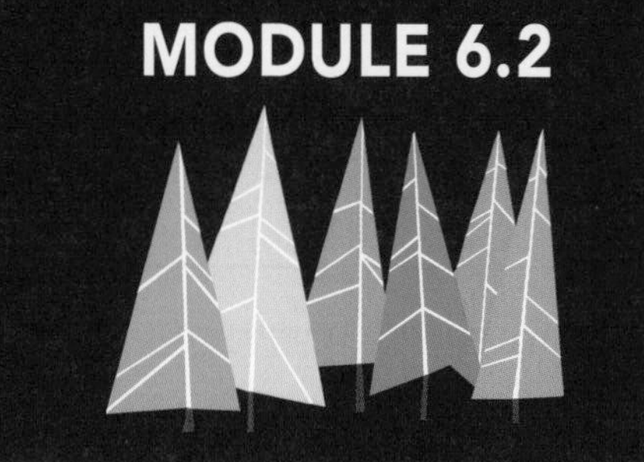

Exchange Rates

In this Module, you will learn to:

- Define the exchange rate, foreign exchange market, currency appreciation, and currency depreciation
- Explain how currencies are valued relative to one another
- Calculate the value of one currency relative to another
- Explain the concept of purchasing power parity
- Explain the difference between nominal and real exchange rates

We have just seen how spending on goods and services and investment in assets between countries affects international capital flows. We've also learned that a country's balance of payments on the current account plus its balance of payments on the capital and financial account add up to zero: a country that receives net capital inflows must run a matching current account deficit, and a country that generates net capital outflows must run a matching current account surplus.

The behavior of the capital and financial account – reflecting inflows or outflows of capital – is determined by demand and supply in international markets for financial capital. At the same time, the balance of payments on goods and services, the main component of the current account, is determined by decisions in the international markets for goods and services. Given that the capital and financial account reflects the movement of financial capital and the current account reflects the movement of goods and services, what ensures that the balance of payments really does balance? That is, what ensures that the two accounts actually offset each other?

The answer lies in the role of the *exchange rate*, which is determined in the *foreign exchange market.*

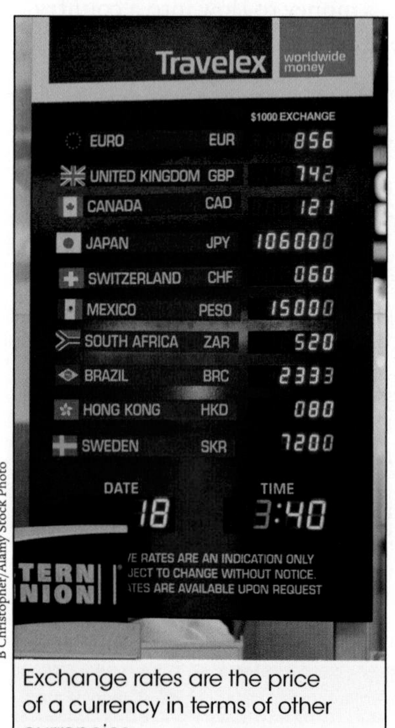

B Christopher/Alamy Stock Photo

Exchange rates are the price of a currency in terms of other currencies.

Understanding Exchange Rates

In general, goods, services, and assets produced in a country must be paid for in that country's currency. U.S. products must be paid for in U.S. dollars; most European products must be paid for in euros; Japanese products must be paid for in yen. Occasionally, sellers will accept payment in foreign currency, but they will then exchange that currency for domestic money.

International transactions, then, require a market – the **foreign exchange market** – in which currencies can be exchanged for each other. This market determines **exchange rates**, the prices at which currencies trade. (The foreign exchange market, in fact, is not located in any one geographic spot. Rather, it is a global electronic market that traders around the world use to buy and sell currencies.)

Currencies are traded in the **foreign exchange market**.

The prices at which currencies trade are known as **exchange rates**.

Table 6.2-1 shows exchange rates among three of the world's most important currencies in January 2022. Each entry shows the price of the "row" currency in terms of the "column" currency. For example, at that time, US$1 exchanged for €0.88, so it took €0.88 to buy US$1. Similarly, it took US$1.13 to buy €1. These two numbers reflect the same rate of exchange between the euro and the U.S. dollar: 1/1.13 = €0.88.

There are two ways to write any given exchange rate. In this case, there were €0.88 to US$1 and US$1.13 to €1. Which is the correct way to write it? The answer is that there is no fixed rule. In most countries, people tend to express the exchange rate as the price of a U.S. dollar in domestic currency. However, this rule isn't universal, and the U.S. dollar–euro rate is commonly quoted both ways. The important thing is to be sure you know which one you are using!

Table 6.2-1	Exchange Rates, January 2022		
	U.S. dollars	Yen	Euros
One U.S. dollar exchanged for	1	113.67	0.88
One yen exchanged for	0.009	1	0.008
One euro exchanged for	1.13	128.98	1

When discussing movements in exchange rates, economists use specialized terms to avoid confusion. When a currency becomes more valuable in terms of other currencies, economists say that the currency **appreciates**. When a currency becomes less valuable in terms of other currencies, it **depreciates**. Suppose, for example, that the value of €1 went from $1 to $1.25, which means that the value of US$1 went from €1 to €0.80 (because 1/1.25 = 0.80). In this case, we would say that the euro appreciated and the U.S. dollar depreciated.

Movements in exchange rates, other things equal, affect the relative prices of goods, services, and assets in different countries. Appreciation of a currency causes the country's net exports to decrease, and depreciation causes the country's net exports to increase. Suppose, for example, that the price of a hotel room in New York City is US$100 and the price of a hotel room in Paris is €100. If the exchange rate is €1 = US$1, these hotel rooms have the same price. If the exchange rate is €1.25 = US$1, however, the French hotel room is 20% cheaper than the American hotel room (because at this rate, €100 equals $80). If the exchange rate is €0.80 = US$1, the French hotel room is 25% more expensive than the American hotel room (because at this rate, €100 equals $125).

AP® ECON TIP

Be able to calculate the value of one currency relative to another and understand that when one currency depreciates, the other will appreciate. On the AP® exam, it is typical to label the exchange rate in terms of 1 unit of the domestic currency. For example, in the United States, the exchange rate will be expressed as the number of units of the other currency per U.S. dollar, or (Units of Foreign Currency/ U.S. dollars).

Gainers and Losers from Currency Depreciation

When the value of the U.S. dollar depreciates, then people who want to exchange it for another currency will need to spend more because the value of each dollar has decreased. For this reason, depreciation is said to *weaken* a currency. When one currency depreciates, another must appreciate. When the value of a currency appreciates, then people who want to exchange it for U.S. dollars can now buy U.S. dollars using less of their currency. Appreciation is said to *strengthen* a currency.

So who gains and who loses when a currency depreciates and, therefore, another currency appreciates? **Table 6.2-2** lists examples of people who gain and lose from depreciation of the U.S. dollar relative to the Mexican peso. Holders of U.S. dollars who need to exchange them for Mexican pesos will lose as a result of depreciation of the U.S. dollar, and holders of Mexican pesos who need to exchange them for U.S. dollars will gain as a result of depreciation of the U.S. dollar.

When a currency becomes more valuable in terms of other currencies, it **appreciates**.

When a currency becomes less valuable in terms of other currencies, it **depreciates**.

Table 6.2-2 Gainers and Losers from Depreciation of the U.S. Dollar

Losers *Holders of U.S. dollars (exchanging for pesos)*	Gainers *Holders of Mexican pesos (exchanging for U.S. dollars)*
U.S. tourists traveling to Mexico	Mexican tourists traveling to the U.S.
U.S. importers of Mexican goods	Mexican importers of U.S. goods
Mexican exporters to the U.S.	U.S. exporters to Mexico
U.S. investors who want to invest in Mexico	Mexican investors who want to invest in the U.S.

When traveling to Mexico, U.S. tourists need to exchange their U.S. dollars for Mexican pesos, but a depreciated U.S. dollar buys fewer pesos than it previously did. Conversely, Mexican tourists traveling to the United States have to exchange their pesos for U.S. dollars, and the appreciated peso will purchase more U.S. dollars. Therefore, U.S. tourists lose from depreciation of the U.S. dollar, while Mexican tourists gain.

Similarly, importers must have the currency of the other country to buy the goods they import. U.S. importers must exchange U.S. dollars for pesos in order to

Avigator Fortuner/Shutterstock

buy Mexican goods. Depreciated U.S. dollars will not buy as many pesos, and therefore the importer can't import as many goods. Mexican importers must trade their pesos for U.S. dollars in order to buy U.S. goods. The appreciated pesos will buy more U.S. dollars and therefore more U.S. goods. U.S. importers lose from depreciation, and Mexican importers gain.

On the other hand, Mexican exporters to the United States are paid for their exports in U.S. dollars, which they must exchange for pesos to spend in their country. When the U.S. dollar depreciates, Mexican exporters will receive fewer pesos for their exports. But U.S. exporters to Mexico are paid with stronger pesos, so they receive more U.S. dollars for their exports than they would have before depreciation. U.S. exporters gain from depreciation of the U.S. dollar, and Mexican exporters lose.

Finally, U.S. investors who want to invest in Mexico, for example if the interest rate in Mexico is higher than in the United States, must make their investments in pesos. A depreciated U.S. dollar will not buy as many of the pesos needed to make a financial investment in Mexico. But a Mexican investor can exchange an appreciated peso for more U.S. dollars for financial investment in the United States. Mexican investors in the United States gain from depreciation of the dollar, and U.S. investors in Mexico lose.

Any change in the exchange rate between two currencies will create winners and losers. But exchange rates can also affect the overall economy. Next, we consider exchange rates in the economy using two important concepts: purchasing power parity and the difference between nominal and real exchange rates.

Purchasing Power Parity

The **purchasing power parity** between two countries' currencies is the nominal exchange rate at which a given basket of goods and services would cost the same amount in each country.

A useful tool for analyzing exchange rates is known as *purchasing power parity*. The **purchasing power parity** between two countries' currencies is the nominal exchange rate at which a given basket of goods and services would cost the same amount in each country. For example, suppose that a basket of goods and services that costs \$100 in the United States costs 1,000 pesos in Mexico. Then the purchasing power parity is 10 pesos per U.S. dollar: at that exchange rate, 1,000 pesos = \$100, so the market basket costs the same amount in both countries.

Calculations of purchasing power parities are usually made by estimating the cost of buying broad market baskets containing many goods and services – everything from automobiles and groceries to housing and telephone calls. As we saw in the Unit introduction, once a year the magazine *The Economist* publishes their list of purchasing power parities based on the cost of buying a market basket that contains only one item – a McDonald's Big Mac.

Nominal exchange rates almost always differ from purchasing power parities. Some of these differences are systematic: in general, aggregate price levels are lower in low-income countries than in high-income countries because services tend to be cheaper in low-income countries. But even among countries at roughly the same level of economic development, nominal exchange rates vary quite a lot from purchasing power parity. **Figure 6.2-1** shows the nominal exchange rate between the Canadian dollar and the U.S. dollar, measured as the number of Canadian dollars per U.S. dollar, from 1990 to 2020, together with an estimate of the purchasing power parity exchange rate between the United States and Canada over the same period. The purchasing power parity didn't change much over this whole period because the United States and Canada had about the same rate of inflation. But at the beginning of the period, the nominal exchange rate was below purchasing power parity, so a given market basket was more expensive in Canada than in the United States. By 2002, the nominal exchange rate was far above the purchasing power parity, so a market basket was much cheaper in Canada than in the United States.

FIGURE 6.2-1 Purchasing Power Parity Versus the Nominal Exchange Rate, 1990–2020

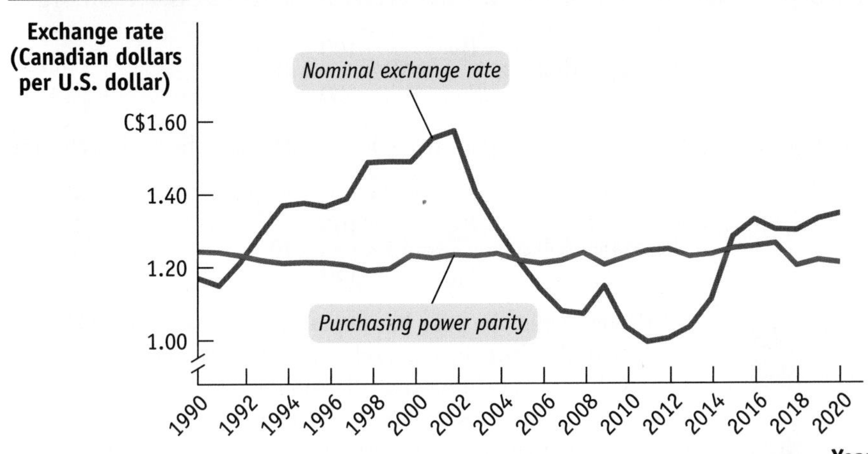

The purchasing power parity between the United States and Canada—the exchange rate at which a basket of goods and services would have cost the same amount in both countries—changed very little over the period shown, staying near CAD1.20 per US$1. But the nominal exchange rate fluctuated widely.
Data Source: OECD.

Over the long run, however, purchasing power parities are pretty good at predicting actual changes in nominal exchange rates. In particular, nominal exchange rates between countries at similar levels of economic development tend to fluctuate around levels that lead to similar costs for a given market basket. In fact, by July 2005, the nominal exchange rate between the United States and Canada was CAD1.22 per US$1—just about the purchasing power parity. In 2015, the nominal exchange rate was close to purchasing power parity, and the two values have remained close in the years since.

Inflation and Real Exchange Rates

In 1994, on average, one U.S. dollar exchanged for 3.4 Mexican pesos. By 2022, the peso had fallen against the dollar by about 83%, with an average exchange rate in early 2022 of 20.47 pesos per U.S. dollar. Did Mexican products also become much cheaper relative to U.S. products over that 28-year period? Did the price of Mexican products expressed in terms of U.S. dollars also fall by 83%? The answer to both questions is no, because Mexico had higher inflation than the United States over that period. Inflation in Mexico hit almost 35% in 1995 and remained significantly higher than inflation in the United States through 2014. In fact, the relative price of U.S. and Mexican products changed little between 1994 and 2014, although the exchange rate changed a lot.

To account for the effects of differences in inflation rates between countries, economists calculate **real exchange rates**, exchange rates adjusted for international differences in aggregate price levels. Suppose that the exchange rate we are looking at is the number of Mexican pesos per U.S. dollar. Let P_{US} and P_{Mex} be indexes of the aggregate price levels in the United States and Mexico, respectively. Then the real exchange rate between the Mexican peso and the U.S. dollar is defined as:

Real exchange rates are exchange rates adjusted for international differences in aggregate price levels.

$$\textbf{(6.2-1)}\quad \text{Real exchange rate} = \text{Mexican pesos per U.S. dollar} \times \frac{P_{US}}{P_{Mex}}$$

To distinguish it from the real exchange rate, the exchange rate *unadjusted* for aggregate price levels is sometimes called the *nominal* exchange rate.

To understand the significance of the difference between the real and nominal exchange rates, let's consider the following example. Suppose that the Mexican peso depreciates against the U.S. dollar, with the exchange rate going from 10 pesos per U.S. dollar to 15 pesos per U.S. dollar, a 50% change. But suppose that at the same time the price of everything in Mexico, measured in pesos, increases by 50%, so that the Mexican

AP® ECON TIP

As with the value of other real variables, the value of real exchange rates are equal to the nominal rate adjusted for changes in the price level.

price index rises from 100 to 150. We'll assume that there is no change in U.S. prices, so that the U.S. price index remains at 100. The initial real exchange rate is:

$$\text{Pesos per dollar} \times \frac{P_{US}}{P_{Mex}} = 10 \times \frac{100}{100} = 10$$

After the peso depreciates and the Mexican price level increases, the real exchange rate is:

$$\text{Pesos per dollar} \times \frac{P_{US}}{P_{Mex}} = 15 \times \frac{100}{150} = 10$$

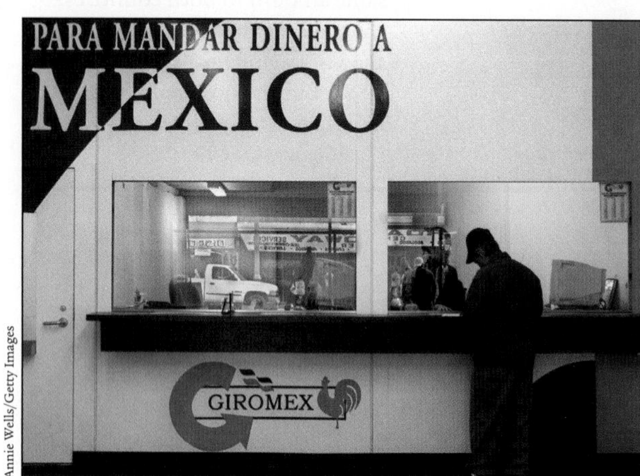

Mexican consumers can exchange their pesos for other currencies.

In this example, the peso has depreciated substantially in terms of the U.S. dollar, but the *real* exchange rate between the peso and the U.S. dollar hasn't changed at all. And because the real peso–U.S. dollar exchange rate hasn't changed, the nominal depreciation of the peso against the U.S. dollar will have no effect either on the quantity of goods and services exported by Mexico to the United States, or on the quantity of goods and services imported by Mexico from the United States. To see why, consider again the example of a hotel room. Suppose that this room initially costs 1,000 pesos per night, which is $100 at an exchange rate of 10 pesos per dollar. After both Mexican prices and the number of pesos per dollar rise by 50%, the hotel room costs 1,500 pesos per night—but 1,500 pesos divided by 15 pesos per dollar is $100, so the Mexican hotel room still costs $100. As a result, a U.S. tourist considering a trip to Mexico will have no reason to change plans.

The same is true for all goods and services that enter into trade: *the current account responds only to changes in the real exchange rate, not the nominal exchange rate.* A country's products become cheaper to foreigners only when that country's currency depreciates in real terms, and those products become more expensive to foreigners only when the currency appreciates in real terms. As a consequence, economists who analyze movements in exports and imports of goods and services focus on the real exchange rate, not the nominal exchange rate.

Figure 6.2-2 illustrates just how important it can be to distinguish between nominal and real exchange rates. Between 1990 and 2013, Mexico's aggregate price level increased relative to the United States' level while the peso depreciated. The line labeled "Nominal exchange rate" shows the number of pesos exchanged for a U.S. dollar from

FIGURE 6.2-2 Real Versus Nominal Exchange Rates, 1990–2013

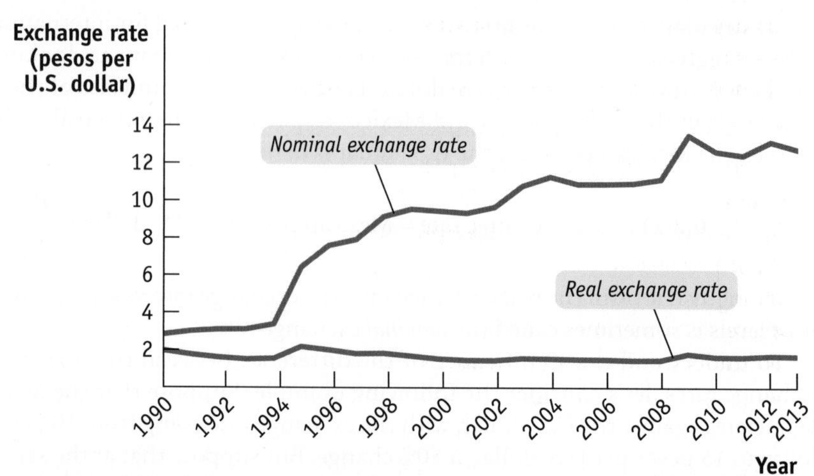

Between 1990 and 2013, the price of a dollar in Mexican pesos increased dramatically. But because Mexico had higher inflation than the United States, the real exchange rate, which accounts for the relative price of Mexican goods and services, ended up roughly where it started.
Data Source: OECD.

1990 to 2013. As you can see, the peso depreciated massively over that period. But the line labeled "Real exchange rate" indicates the cost of Mexican products to U.S. consumers: it was calculated using Equation 6.2-1, with price indexes for both Mexico and the United States set so that the value in 1990 was 100. In real terms, the peso depreciated in 1994 and 1995, and again in 2008, but not by nearly as much as the nominal depreciation. By 2013, the real peso–U.S. dollar exchange rate was just about back where it started.

Now that we understand exchange rates, we can look more closely in the next Module at how equilibrium exchange rates are determined in the foreign exchange market.

Watch the video: ***Exchange Rates***

Module 6.2 Review

Check Your Understanding

1. Suppose Mexico discovers huge reserves of oil and starts exporting oil to the United States. Describe how this event would affect the following:
   a. the nominal peso–U.S. dollar exchange rate
   b. Mexican exports of other goods and services
   c. Mexican imports of goods and services
2. Suppose a basket of goods and services costs $100 in the United States and costs 800 pesos in Mexico, and the current nominal exchange rate is 10 pesos per U.S. dollar. Over the next five years, the cost of that market basket rises to $120 in the United States and to 1,200 pesos in Mexico, although the nominal exchange rate remains at 10 pesos per U.S. dollar. Calculate the real exchange rate now and five years from now, if today's price index in both countries is 100. [Reminder: Equation 2.4-1 provides the price index formula: (Cost of market basket in a given year/Cost of market basket in base year) × 100. For this problem, use the current year as the base year.]

Tackle the AP® Test: Multiple-Choice Questions

1. When the U.S. dollar buys more Japanese yen, what has happened to the value of the U.S. dollar and the Japanese yen?

	USD	*Yen*
a.	appreciated	appreciated
b.	appreciated	depreciated
c.	depreciated	appreciated
d.	depreciated	depreciated
e.	depreciated	not changed

2. The nominal exchange rate at which a given basket of goods and services would cost the same in each country describes
   a. the international consumer price index.
   b. appreciation.
   c. depreciation.
   d. purchasing power parity.
   e. the balance of payments on the current account.
3. What happens to the real exchange rate between the euro and the U.S. dollar (expressed as euros per dollar) if the aggregate price levels in Europe and the United States both fall by the same amount?
   a. It is unaffected.
   b. It increases.
   c. It decreases.
   d. It may increase, decrease, or stay the same.
   e. It cannot be calculated.
4. Which of the following would cause the exchange rate between pesos and U.S. dollars (in terms of pesos per dollar) to decrease?
   a. an increase in net capital flows from Mexico to the United States
   b. an increase in the real interest rate in Mexico relative to the United States
   c. a doubling of prices in both Mexico and the United States
   d. a decrease in oil exports from Mexico to the United States
   e. an increase in the balance of payments on the current account in the United States

5. Which of the following groups will gain from depreciation of the domestic currency?
   a. travelers going to other countries
   b. tourists visiting from other countries
   c. importers
   d. workers
   e. investors in foreign countries
6. Which of the following groups will gain from appreciation of the domestic currency?
   a. tourists visiting from other countries
   b. exporters
   c. investors in foreign countries
   d. workers
   e. domestic investors
7. If the value of €1 went from US$1 to $0.80, then the value of $1 went from €1 to €__________, and the euro has __________.
   a. 1.25; depreciated
   b. 0.80; depreciated
   c. 0.80; appreciated
   d. 0.20; depreciated
   e. 0.20; appreciated

Tackle the AP® Test: Free-Response Questions

1. Give an example of 4 groups that have Korean Won (₩) and want U.S. dollars ($) and 4 groups that have U.S. dollars and want Korean Won.

Rubric for FRQ 1 (8 points)

1 point: Korean tourists traveling to the U.S.
1 point: Korean importers of U.S. goods
1 point: U.S. exporters to Korea
1 point: Korean investors who want to invest in the U.S.
1 point: U.S. tourists traveling to Korea
1 point: U.S. importers of Korean goods
1 point: Korean exporters to the U.S.
1 point: U.S. investors who want to invest in Korea

2. Assume that the price of a Canadian bicycle is CAD100, the price of a German bicycle is €100, and the nominal exchange rate is €1 = CAD1.
   a. In which country is the bicycle cheaper? Explain using the value of the exchange rate.
   b. If the exchange rate changes to €1.25 = CAD1, in which country is the bicycle cheaper? Explain using the value of the exchange rate. **(4 points)**

The Foreign Exchange Market

MODULE 6.3

In this Module, you will learn to:

- Explain the inverse relationship between the exchange rate and the quantity of currency demanded, and the positive relationship between the exchange rate and the quantity supplied
- Explain the relationship between the demand for a currency and the demand for a country's goods and services
- Understand that to make payments in another currency will increase the demand for the foreign currency and the supply of the domestic currency
- Draw a correctly labeled graph of the foreign exchange market indicating the equilibrium exchange rate and quantity of currency on the axes
- Use a correctly labeled graph of the foreign exchange market to explain how exchange rates adjust to restore equilibrium in the foreign exchange market
- Use a graph of the foreign exchange market to illustrate the effect of changes in demand or supply on the equilibrium exchange rate

Demand and Supply in the Foreign Exchange Market

For the sake of simplicity, imagine that there are only two currencies in the world: U.S. dollars and euros. Europeans who want to purchase American goods, services, and assets come to the foreign exchange market to exchange euros for U.S. dollars. That is, Europeans demand U.S. dollars from the foreign exchange market and, correspondingly, supply euros to that market. Americans who want to buy European goods, services, and assets come to the foreign exchange market to exchange U.S. dollars for euros. That is, Americans supply U.S. dollars to the foreign exchange market and, correspondingly, demand euros from that market. International transfers and payments of factor income also enter into the foreign exchange market, but to make things simple, we'll ignore these.

Through the foreign exchange market, U.S. consumers are matched to suppliers of Belgian chocolates.

Hemis/Alamy Stock Photo

Figure 6.3-1 shows how this foreign exchange market works. The quantity of dollars demanded and supplied at any given euro–U.S. dollar exchange rate is shown on the horizontal axis, and the euro–U.S. dollar exchange rate is shown on the vertical axis. The exchange rate plays the same role as the price of a good or service in an ordinary supply and demand diagram.

Equilibrium in the Foreign Exchange Market

Figure 6.3-1 shows two curves, the demand curve for U.S. dollars and the supply curve for U.S. dollars. The key to understanding the slopes of these curves is that the level of the exchange rate affects exports and imports. When a country's currency appreciates (becomes more valuable), exports fall and imports rise. When a country's currency depreciates (becomes less valuable), exports rise and imports fall. To understand why the demand curve for U.S. dollars slopes downward, recall that the

FIGURE 6.3-1 The Foreign Exchange Market

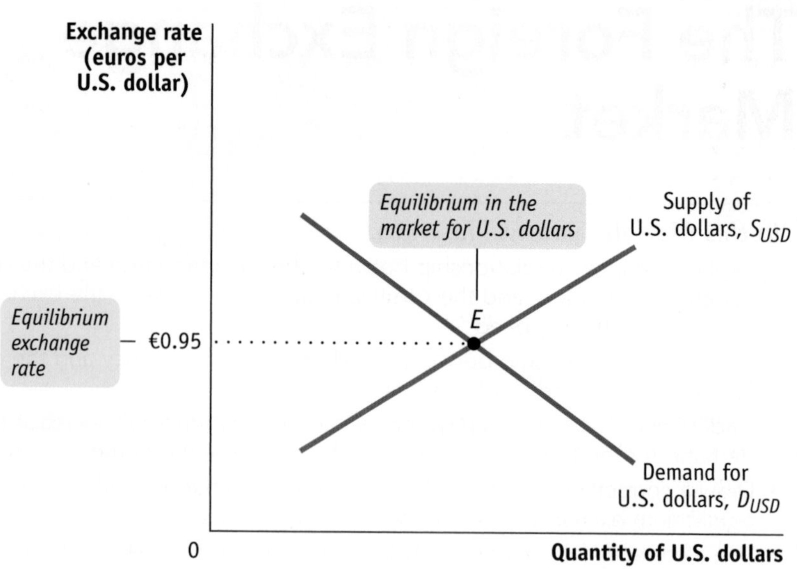

The foreign exchange market matches up the demand for a currency from foreigners who want to buy domestic goods, services, and assets with the supply of a currency from domestic residents who want to buy foreign goods, services, and financial assets. Here the equilibrium in the market for dollars is at point *E*, corresponding to an equilibrium exchange rate of €0.95 per US$1.

AP® ECON TIP

Graph changes in supply or demand in the foreign exchange market to identify their effect on the equilibrium exchange rate. Make sure you can correctly label the exchange rate on the vertical axis using the currencies of the two countries. The quantity on the horizontal axis will be the denominator of the label on the vertical axis. For example, in the graph of the foreign exchange market for British pounds, the quantity of pounds is on the horizontal axis and the vertical axis is labeled U.S. dollars/pound.

The **equilibrium exchange rate** is the exchange rate at which the quantity of a currency demanded in the foreign exchange market is equal to the quantity supplied.

exchange rate, other things equal, determines the prices of American goods, services, and assets relative to those of European goods, services, and assets. If the U.S. dollar rises against the euro (the dollar appreciates), American products will become more expensive to Europeans relative to European products. So Europeans will buy less from the United States and will acquire fewer dollars in the foreign exchange market: the quantity of U.S. dollars demanded falls as the number of euros needed to buy a U.S. dollar rises. If the U.S. dollar falls against the euro (the dollar depreciates), American products will become relatively cheaper for Europeans. Europeans will respond by buying more from the United States and acquiring more dollars in the foreign exchange market: the quantity of U.S. dollars demanded rises as the number of euros needed to buy a U.S. dollar falls.

A similar argument explains why the supply curve of U.S. dollars in Figure 6.3-1 slopes upward: the more euros required to buy a U.S. dollar, the more dollars Americans will supply. Again, the reason is the effect of the exchange rate on relative prices. If the U.S. dollar rises against the euro, European products look cheaper to Americans—who will demand more of them. This will require Americans to convert more dollars into euros.

The **equilibrium exchange rate** is the exchange rate at which the quantity of U.S. dollars demanded in the foreign exchange market is equal to the quantity of U.S. dollars supplied. In Figure 6.3-1, the equilibrium is at point *E*, and the equilibrium exchange rate is €0.95. That is, at an exchange rate of €0.95 per US$1, the quantity of U.S. dollars supplied to the foreign exchange market is equal to the quantity of U.S. dollars demanded.

To understand the significance of the equilibrium exchange rate, it's helpful to consider a numerical example of what equilibrium in the foreign exchange market looks like. Such an example is shown in **Table 6.3-1**. (This is a hypothetical table that isn't intended to match real numbers.) The first row shows European purchases of U.S. dollars, either to buy U.S. goods and services or to buy U.S. assets, such as real estate or shares of stock in U.S. companies. The second row shows U.S. sales of U.S. dollars, either to buy European goods and services or to buy European assets. At the equilibrium exchange rate, the total quantity of U.S. dollars Europeans want to buy is equal to the total quantity of U.S. dollars Americans want to sell.

Table 6.3-1 Equilibrium in the Foreign Exchange Market: A Hypothetical Example

European purchases of U.S. dollars (trillions of U.S. dollars) . . .	. . . to buy U.S. goods and services: 1.0	. . . to buy U.S. assets: 1.0	**Total purchases of U.S. dollars: 2.0**
U.S. sales of U.S. dollars (trillions of U.S. dollars) . . .	. . . to buy European goods and services: 1.5	. . . to buy European assets: 0.5	**Total sales of U.S. dollars: 2.0**
	U.S. balance of payments on the current account (*CA*): –0.5	**U.S. balance of payments on the capital and financial account (*CFA*): +0.5**	$CA + CFA = 0$

Remember that the balance of payments accounts divide international transactions into two types. Purchases and sales of goods and services are counted in the current account. (Again, we're leaving out transfers and factor income to keep things simple.) Purchases and sales of financial assets are counted in the capital and financial account. At the equilibrium exchange rate, then, we have the situation shown in Table 6.3-1: the sum of the balance of payments on the current account plus the balance of payments on the capital and financial account is zero.

Any shift of the supply or demand for a currency in a foreign exchange market will create a temporary disequilibrium, surplus, or shortage, before moving the market to a new equilibrium exchange rate. Consider the foreign exchange market shown in **Figure 6.3-2**. An increase in the demand for U.S. dollars from D_{USD} to D_{USD1} initially creates a shortage in the market for U.S. dollars equal to $(Q_1 - Q)$. The shortage causes the exchange rate to increase until the quantity of U.S. dollars demanded is equal to the quantity of U.S. dollars supplied at a new equilibrium exchange rate above €0.95 (XR_1). A decrease in the demand for U.S. dollars from D_{USD} to D_{USD2} initially creates a surplus of U.S. dollars equal to $(Q - Q_2)$. The surplus causes the exchange rate to decrease until the quantity of U.S. dollars demanded equals the quantity of U.S. dollars supplied at a new equilibrium exchange rate below €0.95 (XR_2).

FIGURE 6.3-2 Disequilibrium in the Foreign Exchange Market

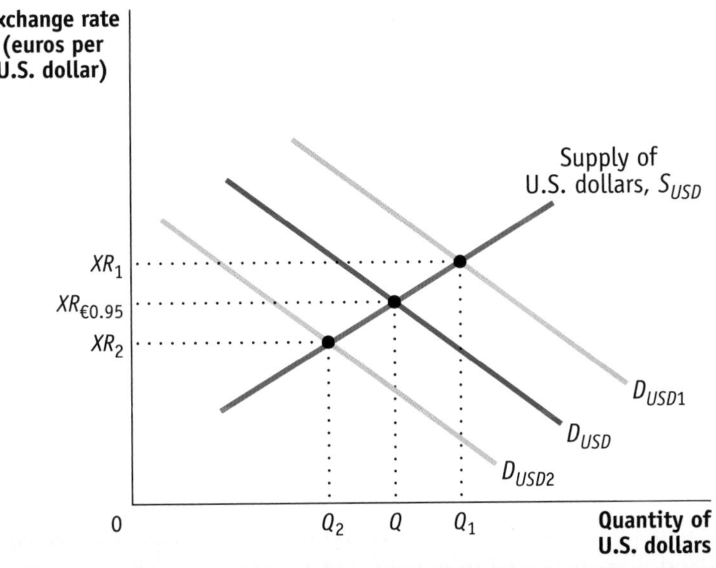

An increase in the demand for U.S. dollars, from D_{USD} to D_{USD1}, will initially lead to a shortage of U.S. dollars. The shortage will move the exchange rate back to equilibrium where D_{USD1} intersects the supply of U.S. dollars at a higher exchange rate. A decrease in the demand for U.S. dollars, from D_{USD} to D_{USD2}, will initially lead to a surplus of U.S. dollars. The surplus will move the exchange rate back to equilibrium, where D_{USD2} intersects the supply of U.S. dollars at a lower exchange rate.

> **AP® ECON TIP**
>
> You should be able to recognize how a change in the demand for goods, services, or financial assets can affect the demand for a currency. For example, changes in the relative price level, relative GDP, or relative attractiveness of investment opportunities, tourism, or speculation will affect demand in the foreign exchange market. Remember that when the demand for one currency changes, there will be a corresponding change in the supply of the other currency.

Shifts of Demand and Supply in the Foreign Exchange Market

Now let's consider how a shift in the demand for U.S. dollars affects equilibrium in the foreign exchange market for both currencies. Remember that a change in the demand for U.S. dollars corresponds to a change in the supply of another currency since other currencies are used to purchase U.S. dollars. For example, the demand for U.S. dollars could increase as a result of an increase in the international demand for U.S. goods, services, or financial assets. The effects of an increase in the demand for U.S. dollars is shown in panel (a) of **Figure 6.3-3**. Note that the increase in the demand for U.S. dollars corresponds to an increase in the supply of euros, shown in panel (b). The demand for U.S. dollars in the foreign exchange market increases as Europeans convert euros into dollars to fund their new purchases or investments in the United States. This effect is shown by the shift of the demand curve from D_{USD1} to D_{USD2}. As a result, the U.S. dollar appreciates: the number of euros per U.S. dollar at the equilibrium exchange rate rises from XR_1 to XR_2. In the market for euros, Europeans supply euros in exchange for U.S. dollars, shifting the supply of euros from S_{EUROS1} to S_{EUROS2}. As a result, the euro depreciates; the number of U.S. dollars per euro at the equilibrium exchange rate falls from XR_1 to XR_2.

FIGURE 6.3-3 An Increase in the Demand for U.S. Dollars

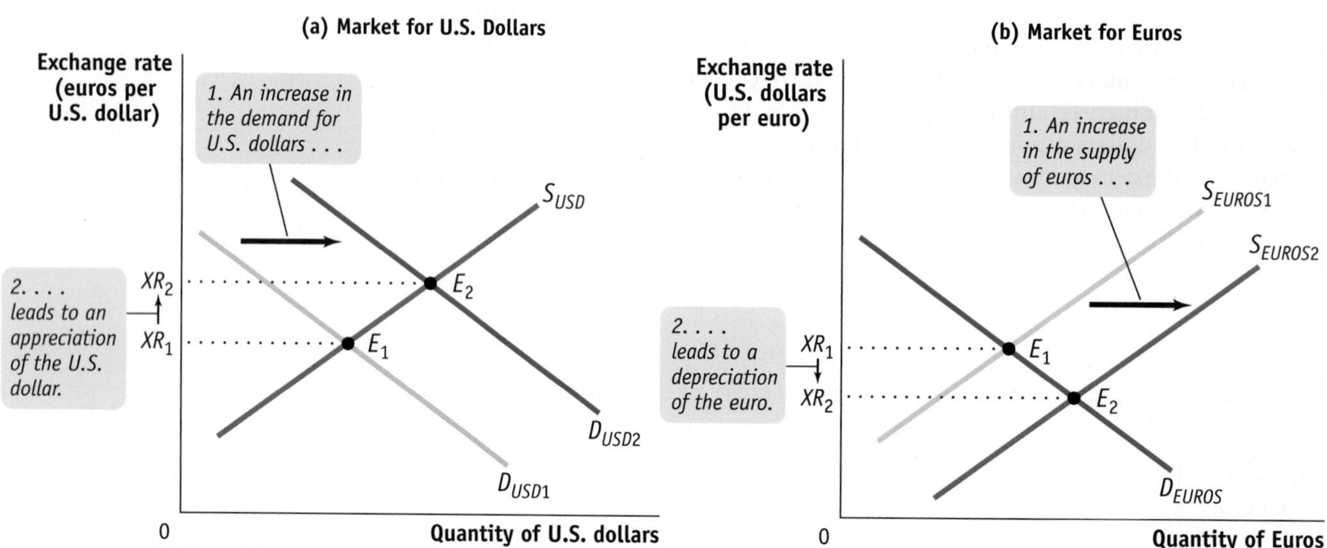

In panel (a), the demand curve for U.S. dollars shifts from D_{USD1} to D_{USD2}. So the equilibrium number of euros per U.S. dollar rises—the dollar *appreciates*. At the same time, the supply curve for euros shifts from S_{EUROS1} to S_{EUROS2}, as shown in panel (b). So the equilibrium number of U.S. dollars per euro falls—the euro *depreciates*.

Figure 6.3-3 illustrates the effect of a shift in demand for U.S. dollars, while **Figure 6.3-4** illustrates how a shift in the supply of U.S. dollars affects the equilibrium in the foreign exchange market. The supply of a currency in a foreign exchange market is the result of the need to make payments in other currencies. Remember that a change in the supply of U.S. dollars corresponds to a change in the demand for another currency. For example, assume the supply of U.S. dollars decreases because there are fewer payments being made in other currencies. The effects of a decrease in the supply of U.S. dollars is shown in panel (a) of Figure 6.3-4. The decrease in

FIGURE 6.3-4 A Decrease in the Supply of U.S. Dollars

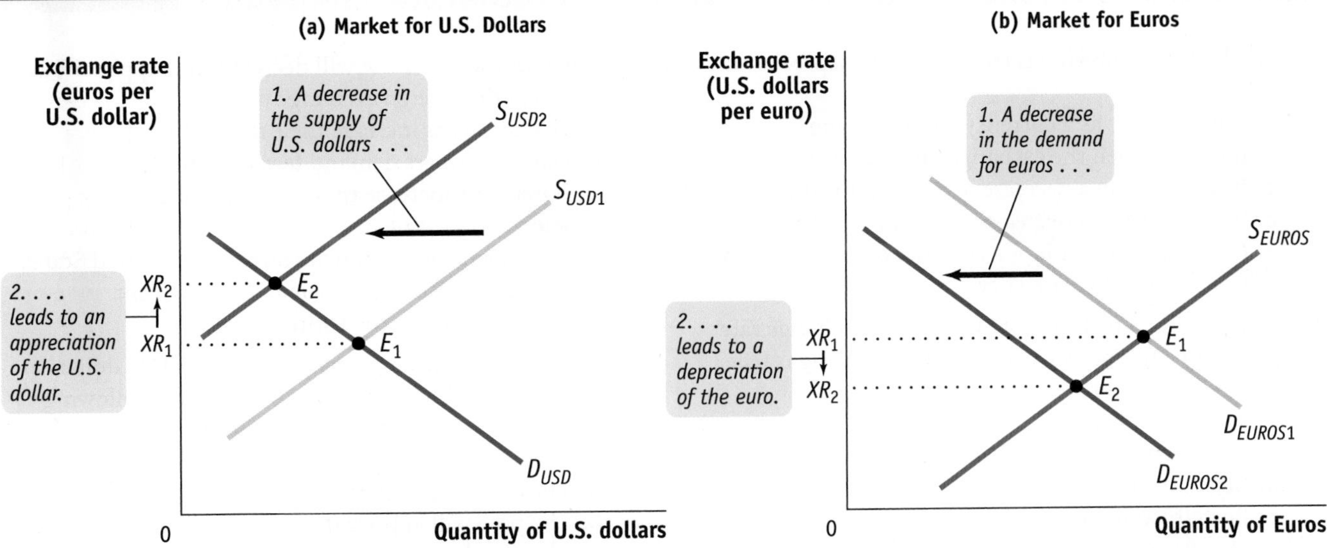

In panel (a), the supply curve for U.S. dollars shifts from S_{USD1} to S_{USD2}. So the equilibrium number of euros per U.S. dollar rises – the dollar *appreciates*. At the same time, the demand curve for euros shifts from D_{EUROS1} to D_{EUROS2}, as shown in panel (b). So the equilibrium number of U.S. dollars per euro falls – the euro *depreciates*.

the supply of U.S. dollars corresponds to a decrease in the demand for euros, shown in panel (b). This decrease is shown by the shift of the supply curve from S_{USD1} to S_{USD2} in panel (a). As a result, the U.S. dollar appreciates: the number of euros per U.S. dollar at the equilibrium exchange rate rises from XR_1 to XR_2. In the market for euros, shown in panel (b), Americans demand fewer euros in exchange for U.S. dollars, shifting the demand for euros from D_{EUROS1} to D_{EUROS2}. As a result, the euro depreciates; the number of U.S. dollars per euro at the equilibrium exchange rate falls from XR_1 to XR_2.

The demand for a country's goods, services, or financial assets will affect supply and demand in foreign exchange markets, increasing or decreasing the equilibrium exchange rate. In the next Modules, we look more closely at the determinants of currency demand and supply, how fiscal and monetary policy can also affect foreign exchange markets, and how those changes affect net exports and our *AD–AS* model. In Module 6.4, we focus on each of the factors that shift demand and supply in foreign exchange markets.

KrakenPlaces/Getty Images

Module 6.3 Review

Check Your Understanding

1. Explain how an increase in the exchange rate signifies depreciation of a currency and how a decrease in the exchange rate signifies appreciation of a currency.
2. Why do people demand and supply currency in foreign exchange markets?

Tackle the AP® Test: Multiple-Choice Questions

1. Which of the following is true regarding depreciation of a currency?
   a. It is the same as a currency strengthening.
   b. It occurs when the exchange rate increases.
   c. It results from a decrease in demand for the currency.
   d. It results from a decrease in the supply of a currency.
   e. It means that a unit of a currency exchanges for more units of another currency.
2. If the Brazilian real (BR) per U.S. dollar exchange rate goes from 5.00 to 5.50, which of the following is true?
   a. The Brazilian real has appreciated.
   b. The U.S. dollar has appreciated.
   c. The Brazilian real has depreciated.
   d. Both (a) and (b).
   e. Both (b) and (c).
3. A decrease in Australian interest rates relative to interest rates in other countries will lead to which of the following?
   a. an increase in the demand for the Australian dollar
   b. a decrease in the demand for the Australian dollar
   c. a decrease in the supply of Australian dollars
   d. an increase in exchange rates for the Australian dollar
   e. a decrease in the demand for other currencies
4. Which of the following will lead to an increase in the supply of Chinese yuan?
   a. an increase in the demand for Chinese goods
   b. an increase in the interest rate in China relative to other countries
   c. an increase in the exchange rate
   d. an increase in the demand for Chinese financial assets
   e. an increase in China's demand for foreign imports
5. Which of the following will decrease the supply of U.S. dollars in the foreign exchange market?
   a. U.S. residents increase their travel abroad.
   b. U.S. consumers demand fewer imports.
   c. Foreigners increase their demand for U.S. goods.
   d. Foreigners increase their travel to the United States.
   e. Foreign investors see increased investment opportunities in the United States.
6. In the foreign exchange market in which U.S. dollars are exchanged for Mexican pesos, which of the following will occur when the demand for the U.S. dollar increases?
   a. The dollar will depreciate.
   b. The peso will appreciate.
   c. The supply of pesos will shift to the right.
   d. The demand for the dollar will shift to the left.
   e. The real exchange rate will decrease.
7. Which of the following will cause a decrease in the demand for U.S. dollars?
   a. a decrease in the relative price level in the United States
   b. a worldwide recession
   c. more foreigners visiting the United States
   d. an increase in the relative interest rate in the United States
   e. an increase in the United States' real GDP

Tackle the AP® Test: Free-Response Questions

1. Draw a correctly labeled graph of the USD foreign exchange market showing the effect on the equilibrium exchange rate between the United States and Japan (the number of yen per U.S. dollar) if capital flows from Japan to the United States decrease due to a change in the preferences of Japanese investors. Has the U.S. dollar appreciated or depreciated? Explain.

Rubric for FRQ 1 (10 points)

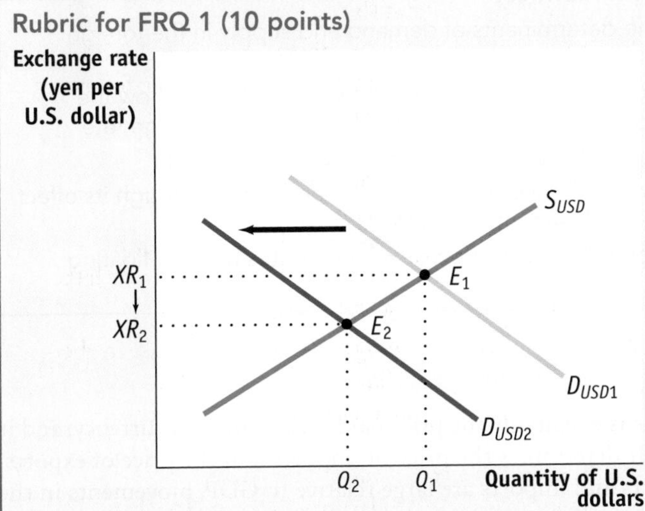

1 point: The vertical axis is labeled "Exchange rate (yen per U.S. dollar)."

1 point: The horizontal axis is labeled "Quantity of U.S. dollars."

1 point: The supply of U.S. dollars is labeled and slopes upward.

1 point: The demand for U.S. dollars is labeled and slopes downward.

1 point: The initial equilibrium exchange rate is found at the intersection of the initial supply and demand curves and is labeled on the vertical axis.

1 point: The initial equilibrium quantity of U.S. dollars is found at the intersection of the initial supply and demand curves and is labeled on the horizontal axis.

1 point: The new demand for U.S. dollars is labeled and to the left of the initial demand.

1 point: The new equilibrium exchange rate is found where the initial supply curve and new demand curve intersect and is labeled on the vertical axis.

1 point: The U.S. dollar has depreciated.

1 point: Because the exchange rate has decreased.

2. Use a correctly labeled graph of the foreign exchange market between the U.S. dollar and the euro to show what would happen to the value of the U.S. dollar if there were an increase in the U.S. demand for imports from Europe. Explain your answer. **(5 points)**

MODULE 6.4

Policies, Economic Conditions, and the Foreign Exchange Market

In this Module, you will learn to:

- Identify and explain the determinants of demand and supply in the foreign exchange market
- Use a correctly labeled graph of the foreign exchange market to show the effect of a change of demand or supply on the equilibrium exchange rate
- Explain how tariffs and quotas affect the equilibrium exchange rate
- Explain how monetary and fiscal policy affects exchange rates through its effect on real GDP, the price level, and interest rates
- Explain how macroeconomic policy affects exchange rates under a floating exchange rate regime

Hossein Lohinejadian/Alamy

The nominal exchange rate is essentially the price paid for a country's currency, and it is a very important price. It determines the price of imports and the price of exports. In economies where exports and imports are large relative to GDP, movements in the exchange rate can have major effects on aggregate output and the aggregate price level. What influences this important price?

In market economies, the nominal exchange rate is determined by market forces – supply and demand in the foreign exchange market – but at different times and in different places, governments have adopted a variety of *exchange rate regimes*. In this Module, we will first distinguish between the two most common exchange rate regimes, fixed and floating, and then we will focus on the market forces that determine floating exchange rates.

Fixed Versus Floating Exchange Rates

An *exchange rate regime* is a rule governing a country's policy toward the exchange rate. There are two main kinds of exchange rate regimes. A country has a *fixed exchange rate* when the government keeps the exchange rate against some other currency at or near a particular target. In 2019, the International Monetary Fund released a report identifying 26 countries with fixed exchange rates, including Denmark, Hong Kong, and Saudi Arabia. The countries with fixed exchange rates tend to be small, and they most commonly tie their currency to the U.S. dollar or the euro. A country has a *floating exchange rate* when the government lets the exchange rate go wherever the market takes it. The majority of countries – including Britain, Canada, and the United States – follow a floating exchange rate policy.

A **devaluation** is a reduction in the value of a currency that is set under a fixed exchange rate regime.

With a fixed exchange rate system, the exchange rate does not change in response to market forces – it changes only when the government decides to change it. When the government reduces the value of a currency that is set under a fixed exchange rate regime, it is called a **devaluation**. As we've already learned, a *depreciation* is a downward move in a currency. A devaluation is a depreciation that is due to a revision in a fixed exchange rate target. An increase in the value of a currency that is set under a fixed exchange rate regime is called a **revaluation**.

A **revaluation** is an increase in the value of a currency that is set under a fixed exchange rate regime.

A devaluation, like any depreciation, makes domestic goods cheaper in terms of foreign currency, which leads to higher exports. At the same time, it makes foreign goods more expensive in terms of domestic currency, which reduces imports. The effect is to increase the balance of payments on the current account. Similarly, a revaluation makes domestic goods more expensive in terms of foreign currency, which reduces exports, and makes foreign goods cheaper in domestic currency, which increases imports. So a revaluation reduces the balance of payments on the current account.

Devaluations and revaluations serve two purposes under a fixed exchange rate regime. First, they can be used to eliminate shortages or surpluses in the foreign exchange market. When there is a shortage in the foreign exchange market, exchange rates will rise; when there is a surplus in the foreign exchange market, exchange rates will fall. Second, devaluation and revaluation can be used as tools of macroeconomic policy. By increasing exports and reducing imports, a devaluation increases aggregate demand. A revaluation has the opposite effect, reducing aggregate demand.

Benefits and Costs of a Fixed Exchange Rate

There are many arguments both for and against a country adopting a fixed or a floating exchange rate. To understand the case for a fixed exchange rate, consider for a moment how easy it is to conduct business across state lines in the United States. There are a number of things that make interstate commerce trouble-free, but one of them is the absence of any uncertainty about the value of money: a dollar is a dollar, in both New York City and Los Angeles.

By contrast, a dollar isn't a dollar in transactions between New York City and Toronto. The exchange rate between the Canadian dollar and the U.S. dollar fluctuates, sometimes widely. If a U.S. firm promises to pay a Canadian firm a given number of U.S. dollars a year from now, the value of that promise in Canadian currency can vary by 10% or more. This uncertainty has the effect of deterring trade between the two countries. So one benefit of a fixed exchange rate is certainty about the future value of a currency.

Once you cross the border into Canada, a dollar is no longer worth a dollar.

Robert Nickelsberg/Getty Images

In some cases, there is an additional benefit to adopting a fixed exchange rate: by committing itself to a fixed rate, a country is also committing itself not to engage in inflationary policies because such policies would destabilize the exchange rate. For example, in 1991, Argentina, which had a long history of irresponsible policies leading to severe inflation, adopted a fixed exchange rate of US$1 per Argentine peso in an attempt to commit itself to noninflationary policies in the future. (Argentina's fixed exchange rate regime collapsed disastrously in late 2001. But that's another story.)

The point is that there is some economic value in having a stable exchange rate. Indeed, the presumed benefits of stable exchange rates motivated the international system of fixed exchange rates created after World War II. It was also a major reason for the creation of the euro.

However, there are also costs to fixing the exchange rate. To stabilize an exchange rate through intervention, a country must keep large quantities of foreign currency on hand, and that currency is usually a low-return investment. Furthermore, even large reserves can be quickly exhausted when there are large capital flows out of a country. If a country chooses to stabilize an exchange rate by adjusting monetary policy rather than through intervention, it must divert monetary policy from other goals, notably stabilizing the economy and managing the inflation rate. Finally, foreign exchange controls, such as import quotas and tariffs, discussed next, distort incentives for importing and exporting goods and services. They can also create substantial costs in terms of red tape and corruption.

So there's a dilemma. Should a country let its currency float, which leaves monetary policy available for macroeconomic stabilization but creates uncertainty for everyone affected by trade? Or should it fix the exchange rate, which eliminates the uncertainty but means giving up monetary policy, adopting exchange controls, or both? Different countries reach different conclusions at different times.

Exchange Rate Determination Under a Floating Exchange Rate Regime

In a floating exchange rate regime, the equilibrium exchange rate in a foreign exchange market is determined by the interaction of currency demand and supply. **Table 6.4-1** highlights the determinants of demand and supply in foreign exchange markets. As we learned in Module 6.3, the demand for a country's currency comes from the demand for that country's goods (and the need to pay for them with the domestic currency). Recall that when someone purchases another currency, they pay for it using their domestic currency. So a change in the demand for a foreign currency will necessarily change the supply of the domestic currency.

Table 6.4-1 The Determinants of Currency Demand and Supply in the Foreign Exchange Market

Determinants of Demand	Determinants of Supply	Determinants of Demand and Supply
Demand for domestic goods	Demand for foreign goods	Tariffs on imports
Demand for domestic services	Demand for foreign services	Quotas for imports
Demand for domestic financial assets	Demand for foreign financial assets	Fiscal policy
		Monetary policy

We have seen that the demand for goods, services, and financial assets determines the demand for a currency in a foreign exchange market because buyers need to pay for them with the domestic currency. People supply a currency in the foreign exchange market when they need to buy a foreign currency in order to pay for foreign goods, services, or financial assets. In addition, the supply of a currency is affected by the country's international trade policies.

Protectionism is the practice of limiting trade to protect domestic industries.

Tariffs are taxes on imports.

An **import quota** is a limit on the quantity of a good that can be imported within a given period.

Governments often practice some degree of **protectionism**, the practice of limiting trade to protect domestic industries. Protectionism includes the imposition of **tariffs** and **import quotas**. The imposition of tariffs, which are taxes on imports, helps domestic industries and provides revenue for the government. The bad news is that tariffs make prices higher for domestic consumers and can spark trade wars. Import quotas limit the quantity of imports from other countries.

Both tariffs and quotas will affect the supply of the domestic currency in the foreign exchange market. Whenever a country imposes a tariff on another country, or limits imports from another country, it decreases the demand for the other country's goods and services. The decreased demand for the other country's goods and services will decrease the demand for the other country's currency. A decreased demand for foreign currency means a decreased supply of the domestic currency in foreign exchange markets.

Next, we consider how macroeconomic policy under a floating exchange rate regime affects the equilibrium exchange rate in foreign exchange markets.

Exchange Rates and Macroeconomic Policy

As we noted at the beginning of this Module, the nominal exchange rate is the price of a country's currency. Like other prices, it is determined by supply and demand. Unlike the price of wheat or oil, however, the exchange rate is the price of a country's currency *in terms of another country's currency*. Currency isn't a good or service produced by the private sector; it's an asset whose quantity is determined by government policy. For example, the Federal Reserve system determines the quantity of U.S. dollars. As a result, governments have much more power to influence nominal exchange rates than they have to influence ordinary prices.

As this discussion suggests, the fact that modern economies are open to international trade and capital flows adds a new level of complication to our analysis of macroeconomic policy.

Fiscal Policy Under a Floating Exchange Rate Regime

Fiscal policy can affect the equilibrium exchange rate in foreign exchange markets through its effect on incomes, prices, and interest rates in the economy. When the government uses expansionary fiscal policy, through increased government spending or decreased taxes, it increases household income. When the government uses contractionary fiscal policy, through decreased government spending and increased taxes, it decreases household income. Increased income leads to higher consumption of both domestic and imported goods and services. The increased demand for imports leads to an increase in the demand for foreign currencies, which results in an increase in the supply of domestic currencies. Decreased income, on the other hand, leads to lower consumption of both domestic and imported goods and services, decreasing the demand for foreign currencies, and therefore decreasing the supply of domestic currency.

Recall that expansionary and contractionary fiscal policy affect not only income, but also the price level in the economy, as shown in Figures 3.8-1 and 3.8-2. An increase in the domestic price level makes domestic goods more expensive relative to imported goods, which increases the demand for imported goods. An increased demand for imported goods will increase the demand for foreign currencies (and the supply of domestic currency). A decrease in the price level as a result of fiscal policy will do the opposite – decrease the demand for imported goods and therefore decrease the demand for foreign currency.

Finally, fiscal policy can affect the equilibrium exchange rate through changes in interest rates. Recall from Module 3.8 that deficit spending for expansionary fiscal policy requires the government to issue bonds, which raises interest rates. Because foreign investors are attracted to higher interest rates, investment in domestic financial assets increases, which leads to an increase in the demand for the domestic currency (and the supply of the foreign currency).

Monetary Policy Under a Floating Exchange Rate Regime

Under a floating exchange rate regime, a country's central bank retains its ability to pursue independent monetary policy: it can increase aggregate demand by cutting the interest rate, or it can decrease aggregate demand by raising the interest rate. But the exchange rate adds another dimension to the effects of monetary policy. Like fiscal policy, expansionary or contractionary monetary policy can affect the equilibrium exchange rate through its effects on income, prices, and interest rates in the economy. To see why, let's visit the hypothetical country of Genovia, with its currency, the geno.

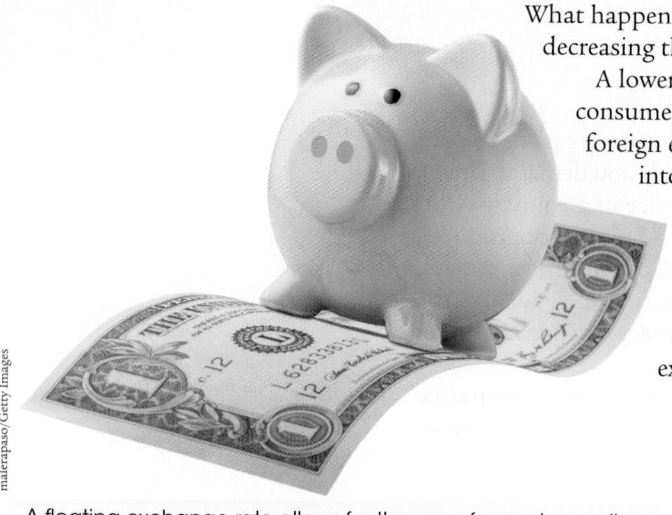

malerapaso/Getty Images

A floating exchange rate allows for the use of monetary policy to stabilize the economy, but also increases uncertainty around trade.

What happens if its central bank pursues expansionary monetary policy by decreasing the interest rate.

A lower interest rate leads to higher investment spending and higher consumer spending. But the decline in the interest rate also affects the foreign exchange market. Foreigners have less incentive to move funds into Genovia because they will receive a lower rate of return on their loans. As a result, they have less need to exchange U.S. dollars for genos, so the demand for genos falls. At the same time, Genovians have *more* incentive to move funds abroad because the rate of return on loans at home has fallen, making investments outside the country more attractive. Thus, they need to exchange more genos for U.S. dollars, and the supply of genos rises.

Figure 6.4-1 shows the effect of an interest rate reduction on the foreign exchange market. The demand curve for genos shifts leftward, from D_{G1} to D_{G2}, and the supply curve shifts rightward, from S_{G1} to S_{G2}. The equilibrium exchange rate, as measured in U.S. dollars per geno, falls from XR_1 to XR_2. That is, a reduction in the Genovian interest rate causes the geno to *depreciate*.

FIGURE 6.4-1 Monetary Policy and the Exchange Rate

Here we show what happens in the foreign exchange market if Genovia cuts its interest rate. Residents of Genovia have a reduced incentive to keep their funds at home, so they invest more abroad. As a result, the supply of genos shifts rightward, from S_{G1} to S_{G2}. Meanwhile, foreigners have less incentive to put funds into Genovia, so the demand for genos shifts leftward, from D_{G1} to D_{G2}. The geno depreciates: the equilibrium exchange rate falls from XR_1 to XR_2.

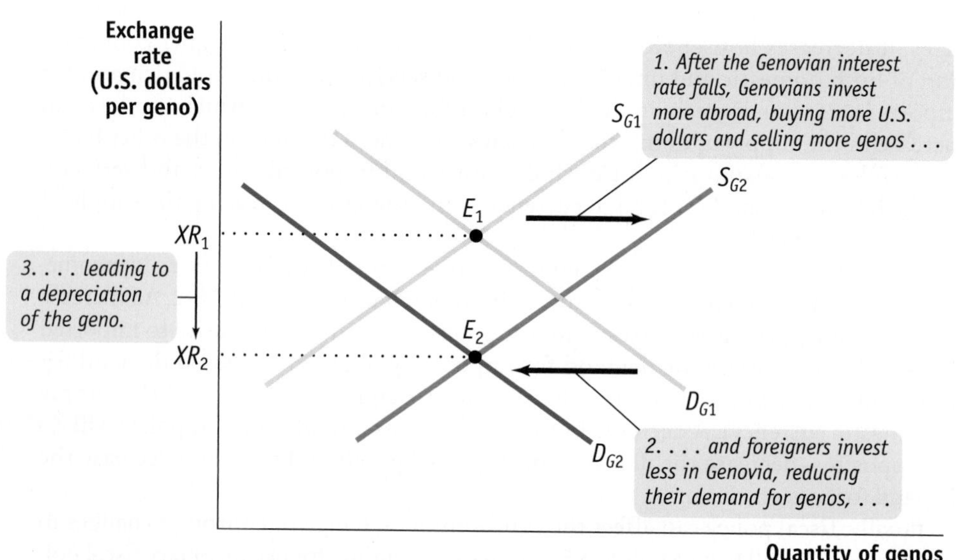

In other words, monetary policy under floating rates has effects beyond those we've described in looking at closed economies.

International Business Cycles

Up to this point, we have discussed macroeconomics, even in an open economy, as if all demand changes, or *shocks*, originated from the domestic economy. In reality, however, economies sometimes face shocks coming from abroad. For example, recessions in the United States have historically led to recessions in Mexico as a result of the close trade relationship between the two countries.

The key point is that changes in aggregate demand affect the demand for goods and services produced abroad as well as at home: other things equal, a recession leads to a fall in imports and an expansion leads to a rise in imports because changes in income affect the demand for *all* goods and services regardless of where they were produced. And one country's imports are another country's exports. This link between aggregate demand in different national economies is one reason business cycles in different countries sometimes—but not always—seem to be synchronized. The prime example is the Great Depression, which affected countries around the world.

Module 6.4 Review

Check Your Understanding

1. Explain how tariffs and import quotas affect the supply of currency in foreign exchange markets.
2. Fiscal and monetary policy affect equilibrium exchange rates in foreign exchange markets through their effect of what three economic variables?

Tackle the AP® Test: Multiple-Choice Questions

1. An increase in the supply of a currency with a floating exchange rate will cause which of the following?
   a. an increase in the demand for the currency
   b. appreciation of the currency
   c. depreciation of the currency
   d. the government to buy more of the currency
   e. the government to buy less of the currency
2. The United States has which of the following exchange rate regimes?
   a. fixed
   b. floating
   c. fixed, but adjusted frequently
   d. fixed, but managed
   e. floating within a target zone
3. Expansionary fiscal policy will result in which of the following?
   a. lower household income
   b. deflation
   c. lower interest rates
   d. increased demand for foreign currency
   e. decreased supply of domestic currency
4. Devaluation of a currency is used to achieve which of the following?
   a. the elimination of a surplus in the foreign exchange market
   b. the elimination of a shortage in the foreign exchange market
   c. a reduction in aggregate demand
   d. a lower inflation rate
   e. a floating exchange rate
5. Monetary policy that reduces the interest rate will do which of the following?
   a. appreciate the domestic currency
   b. decrease exports
   c. increase imports
   d. depreciate the domestic currency
   e. prevent inflation
6. Which of the following would result from a U.S. tariff on imported cars?
   a. The profit of U.S. car manufacturers would decrease.
   b. The price paid for cars in the United States would increase.
   c. More cars would be imported.
   d. Fewer domestically made cars would be sold in the United States.
   e. More cars from all sources would be sold in the United States.
7. An import quota is a
   a. minimum quantity of a good that may be imported.
   b. minimum quantity of a good that a factory must produce and sell overseas.
   c. maximum quantity of a good that may be imported.
   d. maximum quantity of a good that a factory may produce and sell overseas.
   e. maximum price that a company can charge for imports.

Tackle the AP® Test: Free-Response Questions

1. Suppose the United States and India were the only two countries in the world. The currency in India is the rupee.
   a. Draw a correctly labeled graph of the foreign exchange market for U.S. dollars showing the equilibrium in the market.
   b. Will contractionary fiscal policy in the United States increase, decrease, or not change income, the price level, and interest rates in the United States?
   c. Assume the U.S. central bank, the Fed, pursues expansionary monetary policy.
      i. How will expansionary monetary policy affect the supply of rupees in the market for India rupees?
      ii. Explain how expansionary monetary policy will affect the demand for U.S. dollars.
      iii. Show the change in the demand for U.S. dollars that results from expansionary monetary policy on your graph.

Rubric for FRQ 1 (10 points)

1 point: The vertical axis is labeled "Exchange rate (Indian rupees per U.S. dollar)" and the horizontal axis is labeled "Quantity of U.S. dollars."

1 point: Demand is downward-sloping and labeled; supply is upward-sloping and labeled.

1 point: The equilibrium exchange rate is labeled on the vertical axis at the point where the supply and demand curves intersect.

1 point: The equilibrium quantity of dollars is labeled on the horizontal axis at the point where the supply and demand curves intersect.

1 point: Decrease income.

1 point: Decrease the price level.

1 point: Decrease interest rates.

1 point: The supply of Indian rupees will decrease.

1 point: The demand for U.S. dollars will decrease because foreign investors want to decrease financial investment in the U.S. due to lower interest rates.

1 point: The graph shows a new demand curve to the left of the old demand curve.

2. Refer to the graph provided showing the foreign exchange market for genos, the currency of the country of Genovia.

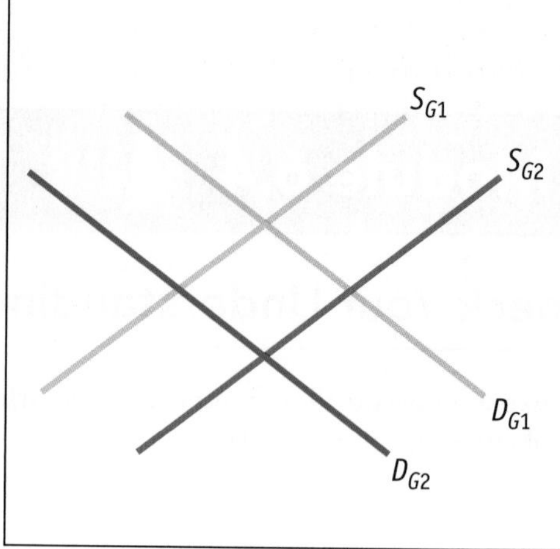

   a. What change in the demand for U.S. imports would lead to the shift from SG_1 to SG_2?
   b. Identify three changes that could lead to the shift from DG_1 to DG_2.
   c. If demand and supply in the market for genos shift from SG_1 to SG_2 and from DG_1 to DG_2, what happens to the value of the geno? **(5 points)**

The Foreign Exchange Market and Net Exports

MODULE 6.5

In this Module, you will learn to:

- Describe the relationship between the value of a country's currency and its imports and exports
- Explain how currency appreciation or depreciation affects a country's net exports
- Use a correctly labeled graph to illustrate how a change in a country's exchange rate and net exports will affect its aggregate demand

Why Trade?

It's natural for the citizens of a country to say, "We can make food, clothing, and almost everything we need. Why should we buy these goods from other countries and send our money overseas?" Module 1.3 explained the answer to this question: because specialization and trade make larger quantities of goods and services available to consumers. Yet the gains from trade are often overlooked, and many countries have experimented with a closed economy. The outcomes of these experiments were disappointing. By trying to make too many different products, countries failed to specialize in what they were best at making; as a result, they ended up with less of most goods than trade would have provided.

Every country today has an open economy, although some economies are more open than others. **Figure 6.5-1** shows expenditures on imports as a percentage of GDP for select countries in 2020, which ranged from 13.3% in the United States to 144.3% in Singapore. Several factors affect a country's approach to trade. Beyond the natural tendency for each country to want to be self-sufficient, special circumstances can limit the options for trade. For example, high transportation costs hinder trade for

FIGURE 6.5-1 Imports of Goods and Services as a Percentage of GDP, 2020

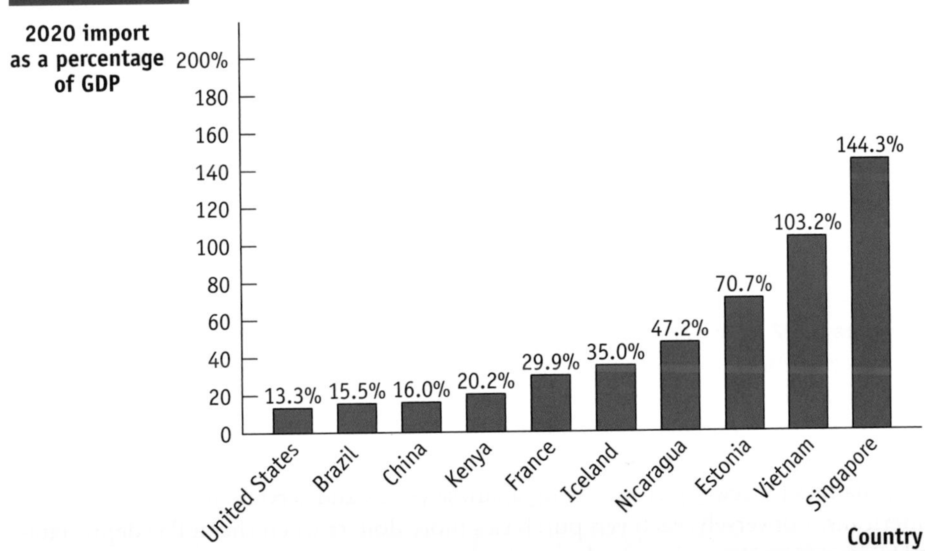

International trade is an important part of every country's economy, but some economies are more open than others. In 2020, imports as a percentage of GDP ranged from 13.3% in the United States to 144.3% in Singapore. *Data Source:* The World Bank.

SOPA Images/Getty Images

A lack of transportation infrastructure can be a hindrance to trade for some countries.

countries with underdeveloped transportation systems as well as for countries that specialize in heavy, low-priced commodities such as bricks, drinking water, watermelons, or sand. Countries are wary of specialization that would make them overly reliant on other countries, because relationships with those countries could sour. And, as a matter of national pride, countries may prefer to make certain products on their own, such as food, art, weapons, and products that showcase technical know-how, despite comparative disadvantages.

International trade can also have its casualties. As production shifts toward a country's comparative advantage, many workers in declining industries will lose their jobs and will remain structurally unemployed until or unless they can obtain the skills required in other industries. For example, as the United States imported more clothing from countries with a comparative advantage in textiles, workers in a Fruit of the Loom factory in Campbellsville, Kentucky, were among many who lost their jobs. Fortunately, the unemployment rates in Campbellsville and in the United States as a whole rose only temporarily. Many of these workers were able to adapt to the requirements of growing industries such as construction, automotive parts, health care, and software design, and were able to secure new jobs as a result.

The value of imports and exports measure a country's level of international trade, while the *difference* between a country's exports and imports determines its net exports. Recall from Module 3.1 that aggregate demand is made up of four components, as shown in Equation 6.5-1, one of which is net exports $(X - M)$ – in addition to consumption (C), investment (I), and government spending (G). We are now finally able to look in detail at how changes in net exports affect aggregate demand:

$$\textbf{(6.5-1)} \quad AD = C + I + G + (X - M)$$

And any change in aggregate demand will result in a new equilibrium in the aggregate demand–aggregate supply model, so we can now see how exchange rates affect the equilibrium output, employment, and price level. But first, let's look at their impact on net exports.

The Effect of the Exchange Rate on Net Exports

The exchange rate for a country's currency is a key determinant of its net exports. The exchange rate determines the price of imports in terms of the domestic currency. When a country's exchange rate changes, it changes the relative price of domestic and imported goods and services. We discussed the factors that cause a currency to depreciate in Module 6.3 – for example, anything that causes either a decrease in the demand or an increase in the supply of a country's currency will cause that currency to depreciate. Currency depreciation makes the domestic currency weaker such that it trades for less foreign currency, making imports more expensive and, therefore, causing imports to decrease. At the same time, depreciation of domestic currency makes foreign currency stronger such that the country's exports are cheaper, therefore, causing exports to increase.

Figure 6.5-2 shows graphs of the foreign exchange market between U.S. dollars and Japanese yen. Panel (a) shows the exchange rate for U.S. dollars decreasing as the result of a decrease in the demand for U.S. dollars, and panel (b) shows the exchange rate for U.S. dollars decreasing as the result of an increase in the supply of U.S. dollars. In both cases, the yen per dollar exchange rate decreases, which means that each dollar exchanges for fewer yen – making Japanese goods and services more expensive for Americans. Conversely, each yen purchases more dollars when the dollar depreciates, so U.S. exports to Japan become less expensive.

FIGURE 6.5-2 Depreciation in the Market for U.S. Dollars

(a) Decrease in Demand for U.S. Dollars

Exchange rate (yen per U.S. dollar)

1. A decrease in the demand for the U.S. dollar . . .

2. . . . leads to a depreciation of the U.S. dollar.

XR_1, XR_2, E_1, E_2, S_{USD}, D_{USD1}, D_{USD2}, Q_2, Q_1

Quantity of U.S. dollars

(b) Increase in Supply of U.S. Dollars

Exchange rate (yen per U.S. dollar)

1. A increase in the supply of the U.S. dollar . . .

2. . . . leads to a depreciation of the U.S. dollar.

XR_1, XR_2, E_1, E_2, S_{USD1}, S_{USD2}, D_{USD}, Q_1, Q_2

Quantity of U.S. dollars

Panel (a) shows depreciation of the U.S. dollar resulting from a decrease in the demand for U.S. dollars. Panel (b) shows depreciation of the dollar resulting from an increase in the supply of U.S. dollars.

Appreciation of a country's currency, caused by either an increase in its demand or a decrease in its supply, will cause the country's exports to decrease and its imports to increase. Recall the factors that cause a currency to appreciate from Module 6.3. In contrast to depreciation, currency appreciation makes the domestic currency stronger such that it trades for more foreign currency, making imports less expensive and causing imports to increase. At the same time, it makes foreign currency weaker such that a country's exports are more expensive, causing exports to decrease.

Thomas Trutschel/Getty Images

Let's return to the foreign exchange market between U.S. dollars and Japanese yen, shown in **Figure 6.5-3**. Panel (a) shows the exchange rate for U.S. dollars increasing as the result of an increase in the demand for U.S. dollars, and panel (b) shows the exchange rate for U.S. dollars increasing as the result of a decrease in the supply of U.S. dollars. In both cases, the yen per dollar exchange rate increases,

FIGURE 6.5-3 Appreciation in the Market for U.S. Dollars

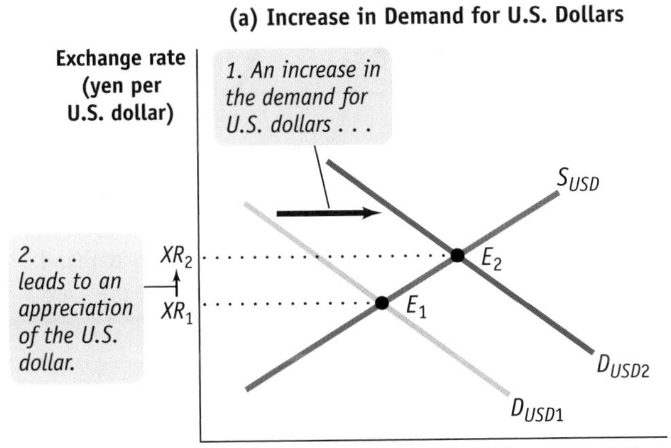

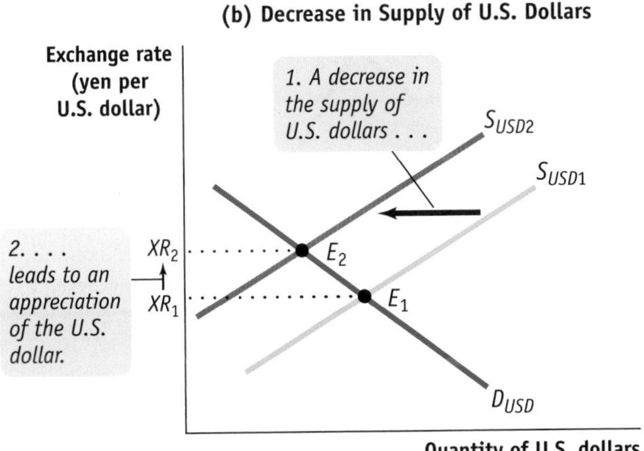

Panel (a) shows appreciation of the U.S. dollar resulting from an increase in the demand for U.S. dollars. Panel (b) shows appreciation of the U.S. dollar resulting from a decrease in the supply of U.S. dollars.

which means that each dollar exchanges for more yen – making Japanese goods and services less expensive for Americans. Conversely, each yen purchases fewer dollars when the dollar appreciates, so U.S. exports to Japan become more expensive.

When the dollar depreciates, imports decrease and exports increase, causing net exports to increase. When the dollar appreciates, imports increase and exports decrease, causing net exports to decrease. Next, we will look at how a change in net exports will cause the aggregate demand curve to shift, leading to a new equilibrium output, employment, and price level in the aggregate demand and aggregate supply model.

The Effect of Net Exports on the Equilibrium Output, Employment, and Price Level

Now that we have seen how exchange rates affect a country's net exports, we can look at how the change in net exports shifts the aggregate demand curve and changes the equilibrium real GDP and price level. Panel (a) of **Figure 6.5-4** shows how a decrease in net exports will decrease aggregate demand, shifting the aggregate demand curve to the left. The new equilibrium is at a lower level of real GDP (it falls from Y_1 to Y_2) and a lower price level (it falls from PL_1 to PL_2). A decrease in net exports has a contractionary effect on aggregate demand and the economy, leading to a decrease in output, price level, and employment. Panel (b), on the other hand, shows how an increase in net exports will increase aggregate demand, shifting the aggregate demand curve to the right. The new equilibrium is at a higher level of real GDP (it rises from Y_1 to Y_2) and a higher price level (it rises from PL_1 to PL_2). An increase in net exports has an expansionary effect on aggregate demand and the economy, leading to an increase in output, price level, and employment.

FIGURE 6.5-4 The Effect of Net Exports on Aggregate Demand, Output, Employment, and the Price Level

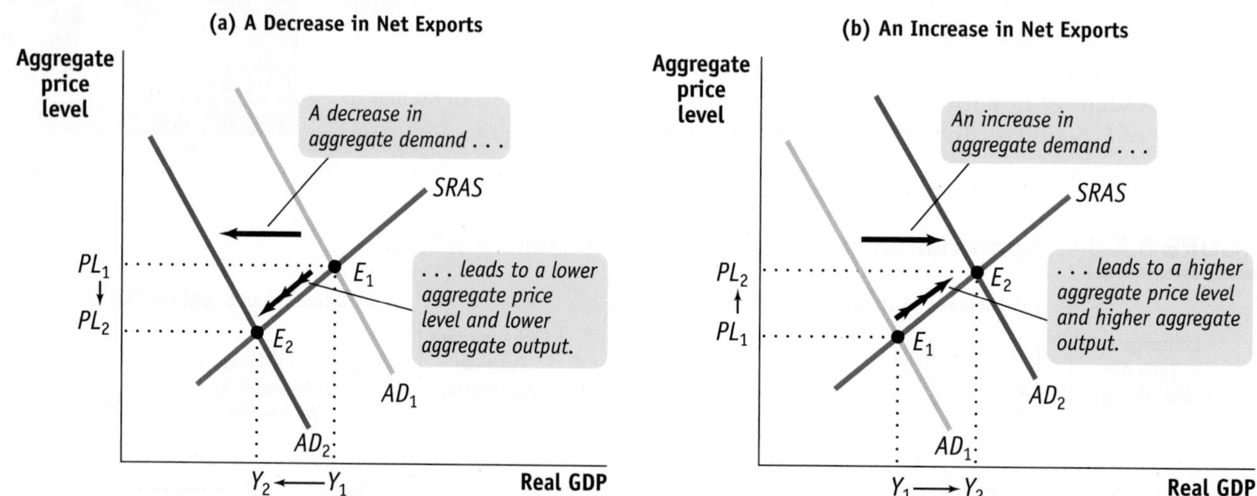

In panel (a), a decrease in net exports decreases aggregate demand, leading to a decrease in output, employment, and the price level. In panel (b), an increase in net exports increases aggregate demand, leading to an increase in output, employment, and the price level.

Figure 6.5-5 diagrams the causal linkages between the appreciation and depreciation of currency and real GDP, employment, and the price level.

In an open economy, the exchange rate for a country's currency, determined in the foreign exchange market, affects the country's net exports, which affect the equilibrium real GDP, employment, and the price level in the economy.

FIGURE 6.5-5 Chain of Causation from Changes in Currency Value

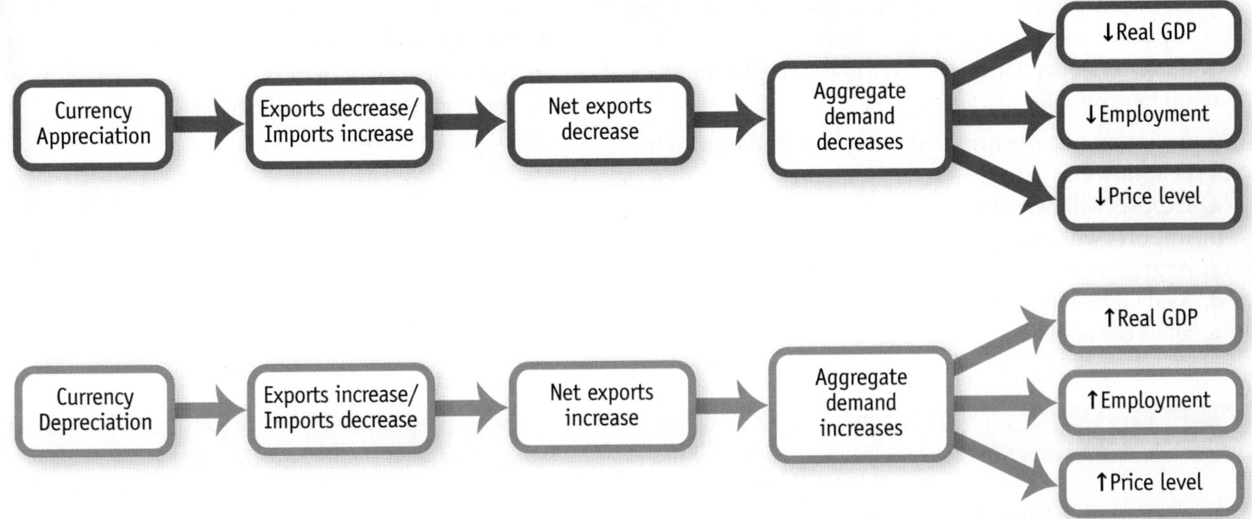

A change in a country's exchange rate will initiate a chain of events that ultimately affects the country's real GDP, employment (and therefore unemployment), and price level. Changes in the exchange rate affect the aggregate economy through their effect on net exports and aggregate demand. All other things held constant, currency appreciation will decrease output, employment, and the price level, while depreciation will increase output, employment, and the price level.

Module 6.5 Review

Check Your Understanding

1. What factors can affect the equilibrium exchange rate determined in foreign exchange markets?
2. Explain how depreciation and appreciation of a country's currency affect its net exports and aggregate demand.

Tackle the AP® Test: Multiple-Choice Questions

1. Which of the following will cause a currency to depreciate?
   a. an increase in currency demand
   b. a decrease in currency supply
   c. an increase in currency supply
   d. an increase in the exchange rate
   e. an increase in net exports
2. How will a decrease in the supply of a currency affect the exchange rate?
   a. It will increase.
   b. It will depreciate.
   c. It will decrease.
   d. It will not change.
   e. It will be unaffected.
3. Net exports will decrease as a result of which of the following?
   a. an increase in imports
   b. an increase in exports
   c. a decrease in imports
   d. currency depreciation
   e. a decrease in aggregate demand
4. If exports and imports both increase, which will happen to net exports? They will
   a. increase.
   b. decrease.
   c. not change.
   d. double.
   e. answer cannot be determined

5. An increase in aggregate demand will cause which of the following?
   a. an increase in net exports
   b. currency appreciation
   c. higher real GDP
   d. a decrease in the price level
   e. lower employment

6. Appreciation of a country's currency will lead to which of the following?
   a. Exports will decrease.
   b. Imports will increase.
   c. Aggregate demand will decrease.
   d. Real GDP will decrease.
   e. all of the above

7. When a country's exchange rate decreases, which of the following will result?
   a. Exports will decrease.
   b. Imports will increase.
   c. Net exports will increase.
   d. Aggregate demand will decrease.
   e. all of the above

Tackle the AP® Test: Free-Response Questions

1. Draw a correctly labeled graph of the foreign exchange market for U.S. dollars in terms of Japanese yen.
   a. On your graph, show the equilibrium exchange rate and quantity, labeled XR_1 and Q_1.
   b. Show the effect of an increase in Americans' preference for Japanese products on the equilibrium exchange rate in the market for dollars. Explain why the preference for Japanese products has this effect.
   c. How will the change in the exchange rate shown in part b affect U.S. net exports and aggregate demand? Explain.

2. Draw a correctly labeled short-run aggregate demand and supply graph showing the equilibrium real GDP and price level, labeled Y_1 and P_1.
   a. Show the effect of depreciation of the domestic currency on the equilibrium real GDP and price level, labeled Y_2 and P_2.
   b. Explain how depreciation of the domestic currency results in the change you show in part a. **(5 points)**

Rubric for FRQ 1 (10 points)

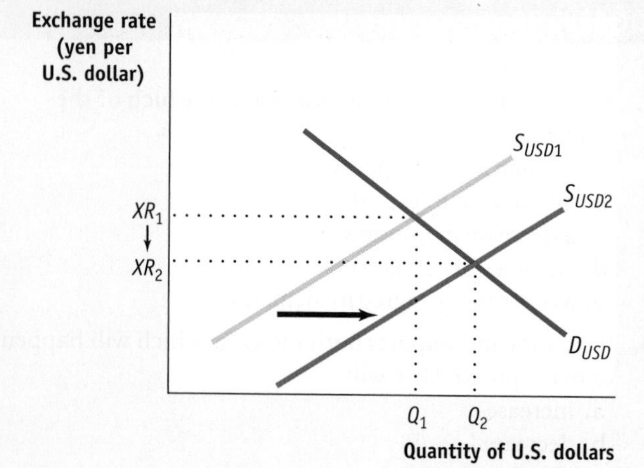

Exchange rate (yen per U.S. dollar)
XR_1
XR_2
S_{USD1}
S_{USD2}
D_{USD}
Q_1 Q_2
Quantity of U.S. dollars

1 point: Vertical axis is labeled yen/U.S. dollar and horizontal axis is labeled quantity of U.S. dollars.

1 point: Downward-sloping and labeled demand curve and upward-sloping and labeled supply curve.

1 point: Equilibrium exchange rate and quantity of dollars are found on the axes where supply and demand cross.

1 point: The new supply of dollars is labeled and to the right of the original supply curve.

1 point: The new equilibrium exchange rate and quantity of dollars are found on the axes where the new supply curve crosses the demand curve.

1 point: Because U.S. consumers need more yen to purchase more Japanese products, the supply of dollars increases.

1 point: Net exports increase.

1 point: Because the exchange rate decreases (the dollar depreciates).

1 point: Aggregate demand increases.

1 point: Because net exports increase.

Real Interest Rates and International Capital Flows

MODULE 6.6

In this Module, you will learn to:

- Explain how real interest rates affect international capital flows
- Use a correctly labeled graph to show how differences in real interest rates across countries affect financial capital flows and exchange rates
- Use a correctly labeled graph to show and explain how real interest rate differentials affect loanable funds markets
- Explain how central banks can influence the domestic interest rate in the short run, thereby affecting net capital inflows

revers/Shutterstock

In this Unit, we have further developed the aggregate demand and aggregate supply model to include an open economy—adding the effects of the flow of goods, services, and financial capital between countries. Each country interacts with the rest of the world through both product and financial markets. Changes in economic activity affect the market for a country's currency and subsequently the value of that currency. Economic policy, including both fiscal and monetary policy, also affects the economy through changes in exchange rates, net exports, and capital flows.

In Modules 6.4 and 6.5 we considered how changes in government policies affect equilibrium exchange rates and how changes in the exchange rate affect a country's net exports. In this Module, we look more closely at how changes in the relative real interest rates between two countries affect financial capital flows, foreign exchange markets, and the loanable funds market. By the end of this Module, we will be able to describe the cause-and-effect chains that explain the connections between macroeconomic variables and the international movements of goods, services, and financial capital.

International Capital Flows and the Loanable Funds Model

We can gain insight into the motivations for capital flows that are the result of private decisions by using the *loanable funds model* developed in Module 4.7. In using this model, we make two important simplifications:

- We simplify the reality of international capital flows by assuming that all flows are in the form of loans. In reality, capital flows take many forms, including purchases of shares of stock in foreign companies and foreign real estate as well as *foreign direct investment*, in which companies build factories or acquire other productive assets abroad.
- We also ignore the effects of expected changes in *exchange rates* and assume that everything else remains constant when we look at changes in countries' relative interest rates.

Figure 6.6-1 recaps the loanable funds model for a closed economy. Equilibrium corresponds to point *E*, at an interest rate of 4%, at which the supply curve for loanable funds (S_{LF}) intersects the demand curve for loanable funds (D_{LF}). If international capital flows are possible, this diagram changes, and *E* will no longer be the equilibrium.

FIGURE 6.6-1 The Loanable Funds Model Revisited

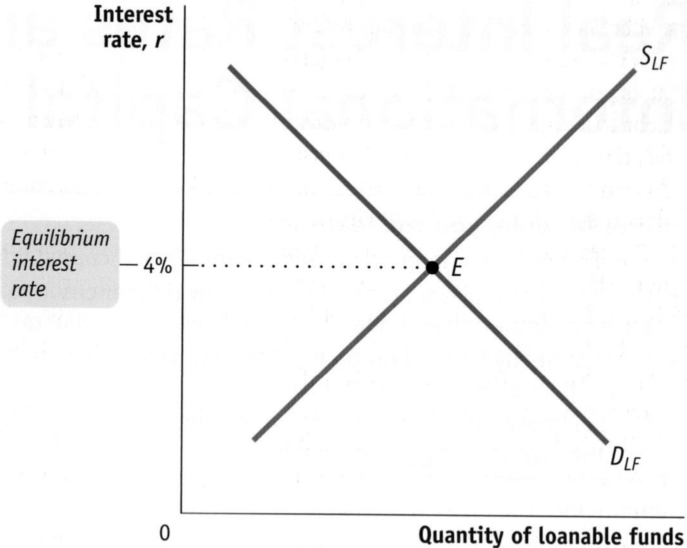

According to the loanable funds model of the interest rate, the equilibrium interest rate is determined by the intersection of the supply curve for loanable funds, S_{LF}, and the demand curve for loanable funds, D_{LF}. At point E, the equilibrium interest rate is 4%.

We can analyze the causes and effects of international capital flows using **Figure 6.6-2**, which places the loanable funds market diagrams for two countries side by side. This figure illustrates a world consisting of only two countries, the United States and Nigeria, assuming there are currently no capital flows between the two countries. Panel (a) shows the loanable funds market in the United States, where the equilibrium in the absence of international capital flows is at point E_{US} with an interest rate of 6%. Panel (b) shows the loanable funds market in Nigeria, where the equilibrium in the absence of international capital flows is at point E_N with an interest rate of 2%.

Will the actual interest rate in the United States remain at 6% and that in Nigeria at 2%? Not if it is easy for Nigerian residents to make loans to Americans. In that case, Nigerian lenders, attracted by relatively high U.S. interest rates, will send some of their loanable funds to the United States. This capital inflow will increase the supply of loanable funds available to American borrowers, pushing the U.S. interest rate down. At the

FIGURE 6.6-2 Loanable Funds Markets in Two Countries

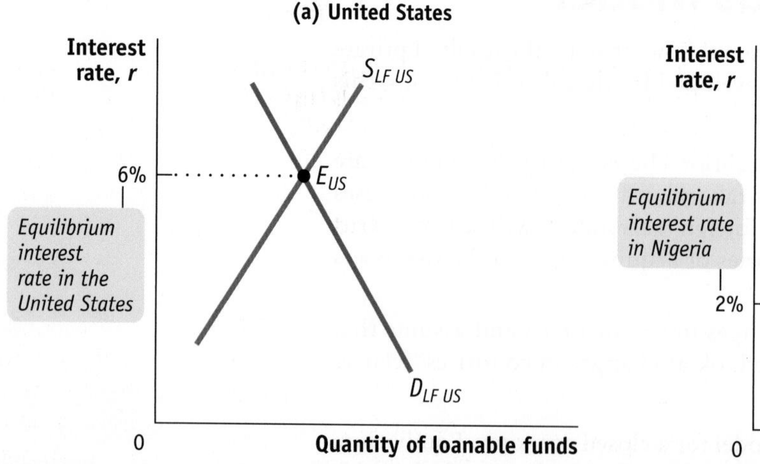

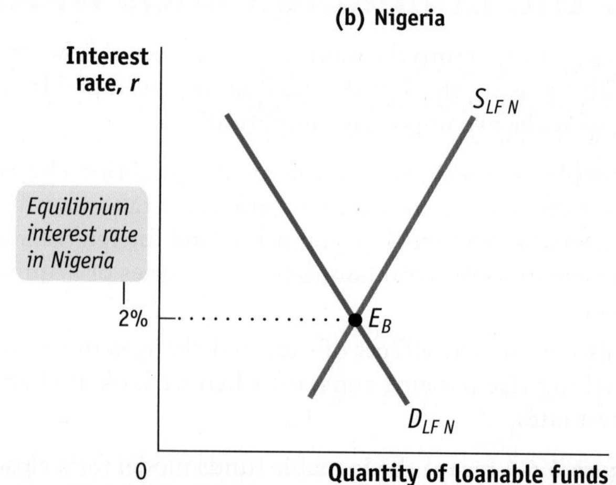

Here we show two countries, the United States and Nigeria, each with its own loanable funds market. The equilibrium interest rate is 6% in the U.S. market but only 2% in the Nigerian market. This creates an incentive for capital to flow from Nigeria to the United States.

same time, it will reduce the supply of loanable funds available to Nigerian borrowers, pushing the Nigerian interest rate up. So international capital flows will narrow the gap between U.S. and Nigerian interest rates.

Let's further suppose that Nigerian lenders regard a loan to an American as being just as good as a loan to one of their own compatriots, and American borrowers regard a debt to a Nigerian lender as no more costly than a debt to an American lender. In that case, the flow of funds from Nigeria to the United States will continue until the gap between their interest rates is eliminated. In other words, international capital flows will equalize the interest rates in the two countries.

Figure 6.6-3 shows an international equilibrium in the loanable funds markets where the equilibrium interest rate is 4% in both the United States and Nigeria. At this interest rate, the quantity of loanable funds demanded by American borrowers exceeds the quantity of loanable funds supplied by American lenders. This gap is filled by "imported" funds—a capital inflow from Nigeria. At the same time, the quantity of loanable funds supplied by Nigerian lenders is greater than the quantity of loanable funds demanded by Nigerian borrowers. This excess is "exported" in the form of a capital outflow to the United States. And the two markets are in equilibrium at a common interest rate of 4%. At that interest rate, the total quantity of loans demanded by borrowers across the two markets is equal to the total quantity of loans supplied by lenders across the two markets.

FIGURE 6.6-3 International Capital Flows

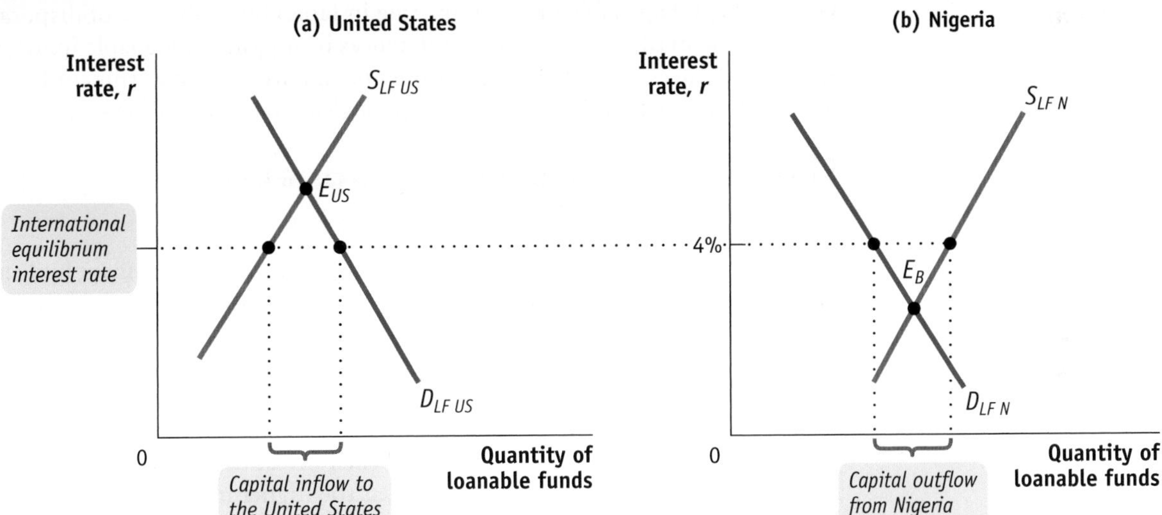

Nigerian lenders lend to borrowers in the United States, leading to equalization of interest rates at 4% in both countries. At that rate, American borrowing exceeds American lending; the difference is made up by capital inflows to the United States. Meanwhile, Nigerian lending exceeds Nigerian borrowing; the excess is a capital outflow from Nigeria.

In short, international capital will flow from countries with relatively low interest rates to countries with relatively high interest rates.

> **AP® ECON TIP**
>
> The capital and financial account will have capital inflows and capital outflows based on changes in interest rates. Financial capital will flow into countries with higher interest rates and out of countries with lower interest rates.

Underlying Determinants of International Capital Flows

The open-economy version of the loanable funds model helps us understand international capital flows in terms of the supply and demand for loanable funds. For example, demand and supply in the loanable funds markets in two countries depend on each country's investment opportunities, savings rates, and government budget deficits.

John Parrot/Stocktrek Images/Getty Images

Loanable funds flow from countries with large amounts of savings to countries with large amounts of investment opportunities, as was the case between Britain and the United States at the turn of the 20th century.

International differences in the demand for loanable funds reflect underlying differences in investment opportunities. In particular, a country with a rapidly growing economy, other things equal, tends to offer more investment opportunities than a country with a slowly growing economy. So a rapidly growing economy typically—though not always—has a higher demand for capital and offers higher returns to investors than a slowly growing economy in the absence of capital flows. As a result, capital tends to flow from slowly growing economies to rapidly growing ones.

The classic example of this tendency is the flow of capital from Britain to the United States, among other countries, between 1870 and 1914. During that era, the U.S. economy was growing rapidly as the population increased and spread westward, and as the nation industrialized. This expansion created a demand for investment spending on railroads, factories, and so on. Meanwhile, Britain had a much more slowly growing population, was already industrialized, and already had a railroad network covering the country. This left Britain with savings to spare, much of which were lent to the United States and other New World economies.

International differences in the supply of loanable funds reflect differences in savings across countries, which may be the result of differences in private savings rates, which vary widely among countries. For example, in October 2021, private savings were 29.5% of disposable personal income in Japan but only 7.1% of disposable personal income in the United States. Differences in supplies of loanable funds may also reflect differences in savings by governments. In particular, government budget deficits, which reduce overall national savings, can lead to capital inflows.

The Effect of Domestic Monetary Policy on Net Capital Inflows

In addition to investment opportunities, savings rates, and government budgets, monetary policy can influence interest rates. Recall from Module 4.6 that central banks can influence domestic interest rates in the short run, which in turn will affect net capital inflows. Contractionary monetary policy leads to an increase in interest rates in the short run. In addition to the effect of higher interest rates on the investment and consumption in the domestic economy, higher interest rates increase capital inflows as foreign investors seek a higher return on their investment. Because foreign investors need domestic currency in order to invest at the higher interest rate, the demand for domestic currency will increase, leading to an increase in the exchange rate. Increased capital inflows increase the quantity of loanable funds supplied in the domestic economy, decreasing the domestic interest rate, eventually equalizing interest rates across countries.

Conversely, expansionary monetary policy leads to a decrease in interest rates in the short run. Lower interest rates decrease capital inflows and increase capital outflows as investors seek a higher return in the other country. Because investors need foreign currency in order to invest at the higher interest rate abroad, the supply of domestic currency increases, leading to a decrease in the exchange rate. Decreased foreign investment decreases the quantity of loanable funds supplied in the domestic economy, increasing the domestic interest rate, and eventually equalizing interest rates across countries. The chain of causation stemming from contractionary and expansionary monetary policy is illustrated in **Figure 6.6-4**.

In an open economy, differences in real interest rates across countries change the relative return on financial investments in those countries. Financial capital will flow toward the country with a relatively higher real interest rate. Changes in net capital

FIGURE 6.6-4 Chain of Causation from Monetary Policy to Capital Flows

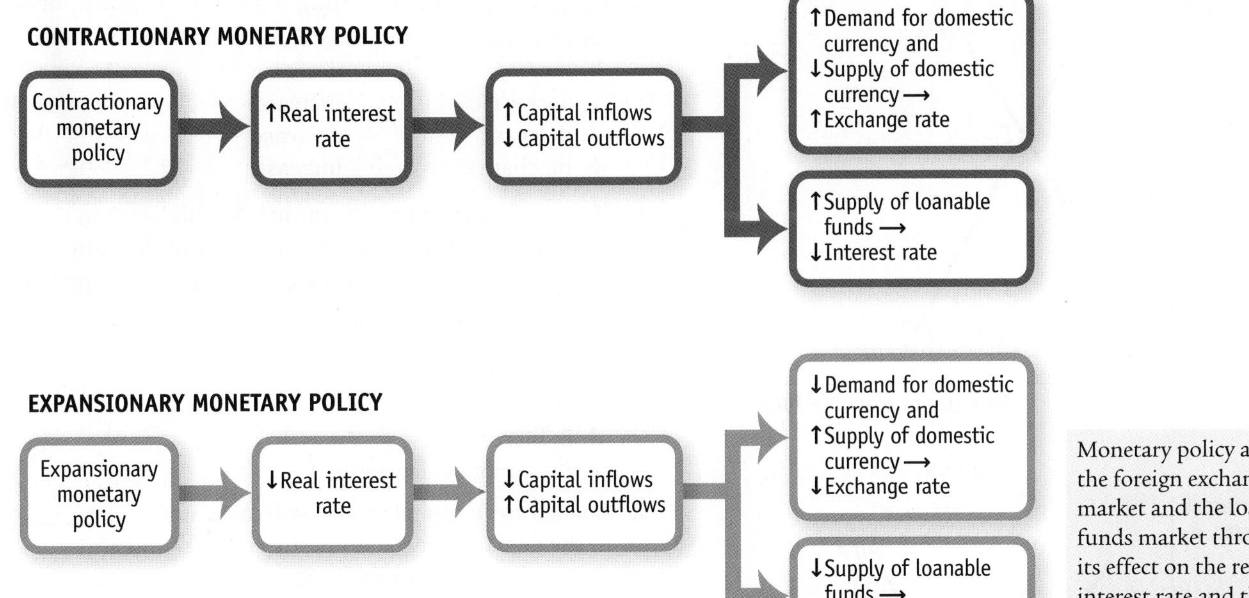

Monetary policy affects the foreign exchange market and the loanable funds market through its effect on the real interest rate and therefore flows of financial capital.

flows will have a further impact in a country's foreign exchange and loanable funds markets.

Now that we have fully developed the aggregate demand and aggregate supply model for an open economy, it is possible to put the entire model together to answer a variety of important macroeconomic questions. The Unit 6 Appendix looks at how to apply the aggregate demand and aggregate supply model for an open economy to answer AP® Macroeconomics exam free response questions.

Module 6.6 Review

Check Your Understanding

1. Explain how differences in real interest rates across countries change the relative values of domestic and foreign assets.
2. Explain how a change in capital inflows affects a country's foreign exchange market.

Tackle the AP® Test: Multiple-Choice Questions

1. Which of the following will increase the demand for loanable funds in a country?
   a. economic growth
   b. decreased investment opportunities
   c. a recession
   d. decreased private savings rates
   e. government budget surpluses

Questions 2 and 3 refer to panels (a) and (b) in the figure below.

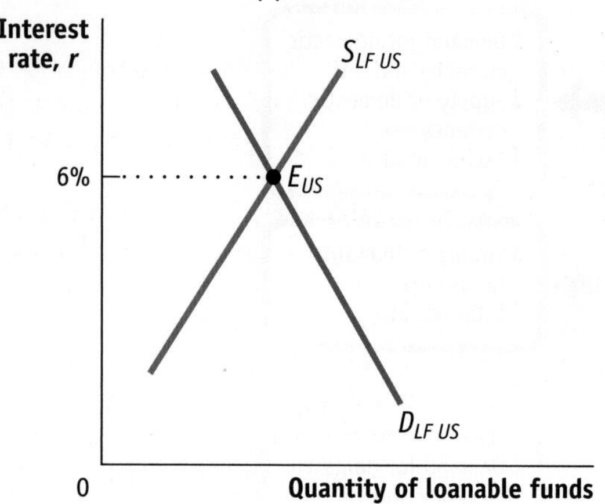

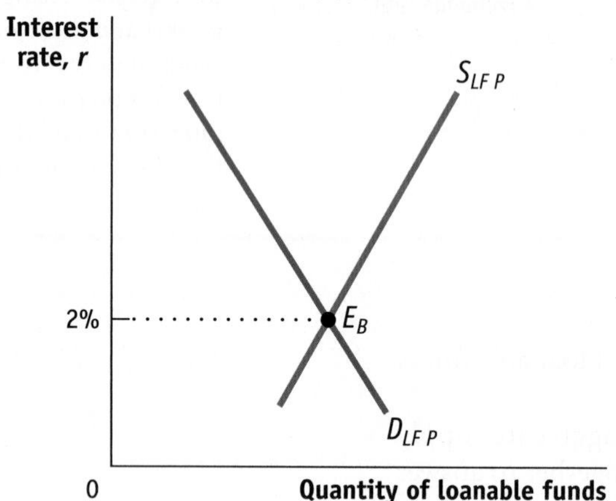

2. The situation shown in these figures will lead to which of the following?
- **a.** capital inflows into the United States
- **b.** capital inflows into Peru
- **c.** increased exports to Peru
- **d.** increased imports to the United States
- **e.** capital outflows from the United States

3. In the long run, what will happen to interest rates in the United States and Peru?

	United States	*Peru*
a.	increase	increase
b.	increase	decrease
c.	decrease	increase
d.	decrease	decrease
e.	no change	increase

4. If the real interest rate in country A is higher than the real interest rate in country B, capital will flow into country __________, causing the real interest rate in country A to __________.
- **a.** A; decrease
- **b.** B; decrease
- **c.** A; increase
- **d.** B; increase
- **e.** B; cannot be determined

5. An increase in capital inflows will cause a(n) __________ in the demand for the domestic currency and a(n) __________ in the exchange rate.
- **a.** increase; increase
- **b.** increase; decrease
- **c.** decrease; increase
- **d.** decrease; decrease
- **e.** no change; increase

6. Which central bank policy will lead to a decrease in capital inflows?
- **a.** raising the interest rate
- **b.** lowering the interest rate
- **c.** raising the interest paid on bank reserves
- **d.** contractionary monetary policy
- **e.** selling bonds

7. Which of the following will lead to an increase in a country's real interest rates and capital inflows?
- **a.** a fast-growing economy
- **b.** an increase in private savings rates
- **c.** a government budget surplus
- **d.** expansionary monetary policy
- **e.** all of the above

Tackle the AP® Test: Free-Response Questions

1. Draw two correctly labeled side-by-side graphs of the loanable funds market in the United States and China, showing a higher interest rate in the United States.
   a. Explain how the higher interest rate in the United States will affect capital flows between the two countries.
   b. On your graphs, label the international equilibrium interest rate and the size of the capital inflows and outflows.

Rubric for FRQ 1 (5 points)

1 point: Two loanable funds market graphs, labeled U.S. and China, with interest rate on the vertical axis and quantity of loanable funds on the horizontal axis.

1 point: Equilibrium interest rate is shown on the vertical axis where upward-sloping supply and downward-sloping demand curves for loanable funds intersect. Equilibrium interest rate is higher in the U.S. than in China.

1 point: Capital will flow into the U.S. because investors seek a higher return on their financial investments.

1 point: The international equilibrium interest rate is shown between the two graphs.

1 point: The size of capital inflow in the U.S. and outflow in China are shown on the graphs.

2. Suppose the United States and Australia were the only two countries in the world, and that both countries pursued a floating exchange rate regime. Note that the currency in Australia is the Australian dollar.
   a. Draw a correctly labeled graph showing equilibrium in the foreign exchange market for U.S. dollars.
   b. If the Federal Reserve pursues expansionary monetary policy, what will happen to the U.S. interest rate and international capital flows? Explain.
   c. On your graph of the foreign exchange market, show the effect of the Fed's policy on the supply of U.S. dollars, the demand for U.S. dollars, and the equilibrium exchange rate.
   d. How does the Fed's monetary policy affect U.S. aggregate demand? Explain. **(10 points)**

UNIT 6 Review

UNIT 6 Review Video

Adventures in AP® Economics Videos

Mod 6.2: Exchange Rates

economics by example

Is Globalization a Bad Word?

Module 6.1

1. A country's **balance of payments accounts** summarize its transactions with the rest of the world.
2. The **current account**, includes the **balance of payments on goods and services** together with balances on factor income and transfers. The **financial account**, measures a country's net sale of assets. The **capital account** measures a country's net flow of investments and loans. By definition, the balance of payments on the current account plus the balance of payments on the **capital and financial account** is zero.

Module 6.2

3. Currencies are traded in the **foreign exchange market**; the prices at which they are traded are **exchange rates**. When a currency rises against another currency, it **appreciates**; when it falls, it **depreciates**. The **equilibrium exchange rate** matches the quantity of that currency supplied to the foreign exchange market to the quantity demanded.
4. To correct for international differences in inflation rates, economists calculate **real exchange rates**, which multiply the exchange rate between two countries' respective currencies by the ratio of the countries' price levels. The current account responds only to changes in the real exchange rate, not the nominal exchange rate. **Purchasing power parity** is the exchange rate that makes the cost of a basket of goods and services equal in two countries. While purchasing power parity and the nominal exchange rate almost always differ, purchasing power parity is a good predictor of actual changes in the nominal exchange rate.

Module 6.3

5. Countries adopt different exchange rate regimes, rules governing exchange rate policy. The main types are fixed exchange rates, where the government takes action to keep the exchange rate at a target level, and floating exchange rates, where the exchange rate is free to fluctuate.
6. Exchange rate policy poses a dilemma: there are economic payoffs to stable exchange rates, but the policies used to fix the exchange rate have costs. Exchange market intervention requires large reserves, and exchange controls distort incentives. If monetary policy is used to help fix the exchange rate, it isn't available to use for domestic policy.
7. Fixed exchange rates aren't always permanent commitments: countries with a fixed exchange rate sometimes engage in **devaluations** or **revaluations**. In addition to helping eliminate a surplus of domestic currency on the foreign exchange market, a devaluation increases aggregate demand. Similarly, a revaluation reduces shortages of domestic currency and reduces aggregate demand.
8. Under floating exchange rates, expansionary monetary policy works in part through the exchange rate: cutting domestic interest rates leads to a depreciation, and through that to higher exports and lower imports, which increases aggregate demand. Contractionary monetary policy has the reverse effect.
9. The fact that one country's imports are another country's exports creates a link between the business cycles in different countries. Floating exchange rates, however, may reduce the strength of that link.

Module 6.4

10. Changes in the determinants of demand and supply in the foreign exchange market affect the equilibrium exchange rate.
11. **Protectionism** is the practice of limiting trade to protect domestic industries. The idea is to allow domestic producers to gain enough strength to compete

in global markets. Taxes on imports, known as **tariffs**, and limits on the quantities of goods that can be imported, known as **import quotas**, are the primary tools of protectionism. Tariffs and quotas affect the equilibrium exchange rate in the foreign exchange market.

12. Fiscal and monetary policy influence aggregate demand, real output, employment, the price level, and interest rates, thereby affecting exchange rates.

Module 6.5

13. Changes in the equilibrium exchange rate in the foreign exchange market can lead to changes in a country's net exports and aggregate demand, real output, employment, and the price level.

Module 6.6

14. Capital flows respond to international differences in interest rates and other rates of return; they can be usefully analyzed using an international version of the loanable funds model, which shows how a country where the interest rate would be low in the absence of capital flows sends funds to a country where the interest rate would be high in the absence of capital flows. The underlying determinants of capital flows are international differences in savings and opportunities for investment spending.
15. Central banks can influence the domestic interest rate, which affects net capital inflows.

Key Terms

AP® Exam Practice Questions

Multiple-Choice Questions

1. Which of the following transactions is counted in the U.S. balance of trade?
   a. A French importer buys a case of California wine.
   b. An American working for a Brazilian company deposits her paycheck.
   c. An American buys a bond from a Kenyan company.
   d. An American charity sends money to an Iraqi aid agency.
   e. A Chinese national buys stock in a U.S. company.
2. The difference between a country's exports and imports of goods is that country's
   a. balance of payments on its current account.
   b. balance of payments on its financial account.
   c. balance of payments on its capital account.
   d. merchandise trade balance.
   e. balance of payments on goods and services.
3. Which of the following relationships between the current account (*CA*) and the capital and financial account (*CFA*) must be true?
   a. $CA - CFA = 0$
   b. $CA + CFA = 0$
   c. $CA = CFA$
   d. $CA = 1/CFA$
   e. $(CA)(CFA) = 1$
4. Which of the following is a reason for capital to flow into a country?
   a. a rapidly growing economy
   b. government budget surpluses
   c. higher savings rates
   d. lower interest rates
   e. a relatively high supply of loanable funds

Refer to the following graphs and information for Questions 5–7.

Suppose that Northlandia and Southlandia are the only two trading countries in the world, that each nation runs a balance of payments on both the current account and the capital and financial account equal to zero, and that each nation sees the other's assets as identical to its own.

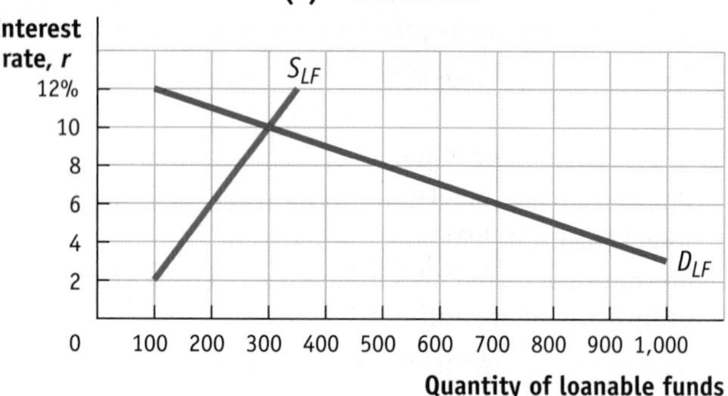

(b) Southlandia

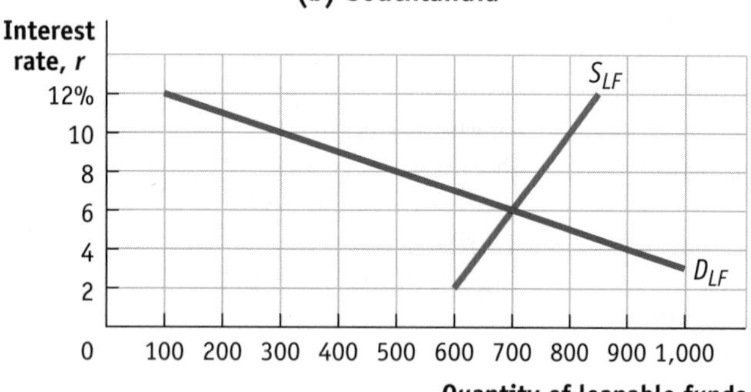

5. Given the situation depicted in the graphs, which of the following will happen?
  a. The interest rate in Northlandia will rise.
  b. The interest rate in Southlandia will fall.
  c. Capital will flow into Northlandia.
  d. Capital will flow into Southlandia.
  e. Southlandia will experience a balance of trade deficit.

6. Which of the following will happen in Southlandia?
  a. The quantity of loanable funds supplied will decrease.
  b. The supply of loanable funds will increase.
  c. The demand for loanable funds will decrease.
  d. The supply of loanable funds will decrease.
  e. The interest rate will decrease.

7. If the international equilibrium interest rate is 8%, which of the following will be true?
  a. Southlandia will experience a capital outflow of $250.
  b. Southlandia will experience a capital outflow of $700.
  c. Northlandia will experience a capital outflow of $250.
  d. Northlandia will experience a capital outflow of $300.
  e. The international equilibrium quantity of loanable funds will be $1,200.

8. Which of the following is traded in a foreign exchange market?
  a. imported goods only
  b. exported goods only
  c. both imported and exported goods
  d. international stocks and bonds
  e. currency

9. Which of the following will occur in the foreign exchange market as a result of capital inflow to the United States?
  a. a decrease in the demand for dollars
  b. a decrease in the dollar exchange rate
  c. an increase in the supply of dollars
  d. appreciation of the dollar
  e. a decrease in the quantity of dollars exchanged

10. The price in a foreign exchange market is a(n)
  a. real interest rate.
  b. nominal interest rate.
  c. tariff.
  d. exchange rate.
  e. discount rate.

Refer to the following graph and information for Questions 11–12.

The graph shows the foreign exchange market for the bern, the currency used in the country of Albernia.

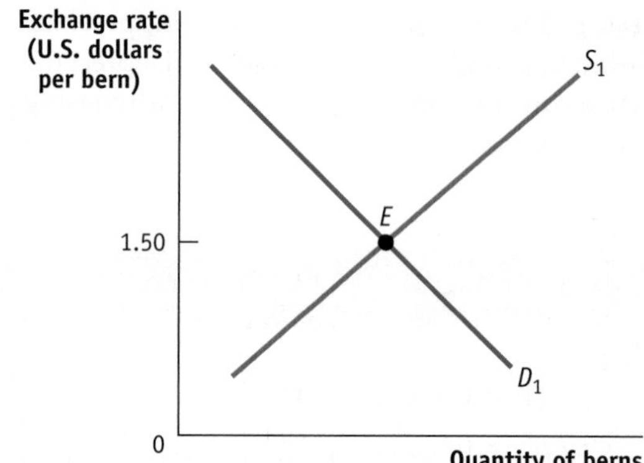

11. Given the equilibrium exchange rate on the graph, which of the following is true regarding the bern?
  a. It takes $1.50 to buy a bern.
  b. It takes $0.75 to buy a bern.
  c. It takes $0.67 to buy a bern.
  d. It takes 1.50 bern to buy a dollar.
  e. It takes 0.75 bern to buy a dollar.

12. How could depreciation of the bern be shown on the graph?
  a. a movement of the equilibrium exchange rate to 2
  b. a movement of the equilibrium exchange rate to 1
  c. a decrease in the equilibrium quantity of berns
  d. a rightward shift of the demand for berns
  e. a leftward shift of the supply of berns

13. Real exchange rates are adjusted for international differences in

a. exchange rates.
b. aggregate price levels.
c. GDP per capita.
d. capital flows.
e. income.

14. Which of the following is true if two countries have purchasing power parity?

a. The two countries' real GDP per capita is the same.
b. The two countries' imports equal their exports.
c. The nominal exchange rate ensures that goods cost the same amount in each country.
d. There are no capital inflows or outflows between the two countries.
e. The countries' exchange rates do not appreciate or depreciate.

15. When a government lets exchange rates be determined by foreign exchange markets, it is called

a. an exchange rate regime.
b. a fixed exchange rate.
c. a floating exchange rate.
d. a market exchange rate.
e. a foreign exchange control.

16. Governments intervene to keep the value of their currency down in order to

a. make domestic goods cheaper in the world market.
b. decrease the price of imported goods.
c. promote capital inflows.
d. decrease exports.
e. reduce aggregate demand.

17. A decrease in domestic interest rates will necessarily have which of the following effects in the foreign exchange market?

a. The supply of the domestic currency will decrease.
b. The demand for the domestic currency will decrease.
c. The exchange rate will increase.
d. The quantity of the domestic currency exchanged will rise.
e. The quantity of the domestic currency exchanged will fall.

18. An import quota on a good will do which of the following?

a. It will raise revenue for the government.
b. It will reduce the domestic price of the good.
c. It will raise the international price of the good.
d. It will reduce the quantity of the good sold domestically.
e. It will decrease domestic production of the good.

19. Which of the following is true of tariffs?

a. They are limits on the quantity of a good that can be imported.
b. They account for over 10% of federal government revenue in the United States.
c. They can result in trade wars between countries.
d. They do not protect domestic industries from competition.
e. They decrease the price of goods.

20. A goal of protectionism is to

a. generate revenue for the federal government.
b. lower the price of goods for domestic consumers.
c. increase world output through specialization and comparative advantage.
d. decrease competition for domestic industries.
e. raise the price of imported goods.

Questions 21 and 22 refer to the following graph.

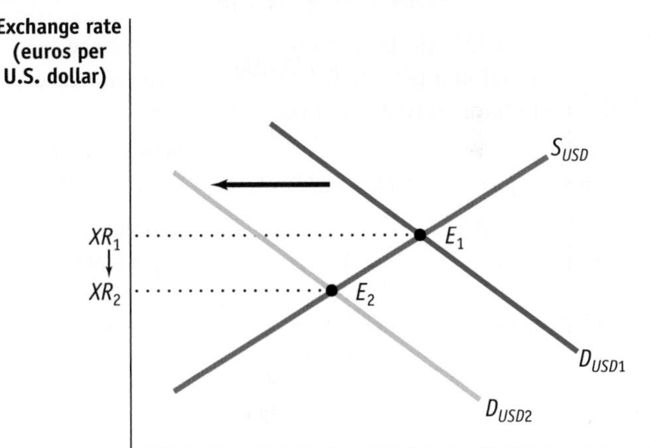

21. Which of the following could cause the movement from D_{USD1} to D_{USD2}?

a. More Americans travel to Europe.
b. The aggregate price level in the United States falls.
c. Exports from the United States increase.
d. Interest rates in the United States rise.
e. Europe goes into a recession.

22. When the exchange rate moves from XR_1 to XR_2, the U.S. dollar has

a. appreciated.
b. depreciated.
c. revalued.
d. become more valuable.
e. caused the relative price level in the United States to rise.

23. Assume the aggregate price level in Mexico increases relative to the aggregate price level in Canada. What will happen to the exchange rate between Mexico and Canada (expressed as Mexican pesos per Canadian dollar)?
   a. It will increase.
   b. It will decrease.
   c. It will remain unchanged.
   d. It will depreciate.
   e. The effect on the exchange rate cannot be determined.

24. Which of the following will result from the imposition of an import quota?
   a. an increase in government revenue
   b. an increase in imports
   c. a decrease in domestic supply
   d. an increase in domestic demand
   e. an increase in domestic price

25. Assume the U.S. dollar (USD) is exchanged for the Australian dollar (AUD). If GDP in Australia increases, what will happen to each of the following?

Demand for USD	*Demand for AUD*	*International Value of AUD*
a. no change	decreases	depreciates
b. increases	no change	depreciates
c. no change	decreases	appreciates
d. decreases	no change	depreciates
e. increase	increases	appreciates

Free-Response Questions

1. Draw a correctly labeled graph showing equilibrium in the market for Chinese yuan being exchanged for U.S. dollars (USD).
   a. Assume the real interest rate in China falls relative to the real interest rate in the United States. Show the impact of the change in the real interest rate on your graph.
   b. How will the change in relative interest rates from part a affect the value of Chinese yuan relative to the U.S. dollar?
   c. Assume that the U.S. current account balance is zero. Based on the change in the value of the yuan, will the U.S. current account balance move to a surplus, move to a deficit, or stay the same? Explain. **(5 points)**

2. Assume the two countries, Xenia and Yania, have flexible exchange rates. The currency in Xenia is the xen dollar (XD), and the currency in Yania is the yan dollar (YD).
   a. Assume the current account in Yania is in deficit and the price level declines. Use a correctly labeled graph of the foreign exchange market to show the effect on the value of the YD.
   b. Will the current account deficit in Yania increase, decrease, or remain unchanged? Explain. **(5 points)**

3. Assume the economy of the country of Mininia is in a recession.
   a. Use a correctly labeled graph of *AD*, *SRAS*, and *LRAS* to illustrate each of the following:
      i. the equilibrium output and price level, labeled Y_1 and PL_1
      ii. the long-run equilibrium output, labeled Y_f
   b. Show the effect of an expansionary fiscal policy on your graph from part a. Label the new output level Y_2.
   c. Draw a correctly labeled graph of the foreign exchange market for the country's currency, the mina, relative to the U.S. dollar.
   d. How will the value of the mina be affected by the change in output shown on your graph from part b? Show the effect on your graph from part c and explain. **(8 points)**

Putting It All Together

MACRO APPENDIX

In this Appendix, you will learn to:

- Use macroeconomic models to conduct policy analysis
- Improve your approach to free-response macroeconomics questions

alexsl/Getty Images

Having completed our study of basic macroeconomic models, we can use them to analyze scenarios and evaluate policy recommendations. In this Appendix, we develop a step-by-step approach to macroeconomic analysis. You can adapt this approach to problems involving any macroeconomic model, including models of aggregate demand and supply, production possibilities, money markets, and the Phillips curve. By the end of this Appendix, you will be able to combine mastery of the principles of macroeconomics with problem-solving skills to analyze a new scenario on your own.

A Structure for Macroeconomic Analysis

In our study of macroeconomics, we have seen questions about the macroeconomy take many different forms. No matter what the specific question, most macroeconomic problems have the following components:

1. *A starting point.* To analyze any situation, you have to know where to start.
2. *A pivotal event.* This might be a change in the economy or a policy response to the initial situation.
3. *Initial effects of the event.* An event will generally have some initial, short-run effects.
4. *Secondary and long-run effects of the event.* After the short-run effects run their course, there are typically secondary effects, and the economy will move toward its long-run equilibrium.

For example, you might be asked to consider the following scenario and answer the associated questions:

Assume the economy is currently operating at an aggregate output level above potential output.

a. Draw a correctly labeled aggregate supply and demand graph showing each of the following:

  i. the short-run equilibrium real output and price level, labelled Y_1 and PL_1

  ii. the full-employment level of output, labelled Y_P

b. What problem exists in the economy?

Now assume that the central bank closes the output gap using contractionary monetary policy.

c. Will the central bank increase or decrease interest rates?

d. Show the short-run effect of the change in interest rates on your graph from part a. Label the new short-run equilibrium real output and price level as Y_2 and PL_2, respectively.

e. Assume the country's currency is called the "ounce" and Canada is the country's largest trading partner. Draw a correctly labeled graph of the foreign exchange market for the ounce and show how the change in the interest rate you previously identified will affect the demand for ounces and the international value of the ounce relative to the Canadian dollar. Based solely on the change in the exchange rate you identified in your graph, will the country's exports increase, decrease, or stay the same? Explain.

f. How will contractionary monetary policy affect the country's real interest rate in the long run? Explain.

Taken as a whole, this scenario and the associated questions can seem overwhelming. Let's start by breaking down our analysis into four components.

Kwanchai Lerttanapunyaporn/EyeEm/ Getty Images

How will the central bank's monetary policy change nominal interest rates?

1. **The starting point**
   Assume the economy is currently operating at an aggregate output level above potential output.

2. **The pivotal event**
   Now assume that the central bank closes the output gap using contractionary monetary policy.

3. **Initial effects of the event**
   Show the short-run effect of the change in interest rates on your graph from part a. Label the new short-run equilibrium real output and price level as Y_2 and PL_2, respectively.

4. **Secondary and long-run effects of the event**
   Assume the country's currency is called the "ounce" and Canada is the country's largest trading partner. Draw a correctly labeled graph of the foreign exchange market for the ounce and show how the change in the interest rate you previously identified will affect the demand for ounces and the international value of the ounce relative to the Canadian dollar. Based solely on the change in the exchange rate you identified in your graph, will the country's exports increase, decrease, or stay the same? Explain.

   How will contractionary monetary policy affect the country's real interest rate in the long run? Explain.

Now we are ready to look at each of the steps and untangle this scenario.

The Starting Point

Assume the economy is currently operating at an aggregate output level above potential output.

a. Draw a correctly labeled aggregate supply and demand graph showing each of the following:

- **i.** the short-run equilibrium real output and price level, labelled Y_1 and PL_1
- **ii.** the full-employment level of output, labelled Y_P

b. What problem exists in the economy?

To analyze a situation, you have to know where to start. You will frequently use the aggregate demand–aggregate supply (*AD–AS*) model to evaluate macroeconomic scenarios. In this model, there are three possible starting points: long-run macroeconomic equilibrium, a recessionary gap, and an inflationary gap. This means that there are three possible "starting-point" graphs, as shown in **Figure A-1**. The economy can be in long-run macroeconomic equilibrium with production at potential output, as in panel (a); it can be in short-run macroeconomic equilibrium at an aggregate output level below potential output (creating a recessionary gap), as in panel (b); or it can be in short-run macroeconomic equilibrium at an aggregate output level above potential output (creating an inflationary gap), as in panel (c) and in our scenario.

FIGURE A-1 Analysis Starting Points

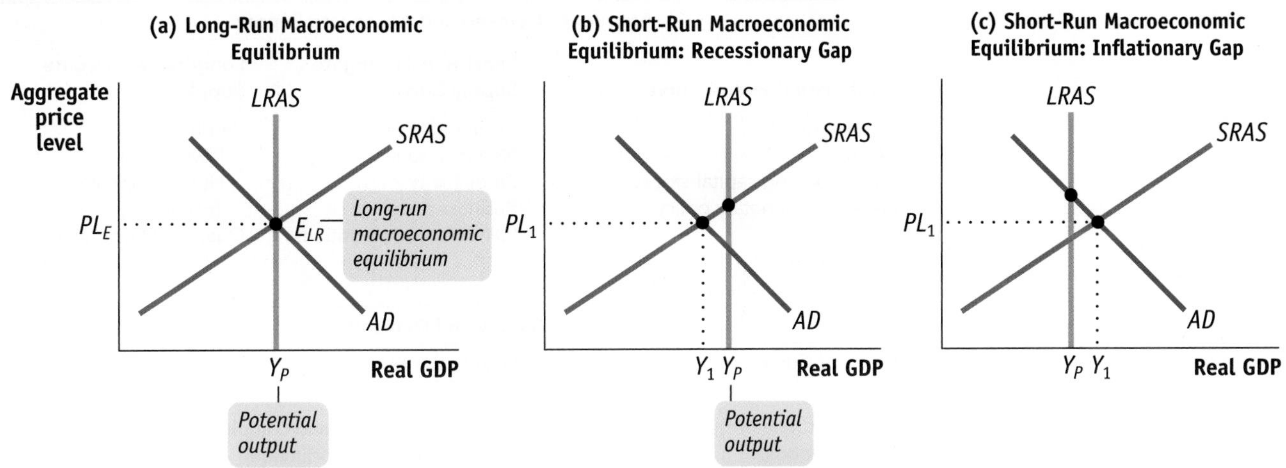

Panels (a), (b), and (c) represent the three basic starting points for analysis using the aggregate demand–aggregate supply model.

The Pivotal Event

Now assume that the central bank closes the output gap using contractionary monetary policy. Will the central bank increase or decrease interest rates?

It is the events in a scenario that make it interesting. Perhaps a country goes into or recovers from a recession, inflation catches consumers off guard or becomes expected, consumers or businesses become more or less confident, holdings of money or wealth change, trading partners prosper or falter, or oil prices plummet or spike. The event can also be expansionary or contractionary monetary or fiscal policy.

While it's impossible to foresee all of the scenarios you might encounter on the AP® exam, we can group the determinants of change into a reasonably small set of major factors that influence macroeconomic models. **Table A-1** matches major factors with the curves they affect. With these influences in mind, it is relatively easy to proceed through a problem by identifying how the given events affect these factors. Most hypothetical scenarios involve changes in just one or two major factors. Although the real world is more complex, it is largely the same factors that change—there are just more of them changing at once.

As shown in Table A-1, many curves are shifted by changes in only a small number of major factors. Even for the aggregate demand curve, which has the largest number of associated factors, you can simplify the task further by asking yourself, "Does the event influence consumer spending, investment spending, government spending, or net exports?" If so, aggregate demand shifts. A shift of the long-run aggregate supply curve is caused only by events that affect labor productivity or the number of workers.

In the supply and demand model, there are five major factors that shift the demand curve and five major factors that shift the supply curve. Most examples using this model will represent a change in one of these 10 factors. The loanable funds market, money market, and foreign exchange market have their own clearly identified factors that affect supply or demand. With this information you can link specific events to relevant factors in the models to see what changes will occur. Remember that having correctly labeled axes on your graphs is crucial to a correct analysis.

Often, as in our scenario, the event is a policy response to an undesirable starting point such as a recessionary or inflationary gap. Expansionary policy is used to combat a recession, and contractionary policy is used to combat inflationary pressures. To begin analyzing a policy response, you need to fully understand how the central bank can implement each type of monetary policy (e.g., increase or decrease the interest rate)

AP® ECON TIP

With the infinite number of possible changes in policy, politics, the economy, and markets, don't expect to analyze a familiar scenario on the AP® exam. But if you understand how to use the macroeconomic models (as we discuss in this Appendix), you will be ready for whatever scenarios you face!

Table A-1 Major Factors That Shift Curves in Each Model

Aggregate Demand and Aggregate Supply		
Aggregate Demand Curve	**Short-Run Aggregate Supply Curve**	**Long-Run Aggregate Supply Curve**
Expectations Wealth Size of existing capital stock Fiscal and monetary policy Net exports Interest rates Investment spending	Commodity prices Nominal wages Productivity Business taxes Inflationary expectations	Productivity Physical capital Human capital Technology Quantity of resources

Supply and Demand	
Demand Curve	**Supply Curve**
Income Prices of substitutes and complements (related goods) Tastes Consumer expectations Number of consumers	Input prices Prices of substitutes and complements (related goods) in production Technology Producer expectations Number of producers

Loanable Funds Market	
Demand Curve	**Supply Curve**
Investment opportunities Government borrowing	Private saving behavior Capital inflows

Money Market	
Demand Curve	**Supply Curve**
Aggregate price level Real GDP Technology (related to money market) Institutions (related to money market)	Affected by the central bank

Foreign Exchange Market	
Demand Curve	**Supply Curve**
Foreigners' purchases of domestic Goods Services Assets	Domestic residents' purchases of foreign Goods Services Assets

and how that policy eventually affects the economy. You also need to understand how the government can implement expansionary or contractionary fiscal policy by raising or lowering taxes or government spending.

The Initial Effect of the Event

Show the short-run effect of the change in interest rates on your graph from part a. Label the new short-run equilibrium real output and price level as Y_2 and PL_2, respectively.

We have seen that events will create short-run effects in our models. In the short run, fiscal and monetary policy both affect the economy by shifting the aggregate demand curve. As shown in panel (a) of **Figure A-2**, expansionary policy shifts aggregate demand to the right, and as shown in panel (b), contractionary policy shifts aggregate demand to the left. To illustrate the effect of a policy response, shift the aggregate demand curve on your starting point graph and indicate the effects of the shift on the aggregate price level and aggregate output.

Secondary and Long-Run Effects of the Event

Assume the country's currency is called the "ounce" and Canada is the country's largest trading partner. Draw a correctly labeled graph of the foreign exchange market for the ounce and

FIGURE A-2 Monetary and Fiscal Policy Close Output Gaps

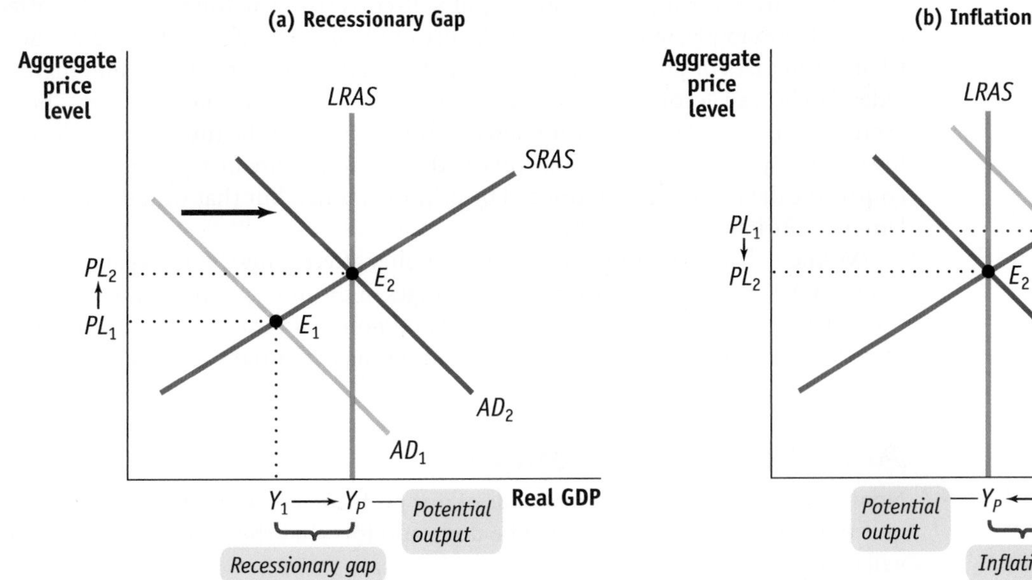

By shifting the aggregate demand curve, monetary and fiscal policy can close output gaps in the economy, as shown in panel (a) for a recessionary gap and panel (b) for an inflationary gap.

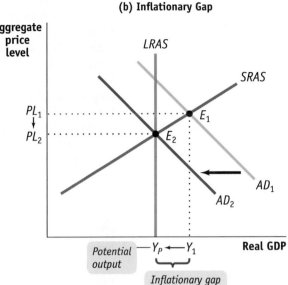

show how the change in the interest rate you previously identified will affect the demand for ounces and the international value of the ounce relative to the Canadian dollar. Based solely on the change in the exchange rate you identified in your graph, will the country's exports increase, decrease, or stay the same? Explain.

How will contractionary monetary policy affect the country's real interest rate in the long run? Explain.

Secondary Effects

In addition to the initial, short-run effects of any event, there will be secondary effects and the economy will move to its long-run equilibrium after the short-run effects run their course.

We have seen that negative or positive demand shocks (including those created by inappropriate monetary or fiscal policy) move the economy away from long-run macroeconomic equilibrium. As explained in Module 3.7 in the absence of policy responses, such events will eventually be offset through changes in short-run aggregate supply resulting from changes in nominal wage rates. This will move the economy back to long-run macroeconomic equilibrium.

If the short-run effects of an action result in changes in real interest rates, the aggregate price level, or real GDP, there will also be secondary effects throughout the open economy. International capital flows and international trade can be affected as a result of the initial effects experienced in the economy. For example, a change in the interest rate, as in our scenario, will lead to a change in international capital flows. Changes in capital flows affect the demand for a currency and therefore its equilibrium exchange rate. Interest rate changes also affect aggregate demand through changes in imports or exports caused by currency appreciation and depreciation. A change in the price level will affect the relative price of imports and exports, and therefore will also affect the value of net exports. These secondary effects act to reinforce the effects of monetary policy.

MANDEL NGAN/Getty Images

You've seen the speech; now, how would you analyze the proposed policy?

Long-Run Effects

While deviations from potential output self-correct in the long run, other effects remain. For example, in the long run, the use of fiscal policy affects the federal budget. Changes in taxes or government spending that lead to budget deficits (and increased federal debt) can "crowd out" private investment spending in the long run. The government's increased demand for loanable funds drives up the interest rate, decreases investment spending, and partially offsets the initial increase in aggregate demand. Of course, the deficit could be addressed by printing money, but that would lead to problems with inflation in the long run.

We know that in the long run, monetary policy affects only the aggregate price level, not real GDP. Because money is neutral, changes in the money supply have no effect on the real economy. The aggregate price level and nominal values will be affected by the same proportion, leaving real values (including the real interest rate as mentioned in our scenario) unchanged.

Analyzing Our Scenario

Now let's address the specific demands of our problem. Focus on the verbs used in the question — they tell you what must be done and for what the points in the questions will be awarded.

Assume the economy is currently operating at an aggregate output level above potential output.

a. Draw a correctly labeled aggregate supply and demand graph showing each of the following:

i. the short-run equilibrium real output and price level, labelled Y_1 and PL_1

ii. the full-employment level of output, labelled Y_P

b. What problem exists in the economy?

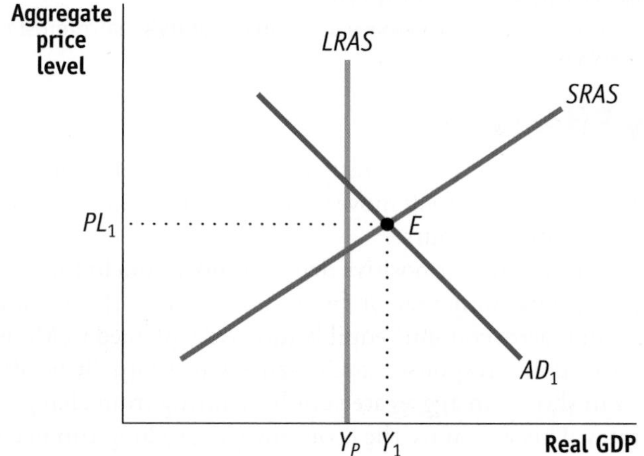

The economy is experiencing inflation.

Now assume that the central bank closes the output gap using contractionary monetary policy.

c. Will the central bank increase or decrease interest rates?

d. Show the short-run effect of the change in interest rate on your graph from part a. Label the new short-run equilibrium real output and price level as Y_2 and PL_2, respectively.

The central bank will increase the interest rate. A higher interest rate will lead to decreased investment and consumer spending, decreasing aggregate demand. The equilibrium price level will decrease to PL_2 and real GDP will decrease to Y_P to close the output gap.

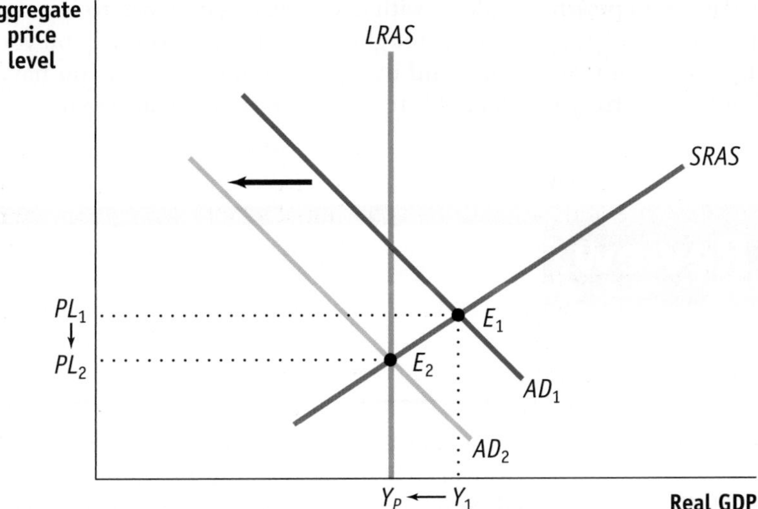

- Assume the country's currency is called the "ounce" and Canada is the country's largest trading partner. Draw a correctly labeled graph of the foreign exchange market for the ounce and show how the change in the interest rate you previously identified will affect the demand for ounces and the international value of the ounce relative to the Canadian dollar.

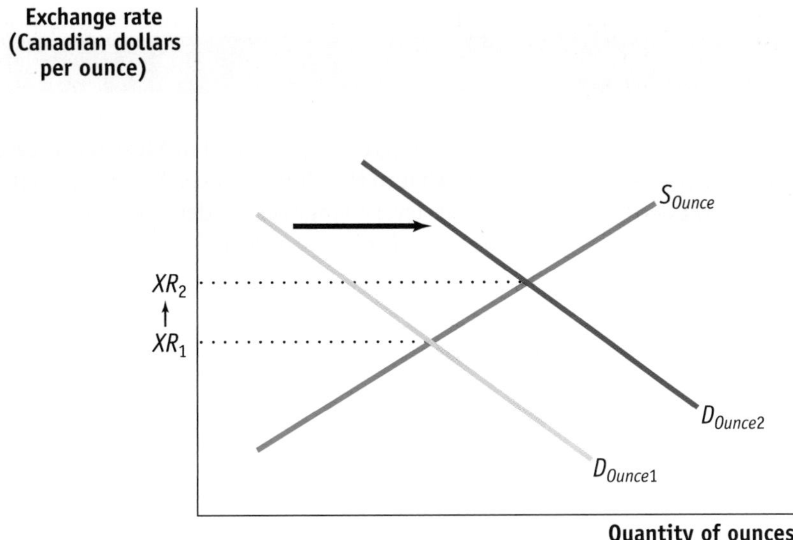

The increase in the country's interest rate will increase the demand for ounces as investors need ounces in order to invest at the country's higher interest rate. The ounce appreciates relative to the Canadian dollar.

- Based solely on the change in the exchange rate you identified in your graph, will the country's exports increase, decrease, or stay the same? Explain.

The appreciation of the ounce/depreciation of the Canadian dollar means that the country's exports to Canada will decrease because Canadians will need more Canadian dollars to purchase the country's exports.

- How will contractionary monetary policy affect the country's real interest rate in the long run? Explain.

There will be no effect on the real interest rate in the long run because, due to the neutrality of money, changes in the money supply do not affect real values in the long run.

Each AP® exam presents students with new scenarios designed to test their understanding of the models presented throughout this book. If you rely on your understanding of economic principles and use the economic models you have studied throughout the course, you will be able to analyze any unfamiliar scenario!

Appendix Review

Check Your Understanding

1. The economy is operating in long-run macroeconomic equilibrium.
   a. Show this situation using a correctly labeled aggregate demand–aggregate supply graph.
   b. Use your graph to show the short-run effect on real GDP and the aggregate price level if there is a decrease in government spending.
   c. What will happen to the aggregate price level and real GDP in the long run? Explain.
   d. Suppose the government is experiencing a persistent budget deficit. How will the decrease in government spending affect that deficit? Use a correctly labeled graph of the loanable funds market to show the effect of a decrease in government spending on the real interest rate.

Tackle the AP® Test: Multiple-Choice Questions

Questions 1–7 refer to the following scenario:

The United States and Mexico are trading partners. Suppose a flu outbreak significantly decreases U.S. tourism in Mexico and causes the Mexican economy to enter a recession. Assume that the money that would have been spent by U.S. tourists in Mexico is, instead, not spent at all.

1. Which of the following occurs as a result of the recession in Mexico?
   a. Output in Mexico increases.
   b. Aggregate demand in the United States decreases.
   c. The price level in Mexico increases.
   d. Output in the United States increases.
   e. The price level in the United States increases.

2. What is the effect of Mexico's falling income on the demand for money and the nominal interest rate in Mexico?

Demand for money	*Nominal interest rate*
a. increases	decreases
b. decreases	decreases
c. increases	increases
d. decreases	increases
e. increases	no change

3. Given what happens to the nominal interest rate, if the aggregate price level in Mexico decreases, what will happen to the real interest rate?
   a. It will increase.
   b. It will decrease.
   c. It will not change.
   d. It will stabilize.
   e. The effect cannot be determined.

4. Suppose the aggregate price level in Mexico decreases relative to that in the United States. What is the effect of this price level change on the demand, and on the exchange rate, for Mexican pesos?

Demand for pesos	*Exchange rate*
a. increases	appreciates
b. increases	depreciates
c. decreases	appreciates
d. decreases	depreciates
e. decreases	no change

5. If the Mexican government pursues expansionary fiscal policy in response to the recession, what will happen to aggregate demand and aggregate supply in Mexico in the short run?

Aggregate demand	*Short-run aggregate supply*
a. increases	increases
b. increases	decreases
c. decreases	increases
d. decreases	decreases
e. increases	no change

6. Suppose the government of Mexico pursues an expansionary fiscal policy leading to an increased budget deficit and national debt. If the government borrows to finance the debt, what will happen in the market for loanable funds?

	Interest rate	*Quantity of loanable funds*
a.	increase	increase
b.	increase	decrease
c.	decrease	increase
d.	decrease	decrease
e.	increase	no change

7. How will a decrease in U.S. tourism to Mexico resulting from a flu outbreak affect Mexico's *LRAS* curve and long-run economic growth?

	LRAS	*Long-run growth*
a.	shift to the right	increase
b.	shift to the left	decrease
c.	shift to the right	decrease
d.	shift to the left	increase
e.	no change	no change

Tackle the AP® Test: Free-Response Questions

1. Suppose the U.S. economy is experiencing a recession.
   a. Draw a correctly labeled aggregate demand–aggregate supply graph showing the aggregate demand, short-run aggregate supply, long-run aggregate supply, equilibrium output, and aggregate price level.
   b. Assume that energy prices increase in the United States. Show the effects of this increase on the equilibrium in your graph from part a.
   c. According to your graph, how does the increase in energy prices affect unemployment and inflation in the economy?
   d. Assume the United States and Canada are the only two countries in an open economy and that energy prices have remained unchanged in Canada. Draw a correctly labeled graph of the foreign exchange market for U.S. dollars, and use it to show the effect of increased U.S. energy prices on the demand for U.S. dollars. Explain.

Rubric for FRQ 1 (10 points)

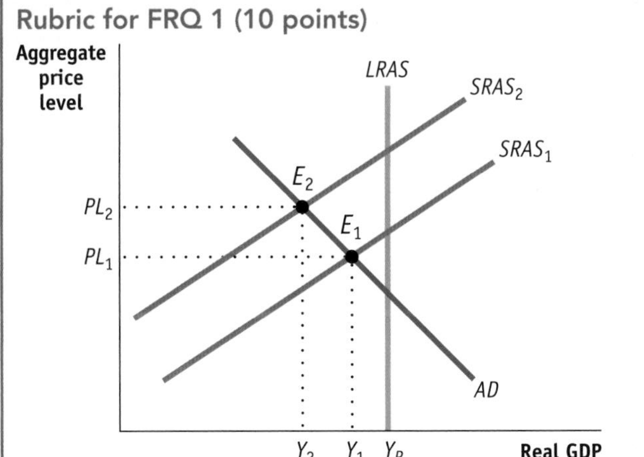

1 point: The vertical axis is labeled "Aggregate price level" and the horizontal axis is labeled "Aggregate output" or "Real GDP." The *AD* curve slopes downward, the *SRAS* curve slopes upward, and the *LRAS* curve is vertical.

1 point: The equilibrium is found where the *SRAS* curve crosses the *AD* curve, and the equilibrium aggregate price level and aggregate output are shown on the axes at this point.

1 point: The equilibrium is to the left of the *LRAS* curve.

1 point: The *SRAS* curve shifts to the left and the equilibrium aggregate price level and output are shown on the axes at the new equilibrium (increased aggregate price level, decreased aggregate output).

1 point: It increases unemployment.

1 point: It increases the aggregate price level (inflation).

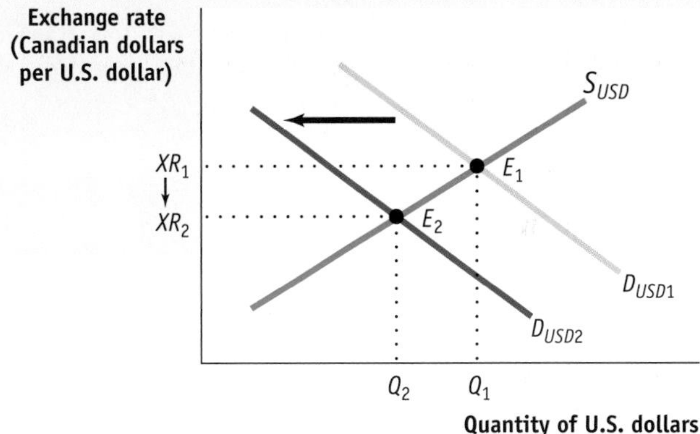

1 point: The vertical axis is labeled "Exchange rate (Canadian dollars per U.S. dollar)" and the horizontal axis is labeled "Quantity of U.S. dollars." Demand for U.S. dollars slopes downward and is labeled; supply of U.S. dollars slopes upward and is labeled.

1 point: The equilibrium exchange rate and quantity of U.S. dollars are shown on the axes at the intersection of the demand and supply curves.

1 point: The demand for U.S. dollars will decrease.

1 point: The inflation in the United States will lead to a decrease in the demand for U.S. exports (which must be purchased with U.S. dollars).

2. Assume the United States is operating below potential output.
   a. Draw a correctly labeled aggregate demand–aggregate supply graph showing equilibrium in the economy.
   b. Suppose the government decreases taxes. On your graph, show how the decrease in taxes will affect *AD*, *SRAS*, *LRAS*, equilibrium aggregate price level, and output.
   c. Assume the decrease in taxes led to an increased budget deficit and that the deficit spending was funded through government borrowing from the public. Use a correctly labeled graph of the market for loanable funds to show the effect of increased borrowing on the interest rate.
   d. Given the effect on the interest rate from part c, draw a correctly labeled graph of the foreign exchange market showing the effect of the change in the interest rate on the supply of U.S. dollars. Explain how the interest rate affects the supply of U.S. dollars.
   e. According to your graph from part d, what has happened to the international value of the U.S. dollar? How will this affect U.S. exports and aggregate demand? **(10 points)**

AP® Macroeconomics Exam
Practice Test

Multiple-Choice Questions

Refer to the figure below to answer Question 1.

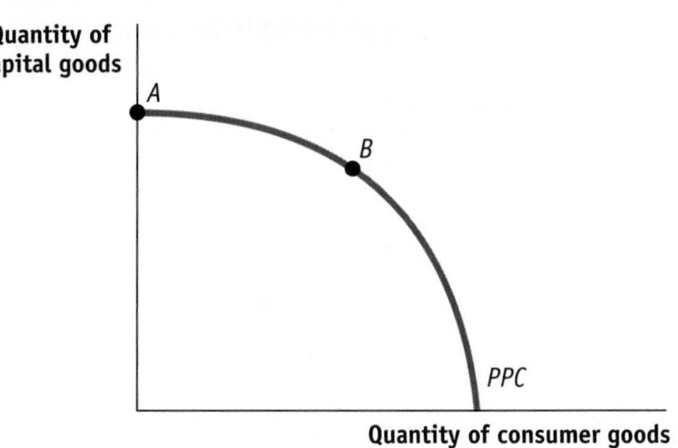

1. A movement from point *B* to point *A* illustrates which of the following?
   a. a choice to produce only capital goods
   b. an advance in technology
   c. a decrease in available resources used to produce consumer goods
   d. an increase in the price of capital goods
   e. an increase in efficiency

Refer to the figure below to answer Question 2.

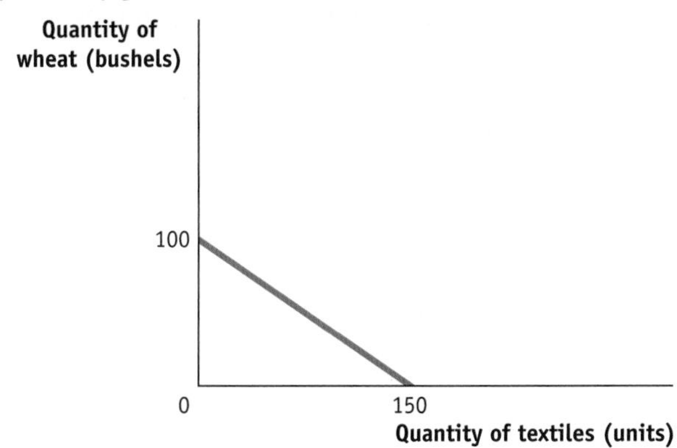

2. A country can produce either 100 bushels of wheat or 150 units of textiles, as shown on the graph above. If an advance in technology affects only the production of wheat, what happens to the slope of the production possibilities curve and the opportunity cost of wheat?

	Slope	*Opportunity cost of wheat*
a.	no change	no change
b.	decrease	decrease
c.	increase	decrease
d.	no change	increase
e.	decrease	increase

3. According to the concept of comparative advantage, which of the following is true when countries specialize and trade?
   a. Each country obtains an absolute advantage.
   b. Total world output increases.
   c. The production possibilities curve for both countries shifts outward.
   d. Prices fall in both countries.
   e. Deadweight loss is created.

Refer to the figure below to answer Question 4.

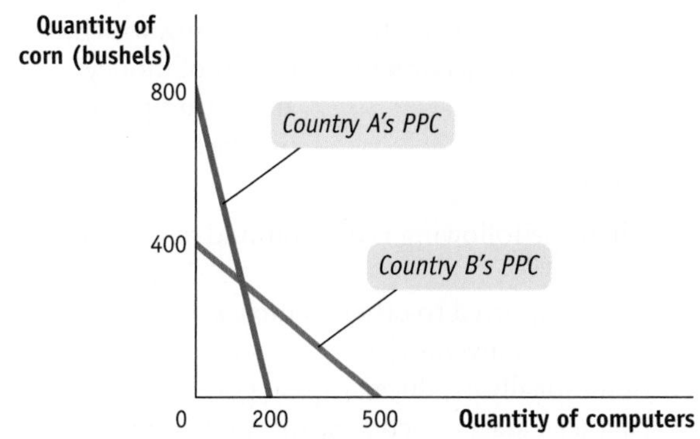

4. Using equal amounts of labor hours, two countries, Country A and Country B, can produce corn and computers as shown. Based on the information provided, which of the following is true?
   a. Country A has an absolute advantage in the production of corn and computers.
   b. Country B has an absolute advantage in the production of corn and computers.
   c. Country A has a comparative advantage in the production of computers.
   d. Country B has a comparative advantage in the production of corn.
   e. Country A has an absolute advantage in the production of corn.

5. If the price of a complementary good increases, which of the following will happen to the price and the quantity sold in a market?

	Price	*Quantity sold*
a.	increase	increase
b.	increase	decrease
c.	decrease	increase
d.	decrease	decrease
e.	increase	no change

6. If the wages of workers producing a good decrease, the price and quantity of the good sold will change in which of the following ways?

	Price	*Quantity*
a.	increase	increase
b.	increase	decrease
c.	decrease	increase
d.	decrease	decrease
e.	increase	no change

7. If real gross domestic product is declining, the economy is most likely experiencing which of the following?

a. increasing unemployment
b. negative long-run economic growth
c. inflationary pressures
d. an increase in aggregate demand
e. a recovery

8. In the circular-flow model of an economy, which of the following is an injection into the flow of money?

a. savings
b. imports
c. exports
d. consumption
e. taxes

9. Which of the following is not counted in a country's GDP?

a. goods exported to other countries
b. changes in inventories
c. domestically produced capital goods
d. financial assets, such as stocks and bonds
e. newly produced services

10. Which of the following is true of the relationship between real GDP and nominal GDP?

a. Real GDP is higher than nominal GDP when there is inflation in the economy.
b. Real GDP is equal to nominal GDP when the economy is at full employment.
c. Real GDP minus nominal GDP equals the rate of inflation.
d. Real GDP is nominal GDP adjusted for changes in the price level.
e. Real GDP increases when nominal GDP increases.

11. Which of the following transactions would be included in the calculation of GDP?

a. Lei buys a used car.
b. Makena buys a new softball bat.
c. Eric mows his own lawn rather than paying someone else $25 to mow it.
d. Paola resells her ticket to a football game.
e. Kumar volunteers for 3 hours per week as a tutor at the local high school.

12. If the real interest rate is 1% and the nominal interest rate is 4%, the expected rate of inflation is

a. 0%.
b. 1%.
c. 2%.
d. 3%.
e. 5%.

13. Suppose that last year the price level increased and the production of goods and services increased. Nominal GDP has necessarily

a. increased, but real GDP decreased.
b. increased, but the value of real GDP cannot be determined.
c. stayed the same, but real GDP increased.
d. increased, and real GDP increased.
e. decreased, but real GDP increased.

14. Given the information provided below, what are the number of unemployed and the labor force participation rate (*LFPR*)?

Population	1,000
Labor force	800
Employment	600

	Unemployed	*LFPR*
a.	200	80%
b.	400	80%
c.	200	25%
d.	400	60%
e.	400	25%

15. A worker who is laid off due to a recession is experiencing which type of unemployment?

a. temporary
b. frictional
c. cyclical
d. structural
e. seasonal

16. Which of the following could lead the unemployment rate to be overstated?

a. discouraged workers
b. teenage workers
c. part-time workers
d. retired workers
e. workers taking time to choose a job offer

17. Substitution bias results when

a. discouraged workers leave the labor force.
b. expected inflation reduces real interest rates.
c. consumers purchase alternative goods in response to price changes.
d. the demand for one good affects the price of a related good.
e. buyers choose imports over domestically produced goods and services.

18. If the general price level doubles and at the same time a worker's real wage rate increases, what must be true of the worker's nominal wage rate?

a. It doubled.
b. It increased by less than double.
c. It increased by more than double.
d. It decreased.
e. It did not change.

19. Which of the following is true of the natural rate of unemployment?
- **a.** It equals the actual rate of unemployment in short-run equilibrium.
- **b.** It includes both frictional and structural unemployment.
- **c.** It measures cyclical unemployment.
- **d.** It changes with the business cycle.
- **e.** It increases over time.

20. A Canadian recession will affect the United States' aggregate supply and demand in which of the following ways?

	Aggregate supply	*Aggregate demand*
a.	increase	increase
b.	increase	decrease
c.	decrease	increase
d.	decrease	decrease
e.	no change	decrease

21. Which of the following will shift the aggregate demand curve to the right?
- **a.** contractionary monetary policy
- **b.** a decrease in the aggregate price level
- **c.** a decrease in the value of household assets
- **d.** a decrease in the consumer confidence index
- **e.** an increase in planned business investment

22. If the marginal propensity to consume in an economy is 0.8 and the government increases spending by $5 million, GDP will increase by how much?
- **a.** $1 million
- **b.** $5 million
- **c.** $25 million
- **d.** $50 million
- **e.** $100 million

23. In the short run, a decrease in aggregate demand will change the price level and aggregate output in which of the following ways?

	Price level	*Aggregate output*
a.	increase	increase
b.	increase	decrease
c.	decrease	increase
d.	decrease	decrease
e.	increase	no change

24. Which of the following is most likely to cause a leftward shift in the long-run aggregate supply curve?
- **a.** a decrease in the wage rate
- **b.** a decrease in short-run aggregate supply
- **c.** contractionary fiscal policy
- **d.** a deadly disease that decreases the size of the labor force
- **e.** a long-term decrease in demand

25. If an economy is in long-run equilibrium, how will an increase in aggregate demand affect real GDP and nominal wages in the long run?

	Real GDP	*Nominal wages*
a.	increase	increase
b.	increase	decrease
c.	decrease	increase
d.	decrease	decrease
e.	no change	increase

26. The long-run aggregate supply curve is always
- **a.** vertical and below potential output.
- **b.** horizontal and at potential output.
- **c.** upward-sloping at all output levels.
- **d.** vertical and at potential output.
- **e.** horizontal at all output levels.

27. An economy experiences inflationary pressures when the equilibrium level of output is
- **a.** too low.
- **b.** above the full employment level of output.
- **c.** equal to the full employment level of output.
- **d.** decreasing.
- **e.** in long-run equilibrium.

28. Which of the following policies might provide a remedy when the equilibrium output in an economy is above the potential level of output?
- **a.** Increase government spending.
- **b.** Decrease the overnight interbank lending rate.
- **c.** Increase transfer payments.
- **d.** Raise taxes.
- **e.** Buy more government securities.

29. Which of the following would cause the aggregate demand curve to shift to the right?
- **a.** an increase in taxes
- **b.** a decrease in consumer wealth
- **c.** an increase in consumer confidence
- **d.** a decrease in exports
- **e.** an increase in savings

30. Which of the following is a liability for a commercial bank?
- **a.** deposits
- **b.** loans
- **c.** reserves
- **d.** Treasury securities
- **e.** its building and equipment

31. Which of the following is a commercial bank's opportunity cost of loaning out its excess reserves?
- **a.** the nominal interest rate paid by borrowers
- **b.** the real interest rate paid by borrowers
- **c.** the interest on reserve balances paid by the central bank
- **d.** the rate of return on investments made by businesses
- **e.** the average return on stock market investments

32. Which of the following is an example of an automatic stabilizer supporting the economy during a recession?
- **a.** The government cuts spending to balance the federal budget.
- **b.** Marginal tax rates are increased to generate revenue.
- **c.** The number of people eligible for transfer payments declines as incomes decline.
- **d.** Tax revenues decline as incomes decline.
- **e.** The eligibility period for unemployment compensation ends.

33. Which of the following will decrease the ability of the banking system to create money?
- **a.** a decrease in the amount of cash people hold
- **b.** a decrease in the reserve requirement
- **c.** an increase in the amount of excess reserves held by banks
- **d.** an increase in banks' willingness to make loans
- **e.** a decrease in the discount rate

34. If the reserve ratio is 10%, what is the maximum amount of money that could be created by a new deposit of $1,000?
- **a.** $1,000
- **b.** $1,010
- **c.** $1,100
- **d.** $10,000
- **e.** $20,000

35. Advances in information technology such as digital payment systems have had what effect on the demand for money and the interest rate?

	Money demand	*Interest rate*
a.	increase	increase
b.	increase	decrease
c.	decrease	increase
d.	decrease	decrease
e.	no change	decrease

36. Which of the following will decrease the demand for money?
- **a.** an increase in the aggregate price level
- **b.** a decrease in the use of mobile devices for payments
- **c.** an increase in the interest rate
- **d.** a decrease in the supply of money
- **e.** a decrease in real GDP

37. Which of the following will increase the interest rate in the market for loanable funds?
- **a.** a decrease in the expected rate of return from investment spending
- **b.** an increase in government budget deficits
- **c.** an increase in the aggregate savings rate
- **d.** a decrease in expected inflation
- **e.** an increase in capital inflows

38. Which of the following is true of the money supply curve?
- **a.** It shifts to the right when the interest rate increases.
- **b.** It shifts to the left when the savings rate decreases.
- **c.** It is vertical.
- **d.** It shows a positive relationship between the interest rate and the quantity of loanable funds.
- **e.** It shifts to the left when the central bank buys government bonds.

39. Crowding out occurs when government borrowing leads to an increase in
- **a.** real GDP.
- **b.** inflation.
- **c.** consumer confidence.
- **d.** unemployment.
- **e.** interest rates.

40. According to the Quantity Theory of Money, the money supply multiplied by the velocity of money is equal to
- **a.** nominal GDP.
- **b.** real GDP.
- **c.** full-employment real GDP.
- **d.** the price level.
- **e.** a constant value.

41. An open market purchase of securities by a central bank will lead to which of the following?
- **a.** a decrease in the demand for money
- **b.** a decrease in interest rates
- **c.** an increase in investment demand
- **d.** a decrease in aggregate demand
- **e.** a decrease in the price level

42. The Federal Reserve will take action to decrease the federal funds rate in an attempt to
- **a.** increase unemployment.
- **b.** increase the money supply.
- **c.** reduce inflation.
- **d.** increase real GDP.
- **e.** discourage investment.

43. An increase in expected inflation is likely to have which of the following effects?
- **a.** shift the long-run Phillips curve to the right
- **b.** shift the short-run Phillips curve downward
- **c.** increase the actual inflation rate
- **d.** decrease the natural unemployment rate
- **e.** shift the short-run aggregate supply curve to the right

44. Which of the following policies could the Federal Reserve implement to combat inflation?
- **a.** Raise the interest rate on reserves.
- **b.** Conduct quantitative easing.
- **c.** Buy Treasury securities.
- **d.** Raise taxes.
- **e.** Reduce government spending.

45. Which of the following is a contractionary fiscal policy?
- **a.** raising the reserve requirement
- **b.** decreasing transfer payments
- **c.** decreasing taxes
- **d.** raising government spending
- **e.** increasing the federal funds rate

46. If a country currently has a positive national debt and a balanced budget, how would a decrease in taxes affect the country's deficit and debt?

	Deficit	*Debt*
a.	increase	increase
b.	increase	decrease
c.	decrease	increase
d.	decrease	decrease
e.	decrease	no change

47. A country's national debt is
   a. the amount the country owes to foreigners.
   b. the difference between the country's tax revenue and government spending in a given year.
   c. the sum of the country's past deficits and surpluses.
   d. always positive.
   e. higher when gross domestic product is increasing.

48. Which of the following is an example of contractionary monetary policy?
   a. raising taxes
   b. increasing government spending
   c. raising reserve requirements
   d. lowering the rate on repurchase agreements
   e. buying Treasury securities

49. During a recession, the central bank might ________ its purchase of bonds in order to ________ the overnight interbank interest rate and ________ aggregate demand.

Bond purchases	*Overnight interbank interest rate*	*Aggregate demand*
a. increase	decrease	increase
b. increase	decrease	decrease
c. decrease	decrease	increase
d. decrease	increase	increase
e. decrease	increase	decrease

50. The short-run Phillips curve shows a ________ relationship between the rate of inflation and the ________ rate.

a. negative	unemployment
b. positive	interest
c. negative	employment
d. positive	GDP growth
e. negative	inflation

51. Which of the following is true of the long-run Phillips curve?
   a. It shows a negative relationship between the unemployment rate and the inflation rate.
   b. It shows a negative relationship between the unemployment rate and the interest rate.
   c. It shifts upward when expected inflation increases.
   d. It is vertical at the natural rate of unemployment.
   e. It shifts to the right when a central bank pursues expansionary monetary policy.

52. An increase in which of the following over time best describes economic growth?
   a. nominal GDP
   b. real GDP per capita
   c. nominal GDP per capita
   d. the labor force
   e. aggregate demand

53. Which of the following is true of an increase in labor productivity in an economy?
   a. It will shift the long-run aggregate supply curve to the left.
   b. It will decrease the wages of workers.
   c. It will reduce the size of the labor force.
   d. It will shift the production possibilities curve outward.
   e. It results from a decrease in the availability of capital.

54. Which of the following is most likely to lead to long-run economic growth?
   a. a more restrictive immigration policy
   b. higher trade barriers
   c. increased government funding of education
   d. contractionary fiscal policy
   e. negative net investment

55. Which of the following transactions will be recorded in the financial account of the United States?
   a. A U.S. firm sells $100 million worth of its product to Mexico.
   b. Chinese imports to the United States increase by $200 million.
   c. The wages paid by U.S. firms to workers in India increase by $20 million.
   d. Canada purchases $50 million of new U.S. Treasury bills.
   e. The United States' trade balance moves from deficit to surplus.

56. The exchange rate is the price of
   a. goods expressed in terms of another nation's currency.
   b. one nation's currency expressed in terms of another country's currency.
   c. the same basket of goods purchased in two countries.
   d. exported goods, adjusted for inflation.
   e. imported goods expressed in the other country's currency.

57. Which of the following would cause the U.S. dollar to depreciate relative to the Canadian dollar?
   a. an increase in net capital flows from Canada to the United States
   b. an increase in the real interest rate in Canada relative to the United States
   c. an increase in the balance of payments on the current account in the United States
   d. a doubling of prices in both Canada and the United States
   e. a decrease in exports from Canada to the United States

58. If a country's inflation rate rises, which of the following will happen to the demand for and value of the country's currency on the foreign exchange market?

Demand	*Value*
a. shift right	depreciate
b. shift right	appreciate
c. shift left	appreciate
d. shift left	depreciate
e. no change	depreciate

59. If foreign investors decrease investment in the United States, what will happen to the value of the dollar in the foreign exchange market and to U.S. net exports?

	Value of the U.S. dollar	*U.S. net exports*
a.	appreciate	increase
b.	appreciate	decrease
c.	depreciate	increase
d.	depreciate	decrease
e.	no change	no change

60. Which of the following is an example of U.S. foreign direct investment?

a. A U.S. citizen spends money while traveling abroad.
b. A U.S. manufacturer builds a factory in another country.
c. A U.S. investor purchases corporate bonds from a Mexican company.
d. A U.S. worker sends money to a family member living abroad.
e. A U.S. bank loans money to an international company.

Free-Response Questions

1. Assume the country of Boland is currently in long-run equilibrium.

a. Draw a correctly labeled production possibilities curve if Boland produces only corn and textiles. On your graph, label point X, a point that illustrates a productively efficient output combination for Boland.

b. Draw a correctly labeled aggregate supply and aggregate demand graph for Boland. Show each of the following:

i. equilibrium output, labeled Y_1

ii. equilibrium price level, labeled PL_1

c. Assume the government of Boland has a balanced budget and decides to raise government spending.

i. What effect will the increase in spending have on Boland's budget?

ii. Show the short-run effect of the increase in spending on your graph from part b, labeling the new equilibrium output and price level Y_2 and PL_2, respectively.

d. Draw a correctly labeled graph of the loanable funds market. Suppose the government of Boland borrows money to pay for the increased spending. Show the effect of this borrowing on your graph.

i. Label the equilibrium interest rate before the government borrowing i_1.

ii. Label the equilibrium interest rate after the government borrowing i_2.

e. How will the change in the interest rate in your graph from part d affect real GDP in the long run? Explain. **(10 points)**

2. Suppose a firm in the United States sells \$5 million worth of its output to consumers in Argentina.

a. How will this transaction affect each of the following?

i. Argentina's current account balance

ii. the United States' current account balance

iii. aggregate demand in Argentina

b. Suppose there is an increase in U.S. financial investment in Argentina.

i. Draw a correctly labeled graph of the foreign exchange market for Argentine pesos and show how an increase in U.S. financial investment in Argentina affects equilibrium in the market.

ii. What happens to the value of the Argentine peso relative to the U.S. dollar? **(6 points)**

3. Assume the expected rate of inflation is zero.

a. Draw a correctly labeled graph showing the short-run and long-run Phillips curves. On your graph, identify each of the following:

i. the nonaccelerating inflation rate of unemployment, labeled N

ii. a point on the short-run Phillips curve indicating an unemployment rate below the natural rate of unemployment, labeled A

b. Now assume the inflation rate associated with point A is incorporated into inflationary expectations. Show the effect of this change in expectations on your graph from part a. **(5 points)**

EM
MACRO

Macro Enrichment Modules

Hopefully this introductory course in economics has kindled your interest in studying economics beyond the AP® exam. If you are interested in how the AD-AS model you have learned about can be used to explain the recent Pandemic Recession in the United States, you will enjoy Enrichment Module A, which describes the U.S. economy leading up to, during, and after the short but deep recession in 2020.

Enrichment Module B is an in-depth examination of modern U.S. monetary policy and recent changes in how the Federal Reserve implements its target interest rate. Each of these Enrichment Modules provides a recent, real-world application of the macroeconomic theory and models that have been developed throughout your AP® Macroeconomics course.

EM A

Recession and Recovery During the Pandemic

In this Module, you will learn to:
- Describe the changes in U.S. macroeconomic measures during the Pandemic Recession
- Discuss the differential effects of the Pandemic Recession on different demographic groups in the United States

The Pandemic and the Economy

In January 2020, the United States declared a public health emergency in response to the spread of the COVID-19 virus. February 2020 marked the beginning of the pandemic in the United States, and it also marked the end of the longest period of economic expansion in U.S. history. On March 13, 2020, President Trump declared a national emergency. In response, local governments advised people to shelter in place, schools shut-down, and nonessential businesses were closed in an effort to prevent the spread of the virus.

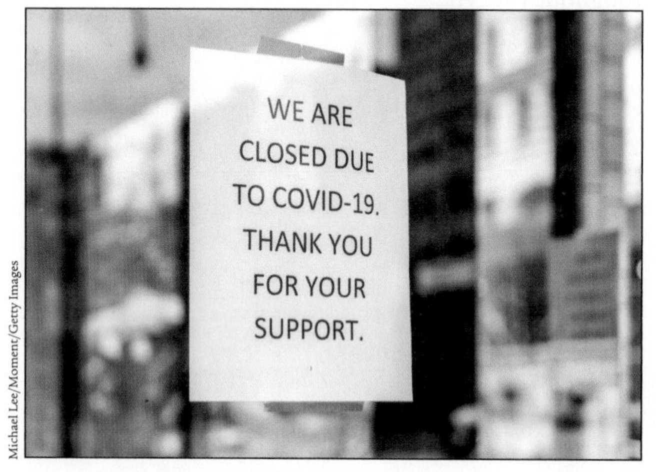

Michael Lee/Moment/Getty Images

In the second quarter of 2020, real GDP growth was −31.2% and the unemployment rate rose to 14.8%, the highest since data collection began in 1948 and reminiscent of estimates for those values during the Great Depression. The government-ordered shut-downs slowed both the spread of the outbreak and economic activity as incomes and consumer spending were reduced.

Figure A-1 shows the GDP-Based Recession Indicator Index (RII) for the United States, provided by the Federal Reserve Bank of St. Louis. This index measures the probability that the economy is in a recession. Unlike the NBER process for declaring the official start and end of recessions (see Unit 3), which

FIGURE A-1 GDP-Based Recession Indicator Index (RII) for the United States 2005–2020

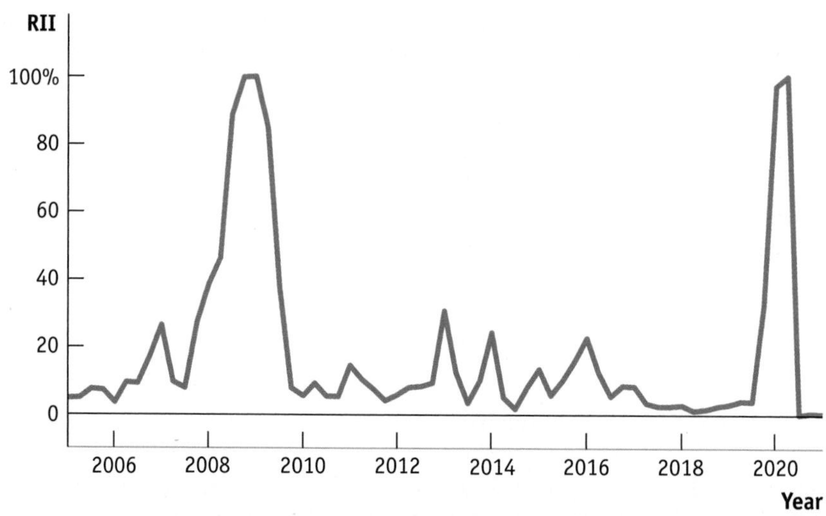

The RII provides a measure of the probability (measured in percentages) that the economy was in recession during a given quarter. The NBER business cycle dates are based on a subjective assessment of a variety of indicators often available only years later. The RII is different in that it is based entirely on currently available GDP data, making it a more objective measure. The RII is reported every quarter.

is based on subjective assessment of data after the fact, the Recession Indicator Index is an objective calculation based on data available when it is calculated. The two high peaks on the Figure A-1 graph represent the 2008–2009 recession and the 2020 recession, which are the two deepest recessions in U.S. history since the Great Depression. The index for the 2008–2009 recession reached a high of 99.7% in the first quarter of 2009, indicating a near certainty that the economy was in recession while the index reached a 100% probability of recession in the second quarter of 2020.

The period between these two recessions, from 2009 to 2019, was the longest U.S. economic expansion on record. Until 2020, the Great Recession of 2007–2008 had been the worst economic downturn since the Great Depression. It was an 18-month contraction of the U.S. economy, shown in Figure A-1 as a climbing and then falling RII that exceeded 50% between the second quarter of 2008 and the third quarter of 2009. The Great Recession was followed by the 73-month expansion from 2009 to 2019, during which annual average real GDP grew by around 2% and the RII stayed below 31%. With GDP growth of 3.5% and an RII of 32%, February 2020 became the business cycle peak, as real GDP went on to *fall* by 3.5% in 2020 and the RII rose to 100% in the second quarter.

The extreme economic decline, which we call the Pandemic Recession, has been estimated to be three times as severe as the Great Recession. It started with the COVID-19 pandemic and ended relatively abruptly in April 2020. The RII fell to zero in the third quarter of 2020 and the NBER identified the recession as lasting only 2 months—March and April 2020. Between the second quarter of 2020 and the first quarter of 2021, real GDP grew by 14.1%, the highest ever U.S. real GDP growth rate. Correspondingly, the unemployment rate fell to 5.4% in July 2021. This rapid turnaround is largely attributed to government stimulus efforts that replaced much of income and spending lost as a result of the pandemic shut-down. Congress passed three acts during the COVID-19 crisis that provided financial aid to families and businesses.

1. The Coronavirus Preparedness and Response Supplemental Appropriations Act (CPRSAA) provided $8.3 billion to federal agencies for response to the pandemic.
2. The Families First Coronavirus Response Act (FFCRA) provided $3.5 billion in paid sick leave, insurance coverage for coronavirus testing, and unemployment benefits.
3. The Coronavirus Aid, Relief, and Economic Security Act, aka the CARES Act, was a $2 trillion aid package providing funding for households, businesses, and local governments.

The 2020 recession was relatively deep and short. Both the cause of and response to the pandemic were unprecedented. As predicted by our aggregate demand and aggregate supply model, abrupt and significant changes in income and consumer spending (and the multiplier process that follows them) contributed to both the steep decline and relatively sudden recovery/expansion. In some ways, the 2020 recession was another example of how a negative demand shock can cause recessions and how fiscal policy can reverse them. However, both the major cause of the 2020 demand shock—the pandemic—and the fiscal policy used to reverse it were unique. In addition, the effects of the 2020 recession were not equal for all groups within the U.S. economy, nor were they all alleviated with the end of the recession in April 2020.

Next, let's look more closely at the fiscal policy used to address the Pandemic Recession, and then we can disaggregate some of the effects of the 2020 recession and consider how the pandemic will have a lasting impact on particular sectors of the U.S. economy.

Fiscal Policy in Response to the Pandemic Recession

We have seen in Unit 3 that expansionary fiscal policy can include increases in government spending, increases in transfer payments, and/or decreases in taxes that increase aggregate demand, shifting the *AD* curve to the right. Congress and the U.S. president are responsible for determining which fiscal policy tool(s) will be changed and by how much.

The policy approach to the Pandemic Recession was somewhat different from the responses to the Great Depression and the Great Recession.

During the 1930s the government increased spending, including spending on the New Deal, which included a series of public works projects that increased employment and income. The increase in government spending was expansionary, but the effect was small relative to the depth of the economic downturn. At the same time, the government enacted tax increases that were contractionary and offset the spending stimulus. These contradictory fiscal policies did not alleviate the severe economic downturn in the 1930s. Most historians cite the huge increase in government spending to finance World War II as the reason for the end to the Great Depression. The Congressional Research Service estimates that, in today's dollars, government spending on World War II was about $4.1 trillion on goods and services related to the war effort. This huge increase in spending was the significant expansionary fiscal policy required to stimulate the economy enough to end the Great Depression.

In response to the financial crisis that set off the Great Recession of 2007–2008, the government enacted two important laws: the Troubled Asset Relief Program (TARP), passed in 2008, and the American Recovery and Reinvestment Act (ARRA), passed in 2009. TARP included several programs run by the U.S. Treasury, including the purchase of troubled companies' assets and equity in order to decrease foreclosures and restore economic growth following the financial crisis. The ARRA included funding for projects that would save and create jobs and enhance the nation's infrastructure. Job creation provided an economic stimulus, while the focus on infrastructure facilitated future economic growth. Funding for the TARP and ARRA was almost $1.5 trillion, and it was spent on purchasing company assets and building infrastructure. These laws represented a significant, and swift, use of expansionary fiscal policy to address the relatively sudden economic downturn.

During the pandemic, government spending increases took two major forms. First, funding was required to fight the pandemic — for example, vaccine development and administration, virus testing, and health care. Second, funding was required to support employment and income — for example, support for businesses to keep workers employed, creation of expanded unemployment compensation, and funding for food security programs and direct cash payments to households. The first form of spending was focused on addressing the spread of the COVID-19 virus — the major cause of the sudden recession. The second form of funding was expansionary fiscal policy focused on providing for people's immediate needs and promoting increased employment.

The Coronavirus Preparedness and Response Supplemental Appropriations Act (CPRSAA) was enacted on March 6, 2020. This law provided $8.3 billion to federal agencies for response to the pandemic, including funds for vaccine development, support for state and local governments, and assistance for small businesses. The Families First Coronavirus Response Act (FFCRA) was enacted on March 18, 2020. It addressed the effects of the pandemic by providing paid sick leave, expanded medical leave, free coronavirus testing, enhanced unemployment insurance, expanded food security initiatives, and increased Medicaid funding. At the time it was passed, the Congressional Budget Office estimated that the FFCRA would add $192 billion to the federal deficit. Finally, the Coronavirus Aid, Relief, and Economic Security Act (CARES Act), enacted on March 27, 2020, was a $2.3 trillion aid package that provided funding for households, businesses, and local governments. This package included extended unemployment benefits, $1,200-per-person checks to most Americans, incentives for businesses to keep workers employed, new loans and grants to businesses, and increased aid to states and hospitals.

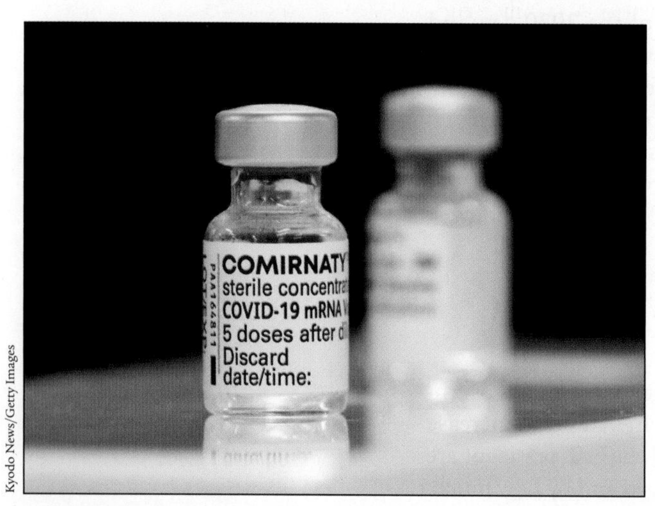

Kyodo News/Getty Images

In 2020, the U.S. government used the pandemic stimulus packages that included increases in transfer payments to increase support to households and promote income and consumption in the economy in an effort to increase aggregate demand in the face of shelter-at-home restrictions and business shut-downs that sent the economy into recession. Government transfer payments, which were $2,418 billion in the first quarter of 2020, rose to $4,767 billion in the second quarter of 2020 (and further to $5,071 billion in the first quarter of 2021).

Luis Alvarez/Getty Images

In each case — the Great Depression, the Great Recession, and the Pandemic Recession — the government implemented expansionary fiscal policy to address the severe economic downturn. In each case, the spending increase was large — commensurate with the size of these largest recessions. However, the specific type of spending differed based on the current situation in the economy and society. World War II required government spending on the war effort that led to an expansion of the economy that the New Deal was not large enough to create. The financial crisis in 2008 required the federal government to address problems in financial markets that led to the Great Recession through spending to purchase "troubled assets" and prevent foreclosures and bankruptcies. After addressing the financial markets with the TARP, additional government spending targeted job and infrastructure creation to reduce unemployment and facilitate economic growth. During the Pandemic Recession, the government focused on spending to alleviate the pandemic and provide transfer payments to support households and businesses affected during the initial shut-downs and subsequent slowdown.

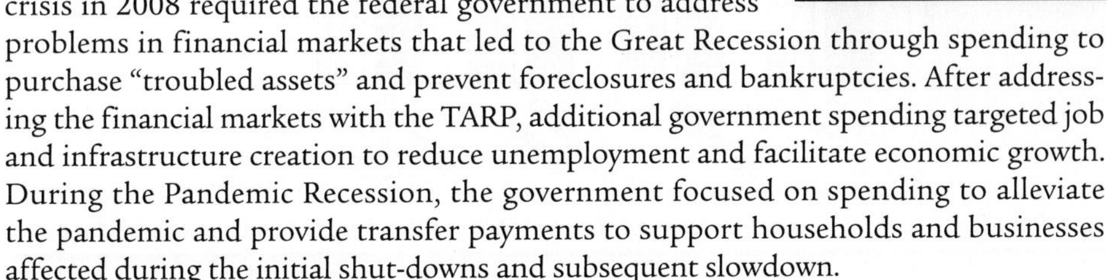

Each of these fiscal policies worked to end the recession and increase economic activity. But economic recessions and recoveries do not impact all groups in the economy equally. Tracking economic contractions and expansions tells us what is happening in the economy as a whole, but a closer look at the data can show how different groups in the economy are affected differently throughout business cycles.

Disaggregated Effects of the Pandemic Recession

The Pandemic Recession had a significant negative impact on the entire economy — no one was left unaffected. However, the pandemic had a disproportionate effect on some groups in the economy — the aggregate data don't tell the whole story. For example, unemployment increased to over 14% during the Pandemic Recession, but some industries and occupations were hit harder than others. The leisure and hospitality industry was the hardest hit, losing nearly half of its jobs in March and April 2020. Occupations including food preparation and serving, and personal care and service, were also greatly affected. In contrast, the financial services sector and the government sector saw only slight increases in unemployment as a result of the pandemic. People who could work from home during the shut-down saw smaller effects than people who worked in jobs that required interactions with the general public.

In addition to the differential impacts on industries and occupations, family structure played an important role in determining the impact of the pandemic on individuals. For example, virtual instruction and lack of daycare negatively affected families with school-aged children. Prior to the pandemic, the U.S. labor force was at its highest ever, at 165 million in February 2020. By April 2020 the labor force had decreased to 156 million, in part because care for children and other family members was no longer available outside the home during the shut-down, and virtual instruction for younger school-aged children required supervision.

We can consider some of the differential impacts of the pandemic based on gender, race, and age by looking at unemployment rates during the pandemic broken down by education level. Disaggregating the data by education level for each group highlights the way that economic downturns affect less educated workers regardless of age, race, or gender. The negative effect of the Pandemic Recession was clearly more pronounced among the less educated than among highly educated workers. Historically, less-educated workers have experienced larger increases in unemployment over business cycles, but the adverse effect of the 2020 recession on these workers was obviously even more pronounced.

Figure A-2 shows Pandemic Recession unemployment rates in April 2020, broken down by education and gender.

FIGURE A-2 Pandemic Recession Unemployment Rates by Education and Gender (April 2020)

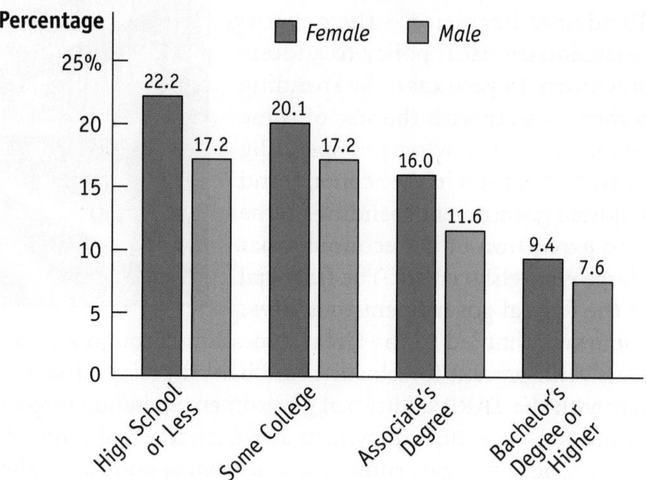

Data from: https://cew.georgetown.edu/cew-reports/jobtracker/#unemployment-tracking

Prior to 2020, unemployment increases during recessions were either higher for men or were roughly equal for men and women. But during the Pandemic Recession, unemployment was much higher for women, causing some to refer to it as a "She-cession." Figure A-2 shows the difference between the male and female unemployment rates at the peak of the recession was between 2% and 5% (and was highest for those with the least education).

There are two main reasons why women experienced higher unemployment. For one, more women are employed in occupations that are relatively stable in typical business cycles but were more affected by the pandemic shut-down – including occupations that require contact with the general public. Second, schools and daycare centers shut down during the pandemic, and because women provide the majority of childcare, many women had to stop working to care for children.

Figure A-3 breaks down the unemployment rate at the peak of the recession by education and race.

FIGURE A-3 Pandemic Recession Unemployment Rates by Education and Race (April 2020)

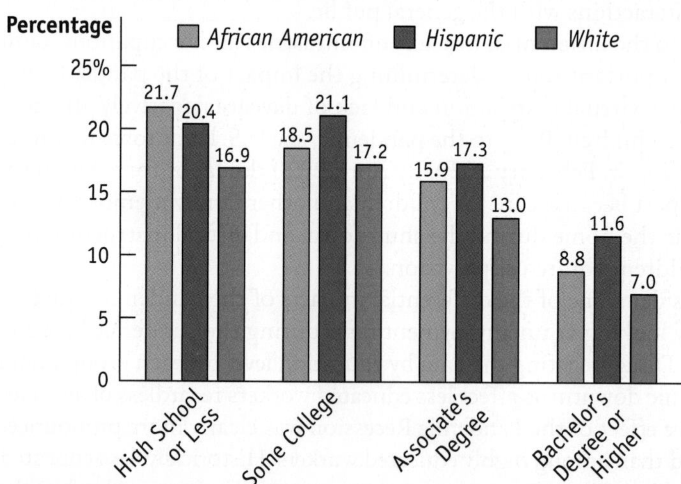

Data from: https://cew.georgetown.edu/cew-reports/jobtracker/#unemployment-tracking

Figure A-3 shows unemployment rates for African Americans, Hispanics, and Whites during the height of the Pandemic Recession. For comparison, immediately preceding the pandemic, approximately 10% of African American and Hispanic workers were unemployed. In April 2020, a couple of months into the pandemic, African American unemployment ranged from 8.8% to 21.7%, with higher unemployment for those with less education. For Hispanic workers, unemployment ranged from 7% to 16.9%, again showing decreased unemployment at higher levels of education. African American and Hispanic workers tend to be employed in the sectors and occupations hardest hit by the pandemic shut-down, and this is captured by the unemployment data.

The unemployment rates for African Americans and Hispanics reported in Figure A-3 may understate the differences between unemployment rates across racial groups. These data don't take into consideration the decreases in labor force participation as a result of the pandemic. Between February 2020 and February 2021, the female labor force decreased by 2.4 million. African American and Hispanic women accounted for 46% of that decrease (while making up only 33% of the female labor force). As we learned in Unit 3, when workers leave the labor force (as in the case of discouraged workers), the unemployment rate decreases. But in this case, women left the labor force as a result of a pandemic. Without the pandemic, these women would have continued working.

Finally, **Figure A-4** shows the unemployment data broken down by education and age. Once again, unemployment rates tend to be higher for less educated workers.

FIGURE A-4 **Pandemic Recession Unemployment Rates by Education and Age (April 2020)**

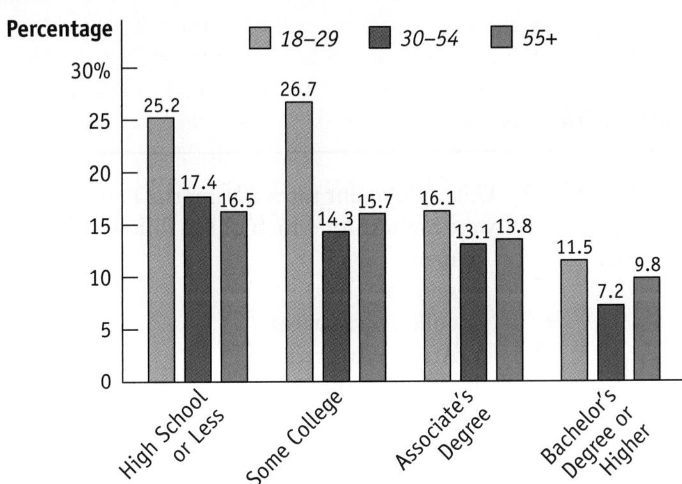

Data from: https://cew.georgetown.edu/cew-reports/jobtracker/#unemployment-tracking

During the Pandemic Recession, younger workers experienced the largest increase in unemployment. Younger workers tend to be employed in the industries and occupations hardest hit by the pandemic. They also tend to have less experience and seniority, and therefore, they are often the first to be let go during a downturn.

These data illustrate the differential effect of the pandemic on unemployment rates across education levels independently for different ages, races, and genders. But the impact is even greater for workers who fall into multiple higher unemployment categories. For example, the unemployment rate for African American women aged 20–24 was 27.5% in the second quarter of 2020.

The Pandemic Recession and the Future

Compared to previous economic downturns, the Pandemic Recession was about three times as bad as the Great Recession (based on the annual decrease in GDP), but not as bad as the Great Depression. While all three downturns began with a significant negative demand shock and were alleviated by expansionary fiscal policy, the cause, consequences, and response to the Pandemic Recession differed in many ways from the previous two extreme downturns. While the economy has recovered from the height of the Pandemic Recession, the effects will continue to be felt by some industries and groups for years to come. It will take years for society to fully adjust to the shock of the COVID-19 pandemic, and the economy will certainly experience long-run changes as a result. Economists have begun to predict possible long-term changes that may result from the pandemic, including new ways of working and learning, a transformed health care industry, the substitution of capital for labor in crowded workspaces, a decrease in urbanization/move to the suburbs, a change in the travel industry including reduced business travel, and a move toward a more green economy.

Enrichment Module A  Review

Check Your Understanding

1. How did the COVID-19 pandemic lead to the sharp recession in early 2020?
2. How did the federal government use fiscal policy to respond to the economic downturn created by the pandemic?
3. What demographic groups were disproportionately affected by the Pandemic Recession?

Multiple-Choice Review Questions

1. Relative to the Great Recession, the Pandemic Recession
   a. lasted longer.
   b. was more severe.
   c. affected less of the world.
   d. affected fewer people.
   e. affected everyone the same.

2. The Pandemic Recession was created by which of the following?
   a. a negative demand shock
   b. a positive demand shock
   c. a negative supply shock
   d. a positive supply shock
   e. excessive fiscal policy

3. Which of the following was used to address the Pandemic Recession?
   a. spending to combat the pandemic
   b. spending to support employment and income
   c. the Troubled Asset Relief Program (TARP)
   d. both a and b
   e. all of the above

4. Which of the following is an example of expansionary fiscal policy used during the Pandemic Recession?
   a. the FOMC decreasing the federal funds rate to zero
   b. increased production of masks
   c. the CARES Act
   d. the TARP program
   e. all of the above

5. Unemployment rates during the Pandemic Recession were highest for which of the following groups?
   a. men
   b. seniors
   c. college graduates
   d. African Americans
   e. all of the above

6. What was the relationship between unemployment and education level during the Pandemic Recession?
   a. positive
   b. negative
   c. direct
   d. independent
   e. no relationship

7. The effect of increased government spending during the pandemic was made even larger due to which of the following?
   a. the COVID-19 virus
   b. stay-at-home-orders
   c. increased health care expenditures
   d. progressive income taxes
   e. the multiplier effect

Free-Response Review Questions

1. Draw a correctly labeled aggregate demand and aggregate supply graph showing an economy in long-run equilibrium.
   a. Assume a pandemic hits the country. Illustrate the effect of a stay-at-home order on your graph. Label the new equilibrium price level and level of real GDP.
   b. i. The pandemic moves the economy into what phase of the business cycle?
      ii. How can the government change spending to address the change in part a?
      iii. How can the government change taxes to address the change in part a?
      iv. How will the change in government spending and taxes each affect aggregate demand? Explain.
   (10 points)

2. How was the unemployment in each of the following groups affected during the pandemic, relative to the overall change in the unemployment rate? Explain.
   a. women
   b. Hispanics
   c. younger workers
   d. less educated workers **(5 points)**

Discussion Starters

1. How is the GDP-based Recession Indicator Index better than the NBER for dating recessions? How is the NBER approach better?
2. How does the Pandemic Recession compare to the Great Recession and the Great Depression?
3. Why were some groups affected by the Pandemic Recession more than other groups?

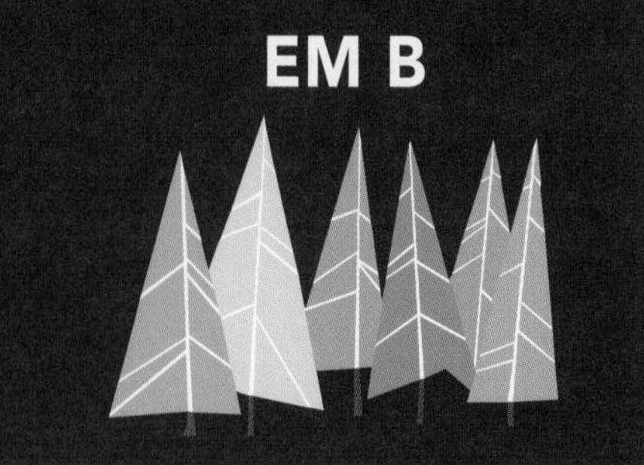

Federal Reserve Monetary Policy with Ample Reserves

In this Module, you will learn to:

- Describe the implementation of monetary policy in an ample-reserves environment
- Use a graph of the market for reserves to show how the federal funds rate is set by the Federal Reserve

In Units 4 and 5, we discuss how central bank monetary policy can be used to shift aggregate demand in order to move the economy to full employment (thereby addressing recessions and inflation). Unit 4 presents the transmission mechanism that translates the change of a monetary policy tool into a change in aggregate demand to stabilize the economy with both **limited reserves** and **ample reserves**.

In an economy with **limited reserves**, in which reserves are scarce, relatively small changes in the supply of reserves will change the nominal interest rate.

In an economy with **ample reserves**, in which reserves are plentiful, changes in the supply of reserves do not affect the nominal interest rate. The Fed instead uses administered rates to set the target federal funds rate.

In January 2019, the United States Federal Reserve announced its plans to remain in an ample-reserve regime and conduct monetary policy using administered rates. In this Enrichment Module, we describe the Fed's transition to an ample-reserves monetary policy regime over the decade since the Great Recession of 2007–2008. We also expand upon our discussion from Unit 4 on how the Federal Reserve uses administered rates, including the interest paid on reserves and the repurchase agreement rate, to conduct monetary policy in the United States. To begin, we'll reconsider monetary policy with limited reserves. Then we will go on to describe how the Federal Reserve conducts monetary policy when there are ample reserves in the economy.

Monetary Policy with Limited Reserves

Prior to the Great Recession of 2007–2008, open market operations (OMOs) were the Fed's most frequently used monetary policy tool. With limited reserves in the banking system, the daily use of OMOs by the Federal Reserve Bank of New York (FRBNY) set interest rates within a target range determined by the Federal Open Market Committee (FOMC). Relatively small changes in reserves caused by open-market purchases or sales of government securities could be used to adjust the federal funds rate up or down as required to hit the policy target.

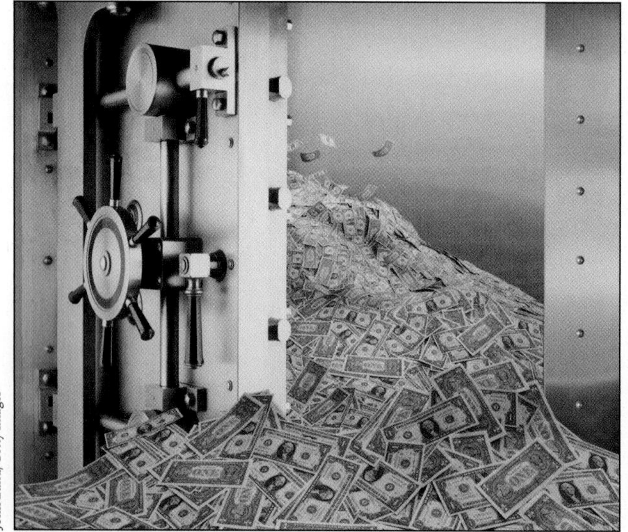
John Lund/Getty Images

Open Market Operations as the Primary Monetary Policy Tool

The use of OMOs was discovered as a monetary policy tool accidentally. In 1922, shortly after World War I, Federal Reserve banks responded to the effect of an economic slowdown on their own balance sheets by purchasing government securities. The Fed soon realized that these purchases affected general credit conditions in the economy and could be used to regulate the economy. In the 1930s, the FOMC was created to oversee OMOs and became the policy-making body for the Federal Reserve. Until the 2007–2008 financial crisis, the Fed used OMOs as its key tool to implement monetary policy with the limited reserves in the banking system.

Innovative Use of Monetary Policy Tools During the 2007–2008 Financial Crisis

The 2007–2008 financial crisis required the Fed to use innovative liquidity tools to fend off the Great Recession. During the crisis, the Fed was unable to use traditional monetary policy tools because it was up against the **zero-bound**, the inability to lower the federal funds rate below zero. In addition, the way that financial markets had evolved to be more diverse and interconnected made traditional approaches less effective. The Fed had to make substantial changes to its monetary policy tools including: providing liquidity to non-depository financial institutions in addition to depository institutions (e.g., banks), removing the stigma associated with borrowing from the Fed's discount window, and increasing transparency with respect to its policy actions.

The **zero-bound** is a limit to expansionary monetary policy resulting from the inability to lower the policy rate below zero. Further economic stimulus, if needed, requires the central bank to pursue other policies.

Quantitative easing, the large-scale purchase of assets by central banks to stimulate the economy (or combat deflation) by providing liquidity, was an important monetary policy tool during the 2007–2008 crisis. Two additional monetary policy tools were also used: interest on reserves (IOR; discussed in Unit 4) and overnight reverse repurchase agreements. These additional policy tools enabled the Fed to provide economic stimulus despite near zero effective federal funds rates between 2008 and 2015 and again in 2020, as shown in **Figure B-1**.

Quantitative easing is an expansionary monetary policy that involves central banks purchasing government bonds and other financial assets.

FIGURE B-1 Effective Federal Funds Rate, 1955–2021

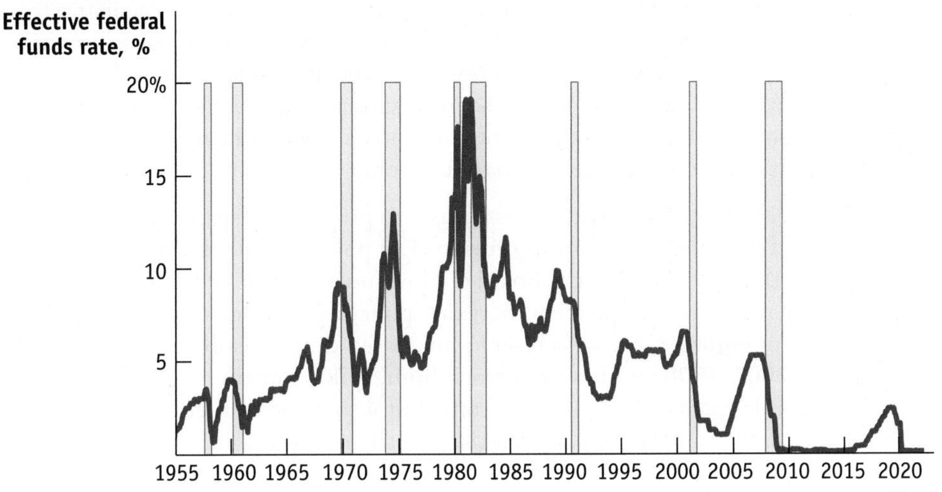

*Shaded bars indicate recessions.

The FOMC sets the target federal funds rate to affect short-term interest rates and pursue the dual mandate of stable prices and maximum sustainable employment. During the Great Recession in 2007–2008, the federal funds rate was decreased to near zero. It was again lowered to near zero during the 2020 pandemic recession.

At times, other central banks, including the Swiss National Bank, Swedish Riksbank, European Central Bank, Danish Nationalbank, and Bank of Japan, have all set negative policy rate targets. The Danish Nationalbank and Swiss National Bank, in particular, have set their policy rates as low as −0.75%.

Setting the effective federal funds rate below zero can be accomplished by charging institutions a fee to hold federal funds deposits at the Fed. The convenience of conducting transactions in the federal funds market will assure there would be trades, even with fees that result in negative rates. In testimony before Congress in 2016, when asked about the possibility of a negative federal funds rate, Fed Chair Yellen stated, "I'm not aware of anything that would prevent us from doing it," but also noted there would be legal questions and technical issues related to such a decision. So it is possible that a negative federal funds rate could be considered as a tool of the Fed in response to a future monetary policy challenge.

Next, we consider monetary policy with ample reserves.

Monetary Policy with Ample Reserves

Since the 2007–2008 financial crisis, the Fed has purposefully changed the way it implements U.S. monetary policy. In a statement released in 2019, the Board of Governors of the Fed described its intent to provide ample reserves in the banking system and

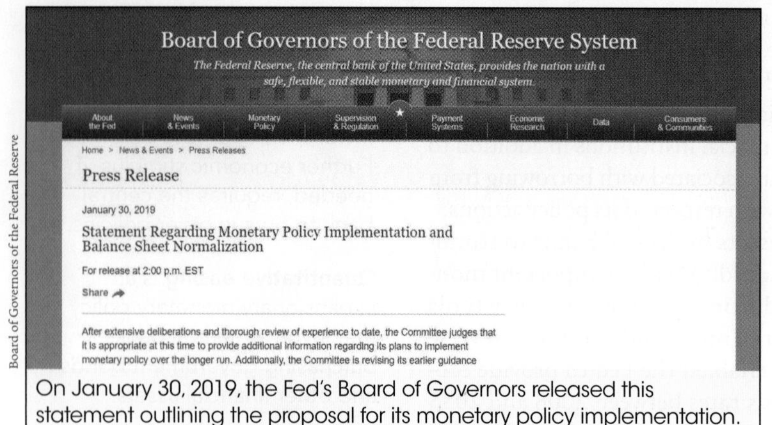

Board of Governors of the Federal Reserve System

The Federal Reserve, the central bank of the United States, provides the nation with a safe, flexible, and stable monetary and financial system.

About the Fed | News & Events | Monetary Policy | Supervision & Regulation | Payment Systems | Economic Research | Data | Consumers & Communities

Home > News & Events > Press Releases

Press Release

January 30, 2019

Statement Regarding Monetary Policy Implementation and Balance Sheet Normalization

For release at 2:00 p.m. EST

Share

After extensive deliberations and thorough review of experience to date, the Committee judges that it is appropriate at this time to provide additional information regarding its plans to implement monetary policy over the longer run. Additionally, the Committee is revising its earlier guidance

Board of Governors of the Federal Reserve

On January 30, 2019, the Fed's Board of Governors released this statement outlining the proposal for its monetary policy implementation.

rely on administering interest rates to conduct monetary policy. In addition, the Fed says it is prepared to use quantitative easing should economic conditions require expansionary policy beyond what can be achieved by lowering interest rates.

The Board of Governors' January 2019 statement on monetary policy implementation reads, in part:

> The Committee intends to continue to implement monetary policy in a regime in which an ample supply of reserves ensures that control over the level of the federal funds rate and other short-term interest rates is exercised primarily through the setting of the Federal Reserve's administered rates, and in which active management of the supply of reserves is not required.
>
> The Committee continues to view changes in the target range for the federal funds rate as its primary means of adjusting the stance of monetary policy. The Committee is prepared to adjust any of the details for completing balance sheet normalization in light of economic and financial developments. Moreover, the Committee would be prepared to use its full range of tools, including altering the size and composition of its balance sheet, if future economic conditions were to warrant a more accommodative monetary policy than can be achieved solely by reducing the federal funds rate.

The Federal Reserve issues such press releases to provide transparency and communicate updated information regarding current Fed policies and intentions for future Fed policy. In this press release, the Board of Governors provides additional information regarding its plans to implement monetary policy over the longer run.

As shown in **Figure B-2**, excess reserves increased dramatically during the Great Recession in 2007–2008 and have remained high, spiking again in 2020 during the COVID-19 Pandemic Recession. Recall from Unit 4 that the Fed reduced the reserve requirement to 0% in March 2020. But despite the reduction in required reserves, banks continue to hold significant (excess) reserves. With such high excess reserves in the banking system, the Fed can no longer use changes in reserves to effectively manage

FIGURE B-2 **Excess Reserves of Depository Institutions, 1985–2020**

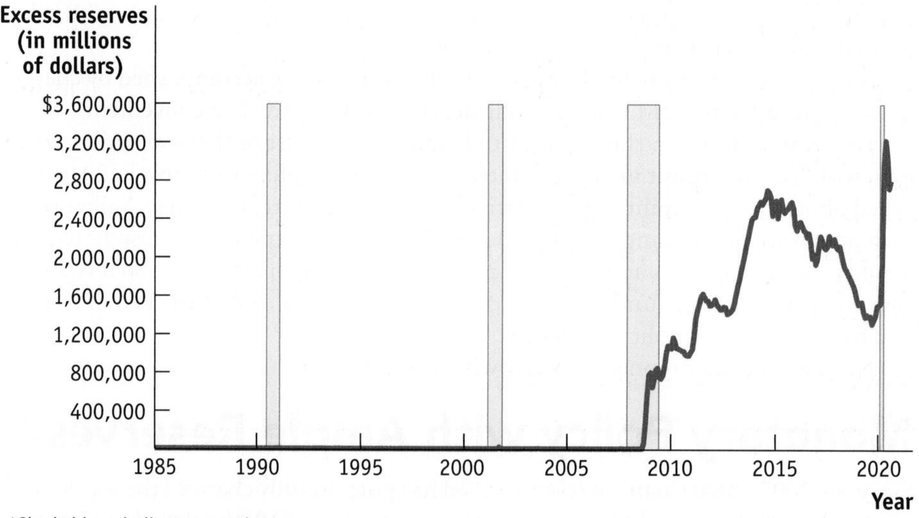

Following the start of the financial crisis in 2007, excess reserves, which had remained very low for the more than two decades shown on the graph, increased sharply. The increases continued until 2014, when excess reserves began to decline. Excess reserves increased dramatically again when the pandemic recession hit in 2020.

the federal funds rate. Instead, the Fed relies on the two tools of monetary policy mentioned above—*interest rates on reserves* and *rates on reverse repurchase agreements*—to maintain the target federal funds rate.

Administered Interest Rates

The primary rates administered by the Federal Reserve are the discount rate, the interest rate paid on reserves, and the rate on reverse repurchase agreements. We have already learned about the discount rate in Unit 4. Here we discuss in detail the use of the Fed's other two important administered rates.

Interest on Reserve Balances

In addition to making loans, banks have a variety of other short-term investment options, as shown in **Figure B-3**.

FIGURE B-3 Examples of Banks' Short-Term Investment Options

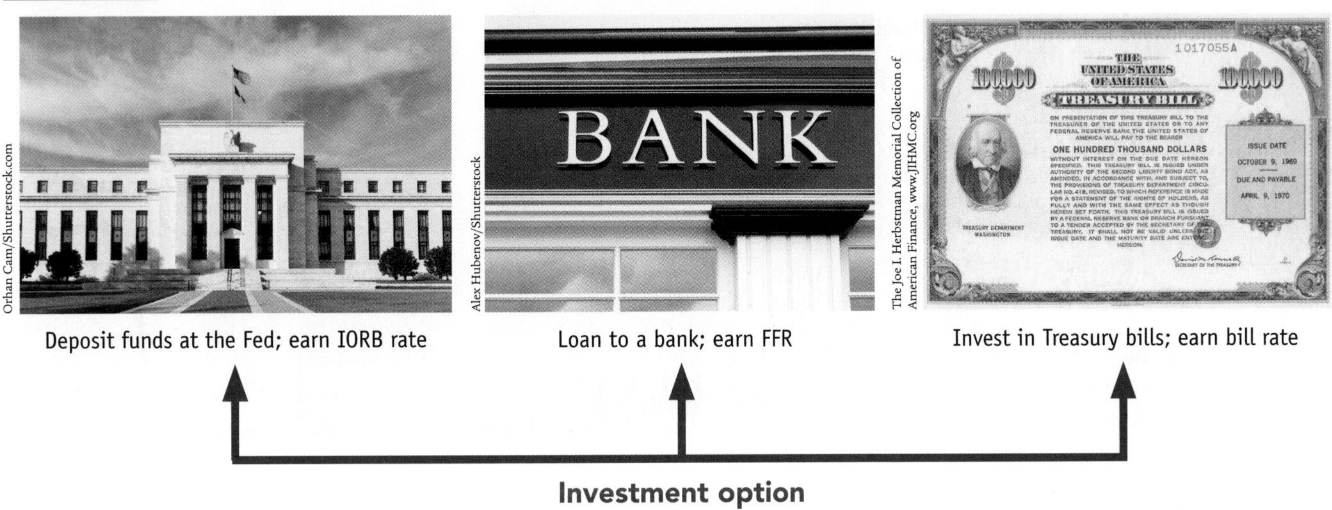

The **interest on reserve balances (IORB)** is the rate the Federal Reserve pays in interest when banks choose to hold its cash as reserves. Earning interest on reserves reduces banks' opportunity cost from holding reserves rather than holding other financial assets. When the Fed pays interest on reserves, it reduces the incentive for banks to lend at rates below the IORB because banks would earn less from loaning their cash than they would by simply holding it as reserves.

The **interest on reserve balances (IORB)** is the rate the Federal Reserve pays in interest on reserves held by banks.

The IORB rate offers banks a safe investment option, so they are unlikely to lend reserves in the federal funds market for less than the IORB rate. Therefore, the IORB rate serves as the lowest rate that banks will accept for making a loan. However, not all financial institutions can hold reserves with the Fed and earn interest. So, in 2014, the FOMC announced that it would use overnight reverse repurchase agreements with some of these institutions to conduct monetary policy.

Reverse Repurchase Agreements

Repurchase agreements and reverse repurchase agreements are temporary OMOs used to address transitory reserve needs. A *repurchase agreement* (RA) is a securities purchase from a **counterparty** made by the Fed with an agreement to resell the securities at a later date. The RA functions as a loan to the counterparty, with the securities used as collateral, and it increases the reserves in the banking

A **counterparty** is the other party participating in a financial transaction.

system because banks have cash instead of securities for the duration of the agreement. The difference between the purchase and sale prices reflects the interest on the loan. The FRBNY has not conducted a significant level of RAs since December 2008.

Reverse repurchase agreements (RRAs) are the sales of securities by the Fed to a counterparty with an agreement to repurchase the securities at a later date.

A **reverse repurchase agreement (RRA)** is a sale of securities by the Fed to a counterparty with an agreement to repurchase the securities at a later date. The difference between the sale and purchase prices reflects the interest on the loan. RRAs temporarily *reduce* reserves in the banking system because banks hold securities instead of cash for the duration of the agreement. The Federal Reserve established an overnight reverse repurchase facility in 2013 to facilitate RRAs for a variety of counterparties, the number of which is expected to remain around 150. **Figure B-4** shows the increase in RRAs by the Fed's overnight reverse repurchase facility from 2017 to 2022.

FIGURE B-4 Overnight Reverse Repurchase Agreements, 2017–2022

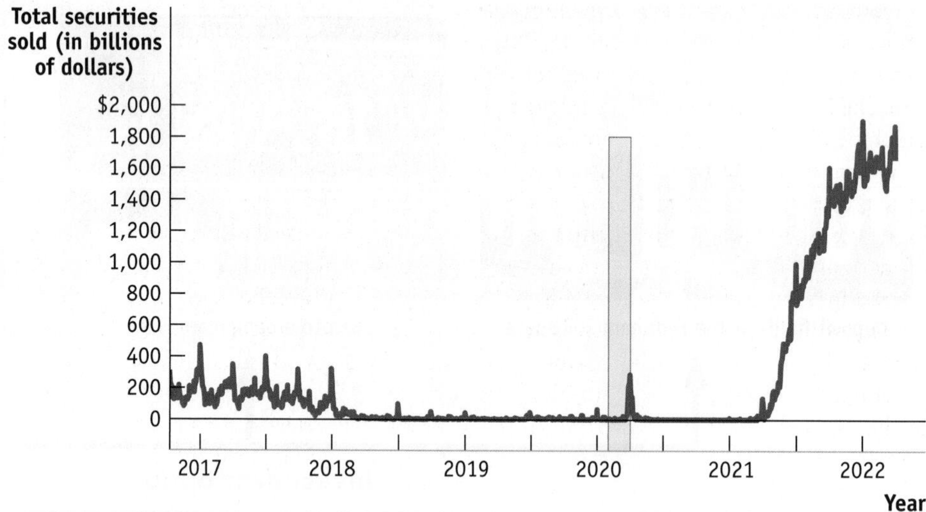

The total value of overnight RRAs stayed relatively low from 2018 to 2022, but spiked during the 2022 pandemic recession. It increased again starting in April 2021 and continued to increase through 2021.

To be eligible to become an RRA counterparty, a firm must be a state or federally chartered bank or savings association with a minimum level of assets, an SEC-registered investment fund, for example a money market fund with a minimum level of net assets, or a government-sponsored enterprise (GSE).

A GSE is a quasi-governmental entity created by Congress to enhance the flow of credit to specific sectors of the U.S. economy, such as education, agriculture, and housing. GSEs facilitate borrowing by individuals from certain groups including students, farmers, and homeowners. Examples of GSEs include the Federal Home Loan Mortgage Bank (Freddie Mac), the Federal National Mortgage Association (Fannie Mae), the Federal Agricultural Mortgage Corporation (Farmer Mac), and a variety of federal home loan banks. RAs and RRAs allow the Fed to affect reserves in the economy through transactions with an expanded list of counterparties, in addition to banks and other depository institutions.

The IORB and RRA rates are two of the administered interest rates referenced in the Federal Reserve press release quoted earlier in this Module. Next, we will consider in more detail how administered rates can be used to set the target federal funds rate.

Administered Interest Rates as the Primary Monetary Policy Tool

In 2019, Jerome Powell, Chair of the FOMC, explained, "The Federal Reserve sets two overnight interest rates: the interest rate paid on banks' reserve balances and the rate on our reverse repurchase agreements. We use these two administered rates to keep a market-determined rate, the federal funds rate, within a target range set by the FOMC." With ample reserves, these two rates administered by the Fed are used to create a range for the federal funds rate, making the IORB the primary tool, and RRAs a supplemental tool, for setting the federal funds rate.

At high levels of reserves, the federal funds rate will move with the interest rate the Fed pays on reserve balances (the IORB) while the rate for RRAs acts as a lower bound for the federal funds rate. Let's consider why the federal funds rate moves with the IORB. Eventually, banks reach a level of reserves at which there is only one way to benefit from holding additional reserves: earning interest from the Fed. At that level of reserves, if the federal funds rate were to fall below the interest rate paid on reserves, banks can borrow from the federal funds market at the lower interest rate and hold the borrowed funds as reserves at the higher interest rate, earning the difference as profits. This is a bank reserves version of the "buy low, sell high" strategy known as **arbitrage**. Arbitrage in the federal funds market would increase the federal funds rate and eliminate the interest rate gap. So arbitrage ensures that the federal funds rate will not fall much below the interest rate on reserves.

Arbitrage is taking advantage of a price difference between two markets.

Why does the rate on RRAs act as a lower bound for the federal funds rate? Nondepository financial institutions cannot earn interest on reserves, but they can participate in the Fed's overnight reverse repurchase program. These financial institutions will not loan funds at an interest rate less than what they can earn through RRAs; therefore, short-term interest rates, including the federal funds rate, will remain above the overnight RRA rate.

Figure B-5 shows the transmission mechanism for monetary policy presented in Unit 4. The causal chain is the same with both limited and ample reserves, but the way in which the FOMC policy is implemented differs. When there were limited reserves in the U.S. economy, the Fed primarily used OMOs to achieve the target federal funds rate. In the current ample-reserves environment, IORB and overnight RRAs are the key policy tools used to achieve the target.

FIGURE B-5 Monetary Policy Transmission Mechanism

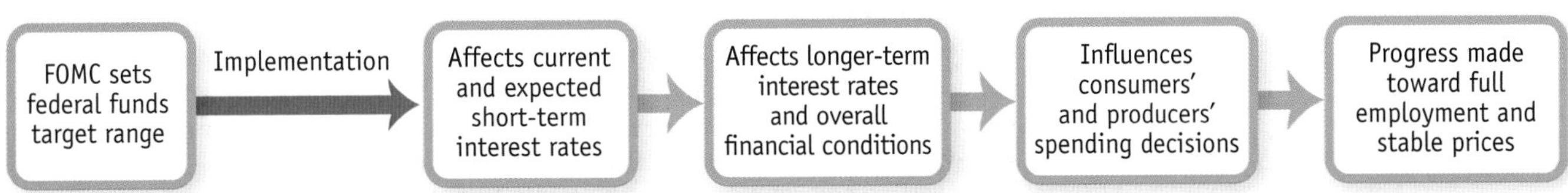

The chain of events that shows how monetary policy ultimately results in a movement of equilibrium toward full employment output is illustrated by the transmission mechanism shown here. The transmission is the same for both limited-reserve and ample-reserve monetary policy tools—only the way that the adjustment of short-term interest rates is achieved is different.

Next, we use the market for reserves to compare the Fed's implementation of monetary policy in limited- and ample-reserve environments.

Monetary Policy and the Market for Reserves

We can use a graph of the market for reserves to illustrate the difference between implementation of monetary policy with limited reserves and ample reserves.

The Market for Reserves with Limited Reserves

The graph of the market for reserves in **Figure B-6** measures the federal funds rate, shown on the vertical axis, and the quantity of reserves held by depository institutions, shown on the horizontal axis.

FIGURE B-6 The Market for Reserves with Limited Reserves

The demand curve for reserves is generally downward sloping in a limited-reserves regime. The intersection of supply and demand in the market for reserves determines the equilibrium federal funds rate (*FFR*), identified on the vertical axis. OMOs can change the supply of reserves and lead to changes in the federal funds rate.

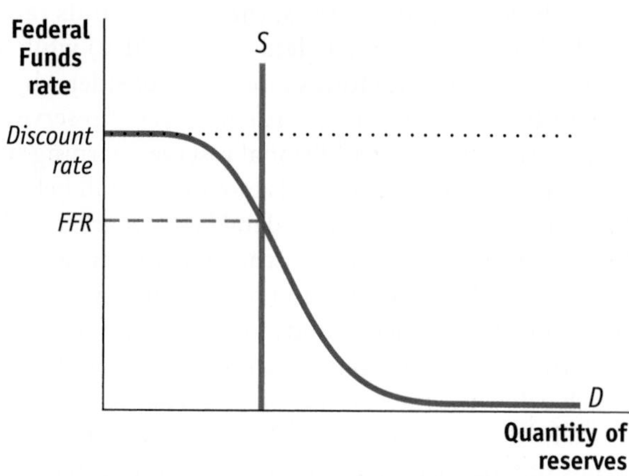

The demand curve in the market for reserves has three distinct segments. The flat section at very low levels of reserves is defined by the discount rate, which is the ceiling for the federal funds rate. Banks will borrow from the Fed, rather than from the federal funds market, if the federal funds rate is above the discount rate. The downward-sloping section in the middle range for reserve levels shows a negative relationship between the federal funds rate and the quantity of reserves demanded – that is, banks will demand more reserves at a lower interest rate and less reserves at a higher interest rate. The third segment of the demand curve for reserves represents the zero bound. The economy operates in the middle segment of the demand curve for reserves in a limited-reserves environment.

The supply of reserves, managed by the Fed, is not dependent on the federal funds rate and therefore the supply curve in the market for reserves is vertical. The equilibrium interest rate is found on the vertical axis where the vertical supply curve intersects the downward-sloping demand curve for reserves at a limited level of reserves. When the economy had limited reserves, changes in the supply of reserves led to changes in the equilibrium federal funds rate so the Fed could set the target federal funds rate using OMOs.

The Market for Reserves with Ample Reserves

Figure B-7 shows the market for reserves in an ample-reserves environment. With ample reserves, the Fed sets the target federal funds rate using its administered rates. The IORB and RRA rates set the lower bound for the federal funds rate. When there are ample reserves in the economy (i.e., on the horizontal portion of the demand curve for reserves shown in Figure B-7), changes in the supply of reserves do not affect the equilibrium federal funds rate. The federal funds rate will stay close to the IORB and remain above the rate on RRAs. The vertical supply curve will intersect the demand curve in its third, flat section and the federal funds rate will remain in that target range.

FIGURE B-7 The Market for Reserves Under an Ample-Reserve Regime

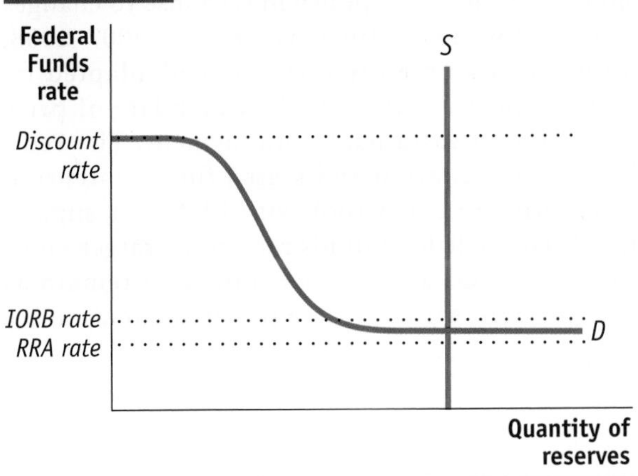

In an environment with ample reserves, the Fed's administered rates will determine the equilibrium federal funds rate, which will remain very close to the IORB (and above the rate for RRAs).

A Comparison of Monetary Policy with Limited and Ample Reserves

Figure B-8 shows a comparison of the market for reserves under the two reserve environments. In panel (a), which shows a relatively low (limited) supply of reserves, small shifts in the supply curve will cause the federal funds rate to increase or decrease so that the use of OMOs would allow the Fed to keep the federal funds rate in the target range or adjust it based on a directive from the FOMC. In panel (b), which shows a relatively high (ample) level of reserves, a small shift of the supply curve will not affect the federal funds rate because equilibrium occurs on the horizontal portion of the demand curve. As we've learned, to shift the federal funds rate in this environment, the Fed must use changes in its administered interest rates. Increasing or decreasing the interest rate paid on reserves will shift the horizontal portion of the demand curve, increasing or decreasing the federal funds rate.

FIGURE B-8 A Comparison of the Monetary Policy with Limited Reserves and Ample Reserves

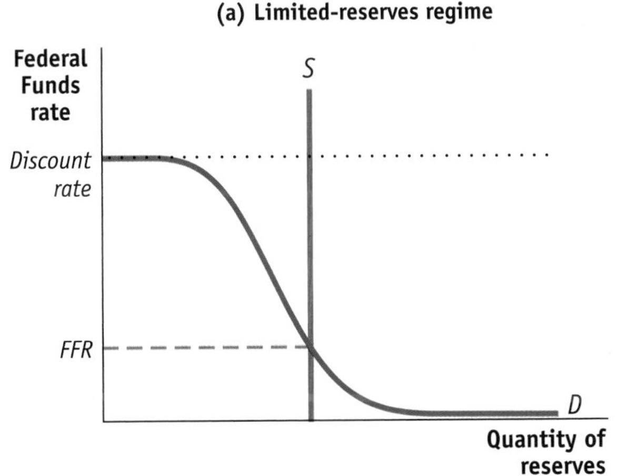

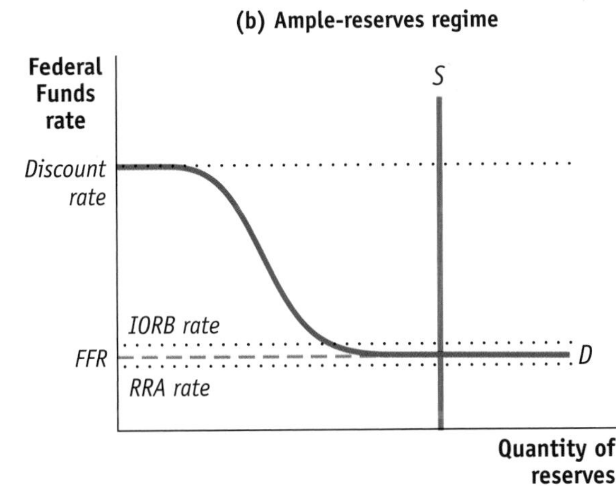

Panel (a) shows the determination of the equilibrium federal funds rate in the market for reserves with limited reserves. Panel (b) shows the determination of the federal funds rate by the administrative interest rates set by the Fed with ample reserves.

Andrew Harrer/Bloomberg/Getty Images

Since its creation in 1913, the Fed has adapted its tools to effectively implement monetary policy in response to changes in the economy. Following the financial crisis in 2007–2008, in an environment of ample reserves, the Fed adapted its monetary policy tools to pursue its dual mandate of price stability and maximum sustainable employment. The Fed's current policy implementation and stated future intention uses IORB as its primary policy tool, with RRAs as a supplemental tool, to keep the federal funds rate in the target range set by the FOMC. OMOs and the discount rate remain as supporting policy tools, with a reserve requirement set at 0% in 2020.

Enrichment Module B 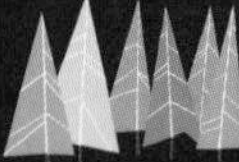 Review

Check Your Understanding

1. How did the Fed set the target federal funds rate with limited reserves?
2. How does the Fed set the target federal funds rate with ample reserves?
3. Use a single graph of the market for reserves to compare equilibrium with limited reserves versus equilibrium with ample reserves. Include two alternative supply curves.

Multiple-Choice Review Questions

1. With ample reserves, the Fed sets the target federal funds rate primarily using which of the following?
   - **a.** quantitative easing
   - **b.** open market operations
   - **c.** the discount rate
   - **d.** interest rates on reserve balances
   - **e.** reserve requirements
2. The Fed's administered rates include which of the following?
   - **a.** the prime interest rate
   - **b.** the rate on reverse repurchase agreements
   - **c.** the federal funds rate
   - **d.** the reserve requirement
   - **e.** all of the above
3. In 2020, the Fed set the reserve requirement at
   - **a.** 0%.
   - **b.** 1%.
   - **c.** 2%.
   - **d.** 5%.
   - **e.** 10%.
4. Compared to earlier years, excess reserves in the United States since 2009 have been
   - **a.** negative.
   - **b.** zero.
   - **c.** falling.
   - **d.** high.
   - **e.** unchanged.
5. How will the Fed decrease the federal funds rate with ample reserves?
   - **a.** buy bonds
   - **b.** lower reserve requirements
   - **c.** decrease the interest paid on reserves
   - **d.** raise the rate for reverse repurchase agreements
   - **e.** all of the above
6. When a bank borrows from the federal funds market in order to earn a higher interest rate holding the funds as reserves, the bank has engaged in which of the following?
   - **a.** arbitrage
   - **b.** entrepreneurship
   - **c.** a criminal act
   - **d.** compounding
   - **e.** fraud
7. The Fed conducts a reverse repurchase agreement with a
   - **a.** bank.
   - **b.** customer.
   - **c.** partner.
   - **d.** counterparty.
   - **e.** financial institution.

Free-Response Review Questions

1. Assume the U.S. economy is currently experiencing inflation.
   a. To combat inflation, will the Fed increase, decrease, or not change each of the following?
      i. purchases of bonds
      ii. the reserve requirement
      iii. the interest rate on reserve balances
      iv. the rate on RRAs
   b. Draw a correctly labeled graph of the market for reserves and show how implementation of an effective monetary policy will change the federal funds rate. **(9 points)**

2. The interest rate the Fed pays for reserves is equal to the federal funds rate.
   a. What will banks do if the federal funds rate falls below the interest rate paid on reserves? Explain.
   b. What is it called when a bank borrows funds at a lower interest rate in order to simultaneously earn a higher interest rate on those funds in a different market?
   c. Draw a correctly labeled graph of the market for reserves. Indicate each of the following on your graph:
      i. the equilibrium federal funds rate
      ii. the effect in the market if banks increase their demand for reserves **(5 points)**

Discussion Starters

1. How does a repurchase agreement affect the supply of reserves? What about a reverse repurchase agreement?
2. Why won't the traditional tools of monetary policy be effective in an ample-reserves environment?
3. When would the discount rate become important for conducting monetary policy?

MICROECONOMICS

Basic Economic Concepts

AP® Economics Skills

1. Principles and Models, 1.A, 1.C, 1.D
2. Interpretation, 2.C
4. Graphing and Visuals, 4.A

Economics: What's It All About?

Did you know that economics is about far more than money? Consider your breakfast this morning. Did you take the time to assemble a balanced meal of fruits, grains, and protein, or did you grab a quick snack before heading out the door? Did you eat cereal purchased in bulk days before, or did you buy a breakfast sandwich at an eatery on the way to school? Were you in such a hurry that you skipped breakfast altogether, or did you arrive at school early to take advantage of their breakfast offerings? Each of these options comes with its own costs in terms of time, money, and resources. Similar considerations attend decisions related to sports, food, the environment, families, health, tourism, and many elements of your daily life. Economics can help you understand the necessary trade-offs and make better choices.

In this course, you will learn a set of economic principles that apply to a broad range of issues. Some of these principles involve *individual choice*. Do you choose to work during the summer or take a rafting trip? Do you watch videos or read your textbook? These dilemmas involve *making a choice* from among a limited number of alternatives — limited by constraints on time, money, and resources. At its most basic level, every question in economics involves individuals making choices.

To understand how an economy works, you need to understand that your choices are shaped by the decisions of others. In our global economy, even the simplest decisions you make — say, what to have for breakfast — are shaped by the decisions of thousands of other people, from the farmer in Costa Rica who decided to grow bananas rather than beets, to the landowner in Iowa who decided to use their land as a dairy farm instead of a housing development. Because each of us depends on so many others — and they, in turn, depend on us — our choices are interdependent. So, although economics at a basic level is about individual choice, in order to understand behavior within an economy, you must also understand the *interactions* between your choices and the choices of others.

Microeconomics helps us understand many important economic interactions by looking at individual choice and the markets for individual goods — for example, the market for bananas. *Macroeconomics*, on the other hand, is our window into economy-wide interactions that shows us how they lead to the ups and downs in the economy as a whole.

In this Unit, we discuss the implications of scarcity to the study of microeconomics and macroeconomics. We introduce several economic systems and their roles in allocating resources. We present the *production possibilities curve* model and use it to understand the gains from trade. Finally, we look at how consumers can weigh costs against benefits to make optimal choices in the face of binding constraints. Because graphical models are central to the study of economics and feature heavily on the AP® exam, they will be emphasized throughout this course. For further review, an appendix on the use of graphs is available at the end of this book.

PhotoTalk/E+/Getty Images

MODULE 1.1

Scarcity and Choice

In this Module, you will learn to:
- Explain how scarcity and choice are central to the study of economics
- Define each category of resources
- Discuss the importance of opportunity cost to decision making
- Distinguish between different types of economics

Scarcity and Choice: The Core of Economics

Economics is the study of scarcity and choice.

Economics is the study of scarcity and choice. We can appreciate the breadth of economics by considering how few things *are not* scarce. To be scarce, something must be desired in quantities beyond the available supply. Can you think of goods or services that are available to everyone in unlimited supplies? Air, perhaps, although pollution and airborne diseases have limited the availability of clean air.

Some information of value to consumers and producers is not scarce. *Established knowledge* is knowledge that is both widespread and useful. For example, unlike your favorite sports team's strategy for an upcoming match and the recipe for Coca-Cola, the knowledge that heat melts iron or that wheels assist with transportation is no secret. Such knowledge is widespread, in part because it is *non-rival in consumption*, meaning that one person's use of the knowledge does not hinder other people's use of it. Peanut butter is *rival in consumption* because if you eat my peanut butter, I can't eat it. But if you use the established knowledge that peanut butter and jelly combine to make a good sandwich, that doesn't affect my ability to use the same knowledge. I would happily share my sandwich recipe with you. Likewise, any established knowledge that is shared freely need not be scarce.

Marek Slusarczyk/Alamy

Convenience stores often provide the only easily accessed option for busy urban dwellers.

Everything, from art museums to zippers, are limited in supply – that is, they are scarce. So the principles of economics apply to most things. Let's take a closer look at the causes and implications of scarcity.

Resources Are Scarce

You make a **trade-off** when you give up something to get something else.

You can't always get what you want. You might like to have a beautiful bike, the best smartphone, the finest shoes, and the latest equipment for your hobbies. But not many people can afford all of that. So each individual faces trade-offs. You make a **trade-off** when you give up something in order to have something else. Perhaps you can buy a bike this year if you don't upgrade your phone, or you can buy a new pair of shoes if you don't buy a new fishing pole.

Limited income isn't the only barrier to people having everything they want. Time is also in limited supply: there are only 24 hours in a day. And because the time we have is limited, choosing to spend time on one activity also means choosing not to spend time on a different activity – spending a night studying for an exam means forgoing a night at the movies. Indeed, many people feel so limited by the number of hours in the day that they are willing to trade money for time. For example, convenience stores usually charge higher prices than larger supermarkets. The closer, smaller convenience stores often appeal to customers who would rather pay more than spend extra time traveling to a supermarket where they might also have to wait in longer lines.

Individual choices are decisions by individuals about what to do, which necessitate decisions about what not to do.

Every economic issue involves **individual choice** – decisions by individuals about what to do and what *not* to do. Why do individuals have to make choices?

The ultimate reason is that, with few exceptions, *resources are scarce*. A **resource** is anything that can be used to produce something else. The economy's resources, also called **factors of production**, can be classified into four categories: **land** (all resources that come from nature, including plants, water, and minerals), **labor** (the effort of workers), **capital** (manufactured goods used to make other goods and services, such as machinery, buildings, and tools), and **entrepreneurship** (risk taking, innovation, and the organization of resources for production). A resource is **scarce** when there is not enough of it available to satisfy all of the various ways a society wants to use it. For example, there are limited supplies of oil and coal, which currently provide most of the energy used to produce and deliver everything we buy.

A **resource** or **factor of production** is anything that can be used to produce something else.

Land refers to all resources that come from nature, such as timber, wind, and petroleum.

Labor is the effort of workers.

Capital refers to manufactured goods used to make other goods and services.

Entrepreneurship describes the efforts of entrepreneurs in organizing resources for production, taking risks to create new enterprises, and innovating to develop new products and production processes.

A **scarce** resource is not available in sufficient quantities to satisfy all the various ways a society wants to use it.

Just as individuals must make choices, the scarcity of resources means that society as a whole must make choices. One way for a society to make choices is simply to allow them to emerge out of many individual choices. For example, there are only 168 hours in a week, and Americans must decide how to spend their time. How many hours will they spend going to supermarkets to get lower prices rather than saving time by shopping at convenience stores? The answer is the sum of individual decisions: society's choice about where to shop is simply the sum of the choices made by the millions of individuals in the economy.

Some decisions are best not left to individual choice. For example, the authors of this book live in areas that until recently were mainly farmland but are now being rapidly developed for housing and industry. Most local residents feel that their communities would be more pleasant places to live if some land were left undeveloped. But the benefit an individual landowner receives from undeveloped land is often small relative to the financial incentive to sell the land to a developer. To avoid individual choices that work against community interests, local governments in many communities across the United States have purchased undeveloped land to preserve as open space, such as parks, with broad appeal to residents and visitors. Decisions about how to use scarce resources are often best left to individuals, but sometimes should be made at a community level.

AP® ECON TIP

Be careful when you see key terms you think you already know, because economists have special meanings for many words. For example, economists use the term *land* in reference to all sorts of natural resources and raw materials such as silicon, cotton, and even water.

The principles of economics provide guidance for anyone making a decision. The decisions of what to do with the next hour of free time, the next dollar of spending money, and the next tree are *marginal decisions*. They involve trade-offs at the margin: comparing the costs and benefits of doing a little bit more of an activity versus a little bit less. The gain from doing something one more time is called the *marginal benefit*. The cost of doing something one more time is the *marginal cost*. If the marginal benefit of reading another page, buying another bag of chips, or cutting down another tree exceeds the marginal cost, the activity should continue. But if the cost of one more exceeds the benefit of one more—that is, if the marginal cost exceeds the marginal benefit—the activity should stop. The study of such decisions, known as **marginal analysis**, plays a central role in economics because doing things until the marginal benefit no longer exceeds the marginal cost is the key to deciding "how much" to do of any activity.

AP® ECON TIP

Questions on the AP® exam generally use the term *capital* to refer to the category of factors of production made up of manufactured goods used to make other goods and services. Don't confuse this type of capital with *financial capital* such as money, stocks, and bonds.

Opportunity Cost: The Real Cost of Something Is What You Must Give Up to Get It

Suppose it is your last year of high school and you are deciding which college to attend. You have narrowed your choices to a small college near home or a large state university several hours away. If you decide to attend the local liberal arts college, what is the cost of that decision? Of course, you will have to pay for tuition, textbooks, and housing no matter which college you choose. Added to the cost of choosing the local college is the forgone opportunity to attend the large state university,

Marginal analysis is the study of the costs and benefits of doing a little bit more of an activity versus a little bit less.

your next best alternative. The value of going to the state university may be small or large, depending on your interests and preferences. Economists call the value of the next best alternative that you must give up when you make a particular choice an **opportunity cost**.

The real cost of an item is its **opportunity cost**: the value of the next best alternative that you must give up in order to get the item.

Opportunity costs are crucial to individual choice because, in the end, all costs are opportunity costs. That's because with every choice, an alternative is forgone – money or time spent on one thing can't be spent on another. If you spend $10 on a pizza, you forgo the opportunity to spend that $10 on a hamburger. If you spend Saturday afternoon at the park, you can't spend Saturday afternoon doing homework. And if you attend one school, you can't attend another.

The park and school examples show that economists are concerned with more than just costs paid in dollars and cents. The forgone opportunity to do homework has no direct monetary cost, but it is an opportunity cost nonetheless. And if the local college and the state university have the same tuition and fees, the cost of choosing one school over the other has nothing to do with payments and everything to do with forgone opportunities.

Now, suppose tuition and fees at the state university are $5,000 less than at the local college. In that case, the next-best alternative to attending the local college is to attend the state university *and* to have $5,000 to spend on other things. The opportunity cost of choosing the college is the combined value of these forgone alternatives. So the opportunity cost of a choice captures the full value of the best forgone alternative – whether or not money is involved.

Cory Knowlton/ZUMA Press, Inc./Alamy

Mallory Pugh understood the concept of opportunity cost.

The choice to go to college *at all* provides another important example of opportunity costs. High school graduates can either go to college or seek immediate employment. Even with a full scholarship that would make college "free" in terms of monetary costs, going to college would still be an expensive proposition because the time spent on schoolwork can't be spent earning money. By going to college, students forgo the income they could have earned if they had gone straight to work instead. Therefore, the opportunity cost of attending college is the value of all necessary monetary payments for tuition and fees *plus* the forgone income from the best available job that could take the place of going to college.

The opportunity cost of going to college is high for people who could earn a lot during what would otherwise be their college years. Soccer standout Mallory Pugh withdrew from her first year in college because the opportunity cost of continuing would have included her salary and Nike endorsement deal as a professional soccer player. Facebook co-founder Mark Zuckerberg, Dropbox co-founder Arash Ferdowsi, and singer Taylor Swift are among the high achievers who decided that the opportunity cost of completing college was prohibitive. Despite these notable exceptions, however, for most people the value of a college degree far exceeds the value of alternative earnings.

AP® ECON TIP

Students of microeconomics should pay close attention to *marginal analysis*, as it is often tested on the AP® exam. Any time you see "marginal," think "additional."

Microeconomics Versus Macroeconomics

We have presented economics as the study of scarcity and choice and described how, at its most basic level, economics is about individual choice. The branch of economics concerned with how individuals make decisions and how those decisions interact is called **microeconomics**. Microeconomics focuses on choices made by individuals, households, or firms – the smaller parts that make up the economy as a whole. A **household** is a person or group of people who share their income. If you have a parent or guardian who provides your food and housing, the two of you are members of the same household. A **firm** is any organization that produces goods or services for sale, such as a hair salon, bank, software company, grocery store, or carrot farm.

Microeconomics is the study of how individuals, households, and firms make decisions and how those decisions interact.

A **household** is a person or group of people who share their income.

A **firm** is any organization that produces goods or services for sale.

If the economy were a national park, microeconomics would be the study of individual trees and macroeconomics would be the study of the entire forest. **Macroeconomics** focuses on the bigger picture – the overall ups and downs of the economy. When you study macroeconomics, you learn how economists explain these fluctuations and how governments can use economic policy to minimize the resulting damage. Macroeconomics focuses on *economic aggregates* – economic measures such as the unemployment rate, the inflation rate, and gross domestic product – that summarize data across many different markets.

Abstract Aerial Art/DigitalVision/Getty Images

Table 1.1-1 lists some typical questions that involve economics. A microeconomic version of the question appears on the left, paired with a similar macroeconomic question on the right. By comparing the questions, you can begin to get a sense of the difference between microeconomics and macroeconomics.

Macroeconomics is concerned with the overall ups and downs of the economy.

Table 1.1-1 Microeconomic Versus Macroeconomic Questions

Microeconomic Questions	Macroeconomic Questions
How many years of education should I receive before I start my career?	How many people are employed in the economy as a whole this year?
What determines the salary that Citibank offers to a new college graduate?	What determines the average salary paid to workers in the economy?
What is the cost to a high school of offering a new course?	What is the overall level of prices in the economy as a whole?
What government policies would encourage more students to choose to attend college?	What government policies would promote employment and growth in the economy as a whole?
What determines the number of iPhones exported to France?	What determines the overall trade in goods, services, and financial assets between the United States and the rest of the world?

As these questions illustrate, microeconomics focuses on how individuals and firms make decisions, and the consequences of those decisions. For example, a school will use microeconomics to determine how much it would cost to offer a new course, which includes the instructor's salary, the cost of class materials, and so on. By weighing the costs and benefits, the school can then decide whether or not to offer the course. Macroeconomics, in contrast, examines the *overall* behavior of the economy – how the actions of all of the individuals and firms in the economy interact to produce a particular economy-wide level of economic performance. For example, macroeconomics is concerned with the general level of prices in the economy and how high or low they are relative to prices last year, rather than with the price of a particular good or service.

Positive Versus Normative Economics

Economic analysis draws on a set of basic economic principles. How these principles are applied depends on the purpose of the analysis. Economic analysis that is used to answer questions about the way the economy works – questions that have definite right and wrong answers – is known as *positive economics.* In contrast, economic analysis that involves saying how the economy *should* work is known as *normative economics.*

Imagine you are an economic adviser to the governor of your state, and the governor is considering an increase in the toll charged along the state turnpike. Below are three questions the governor might ask you.

1. How much revenue will the tolls yield next year without an increase?
2. How much higher would that revenue be if the toll were raised from $2.00 to $3.00?
3. Should the toll be raised, bearing in mind that a toll increase would lower the volume of traffic and air pollution in the area but impose a financial hardship on frequent commuters?

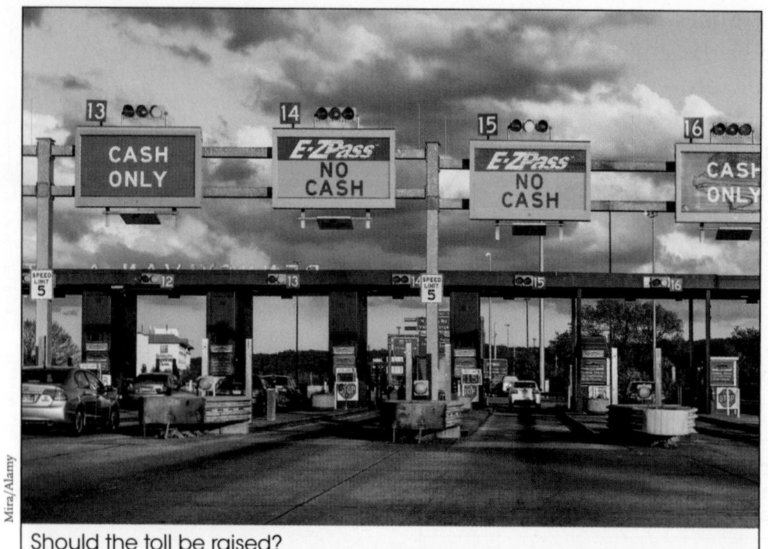

Mira/Alamy

Should the toll be raised?

There is a notable difference between the first two questions and the third one. The first two are questions about facts. Your forecast of next year's toll revenue without any increase will be proved right or wrong when the numbers actually come in. Your estimate of the impact of a change in the toll is a little harder to check – the increase in revenue depends on other factors besides the toll, and it may be hard to disentangle the causes of any change in revenue. Still, in principle there is only one right answer.

But the question of whether or not tolls should be raised may not have a "right" answer – two people who agree on the effects of a higher toll could still disagree about whether raising the toll is a good idea. For example, someone who lives near the turnpike but doesn't commute on it will care a lot about noise and air pollution but not so much about commuting costs. A regular commuter who doesn't live near the turnpike will have the opposite priorities.

This example highlights a key distinction between the two roles of economic analysis and presents another way to think about the distinction between positive and normative analysis: positive economics is about description, and normative economics is about prescription. Positive economics occupies most of the time and effort of economists.

Looking back at the three questions the governor might ask, it is worth noting a subtle but important difference between questions 1 and 2. Question 1 asks for a simple prediction about next year's revenue – a forecast. Question 2 is a "what if" question, asking how revenue would change if the toll were to increase. Economists are often called upon to answer both types of questions. Economic *models*, which provide simplified representations of reality using, for example, graphs or equations, are especially useful for answering "what if" questions.

The answers to such questions often serve as a guide to policy, but they are still predictions, not prescriptions. That is, they attempt to tell you what will happen if a policy is changed, but they don't tell you whether or not that result is good. Suppose that your economic model tells you that the governor's proposed increase in highway tolls will likely raise property values in communities near the road but will tax or inconvenience people who currently use the turnpike to get to work. Does that information make this proposed toll increase a good idea or a bad one? It depends on whom you ask. As we've just seen, someone who is very concerned with the communities near the road will support the increase, but someone who is very concerned with the welfare of drivers will feel differently. That's a value judgment – it's not a question of positive economic analysis.

Still, economists often do engage in normative economics and give policy advice. How is this possible when there may be no "right" answer? It is possible, in part, because economists are also citizens, and we all have our opinions. But economic analysis can often be used to show that some policies are clearly better than others, regardless of individual opinions.

Suppose that policies A and B achieve the same goal, but everyone will be better off with policy A than with policy B – or at least policy A makes some people better off without making other people worse off, while policy B does the opposite. Then A is clearly more beneficial than B. That's not a value judgment: we're talking about how best to achieve a goal, not about the goal itself.

Consider the goal of making housing affordable for more families. Two different policies have been used to help low-income families obtain housing: rent control, which limits the rents landlords are allowed to charge, and rent subsidies, which provide families with additional money with which to pay rent. As we'll see later in this book, rent control decreases the quantity and quality of available housing while rent subsidies do not. So the great majority of economists, whatever their personal politics, favor subsidies over rent control.

Likewise, the study of economics may provide you with clarity on both the way the economy works and the best decisions going forward.

Module 1.1  Review

Check Your Understanding

1. What is it about most resources that forces everyone to make choices?
2. Under which category does each of the following resources fall?
   - **a.** time spent making pizzas at a restaurant
   - **b.** a bulldozer
   - **c.** a river
3. You make $45,000 per year at your current job with Whiz Kids Consultants. You are considering a job offer from Brainiacs, Inc., which would pay you $50,000 per year and you must consider the trade-offs. Is each of the following elements an opportunity cost of accepting the new job at Brainiacs, Inc.? Answer yes or no, and explain your answer.
   - **a.** the increased time spent commuting to your new job
   - **b.** the $45,000 salary from your old job
   - **c.** the more spacious office at your new job

Tackle the AP® Test: Multiple-Choice Questions

1. Which of the following is an example of capital?
   - **a.** a cheeseburger dinner
   - **b.** a construction worker
   - **c.** petroleum
   - **d.** a factory
   - **e.** an acre of farmland
2. Which of the following is not an example of resource scarcity?
   - **a.** There is a finite amount of petroleum in the world.
   - **b.** Farming communities are experiencing droughts.
   - **c.** There are not enough physicians to satisfy all desires for health care in the United States.
   - **d.** Cassette tapes are no longer being produced.
   - **e.** Teachers would like to have more instructional technology in their classrooms.
3. Suppose that you prefer reading a book you already own to watching videos and that you prefer watching videos to listening to music. If these are your only three choices, what is the opportunity cost of reading?
   - **a.** watching videos and listening to music
   - **b.** watching videos
   - **c.** listening to music
   - **d.** sleeping
   - **e.** the price of the book
4. Which of the following statements is normative?
   - **a.** The price of gasoline is rising.
   - **b.** The price of gasoline is too high.
   - **c.** Gas prices are expected to fall in the near future.
   - **d.** Cars can run on gasoline, electricity, or diesel fuel.
   - **e.** When the price of gasoline rises, drivers buy less gasoline.
5. Which of the following questions is studied in microeconomics?
   - **a.** Should I go to college or get a job after I graduate?
   - **b.** What government policies should be adopted to promote employment in the economy?
   - **c.** How many people are employed in the economy this year?
   - **d.** Has the overall level of prices in the economy increased or decreased this year?
   - **e.** What determines the overall salary levels paid to workers in a given year?
6. An activity should certainly continue if the
   - **a.** marginal benefit is positive.
   - **b.** marginal cost is negative.
   - **c.** marginal cost exceeds the marginal benefit.
   - **d.** marginal benefit equals the marginal cost.
   - **e.** marginal benefit exceeds the marginal cost.
7. All opportunity costs are
   - **a.** nonmonetary.
   - **b.** forgone monetary payments.
   - **c.** losses of time.
   - **d.** values of alternatives that must be given up.
   - **e.** related to educational opportunities.

Tackle the AP® Test: Free-Response Questions

1. Define the term *economics* and explain why that definition encompasses much more than money. Then define the term *resources* and list the four categories of resources.

2. In what type of economic analysis do questions have a "right" or "wrong" answer? In what type of economic analysis might an economist say, "I believe this policy should be adopted"? What type of economics focuses on the big picture in the economy? What type of economics focuses on individuals, households, and firms? Define marginal analysis. **(5 points)**

Rubric for FRQ 1 (6 points)

1 point: Economics is the study of scarcity and choice.

1 point: Almost everything is scarce, so economics can apply to almost everything.

1 point: Resources are anything that can be used to produce something else.

1 point each: The four categories of the economy's resources are land, labor, capital, and entrepreneurship.

Economic Systems

MODULE 1.2

In this Module, you will learn to:

- Describe the purpose of an economy
- Identify the three basic economic questions
- Summarize how resources are allocated under various economic systems
- Explain why most countries have a mixed economy
- Discuss the importance of incentives to behavioral change

Amazon offers more than 12 million products for sale through its online catalog. But it is extremely unlikely that you – or anyone else – could afford to buy everything you desire. Besides, there's only so much space in your home. Given the limitations on your budget and your living space, you must choose which products to buy and which to pass up. Other choices preceded your ability to consider those products: manufacturers chose to devote resources to making them, and retailers chose to sell them.

An **economy** is a system that coordinates a society's choices about production and consumption. In this Module, we will examine the workings of several economic systems.

An **economy** is a system for coordinating a society's productive and consumptive activities.

How Economic Systems Address the Three Basic Economic Questions

Every economy must address three basic questions about *resource allocation*:

1. What goods and services will be produced?
2. How will those goods and services be produced?
3. Who will receive the goods and services?

Consider the allocation of harvested trees. Those trees could become products as diverse as paper, toys, furniture, and homes. The chosen products could be made using a variety of processes, such as mostly by hand or mostly with machines. And the products could be distributed in ways that include by markets where goods are bought and sold, by auction, by lottery, by government decree, or according to need.

Ideally, the answers to the *What? How?* and *Who?* questions are *efficient* in the sense that no alternative allocation of resources could make some people better off without making other people worse off. It would be inefficient to produce mostly log cabins if most people prefer modern architecture. It would be inefficient to use machine-intensive production methods in an economy with few machines and plenty of idle workers. And it would be inefficient to distribute wooden toys with a lottery because they might go to retirees rather than children. Different economic systems address the basic economic questions in very different ways.

Traditional Economies

In a **traditional economy**, the three basic questions are answered on the basis of precedent. Visit an Amish community in the United States or a small village in many parts of the world, and you will see the production of traditional goods and services using methods passed down for generations. Even the distribution of

In a **traditional economy**, production and consumption decisions are based on precedent.

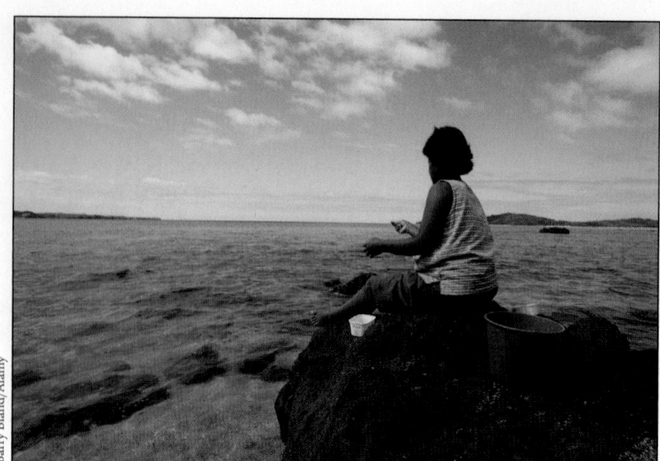
Barry Bland/Alamy

Tradition has a strong influence on the decisions of what, how, and for whom to produce in the Fijian village where this woman fishes, and perhaps in your household as well.

goods and services to leaders, elders, women, men, and children is likely to follow tradition. In a traditional Fijian village, you can see women fishing, men farming, children making crafts, and elders dispensing wisdom just as they have for centuries.

Consider your own household. Are some of the decisions about what is done, how it is done, and who gets what based on tradition? Due to the ease and familiarity of doing things as they have been done before, and the reliability of time-tested methods, elements of tradition continue to exist within every economy, if not every household.

Market Economies

In a **market economy**, the factors of production are privately owned and the decisions of individual producers and consumers largely determine what, how, and for whom to produce.

In a **market economy**, production and consumption are the result of decentralized decisions made by many firms and individuals. Market economies are also described as *capitalist*, which means that the factors of production are owned by private households rather than by the government. There is no central authority telling people what to produce or who should receive it. Each firm can make whatever products or services it thinks will be most profitable, and each consumer can choose what to buy on the basis of their needs, wants, and financial constraints. Buyers and sellers come together in markets to trade at prices determined largely by supply and demand. Goods and services are allocated to the consumers who are willing to pay the going prices for them. The term *free enterprise* applies to a market economy with minimal government involvement.

AP® ECON TIP

Don't be confused by the multiple terms sometimes used to describe the same economy. The descriptors *market*, *capitalist*, and *free enterprise* all indicate that an economy is not a command economy, but highlight different aspects of the distinction. Calling it a *market economy* emphasizes that market forces determine economic outcomes. Calling it *capitalist* stresses that capital and other resources are privately owned. And applying the term *free enterprise* indicates minimal government oversight.

Command Economies

In a **command economy**, the factors of production are publicly owned and a central authority makes production and consumption decisions.

In a **command economy**, the factors of production are publicly owned and central authorities *do* make production and consumption decisions. For example, under *communism*, legislators from a single political party – the Communist Party – determine production levels and wages. Their aim is to distribute goods and services according to citizens' needs. Under *socialism*, the distribution mechanism is different. Assemblies of elected representatives and councils of workers and consumers make economic decisions, often with oversight from a central government.

Command economies have been tried, notably in the Soviet Union between 1917 and 1991 and in North Korea today, but they don't work very well. For example, producers in the Soviet Union routinely found themselves unable to meet national production targets because the economic system did not provide adequate supplies of crucial resources. In other cases, production went as planned, but the central authorities failed to order the goods and services people most wanted. As a result, consumers struggled to find necessary items such as food, clothing, and health care products. Wages were low, and shops often had long lines of customers seeking short supplies of goods.

Mixed Economies

A **mixed economy** combines elements of traditional, market, and command economies.

Pure forms of traditional, market, and command economies leave something to be desired. Among other drawbacks, traditional economies are rigid, market economies bring about income inequality, and command economies have difficulty meeting consumer needs with centralized production decisions. Most countries today, including the United States, have a **mixed economy**, meaning one with characteristics of traditional, market, and command economies.

Traditional work schedules, production decisions, and purchases are common in modern economies due to the ease of following cultural norms, the entrenchment of gender roles, and the familiarity of customs and rituals. Among primarily market-based economies, notable socialist elements appear in the forms of publicly owned schools, police and fire departments, national defense forces, transportation systems, and programs to assist low-income, disabled, and elderly residents. Most of the countries that had command economies in the past, including China, Cuba, Russia, and Vietnam, have evolved to allow at least some private control of businesses. By transitioning to mixed economies, these countries have added popular freedoms and harnessed market forces to address societal needs with generous portions of something deemed critical by economists: incentives.

Norm Betts/Bloomberg/Getty Images

In a market economy, entrepreneurs seek to make the products that consumers are most eager to buy.

Incentives Matter

The success or failure of an economic system often comes down to the incentives it provides. **Incentives** are rewards or punishments that motivate particular choices. Many of the shortcomings of command economies result from inadequate incentives for producers to satisfy consumers' needs. In market economies, producers are free to raise the price when there is a shortage of a product and to keep the resulting profits. Profits provide an incentive for producers to make more of the most-needed goods and services and thus to eliminate shortages.

In fact, economists tend to be skeptical of any attempt to change people's behavior that doesn't change their incentives. For example, a plan that calls on manufacturers to voluntarily reduce pollution is likely to be ineffective unless it is accompanied by incentives, such as tax breaks or the avoidance of fines.

Property rights, which establish ownership and grant individuals the right to trade goods and services with each other, create many of the incentives in market economies. Property rights can apply to resources, goods, firms, and intellectual property, such as inventions and works of art. With the right to own property comes the incentive to produce things of value, either to keep, or to trade for things of even greater value. Ownership also creates an incentive to put resources to their best possible use. Property rights to a lake, for example, give the owners an incentive not to pollute that lake if its use for recreation, serenity, or sale has significant value.

AP® ECON TIP

An exam question might hint at a type of economy by saying who owns the factors of production (resources), such as capital. Remember that these things are owned privately by households in a market economy and publicly (which could also be described as "collectively" or "by the government") in a command economy.

Incentives are rewards or punishments that motivate particular choices.

Property rights establish ownership and grant individuals the right to trade goods and services with each other.

Module 1.2  Review

Check Your Understanding

1. Explain why incentives matter in an economy.
2. Explain how economic decisions are made in a market economy.

Tackle the AP® Test: Multiple-Choice Questions

1. The system that coordinates a society's choices about production and consumption is in every case its
   a. central authority.
   b. market.
   c. government.
   d. free enterprise.
   e. economy.

2. One of the three basic economic questions is:
   a. How much will it cost?
   b. With which countries will we trade?
   c. Who will receive the goods and services?
   d. What will the wage rate be?
   e. What is the rate of unemployment?

3. Who owns the factors of production in a market economy?
   a. the government
   b. households
   c. general assemblies
   d. councils of workers
   e. public firms

4. In which type of economy would you be most likely to see children following the same career path as their parents?
   a. a socialist economy
   b. a market economy
   c. a mixed economy
   d. a traditional economy
   e. a command economy

5. Which two types of systems are both considered command economies?
   a. market and traditional
   b. traditional and socialist
   c. socialist and communist
   d. communist and market
   e. market and capitalist

6. Most countries today have a
   a. market economy.
   b. socialist economy.
   c. command economy.
   d. traditional economy.
   e. mixed economy.

7. Which of the following exist(s) in a command economy but not in a market economy?
   a. property rights for individuals
   b. land, labor, capital, and entrepreneurship
   c. plenty of incentives to motivate firms to produce what consumers need
   d. easy access to desired goods and services
   e. a central authority making production and consumption decisions

Tackle the AP® Test: Free-Response Questions

1. Define *property rights* and *incentives*. Describe how property rights help to create incentives for productivity.

2. Explain two ways in which *command economies* differ from *market economies*. **(2 points)**

Rubric for FRQ 1 (3 points)

1 point: Property rights establish ownership and grant individuals the right to trade goods and services with each other.

1 point: Incentives are rewards or punishments that motivate particular choices.

1 point: Property rights incentivize productivity because they allow producers to benefit from their work, either by keeping what they produce or by selling it to others to acquire things of greater value.

The Production Possibilities Curve Model

MODULE 1.3

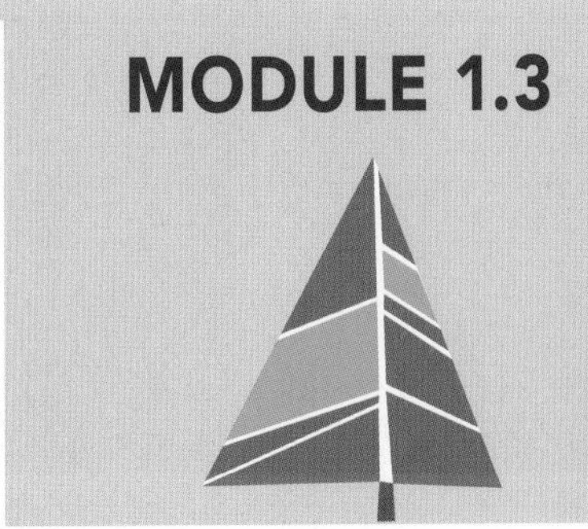

> **In this Module, you will learn to:**
> - Summarize the crucial role of models as simplified representations of economic realities
> - Explain how the production possibilities curve graph illustrates necessary trade-offs
> - Describe what the production possibilities curve model tells us about scarcity, efficiency, and opportunity cost
> - Explain how changes in technology and the availability of resources influence economic growth and the production possibilities curve

A good economic model, like a good street map app, can be a tremendous aid when navigating complex situations. In this Module, we look at the *production possibilities curve*, a model that helps economists think about the trade-offs necessary in every economy. The production possibilities curve helps us understand three important aspects of the real economy: efficiency, opportunity cost, and economic growth.

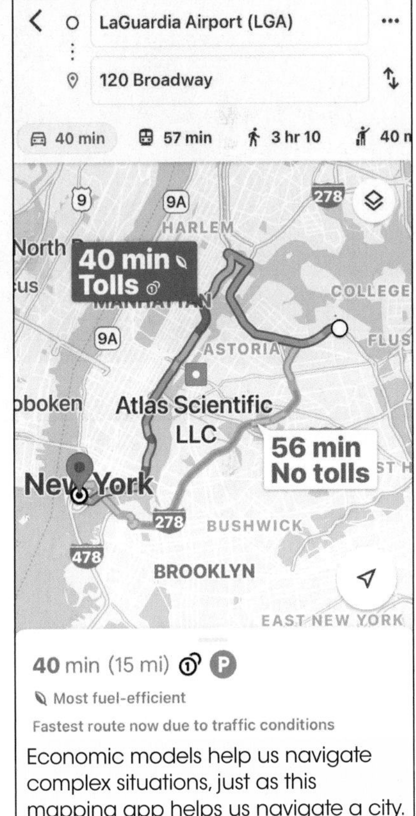

Economic models help us navigate complex situations, just as this mapping app helps us navigate a city.

The Use of Models in Economics

In 1901, one year after their first glider flights at Kitty Hawk, the Wright brothers built something else that would change the world – a wind tunnel. This apparatus let them experiment with many different designs for wings and control surfaces. These experiments gave them knowledge that would make heavier-than-air flight possible. Needless to say, testing an airplane design in a wind tunnel is cheaper and safer than building a full-scale version and hoping it will fly. Today, pilots train with flight simulators and cockpit models that allow them to practice maneuvers without ever leaving the ground. Likewise, models play a crucial role in almost all scientific research – economics included.

A **model** is any simplified version of reality used to better understand a real-life situation. But how do we create a simplified representation of an economic situation? One possibility – an economist's equivalent of a wind tunnel – is to find or create a real but simplified economy. For example, economists interested in the role of money have studied the system of exchange that developed in World War II prison camps, in which cigarettes became a universally accepted form of payment, even among prisoners who didn't smoke.

A **model** is a simplified representation used to better understand a real-life situation.

The workings of the economy can modeled on a computer. For example, when changes in tax law are proposed, government officials use *tax models* – large mathematical computer programs – to assess how the proposed changes would affect different groups of people. Economists particularly like to create models with graphs and equations.

Models are important because their simplicity allows economists to focus on the influence of only one change at a time. That is, they allow us to hold everything else constant and study how one change affects the overall economic outcome. So when building economic models, it is important to make the **other things equal assumption**, which means that all other relevant factors remain unchanged. Sometimes the Latin phrase *ceteris paribus*, which means "other things equal," is used.

The **other things equal assumption** means that all other relevant factors remain unchanged. This is also known as the *ceteris paribus* assumption.

It isn't always possible to find or create a small-scale version of the whole economy, and a computer program is only as good as the data it uses. (Programmers have a saying: garbage in, garbage out.) For many purposes, the most effective form of economic modeling is the construction of "thought experiments": simplified, hypothetical versions of real-life situations.

Throughout this book, starting in this Module, you will see how graphical models illustrate the relationships between variables and reveal the effects of changes in the economy. One such graph is the *production possibilities curve*, a model that helps economists think about the choices to be made in every economy.

Trade-offs: The Production Possibilities Curve

The true story of Alexander Selkirk may have inspired Daniel Defoe's 1719 novel about shipwrecked hero Robinson Crusoe. In 1704, Selkirk was a crew member on a ship that he correctly feared was not seaworthy. Before the ship met its fate at the bottom of the sea, Selkirk quarreled with the captain about the need for repairs, and then abandoned the ship during a stop at a deserted island near Chile. As in the story of Robinson Crusoe, Selkirk was alone and had limited resources: the natural resources of the island, a few items he brought from the ship, and, of course, his own time and effort. With that, he had to make a life for four and a half years. In effect, he became a one-man economy.

SJ Travel Photo and Video/Shutterstock

In Module 1.1, we introduced one of the important principles of economics: resources are generally scarce. As a result, participants in any economy—whether it contains one person or millions of people—face trade-offs. For example, if castaways on a tropical island devote more resources to catching fish, they benefit by catching more fish, but they cannot use those same resources to gather coconuts, so the trade-off is that they have fewer coconuts.

To think about the trade-offs necessary in any economy, economists often use the **production possibilities curve** model. The idea behind this model is to improve our understanding of trade-offs by considering a simplified economy that produces only two goods. This simplification enables us to show the trade-offs graphically.

The **production possibilities curve** illustrates the necessary trade-offs in an economy that produces only two goods. It shows the maximum quantity of one good that can be produced for each possible quantity of the other good produced.

Figure 1.3-1 shows a hypothetical production possibilities curve for Alexis, a castaway alone on an island, who must make a trade-off between fish production and coconut production. The curve shows the maximum quantity of fish Alexis can catch during a week *given* the quantity of coconuts she gathers, and vice versa. That is, it answers questions of the form, "What is the maximum quantity of fish Alexis can catch if she also gathers 9 (or 15, or 30) coconuts?"

There is a crucial distinction between points *inside* or *on* the production possibilities curve (the shaded area in Figure 1.3-1) and points *outside* the curve. If a production point lies inside or on the curve—like point *C*, at which Alexis catches 20 fish and gathers 9 coconuts—it is feasible. After all, the curve tells us that if Alexis catches 20 fish, she could also gather a maximum of 15 coconuts, so she could certainly gather 9 coconuts. Production inside the curve indicates that resources are underutilized, which can mean that land or capital lies idle or that workers are unemployed. A production point outside the curve—such as point *D*, which would have Alexis catching 40 fish and gathering 30 coconuts—isn't feasible because the economy's resources and technology are not sufficient to reach that point.

In Figure 1.3-1, the production possibilities curve intersects the horizontal axis at 40 fish. This means that if Alexis devoted all her resources to catching fish, she would catch 40 fish per week but would have no resources left over to gather coconuts. The

FIGURE 1.3-1 The Production Possibilities Curve

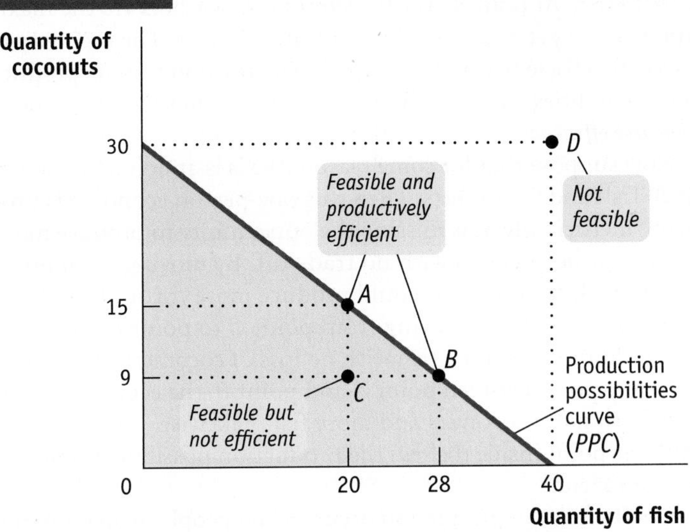

The production possibilities curve illustrates the trade-offs facing an economy that produces two goods. It shows the maximum quantity of one good that can be produced, given the quantity of the other good produced. Here, the maximum quantity of coconuts that Alexis can gather depends on the quantity of fish she catches, and vice versa. Her feasible production is shown by the area *inside* or *on* the curve. Production at point *D* is not feasible. Production at point *C* is feasible but not efficient and indicates underutilized resources. Points *A* and *B* are feasible and *productively efficient*, meaning resources are fully utilized and the only way to make more of one good is to make less of the other good.

production possibilities curve intersects the vertical axis at 30 coconuts. This means that if Alexis devoted all her resources to gathering coconuts, she could gather 30 coconuts per week but would have no resources left over to catch fish. Thus, if Alexis wants 30 coconuts, the trade-off is that she can't have any fish.

The curve also shows less extreme trade-offs. For example, if Alexis decides to catch 20 fish, she would be able to gather at most 15 coconuts; this production choice is illustrated by point *A*. If Alexis decides to catch 28 fish, she could gather at most 9 coconuts, as shown by point *B*.

Thinking in terms of a production possibilities curve simplifies the complexities of reality. The real-world economy produces millions of different goods. Even a castaway on an island would produce more than two different items (for example, Alexis would need clothing and housing as well as food). But in this model we imagine an economy that produces only two goods, because in a model with many goods, it would be much harder to study trade-offs, efficiency, and economic growth.

Efficiency

The production possibilities curve is useful for illustrating the general economic concept of efficiency. An economy is **efficient** if there are no missed opportunities—meaning that there is no way to make some people better off without making other people worse off. For example, suppose a course you are taking meets in a classroom that is too small for the number of students—some may be forced to sit on the floor or stand—while a larger classroom nearby sits empty. Economists would say that this is an *inefficient* use of resources because there is a way to make some people better off without making anyone worse off—after all, the larger classroom is empty. The school is not using its resources efficiently. When an economy is using all of its resources efficiently, the only way to make one person better off is to change the use of resources in a way that makes someone else worse off. So in our classroom example, if all larger classrooms were already fully occupied, we could say that the school was run in an efficient way; your classmates could be made better off only by making people in the larger classroom worse off—by moving them to the room that is too small.

An economy is **efficient** if there is no way to make anyone better off without making at least one person worse off.

Returning to our castaway example, as long as Alexis produces a combination of coconuts and fish that is on the production possibilities curve, her production is efficient. No resources are being wasted, so there is no way to make more of one good without making less of the other. For example, at point *A*, the 15 coconuts she gathers

David Grossman/Alamy

A crowded classroom reflects inefficiency if switching to a larger classroom would make some students better off without making anyone worse off.

are the maximum quantity she can get *given* that she has chosen to catch 20 fish. At point *B*, the 9 coconuts she gathers are the maximum she can get *given* her choice to catch 28 fish. The economy is producing efficiently if it is producing at any point on its production possibilities curve. Fittingly, economists call this achievement *productive efficiency*.

Now suppose that for some reason Alexis is at point *C*, producing 20 fish and 9 coconuts. Then this one-person economy is producing inefficiently: it is missing the opportunity to produce more of either or both goods with no trade-off. By moving from point *C* to point *A*, the economy could produce more coconuts without giving up any fish. By moving from point *C* to point *B*, the economy could produce more fish with no loss of coconuts. Or by moving to any point between point *A* and point *B*, the economy could make both more coconuts and more fish. Likewise, production at any other point inside (below) the production possibilities curve is also inefficient.

Another example of inefficiency in production occurs when people in an economy are involuntarily unemployed: they want to work but are unable to find jobs. When that happens, the economy is not productively efficient because it could produce more output if those people were employed. The production possibilities curve shows all the combinations of two goods that could be produced if all resources were fully employed. Changes in unemployment move the economy closer to, or further away from, the production possibilities curve (*PPC*). But the curve itself is determined by what would be possible if there were no unemployment in the economy. Greater unemployment is represented by points farther below the *PPC*—the economy is not reaching its possibilities if it is not using all of its resources. Lower unemployment is represented by points closer to the *PPC*—as unemployment decreases, the economy moves closer to reaching its possibilities.

Productive efficiency is only *part* of what's required for the economy as a whole to be efficient. The allocation of resources between the two goods can also be efficient or inefficient, depending on whether the quantities of each good produced make consumers as well off as possible. If an economy produces at the point along its production possibilities curve that is preferred by consumers, we say that it has achieved *allocative efficiency*. To see why allocative efficiency is important, notice that points *A* and *B* in Figure 1.3-1 both represent situations in which the economy is productively efficient, because in each case it can't produce more of one good without producing less of the other. But these two situations may not be equally desirable. Suppose Alexis prefers point *B* to point *A*—that is, she would rather consume 28 fish and 9 coconuts than 20 fish and 15 coconuts. Then point *A* represents an inefficient allocation of resources because it is possible to make Alexis better off without making anyone else worse off. (Of course, in this castaway economy, there isn't anyone else; Alexis is all alone.)

This example shows that efficiency for the economy as a whole requires *both* productive and allocative efficiency. To be efficient, an economy must produce as much of each good as it can, given the production levels of other goods, and it must produce the mix of goods that people most want to consume. We will discuss both types of efficiency more in Module 3.7.

Opportunity Cost

AP® ECON TIP

Opportunity Cost = Opportunity Lost (the financial or nonfinancial cost of a choice not taken)

The production possibilities curve reminds us that the true cost of any good is not only its price, but also everything else in addition to money that must be given up in order to get that good—the *opportunity cost*. If, for example, Alexis decides to go from point *A* to point *B*, she will produce 8 more fish but 6 fewer coconuts. So the opportunity cost of those 8 fish is the 6 coconuts not gathered. Since 8 extra fish have an opportunity cost of 6 coconuts, 1 fish has an opportunity cost of $6/8 = 3/4$ of a coconut.

Is the opportunity cost of an extra fish in terms of coconuts always the same, no matter how many fish Alexis catches? In the example illustrated by Figure 1.3-1, the answer is yes. If Alexis increases her catch from 28 to 40 fish, an increase of 12, the number of coconuts she gathers falls from 9 to zero. So her opportunity cost per additional fish is $\frac{9}{12} = \frac{3}{4}$ of a coconut, the same as it was when her catch went from 20 fish to 28. However, the unchanging opportunity cost of an additional fish in this example is a result of an assumption we've made, an assumption that's reflected in the way Figure 1.3-1 is drawn. Specifically, whenever we assume that the opportunity cost of an additional unit of a good doesn't change regardless of the output mix, the production possibilities curve is a straight line.

Creativ Studio Heinemann/Getty Images

Moreover, as you might have already guessed, the slope of a straight-line production possibilities curve is equal to the opportunity cost—specifically, the opportunity cost for the good measured on the horizontal axis in terms of the good measured on the vertical axis. In Figure 1.3-1, the production possibilities curve has a *constant slope* of $-\frac{3}{4}$, implying that Alexis faces a *constant opportunity cost* per fish equal to $\frac{3}{4}$ of a coconut. (A review of how to calculate the slope of a straight line is found in the Appendix.) This is the simplest case, but the production possibilities curve model can also be used to examine situations in which opportunity costs change as the mix of output changes.

Figure 1.3-2 illustrates a different assumption, a case in which Alexis faces *increasing opportunity cost*. Here, the more fish she catches, the more coconuts she has to give up, and vice versa. For example, to go from producing zero fish to producing 20 fish, she has to give up 5 coconuts. So the opportunity cost of those 20 fish is 5 coconuts. But to increase her fish production from 20 to 40—that is, to produce an additional 20 fish—she must give up 25 more coconuts, a much higher opportunity cost. As you can see in Figure 1.3-2, when opportunity costs are increasing rather than constant, the production possibilities curve is a concave-shaped (bowed-out) curve rather than a straight line. Though it is not likely, if the opportunity costs are decreasing, the production possibility curve would instead be convex-shaped (bowed in).

Although it's often useful to work with the simple assumption that the production possibilities curve is a straight line, in reality, opportunity costs are typically increasing. When only a small amount of a good is produced, the opportunity cost of producing that good is relatively low because the economy needs to use only those resources that are especially well suited for its production. For instance, if an economy grows only a

> **AP® ECON TIP**
>
> The use of specialized resources makes the production possibilities curve *concave to the origin*, meaning that it is bowed out as shown in Figure 1.3-2. When there is *no* specialization of resources for the production of the goods, there is *no* increase in the opportunity cost of making more of either good and *no* change in the slope of the production possibilities curve—it is a straight line.

FIGURE 1.3-2 Increasing Opportunity Cost

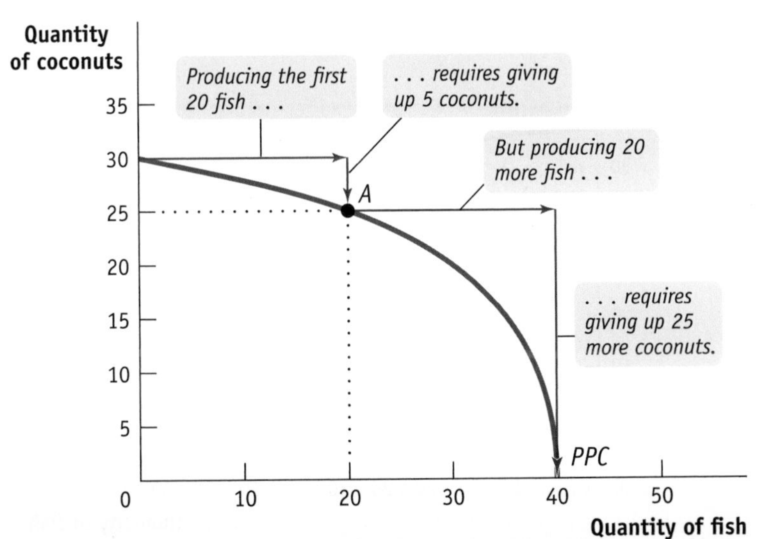

The concave (bowed-out) shape of the production possibilities curve reflects increasing opportunity cost. In this example, to produce the first 20 fish, Alexis must give up 5 coconuts. But to produce an additional 20 fish, she must give up 25 more coconuts. The opportunity cost of fish increases because as Alexis catches more fish, she must make increasing use of resources specialized for coconut production. In the unlikely event that opportunity costs are decreasing, the production possibilities curve is instead convex (bowed in).

small amount of corn, that corn can be grown in places where the soil and climate are perfect for growing corn but less suitable for growing another crop, such as wheat. So growing that corn involves giving up only a small amount of wheat production. Once the economy grows a lot of corn, however, land that is well suited for wheat but isn't so great for corn must be used to produce corn anyway. As a result, increases in corn production involve sacrificing more and more wheat per unit of corn. In other words, as more of a good is produced, its opportunity cost typically rises because resources specialized for the production of that good are used up and resources specialized for the production of the other good must be used instead.

In some cases, there is no specialization of resources, meaning that all resources are equally suitable for the production of each good. That might be the case when the two goods are leather belts and leather hats, pizzas and calzones, or cappuccinos and lattes. When there is no specialization of resources, the opportunity cost of each unit remains the same as more of a good is made. For example, assuming that two leather belts could be made with the labor, leather, and other resources needed to make one leather hat, the opportunity cost of *each* leather hat is two belts. When no resources are specialized for the production of either good, the production possibilities curve is a straight, downward-sloping line like the one in Figure 1.3-1.

Economic Growth

Economic growth is an increase in the maximum amount of goods and services an economy can produce.

Finally, the production possibilities curve helps us understand what it means to talk about **economic growth**, which is an increase in the maximum possible output of an economy. When are we justified in saying that an economy has grown over time? After all, although the U.S. economy today produces more of many things than it did a century ago, it produces less of other things, such as horse-drawn carriages. In other words, production of many goods is actually down. So how can we say for sure that the economy as a whole has grown?

The answer, illustrated in **Figure 1.3-3**, is that economic growth means an *expansion of the economy's production possibilities*: the economy *can* produce more of everything. For example, if Alexis's production is initially at point *A* (20 fish and 25 coconuts), with economic growth she could move to point *E* (25 fish and 30 coconuts). Point *E* lies outside the original curve, so in the production possibilities curve model, growth is shown as an outward shift of the curve. Unless the *PPC* shifts outward, the points beyond the *PPC* are unattainable because they are beyond the economy's production possibilities.

What can cause the production possibilities curve to shift outward? There are two general sources of economic growth. One is an increase in the availability of resources

FIGURE 1.3-3 Economic Growth

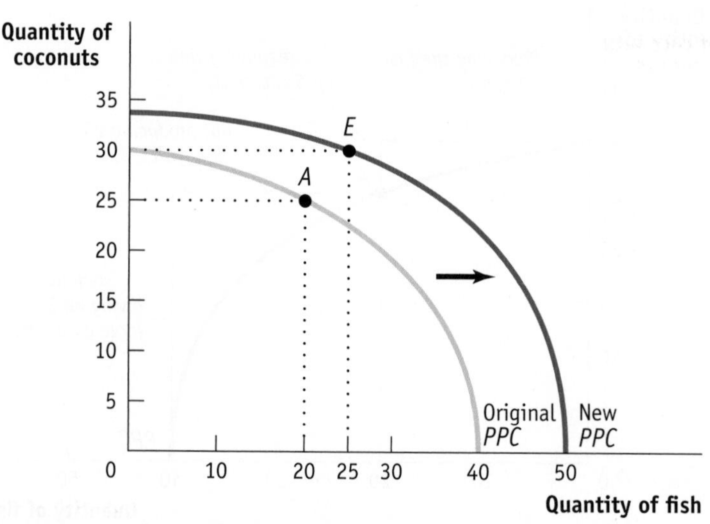

Economic growth results in an *outward shift* of the production possibilities curve because production possibilities are expanded. The economy can now produce more of everything. For example, if production is initially at point *A* (20 fish and 25 coconuts), with sufficient economic growth it could move to point *E* (25 fish and 30 coconuts).

(also called factors of production) used to produce goods and services: labor, land, capital, and entrepreneurship. To see how adding to an economy's resources leads to economic growth, suppose that fish become more abundant in the waters around Alexis's island. She can then catch more fish in the course of a day spent fishing. The number of additional fish Alexis catches depends on how much time she decides to spend fishing now that there are more fish in her part of the sea. But because the increased fish population makes her fishing more productive, she can catch more fish without reducing the number of coconuts she gathers, or she can gather more coconuts without reducing her fish catch. So her production possibilities curve shifts outward.

Fuse/Getty Images

The other source of economic growth is improved **technology**, the technical means for the production of goods and services. Suppose Alexis figures out a better way either to catch fish or to gather coconuts – say, by inventing a fishing net or a wagon for transporting coconuts. Either invention would shift her production possibilities curve outward. However, the shift would not be a simple outward expansion of every point along the *PPC*. Technology specific to the production of only one good has no effect if all resources are devoted to the other good: a fishing net will be of no use if Alexis produces nothing but coconuts. So the point on the *PPC* that represents the number of coconuts that can be produced if there is no fishing will not change. In real-world economies, innovations in the techniques we use to produce goods and services have been a crucial force behind economic growth.

Technology is the technical means for producing goods and services.

Remember, economic growth means an increase in what the economy *can* produce. What the economy actually produces depends on the choices people make. After her production possibilities expand, Alexis might not choose to produce both more fish and more coconuts; she might choose to increase production of only one good, or she might even choose to produce less of one good. For example, if she gets better at catching fish, she might decide to go on an all-fish diet and skip the coconuts, just as the introduction of motor vehicles led most people to give up horse-drawn carriages. But even if, for some reason, she chooses to produce either fewer coconuts or fewer fish than before, we would still say that her economy has grown, because she *could* have produced more of everything.

If an economy's production possibilities curve shifts inward, the economy has become smaller. This could happen if the economy loses resources or technology, as could result from war or natural disaster. **Figure 1.3-4** shows what could happen if a hurricane destroyed some of the trees and fishing nets on the island. If Alexis's production is initially at point *A* (20 fish and 25 coconuts), the storm could drive production down to point *F* (15 fish and 20 coconuts). Point *F* lies inside the original curve, so the shrinkage of the economy is shown as an inward shift of the production possibilities curve.

FIGURE 1.3-4 A Shrinking Economy

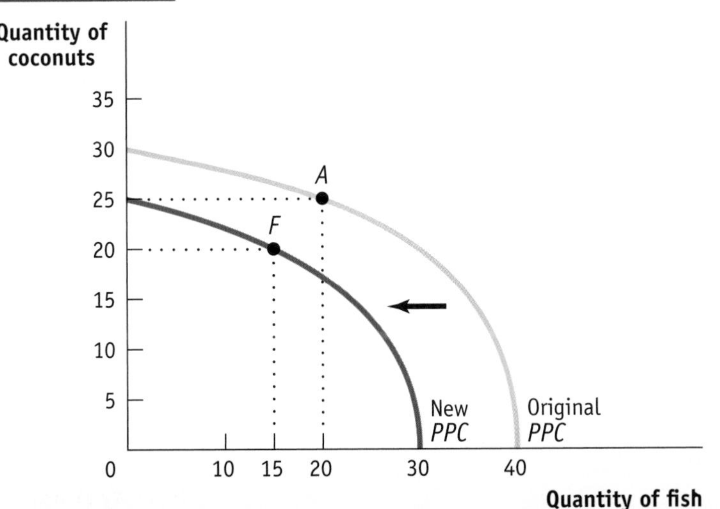

A shrinking economy results in an *inward shift* of the production possibilities curve because production possibilities have diminished. The economy cannot produce as much of either good as it could before. For example, if production starts at point *A* (20 fish and 25 coconuts), after the shrinkage, production could move to point *F* (15 fish and 20 coconuts).

The production possibilities curve is a very simplified model of an economy, yet it teaches us important lessons about real-life economies. It gives us our first clear sense of what constitutes economic efficiency, it illustrates the concept of opportunity cost, and it shows what economic growth is all about.

Watch the Video:
Production Possibilities Curve

Module 1.3  Review

Check Your Understanding

1. True or false? Explain your answer.
   a. An increase in the amount of resources available to Alexis for use in producing coconuts and fish does not change her production possibilities curve.
   b. A technological change that allows Alexis to catch more fish relative to any amount of coconuts gathered results in a change in her production possibilities curve.
   c. Points inside a production possibilities curve are efficient, and points outside a production possibilities curve are inefficient.

Tackle the AP® Test: Multiple-Choice Questions

Refer to the graph to answer Questions 1–5.

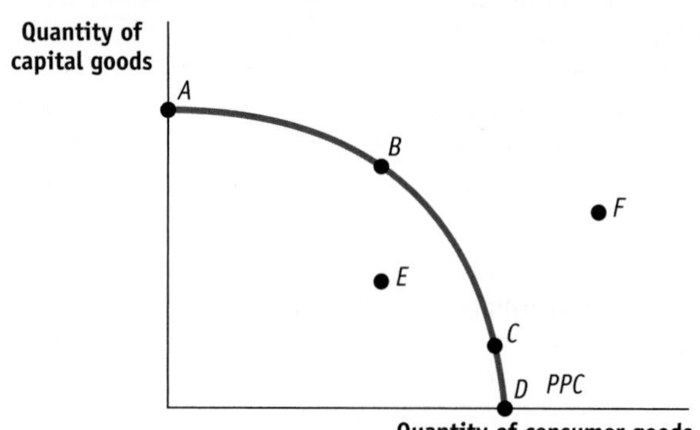

1. Which point(s) on the graph represent efficiency in production?
   a. *B* and *C*
   b. *A* and *D*
   c. *A*, *B*, *C*, and *D*
   d. *A*, *B*, *C*, *D*, and *E*
   e. *A*, *B*, *C*, *D*, *E*, and *F*
2. For this economy, an increase in the quantity of capital goods (such as hammers) without a decrease in the quantity of consumer goods (such as shirts)
   a. cannot happen because there is always an opportunity cost.
   b. is represented by a movement from point *E* to point *A*.
   c. is represented by a movement from point *C* to point *B*.
   d. is represented by a movement from point *E* to point *B*.
   e. is possible only with an increase in resources or technology.
3. An increase in unemployment could be represented by a movement from point
   a. *D* to point *C*.
   b. *B* to point *A*.
   c. *C* to point *F*.
   d. *B* to point *E*.
   e. *E* to point *B*.
4. Which of the following might allow economic growth and a movement from point *B* to point *F*?
   a. more workers
   b. discovery of new resources
   c. building new factories
   d. technological advances
   e. all of the above
5. This production possibilities curve shows the trade-off between consumer goods and capital goods. Since capital goods are a resource, an increase in the production of capital goods today will increase the economy's production possibilities in the future. Therefore, all other things equal (*ceteris paribus*), producing at which point today will result in the largest outward shift of the *PPC* in the future?
   a. *A*
   b. *B*
   c. *C*
   d. *D*
   e. *E*

6. The production possibilities curve will certainly be straight if
   a. making more of one good means that less of the other good can be made.
   b. the opportunity cost of making each good increases as more is made.
   c. no resources are specialized for the production of either good.
   d. the opportunity cost of making the first unit of each good is the same.
   e. the economy experiences decreasing opportunity costs for the production of both goods.
7. The allocation of resources in the economy is efficient
   a. at every point along a production possibilities curve.
   b. at every point above a production possibilities curve.
   c. at every point below a production possibilities curve.
   d. at the point on a production possibilities curve that minimizes the use of resources.
   e. at the point along a production possibilities curve that makes consumers as well off as possible.
8. Which of the following could not be considered an economic model?
   a. a graph
   b. an equation
   c. a computer simulation
   d. the economy itself
   e. a real but simplified economy
9. The "other things equal" assumption allows economists to
   a. avoid making assumptions about reality.
   b. focus on the effects of only one change at a time.
   c. avoid making the *ceteris paribus* assumption.
   d. allow nothing to change in their model.
   e. reflect all aspects of the real world in their model.

Tackle the AP® Test: Free-Response Questions

1. Refer to the graph. Assume that the country is producing at point *C*.

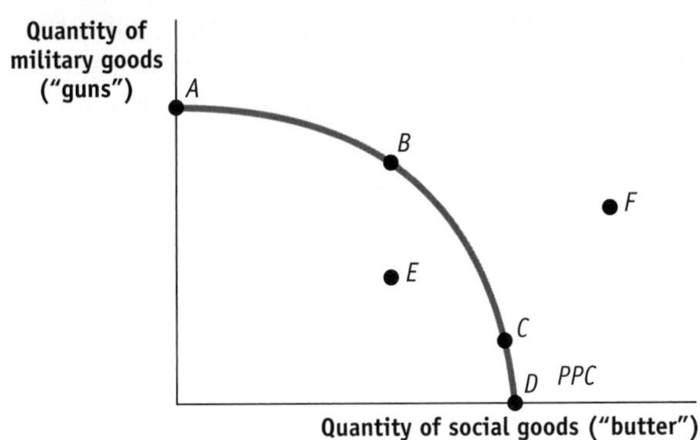

   a. Does this country's production possibilities curve exhibit increasing opportunity costs? Explain.
   b. Suppose point *C* initially represents the best allocation of resources for this country, but then the country goes to war. Before any of the country's resources are lost in the fighting, which point is the most likely to represent an efficient allocation of resources for the country when it is at war? Explain.
   c. If the economy experiences a major hurricane that severely disrupts production, the country would move from point *C* to which point? Explain.

Rubric for FRQ 1 (6 points)

1 point: Yes

1 point: The *PPC* is concave (bowed outward), so with each additional unit of butter produced, the opportunity cost in terms of gun production (indicated by the slope of the line) increases. Likewise, as more guns are produced, the opportunity cost in terms of butter increases.

1 point: *B*

1 point: The country would choose an efficient point with more (but not all) military goods with which to fight the war. Point *A* would be an unlikely choice because at that point there is no production of any social goods, some of which are needed to maintain a minimal standard of living.

1 point: *E*

1 point: A recession, which causes unemployment, is represented by a point below the *PPC*.

2. Assume that an economy can choose between producing food and producing shelter at a constant opportunity cost. Draw a correctly labeled production possibilities curve for the economy. On your graph:
   a. Use the letter *E* to label one of the points at which production is efficient.
   b. Use the letter *U* to label one of the points at which there might be unemployment.
   c. Use the letter *I* to label one of the points that is not feasible. **(5 points)**

MODULE 1.4

Comparative Advantage and Trade

In this Module, you will learn to:

- Explain how trade leads to gains for individuals and economies
- Define absolute advantage and comparative advantage
- Use production possibilities curves to determine absolute and comparative advantages
- Describe how comparative advantage determines how trading partners should specialize
- Calculate mutually beneficial terms of trade

Gains from Trade

A family could try to take care of all its own needs—growing its own food, sewing its own clothing, providing itself with entertainment, and writing its own economics textbooks. But trying to live that way would be hard. A much higher standard of living can be attained for everyone by dividing tasks such that each person provides one or more goods or services in return for different desired goods and services. This system describes **trade**.

In a market economy, individuals engage in **trade**: they provide goods and services to others and receive goods and services in return.

The gains from trade come from **specialization**: each person specializes in the task that they are good at performing.

The reason we have an economy, rather than many self-sufficient individuals, is to take advantage of the gains from trade: by dividing tasks and trading, two people (or 7 billion people) can each get more of what they want than they could get by being self-sufficient. The division of tasks that allows gains from trade is known as **specialization**, which allows each person to engage in a task that they are particularly good at performing.

The advantages of specialization, and the resulting gains from trade, were the starting point for Adam Smith's 1776 book *The Wealth of Nations*, which many regard as the beginning of economics as a discipline. Smith's book begins with a description of an eighteenth-century pin factory where, rather than each of the 10 workers making a pin from start to finish, each worker specialized in one of the many steps in pin-making:

> One man draws out the wire, another straights it, a third cuts it, a fourth points it, a fifth grinds it at the top for receiving the head; to make the head requires two or three distinct operations; to put it on, is a particular business, to whiten the pins is another; it is even a trade by itself to put them into the paper; and the important business of making a pin is, in this manner, divided into about eighteen distinct operations. . . . Those ten persons, therefore, could make among them upwards of forty-eight thousand pins in a day. But if they had all wrought separately and independently, and without any of them having been educated to this particular business, they certainly could not each of them have made twenty, perhaps not one pin a day. . . .

Ryan Pyle/Corbis/Getty Images

The concept of specialization allows for the mass production of most of the devices and appliances that we use today, like the car engine pictured here.

The same principle applies when we look at how people divide tasks among themselves and trade in an economy. The economy as a whole can produce more when each person *specializes* in a task and *trades* with others.

The benefits of specialization are the reason a person typically focuses on the production of only one type of good or service. It takes many years of study and experience to become a doctor; it also takes many years of study and experience to become a commercial airline pilot. Many doctors might have the potential to become excellent pilots, and vice versa, but it is very unlikely that anyone who decided to pursue both careers would be as good a pilot or as good a doctor as someone who specialized in only one of those professions. So it is to everyone's advantage when individuals specialize in their career choices.

Markets are what allow a doctor and a pilot to specialize in their respective fields. Because markets for commercial flights and for doctors' services exist, a doctor is assured to find a flight and a pilot is assured to find a doctor. As long as individuals know they can find the goods and services they want in the market, they are willing to forgo self-sufficiency and specialize instead.

Comparative Advantage and Gains from Trade

The production possibilities curve model is particularly useful for illustrating gains from trade – trade based on *comparative advantage*. Let's stick with Alexis being stranded on her island, but now we'll suppose that a second castaway, Jacob, has washed ashore. Can Alexis and Jacob benefit from trading with each other?

It's obvious that there will be potential gains from trade if the two castaways do different things particularly well. For example, if Alexis is a skilled fisher and Jacob is very good at climbing trees, clearly it makes sense for Alexis to catch fish and Jacob to gather coconuts – and for both castaways to trade the products of their efforts.

But one of the most important insights in all of economics is that there are gains from trade even if one of the trading parties isn't especially good at anything. Suppose, for example, that Jacob is less well suited to primitive life than Alexis; he's not nearly as good at catching fish, and compared to Alexis, even his coconut gathering leaves something to be desired. Nonetheless, what we'll see is that both Alexis and Jacob can live better by trading with each other than either could alone.

Roderick Chen/Design Pics Inc/Alamy

For the purposes of this example, let's go back to the simple case of straight-line production possibilities curves. Alexis's production possibilities are represented by the production possibilities curve in panel (a) of **Figure 1.4-1**, which is the same as the production possibilities curve in Figure 1.3-1. According to this *PPC*, Alexis could catch 40 fish, but only if she gathered no coconuts, and she could gather 30 coconuts, but only if she caught no fish. Recall that this means the slope of her production possibilities curve is $-3/4$: her opportunity cost of 1 fish is $3/4$ of a coconut.

FIGURE 1.4-1 Production Possibilities for Two Castaways

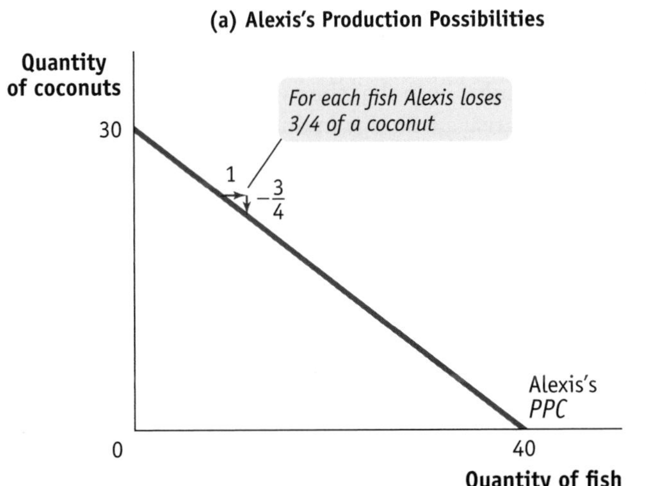

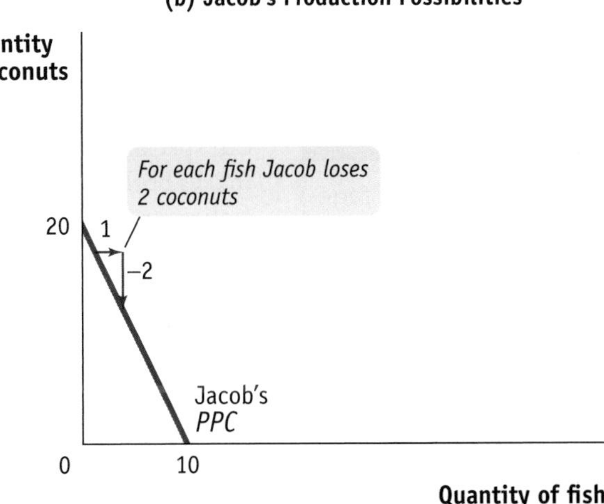

Here, each of the two castaways has a constant opportunity cost of fish, and therefore a straight-line production possibilities curve. In Alexis's case, each fish has an opportunity cost of $3/4$ of a coconut. In Jacob's case, each fish has an opportunity cost of 2 coconuts.

Panel (b) of Figure 1.4-1 shows Jacob's production possibilities. Like that of Alexis, Jacob's production possibilities curve is a straight line, implying a constant opportunity cost of fish in terms of coconuts. His production possibilities curve has a constant slope of –2. Jacob is less productive all around: at most he can produce 10 fish or 20 coconuts. But he is particularly bad at fishing: whereas Alexis sacrifices ¾ of a coconut per fish caught, for Jacob, the opportunity cost of a fish is 2 whole coconuts. **Table 1.4-1** summarizes the two castaways' opportunity costs of fish and coconuts.

Table 1.4-1 Alexis's and Jacob's Opportunity Costs of Fish and Coconuts

	Alexis's Opportunity Cost	Jacob's Opportunity Cost
One fish	¾ coconut	2 coconuts
One coconut	4/3 fish	½ fish

An individual has a **comparative advantage** in producing a good or service if that person's opportunity cost is the lowest among the people who could produce that good or service.

With information on opportunity costs we can determine who has the *comparative advantage* in producing each good. An individual has a **comparative advantage** in producing something if they have the lowest opportunity cost among the producers. In other words, Jacob has a comparative advantage over Alexis in producing a particular good or service if Jacob's opportunity cost of producing that good or service is lower than Alexis's opportunity cost. In this case, Jacob has a comparative advantage in gathering coconuts because his opportunity cost of ½ fish is lower than Alexis's opportunity cost of 4/3 fish, and Alexis has a comparative advantage in catching fish because her opportunity cost of ¾ coconut is lower than Jacob's opportunity cost of 2 coconuts.

Notice that Alexis is better than Jacob at producing both goods: If both castaways devoted their efforts to catching fish, Alexis would catch 40 fish per week while Jacob caught 10, and if they devoted their efforts to gathering coconuts, Alexis would gather 30 coconuts per week while Jacob gathered 20. Information on possible output levels allows us to determine absolute advantages. An individual has an **absolute advantage** in producing something if that person can produce more of it with a given amount of time and resources. Since Alexis can make more of either good than Jacob, Alexis has an absolute advantage in both activities.

An individual has an **absolute advantage** in producing a good or service if they can make more of it with a given amount of time and resources.

To examine the gains from trade, our point of comparison will be the alternative to trade: Alexis and Jacob could go their separate ways, each living on their own side of the island, catching their own fish and gathering their own coconuts. Let's suppose they start out that way and make the consumption choices shown in **Figure 1.4-2**: in the absence of trade, Alexis consumes 28 fish and 9 coconuts per week, while Jacob consumes 6 fish and 8 coconuts.

Is this the best they can do? No, it isn't. Given that the two castaways have different opportunity costs, each has a comparative advantage in one good or the other. They can specialize on the basis of their comparative advantages and strike a trade deal that makes both of them better off. **Table 1.4-2** shows how such a deal can work: Alexis specializes in the production of fish, catching 40 per week, and gives 10 to Jacob. Meanwhile, Jacob specializes in the production of coconuts, gathering 20 per week, and gives 10 to Alexis. The result is shown by the points above the *PPC*s in Figure 1.4-2. Alexis now consumes more of both goods than before: instead of 28 fish and 9 coconuts, she consumes 30 fish and 10 coconuts. Jacob also consumes more, going from 6 fish and 8 coconuts to 10 fish and 10 coconuts. As Table 1.4-2 also shows, both Alexis and Jacob experience gains from trade: Alexis's consumption of fish increases by two, and her consumption of coconuts increases by one. Jacob's consumption of fish increases by four, and his consumption of coconuts increases by two.

AP® ECON TIP

Having an *absolute* advantage is not the same thing as having a *comparative* advantage. For example, it is quite possible to be able to make more of something than other producers (that is, to have an absolute advantage) but to have a higher opportunity cost than other producers (that is, to have a comparative *dis*advantage).

So both castaways are better off when they each specialize in what they are good at and trade with each other. It's a good idea for Alexis to catch the fish for both of them, because her opportunity cost of catching a fish is relatively low and she therefore has a

FIGURE 1.4-2 Comparative Advantage and Gains from Trade

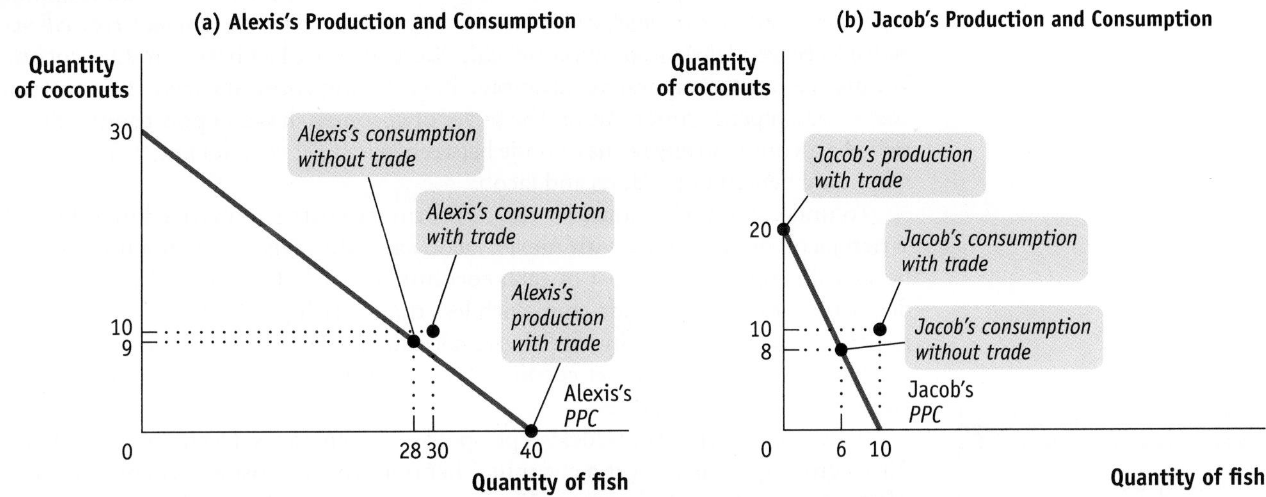

By specializing and trading, the two castaways can produce and consume more of both goods. Alexis specializes in catching fish, her comparative advantage, and Jacob—who has an *absolute* disadvantage in both goods but a *comparative* advantage in coconuts—specializes in gathering coconuts. The result is that each castaway can consume more of both goods than either could without trade.

Table 1.4-2 How the Castaways Gain from Trade

		Without Trade		With Trade		Gains from Trade
		Production	Consumption	Production	Consumption	
Alexis	Fish	28	28	40	30	+2
	Coconuts	9	9	0	10	+1
Jacob	Fish	6	6	0	10	+4
	Coconuts	8	8	20	10	+2

comparative advantage in catching fish. Correspondingly, it's a good idea for Jacob to gather coconuts for both of them.

Or we could describe the situation in a different way. Because Alexis is so good at catching fish, her opportunity cost of gathering coconuts is relatively high, which gives her a comparative disadvantage in gathering coconuts. Because Jacob is a relatively bad at fishing, his opportunity cost of gathering coconuts is much lower, giving him a comparative advantage in gathering coconuts.

At first, it might seem as though Alexis has nothing to gain from trading with less competent Jacob. But we've just seen that Alexis can indeed benefit from a deal with Jacob because *comparative*, not *absolute*, advantage is the basis for mutual gain. It doesn't matter that it takes Jacob more time to gather a coconut; what matters is that for him, the opportunity cost of that coconut in terms of fish is lower. So, despite his absolute disadvantage in both activities, Jacob's comparative advantage in coconut gathering makes mutually beneficial trade possible.

Mutually Beneficial Terms of Trade

The **terms of trade** indicate the rate at which one good can be exchanged for another. In our story, Alexis and Jacob traded 10 coconuts for 10 fish, so each coconut traded for 1 fish. Why not some other terms of trade, such as $\frac{3}{4}$ fish per coconut? Indeed, there are many terms of trade that would make both Alexis and Jacob better off than if they didn't trade. There are also terms that Alexis or Jacob would certainly reject. For example, Alexis would not trade 2 fish per coconut, because she only gives up $\frac{4}{3}$ fish per coconut without trade.

The **terms of trade** indicate the rate at which one good can be exchanged for another.

To find the range of mutually beneficial terms of trade for a coconut, look at each person's opportunity cost of producing a coconut. *Any price per coconut between the opportunity cost of the coconut producer and the opportunity cost of the coconut buyer will make both sides better off than in the absence of trade.* We know that Jacob will produce coconuts because he has a comparative advantage in gathering coconuts. Jacob's opportunity cost is ½ fish per coconut. Alexis, the buyer of coconuts, has an opportunity cost of $\frac{4}{3}$ fish per coconut. So any terms of trade between ½ fish per coconut and $\frac{4}{3}$ fish per coconut would benefit both Alexis and Jacob.

To understand why, consider the opportunity costs summarized in Table 1.4-1 When Jacob doesn't trade with Alexis, Jacob can gain ½ fish by giving up a coconut, because his opportunity cost of each coconut is ½ fish. Jacob will clearly reject any deal with Alexis that provides him with less than ½ fish per coconut—he's better off not trading at all and getting ½ fish per coconut. But Jacob benefits from trade if he receives more than ½ fish per coconut. So the terms of 1 fish per coconut, as in our story, are acceptable to Jacob.

AP® ECON TIP

The mutually beneficial terms of trade for a good fall between the producer's opportunity cost for the good and the buyer's opportunity cost for the good.

It also makes sense from Alexis's perspective. When Alexis doesn't trade with Jacob, Alexis gives up $\frac{4}{3}$ fish to get a coconut—her opportunity cost of a coconut is $\frac{4}{3}$ fish. Alexis will reject any deal that requires her to pay more than $\frac{4}{3}$ fish per coconut. But Alexis benefits from trade if she pays less than $\frac{4}{3}$ fish per coconut. The terms of 1 fish per coconut are thus acceptable to Alexis as well. Both islanders would also be made better off by terms of ¾ fish per coconut or $\frac{5}{4}$ fish per coconut or any other price between ½ fish and $\frac{4}{3}$ fish per coconut. Their negotiation skills determine where the terms of trade fall within that range.

So remember, Alexis and Jacob will engage in trade only if the "price" of the good each person obtains from trade is less than their own opportunity cost of producing the good. The same is true for international trade. Whenever two parties trade voluntarily, the terms of trade for each good are found between the opportunity cost of the producer and the opportunity cost of the buyer.

The story of Alexis and Jacob clearly simplifies reality. Yet it teaches us some very important lessons that also apply to the real economy. First, the story illustrates the gains from trade. By agreeing to specialize and trade, Alexis and Jacob can each consume more of both goods than if each tried to be self-sufficient. Second, the story demonstrates a key point that is often overlooked in real-world arguments: as long as potential trading partners have different opportunity costs, *each has a comparative advantage in something and each has a comparative disadvantage in something else, so each can benefit from trade.*

The idea of comparative advantage applies to many activities in the economy. Perhaps its most important application is in trade—not between individuals, but between countries. So let's look briefly at how the model of comparative advantage helps us understand both the causes and the effects of international trade.

Comparative Advantage and International Trade

AP® ECON TIP

The producer with the *absolute advantage* can produce the largest quantity of the good. However, it is the producer with the *comparative advantage*, and not necessarily the one with the absolute advantage, who should specialize in the production of that good to achieve mutual gains from trade.

International trade provides much of what we buy. Look at the label on most manufactured goods sold in the United States, and you will probably find it was produced in some other country—in China, Japan, or even Canada. On the other hand, many U.S. industries sell a large portion of their output overseas. This is particularly true for the agriculture, high technology, and entertainment industries.

Should we celebrate this international exchange of goods and services, or should it cause us concern? Politicians and the public sometimes question the desirability of international trade, arguing that the nation should produce goods for itself rather than buy them from other countries. Industries around the world demand protection from foreign competition: Japanese farmers want to keep out American rice, and American steelworkers want to keep out European steel. These demands are often supported by public opinion.

Economists, however, have a very positive view of international trade. Why? Because they view it in terms of comparative advantage. **Figure 1.4-3** shows how international trade can be interpreted in terms of comparative advantage. Although the example is hypothetical, it is based on an actual pattern of international trade: American exports of pork to Canada and Canadian exports of aircraft to the United States. Panels (a) and (b) illustrate hypothetical production possibilities curves for the United States and Canada, with pork measured on the horizontal axis and aircraft measured on the vertical axis. The U.S. production possibilities curve is flatter than the Canadian production possibilities curve, implying that producing one more ton of pork costs fewer aircraft in the United States than it does in Canada. This means that the United States has a comparative advantage in pork, and Canada has a comparative advantage in aircraft.

Canada has a comparative advantage in this jacket.

Steve Russell/Toronto Star/Getty Images

FIGURE 1.4-3 Comparative Advantage and International Trade

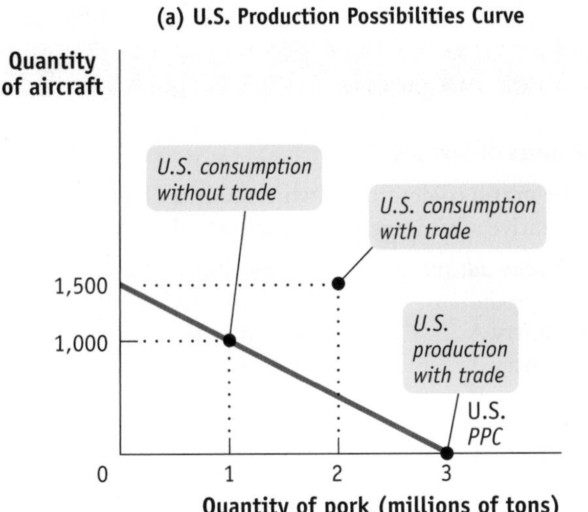

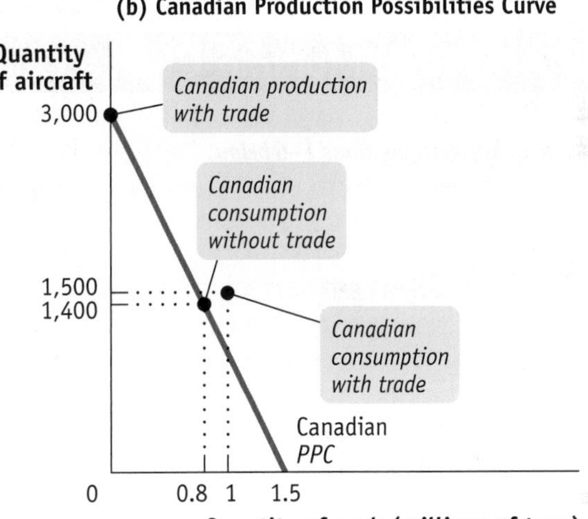

In this hypothetical example, Canada and the United States produce only two goods: pork and aircraft. Aircraft are measured on the vertical axis and pork on the horizontal axis. Panel (a) shows the U.S. production possibilities curve. It is relatively flat, implying that the United States has a comparative advantage in pork production. Panel (b) shows the Canadian production possibilities curve. It is relatively steep, implying that Canada has a comparative advantage in aircraft production. Just like two individuals, both countries gain from specialization and trade.

Although the consumption points in Figure 1.4-3 are hypothetical, they illustrate a general principle: as in the example of Alexis and Jacob, the United States and Canada can both achieve mutual gains from trade. If the United States concentrates on producing pork and sells some of its output to Canada, while Canada concentrates on aircraft and sells some of its output to the United States, both countries can consume more than if they insisted on being self-sufficient. For example, the United States could trade 1 million tons of pork for 1,500 aircraft from Canada. This would allow both countries to consume at a point outside of their production possibilities curves.

Moreover, these mutual gains don't depend on each country's being better at producing one kind of good. Even if, say, one country has remarkably productive workers who give it an absolute advantage in both industries, there are still mutual gains from trade.

Module 1.4  Review

> **Adventures in AP® Economics**
> Watch the Video:
> ***Comparative Advantage and Absolute Advantage***

Check Your Understanding

1. In the country of Imsmall, an automobile can be produced by 8 workers in one day and a washing machine by 3 workers in one day. In the country of Sosmall, an automobile can be produced by 6 workers in one day, and a washing machine by 2 workers in one day. Suppose each country has 24 workers.
   a. How many automobiles could each country make if it made nothing else?
   b. How many washing machines could each country make if it made nothing else?
   c. Which country has an absolute advantage in the production of automobiles? In washing machines?
   d. Which country has a comparative advantage in the production of washing machines? In automobiles?
   e. What type of specialization results in the greatest gains from trade between the two countries?
2. Refer to the story of Alexis and Jacob illustrated by Figure 1.4-1 in the text. Explain why Alexis and Jacob are willing to engage in a trade of 1 fish for 1½ coconuts.

Tackle the AP® Test: Multiple-Choice Questions

Refer to the graph below to answer Questions 1–6 below.

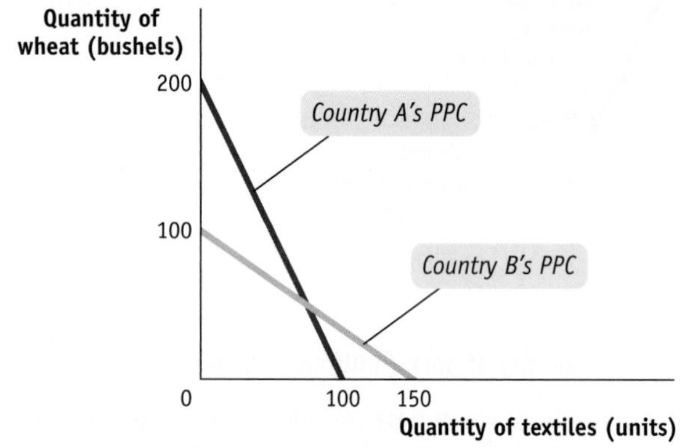

1. Use the graph to determine which country has an absolute advantage in producing each good.

Absolute advantage in wheat production	*Absolute advantage in textile production*
a. Country A	Country B
b. Country A	Country A
c. Country B	Country A
d. Country B	Country B
e. Country A	Neither country

2. For Country A, the opportunity cost of a bushel of wheat is
   a. ½ unit of textiles.
   b. ⅔ unit of textiles.
   c. 1⅓ units of textiles.
   d. 1½ units of textiles.
   e. 2 units of textiles.
3. Use the graph to determine which country has a comparative advantage in producing each good.

Comparative advantage in wheat production	*Comparative advantage in textile production*
a. Country A	Country B
b. Country A	Country A
c. Country B	Country A
d. Country B	Country B
e. Country A	Neither country

4. If the two countries specialize and trade, which of the choices below describes the countries' imports?

Import wheat	*Import textiles*
a. Country A	Country A
b. Country A	Country B
c. Country B	Country B
d. Country B	Country A
e. Neither country	Country B

5. What is the highest price Country B is willing to pay to buy wheat from Country A?
   a. ½ unit of textiles
   b. ⅔ unit of textiles
   c. 1 unit of textiles
   d. 1½ units of textiles
   e. 2 units of textiles

6. What are the mutually beneficial terms of trade, measured in units of wheat from Country A per unit of textiles from Country B?
   a. between 1 and 2
   b. between ⅔ and 2
   c. between ½ and 1½
   d. between ⅔ and 1½
   e. between ½ and 2

7. There are opportunities for mutually beneficial trade between two countries whenever
   a. one can produce more of everything than the other.
   b. the production possibilities curves of the two countries are identical.
   c. each country has a comparative advantage in making something.
   d. the countries are similar in size.
   e. no country has an absolute advantage in producing both goods.

Tackle the AP® Test: Free-Response Questions

1. Refer to the graph below to answer the following questions.

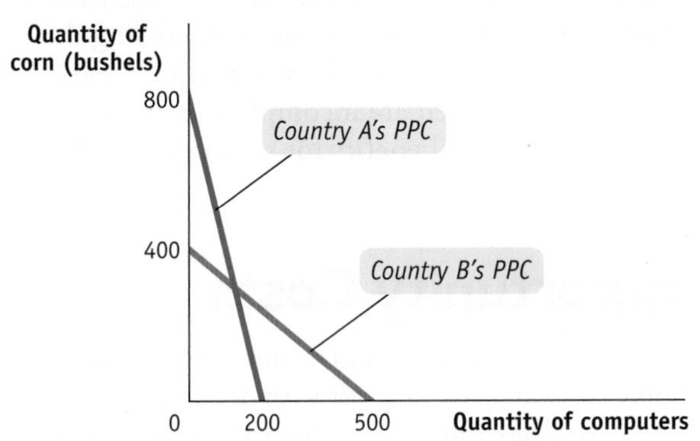

   a. What is the opportunity cost of a bushel of corn in each country?
   b. Which country has an absolute advantage in computer production? Explain.
   c. Which country has a comparative advantage in corn production? Explain.
   d. If each country specializes, what good will Country B import? Explain.
   e. What is the minimum price Country A will accept to export corn to Country B? Explain.
   f. What is the maximum price Country B will pay to import corn from Country A?

Rubric for FRQ 1 (10 points)

1 point: Country A, ¼ computer; Country B, 1¼ computers

1 point: Country B

1 point: Because Country B can produce more computers than Country A (500 versus 200)

1 point: Country A

1 point: Because Country A can produce corn at a lower opportunity cost (¼ computer versus 1¼ computers)

1 point: Corn

1 point: Country B has a comparative advantage in the production of computers, so it will produce computers and import corn (Country A has a comparative advantage in corn production, so it will specialize in corn and import computers from Country B).

1 point: ¼ computer

1 point: Country A's opportunity cost of producing corn is ¼ computer, so that is the lowest price it will accept to sell corn to Country B.

1 point: 1¼ computers

2. Refer to the table below to answer the following questions. These two countries are producing textiles and wheat using equal amounts of resources. The table indicates the maximum weekly output for workers who produce wheat or textiles.

	Weekly output per worker	
	Country A	**Country B**
Bushels of wheat	15	10
Units of textiles	60	60

   a. What is the opportunity cost of producing a bushel of wheat for each country?
   b. Which country has the absolute advantage in wheat production?
   c. Which country has the comparative advantage in textile production? Explain. **(5 points)**

MODULE 1.5

Cost-Benefit Analysis

In this Module, you will learn to:

- Calculate the opportunity cost of a decision
- Define utility and revenue, the benefits sought by consumers and firms
- Conduct cost-benefit analysis
- Explain why some decisions are based on comparisons of marginal values while others are based on comparisons of total values

Module 1.4 explained how differences in opportunity costs across countries reveal advantages in the context of trade. Here we will discuss appropriate measures and comparisons of the costs and benefits felt by individual decision makers—a process called *cost-benefit analysis.* We begin our dive into cost-benefit analysis by discussing the types of costs and benefits that influence decisions by consumers and firms. Cost-benefit analysis is flawed if the costs or benefits analyzed are incomplete or exaggerated. In Unit 6, we will examine situations with costs or benefits for society that differ from those of decision makers.

All Costs Are Opportunity Costs

Module 1.1 introduced opportunity cost as the value of the next-best alternative forgone when a decision is made. Some costs are paid *explicitly* with dollars; others are paid *implicitly* with time and missed opportunities; but all such costs represent opportunity costs. Money spent on one purchase can't be spent on another purchase. Time spent on one activity can't be spent on another activity. And resources devoted to one use can't be used for something else. When economists talk about the cost of something, they generally mean the opportunity cost, because they want to consider the value of everything sacrificed for a decision. **Rational agents**, meaning consumers, producers, and others who behave rationally and make optimal decisions, incorporate their opportunity costs into the decision-making process, whether those costs are explicit or implicit.

Rational agents are consumers, producers, and others who behave rationally and make optimal decisions.

Suppose you're at a baseball game and a vendor is selling hot dogs, large drinks, and ice cream sundaes, each for $5. With the $5 you brought to spend on a snack, you can pick any one of the three items. The opportunity cost of a hot dog is not the value of a large drink *and* the value of an ice cream sundae, because you can't have both instead of a hot dog. The opportunity cost of a hot dog is the value of the one alternative you would purchase with your $5 if you didn't buy the hot dog. If your best alternative to a hot dog is a large drink, the opportunity cost of a hot dog is the value of a large drink. By choosing the item with the greatest value to you, your opportunity cost is minimized and your choice is optimized.

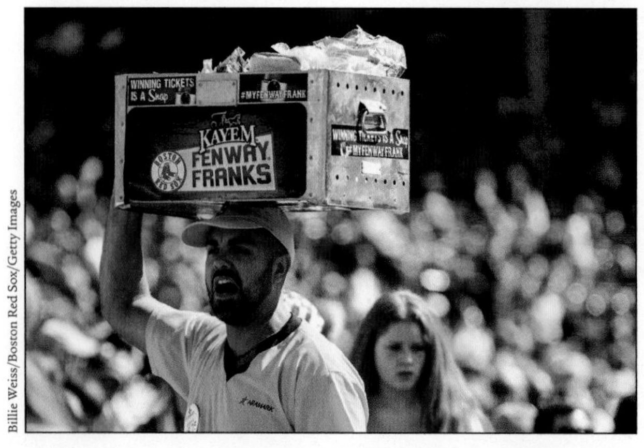

Billie Weiss/Boston Red Sox/Getty Images

Money need not be involved in the calculation of an opportunity cost. Consider the service on an airplane, where, unlike at a baseball game, the beverages are free. A flight attendant comes down the aisle offering everyone a drink. Suppose you could choose a soda, a sparkling water, an orange juice, or a milk. There is an opportunity cost of choosing each beverage even though the drinks are free. If milk is the best alternative to orange juice, your opportunity cost of choosing an orange juice is the value of a milk. This cost is not paid in dollars, but it is possible to express its value in dollars for convenience in making comparison with other values. To do so, ask yourself, "What is the most I would be willing to pay for a milk?" If you would be willing to pay up to $3 for a milk, the opportunity cost of an orange juice is $3 – the value of the forgone milk.

Some situations involve a combination of explicit and implicit costs. Suppose Isha earns a salary of $50,000 per year to manage an ice cream shop, but someone has offered her $60,000 a year to deliver seafood from a distribution center to restaurants. The delivery job would require Isha to rent a truck for $7,000 per year. The delivery job would also require Isha to start working weekends, a fate she would be willing to pay $5,000 a year to avoid. What should Isha do? The annual opportunity cost of staying at the ice cream shop is the value of her forgone $60,000 salary in the delivery job, minus the $7,000 cost of a truck rental, minus the $5,000 value of having to work weekends:

$$\$60{,}000 - \$7{,}000 - \$5{,}000 = \$48{,}000.$$

Since her $48,000 annual opportunity cost of staying is less than the $50,000 salary she would forgo by switching jobs, Isha should continue to manage the ice cream shop.

AP® ECON TIP

If asked to calculate the opportunity cost of a decision, include the value of everything lost if the decision is made, whether it is paid explicitly in dollars or not. Do not include costs incurred regardless of the decision. For instance, if the choice is between two colleges and both have a room-and-board fee of $15,000, that fee is not part of the opportunity cost of going to one school rather than the other.

The Benefit Consumers Seek

When we analyze consumer behavior, we examine how people pursue their needs and wants and the subjective feelings that motivate purchases. Consumers seek happiness and satisfaction. Yet there is no simple way to measure subjective feelings. How much satisfaction do I get from eating my third cookie? Is it less or more than the satisfaction you receive from eating your third cookie? Does it even make sense to ask that question?

Luckily, we don't need to make comparisons between your feelings and mine. We can analyze consumers' choices with only the assumption that individuals try to maximize some personal measure of the satisfaction gained from consumption. That measure of satisfaction is known as **utility**. Don't worry about trying to measure utility. Economists use the concept of utility to understand consumer behavior, but don't measure it explicitly in practice. When talking about utility, it is useful to suppose that we can measure it in hypothetical units called – what else? – **utils**. Economists make up numbers of utils to provide examples. What matters is not the number but the concept that it is better to have a higher number of utils. That is, whether you get 1,000 utils from the second cookie and 600 from the third, or 5 utils from the second cookie and 3 utils from the third, the important thing is that the third cookie gives you less satisfaction than the second cookie.

Design Pics Inc/Alamy

Utility is a measure of personal satisfaction.

A **util** is a unit of utility.

The Benefit Firms Seek

Firms have a different agenda than consumers. Firms generally seek to maximize *profit*, which is the difference between the total amount of money received in exchange for goods and services and the total cost. Economists refer to the money a firm receives as *revenue*. So while consumers seek the benefit of utility, firms seek the benefit of revenue. The sales reports that business managers peruse are largely stories about the total revenue received from customers, found by multiplying the price of each product by the quantity sold. But no amount of total revenue alone is cause for celebration, because the objective is profit, and the determination of profit requires *cost-benefit analysis*.

Comparisons of Total Benefit and Total Cost

Consumers and firms share the common objective of maximizing the difference between their *total benefit* and their *total cost*. **Cost-benefit analysis** is the process of comparing costs with benefits to inform a decision. When a firm is simply deciding whether to do something or not, it is best to proceed if the total benefit exceeds the total cost and not proceed if the total cost exceeds the total benefit. Decision makers would be indifferent about doing something with a total cost that equals its total benefit.

Cost-benefit analysis is the process of comparing the costs and the benefits of an option.

When you shop, you are surrounded with opportunities to receive the value of a good in exchange for the price of that good. You wouldn't pay $40 for pajamas that would give you $10 worth of utility, but you would pay $12 for a pizza worth $15 to you. Those decisions are based on cost-benefit analysis. Similarly, a seafood distributor will hire a new delivery worker who must be paid $60,000 a year if her work increases total revenue by $65,000 year. For all such questions of, "Should I do this?" a comparison of total cost and total benefit will indicate the answer. A similar cost-benefit analysis can be applied to decisions of whether to take a trip, whether to run a marathon, and whether to start a new business. Next, we'll see how the appropriate approach differs when the question is, "How many?" "How much?" or "For how long?"

Comparisons of Marginal Benefit and Marginal Cost

Often we have more than two options. We must decide how many pairs of shoes to buy, how much to exercise, and how long to study. Firms must decide how many workers to hire, how much cheese to produce, and how long they should continue a sale. In these examples, it is still true that nothing should be done if the total cost exceeds the total benefit. That is, if you're sure no amount of cheesecake is worth the cost, you don't need to worry about how many pieces to eat—just walk away from the display case. But if the total benefit of something exceeds the total cost, the best decision is to choose the amount that maximizes the difference between the total benefit and the total cost.

leezsnow/E+/Getty Images

To see how this difference is determined, consider a private college's decision of whether to add new sports teams. Should a school with a few traditional sports teams add lacrosse, rugby, bowling, cycling, and crew? New teams attract more college-bound high school athletes, whose tuition payments benefit the school with added revenue. The first new team generates a lot of excitement, showing that the school is evolving and helping it keep pace with more prestigious colleges. Subsequent new teams draw less and less attention, although each brings in some student-athletes and reinforces the school's image as a vibrant place. Of course, new teams are not cheap. Each added sport requires the school to pay for coaches, team travel, insurance, and facilities. The cost per additional team might start out relatively low if new teams fit into existing spaces, but as new locker rooms, fields, and staff are required, the cost per new team rises.

Any question that asks *how many*, *how much*, or *for how long* is best addressed with the type of cost-benefit analysis described in Module 1.1: *marginal analysis*, which is a comparison of the costs and benefits of one more versus one less. The added cost of one more is the *marginal cost*. The added benefit of one more is the *marginal benefit*. **Table 1.5-1** indicates the annual marginal cost, marginal benefit, total cost, and total

Table 1.5-1 The Costs and Benefits of New Sports Teams at a Private College

Quantity of New Teams	Marginal Cost	Marginal Benefit	Total Cost	Total Benefit	Profit (net gain)
1	$100,000	$500,000	$100,000	$500,000	$400,000
2	$120,000	$300,000	$220,000	$800,000	$580,000
3	$150,000	$160,000	$370,000	$960,000	$590,000
4	$200,000	$120,000	$570,000	$1,080,000	$510,000
5	$280,000	$90,000	$850,000	$1,170,000	$320,000

benefit of the first five new sports teams for our fictional college. In this simple example, we are looking only at the costs and benefits of adding teams, so the costs and benefits associated with having a sports program to begin with—an athletic director, a sports complex, and so on—are not considered. We will also suppose that the cost and benefit of a new team depend on how many teams have already been added, and not on which sport it is.

The total cost for a particular quantity of new teams is found by adding the marginal costs of each team up to that quantity. For example, the total cost of three new teams is the sum of the marginal costs of the first three teams: $100,000 + $120,000 + $150,000 = $370,000. If there were additional costs that did not rise with the number of teams, such as the cost of a consultant hired to advise the college on this matter, those costs would be included when calculating the total cost as well.

If we knew only the total cost for each quantity, we could determine the marginal cost for any new team by subtracting the total cost for one-fewer teams from the total cost for the quantity we're considering. For example, we could find the marginal cost of the fourth new team by subtracting the total cost for three teams from the total cost for four teams: $850,000 – $570,000 = $280,000.

Calculations of total benefit and marginal benefit work similarly. The total benefit for any quantity is found by adding the marginal benefits for the teams up to that quantity. So the total benefit of two new teams is $500,000 + $300,000 = $800,000. With only information on total benefits, we could find the marginal benefit of any new team by subtracting the total benefit of one-fewer teams from the total benefit of the quantity we're considering. For example, the marginal benefit of the fifth team is the total benefit of five teams minus the total benefit of the first four teams: $1,170,000 – $1,080,000 = $90,000.

At this point, however, our analysis is incomplete. What the school really cares about is not just cost or benefit, but the net gain (or profit) from the added sports. Here's where the virtues of marginal analysis come to light. Suppose the athletic director argues that five teams should be added because the total benefit of five new teams exceeds the total cost, resulting in a profit of $320,000. Does this cost-benefit analysis justify the addition of five teams? No, because although there would indeed be a positive profit with five new teams, a greater profit could be achieved with fewer new teams. Notice that the profit is highest with three new teams and decreases after that because the marginal benefit of the fourth and fifth teams exceeds the marginal cost.

For all-or-nothing questions such as whether to buy a product, take a job, or engage in an activity, comparisons of total benefit and total cost guide wise decisions. When a decision involves choices among several quantities, amounts, or times, it is best to keep adding until the next unit would have a marginal cost that exceeds the marginal benefit. Due to the insights gained from marginal analysis, you will encounter many related applications in the study of economics. You will learn more about why the marginal cost tends to rise and the marginal benefit tends to fall. You will see how market forces can lead to the outcomes prescribed by marginal analysis. And in the next Module, you will discover the marginal analysis consumers use to maximize their utility.

AP® ECON TIP

When determining how many units of something is optimal, don't choose the largest quantity just because the total benefit of that quantity exceeds the total cost. A smaller quantity might increase the net gain. The correct approach is to conduct marginal analysis and increase the quantity until the marginal cost of another unit would exceed the marginal benefit.

Sunk Costs

Although we have devoted much attention to costs that should be taken into account when making decisions, some costs should be ignored when doing so. This section presents these kinds of costs—what economists call *sunk costs*—and explains why they should be ignored.

To gain some intuition, consider the following scenario. You own a car that is a few years old, and you have just replaced the brake pads at a cost of $250. But then you find out that the entire brake system is defective and also must be replaced. This work will

Monty Rakusen/Image Source/Getty Images

cost you an additional $1,500. Alternatively, you could sell the car and buy another of comparable quality, but with no brake defects, by spending $1,600. What should you do: fix your old car, or sell it and buy another?

Some might say that you should take the latter option. After all, this line of reasoning goes, if you repair your car, you will end up having spent $1,750: $1,500 for the brake system and $250 for the brake pads. If you were instead to sell your old car and buy another, you would spend only $1,600.

This reasoning might sound plausible, but it is wrong. It ignores the fact that you have *already* spent $250 on brake pads, and that $250 is *nonrecoverable.* Because this $250 has already been spent and you cannot get it back, it should have no effect on your decision whether to repair your car and keep it or not. From a rational viewpoint, the real cost at this time of repairing and keeping your car is $1,500, not $1,750. So, the correct decision is to repair your car and keep it rather than spend $1,600 on another car.

A **sunk cost** is a cost that has already been incurred and is nonrecoverable. A sunk cost should be ignored in a decision about future actions.

In this example, the $250 that has already been spent and cannot be recovered is what economists call a **sunk cost**. Sunk costs should be ignored in making decisions because they have no influence on future costs and benefits. It's like the old saying, "There's no use crying over spilled milk": once something can't be recovered, it is irrelevant in making decisions about what to do in the future. This logic applies equally to individuals, firms, and governments: regardless of how much has been spent on a project in the past, if the future costs exceed the future benefits, the project should not continue.

It is often psychologically hard to ignore sunk costs. And if, in fact, you haven't yet incurred the costs, then you *should* take them into consideration. That is, if you had known at the beginning that it would cost $1,750 to repair your car, then the right choice *at that time* would have been to buy another car for $1,600. But once you have already paid the $250 for brake pads, you should no longer include that cost in your decision making about your next actions. It may be hard to "let bygones be bygones," but it is the right way to make a decision.

Module 1.5  Review

Check Your Understanding

1. Suppose that, if you attend a local concert, you must pay $55 for a ticket and lose $40 of pay at work due to taking the night of the concert off. Whether or not you go to the concert, you must pay $15 for dinner that evening. What is the opportunity cost of going to the concert?

2. Explain when it is appropriate to conduct marginal analysis rather than comparing the total benefit and the total cost.

Tackle the AP® Test: Multiple-Choice Questions

Consider the following scenario: Tariq has five hours of study time to allocate between economics and chemistry. His objective is to maximize the combined total number of points earned on the tests in each class. The benefit of spending more time studying economics is more points on the economics test. The cost of spending more time studying economics is points lost on the chemistry test. Answer questions 1–5 based on the table below, which indicates the costs and benefits of each possible quantity of hours spent studying economics in terms of points.

Quantity (hours)	Marginal Cost	Marginal Benefit	Total Cost	Total Benefit
0	—	—	0	0
1	5	40		40
2	7	30	12	
3	10	20	22	
4		10	37	100
5	25		62	100

1. What is the marginal benefit of the fifth hour spent studying economics?
   a. 0
   b. 10
   c. 25
   d. 30
   e. 100

2. Which hour of studying economics adds the most to the combined total number of points on the two exams?
   a. first
   b. second
   c. third
   d. fourth
   e. fifth

3. What is the total benefit of studying economics for two hours?
   a. 7
   b. 23
   c. 30
   d. 40
   e. 70

4. How many points does Tariq add to his combined total for the two exams if he studies economics for four hours rather than zero hours?
   a. 0
   b. 10
   c. 47
   d. 63
   e. 100

5. How many hours should Tariq spend studying economics?
   a. 1
   b. 2
   c. 3
   d. 4
   e. 5

6. Opportunity costs include costs that are
   a. implicit only.
   b. explicit only.
   c. losses of time only.
   d. monetary only.
   e. explicit and implicit.

7. Economists generally measure total benefit in terms of ________ for consumers and ________ for firms.
   a. revenue profit
   b. utility revenue
   c. profit revenue
   d. utility profit
   e. revenue utility

8. When making decisions, which of the following costs should be ignored?
   a. implicit costs
   b. total costs
   c. marginal costs
   d. sunk costs
   e. None of the above – no costs should be ignored.

Tackle the AP® Test: Free-Response Questions

1. Next summer Mariana could be a camp counselor in July and August and earn $1,000, or she could pay $500 to take a computer programming class in July and then work as a computer programmer earning $2,000 for the entire month of August. Her room and board are free for both the counseling job and the class, but if she ends up programming in August, she will spend a total of $600 on room and board for that month. She would enjoy the activities in both roles equally.
   a. What is the opportunity cost of taking the class and being a programmer?
   b. What is the opportunity cost of being a camp counselor?
   c. What is the explicit cost of taking the class and being a programmer?
   d. What is the best choice for Mariana? Explain.
   e. Does Mariana's decision require marginal analysis? Explain.

Rubric for FRQ 1 (6 points)

1 point: Mariana would forgo the $1,000 she would otherwise earn as a camp counselor as well as the opportunity to spend the $500 class fee and the $600 room and board expense on something else: $\$1,000 + \$500 + \$600 = \$2,100$.

1 point: Mariana would forgo the $2,000 income as a programmer, minus her $1,100 worth of class, room, and board expenses: $\$2,000 - \$500 - \$600 = \$900$.

1 point: The explicit cost of taking the class and being a programmer—the cost actually paid with money—is $500 for the class and $600 for room and board: $\$500 + \$600 = \$1,100$.

1 point: Mariana should be a camp counselor.

1 point: Mariana's opportunity cost of being a camp counselor, $900, is less than her benefit from being a camp counselor, $1,000.

1 point: No. There are only two options, so a comparison of the total cost and the total benefit of either option is all that is required to determine the best choice.

2. Suppose a software company could run up to three advertisements for its new app. The only cost of advertising is the $20,000 cost of each ad. Answer the questions using the information on advertisement costs and benefits in the table below.

Quantity of Advertisements	Marginal Benefit
1	$50,000
2	$30,000
3	$12,000

   a. What is the marginal cost of the third advertisement?
   b. What is the total benefit of three advertisements?
   c. How much does the first advertisement contribute to the company's profit?
   d. How many advertisements should the company run? Explain. **(5 points)**

Consumer Choice

MODULE 1.6

> ***In this Module, you will learn to:***
> - Describe how rational consumers make choices about goods and services
> - Discuss the assumptions of consumer choice theory
> - Explain why the principle of diminishing marginal utility applies to the consumption of most goods and services
> - Calculate marginal values and use marginal analysis to find the optimal consumption bundle for a rational consumer

In Module 1.5, we saw how marginal analysis informs decisions about how far to take something, whether it is advertising, studying, or adding sports teams to a private college. We also identified *utility* as the metric economists use to discuss consumers' level of satisfaction. This Module applies insights about marginal analysis to the behavior of rational consumers and their quest to maximize utility.

Utility and Consumption

We can think of consumers as using consumption to "produce" utility, much as firms use inputs to produce output. As consumers, we do not make explicit calculations of the utility generated by consumption choices. Even so, we must make choices, and we usually base our choices on at least an attempt to achieve greater satisfaction. You can have either soup or salad with your meal. Which would you enjoy more? You can go to a concert or put the money toward a new laptop computer. Which would make you happier? These are the types of questions that go into utility maximization.

The concept of utility is useful in our study of choices made in a more or less rational way. A *utility function* shows the relationship between a consumer's utility and the combination of goods and services – the *consumption bundle* – the individual consumes. **Figure 1.6-1** illustrates a utility function. It shows the total utility that Olivia, who likes cookies, gets from the bite-sized cookies at her school cafeteria's all-you-can-eat lunch buffet. We suppose her consumption bundle consists of a serving of tuna casserole plus a number of cookies to be determined. The table that accompanies the figure shows how Olivia's total utility depends on the number of cookies; the curve in panel (a) of the figure shows that same information graphically.

LauriPatterson/E+/Getty Images

Olivia's utility function slopes upward over most of the range shown, but it gets flatter as the number of cookies consumed increases. In this example it eventually turns downward. According to the information in the table in Figure 1.6-1, nine cookies is a cookie too far. Adding that additional cookie actually makes Olivia worse off: it would hurt her stomach and lower her total utility. If she's rational, of course, Olivia will realize that and not consume the ninth cookie.

So when Olivia chooses how many cookies to consume, she will make this decision by considering the *change* in her total utility from consuming one more cookie. This consideration illustrates the general point: to maximize *total* utility, consumers must focus on *marginal* utility.

The Principle of Diminishing Marginal Utility

In addition to showing how Olivia's total utility depends on the number of cookies she consumes, the table in Figure 1.6-1 also shows the *marginal utility* generated by consuming each additional cookie. The marginal utility values are placed between the total utility values to emphasize that **marginal utility** is the *change* in total utility when

The **marginal utility** of a good or service is the change in total utility generated by consuming one additional unit of that good or service.

FIGURE 1.6-1 Olivia's Total Utility and Marginal Utility

(a) Olivia's Utility Function

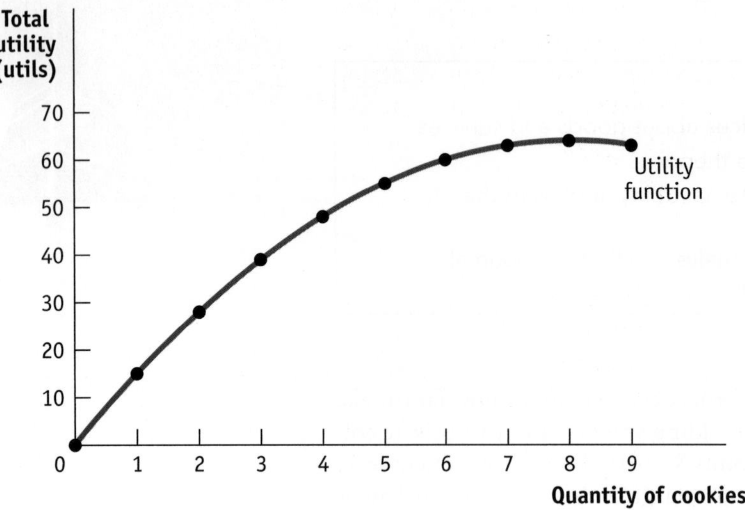

Quantity of cookies	Total utility (utils)	Marginal utility per cookie (utils)
0	0	
		15
1	15	
		13
2	28	
		11
3	39	
		9
4	48	
		7
5	55	
		5
6	60	
		3
7	63	
		1
8	64	
		−1
9	63	

(b) Olivia's Marginal Utility Curve

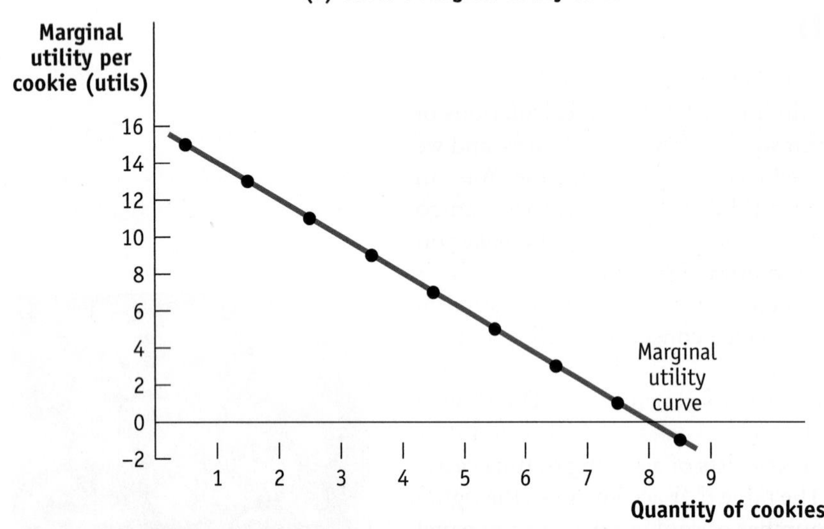

Panel (a) shows how Olivia's total utility depends on her consumption of cookies. It increases until it reaches its maximum utility level of 64 utils at 8 cookies consumed and decreases after that. The table shows how Olivia's marginal utility for each cookie is calculated based on her total utility levels. Each marginal utility value is shown in between two total utility values to emphasize that marginal utility is the increase in total utility when one more unit is added. Panel (b) shows the marginal utility curve, which slopes downward due to diminishing marginal utility. That is, each additional cookie gives Olivia less utility than the previous cookie.

The **marginal utility curve** shows how marginal utility depends on the quantity of a good or service consumed.

one more unit of the good is consumed. The **marginal utility curve** shows how marginal utility depends on the quantity of cookies consumed. The curve is constructed by plotting points at the midpoint between the numbered quantities since marginal utility is found as consumption levels change. For example, when consumption rises from 1 to 2 cookies, marginal utility is 13. Therefore, we place the point corresponding to the marginal utility of 13 halfway between 1 and 2 cookies.

The marginal utility curve slopes downward because each successive cookie adds less to total utility than the previous cookie. This is reflected in the table: marginal utility falls from a high of 15 utils for the first cookie consumed to a low of −1 for the ninth cookie consumed. The fact that the ninth cookie has negative marginal utility means that consuming it actually reduces total utility. (Restaurants that offer all-you-can-eat meals depend on the proposition that you can have too much of a good thing!) Not all marginal utility curves eventually become negative, but it is generally accepted that marginal utility curves do slope downward. In other words, consumption of most goods and services is subject to *diminishing marginal utility*.

The **principle of diminishing marginal utility** says that the additional satisfaction a consumer gets from one more unit of a good or service declines as the amount of that good or service consumed rises. Or, to put it slightly differently, the more of a good or service you consume, the closer you are to being satiated—reaching a point at which an additional unit of the good adds nothing to your satisfaction. For someone who almost never gets to eat a banana, the occasional banana is a marvelous treat (as it was in Eastern Europe before the fall of communism, when bananas were very hard to find). For someone who eats them all the time, a banana is, well, just a banana.

According to the **principle of diminishing marginal utility,** each successive unit of a good or service consumed adds less to total utility than does the previous unit.

The Occasional Ups and Downs of Marginal Utility

Diminishing marginal utility is the norm, but it is not universal. In fact, there are a number of goods for which, at least over some range, marginal utility is surely *increasing*. For example, there are goods that require some experience to enjoy. The first time skateboarding might involve a lot more falling down than fun. It becomes a pleasurable activity only if you do it enough to become reasonably competent. Even some less strenuous forms of consumption take practice; people who are not accustomed to drinking coffee say it has a bitter taste and can't understand its appeal. (The authors, on the other hand, regard coffee as one of the basic food groups.)

Fabio Principe/Alamy

Another example would be goods that deliver only positive utility if you buy a sufficient quantity. The great Victorian economist Alfred Marshall, who more or less invented the supply and demand model that we will encounter in Unit 2, gave the example of wallpaper: buying only enough to do half a room is worse than useless. If you need two rolls of wallpaper to finish a room, the marginal utility of the second roll is larger than the marginal utility of the first roll.

So why does it make sense to assume diminishing marginal utility? For one thing, most goods don't suffer from these qualifications: nobody needs to learn to like ice cream. Also, although most people don't skateboard and some people don't drink coffee, those who do skateboard or drink coffee do enough of it that the marginal utility of one more jump or one more cup is less than that of the last. So *in the relevant range* of consumption, marginal utility is still diminishing.

The principle of diminishing marginal utility doesn't always apply, but it does apply in the great majority of cases, enough to serve as a foundation for our analysis of consumer behavior.

Budgets and Optimal Consumption

The principle of diminishing marginal utility explains why most people eventually reach a limit, even at an all-you-can-eat buffet where the cost of another cookie is measured only in future indigestion. Under ordinary circumstances, however, it costs some additional resources to consume more of a good, and consumers must take that cost into account when making choices.

What do we mean by cost in this scenario? As always, the fundamental measure of cost is *opportunity cost.* Because the amount of money a consumer can spend is limited, a decision to consume more of one good is also a decision to consume less of some other good.

Budget Constraints and Budget Lines

Consider Sebastian, whose appetite is exclusively for cookies and tofu. (There's no accounting for tastes.) He has a weekly income of $20 and since, given his appetite, more of either good is better than less, he spends all of it on cookies and tofu. We will assume that cookies cost $4 per pound and tofu costs $2 per pound. What are his possible choices?

Whatever Sebastian chooses, we know that the cost of his consumption bundle cannot exceed the amount of money he has to spend. That is,

(1.6-1) Expenditure on cookies + Expenditure on tofu ≤ Total income

A **budget constraint** limits the cost of a consumer's consumption bundle to no more than the consumer's income.

Consumers always have limited income, which constrains how much they can consume. So the requirement illustrated by equation 1.6-1 – that a consumer must choose a consumption bundle that costs no more than their income – is known as the consumer's **budget constraint**. It's a simple way of saying that a consumer can't spend more than the total amount of income available to them. In other words, consumption bundles are affordable when they obey the budget constraint. We call the set of all of Sebastian's affordable consumption bundles his *consumption possibilities*. In general, whether or not a particular consumption bundle is included in a consumer's consumption possibilities depends on the consumer's income and the prices of goods and services.

A consumer's **budget line (*BL*)** shows the consumption bundles available to a consumer who spends all of their income.

Figure 1.6-2 shows Sebastian's consumption possibilities. The quantity of cookies in his consumption bundle is measured on the horizontal axis and the quantity of tofu on the vertical axis. The downward-sloping **budget line (*BL*)** shows all the consumption bundles available to Sebastian when he spends all of his income. Every bundle on or inside this line (the shaded area) is affordable; every bundle outside this line is unaffordable. As an example, point *C* on the budget line represents 2 pounds of cookies and 6 pounds of tofu. Let's verify that it satisfies Sebastian budget constraint. The cost of bundle *C* is 6 pounds of tofu × $2 per pound + 2 pounds of cookies × $4 per pound = $12 + $8 = $20. So bundle *C* does indeed satisfy Sebastian's budget constraint: it costs no more than his weekly income of $20. In fact, bundle *C* costs exactly as much as Sebastian's income. With a bit of arithmetic you can check that all the other bundles along the budget line cost exactly $20. At the extremes, if Sebastian spends all of his income on cookies (bundle *F*), he can purchase 5 pounds of cookies; if he spends all of his income on tofu (bundle *A*), he can purchase 10 pounds of tofu.

FIGURE 1.6-2 The Budget Line

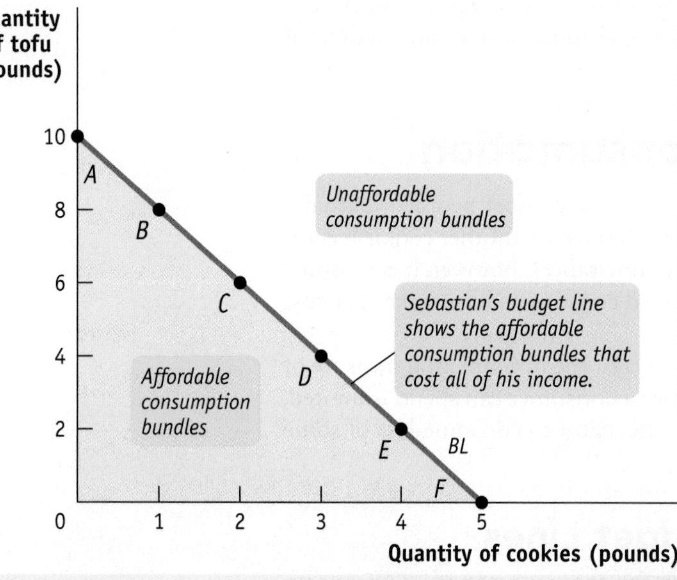

Consumption bundle	Quantity of cookies (pounds)	Quantity of tofu (pounds)
A	0	10
B	1	8
C	2	6
D	3	4
E	4	2
F	5	0

The *budget line (BL)* represents all the combinations of quantities of tofu and cookies that Sebastian can purchase if he spends all of his income. It is the boundary between the set of affordable consumption bundles and the unaffordable ones.

The budget line is downward-sloping because when Sebastian spends all of his income, in order to consume more pounds of cookies, he must consume fewer pounds of tofu. For example, if he starts out consuming at point *A* and he wants more cookies, he must move to a point further down, like *B*, where he has more cookies but less tofu. So when Sebastian is on his budget line, the opportunity cost of consuming more pounds of cookies is consuming fewer pounds of tofu, and vice versa.

Do we need to consider the other bundles in Sebastian's consumption possibilities – the ones that lie *within* the shaded region in Figure 1.6-2 bounded by the budget line? The answer, for all practical situations, is no: as long as Sebastian doesn't get satiated – that is, as long as his marginal utility from consuming either good is always positive – and he doesn't get any utility from saving income rather than spending it, he will always choose to consume a bundle that lies on his budget line.

Given Sebastian's $20 per week budget, next we can consider the culinary dilemma of what point on his budget line Sebastian will choose.

The Optimal Consumption Bundle

Because Sebastian's budget constrains him to a consumption bundle somewhere along the budget line, a choice to consume a given quantity of cookies also determines his tofu consumption, and vice versa. We want to find the consumption bundle – represented by a point on the budget line – that maximizes Sebastian's total utility. This bundle is Sebastian's **optimal consumption bundle**.

A consumer's **optimal consumption bundle** is the consumption bundle that maximizes the consumer's total utility given their budget constraint.

Table 1.6-1 shows hypothetical levels of utility Sebastian gets from consuming various quantities of cookies and tofu, respectively. The table indicates that Sebastian has a healthy appetite; the more of either good he consumes, the higher his utility. But because he has a limited budget, he must make a trade-off: the more pounds of cookies he consumes, the fewer pounds of tofu, and vice versa. That is, he must choose a point on his budget line.

Table 1.6-1 Sebastian's Utility from Cookie and Tofu Consumption

Utility from cookie consumption		Utility from tofu consumption	
Quantity of cookies (pounds)	Utility from cookies (utils)	Quantity of tofu (pounds)	Utility from tofu (utils)
0	0	0	0
1	15	1	11.5
2	25	2	21.4
3	31	3	29.8
4	34	4	36.8
5	36	5	42.5
		6	47.0
		7	50.5
		8	53.2
		9	55.2
		10	56.7

Table 1.6-2 shows how his total utility varies for the different consumption bundles along his budget line. Each of six possible consumption bundles, *A* through *F* from Figure 1.6-2, is given in the first column. The second column shows the level of cookie consumption corresponding to each choice. The third column shows the utility Sebastian gets from consuming those cookies. The fourth column shows the quantity of tofu Sebastian can afford *given* the level of cookie consumption; this quantity goes down as his cookie consumption goes up

Table 1.6-2 Sebastian's Budget and Total Utility

Consumption bundle	Quantity of cookies (pounds)	Utility from cookies (utils)	Quantity of tofu (pounds)	Utility from tofu (utils)	Total utility (utils)
A	0	0	10	56.7	56.7
B	1	15	8	53.2	68.2
C	2	25	6	47.0	72.0
D	3	31	4	36.8	67.8
E	4	34	2	21.4	55.4
F	5	36	0	0	36.0

because he is sliding down the budget line. The fifth column shows the utility he gets from consuming tofu. And the final column shows his *total utility*. In this example, Sebastian's total utility is the sum of the utility he gets from cookies and the utility he gets from tofu.

Figure 1.6-3 gives a visual representation of the data in Table 1.6-2. Panel (a) shows Sebastian's budget line, to remind us that a decision to consume more cookies is also a decision to consume less tofu. Panel (b) then shows how his total utility depends on that choice. The horizontal axis in panel (b) has two sets of labels: it shows both the quantity of cookies, increasing from left to right, and the quantity of tofu, increasing from right to left. The reason we can use the same axis to represent consumption of both goods is that Sebastian is constrained by the budget line: the more pounds of cookies he consumes, the fewer pounds of tofu he can afford, and vice versa.

Ngoc To Vy Nguyen / EyeEm/Getty Images

Clearly, the consumption bundle that makes the best of the trade-off between cookie consumption and tofu consumption – the optimal consumption bundle – is the one that maximizes Sebastian's total utility. That is, Sebastian's optimal consumption bundle puts him at the top of the total utility curve.

Just by looking at Figure 1.6-3, we can see that Sebastian's total utility is maximized at point *C* – that his optimal consumption bundle contains 2 pounds of cookies and 6 pounds of tofu. But we usually gain more insight into "how much" problems when we use marginal analysis. So next, we represent and solve the optimal consumption choice problem with marginal analysis.

Spending the Marginal Dollar

As we've just seen, we can find Sebastian's optimal consumption choice by finding the total utility he receives from each consumption bundle on his budget line and then choosing the bundle that maximizes total utility. But we can use marginal analysis instead, which leads to some useful guidelines for how much to buy. How do we do this? By looking at the choice of an optimal consumption bundle as a problem of *how much to spend on each good*. Using marginal analysis, this becomes a question of how to *spend the marginal dollar* – how to allocate an additional dollar between cookies and tofu in a way that maximizes utility.

Our first step in applying marginal analysis is to ask if Sebastian is made better off by spending an additional dollar on either good; and if so, by how much is he better off. To answer this question, we must calculate the *marginal utility per dollar* spent on either cookies or tofu – how much additional utility Sebastian gets from spending an additional dollar on either good.

FIGURE 1.6-3 Optimal Consumption Bundle

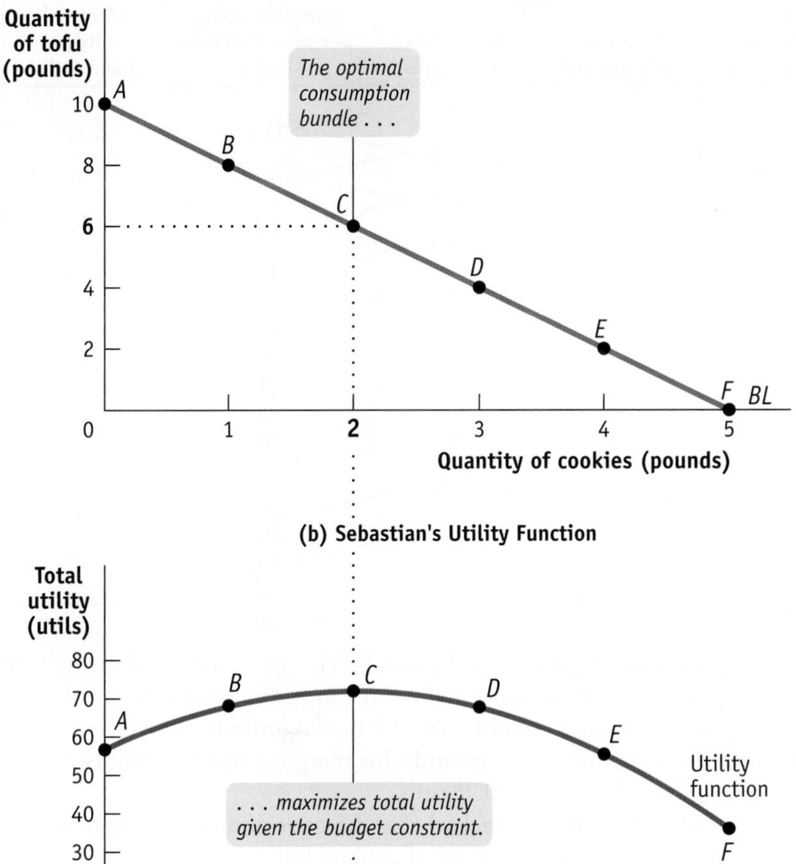

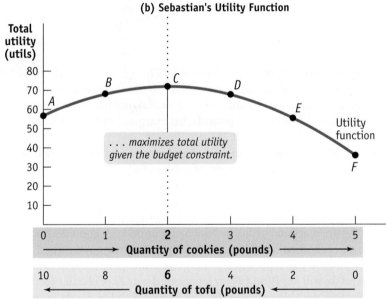

Panel (a) shows Sebastian's budget line and his six possible consumption bundles. Panel (b) shows how his total utility is affected by his consumption bundle, which must lie on his budget line. The quantity of cookies is measured from left to right on the horizontal axis, and the quantity of tofu is measured from right to left. As he consumes more cookies, due to his fixed budget, he must consume less tofu. As a result, the quantity of tofu decreases as the quantity of cookies increases. His total utility is maximized at bundle C, where he consumes 2 pounds of cookies and 6 pounds of tofu. This is Sebastian's *optimal consumption bundle*.

Marginal Utility per Dollar

We've already introduced the concept of marginal utility, the additional utility a consumer gets from consuming one more unit of a good or service; now let's use this concept to derive the related measure of marginal utility per dollar.

Table 1.6-3 shows how to calculate the marginal utility per dollar spent on cookies and tofu, respectively.

In panel (a) of the table, the first column shows different possible amounts of cookie consumption. The second column shows the utility Sebastian derives from each amount of cookie consumption; the third column shows the marginal utility, the increase in utility Sebastian gets from consuming an additional pound of cookies. Panel (b) provides the same information for tofu. The next step is to derive marginal utility *per dollar* for each good. To do this, we just divide the marginal utility of the good by its price in dollars.

It's important to divide marginal utility by price because gains in utility from the two goods have differing prices. Consider what happens if Sebastian increases

AP® ECON TIP

You may need to fill in or interpret a marginal utility table like Table 1.6-3 for the AP® exam. You may also be asked to determine how a change in price affects the quantity demanded for each good.

Table 1.6-3 Sebastian's Marginal Utility per Dollar

(a) Cookies (price of cookies = \$4 per pound)

Quantity of cookies (pounds)	Utility from cookies (utils)	Marginal utility per pound of cookies (utils)	Marginal utility per dollar (utils)
0	0		
		15	3.75
1	15		
		10	2.50
2	25		
		6	1.50
3	31		
		3	0.75
4	34		
		2	0.50
5	36		

(b) Tofu (price of tofu = \$2 per pound)

Quantity of tofu (pounds)	Utility from tofu (utils)	Marginal utility per pound of tofu (utils)	Marginal utility per dollar (utils)
0	0		
		11.5	5.75
1	11.5		
		9.9	4.95
2	21.4		
		8.4	4.20
3	29.8		
		7.0	3.50
4	36.8		
		5.7	2.85
5	42.5		
		4.5	2.25
6	47.0		
		3.5	1.75
7	50.5		
		2.7	1.35
8	53.2		
		2.0	1.00
9	55.2		
		1.5	0.75
10	56.7		

AP® ECON TIP

To determine whether a consumer should buy more of one good or another, compare the marginal utility *per dollar* received from each good, not just the marginal utility received from each good.

his cookie consumption from 2 pounds to 3 pounds. This raises his total utility by 6 utils. But he must spend \$4 for that additional 6 utils, so the increase in his utility per additional dollar spent on cookies is 6 utils/\$4 = 1.5 utils. Similarly, if he increases his cookie consumption from 3 pounds to 4 pounds, his marginal utility is 3 utils but his marginal utility per dollar is 3 utils/\$4 = 0.75 utils.

Notice in the last two columns of panel (a) that, because of diminishing marginal utility, Sebastian's marginal utility per pound of cookies falls as the quantity of cookies he consumes rises. As a result, his marginal utility per dollar spent on cookies also falls as the quantity of cookies he consumes rises. Similarly, the last column of panel (b) shows how his marginal utility per dollar spent on tofu depends on the quantity of tofu he consumes. Again, marginal utility per dollar spent on each good declines as the quantity of that good consumed rises because of diminishing marginal utility.

We will use MU_C and MU_T to represent the marginal utility per pound of cookies and tofu, respectively. And we will use P_C and P_T to represent the price of cookies (per pound) and the price of tofu (per pound), respectively. The marginal utility per dollar spent on cookies is $\frac{MU_C}{P_C}$ and the marginal utility per dollar spent on tofu is $\frac{MU_T}{P_T}$. In general, the additional utility generated from an additional dollar spent on a good is equal to

$$\text{(1.6-2)} \quad \text{Marginal utility per dollar spent on a good} = \frac{\text{Marginal utility of one unit of the good}}{\text{Price of one unit of the good}} = \frac{MU_{good}}{P_{good}}$$

Next, we'll see how this concept helps us determine a consumer's optimal consumption bundle using marginal analysis.

Optimal Consumption

When you're deciding how much of one particular good to purchase, it's wise to buy more as long as the value of the marginal utility you receive from that good exceeds its price. When you're choosing the quantities of two goods to buy, there's another trick for finding the optimal consumption bundle. Let's consider **Figure 1.6-4**. As in Figure 1.6-3, we can measure both the quantity of cookies and the quantity of tofu on the horizontal axis thanks to the budget constraint that forces more of one to mean less of the other. Along the horizontal axis of Figure 1.6-4 – also as in Figure 1.6-3 – the quantity of cookies increases as you move from left to right, and the quantity of tofu increases as you move from right to left. The curve labeled $\frac{MU_C}{P_C}$ in Figure 1.6-4 shows Sebastian's marginal utility per dollar spent on cookies as derived in Table 1.6-3. Likewise, the curve labeled $\frac{MU_T}{P_T}$ shows his marginal utility per dollar spent on tofu. Notice that the two curves, and $\frac{MU_T}{P_T}$, cross at the optimal consumption bundle, point C, consisting of 2 pounds of cookies and 6 pounds of tofu.

Beyond that, Figure 1.6-4 illustrates an important feature of Sebastian's optimal consumption bundle: when Sebastian consumes 2 pounds of cookies and 6 pounds of tofu, his marginal utility per dollar spent is the same, 2, for both goods. So at the optimal consumption bundle, $\frac{MU_C}{P_C} = \frac{MU_T}{P_T} = 2$.

FIGURE 1.6-4 Marginal Utility per Dollar

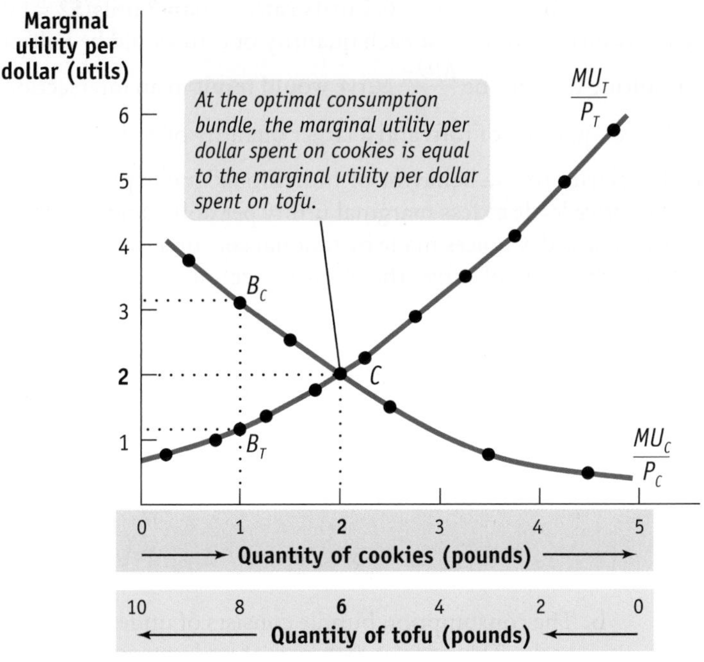

Sebastian's optimal consumption bundle is at point C, where his marginal utility per dollar spent on cookies, $\frac{MU_C}{P_C}$, is equal to his marginal utility per dollar spent on tofu, $\frac{MU_T}{P_T}$. This illustrates the optimal consumption rule: *at the optimal consumption bundle, the marginal utility per dollar spent on each good and service is the same.* At any other consumption bundle on Sebastian's budget line, such as bundle *B* in Figure 1.6-3, represented here by points B_C and B_T, consumption is not optimal: Sebastian can increase his utility at no additional cost by reallocating his spending.

This result isn't an accident. Consider another one of Sebastian's possible consumption bundles – say, *B* in Figure 1.6-3, at which he consumes 1 pound of cookies and 8 pounds of tofu. The marginal utility per dollar spent on each good is shown by points B_C and B_T in Figure 1.6-4. At that consumption bundle, Sebastian's marginal utility per dollar spent on cookies would be approximately 3, but his marginal utility per dollar spent on tofu would be only approximately 1. This shows that he has made a mistake: he is consuming too much tofu and not enough cookies.

How do we know this? If Sebastian's marginal utility per dollar spent on cookies is higher than his marginal utility per dollar spent on tofu, he has a simple way to make himself better off while staying within his budget: spend \$1 less on tofu and \$1 more on cookies. By spending an additional dollar on cookies, he adds about 3 utils to his total utility; meanwhile, by spending \$1 less on tofu, he subtracts only about 1 util from his total utility. Because his marginal utility per dollar spent is higher for cookies than for tofu, reallocating his spending toward cookies and away from tofu would increase his total utility. On the other hand, if his marginal utility per dollar spent on tofu is higher, he can increase his utility by spending less on cookies and more on tofu. So if Sebastian has in fact chosen his optimal consumption bundle, his marginal utility per dollar spent on cookies and tofu must be equal.

The **optimal consumption rule** says that in order to maximize utility, a consumer must equate the marginal utility per dollar spent on each good and service in the consumption bundle.

This is a general principle known as the **optimal consumption rule**: *when a consumer maximizes utility in the face of a budget constraint, the marginal utility per dollar spent on each good or service in the consumption bundle is the same.* That is, for any two goods *C* and *T*, the optimal consumption rule says that at the optimal consumption bundle

$$\textbf{(1.6-3)} \quad \frac{MU_C}{P_C} = \frac{MU_T}{P_T}$$

It's easiest to understand the optimal consumption rule using examples in which the consumption bundle contains only two goods, but it applies no matter how many goods or services a consumer buys: the marginal utilities per dollar spent for each and every good or service in the optimal consumption bundle are equal.

When the price of a good changes, the marginal utility per dollar spent on the good changes and so does the optimal consumption bundle. Suppose the price of tofu doubled from \$2 per pound to \$4 per pound. The marginal utility per dollar for, say, the ninth pound of tofu would now be 2 utils/\$4 = 0.5 utils rather than 2 utils/\$2 = 1.0 util. Likewise, the marginal utility per dollar for each quantity of tofu would be half of what it used to be. The resulting drop in the $\frac{MU_T}{P_T}$ curve would result in an intersection with the $\frac{MU_C}{P_C}$ curve at a lower quantity of tofu and a larger quantity of cookies.

Marginal analysis adds clarity to the behavior of individuals and explains more precisely how an increase in price leads to less marginal utility per dollar and therefore a decrease in the quantity demanded. Choices made by rational consumers on the basis of marginal analysis underpin the demand curves that we will encounter in Module 2.1.

Module 1. 6  Review

Check Your Understanding

1. Explain why a rational consumer who has diminishing marginal utility for a good would not consume an additional unit when it generates negative marginal utility, even when that unit is free.
2. In the following two examples, find all the consumption bundles that lie on the consumer's budget line. Illustrate these consumption possibilities in a diagram, and draw the budget line through them.
   a. The consumption bundle consists of movie tickets and buckets of popcorn. The price of each ticket is \$10, the price of each bucket of popcorn is \$5, and the consumer's income is \$20. In your diagram, put movie tickets on the vertical axis and buckets of popcorn on the horizontal axis.
   b. The consumption bundle consists of underwear and socks. The price of each pair of underwear is \$4, the price of each pair of socks is \$2, and the consumer's income is \$12. In your diagram, put pairs of socks on the vertical axis and pairs of underwear on the horizontal axis.
3. In Table 1.6-3 you can see that the marginal utility per dollar spent on cookies and the marginal utility per dollar spent on tofu are equal when Sebastian increases his consumption of cookies from 3 pounds to 4 pounds and his consumption of tofu from 9 pounds to 10 pounds. Explain why 4 cookies and 10 pounds of tofu is not Sebastian's optimal consumption bundle. Illustrate your answer using a budget line like the one in Figure 1.6-3.

Tackle the AP® Test: Multiple-Choice Questions

1. Typically, each successive unit of a good consumed will cause marginal utility to
   - a. increase at an increasing rate.
   - b. increase at a decreasing rate.
   - c. increase at a constant rate.
   - d. decrease.
   - e. either increase or decrease.

2. Assume there are two goods, good X and good Y. Good X costs $5 and good Y costs $10. If your income is $200, which of the following combinations of good X and good Y is on your budget line?
   - a. 0 units of good X and 18 units of good Y
   - b. 0 units of good X and 20 units of good Y
   - c. 20 units of good X and 0 units of good Y
   - d. 10 units of good X and 12 units of good Y
   - e. all of the above

3. The optimal consumption rule states that total utility is maximized when all income is spent and
   - a. *MU/P* is equal for all goods.
   - b. *MU* is equal for all goods.
   - c. *P/MU* is equal for all goods.
   - d. *MU* is as high as possible for all goods.
   - e. the amount spent on each good is equal.

4. A consumer is spending all of her income and receiving 100 utils from the last unit of good A and 80 utils from the last unit of good B. If the price of good A is $2 and the price of good B is $1, to maximize total utility the consumer should buy
   - a. more of good A.
   - b. more of good B.
   - c. less of good B.
   - d. more of both goods.
   - e. less of both goods.

5. The optimal consumption bundle is always represented by a point
   - a. inside the consumer's budget line.
   - b. outside the consumer's budget line.
   - c. at the highest point on the consumer's budget line.
   - d. on the consumer's budget line.
   - e. at the horizontal intercept of the consumer's budget line.

6. Suppose the seventh carrot you consume provides a marginal utility of 3 utils and the eighth carrot provides a marginal utility of 2 utils. If you consume the eighth carrot, your total utility will
   - a. decrease by 1.
   - b. increase by 1.
   - c. decrease by 2.
   - d. increase by 2.
   - e. decrease by 5.

7. A second of which of the following is the most likely to provide more marginal utility than the first?
   - a. refrigerator
   - b. shoe
   - c. car
   - d. t-shirt
   - e. mailbox

Tackle the AP® Test: Free-Response Questions

1. Refer to the table provided. Assume you have $20 to spend.

Snacks (price = $4)		Drinks (price = $2)	
Quantity	Total utility (utils)	Quantity	Total utility (utils)
1	15	1	12
2	25	2	21
3	31	3	29
4	34	4	36
5	36	5	42
		6	47
		7	50
		8	52

   a. Draw a correctly labeled budget line.
   b. Determine the marginal utility and the marginal utility per dollar spent on the fourth drink.
   c. What is the optimal consumption rule?
   d. How many drinks and snacks should you purchase to maximize your total utility?

Rubric for FRQ 1 (6 points)

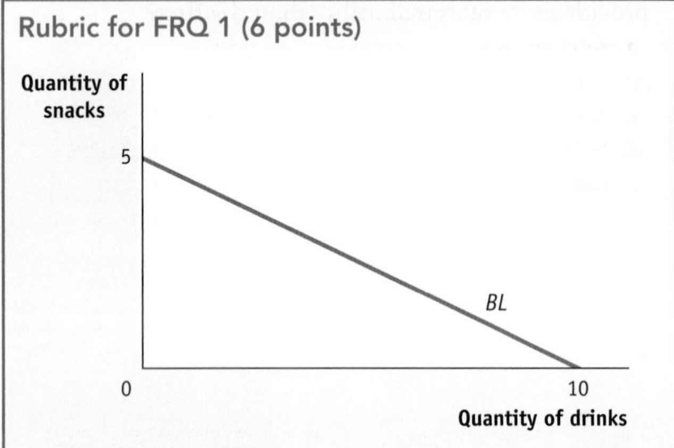

1 point: Graph with "Quantity of snacks" and "Quantity of drinks" as axis labels

1 point: Straight budget line with intercepts at 5 snacks and 0 drinks and at 0 snacks and 10 drinks

1 point: *MU* = 7 utils

1 point: *MU*/*P* = 3.5 utils per dollar

1 point: Total utility is maximized when the marginal utility per dollar is equal for all goods.

1 point: 6 drinks, 2 snacks

2. Assume you have an income of $100. The price of good X is $5, and the price of good Y is $20.
   a. Draw a correctly labeled budget line with "Quantity of good X" on the horizontal axis and "Quantity of good Y" on the vertical axis. Be sure to correctly label the horizontal and vertical intercepts.
   b. With your current consumption bundle, you spend all of your income and receive 100 utils from consuming your last unit of good X and 400 utils from consuming your last unit of good Y. Are you maximizing your total utility? Explain.
   c. What will happen to the marginal utility and the total utility you receive just from consuming good X if you decide to consume another unit of good X? Explain.
   (6 points)

UNIT 1

Review

Adventures in AP® Economics Videos

Mod 1.3: Production Possibilities Curves
Mod 1.4: Comparative Advantage and Absolute Advantage

UNIT 1 Review Video

economics by example
What's to Love About Economics?

Module 1.1

1. Everyone has to make choices about what to do and what *not* to do. **Individual choice** is the basis of **economics**—if it doesn't involve choice, it isn't economics.
2. The reason choices must be made is that **resources**—anything that can be used to produce something else—are **scarce**. The four categories of resources, also called **factors of production**, are **land**, **labor**, **capital**, and **entrepreneurship**. Individuals are limited in their choices by money and time; economies are limited by their supplies of resources.
3. Economic decisions are informed by **marginal analysis**—the study of the costs and benefits of doing something a little bit more or a little bit less.
4. Because you must choose among limited alternatives, the true cost of anything is what you must give up to get it—all costs are **opportunity costs**.
5. **Microeconomics** is the branch of economics that focuses on how choices are made by individuals, **households**, and **firms**. **Macroeconomics** is concerned with the overall ups and downs of the economy and focuses on economic aggregates, such as the unemployment rate and gross domestic product, that summarize data across many different markets.
6. Economists use economic models for positive economics, which describes how the economy works, and for normative economics, which prescribes how the economy *should* work. Positive economics often involves making forecasts. Economics can determine correct answers for positive questions, but typically not for normative questions, which involve value judgments. Exceptions occur when policies designed to achieve a certain prescription can be clearly ranked in terms of preference.

Module 1.2

7. The **economy** is a system that coordinates choices about production and consumption. Three fundamental questions must be answered in each economy: What will be produced? How will it be produced? and Who will receive it?
8. In a **traditional economy**, those questions are answered based on precedent. In a **market economy**, these choices are made by many individuals, households, and firms. In a **command economy**, these choices are made by a central authority. A **mixed economy** shares characteristics of traditional, market, and command economies.
9. **Incentives** are rewards or punishments that motivate particular choices and can be lacking in a command economy where producers cannot set their own prices or keep their own profits.
10. **Property rights** create incentives in market economies by establishing ownership and granting individuals the right to trade goods and services for mutual gain.

Module 1.3

11. Almost all economics is based on **models**, "thought experiments" or simplified versions of reality, many of which use analytical tools such as mathematics and graphs. An important assumption in economic models is the **"other things equal" (ceteris paribus) assumption**, which allows analysis of the effect of change in one factor by holding all other relevant factors unchanged.
12. One important economic model is the **production possibilities curve**, which illustrates the **trade-offs** facing an economy that produces only two goods. The production possibilities curve illustrates three elements: opportunity cost (showing how much less of one good must be produced if more of the other good is produced), **efficiency** (an economy produces efficiently if it produces on the production possibilities curve and allocates resources efficiently if it produces the mix of goods and services that people most want to consume), and **economic growth** (an increase

in the economy's maximum possible output shown by an outward shift of the production possibilities curve).

13. There are two basic sources of growth in the production possibilities curve model: an increase in resources and improved **technology**.

Module 1.4

14. There are **gains from trade**: by engaging in the **trade** of goods and services with one another, the members of an economy can all be made better off. Underlying gains from trade are the advantages of **specialization**, of having individuals specialize in the tasks they are comparatively good at.

15. The existence of **comparative advantages** explains the source of gains from trade between individuals and countries. Having a comparative advantage means that you can make a good or service at a lower opportunity cost than everyone else. This is often confused with an **absolute advantage**, which is an ability to produce more of a particular good or service or to use fewer resources to produce a particular good or service than anyone else. This confusion leads some to erroneously conclude that there are no gains from trade between people or countries.

16. As long as a comparative advantage exists between two parties, there are opportunities for mutually beneficial trade. The **terms of trade** indicate the rate at which one good can be exchanged for another. The range of mutually beneficial terms of trade for a good are found between the producer's opportunity cost of making the good and the buyer's opportunity cost of making the same good.

Module 1.5

17. **Rational agents** include consumers, producers, and others who behave rationally and make optimal decisions. Consumers maximize a measure of satisfaction called **utility**. We measure utility in hypothetical units called **utils**. Firms generally maximize profit, which is the difference between the revenue they take in from sales and the costs they incur.

18. **Cost-benefit analysis** is the process of comparing costs with benefits to inform a decision. When the decision is simply whether to do something or not, it is best to proceed if the total benefit exceeds the total cost, and not to proceed if the total cost exceeds the total benefit.

19. Questions involving more than two options, such as How many? How much? or For how long? are best answered with a variant of cost-benefit analysis called *marginal analysis*. It is advisable to continue an activity such as production or consumption until the additional or *marginal benefit* of one more unit would fall below the additional or *marginal cost*.

20. **Sunk costs** are expenditures that have already been made and cannot be recovered. Sunk costs should be ignored when making decisions about future actions, because what is important in these decisions is a comparison of future costs and future benefits.

Module 1.6

21. The **marginal utility** of a good or service is the additional utility generated by consuming one more unit of the good or service. We usually assume that the **principle of diminishing marginal utility** holds: consumption of another unit of a good or service yields less additional utility than the previous unit. As a result, the **marginal utility curve** slopes downward.

22. A **budget constraint** limits a consumer's spending to no more than their income. It defines the consumer's consumption possibilities, the set of all affordable consumption bundles. A consumer who spends all of their income will choose a consumption bundle on the **budget line**. An individual chooses the consumption bundle that maximizes total utility, the **optimal consumption bundle**.

23. We use marginal analysis to find the optimal consumption bundle by analyzing how to allocate the marginal dollar. According to the **optimal consumption rule**, with the optimal consumption bundle, the marginal utility per dollar spent on each good and service—the marginal utility of a good divided by its price—is the same.

Key Terms

AP® Exam Practice Questions

Multiple-Choice Questions

1. In a market economy, most choices about production and consumption are made by which of the following?
 a. politicians
 b. many individuals and firms
 c. the government
 d. managers
 e. economists

2. Which of the following pairs indicates a category of resources and an example of that resource?

	Category	*Example*
a.	money	investment
b.	capital	money
c.	capital	minerals
d.	land	factory
e.	land	timber

3. You can either go to a movie or study for an exam. Which of the following is an opportunity cost of studying for the exam?
 a. a higher grade on the exam
 b. the price of a movie ticket
 c. the cost of paper, pens, books, and other study materials
 d. the enjoyment from seeing the movie
 e. the sense of achievement from learning

4. Which of the following situations is explained by increasing opportunity costs?
 a. More people go to college when the job market is good.
 b. More people do their own home repairs when hourly wages fall.
 c. There are more parks in crowded cities than in suburban areas.
 d. Convenience stores cater to busy people.
 e. People with higher wages are more likely to mow their own lawns.

5. Which of the following is a microeconomic issue?
 a. the unemployment rate in your country
 b. the gross domestic product for France
 c. the wage rate for employees at your school
 d. the national rate of inflation
 e. government efforts to end a recession

6. Amal likes to eat peaches. She would maximize her utility by eating peaches until, for one more peach,
 a. the total cost would exceed the total benefit.
 b. the total benefit would exceed the total cost.
 c. the total benefit would equal the total cost.
 d. the marginal benefit would exceed the marginal cost.
 e. the marginal cost would exceed the marginal benefit.

7. An economic system that combined elements of traditional, market-based, and command economies is called a
   a. rarity.
   b. trad-mar-com economy.
   c. varied economy.
   d. mixed economy.
   e. combo economy.

Refer to the following table and information for Questions 8–11.

Suppose that Atlantis is a small, isolated island in the South Atlantic. The inhabitants grow potatoes and catch fish. The following table shows the maximum annual output combinations of potatoes and fish that can be produced.

Maximum annual output options	Quantity of potatoes (pounds)	Quantity of fish (pounds)
A	1,000	0
B	800	300
C	600	500
D	400	600
E	200	650
F	0	675

8. Atlantis can produce which of the following combinations of output?

Pounds of potatoes	*Pounds of fish*
a. 1,000	675
b. 600	600
c. 400	600
d. 300	800
e. 200	675

9. If Atlantis is efficient in production, what is the opportunity cost of increasing the annual output of potatoes from 600 to 800 pounds?
   a. 200 pounds of fish
   b. 300 pounds of fish
   c. 500 pounds of fish
   d. 675 pounds of fish
   e. 800 pounds of fish

10. As Atlantis produces more potatoes, what is true about the opportunity cost of producing potatoes?
   a. It stays the same.
   b. It continually increases.
   c. It continually decreases.
   d. It increases and then decreases.
   e. It decreases and then increases.

11. Which of the following combinations of output is efficient?

Pounds of potatoes	*Pounds of fish*
a. 1,000	0
b. 600	600
c. 400	500
d. 300	400
e. 0	0

Refer to the following information for Questions 12–13.

In the ancient country of Roma, only two goods – spaghetti and meatballs – are produced. There are two tribes in Roma, the Tivoli and the Frivoli. By themselves, in a given month, the Tivoli can produce 30 pounds of spaghetti and no meatballs, 50 pounds of meatballs and no spaghetti, or any combination in between. In the same month, the Frivoli can produce 40 pounds of spaghetti and no meatballs, 30 pounds of meatballs and no spaghetti, or any combination in between.

12. Which tribe has a comparative advantage in meatball and spaghetti production?

Meatballs	*Spaghetti*
a. Tivoli	Tivoli
b. Frivoli	Frivoli
c. Tivoli	Frivoli
d. Frivoli	Tivoli
e. Neither	both

13. In AD 100, the Frivoli discovered a new technique for making meatballs and doubled the quantity of meatballs they could produce each month. After the discovery of this new technique in Frivoli only, which tribe had an absolute advantage in meatball production, and which had a comparative advantage in meatball production?

Absolute advantage	*Comparative advantage*
a. Tivoli	Tivoli
b. Frivoli	Frivoli
c. Tivoli	Frivoli
d. Frivoli	Tivoli
e. Frivoli	both

14. Which of the following is a basic source of economic growth in the production possibilities model?
   a. specialization
   b. efficiency
   c. opportunity cost
   d. trade-offs
   e. improved technology

15. Comparative advantage explains which of the following?
   a. a country's ability to produce more of a particular good or service
   b. when production is considered efficient
   c. why the production possibilities curve is bowed outward
   d. the source of gains from trade
   e. why the production possibilities curve shifts outward

16. If there is no specialization of resources in the production of milk and cream, the production possibilities curve for an economy that produces these two goods is
   a. bowed out and downward-sloping.
   b. straight and downward-sloping.
   c. bowed in and downward-sloping.
   d. horizontal.
   e. vertical.

17. Suppose that in a day Nigel can make three placemats or one gallon of maple syrup, and Pauline can make two placemats or two gallons of maple syrup. Which of the following terms of trade would be mutually beneficial for Nigel and Pauline?
- **a.** Nigel trades one placemat for ½ gallon of maple syrup from Pauline.
- **b.** Pauline trades one placemat for ½ gallon of maple syrup from Nigel.
- **c.** Nigel trades one placemat for two gallons of maple syrup from Pauline.
- **d.** Pauline trades one placemat for two gallons of maple syrup from Nigel.
- **e.** Nigel trades one placemat for ¼ gallon of maple syrup from Pauline.

18. If Country A has an absolute advantage in making butter and is considering trade with Country B, we know that
- **a.** Country A also has a comparative advantage in making butter.
- **b.** Country B has a comparative advantage in making butter.
- **c.** Country A can make more butter than Country B can with a given amount of input.
- **d.** if the two countries trade, Country A should specialize in making butter.
- **e.** if the two countries trade, Country B should specialize in making butter.

19. Economic growth is defined as an increase in
- **a.** the output of an economy.
- **b.** the employment level in an economy.
- **c.** the spending level in an economy.
- **d.** the quality of life in an economy.
- **e.** the maximum possible output of an economy.

20. The study of the costs and benefits of doing a little bit more of an activity instead of a little bit less is called
- **a.** economics.
- **b.** microeconomics.
- **c.** macroeconomics.
- **d.** marginal analysis.
- **e.** market analysis.

21. The fundamental problem with command economies is a lack of
- **a.** central authority.
- **b.** workers.
- **c.** incentives.
- **d.** land.
- **e.** opportunity cost.

22. The three basic questions that must be answered in every economy are:
- **a.** What will be produced? How will it be produced? Who will receive it?
- **b.** When will production occur? Where will it occur? Who will the producers be?
- **c.** Who will receive money? How will they receive it? When will they receive it?
- **d.** What resources will go toward food? What resources will go toward capital? What resources will go toward clothing?
- **e.** What will be taxed? How much will it be taxed? Who will pay the tax?

23. __________ incentivize productivity because they allow individuals to benefit from the production and trade of goods and services.
- **a.** Marginal costs
- **b.** Production possibilities frontiers
- **c.** Opportunity costs
- **d.** Models
- **e.** Property rights

24. The country of Sneedleham makes needles and ham at a constant opportunity cost. If Sneedleham acquires more resources but the opportunity cost of producing each good remains the same, how will the country's production possibilities curve change?
- **a.** It will shift inward and become steeper.
- **b.** It will shift outward and become steeper.
- **c.** It will change from being linear to being bowed outward.
- **d.** It will shift inward with no change in slope.
- **e.** It will shift outward with no change in slope.

25. Which of the following is true about the *ceteris paribus* assumption?
- **a.** It makes the use of more complicated but more rewarding models.
- **b.** It means "maximize profit at all costs."
- **c.** It simplifies the study of how a single change affects an economy.
- **d.** It means "the customer is always right."
- **e.** It means "people behave rationally."

26. Kateryna spends all of her income on milk and bananas and receives 12 utils from the last unit of milk and 8 utils from the last unit of bananas. If the price of milk is \$3 and the price of bananas is \$2, to maximize her total utility, Kateryna should
- **a.** buy more milk.
- **b.** buy more bananas.
- **c.** buy fewer bananas.
- **d.** buy more of both goods.
- **e.** make no change in her consumption.

Free-Response Questions

1. The Hatfield family lives on the east side of the Hatatoochie River, and the McCoy family lives on the west side. Each family's diet consists of fried chicken and corn-on-the-cob, and each is self-sufficient, raising its own chickens and growing its own corn.

   Assume the Hatfield family has a comparative advantage in the production of corn.

   a. Draw a correctly labeled graph showing a hypothetical production possibilities curve for the McCoy family.

   b. Which family has the comparative advantage in the production of chickens? Explain.

   c. Assuming that each family is producing efficiently, how can the two families increase their consumption of both chicken and corn? **(5 points)**

2. Suppose the country of Lunchland produces only peanut butter and jelly using resources that are not equally useful for producing both goods.

   a. Draw a correctly labeled production possibilities curve graph for Lunchland and label the following:

   i. point *A*, indicating an inefficient use of resources.

   ii. point *B*, indicating quantities of peanut butter and jelly that are currently not possible.

   b. Identify two things that could happen to enable Lunchland to produce or consume the quantities identified in part a (ii). **(5 points)**

3. Fields Farm and Romano Farm have identical resources and produce oranges and/or peaches at a constant opportunity cost. The table below shows the maximum quantity of oranges and peaches each farm could produce if it devoted all of its resources to that fruit.

	Output (bushels per day)	
	Oranges	**Peaches**
Fields Farm	80	40
Romano Farm	60	20

   a. On a correctly labeled graph and using the numbers in the table, draw the production possibilities curve for Romano Farm.

   b. What is Fields Farm's opportunity cost of producing one bushel of peaches?

   c. Suppose each farm agrees to specialize in one good and trade for the other good.

   i. Which farm should specialize in peaches? Explain.

   ii. If the farms specialize as indicated in part c (i), would the terms of trade of four oranges in exchange for one peach be acceptable to both farms? Explain.

   d. Now suppose Romano Farm obtains new technology used only for the production of peaches. Show the effect of this change on the graph drawn for part a. **(5 points)**

Supply and Demand

AP® Economics Skills

2. Interpretation (2.A)
3. Manipulation (3.A, 3.C)
4. Graphing and Visuals (4.A, 4.C)

Board Feet and Beetles

The floors you walk on, the building you live in, the table you dine on, and the bed you sleep in may be made of wood. The prices of wooden flooring, homes, and furniture rise and fall with the price of lumber, which is wood cut into pieces for construction purposes. Lumber is measured in board feet, with one board foot being one foot long, one foot wide, and one inch thick. The price per board foot of lumber has had its share of ups and downs. From 1990 until 2018, that price bounced around between just under 20 cents to just over 40 cents. Then the price took a more dramatic roller coaster ride, rising as high as 60 cents in 2018, 93 cents in 2020, and $1.50 (!) in 2021 before dropping below 50 cents later that year.

Why did lumber prices climb so high? Two culprits are to blame: supply and demand. The supply of lumber was constrained by shortages of workers and sawmill equipment, along with a plague of tiny beetles that destroyed enough trees to build several million homes. On the demand side, new housing and other construction projects fueled the desire for more lumber than usual. Most notably, the COVID-19 pandemic kept people at home in early 2020, where they craved larger homes to make quarantine more bearable. Later in 2020 and 2021, low interest rates made home loans cheap and drove the construction of new homes to its highest level in 14 years. Every new home needed floors, furniture, and a roof, so the demand for lumber soared.

Wait a minute: how, exactly, do pandemics and pests raise the price of wood? It's a matter of supply and demand – but what does that mean? Many people use "supply and demand" as a catchphrase to mean "the laws of the marketplace at work." To economists, however, the concept of supply and demand has a precise meaning: it is a *model* of market behavior that is extremely useful for understanding many – but not all – markets.

In this Unit, we lay out the pieces that make up the *supply and demand model*, put them together, and show how this model can be used to understand how most markets behave.

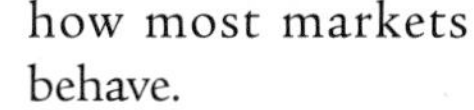

Hill Street Studios/Stone/Getty Images

MODULE 2.1

Demand

In this Module, you will learn to:
- Draw a demand curve and interpret its meaning
- Define the law of demand
- Discuss the difference between movements along a demand curve and changes in demand
- Explain how incentives and constraints affect demand

Introduction to Demand

Module 1.1 explained that a well-defined system of property rights creates incentives for producers to provide goods and services of value to consumers. In this Module, we examine consumers' demand for those goods and services and the influences on that demand in a market system. Lumber sellers and lumber buyers constitute a *market*—a group of producers and consumers who exchange a good or service for payment. We'll focus on a particular type of market known as a *perfectly competitive market*. Module 3.7 describes a perfectly competitive market as one in which there are many buyers and sellers of the same good or service. The key feature of a perfectly competitive market is that no individual's actions have a noticeable effect on the price at which the good or service is sold.

Chih-Chung Johnny Chang/Alamy

The market for lumber is perfectly competitive: No individual buyer or seller can have a noticeable influence on the price of lumber.

It's important to understand, however, that many markets do not resemble this description. For example, the market for cola beverages is very different. In that market, Coca-Cola and Pepsi account for such a large proportion of total sales that they are able to influence the price at which cola beverages are bought and sold. The market for lumber, in contrast, can be more accurately described as perfectly competitive: It is so huge that even the largest lumber, flooring, construction, and furniture companies account for only a tiny fraction of transactions, giving them little power to influence the price at which lumber is bought and sold.

The **supply and demand model** is a model of how a perfectly competitive market works.

For markets with enough competition to resemble perfectly competitive markets, their behavior is well described by the **supply and demand model**. Because many markets *are* very competitive, the supply and demand model is a useful one indeed.

There are six key elements in the supply and demand model:

- The *demand curve*
- The set of factors that cause the demand curve to shift
- The *supply curve*
- The set of factors that cause the supply curve to shift
- The *market equilibrium*, which includes the *equilibrium price* and *equilibrium quantity*
- The way the market equilibrium changes when the supply curve or demand curve shifts

To explain the supply and demand model, we will examine each of these elements in turn. In this Module we begin with the demand curve and then discuss the factors that cause the demand curve to shift.

The Demand Curve

How many board feet of lumber, nailed together into new homes, do consumers around the world want to buy in a given year? You might at first think that we can answer this question by multiplying the number of new homes purchased around the world each year by the amount of lumber it takes to make the average home. But that's not enough to answer the question, because how many homes—and thus how many board feet of lumber—consumers want to buy depends on the price of lumber. When the price of lumber rises, as it did in 2021, some people will respond to the higher price by either forgoing the purchase of a new home or having their home built with wood substitutes, such as plastic composites or steel. In general, the quantity of lumber, or of any good or service that people *want* to buy (taking "want" to mean they are willing and able to buy it), depends on the price. The higher the price, the less of the good or service people want to purchase; alternatively, the lower the price, the more they want to purchase.

So the answer to the question "How many board feet of lumber do consumers want to buy?" depends on the price of lumber. If you don't yet know what the price will be, you can start by making a table of how much lumber people would want to buy at a number of different prices. Such a table is known as a *demand schedule*. This demand schedule, in turn, can be used to draw a *demand curve*, which is one of the key elements of the supply and demand model.

AP® ECON TIP

In several common economics graphs, including the graph of supply and demand, the independent variable is on the vertical axis and the dependent variable is on the horizontal axis. You may have learned the opposite convention in math and science class, but don't let that confuse you—economists go their own way.

The Demand Schedule and the Demand Curve

A **demand schedule** is a table that shows how much of a good or service consumers will want to buy at different prices. On the right side of **Figure 2.1-1**, we show a hypothetical demand schedule for lumber. It's hypothetical in that it doesn't use actual data on the world demand for lumber. The demand schedule assumes that all lumber is standardized, although in reality there are various grades and sizes.

A **demand schedule** is a table that shows how much of a good or service consumers will be willing and able to buy at different prices.

FIGURE 2.1-1 The Demand Schedule and the Demand Curve

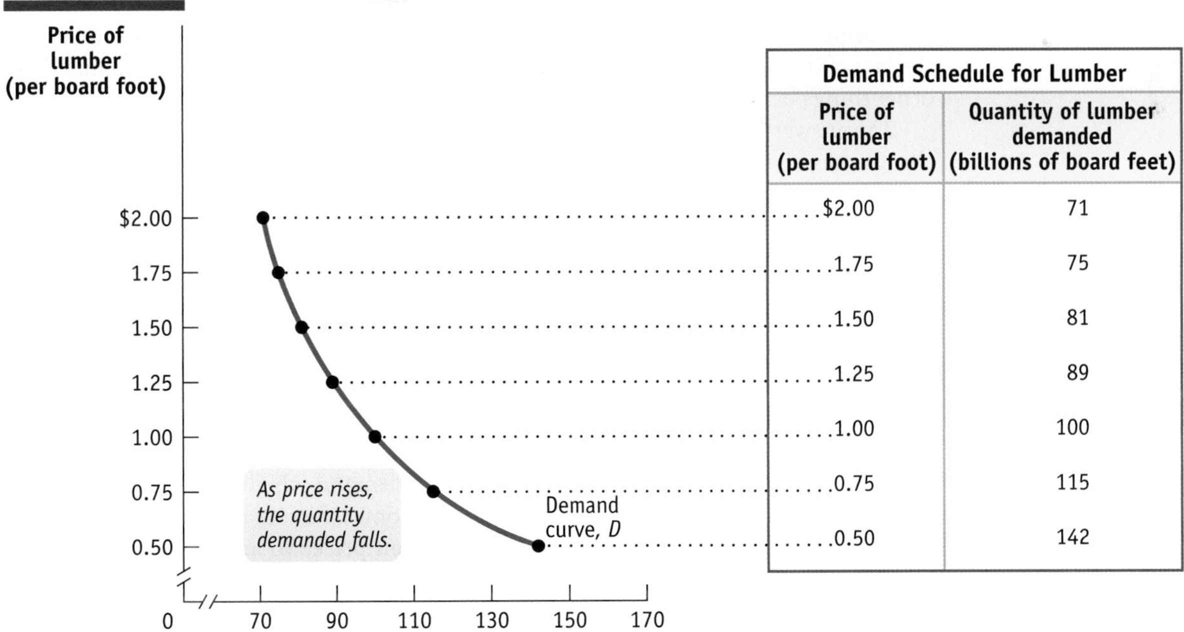

Demand Schedule for Lumber

Price of lumber (per board foot)	Quantity of lumber demanded (billions of board feet)
$2.00	71
1.75	75
1.50	81
1.25	89
1.00	100
0.75	115
0.50	142

The demand schedule for lumber yields the corresponding demand curve, which shows how much of a good or service consumers want to buy at any given price. The demand curve and the demand schedule reflect the law of demand: As price rises, the quantity demanded falls. Similarly, a decrease in price raises the quantity demanded. As a result, the demand curve is downward-sloping.

The **quantity demanded** is the actual amount of a good or service consumers are willing and able to buy at some specific price. It is shown as a single point in a demand schedule or along a demand curve.

A **demand curve** is a graphical representation of the demand schedule. It shows the relationship between quantity demanded and price.

The **law of demand** says that a higher price for a good or service, all other things being equal, leads people to demand a smaller quantity of that good or service.

According to the table, if lumber costs $1.00 per board foot, consumers around the world will want to purchase 100 billion board feet of lumber over the course of a year. If the price is $1.25 a board foot, they will want to buy only 89 billion board feet; if the price is only $0.75 a board foot, they will want to buy 115 billion board feet; and so on. So the higher the price, the fewer board feet of lumber consumers will want to purchase. In other words, as the price rises, the **quantity demanded** of lumber – the actual amount consumers are willing and able to buy at a specific price – falls.

The graph in Figure 2.1-1 is a visual representation of the demand schedule. The vertical axis shows the price of a board foot of lumber, and the horizontal axis shows the quantity of lumber in board feet. Each point on the graph corresponds to one of the entries in the table. The curve that connects these points is a **demand curve**, which is another way of showing the relationship between the quantity demanded and the price.

Note that the demand curve shown in Figure 2.1-1 slopes downward. This reflects the general proposition that a higher price reduces the quantity demanded. For example, construction companies know they will sell fewer homes when their price is higher, reflecting a $2.00 price per board foot of lumber, compared to the number they will sell when the price is lower, reflecting a price of only $1.00 per board foot of lumber. When home prices are relatively high, some people will decide not to build a new home, delay the construction of their home, build a smaller home, or use less wood in their home.

In the real world, demand curves almost always slope downward. It is so likely that, all other things being equal, a higher price for a good will lead people to demand a smaller quantity of it, that economists are willing to call it a "law" – the **law of demand**. The principle of diminishing marginal utility discussed in Module 1.6 helps to explain the law of demand: If consumers get less and less satisfaction out of additional units of a good or service, a higher price will make fewer units worthwhile to purchase. In Module 2.3, we will see how the *income effect* and the *substitution effect* of a price change also contribute to the demand curve's downward slope.

Shifts of the Demand Curve

Even though lumber prices were higher in 2021 than they had been in 2020, the total consumption of lumber was also higher in 2021. How can we reconcile this fact with the law of demand, which says that a higher price reduces the quantity demanded, all other things being equal?

The answer lies in the crucial phrase *all other things being equal*. In this case, all other things weren't equal: there were changes between 2020 and 2021 that increased the quantity of lumber demanded at any given price. To begin with, the COVID-19 pandemic changed consumers' tastes for homes, and the relaxation of COVID-19 restrictions improved buyers' ability to arrange for new construction. In addition, rising incomes in countries like China allowed people to buy more homes than before. These changes led to an increase in the quantity of lumber demanded at any given price. **Figure 2.1-2** illustrates this phenomenon using the demand schedule and demand curve for lumber. (As before, the numbers in Figure 2.1-2 are hypothetical.)

The table in Figure 2.1-2 shows two demand schedules. The first is a demand schedule for 2020, the same one shown in Figure 2.1-1. The second is a demand schedule for 2021. That schedule differs from the 2020 demand schedule due to factors such as changing tastes for new homes and higher incomes, factors that led to an increase in the quantity of lumber demanded at any given price. So at each price, the 2021 schedule shows a larger quantity demanded than the 2020 schedule. For example, the quantity of lumber consumers wanted to buy at a price of $1 per board foot increased from 100 billion to 120 billion board feet per year, the quantity demanded at $1.25 per board foot went from 89 billion to 107 billion board feet, and so on.

What is clear from this example is that the changes that occurred between 2020 and 2021 generated a *new* demand schedule, one in which the quantity demanded was greater at any given price than in the original demand schedule. The two curves in Figure 2.1-2 show the same information graphically. As you can see, the demand

FIGURE 2.1-2 An Increase in Demand

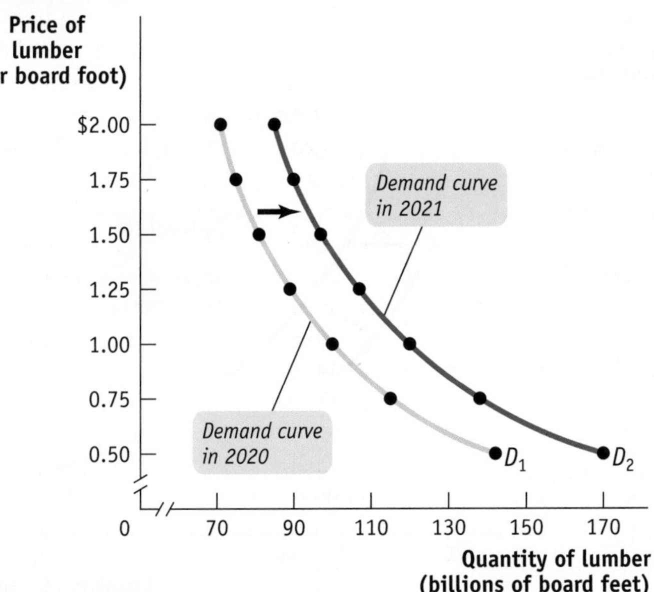

Demand Schedules for Lumber		
Price of lumber (per board foot)	Quantity of lumber demanded (billions of board feet)	
	in 2020	in 2021
$2.00	71	85
1.75	75	90
1.50	81	97
1.25	89	107
1.00	100	120
0.75	115	138
0.50	142	170

Changes in tastes and increases in income, among other changes, generate an increase in demand – a rise in the quantity demanded at any given price. This is represented by the two demand schedules – one showing demand in 2020 (D_1), and the other showing demand in 2021 (D_2), after the rise in population and income – and their corresponding demand curves. The increase in demand shifts the demand curve to the right.

schedule for 2021 corresponds to a new demand curve, D_2, that is to the right of the demand curve for 2020, D_1. This **change in demand** shows the increase in the quantity demanded at any given price, represented by the shift in position of the original demand curve, D_1, to its new location at D_2.

It's crucial to make the distinction between such changes in demand and **movements along the demand curve**, which are changes in the quantity demanded of a good that result from a change in that good's price. **Figure 2.1-3** illustrates the difference.

The movement from point *A* to point *B* is a movement along the demand curve: the quantity demanded rises due to a fall in price as you move down D_1. Here, a fall in the price of lumber from $1.50 to $1 per board foot generates a rise in the quantity demanded from 81 billion to 100 billion board feet per year. But the quantity demanded can also rise when the price is unchanged if there is an *increase in demand* – a rightward shift of the demand curve. This is illustrated in Figure 2.1-3 by the shift of the demand curve from D_1 to D_2. Holding the price constant at $1.50 per board foot, the quantity demanded rises from 81 billion board feet at point *A* on D_1 to 97 billion board feet at point *C* on D_2.

When economists talk about a "change in demand," saying "the demand for *X* increased" or "the demand for *Y* decreased," they mean that the demand curve for *X* or *Y* shifted – *not* that the quantity demanded rose or fell because of a change in the price.

A **change in demand** is a shift of the demand curve, which changes the quantity demanded at any given price.

A **movement along the demand curve** is a change in the quantity demanded of a good that is the result of a change in that good's price.

AP® ECON TIP

A price change causes a change in the quantity demanded, shown by a movement along the demand curve. When a nonprice determinant of demand changes, this changes demand, and therefore shifts the demand curve. It is correct to say that an increase in the price of apples decreases the *quantity of apples demanded*; it is incorrect to say that an increase in the price of apples *decreases the demand for apples.*

Understanding Shifts of the Demand Curve

Figure 2.1-4 illustrates the two basic ways in which demand curves can shift. When economists talk about an "increase in demand," they mean a *rightward* shift of the demand curve: at any given price, consumers demand a larger quantity of the good or service than before. This is shown in our figure by the rightward shift of the original demand curve D_1 to D_2. And when economists talk about a "decrease in demand," they mean a *leftward* shift of the demand curve: at any given price, consumers demand a smaller quantity of the good or service than before. This is shown by the leftward shift of the original demand curve D_1 to D_3.

FIGURE 2.1-3 A Movement Along the Demand Curve Versus a Shift of the Demand Curve

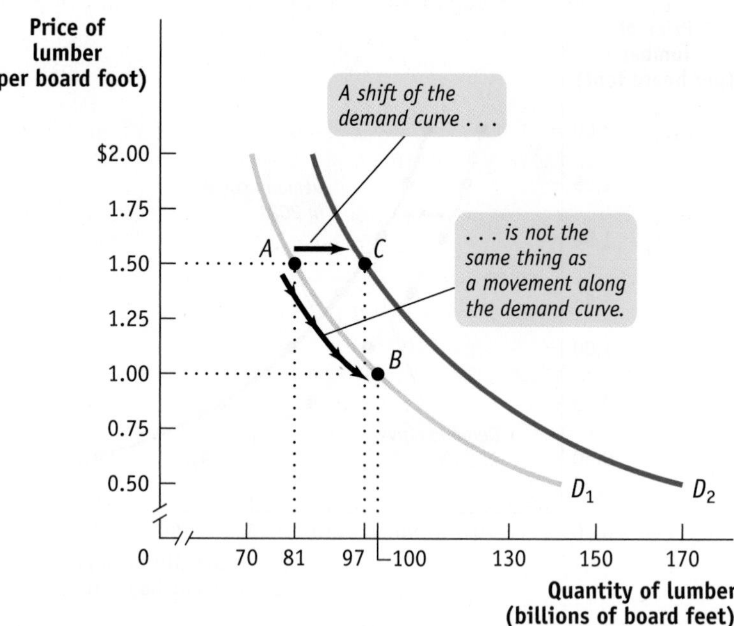

The rise in the quantity demanded when going from point *A* to point *B* reflects a movement along the demand curve: it is the result of a fall in the price of the good. The rise in the quantity demanded when going from point *A* to point *C* reflects a change in demand: this shift to the right, from D_1 to D_2, is the result of a rise in the quantity demanded at any given price.

FIGURE 2.1-4 Shifts of the Demand Curve

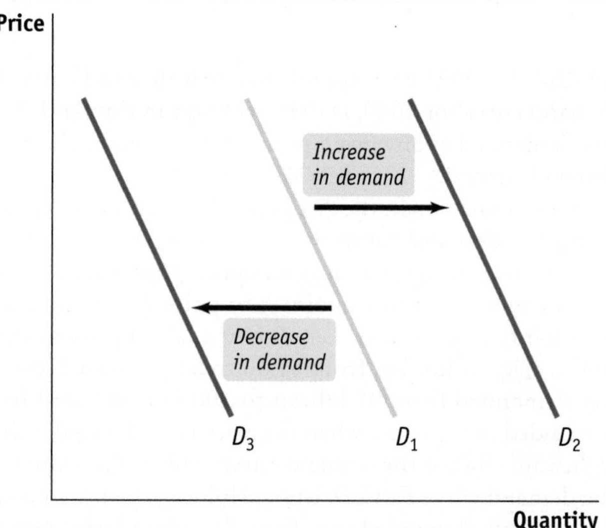

Any event that increases demand shifts the demand curve to the right, reflecting a rise in the quantity demanded at any given price. Any event that decreases demand shifts the demand curve to the left, reflecting a fall in the quantity demanded at any given price.

AP® ECON TIP

When shifting curves, a decrease is shown as a movement to the left and an increase is shown as a movement to the right. Quantity is measured on the horizontal axis and is lower to the left and higher to the right. Remember: *left is less and right is more.*

What caused the demand curve for lumber to shift? We have already mentioned reasons that include changes in tastes and income. If you think about it, you can come up with other things that would be likely to shift the demand curve for lumber. For example, suppose the price of house rentals rises. This will induce some people who were previously content renting to buy a new home instead, increasing the demand for lumber.

There are five principal factors that shift the demand curve for a good or service:

- Changes in tastes
- Changes in the prices of related goods or services
- Changes in income
- Changes in the number of consumers (buyers)
- Changes in expectations

Although this is not an exhaustive list, it contains the five most important factors that can shift demand curves. Changes in demand can generally be viewed as a change in one of these factors. When we say that the quantity of a good or service demanded falls as its price rises, *all other things being equal*, we are in fact stating that the factors that shift demand are remaining unchanged.

Table 2.1-1 gives an overview of the ways that these five factors can shift demand. Next, we explore in detail *how* these factors shift the demand curve.

> **AP® ECON TIP**
>
> The mnemonic *TRIBE* can help you remember the factors that shift demand. Demand is shifted by changes in . . . **T**astes, prices of **R**elated goods, **I**ncome, the number of **B**uyers, and **E**xpectations.

Changes in Tastes Why do people want what they want? Fortunately, we don't need to answer that question—we just need to acknowledge that people have certain preferences, or tastes, that determine what they choose to consume and that these tastes can change. Economists usually lump together changes in demand due to fads, beliefs, cultural shifts, and so on under the heading of changes in *tastes*.

incamerastock/Alamy

Consider this example: From the 1950s through the 1970s, vinyl records dominated the personal music market. Then came cassettes and CDs in the 1980s and 1990s, which were more portable and easier to store, and the demand for vinyl records decreased. In the 2000s, as digital downloads and streaming music became popular, the demand for CDs decreased. At the same time, vinyl records made a comeback, purely as a matter of taste. The demand for vinyl records has increased so much that most artists now release their music on vinyl, and you can probably find records at your favorite big-box or online store.

Economists have little to say about the forces that influence consumers' tastes. (Marketers and advertisers, however, have plenty to say about them!) However, a *change* in tastes has a predictable impact on demand. When tastes change in favor of a good, more people want to buy it at any given price, so the demand curve shifts to the right. When tastes change against a good, fewer people want to buy it at any given price, so the demand curve shifts to the left.

Changes in the Prices of Related Goods or Services While there's nothing quite like a comfortable pair of all-cotton blue jeans, for some purposes, khakis—typically made from polyester blends—aren't a bad alternative. Khakis are what economists call a *substitute* for jeans. A pair of goods are **substitutes** if a rise in the price of one good (jeans) makes consumers more willing to buy the other good (polyester-blend khakis). Substitutes are usually goods that in some way serve a similar function: coffee and tea, muffins and doughnuts, train rides and airplane rides, lumber and plastic composites. A rise in the price of the alternative good provides an incentive for some consumers to purchase the original good *instead* of the alternative good, shifting demand for the original good to the right. Likewise, when the price of the alternative good falls, some consumers switch from the original good to the alternative, shifting the demand curve for the original good to the left.

Two goods are **substitutes** if a rise in the price of one of the goods leads to an increase in the demand for the other good.

But sometimes a fall in the price of one good makes consumers *more* willing to buy another good. Such pairs of goods are known as **complements**. Complements are goods that in some sense are consumed together: smartphones and apps, cookies and milk, cars and gasoline. Because consumers like to consume a good and its complement together, a change in the price of one of the goods will affect the demand for its complement. In particular, when the price of one good rises, the demand for its complement decreases, shifting the demand curve for the complement to the left. So a rise in the price of cookies is likely to cause a leftward shift in the demand curve for milk, as people consume fewer snacks of cookies and milk. Likewise, when the price of one good falls, the demand for its complement increases, shifting the demand curve for the complement to the right. This means that if, for some reason, the price of cookies falls, we should see a rightward shift in the demand curve for milk, as people consume more cookies *and* more milk.

Two goods are **complements** if a rise in the price of one of the goods leads to a decrease in the demand for the other good.

Table 2.1-1 Factors That Shift Demand

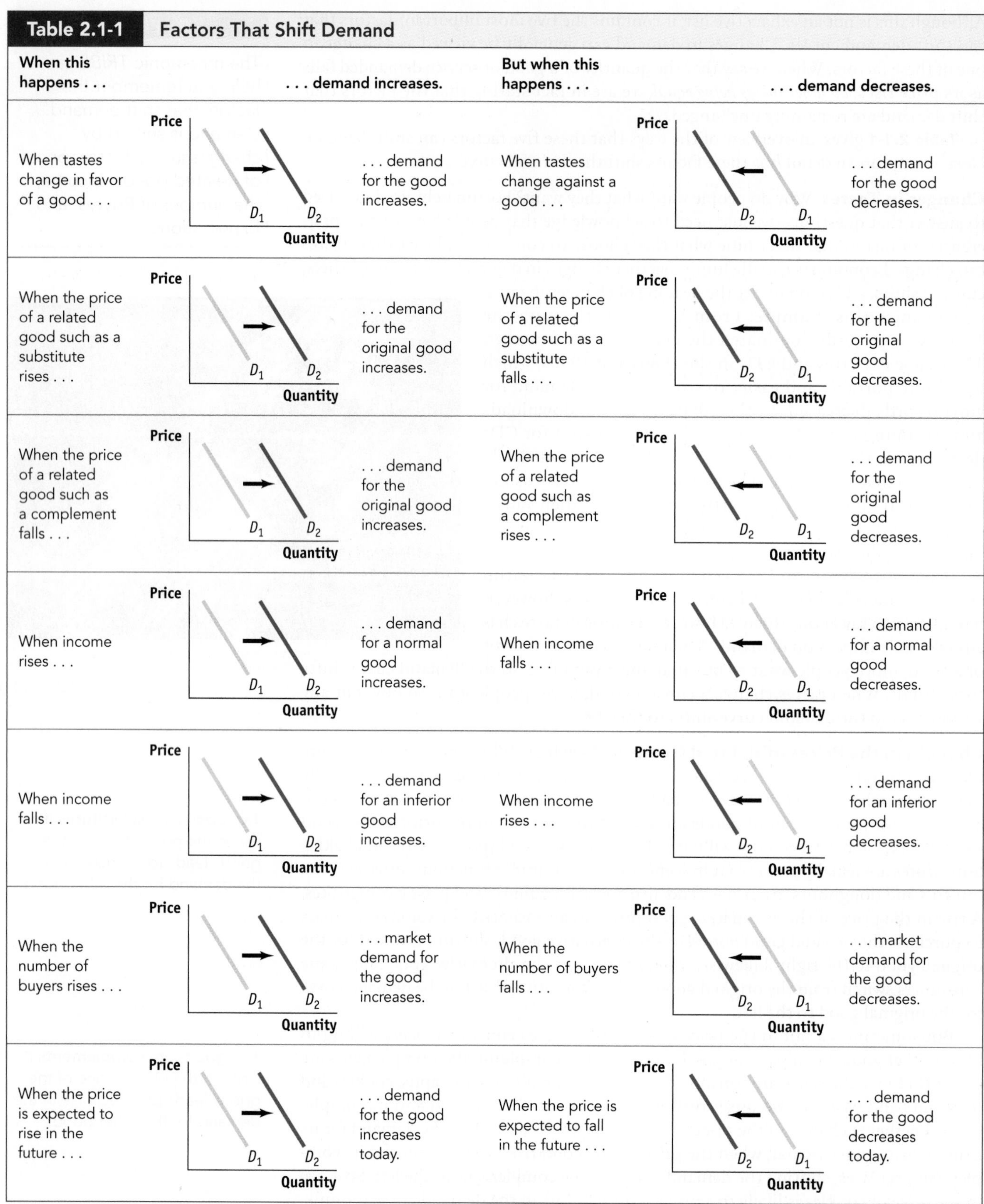

When this happens . . .	. . . demand increases.	But when this happens . . .	. . . demand decreases.
When tastes change in favor of a good . . .	. . . demand for the good increases.	When tastes change against a good . . .	. . . demand for the good decreases.
When the price of a related good such as a substitute rises . . .	. . . demand for the original good increases.	When the price of a related good such as a substitute falls . . .	. . . demand for the original good decreases.
When the price of a related good such as a complement falls . . .	. . . demand for the original good increases.	When the price of a related good such as a complement rises . . .	. . . demand for the original good decreases.
When income rises . . .	. . . demand for a normal good increases.	When income falls . . .	. . . demand for a normal good decreases.
When income falls . . .	. . . demand for an inferior good increases.	When income rises . . .	. . . demand for an inferior good decreases.
When the number of buyers rises . . .	. . . market demand for the good increases.	When the number of buyers falls . . .	. . . market demand for the good decreases.
When the price is expected to rise in the future . . .	. . . demand for the good increases today.	When the price is expected to fall in the future . . .	. . . demand for the good decreases today.

Changes in Income Limited income is a constraint on consumers' purchasing decisions. When individuals have more income, they are normally more likely to purchase a good or service at any given price. For example, if a family's income rises, it is more likely to take that summer trip to Disney World – and therefore also more likely to buy plane tickets. So a rise in consumer incomes will cause the demand curves for most goods to shift to the right.

Why do we say "most goods," rather than "all goods"? Most goods are **normal goods** – the demand for them increases when consumer incomes rise. However, the demand for some goods decreases when incomes rise – these goods are known as **inferior goods**. Usually an inferior good is one that is considered less desirable than more expensive alternatives – such as a bus ride versus a taxi ride. When they can afford to, people stop buying an inferior good and switch their consumption to the preferred, more expensive alternative. So when a good is inferior, a rise in income shifts the demand curve to the left. And, not surprisingly, a fall in income shifts the demand curve to the right.

When a rise in income increases the demand for a good—the normal case—it is a **normal good**. When a rise in income decreases the demand for a good, it is an **inferior good**.

Consider the difference between so-called casual-dining restaurants such as Applebee's and Olive Garden and fast-food chains such as McDonald's and KFC. When their incomes rise, Americans tend to eat out more at casual-dining restaurants. However, some of this increased dining out comes at the expense of fast-food venues – to some extent, people visit McDonald's less once they can afford to move upscale. So casual dining is a normal good, while fast food appears to be an inferior good.

MediaNews Group/Orange County Register/Getty Images

When their incomes increase, some people switch from eating at fast food restaurants to eating at casual-dining restaurants like Applebee's.

Changes in the Number of Consumers (Buyers) A growing world population increases the demand for most things, including fast food, clothing, and lumber. With more people needing housing and furniture, the overall demand for lumber rises and the lumber demand curve shifts to the right, even if each individual's demand for lumber remains unchanged. How the number of consumers affects the market demand curve is described in detail shortly.

Changes in Expectations When consumers have some choice about when to make a purchase, current demand for a good or service is often affected by expectations about its future price. For example, savvy shoppers often wait for seasonal sales – say, buying next year's holiday gifts during the post-holiday markdowns. In this case, expectations of a future drop in price lead to a decrease in demand today. Alternatively, expectations of a future rise in price are likely to cause an increase in demand today. For example, if you heard that the price of jeans would increase next year, you might go out and buy an extra pair now.

Changes in expectations about future income can also lead to changes in demand. If you learned today that you would inherit a large sum of money sometime in the future, you might borrow some money today and increase your demand for certain goods. Maybe you would buy more electronics, jewelry, or sports equipment. On the other hand, if you learned that you would earn less in the future than you thought, you might reduce your demand for those goods and save more money today. *Consumption smoothing* of this type shifts your demand curves for those goods to the right when your expected future income increases, and to the left when your expected future income decreases. Your own demand curves for goods and services are known as *individual demand curves*, which we'll explore next.

Individual Versus Market Demand Curves

An **individual demand curve** illustrates the relationship between quantity demanded and price for an individual consumer.

We have discussed both the demand of individuals and the market demand for various goods. Now let's distinguish between an **individual demand curve**, which shows the relationship between quantity demanded and price for an individual consumer, and a market demand curve, which shows the combined demand by all consumers. Suppose that Darla is a consumer of blue jeans. Also suppose that all blue jeans are the same, so they sell for the same price. Panel (a) of **Figure 2.1-5** shows how many pairs of jeans she will buy per year at any given price per pair. Then D_{Darla} is Darla's individual demand curve.

FIGURE 2.1-5 Individual Demand Curves and the Market Demand Curve

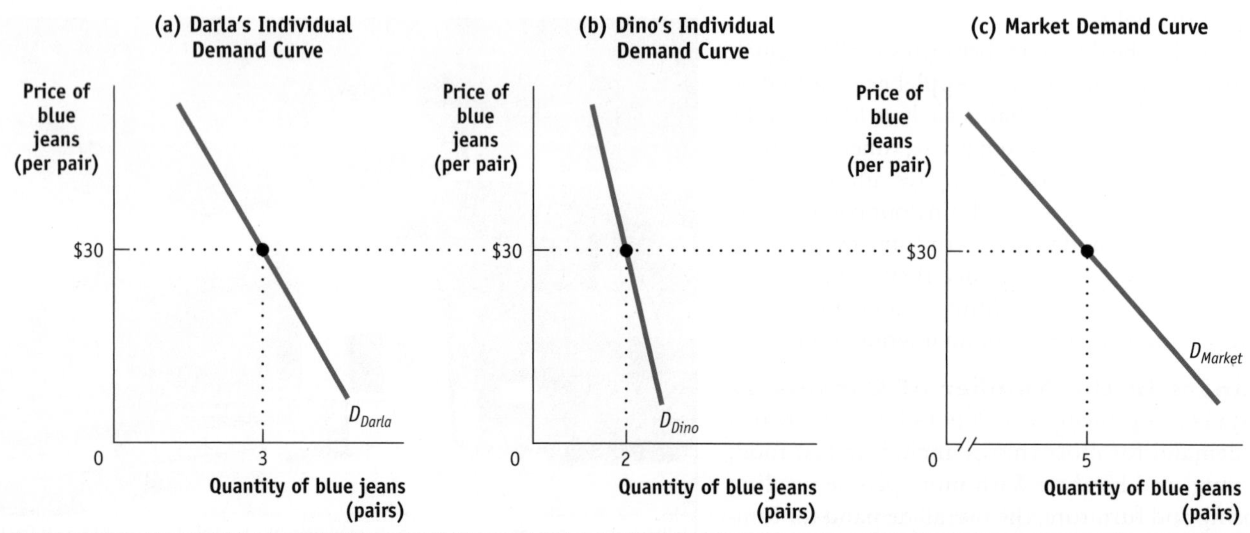

Darla and Dino are the only two consumers of blue jeans in the market. Panel (a) shows Darla's individual demand curve: the number of pairs of jeans she will buy per year at any given price. Panel (b) shows Dino's individual demand curve. Given that Darla and Dino are the only two consumers, the *market demand curve*, which shows the quantity of blue jeans demanded by all consumers at any given price, is shown in panel (c). The market demand curve is the *horizontal sum* of the individual demand curves of all consumers. In this case, at any given price, the quantity demanded by the market is the sum of the quantities demanded by Darla and Dino.

The *market demand curve* shows how the combined quantity demanded by all consumers depends on the market price of that good. (Most of the time, when economists refer to the demand curve, they mean the market demand curve.) The market demand curve is the *horizontal sum* of the individual demand curves of all consumers in that market. To see what we mean by the term *horizontal sum*, assume for a moment that there are only two consumers of blue jeans, Darla and Dino. Dino's individual demand curve, D_{Dino}, is shown in panel (b). Panel (c) shows the market demand curve. At any given price, the quantity demanded by the market is the sum of the quantities demanded by Darla and Dino. For example, at a price of $30 per pair, Darla demands three pairs of jeans per year and Dino demands two pairs per year. So the quantity demanded by the market is five pairs per year.

Clearly, the quantity demanded by the market at any given price is larger with Dino present than it would be if Darla were the only consumer. The quantity demanded at any given price would be even larger if we added a third consumer, then a fourth, and so on. So an increase in the number of consumers leads to an increase in demand.

Module 2.1  Review

Adventures in AP® Economics

Watch the video: ***Demand***

Check Your Understanding

1. Explain whether each of the following events represents (i) a *change in* demand (a *shift* of the demand curve) or (ii) a *movement along* the demand curve (a *change in the quantity demanded*).
   - **a.** A store owner finds that customers are willing to pay more for umbrellas on rainy days.
   - **b.** When XYZ Mobile, a cellular plan provider, offered reduced rates on data charges, its volume data usage by users increased sharply.
   - **c.** People buy more long-stem roses the week of Valentine's Day, even though the prices are higher than at other times during the year.
   - **d.** A sharp rise in the price of gasoline leads many commuters to join carpools in order to reduce their gasoline purchases.

Tackle the AP® Test: Multiple-Choice Questions

1. The supply and demand model shows the workings of a perfectly competitive market in which
   - **a.** there are many buyers and sellers.
   - **b.** each firm sells a different variety of the product.
   - **c.** buyers can influence the market price.
   - **d.** sellers can influence the market price.
   - **e.** all of the above
2. The law of demand states that the relationship between price and the quantity demanded is
   - **a.** positive.
   - **b.** negative.
   - **c.** direct.
   - **d.** unclear.
   - **e.** weak.
3. Which of the following would increase demand for a normal good? A decrease in
   - **a.** price.
   - **b.** income.
   - **c.** the price of a substitute.
   - **d.** consumer taste for a good.
   - **e.** the price of a complement.
4. A decrease in the price of butter would most likely decrease the demand for
   - **a.** margarine.
   - **b.** bagels.
   - **c.** jelly.
   - **d.** milk.
   - **e.** syrup.
5. If an increase in income leads to a decrease in demand, the good is
   - **a.** a complement.
   - **b.** a substitute.
   - **c.** inferior.
   - **d.** abnormal.
   - **e.** normal.
6. Which of the following will occur if consumers expect the price of a good to fall in the coming months?
   - **a.** The quantity demanded will rise today.
   - **b.** The quantity demanded will remain the same today.
   - **c.** Demand will increase today.
   - **d.** Demand will decrease today.
   - **e.** No change will occur today.
7. Which of the following will increase the demand for disposable diapers?
   - **a.** a new "baby boom"
   - **b.** concern over the environmental effect of landfills
   - **c.** a decrease in the price of cloth diapers
   - **d.** a move toward earlier potty training of children
   - **e.** a decrease in the price of disposable diapers

Tackle the AP® Test: Free-Response Questions

1. Create a table with two hypothetical prices for a good and two corresponding quantities demanded. Choose the prices and quantities so that they illustrate the law of demand. Using your data, draw a correctly labeled graph showing the demand curve for the good. Using the same graph, illustrate an increase in demand for the good.

Rubric for FRQ 1 (6 points)

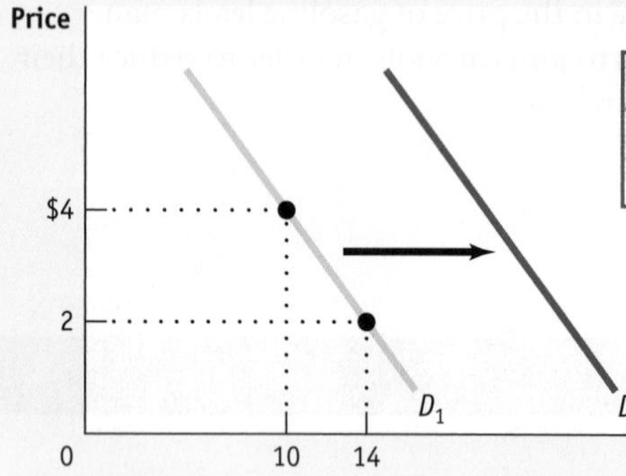

Price
$4
2
0
10 14
Quantity
D_1
D_2

Price	Quantity
$4	10
2	14

1 point: Table with data labeled "Price" (or "P") and "Quantity" (or "Q")

1 point: Values in the table show a negative relationship between *P* and *Q*

1 point: Graph with "Price" on the vertical axis and "Quantity" on the horizontal axis

1 point: Negatively sloped curve labeled "Demand" or "D"

1 point: Demand curve correctly plots the data from the table

1 point: A second demand curve (with a label such as D_2) shown to the right of the original demand curve

2. Draw a correctly labeled graph showing the demand for apples. On your graph, illustrate what happens to the demand for apples if a new report from the Surgeon General finds that an apple a day really *does* keep the doctor away. **(3 points)**

Supply

In this Module, you will learn to:

- Draw a supply curve and interpret its meaning
- Define the law of supply
- Discuss the difference between movements along the supply curve and changes in supply
- Explain how producers' responses to incentives and technology affect supply

The Supply Curve

Blink Photo/Alamy

Some parts of the world are especially well suited to growing hardwood trees for lumber production, and the United States is among them. But even in the United States, some land is better suited to growing hardwood trees than other land. Whether American tree farmers restrict their tree-growing to only the most ideal locations or expand it to less suitable land depends on the price they expect to get for their logs, which depends on the price sawmills can get for their lumber. Moreover, there are many other areas in the world where hardwood trees could be grown – such as China, Canada, and Germany. The number of hardwood trees actually grown and harvested there depends, again, on the price.

So just as the quantity of lumber that consumers want to buy depends on the price they have to pay, the quantity that producers are willing to produce and sell – the **quantity supplied** – depends on the price they are offered.

The **quantity supplied** is the actual amount of a good or service people are willing to sell at some specific price.

The Supply Schedule and the Supply Curve

The table in **Figure 2.2-1** shows how the quantity of lumber made available varies with the price – that is, it shows a hypothetical **supply schedule** for lumber.

A supply schedule works the same way as the demand schedule shown in Figure 2.1-1: in this case, the table shows the number of board feet of lumber sawmills are willing to sell at different prices. At a price of $0.50 per board foot, sawmills are willing to sell only 80 billion board feet of lumber per year. At $0.75 per board foot, they're willing to sell 91 billion board feet. At $1, they're willing to sell 100 billion board feet, and so on.

In the same way that a demand schedule can be represented graphically by a demand curve, a supply schedule can be represented by a **supply curve**, as shown in Figure 2.2-1. Each point on the curve represents an entry from the table.

Suppose that the price of lumber rises from $1 to $1.25; we can see that the quantity of lumber sawmills are willing to sell rises from 100 billion to 107 billion board feet. This is the normal situation for a supply curve: a higher price leads to a higher quantity supplied. Some economists refer to this positive relationship as the **law of supply**. So just as demand curves normally slope downward, supply curves normally slope upward: the higher the price being offered, the more of any good or service producers will be willing to sell.

A **supply schedule** shows how much of a good or service producers would supply at different prices.

A **supply curve** shows the relationship between the quantity supplied and the price.

The **law of supply** says that, other things being equal, the price and quantity supplied of a good are positively related.

AP® ECON TIP

A change in demand does not affect supply (either the supply schedule or the supply curve). However, if a change in demand causes a change in price, it will affect the quantity supplied by causing a movement along the supply curve.

Shifts of the Supply Curve

For many decades following World War II, lumber remained relatively cheap. One reason is that the number of trees harvested for lumber production increased. Another factor accounting for lumber's relative cheapness was advances in sawmill

FIGURE 2.2-1 The Supply Schedule and the Supply Curve

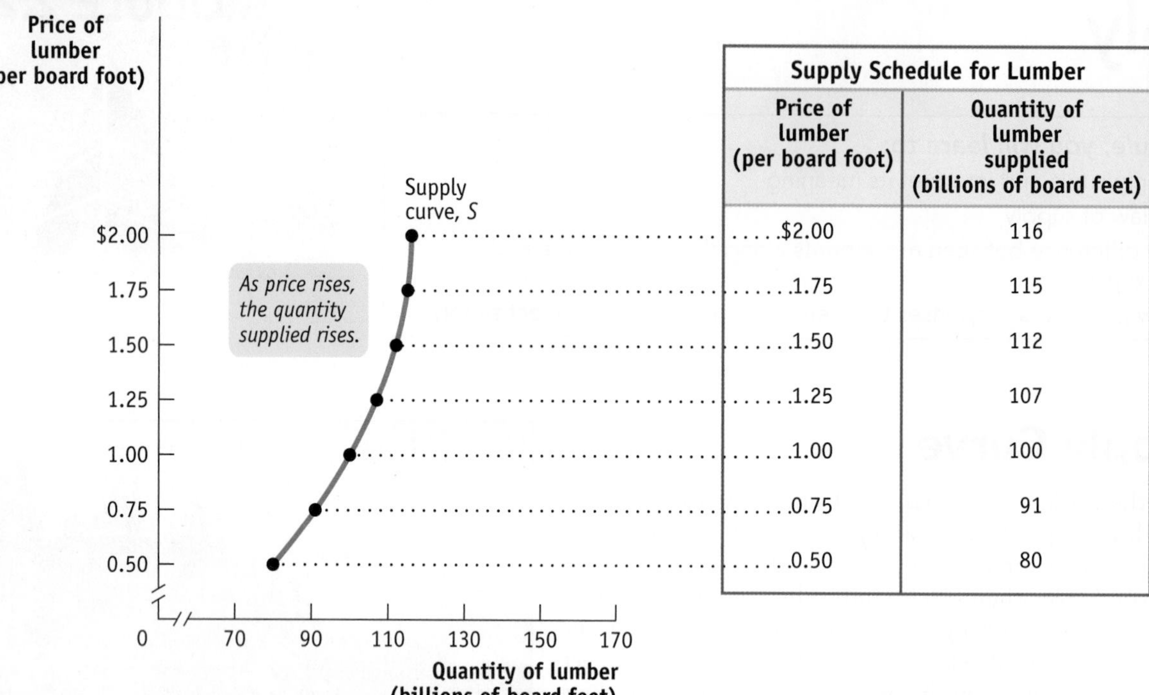

Supply Schedule for Lumber	
Price of lumber (per board foot)	Quantity of lumber supplied (billions of board feet)
$2.00	116
1.75	115
1.50	112
1.25	107
1.00	100
0.75	91
0.50	80

The supply schedule for lumber is plotted to yield the corresponding supply curve, which shows how much lumber producers are willing to sell at any given price. The supply curve and the supply schedule reflect the fact that supply curves are usually upward-sloping: the quantity supplied rises when the price rises.

Lumber production isn't what it used to be. Advancements in sawmill technology helped to keep lumber prices low for decades

technology, including the automation of many difficult and dangerous sawing processes. **Figure 2.2-2** illustrates how these events affected the supply schedule and the supply curve for lumber.

The table in Figure 2.2-2 shows two supply schedules. The schedule for before improved sawmill technology was adopted is the same one as in Figure 2.2-1. The second schedule shows the supply of lumber *after* the improved technology was adopted. When technology or anything else changes the quantity supplied at each price, this change in the supply schedule constitutes a **change in supply** and is illustrated by a shift in the supply curve. Figure 2.2-2 shows the shift of the supply curve from S_1, its position before the adoption of new sawmill technology, to S_2, its position after the adoption of new sawmill technology. Notice that S_2 lies to the right of S_1, reflecting the fact that the quantity supplied rises at any given price.

A **change in supply** is a shift of the supply curve, which indicates a change in the quantity supplied at any given price.

A **movement along the supply curve** is a change in the quantity supplied of a good arising from a change in the good's price.

As in the analysis of demand, it's crucial to draw a distinction between such changes in supply and **movements along the supply curve**—changes in the quantity supplied arising from a change in price. We can see this difference in **Figure 2.2-3**. The movement from point *A* to point *B* is a movement along the supply curve: the quantity supplied rises along S_1 due to a rise in price. Here, a rise in price from $1 to $1.50 leads to a rise in the quantity supplied from 100 billion to 112 billion board feet of lumber. But the quantity supplied can also rise when the price is unchanged if there is an increase in supply—a rightward shift of the supply curve. This is shown by the rightward shift of the supply curve from S_1 to S_2. Holding the price

FIGURE 2.2-2 An Increase in Supply

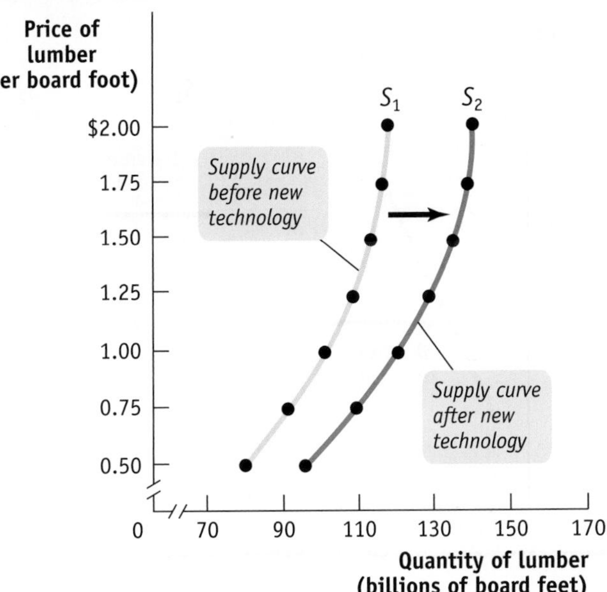

Supply Schedules for Lumber		
Price of lumber (per board foot)	Quantity of lumber supplied (billions of board feet)	
	Before new technology	After new technology
$2.00	116	139
1.75	115	138
1.50	112	134
1.25	107	128
1.00	100	120
0.75	91	109
0.50	80	96

The adoption of improved sawmill technology generated an increase in supply—a rise in the quantity supplied at any given price. This event is represented by the two supply schedules—one showing supply before the new technology was adopted (S_1), the other showing supply after the new technology was adopted (S_2)—and their corresponding supply curves. The increase in supply shifts the supply curve to the right.

FIGURE 2.2-3 A Movement Along the Supply Curve Versus a Shift of the Supply Curve

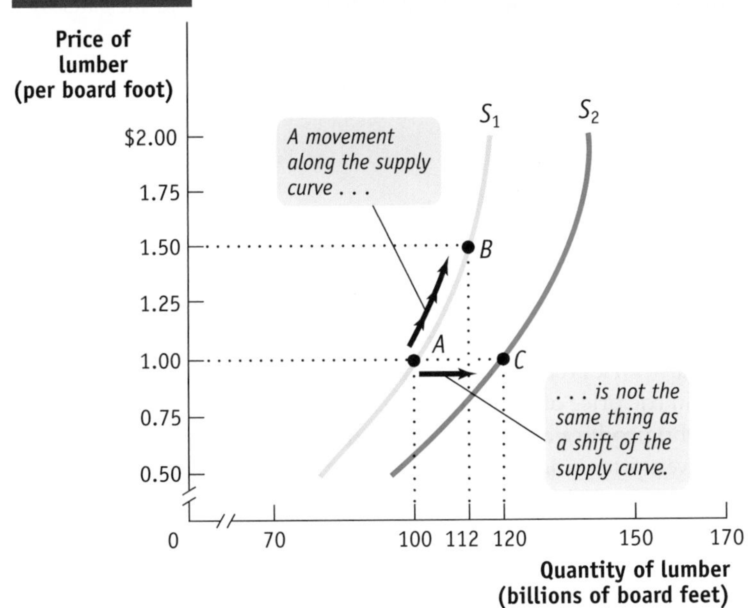

The increase in quantity supplied when going from point *A* to point *B* reflects a movement along the supply curve: it is the result of a rise in the price of the good. The increase in quantity supplied when going from point *A* to point *C* reflects a shift of the supply curve from S_1 to S_2: it is the result of an increase in the quantity supplied at any given price.

constant at $1, the quantity supplied rises from 100 billion board feet at point *A* on S_1 to 120 billion board feet at point *C* on S_2.

Understanding Shifts of the Supply Curve

Figure 2.2-4 illustrates the two basic ways in which supply curves can shift. When economists talk about an "increase in supply," they mean a *rightward* shift of the supply

FIGURE 2.2-4 Shifts of the Supply Curve

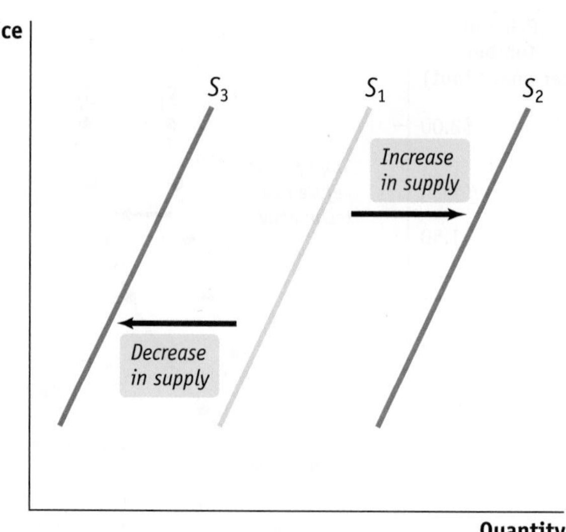

Any event that increases supply shifts the supply curve to the right, reflecting a rise in the quantity supplied at any given price. Any event that decreases supply shifts the supply curve to the left, reflecting a fall in the quantity supplied at any given price.

> **AP® ECON TIP**
>
> A price change causes a change in the quantity supplied, shown by a movement along the supply curve. When a nonprice determinant of supply changes, this changes supply and therefore shifts the supply curve. It is correct to say that an increase in the price of apples increases the *quantity of apples supplied*; it is incorrect to say that an increase in the price of apples *increases the supply of apples*.

An **input** is a good or service that is used to produce another good or service.

curve: at any given price, producers supply a larger quantity of the good than before. This is shown in Figure 2.2-4 by the rightward shift of the original supply curve S_1 to S_2. And when economists talk about a "decrease in supply," they mean a *leftward* shift of the supply curve: at any given price, producers supply a smaller quantity of the good than before. This is represented by the leftward shift of S_1 to S_3.

Shifts of the supply curve for a good or service are typically the result of a change in one of five factors (though, as in the case of demand, there are other possible causes):

- input prices
- the prices of related goods or services
- producer expectations
- the number of producers
- technology

Table 2.2-1 provides an overview of the factors that shift supply.

Changes in Input Prices To produce output, you need *inputs*. An **input** is any good or service used to produce another good or service. For example, to make vanilla ice cream, you need vanilla beans, cream, sugar, and so on. Inputs, like outputs, have prices. And an increase in the price of an input makes the production of the final good more costly for those who produce and sell it. So producers are less willing to supply the final good at any given price, and the supply curve shifts to the left. For example, when lumber prices surged in 2021, construction companies began cutting back on new projects. Similarly, a fall in the price of an input makes the production of the final good less costly for sellers. They are more willing to supply the good at any given price, and the supply curve shifts to the right.

Changes in the Prices of Related Goods or Services A single producer often produces a mix of goods rather than a single product. For example, an oil refinery produces gasoline from crude oil, but it also produces heating oil and other products from the same raw material. When a producer sells several products, the quantity of any one good it is willing to supply at any given price depends on the prices of its other co-produced goods.

How a price change for one of the goods affects the supply of a related good depends on the relationship between the goods. When a producer can use the same inputs to

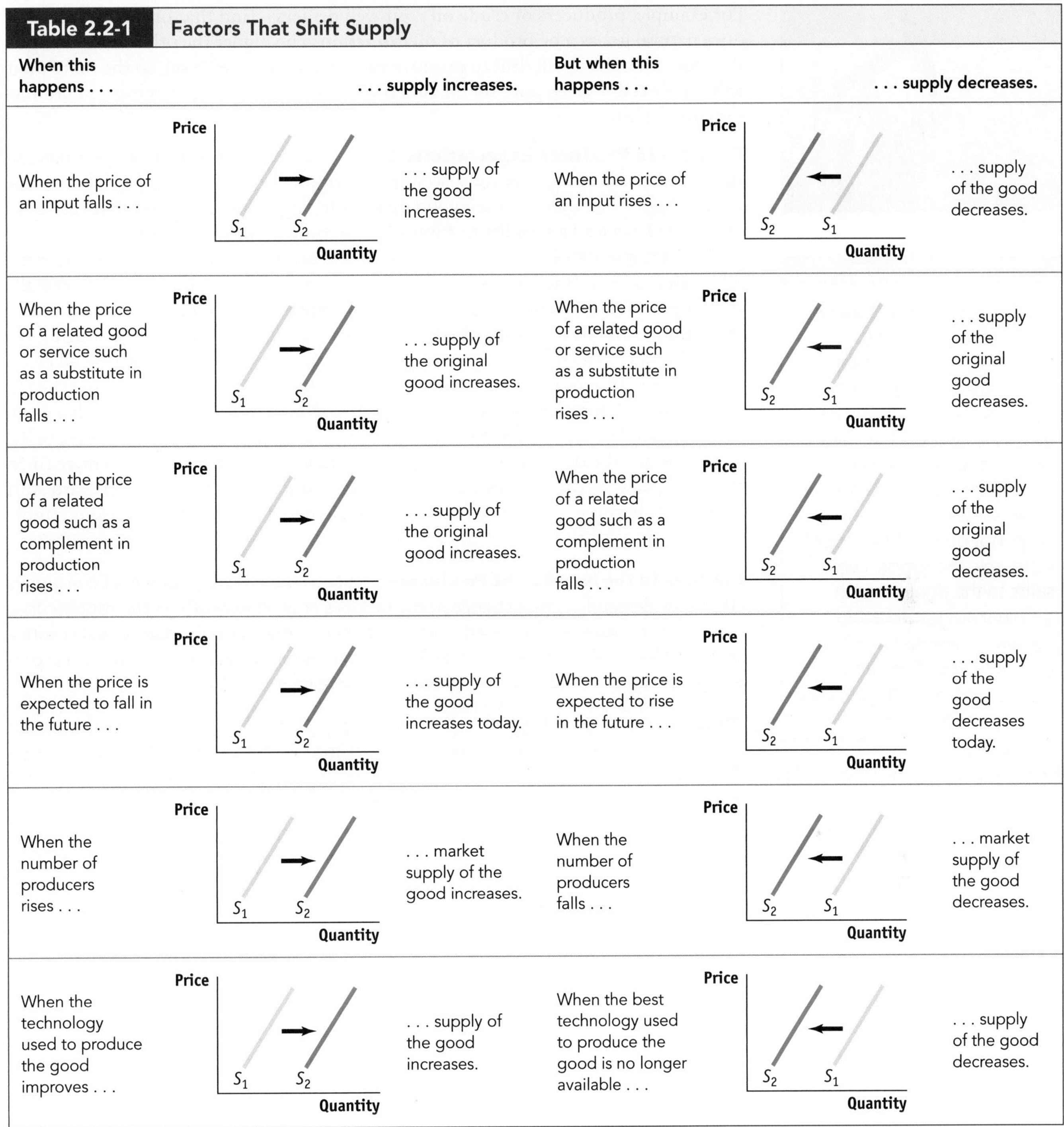

Table 2.2-1 Factors That Shift Supply

When this happens . . .	. . . supply increases.	But when this happens . . .	. . . supply decreases.
When the price of an input falls . . .	. . . supply of the good increases.	When the price of an input rises . . .	. . . supply of the good decreases.
When the price of a related good or service such as a substitute in production falls . . .	. . . supply of the original good increases.	When the price of a related good or service such as a substitute in production rises . . .	. . . supply of the original good decreases.
When the price of a related good such as a complement in production rises . . .	. . . supply of the original good increases.	When the price of a related good such as a complement in production falls . . .	. . . supply of the original good decreases.
When the price is expected to fall in the future . . .	. . . supply of the good increases today.	When the price is expected to rise in the future . . .	. . . supply of the good decreases today.
When the number of producers rises . . .	. . . market supply of the good increases.	When the number of producers falls . . .	. . . market supply of the good decreases.
When the technology used to produce the good improves . . .	. . . supply of the good increases.	When the best technology used to produce the good is no longer available . . .	. . . supply of the good decreases.

make either one good or the other, the two goods are **substitutes in production**. For such goods, an increase in the price of one good creates an incentive for the producer to use more inputs to produce the good whose price has risen and to supply less of the other good. For example, when the price of heating oil rises, an oil refiner will use more crude oil to make heating oil and supply less gasoline at any given price, shifting the supply curve for gasoline to the left. When the price of heating oil falls, the oil refiner will supply more gasoline at any given price, shifting the supply curve for gasoline to the right.

When two goods are jointly produced, meaning that increased production of either of the goods creates more of the other good, the two goods are **complements in production**.

Two goods are **substitutes in production** if producers can use the same inputs to make either one good or the other.

Two goods are **complements in production** if increased production of either good creates more of the other.

For example, producers of crude oil – oil-well drillers – find that oil wells often produce natural gas as a by-product of oil extraction. The higher the price of natural gas, the more oil wells it will drill to produce natural gas along with oil, so the more oil it will supply at any given price for oil. As a result, natural gas is a complement in production for crude oil.

Changes in Producer Expectations Just as changes in consumer expectations can shift the demand curve, they can also shift the supply curve. When suppliers have some choice about when they put their good up for sale, changes in the expected future price of the good can lead a supplier to supply less or more of the good today.

For example, gasoline and other oil products are often stored for significant periods of time at oil refineries before being sold to consumers. In fact, storage is normally part of producers' business strategy. Knowing that the demand for gasoline peaks in the summer, oil refiners normally reserve some of their gasoline produced during the spring for sale in the summer. Similarly, knowing that the demand for heating oil peaks in the winter, they normally reserve some of their heating oil produced during the fall for sale in the winter. In each case, producers make a decision of when to sell a given product based on a comparison of the current price versus the expected future price. This example illustrates how changes in expectations can alter supply: an increase in the anticipated future price of a good or service reduces supply today, a leftward shift of the supply curve. Similarly, a fall in the anticipated future price increases supply today, a rightward shift of the supply curve.

AP® ECON TIP

A change in supply is shown by a shift of the curve, indicating a change in the quantity supplied at every price. Remember: *left is less and right is more*. But looks can be deceiving. When supply decreases, the supply curve shifts to the left—which is up, not down. When supply increases, the supply curve shifts to the right—which is down, not up. To avoid confusion, always think "right" and "left" (not "up" and "down") when shifting supply and demand curves.

Changes in the Number of Producers Just as a change in the number of consumers affects the demand curve, a change in the number of producers affects the supply curve. A market with many producers will supply a larger quantity of a good than a market with a single producer, all other things equal. For example, when the patent runs out on a profitable pharmaceutical drug, new suppliers enter the market, and the supply increases.

Changes in Technology When economists talk about "technology," they mean all the methods people can use to turn inputs into useful goods and services. In that sense, the whole complex sequence of activities that turn lumber harvested and milled in Canada into the shelves in your closet is technology.

Improvements in technology enable producers to spend less on inputs yet still produce the same output. When a better technology becomes available, reducing the cost of production, supply increases, and the supply curve shifts to the right. As we have already mentioned, improved technology enabled sawmills to keep lumber prices low for decades, even as worldwide demand grew.

AP® ECON TIP

The mnemonic *I-RENT* can help you remember the factors that shift supply. Supply is shifted by changes in . . . **I**nput (resource) prices, prices of **R**elated goods and services, producer **E**xpectations, the **N**umber of producers, and **T**echnology.

Individual Versus Market Supply Curves

Now that we have introduced the market supply curve, let's examine how it relates to a producer's **individual supply curve**. Look at panel (a) in **Figure 2.2-5**. The individual supply curve shows the relationship between quantity supplied and price for an individual producer. For example, suppose that Mr. Silva owns a sawmill in Brazil and that panel (a) of Figure 2.2-5 shows how many board feet of lumber he will supply per year at any given price. Then S_{Silva} is his individual supply curve.

An **individual supply curve** illustrates the relationship between quantity supplied and price for an individual producer.

The *market supply curve* shows how the combined total quantity supplied by all individual producers in the market depends on the market price of that good. Just as the market demand curve is the horizontal sum of the individual demand curves of all consumers, the market supply curve is the horizontal sum of the individual supply curves of all producers. Assume for a moment that there are only two producers of lumber, Mr. Silva and Ms. Liu, who operates a sawmill in China. Ms. Liu's individual supply curve is shown in panel (b). Panel (c) shows the market supply curve. At any given price, the quantity supplied to the market is the sum of the quantities supplied by Mr. Silva and Ms. Liu. For example, at a price of $2 per board foot, Mr. Silva supplies 30,000 board feet of lumber per year and Ms. Liu supplies 20,000 board feet per year, making the quantity supplied to the market 50,000 board feet.

FIGURE 2.2-5 Individual Supply Curves and the Market Supply Curve

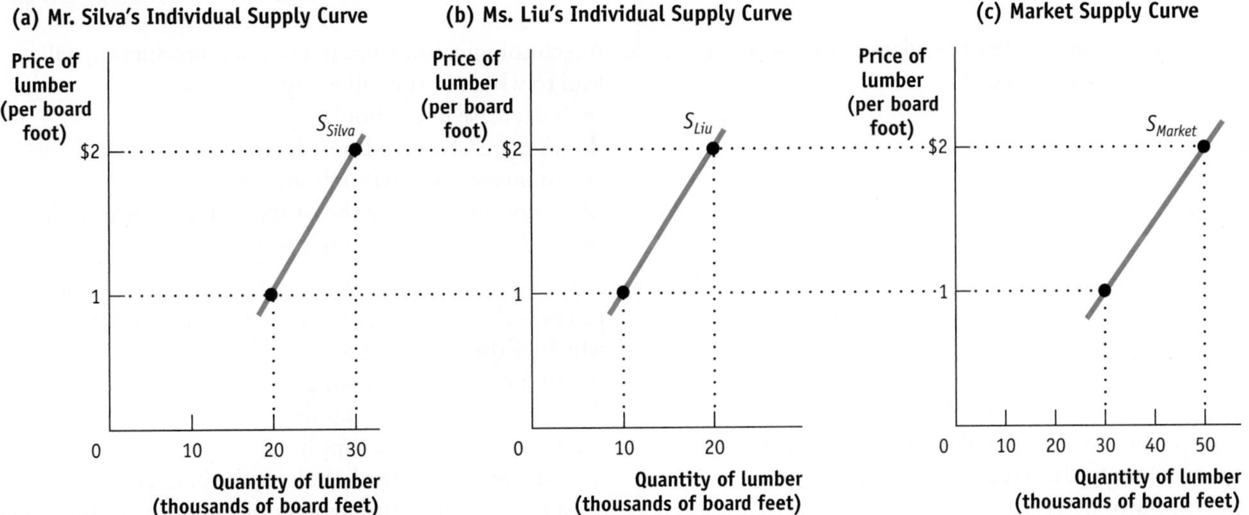

Panel (a) shows the individual supply curve for Mr. Silva, S_{Silva}, which indicates the quantity of lumber he will sell at any given price. Panel (b) shows the individual supply curve for Ms. Liu, S_{Liu}. The *market supply curve*, which shows the quantity of lumber supplied by all producers at any given price, is in panel (c). The market supply curve is the *horizontal sum* of the individual supply curves of all producers.

Clearly, the quantity supplied to the market at any given price is larger with Ms. Liu present than it would be if Mr. Silva were the only supplier. The quantity supplied at a given price would be even larger if we added a third producer, then a fourth, and so on. So an increase in the number of producers leads to an increase in supply and a rightward shift of the supply curve.

Adventures in AP® Economics

Watch the video: ***Supply***

Module 2.2  Review

Check Your Understanding

1. Explain whether each of the following events represents (i) a *change in* supply (a *shift* in the supply curve) or (ii) a *movement along* the supply curve (a *change in the quantity supplied*).
   a. During a real estate boom that causes home prices to rise, more homeowners put their homes up for sale.
   b. Many strawberry farmers open temporary roadside stands during harvest season, even though prices are usually low at that time.
   c. Immediately after the school year begins, fewer young people are available to work. Fast-food chains must raise wages, which represent the price of labor, to attract workers.
   d. Many construction workers temporarily move to areas that have suffered hurricane damage, lured by higher wages.
   e. Since new technologies have made it possible to build larger cruise ships (which are cheaper to run per passenger), Caribbean cruise lines have offered more cabins, at lower prices, than before.
2. After each of the following events, will the supply curve for the good that is mentioned shift to the left, shift to the right, or remain unchanged?
   a. The coffee berry borer beetle destroys large quantities of coffee berries.
   b. Consumers demand more bike helmets than ever.
   c. The number of tea producers increases.
   d. The price of leather, an input in wallet production, increases.

Tackle the AP® Test: Multiple-Choice Questions

1. The law of supply states that the relationship between price and quantity supplied is
   a. positive.
   b. negative.
   c. indirect.
   d. unclear.
   e. weak.

2. Because the market supply curve is the sum of individual producers' supply curves, an increase in the number of producers will cause which of the following?
   a. the supply curve to shift to the left
   b. the supply curve to shift to the right
   c. a movement to the right along the supply curve
   d. a movement to the left along the supply curve
   e. the supply to decrease

3. Which of the following will decrease the supply of rice?
   a. There is a technological advance that affects the production of *all* goods.
   b. The price of rice falls.
   c. The price of corn (which consumers regard as a substitute for rice) decreases.
   d. The wages of workers producing rice increase.
   e. The demand for rice decreases.

4. An increase in the demand for steak, which increases the price of steak, will lead to an increase in which of the following?
   a. the supply of steak
   b. the supply of hamburger (a substitute in production)
   c. the supply of chicken (a substitute in consumption)
   d. the supply of leather (a complement in production)
   e. the demand for leather

5. A technological advance in textbook production will lead to which of the following?
   a. a decrease in textbook supply
   b. an increase in textbook demand
   c. an increase in textbook supply
   d. a movement along the supply curve for textbooks
   e. an increase in textbook prices

6. Expectations among hiking-boot makers that boot prices will rise significantly in the future will lead to which of the following now?
   a. an increase in boot supply
   b. no change in boot supply
   c. a decrease in boot supply
   d. a movement to the left along the boot supply curve
   e. a movement to the right along the boot supply curve

7. Starch from the stalks of potato plants is used to make packing peanuts, a complement in production. A decrease in potato demand that lowers potato prices will cause which of the following in the packing-peanut market?
   a. an increase in supply and no change in demand
   b. an increase in supply and a decrease in demand
   c. a decrease in both demand and supply
   d. a decrease in supply and no change in demand
   e. a decrease in supply and an increase in demand

Tackle the AP® Test: Free-Response Questions

1. Tesla Motors makes sports cars powered by lithium batteries.
   a. Draw a correctly labeled graph showing a hypothetical supply curve for Tesla sports cars.
   b. On the same graph, show the effect of a major new discovery of lithium that lowers the price of lithium.
   c. Suppose Tesla Motors expects to be able to sell its cars for a higher price next month. Explain the effect that will have on the supply of Tesla cars this month.

Rubric for FRQ 1 (4 points)

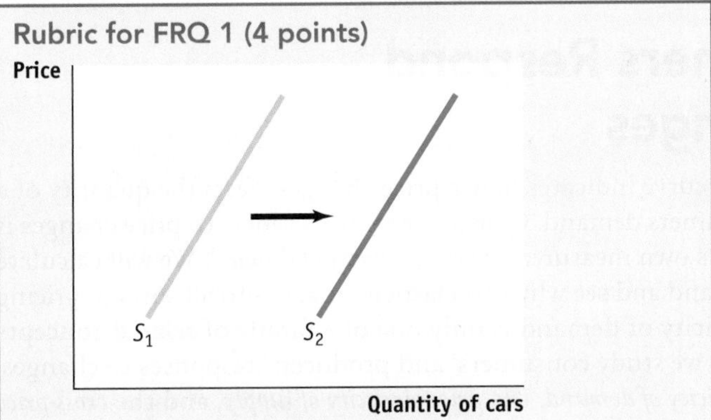

1 point: Graph with "Price" or "P" on the vertical axis and "Quantity" or "Q" on the horizontal axis

1 point: A positively sloped curve labeled "Supply" or "S"

1 point: A second supply curve shown to the right of the original supply curve with a label such as S_2, indicating that it is the new supply curve

1 point: Correct explanation that the expectation of higher prices next month would lead to a decrease in the supply of Tesla cars this month because the company will want to sell more of its cars when the price is higher

2. Suppose AP® Economics students at your school offer tutoring services to students in regular economics courses.
   a. Draw a correctly labeled graph showing the supply curve for tutoring services measured in hours. Label the supply curve "S_1."
   b. Suppose the wage paid for babysitting, an alternative activity for AP® Economics students, increases. Show the effect of this wage increase on the graph you drew for part a. Label the new supply curve "S_2."
   c. Suppose instead that the number of AP® Economics students increases. Show the effect of this increase in AP® Economics students on the same graph you drew for parts a and b. Label the new supply curve "S_3." **(5 points)**

MODULE 2.3

Price Elasticity of Demand

In this Module, you will learn to:
- Discuss the role of substitution and income effects
- Define elasticity
- Explain measures of elasticity using graphs
- Describe the relationship between elasticity and total revenue
- Calculate the price elasticity of demand and identify its determinants

How Consumers Respond to Price Changes

The shape of the demand curve indicates how a price change affects the quantity of a good or service that consumers demand. Consumer responsiveness to price changes is so important that it has its own measure: *the price elasticity of demand.* We will calculate the price elasticity of demand and see why this elasticity matters to all sorts of pricing decisions. The price elasticity of demand is only one of a family of related concepts that we will find useful as we study consumers' and producers' responses to changes, including the *income elasticity of demand*, the *price elasticity of supply*, and the *cross-price elasticity of demand.*

We begin with the *substitution* and *income effects*, which give the demand curve its shape.

The Substitution Effect

When the price of a good increases, an individual will normally buy less of that good and more of other goods. And when the price of a good decreases, an individual will normally buy more of that good and less of other goods. This explains why the individual demand curve, which relates an individual's consumption of a good to the price of that good, normally obeys the law of demand and slopes downward.

Another way to think about why demand curves slope downward is to focus on opportunity costs. For simplicity, let's suppose there are only two goods between which to choose: Good 1 and Good 2. When the price of Good 1 decreases, an individual doesn't have to give up as many units of Good 2 in order to buy one more unit of Good 1. That makes it attractive to buy more of Good 1, whose price has gone down. Conversely, when the price of Good 1 increases, one must give up more units of Good 2 to buy one more unit of Good 1, so consuming Good 1 becomes less attractive and the consumer buys fewer.

The change in the quantity demanded as the good that has become relatively cheaper is substituted for the good that has become relatively more expensive is known as the **substitution effect**. When a good absorbs only a small share of the typical consumer's income, as with pillowcases and kites, the substitution effect is essentially the sole explanation of why the market demand curve slopes downward. However, there are some goods, like food and housing, that account for a substantial share of many consumers' incomes. In such cases, another effect, called the *income effect,* also comes into play.

The **substitution effect** of a change in the price of a good is the change in the quantity of that good demanded as the consumer substitutes the good that has become relatively cheaper for the good that has become relatively more expensive.

The Income Effect

Consider the case of a family that spends half of its income on rental housing. Now suppose that the price of housing increases everywhere. This change will have a substitution effect on the family's demand: other things equal, the family will have an incentive to consume less housing—say, by moving to a smaller apartment—and more of other goods. But, in a real sense, the family will also be made poorer by that higher housing price—its income will buy less housing than before. When income is adjusted to reflect its true purchasing power, it is called *real income*, in contrast to *money income* or *nominal income*, which has not been adjusted.

This reduction in a consumer's real income will have an additional effect, beyond the substitution effect, on the amount of housing and other goods the family chooses to buy. The **income effect** of a change in the price of a good is the change in the quantity of that good demanded that results from a change in the overall purchasing power of the consumer's income when the price of the good changes.

For the majority of goods, the income effect of a price change is not important and has no significant effect on individual consumption. Thus, most market demand curves slope downward solely because of the substitution effect—end of story. When it does matter, the income effect usually reinforces the substitution effect. That is, when the price rises on a good that absorbs a substantial share of income, consumers of that good feel poorer because their purchasing power falls. And for all *normal* goods—goods for which demand decreases when income falls—this reduction in real income leads to a reduction in the quantity demanded and reinforces the substitution effect.

Module 2.1 introduced both normal goods and *inferior goods*—those goods, such as canned meat and ramen noodles, for which demand increases when income falls. In the case of an inferior good, the income and substitution effects work in opposite directions. For example, suppose the price of canned meat increases. The resulting substitution effect is a decrease in the quantity of canned meat demanded, because for both normal and inferior goods, the substitution effect of a price increase is a decrease in the quantity demanded of the good whose price has risen. But the income effect of a price increase for canned meat is an *increase* in the quantity demanded. This makes sense because the price increase lowers the real income of the consumer, and as real income decreases, the demand for an inferior good increases.

Could the *total effect* of a price increase—the combination of the income effect and the substitution effect—ever be an increase in the quantity demanded? In other words, might we see an increase in the price of ramen noodles lead to an increase in the quantity of ramen noodles demanded? It is conceivable. If a good were so inferior that the income effect exceeded the substitution effect, an increase in the price of that good would lead to an increase in the quantity of that good that is demanded. There is controversy over whether such goods, known as "Giffen goods," exist at all. If they do, they are very rare. You can generally assume that the income effect for an inferior good is smaller than the substitution effect, and so a price increase will lead to a decrease in the quantity demanded.

Next, we will discuss elasticity as a measure of the responsiveness of the quantity demanded to price changes.

AP® ECON TIP

When two terms are similar, you can more easily distinguish them by looking at the definitions next to each other: The *substitution effect* comes from a change in the price of one good relative to the price of another good. The *income effect* of a price change comes from a change in the purchasing power of income. An income effect can also result from a change in the actual income received.

The **income effect** of a change in the price of a good is the change in the quantity of that good demanded that results from a change in the consumer's purchasing power when the price of the good changes.

Kimberly Whitaker/Moment/Getty Images

A price hike on kites does not trigger a significant income effect because expenditures on kites are such a small portion of consumers' income. A price hike on homes, on the other hand, does cause a sizable income effect because consumers spend a large portion of their income on housing.

Defining and Measuring Elasticity

If the price of a good or service increases, we know from the law of demand that the quantity demanded will decrease. But *by how much* will the quantity demanded decrease if the price goes up? A firm considering a price change would certainly want to know! Economists use the *price elasticity of demand* to measure the responsiveness of the quantity demanded to changes in the price. Elasticity can also be used to measure the responsiveness of any other variable to changes in a related variable. We will start by looking at the price elasticity of demand and then consider three other types of elasticities in the next two Modules.

Consider a pharmaceutical company that would like to know whether it could raise its revenue by raising the price of its drugs. To know this, the company would have to know whether the price increase would decrease the quantity demanded by a lot or a little. That is, it would have to know the price elasticity of demand for its products.

Calculating the Price Elasticity of Demand

Figure 2.3-1 shows a hypothetical demand curve for a potentially life-saving medical product purchased by millions of Americans each year, flu vaccinations. At a price of \$20 per vaccination, consumers would demand 10 million vaccinations per year (point *A*); at a price of \$21, the quantity demanded would fall to 9.9 million vaccinations per year (point *B*).

FIGURE 2.3-1 The Demand for Vaccinations

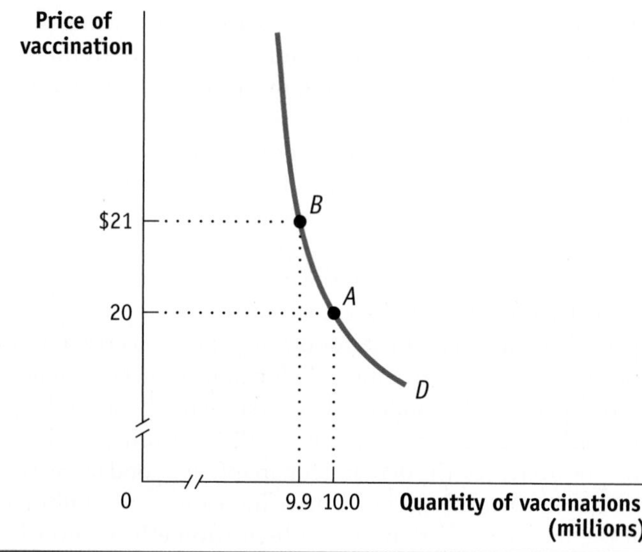

At a price of \$20 per vaccination, the quantity of vaccinations demanded is 10 million per year (point *A*). When price rises to \$21 per vaccination, the quantity demanded falls to 9.9 million vaccinations per year (point *B*). With the price elasticity of demand, one can measure the influence of price changes on the quantity demanded.

Figure 2.3-1, then, tells us the change in the quantity demanded for a particular change in the price. But how can we turn this information into a measure of price responsiveness? The answer is to calculate the price elasticity of demand. The **price elasticity of demand** compares the *percentage change in quantity demanded* to the *percentage change in price* as we move along the demand curve. As we'll see later, economists use percentage changes to get a measure that doesn't depend on the units involved (say, a child-sized dose versus an adult-sized dose of vaccine). But before we get to that, let's look at how elasticity is calculated.

The **price elasticity of demand** is the ratio of the percentage change in the quantity demanded to the percentage change in the price as we move along the demand curve (dropping the minus sign).

To calculate the price elasticity of demand, we first calculate the percentage change in the quantity demanded and the corresponding percentage change in the price as we move along the demand curve. The easiest way to do this, which we will describe as the *simple method* to distinguish it from the *midpoint method* to be discussed a bit later, is as follows:

$$\textbf{(2.3-1)} \quad \% \text{ change in quantity demanded} = \frac{\text{Change in quantity demanded}}{\text{Initial quantity demanded}} \times 100$$

and

$$\textbf{(2.3-2)} \quad \% \text{ change in price} = \frac{\text{Change in price}}{\text{Initial price}} \times 100$$

In Figure 2.3-1, we see that when the price rises from \$20 to \$21, the quantity demanded falls from 10 million to 9.9 million vaccinations, yielding a change in the quantity demanded of 0.1 million vaccinations. So the percentage change in the quantity demanded is

$$\text{\% change in quantity demanded} = \frac{-0.1 \text{ million vaccinations}}{10 \text{ million vaccinations}} \times 100 = -1\%$$

The initial price is \$20 and the change in the price is \$1, so the percentage change in the price is

$$\text{\% change in price} = \frac{\$1}{\$20} \times 100 = 5\%$$

To calculate the price elasticity of demand, we find the ratio of the percentage change in the quantity demanded to the percentage change in the price:

$$\textbf{(2.3-3)} \quad \text{Price elasticity of demand} = \frac{\text{\% change in quantity demanded}}{\text{\% change in price}}$$

In Figure 2.3-1, the price elasticity of demand is therefore

$$\text{Price elasticity of demand} = \frac{1\%}{5\%} = 0.2$$

Notice that we have dropped the minus sign that had been on the percentage change in quantity. The *law of demand* tells us that a positive percentage change in the price (a rise in the price) leads to a negative percentage change in the quantity demanded, and a negative percentage change in the price (a fall in the price) leads to a positive percentage change in the quantity demanded. This makes the price elasticity of demand a negative number. However, when economists talk about the price elasticity of demand, they usually drop the minus sign for convenience and report the absolute value of the price elasticity of demand. In this case, for example, economists would usually say "the price elasticity of demand is 0.2," a kind of shorthand for *minus* 0.2. We follow that convention here.

AP® ECON TIP

Among other useful interpretations, the value of the price elasticity of demand indicates the number of percentage points by which the quantity demanded decreases as a result of a one-percent increase in the price.

To arrive at a more general formula for the price elasticity of demand based on the simple method, suppose that we have data for two points on a demand curve. At point 1, the quantity demanded and the price are (Q_1, P_1); at point 2, they are (Q_2, P_2). Then the simple formula for calculating the price elasticity of demand is

$$\textbf{(2.3-4)} \quad \text{Price elasticity of demand} = \frac{\dfrac{Q_2 - Q_1}{Q_1}}{\dfrac{P_2 - P_1}{P_1}}$$

And don't forget to drop the minus sign!

AP® ECON TIP

Be sure to use *absolute values* when computing the price elasticity of demand. In other words, always write the price elasticity of demand as a positive number.

The larger the price elasticity of demand, the more responsive the quantity demanded is to the price. When the price elasticity of demand is large—when consumers change their quantity demanded by a large percentage compared with the percentage change in the price—economists say that demand is highly elastic.

As we'll see shortly, a price elasticity of 0.2 indicates a small response of the quantity demanded to the price. That is, the quantity demanded will fall by a relatively small amount when the price rises. This is what economists call *inelastic* demand. Later in this Module, we'll see why inelastic demand is exactly what a pharmaceutical company needs to succeed with a strategy to increase revenue by raising the price of its flu vaccines.

An Alternative Way to Calculate Elasticities: The Midpoint Method

At this point we need to discuss a technical issue that arises when you calculate percentage changes in variables and how economists deal with it. In our previous example, we found an elasticity of demand for vaccinations of 0.200 when considering a movement from point *A* to point *B*. However, when going from point *B* to point *A*, the same elasticity formula would indicate an elasticity of 0.212 (for useful practice, try this calculation). This is a nuisance: we'd like to have an elasticity measure that doesn't depend on the direction of change. A good way to avoid computing different elasticities for rising and falling prices is to use the *midpoint method* (sometimes called the *arc method*).

Using the midpoint method, we calculate the percentage change by dividing the change in a variable by the average, or midpoint, of the initial and final values of that variable. So the average value of a variable, *X*, is defined as

$$\text{Average value of } X = \frac{\text{Initial value of } X + \text{Final value of } X}{2}$$

When calculating the price elasticity of demand using the midpoint method, both the percentage change in the price and the percentage change in the quantity demanded are found using average values in this way. To see how this method works, suppose you have the following data for chocolate bars:

	Price	Quantity demanded
Situation A	$0.90	1,100
Situation B	$1.10	900

To calculate the percentage change in quantity going from situation A to situation B, we compare the change in the quantity demanded—a fall of 200 units—with the *average* of the quantity demanded in the two situations. So we calculate

$$\%\text{ change in quantity demanded} = \frac{-200}{(1{,}100+900)/2} \times 100 = \frac{-200}{1{,}000} \times 100 = -20\%$$

In the same way, we calculate the percentage change in price as

$$\%\text{ change in price} = \frac{\$0.20}{(\$0.90+\$1.10)/2} \times 100 = \frac{\$0.20}{\$1.00} \times 100 = 20\%$$

So in this case we would calculate the price elasticity of demand to be

$$\text{Price elasticity of demand} = \frac{\%\text{ change in quantity demanded}}{\%\text{ change in price}} = \frac{20\%}{20\%} = 1$$

Again, we have dropped the minus sign.

The important point is that we would get the same result, a price elasticity of demand of 1, whether we went up the demand curve from situation A to situation B or down from situation B to situation A.

AP® ECON TIP

If an exam question requires you to calculate an elasticity and does not indicate which formula to use, that typically means the graders will accept the use of either formula, and you can use whichever formula you are most comfortable with.

The general formula for the price elasticity of demand based on the midpoint method, moving between point 1, where the quantity demanded and the price are (Q_1, P_1) and point 2, where they are (Q_2, P_2), is

$$\textbf{(2.3-5)} \quad \text{Price elasticity of demand} = \frac{\dfrac{Q_2 - Q_1}{(Q_1 + Q_2)/2}}{\dfrac{P_2 - P_1}{(P_1 + P_2)/2}}$$

You guessed it—minus the minus sign.

Elasticity Estimates

In 1970, economists Hendrik S. Houthakker and Lester D. Taylor published a comprehensive study that estimated the price elasticities of demand for a wide variety of goods. Some of their results are summarized in **Table 2.3-1**. These estimates show a wide range of price elasticities. There are some goods, such as eggs, for which demand hardly responds at all to changes in the price; there are other goods, most notably foreign travel, for which the quantity demanded is very sensitive to the price.

Notice that Table 2.3-1 is divided into two parts: inelastic demand and elastic demand. Inelastic demand is *less responsive* to price changes than elastic demand. We'll explain the significance of that division next.

Table 2.3-1 Some Estimated Price Elasticities of Demand

Good	Price elasticity of demand
Inelastic demand	
Eggs	0.1
Beef	0.4
Stationery	0.5
Gasoline	0.5
Elastic demand	
Housing	1.2
Restaurant meals	2.3
Airline travel	2.4
Foreign travel	4.1

Data from: Hendrick S. Houthakker and Lester D. Taylor, *Consumer Demand in the United States, 1929–1970* (Harvard University Press, 1970).

What the Price Elasticity of Demand Tells Us

Well into the coronavirus pandemic, Pfizer-BioNTech raised the price of its COVID-19 vaccine by about 25% in some countries because the price elasticity of demand was low. But what does that mean? How low does a price elasticity have to be for it to be classified as low? How high does it have to be for it to be considered high? And what determines whether the price elasticity of demand is high or low? To answer these questions, we need to look more deeply at the price elasticity of demand.

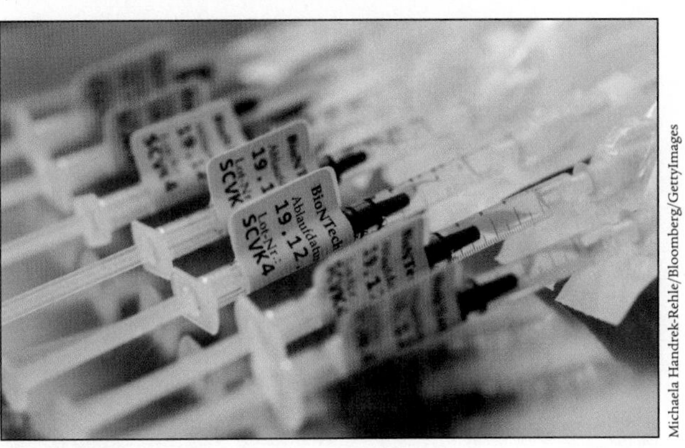

Michaela Handrek-Rehle/Bloomberg/Getty Images

How Elastic Is Elastic?

As a first step toward classifying price elasticities of demand, let's look at two extreme cases. First, consider the demand for a good when people pay no attention to its price. Suppose, for example, that consumers would buy 1 million heart bypass surgeries per year regardless of the price. If that were true, the demand curve for these surgeries would look like the curve shown in panel (a) of **Figure 2.3-2**: it would be a vertical line at 1 million heart bypass surgeries. Since the percentage change in the quantity demanded is zero for *any* change in the price, the price elasticity of demand

FIGURE 2.3-2 Two Extreme Cases of Price Elasticity of Demand

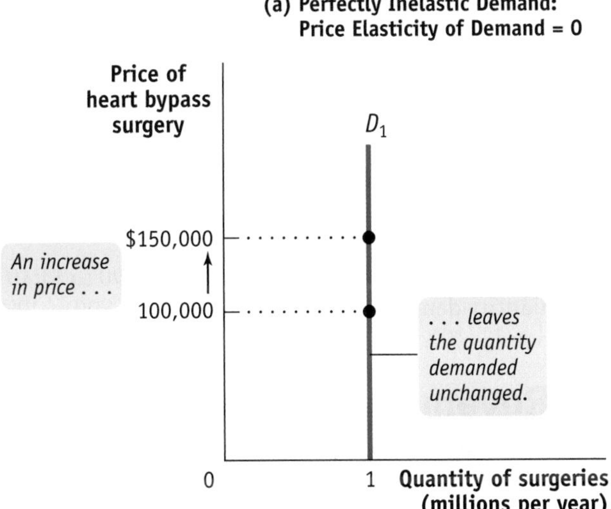

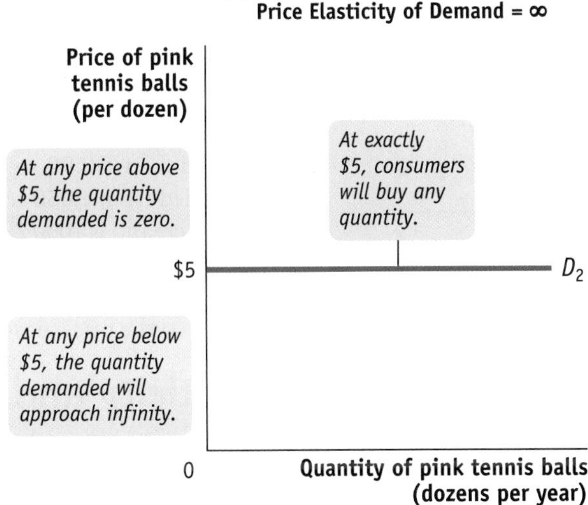

Panel (a) shows a perfectly inelastic demand curve, which is a vertical line. The quantity of heart bypass surgeries demanded is always 1 million, regardless of the price. As a result, the price elasticity of demand is zero—the quantity demanded is unaffected by the price. Panel (b) shows a perfectly elastic demand curve, which is a horizontal line. At a price of $5, consumers will buy any quantity of pink tennis balls, but they will buy none at a price above $5. As a result, the price elasticity of demand is infinite.

Demand is **perfectly inelastic** when the quantity demanded does not respond at all to changes in the price. When demand is perfectly inelastic, the demand curve is a vertical line.

Demand is **perfectly elastic** when any price increase will cause the quantity demanded to drop to zero. When demand is perfectly elastic, the demand curve is a horizontal line.

Demand is **elastic** if the price elasticity of demand is greater than 1, **inelastic** if the price elasticity of demand is less than 1, and **unit-elastic** if the price elasticity of demand is exactly 1.

in this case is zero. The case of a zero price elasticity of demand is known as **perfectly inelastic** demand.

The opposite extreme occurs when even a tiny rise in the price will cause the quantity demanded to drop to zero or when even a tiny fall in the price will cause the quantity demanded to get extremely large. Panel (b) of Figure 2.3-2 shows the case of pink tennis balls; we suppose that tennis players don't have a color preference, and that other tennis ball colors, such as neon green and vivid yellow, are available at $5 per dozen balls. In this case, consumers will buy no pink tennis balls if they cost more than $5 per dozen. But if pink tennis balls cost less than $5 per dozen, consumers will buy no other color. The demand curve will therefore be a horizontal line at a price of $5 per dozen. If the price falls from above $5 to below $5, the quantity demanded will rise from zero to a number approaching infinity. So a horizontal demand curve implies an infinite price elasticity of demand. When the price elasticity of demand is infinite, economists say that demand is **perfectly elastic**.

The price elasticity of demand for the vast majority of goods is somewhere between these two extreme cases. Economists use one level of magnitude for classifying these intermediate cases: they ask whether the price elasticity of demand is greater or less than 1. When the price elasticity of demand is greater than 1, economists say that demand is **elastic**. When the price elasticity of demand is less than 1, they say that demand is **inelastic**. The borderline case is **unit-elastic** demand, where the price elasticity of demand is—surprise—exactly 1.

PR images/Alamy

When the Washington State Transportation Commission decided to raise the toll for the SR 520 bridge in 2023, at issue was the price elasticity of demand, which would determine the resulting drop in use.

To see why a price elasticity of demand equal to 1 is a useful dividing line, let's consider a hypothetical example: a toll bridge operated by the state highway department. Other things equal, the number of drivers who use the bridge depends on the toll, the price the highway department charges for crossing the bridge: the higher the toll, the fewer the drivers who use the bridge.

Figure 2.3-3 shows three hypothetical demand curves that exhibit unit-elastic demand, inelastic demand, and elastic demand, respectively. In each case, point *A* shows the quantity demanded if the toll is $0.90, and point *B* shows the quantity demanded if the toll is $1.10. An increase in the toll from $0.90 to $1.10 is a 20% increase if we use the midpoint method to calculate the percentage change.

Panel (a) shows what happens when the toll is raised from $0.90 to $1.10 and the demand curve is unit-elastic. Here the 20% increase in price leads to a fall in the quantity of cars using the bridge each day from 1,100 to 900, a 20% decline (again using the midpoint method). So the price elasticity of demand is 20%/20% = 1.

Panel (b) shows a case of inelastic demand when the toll is raised from $0.90 to $1.10. The same 20% increase in price reduces the quantity demanded from 1,050 to 950. That's only a 10% decline, so in this case the price elasticity of demand is 10%/20% = 0.5.

Panel (c) shows a case of elastic demand when the toll is raised from $0.90 to $1.10. The 20% price increase causes the quantity demanded to fall from 1,200 to 800, a 40% decline, so the price elasticity of demand is 40%/20% = 2.

Elasticity and Total Revenue

Why does it matter whether demand is unit-elastic, inelastic, or elastic? Because this classification indicates how changes in the price of a good will affect the *total revenue* earned by producers from the sale of that good. In many real-life situations, such as the one faced by Pfizer-BioNTech, it is crucial to know how price changes affect total revenue. **Total revenue** is defined as the total value of sales of a good or service: the price multiplied by the quantity sold.

Total revenue is the total value of sales of a good or service. It is equal to the price multiplied by the quantity sold.

(2.3-5) Total revenue = Price × Quantity sold

FIGURE 2.3-3 Unit-Elastic Demand, Inelastic Demand, and Elastic Demand

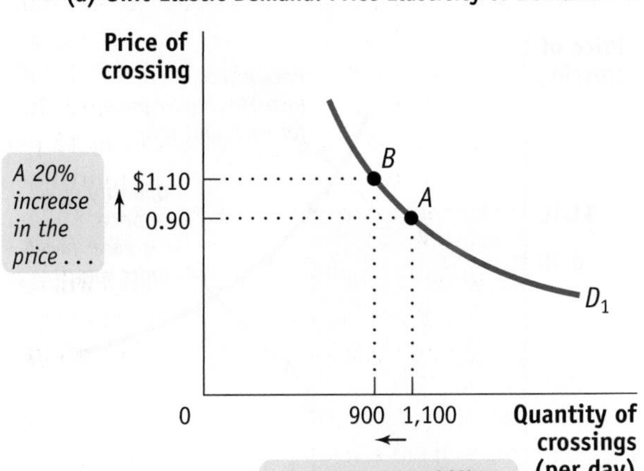

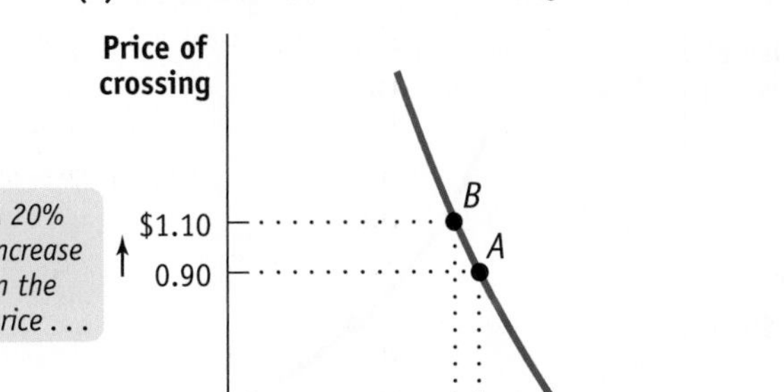

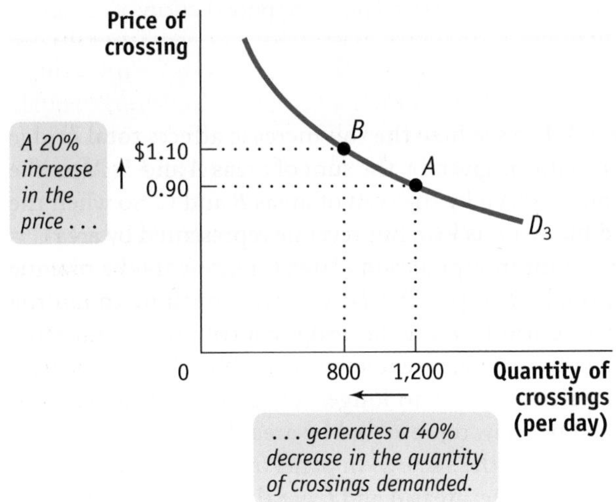

Panel (a) shows a case of unit-elastic demand: a 20% increase in price generates a 20% decline in quantity demanded, implying a price elasticity of demand of 1. Panel (b) shows a case of inelastic demand: a 20% increase in price generates a 10% decline in quantity demanded, implying a price elasticity of demand of 0.5. Panel (c) shows a case of elastic demand: a 20% increase in price causes a 40% decline in quantity demanded, implying a price elasticity of demand of 2. All percentages are calculated using the midpoint method.

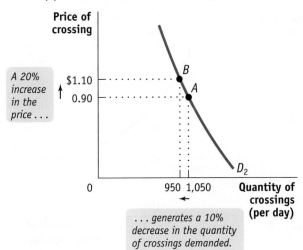

A useful graphical representation can help us understand why knowing the price elasticity of demand is crucial when we ask whether an increase in price will increase or decrease total revenue. Panel (a) of **Figure 2.3-4** shows the same demand curve as panel (a) of Figure 2.3-3. We see that 1,100 drivers will use the bridge if the toll is $0.90. So the total revenue at a price of $0.90 is $\$0.90 \times 1{,}100 = \$990$. This value is equal to the area of the green rectangle, which is drawn with the bottom left corner at the point (0, 0) and the top right corner at (1,100, 0.90). In general, the total revenue at any given price is equal to the area of a rectangle whose height is the price and whose width is the quantity demanded at that price.

To get an idea of why total revenue is important, consider the following scenario. Suppose that the toll on the bridge is currently $0.90 but that the highway department must raise extra money for road repairs. One way to do this is to raise the toll on the bridge. But this plan might backfire, since a higher toll will reduce the number of drivers who use the bridge. And if traffic on the bridge dropped by a high enough percentage, a higher toll would actually reduce total revenue instead of increasing it. So it's important for the highway department to know how drivers will respond to a toll increase.

AP® ECON TIP

When thinking of perfectly inelastic demand, think *I = Inelastic*, with the I representing the vertical perfectly inelastic demand curve. When thinking of perfectly elastic demand, think *E = Elastic*, with the horizontal middle line of the E representing the horizontal perfectly elastic demand curve.

FIGURE 2.3-4 Total Revenue

(a) Total Revenue by Area

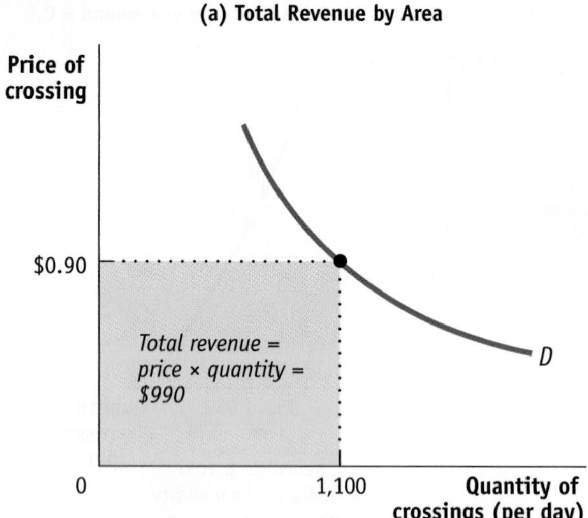

(b) Effect of a Price Increase on Total Revenue

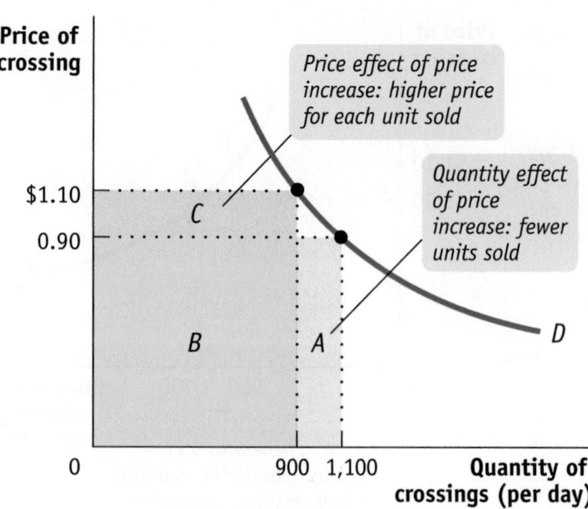

The green rectangle in panel (a) represents the total revenue generated from 1,100 drivers who each pay a toll of $0.90. Panel (b) shows how total revenue is affected when the price increases from $0.90 to $1.10. Due to the quantity effect, total revenue falls by area *A*. Due to the price effect, total revenue increases by area *C*. In general, the net effect can go either way, depending on the price elasticity of demand.

Examine panel (b) of Figure 2.3-4 to see how the toll increase affects total bridge revenue. At a toll of $0.90, total revenue is given by the sum of areas *A* and *B*. After the toll is raised to $1.10, total revenue is given by the sum of areas *B* and *C*. So when the toll is raised, revenue represented by area *A* is lost, but revenue represented by area *C* is gained. These two areas have important interpretations. Area *C* represents the revenue gain that comes from the additional $0.20 paid by drivers who continue to use the bridge. That is, the 900 drivers who continue to use the bridge contribute an additional $0.20 × 900 = $180 per day to total revenue, represented by area *C*. But 200 drivers who would have used the bridge at a price of $0.90 no longer do so, generating a loss to total revenue of $0.90 × 200 = $180 per day, represented by area *A*. (In this particular example, because demand is unit-elastic—the same as in panel (a) of Figure 2.3-3—the rise in the toll has no effect on total revenue; areas *A* and *C* are the same size.)

Except in the rare case of a good with perfectly elastic or perfectly inelastic demand, when a seller raises the price of a good, two countervailing effects are present:

- *A price effect.* After a price increase, each unit sold sells at a higher price, which tends to raise revenue.
- *A quantity effect.* After a price increase, fewer units are sold, which tends to lower revenue.

AP® ECON TIP

Don't confuse revenue with profit. Revenue is what the firm receives; profit is what the firm receives minus the firm's costs.

But what is the net effect on total revenue of a price increase: does it go up or down? The answer is that, in general, total revenue can go either way—an increase in price may either increase total revenue or decrease it. If the price effect, which tends to raise total revenue, is the stronger of the two effects, then total revenue goes up. If the quantity effect, which tends to reduce total revenue, is stronger, then total revenue goes down. And if the strengths of the two effects are exactly equal—as in our toll bridge example, where a $180 gain offsets a $180 loss—total revenue is unchanged by the price increase.

How do we know which effect, if either, is stronger? The size of the price elasticity of demand tells us. Specifically:

- If demand for a good is *unit-elastic* (the price elasticity of demand is 1), an increase in price does not change total revenue. In this case, the quantity effect and the price effect exactly offset each other.

- If demand for a good is *inelastic* (the price elasticity of demand is less than 1), a higher price increases total revenue. In this case, the price effect is stronger than the quantity effect.
- If demand for a good is *elastic* (the price elasticity of demand is greater than 1), an increase in price reduces total revenue. In this case, the quantity effect is stronger than the price effect.

Table 2.3-2 shows how the effect of a price increase on total revenue depends on the price elasticity of demand, using the same data as in Figure 2.3-3. When demand is unit-elastic, an increase in the price from $0.90 to $1.10 leaves total revenue unchanged at $990. When demand is inelastic, the price effect dominates the quantity effect; the same price increase leads to an increase in total revenue from $945 to $1,045. And when demand is elastic, the quantity effect dominates the price effect; the price increase leads to a decline in total revenue from $1,080 to $880.

Table 2.3-2 **Price Elasticity of Demand and Total Revenue**

	Price of crossing = $0.90	Price of crossing = $1.10
Unit-elastic demand (price elasticity of demand = 1)		
Quantity demanded	1,100	900
Total revenue	$990	$990
Inelastic demand (price elasticity of demand = 0.5)		
Quantity demanded	1,050	950
Total revenue	$945	$1,045
Elastic demand (price elasticity of demand = 2)		
Quantity demanded	1,200	800
Total revenue	$1,080	$880

AP® ECON TIP

If total revenue and price move in the same direction, the good is inelastic. If total revenue and price move in opposite directions, the good is elastic. If total revenue does not change when price changes, the good is unit-elastic.

The price elasticity of demand also predicts the effect of a *fall* in price on total revenue. When the price falls, the same two countervailing effects are present, but they work in the opposite directions as compared to the case of an increase in price.

Price Elasticity Along the Demand Curve

Suppose an economist says that "the price elasticity of demand for coffee is 0.25." What they mean is that *at the current price*, the elasticity is 0.25. In the previous discussion of the toll bridge, what we were really describing was the elasticity *at the price* of $0.90. Why this qualification? Because for the vast majority of demand curves, the price elasticity of demand at one point along the curve is different from the price elasticity of demand at other points along the same curve.

To see this, consider the table in **Figure 2.3-5**, which shows a hypothetical demand schedule. It also shows in the last column the total revenue generated at each price. The upper panel of the graph shows the corresponding demand curve. The lower panel illustrates the same data on total revenue: the height of a bar at each quantity demanded—which corresponds to a particular price—measures the total revenue generated at that price.

In Figure 2.3-5, you can see that when the price is low, raising the price increases total revenue: starting at a price of $1, raising the price to $2 increases total revenue from $9 to $16. This means that when the price is low, demand is inelastic. Moreover, you can see that demand is inelastic on the entire section of the demand curve where the price is below $5.

When the price is high, however, raising it further reduces total revenue: starting at a price of $8, for example, raising the price to $9 reduces total revenue from

FIGURE 2.3-5 The Price Elasticity of Demand Changes Along the Demand Curve

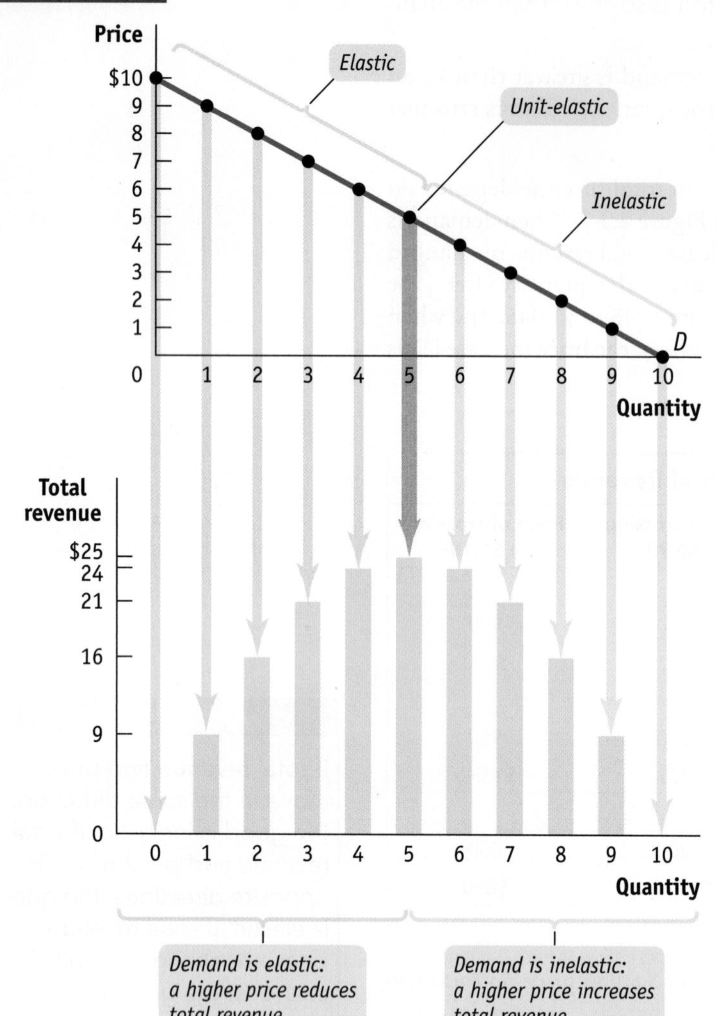

Demand Schedule and Total Revenue for a Linear Demand Curve

Price	Quantity demanded	Total revenue
$0	10	$0
1	9	9
2	8	16
3	7	21
4	6	24
5	5	25
6	4	24
7	3	21
8	2	16
9	1	9
10	0	0

The upper panel shows a demand curve corresponding to the demand schedule in the table. The lower panel shows how total revenue changes along that demand curve: at each price and quantity combination, the height of the bar represents the total revenue generated. You can see that at a low price, raising the price increases total revenue. So demand is inelastic at low prices. At a high price, however, a rise in price reduces total revenue. So demand is elastic at high prices.

AP® ECON TIP

For a straight, downward-sloping demand curve, the upper left segment of the demand curve is elastic and the bottom right segment is inelastic.

$16 to $9. This means that when the price is high, demand is elastic. Furthermore, you can see that demand is elastic over the section of the demand curve where the price exceeds $5.

For the vast majority of goods, the price elasticity of demand changes along the demand curve. So whenever you measure a good's elasticity, you are really measuring it at a particular point or section of the good's demand curve.

What Factors Determine the Price Elasticity of Demand?

Pfizer-BioNTech was able to significantly raise its price for COVID-19 vaccines for several important reasons: there were few substitutes, the price was a small fraction of the typical consumer's income, and many people considered them a medical necessity. Over time, some people were able to find providers of alternative vaccines with lower prices. This experience illustrates the four main factors that determine elasticity: whether close substitutes are available, the share of income a consumer spends on the good, whether the good is a necessity or a luxury, and how much time has elapsed since the price change. Let's look at each of these factors in detail.

Whether Close Substitutes Are Available

The price elasticity of demand tends to be high if there are other goods that consumers regard as similar and would be willing to consume instead. The price elasticity of demand tends to be low if there are no close substitutes.

Share of Income Spent on the Good

The price elasticity of demand tends to be low when spending on a good accounts for a small share of a consumer's income. In that case, a significant change in the price of the good has little impact on how much the consumer spends. In contrast, when a good accounts for a significant share of a consumer's spending, the consumer is likely to be very responsive to a change in price. In this case, the price elasticity of demand is high.

Mariusz Burcz/Alamy

You may want a Tesla Roadster, but you don't need one, so your price elasticity of demand for a Roadster is probably high.

Whether the Good Is a Necessity or a Luxury

The price elasticity of demand tends to be low if a good is something you must have, like a life-saving medicine, or something you feel like you must have due to an addiction. The price elasticity of demand tends to be high if the good is a luxury—something you can easily live without.

Time

In general, the price elasticity of demand tends to increase as consumers have more time to adjust to a price change. This means that the long-run price elasticity of demand is often higher than the short-run elasticity.

A good illustration of the effect of time on the elasticity of demand is drawn from dramatic increases in gasoline prices, which occurred in the United States in 2011 and 2021. Initially, consumption fell very little because there were no close substitutes for gasoline and because people needed to drive their cars to carry out the ordinary tasks of life. Over time, however, Americans changed their car-buying and driving habits in ways that enabled them to gradually reduce their gasoline consumption. Within two years of the 2011 increase, the average household used 19% less gasoline, and the average vehicle used 14% less gasoline than they had a decade earlier, confirming that the long-run price elasticity of demand for gasoline was indeed much higher than the short-run elasticity. The 2021 increase was followed by burgeoning interest in electric vehicles.

AP® ECON TIP

Use the mnemonic *SPLAT* to help remember that the determinants of price elasticity of demand are: **S**ubstitutes, **P**roportion of income, **L**uxury or necessity, **A**ddictive or habit forming, and **T**ime.

Module 2.3  Review

Check Your Understanding

1. The price of strawberries falls from $1.50 to $1.00 per carton and the quantity demanded goes from 100,000 to 200,000 cartons. Use the simple method to find the price elasticity of demand.

2. The price elasticity of demand for movie tickets is 1 at the current price of $10 per ticket and the current consumption level of 4,000 tickets. Using the midpoint method, calculate the percentage by which the owners of movie theaters must reduce the price in order to sell 5,000 tickets.

3. For each case, choose the condition that characterizes demand: elastic demand, inelastic demand, or unit-elastic demand.
   a. Total revenue decreases when price increases.
   b. When price falls, the additional revenue generated by the increase in the quantity sold is exactly offset by the revenue lost from the fall in the price received per unit.
   c. Total revenue falls when output increases.
   d. Producers in an industry find they can increase their total revenues by working together to reduce industry output.

4. For the following goods, would you expect the demand to be elastic, inelastic, or unit-elastic? Explain.
   a. demand by a snake-bite victim for an antidote
   b. demand by students for blue pencils
   c. demand by the chess club, which has a fixed budget, for chess sets

Tackle the AP® Test: Multiple-Choice Questions

1. Which of the following statements is true?
   a. When a good absorbs only a small share of the typical consumer's income, the income effect explains the demand curve's negative slope.
   b. A change in consumption brought about by a change in purchasing power describes the substitution effect.
   c. In the case of an inferior good, the income effect is usually larger than the substitution effect.
   d. In the case of an inferior good, the income and substitution effects work in opposite directions.
   e. Normal goods and inferior goods differ in regard to the direction of the substitution effect caused by a price increase.

2. If there is an increase in the price of an inferior good on which consumers spend a large share of their income, which of the following will decrease the quantity of that good demanded?
   a. the Giffen effect
   b. the income effect only
   c. the substitution effect only
   d. the income effect and the substitution effect
   e. neither the income effect nor the substitution effect

3. If a decrease in price from $2 to $1 causes an increase in quantity demanded from 100 to 120, using the midpoint method, price elasticity of demand equals
   a. 0.17.
   b. 0.27.
   c. 0.40.
   d. 2.5.
   e. 3.72.

4. Which of the following is likely to have the highest price elasticity of demand?
   a. eggs
   b. beef
   c. housing
   d. gasoline
   e. foreign travel

5. If a 2% change in the price of a good leads to a 10% change in the quantity demanded of a good, what is the price elasticity of demand?
   a. 0.02
   b. 0.2
   c. 5
   d. 10
   e. 20

6. A perfectly elastic demand curve is
   a. upward-sloping.
   b. vertical.
   c. not a straight line.
   d. horizontal.
   e. downward-sloping.

7. Which of the following would cause the demand for a good to be relatively inelastic?
   a. The good has a large number of close substitutes.
   b. Expenditures on the good represent a large share of consumer income.
   c. There is ample time to adjust to price changes.
   d. The good is a necessity.
   e. The price of the good is in the upper left section of a linear demand curve.

8. Which of the following is correct for a price increase? When demand is ____________, total revenue will ____________.

	Demand	*Total Revenue*
a.	inelastic	decrease
b.	elastic	decrease
c.	unit-elastic	increase
d.	unit-elastic	decrease
e.	elastic	increase

9. Total revenue is maximized when demand is
   a. elastic.
   b. inelastic.
   c. unit-elastic.
   d. zero.
   e. infinite.

10. If you are addicted to chocolate cake such that you buy one piece per day regardless of the price, your price elasticity of demand for chocolate cake is
    a. infinity.
    b. 1.
    c. more than 1 but less than infinity.
    d. 0.
    e. more than 0 but less than 1.

Tackle the AP® Test: Free-Response Questions

1. Draw a correctly labeled graph of a perfectly inelastic demand curve.
   a. What is the price elasticity of demand for this good?
   b. What is the slope of the demand curve for this good?
   c. Is this good more likely to be a luxury or a necessity? Explain.

Rubric for FRQ 1 (5 points)

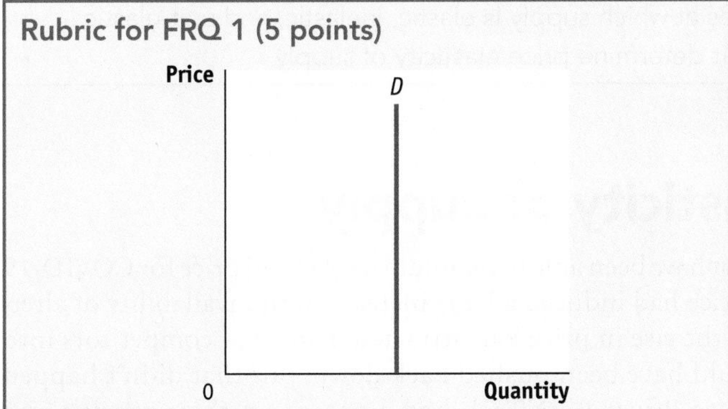

1 point: A graph with "Price" (or "P") on the vertical axis, "Quantity" (or "Q") on the horizontal axis, and a vertical line labeled "Demand" (or "D")

1 point: Zero

1 point: Infinite or undefined

1 point: Necessity

1 point: Since you have to have a necessity (such as a life-saving medicine), you do not change the quantity you purchase when the price changes.

2. Assume the price of an inferior good increases.
   a. In what direction will the substitution effect change the quantity demanded? Explain.
   b. In what direction will the income effect change the quantity demanded? Explain.
   c. Given that the demand curve for the good slopes downward, what is true of the relative sizes of the income and substitution effects for the inferior good? Explain. **(6 points)**

3. Draw a correctly labeled graph illustrating a demand curve that is a straight line and is neither perfectly elastic nor perfectly inelastic.
   a. On your graph, indicate the half of the demand curve along which demand is elastic.
   b. In the elastic range, how will an increase in price affect total revenue? Explain. **(4 points)**

MODULE 2.4

Price Elasticity of Supply

In this Module, you will learn to:

- Define the price elasticity of supply
- Explain the price elasticity of supply using graphs
- Calculate the price elasticity of supply
- Identify elasticity values at which supply is elastic, inelastic, and unit-elastic
- Identify the factors that determine price elasticity of supply

The Price Elasticity of Supply

Pfizer-BioNTech would not have been able to maintain its elevated price for COVID-19 vaccinations if a higher price had induced a large increase in the availability of alternative vaccines. In fact, if the rise in price had attracted many new competitors into the market, the price would have been pushed back down. But that didn't happen because Pfizer-BioNTech had a patent on their vaccine and only a small number of competing vaccines were available. This was another critical element in the ability of a few producers, including Pfizer-BioNTech, to get significantly higher prices for their products: a low responsiveness in the quantity of output supplied to the higher price of vaccinations. To determine the magnitude of producers' response to price changes, we need a measure parallel to the price elasticity of demand – the *price elasticity of supply*.

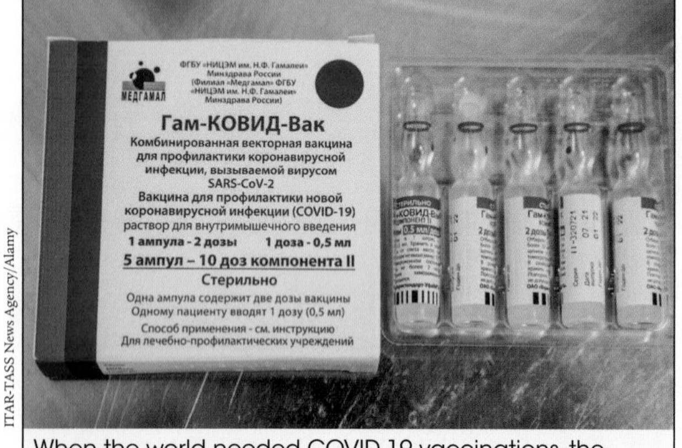

ITAR-TASS News Agency/Alamy

When the world needed COVID-19 vaccinations, the supply response was slow because the small number of producers lacked the resources needed to increase output rapidly.

Measuring the Price Elasticity of Supply

The **price elasticity of supply** is a measure of the responsiveness of the quantity of a good supplied to changes in the price of that good. The formula for the price elasticity of supply is the same as the formula for the price elasticity of demand (although there is no minus sign to be eliminated here):

The **price elasticity of supply** is a measure of the responsiveness of the quantity of a good supplied to changes in the price of that good. It is the ratio of the percentage change in the quantity supplied to the percentage change in the price as we move along the supply curve.

$$\textbf{(2.4-1)}\quad \text{Price elasticity of supply} = \frac{\text{\% change in quantity supplied}}{\text{\% change in price}}$$

The only difference is that here we consider movements along the supply curve rather than movements along the demand curve. Recall from Module 2.4 that the *simple method* for finding the percentage change is to divide the change by the original value. You again have the option of using the *midpoint method* and dividing the change by the average of the values.

Suppose the price of hand soap rises by 10%. If the quantity of hand soap supplied also increases by 10% in response, the price elasticity of supply of hand soap is 10%/10% = 1, so supply is *unit-elastic*. If the quantity supplied increases by 5%, the price elasticity of supply is 0.5 and supply is *inelastic*; if the quantity increases by 20%, the price elasticity of supply is 2 and supply is *elastic*.

Let's consider another example. **Figure 2.4-1** shows a hypothetical supply curve for sweatshirts. An increase in the price from \$25 to \$30 causes an increase in the quantity supplied from 40 sweatshirts per day to 50 sweatshirts per day. Using the simple

FIGURE 2.4-1 Elastic Supply

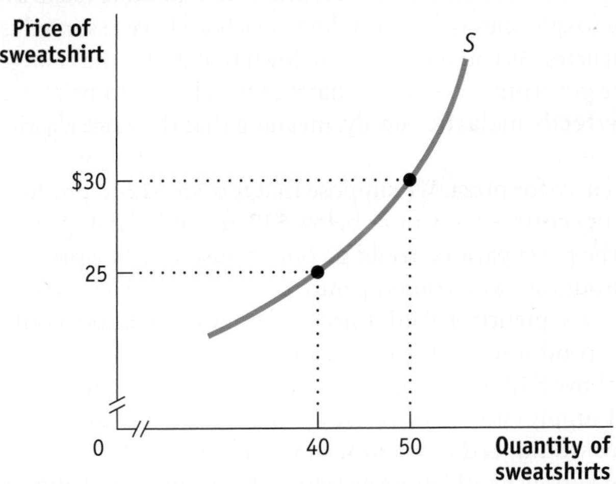

At a price of \$25, a firm supplies 40 sweatshirts per day. When the price rises to \$30, the firm supplies 50 sweatshirts per day. The price change of $(30-25)/25 \times 100 = 20\%$ changes the quantity supplied by $(50-40)/40 \times 100 = 25\%$, so the price elasticity of supply is $25\%/20\% = 1.25$ and the supply is elastic.

method, the percentage change in the quantity supplied is $(50-40)/40 \times 100 = 25\%$. The percentage change in price is $(30-25)/25 \times 100 = 20\%$. So the price elasticity of supply is $25\%/20\% = 1.25$ and the supply is elastic. This elasticity makes sense because the inputs used to make sweatshirts are readily available in many countries, and if the traditional cotton fabric were in short supply, available substitutes include polyester, nylon, and bamboo.

As in the case of demand, the extreme values of the price elasticity of supply have a simple graphical representation. Panel (a) of **Figure 2.4-2** shows the supply of cell phone frequencies, the portion of the radio spectrum that is suitable for sending and receiving cell phone signals. Governments own the right to sell the use of this part of the radio spectrum to cell phone operators inside their borders. But governments can't

FIGURE 2.4-2 Two Extreme Cases of Price Elasticity of Supply

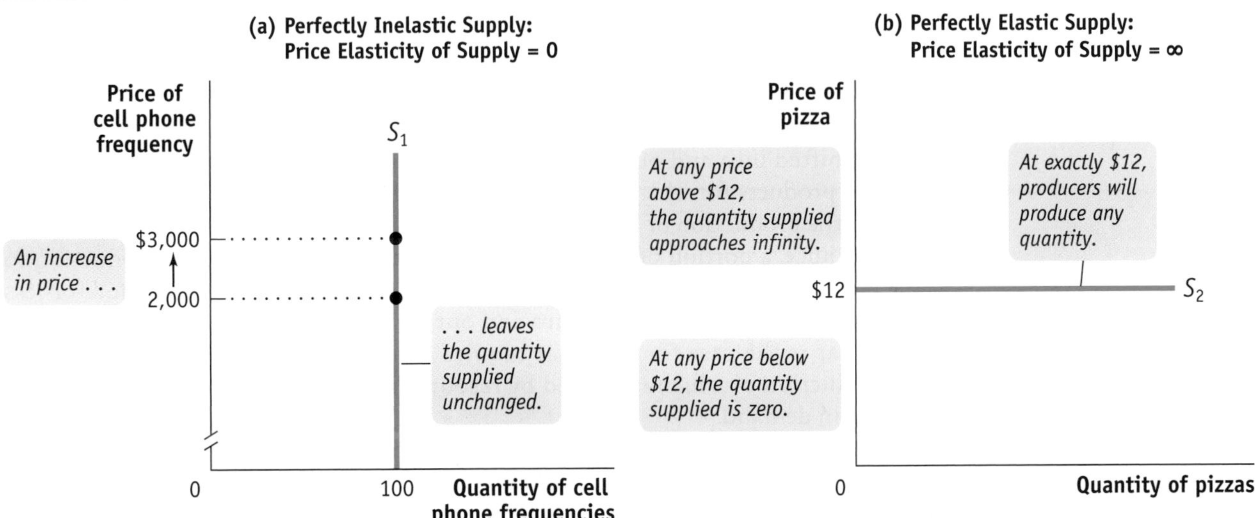

Panel (a) shows a perfectly inelastic supply curve, which is a vertical line. The price elasticity of supply is zero: the quantity supplied is always the same, regardless of price. Panel (b) shows a perfectly elastic supply curve, which is a horizontal line. At a price of \$12, producers will supply any quantity, but they will supply none at a price below \$12. If the price rises above \$12, they will supply an extremely large quantity.

increase or decrease the number of cell phone frequencies they have to offer—for technical reasons, the quantity of frequencies suitable for cell phone operation is fixed. So the supply curve for cell phone frequencies is a vertical line, which we have assumed is set at the quantity of 100 frequencies. As you move up and down that curve, the change in the quantity supplied by the government is zero, whatever the change in price. So panel (a) illustrates a case of **perfectly inelastic supply**, meaning that the price elasticity of supply is zero.

There is **perfectly inelastic supply** when the price elasticity of supply is zero, so that changes in the price of the good have no effect on the quantity supplied. A perfectly inelastic supply curve is a vertical line.

Panel (b) shows the supply curve for pizza. We suppose that it costs $12 to produce a pizza, including all opportunity costs. At any price below $12, it would be unprofitable to produce pizza, and all the pizza parlors would go out of business. At a price of $12 or more, there are many producers who could operate pizza parlors. The ingredients—flour, tomatoes, cheese—are plentiful. And if necessary, more tomatoes could be grown, more milk could be produced to make mozzarella cheese, and so on. So by allowing profits, any price above $12 would elicit the supply of an extremely large quantity of pizzas. The implied supply curve is therefore a horizontal line at $12. Since even a tiny increase in the price would lead to an enormous increase in the quantity supplied, the price elasticity of supply would approach infinity. A horizontal supply curve such as this represents a case of **perfectly elastic supply**.

There is **perfectly elastic supply** if the quantity supplied is zero below some price and approaches infinity above that price. A perfectly elastic supply curve is a horizontal line.

As our cell phone frequencies and pizza examples suggest, real-world instances of both perfectly inelastic and perfectly elastic supply are easier to find than their counterparts in demand. Unlike the price elasticity of demand, the price elasticity of supply does not indicate whether a price increase raises or lowers total revenue. If supply is perfectly inelastic, total revenue increases exactly in proportion to the price. For example, if the price doubles, total revenue doubles, because twice as much money is received for the same quantity of goods. If the supply is anything other than perfectly inelastic, the total revenue increases more than in proportion to the price. If the price doubles, total revenue more than doubles. This is because both the price and the quantity sold are increasing, so the increase in the quantity amplifies the effect on total revenue of the increase in price.

AP® ECON TIP

If a straight-line supply curve intersects the horizontal axis, supply is inelastic; if it intersects the vertical axis, supply is elastic; if it intersects the origin, supply is unit-elastic.

What Factors Determine the Price Elasticity of Supply?

Our examples tell us the main determinant of the price elasticity of supply: the availability of inputs. As with the price elasticity of demand, time may play a role in the price elasticity of supply. And the size of existing inventories affects the ability of firms to respond to higher prices. Here we briefly summarize these factors.

The Availability of Inputs

The price elasticity of supply tends to be high when inputs are readily available and can be shifted into and out of production at a relatively low cost. That is the case for food products for which ingredients can be diverted from the production of one good to the production of another. If the price of grape jelly rises relative to the price of grape juice, a portion of the grape crop can be switched from juice production to jelly production. It tends to be low when inputs are available only in a more-or-less fixed quantity or can be shifted into and out of production only at a relatively high cost. That is the case for cars that require lithium batteries or computer chips, the production of which is limited by resource availability and slow to respond to changes in demand.

The price elasticity of pizza supply is very high because the inputs needed to make more pizza are readily available. The price elasticity of cell phone frequencies is zero because an essential input—the radio spectrum—cannot be increased at all.

Many industries are like pizza and have high price elasticities of supply: they can be readily expanded because they don't require any hard-to-obtain resources. On the other hand, the price elasticity of supply is usually substantially less than perfectly elastic for goods that involve limited natural resources: minerals like gold or copper, agricultural products like coffee trees that mature slowly and only in particular types of soil, and renewable resources like ocean fish that can be exploited only up to a point without destroying the resource.

Kuznetsov Alexey/Shutterstock

The supply of coffee responds slowly to price changes because coffee trees take three to five years to mature and require rich, porous soil.

The Substitutability of Inputs

There may be several different inputs that could serve the same purpose in a production process. For instance, soda can be sweetened with sugar or corn syrup, and pizza crusts can be made with several types of flour. If the price of a product increases but the input currently used to make it isn't readily available, the price elasticity of supply might still be high if an alternative input can be substituted at a reasonable price.

In 2020, the supplies of many products were threatened by work stoppages and worker shortages due to the pandemic. During that period, to improve producers' ability to substitute inputs in response to rising prices for critical goods and services, the Food and Drug Administration temporarily loosened the requirement that all ingredients be listed on food packages. For example, when the bleaching agent used to make bleached flour was in short supply, this policy allowed unbleached flour to be substituted as an input in baked goods.

Time

The price elasticity of supply tends to increase as producers have more time to respond to a price change by increasing productive capacity, adopting new technology, or finding new supplies of inputs. Adjustments of these types allowed the quantity of COVID-19 vaccines supplied to increase dramatically as the pandemic progressed into its second year. The benefits of having more time to respond make the long-run price elasticity of supply higher in most cases than the short-run elasticity. Given enough time, producers are often able to significantly change the amount they produce in response to a price change, even when production involves a limited natural resource. For example, given a few years, new gold deposits can be discovered and mined, new coffee trees can bear fruit, and new fisheries can be established.

AP® ECON TIP

Time gives firms a chance to adjust their size and find new sources of inputs. So the more time, the more ability to respond to price changes and the greater the elasticity of supply.

Existing Inventories

Firms can respond quickly to a price increase regardless of the availability of inputs if they have a large quantity of products on hand, stored as *inventories*. For example, some automobile dealers hold large inventories of cars and can increase the quantity sold immediately in response to an increase in car prices. In contrast, firms selling perishable goods such as fish and fresh vegetables tend not to hold large inventories and cannot respond quickly to price fluctuations.

Excess Capacity

A final determinant of the price elasticity of supply is the producers' *excess capacity*, which is their ability to increase output in their current facilities. Many colleges have excess capacity, meaning they could provide more educations on their existing campuses if more students were willing and able to pay a high enough price in the form of tuition. Among other examples, the steel industry in many countries including the United States has considerable excess capacity. The more excess capacity, the more output could grow in the short run in response to a price increase, and the higher the price elasticity of supply.

AP® ECON TIP

The mnemonic *TEASE* can help you remember the factors that influence the price elasticity of supply. The elasticity of supply is higher when there is more of the following: **T**ime, **E**xcess capacity, **A**vailability of inputs, **S**ubstitutability of inputs, and **E**xisting inventories.

Module 2.4  Review

Check Your Understanding

1. Identify five reasons a good would have a low price elasticity of supply.
2. Using the simple method, calculate the price elasticity of supply for web-design services when the price per hour rises from $100 to $150 and the number of hours supplied increases from 400,000 hours to 500,000. Is supply elastic, inelastic, or unit-elastic?

Tackle the AP® Test: Multiple-Choice Questions

1. Which of the following statements is true?
   a. The formula for the price elasticity of supply is the percentage change in price divided by the percentage change in the quantity supplied.
   b. The number that comes out of the price elasticity of supply formula is a price.
   c. The price elasticity of supply depends on the price elasticity of demand.
   d. When supply is perfectly inelastic, total revenue increases by the same proportion as the price.
   e. The price elasticity of supply is always negative.
2. You're special! There's only one of you regardless of the amount people might pay for your work. The price elasticity of supply for you is
   a. virtually infinite.
   b. 1.
   c. more than 1 but less than 100.
   d. 0.
   e. more than 0 but less than 1.
3. If a 4% change in the price of a good leads to a 10% change in the quantity supply of a good, what is the price elasticity of supply?
   a. 0.4
   b. 0.25
   c. 2.5
   d. 4
   e. 10
4. If an increase in price from $2 to $3 causes an increase in quantity supplied from 100 to 120, using the simple method, the price elasticity of supply is
   a. 0.20.
   b. 0.40.
   c. 0.50.
   d. 2.50.
   e. 3.72.
5. A perfectly elastic supply curve
   a. increases from left to right.
   b. decreases from left to right.
   c. is horizontal.
   d. is vertical.
   e. is U-shaped.
6. Which of the following leads to a more inelastic price elasticity of supply?
   a. a small demand for the good
   b. a high degree of substitutability between inputs
   c. the use of inputs that are easily obtained
   d. a more inelastic price elasticity of demand
   e. a shorter time period in which to supply the good
7. If farmers would supply an unlimited quantity of asparagus for $3 per pound, but none for less than that, the price elasticity of supply for asparagus is
   a. virtually infinite.
   b. 1.
   c. more than 1 but less than 100.
   d. 0.
   e. more than 0 but less than 1.

Tackle the AP® Test: Free-Response Questions

1. Suppose a firm with a straight supply curve will supply 0 units for a price of $0, 1 unit for a price of $0.50, and 2 units for a price of $1.00. Draw a correctly labeled graph of the supply curve for this firm.
   a. What is the price elasticity of supply for this firm?
   b. What is the slope of the supply curve for this firm?
   c. Shade the area on the graph that represents the total revenue from selling one unit.
   d. Does total revenue increase in proportion to the price for this firm? Explain.

Rubric for FRQ 1 (5 points)

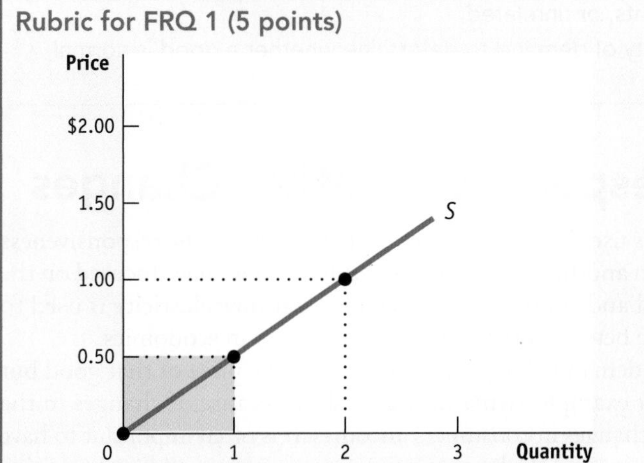

1 point: A graph with "Price" (or "P") on the vertical axis, "Quantity" (or "Q") on the horizontal axis, and a straight line starting at the origin and going through the points (1, ½) and (2, 1) labeled "Supply" (or "S")

1 point: The price elasticity of supply is 1.

1 point: The slope of the supply curve is ½.

1 point: The square area from the origin up to a height of ½ and over to a quantity of 1 is shaded.

1 point: No. The total revenue is price times quantity and would increase in proportion to the price only if the quantity didn't change. Here total revenue increases more than in proportion to the price because as the price increases, the quantity also increases.

2. Assume the price of corn rises by 20% and this causes suppliers to increase the quantity of corn supplied by 40%.
   a. Calculate the price elasticity of supply.
   b. In this case, is supply elastic or inelastic?
   c. Draw a correctly labeled graph of a supply curve illustrating the most extreme case of the category of elasticity you found in part b (either perfectly elastic or perfectly inelastic supply).
   d. What would likely be true of the availability of inputs for a firm with the supply curve you drew in part c? Explain. **(5 points)**

MODULE 2.5

Cross-Price Elasticity and Income Elasticity

In this Module, you will learn to:

- Measure the responsiveness of the demand for one good to changes in the price of another good using the cross-price elasticity of demand
- Measure the responsiveness of demand to changes in income using the income elasticity of demand
- Use the cross-price elasticity of demand to determine whether two goods are substitutes, complements, or unrelated
- Use the income elasticity of demand to determine whether a good is normal, inferior, or neither

Measuring Responses to Other Changes

You've seen that economists use the concept of *elasticity* to measure the responsiveness of one variable to changes in another. However, up to this point we have focused on the price elasticities of demand and supply. Now we can look at how elasticity is used to understand the relationship between other important variables in economics.

The quantity of a good demanded depends not only on the price of that good but also on other variables. For example, demand curves shift because of changes in the prices of related goods and changes in consumers' incomes. It is often important to have a measure of these other effects, and the best measures are—you guessed it—elasticities. Specifically, we can best measure how the demand for a good is affected by prices of other goods using a measure called the *cross-price elasticity of demand*, and we can best measure how demand is affected by changes in income using the *income elasticity of demand*.

The **cross-price elasticity of demand** between two goods measures the effect of a change in one good's price on the quantity demanded of the other good. It is equal to the percentage change in the quantity demanded of one good divided by the percentage change in the other good's price.

The Cross-Price Elasticity of Demand

The demand for a good is often affected by the prices of other, related goods that are either substitutes or complements. A change in the price of a related good shifts the demand curve of the original good, reflecting a change in the quantity demanded at any given price. The strength of such a "cross" effect on demand can be measured by the **cross-price elasticity of demand**, defined as the ratio of the percentage change in the quantity demanded of one good to the percentage change in the price of another.

$$\textbf{(2.5-1)} \quad \begin{array}{c}\text{Cross-price elasticity}\\ \text{of demand between}\\ \text{goods A and B}\end{array} = \frac{\%\text{ change in quantity of A demanded}}{\%\text{ change in price of B}}$$

When two goods are substitutes in consumption, like hot dogs and hamburgers, the cross-price elasticity of demand is positive: a rise in the price of hot dogs increases the demand for hamburgers—that is, it causes a rightward shift of the demand curve for hamburgers. If the goods are close substitutes, like two brands of colas, the cross-price elasticity will be positive and large; if they are not close substitutes, like cola and juice, the cross-price elasticity will be positive and small. So when the cross-price elasticity of demand is positive, its size is a measure of how substitutable the two goods are.

AdShooter/iStock

When two goods are complements in consumption, like hot dogs and hot dog buns, the cross-price elasticity is negative: a rise in the price of hot dogs decreases the demand for hot dog buns—that is, it causes a leftward shift of the demand curve for hot dog buns. As with substitutes, the size of the cross-price elasticity of demand between two complements tells us how strongly complementary they are. If the cross-price elasticity is only slightly below zero, they are weak complements, such as movie tickets and gasoline; if it is a large negative number, they are strong complements, such as smartphones and smartphone cases. If the cross-price elasticity is zero, the two goods are unrelated in the sense that they are neither substitutes nor complements.

Note that in the case of the cross-price elasticity of demand, the sign (plus or minus) is very important: it tells us whether the two goods are complements or substitutes. So we cannot drop the minus sign as we did for the price elasticity of demand.

Remember that elasticity is a *unit-free* measure—that is, it doesn't depend on the units in which goods are measured. To see the potential problem with units, suppose someone told you that "if the price of hot dog buns rises by \$0.30, Americans will buy 10 million fewer hot dogs this year." If you've ever bought hot dog buns, you'll immediately wonder: is that a \$0.30 increase in the price *per bun*, or is it a \$0.30 increase in the price *per package* of buns? It makes a big difference what units we are talking about! However, if someone says that the cross-price elasticity of demand between buns and hot dogs is –0.3, you'll know that a 1% increase in the price of buns causes a 0.3% decrease in the quantity of hot dogs demanded, regardless of whether buns are sold individually or by the package. So elasticity is defined as a ratio of percentage changes, which avoids confusion over units.

Suppose a decrease in the price of tuna fish from \$1.60 per can to \$1.20 per can led to an increase in the quantity demanded of sliced bread, from 50 loaves per day to 70 loaves per day. The percentage change in the quantity demanded is $[(70 - 50)/50] \times 100 = 40\%$ and the percentage change in the price is $[(\$1.20 - \$1.60)/\$1.60] \times 100 = -25\%$. The cross-price elasticity of demand for sliced bread and tuna fish is then $40\%/-25\% = -1.6$, and the two goods are complements. As with all of the elasticities, the midpoint formula is also an option.

AP® ECON TIP

When interpreting elasticities, remember that a negative cross-price elasticity identifies a complement (one you buy less of when the price of the other goes up). A positive cross-price elasticity identifies a substitute (one you buy more of when the price of the other goes up).

The Income Elasticity of Demand

The **income elasticity of demand** measures how changes in income affect the demand for a good. It indicates whether a good is normal or inferior and specifies how responsive demand for the good is to changes in income. Having learned the price and cross-price elasticity formulas, the income elasticity formula will look familiar:

$$\textbf{(2.5-2)} \quad \text{Income elasticity of demand} = \frac{\%\text{ change in quantity demanded}}{\%\text{ change in income}}$$

The **income elasticity of demand** is the percentage change in the quantity of a good demanded when a consumer's income changes divided by the percentage change in the consumer's income; it measures how changes in income affect the demand for a good.

Just as the cross-price elasticity of demand between two goods can be either positive or negative, depending on whether the goods are substitutes or complements, the income elasticity of demand for a good can also be either positive or negative. Recall that there are *normal goods*, for which demand increases when income rises, and *inferior goods*, for which demand decreases when income rises. These definitions relate directly to the sign of the income elasticity of demand:

- When the income elasticity of demand is positive, the good is a normal good.
- When the income elasticity of demand is negative, the good is an inferior good.

An income elasticity of demand of zero would indicate that the consumer's income does not affect the quantity of the good demanded.

Economists often use estimates of the income elasticity of demand to predict which industries will grow most rapidly as the incomes of consumers grow over time. In doing this, they often find it useful to make a further distinction among normal goods, identifying which are *income-elastic* and which are *income-inelastic.*

The demand for a good is **income-elastic** if the income elasticity of demand for that good is greater than 1. When income rises, the demand for income-elastic goods rises *faster* than income. Luxury goods, such as second homes and international travel, tend to be income-elastic. The demand for a good is **income-inelastic** if the income elasticity of demand for that good is positive but less than 1. When income rises, the demand for income-inelastic goods rises as well, but more slowly than income. Necessities such as food and clothing tend to be income-inelastic.

AP® ECON TIP

A negative income elasticity identifies an inferior good (one you buy less of when your income goes up). A positive income elasticity identifies a normal good (one you buy more of when your income goes up).

The demand for a good is **income-elastic** if the income elasticity of demand for that good is greater than 1. The demand for a good is **income-inelastic** if the income elasticity of demand for that good is positive but less than 1.

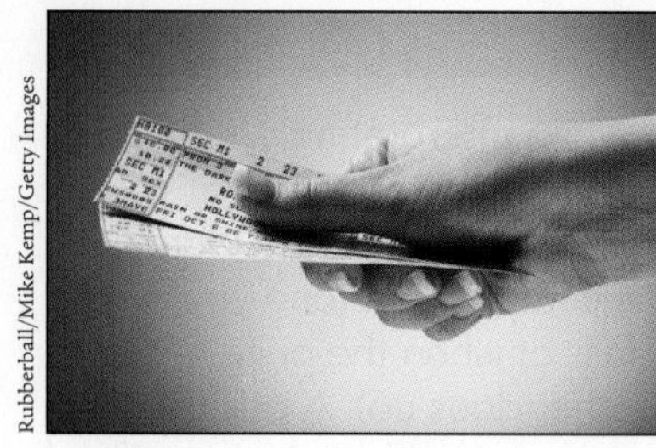
Rubberball/Mike Kemp/Getty Images

As a numerical example, suppose that an increase in Rita's income from $50,000 per year to $60,000 per year would lead her to increase her purchases of concert tickets from 2 tickets per year to 3 tickets per year. The percentage change in her quantity demanded is $[(3-2)/2] \times 100 = 50\%$ and the percentage change in her income is $[(\$60{,}000 - \$50{,}000)/\$50{,}000] \times 100 = 20\%$. So Rita's income elasticity of demand for concert tickets is $50\%/20\% = 2.5$. Concerts are a normal good for Rita because she purchases more when her income increases, and her demand is income-elastic because her income elasticity of demand is greater than 1.

An Elasticity Menagerie

Over the last three Modules, we've run through several different types of elasticity. Keeping them all straight can be a challenge, but the formulas are quite similar, and all of these elasticities are important. **Table 2.5-1** provides a summary of all the types of elasticity we have discussed and their implications.

Table 2.5-1 An Elasticity Menagerie

Name	Elasticity values	Significance
Price elasticity of demand = $\frac{\text{\% change in quantity demanded}}{\text{\% change in price}}$ (dropping the minus sign)		
Perfectly inelastic demand	0	Price has no effect on quantity demanded (vertical demand curve).
Inelastic demand	Between 0 and 1	A rise in price increases total revenue.
Unit-elastic demand	Exactly 1	Changes in price have no effect on total revenue.
Elastic demand	Greater than 1, less than ∞	A rise in price reduces total revenue.
Perfectly elastic demand	∞	A rise in price causes quantity demanded to fall to 0. A fall in price leads to a quantity demanded that approaches infinity (horizontal demand curve).
Cross-price elasticity of demand = $\frac{\text{\% change in quantity of } \textit{one good} \text{ demanded}}{\text{\% change in price of } \textit{another good}}$		
Complements	Negative	Quantity demanded of one good falls when the price of another rises.
Substitutes	Positive	Quantity demanded of one good rises when the price of another rises.
Income elasticity of demand = $\frac{\text{\% change in quantity demanded}}{\text{\% change in income}}$		
Inferior good	Negative	Quantity demanded falls when income rises.
Normal good, income-inelastic	Positive, less than 1	Quantity demanded rises when income rises, but not as rapidly as income.
Normal good, income-elastic	Greater than 1	Quantity demanded rises when income rises, and more rapidly than income.
Price elasticity of supply = $\frac{\text{\% change in quantity supplied}}{\text{\% change in price}}$		
Perfectly inelastic supply	0	Price has no effect on quantity supplied (vertical supply curve).
Inelastic supply	Between 0 and 1	Quantity supplied rises by a smaller percentage than price.
Unit-elastic supply	Exactly 1	Quantity supplied rises by the same percentage as price.
Elastic supply	Greater than 1, less than ∞	Quantity supplied rises by a larger percentage than price.
Perfectly elastic supply	∞	Any fall in price causes quantity supplied to fall to 0. Any rise in price elicits a quantity supplied that approaches infinity (horizontal supply curve).

Module 2.5  Review

Adventures in AP® Economics
Watch the video: ***Elasticity***

Check Your Understanding

1. After Chelsea's income increased from $12,000 to $18,000 a year, her purchases of submarine sandwiches increased from 10 to 40 per year. Calculate Chelsea's income elasticity of demand for submarine sandwiches using the simple method.

2. As the price of margarine rises by 20%, a manufacturer of baked goods increases its quantity of butter demanded by 5%. Calculate the cross-price elasticity of demand between butter and margarine. Are butter and margarine substitutes or complements for this manufacturer?

Tackle the AP® Test: Multiple-Choice Questions

1. If the cross-price elasticity between two goods is negative, this means that the two goods are
   a. substitutes.
   b. complements.
   c. normal.
   d. inferior.
   e. luxuries.

2. If Kylie buys 200 units of Good X when her income is $20,000 and 300 units of Good X when her income increases to $25,000, her income elasticity of demand, using the simple method, is
   a. 0.06.
   b. 0.5.
   c. 1.65.
   d. 1.8.
   e. 2.0.

3. The income elasticity of demand for every normal good is
   a. 0.
   b. 1.
   c. infinite.
   d. positive.
   e. negative.

4. If the cross-price elasticity between two goods is zero, this means that the two goods are
   a. strong substitutes.
   b. weak complements.
   c. income-elastic.
   d. income-inelastic.
   e. unrelated.

5. When the price of 5K races goes down by 30%, Willie's purchases of running shoes increase by 15%. Willie's cross-price elasticity of demand is
   a. −1/2.
   b. −1.
   c. −2.
   d. −4.
   e. −12.

6. Tayo buys more cereal when his income falls. For Tayo, cereal
   a. is a normal good.
   b. has a positive income elasticity of demand.
   c. has a negative income elasticity of demand.
   d. has income-inelastic demand.
   e. has income-elastic demand.

7. It is appropriate to drop the negative sign on the
   a. price elasticity of demand.
   b. price elasticity of supply.
   c. cross-price elasticity of demand.
   d. income elasticity of demand.
   e. value of every type of elasticity.

Tackle the AP® Test: Free-Response Questions

1. Refer to the table below to answer the following questions.

Price of good A	Quantity of good A demanded	Quantity of good B demanded
$10	90	5
$8	100	10

   a. Using the simple method, calculate the price elasticity of demand for good A for an increase in price from $8 to $10.

   b. Indicate any version of the formula for calculating the cross-price elasticity of demand for good B with respect to the price of good A.

   c. Using the simple method, calculate the cross-price elasticity of demand between good B and good A for a decrease in the price of good A from $10 to $8.

   d. What does your answer for part c tell you about the relationship between the two goods? Explain.

Rubric for FRQ 1 (5 points)

1 point: 0.40

1 point: % change in quantity of good B demanded/% change in price of good A or (change in Q_B/original Q_B)/(change in P_A/original P_A) or (change in Q_B/average Q_B)/(change in P_A/average P_A)

1 point: –5

1 point: They are complements.

1 point: Cross-price elasticity is negative—when the price of good A goes down, in addition to buying more of good A, people buy more of good B to go along with it.

2. When Tongyao's annual income rises from $30,000 to $40,000, she increases her hamburger consumption from 36 to 45 per year, but when her income rises from $40,000 to $50,000 per year, she decreases her hamburger consumption from 45 to 40 per year, choosing to purchase more steaks instead.

   a. Calculate Tongyao's income elasticity of demand for an increase in income from $30,000 to $40,000.

   b. For an increase in income from $30,000 to $40,000, is Tongyao's demand for hamburgers income elastic, income inelastic, or neither?

   c. For the second increase in income, are hamburgers a normal good or an inferior good for Tongyao?

   d. Explain how you can determine the answer to part c without calculating the income elasticity of demand.

   e. Describe what happens to Tongyao's demand curve for hamburgers as her income increases from $30,000 to $40,000 and from $40,000 to $50,000. **(5 points)**

Consumer Surplus, Producer Surplus, and Market Equilibrium

MODULE 2.6

In this Module, you will learn to:

- Define consumer surplus and explain its relationship to the demand curve
- Define producer surplus and explain its relationship to the supply curve
- Calculate the consumer surplus and the producer surplus using areas on a graph
- Define market equilibrium and explain how the equilibrium price and quantity are determined

There is a lively market in second-hand college textbooks. At the end of each term, some students decide the money they can make by selling their used books is worth more to them than keeping the books. And some students prefer to buy a somewhat battered but less expensive used textbook rather than pay full price for a new one.

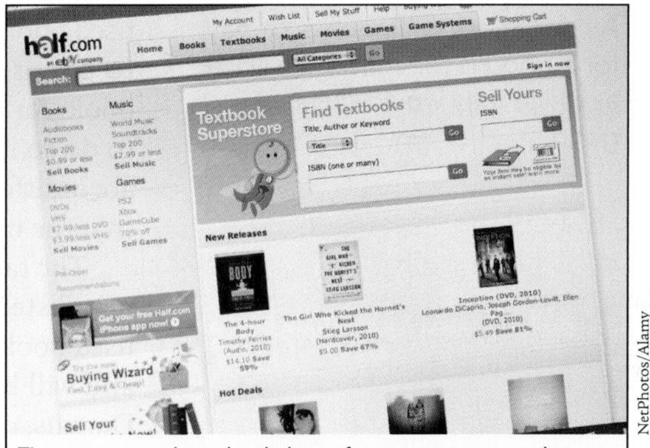

NetPhotos/Alamy

The economic principles of consumer surplus, producer surplus, and market equilibrium are all illustrated in an analysis of the used-textbook market.

Textbook publishers and authors are not happy about these transactions because they cut into sales of new books. But both the students who sell used books and those who buy them clearly benefit from the existence of the used-book market. That is why many college bookstores and online stores facilitate their trade, buying used textbooks and selling them alongside the new books.

Can we determine *how much* the buyers and sellers of textbooks gain from the existence of the used-book market? Yes, we can. In this Module we will see how to measure the benefits from being able to purchase a good, such as those enjoyed by buyers of used textbooks. These benefits are known as *consumer surplus*. And we will see that there is a corresponding measure, *producer surplus*, of the benefits sellers receive from being able to sell a good.

AP® ECON TIP

On the AP® exam you may be asked to draw a graph and shade the areas that represent consumer and producer surplus.

The concepts of consumer surplus and producer surplus are useful for analyzing a wide variety of economic issues. They let us quantify the benefits producers and consumers receive from the existence of a market. These surpluses also allow us to calculate how the welfare of consumers and producers is affected by changes in market prices. Such calculations play a crucial role in the evaluation of many economic policies.

What information do we need to calculate consumer and producer surplus? Surprisingly, all we need are the demand and supply curves for a good. That is, the supply and demand model isn't just a model of how a competitive market works—it's also a model of how much consumers and producers gain from participating in that market. So our first step will be to learn how consumer and producer surplus can be derived from the demand and supply curves. We will then see how these concepts can be applied to actual economic issues.

Consumer Surplus and the Demand Curve

First-year college students are often surprised by the prices of the textbooks required for their classes. But at the end of the semester, students might again be surprised to find they can sell back at least some of their textbooks for a sizable portion of the purchase price. The ability to purchase used textbooks at the start of the semester and to sell back used textbooks at the end of the semester is beneficial to students who want to save money.

The market for used textbooks provides a convenient starting point for us to develop the concepts of consumer and producer surplus. We'll use these concepts to understand exactly how buyers and sellers benefit from a competitive market and how big those benefits are. In addition, these concepts assist in the analysis of what happens when competitive markets don't work well or there is interference in the market.

Let's begin by looking at the market for used textbooks, starting with the buyers. We will see that the demand curve is derived from their tastes or preferences—and those same preferences also determine how much they gain from the opportunity to buy used books.

Willingness to Pay and the Demand Curve

A consumer's **willingness to pay** for a good is the maximum price at which they would buy that good.

A used book is not as good as a new book—it will be battered and coffee-stained, may include someone else's highlighting, and may not be completely up to date. How much this bothers you depends on your preferences. Some students would prefer to buy the used book even if it is only slightly cheaper than a new one, while others would buy the used book only if it is considerably cheaper. Let's define a potential buyer's **willingness to pay** as the maximum price at which they would buy a good, in this case a used textbook. An individual won't buy the good if it costs more than this amount but is eager to do so if it costs less. If the price is equal to an individual's willingness to pay, they are indifferent between buying and not buying. For the sake of simplicity, we'll assume that the individual buys the good in this case.

The table in **Figure 2.6-1** shows five potential buyers of a used book that costs $200 new, listed in order of their willingness to pay. At one extreme is Ally, who will buy a used book even if the price is as high as $118. Bassel is less willing to have a used book and will buy one only if the price is $90 or less. Cierra is willing to pay only $70, and Darrius, only $50. Emma, who really doesn't like the idea of a used book, will buy one only if it costs no more than $20.

FIGURE 2.6-1 The Demand Curve for Used Textbooks

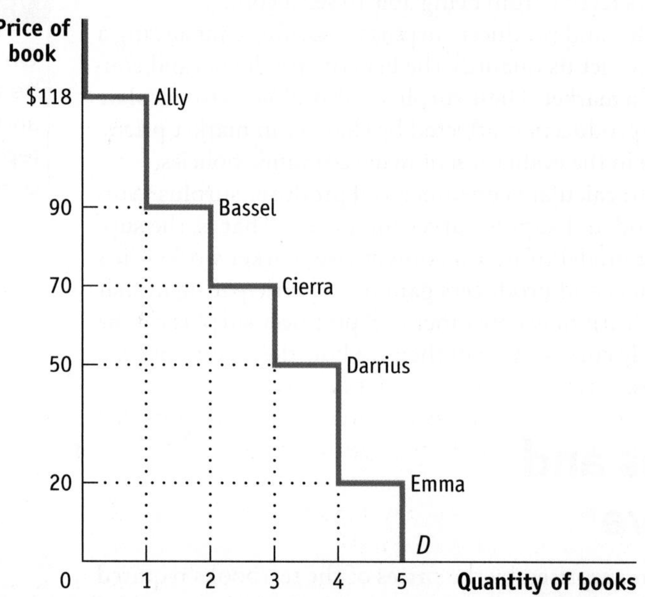

Potential buyers	Willingness to pay
Ally	$118
Bassel	90
Cierra	70
Darrius	50
Emma	20

With only five potential consumers in this market, the demand curve is step-shaped. Each step represents one consumer, and its height indicates that consumer's willingness to pay—the maximum price at which each will buy a used textbook—as indicated in the table.

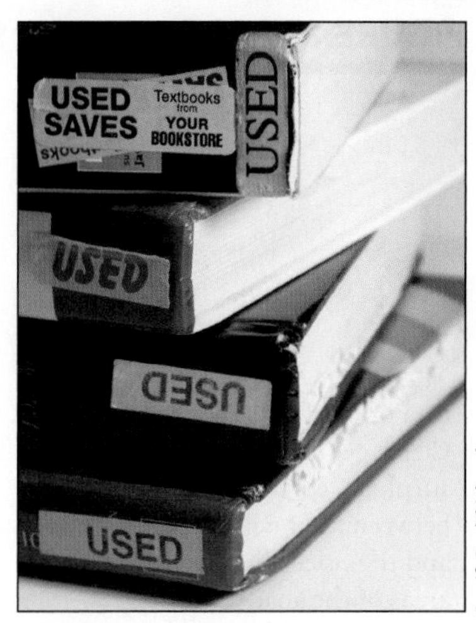

JenniferRae/Thinkstock

How many of these five students will actually buy a used book? It depends on the price. If the price of a used book is $110, only Ally buys one; if the price is $80, Ally and Bassel both buy used books, and so on, until you reach a price of $20, at which all five students are willing to purchase a book. So the information in the table can be used to construct the *demand schedule* for used textbooks.

We can use this demand schedule to derive the market demand curve shown in Figure 2.6-1. Because we are considering only a small number of consumers, this curve doesn't look like the smooth demand curves we have seen previously for markets that contained hundreds or thousands of consumers. This demand curve is step-shaped, with alternating horizontal and vertical segments. Each horizontal segment—each step—corresponds to one potential buyer's willingness to pay. However, we'll see shortly that for the analysis of consumer surplus, it doesn't matter whether the demand curve is step-shaped, as in this figure, or whether there are so many consumers that the steps are tiny and the curve appears smooth.

Willingness to Pay and Consumer Surplus

Suppose that the campus bookstore makes used textbooks available at a price of $60. In that case, Ally, Bassel, and Cierra will buy books. Do they gain from their purchases, and if so, how much?

The answer, shown in **Table 2.6-1**, is that each student who purchases a book does achieve a net gain, but the amount of the gain differs among students. Ally would have been willing to pay $118, so her net gain is $118 – $60 = $58. Bassel would have been willing to pay $90, so his net gain is $90 – $60 = $30. Cierra would have been willing to pay $70, so her net gain is $70 – $60 = $10. Darrius and Emma, however, won't be willing to buy a used book at a price of $60, so they neither gain nor lose.

Table 2.6-1 Consumer Surplus When the Price of a Used Textbook Is $60

Potential buyer	Willingness to pay	Price paid	Individual consumer surplus = Willingness to pay – Price paid
Ally	$118	$60	$58
Bassel	90	60	30
Cierra	70	60	10
Darrius	50	—	—
Emma	20	—	—
All buyers			**Total consumer surplus = $98**

The net gain a buyer achieves from the purchase of a good is called that buyer's *individual consumer surplus*. It is equal to the difference between the buyer's willingness to pay and the price paid. Whenever a buyer pays a price less than their willingness to pay, the buyer achieves some individual consumer surplus.

The sum of the individual consumer surpluses achieved by all the buyers of a good is known as the *total consumer surplus* achieved in the market. In Table 2.6-1, the total consumer surplus is the sum of the individual consumer surpluses achieved by Ally, Bassel, and Cierra: $58 + $30 + $10 = $98.

Economists often use the term **consumer surplus** to refer to both individual and total consumer surplus. We will follow this practice; it will always be clear from the context whether we are referring to the consumer surplus achieved by an individual or by all buyers.

The term **consumer surplus** can be used to refer to both individual and total consumer surplus. It is the difference between the amount paid for a good and the consumer's (or consumers') willingness to pay for the units purchased.

Total consumer surplus can be represented graphically. **Figure 2.6-2** reproduces the demand curve from Figure 2.6-1. Each step in that demand curve is one book wide and represents one consumer. For example, the height of Ally's step is $118, her willingness to pay. This step forms the top of a rectangle, the bottom of which lies on the

FIGURE 2.6-2 Consumer Surplus in the Used-Textbook Market

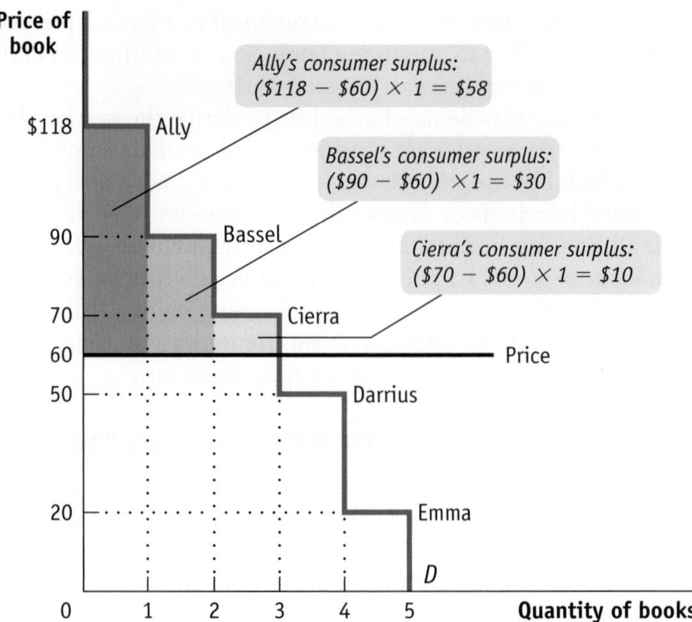

At a price of $60, Ally, Bassel, and Cierra get individual consumer surpluses equal to the difference between their willingness to pay and the price, illustrated by the areas of the shaded rectangles. Both Darrius and Emma have a willingness to pay that is less than $60, so they are unwilling to buy a book in this market; they receive no consumer surplus. The total consumer surplus is given by the entire shaded area.

price line showing the $60 price she actually pays for a book. The area of Ally's rectangle, ($118 − $60) × 1 = $58, is her consumer surplus from purchasing one book at $60. So the individual consumer surplus Ally gains is the *area of the dark blue rectangle* shown in Figure 2.6-2.

In addition to Ally, Bassel and Cierra will also each buy a book when the price is $60. Like Ally, they benefit from their purchases, though not as much, because they each have a lower willingness to pay. Figure 2.6-2 shows the consumer surplus gained by Bassel and Cierra as rectangles shaded with lighter blues. Darrius and Emma receive no consumer surplus because they do not buy books at a price of $60.

The total consumer surplus achieved in this market is just the sum of the individual consumer surpluses received by Ally, Bassel, and Cierra. So the total consumer surplus is equal to the combined area of the three shaded rectangles in Figure 2.6-2, $98. Another way to say this is that total consumer surplus is equal to the area below the demand curve but above the price.

This is worth repeating as a general principle: *The total consumer surplus generated by purchases of a good at a given price is equal to the area below the demand curve but above that price.* The same principle applies regardless of the number of consumers.

When we consider large markets, this graphical representation becomes particularly helpful. Consider, for example, the sales of laptop computers to millions of potential buyers. Each potential buyer has a maximum price that he or she is willing to pay. With so many potential buyers, the step representing each buyer's willingness to pay becomes very narrow and the demand curve appears smooth, like the one shown in **Figure 2.6-3**.

AP® ECON TIP

You may be asked to calculate the size of the area that represents consumer surplus, which is bounded by the demand curve, the price line, and the vertical axis. Remember: the area of a triangle = ½ × base × height.

Suppose that at a price of $1,500, a total of 1 million laptops are purchased. How much do consumers gain from being able to buy those 1 million laptops? We could answer that question by calculating the individual consumer surplus of each buyer and then adding these numbers up to arrive at a total. But it is much easier just to look at Figure 2.6-3 and use the fact that total consumer surplus is equal to the shaded area below the demand curve but above the price. Recall that the area of a triangle is ½ × the base of the triangle × the height of the triangle. So the total consumer surplus in this case is ½ × 1 million × $3,500 = $1.75 billion.

FIGURE 2.6-3 Consumer Surplus

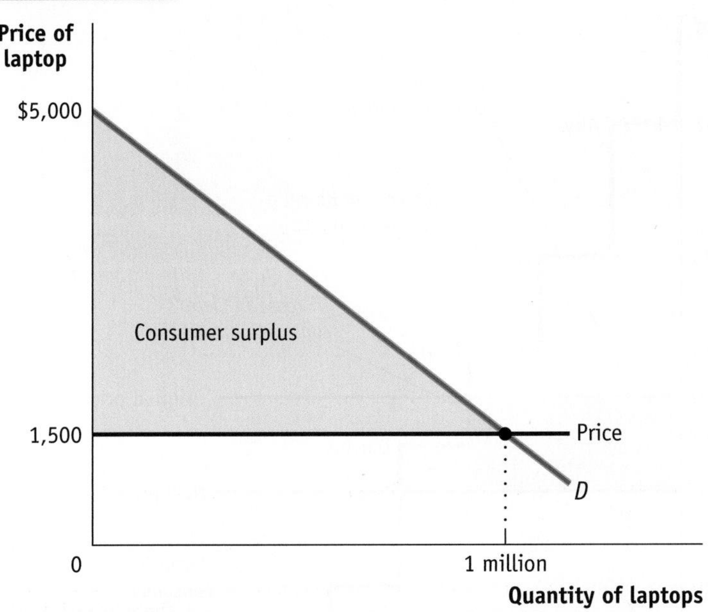

The demand curve for laptop computers is smooth because there are many potential buyers. At a price of $1,500, 1 million laptops are demanded. The consumer surplus at this price is equal to the shaded area: the area below the demand curve but above the price. The area of a triangle is ½ × the base of the triangle × the height of the triangle. So the total consumer surplus in this case is ½ × 1 million × $3,500 = $1.75 billion. This is the total net gain to consumers generated from buying and consuming laptops when the price is $1,500.

How Changing Prices Affect Consumer Surplus

It is often important to know how price *changes* affect consumer surplus. For example, we may want to know the harm to consumers from a frost in Florida that drives up the price of oranges, or consumers' gain from the introduction of fish farming that makes salmon steaks less expensive. The same approach we have used to derive consumer surplus can be used to answer questions about how changes in prices affect consumers.

Let's return to the example of the market for used textbooks. Suppose the bookstore decided to sell used textbooks for $40 instead of $60. By how much would this fall in price increase consumer surplus?

The answer is illustrated in **Figure 2.6-4**. As shown in the figure, there are two parts to the increase in consumer surplus. The first part, shaded dark blue, is the gain of those who would have bought books even at the higher price of $60. Each of the students who would have bought books at $60 – Ally, Bassel, and Cierra – now pays $20 less, and therefore each gains $20 in consumer surplus from the fall in price to $40. So the dark blue area represents the $20 × 3 = $60 increase in consumer surplus to those three buyers. The second part, shaded light blue, is the gain to those who would not have bought a book at $60 but are willing to pay more than $40. In this case that gain goes to Darrius, who would not have bought a book at $60 but does buy one at $40. He gains $10 – the difference between his willingness to pay of $50 and the new price of $40. So the light blue area represents a further $10 gain in consumer surplus. The total increase in consumer surplus is the sum of the shaded areas, $70. Likewise, a rise in price from $40 to $60 would decrease consumer surplus by an amount equal to the sum of the shaded areas.

Producer Surplus and the Supply Curve

Just as some buyers of a good would have been willing to pay more for their purchase than the price they actually pay, some sellers of a good would have been willing to sell it for less than the price they actually receive. We can therefore carry out an analysis of producer surplus and the supply curve that is almost exactly parallel to that of consumer surplus and the demand curve.

FIGURE 2.6-4 Consumer Surplus and a Fall in the Price of Used Textbooks

There are two parts to the increase in consumer surplus generated by a fall in price from $60 to $40. The first part is the dark blue rectangle that represents the $20 increase in consumer surplus for each person who would have bought a used textbook at the original price of $60. The second part is the light blue area that represents the increase in consumer surplus for those who would *not* have bought a used textbook at the original price of $60 but who buy at the new price of $40—namely, Darrius's increase in consumer surplus of $10. The total increase in consumer surplus is $3 \times \$20 + \$10 = \$70$, represented by the sum of the shaded areas.

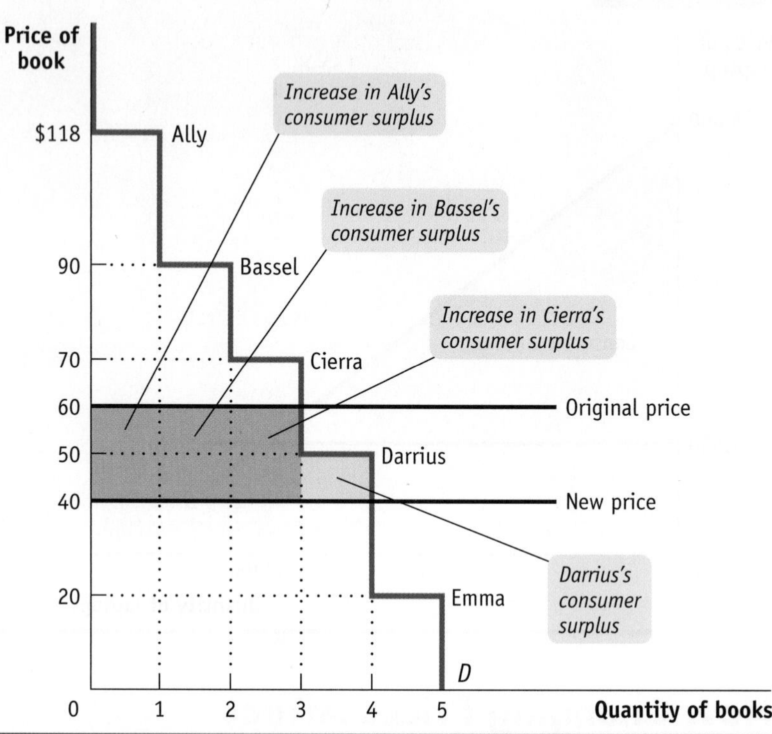

Cost

Before we can find the producer surplus, we must examine the underlying cost. Consider a group of students who are potential sellers of used textbooks. Because they have different preferences, the various potential sellers differ in regard to the lowest price they would accept for their books. The table in **Figure 2.6-5** shows the prices at which several different students would be willing to sell. Andrew is willing to sell the book as long as he can get at least $10; Bina won't sell unless she can get at least $30; Carlos requires $50; Donna requires $70; Emir requires $90.

A seller's **cost** is the lowest price at which they are willing to sell a good.

The lowest price at which a potential seller is willing to sell is called the seller's **cost**. So Andrew's cost is $10, Bina's is $30, and so on.

Using the term *cost*, which people normally associate with the monetary cost of producing a good, may sound a little strange when applied to sellers of used textbooks. The students don't have to manufacture the books, so it doesn't cost the student who sells a book anything to make that book available for sale, does it?

Yes, it does. A student who sells a book won't have it later, as part of their personal collection. So there is an *opportunity cost* to selling a textbook, even if the owner has completed the course for which it was required. And remember that one of the basic principles of economics is that the true measure of the cost of doing something is always its opportunity cost. That is, the real cost of something is what you must give up to get it.

So it is appropriate to refer to the minimum price at which someone will sell a good as the "cost" of selling that good, even if that person doesn't spend any money to make the good available for sale. Of course, in most real-world markets the sellers either produce the good or purchase it from producers, and therefore *do* spend money to make the good available for sale. In this case the cost of making the good available for sale *includes* monetary costs, but it may also include other opportunity costs.

FIGURE 2.6-5 The Supply Curve for Used Textbooks

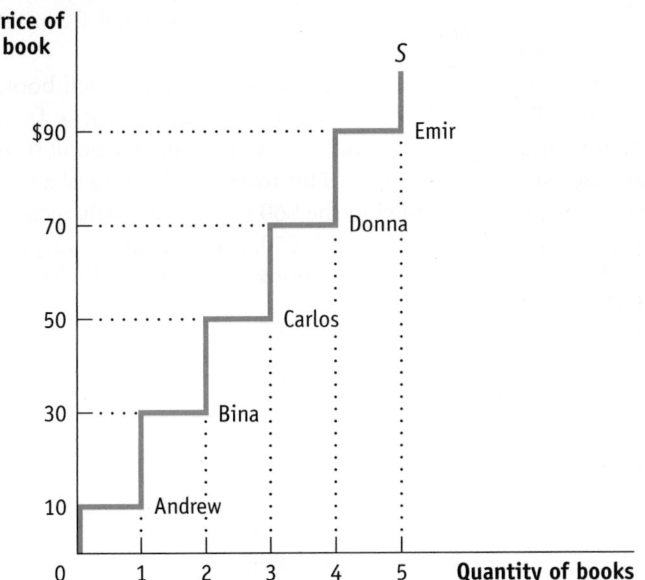

Potential sellers	Cost
Andrew	$10
Bina	30
Carlos	50
Donna	70
Emir	90

The supply curve illustrates sellers' cost, the lowest price at which a potential seller is willing to sell the good, and the quantity supplied at that price. Each of the five students has one book to sell and each has a different cost, as indicated in the accompanying table.

Producer Surplus

Now we're ready to find the producer surplus. Suppose that Andrew sells his book for $60. Clearly he has gained from the transaction: he would have been willing to sell for only $10, so he has gained $50. This net gain, the difference between the price he actually gets and his cost – the minimum price at which he would have been willing to sell – is known as his *individual producer surplus*.

Just as we derived the demand curve from the willingness to pay of different consumers, we can derive the supply curve from the cost of different producers. The step-shaped curve in Figure 2.6-5 shows the supply curve implied by the costs shown in the accompanying table. At a price less than $10, none of the students are willing to sell; at a price between $10 and $30, only Andrew is willing to sell, and so on until you reach $90, the price at which all five students are willing to sell.

As in the case of consumer surplus, we can add the individual producer surpluses of each seller to calculate the *total producer surplus*, the total net gain to all sellers in the market. Economists use the term **producer surplus** to refer to either total or individual producer surplus. **Table 2.6-2** shows the net gain to each of the students who would sell a used book at a price of $60: $50 for Andrew, $30 for Bina, and $10 for Carlos. The total producer surplus is $50 + $30 + $10 = $90.

Economists use the term **producer surplus** to refer to both individual and total producer surplus. It is the difference between the price received and the seller's (or sellers') cost.

Table 2.6-2 Producer Surplus When the Price of a Used Textbook Is $60

Potential seller	Cost	Price received	Individual producer surplus = Price received – Cost
Andrew	$10	$60	$50
Bina	30	60	30
Carlos	50	60	10
Donna	70	—	—
Emir	90	—	—
All sellers			**Total producer surplus = $90**

In upcoming Modules we will discuss *profit.* For now, we should note that in most cases, producer surplus differs from profit because more types of costs – not just the lowest price at which the seller would provide the good – are subtracted from the amount sellers receive in the calculation of profit.

As with consumer surplus, the producer surplus gained by those who sell books can be represented graphically. **Figure 2.6-6** reproduces the supply curve from Figure 2.6-5. Each step in that supply curve has a width that represents one book from one seller. The height of Andrew's step is $10, his cost. This forms the bottom of a rectangle, the top of which lies on the price line showing the $60 price he actually receives for his book. The area of this rectangle, ($60 – $10) × 1 = $50, is his producer surplus. So the producer surplus Andrew gains from selling his book is the *area of the dark red rectangle* shown in the figure.

FIGURE 2.6-6 **Producer Surplus in the Used-Textbook Market**

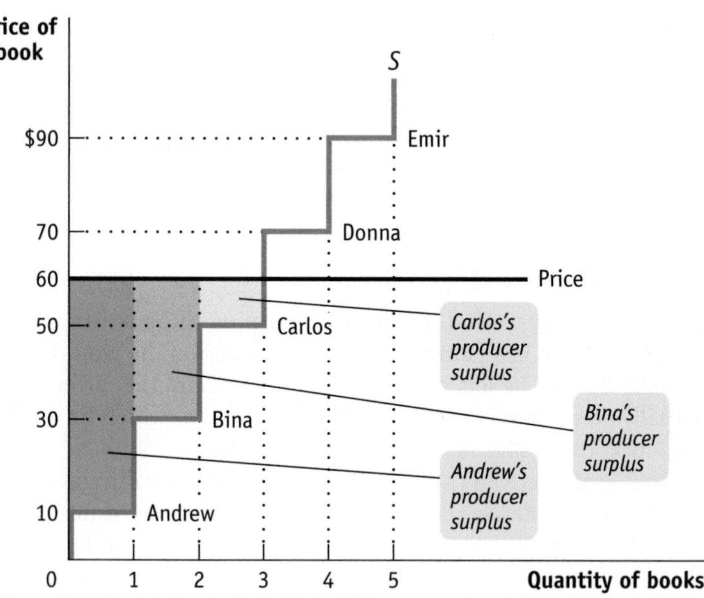

At a price of $60, Andrew, Bina, and Carlos each sell a book but Donna and Emir do not. Andrew, Bina, and Carlos get individual producer surpluses equal to the difference between the price and their cost, illustrated here by the shaded rectangles. Donna and Emir each have a cost that is greater than the price of $60, so they are unwilling to sell a book and so receive no producer surplus. The total producer surplus is given by the entire shaded area.

Let's assume that the campus bookstore is willing to buy all the used copies of this book that students are willing to sell at a price of $60. Then, in addition to Andrew, Bina and Carlos will also sell their books. They will benefit from their sales, though not as much as Andrew, because they have higher costs. Andrew, as we have seen, gains $50. Bina gains a smaller amount: since her cost is $30, she gains only $30. Carlos gains even less, only $10. Donna and Emir will not sell a book because their cost exceeds the price. The total producer surplus of $90 is represented in Figure 2.6-6 by the combined area of the three shaded rectangles.

As with consumer surplus, we have a general rule for determining the total producer surplus from sales of a good: *The total producer surplus from sales of a good at a given price is the area above the supply curve but below that price.*

This rule applies both to examples like the one shown in Figure 2.6-6, where there are a small number of producers and a step-shaped supply curve, and to more realistic examples, where there are many producers and the supply curve is more or less smooth.

Consider, for example, the supply of wheat. **Figure 2.6-7** shows how producer surplus depends on the price per bushel. Suppose that, as shown in the figure, the price is $5 per bushel and farmers supply 1 million bushels. What is the benefit to the farmers from selling their wheat at a price of $5? Their producer surplus is equal to the shaded area above the supply curve but below the price of $5 per bushel: $\frac{1}{2}$ × 1 million × $4 = $2 million.

AP® ECON TIP

The area on a graph that represents producer surplus is bounded by the supply curve, the price line, and the vertical axis.

FIGURE 2.6-7 Producer Surplus

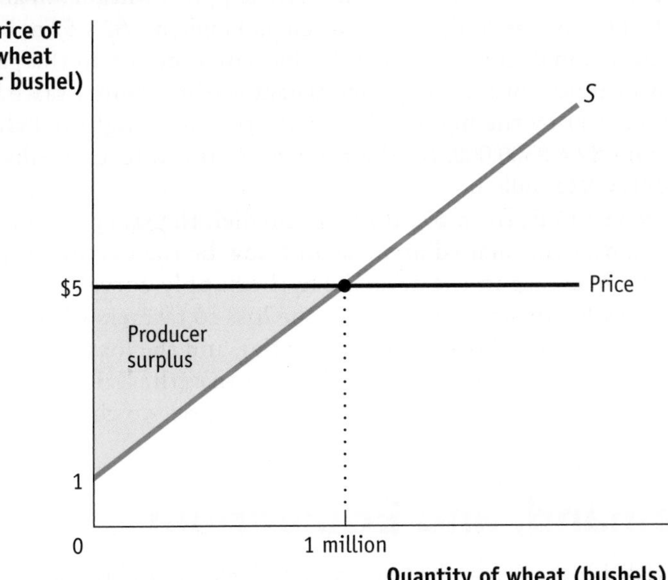

At a price of \$5 per bushel, farmers supply 1 million bushels of wheat. The producer surplus at this price is equal to the shaded area above the supply curve but below the price: $\frac{1}{2} \times 1 \text{ million} \times \$4 = \$2 \text{ million}$.

How Changing Prices Affect Producer Surplus

As in the case of consumer surplus, a change in price alters producer surplus. However, although a fall in price increases consumer surplus, it reduces producer surplus. Similarly, a rise in price reduces consumer surplus but increases producer surplus.

To see this, let's first consider a rise in the price of the good. Producers of the good will experience an increase in producer surplus, though not all producers gain the same amount. Some producers would have produced the good even at the original, lower price; they will gain the entire price increase on every unit they produce. Other producers will enter the market because of the higher price; they will gain only the difference between the new price and their cost.

Figure 2.6-8 shows the effect on producer surplus of a rise in the price of wheat from \$5 to \$7 per bushel. The increase in producer surplus is the sum of the

FIGURE 2.6-8 A Rise in the Price Increases Producer Surplus

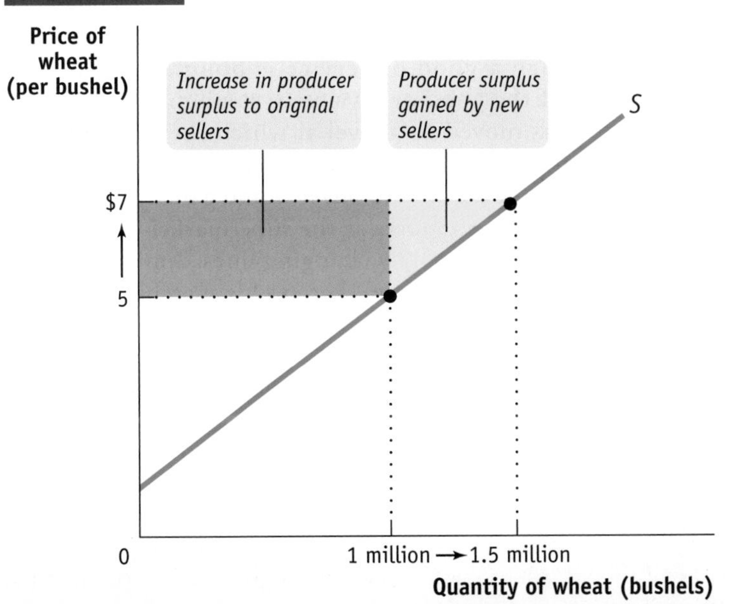

A rise in the price of wheat from \$5 to \$7 leads to an increase in the quantity supplied and an increase in producer surplus. The change in total producer surplus is given by the sum of the shaded areas: the total area above the supply curve but between the old and new prices. The dark red area represents the gain to the farmers who would have supplied 1 million bushels at the original price of \$5; the triangular light red area represents the increase in producer surplus achieved by the farmers who supply the additional 500,000 bushels because of the higher price.

shaded areas, which consists of two parts. First, there is a dark red rectangle corresponding to the gains to those farmers who would have supplied wheat even at the original $5 price. The area of the dark red rectangle is 1 million × $2 = $2 million. Second, there is an additional light red triangle that corresponds to the gains to those farmers who would not have supplied wheat at the original price but are drawn into the market by the higher price. The area of the light red triangle is ½ × 0.5 million × $2 = $500,000. So the total gain in producer surplus is $2 million + $500,000 = $2.5 million.

If the price were to fall from $7 to $5 per bushel, the story would run in reverse. The sum of the shaded areas would now be the decline in producer surplus, the decrease in the area above the supply curve but below the price. The loss would consist of two parts: the loss to farmers who would still grow wheat at a price of $5 (the dark red rectangle), and the loss to farmers who would no longer grow wheat because of the lower price (the light red triangle). But what determines the price? And what causes the price to change? We'll examine that next.

Belinka/Shutterstock

Supply, Demand, and Equilibrium

We are already familiar with the demand curve, the supply curve, and the set of factors that shift each curve. We can put these elements together to show how they determine the price of the good, the quantity sold, and the resulting consumer and producer surplus.

Randy Duchaine/Alamy

Just as supermarket checkout lines tend to balance out, price and quantity in a competitive market tend to move toward a state of equilibrium.

In competitive markets, the forces of supply and demand tend to move price and quantity toward what economists call *equilibrium*. An economic situation is in **equilibrium** when no individual would be better off doing something different. Imagine a busy afternoon at your local supermarket; there are long lines at the checkout counters. Then one of the previously closed registers opens. The first thing that happens is a rush to the newly opened register. But soon enough, things settle down and shoppers have rearranged themselves so that the line at the newly opened register is about as long as all the others. When all the checkout lines are the same length, and none of the shoppers can be better off by doing something different, this situation is in equilibrium.

The concept of equilibrium helps us understand the price at which a good or service is bought and sold as well as the quantity transacted of the good or service. A competitive market is in equilibrium when the price has moved to a level at which the quantity of a good demanded equals the quantity supplied. At that price, no seller would gain by offering to sell more or less of the good, and no buyer would gain by offering to buy more or less of the good. Recall the shoppers at the supermarket who cannot make themselves better off (cannot save time) by changing lines. Similarly, at the market equilibrium, the price has moved to a level that exactly matches the quantity demanded by consumers to the quantity supplied by sellers.

The price that matches the quantity supplied and the quantity demanded is the **equilibrium price**; the quantity bought and sold at that price is the **equilibrium quantity**. The equilibrium price is also known as the *market-clearing price*: it is the price that "clears the market" by ensuring that every buyer willing to pay that price finds a seller willing to sell at that price, and vice versa. So how do we find the equilibrium price and quantity?

An economic situation is in **equilibrium** when no individual would be better off doing something different. Equilibrium in a competitive market occurs where the supply and demand curves intersect.

A competitive market is in equilibrium when the price has moved to a level at which the quantity demanded of a good equals the quantity supplied of that good. The price at which this takes place is the **equilibrium price**, also referred to as the *market-clearing price*. The quantity of the good bought and sold at that price is the **equilibrium quantity**.

Finding the Equilibrium Price and Quantity

The easiest way to determine the equilibrium price and quantity in a market is by putting the supply curve and the demand curve on the same diagram. Since the supply curve shows the quantity supplied at any given price and the demand curve shows the quantity demanded at any given price, the price at which the two curves cross is the equilibrium price: the price at which quantity supplied equals quantity demanded.

Figure 2.6-9 combines the supply curve from Figure 2.6-8 with a hypothetical demand curve for wheat. The supply and demand curves intersect at point *E*, which is the equilibrium of this market; $5 is the equilibrium price, and 1 million bushels is the equilibrium quantity. When this market is in equilibrium, the area above the price line and below the demand curve represents consumer surplus, and the area below the price line and above the supply curve represents producer surplus.

Let's confirm that point *E* fits our definition of equilibrium. At a price of $5 per bushel, farmers are willing to sell 1 million bushels of wheat and wheat consumers want to buy 1 million bushels. So at the price of $5 per bushel, the quantity of wheat supplied equals the quantity demanded. Notice that at any other price, the market would not clear: some willing buyers would not be able to find a willing seller, or vice versa. More specifically, if the price were more than $5, the quantity supplied would exceed the quantity demanded; if the price were less than $5, the quantity demanded would exceed the quantity supplied.

Given the demand and supply curves shown in Figure 2.6-9, our model predicts that 1 million bushels of wheat would change hands at a price of $5 per bushel. The consumer surplus would be $\frac{1}{2} \times 1$ million $\times \$3 = \$1.5$ million, and the producer surplus would be $\frac{1}{2} \times 1$ million $\times \$4 = \$2$ million. Module 2.8A discusses the efficiency of equilibrium in a perfectly competitive market due to its maximization of *total surplus*, which is the sum of consumer surplus and producer surplus. But how can we be sure that the market will arrive at the equilibrium price? We begin the next Module by answering that question.

AP® ECON TIP

The term *equilibrium* is used in a variety of situations to indicate *balance* or *no tendency for change*. In the supply and demand model, when a market is in equilibrium, the quantity supplied equals the quantity demanded and there is no shortage or surplus, so there is no tendency for the price to change.

AP® ECON TIP

Equilibrium price and quantity are found where the supply and demand curves intersect on the graph, but the values for price and quantity must be shown on the axes. Points labeled inside the graph are unlikely to receive points when students are asked to show equilibrium price and quantity on the AP® exam.

FIGURE 2.6-9 Market Equilibrium

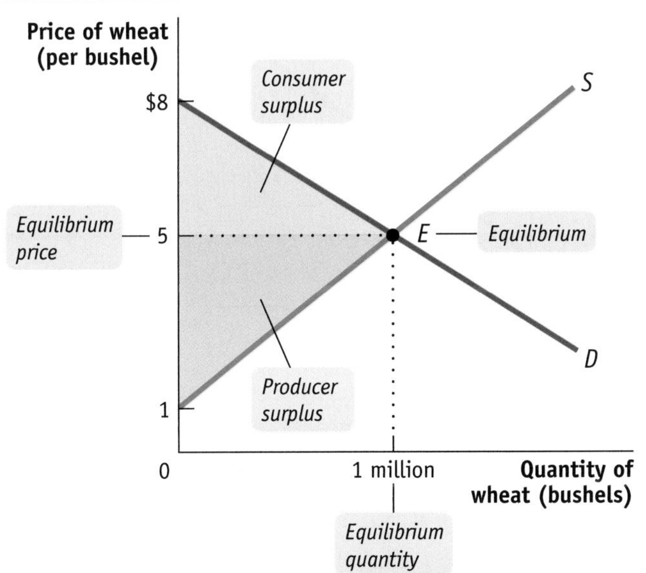

Market equilibrium occurs at point *E*, where the supply curve and the demand curve intersect. In equilibrium, the quantity demanded is equal to the quantity supplied. In this market, $5 is the equilibrium price, and 1 million bushels is the equilibrium quantity. The area above the price line and below the demand curve represents consumer surplus, and the area below the price line and above the supply curve represents producer surplus.

Adventures in AP® Economics

Watch the video: *Consumer and Producer Surplus*

Module 2.6  Review

Check Your Understanding

1. Consider the market for cheese-stuffed jalapeño peppers. There are two consumers, Casey and Josey, and their willingness to pay for each pepper is given in the accompanying table. (Neither is willing to consume more than four peppers at any price.) Use the table (a) to construct the market demand schedule for peppers for prices of $0.00, $0.10, and so on, up to $0.90, and (b) to calculate the total consumer surplus when the price of a pepper is $0.40.

Quantity of peppers	Casey's willingness to pay	Josey's willingness to pay
1st pepper	$0.90	$0.80
2nd pepper	0.70	0.60
3rd pepper	0.50	0.40
4th pepper	0.30	0.30

2. Again consider the market for cheese-stuffed jalapeño peppers. There are two producers, Cara and Jamie, and their costs of producing each pepper are given in the accompanying table. (Neither is willing to produce more than four peppers at any price.) Use the table (a) to construct the market supply schedule for peppers for prices of $0.00, $0.10, and so on, up to $0.90, and (b) to calculate the total producer surplus when the price of a pepper is $0.70.

Quantity of peppers	Cara's cost	Jamie's cost
1st pepper	$0.10	$0.30
2nd pepper	0.10	0.50
3rd pepper	0.40	0.70
4th pepper	0.60	0.90

Tackle the AP® Test: Multiple-Choice Questions

1. Refer to the graph below. What is the value of consumer surplus when the market price is $4?

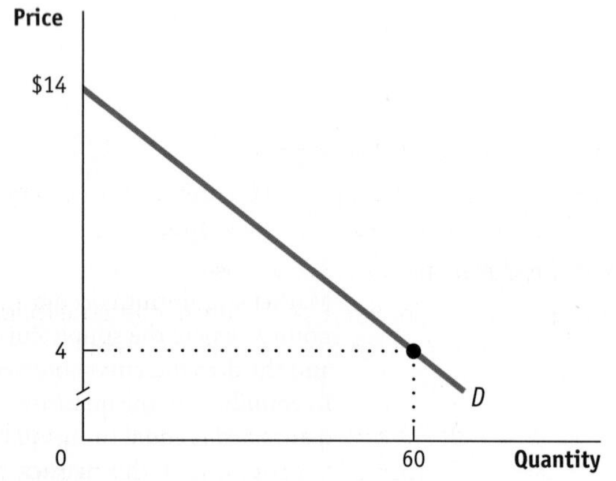

a. $60
b. $240
c. $300
d. $540
e. $600

2. Refer to the graph below. What is the value of producer surplus when the market price is $60?

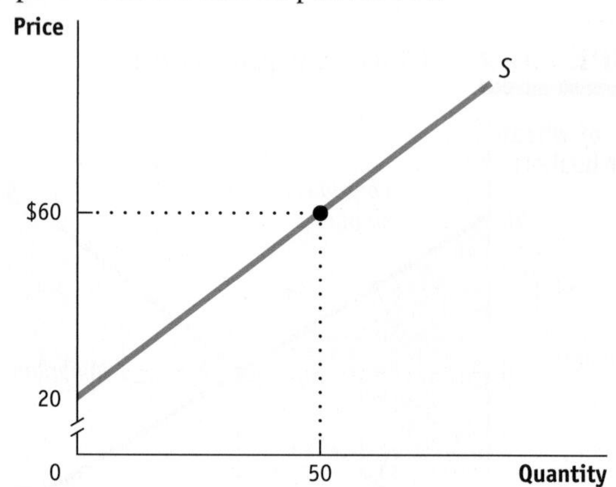

a. $100
b. $150
c. $1,000
d. $1,500
e. $3,000

3. Which of the following is true when a competitive market is in equilibrium?
   a. The producer surplus is maximized.
   b. The consumer surplus is maximized.
   c. The price is halfway between the ideal price for buyers and the ideal price for sellers.
   d. Every buyer willing to pay the current price can find a seller willing to sell at that price.
   e. The demand curve and the supply curve have the same slope.
4. Consumer surplus is found as the area
   a. above the supply curve but below the price.
   b. below the demand curve but above the price.
   c. above the demand curve but below the price.
   d. below the supply curve but above the price.
   e. below the supply curve but above the demand curve.
5. Suppose a new policy allocates kidneys to patients needing a kidney transplant on the basis of who would receive the highest net benefit in terms of the expected increase in life span from a transplant. This policy would essentially be an attempt to maximize
   a. consumer surplus.
   b. producer surplus.
   c. profit.
   d. equity.
   e. respect for elders.
6. Producer surplus is shown on a graph by the area
   a. above the supply curve but below the price.
   b. below the demand curve but above the price.
   c. above the demand curve but below the price.
   d. below the supply curve but above the price.
   e. below the supply curve but above the demand curve.
7. Suppose there is a decrease in the price of swimsuits and no change in the market demand curve for swimsuits. Who receives the resulting increase in consumer surplus?
   a. only buyers who purchased swimsuits at the original price
   b. only buyers who did not purchase swimsuits at the original price
   c. only sellers who sold swimsuits at the original price
   d. everyone who bought or sold swimsuits at the original price
   e. buyers who did, and who did not, purchase swimsuits at the original price

Tackle the AP® Test: Free-Response Questions

1. Refer to the graph provided.

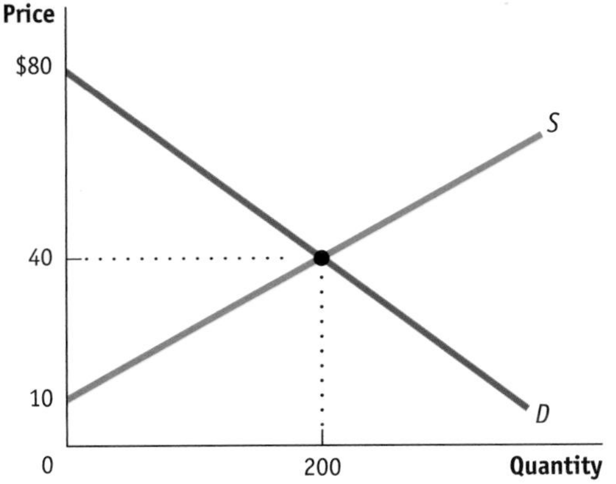

   a. Calculate consumer surplus.
   b. Calculate producer surplus.
   c. If supply increases, what will happen to consumer surplus? Explain.
   d. If demand decreases, what will happen to producer surplus? Explain.

Rubric for FRQ 1 (6 points)

1 point: $4,000

1 point: $3,000

1 point: Consumer surplus will increase.

1 point: An increase in supply lowers the equilibrium price, which causes consumer surplus to increase.

1 point: Producer surplus will decrease.

1 point: A decrease in demand decreases the equilibrium price, which causes producer surplus to decrease.

2. Draw a correctly labeled graph showing a competitive market in equilibrium. On your graph, clearly indicate and label the area of consumer surplus and the area of producer surplus. **(3 points)**

MODULE 2.7

Market Disequilibrium and Changing Market Conditions

In this Module, you will learn to:

- Define a surplus and a shortage
- Explain how changes in a competitive market affect equilibrium price, equilibrium quantity, consumer surplus, and producer surplus
- Calculate the change in consumer and producer surplus that results from a change in market conditions

In Module 2.6 we found that the price and quantity in a competitive market are determined by the market equilibrium, which is located at the intersection of the supply curve and the demand curve. We begin this Module by answering three relevant questions:

1. Why do all sales and purchases in a market take place at the same price?
2. Why does the market price fall if it is above the equilibrium price?
3. Why does the market price rise if it is below the equilibrium price?

Why Do All Sales and Purchases in a Market Take Place at the Same Price?

Gary Yeowell/DigitalVision/Getty Images

Prices for souvenirs vary widely in places where visitors don't have time to comparison shop.

There are some markets where the same good can sell for many different prices, depending on who is selling or who is buying. For example, have you ever bought a souvenir in a popular tourist destination and then seen the same item on sale somewhere else (perhaps even in the shop next door) for a lower price? Because tourists don't know which shops offer the best deals and don't have time for comparison shopping, sellers in tourist areas can charge different prices for the same good.

But in any market in which the buyers and sellers have both been around for some time, sales and purchases tend to converge at a generally uniform price, so we can safely talk about *the* market price. It's easy to see why. Suppose a seller offered a potential buyer a price noticeably above what the buyer knew other people were paying. The buyer would clearly be better off shopping elsewhere—unless the seller were prepared to offer a better deal. Conversely, a seller would not be willing to sell for significantly less than the amount that seller knew most buyers were paying; the seller would be better off waiting to get a more reasonable customer. So in any well-established, ongoing market, all sellers receive and all buyers pay approximately the same price. This is what we call the *market price*.

Why Does the Market Price Fall If It Is Above the Equilibrium Price?

A market is in **disequilibrium** when the market price is above or below the price that equates the quantity demanded with the quantity supplied.

Let's revisit the market for lumber introduced earlier in this Unit. **Figure 2.7-1** illustrates the lumber market in **disequilibrium**, meaning that the market price differs from the price that would equate the quantity demanded with the quantity supplied. In this example, the market price of $1.50 is above the equilibrium price of $1. Why can't the price stay there?

FIGURE 2.7-1 Price Above Its Equilibrium Level Creates a Surplus

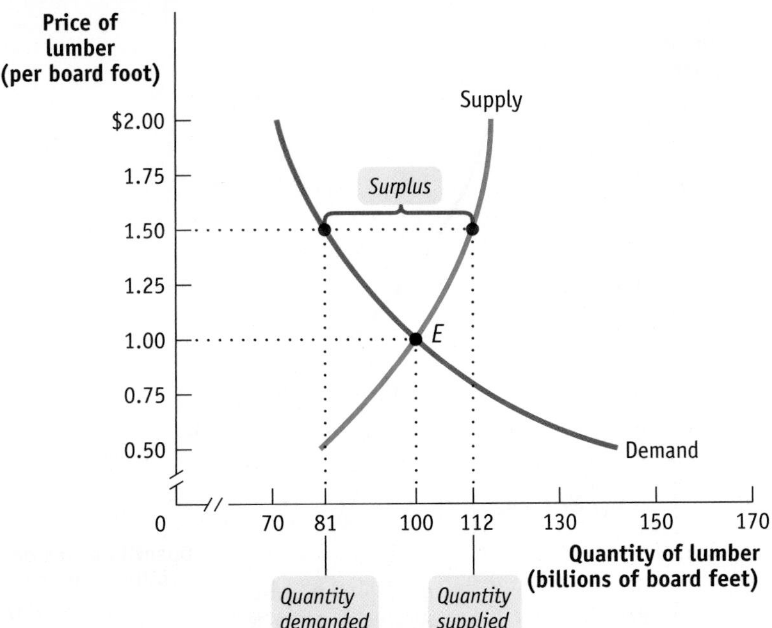

The market price of $1.50 is above the equilibrium price of $1. This places the market in disequilibrium and creates a surplus: at a price of $1.50, producers would like to sell 112 billion board feet but consumers want to buy only 81 billion board feet, so there is a surplus of 31 billion board feet. This surplus will push the price down until it reaches the equilibrium price of $1.

As the figure shows, at a price of $1.50 there would be more board feet of lumber available than consumers wanted to buy: 112 billion board feet would be supplied and 81 billion board feet would be demanded. When the quantity supplied exceeds the quantity demanded, the difference between the quantity supplied and the quantity demanded is described as the **surplus**—also known as the *excess supply*. The difference of 31 billion board feet is the surplus of lumber at a price of $1.50. This surplus of the quantity supplied over the quantity demanded that exists when the market is in disequilibrium should not to be confused with consumer surplus or producer surplus. Consumer surplus and producer surplus constitute net gains from buying or selling a good, and both can exist whether the market is in equilibrium or disequilibrium.

There is a **surplus** of a good or service when the quantity supplied exceeds the quantity demanded. Surpluses occur when the price is above its equilibrium level.

This surplus means that some lumber producers are frustrated: at the current price, they cannot find consumers who want to buy their lumber. The surplus offers an incentive for those frustrated would-be sellers to offer a lower price in order to poach business from other producers and entice more consumers to buy. The result of this price cutting will be to push the prevailing price down until it reaches the equilibrium price. So the price of a good will fall whenever there is a surplus—that is, whenever the market price is above its equilibrium level.

AP® ECON TIP

Consider what you would do if you were selling something for a price that didn't attract enough buyers to purchase the quantity you chose to supply. If you would lower the price, you exemplify the behavior that brings market prices to equilibrium.

Why Does the Market Price Rise If It Is Below the Equilibrium Price?

Now suppose the price is below its equilibrium level—say, at $0.75 per board foot, as shown in **Figure 2.7-2**. In this case, the quantity demanded, 115 billion board feet, exceeds the quantity supplied, 91 billion board feet, implying that there are would-be buyers who cannot find lumber: there is a **shortage**, also known as an *excess demand*, of 24 billion board feet.

There is a **shortage** of a good or service when the quantity demanded exceeds the quantity supplied. Shortages occur when the price is below its equilibrium level.

When there is a shortage, there are frustrated would-be buyers—people who want to purchase lumber but cannot find willing sellers at the current price. In this situation, either buyers will offer more than the prevailing price, or sellers will realize that they can charge higher prices. Either way, the result is to drive up the prevailing price. This bidding up of prices happens whenever there are shortages—and there will be

FIGURE 2.7-2 Price Below Its Equilibrium Level Creates a Shortage

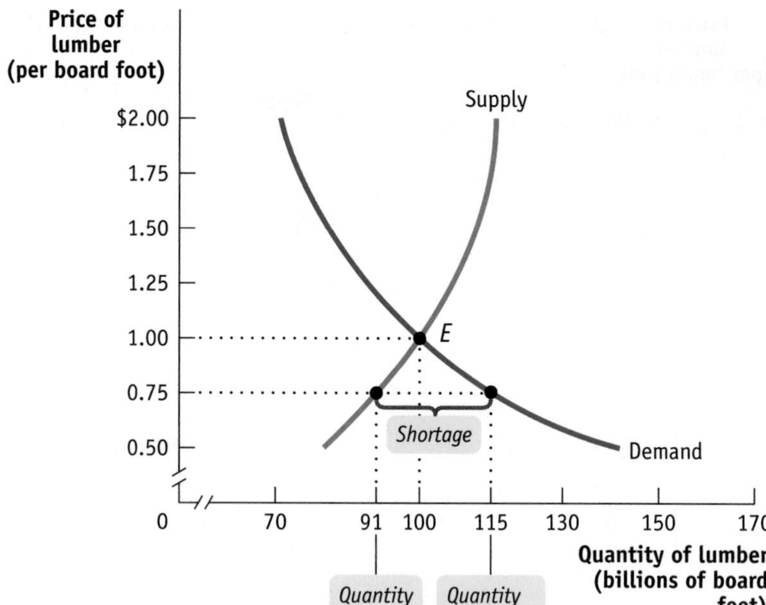

The market price of $0.75 is below the equilibrium price of $1. This creates a shortage: consumers want to buy 115 billion board feet, but only 91 billion board feet are for sale, so there is a shortage of 24 billion board feet. This shortage will push the price up until it reaches the equilibrium price of $1.

shortages whenever the price is below its equilibrium level. So the market price will rise if it is below the equilibrium level.

Using Equilibrium to Describe Markets

We have now seen that a market tends to have a single price, the *equilibrium price.* If the market price is above the equilibrium level, the ensuing surplus leads buyers and sellers to take actions that lower the price. And if the market price is below the equilibrium level, the ensuing shortage leads buyers and sellers to take actions that raise the price. So the market price always *moves toward* the equilibrium price, the price at which there is neither a surplus nor a shortage.

Changes in Supply and Demand

Chris A Selby/Alamy

Pine beetle infestations killed off trees such as this one, decreasing the supply—and increasing the equilibrium price—of lumber.

The devastation of forests by the pine beetle in recent years came as a surprise, but the subsequent increase in the price of lumber was no surprise at all. Suddenly there was a decrease in supply: the quantity of lumber available at any given price fell. Predictably, a decrease in supply raises the equilibrium price.

A beetle infestation is an example of an event that can shift the supply curve for a good without having much effect on the demand curve. There are many such events. There are also events that can shift the demand curve without shifting the supply curve. For example, a medical report that chocolate is good for you increases the demand for chocolate but does not affect the supply. Events generally shift either the supply curve or the demand curve, but not both; it is therefore useful to ask what happens in each case.

What Happens When the Demand Curve Shifts

Wood composites made from plastic and wood fibers are a substitute for lumber. If the price of composites rises, the demand for lumber will increase as more consumers use lumber rather than composites. If the price of composites falls, the demand for lumber will decrease as more consumers are drawn away from lumber by the lower price of composites. But how does the price of composites affect the *market equilibrium* for lumber?

Figure 2.7-3 shows the effect of changes in the price of wood composites on the market for lumber. A rise in the price of composites increases the demand for lumber, and a fall in the price of composites decreases the demand for lumber. Point E_1 shows the equilibrium corresponding to the original demand curve, with P_1 the equilibrium price and Q_1 the equilibrium quantity bought and sold.

FIGURE 2.7-3 Equilibrium and Shifts of the Demand Curve

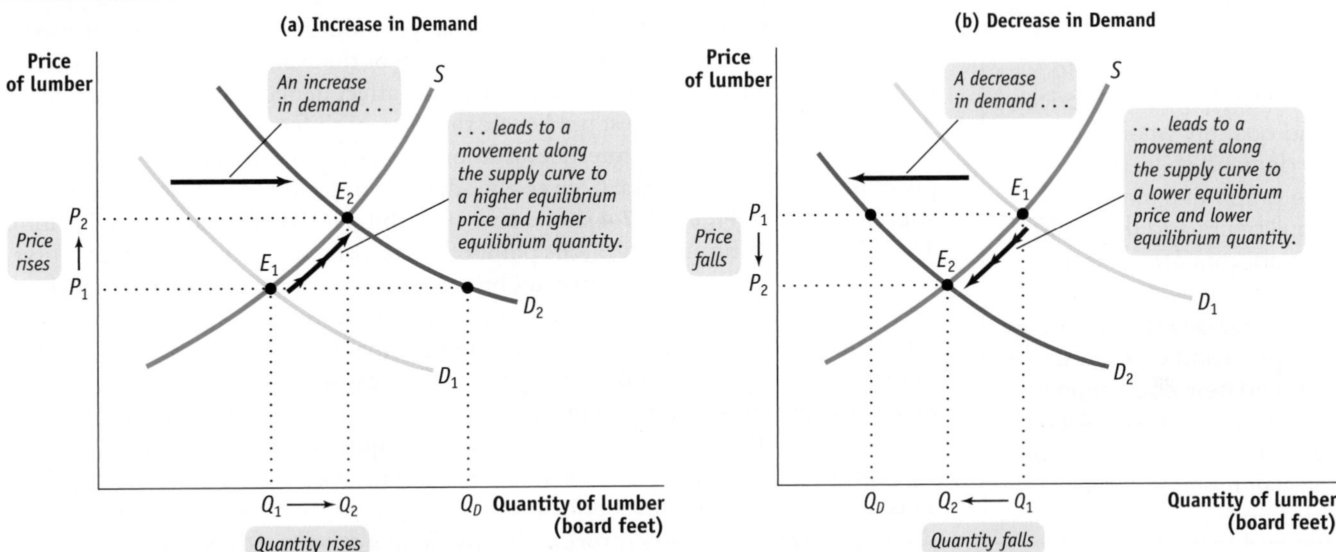

(a) The original equilibrium in the market for lumber is at E_1. A *rise* in the price of wood composites, a lumber substitute, shifts the demand curve D_1 *rightward* to D_2. A *shortage* equal to $(Q_D - Q_1)$ exists at the original price, P_1, causing both the price and quantity supplied to rise, a movement along the supply curve. A new equilibrium is reached at E_2, where quantity demanded is again equal to quantity supplied with a higher equilibrium price, P_2, and a higher equilibrium quantity, Q_2. (b) A *fall* in the price of wood composites shifts the demand curve D_1 *leftward* to D_2. A *surplus* equal to $(Q_1 - Q_D)$ exists at the original price, P_1, causing both the price and quantity supplied to fall, a movement along the supply curve. A new equilibrium is reached at E_2, where quantity demanded is again equal to quantity supplied with a lower equilibrium price, P_2, and a lower equilibrium quantity, Q_2.

An increase in demand is indicated by a *rightward* shift of the demand curve from D_1 to D_2, as shown in panel (a). At the original market price P_1, this market is no longer in equilibrium: a shortage occurs because the quantity demanded, Q_D, exceeds the quantity supplied, Q_1. So the price of lumber rises and generates an increase in the quantity supplied, an upward *movement along the supply curve.* A new equilibrium is established at point E_2, with a higher equilibrium price, P_2, and a higher equilibrium quantity, Q_2.

This sequence of events resulting from a change in demand reflects a general principle: *When demand for a good or service increases, the equilibrium price and the equilibrium quantity of the good or service both rise.*

What would happen in the reverse case of a fall in the price of wood composites? A decrease in demand is indicated by a *leftward* shift of the demand curve from D_1 to D_2, as shown in panel (b) of Figure 2.7-3. At the original market price, P_1, this market is no longer in equilibrium: a surplus occurs because the quantity supplied, Q_1, exceeds the quantity demanded, Q_D. So the price of lumber falls and generates a decrease in the quantity supplied, a downward *movement along the supply curve.* A new equilibrium is established at point E_2, with a lower equilibrium price, P_2, and lower equilibrium quantity, Q_2.

A fall in the price of composites reduces the demand for lumber, shifting the demand curve to the *left*. At the original price, a surplus occurs as quantity supplied exceeds quantity demanded. The price falls and leads to a decrease in the quantity supplied, resulting in a lower equilibrium price and a lower equilibrium quantity. This illustrates another general principle: *When demand for a good or service decreases, the equilibrium price and the equilibrium quantity of the good or service both fall.*

To summarize how a market responds to a change in demand: *An increase in demand leads to a rise in both the equilibrium price and the equilibrium quantity. A decrease in demand leads to a fall in both the equilibrium price and the equilibrium quantity. That is, a change in demand causes equilibrium price and quantity to move in the same direction.*

What Happens When the Supply Curve Shifts

> **AP® ECON TIP**
>
> The graph never lies! To see what happens to price and quantity when supply or demand shifts, draw the graph of a market in equilibrium and then shift the appropriate curve to show the new equilibrium price and quantity. Compare the price and quantity at the old and new equilibriums to find your answer! A quick drawing can even help you answer multiple choice questions.

In the real world, it is a bit easier to predict changes in supply than changes in demand. Physical factors that affect supply, such as weather or the availability of inputs, are easier to get a handle on than the fickle tastes that affect demand. Still, with supply as with demand, what we can best predict are the *effects* of shifts of the supply curve.

As we mentioned earlier, forest devastation by pine beetles sharply reduced the supply of lumber in recent years. Conversely, advances in technology have increased the supply of lumber. **Figure 2.7-4** shows how such shifts affect the market equilibrium. The original equilibrium is at E_1, the point of intersection of the original supply curve, S_1, and the demand curve, with an equilibrium price P_1 and equilibrium quantity Q_1. As a result of insect damage, supply decreases and S_1 shifts *leftward* to S_2, as shown in panel (a). At the original price P_1, a shortage of lumber equal to $(Q_1 - Q_S)$ now exists, and the market is no longer in equilibrium. The shortage causes a rise in price and a fall in quantity demanded, an upward movement along the demand curve. The new equilibrium is at E_2, with an equilibrium price P_2 and an equilibrium quantity Q_2. In the new equilibrium, E_2, the price is higher and the equilibrium quantity is lower than before. This can be stated as a general principle: *When supply of a good or service decreases, the equilibrium price of the good or service rises, and the equilibrium quantity of the good or service falls.*

FIGURE 2.7-4 Equilibrium and Shifts of the Supply Curve

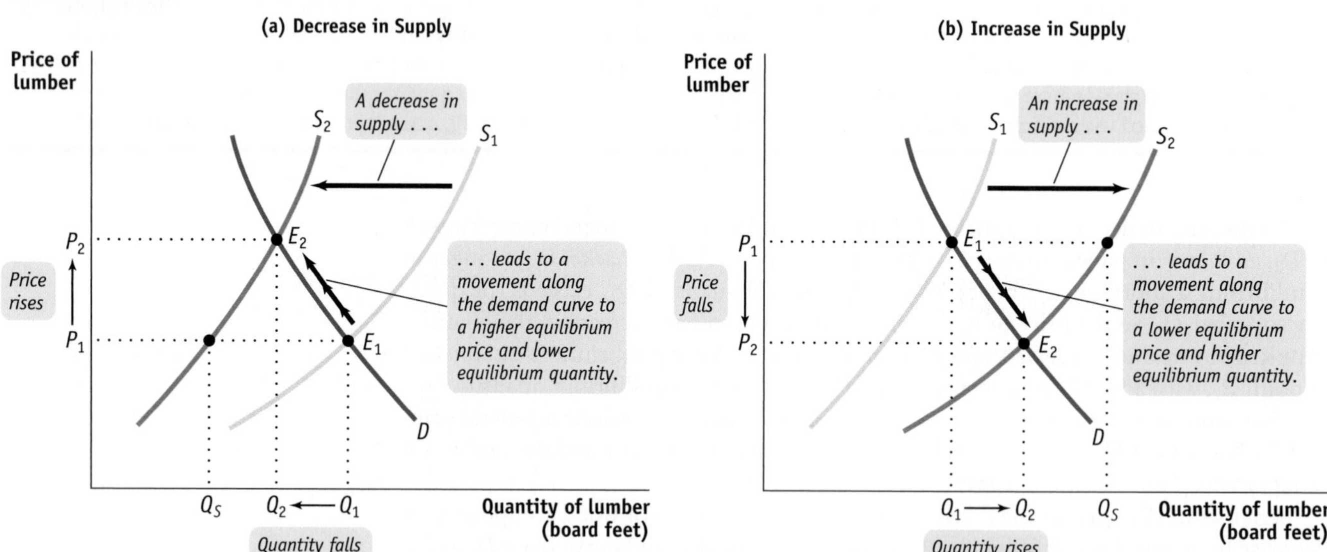

(a) Insect infestation in lumber-growing areas shifts the supply curve *leftward* from S_1 to S_2, creating a *shortage* equal to $(Q_1 - Q_S)$ at the original price, causing an increase in price and a decrease in quantity supplied and a movement along the demand curve. A new equilibrium is established at E_2, where quantity demanded equals quantity supplied with a higher equilibrium price, P_2, and a lower equilibrium quantity, Q_2. (b) The advance in sawmill technology shifts the supply curve *rightward* from S_1 to S_2, creating a *surplus* equal to $(Q_S - Q_1)$ at the original price, causing a decrease in price and an increase in quantity supplied, and a movement along the demand curve. A new equilibrium is established at E_2, where quantity demanded again equals quantity supplied with a lower equilibrium price, P_2, and a higher equilibrium quantity, Q_2.

What happens to the market when supply increases? An increase in supply leads to a *rightward* shift of the supply curve, as shown in panel (b) of Figure 2.7-4. The original equilibrium is at E_1, the point of intersection of the original supply curve, S_1, and the demand curve, with an equilibrium price P_1 and equilibrium quantity Q_1. As a result of an advance in technology, supply increases and S_1 shifts *rightward* to S_2. At the original price, P_1, a surplus of lumber equal to $(Q_S - Q_1)$ now exists and the market is no longer in equilibrium. The surplus causes a fall in price and an increase in quantity demanded, represented by a downward movement along the demand curve. The new equilibrium is at E_2, with an equilibrium price P_2 and an equilibrium quantity Q_2. In the new equilibrium, E_2, the price is lower and the equilibrium quantity is higher than before. This can be stated as a general principle: *When supply of a good or service increases, the equilibrium price of the good or service falls, and the equilibrium quantity of the good or service rises.*

To summarize how a market responds to a change in supply: *An increase in supply leads to a fall in the equilibrium price and a rise in the equilibrium quantity. A decrease in supply leads to a rise in the equilibrium price and a fall in the equilibrium quantity. That is, a change in supply causes equilibrium price and quantity to move in opposite directions.*

AP® ECON TIP

A shift of the demand curve does not cause a shift of the supply curve, and a shift of the supply curve does not cause a shift of the demand curve. A change in the equilibrium price causes a movement *along* the curve that didn't shift.

Changes in Consumer and Producer Surplus

Changes in market conditions cause changes in consumer and producer surplus. **Figure 2.7-5** illustrates how shifts in supply and demand affect the net gains from consumption and production. We have drawn *straight* supply and demand curves to simplify the calculation of each type of surplus.

FIGURE 2.7-5 Shifts and Changes in Consumer and Producer Surplus

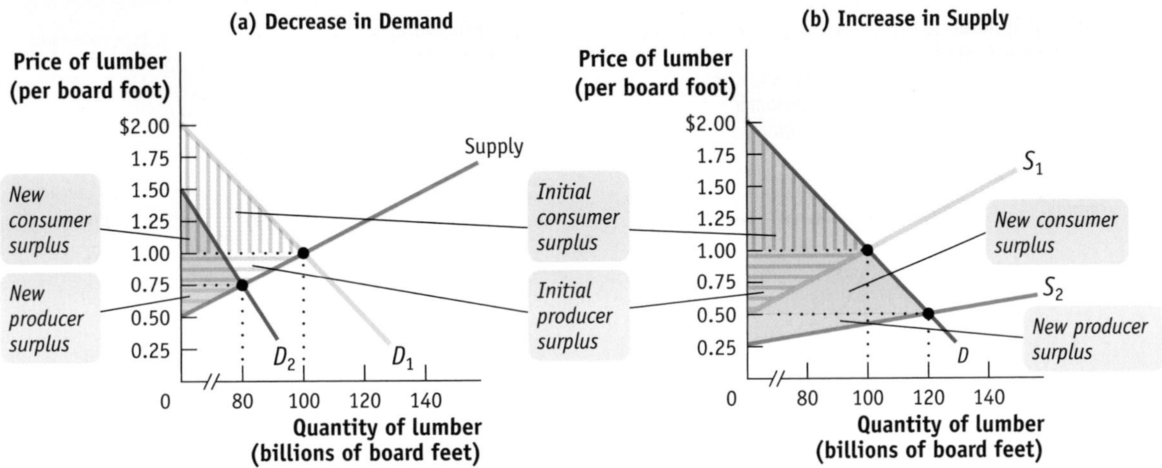

Panel (a) illustrates how a decrease in demand affects consumer and producer surplus. The consumer surplus decreases from ½ × 100 million × \$1.00 = \$50 million to ½ × 80 million × \$0.75 = \$30 million, and the producer surplus decreases from ½ × 100 million × \$0.50 = \$25 million to ½ × 80 million × \$0.25 = \$10 million. Panel (b) illustrates the effect of an increase in supply. Consumer surplus rises from ½ × 100 million × \$1.00 = \$50 million to ½ × 120 million × \$1.50 = \$90 million. Although the quantity rises, the much lower price reduces the producer surplus from ½ × 100 million × \$0.50 = \$25 million to ½ × 120 million × \$0.25 = \$15 million.

Panel (a) shows the effect of a decrease in demand. The initial consumer surplus, marked by vertical blue stripes, is ½ × 100 million × \$1.00 = \$50 million (found using the ½ × base × height formula for a triangle). The initial producer surplus, marked by horizontal red stripes, is ½ × 100 million × \$0.50 = \$25 million. When demand decreases, the price falls from \$1.00 to \$0.75 and the quantity falls from 100 million to 80 million. Both consumers and producers receive a smaller surplus, shaded solid blue and solid red, respectively. The new consumer surplus is ½ × 80 million × \$0.75 = \$30 million, and the new producer surplus is ½ × 80 million × \$0.25 = \$10 million.

Panel (b) shows the effect of an increase in supply. The initial consumer and producer surplus are \$50 million and \$25 million, respectively, as in panel (a). When supply increases, the price falls from \$1.00 to \$0.50 and the quantity increases from 100 million to 120 million. The purchase of a larger quantity at a lower price increases the consumer surplus to the blue shaded area, representing ½ × 120 million × \$1.50 = \$90 million. However, notice that the demand is inelastic in the range of prices from \$1.00 down to \$0.50 – the 50% price drop leads to only a 20% increase in the quantity demanded. The relatively small increase in quantity that follows the large decrease in price, along with the shallow slope of the supply curve, result in a reduction in the producer surplus to the red shaded area representing ½ × 120 million × \$0.25 = \$15 million.

The effects of supply and demand curve shifts on price, quantity, consumer surplus, and producer surplus depend on the price elasticities of supply and demand. To see the importance of these elasticities, we can compare the graphs in Figure 2.7-5 with those in **Figure 2.7-6**, which depict the same shifts but very different elasticities for the curves that do not shift. In panel (a), the supply curve is drawn perfectly elastic. As a result, the price does not change – unlike in panel (a) of Figure 2.7-5. In Figure 2.7-6, there is no producer surplus (that is, there is no difference between the price paid and the lowest price firms would accept) before or after the shift. When the supply is more elastic, the demand shift causes a larger decrease in quantity, and thus a larger decrease in consumer surplus.

FIGURE 2.7-6 Price Elasticities and the Effects of Shifts

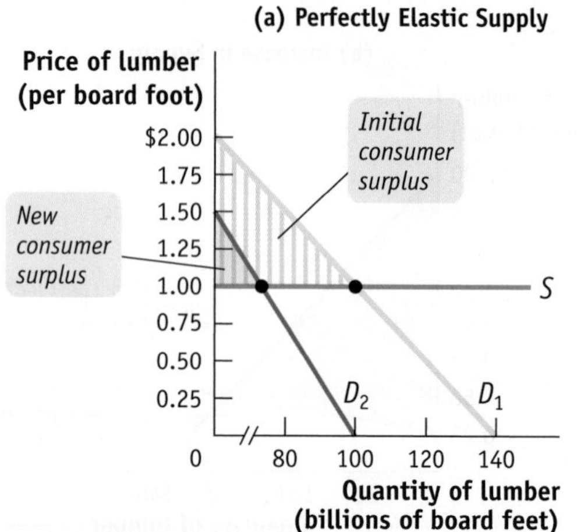

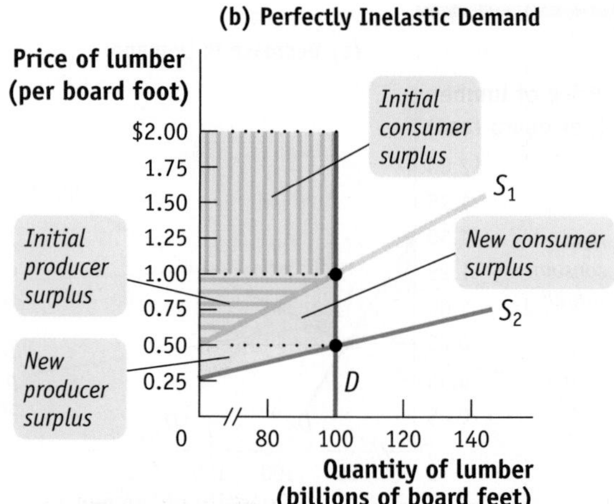

Price elasticities influence the way shifts of supply and demand curves affect price, quantity, consumer surplus, and producer surplus. This figure shows the same shifts depicted in Figure 2.7-5, but the elasticities of the curves that do not shift are very different. In panel (a), the supply curve is perfectly elastic. In this case, there is no producer surplus before or after the shift because consumers pay the lowest price that producers would accept. Relative to when supply was not perfectly elastic, the shift in the demand curve causes a larger decrease in the equilibrium quantity, and thus a larger decrease in consumer surplus. In panel (b), the demand curve is perfectly inelastic up to a price of \$2.00 per board foot. The result is an equilibrium quantity that does not change when the supply curve shifts. Relative to demand that is not perfectly inelastic, the consumer surplus and the price change are larger and the producer surplus is smaller as a result of the shift, because the quantity does not increase.

In panel (b) of Figure 2.7-6, the demand curve is perfectly inelastic up to a price of \$2.00 per board foot. In this case, the equilibrium quantity does not change when the supply curve shifts. The consumer surplus and the price change are larger, and the producer surplus is smaller after the shift, because the quantity does not increase.

The important takeaway is that the elasticities of supply and demand have a large influence on the changes in price, quantity, and surplus that result from a shift in supply or demand.

Simultaneous Shifts of Supply and Demand Curves

It sometimes happens that simultaneous events shift *both* the demand and supply curves at the same time. This is not unusual; in real life, supply curves and demand curves for many goods and services shift quite often because the economic environment continually changes.

Figure 2.7-7 illustrates two examples of simultaneous shifts of the supply and demand curves. In both panels there is an increase in demand—that is, a rightward shift of the demand curve, from D_1 to D_2—for example, representing an increase in the demand for lumber due to changing tastes in home renovations. Notice that the rightward shift in panel (a) is larger than the one in panel (b): we can suppose that panel (a) represents a year in which many more people than usual choose to improve their homes, and panel (b) represents a normal year. Both panels also show a decrease in supply—that is, a leftward shift of the supply curve from S_1 to S_2. Also notice that the leftward shift in panel (b) is larger than the one in panel (a): we can suppose that panel (b) represents the effect of particularly severe beetle infestations, and panel (a) represents the effect of much less severe insect damage.

FIGURE 2.7-7 Simultaneous Shifts of the Demand and Supply Curves

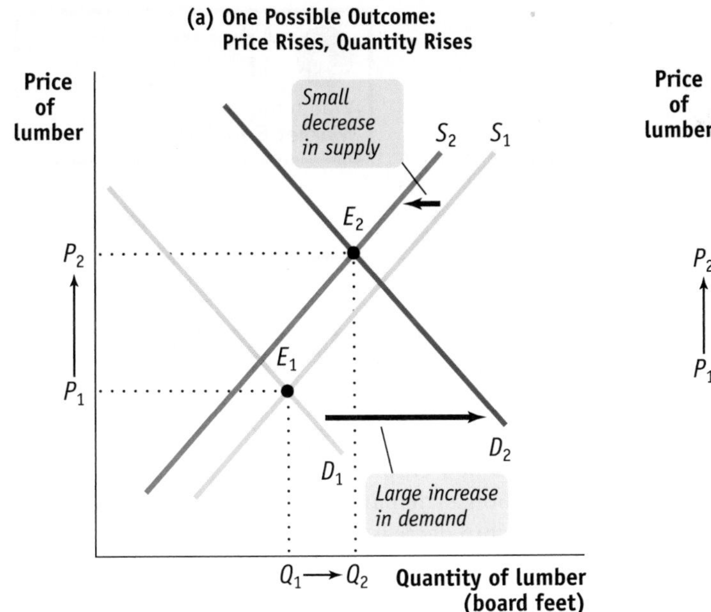

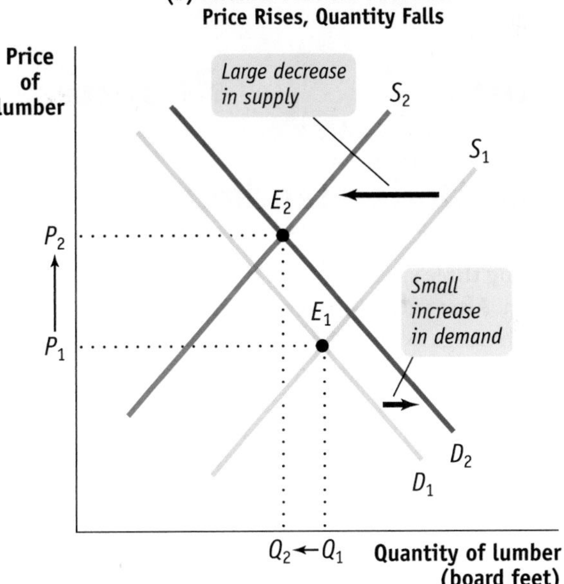

In panel (a) there is a simultaneous rightward shift of the demand curve and leftward shift of the supply curve. Here the increase in demand is sufficiently large relative to the decrease in supply to cause both the equilibrium price and the equilibrium quantity to rise. In panel (b) there is also a simultaneous rightward shift of the demand curve and leftward shift of the supply curve. Here the decrease in supply is large enough relative to the increase in demand to cause the equilibrium quantity to fall while the equilibrium price rises.

In both cases, the equilibrium price rises from P_1 to P_2 as the equilibrium moves from E_1 to E_2. But what happens to the equilibrium quantity, the quantity of lumber bought and sold? In panel (a) the increase in demand is large enough relative to the decrease in supply so that the equilibrium quantity rises as a result. In panel (b), the decrease in supply is sufficiently large relative to the increase in demand to cause the equilibrium quantity to fall as a result. That is, when demand increases and supply decreases, the actual quantity bought and sold can go either way, depending on the *relative sizes* of the shifts in demand and supply.

> **AP® ECON TIP**
>
> To clarify what you know and what you don't know about the effect of simultaneous shifts, treat each shift individually and identify the effect on equilibrium price and quantity. Both shifts will have the same effect on either price or quantity, so you know how that has changed. The shifts will have opposite effects on either price or quantity, so unless you know the relative sizes of the shifts, that result is ambiguous.

In general, when supply and demand shift in opposite directions, we can't predict the ultimate effect on the quantity bought and sold. Without information on the relative sizes of the shifts, we can only make the following prediction about the outcome:

- When demand increases and supply decreases, the equilibrium price rises but the change in the equilibrium quantity is ambiguous.
- When demand decreases and supply increases, the equilibrium price falls but the change in the equilibrium quantity is ambiguous.

Now suppose that the demand and supply curves shift in the same direction. Can we safely make any predictions about the changes in price and quantity? In this situation, the change in quantity bought and sold can be predicted, but the change in price is ambiguous. The two possible outcomes when the supply and demand curves shift in the same direction (which you should check for yourself) are as follows:

- When both demand and supply increase, the equilibrium quantity rises but the change in the equilibrium price is ambiguous.
- When both demand and supply decrease, the equilibrium quantity falls but the change in the equilibrium price is ambiguous.

Module 2.7  Review

Watch the video: ***Market Equilibrium***

Check Your Understanding

1. In the following three situations, the market is initially in equilibrium. After each event described below, does a surplus or shortage exist at the original equilibrium price? What will happen to the equilibrium price as a result?
   a. There is a bumper crop of grapes.
   b. After a hurricane, Florida hoteliers often find that many people cancel their upcoming vacations, leaving them with empty hotel rooms.
   c. After a heavy snowfall, many people want to buy second-hand snowblowers at the local tool shop.
2. For each of the following examples, explain how the indicated change affects supply or demand for the good in question and how the shift you describe affects the equilibrium price and quantity.
   a. As the price of gasoline rose in the United States during the early 2020s, more people bought electric cars.
   b. Technological innovation in the use of recycled paper has lowered the cost of paper production.
   c. When a movie-streaming service lowers its price, local movie theaters have more unfilled seats.
3. Periodically, a computer-chip maker such as Intel introduces a new chip that is faster than the previous one. In response, demand for computers using the earlier chip decreases as customers put off purchases in anticipation of machines containing the new chip. Simultaneously, computer makers increase their production of computers containing the earlier chip in order to clear out their stocks of those chips.

   Draw two diagrams of the market for computers containing the earlier chip: (a) one in which the equilibrium quantity falls in response to these events; and (b) one in which the equilibrium quantity rises. What happens to the equilibrium price in each diagram?

Tackle the AP® Test: Multiple-Choice Questions

1. In a market with an upward-sloping supply curve, in which of the following cases will the producer surplus definitely increase?
   - **a.** There is an increase in demand.
   - **b.** There is an increase in demand and a decrease in supply.
   - **c.** There is an increase in supply.
   - **d.** There is a decrease in demand and an increase in supply.
   - **e.** There is a decrease in supply.
2. Price will tend to fall when
   - **a.** there is a shortage.
   - **b.** quantity demanded is greater than quantity supplied.
   - **c.** quantity supplied is less than quantity demanded.
   - **d.** price is above equilibrium.
   - **e.** price is below equilibrium.
3. Which of the following describes what will happen in the market for tomatoes if a salmonella outbreak is attributed to tainted tomatoes?
   - **a.** Supply will decrease and price will increase.
   - **b.** Supply will decrease and price will decrease.
   - **c.** Demand will decrease and price will increase.
   - **d.** Demand will decrease and price will decrease.
   - **e.** Supply and demand will both decrease.
4. Which of the following will lead to an increase in the equilibrium price of product X? A(n)
   - **a.** increase in consumer incomes if product X is an inferior good.
   - **b.** increase in the price of machinery used to produce product X.
   - **c.** technological advance in the production of good X.
   - **d.** decrease in the price of good Y (a substitute for good X).
   - **e.** expectation by consumers that the price of good X is going to fall.
5. The equilibrium price will rise, but the equilibrium quantity may increase, decrease, or stay the same if
   - **a.** demand increases and supply decreases.
   - **b.** demand increases and supply increases.
   - **c.** demand decreases and supply increases.
   - **d.** demand decreases and supply decreases.
   - **e.** demand increases and supply does not change.
6. An increase in the number of buyers and a technological advance will cause
   - **a.** demand to increase and supply to increase.
   - **b.** demand to increase and supply to decrease.
   - **c.** demand to decrease and supply to increase.
   - **d.** demand to decrease and supply to decrease.
   - **e.** no change in demand and an increase in supply.
7. Which of the following is certainly true if demand and supply increase at the same time?
   - **a.** The equilibrium price will increase.
   - **b.** The equilibrium price will decrease.
   - **c.** The equilibrium quantity will increase.
   - **d.** The equilibrium quantity will decrease.
   - **e.** The equilibrium quantity may increase, decrease, or stay the same.
8. An increase in demand will have the largest effect on the equilibrium quantity when the supply curve is
   - **a.** upward sloping.
   - **b.** downward sloping.
   - **c.** perfectly inelastic.
   - **d.** perfectly elastic.
   - **e.** unit elastic.

Tackle the AP® Test: Free-Response Questions

1. Draw a correctly labeled graph showing the market for tomatoes in equilibrium. Label the equilibrium price "P_E" and the equilibrium quantity "Q_E." On your graph, draw a horizontal line indicating a price, labeled "P_C," that would lead to a shortage of tomatoes. Label the size of the shortage on your graph.

Rubric for FRQ 1 (6 points)

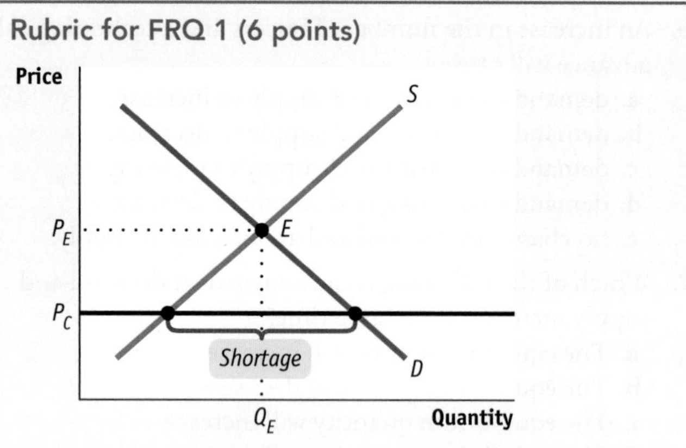

1 point: Graph with the vertical axis labeled "Price" or "P" and the horizontal axis labeled "Quantity" or "Q"

1 point: Downward-sloping demand curve labeled "Demand" or "D"

1 point: Upward-sloping supply curve labeled "Supply" or "S"

1 point: Equilibrium price "P_E" labeled on the vertical axis and quantity "Q_E" labeled on the horizontal axis at the intersection of the supply and demand curves

1 point: Price line at a price "P_C" below the equilibrium price

1 point: Correct indication of the shortage, which is the horizontal distance between the quantity demanded and the quantity supplied at the height of P_C

2. Draw a correctly labeled graph showing the market for cups of coffee in equilibrium. On your graph, show the effect of a decrease in the price of coffee beans on the equilibrium price and the equilibrium quantity in the market for cups of coffee. Use vertical stripes to shade in the initial producer surplus and horizontal stripes to shade in the producer surplus after the price of coffee beans decreases. **(7 points)**

MODULE 2.8A

Government Intervention: Taxes, Subsidies, and Market Efficiency

In this Module, you will learn to:

- Discuss the efficiency of market outcomes
- Use graphs to show how taxes and subsidies can lead to deadweight loss
- Describe how the elasticity of supply and demand affect tax incidence
- Explain how taxes and subsidies affect market outcomes and government budgets

Consumer Surplus, Producer Surplus, and Market Efficiency

Markets are a remarkably effective way to organize economic activity: under the right conditions, they can make society as well off as possible given the available resources. The concepts of consumer and producer surplus that we learned in the previous Modules can help us deepen our understanding of why this is so.

The Gains from Trade

Module 2.6 discussed consumer and producer surplus in a small market for used textbooks. Now consider a much bigger used textbook market—say, one at a large state university. Because it has many potential buyers and sellers of the same textbook, the market is competitive. By lining up students who are potential buyers in the order of their willingness to pay, starting with the student with the highest willingness to pay and ending with the student with the lowest willingness to pay, we can use those values to assemble a demand curve like the one in **Figure 2.8-1**. Similarly, we can line up students who are potential sellers of the book, from the student with the lowest cost of selling it to the student with the highest cost of selling it, to derive a supply curve like the one shown in the figure.

Patrick T. Fallon/AFP/Getty Images

This hypothetical market reaches equilibrium at a price of $60 per book, and 1,000 books are bought and sold at that price. The two shaded triangles show the consumer surplus (blue) and the producer surplus (pink) generated by this market. The sum of consumer and producer surplus, the total net gain to consumers and producers from trading in a market, is known as **total surplus.**

Total surplus is the total net gain to consumers and producers from trading in a market. It is the sum of consumer and producer surplus.

The striking thing about this picture is that both consumers and producers gain—that is, both consumers and producers are better off because there is a market for this good. This illustrates another core principle of economics: *There are gains from trade*. These gains are the reason everyone is better off participating in a market economy than they would be if each individual tried to be self-sufficient. But could the net gains from trade be larger? This is a question of market efficiency.

The Efficiency of Markets

A market is *efficient* if no change in its workings could make some people better off without making other people worse off. Could a change improve the outcome in

FIGURE 2.8-1 Total Surplus

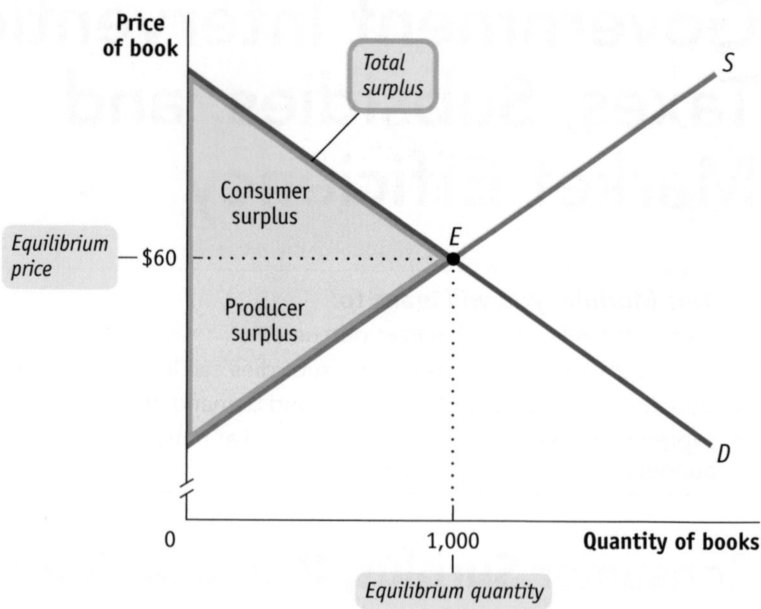

In the market for used textbooks, the equilibrium price is $60 and the equilibrium quantity is 1,000 books. Consumer surplus is given by the blue area, the area below the demand curve but above the price. Producer surplus is given by the pink area, the area above the supply curve but below the price. The sum of the blue and the pink areas is total surplus (indicated by the green triangle), the total benefit to society from the production and consumption of the good.

the textbook market? Imagine a committee whose goal is to replace the outcome determined by market equilibrium with an alternative outcome that would increase total surplus — that is, to increase the total net gain for consumers and producers.

Let's consider three approaches the committee could take:

1. It could reallocate consumption among consumers.
2. It could reallocate sales among sellers.
3. It could change the quantity traded.

The Reallocation of Consumption Among Consumers

The committee might try to increase total surplus by selling the used books to different consumers. **Figure 2.8-2** shows why this will result in lower surplus compared to the market equilibrium outcome. Points *A* and *B* show the positions of potential buyers Ana and Bob, respectively, on the demand curve. As we can see from the figure, Ana is willing to pay $70 for a book, but Bob is willing to pay only $50. Since the market equilibrium price is $60, under the market outcome Ana gets a book and Bob does not.

Now suppose the committee reallocates consumption. This would mean taking the book away from Ana and giving it to Bob. Since the book is worth $70 to Ana but only $50 to Bob, this change *reduces total consumer surplus* by $70 – $50 = $20. Moreover, this result of a decrease in total surplus doesn't depend on which two students we pick. Every student who buys a book at the market equilibrium price has a willingness to pay of $60 or more, and every student who doesn't buy a book has a willingness to pay of less than $60. So reallocating the good among consumers always means taking a book away from a student who values it more and giving it to one who values it less. This necessarily reduces total consumer surplus.

The Reallocation of Sales Among Sellers

The committee might try to increase total surplus by altering who sells their books, taking sales away from sellers who would have sold their books at the market equilibrium price, and compelling those who would not have sold their books at that

FIGURE 2.8-2 Reallocating Consumption Lowers Consumer Surplus

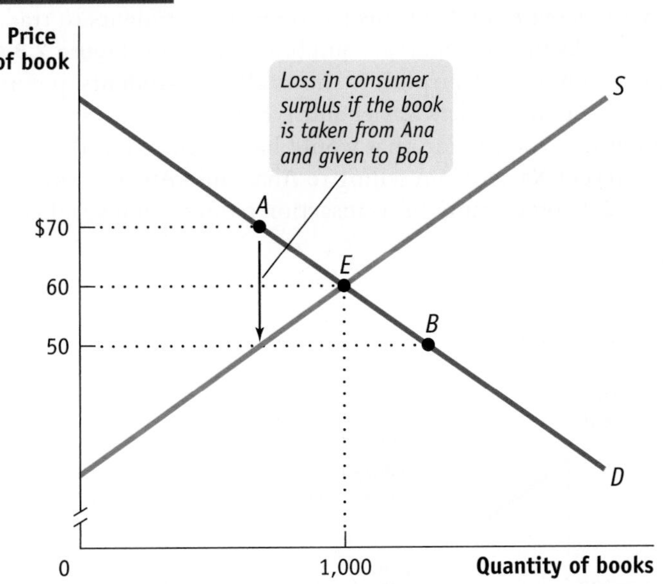

Ana (point *A*) has a willingness to pay of $70. Bob (point *B*) has a willingness to pay of only $50. At the market equilibrium price of $60, Ana purchases a book but Bob does not. If we rearrange consumption by taking a book from Ana and giving it to Bob, consumer surplus declines by $20 and, as a result, total surplus declines by $20. The market equilibrium generates the highest possible consumer surplus by ensuring those who consume the good are those who most value it.

price to do so. **Figure 2.8-3** shows why this will result in lower surplus. Here points *X* and *Y* show the positions on the supply curve of Xavier, who has a cost of $50, and Yvonne, who has a cost of $70. At the equilibrium market price of $60, Xavier would sell his book but Yvonne would not sell hers. If the committee reallocated sales, forcing Xavier to keep his book and Yvonne to sell hers, total producer surplus would be reduced by $70 – $50 = $20. Again, there is a decrease in total surplus no matter which seller and non-seller we choose to switch. Any student who sells a book at the market equilibrium price has a lower cost than any student who keeps a book. So reallocating sales among sellers necessarily increases total cost and reduces total producer surplus.

FIGURE 2.8-3 Reallocating Sales Lowers Producer Surplus

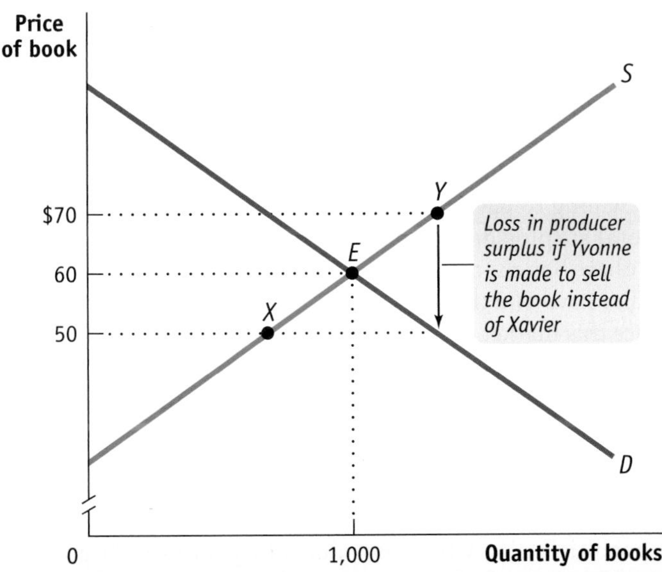

Yvonne (point *Y*) has a cost of $70, $20 more than Xavier (point *X*), who has a cost of $50. At the market equilibrium price of $60, Xavier sells a book but Yvonne does not. If we rearrange sales by preventing Xavier from selling his book and compelling Yvonne to sell hers, producer surplus declines by $20 and, as a result, total surplus declines by $20. The market equilibrium generates the highest possible producer surplus by ensuring that those who sell the good are those who most value the ability to sell it.

Changes in the Quantity Traded

The committee might try to increase total surplus by compelling students to trade either more books or fewer books than the market equilibrium quantity. **Figure 2.8-4** shows why this will result in lower total surplus. It shows all four students: potential buyers Ana and Bob, and potential sellers Xavier and Yvonne. To reduce sales, the committee will have to prevent a transaction that would have occurred in the market equilibrium – that is, prevent Xavier from selling to Ana. Since Ana is willing to pay \$70 and Xavier's cost is \$50, preventing this transaction reduces total surplus by \$70 – \$50 = \$20.

FIGURE 2.8-4 Changing the Quantity Lowers Total Surplus

If Xavier (point *X*) were prevented from selling his book to someone like Ana (point *A*), total surplus would fall by \$20, the difference between Ana's willingness to pay (\$70) and Xavier's cost (\$50). This means that total surplus falls whenever fewer than 1,000 books – the equilibrium quantity – are bought and sold. Likewise, if Yvonne (point *Y*) were compelled to sell her book to someone like Bob (point *B*), total surplus would also fall by \$20, the difference between Yvonne's cost (\$70) and Bob's willingness to pay (\$50). This means that total surplus falls whenever more than 1,000 books are bought and sold.

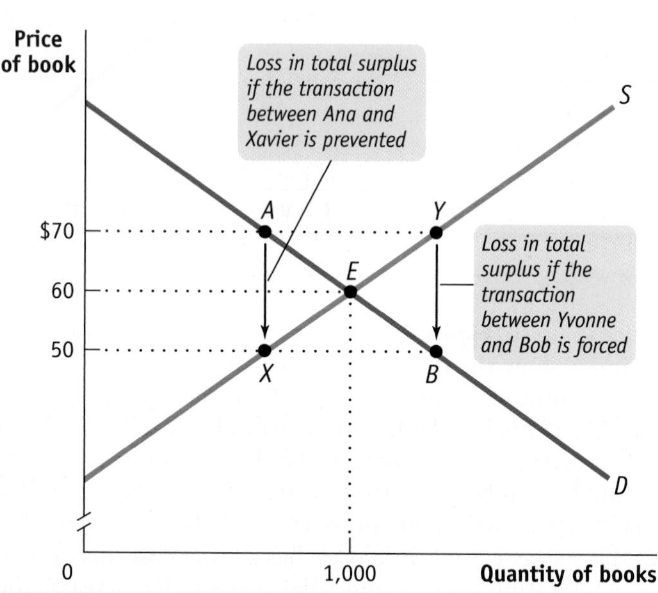

AP® ECON TIP

Anything that prevents the sale of a unit that would have occurred in market equilibrium reduces total surplus.

Once again, this result doesn't depend on which two students we pick: any student who would have sold the book in the market equilibrium has a cost of \$60 or less, and any student who would have purchased the book in the market equilibrium has a willingness to pay of \$60 or more. So preventing any sale that would have occurred in the market equilibrium necessarily reduces total surplus.

Finally, the committee might try to increase sales by forcing Yvonne, who would not have sold her book at the market equilibrium price, to sell it to someone like Bob, who would not have bought a book at the market equilibrium price. Because Yvonne's cost is \$70, but Bob is only willing to pay \$50, this transaction reduces total surplus by \$20. And once again, total surplus decreases no matter which two students we pick – anyone who wouldn't have bought the book has a willingness to pay of less than \$60, and anyone who wouldn't have sold the book has a cost of more than \$60.

The key point is that once this market is in equilibrium, there is no way to increase the gains from trade. Any other outcome reduces total surplus. We can summarize our results by stating that an efficient market performs four important functions:

1. It distributes the good to the potential buyers who most value it, as indicated by the fact that they have the highest willingness to pay. This is called *distributive efficiency*.
2. It allocates sales to the potential sellers who most value the right to sell the good, as indicated by the fact that they have the lowest cost. Producing goods at the lowest possible cost is known as *productive efficiency*.

3. It ensures that every consumer who makes a purchase values the good more than every seller who makes a sale, so that all transactions are mutually beneficial.
4. It ensures that every potential buyer who doesn't make a purchase values the good less than every potential seller who doesn't make a sale, so that no mutually beneficial transactions are missed.

Together, the third and fourth functions allocate resources to the production of all of those units of a good – and only those units – whose value to consumers exceeds the cost of making them. To do this is to achieve *allocative efficiency*. Each of these types of efficiency is discussed further in Module 3.7.

It is important to see that government intervention in a market that does achieve efficiency can lead to inefficient distribution, production, and allocation. There are three caveats, however. First, although a market may be efficient, it isn't necessarily *fair*. In fact, fairness, or *equity*, is often in conflict with efficiency. We'll discuss this in the next section.

The second caveat is that, under some well-defined conditions, markets can fail to deliver efficiency. When this occurs, markets no longer maximize total surplus. We'll take a closer look at market failures in Unit 6.

Third, even when the market equilibrium maximizes total surplus, this does not mean that it results in the best outcome for every *individual* consumer and producer. Shortly, we'll see that if the government intervenes in an efficient market, say by raising or lowering the price, some people will be happier, but society as a whole will be worse off because total surplus would be lower.

Equity and Efficiency

It's easy to get carried away with the idea that markets are always good and that economic policies that interfere with efficiency are bad. Even if all markets were efficient to begin with, the assumption that nothing should change would be misguided because there is another factor to consider: society also cares about equity, or what's "fair."

Edwin Remsberg/The Image Bank/Getty Images

There is often a trade-off between equity and efficiency. Policies that promote equity can come at the cost of decreased efficiency, and policies that promote efficiency can result in decreased equity. So it's important to realize that a society's choice to sacrifice some efficiency for the sake of equity, however it defines equity, may be a valid one. It's also important to understand that fairness, unlike efficiency, can be very hard to define. Fairness is a concept about which well-intentioned people often disagree.

The trade-off between equity and efficiency is at the core of many debates over taxes and subsidies. Consider the question of how the tax burden should vary with individuals' income. All taxes are ultimately paid out of income, so this question is relevant to more than just income taxes. Any tax that has high-income taxpayers pay a smaller percentage of their income than low-income taxpayers is a **regressive tax**. For instance, a sales tax is regressive, because high-income people generally spend a smaller proportion of their income than low-income people, so high-income taxpayers pay the sales tax on a relatively small portion of their income. Any tax that has all taxpayers pay the same percentage of their income is a **proportional tax**. A "flat" income tax of, say, 10% on all income would be an example of a proportional tax. Any tax that has high-income taxpayers pay a larger percentage of their income than low-income taxpayers is a **progressive tax**. The current U.S. income tax system is progressive.

A **regressive tax** rises less than in proportion to income.

A **proportional tax** rises in proportion to income.

A **progressive tax** rises more than in proportion to income.

Unfortunately, the most equitable taxes are generally not the most efficient taxes. For example, advocates of progressive income taxes emphasize the fairness of placing a heavier tax burden on high-income taxpayers. Critics argue that progressive income taxes create a growing disincentive for workers to increase their earnings. Such equity-efficiency trade-offs fuel debates and force tough decisions for policy makers.

Next, we'll see how to measure the efficiency loss caused by some particular taxes; later in this Module, we'll discuss taxes that are efficient but not equitable.

The Effects of Taxes on Total Surplus

An **excise tax** is a tax on sales of a particular good or service.

To understand the economics of taxes, it's helpful to look at a simple type of tax known as an **excise tax**—a tax charged on each unit of a particular good or service that is sold. Most tax revenue in the United States comes from other kinds of taxes, but excise taxes are common. For example, there are federal excise taxes on gasoline, cigarettes, and foreign-made trucks, and many local governments impose excise taxes on services such as hotel room rentals. The lessons we'll learn from studying excise taxes apply to other, more complex taxes as well.

The Effect of an Excise Tax on Quantities and Prices

Suppose that the supply and demand for hotel rooms in the city of Newaygo are as shown in **Figure 2.8-5**. We'll make the simplifying assumption that all hotel rooms are the same. In the absence of taxes, the equilibrium price of a room is $80 per night and the equilibrium quantity of hotel rooms rented is 10,000 per night.

FIGURE 2.8-5 **The Supply and Demand for Hotel Rooms in Newaygo**

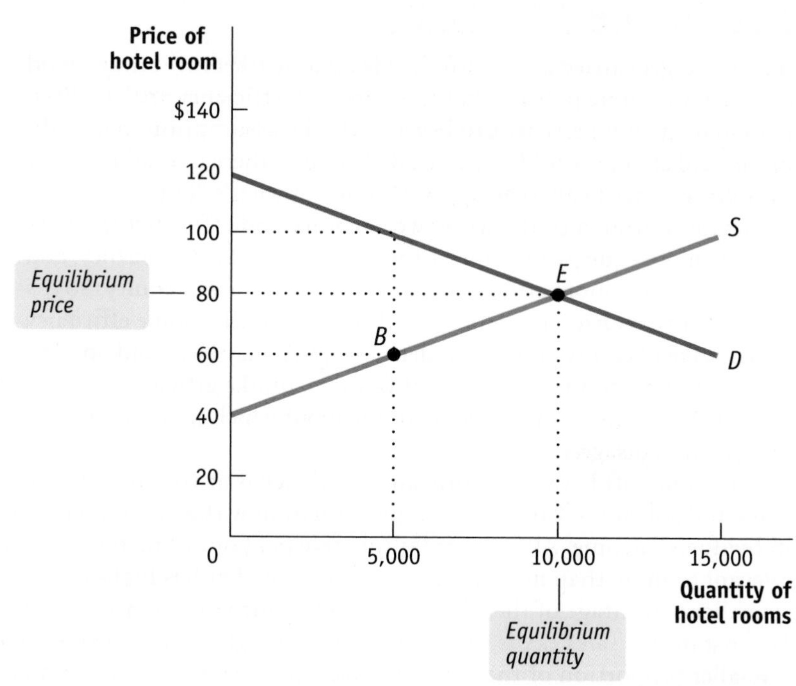

In the absence of taxes, the equilibrium price of hotel rooms is $80 per night, and the equilibrium number of rooms rented is 10,000 per night, as shown by point *E*. The supply curve, *S*, shows the quantity supplied at any given price, pre-tax. At a price of $60 per night, hotel owners are willing to supply 5,000 rooms, as shown by point *B*. But post-tax, hotel owners are willing to supply the same quantity only at a price of $100 per night: $60 for themselves plus $40 paid to the city as tax.

Now suppose that Newaygo's government imposes an excise tax of $40 per night on hotel rooms—that is, every time a room is rented for the night, the owner of the hotel must pay the city $40. For example, if a customer pays $80, $40 of that payment is collected as a tax, leaving the hotel owner with only $40. As a result of this tax, hotel owners are less willing to supply rooms at any given price.

What does this imply about the supply curve for hotel rooms in Newaygo? To answer this question, we must compare the incentives of hotel owners *pre-tax* (before the tax is levied) to their incentives *post-tax* (after the tax is levied). From Figure 2.8-5 we know that pre-tax, hotel owners are willing to supply 5,000 rooms per night at a price of $60 per room. But after the $40 tax per room is levied, they are willing to supply the same quantity, 5,000 rooms, only if they receive $100 per room—$60 for themselves plus $40 paid to the city as tax. Likewise, at every quantity supplied, the price that producers must receive to produce a given quantity has increased by $40. This result implies that the post-tax supply curve lies above the pre-tax supply curve by the amount of the tax.

The upward shift of the supply curve caused by the tax is shown in **Figure 2.8-6**, where S_1 is the pre-tax supply curve and S_2 is the post-tax supply curve. As you can see, the market equilibrium moves from E, at the equilibrium price of $80 per room and 10,000 rooms rented each night, to A, at a market price of $100 per room and only 5,000 rooms rented each night. In this case, $100 is the price consumers pay for 5,000 rooms, but hotel owners receive only $60 after paying the $40 tax. From the point of view of hotel owners, it is as if they were on their original supply curve at point B.

How do we know that 5,000 rooms will be supplied at a price of $100? Because the price *net of tax* is $60, and according to the original supply curve, 5,000 rooms will be supplied at a price of $60, as shown by point B in Figure 2.8-6.

An excise tax effectively *drives a wedge* between the price paid by consumers and the price received by producers. As a result of this wedge, consumers pay more and producers receive less. In our example, consumers—people who rent hotel rooms—end up paying $100 per night, $20 more than the pre-tax price of $80. At the same time, producers—the hotel owners—receive a price net of tax of $60 per room, $20 less than the pre-tax price. In addition, the tax creates missed opportunities: 5,000 potential consumers who would have rented hotel rooms—those willing to pay $80 but not $100 per night—are discouraged from renting

FAIRFIELD INN & SUITES® Marriott | FAIRFIELD INN

Fairfield Inn & Suites®
New York Downtown Manhattan
World trade Center Area

Guest — Room: **1203** Room Type: **KING**

Arrive:	Time:	Depart:	Time:
25Feb18	03:45PM	28Feb18	

Date	Description	Charges
25Feb18	Room Charge	97.00
25Feb18	State Occupancy Tax	8.61
25Feb18	Occupancy Sales Tax	5.70
25Feb18	City Tax	1.50
25Feb18	Tourism Tax	2.00
26Feb18	Room Charge	146.00
26Feb18	State Occupancy Tax	12.96
26Feb18	Occupancy Sales Tax	8.58
26Feb18	City Tax	1.50
26Feb18	Tourism Tax	2.00
27Feb18	Room Charge	264.00
27Feb18	State Occupancy Tax	23.43
27Feb18	Occupancy Sales Tax	15.51
27Feb18	City Tax	1.50
27Feb18	Tourism Tax	2.00

This hotel receipt lists several taxes, each of which drives a wedge between the price paid by the consumer and the price received by the hotel owners.

FIGURE 2.8-6 An Excise Tax Imposed on Hotel Owners

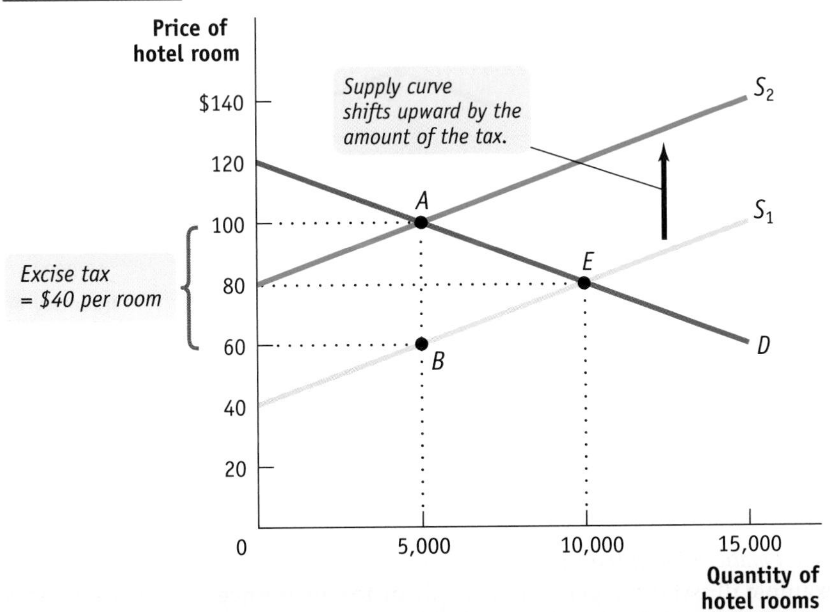

A $40 per room tax imposed on hotel owners shifts the supply curve from S_1 to S_2, an upward shift of $40. The equilibrium price of hotel rooms rises from $80 to $100 per night, and the equilibrium quantity of rooms rented falls from 10,000 to 5,000. Although hotel owners pay the tax, they actually bear only half the burden: the price they receive net of tax falls only $20, from $80 to $60. Guests who rent rooms bear the other half of the burden because the price they pay rises by $20, from $80 to $100.

> **AP® ECON TIP**
>
> A tax of a certain amount or percentage per unit of a good, such as a $1 per unit excise tax or a 5% sales tax, generally increases the equilibrium price and decreases the equilibrium quantity.

rooms. Correspondingly, 5,000 rooms that would have been made available by hotel owners for $80 are not offered when they receive only $60. So this tax leads to inefficiency by distorting incentives and creating missed opportunities for mutually beneficial transactions.

It's important to recognize that as we've described it, Newaygo's hotel tax is a tax on the hotel owners, not their guests—it's a tax on the producers of hotel services, not the consumers. Yet the price received by producers, net of tax, is down by only $20, half the amount of the tax, and the price paid by consumers is up by $20. In effect, half the tax is being paid by consumers.

What would happen if the city levied a tax on consumers instead of producers? Suppose that instead of requiring hotel owners to pay $40 per night for each room they rent, the city required hotel *guests* to pay $40 for each night they stayed in a hotel. **Figure 2.8-7** shows the result. If hotel guests must pay a tax of $40 per night to the government, the amount guests would pay to the hotel for any particular quantity of rooms *not including the tax* falls by $40. For example, if guests would pay up to $100 per room for 5,000 rooms in the absence of a tax, they would only pay the hotel up to $60 per room for 5,000 rooms if they also have to pay a $40 tax per room, making their total payment per room including the tax $100. Likewise, at every quantity demanded, the price that consumers must be offered to demand a given quantity has fallen by $40. So the demand curve shifts *downward* by the amount of the tax, from D_1 to D_2. This shifts the equilibrium from *E* to *B*, where the market price of hotel rooms is $60 and 5,000 hotel rooms are rented. In effect, hotel guests pay $100 when you include the tax. So from the point of view of guests, it is as if they were on their original demand curve at point *A*.

FIGURE 2.8-7 An Excise Tax Imposed on Hotel Guests

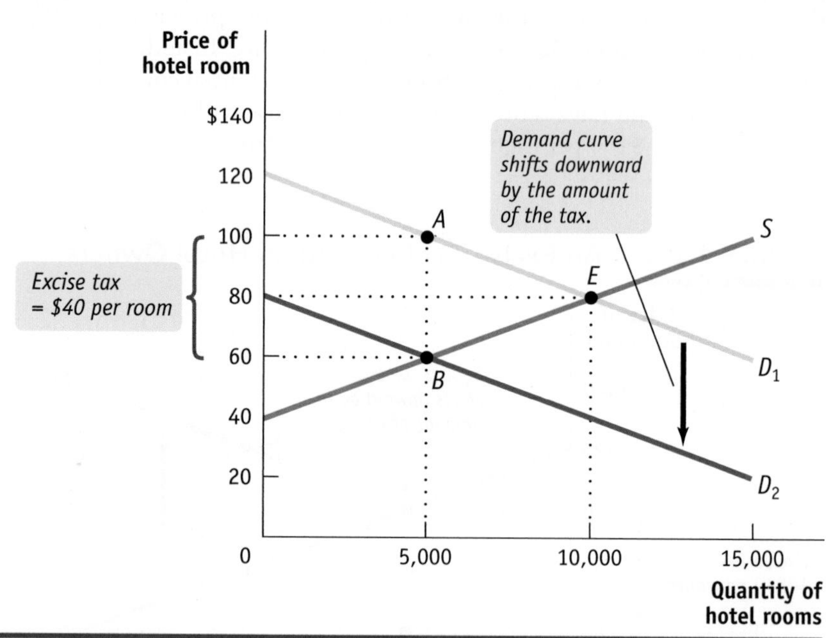

A $40 per room tax imposed on hotel guests shifts the demand curve from D_1 to D_2, a downward shift of $40. The equilibrium price of hotel rooms falls from $80 to $60 per night, and the quantity of rooms rented falls from 10,000 to 5,000. In this case the tax is officially paid by consumers, while in Figure 2.8-6 the tax was paid by producers, but the outcome is the same: after taxes, hotel owners receive $60 per room and guests pay $100.

If you compare Figures 2.8-6 and 2.8-7, you will notice that the effects of the tax are the same even though different curves shifted. In each case, consumers pay $100 per unit (including the tax, if it is their responsibility), producers receive $60 per unit (after paying the tax, if it is their responsibility), and 5,000 hotel rooms are bought and sold. *In fact, it doesn't matter who officially pays the tax—the equilibrium outcome is the same.*

Tax incidence is the distribution of the tax burden.

This example illustrates a general principle of **tax incidence**, a measure of who really pays a tax: the burden of a tax cannot be determined by looking at who writes the check to the government. In this particular case, a $40 tax on hotel rooms brings about a $20 increase in the price paid by consumers and a $20 decrease in the price received by producers. Regardless of whether the tax is levied on consumers or producers, the incidence of the tax is the same. As we will see next, the burden of a tax depends on the price elasticities of supply and demand.

Price Elasticities and Tax Incidence

In the example shown in Figures 2.8-5 through 2.8-7, a tax on hotel rooms falls equally on consumers and producers, no matter on whom the tax is levied. This 50–50 split between consumers and producers is a result of our assumptions in this example. In the real world, the incidence of an excise tax usually falls unevenly between consumers and producers: one group bears more of the burden than the other.

What determines how the burden of an excise tax is allocated between consumers and producers? The answer depends on the shapes of the supply curve and the demand curve. *More specifically, the incidence of an excise tax depends on the price elasticity of supply and the price elasticity of demand.* (Refer back to Table 2.5-1 for a refresher on elasticity.) We can see this by looking first at a case in which consumers pay most of an excise tax, and then at a case in which producers pay most of the tax.

When an Excise Tax Is Paid Mainly by Consumers

Figure 2.8-8 shows an excise tax that falls mainly on consumers: an excise tax on gasoline, which we set at $1 per gallon. (There really is a federal excise tax on gasoline, though it is actually only about $0.18 per gallon in the United States. In addition, some states impose excise taxes between $0.09 and $0.59 per gallon.) According to Figure 2.8-8, in the absence of the tax, gasoline would sell for $2 per gallon.

FIGURE 2.8-8 An Excise Tax Paid Mainly by Consumers

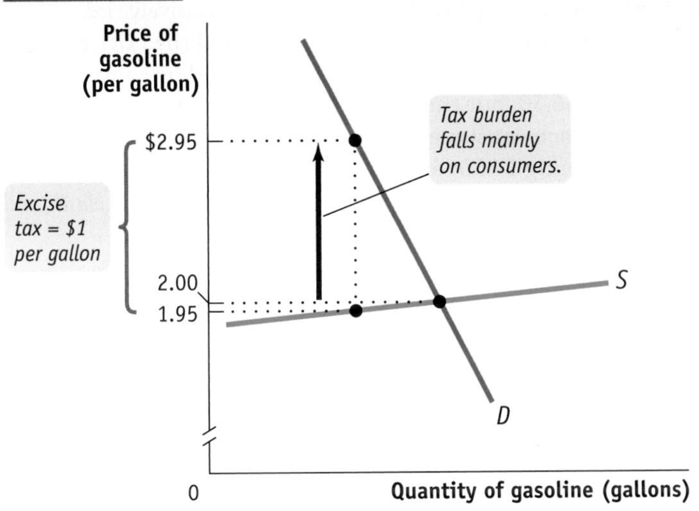

The relatively steep demand curve here reflects a price-inelastic demand for gasoline. The relatively flat supply curve reflects a price-elastic supply. The pre-tax price of a gallon of gasoline is $2.00, and a tax of $1.00 per gallon is imposed. The price paid by consumers rises by $0.95 to $2.95, reflecting the fact that most of the burden of the tax falls on consumers. Only a small portion of the tax is borne by producers: the price they receive falls by only $0.05 to $1.95.

The shapes of the supply and demand curves in Figure 2.8-8 reflect two key assumptions. First, the demand for gasoline is assumed to be price inelastic (that is, the price elasticity of demand is assumed to be less than 1), so the demand curve is relatively steep. Recall that when demand is price inelastic, the quantity demanded changes little in response to a change in price. Second, the supply of gasoline is assumed to be price elastic (the price elasticity of supply is assumed to be greater than 1), so the supply curve is relatively flat. A price-elastic supply means that the quantity supplied changes a lot in response to a change in price.

We have just learned that an excise tax drives a wedge, equal to the size of the tax, between the price paid by consumers and the price received by producers. This wedge drives the price paid by consumers up and the price received by producers down. But as we can see from Figure 2.8-8, in this case those two effects are very unequal in size. The price received by producers falls only slightly, from \$2.00 to \$1.95, but the price paid by consumers rises by a lot, from \$2.00 to \$2.95. This means that consumers bear the greater share of the tax burden.

This example illustrates another general principle of taxation: *When the demand is price inelastic and the supply is price elastic, the burden of an excise tax falls mainly on consumers.* Why? A price-inelastic demand means that consumers have few substitutes and, therefore, little alternative to buying higher-priced gasoline. In contrast, a price-elastic supply results from the fact that producers have many production substitutes for their gasoline (that is, the crude oil from which gasoline is refined can be made into other things, such as plastic). This gives producers much greater flexibility in refusing to accept lower prices for their gasoline. And, not surprisingly, the party with the least flexibility—in this case, consumers—gets stuck paying most of the tax. This is a good description of how the burden is allocated between consumers and producers for most of the excise taxes actually collected in the United States, such as those on cigarettes and alcoholic beverages.

Thinkstock Images/Getty Images

Cavan Images/Getty Images

When an Excise Tax Is Paid Mainly by Producers

Figure 2.8-9 shows an example of an excise tax paid mainly by producers: a \$5.00 per day tax on downtown parking in a small city. In the absence of the tax, the market equilibrium price of parking is \$6.00 per day.

We've assumed in this case that the supply is price inelastic because the lots used for parking have very few alternative uses. This makes the supply curve for parking spaces relatively steep. The demand, however, is assumed to be price elastic. Consumers can easily switch from the downtown spaces to other parking spaces a few minutes' walk from downtown that are not subject to the tax, and some consumers can ride bikes or use public transportation. This makes the demand curve relatively flat.

The tax drives a wedge between the price paid by consumers and the price received by producers. In this example, however, the tax causes the price paid by consumers to rise only slightly, from \$6.00 to \$6.50, but the price received by producers falls a lot, from \$6.00 to \$1.50. In the end, each consumer bears only \$0.50 of the \$5 tax burden, with producers bearing the remaining \$4.50 for each parking space used.

Again, this example illustrates a general principle: *When the demand is price elastic and the supply is price inelastic, the burden of an excise tax falls mainly on producers.*

FIGURE 2.8-9 An Excise Tax Paid Mainly by Producers

The relatively flat demand curve here reflects a price-elastic demand for downtown parking, and the relatively steep supply curve results from a price-inelastic supply. When a tax of \$5.00 per day is imposed on parking spaces, the price received by producers falls a lot, \$4.50, reflecting the fact that they bear most of the tax burden. The price paid by consumers rises a small amount, \$0.50, so they bear very little of the burden.

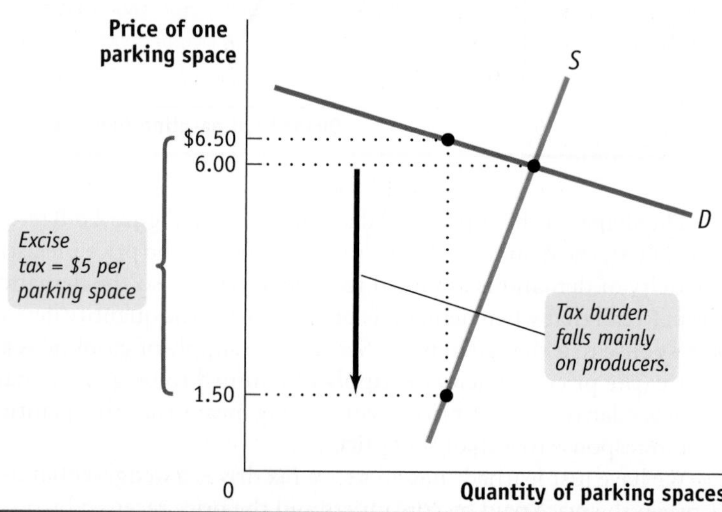

The Benefits and Costs of Taxation

When a government is considering whether to impose a tax or how to design a tax system, it has to weigh the benefit of a tax against its cost. We may not think of a tax as something that is beneficial, but governments need money to provide things people want, such as streets, schools, national defense, and health care for those unable to afford it. The benefit of a tax is the revenue it raises for the government to pay for these services. Unfortunately, this benefit comes at a cost—a cost that is normally larger than the amount consumers and producers pay. Let's look first at what determines how much money a tax raises and then at the cost a tax imposes.

The Revenue from an Excise Tax

How much revenue does the government collect from an excise tax? In our hotel tax example, the revenue is equal to the area of the shaded rectangle in **Figure 2.8-10**.

FIGURE 2.8-10 The Revenue from an Excise Tax

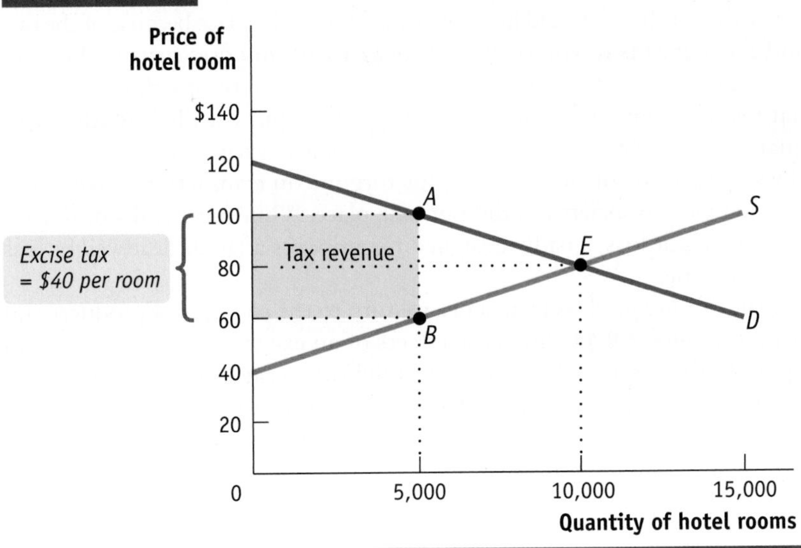

The revenue from a $40 excise tax on hotel rooms is $200,000, equal to the tax rate, $40—the size of the wedge that the tax drives between the price consumers pay and the price producers receive—multiplied by the number of rooms rented, 5,000. This is equal to the area of the shaded rectangle.

To see why this area represents the revenue collected by a $40 tax on hotel rooms, notice that the *height* of the rectangle is $40, equal to the tax per room. As we've seen, it is also the size of the wedge that the tax drives between the price received by producers (sometimes called the *supply price*) and the price paid by consumers (sometimes called the *demand price*). Meanwhile, the *width* of the rectangle is 5,000 rooms, equal to the equilibrium quantity of rooms given the $40 tax. With that information, we can make the following calculations.

The tax revenue collected is

$$\text{Tax revenue} = \$40 \text{ per room} \times 5{,}000 \text{ rooms} = \$200{,}000.$$

The area of the shaded rectangle is

$$\text{Area} = \text{Height} \times \text{Width} = \$40 \text{ per room} \times 5{,}000 \text{ rooms} = \$200{,}000.$$

So,

$$\text{Tax revenue} = \text{Area of shaded rectangle.}$$

This equation summarizes a general principle: *The revenue collected by an excise tax is equal to the area of a rectangle with the height of the tax wedge between the supply price and the demand price and the width of the quantity sold under the tax.*

The Costs of Taxation

What is the cost of a tax? You might be inclined to answer that it is the amount of money taxpayers pay to the government—the tax revenue collected. But suppose the government uses the tax revenue to provide services that taxpayers want. Or suppose that the government simply hands the tax revenue back to taxpayers in the form of a rebate. Would we say in those cases that the tax didn't actually cost anything?

No—because a tax prevents mutually beneficial transactions from occurring. Consider Figure 2.8-10 once more. Here, with a \$40 tax on hotel rooms, guests pay \$100 per room but hotel owners receive only \$60 per room. Because of the decrease in quantity, we know that some transactions didn't occur that would have occurred without the tax. More specifically, we know from the supply and demand curves that there are some potential guests who would be willing to pay almost \$100 per night and some hotel owners who would be willing to supply rooms if they received a bit more than \$60 per night. If these two sets of people were allowed to trade with each other without the tax, they would engage in mutually beneficial transactions—hotel rooms would be rented. But such deals would be illegal because the \$40 tax would not be paid. In our example, 5,000 potential hotel room rentals that would have occurred in the absence of the tax, and would have benefitted both guests and hotel owners, do not take place because of the tax.

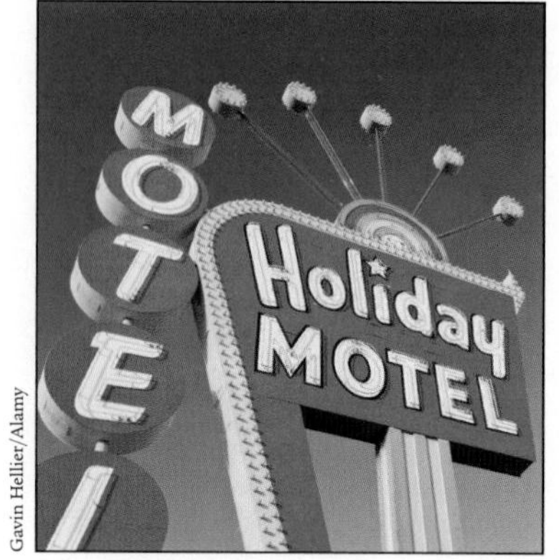

Gavin Hellier/Alamy

So over and above the tax revenue collected, an excise tax imposes costs in the form of inefficiency, because the tax discourages mutually beneficial transactions. The cost to society that results from an inefficient quantity of output is called **deadweight loss**. When quantity is inefficiently low, as is the case when an excise tax is imposed, the deadweight loss is the value of the total surplus forgone on transactions that would have provided a net gain to society but did not take place. While most real-world taxes impose some deadweight loss, a badly designed tax imposes a larger deadweight loss than a well-designed one.

Deadweight loss is the net loss to society resulting from an inefficient quantity of output. When quantity is inefficiently low, that loss is the total surplus forgone on the transactions that would provide a net gain to society but did not occur.

To measure the deadweight loss from a tax, we turn to the concepts of producer and consumer surplus. **Figure 2.8-11** shows the effects of an excise tax on consumer and producer surplus. In the absence of the tax, the equilibrium is at E and the equilibrium price and quantity are P_E and Q_E, respectively. An excise tax drives a wedge equal to the amount of the tax between the price received by producers and the price paid by consumers, reducing the quantity sold. In this case, with a tax of T dollars per unit, the quantity sold falls to Q_T. The price paid by consumers rises to P_C. The price received by producers falls to P_P. The difference between these prices, $P_C - P_P$, is equal to the excise tax, T.

FIGURE 2.8-11 A Tax Reduces Consumer and Producer Surplus

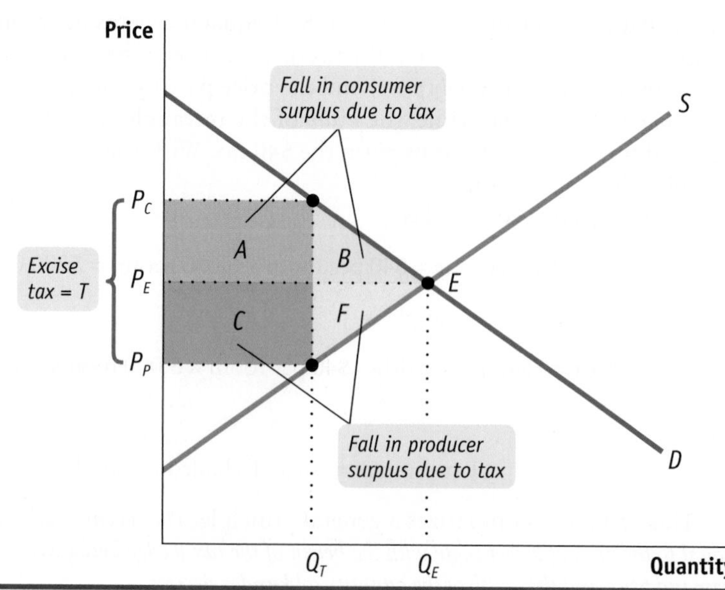

Before the tax, the equilibrium price and quantity are P_E and Q_E, respectively. After an excise tax of T per unit is imposed, the price to consumers rises to P_C and consumer surplus falls by the sum of the dark blue rectangle, labeled A, and the light blue triangle, labeled B. The tax also causes the price to producers to fall to P_P; producer surplus falls by the sum of the red rectangle, labeled C, and the pink triangle, labeled F. The government receives revenue from the tax, $Q_T \times T$, which is given by the sum of the areas A and C. Areas B and F represent the losses to consumer and producer surplus that are not collected by the government as revenue; they are the deadweight loss to society of the tax.

Using the concepts of producer and consumer surplus, we can show exactly how much surplus producers and consumers lose as a result of the tax. We learned previously that a fall in the price of a good generates a gain in consumer surplus that is equal to the sum of the areas of a rectangle and a triangle. Similarly, a price increase causes a loss to consumers that is represented by the sum of the areas of a rectangle and a triangle. In the case of an excise tax, the rise in the price paid by consumers causes a loss equal to the sum of the areas of the dark blue rectangle labeled *A* and the area of the light blue triangle labeled *B* in Figure 2.8-11.

Meanwhile, the fall in the price received by producers leads to a fall in producer surplus. This loss in producer surplus is the sum of the areas of the red rectangle labeled *C* and the pink triangle labeled *F* in Figure 2.8-11.

Of course, although consumers and producers are hurt by the tax, the government gains revenue. The revenue the government collects is equal to the tax per unit sold, *T*, multiplied by the quantity sold, Q_T, or the area of a rectangle Q_T wide and *T* high. In the figure, this area is the sum of rectangles *A* and *C*. So the government gains part of what consumers and producers lose from an excise tax.

A portion of the loss to producers and consumers from the tax is not offset by a gain of tax revenue for the government. Specifically, triangles *B* and *F* represent the deadweight loss caused by the tax. That loss is the amount of total surplus that would have been generated by transactions that now do not take place because of the tax. The deadweight loss is simply lost—it is not transferred or captured in any way by consumers, producers, the government, or anyone else.

Figure 2.8-12 is a version of Figure 2.8-11 that leaves out rectangles *A* (the surplus shifted from consumers to the government) and *C* (the surplus shifted from producers to the government) and shows only the deadweight loss, drawn here as a triangle shaded yellow. The base of that triangle is equal to the tax wedge, *T*; the height of the triangle is equal to the reduction in the quantity transacted due to the tax, $Q_E - Q_T$. Clearly, the larger the tax wedge and the larger the reduction in the quantity transacted, the greater the inefficiency from the tax. But also note an important, contrasting point: if the excise tax somehow *didn't* reduce the quantity bought and sold in this market—if Q_T remained equal to Q_E after the tax was levied—the yellow triangle would disappear and the deadweight loss from the tax would be zero. So it is by discouraging transactions that an excise tax creates deadweight loss. In Module 2.9, we'll see that at the international level, import quotas and tariffs (which are essentially

> **AP® ECON TIP**
> It is useful to practice some problems in which letters represent the values on a graph, and specific numbers are not provided, because you may need to solve problems like that on the AP® exam.

> **AP® ECON TIP**
> On a graph, deadweight loss is represented by a triangle that points in the direction of the efficient quantity.

FIGURE 2.8-12 The Deadweight Loss of a Tax

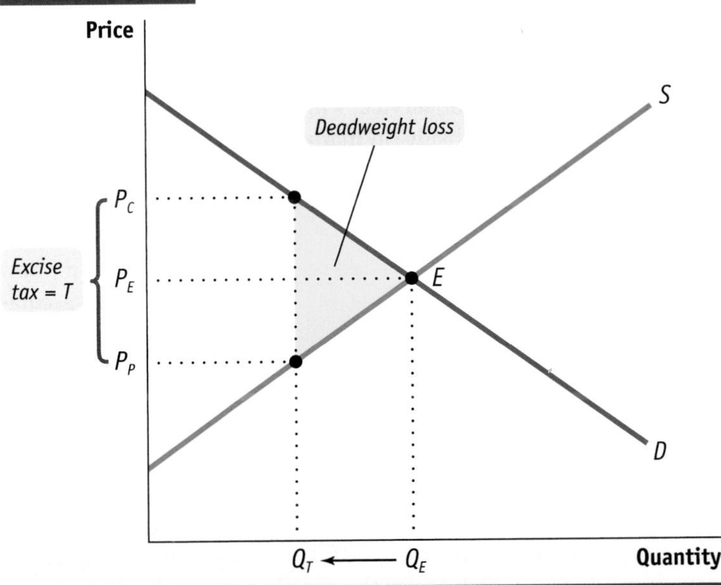

A tax leads to a deadweight loss because it creates inefficiency: some mutually beneficial transactions never take place because of the tax, namely the transactions from Q_T to Q_E. The yellow area in the graph represents the value of the deadweight loss, which is the total surplus that would have been gained from those discouraged transactions.

taxes on imports) discourage transactions between countries, which likewise creates deadweight loss.

Some extreme forms of taxation, such as the regressive *poll tax* instituted by the government of British Prime Minister Margaret Thatcher in 1990 to fund community services, are notably unfair but very efficient. A poll tax is an example of a **lump-sum tax**, a tax that is the same for everyone regardless of any actions people take. A lump-sum tax does not distort incentives because people have to pay the same amount of tax regardless of what they earn, buy, or sell. So lump-sum taxes, although unfair, do not create inefficiencies or deadweight loss. The poll tax in Britain was widely perceived as much less fair than the tax structure it replaced, in which local taxes were proportional to property values.

A **lump-sum tax** is a tax of a fixed amount paid by all taxpayers.

Under the old British tax system, the highest local taxes were paid by the people with the most expensive houses. Because these people tended to be wealthy, they were also best able to bear the burden. But the old system definitely distorted incentives to engage in mutually beneficial transactions and created deadweight loss. People who were considering home improvements knew that by making their property more valuable, such improvements would increase their tax bills. The result, surely, was that some home improvements that would have taken place without the tax did not take place because of it.

AP® ECON TIP

Unless they cause a producer to go out of business, lump-sum taxes do not affect price or quantity, so they do not create deadweight loss.

One element of the inefficiency caused by a tax is not shown in Figure 2.8-12: the resources actually used by the government to collect the tax, and by taxpayers to pay it, beyond the amount of the tax itself. These lost resources are called the **administrative costs** of the tax. The most familiar administrative cost of the U.S. tax system is the time individuals spend filling out their income tax forms, or alternatively, the money they spend on accountants to prepare their tax forms for them. The use of accountants' time is an inefficiency from society's point of view because if they weren't needed to work on taxes, accountants could instead perform other, non-tax-related services. Included in the administrative costs that taxpayers incur are resources used to evade the tax, both legally and illegally. The costs of operating the Internal Revenue Service, the arm of the federal government tasked with collecting the federal income tax, are actually quite small in comparison to the administrative costs paid by taxpayers. The total inefficiency caused by a tax can be measured by the sum of its deadweight loss and its administrative costs.

The **administrative costs** of a tax are the resources used by the government to collect the tax, and by taxpayers to pay (or to evade) it, over and above the amount collected.

Subsidies and Efficiency

The many tools of government policy include a reversal of the tax idea known as a *subsidy*. For our purposes, a **subsidy** is a government payment made to assist or incentivize producers or consumers. The subsidy can be a lump sum that doesn't depend on production or consumption levels, a percentage of the price of a good or service, or a specific amount for each unit of a good or service, which is called a *per-unit subsidy*. Examples include the $7,500-per-vehicle subsidy on many electric vehicles provided to consumers by the U.S. government in the form of a tax deduction. A subsidy is effectively a negative tax and can have the opposite effect of a tax, leading to a larger quantity of a good or service being bought and sold.

A **subsidy** is a government payment made to assist or incentivize producers or consumers.

In Unit 6, we will see how subsidies are used to encourage production or consumption in markets with inefficiently low equilibrium quantities, such as the markets for vaccinations and electric cars. In this Module, we make the assumption that markets are efficient to begin with, which is possible in many agricultural markets in which subsidies are provided for farmers or consumers. Pakistan, Tanzania, and the United States are among the countries that subsidize sunflower farmers, whose seeds are used to make sunflower oil and other products. **Figure 2.8-13** shows a hypothetical market for sunflower seeds. The equilibrium price is $1,000 per ton and the equilibrium quantity is 500 tons.

Matthew Fabilenia/Getty Images

Suppose farmers receive a subsidy of $100 per ton of sunflower seeds they produce. This subsidy shifts the supply curve downward by $100, which you will recall is the opposite effect of a tax on producers, which shifts the supply curve *up* by the amount

FIGURE 2.8-13 The Effects of a Subsidy

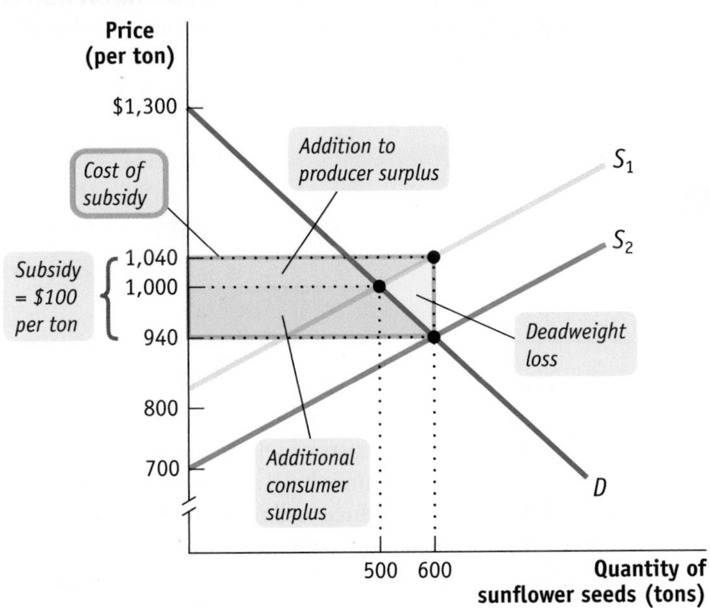

A $100 per ton subsidy in the market for sunflower seeds drives a $100 wedge between the price consumers pay and the price producers receive. The effects are the same whether the subsidy is given to producers or consumers: The subsidy increases the equilibrium quantity from 500 to 600 tons, lowers consumers' price from $1,000 to $940 per ton, and raises producers' price from $1,000 to $1,040 per ton. The area of the orange rectangle indicates the total cost of the subsidy to the government, equal to the subsidy per unit times the quantity sold: $100 × 600 = $60,000. Consumer surplus increases by the area shaded in blue and producer surplus increases by the area shaded in red. Assuming the market was efficient to begin with, the yellow area represents deadweight loss, which in this case is society's net loss from overproduction.

of the tax. Why does the downward shift from S_1 to S_2 make sense? Because the height of the supply curve indicates the lowest price producers would accept for each ton of sunflowers, and they will accept $100 less from consumers for each ton if the government gives them $100 for producing each ton. At the new equilibrium quantity of 600, consumers pay $940 per ton, and producers receive $940 from consumers plus the $100 subsidy for a total of $1,040 per ton.

The cost to the government of subsidizing 600 tons of sunflower seeds at a rate of $100 per ton is 600 × $100 = $60,000. That cost is shown in Figure 2.8-13 by the area of the orange rectangle with a height of $100 and a width of 600. We've seen that consumer surplus, represented by the area below the demand curve and above the price, is ½(500 × $300) = $75,000 without the subsidy. Consumer surplus rises to ½(600 × $360) = $108,000 when the subsidy lowers the price for consumers. The $33,000 increase in consumer surplus is shown in the graph by the area shaded in blue. The producer surplus, represented by the area below the price and above the supply curve, is ½(500 × $200) = $50,000 without the subsidy and increases to ½(600 × $240) = $72,000 when the subsidy raises the price for producers. The $22,000 increase in producer surplus is shown by the area shaded in red.

The orange rectangle in Figure 2.8-13 represents the cost of the subsidy. Comparing this area with the red and blue areas representing increases in consumer or producer surplus, we see that some of the cost of the subsidy—the portion shaded yellow—is not regained as surplus. That yellow triangle represents deadweight loss and amounts to ½(100 × $100) = $5,000. In this case, the deadweight loss is the amount by which the cost of producing the last 100 tons of sunflower seeds exceeds the benefit of those sunflower seeds to society. More generally, if a market equilibrium is efficient in the absence of intervention (such as a subsidy), the deadweight loss from overproduction is represented by the area between the original supply and demand curves stretching from the efficient market equilibrium quantity to the quantity actually produced.

As with a tax, the effects of a subsidy are independent of whether consumers or producers receive the subsidy. Either way, a subsidy drives a wedge between the price consumers pay and the price producers receive. If the $100 per ton subsidy were given to consumers of sunflower seeds rather than producers, the supply shift would be replaced by an *upward* shift by $100 in the demand curve. This makes sense because if consumers receive $100 per ton from the government, they would be willing to pay

AP® ECON TIP

When the quantity is inefficiently high, as in the case of a subsidy, the deadweight loss is the net cost of producing units whose marginal cost to society exceeds the marginal benefit to society.

$100 more for each ton of sunflowers. Everything else would be the same as with a subsidy to producers, including the price consumers pay (their payment to the producers minus the $100 subsidy), the price producers receive, the gain in producer surplus, the gain in consumer surplus, and the deadweight loss.

Module 2.8A  Review

Check Your Understanding

1. Using the tables in Check Your Understanding Questions 1 and 2 in Module 2.6 (reproduced below), find the equilibrium price and quantity in the market for cheese-stuffed jalapeño peppers. What is the total surplus in the equilibrium in this market, and how much of it does each consumer and producer receive?

Quantity of peppers	Casey's willingness to pay	Josey's willingness to pay
1st pepper	$0.90	$0.80
2nd pepper	0.70	0.60
3rd pepper	0.50	0.40
4th pepper	0.30	0.30
Quantity of peppers	**Cara's cost**	**Jamie's cost**
1st pepper	$0.10	$0.30
2nd pepper	0.10	0.50
3rd pepper	0.40	0.70
4th pepper	0.60	0.90

2. Consider the market for butter, shown in the accompanying figure. The government imposes an excise tax of $0.30 per pound of butter. What is the price paid by consumers post-tax? What is the price received by producers post-tax? What is the quantity of butter sold? How is the incidence of the tax allocated between consumers and producers? Show this on the figure.

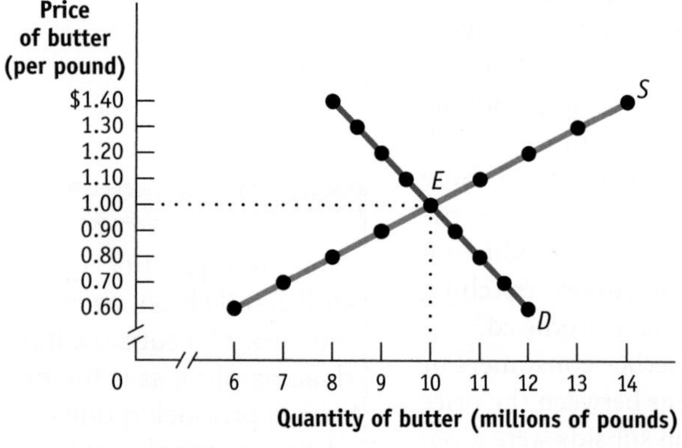

3. The accompanying table shows five consumers' willingness to pay for one can of energy drink each as well as five producers' costs of selling one can of energy drink each. Each consumer buys at most one can of energy drink; each producer sells at most one can of energy drink. The government asks your advice about the effects of an excise tax of $0.40 per can of energy drink. Assume that there are no administrative costs from the tax.

	Consumer willingness to pay		Producer cost
Ana	$0.70	Zhang	$0.10
Bernice	0.60	Yves	0.20
Chizuko	0.50	Xavier	0.30
Dagmar	0.40	Walter	0.40
Ella	0.30	Vern	0.50

a. Without the excise tax, what is the equilibrium price and the equilibrium quantity of energy drink?
b. The excise tax raises the price paid by consumers post-tax to $0.60 and lowers the price received by producers post-tax to $0.20. With the excise tax, what is the quantity of energy drink sold?
c. Without the excise tax, how much consumer surplus does each consumer gain? How much consumer surplus does each consumer gain with the tax? How much total consumer surplus is lost as a result of the tax?
d. Without the excise tax, how much producer surplus does each producer gain? How much producer surplus does each producer gain with the tax? How much total producer surplus is lost as a result of the tax?
e. How much government revenue does the excise tax create?
f. What is the deadweight loss from the imposition of this excise tax?

Tackle the AP® Test: Multiple-Choice Questions

1. At market equilibrium in a competitive market, which of the following is necessarily true?
   a. Consumer surplus is maximized.
   b. Producer surplus is maximized.
   c. Total surplus is maximized.
   d. Some buyers who do not make a purchase value the good more than some buyers who do make a purchase.
   e. The result is the best outcome for every individual seller.

2. Which of the following is true regarding equity and efficiency in competitive markets?
   a. Competitive markets ensure equity and efficiency.
   b. There is often a trade-off between equity and efficiency.
   c. Competitive markets lead to neither equity nor efficiency.
   d. There is general agreement about the level of equity and efficiency in a market.
   e. None of the above is true.

3. An excise tax will be paid mainly by producers when
   a. it is imposed on producers.
   b. it is imposed on consumers.
   c. the price elasticity of supply is low and the price elasticity of demand is high.
   d. the price elasticity of supply is high and the price elasticity of demand is low.
   e. the price elasticity of supply is perfectly elastic.

4. Which of the following is the most likely to be a regressive tax?
   a. a tax of 12% of the value of each individual's property
   b. a personal income tax of 15% of the first $50,000 in income and 20% on all additional income
   c. a 10% tax on yachts
   d. a 25% tax on all income
   e. a 7% state sales tax on all goods

5. A lump-sum tax on the citizens of a country
   a. does not create deadweight loss.
   b. distorts incentives for production.
   c. is considered a progressive tax.
   d. collects taxes in proportion to the wealth of each citizen.
   e. is inferior to excise taxes at promoting economic efficiency.

6. The following graph represents the toothpaste market, which begins with an equilibrium price of P_2 and an equilibrium quantity of Q_2. If an excise tax of $P_3 - P_1$ per unit is imposed on toothpaste sellers, the tax revenue will be represented by area(s) __________ and the deadweight loss will be represented by area(s) __________.

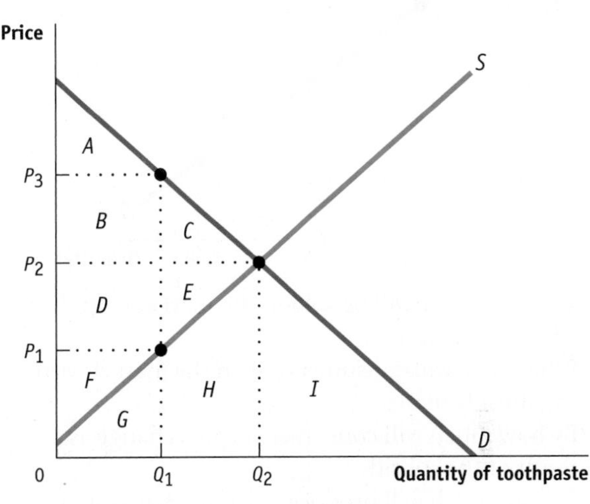

	Tax revenue	*Deadweight loss*
a.	*B*	*E*
b.	*DE*	*GHI*
c.	*BD*	*GHI*
d.	*BD*	*CE*
e.	*DE*	*CE*

7. A per-unit subsidy drives a wedge between the price consumers pay and the price producers receive with a height equal to
   a. the deadweight loss caused by the tax.
   b. the amount of the subsidy per unit.
   c. the total cost of the subsidy to the government.
   d. the pre-subsidy price of the good.
   e. the amount by which the price received by producers increases as a result of the subsidy.

Tackle the AP® Test: Free-Response Questions

1. Refer to the graph. Assume the government provides a subsidy of $60 to producers in this market.

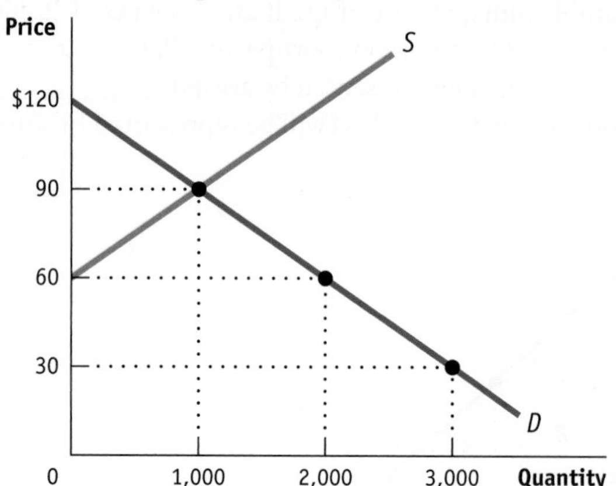

  a. What quantity will be sold in the market with the subsidy in place?
  b. What price will consumers pay in the market with the subsidy in place?
  c. By how much will consumer surplus change as a result of the subsidy?
  d. By how much will producer surplus change as a result of the subsidy?
  e. How much revenue will the government spend on this subsidy?
  f. Assuming the market was initially efficient, calculate the deadweight loss created by the subsidy.

Rubric for FRQ 1 (6 points)

1 point: 2,000

1 point: $60

1 point: Consumer surplus will increase by $45,000, from ½($1,000 × 30) = $15,000 before the subsidy to ½($2,000 × 60) = $60,000 with the subsidy.

1 point: Producer surplus will increase by $45,000, from ½($1, 000 × 30) = $15,000 before the subsidy to ½($2,000 × 60) = $60,000 with the subsidy.

1 point: $60 × 2,000 = $120,000

1 point: ½ × $60 × 1,000 = $30,000

2. Draw a correctly labeled graph of a competitive market in equilibrium. Use your graph to illustrate the effect of an excise tax imposed on consumers. Indicate each of the following on your graph:
  a. the equilibrium price and quantity without the tax, labeled P_E and Q_E
  b. the quantity sold in the market post-tax, labeled Q_T
  c. the price paid by consumers post-tax, labeled P_C
  d. the price received by producers post-tax, labeled P_P
  e. the tax revenue generated by the tax, labeled "Tax revenue"
  f. the deadweight loss resulting from the tax, labeled "DWL" **(7 points)**

Government Intervention: Price and Quantity Controls

MODULE 2.8B

In this Module, you will learn to:

- Explain the workings of price and quantity controls
- Use graphs to show how price controls alter consumer and producer behavior
- Describe how price and quantity controls can lead to market inefficiency

Why Governments Control Prices

As we saw in Module 2.8A, the equilibrium price creates the largest possible total surplus, which is the sum of consumer surplus and producer surplus. Even so, the equilibrium price is actually not the preferred price of either buyers or sellers. After all, buyers would always like to pay less, and sometimes they can make a strong argument for lower prices. Consider the market for apartments in a major city. If the equilibrium between supply and demand for apartments occurs at a rental rate the average worker can't afford, citizens might ask the government to impose limits on the rents landlords can charge.

Sellers, on the other hand, would like to get more money for what they sell, and sometimes they can make a strong case that they should receive higher prices. For example, in the labor market, the price for an hour of a worker's time is called the *wage rate*. What if the equilibrium in the market for less skilled workers leads to wage rates that leave workers impoverished? In that case, workers – the sellers in this case – might ask the government to require employers to pay a rate no lower than some specified minimum wage.

Price controls are legal restrictions on how high or low a market price may go. They can take two forms: **price ceiling**, which is a maximum price sellers are allowed to charge for a good or service, or a **price floor**, which is a minimum price buyers are required to pay for a good or service.

As these cases illustrate, there is often pressure for governments to intervene in markets. When a government intervenes to regulate prices, we say that it imposes **price controls**. These controls typically take the form of either an upper limit, called a **price ceiling**, or a lower limit, called a **price floor**.

There are certain predictable and unpleasant side effects of price controls. To examine them, we make an important assumption in this Module: the markets in question are efficient before price controls are imposed. Some markets are inefficient, as in the case of a market dominated by a *monopolist*, a single seller who has the power to influence the market price. When a market is inefficient, price controls potentially move that market closer to efficiency without necessarily causing problems. In practice, however, price controls often *are* imposed on markets that are efficient – like the rent controls on apartments in several cities including New York. So the analysis in this Module applies to many important real-world situations.

S. Greg Panosian/Getty Images

Price Ceilings

Aside from rent control, there are not many price ceilings in the United States today. But at times they have been widespread. Price ceilings are typically imposed during crises – wars, harvest failures, natural disasters – because these events often lead to sudden price increases that hurt many people but produce big gains for a lucky few. The U.S. government imposed ceilings on many prices during World War II, when steep increases in the demand for raw materials such as aluminum and steel sent prices skyward. Price controls on oil were imposed in 1973, when a group of oil-exporting countries dramatically reduced oil supplies. Price controls were also imposed on California's wholesale electricity market in 2001, when a shortage created big profits for a few power-generating companies but led to higher electricity bills for consumers.

Rent control in New York City began during World War II and remains today. You can rent a one-bedroom apartment in Manhattan on fairly short notice – if you are able and willing to pay several thousand dollars a month. Yet some people pay only a small fraction of this amount for comparable apartments because their landlords face price ceilings that prevent them from raising the rent to the market-equilibrium level. Landlords of *rent-controlled* apartments can raise their rent only at the rate of increases in operating costs as estimated by the city government, and landlords of *rent-stabilized* apartments can increase their rent by a generally larger but still only modest percentage determined by the city. Aside from producing great deals for some renters, however, what are the broader consequences of New York's rent regulation? To answer this question, we turn to the supply and demand model.

How Price Ceilings Cause Inefficiencies

To see what can go wrong when a government imposes a price ceiling on an efficient market, consider **Figure 2.8-14**, which shows a simplified model of the market for apartments in New York. For simplicity, imagine all apartments are identical, so their rental price would be the same in the absence of price controls. The table in the figure shows the demand and supply schedules; the demand and supply curves are shown on the left. We show the quantity of apartments on the horizontal axis and the monthly rent per apartment on the vertical axis. You can see that in an unregulated market, the equilibrium would be at point *E*: 2 million apartments would be rented for $1,400 each per month.

FIGURE 2.8-14 The Market for Apartments Without Government Controls

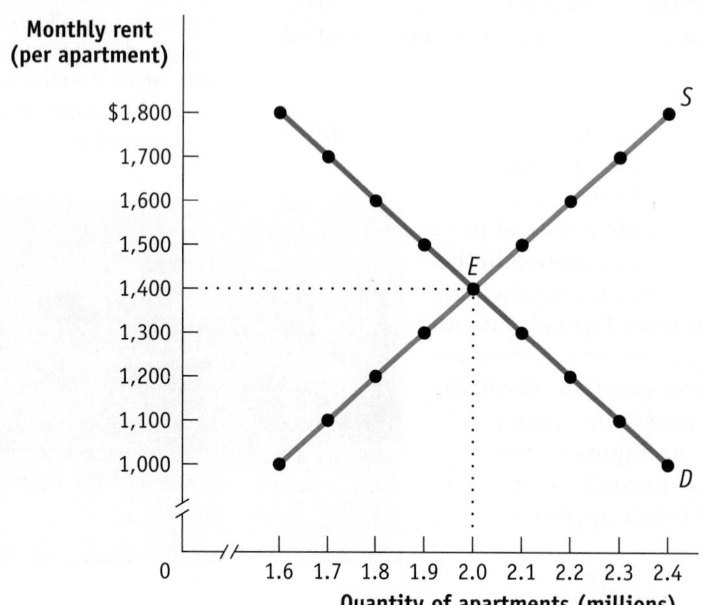

Monthly rent (per apartment)	Quantity of apartments (millions)	
	Quantity demanded	Quantity supplied
$1,800	1.6	2.4
1,700	1.7	2.3
1,600	1.8	2.2
1,500	1.9	2.1
1,400	2.0	2.0
1,300	2.1	1.9
1,200	2.2	1.8
1,100	2.3	1.7
1,000	2.4	1.6

Without government intervention, the market for apartments reaches equilibrium at point *E*. The 2 million people willing and able to rent an apartment for the equilibrium rent of $1,400 per month can all receive one.

Inefficiently low quantity Now suppose that the government imposes a price ceiling on rent of $1,200. **Figure 2.8-15** shows the effect of the price ceiling, represented by the line at $1,200. For $1,200, landlords have less incentive to offer apartments, so they

FIGURE 2.8-15 The Effects of a Price Ceiling

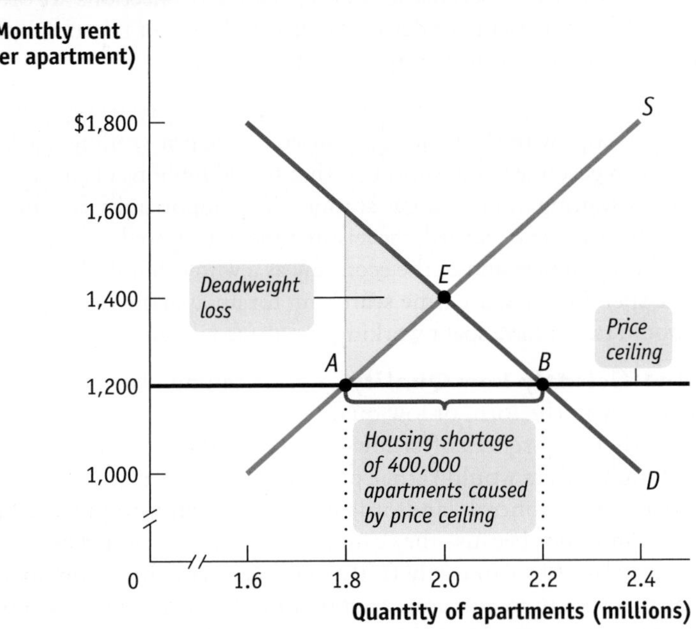

The black horizontal line represents the government-imposed price ceiling on rents of $1,200 per month. This price ceiling reduces the quantity of apartments supplied to 1.8 million, point *A*, and increases the quantity demanded to 2.2 million, point *B*. This creates a shortage of 400,000 units: 400,000 of the people who want apartments at the legal rent of $1,200 cannot get them. The area shaded yellow represents the deadweight loss from the 200,000 apartments that would have provided mutual benefits for renters and landlords at the market equilibrium price of $1,400.

won't be willing to supply as many as they would at the equilibrium rate of $1,400. They will choose point *A* on the supply curve, offering only 1.8 million apartments for rent, 200,000 fewer than in the unregulated market.

At the same time, more people will want to rent apartments for $1,200 than for the equilibrium price of $1,400; as shown at point *B* on the demand curve, at a monthly rent of $1,200, the quantity of apartments demanded rises to 2.2 million, 200,000 more than in the unregulated market and 400,000 more than are actually available at the price of $1,200. So there is a shortage of rental housing at that price because there are 400,000 more people who want to rent than are able to find apartments.

The reduction in quantity leads to deadweight loss because there are lost opportunities for mutually beneficial trade. Generally, when the demand curve lies above the supply curve at the quantity bought and sold, we know there is deadweight loss because consumers' willingness to pay for another unit (as shown by the height of the demand curve) exceeds the cost of providing another unit (as shown by the height of the supply curve). The area shaded yellow in Figure 2.8-15 represents the deadweight loss from the 200,000 apartments that would provide mutual benefits for renters and landlords in the absence of the price ceiling.

Do price ceilings always cause shortages and deadweight loss? No. If a price ceiling is set above the equilibrium price, it won't have any effect. Suppose that the equilibrium rental rate on apartments is $1,400 per month and the city government sets a ceiling of $1,600. Who cares? In this case, the price ceiling won't be binding—it won't actually constrain market behavior—and it will have no effect.

Inefficient Allocation to Consumers Rent control doesn't just lead to a shortage of available apartments. It can also lead to misallocation of the apartments that are available. In the case shown in Figure 2.8-15, 2.2 million people would like to rent an apartment at $1,200 per month, but only 1.8 million apartments are available. Of those 2.2 million who are seeking an apartment, some want an apartment badly and are willing to pay a high price to get one. Others have a less urgent need and are willing only to pay a low price, perhaps because they have many housing options.

An efficient allocation of apartments would reflect differences in needs and wants: the people who most value an apartment will get one and people who aren't all that eager to find an apartment won't. Apartments are distributed inefficiently if some people who are not especially eager to find an apartment get one and others who are very eager to find an apartment can't. Because luck and personal connections are often involved in the allocation of apartments under rent control, the result is generally an inefficient allocation to consumers of the few apartments available.

Wasted Resources Sometimes a price ceiling leads to wasted resources: people expend money, effort, and time to cope with the shortages caused by the price ceiling. Back in 1979, U.S. price controls on gasoline led to shortages that forced millions of Americans to spend hours each week waiting in lines at gas stations. The opportunity cost of the time spent in gas lines – the wages not earned, the leisure time not enjoyed – was a waste from the point of view of consumers and of the economy as a whole. Similarly, because of rent control, people spend their spare time searching for an apartment, time they would rather have spent working or engaged in family activities.

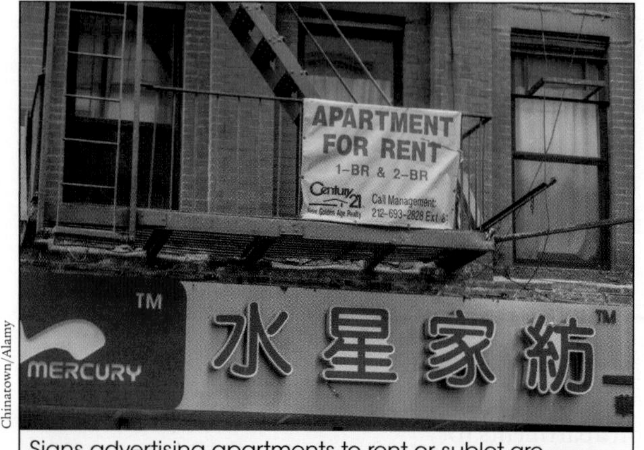

Chinatown/Alamy

Signs advertising apartments to rent or sublet are common in New York City.

Inefficiently Low Quality A price ceiling also causes inefficiency in the form of low quality. The level of quality is inefficiently low if sellers offer low-quality goods at a low price even though buyers would rather pay more for higher quality. In the case of rent control, landlords have no incentive to provide better conditions because they cannot raise rents to cover their repair costs and they can easily find tenants to rent their apartments as they are. In many cases, tenants would be willing to pay much more for improved conditions than it would cost for the landlord to provide them – for example, the upgrade of an antiquated electrical system that cannot safely run air conditioners or computers. But any additional payment for such improvements would be legally considered a rent increase, which is prohibited. Indeed, rent-controlled apartments are notoriously badly maintained, rarely painted, subject to frequent electrical and plumbing problems, and sometimes even hazardous to inhabit.

A **black market** is a market in which goods or services are bought and sold illegally— either because it is illegal to sell them at all or because the prices charged are legally prohibited by a price ceiling.

Black Markets A last notable repercussion of price ceilings is the incentive they provide for illegal activities. A market in which something is bought and sold illegally is called a **black market**. Some people fortunate enough to get a rent-controlled apartment turn around and illegally sublet the apartment to someone else. And sometimes a landlord will say to a potential tenant, "Look, you can have this place if you slip me an extra few hundred in cash each month."

Black markets may help those who are willing to pay the most for apartments to get them, but they also encourage disrespect for the law and bias the opportunities against those who are honest.

So Why Are There Price Ceilings?

Given that price ceilings cause shortages, inefficiency, and black markets, why do governments still sometimes impose them? Why does rent control, in particular, persist in New York City? One answer is that although price ceilings have adverse effects, they do benefit a small group of people. And those who benefit from the controls may be better organized and more vocal than those who are harmed by them. Also, when price ceilings have been in effect for a long time, buyers may not have a realistic idea of what would happen without them. They might have heard about black market transactions at much higher prices, and don't realize that the black market prices are much higher than the price that would prevail in the absence of price controls. A last answer is that government officials often do not understand what you just learned about supply and demand!

AP® ECON TIP

When it comes to price controls, the ceiling is down low and the floor is up high. That is, to have any effect, a price ceiling must be below the equilibrium price, and a price floor must be above the equilibrium price.

Price Floors

Sometimes governments intervene to push market prices up instead of down. *Price floors* have been widely legislated for agricultural products such as wheat and milk to support the incomes of farmers. Historically, there were also price floors on services such as trucking and air travel, although these were phased out by the U.S. government in the 1970s. If you have ever worked in a fast-food restaurant, you are likely to have encountered a price floor. Governments in the United States and many other countries impose a floor on the price of labor called a **minimum wage**.

A **minimum wage** is a legal floor on the hourly wage rate paid for a worker's labor.

Just like price ceilings, price floors help some people but cause undesirable side effects. **Figure 2.8-16** shows hypothetical supply and demand curves for butter. Left to itself, the market would move to equilibrium at point *E*, with 10 million pounds of butter bought and sold at a price of $1 per pound.

FIGURE 2.8-16 The Market for Butter in the Absence of Government Controls

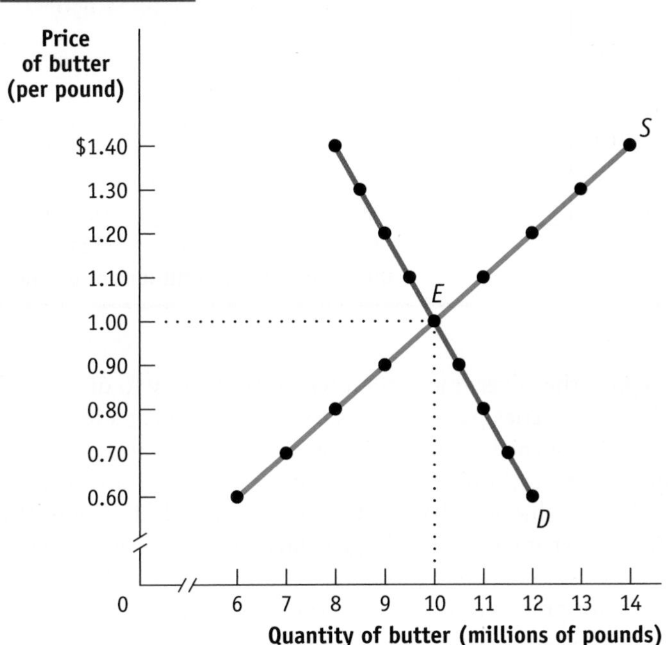

Price of butter (per pound)	Quantity of butter (millions of pounds)	
	Quantity demanded	Quantity supplied
$1.40	8.0	14.0
1.30	8.5	13.0
1.20	9.0	12.0
1.10	9.5	11.0
1.00	10.0	10.0
0.90	10.5	9.0
0.80	11.0	8.0
0.70	11.5	7.0
0.60	12.0	6.0

Without government intervention, the market for butter reaches equilibrium at a price of $1 per pound with 10 million pounds of butter bought and sold.

Now suppose that to help dairy farmers, the government imposes a price floor on butter of $1.20 per pound. The horizontal line at $1.20 in **Figure 2.8-17** represents the price floor. At that price, producers want to supply 12 million pounds (point *B* on the supply curve), but consumers want to buy only 9 million pounds (point *A* on the demand curve). So the price floor leads to a surplus of 3 million pounds of butter. The area shaded yellow represents the deadweight loss from the 1 million pounds of butter that would have provided mutual benefits for buyers and sellers at the market equilibrium price of $1.00, but go unsold with the price floor in place.

Does a price floor always lead to an unwanted surplus and deadweight loss? No. Just as in the case of a price ceiling, the floor may not be binding—it may be irrelevant. For example, if the equilibrium price of butter is $1 per pound but the floor is set at only $0.80, the floor has no effect.

If a price floor *is* binding, what happens to the unwanted surplus? The answer depends on government policy. In the case of agricultural price floors, governments typically buy up the unwanted surplus. For example, the U.S. government has at times found itself warehousing thousands of tons of butter, cheese, and other farm products. The European Commission, which administers price floors for a number of European countries, once found itself the owner of a so-called butter mountain, equal in weight to the entire population of Austria.

FIGURE 2.8-17 The Effects of a Price Floor

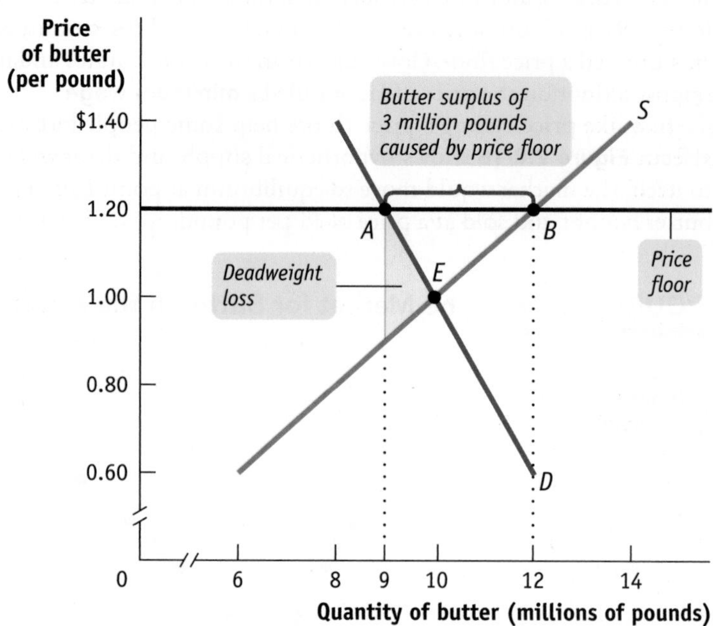

The dark horizontal line represents the government-imposed price floor of $1.20 per pound of butter. At that price the quantity of butter demanded falls to 9 million pounds and the quantity supplied rises to 12 million pounds, generating a surplus of 3 million pounds of butter. The area shaded yellow represents the deadweight loss from the 1 million pounds of butter that would have provide mutual benefits for buyers and sellers at the market equilibrium price of $1.00.

After purchasing a surplus, the government then has to find a way to dispose of these unwanted goods. Some countries pay exporters to sell products at a loss overseas; this is standard procedure for the European Union. The United States gives surplus food to schools, which use it in school lunches. In some cases, governments have actually destroyed the surplus production. To avoid the problem of dealing with the unwanted surplus, the U.S. government typically pays farmers not to produce the products at all.

When the government is not prepared to purchase the unwanted surplus, a price floor means that would-be sellers cannot find buyers. This is what happens when there is a price floor on the wage rate paid for an hour of labor, the *minimum wage*: when the minimum wage is above the equilibrium wage rate, some people who are willing to work—that is, sell labor—cannot find employers who want to hire them—that is, buy labor. The result is *unemployment*—a surplus of workers in the market.

How a Price Floor Causes Inefficiency

The surplus that results from a price floor creates missed opportunities—inefficiencies—that resemble those created by the shortage that results from a price ceiling.

Inefficiently Low Quantity By raising the price of a good, a price floor reduces the quantity of that good demanded. And because sellers can't sell more units of a good than buyers are willing to buy, a price floor reduces the quantity bought and sold below the market equilibrium quantity. Notice that this is the *same* effect as a price ceiling. You might be tempted to think that a price floor and a price ceiling have opposite effects, but both have the effect of reducing the quantity of a good bought and sold.

Inefficient Allocation of Sales Among Sellers Like a price ceiling, a price floor can lead to *inefficient allocation*—but in this case, inefficient allocation of sales among sellers rather than inefficient allocation to consumers. Suppose you would be willing to sell your English tutoring services for $5 per hour, but the minimum wage is $9 per hour. Because you are forced to compete with someone who would tutor for no less than $9 per hour, you risk losing the job to this competitor. In this case, the price floor on wages prevents the worker who would sell tutoring services for the lowest amount from being able to do so.

Wasted Resources Also like a price ceiling, a price floor generates inefficiency by *wasting resources*. The most graphic examples involve government purchases of the unwanted surpluses of agricultural products caused by price floors. When the surplus production is simply destroyed, it is pure waste. Price floors also lead to wasted time and effort. In the case of the minimum wage, would-be workers spend excessive amounts of time searching for jobs due to the surplus of workers.

While price ceilings lead to a degradation of quality, price floors lead suppliers to offer goods of inefficiently high quality. How can this be? Isn't high quality a good thing? Yes, but only if it is worth the cost. In many cases, consumers would rather have producers spend less on quality and offer a lower price. A good example of inefficiently high quality comes from the days when transatlantic airfares were set artificially high by international treaty. Forbidden to compete for customers by offering lower ticket prices, airlines instead tried to lure customers with expensive services, like lavish in-flight meals. At one point the regulators tried to restrict this practice by defining maximum service standards – for example, requiring that snack service consist of no more than a sandwich. One airline then introduced what it called a "Scandinavian Sandwich," a towering affair that forced regulators to convene another conference to define *sandwich*. All of this was wasteful, especially considering that what passengers really wanted was less food and lower airfares.

Fox Photos/Getty Images

Price floors led airlines to compete by offering lavish meals and luxurious comfort, even though many customers just wanted cheaper seats.

Illegal Activity Finally, like price ceilings, price floors provide incentives for illegal activity. For example, in countries where the minimum wage is far above the equilibrium wage rate, workers desperate for jobs sometimes agree to work off the books for employers who conceal their employment from the government – or who bribe the government inspectors. This practice is especially common in southern European countries such as Italy and Spain.

So Why Are There Price Floors?

Why do governments impose price floors when they have the negative side effects of unwanted surpluses, inefficiency, and illegal activity? Government officials often disregard warnings about the consequences of price floors either because they believe the relevant market is poorly described by the supply and demand model or, more often, because they do not understand the model. Above all, just as price ceilings are often imposed because they benefit some influential buyers of a good, price floors are often imposed because they benefit some influential sellers.

Controlling Quantities

In the 1930s, New York City instituted a system of licensing for taxicabs: only taxis with a "medallion" were allowed to pick up passengers. This system was intended to ensure quality, and medallion owners were supposed to maintain certain safety and cleanliness standards. A total of 11,787 medallions were issued when this program began, with taxi owners paying $10 for each medallion. The privilege to sell taxi services gained value as New York swiftly grew into the financial capital of the world, outpacing growth in the number of medallions. The price of medallions skyrocketed, peaking at over $1 million in 2013, but as we discuss below, innovations in ride sharing eroded the value of medallions – an unintended consequence of *quantity control*. In 2022, there were 13,587 medallions worth around $100,000 each.

Ron Adar/Alamy

A taxi medallion system is a form of **quantity control**, or **quota**, by which the government regulates the quantity of a good that can be bought and sold rather than regulating the price. Typically, the government limits quantity in a market

A **quantity control**, or **quota**, is an upper limit on the quantity of some good that can be bought or sold.

A **license** gives its owner the right to supply a good or service.

by issuing **licenses**; only people with a license can legally supply the good. A taxi medallion is just such a license. The government of New York City limits the number of taxi rides that can be sold by limiting the number of taxis to only those who hold medallions. There are many other cases of quantity controls, ranging from limits on how much foreign currency (for instance, British pounds or Mexican pesos) people are allowed to buy, to caps on the quantity of clams New Jersey fishing boats are allowed to catch. Module 2.9 discusses quotas on goods imported from other countries.

Some attempts to control quantities are undertaken for good economic reasons, some for bad ones. In many cases, as we will see, quantity controls introduced to address a temporary problem become politically hard to remove later because the beneficiaries don't want them abolished, even after the original reason for their existence is long gone. Whatever the reasons for such controls, they have certain predictable—and usually undesirable—economic consequences.

AP® ECON TIP

Quantity controls and price controls are graphed differently. Graph a quota as a vertical line at the quantity limit. Graph a price ceiling or floor as a horizontal line at the price limit.

The Anatomy of Quantity Controls

To understand why a New York taxi medallion has value, we consider a simplified version of the market for taxi rides, shown in **Figure 2.8-18**. We will suppose that all taxi rides are the same—ignoring the real-world complication that some taxi rides are longer, and therefore more expensive, than others. The table in the figure shows supply and demand schedules. The equilibrium—indicated by point *E* in the figure and by the shaded entries in the table—is a fare of $5 per ride, with 10 million rides taken per year. (You'll see in a minute why we present the equilibrium this way.)

FIGURE 2.8-18 The Market for Taxi Rides in the Absence of Government Controls

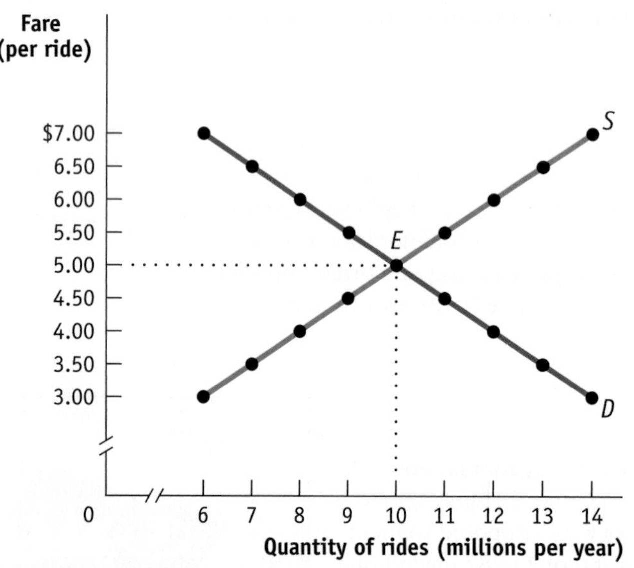

Fare (per ride)	Quantity of rides (millions per year) Quantity demanded	Quantity supplied
$7.00	6	14
6.50	7	13
6.00	8	12
5.50	9	11
5.00	10	10
4.50	11	9
4.00	12	8
3.50	13	7
3.00	14	6

Without government intervention, the market reaches equilibrium with 10 million rides taken per year at a fare of $5 per ride.

The New York medallion system limits the number of taxis, but each taxi driver can offer as many rides as the driver can manage. (Now you know why New York taxi drivers are so aggressive!) To simplify our analysis, however, we will assume that a medallion system limits the number of taxi rides that can legally be given.

Until now, we have derived the demand curve by answering questions of the form: "How many taxi rides will passengers want to take if the price is $5 per ride?" But it is possible to reverse the question and ask instead: "At what price will consumers want to buy 10 million rides per year?" The price at which consumers want to buy a given quantity—in this case, 10 million rides at $5 per ride—is the **demand price** of that quantity. You can see from the demand schedule in Figure 2.8-18 that the demand price of 6 million rides is $7 per ride, the demand price of 7 million rides is $6.50 per ride, and so on.

The **demand price** of a given quantity is the price at which consumers will demand that quantity.

Similarly, the supply curve represents the answer to questions of the form: "How many taxi rides would taxi drivers supply at a price of $5 each?" But we can also reverse this question to ask: "At what price will producers be willing to supply 10 million rides per year?" The price at which producers will supply a given quantity—in this case, 10 million rides at $5 per ride—is the **supply price** of that quantity. We can see from the supply schedule in Figure 2.8-18 that the supply price of 6 million rides is $3 per ride, the supply price of 7 million rides is $3.50 per ride, and so on.

The **supply price** of a given quantity is the price at which producers will supply that quantity.

Now we are ready to understand the effects of a quota. Let's assume that the city government limits the number of taxi rides that can legally be given to 8 million per year. Medallions, each of which carries the right to provide a certain number of taxi rides per year, are made available to selected people in such a way that a total of 8 million rides will be provided. Medallion holders may then either drive their own taxis or rent their medallions to others for a fee.

Figure 2.8-19 shows the resulting market for taxi rides, with the black vertical line at 8 million rides per year representing the quota. Because the quantity of rides is limited to 8 million, the demand price is $6 per ride as shown at point *A* on the demand curve, corresponding to the shaded entry in the demand schedule. Meanwhile, the supply price of 8 million rides is $4 per ride as shown at point *B* on the supply curve, corresponding to the shaded entry in the supply schedule.

FIGURE 2.8-19 Effect of a Quota on the Market for Taxi Rides

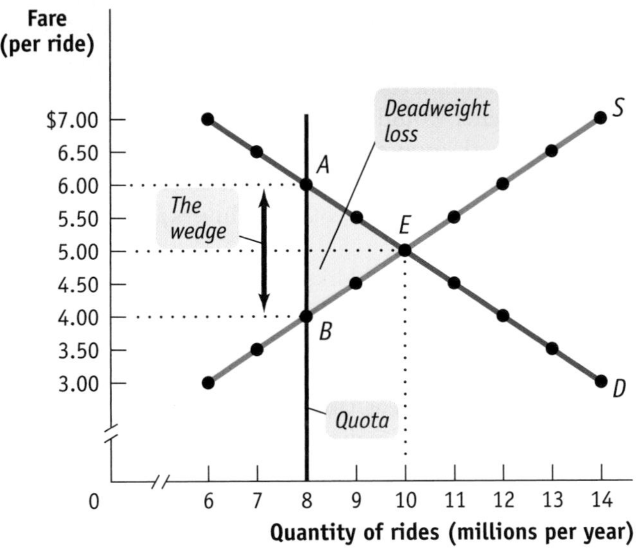

Fare (per ride)	Quantity of rides (millions per year) — Quantity demanded	Quantity supplied
$7.00	6	14
6.50	7	13
6.00	8	12
5.50	9	11
5.00	10	10
4.50	11	9
4.00	12	8
3.50	13	7
3.00	14	6

The table shows the demand price and the supply price corresponding to each quantity: the price at which that quantity would be demanded and supplied, respectively. The city government imposes a quota of 8 million rides by selling enough medallions for only 8 million rides, represented by the black vertical line. The price paid by consumers rises to $6 per ride, the demand price of 8 million rides, shown by point *A*. The supply price of 8 million rides is only $4 per ride, shown by point *B*. The difference between these two prices is the quota rent per ride, the earnings that accrue to the owner of a medallion. The quota rent drives a wedge between the demand price and the supply price. Because the quota discourages mutually beneficial transactions, it creates a *deadweight loss* equal to the shaded triangle.

The difference between the demand and supply price at the quota amount is the **quota rent**, the earnings that accrue to the license-holder from ownership of the right to sell the good or service. It is equal to the market price of the license when the licenses are traded.

In every case in which the supply of a good or service is legally restricted, there is a wedge between the demand price of the quantity transacted and the supply price of the quantity transacted. This wedge, illustrated by the double-headed arrow in Figure 2.8-19, has a special name: the **quota rent**. It is the earnings that accrue to the medallion holder from ownership of a valuable commodity, the medallion. In the taxi case, the quota rent of $2 per ride goes to the owner of the medallion, as does the supply price of $4 that makes up the remainder of the total fare of $6. If the medallion owner were to sell or rent out the medallion, its value would be equivalent to the quota rent times the number of rides for which the ownership was transferred. Since other drivers would be willing to pay up to $2 per ride to rent the medallion, the quota rent is also the owner's opportunity cost of using the medallion instead of allowing another driver to use it.

Quotas – like price ceilings and price floors – don't always have a real effect. If the quota were set at 12 million rides – that is, above the equilibrium quantity in an unregulated market – it would have no effect because it would not be binding.

The Costs of Quantity Controls

Like price controls, quantity controls have some predictable and undesirable side effects. The first is the by-now-familiar problem of inefficiency due to missed opportunities: quantity controls cause deadweight loss by preventing transactions that would benefit both buyers and sellers. In Figure 2.8-19 you can see that, starting at the quota of 8 million rides, New Yorkers would be willing to pay at least $5.50 per ride for an additional 1 million rides and that taxi drivers would require no more than $4.50 per ride for those rides. Those 1 million mutually beneficial rides would have taken place if there had been no quota. The same is true for the next 1 million rides: New Yorkers would be willing to pay at least $5 per ride when the quantity of rides is increased from 9 to 10 million, and taxi drivers would require no more than $5 per ride for those rides. Again, those rides would have occurred without the quota. Only when the market has reached the unregulated market equilibrium quantity of 10 million rides are there no missed opportunities for mutually beneficial rides – the quota of 8 million rides has caused 2 million missed opportunities for rides with a benefit to riders that exceeds the cost to drivers.

There is deadweight loss any time a quota forbids transactions in which a buyer would be willing to pay more than a seller would be willing to accept. Figure 2.8-19 illustrates the deadweight loss caused by the quota on taxi rides with a shaded triangle between the demand and supply curves. This triangle represents the loss experienced by both disappointed would-be riders and frustrated would-be drivers as a result of the quota.

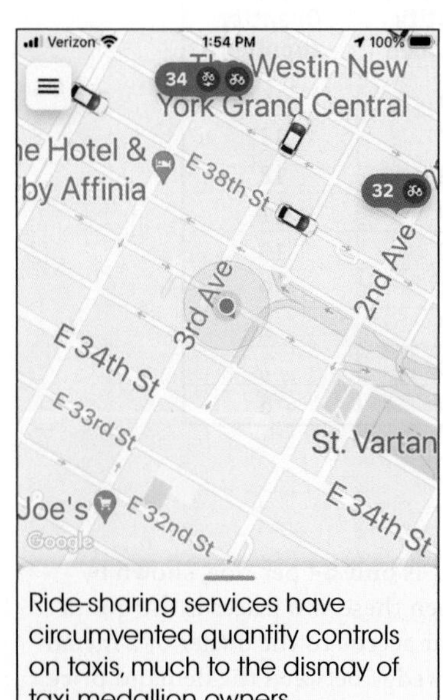

Ride-sharing services have circumvented quantity controls on taxis, much to the dismay of taxi medallion owners.

Because there are transactions that people would like to make but are not allowed to, quantity controls generate an incentive to get around or even break the law. Taxi regulation applies only to those drivers who are hailed by people on the street. A car service that makes prearranged pickups does not need a medallion. This distinction gives an advantage to ride-sharing services such as Uber and Lyft that compete with taxis to provide rides. Ride-sharing services allow registered individuals to provide ride services using their own vehicles and have provided more rides than taxis in New York City since 2016. The competition has driven the value of medallions down to around $100,000, roughly one-tenth of their value a decade ago.

Earlier in the Module, we saw price controls result in black market activity. Here we see quantity controls lead to innovation in the market for taxi rides that diminishes the value of taxi medallions. These examples illustrate the challenges of government control of market forces and the predictable and often undesirable consequences of price and quantity controls.

Module 2.8B  Review

Check Your Understanding

1. On game days, homeowners near Middletown University's stadium used to rent parking spaces in their driveways to fans at a going rate of $11. A new town ordinance now sets a maximum parking fee of $7. Use the accompanying supply and demand diagram to show how each of the following can result from the price ceiling.

Parking fee
$15
11
7
3
0
S
E
D
3,200 3,600 4,000 4,400 4,800
Quantity of parking spaces

   a. Some homeowners now think it's not worth the hassle to rent out spaces.
   b. Some fans who used to carpool to the game now drive alone.
   c. Some fans can't find parking and leave without seeing the game.

   Explain how each of the following adverse effects arises from the price ceiling.

   d. Some fans now arrive several hours early to find parking.
   e. Friends of homeowners near the stadium regularly attend games, even if they aren't big fans. But some serious fans have given up because of the parking situation.
   f. Some homeowners rent spaces for more than $7 but pretend that the buyers are nonpaying friends or family.

2. True or false? Explain your answer. A price ceiling below the equilibrium price in an otherwise efficient market
   a. increases quantity supplied.
   b. makes some people who want to consume the good worse off.
   c. makes all producers worse off.

3. Suppose that the supply and demand for taxi rides is given by Figure 2.8-18 and a quota is set at 6 million rides. Replicate the graph from Figure 2.8-18, and identify each of the following on your graph:
   a. the price of a ride
   b. the quota rent
   c. the deadweight loss resulting from the quota

   Suppose the quota on taxi rides is increased to 9 million.

   d. What happens to the quota rent and the deadweight loss?

Tackle the AP® Test: Multiple-Choice Questions

1. An effective minimum wage law
   a. is an example of a price ceiling.
   b. benefits all workers.
   c. reduces the quantity of labor supplied.
   d. reduces the quantity of labor demanded.
   e. is all of the above.

2. Effective price ceilings are inefficient because they
   a. create shortages.
   b. lead to wasted resources.
   c. decrease quality.
   d. create black markets.
   e. do all of the above.

3. Refer to the graph provided.

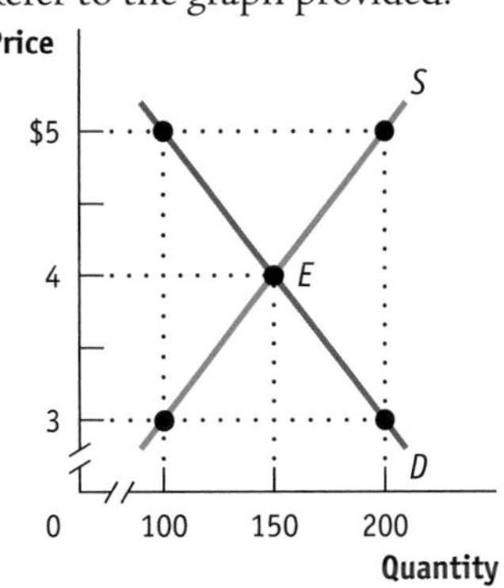

   A price floor set at $5 will result in
   a. a shortage of 100 units.
   b. a surplus of 100 units.
   c. a shortage of 200 units.
   d. a surplus of 200 units.
   e. a surplus of 50 units.

Use the graph provided to answer Questions 4 and 5.

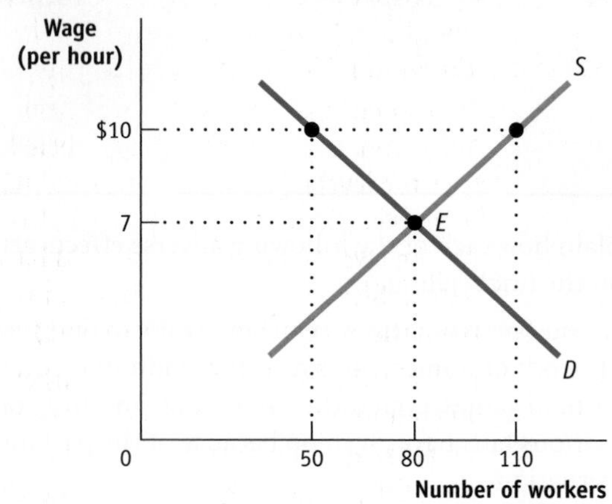

4. If the government establishes a minimum wage at $10, how many workers will benefit from the higher wage?
   a. 30
   b. 50
   c. 60
   d. 80
   e. 110

5. With a minimum wage of $10, how many workers are unemployed (would like to work, but are unable to find a job)?
   a. 30
   b. 50
   c. 60
   d. 80
   e. 110

Refer to the graph provided for Questions 6–8.

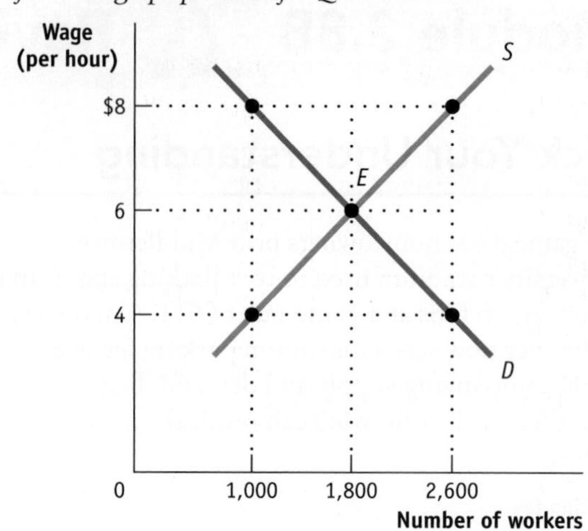

6. If the government established a quota of 1,000 in this market, the demand price would be
   a. less than $4.
   b. $4.
   c. $6.
   d. $8.
   e. more than $8.

7. If the government established a quota of 1,000 in this market, the supply price would be
   a. less than $4.
   b. $4.
   c. $6.
   d. $8.
   e. more than $8.

8. If the government established a quota of 1,000 in this market, the quota rent would be
   a. $2.
   b. $4.
   c. $6.
   d. $8.
   e. more than $8.

Tackle the AP® Test: Free-Response Questions

1. Refer to the graph provided to answer the following questions.

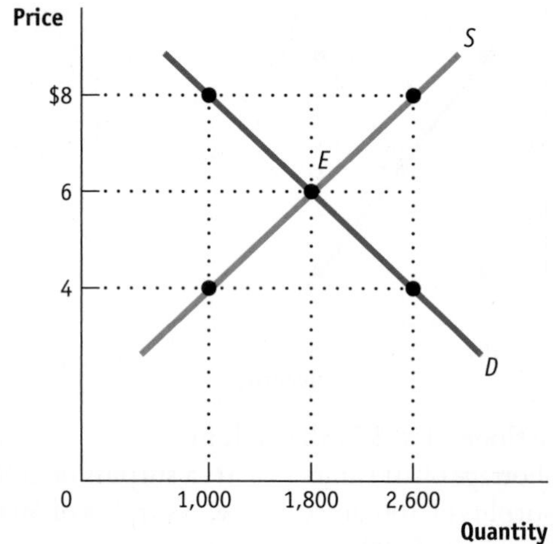

   a. What are the equilibrium wage and quantity of workers in this market?
   b. For it to have an effect, where would the government have to set a minimum wage?
   c. If the government set a minimum wage at $8,
      i. how many workers would supply their labor?
      ii. how many workers would be hired?
      iii. how many workers would want to work that did *not* want to work for the equilibrium wage?
      iv. how many previously employed workers would no longer have a job?

Rubric for FRQ 1 (6 points)

1 point: equilibrium wage = \$6, quantity of labor = 1,800

1 point: The minimum wage will have an effect if it is set anywhere above \$6.

1 point: 2,600 workers would supply their labor

1 point: 1,000 workers would be hired

1 point: 800 (the number of workers who would want to work for \$8 but did not supply labor for \$6)

1 point: 800 (at the equilibrium wage of \$6, 1,800 workers were hired; at a wage of \$8, 1,000 workers would be hired; 1,800 – 1,000 = 800)

2. Draw a correctly labeled graph illustrating hypothetical supply and demand curves for the U.S. automobile market. Label the equilibrium price and quantity. Suppose the government institutes a quota to limit automobile production. Draw a vertical line labeled "$Q_{ineffective}$" to show the level of a quota that would have no effect on the market. Draw a vertical line labeled "$Q_{effective}$" to show the level of a quota that would have an effect on the market. Shade in and label the deadweight loss resulting from the effective quota. **(5 points)**
3. Draw a correctly labeled graph of a housing market in equilibrium. On your graph, illustrate an effective legal limit (ceiling) on rent. Identify the quantity of housing demanded, the quantity of housing supplied, and the size of the resulting surplus or shortage. **(6 points)**

MODULE 2.9

International Trade and Public Policy

In this Module, you will learn to:
- Explain the workings of import tariffs and quotas
- Discuss the pros and cons of restrictions on international trade
- Illustrate the effects of international trade and trade restrictions on a graph

Trade Restrictions

It's natural for the citizens of a country to say, "We can make food, clothing, and almost everything we need. Why should we buy these goods from other countries and send our money overseas?" Module 1.4 explained the answer to this question: because specialization and trade make larger quantities of goods and services available to consumers. Yet the gains from trade are often overlooked, and many countries have experimented with a closed economy. Examples from the last century include Germany in 1933–1945, Spain in 1939–1959, Cambodia in 1975–1979, and Afghanistan in 1996–2001. The outcomes of these experiments were disappointing. By trying to make too many different products, these countries failed to specialize in what they were best at making, and they ended up with less of most goods than trade would have provided.

Every country now has an open economy, although some economies are more open than others. **Figure 2.9-1** shows expenditures on imports as a percentage of GDP for select countries, which ranged from 5% in Sudan to 176% in Luxembourg. Several factors affect a country's approach to trade. Beyond the natural tendency for each country to want to be self-sufficient, special circumstances can limit the options for trade. For example, high transportation costs hinder trade for countries with underdeveloped transportation systems as well as for countries that specialize

FIGURE 2.9-1 Imports of Goods and Services as a Percentage of GDP

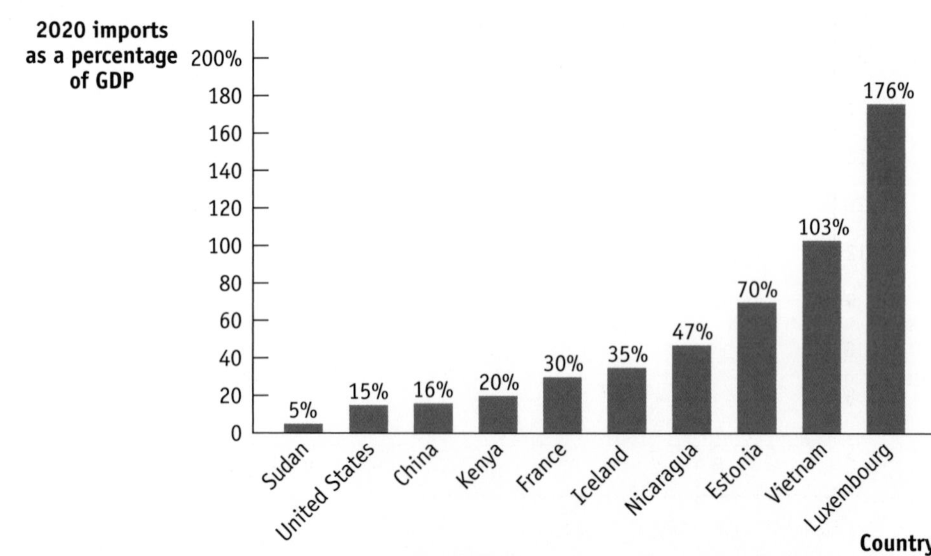

International trade is an important part of every country's economy, but some economies are more open than others. In 2020, imports as a percentage of GDP ranged from 5% in Sudan to 176% in Luxembourg.
Data Source: The World Bank.

in heavy, low-priced commodities such as bricks, drinking water, pineapples, or sand. Countries are wary of specialization that would make them overly reliant on other countries, because relationships with those countries could sour. And, as a matter of national pride, countries may prefer to make certain products on their own, such as food, art, weapons, and products that showcase technical know-how, despite comparative disadvantages.

International trade can also have its casualties. As production shifts toward a country's comparative advantage, many workers in declining industries will lose their jobs and will remain unemployed until or unless they can obtain the skills required in other industries. For example, in the late 1990s, as the United States imported more clothing from countries with a comparative advantage in textiles, workers in the Fruit of the Loom factory in Campbellsville, Kentucky, were among many who lost their jobs. Fortunately, the unemployment rates in Campbellsville and in the United States as a whole rose only temporarily. Many of these workers were able to adapt to the requirements of growing industries such as construction, automotive parts, health care, and software design, and were able to secure new jobs as a result.

Some industries may not initially be competitive at the international level, but they could attain a comparative advantage after a period of protection from lower-priced imports. This is the motivation for **protectionism**, the practice of limiting trade to protect domestic industries. *Tariffs* and *import quotas* are the primary tools of protectionism. Policy makers must weigh arguments for protectionism against the gains from trade.

Protectionism is the practice of limiting trade to protect domestic industries.

Gains from Trade

Consider the U.S. market for ceramic plates, a hypothetical version of which is shown in **Figure 2.9-2**. The upward-sloping supply curve shows the supply from U.S. firms. The demand curve is for U.S. consumers only. If the United States became an *autarky* by having a *closed economy,* meaning there was no free trade, 5 million plates would sell for the no-trade equilibrium price of $15 each. However, suppose that an unlimited quantity of plates could be imported for the equilibrium price in the world market, $9.

FIGURE 2.9-2 The U.S. Ceramic Plate Market with Imports

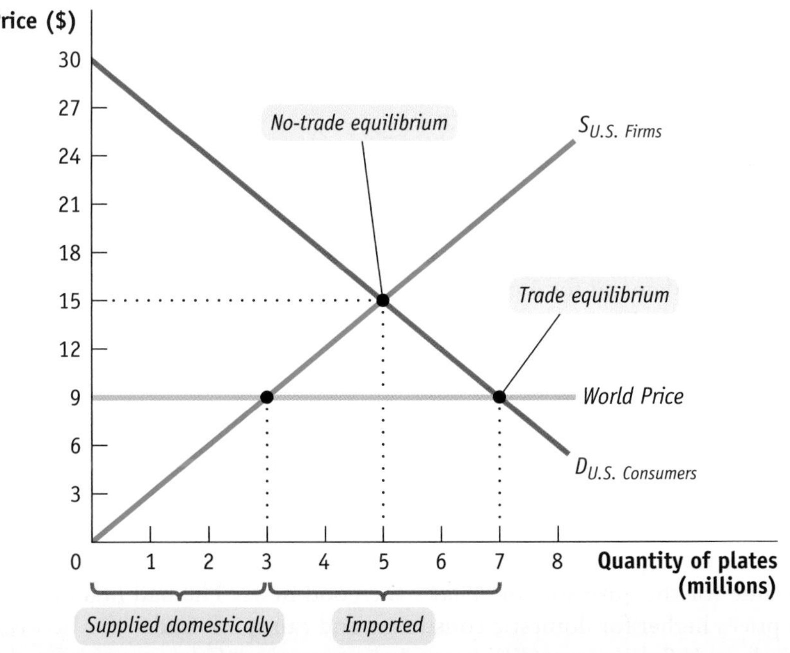

Without trade, 5 million plates would be sold at the no-trade equilibrium price of $15. An unlimited quantity of plates can be imported at the equilibrium world price of $9. With unrestricted trade, domestic firms will be unable to charge more than the world price, for which they are willing to supply 3 million plates. Domestic consumers will demand 7 million plates at a price of $9 each. The difference between the domestic demand and the domestic supply, 4 million plates, will be imported.

In the absence of trade restrictions, domestic firms would be unable to charge more than the world price. At the $9 world price, domestic firms would be willing to supply 3 million plates, but domestic consumers would demand 7 million. Four million imported plates would make up the difference between the 7 million plates demanded and the 3 million supplied in the domestic market.

Figure 2.9-3 shows the effect of international trade on consumer and producer surplus. The shaded blue triangle represents consumer surplus, and the shaded red triangle represents producer surplus with no trade. If international trade provides access to unlimited plates at a world price of $9, the consumer surplus increases to the blue striped triangle, and the producer surplus decreases to the red striped triangle. Total surplus increases by the area of the green triangle. Recall that the value of each these surplus triangles is easily found as ½(base × height). For example, the total surplus increases by ½(4 × $6) = $12.

FIGURE 2.9-3 The Effect of International Trade on Consumer and Producer Surplus

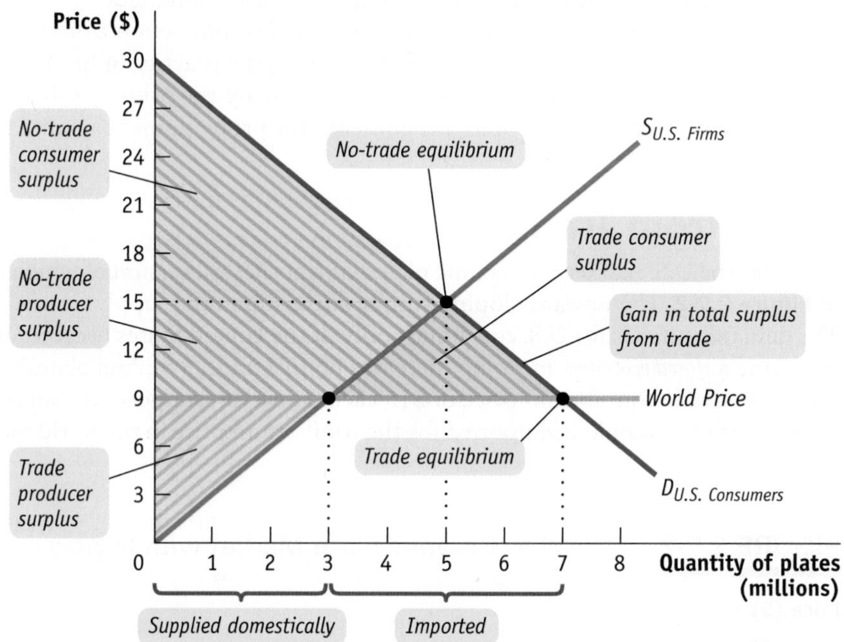

When the economy opens to international trade at a world price of $9, consumer surplus increases from the shaded blue triangle to the striped blue triangle, and producer surplus decreases from the shaded red triangle to the striped red triangle. The green triangle shows the increase in total surplus that results from trade.

The world price could also be higher than the no-trade equilibrium price. **Figure 2.9-4** shows the gains from trade in the case of a world price of $21. Domestic firms will be unwilling to sell plates anywhere for less than $21 because they can sell as many as they want in the world market for $21. The domestic firms will satisfy domestic consumers' demand for 3 million plates at that price and export 4 million plates. Again, the shaded blue triangle represents consumer surplus, and the shaded red triangle represents producer surplus with no trade. International trade at a world price of $21 lowers consumer surplus to the area of the blue striped triangle and raises producer surplus to the area of the red striped triangle. Total surplus increases by the area of the green triangle, ½(4 × $6) = $12.

Tariffs

Tariffs are taxes on imports.

The imposition of **tariffs**, which are taxes on imports, helps domestic industries and provides revenue for the government. That's the good news. The bad news is that tariffs make prices higher for domestic consumers and can spark trade wars between countries. Early in U.S. history, tariffs provided a majority of the revenue for the

FIGURE 2.9-4 A World Price Above the No-Trade Equilibrium Price

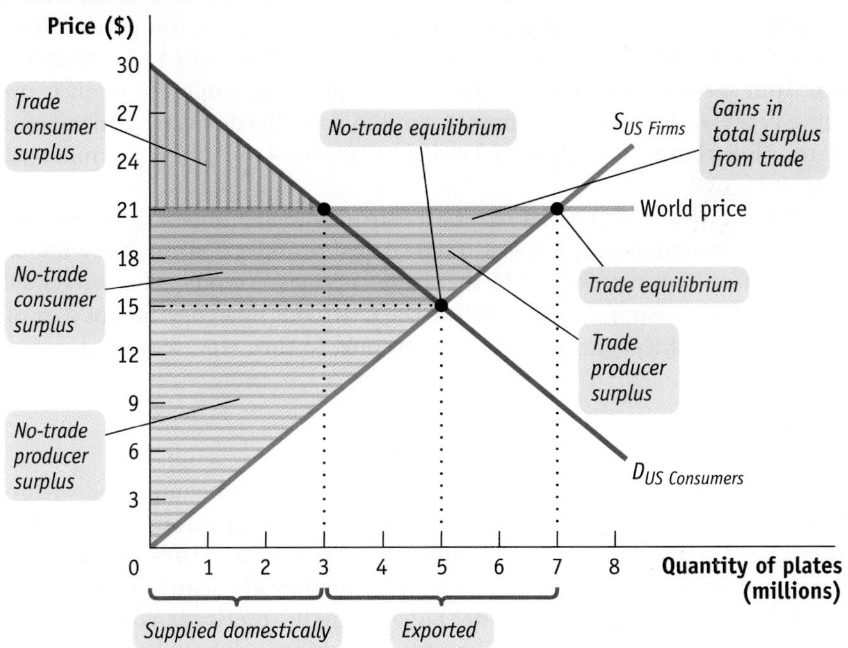

With a world price of $21 that exceeds the no-trade equilibrium price of $15, domestic firms supply 3 million plates to domestic consumers and export 4 million plates. Relative to no trade, international trade decreases consumer surplus from the area of the shaded blue triangle to the area of the striped blue triangle and increases producer surplus from the area of the shaded red triangle to the area of the striped red triangle. The green triangle represents the increase in total surplus from trade.

U.S. government, reaching a high of 97.9% in 1825. As the benefits of free trade came to light, and income and payroll taxes were adopted in the early 1900s, the use of tariffs diminished. By 1944, tariff revenue amounted to only about 1% of federal government revenue, which is still the case today. Nonetheless, many countries, including the United States, impose tariffs on imports.

Suppose the world price is $9 and the U.S. imposes a tariff of $3 per imported ceramic plate. As shown in **Figure 2.9-5**, that effectively raises the price by $3. For every

FIGURE 2.9-5 A Tariff on Ceramic Plates

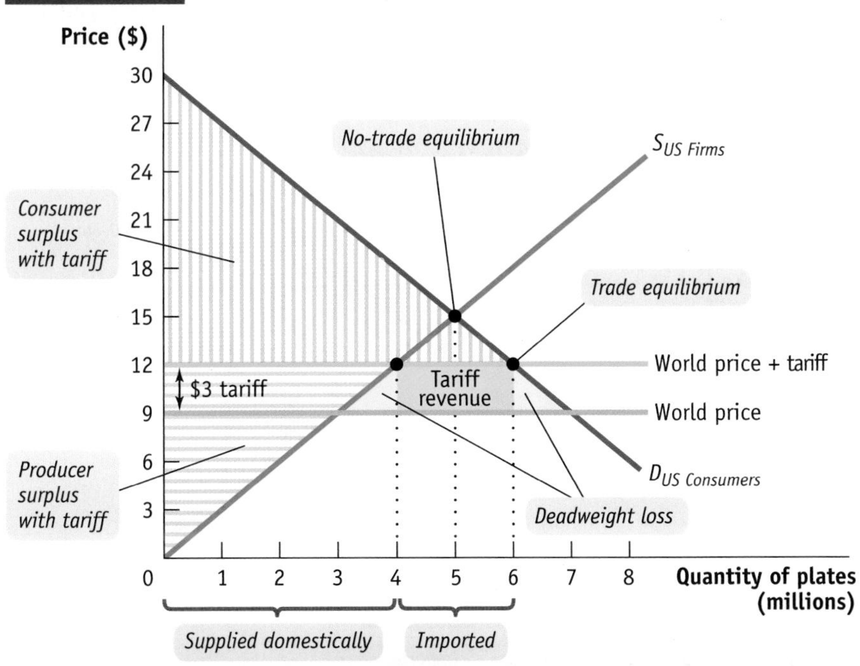

A tariff of $3 per imported ceramic plate effectively raises the price by $3. To receive an imported plate, one must pay $9 to the foreign suppliers plus $3 for the tariff, for a total of $12. Domestic firms can then charge up to $12, for which they are willing to supply 4 million plates. Domestic consumers demand 6 million plates for $12 each. Two million plates will be imported to make up the difference between the domestic supply and the domestic demand. This is 2 million less than the 4 million plates imported without the tariff.

imported plate, the required payment is now \$9 to the foreign suppliers plus \$3 for the tariff, for a total of \$12. Domestic firms are now able to charge up to \$12, for which they are willing to supply 4 million plates, an increase of 1 million compared to the no-tariff situation. Domestic consumers demand 6 million plates for \$12, a decrease of 1 million from the no-tariff situation. Two million plates are imported to make up the difference between the domestic supply of 4 million and the domestic demand of 6 million plates. Note that this is a drop of 2 million from the 4 million plates imported without the tariff.

Figure 2.9-5 shows the post-tariff consumer surplus with a blue striped triangle and the post-tariff producer surplus with a red striped triangle. The tariff revenue is 2 million × \$3 = \$6 million, represented by the shaded orange rectangle. The two yellow triangles were part of consumer surplus before the tariff, but now they are not part of consumer surplus, producer surplus, or tariff revenue, so they represent deadweight loss from the tariff.

Import Quotas

An **import quota** is a limit on the quantity of a good that can be imported within a given period.

AP® ECON TIP

You won't have to draw the import quota graph on the AP® exam, but you will have to understand the implications of quotas, and studying the graph shown in Figure 2.9-6 can provide a better understanding.

An **import quota** is a limit on the quantity of a good that can be imported within a given period. By restricting the supply of imports, import quotas reduce the equilibrium quantity and increase the equilibrium price. Like tariffs, quotas help domestic firms compete with foreign suppliers, but they also cause prices to be higher for domestic consumers. Consider sugar, which Americans consume at a rate of about 11 million tons per year. To protect domestic sugar cane and sugar beet farmers, the U.S. Department of Agriculture (USDA) sets a quota for the amount of sugar that can be imported – 1.2 million tons in 2021 – before a substantial tariff is applied.

Suppose that the United States imposes an import quota of 2 million ceramic plates. That quota would prevent a trade equilibrium at the intersection of U.S. consumers' demand and the supply from the rest of the world because, as we saw in Figure 2.9-2, that equilibrium would require imports of 4 million plates. Instead, consumers would face the pink supply curve in **Figure 2.9-6**, which represents the U.S. supply plus the 2 million plates that could be imported with the quota. Imports would not

FIGURE 2.9-6 A Ceramic Plates Quota

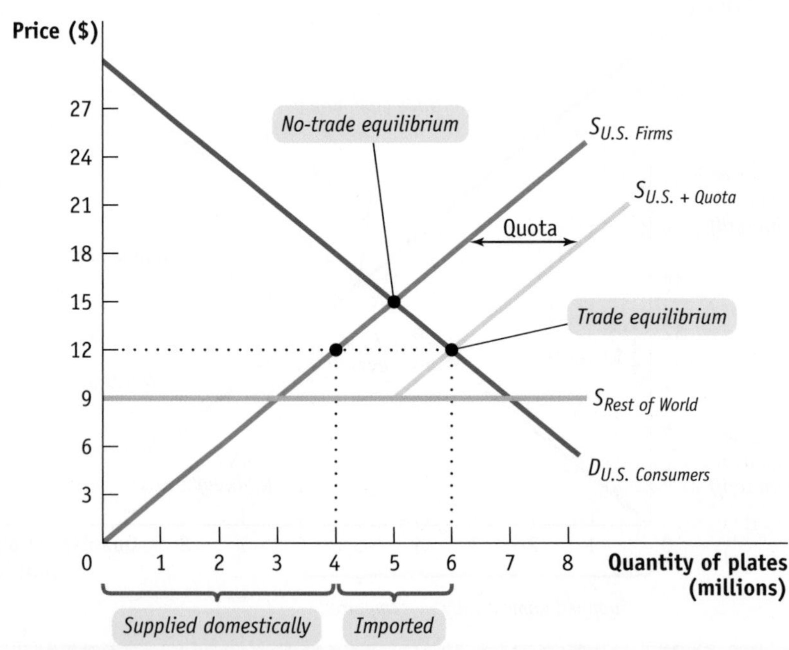

With an import quota of 2 million ceramic plates, consumers face the pink supply curve made up of the U.S. supply plus the 2 million plates that can be imported. Imports are not available for less than \$9, so the pink U.S.-plus-quota supply curve does not extend below \$9. At the \$12 equilibrium price with the quota, a quantity of 6 million plates are purchased, 4 million of which are supplied domestically.

be available for less than $9, so the U.S.-plus-quota supply curve does not extend below a price of $9. The equilibrium price with the quota is $12. Six million plates would be sold at that price, 4 million of which would be made domestically.

The quota of 2 million plates would have the same effect on the price, imports, domestic supply, consumer surplus, producer surplus, and deadweight loss as the $3 tariff. One difference is that with the quota, no tariff revenue would be collected. Instead, as with the quota on taxi rides discussed in Module 2.8B, those who received the licenses to sell plates under the quota would receive additional benefits. Specifically, licensees would gain the difference between the domestic equilibrium price and the trade equilibrium price for each unit sold under the quota, $3 × 2 million = $6 million.

Paresh Nath/CagleCartoons.com

The use of tariffs and import quotas is seldom one-sided. When one country erects a trade barrier against another, retaliation is common. For instance, in 2018, after the Trump administration threatened to impose a tariff on imported steel, European Union leaders threatened to raise tariffs on items imported from the United States, such as bourbon and blue jeans. Escalating trade wars can obliterate the gains from trade, which motivates many countries to move in the opposite direction and negotiate the elimination of trade barriers. Trade agreements such as the Central America-Dominican Republic Free Trade Agreement and the U.S.-Mexico-Canada Agreement limit the use of tariffs, quotas, regulations, and other impediments to trade among the economies involved.

AP® ECON TIP

Tariffs and quotas both affect the price and quantity in a market, but tariffs provide governments with revenues and quotas do not.

Module 2.9  Review

Check Your Understanding

Use the information provided in Figure 2.9-2 to answer the following questions:

1. What is the smallest tariff that would cause all ceramic plates to be supplied by U.S. firms?
2. What is the smallest import quota that would have no effect on international trade? Hint: You can think of the question this way: Every import quota smaller than what level would have an effect on international trade?

Tackle the AP® Test: Multiple-Choice Questions

1. Which of the following is put forth as a reason for trade restrictions?
   a. National pride can take precedence over the gains from trade.
   b. Domestic industries need protection from foreign competition while they develop a comparative advantage.
   c. Citizens don't want to send their money to other countries for goods they could make themselves.
   d. Countries don't want to become overly reliant on other countries.
   e. All of the above are reasons.
2. Relative to autarky, trade at a world price above the domestic equilibrium price leads to a(n)
   a. increase in consumer surplus.
   b. decrease in producer surplus.
   c. increase in deadweight loss.
   d. increase in total surplus.
   e. increase in tariff revenue.

3. Which of the following would result from a U.S. tariff on imported cars?
   a. The profit of U.S. car manufacturers would decrease.
   b. The price paid for cars in the United States would increase.
   c. More cars would be imported.
   d. Fewer domestically made cars would be sold in the United States.
   e. More cars from all sources would be sold in the United States.
4. An import quota is a
   a. minimum quantity of a good that may be imported.
   b. minimum quantity of a good that a factory must produce and sell overseas.
   c. maximum quantity of a good that may be imported.
   d. maximum quantity of a good that a factory may produce and sell overseas.
   e. maximum price that a company can charge for imports.
5. Which of the following would result if China imposed an import quota on cell phones that influenced the amount of trade?
   a. The price of cell phones in China would decrease.
   b. The Chinese government would collect more taxes on imported cell phones.
   c. More cell phones made outside of China would be sold in China.
   d. More cell phones made in China would be sold in China.
   e. More cell phones from all sources would be sold in China.
6. Which of the following is a difference between the effects of a tariff and the effects of a quota relative to the free-trade output?
   a. Domestic supply increases with a quota but not a tariff.
   b. Domestic price decreases with a tariff but not a quota.
   c. Government revenue decreases with a quota but not a tariff.
   d. Government revenue increases with a tariff but not a quota.
   e. Imports increase with a tariff but not a quota.
7. Which of the following is true regarding trade agreements?
   a. They increase tariffs.
   b. They increase regulations.
   c. They decrease impediments to trade.
   d. They enact quotas.
   e. They initiate trade wars.

Tackle the AP® Test: Free-Response Questions

1. Suppose that rice is traded in the world market at a price of US$1 per pound, and that in the absence of trade, the equilibrium price of rice in Mexico is US$1.25 per pound.
   a. Draw a correctly labeled graph that shows the domestic supply and demand for rice in Mexico.
   b. Label the no-trade equilibrium and the trade equilibrium.
   c. Use labeled brackets to indicate the portions of the horizontal axis that represent
      i. the quantity of rice imported at the world price.
      ii. the quantity of rice supplied domestically at the world price.
   d. Suppose that Mexico imposes a tariff of US$0.15 per pound of imported rice.
      i. Label the new trade equilibrium.
      ii. Shade the area that represents the total tariff revenue.
      iii. Shade the area that represents producer surplus with the tariff in place.

Rubric for FRQ 1 (7 points)

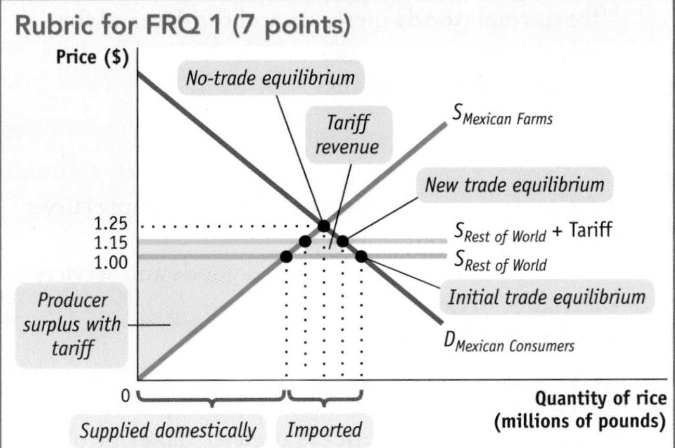

1 point: Graph shows "Price" on the vertical axis, "Quantity of Rice" on the horizontal axis, downward-sloping demand, upward-sloping supply, and the no-trade equilibrium.

1 point: Horizontal world price line and trade equilibrium are presented as shown in the figure.

1 point: Graph shows correct indication of imported quantity.

1 point: Graph shows correct indication of domestically supplied quantity.

1 point: Horizontal world price + tariff line and new trade equilibrium are presented as in the figure.

1 point: Shaded area that represents tariff revenue is presented as in the figure.

1 point: Shaded area that represents producer surplus with the tariff in place as in the figure.

2. Suppose that cheese is traded in the world market at a price of €3 per pound. Assume that France has no trade barriers and has supply and demand curves for cheese as shown in the graph.

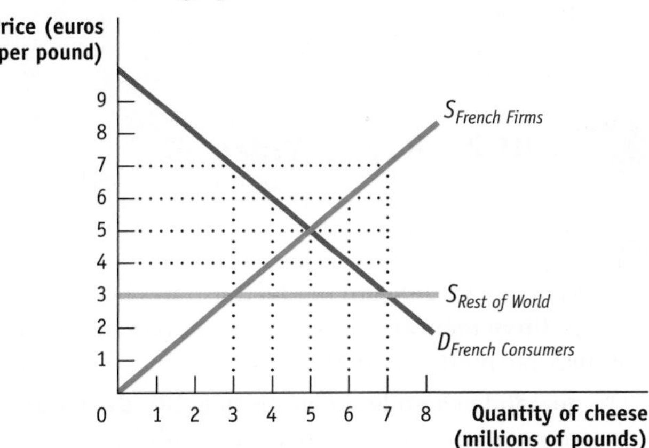

   a. How much cheese does France import?
   b. Suppose that France adopts an import quota of 2 million pounds of cheese.
      i. What will the price be at the new trade equilibrium?
      ii. How much cheese will French suppliers provide domestically with the quota in place?
      iii. If France imposed a tariff instead of a quota to restrict cheese imports, a tariff of what amount per pound would result in imports of 2 million pounds of cheese?
   c. Suppose that instead of any other trade restriction, France imposed a tariff of €4 per pound of cheese. How much cheese would France import? Explain.
   (6 points)

UNIT 2

Review

Adventures in AP® Economics Videos

Mod 2.1: Demand
Mod 2.2: Supply
Mod 2.5: Elasticity
Mod 2.6: Consumer Surplus and Producer Surplus
Mod 2.7: Market Equilibrium

economics by example

The Coffee Market's Hot; Why Are Bean Prices Not?
Why Is a Newspaper Heist So Easy?

UNIT 2 Review Video

Module 2.1

1. The **supply and demand model** illustrates how a **competitive market**, one with many buyers and sellers of the same product, works.
2. The **demand schedule** shows the **quantity demanded** at each price and is represented graphically by a **demand curve**. The **law of demand** says that demand curves slope downward, meaning that as price decreases, the quantity demanded increases.
3. A **movement along the demand curve** occurs when the price changes and causes a change in the quantity demanded. When economists talk of **changes in demand**, they mean shifts of the demand curve—a change in the quantity demanded at any given price. An increase in demand causes a rightward shift of the demand curve. A decrease in demand causes a leftward shift.
4. There are five main factors that shift the demand curve:
   - a change in tastes
   - a change in the prices of related goods, such as **substitutes** or **complements**
   - a change in income: when income rises, the demand for **normal goods** increases and the demand for **inferior goods** decreases
   - a change in expectations

Module 2.2

5. The **supply schedule** shows the **quantity supplied** at each price and is represented graphically by a **supply curve**. According to the **law of supply**, supply curves slope upward, meaning that as price increases, the quantity supplied increases.
6. A **movement along the supply curve** occurs when the price changes and causes a change in the quantity supplied. When economists talk of **changes in supply**, they mean shifts of the supply curve—a change in the quantity supplied at any given price. An increase in supply causes a rightward shift of the supply curve. A decrease in supply causes a leftward shift.
7. There are five main factors that shift the supply curve:
   - a change in **input** prices
   - a change in the prices of related goods and services
   - a change in expectations
   - a change in the number of producers
   - a change in technology

   Two related goods can be **substitutes in production**, meaning that the same inputs used to make one of the goods could instead be used to produce the other, or **complements in production**, which means the two goods are produced together using the same inputs.

Module 2.3

8. Changes in the price of a good affect the quantity consumed as a result of the **substitution effect**, and in some cases the **income effect**. Most goods absorb only a small share of a consumer's spending; for these goods, only the substitution effect—buying less of the good that has become relatively more expensive and more of the good that has become relatively cheaper—is significant. The income effect becomes substantial when there is a change in the price of a good that absorbs a large share of a consumer's spending, thereby changing the purchasing power of the consumer's income.
9. Many economic questions depend on the size of consumer or producer responses to changes in prices or other variables. *Elasticity* is a general measure of responsiveness that can be used to answer such questions.

10. The **price elasticity of demand** – the percentage change in the quantity demanded divided by the percentage change in the price (dropping the minus sign) – is a measure of the responsiveness of the quantity demanded to changes in the price. The *simple method* of finding the price elasticity of demand is to calculate the percentage change in each variable as the change divided by the initial value. To avoid getting different elasticity values depending on the direction of movement along the demand curve, one can use the *midpoint method*, which calculates percentage changes in prices and quantities based on the average of the initial and final values.
11. Demand can fall anywhere in the range from **perfectly inelastic**, meaning the quantity demanded is unaffected by the price, to **perfectly elastic**, meaning there is a unique price at which consumers will buy as much or as little as they are offered. When demand is perfectly inelastic, the demand curve is a vertical line; when it is perfectly elastic, the demand curve is a horizontal line.
12. The price elasticity of demand is classified according to whether it is more or less than 1. If it is greater than 1, demand is **elastic**; if it is less than 1, demand is **inelastic**; if it is exactly 1, demand is **unit-elastic**. This classification determines how **total revenue**, the total value of sales, changes when the price changes. If demand is elastic, total revenue falls when the price increases and rises when the price decreases. If demand is inelastic, total revenue rises when the price increases and falls when the price decreases.
13. The price elasticity of demand depends on whether there are close substitutes for the good in question, whether the good is a necessity or a luxury, the share of income spent on the good, and the length of time that has elapsed since the price change.

Module 2.4

14. The **price elasticity of supply** is the percentage change in the quantity of a good supplied divided by the percentage change in the price. If the quantity supplied does not change at all, we have an instance of **perfectly inelastic supply**; the supply curve is a vertical line. If the quantity supplied is zero below some price but infinite above that price, we have an instance of **perfectly elastic supply**; the supply curve is a horizontal line.
15. The price elasticity of supply depends on the availability of resources to expand production and on time. It is higher when inputs are available at relatively low cost and when more time has elapsed since the price change.

Module 2.5

16. The **cross-price elasticity of demand** measures the effect of a change in one good's price on the quantity of another good demanded. The cross-price elasticity of demand can be positive, in which case the goods are substitutes, or negative, in which case they are complements.
17. The **income elasticity of demand** is the percentage change in the quantity of a good demanded when a consumer's income changes divided by the percentage change in income. The income elasticity of demand indicates how intensely the demand for a good responds to changes in income. It can be negative; in that case the good is an inferior good. Goods with positive income elasticities of demand are normal goods. If the income elasticity is greater than 1, a good is **income-elastic**; if it is positive and less than 1, the good is **income-inelastic**.

Module 2.6

18. The **willingness to pay** of each individual consumer determines the shape of the demand curve. When price is less than or equal to the willingness to pay, the potential consumer purchases the good. The difference between willingness to pay and price is the net gain to the consumer, the individual consumer surplus.
19. Total consumer surplus in a market, which is the sum of all individual consumer surpluses in a market, is equal to the area below the market demand curve but above the price. A rise in the price of a good reduces consumer surplus; a fall in the price increases consumer surplus. The term **consumer surplus** is often used to refer to both individual and total consumer surplus.
20. The **cost** of each potential producer of a good, the lowest price at which he or she is willing to supply a unit of that good, determines the shape of the supply curve. If the price of a good is above a producer's cost, a sale generates a net gain to the producer, known as the individual producer surplus.

21. Total producer surplus in a market, the sum of the individual producer surpluses in a market, is equal to the area above the market supply curve but below the price. A rise in the price of a good increases producer surplus; a fall in the price reduces producer surplus. The term **producer surplus** is often used to refer to both individual and total producer surplus.

22. An economic situation is in **equilibrium** when no individual would be better off doing something different. The supply and demand model is based on the principle that the price in a market moves to its **equilibrium price**, or market-clearing price, the price at which the quantity demanded is equal to the quantity supplied. This quantity is the **equilibrium quantity**.

Module 2.7

23. A market is in **disequilibrium** if the market price is above or below the price that equates the quantity demanded with the quantity supplied. When the price is above its market-clearing level, there is a **surplus** that pushes the price down. When the price is below its market-clearing level, there is a **shortage** that pushes the price up.

24. An increase in demand increases both the equilibrium price and the equilibrium quantity; a decrease in demand has the opposite effect. An increase in supply reduces the equilibrium price and increases the equilibrium quantity; a decrease in supply has the opposite effect.

25. Shifts of the demand curve and the supply curve can happen simultaneously. When they shift in opposite directions, the change in price is predictable but the change in quantity is not. When they shift in the same direction, the change in quantity is predictable but the change in price is not. In general, the curve that shifts the greater distance has a greater effect on the changes in price and quantity.

Module 2.8A

26. **Total surplus**, the total gain to society from the production and consumption of a good, is the sum of consumer and producer surplus.

27. Usually, markets are efficient and achieve the maximum total surplus. Any possible reallocation of consumption or sales, or change in the quantity bought and sold, reduces total surplus. However, society also cares about equity. So government intervention in a market that reduces efficiency but increases equity can be a valid choice by society.

28. A tax that rises more than in proportion to income is a **progressive tax**. A tax that rises less than in proportion to income is a **regressive tax**. A tax that rises in proportion to income is a **proportional tax**.

29. An **excise tax**—a tax on the purchase or sale of a good—raises the price paid by consumers and reduces the price received by producers, driving a wedge between the two. **Tax incidence**—how the burden of the tax is divided between consumers and producers—does not depend on who officially pays the tax.

30. The incidence of an excise tax depends on the price elasticities of supply and demand. If the price elasticity of demand is higher than the price elasticity of supply, the tax falls mainly on producers; if the price elasticity of supply is higher than the price elasticity of demand, the tax falls mainly on consumers.

31. The tax revenue generated by a tax depends on the tax rate and on the number of units sold with the tax. Excise taxes cause inefficiency in the form of **deadweight loss** because they discourage some mutually beneficial transactions. Taxes also impose **administrative costs**: resources used to collect the tax, to pay it (over and above the amount of the tax), and to evade it.

32. An excise tax generates revenue for the government but lowers total surplus. The loss in total surplus exceeds the tax revenue, resulting in a deadweight loss to society. This deadweight loss is represented by a triangle, the area of which equals the value of the transactions discouraged by the tax. If either demand or supply is perfectly inelastic, there is no deadweight loss from a tax.

33. A **lump-sum tax** is a tax of a fixed amount paid by all taxpayers. Because a lump-sum tax does not depend on the behavior of taxpayers, it does not discourage mutually beneficial transactions and therefore causes no deadweight loss.

Module 2.8B

34. Even when a market is efficient, governments often intervene to pursue greater fairness or to please a powerful interest group. Interventions can take the form of **price controls** or quantity controls (quotas), both of which generate predictable and undesirable side effects, consisting of various forms of inefficiency and illegal activity.

35. A **price ceiling**, a maximum market price below the equilibrium price, benefits successful buyers but creates

shortages. Because the price is maintained below the equilibrium price, the quantity demanded is increased and the quantity supplied is decreased compared to the equilibrium quantity. This leads to predictable problems, including inefficient allocation to consumers, wasted resources, and inefficiently low quality. It also encourages illegal activity as people turn to **black markets** to get the good. Because of these problems, price ceilings have generally lost favor as an economic policy tool. But some governments continue to impose them either because they don't understand the effects or because the price ceilings benefit some influential group.

36. A **price floor**, a minimum market price above the equilibrium price, benefits successful sellers but creates a surplus: because the price is maintained above the equilibrium price, the quantity demanded is decreased and the quantity supplied is increased compared to the equilibrium quantity. This leads to predictable problems: inefficiencies in the form of inefficient allocation of sales among sellers, wasted resources, and inefficiently high quality. It also encourages illegal activity and black markets. The most well-known kind of price floor is the **minimum wage**, but price floors are also commonly applied to agricultural products.

37. **Quantity controls**, or **quotas**, limit the quantity of a good that can be bought or sold. The government issues **licenses** to individuals, the right to sell a given quantity of the good. The owner of a license earns a **quota rent**, earnings that accrue from ownership of the right to sell the good. It is equal to the difference between the **demand price** at the quota amount, what consumers are willing to pay for that amount, and the **supply price** at the quota amount, what suppliers are willing to accept for that amount. Economists say that a quota drives a wedge between the demand price and the supply price; this wedge is equal to the **quota rent**. By limiting mutually beneficial transactions, quantity controls generate inefficiency. Like price controls, quantity controls lead to deadweight loss and encourage innovation or illegal activity.

Module 2.9

38. **Protectionism** is the practice of limiting trade to protect domestic industries. The idea is to allow domestic producers to gain enough strength to compete in global markets. Taxes on imports, known as **tariffs**, and limits on the quantities of goods that can be imported, known as **import quotas**, are the primary tools of protectionism.

Key Terms

AP® Exam Practice Questions

Multiple Choice Questions

1. Which of the following changes will most likely result in an increase in the demand for hamburgers in your hometown?
   - **a.** The price of hot dogs decreases.
   - **b.** The price of drinks sold at hamburger restaurants increases.
   - **c.** Income in your town decreases and hamburgers are a normal good.
   - **d.** The local newspaper publishes a story on health problems caused by red meat.
   - **e.** The number of vegetarians in your town decreases and the population size remains the same.

2. Which of the following changes will most likely result in a decrease in the supply of guitars?
   - **a.** The popularity of guitar music increases.
   - **b.** Consumer incomes decrease.
   - **c.** A new firm enters the guitar industry.
   - **d.** The guitar-making process is reengineered to be more efficient.
   - **e.** The wages of guitar makers increase.

3. Which of the following will most likely result in a decrease in the quantity of lemons demanded?
   - **a.** an increase in the price of lemons
   - **b.** an increase in the price of limes
   - **c.** an increase in the price of lemonade
   - **d.** an increase in the number of lemonade stands
   - **e.** a decrease in consumer income

4. If two goods are complements, an increase in the price of one good will cause which of the following?
   - **a.** a decrease in the demand for the other
   - **b.** a decrease in the quantity demanded of the other
   - **c.** an increase in the demand for the other
   - **d.** an increase in the quantity demanded of the other
   - **e.** no change in the demand for the other

5. Which of the following is true at the equilibrium price in a market?
   - **a.** Consumers who purchase the good may be better off buying something else instead.
   - **b.** The market has not yet cleared.
   - **c.** There is a tendency for the price to decrease over time.
   - **d.** There may be either a surplus or a shortage of the good.
   - **e.** The quantity demanded of the good equals the quantity supplied.

6. A survey indicated that chocolate is America's favorite ice cream flavor. Which of the following will lead to a decrease in the price of chocolate ice cream?
   - **a.** A drought in the Midwest causes farmers to reduce the number of dairy cows they raise.
   - **b.** A new report from the American Medical Association concludes that chocolate has significant health benefits.
   - **c.** The price of vanilla ice cream increases.
   - **d.** New freezer technology lowers the cost of producing ice cream.
   - **e.** The price of ice cream toppings decreases.

7. Which of the following events will increase both the price and the quantity of pizza?
   - **a.** The price of mozzarella cheese increases.
   - **b.** New health hazards of eating pizza are widely publicized.
   - **c.** The price of pizza ovens rises.
   - **d.** Consumers expect the price of pizza to fall next week.
   - **e.** Consumer income falls and pizza is an inferior good.

Use the following situation and diagram to answer Questions 8-11.

For the last 70 years, the U.S. government has used price supports to provide income assistance to U.S. farmers. At times, the government has used price floors, which it maintains by buying up the surplus farm products. At other times, it has used target prices, giving the farmer an amount equal to the difference between the market price and the target price for each unit sold.

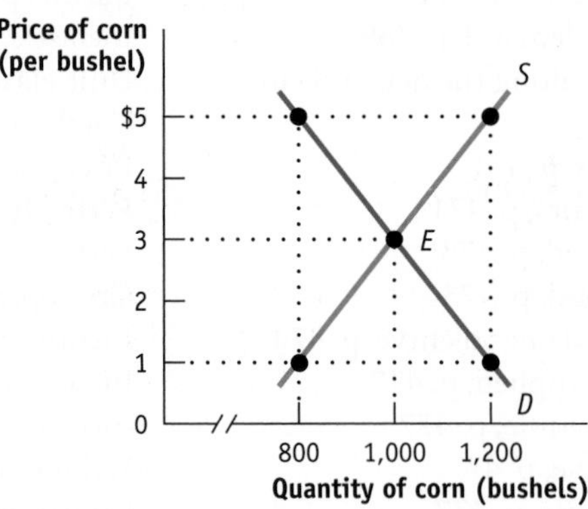

8. What are the equilibrium price and quantity in the market for corn?

	Price	*Quantity*
a.	$1	800
b.	$1	1,200
c.	$3	1,000
d.	$5	800
e.	$5	1,200

9. If the government sets a price floor of $5 per bushel, how many bushels of corn are produced?
a. 0
b. 400
c. 800
d. 1,000
e. 1,200

10. If the government sets a price floor of $5 per bushel, how many bushels of corn are purchased by consumers?
a. 0
b. 400
c. 800
d. 1,000
e. 1,200

11. How much does a price floor of $5 cost the government if it maintains the price floor by buying any surplus corn?
a. $0
b. $2,000
c. $4,000
d. $5,000
e. $6,000

Use the following diagram to answer Questions 12–14.

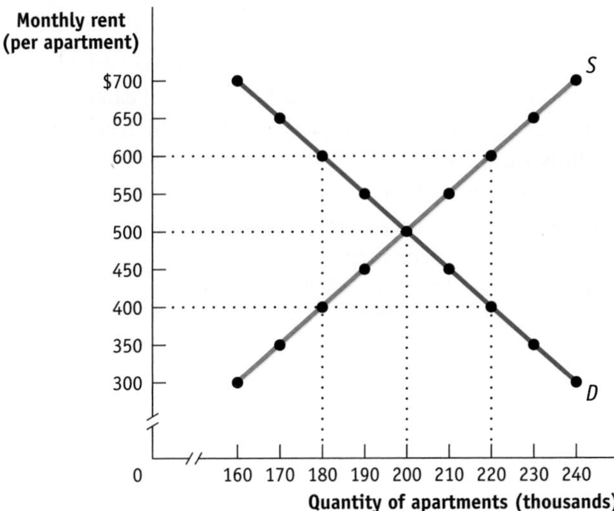

12. Where must an effective price ceiling in this market be set?
a. at $500
b. above $400
c. above $500
d. below $600
e. below $500

13. How many apartments will be offered for rent if the government sets a price ceiling at $400?
a. 0
b. 40,000
c. 180,000
d. 200,000
e. 220,000

14. A price ceiling set at $400 will result in which of the following in the market for apartments?
a. a surplus of 40,000 apartments
b. a surplus of 220,000 apartments
c. no surplus or shortage
d. a shortage of 40,000 apartments
e. a shortage of 220,000 apartments

Refer to the following table and information to answer Questions 15–17.

Only fishing boats licensed by the U.S. government are allowed to catch swordfish in the waters off the North Atlantic coast. The following table shows hypothetical demand and supply schedules for swordfish caught in the United States each year.

	Quantity of swordfish (millions of pounds per year)	
Price of swordfish (per pound)	Quantity demanded	Quantity supplied
$20	6	15
18	7	13
16	8	11
14	9	9
12	10	7

15. If the government establishes a quota of 7 million pounds in the market, what will the demand price of swordfish be (per pound)?
a. $20
b. $18
c. $16
d. $14
e. $12

16. What is the quota rent per pound of swordfish received by licensed fishing boats when the government sets a quota of 7 million pounds?
a. $0
b. $6
c. $12
d. $18
e. $30

17. If there is a quota of 7 million pounds and swordfish fishing licenses are traded in a market, how much will the price of a fishing license be per pound?
a. $0
b. $6
c. $12
d. $18
e. $30

18. When transactions do not occur due to price or quantity controls, what is the term for the lost gains?
a. wasted resources
b. inefficient quality
c. price wedge
d. black market losses
e. deadweight loss

19. Suppose market prices for tomatoes were to increase by 10%, and tomato farmers wanted to know whether or not their overall total revenues would rise or fall as a consequence. The farmers could figure this out by calculating which of the following economic concepts?
a. deadweight loss
b. producer surplus
c. diminishing marginal utility
d. price elasticity of demand
e. administrative costs

20. Suppose Jolene buys apples weekly. If the price of apples were to drop, Jolene would experience a(n) ____________ in ____________.

a.	decrease	total revenue
b.	increase	consumer surplus
c.	decrease	her budget constraint
d.	increase	marginal utility
e.	decrease	willingness to pay

21. Pizza and soda are often consumed together at Daniel's Diner. Suppose that the price of pizza rises from $0.75 a slice to $1.25 a slice, and consequently April sales of pizza drop from 1,050 to 950 slices. Using the midpoint method and this information, an economist could conclude which of the following?
    a. The cross-price elasticity of demand is 0.2.
    b. The price elasticity of supply is 0.1.
    c. The price elasticity of demand is 0.2.
    d. The income elasticity of demand is 0.5.
    e. The unit elasticity of demand is 0.1.

22. If the demand curve is a straight line with a slope of −1, then from the left end of the curve to the right,
    a. demand is unit-elastic.
    b. demand is elastic.
    c. demand is inelastic.
    d. the price elasticity ranges from very high to very low.
    e. the price elasticity ranges from very low to very high.

23. If the price of an inferior good decreases, then consumers' purchasing power ____________, and the income effect alone causes consumers to buy ____________ of the good.

a.	decreases	more
b.	decreases	less
c.	increases	more
d.	increases	less
e.	remains the same	more

Use the following information to answer Questions 24–26.

Suppose the government levies a tax of $0.50 per liter on the buyers of soda. Suppose also that the price elasticity of demand for soda is 1.2 and the price elasticity of supply is 0.7.

24. Because this tax is levied on the sale of a specific good, it is a(n)
    a. excise tax.
    b. progressive tax.
    c. regressive tax.
    d. proportional tax.
    e. lump-sum tax.

25. After this tax is levied, total surplus will ____________, and the price received by producers (not including the tax) will ____________.

a.	increase	increase by exactly $0.50
b.	decrease	fall by exactly $0.50
c.	increase	fall by less than $0.50
d.	decrease	fall by less than $0.50
e.	increase	increase by more than $0.50

26. If economists were to study the tax incidence in this soda market, they would conclude which of the following?
    a. The burden of this tax falls entirely on consumers.
    b. The burden of this tax falls entirely on producers.
    c. The burden of this tax falls equally on consumers and producers.
    d. The burden of this tax falls more on consumers than on producers.
    e. The burden of this tax falls more on producers than on consumers.

27. Julia is willing to sell her used calculator for $20. Her friend Javier is willing to pay $90 for a used calculator. They agree and trade at a price of $50. Which of the following is correct?
    a. Julia's cost is $50.
    b. Javier's consumer surplus is $30.
    c. Julia's producer surplus is $30.
    d. Javier's budget line is $90.
    e. Julia's deadweight loss is $70.

Refer to the figure for Questions 28–34.

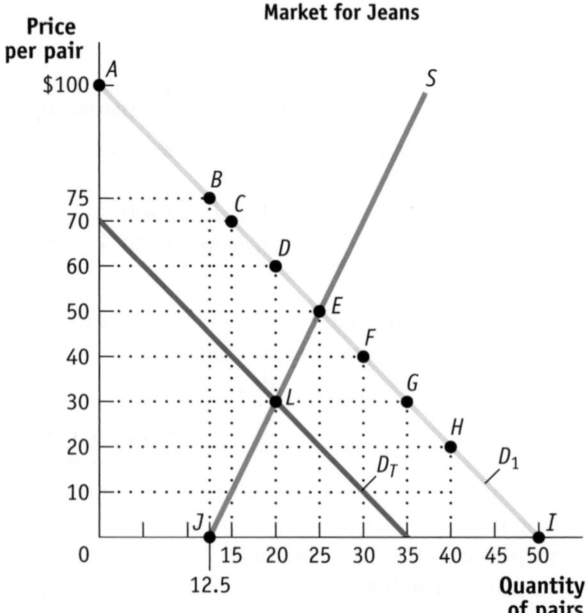

28. Using the simple method, the price elasticity of demand going from point *D* to point *H* is ___________ and economists would classify it as ___________.

a.	0.67	inelastic
b.	1.5	elastic
c.	1	unit-elastic
d.	0.67	elastic
e.	1.5	inelastic

29. Using the simple method, the price elasticity of supply going from point *E* to point *J* is ___________ and economists would classify it as ___________.

a.	0.5	inelastic
b.	0.375	elastic
c.	0	perfectly inelastic
d.	2.00	elastic
e.	5.0	inelastic

30. Which of the following statements about the tax on jeans is true?

a. Buyers bear the entire burden of the tax, since the tax was levied on them.
b. Buyers bear most of the burden of the tax, since the tax was levied on them.
c. Buyers bear most of the burden of the tax, since demand is more *inelastic* than supply.
d. Buyers bear a smaller tax burden than sellers, since demand is more *elastic* than supply.
e. Buyers and sellers share the tax burden equally.

31. How much revenue would the government collect from the tax on jeans?

a. $1,250
b. $1,200
c. $750
d. $600
e. $300

32. Buyers in the jeans market gain ___________ in consumer surplus before the imposition of the tax, and they gain ___________ in consumer surplus after the imposition of the tax.

a.	$625	$400
b.	$400	$225
c.	$400	$625
d.	$625	$225
e.	$225	$400

33. Jeans and product X (not shown) have a cross-price elasticity of 3.7. After the imposition of the tax on jeans, buyers' consumption of product X would ___________ because jeans and product X are ___________.

a.	decrease	normal goods
b.	increase	substitutes
c.	decrease	complements
d.	increase	complements
e.	decrease	substitutes

34. The deadweight loss caused by the tax on jeans is

a. $5.
b. $30.
c. $50.
d. $60.
e. $75.

35. If razors and shaving cream are complements, their cross-price elasticity of demand will necessarily be

a. greater than 1.
b. less than −1.
c. 0.
d. positive.
e. negative.

36. The height of the demand curve at each quantity is determined by

a. consumers' willingness to pay.
b. the price of the good.
c. the location of the supply curve.
d. the marginal cost of production.
e. the availability of inputs for making that good.

37. Suppose the world price for a good is below the domestic equilibrium price and a decrease in protectionism leads to lower tariffs. Which of the following is likely to increase as a result?

a. consumer surplus
b. producer surplus
c. tariff revenue
d. the quantity supplied domestically
e. exports of the good

Free-Response Questions

1. Pablo Picasso painted only 1,000 paintings during his "Blue Period."

a. Draw a correctly labeled graph of the market for Picasso's "Blue Period" paintings showing each of the following:
   i. the supply and demand curves for paintings
   ii. the equilibrium price and quantity of paintings
b. List the five principal factors that will lead to a change in the price of paintings in this market.
c. Show the effect on price in your market for paintings if wealthy art collectors decide that it is essential to acquire Picasso's "Blue Period" paintings for their collections. **(5 points)**

2. On the island of Rockville, the equilibrium quantity of acres of land sold is currently 1,000, and the equilibrium price per acre is $500. Landowners have an elasticity of supply equal to 0. Consumers have an elasticity of demand greater than 1.

   a. Using a correctly labeled graph of supply and demand for acres of land, show the equilibrium price ($500) and equilibrium quantity (1,000).

   Now suppose that the government of Rockville imposes an excise tax of $20 per acre on the buyers of land.

   b. Show the effects of the tax on your graph from part a, and indicate the new equilibrium price and equilibrium quantity.
   c. Calculate the amount of tax revenue that is collected.
   d. Calculate the amount of deadweight loss.
   e. Who bears the burden of this tax? Explain. **(9 points)**

3. Connor sells peanut butter and chocolate at his snack shop.

   a. Consumer demand is such that each day he can sell 50 jars of peanut butter for $4 each or 30 jars for $5 each. Is the price elasticity of demand for peanut butter elastic, inelastic, or unit-elastic? Explain.
   b. When the price of peanut butter is $4, Conner sells 20 chocolate bars per day, and when the price of peanut butter is $5, he sells 15 chocolate bars per day.
      i. Calculate the cross-price elasticity for peanut butter and chocolate. Show your work.
      ii. Based on your answer to part (i), are peanut butter and chocolate substitutes, complements, or unrelated?
   c. Joyah is one of Connor's customers. When Joyah's income increased by 10%, she bought 10% less peanut butter. For Joyah, is peanut butter necessarily a normal good, an inferior good, a luxury, or a necessity? Explain. **(5 points)**

Production Costs, Profit, and Perfect Competition

AP® Economic Skills

1. Principles and Models (1.A, 1.C, 1.D, 2.A)
2. Graphing and Visuals (4.A)

The Cost of Power

In this Unit, we focus on the factors that affect producer choice and the supply side of the supply and demand model introduced in Unit 2. Producers seek profit, which is the difference between total revenue and total cost. We turn to graphs to illustrate the story of what happens to various measures of revenue, cost, and profit as output changes. Different situations lead to different stories.

Consider the Richland Wind Farm in western Iowa, which cost around $67 million to build in 2020. The wind farm's 53 turbines have the capacity to produce 130 megawatts of electricity at a negligible additional cost per kilowatt-hour, because the primary input—wind—is free.

For comparison, Wisconsin's Nemadji Trail Energy Center natural gas-fired power plant, proposed for completion in 2025, will cost an estimated $700 million and have a capacity of up to 550 megawatts. The cost story at Nemadji Trail differs from that at the Richland Wind Farm because each kilowatt-hour of electricity produced at Nemadji Trail will require the use of additional natural gas, which isn't free. But the larger capacity at Nemadji Trail will allow the cost of constructing the plant to be spread across more units of output.

The ability for power plants to cover their costs depends not only on the size of the costs but also on the prices sellers can charge per kilowatt-hour of electricity, which range from 10 cents in Louisiana to 33 cents in Hawaii. Given the complexity of cost and revenue stories, the need to visualize them with graphs is clear. In this Unit, you will learn several analytical tools used to inform production decisions.

Franck Foros/Alamy

We'll start with a discussion of the production function, which shows the relationship between the inputs used for production and the output that is produced. Next, we will consider the costs that influence firms' decisions about supply. Then we'll investigate firms' ultimate goal of profit maximization. The final Modules in this Unit examine a firm's decision to enter or exit a market and expand on the market structure of perfect competition introduced in Unit 2.

MODULE 3.1

The Production Function

In this Module, you will learn to:

- Define fixed inputs and variable inputs
- Summarize the importance of a firm's production function
- Calculate the marginal product of labor
- Explain why production is often subject to diminishing marginal returns to inputs
- Use a graph to show how the production function changes between the short run and the long run

Inputs and Output

To produce goods or services for sale, a firm must transform inputs into output. The quantity of output a firm produces depends on the quantity of inputs; this relationship is known as the firm's **production function**. As we'll see in the next Module, a firm's production function influences its *cost curves*. As a first step in understanding this relationship, let's look at the characteristics of a hypothetical production function.

A **production function** is the relationship between the quantity of inputs a firm uses and the quantity of output it produces.

Production with Fixed and Variable Inputs

To understand the concept of a production function, let's consider a farm that we assume, for the sake of simplicity, produces only one output, wheat, and uses only two inputs, land and labor. This farm is owned by a couple named Mia and Liam. They hire workers to do the actual physical labor on the farm. Moreover, we will assume that all potential workers are of the same quality—they are all equally knowledgeable and capable of performing farmwork.

View Stock/Alamy

Mia and Liam's farm sits on 10 acres of land; no more acres are available to them, and they are currently unable to either increase or decrease the size of their farm by selling, buying, or leasing acreage. Land, in this case, is what economists call a **fixed input**—an input whose quantity is fixed for a period of time and cannot be varied. (As another example, the fixed inputs for a school include the classrooms and school buses.)

Mia and Liam, however, are free to decide how many workers to hire. The labor provided by these workers is called a **variable input**—an input whose quantity the firm can vary at any time. For a school, the variable inputs include electricity, chalk, and teachers.

A **fixed input** is an input whose quantity is fixed for a period of time and cannot be varied.

A **variable input** is an input whose quantity the firm can vary at any time.

The **long run** is the time period in which all inputs can be varied.

The **short run** is the time period in which at least one input is fixed.

In reality, whether or not the quantity of an input is really fixed depends on the time period being considered. Given a long enough period of time, firms can adjust the quantity of any input. Economists define the **long run** as the time period in which all inputs can be varied. So there are no fixed inputs in the long run. In contrast, the **short run** is defined as the time period in which at least one input is fixed. For now, we will restrict our attention to the short run and assume that at least one input (land) is fixed. Later in this Unit, we'll look more carefully at the distinction between the short run and the long run.

Mia and Liam know that the quantity of wheat they produce depends on the number of workers they hire. Using modern farming techniques, one worker can cultivate the 10-acre farm, albeit not very intensively. When an additional worker is added, the land is divided equally among all the workers: each worker has 5 acres to cultivate when 2 workers are employed, each cultivates $3\frac{1}{3}$ acres when 3 are employed, and so on. So, as additional workers are employed, the 10 acres of land are cultivated more intensively and more bushels of wheat are produced.

The relationship between the quantity of labor and the quantity of output, for a given amount of the fixed input, constitutes the farm's production function. The production function for Mia and Liam's farm, where land is the fixed input and labor is the variable input, is shown in the first two columns of the table in **Figure 3.1-1**; the diagram shows the same information graphically. The curve in Figure 3.1-1 shows how the quantity of output depends on the quantity of the variable input for a given quantity of the fixed input; it is called the farm's **total product curve**. The physical quantity of output, bushels of wheat, is measured on the vertical axis; the quantity of the variable input, labor (that is, the number of workers employed), is measured on the horizontal axis. The total product curve here slopes upward, reflecting the fact that more bushels of wheat are produced as more workers are employed.

The **total product curve** shows how the quantity of output depends on the quantity of the variable input for a given quantity of the fixed input.

FIGURE 3.1-1 **The Production Function and the Total Product Curve for Mia and Liam's Farm**

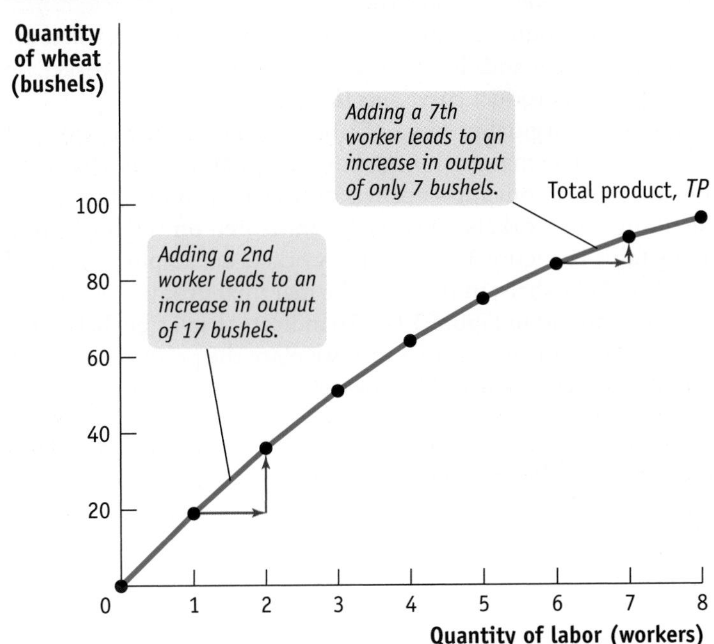

Quantity of labor L (workers)	Quantity of wheat Q (bushels)	Marginal product of labor $MPL = \Delta Q/\Delta L$ (bushels per worker)
0	0	
		19
1	19	
		17
2	36	
		15
3	51	
		13
4	64	
		11
5	75	
		9
6	84	
		7
7	91	
		5
8	96	

The table shows the production function, the relationship between the quantity of the variable input (labor, measured in number of workers) and the quantity of output (wheat, measured in bushels) for a given quantity of the fixed input (10 acres of land). It also shows the marginal product of labor on Mia and Liam's farm. The total product curve shows the production function graphically. It slopes upward because more wheat is produced as more workers are employed. It also becomes flatter because the marginal product of labor declines as more and more workers are employed.

Although the total product curve in Figure 3.1-1 slopes upward along its entire length, the slope isn't constant: as you move up the curve to the right, it flattens out. To understand this changing slope, look at the third column of the table in Figure 3.1-1, which shows the *change in the quantity of output* generated by adding one more worker. That is, it shows the **marginal product** of labor, or *MPL*: the additional quantity of output from using one more unit of labor (one more worker).

The **marginal product** of an input is the additional quantity of output produced by using one more unit of that input.

In this example, we have data at intervals of 1 worker—that is, we have information on the quantity of output when there are 3 workers, 4 workers, and so on. Sometimes data aren't available in increments of 1 unit—for example, you might have information on the quantity of output only when there are 40 workers and when there are 50 workers. In this case, you can use the following equation to calculate the marginal product of labor:

$$\textbf{(3.1-1)} \quad \begin{array}{c}\text{Marginal}\\ \text{product of}\\ \text{labor}\end{array} = \begin{array}{c}\text{Change in quantity of}\\ \text{output produced by one}\\ \text{additional unit of labor}\end{array} = \frac{\text{Change in quantity of output}}{\text{Change in quantity of labor}}$$

Equation 3.1-1 can also be written using the Greek uppercase delta, the triangular symbol Δ, to represent the change in a variable:

$$MPL = \frac{\Delta Q}{\Delta L}$$

Now we can explain the significance of the slope of the total product curve: it is equal to the marginal product of labor. The slope of a line is equal to "rise" over "run." This implies that the slope of the total product curve is the change in the quantity of output (the "rise") divided by the change in the quantity of labor (the "run"). And, as we can see from Equation 3.1-1, this is simply the marginal product of labor. So in Figure 3.1-1, the fact that the marginal product of the first worker is 19 also means that the slope of the total product curve in going from 0 to 1 worker is 19. Similarly, the slope of the total product curve in going from 1 to 2 workers is the same as the marginal product of the second worker, 17, and so on.

In this example, the marginal product of labor steadily declines as more workers are hired—that is, each successive worker adds less to output than the previous worker. So as employment increases, the total product curve gets flatter.

Figure 3.1-2 shows how the marginal product of labor depends on the number of workers employed on the farm. The marginal product of labor, *MPL*, is measured on the vertical axis in units of physical output—bushels of wheat—produced per additional worker, and the number of workers employed is measured on the horizontal axis. You can see from the table in Figure 3.1-1 that if 5 workers are employed instead of 4, output rises from 64 to 75 bushels; in this case the marginal product of labor is 11 bushels—the same number found in Figure 3.1-2. To indicate that 11 bushels is the marginal product when employment rises from 4 to 5, we place the point corresponding to that information halfway between 4 and 5 workers.

FIGURE 3.1-2 **The Marginal Product of Labor Curve for Mia and Liam's Farm**

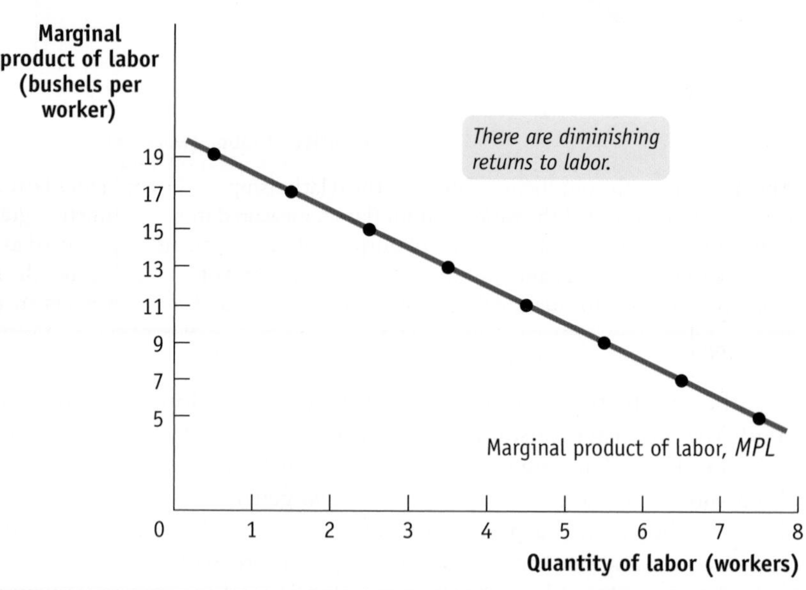

The marginal product of labor curve plots each worker's marginal product, the increase in the quantity of output generated by each additional worker. The change in the quantity of output is measured on the vertical axis and the number of workers employed on the horizontal axis. The first worker employed generates an increase in output of 19 bushels, the second worker generates an increase of 17 bushels, and so on. The curve slopes downward due to diminishing returns to labor.

There are **diminishing returns to an input** when an increase in the quantity of that input, holding the levels of all other inputs fixed, leads to a decline in the marginal product of that input.

In this example, the marginal product of labor falls as the number of workers increases. That is, there are *diminishing returns to labor* on Mia and Liam's farm. In general, there are **diminishing returns to an input** when an increase in the quantity of that input, holding the quantity of all other inputs fixed, reduces that input's marginal product. Due to diminishing returns to labor, the *MPL* curve is negatively sloped.

To grasp why diminishing returns can occur, think about what happens as Mia and Liam add more and more workers without increasing the number of acres farmed. As the number of workers increases, the land is farmed more intensively and the number of bushels increases. But each additional worker is working with a smaller share of the 10 acres—the fixed input—than the previous worker. As a result, output does not increase by as much when an additional worker is hired as it did when the previous worker was hired. So it's not surprising that the marginal product of the additional worker falls.

David Silverman/Getty Images

With diminishing returns to labor, each new worker added to a fixed amount of land contributes less to total output than the previous worker.

The next Module explains that opportunities for specialization among workers can allow the marginal product of labor to increase for the first few workers, but eventually diminishing returns set in as the result of redundancy and congestion. The crucial point to emphasize about diminishing returns is that, like many propositions in economics, it is an "other things equal" proposition: each successive unit of an input will raise production by less than the previous unit *if the quantity of all other inputs is held fixed.*

Production When All Inputs Are Variable

What would happen if the levels of other inputs were allowed to change? You can see the answer illustrated in **Figure 3.1-3**. Panel (a) shows two total product curves, TP_{10} and TP_{20}. TP_{10} is the farm's total product curve when its total area is 10 acres (the same curve as in Figure 3.1-1). TP_{20} is the total product curve when the farm's area has increased to 20 acres. Except when 0 workers are employed, TP_{20} lies everywhere above TP_{10} because with more acres available, any given number of workers produces more output.

> **AP® ECON TIP**
>
> Questions about the short run and the long run can cause confusion. Just remember that in the long run, all inputs are variable, and in the short run, at least one input is fixed.

FIGURE 3.1-3 Total Product, Marginal Product, and the Fixed Input

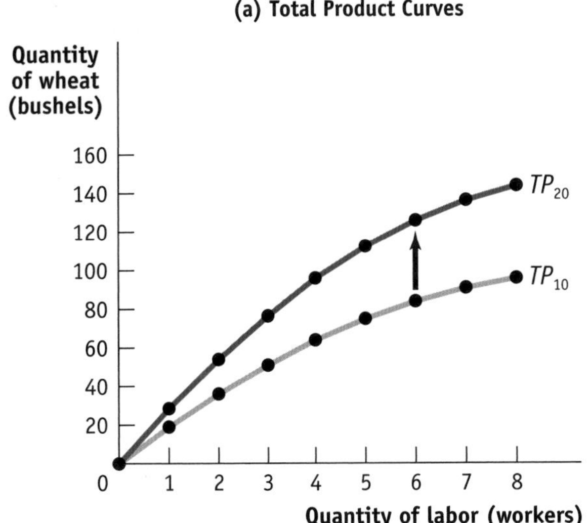

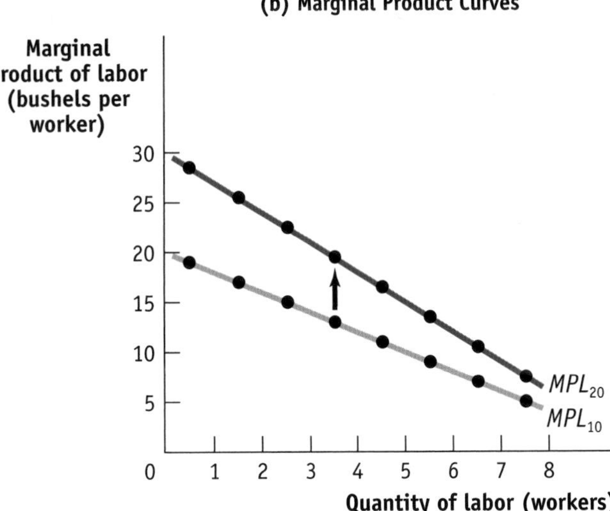

This figure shows how the quantity of output—illustrated by the total product curve—and marginal product depend on the level of the fixed input. Panel (a) shows two total product curves for Mia and Liam's farm, TP_{10} when their farm is 10 acres and TP_{20} when it is 20 acres. With more land, each worker can produce more wheat, so an increase in the fixed input shifts the total product curve up from TP_{10} to TP_{20}. This result also implies that the marginal product of each worker is higher when the farm is 20 acres than when it is 10 acres. As a result, an increase in acreage also shifts the marginal product of labor curve up from MPL_{10} to MPL_{20}. Panel (b) shows the marginal product of labor curves. Note that both marginal product of labor curves still slope downward due to diminishing returns to labor.

> **AP® ECON TIP**
>
> The *MPL* typically falls as more workers are hired because increases in production are limited by a fixed amount of capital or land that must be shared among the growing number of workers. Also, it may be necessary to hire less qualified workers.

Panel (b) shows the corresponding marginal product of labor curves. MPL_{10} is the marginal product of labor curve given 10 acres to cultivate (the same curve as in Figure 3.1-2), and MPL_{20} is the marginal product of labor curve given 20 acres. Both curves slope downward because, in each case, the amount of land is fixed, albeit at different levels. But MPL_{20} lies everywhere above MPL_{10}, reflecting the fact that the marginal product of the same worker is higher when that worker has more of the fixed input to work with.

Figure 3.1-3 demonstrates a general result: *the position of the total product curve depends on the quantities of other inputs.* If you change the quantities of the other inputs, both the total product curve and the marginal product curve of the remaining input will shift. It is important to consider these shifts when making predictions on the basis of diminishing returns. Even Thomas Malthus, the English economist who introduced the principle of diminishing returns to an input back in 1798, was led astray by assumptions that other factors would remain largely unchanged.

Malthus argued that as a country's population grew but its land area remained fixed, it would become increasingly difficult to grow enough food. Though more intensive cultivation of the land could increase crop yields, as the marginal product of labor diminished, each successive farmer would add less to the total than the last. In a country with a small population and abundant land (an accurate description of the United States at the time), Malthus argued, families would be large and the population would grow rapidly. Ultimately, the pressure of population on the land would reduce the condition of most people to a level at which starvation and disease held the population in check. Arguments like this led the historian Thomas Carlyle to dub economics the "dismal science."

Happily, Malthus's predictions have turned out to be wrong. The world population has increased from about 1 billion at the time when Malthus wrote to more than 7.9 billion in 2022, but in most parts of the world people eat better now than ever before. And where they do not, problems with food distribution or government corruption—and not population pressure on the land—are typically to blame. Diminishing returns to labor can be mitigated by investments in capital and improvements in farming technology. Fortunately, since the eighteenth century, rapid capital accumulation and technological progress have relaxed the limits imposed by diminishing returns. Diminishing returns to labor imply that the marginal product declines when *all* other things—including capital and technology—remain the same. So the pleasing fact that Malthus's predictions were wrong does not invalidate the concept of diminishing returns.

Module 3.1  Review

Check Your Understanding

1. Erin's ice-making company produces ice cubes using a 10-ton machine and electricity (along with water, which, for simplicity, we will ignore as an input). The quantity of output, measured in pounds of ice, is given in the table below.

Quantity of electricity (kilowatts)	Quantity of ice (pounds)
0	0
1	1,000
2	1,800
3	2,400
4	2,800

a. What is the fixed input? What is the variable input?

b. Construct a table showing the marginal product of the variable input. Does it show diminishing returns?

c. Suppose a 50% increase in the size of the fixed input increases output by 100% for any given amount of the variable input. Construct a table showing the quantity of output and the marginal product in this case.

Tackle the AP® Test: Multiple-Choice Questions

1. A production function shows the relationship between inputs and
   a. fixed costs.
   b. variable costs.
   c. total revenue.
   d. output.
   e. profit.
2. Which of the following defines the short run?
   a. less than a year
   b. when all inputs are fixed
   c. when no inputs are variable
   d. when only one input is variable
   e. when at least one input is fixed
3. The slope of the total product curve is equal to the
   a. marginal product.
   b. marginal cost.
   c. average product.
   d. average revenue.
   e. profit.
4. When the returns to an input are diminishing and a profit-maximizing firm chooses to hire more of that input, the total product curve has what kind of slope?
   a. negative and decreasing
   b. positive and decreasing
   c. negative and increasing
   d. positive and increasing
   e. positive and constant
5. Historically, the limits imposed by diminishing returns have been alleviated primarily by
   a. investments in capital and technology.
   b. population growth.
   c. new discoveries of land.
   d. the teachings of Thomas Malthus.
   e. the lessons of economic models.
6. Diminishing returns are a common result of
   a. more of one input being added to a fixed quantity of another input.
   b. the quantities of two inputs being decreased at the same time.
   c. the quantities of two inputs being increased at the same time.
   d. the profit of a firm being limited by increasing competition.
   e. the profit of a firm being limited by increasing input costs.
7. A horizontal marginal product curve would indicate that the total product curve is
   a. horizontal.
   b. vertical.
   c. downward-sloping.
   d. upward-sloping.
   e. downward-sloping and then upward-sloping.

Tackle the AP® Test: Free-Response Questions

1. Draw a correctly labeled graph of a production function that exhibits diminishing returns to labor. Assume labor is the variable input and capital is the fixed input. Explain how your graph illustrates diminishing returns to labor.

Rubric for FRQ 1 (4 points)

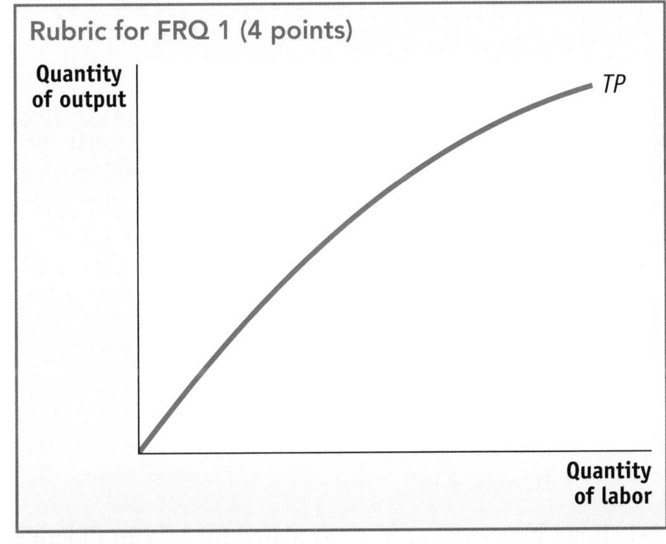

1 point: Graph with vertical axis labeled "Quantity of output" or "Q" and horizontal axis labeled "Quantity of labor" or "L"

1 point: Upward-sloping curve labeled "Total product" or "*TP*"

1 point: The slope of the total product curve is positive and decreasing.

1 point: A positive and decreasing slope illustrates diminishing returns to labor because each additional unit of labor increases total product by less than the previous unit of labor.

2. Use the data in the table below to graph the production function and the marginal product of labor. Do the data illustrate diminishing returns to labor? Explain. **(5 points)**

Quantity of labor	Quantity of output
0	0
1	25
2	47
3	66
4	82
5	95
6	105
7	112
8	116

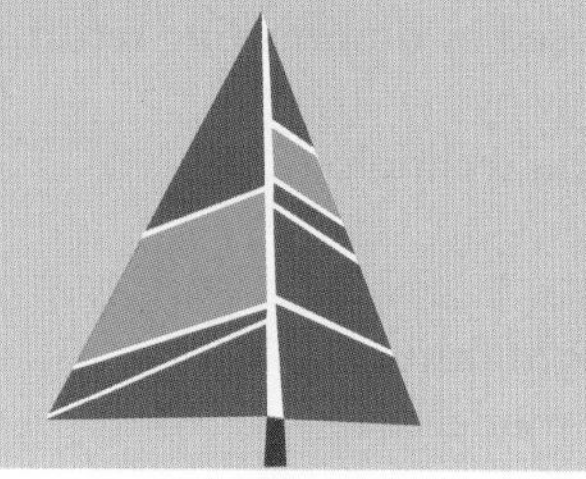

MODULE 3.2

Short-Run Production Costs

In this Module, you will learn to:

- Define and calculate the various types of costs that firms face in the short run
- Explain how a production function with diminishing marginal returns yields an upward-sloping marginal cost curve
- Use a graph to show the relationships among cost curves
- Explain the factors that influence the shape of the cost curves
- Use a graph to illustrate shifts in fixed and variable cost curves

From the Production Function to Cost Curves

Now that we understand a firm's production function, we can use that knowledge to develop its *cost curves.* To see how a firm's production function is related to its cost curves in the short run, let's turn once again to Mia and Liam's farm. Once Mia and Liam know their production function, they know the relationship between inputs of labor and land and output of wheat. But if they want to maximize their profits, they must apply this knowledge about inputs and output to learn the relationship between output and cost. Let's see how they can do this.

Terrance Klassen/AGE Fotostock

To translate information about a firm's production function into information about its cost, we need to know how much the firm must pay for its inputs. We will assume that Mia and Liam face either an explicit or an implicit cost of $400 for the use of the land. It is irrelevant whether Mia and Liam must rent the land for $400 from someone else (an explicit cost) or whether they own the land themselves and forgo earning $400 from renting it to someone else (an implicit cost). Either way, they pay an opportunity cost of $400 by using the land to grow wheat.

Moreover, in this Module we focus on the short run, when the quantity of inputs such as land cannot change. Since land is a fixed input for which Mia and Liam pay $400 whether they grow one bushel of wheat or one hundred, its cost is a **fixed cost (*FC*)**, which is a cost that does not depend on the quantity of output produced. In business, a fixed cost is often referred to as an *overhead cost.*

A **fixed cost (*FC*)** is a cost that does not depend on the quantity of output produced. It is the cost of the fixed input.

A **variable cost (*VC*)** is a cost that depends on the quantity of output produced. It is the cost of the variable input.

The **total cost (*TC*)** of producing a given quantity of output is the sum of the fixed cost and the variable cost of producing that quantity of output.

We also assume that Mia and Liam must pay each worker $200. Using their production function, Mia and Liam know that the number of workers they must hire depends on the amount of wheat they intend to produce. So the cost of labor, which is equal to the number of workers multiplied by $200, is a **variable cost (*VC*)**, which is a cost that depends on the quantity of output produced. Adding the fixed cost and the variable cost of a given quantity of output gives the **total cost (*TC*)** of that quantity of output. We can express the relationship among fixed cost, variable cost, and total cost as an equation:

$$\textbf{(3.2-1)} \quad \text{Total cost} = \text{Fixed cost} + \text{Variable cost}$$

or

$$TC = FC + VC$$

The table in **Figure 3.2-1** shows how total cost is calculated for Mia and Liam's farm. The second column shows the number of workers employed, L. The third column

FIGURE 3.2-1 The Total Cost Curve for Mia and Liam's Farm

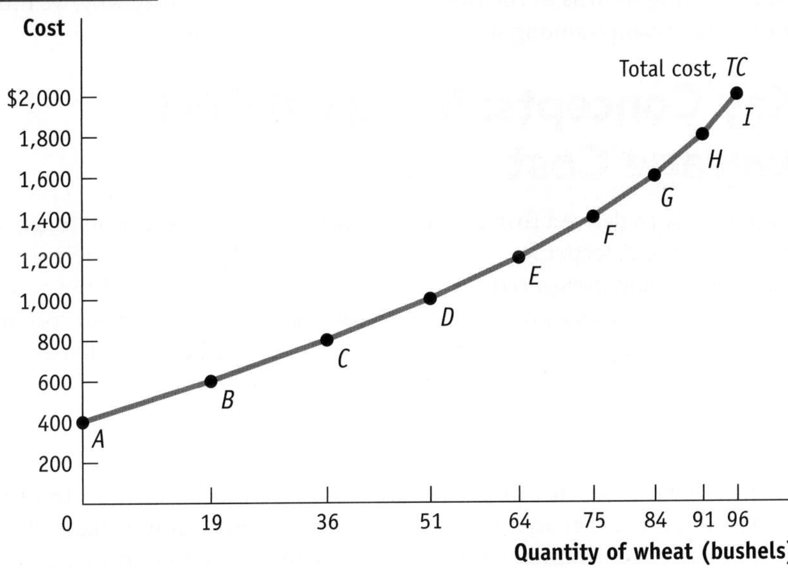

Point on graph	Quantity of labor *L* (workers)	Quantity of wheat *Q* (bushels)	Variable cost *VC*	Fixed cost *FC*	Total cost *TC* = *FC* + *VC*
A	0	0	$0	$400	$400
B	1	19	200	400	600
C	2	36	400	400	800
D	3	51	600	400	1,000
E	4	64	800	400	1,200
F	5	75	1,000	400	1,400
G	6	84	1,200	400	1,600
H	7	91	1,400	400	1,800
I	8	96	1,600	400	2,000

The table shows the variable cost, fixed cost, and total cost for various output quantities on Mia and Liam's 10-acre farm. The total cost curve shows how the total cost (measured on the vertical axis) depends on the quantity of output (measured on the horizontal axis). The labeled points on the curve correspond to the rows of the table. The total cost curve slopes upward because the number of workers employed, and hence the total cost, increases as the quantity of output increases. The curve gets steeper as output increases due to diminishing returns to labor.

shows the corresponding level of output, *Q*, taken from the table in Figure 3.1-1. The fourth column shows the variable cost, *VC*, equal to the number of workers multiplied by $200. The fifth column shows the fixed cost, *FC*, which is $400 regardless of the quantity of wheat produced. The sixth column shows the total cost of output, *TC*, which is the variable cost plus the fixed cost.

The first column labels each row of the table with a letter, from *A* to *I*. These labels will be helpful in understanding our next step: drawing the **total cost curve**, a curve that shows how total cost depends on the quantity of output.

The **total cost curve** shows how total cost depends on the quantity of output.

The graph in Figure 3.2-1 shows Mia and Liam's total cost curve. The horizontal axis measures the quantity of output in bushels of wheat, and the vertical axis measures the total cost. Each point on the curve corresponds to one row of the table in Figure 3.2-1. For example, point *A* shows the situation when 0 workers are employed: output is 0, and the total cost is equal to the fixed cost, $400. Similarly, point *B* shows the situation when 1 worker is employed: output is 19 bushels, and the total cost is $600, equal to the sum of $400 in fixed cost and $200 in variable cost.

Like the total product curve, the total cost curve slopes upward: due to the increasing variable cost, the more output produced, the higher the farm's total cost. But unlike the total product curve, which gets flatter as employment rises, the total cost curve gets *steeper*. That is, the slope of the total cost curve becomes greater as the amount of

AP® ECON TIP

Understanding cost curves is crucial to understanding the market-structure models covered on the AP® exam. Create note cards with definitions and formulas from this Module to aid you in your studies.

output produced increases. As we will soon see, the steepening of the total cost curve is also due to diminishing returns to the variable input. Before we can see why, we must first look at the relationships among several useful measures of cost.

Two Key Concepts: Marginal Cost and Average Cost

We've just learned how to derive a firm's total cost curve from its production function. Our next step is to take a deeper look at total cost by deriving two extremely useful measures: *marginal cost* and *average cost.* As we'll see, these two measures of the cost of production have a somewhat surprising relationship to each other. Marginal cost and average cost will prove to be vitally important in later Modules, where we will use them to analyze the firm's output decision and the market supply curve.

Marginal cost is the cost of producing one more unit of output, which can be found as the increase in total cost when one more unit is made.

Marginal Cost

A firm's **marginal cost** is its cost of producing one more unit of output. In other words, marginal cost is the increase in total cost when one more unit is made. We've already seen that marginal product is easiest to calculate if data on output are available in increments of one unit of input. Similarly, marginal cost is easiest to calculate if data on total cost are available in increments of one unit of output because the increase in total cost for each unit is clear. When the data come in less convenient increments, it's still possible to calculate marginal cost over each interval. But for the sake of simplicity, let's work with an example in which the data come in convenient one-unit increments.

Consider Selena's Gourmet Salsas, which produces bottled salsa and sells it to stores and restaurants by the case. **Table 3.2-1** shows how its costs per day depend on the number of cases of salsa it produces per day. The firm has a fixed cost of $108 per day, shown in the second column, which is the daily rental cost of its salsa-making equipment. The third column shows the variable cost, and the fourth column shows the total cost. Panel (a) of **Figure 3.2-2** plots the total cost curve. Like the total cost curve for Mia and Liam's farm in Figure 3.2-1, this curve slopes upward, getting steeper as quantity increases.

D. Hurst/Alamy

Table 3.2-1 Costs at Selena's Gourmet Salsas

Quantity of salsa Q (cases)	Fixed cost FC	Variable cost VC	Total cost TC = FC + VC	Marginal cost of case MC = ΔTC/ΔQ
0	$108	$0	$108	
				$12
1	108	12	120	
				36
2	108	48	156	
				60
3	108	108	216	
				84
4	108	192	300	
				108
5	108	300	408	
				132
6	108	432	540	
				156
7	108	588	696	
				180
8	108	768	876	
				204
9	108	972	1,080	
				228
10	108	1,200	1,308	

FIGURE 3.2-2 The Total Cost and Marginal Cost Curves for Selena's Gourmet Salsas

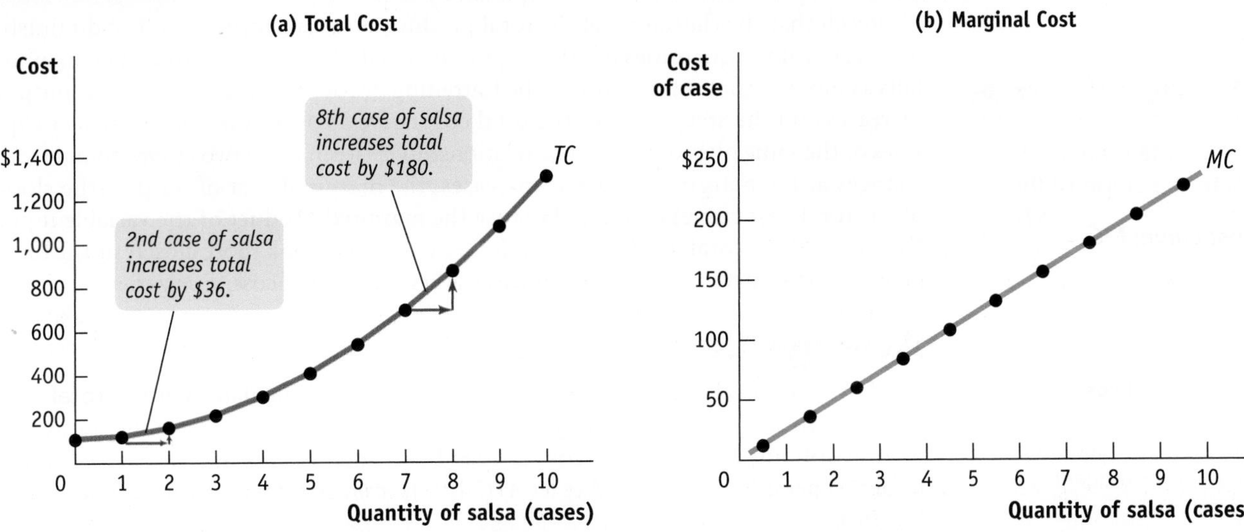

Panel (a) shows the total cost curve from Table 3.2-1. Like the total cost curve in Figure 3.2-1, the curve in panel (a) slopes upward and gets steeper as we move up it to the right. Panel (b) shows the marginal cost curve. It also slopes upward, reflecting diminishing returns to the variable input.

The significance of the slope of the total cost curve is shown by the fifth column of Table 3.2-1, which indicates marginal cost—the additional cost of each additional unit. The general formula for marginal cost is

$$\text{(3.2-2)} \quad \text{Marginal cost} = \begin{matrix}\text{Change in total}\\ \text{cost generated by}\\ \text{one additional unit}\\ \text{of output}\end{matrix} = \frac{\text{Change in total cost}}{\text{Change in quantity of output}}$$

or

$$MC = \frac{\Delta TC}{\Delta Q}$$

As in the case of marginal product, marginal cost is equal to "rise" (the increase in total cost) divided by "run" (the increase in the quantity of output). So just as marginal product is equal to the slope of the total product curve, marginal cost is equal to the slope of the total cost curve.

Now we can understand why the total cost curve gets steeper as it increases from left to right: as you can see in Table 3.2-1, marginal cost at Selena's Gourmet Salsas rises as output increases. And because marginal cost equals the slope of the total cost curve, a higher marginal cost means a steeper slope. Panel (b) of Figure 3.2-2 shows the corresponding **marginal cost curve**, *MC*, which illustrates the relationship between marginal cost and output. Notice that we plot the marginal cost for increasing output from 0 to 1 case of salsa halfway between 0 and 1, the marginal cost for increasing output from 1 to 2 cases of salsa halfway between 1 and 2, and so on.

The **marginal cost curve** shows how the cost of producing one more unit depends on the quantity that has already been produced.

Why does our marginal cost curve slope upward? Because in this example, there are diminishing returns to inputs. The fixed cost is, well, fixed, so the change in the total cost that constitutes the marginal cost is simply the increase in the variable cost, which is the cost of the variable input. As more of the variable input is used to make larger quantities of output, the marginal product of the variable input decreases, just as we saw in Module 3.1 for Mia and Liam's farm. This implies that as the quantity of output grows, more and more of the variable input must be used to produce each additional unit of output. And since each unit of the variable input must be paid for, the additional cost per additional unit of output also rises.

Recall that the flattening of the total product curve is another result of diminishing returns: if the quantities of other inputs are fixed, the marginal product of an input falls as more of that input is used. The flattening of the total product curve as output increases and the steepening of the total cost curve as output increases are just flipsides of the same phenomenon. The relationship between these two curves comes from changes at the margin: As output increases, the marginal cost of output (the slope of the total cost curve) increases because the marginal product of the variable input (the slope of the total product curve) decreases. We will look more closely at the links between these curves after we introduce another measure of cost: *average cost.*

AP® ECON TIP

Remember: Marginal cost is equal to the slope of the total cost curve: $MC = \frac{\Delta TC}{\Delta Q}$.

Average Cost

The **average total cost (*ATC*)**, often referred to simply as the **average cost**, is the total cost divided by the quantity of output produced.

In addition to total cost and marginal cost, it's useful to calculate **average total cost (*ATC*)**, often simply called **average cost**. The average total cost of producing a given quantity of output is the total cost divided by the quantity; that is, it is equal to the total cost per unit of output. If we let *ATC* denote average total cost, the equation looks like this:

$$\textbf{(3.2-3)} \quad ATC = \frac{\text{Total cost}}{\text{Quantity of output}} = \frac{TC}{Q}$$

Average total cost is important because it tells the producer how much the *average* or *typical* unit of output costs to produce. Marginal cost, meanwhile, tells the producer how much *one more* unit of output costs to produce. Although they may look very similar, these two measures of cost typically differ—and confusion between them can cause problems in the classroom and in real life, so let's see how the average total cost differs from the marginal cost.

Table 3.2-2 uses data from Selena's Gourmet Salsas to calculate average total cost. For example, the total cost of producing 4 cases of salsa is \$300, consisting of \$108 in fixed cost and \$192 in variable cost (from Table 3.2-1). So the average total cost of producing 4 cases of salsa is \$300/4 = \$75. You can see from Table 3.2-2 that as the quantity of output increases, the average total cost first falls, then rises.

Table 3.2-2 Average Costs for Selena's Gourmet Salsas

Quantity of salsa Q (cases)	Total cost *TC*	Average total cost of case *ATC = TC/Q*	Average fixed cost of case *AFC = FC/Q*	Average variable cost of case *AVC = VC/Q*
1	\$120	\$120.00	\$108.00	\$12.00
2	156	78.00	54.00	24.00
3	216	72.00	36.00	36.00
4	300	75.00	27.00	48.00
5	408	81.60	21.60	60.00
6	540	90.00	18.00	72.00
7	696	99.43	15.43	84.00
8	876	109.50	13.50	96.00
9	1,080	120.00	12.00	108.00
10	1,308	130.80	10.80	120.00

Figure 3.2-3 plots the *ATC* data from Table 3.2-2 to yield the *average total cost curve*, which shows how average total cost depends on output. As before, the cost is measured on the vertical axis, and the quantity of output is measured on the horizontal axis. The average total cost curve has a distinctive U shape that corresponds to

FIGURE 3.2-3 The Average Total Cost Curve for Selena's Gourmet Salsas

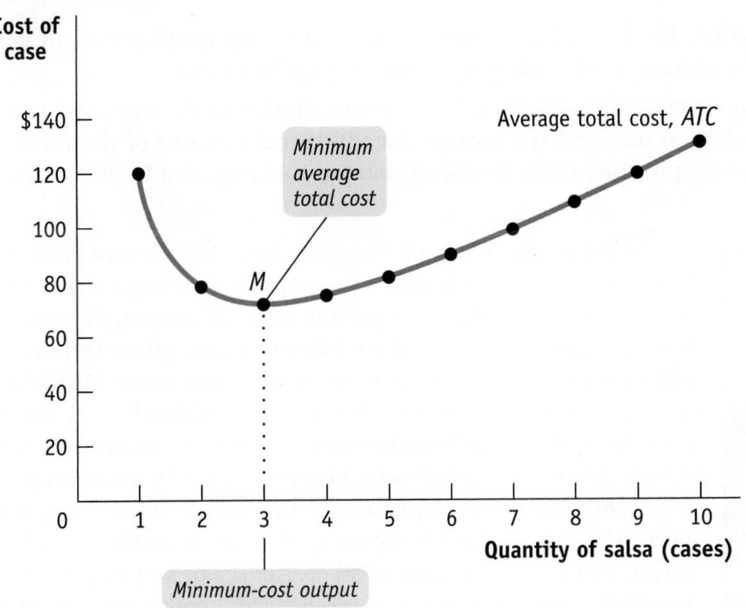

The average total cost curve at Selena's Gourmet Salsas is U-shaped. At low levels of output, the average total cost falls because the "spreading effect" of falling average fixed cost dominates the "diminishing returns effect" of rising average variable cost. At higher levels of output, the opposite is true and the average total cost rises. At point *M*, corresponding to an output of three cases of salsa per day, the average total cost is at its minimum level, the minimum average total cost.

how the average total cost first falls and then rises as output increases. Economists believe that such U-shaped average total cost curves are the norm for firms in many industries.

To help our understanding of why the average total cost curve is U-shaped, Table 3.2-2 breaks average total cost into its two underlying components, *average fixed cost* and *average variable cost.* The **average fixed cost (*AFC*)** is the fixed cost divided by the quantity of output, also known as the fixed cost per unit of output. For example, if Selena's Gourmet Salsas produces 4 cases of salsa, the average fixed cost is $108/4 = $27 per case. The **average variable cost (*AVC*)** is the variable cost divided by the quantity of output, also known as the variable cost per unit of output. At an output of 4 cases, the average variable cost is $192/4 = $48 per case. Writing these in the form of equations:

The **average fixed cost (*AFC*)** is the fixed cost per unit of output.

The **average variable cost (*AVC*)** is the variable cost per unit of output.

$$\textbf{(3.2-4)}\quad AFC = \frac{\text{Fixed cost}}{\text{Quantity of output}} = \frac{FC}{Q}$$

$$AVC = \frac{\text{Variable cost}}{\text{Quantity of output}} = \frac{VC}{Q}$$

The average total cost (*ATC*) is the sum of the average fixed cost (*AFC*) and the average variable cost (*AVC*). The average total cost curve has a U shape because these components move in opposite directions as output rises.

The average fixed cost falls as more output is produced because the numerator (the fixed cost) is a fixed number but the denominator (the quantity of output) increases as more is produced. Another way to think about this relationship is that, as more output is produced, the fixed cost is spread over more units of output; the end result is that the fixed cost *per unit of output*—the average fixed cost—falls. You can see this spreading effect in the fourth column of Table 3.2-2: the average fixed cost drops continuously as output increases.

The average variable cost, in contrast, rises as output increases. As we've seen, this fact reflects diminishing returns to the variable input: each additional unit of output adds more to the variable cost than the previous unit because increasing amounts of the variable input are required to make another unit.

So increasing output has two opposing effects on average total cost—the "spreading effect" and the "diminishing returns effect":

- *The spreading effect:* The larger the output, the greater the quantity of output over which the fixed cost is spread, leading to a lower average fixed cost.
- *The diminishing returns effect:* The larger the output, the lower the marginal product of the variable input, and the greater the additional amount of the variable input required to produce another unit of output, leading to a higher average variable cost.

Oliver Bunic/Bloomberg/Getty Images

When output increases, the average fixed cost falls because the fixed cost is spread over more units of output. But sooner or later, the average variable cost increases due to diminishing returns.

At low levels of output, the spreading effect is very powerful because even small increases in output cause large reductions in the average fixed cost. So at low levels of output, the spreading effect dominates the diminishing returns effect and causes the average total cost curve to slope downward. But when output is large, the average fixed cost is already quite small, so increasing output further has only a very small spreading effect. Diminishing returns, however, usually grow increasingly important as output rises. As a result, when output is large, the diminishing returns effect dominates the spreading effect, causing the average total cost curve to slope upward. At the bottom of the U-shaped average total cost curve, point *M* in Figure 3.2-3, the two effects exactly balance each other. At this point the average total cost is at its minimum level, the *minimum average total cost.*

Figure 3.2-4 brings together in a single picture the four cost curves that we have derived from the total cost curve for Selena's Gourmet Salsas: the marginal cost curve (*MC*), the average total cost curve (*ATC*), the average variable cost curve (*AVC*), and the average fixed cost curve (*AFC*). All are based on the information in Tables 3.2-1 and 3.2-2. As before, the cost is measured on the vertical axis, and the quantity of output is measured on the horizontal axis.

FIGURE 3.2-4 The Marginal and Average Cost Curves for Selena's Gourmet Salsas

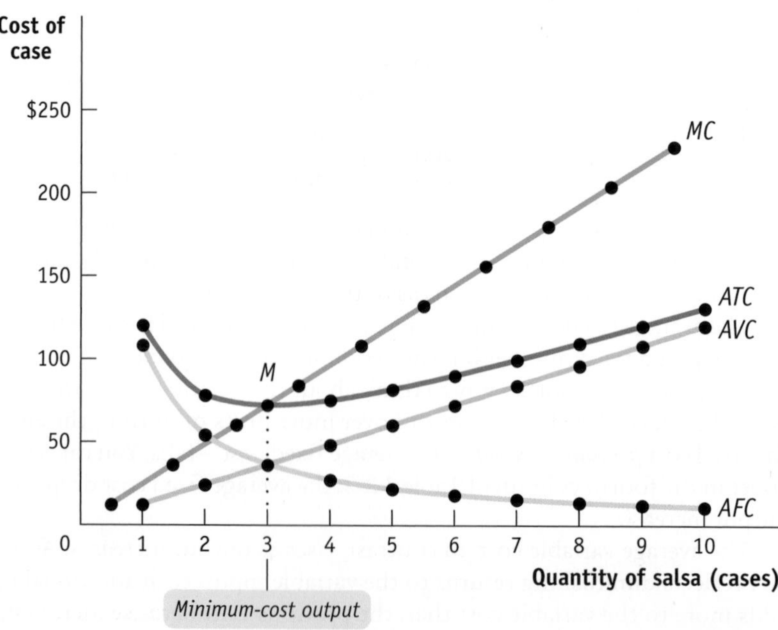

Here we have the family of cost curves for Selena's Gourmet Salsas: the marginal cost curve (*MC*), the average total cost curve (*ATC*), the average variable cost curve (*AVC*), and the average fixed cost curve (*AFC*). Note that the average total cost curve is U-shaped and the marginal cost curve crosses the average total cost curve at the bottom of the U, point *M*, corresponding to the minimum average total cost from Table 3.2-2 and Figure 3.2-3.

Let's take a moment to note some features of the various cost curves. First of all, the marginal cost curve (*MC*) slopes upward – the result of diminishing returns that make an additional unit of output more costly to produce than the one before. The average variable cost curve (*AVC*) also slopes upward – again, due to diminishing returns – but is flatter than the marginal cost curve. This is because the higher cost of an additional unit of output is averaged across all units, not just the additional unit, in the average variable cost measure. Meanwhile, the average fixed cost curve (*AFC*) slopes downward because of the spreading effect.

Finally, notice that the marginal cost curve (*MC*) intersects the average total cost curve (*ATC*) at its lowest point, point *M* in Figure 3.2-4. This last feature is our next subject of study.

Minimum Average Total Cost

For a U-shaped average total cost curve, the average total cost is at its minimum level at the bottom of the U. Economists call the quantity of output that corresponds to the minimum average total cost the **minimum-cost output**. In the case of Selena's Gourmet Salsas, the minimum-cost output is three cases of salsa per day.

The **minimum-cost output** is the quantity of output at which the average total cost is lowest—it corresponds to the bottom of the U-shaped average total cost curve.

In Figure 3.2-4, the bottom of the U is at the level of output at which the marginal cost curve crosses the average total cost curve from below. Is this an accident? No – it reflects general principles that are always true about a firm's marginal cost and average total cost curves:

- At the minimum-cost output, the average total cost *is equal to* the marginal cost.
- At output less than the minimum-cost output, the marginal cost *is less than* the average total cost and the average total cost is falling.
- And at output greater than the minimum-cost output, the marginal cost *is greater than* the average total cost and the average total cost is rising.

To understand these principles, think about how your grade in one course – say, a 3.0 in physics – affects your overall grade point average. If your GPA before receiving that grade was more than 3.0, the new grade lowers your average. Similarly, if the marginal cost – the cost of producing one more unit – is less than the average total cost, producing that extra unit lowers the average total cost. This change in average total cost is shown in **Figure 3.2-5** by the movement from A_1 to A_2. In this case, the marginal

FIGURE 3.2-5 **The Relationship Between the Average Total Cost Curve and the Marginal Cost Curve**

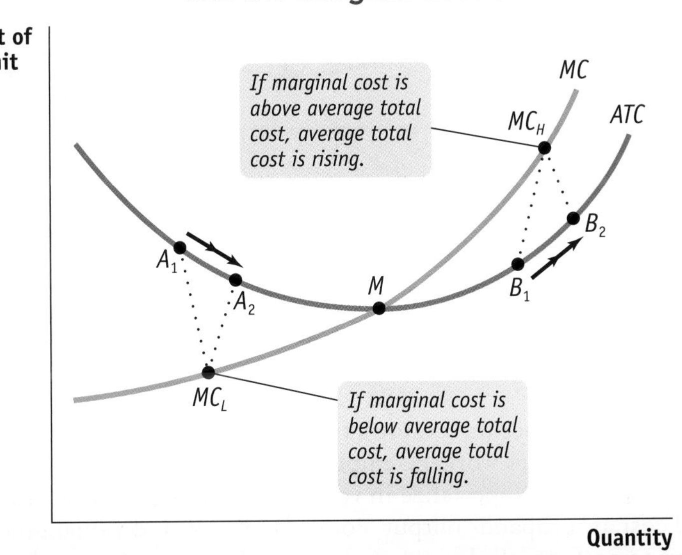
Cost of unit
MC
ATC
If marginal cost is above average total cost, average total cost is rising.
MC_H
B_2
A_1
A_2
M
B_1
MC_L
If marginal cost is below average total cost, average total cost is falling.
Quantity

To see why the marginal cost curve (*MC*) must cut through the average total cost curve at the minimum average total cost (point *M*), corresponding to the minimum-cost output, we look at what happens if the marginal cost is different from the average total cost. If the marginal cost (*MC*) is *less* than the average total cost (*ATC*), an increase in output must reduce the average total cost, as in the movement from A_1 to A_2. If the marginal cost is *greater* than the average total cost, an increase in output must increase the average total cost, as in the movement from B_1 to B_2.

cost of producing an additional unit of output is low, as indicated by the point MC_L on the marginal cost curve. When the cost of producing the next unit of output is less than the average total cost, increasing production reduces the average total cost. So any quantity of output at which the marginal cost is less than the average total cost must be on the downward-sloping segment of the U.

But if your grade in physics is more than the average of your previous grades, this new grade raises your GPA. Similarly, if the marginal cost is greater than the average total cost, producing that extra unit raises the average total cost. This change is illustrated by the movement from B_1 to B_2 in Figure 3.2-5, where the marginal cost, MC_H, is higher than the average total cost. Any quantity of output at which the marginal cost is greater than the average total cost must be on the upward-sloping segment of the U.

AP® ECON TIP

When drawing cost curves, be sure to have the marginal cost curve intersect the average total cost curve at the lowest point on the average total cost curve.

Finally, if a new grade is exactly equal to your previous GPA, the additional grade neither raises nor lowers that average—it stays the same. This corresponds to point *M* in Figure 3.2-5: when the marginal cost equals the average total cost, we must be at the bottom of the U because only at that point is the average total cost neither falling nor rising.

Does the Marginal Cost Curve Always Slope Upward?

Up to this point, we have emphasized the importance of diminishing returns, which lead to a marginal product curve that always slopes downward and a marginal cost curve that always slopes upward. In practice, however, economists believe that marginal cost curves often slope *downward* as a firm increases its production from zero up to some low level, sloping upward only at higher levels of production: realistic marginal cost curves, therefore, look like the curve labeled *MC* in **Figure 3.2-6**.

FIGURE 3.2-6 More Realistic Cost Curves

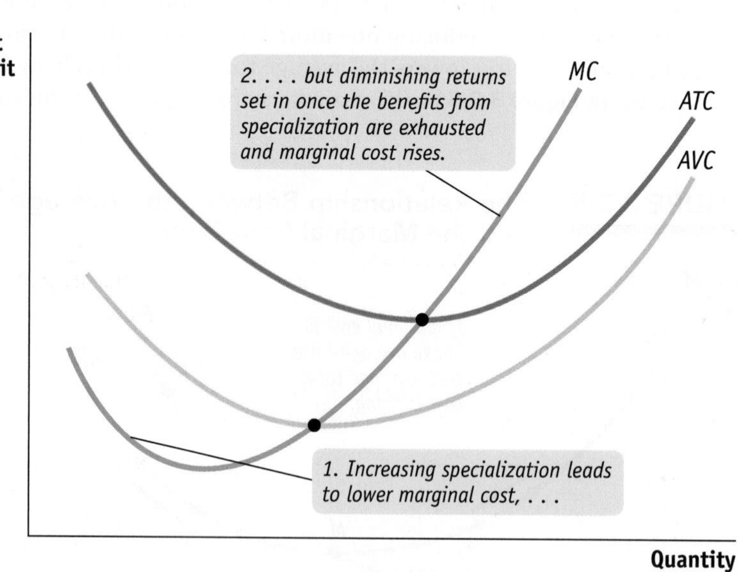

A realistic marginal cost curve has a "swoosh" shape. Starting from a very low output level, the marginal cost often falls as the firm increases output. That's because hiring additional workers allows greater specialization of their tasks and leads to increasing returns. Once specialization is achieved, however, diminishing returns to additional workers set in and the marginal cost rises. The corresponding average variable cost curve is now U-shaped, like the average total cost curve.

This initial downward slope occurs because a firm often finds that, when it starts with only a very small number of workers, employing more workers and expanding output allows its workers to specialize in various tasks. This, in turn, lowers the firm's marginal cost as it expands output. For example, one individual producing salsa would have to perform all the tasks involved: selecting and preparing the ingredients, mixing the salsa, bottling and labeling it, packing it into cases, and so on. As more workers are employed, they can divide the tasks, with each worker specializing in one aspect or a few aspects of salsa-making. This specialization leads to *increasing returns* to the hiring of additional workers and results in a marginal product of labor curve that initially slopes upward and a marginal cost curve that initially slopes downward. Once there are enough workers to have completely exhausted the benefits of further specialization, diminishing returns to labor set in, and the marginal cost curve changes direction and slopes upward. So typical marginal cost curves actually have the "swoosh" shape shown by *MC* in Figure 3.2-6. For the same reason, average variable cost curves typically look like *AVC* in Figure 3.2-6: they are U-shaped rather than strictly upward-sloping.

However, as Figure 3.2-6 also shows, the key features we saw from the example of Selena's Gourmet Salsas remain true: the average total cost curve is U-shaped, and the marginal cost curve passes through the minimum point of the average total cost curve.

Figure 3.2-7 shows the relationship between the marginal product of labor (*MPL*) curve and the marginal cost (*MC*) curve under the assumptions that labor is the only variable input and the wage rate remains unchanged. The horizontal axis on the top graph measures the quantity of labor; the horizontal axis on the bottom graph measures the quantity of output produced by the quantity of labor shown in the top graph. As the marginal product curve rises to its peak at the dotted line, the marginal cost falls, because less and less additional labor is needed to make each additional unit of

AP® ECON TIP

As is true for the average total cost curve, the marginal cost curve intersects the average variable cost curve at the lowest point on the average variable cost curve.

FIGURE 3.2-7 **Links Between Productivity and Cost**

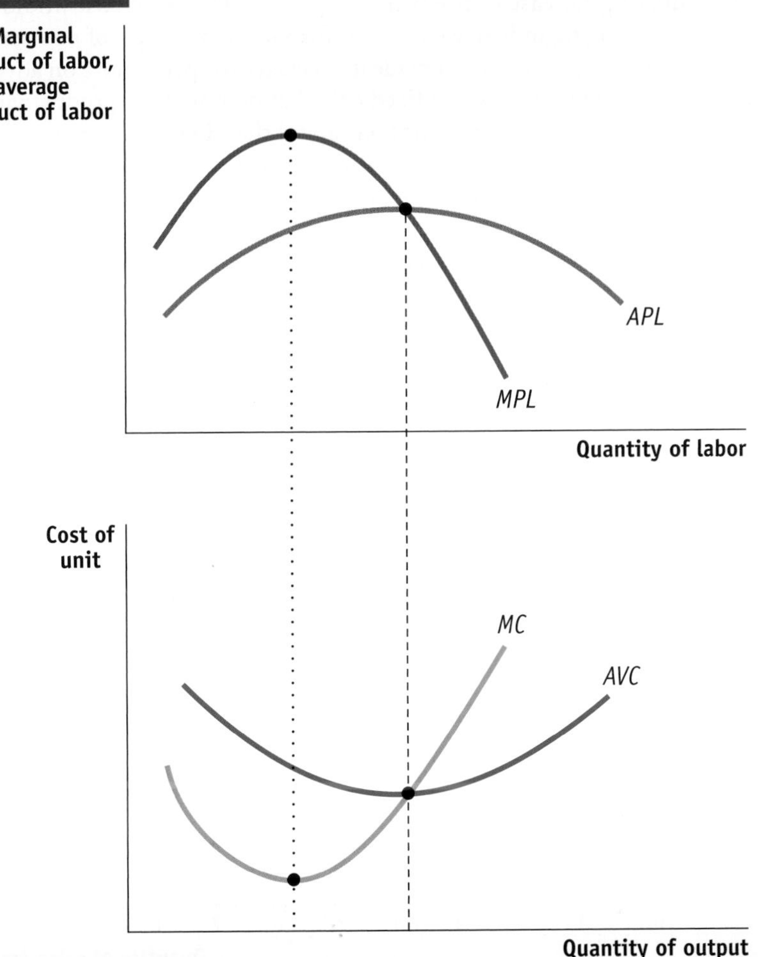

If labor is the only variable input and the wage rate remains unchanged, the marginal cost (*MC*) falls as the marginal product (*MPL*) rises, and the marginal cost rises as the marginal product falls. Similarly, the average variable cost (*AVC*) rises as the average product (*APL*) falls, and the average variable cost falls as the average product rises.

output. To the right of this dotted line, the marginal cost rises as the marginal product falls, because more and more additional labor is needed to make each additional unit of output. The marginal product and the marginal cost go in opposite directions.

The **average product** of an input is the total product divided by the quantity of the input.

The **average product curve** for an input shows the relationship between the average product and the quantity of the input.

The **average product** of an input is the total product divided by the quantity of the input. For example, if 5 workers produce 75 bushels of wheat, the average product of labor is 75/5 = 15 bushels. The **average product curve** for labor, labeled *APL* in Figure 3.2-7, shows the relationship between the average product of labor and the quantity of labor. With labor as the only variable input and a fixed wage rate, the average product and the average variable cost go in opposite directions, just like the marginal product and the marginal cost. To the left of the dashed (not dotted) line in Figure 3.2-7, the average product is rising and the average variable cost is falling, while to the right of this dashed line, the average product is falling and the average variable cost is rising.

Cost Shifters

Firms are always looking for ways to lower their costs. We've seen that technology and other determinants of productivity affect costs, as do input prices, taxes, subsidies, and outside influences such as weather, wars, and natural disasters. How a change in cost shifts cost curves depends on the size and direction of the change, but also on which type of cost has changed, as we'll examine next.

A Change in Fixed Cost

Suppose the owner of the building where Selena makes her gourmet salsas raises her rent. This constitutes an increase in the firm's fixed cost. The fixed cost would also increase if, for example, rising industry standards forced the purchase of new sanitizing equipment or if growing competition made it necessary to spend more on advertising. For now, we will consider increases in fixed cost that do not affect productivity. In the next Module, we will look at expenditures on capital that do increase productivity.

Let's consider a rent increase that doubles Selena's fixed cost from \$108 per day to \$216 per day. This \$108 increase in fixed cost will also increase total cost by \$108 per day because total cost equals variable cost (which is unchanged) plus fixed cost (which has increased by \$108). **Figure 3.2-8** shows how this cost increase affects Selena's average fixed cost and average total cost curves. If only one case of salsa is produced, the

FIGURE 3.2-8 Shifts Caused by a Change in Fixed Cost

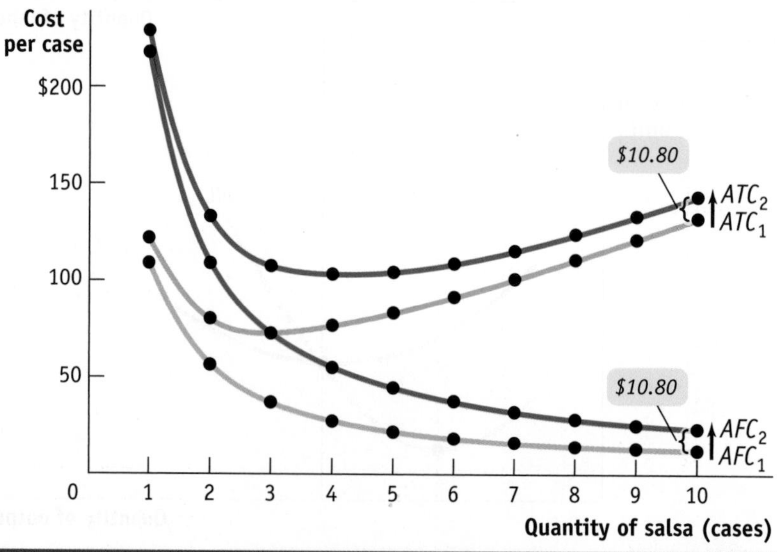

An increase in fixed cost shifts the average fixed cost and average total cost curves upward, from AFC_1 and ATC_1 to AFC_2 and ATC_2. Unless the change in fixed cost involves a change in productivity, the marginal cost curve and the average variable cost curve (not shown) are unaffected by a change in fixed cost.

higher fixed cost increases the average fixed cost by $\$108/1 = \$108$. But as the cost increase is spread across more and more units of output, the size of the shift in average fixed cost gets smaller and smaller. As can be seen in the figure, for the 10th unit, the new average fixed cost curve, AFC_2, is only above the old curve, AFC_1, by $\$108/10 = \$10.80$.

The average total cost curve rises by the same amount as the average fixed cost curve at each quantity—represented in the figure by the difference between ATC_1 and ATC_2—because the average total cost is the (unchanged) average variable cost plus the average fixed cost. This change in the fixed cost of rent, however, does not affect productivity, so the variable cost and the corresponding average variable cost curve and marginal cost curve are unaffected. (For simplicity, those cost curves are not shown on the graph.)

To summarize, a change in fixed cost also affects average fixed cost, total cost, and average total cost. If the change does not influence productivity, it will not affect variable cost, average variable cost, or marginal cost.

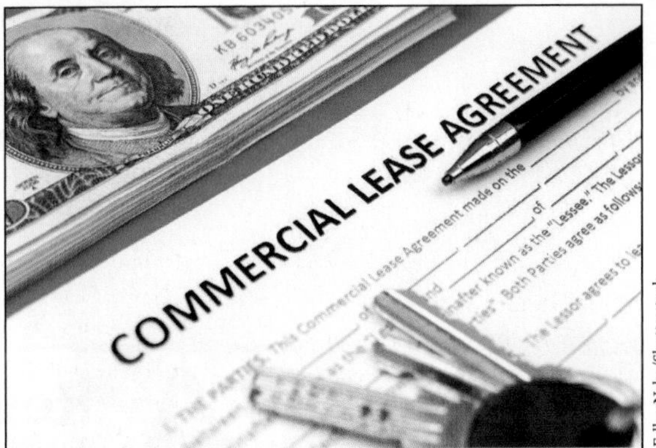

FellowNeko/Shutterstock

A rent increase affects fixed cost—and thus average fixed cost, total cost, and average total cost—but not variable cost, average variable cost, or marginal cost.

A Change in Variable Cost

Now suppose that instead of an increase in rent (a fixed cost), the cost of bottles increases such that each case costs \$40 more to produce. Because the added cost of this change depends on quantity of cases produced, it is an increase in variable cost. A similar increase in variable cost could result, for example, from a per-unit tax or an increase in shipping costs.

Figure 3.2-9 shows how this increase in variable cost affects Selena's cost curves. The \$40 increase in the cost of producing each unit shifts the marginal cost curve up by \$40, represented by the shift from MC_1 to MC_2. The average variable cost curve (not shown in this figure) also shifts up by \$40. As the sum of the (unchanged) average fixed cost and the average variable cost, the average total cost curve shifts up by \$40 as well, from ATC_1 to ATC_2. The average fixed cost curve remains unchanged because there has been no change in the fixed cost. The total cost increases by \$40 times the quantity of cases produced. So as this example illustrates, a change in variable cost also affects marginal cost, average variable cost, total cost, and average total cost, but not fixed cost or average fixed cost.

Changes in the opposite direction—a decrease in fixed cost or variable cost—would shift the relevant curves downward instead of upward. That is, a decrease in fixed cost

FIGURE 3.2-9 **Shifts Caused by a Change in Variable Cost**

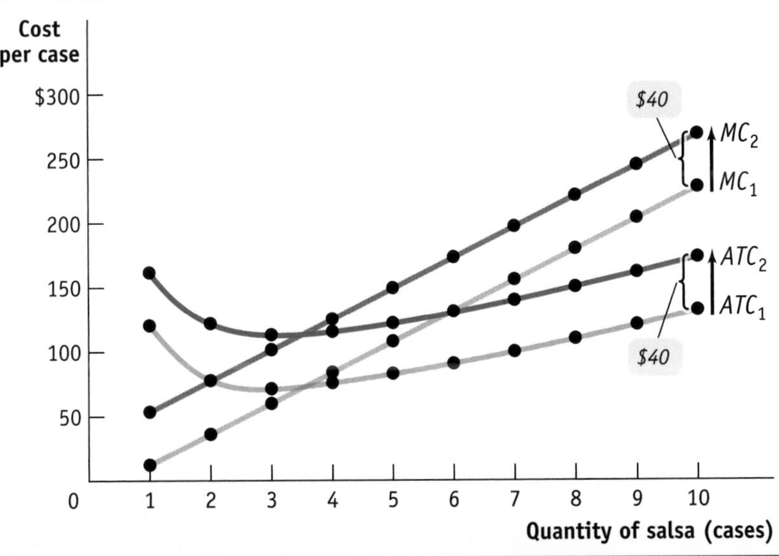

Here we see how a \$40 increase in the cost of producing each unit affects the marginal cost curve and the average total cost curve, from ATC_1 and MC_1 to ATC_2 and MC_2. These curves shift upward by \$40, as does the average variable cost curve. The average fixed cost curve (not shown) is unaffected by a change in variable cost.

would shift the fixed cost (*FC*), average fixed cost (*AFC*), and average total cost (*ATC*) curves downward, and a decrease in variable cost would shift the variable cost (*VC*), marginal cost (*MC*), average variable cost (*AVC*), and average total cost (*ATC*) curves downward. In the next Module, we'll see how costs differ in the short run and in the long run.

Adventures in AP® Economics

Watch the video: ***Production Costs***

Module 3.2  Review

Check Your Understanding

1. Alicia sells apple pies out of a food truck. Alicia must pay $9.00 per day to rent a parking space for her truck. It costs her $1.00 to produce the first pie of the day; each subsequent pie costs 50% more to produce than the one before. For example, the second pie costs $\$1.00 \times 1.5 = \$1.50$ to produce, the third pie costs $\$1.50 \times 1.5 = \$2.25$ to produce, and so on.
   a. Calculate Alicia's marginal cost, variable cost, average fixed cost, average variable cost, and average total cost as her daily pie output rises from 0 to 6. (*Hint:* The variable cost of two pies is just the marginal cost of the first pie, plus the marginal cost of the second, and so on.)
   b. Indicate the range of pies for which the spreading effect dominates and the range for which the diminishing returns effect dominates.
   c. What is Alicia's minimum-cost output? Explain why making one more pie lowers Alicia's average total cost when output is lower than the minimum-cost output. Similarly, explain why making one more pie raises Alicia's average total cost when output is greater than the minimum-cost output.

Tackle the AP® Test: Multiple-Choice Questions

1. When a firm is producing zero output, the total cost equals
   a. zero.
   b. the variable cost.
   c. the fixed cost.
   d. the average total cost.
   e. the marginal cost.

2. Marginal cost can be found at the change in either of which two types of cost when output increases by one?
   a. average variable cost or average total cost
   b. average fixed cost or average total cost
   c. total cost or fixed cost
   d. variable cost or fixed cost
   e. variable cost or total cost

3. Which of the following statements is correct about costs?
   a. *AVC* is the change in total cost generated by one additional unit of output.
   b. $MC = TC/Q$
   c. The average cost curve crosses at the minimum of the marginal cost curve.
   d. The *AFC* curve slopes upward.
   e. $AVC = ATC - AFC$

4. The slope of the total cost curve equals the
   a. variable cost.
   b. average variable cost.
   c. average total cost.
   d. average fixed cost.
   e. marginal cost.

5. On the basis of the data in the table below, what is the marginal cost of the third unit of output?

Quantity	Variable cost	Total cost
0	$0	$40
1	20	60
2	50	90
3	90	130
4	140	180
5	200	240

   a. $40
   b. $50
   c. $60
   d. $90
   e. $130

6. Which of the following always decreases when the quantity of output increases?
   a. average variable cost
   b. marginal cost
   c. average fixed cost
   d. average total cost
   e. average product of labor

7. If labor is the only variable input and the wage rate is fixed, which of the following move in opposite directions each time the quantity of output increases?
   a. marginal cost and average variable cost
   b. average product of labor and marginal product of labor
   c. marginal cost and average product of labor
   d. marginal product of labor and average variable cost
   e. marginal cost and marginal product of labor

Tackle the AP® Test: Free-Response Questions

1. Use the information in the table below to answer the following questions.

Quantity	Variable cost	Total cost
0	$0	$40
1	20	60
2	50	90
3	90	130
4	140	180
5	200	240

   a. What is the firm's fixed cost? Explain how you know.
   b. Draw one correctly labeled graph showing the firm's marginal and average total cost curves.
   c. Show how the curves on this graph would shift if the fixed cost increased by $10 due to an increase in property taxes. Add a "2" subscript to the label of any curve that has shifted.

Rubric for FRQ 1 (7 points)

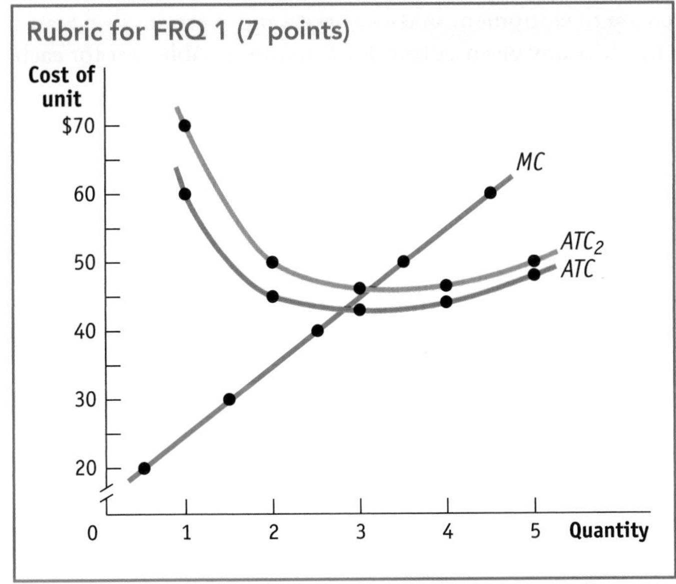

1 point: $FC = \$40$

1 point: We can identify the fixed cost as $40 because when the firm is not producing, it still incurs a cost of $40. This could only be the result of a fixed cost because the variable cost is zero when output is zero.

1 point: Graph with correct labels ("Cost of unit" on vertical axis; "Quantity" on horizontal axis)

1 point: Upward-sloping curve plotted according to data, labeled "*MC*"

1 point: U-shaped curve plotted according to the provided data, labeled "*ATC*"

1 point: *MC* curve crossing at minimum of *ATC* curve (Note: We have simplified this graph by drawing smooth lines between discrete points. If we had drawn the *MC* curve as a step function instead, the *MC* curve would have crossed the *ATC* curve exactly at its minimum point.)

1 point: An ATC_2 curve above the original *ATC* curve, but no shift in the *MC* curve.

2. Draw a correctly labeled graph showing a firm with a realistic "swoosh"-shaped *MC* curve and *ATC*, *AVC*, and *AFC* curves with their typical shapes. **(6 points)**

MODULE 3.3

Long-Run Production Costs

In this Module, you will learn to:

- Explain why all costs become variable in the long run
- Define increasing, decreasing, and constant returns to scale
- Use a graph to illustrate economies of scale and diseconomies of scale
- Explain the significance of the minimum efficient scale

Until now we have focused on the short run, a period during which the cost of at least one input is set in stone. In the long run, the abundance of time changes the rules—all inputs are variable. This means that *in the long run, a firm's fixed cost becomes a variable it can choose.* For example, given time, Selena's Gourmet Salsas can acquire additional food-preparation equipment or dispose of some of its existing equipment. In this Module, we will study how a firm's costs differ in the short run and in the long run. We will also examine how costs might change in response to increases in inputs and in output.

REDA &CO srl/Alamy

Short-Run Costs

Suppose that Selena's Gourmet Salsas is considering an acquisition of capital in the form of food-preparation equipment. Obtaining the new capital will affect the firm's total cost in two ways. The first resembles the effect of higher building rent that we examined in Module 3.2: Whether the firm rents or buys the additional equipment, the acquisition will mean a higher fixed cost in the short run. Second, unlike an increase in rent, an increase in equipment makes workers more productive: Fewer workers will be needed to produce any given output level, so the variable cost for each output level will be reduced.

The table in **Figure 3.3-1** shows how acquiring additional equipment affects costs. In our original example, we assumed that Selena's Gourmet Salsas had a fixed cost of \$108. The left half of the table shows variable cost as well as total cost and average total cost assuming a fixed cost of \$108. The average total cost curve for this level of fixed cost is given by ATC_1 in Figure 3.3-1. Let's compare that to a situation in which the firm buys additional food-preparation equipment, doubling its fixed cost to \$216 but reducing its variable cost at any given level of output. The right half of the table shows the firm's variable cost, total cost, and average total cost with this higher level of fixed cost. The average total cost curve corresponding to \$216 in fixed cost is given by ATC_2 in Figure 3.3-1.

From the figure you can see that when output is small—4 cases of salsa per day or fewer—average total cost is smaller when Selena forgoes the additional equipment and maintains the lower fixed cost of \$108: ATC_1 lies below ATC_2. For example, at 3 cases per day, the average total cost is \$72 without the additional equipment and \$90 with the additional equipment. But as output increases beyond 4 cases per day, the firm's average total cost is lower if it acquires the additional equipment, raising its fixed cost to \$216. For example, at 9 cases of salsa per day, the average total cost is \$120 when fixed cost is \$108, but only \$78 when fixed cost is \$216.

How can a higher fixed cost sometimes raise and sometimes lower average total cost? When output is low, the increase in fixed cost from the additional equipment outweighs the reduction in variable cost from higher worker productivity—that is,

FIGURE 3.3-1 Choosing the Level of Fixed Cost for Selena's Gourmet Salsas

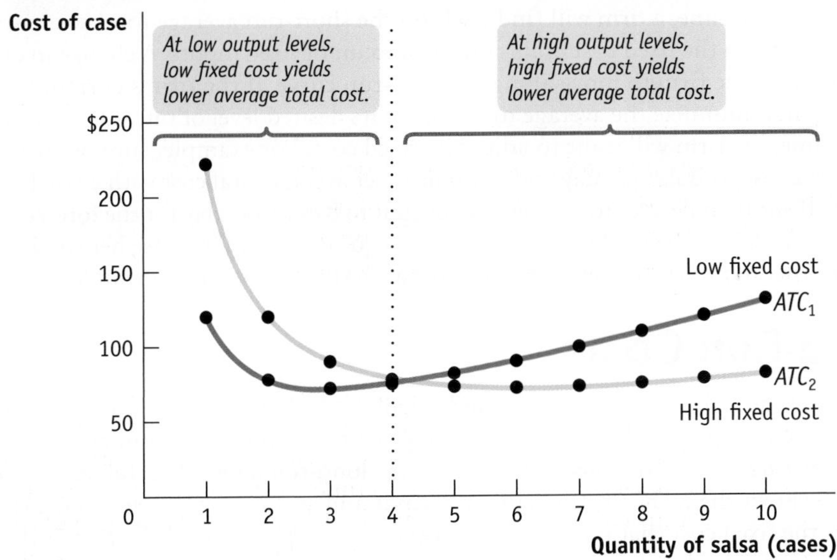

	Low fixed cost (*FC* = $108)			High fixed cost (*FC* = $216)		
Quantity of salsa (cases)	High variable cost	Total cost	Average total cost of case ATC_1	Low variable cost	Total cost	Average total cost of case ATC_2
1	$12	$120	$120.00	$6	$222	$222.00
2	48	156	78.00	24	240	120.00
3	108	216	72.00	54	270	90.00
4	192	300	75.00	96	312	78.00
5	300	408	81.60	150	366	73.20
6	432	540	90.00	216	432	72.00
7	588	696	99.43	294	510	72.86
8	768	876	109.50	384	600	75.00
9	972	1,080	120.00	486	702	78.00
10	1,200	1,308	130.80	600	816	81.60

The left side of the table shows prices per unit when fixed cost is low ($108). Expenditures on equipment and other capital that increases productivity raise the fixed cost but lower the variable cost, as shown on the right side of the table. The effect of these expenditures on average total cost depends on the level of output. In the graph, ATC_1 is the average total cost curve corresponding to a relatively low fixed cost of $108; ATC_2 is the average total cost curve corresponding to a higher fixed cost of $216 resulting from the purchase of additional equipment that lowers the variable cost. At low output levels—4 or fewer cases of salsa per day—ATC_1 lies below ATC_2, meaning that the average total cost is lower with less equipment and only $108 in fixed cost. But as output goes up, the average total cost is lower with the $216 in fixed cost due to the relatively large productivity gains from added equipment at higher output levels. Specifically, at more than 4 cases of salsa per day, ATC_2 lies below ATC_1.

there are too few units of output over which to spread the additional fixed cost. So if Selena plans to produce 4 or fewer cases per day, she would be better off choosing the lower level of fixed cost to achieve a lower average total cost of production. When planned output is high, however, the lower variable cost outweighs the higher fixed cost, in which case Selena should acquire the additional equipment.

In general, for each output level there is some amount of fixed inputs such as capital and land—and a corresponding fixed cost—that minimizes the firm's average total cost for that output level. When the firm has a desired output level that it expects to maintain over time, it should choose the optimal fixed cost for that level—that is, the level of fixed cost that minimizes its average total cost.

Now that we are studying a situation in which fixed cost can change, we need to take *time* into account when discussing average total cost. All of the average total cost curves we have considered until now are defined for a given level of fixed cost—that is, they are defined for the short run, the period of time over which fixed cost doesn't vary. To reinforce that distinction, for the rest of this Module we will refer to these average total cost curves as "short-run average total cost curves."

For most firms, it is realistic to assume that there are many possible choices of fixed cost, not just two. The implication: for such a firm, many possible short-run average total cost curves will exist, each corresponding to a different choice of fixed cost and so giving rise to what is called a firm's "family" of short-run average total cost curves.

At any given time, a firm will find itself on the short-run average total cost curve corresponding to the fixed cost of its current amount of fixed inputs. A change in output will cause the firm to move along its short-run curve. If the firm's current fixed cost does not minimize the average total cost of its desired level of output, given sufficient time, the firm will want to adjust its fixed cost. For example, suppose Selena produces 2 cases of salsa per day and minimizes her average total cost with a fixed cost of $108. If she then decides to increase her output to 8 cases per day for the foreseeable future, in the long run she should acquire more equipment and increase her fixed cost to a level that minimizes her average total cost at the 8-cases-per-day output level.

Long-Run Costs

The **long-run average total cost curve (*LRATC*)** shows the relationship between output and average total cost when fixed cost is chosen to minimize average total cost for each level of output.

Suppose we do a thought experiment and calculate the lowest possible average total cost for each output level. Economists have given this thought experiment a name: the *long-run average total cost curve.* Specifically, the **long-run average total cost curve (*LRATC*)** shows the relationship between output and average total cost when a firm chooses the fixed cost that minimizes average total cost *for each level of output.* If there are many possible choices of fixed cost—for example, many options for the scale of buildings or the amount of equipment—then the long-run average total cost curve will have the familiar, smooth U shape, as shown by *LRATC* in **Figure 3.3-2**.

FIGURE 3.3-2 Short-Run and Long-Run Average Total Cost Curves

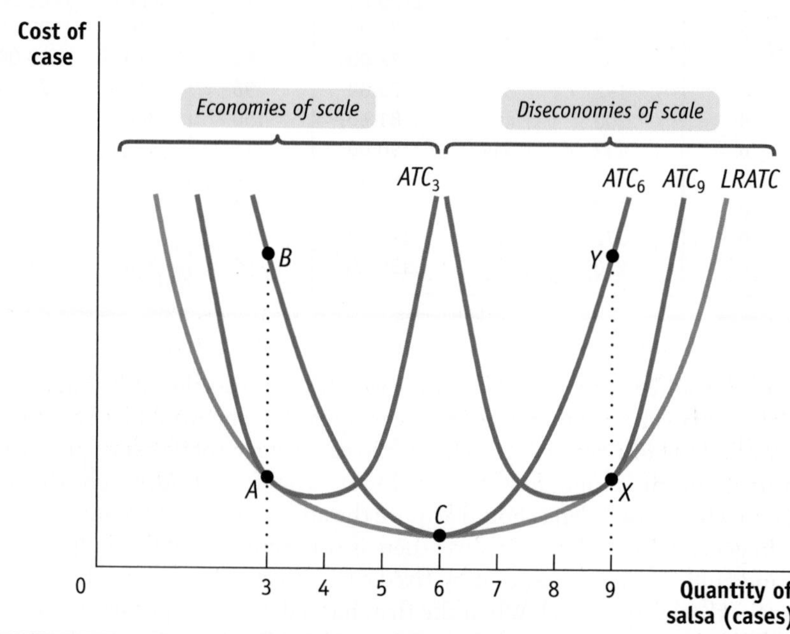

Short-run and long-run average total cost curves differ because a firm can choose its fixed cost in the long run. If Selena has the level of fixed cost that minimizes short-run average total cost at an output of 6 cases, and actually produces 6 cases, then she will be at point *C* on *LRATC* and ATC_6. But if she produces only 3 cases, she will move to point *B*. If she expects to produce only 3 cases for a long time, in the long run she will use less capital to reduce her fixed cost and move to point *A* on ATC_3. Likewise, if she produces 9 cases (putting her at point *Y*) and expects to continue this for a long time, she will increase her fixed cost in the long run and move to point *X* on ATC_9.

We can now draw the distinction between the short run and the long run more fully. In the long run, when a firm has had time to choose the fixed cost appropriate for its desired level of output, that firm will be at some point on the long-run average total cost curve. But if the output level is altered, the firm will no longer be on its long-run average total cost curve and will instead move along its current short-run average total cost curve. It will not be on its long-run average total cost curve again until it readjusts its fixed cost for its new output level.

Figure 3.3-2 illustrates this point. The curve ATC_3 shows the short-run average total cost if Selena has chosen the level of fixed cost that minimizes average total cost at an output of 3 cases of salsa per day. This is confirmed by the fact that at 3 cases per day, ATC_3 touches *LRATC*, the long-run average total cost curve. Similarly, ATC_6 shows the short-run average total cost if Selena's fixed cost minimizes the average total cost of producing 6 cases per day. We know this because ATC_6 touches *LRATC* at 6 cases per day. And ATC_9 shows the short-run average total cost if Selena's fixed cost minimizes the average total cost of producing 9 cases per day. It touches *LRATC* at 9 cases per day.

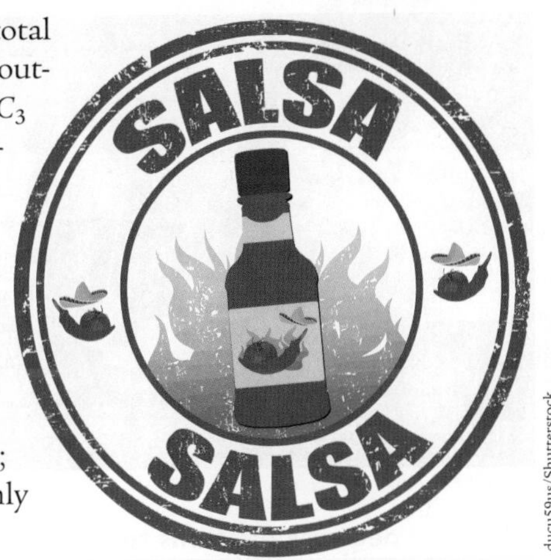

ducu59us/Shutterstock

When output levels change significantly, so does the amount of capital that minimizes long-run average total cost.

Suppose that Selena initially chose to be on ATC_6. If she actually produces 6 cases of salsa per day, her firm will be at point *C* on both its short-run and long-run average total cost curves. But what if Selena ends up producing only 3 cases of salsa per day? In the short run, her average total cost is indicated by point *B* on ATC_6; it is no longer on the *LRATC*. If Selena had known that she would be producing only 3 cases per day, she would have been better off acquiring less equipment and lowering her fixed cost to the one corresponding to ATC_3, thereby achieving a lower average total cost. Then her firm would have found itself at point *A* on the long-run average total cost curve, which lies below point *B*.

Suppose, conversely, that Selena ends up producing 9 cases per day even though she initially chose to be on ATC_6. In the short run her average total cost is indicated by point *Y* on ATC_6. But she would be better off purchasing more equipment and incurring a higher fixed cost in order to reduce her variable cost and move to ATC_9. This would allow her to reach point *X* on the long-run average total cost curve, which lies below *Y*. The distinction between short-run and long-run average total costs is extremely important in making sense of how real firms operate over time. A company that has to increase output suddenly to meet a surge in demand will typically find that in the short run, its average total cost rises sharply because it is hard to get extra production out of existing facilities. But given time to build new factories or add machinery, short-run average total cost falls.

AP® ECON TIP

Remember that the long run and the short run don't refer to predetermined periods of time. They are defined by whether or not all inputs are variable. In the short run, at least one input is not variable, but in the long run, all inputs are variable.

Returns to Scale

What determines the shape of the long-run average total cost curve? It is the influence of *scale*—the size of a firm's operations—on its long-run average total cost of production. Firms that experience *scale effects* in production find that their long-run average total cost changes substantially depending on the quantity of output they produce.

Economies of scale exist when long-run average total cost declines as output increases. As you can see in Figure 3.3-2, Selena's Gourmet Salsas experiences economies of scale over output levels ranging from 0 up to 6 cases of salsa per day—the output levels over which the long-run average total cost curve is declining. Economies of scale can result from **increasing returns to scale**, which exist when output increases more than in proportion to an increase in all inputs. For example, if Selena could double all of her inputs and make more than twice as much salsa, she would be experiencing increasing returns to scale. With twice the inputs (and costs) and more than twice the salsa, she would be enjoying decreasing long-run average total cost, and thus economies of scale. Increasing returns to scale therefore imply economies of scale, although economies of scale exist whenever long-run average total cost is falling, whether or not all inputs are increasing by the same proportion.

There are **economies of scale** when long-run average total cost declines as output increases.

There are **increasing returns to scale** when output increases more than in proportion to an increase in all inputs. For example, with increasing returns to scale, doubling all inputs would cause output to more than double.

When economies of scale end, the firm has reached its **minimum efficient scale**, which is the smallest quantity at which the firm's long-run average total cost is minimized. Selena's minimum efficient scale is 6, as shown by point *C* in Figure 3.3-2. The minimum efficient scale has a bearing on the number of firms in a market. As we will see in Unit 4, if the minimum efficient scale for a good is quite large, it is natural for the market to have only one firm, known as a *monopoly*. When the minimum efficient scale is small, the market is likely to be competitive because many small firms can all achieve the minimum efficient scale.

The **minimum efficient scale** is the smallest quantity at which a firm's long-run average total cost is minimized.

There are **diseconomies of scale** when long-run average total cost increases as output increases. Selena's Gourmet Salsas faces decreasing returns to scale at output levels

There are **diseconomies of scale** when long-run average total cost increases as output increases.

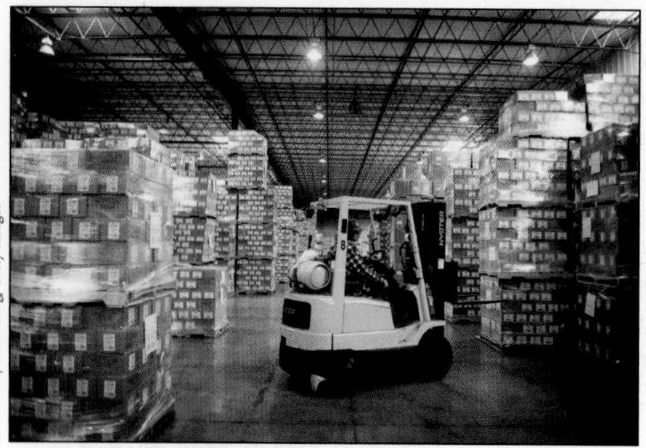
Leah Nash/Bloomberg/Getty Images

greater than 6 cases, the output levels over which its long-run average total cost curve is rising. Diseconomies of scale can result from **decreasing returns to scale**, which exist when output increases less than in proportion to an increase in all inputs—for example, doubling the inputs results in less than double the output. When output increases directly in proportion to an increase in all inputs—for example, doubling the inputs results in double the output—the firm is experiencing **constant returns to scale**.

There are **decreasing returns to scale** when output increases less than in proportion to an increase in all inputs.

There are **constant returns to scale** when output increases directly in proportion to an increase in all inputs.

What explains these scale effects in production? The answer ultimately lies in the firm's technology of production. Economies of scale often arise from the increased *specialization* that larger output levels allow—in a larger scale of operation, individual workers can limit themselves to more specialized tasks, becoming more skilled and efficient at doing them. Another source of economies of scale is a very large initial setup cost; in some industries—such as auto manufacturing, electricity generating, petroleum refining, and wireless communications—it is necessary to pay a high fixed cost in the form of plant and equipment before producing any output. As we'll see when we study monopoly in Unit 4, economies of scale have important implications for how firms and industries behave and interact.

Diseconomies of scale—the opposite scenario—typically arise in large firms due to problems of coordination and communication: as a firm grows in size, it becomes ever more difficult and therefore more costly to communicate and to organize activities. Although economies of scale induce firms to grow larger, diseconomies of scale tend to limit their size.

Summing Up Costs: The Short and Long of It

If a firm is to make the best decisions about how much to produce, it has to understand how its costs relate to the quantity of output it chooses to produce. **Table 3.3-1** provides a quick summary of the concepts and measures of cost you have learned about. In the next Module, we'll see that an understanding of cost is critical to the maximization of profit, which is the primary goal of most firms.

AP® ECON TIP

Don't mix up the concepts of diminishing returns and returns to scale. Diminishing returns is a short-run concept because at least one input is being held constant. Returns to scale is a long-run concept because all inputs are variable.

Table 3.3-1 Concepts and Measures of Cost

	Measurement	Definition	Mathematical term
Short run	Fixed cost	Cost that does not depend on the quantity of output produced	*FC*
	Average fixed cost	Fixed cost per unit of output	$AFC = FC/Q$
Short run and long run	Variable cost	Cost that depends on the quantity of output produced	*VC*
	Average variable cost	Variable cost per unit of output	$AVC = VC/Q$
	Total cost	The sum of fixed cost (short run) and variable cost	$TC = FC$ (*short run*) $+ VC$
	Average total cost (average cost)	Total cost per unit of output	$ATC = TC/Q$
	Marginal cost	The change in total cost generated by producing one more unit of output	$MC = \Delta TC/\Delta Q$
Long run	Long-run average total cost	Average total cost when fixed cost has been chosen to minimize average total cost for each level of output	*LRATC*

Module 3.3  Review

Adventures in AP® Economics
Watch the video:
Returns to Scale

Check Your Understanding

1. The accompanying table shows three possible combinations of fixed cost and average variable cost. For each choice, average variable cost is constant (it does not vary with the quantity of output produced).

Choice	Fixed cost	Average variable cost
1	$8,000	$1.00
2	12,000	0.75
3	24,000	0.25

   a. For each of the three choices, calculate the average total cost of producing 12,000, 22,000, and 30,000 units. For each of these quantities, which choice results in the lowest average total cost?
   b. Suppose that the firm, which has historically produced 12,000 units, experiences a sharp, permanent increase in demand that leads it to produce 22,000 units. Explain how its average total cost will change in the short run and in the long run.
   c. Explain what the firm should do instead if it believes the change in demand is temporary.

2. In each of the following cases, explain whether the firm is likely to experience economies of scale or diseconomies of scale and why.
   a. an interior design firm in which design projects are based on the expertise of the firm's owner
   b. a diamond-mining company

Tackle the AP® Test: Multiple-Choice Questions

1. In the long run,
   a. all inputs are variable.
   b. all inputs are fixed.
   c. some inputs are variable and others are fixed.
   d. a firm will go out of business.
   e. firms increase in size.

2. Which of the following is always considered the long run?
   a. 1 month
   b. 1 year
   c. 2 years
   d. 5 years
   e. none of the above

3. Which of the following statements is generally correct?
   a. Firms tend to experience economies of scale at high levels of output and diseconomies of scale at low levels of output.
   b. Fixed costs are the greatest in the long run.
   c. The average total cost of producing a particular quantity of output is the same in the short run and in the long run.
   d. The short-run average total cost curve intersects the long-run average total cost curve at its minimum point.
   e. The long-run average total cost curve is U-shaped.

4. Suppose *WhatTime* makes watches and its total costs in the long run are as shown in the table. What is *WhatTime*'s minimum efficient scale?

Quantity of Watches	Long-run total cost
1	200
2	250
3	300
4	400
5	600

   a. 1
   b. 2
   c. 3
   d. 4
   e. 5

5. There is a different short-run average total cost curve for each level of
   a. variable cost.
   b. variable inputs.
   c. fixed cost.
   d. long-run average total cost.
   e. output prices.

6. If the long-run average total cost decreases as the quantity of output increases, the firm is necessarily experiencing
   a. constant returns to scale.
   b. increasing returns to scale.
   c. economies of scale.
   d. diminishing returns.
   e. decreasing returns to scale.

7. When the current amount of fixed cost minimizes the long-run average total cost for the quantity of output being produced, the short-run average total cost curve is necessarily
   a. horizontal.
   b. downward-sloping.
   c. above the long-run average total cost curve.
   d. below the long-run average total cost curve.
   e. touching the long-run average total cost curve.

Tackle the AP® Test: Free-Response Questions

1. Refer to the graph provided to answer the following questions.

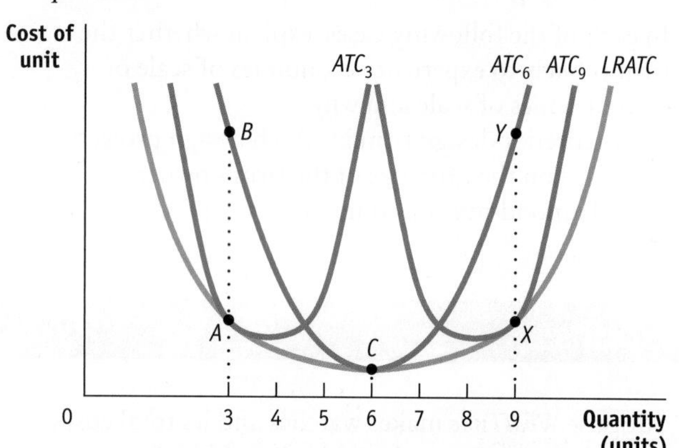

   a. The level of fixed cost that puts the firm at point *B* when the quantity is 3 minimizes short-run average total cost for what output level?
   b. At an output level of 3, is the firm experiencing economies or diseconomies of scale? Explain.
   c. In the long run, if the firm expects to produce an output of 9, the firm will produce on which short-run average total cost curve and at which point on the graph?

Rubric for FRQ 1 (5 points)

1 point: 6
1 point: Economies of scale
1 point: At an output of 3, the *LRATC* is decreasing.
1 point: In the long run the firm will produce on ATC_9.
1 point: In the long run the firm will produce at point *X*.

2. Draw a correctly labeled graph showing a short-run average total cost curve and the corresponding long-run average total cost curve. On your graph, identify the areas of economies and diseconomies of scale. **(5 points)**

Types of Profit

MODULE 3.4

In this Module, you will learn to:

- Describe the different types of profit, including accounting profit, economic profit, and normal profit
- Explain the difference between explicit and implicit costs and their importance in decision making
- Calculate a firm's profit or loss
- Explain how firms respond to positive, zero, and negative economic profit

Understanding Profit

The primary goal of most firms is to maximize profit. Other goals, such as maximizing market share or protecting the environment, may also figure into a firm's mission. Economic models generally start with the assumption that firms attempt to maximize profit, so we will begin with an explanation of how economists define and calculate profit. In the next Module, we will look at how firms go about maximizing their profit.

A firm's profit is equal to its *total revenue* (the price of the output times the quantity sold, or $P \times Q$) minus its *total cost* (the cost of all the inputs used to produce its output):

$$\text{Profit} = \text{Total Revenue} - \text{Total Cost}$$

However, there are different types of cost that may be used to calculate different types of profit. Module 3.2 explained cost categories that depend on what is purchased. Now we will look at cost categories that depend on whether money is actually exchanged.

Explicit Versus Implicit Cost

Suppose that, after graduating from high school, you have two options: go to college or take a job immediately. You would like to continue your education but are concerned about the cost.

What exactly is the cost of attending college? Here it is important to remember the concept of *opportunity cost*, because the cost of getting a degree includes the income you forgo while in college. The opportunity cost of additional education, like any cost, can be broken into two parts: the *explicit cost* and the *implicit cost*.

mphillips007/iStock/Getty Images

College students incur not only explicit costs, such as tuition, but also the implicit cost of forgone income.

An **explicit cost** is a cost that requires an outlay of money. For example, the explicit cost of a year of college includes tuition. In contrast, an **implicit cost** does not involve an outlay of money; instead, it is measured by the value, in dollar terms, of the benefits that are forgone. For example, the implicit cost of a year spent in college includes the additional income you would have earned if you had taken a full-time job instead.

An **explicit cost** is a cost that involves actually paying out money. An **implicit cost** does not require an outlay of money; it is measured by the value, in dollar terms, of benefits that are forgone.

A common mistake, both in economic analysis and in real business situations, is to ignore implicit costs and focus exclusively on explicit costs. That's problematic because the implicit cost of many activities is quite substantial—indeed, sometimes it is much larger than the explicit cost.

Table 3.4-1 gives a breakdown of hypothetical explicit and implicit costs associated with attending college for a year instead of working. The explicit cost consists of tuition, books, supplies, and a computer for doing assignments—all of which require you to spend money. The implicit cost is the salary you would have earned if you had taken a full-time job instead. In this example, the implicit cost of the forgone salary, $32,000,

Table 3.4-1	Opportunity Cost of a Year of College		
Explicit cost		**Implicit cost**	
Tuition	$17,000	Forgone salary	$32,000
Books and supplies	1,000		
Computer	1,500		
Total explicit cost	19,500	Total implicit cost	32,000
Total opportunity cost = Total explicit cost + Total implicit cost = $51,500			

is even larger than the explicit cost of attending college, $19,500. This illustrates the importance of considering the implicit cost.

A slightly different way of looking at the implicit cost in this example can deepen our understanding of opportunity cost. The forgone salary is the cost of using your own resources – your time – in going to college rather than working. The use of your *time* for more education, despite the fact that you don't have to spend any money, is still costly to you. This decision exemplifies an important aspect of opportunity cost: in considering the cost of an activity, you should include the cost of using any of your own resources for that activity. You can calculate the cost of using your own resources by determining what they would have earned in their next best alternative use.

Accounting Profit Versus Economic Profit

As the example of going to college suggests, taking account of implicit as well as explicit costs can be very important when making decisions. This is true whether the decisions affect individuals, groups, governments, or firms.

Jon Arnold Images Ltd/Alamy

Consider the case of Babette's Cajun Café, a small restaurant in New Orleans. Suppose that this year Babette received $110,000 in revenue. Out of that revenue, she paid $60,000 in expenses: the cost of food ingredients and other supplies, the cost of wages for her employees, and the rent for her restaurant space. We assume that Babette owns her restaurant equipment – items such as appliances and furnishings. The question is: Is Babette's restaurant profitable?

At first, it might seem that the answer is obviously yes: she receives $110,000 from her customers and has expenses of only $60,000. Doesn't this mean she has a profit of $50,000? Not according to her accountant, who reduces the number by $5,000 for the yearly *depreciation* (reduction in value) of the restaurant equipment. Depreciation occurs because equipment wears out over time. As a consequence, every few years Babette must replace her appliances and furnishings. The yearly depreciation amount reflects what an accountant estimates to be the reduction in the value of the machines due to wear and tear that year. This leaves $45,000, which is the business's **accounting profit**. That is, the accounting profit of a business is its total revenue minus its *explicit* cost and depreciation. The accounting profit is the number that Babette has to report on her income tax forms and that she would be obliged to report to anyone thinking of investing in her business.

The **accounting profit** of a business is the business's total revenue minus the explicit cost and depreciation.

The **economic profit** of a business is the business's total revenue minus the opportunity cost of its resources. It is usually less than the accounting profit.

Accounting profit is a useful number, but suppose that Babette wants to decide whether to keep her restaurant open or to take a different career path. To make this decision, she will need to calculate her **economic profit** – the total revenue she receives minus her *opportunity* cost, which includes implicit as well as explicit costs. In general, when economists use the simple term *profit*, they are referring to economic profit. (We adopt that simplification in this book.)

Why does Babette's economic profit differ from her accounting profit? Because she has an implicit cost over and above the explicit cost her accountant has calculated. Businesses can face an implicit cost for two reasons. First, if the business owns its capital – its equipment, buildings, tools, inventory, and financial assets – it does not pay any money for its use, but it pays an implicit cost because it does not use the capital in some other way. Second, the owner devotes time and energy to the business that could have been used elsewhere – a particularly important factor in small businesses, whose owners tend to put in many long hours.

If Babette had rented her appliances and furnishings instead of owning them, her rent would have been an explicit cost. But because Babette owns her own equipment, she does not pay rent on it, and her accountant deducts an estimate of its depreciation in the profit statement. However, this does not account for the opportunity cost of the equipment – what Babette forgoes by using it. Suppose that if she doesn't use the equipment in her own restaurant, Babette's most lucrative alternative is to sell the equipment for $55,000 and put the money into a bank account where it would earn yearly interest of $3,000. This $3,000 is an implicit cost of running the business. The **implicit cost of capital** is the opportunity cost of the capital used by a business; it reflects the income that could have been earned if the capital had been used in its next best alternative way. It is just as much a true cost as if Babette had rented her equipment instead of owning it.

Finally, Babette should take into account the opportunity cost of her own time. Suppose that instead of running her own restaurant, she could earn $44,000 each year as a chef in someone else's restaurant. That $44,000 is also an implicit cost of her business.

AP® ECON TIP

Accounting profit, often discussed by the media and business community, is calculated without subtracting implicit costs. When economists or the AP® exam mention profit, they generally mean *economic profit*, which accounts for both implicit and explicit costs.

The **implicit cost of capital** is the opportunity cost of the capital used by a business—the income the owner could have realized from that capital if it had been used in its next best alternative way.

Table 3.4-2 summarizes the accounting for Babette's Cajun Café, taking both explicit and implicit costs into account. The column titled Case 1 shows that, although the business makes an accounting profit of $45,000, its economic profit is actually negative. This means that Babette would be better off financially if she closed the restaurant and devoted her time and capital to something else. If, however, some of Babette's cost should fall sufficiently, she could earn a positive economic profit. In that case, she would be better off financially if she continued to operate the restaurant. For instance, consider the Case 2 column: here we assume that the salary Babette could earn as a chef employed by someone else has dropped to $39,000 (say, due to an increase in the availability of chefs). In this case, her economic profit is positive: she is earning more than her explicit and implicit costs, and she should keep her restaurant open.

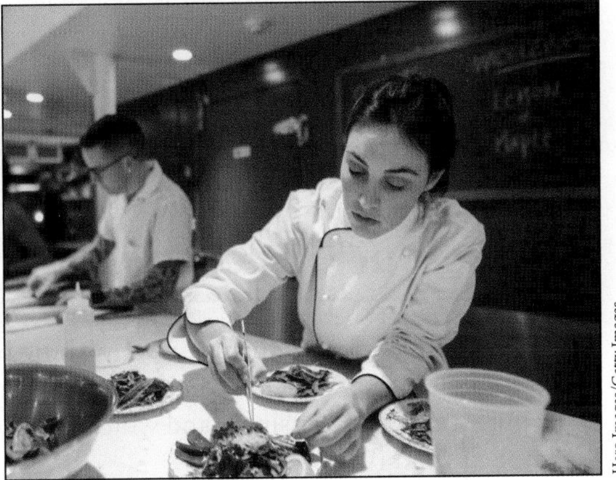

Hero Images/Getty Images

Table 3.4-2 Profit at Babette's Cajun Café

	Case 1	Case 2
Revenue	$110,000	$110,000
Explicit cost	−60,000	−60,000
Depreciation	−5,000	−5,000
Accounting profit	**45,000**	**45,000**
Implicit cost of business		
Income Babette could have earned on capital used in the next best way	−3,000	−3,000
Income Babette could have earned as a chef in someone else's restaurant	−44,000	−39,000
Economic profit	**−2,000**	**3,000**

In real life, discrepancies between accounting profit and economic profit are extremely common. For example, farmers are well aware of the opportunity cost of farming their land rather than selling it to developers.

AP® ECON TIP

Economic profit can be negative. You would be correct in saying that a firm is incurring a *loss* when economic profit is negative.

Normal Profit

An economic profit equal to zero is also known as a **normal profit**. It is an economic profit just high enough to keep a firm engaged in its current activity.

In the previous example, when Babette is earning an economic profit, her total revenue is higher than the sum of her implicit and explicit costs. This means that operating her restaurant makes Babette better off financially than she would be using her resources in any other activity. When Babette earns a negative economic profit (which can also be described as a *loss*), it means that Babette would be better off financially if she devoted her resources to her next best alternative. As this example illustrates, economic profits signal the best use of resources. A positive economic profit indicates that the current use is the best use of resources. A negative economic profit indicates that there is a better alternative use for resources.

What about an economic profit *equal to zero*? It's tempting to think that earning zero profit is a bad thing. After all, the goal of most firms is to maximize profit. However, an economic profit equal to zero is not bad at all. An economic profit of zero means that the firm could not do any better using its resources in any alternative activity. Another name for an economic profit of zero is a **normal profit**. A firm earning a normal profit is earning just enough to keep it using its resources in its current activity. After all, it can't do any better in any other activity! In Module 3.6, we'll see that firms earning negative economic profit can sometimes minimize their losses by staying open for a while, but all such firms will close in the long run unless conditions change. But first, in the next Module, we look at the analysis that firms make when seeking to maximize profit.

AP® ECON TIP

Remember that a firm with zero economic profit earns just enough to cover its implicit and explicit costs. The firm may have zero economic profit and a positive accounting profit.

Module 3.4  Review

Check Your Understanding

1. Karma and Don run a furniture-refinishing business from their home. Which of the following represent an explicit cost of the business and which represent an implicit cost?
   a. supplies such as paint stripper, varnish, polish, and sandpaper
   b. basement space used as a workroom, which could otherwise be rented out as an apartment
   c. wages paid to a part-time helper
   d. a van that they inherited and use only for transporting furniture
   e. the job at a larger furniture restorer that Karma gave up in order to run the business
2. **a.** Suppose you are in business earning an accounting profit of $25,000. What is your economic profit if the implicit cost of your capital is $2,000 and the opportunity cost of your time is $23,000? Explain your answer.
   b. What does your answer to part a tell you about the advisability of devoting your time and capital to this business?

Tackle the AP® Test: Multiple-Choice Questions

1. Which of the following is an example of an *implicit* cost of going out for lunch?
   a. the amount of the tip you leave the waiter
   b. the total bill you charge to your credit card
   c. the cost of gas to drive to the restaurant
   d. the value of the time you spent eating lunch
   e. all of the above
2. Which of the following is an *implicit* cost of taking swimming lessons on Saturdays rather than working at a restaurant?
   a. the fee for the lessons
   b. the cost of the swimsuit
   c. your future earnings as a lifeguard, a job that requires swimming skills
   d. the cost of transportation to the swimming pool
   e. forgone wages at the restaurant

3. Accounting profit equals total revenue minus depreciation and total
   a. explicit cost only.
   b. implicit cost only.
   c. explicit cost plus total implicit cost.
   d. opportunity cost.
   e. explicit cost plus total opportunity cost.

4. Which of the following is considered when calculating economic profit but not accounting profit?
   a. implicit cost
   b. explicit cost
   c. total revenue
   d. marginal cost
   e. All of the above are also considered when calculating accounting profit.

5. You sell T-shirts at your school's football games. Each shirt costs $5 to make and sells for $10. Each game lasts two hours, and you sell 100 shirts per game. During this time, you could be earning $12 per hour at your other job. What are your accounting profit and economic profit from selling shirts at a game?

	Accounting profit	*Economic profit*
a.	$1,000	$500
b.	$500	$1,000
c.	$500	$476
d.	$476	$500
e.	$500	$500

6. Opportunity costs include
   a. implicit costs only.
   b. explicit costs only.
   c. depreciation costs and explicit costs only.
   d. implicit costs and explicit costs.
   e. implicit costs and accounting profit only.

7. Earning an economic profit of zero is
   a. acceptable because the firm could make no better alternative use of its resources.
   b. a sign that the firm should shut down.
   c. acceptable during a recession but otherwise not.
   d. less desirable to a firm than earning an accounting profit of zero.
   e. equivalent to earning an accounting profit of zero if implicit costs exist.

Tackle the AP® Test: Free-Response Questions

1. Your firm is selling 10,000 units of output at a price of $10 per unit. Your firm's total explicit cost is $70,000. Your firm's implicit cost of capital is $10,000, and your opportunity cost is $20,000.
   a. Calculate total revenue. Show your work.
   b. Calculate total implicit cost. Show your work.
   c. Calculate your accounting profit. Show your work.
   d. Calculate your economic profit. Show your work.
   e. Given the value of your economic profit calculated in part d, might there be a better use of your resources? Explain your answer.

Rubric for FRQ 1 (5 points)

1 point: Total revenue = $10 × 10,000 = $100,000

1 point: Total implicit cost = $10,000 + $20,000 = $30,000

1 point: Accounting profit = $100,000 – $70,000 = $30,000

1 point: Economic profit = $100,000 – $70,000 – $10,000 – $20,000 = $0

1 point: No. Because your firm earns normal profit, there is no better alternative use for your resources.

2. Malik owns and operates Malik's Meatloaf Stand, which sells meatloaf by the slice. Use the data in the table provided to answer the questions below.

Malik's Meatloaf Stand: January	
Price per slice	$2
Slices sold	2,000
Explicit cost	$400
Depreciation	$100
Implicit cost of capital	$200

   a. Calculate Malik's Meatloaf Stand's total revenue for January.
   b. Calculate Malik's Meatloaf Stand's accounting profit for January.
   c. What additional information does Malik need in order to determine whether or not to continue operating the Meatloaf Stand?
   d. Suppose these numbers remain unchanged in the long run. Explain how Malik will determine whether or not to continue operating the business in the long run on the basis of these numbers. **(4 points)**

MODULE 3.5 Profit Maximization

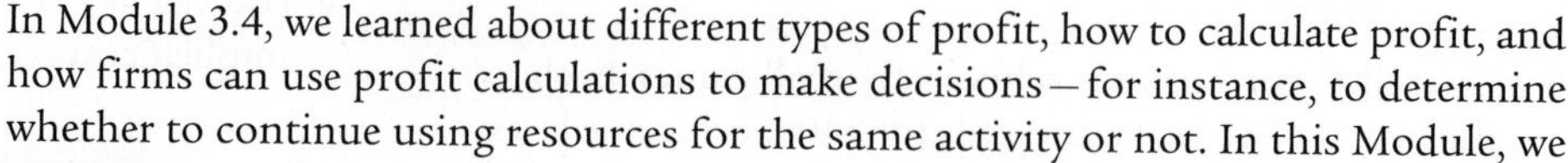

In this Module, you will learn to:

- Define marginal revenue
- Apply the profit-maximizing rule to output decisions and use a graph to show the profit-maximizing level of output

Maximizing Profit

In Module 3.4, we learned about different types of profit, how to calculate profit, and how firms can use profit calculations to make decisions—for instance, to determine whether to continue using resources for the same activity or not. In this Module, we ask the question: what quantity of output would maximize the producer's profit? First, we will find the profit-maximizing quantity by calculating the total profit at each quantity for comparison. Then we will use marginal analysis to determine the *profit-maximizing rule*, which turns out to be simple: as our discussion of marginal analysis in Module 1.1 suggested, a producer should increase production until marginal benefit equals marginal cost.

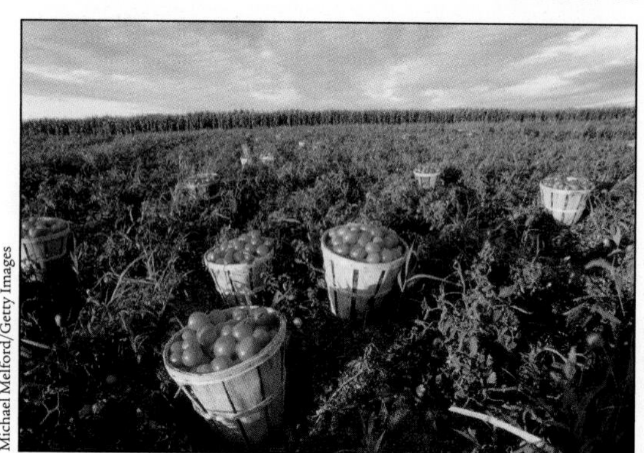
Michael Melford/Getty Images

Consider Jennifer and Jayden, who run an organic tomato farm. Suppose that the market price of organic tomatoes is $18 per bushel and that Jennifer and Jayden can sell as many tomatoes as they would like at that price. We can use the data in **Table 3.5-1** to find their profit-maximizing level of output.

Table 3.5-1 Profit for Jennifer and Jayden's Farm When Market Price Is $18

Quantity of tomatoes Q (bushels)	Total revenue *TR*	Total cost *TC*	Profit *TR* – *TC*
0	$0	$14	–$14
1	18	30	–$12
2	36	36	0
3	54	44	10
4	72	56	16
5	90	72	18
6	108	92	16
7	126	116	10

The first column shows the quantity of output in bushels, and the second column shows Jennifer and Jayden's total revenue from their output: the market value of their output. Total revenue (*TR*) is equal to the market price multiplied by the quantity of output:

$$\textbf{(3.5-1)} \quad TR = P \times Q$$

In this example, total revenue is equal to $18 per bushel times the quantity of output in bushels.

The third column of Table 3.5-1 shows Jennifer and Jayden's total cost, *TC*. Even if they don't grow any tomatoes, Jennifer and Jayden must pay $14 to rent the land for their farm. As the quantity of tomatoes increases, so does the total cost of seeds, fertilizer, labor, and other inputs.

The fourth column shows their profit, equal to total revenue minus total cost:

$$\textbf{(3.5-2)} \quad \text{Profit} = TR - TC$$

As indicated by the numbers in the table, profit is maximized at an output of five bushels, where profit is equal to $18. Next, we will gain more insight into the profit-maximizing choice of output by viewing it as a problem of marginal analysis.

Using Marginal Analysis to Choose the Profit-Maximizing Quantity of Output

The **principle of marginal analysis** provides a clear message about when to stop doing anything: proceed until the *marginal benefit* equals the *marginal cost*. To apply this principle, consider the effect on a producer's profit of increasing output by one unit. The marginal benefit of that unit is the additional revenue generated by selling it; this measure is called the **marginal revenue** of that output. The general formula for marginal revenue is

$$\textbf{(3.5-3)} \quad \text{Marginal revenue} = \begin{array}{l}\text{Change in total}\\ \text{revenue generated}\\ \text{by one additional}\\ \text{unit of output}\end{array} = \frac{\text{Change in total revenue}}{\text{Change in quantity of output}}$$

or

$$MR = \Delta TR/\Delta Q$$

According to the **principle of marginal analysis**, every activity should continue until the marginal benefit equals the marginal cost.

Marginal revenue is the change in total revenue generated by an additional unit of output.

The **profit-maximizing rule**—also called the *optimal output rule*—applies the principle of marginal analysis to the producer's decision of how much to produce. This rule states that profit is maximized by producing the quantity at which the marginal revenue of the last unit produced is equal to its marginal cost. Note that there may not be any particular quantity at which the marginal revenue exactly equals the marginal cost. We see an example of this in **Table 3.5-2**, which provides cost and revenue data for Jennifer and Jayden's farm. In this case, the producer should produce until one more unit would cause the marginal cost to rise above the marginal revenue, which producing the sixth unit would do for Jennifer and Jayden.

As a common simplification, we can think of marginal cost as rising steadily, rather than jumping from one level at one quantity to a different level at the next quantity.

The **profit-maximizing rule** says that profit is maximized by producing the quantity of output at which the marginal revenue of the last unit produced is equal to its marginal cost.

AP® ECON TIP

The quantity of output at which $MR = MC$ is the focus of firms and wise AP® exam takers because it is this quantity that maximizes profit for firms in every type of market structure. If there is no output level at which $MR = MC$, the firm should produce the largest quantity at which MR is greater than MC.

Table 3.5-2 Short-Run Costs for Jennifer and Jayden's Farm

Quantity of tomatoes Q (bushels)	Total cost TC	Marginal cost of bushel $MC = \Delta TC/\Delta Q$	Marginal revenue of bushel MR	Net gain of bushel = MR − MC
0	$14			
		$16	$18	$2
1	30			
		6	18	12
2	36			
		8	18	10
3	44			
		12	18	6
4	56			
		16	18	2
5	72			
		20	18	−2
6	92			
		24	18	−6
7	116			

This ensures that the marginal cost will equal the marginal revenue at some quantity. We employ this simplified approach when we graph the data for Jennifer and Jayden's farm in **Figure 3.5-1**.

FIGURE 3.5-1 **The Firm's Profit-Maximizing Quantity of Output**

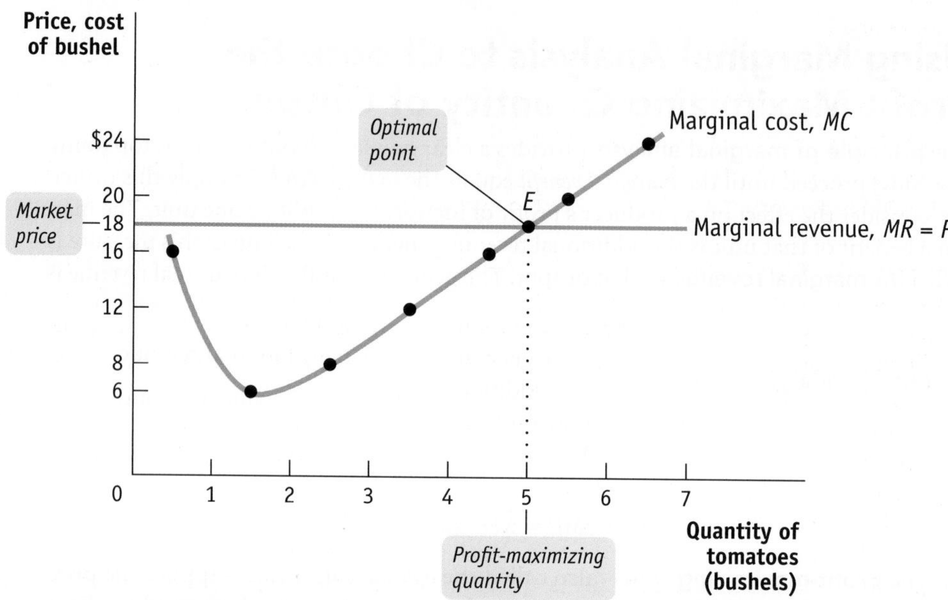

At the profit-maximizing quantity of output, the marginal revenue is equal to the marginal cost. It is located on the quantity axis below point *E*, where the marginal cost curve crosses the marginal revenue curve. Here, the profit-maximizing output is 5 bushels.

C Squared Studios/Getty Images

The second column of Table 3.5-2 contains the farm's total cost of output. The third column shows their marginal cost. Notice that, in this example, marginal cost initially falls as output rises but then begins to increase, so that the marginal cost curve has the "swoosh" shape discussed in Module 3.2 and seen in Figure 3.5-1.

The fourth column contains the farm's marginal revenue, which has an important feature: Jennifer and Jayden's marginal revenue is assumed to be constant at $18 for every output level. The assumption holds true for a particular type of market—a perfectly competitive market—which we will examine closely in Module 3.7. For now, we use this assumption just to make the calculations easier. The fifth and final column shows the calculation of the net gain per bushel of tomatoes, which is equal to the marginal revenue minus the marginal cost. As you can see, net gain is positive for the first through fifth bushels: producing each of these bushels raises Jennifer and Jayden's profit. For the sixth and seventh bushels, however, the net gain is negative: producing them would decrease, not increase, profit. (You can verify this by reexamining Table 3.5-1.) So five bushels are Jennifer and Jayden's optimal (profit-maximizing) output; if they produced one more unit, the marginal cost would rise above the market price, $18.

Figure 3.5-1 shows that Jennifer and Jayden's profit-maximizing quantity of output is, indeed, the number of bushels at which the steadily rising marginal cost of production is equal to the marginal revenue (which is equivalent to the price in perfectly competitive markets). We plot the marginal cost of increasing output from one to two bushels halfway between one and two, and so on. The horizontal line at $18 is Jennifer and Jayden's **marginal revenue curve**, which shows the relationship between marginal revenue and output. Note that the marginal revenue stays the same regardless of how much Jennifer and Jayden sell because we have assumed that marginal revenue is constant.

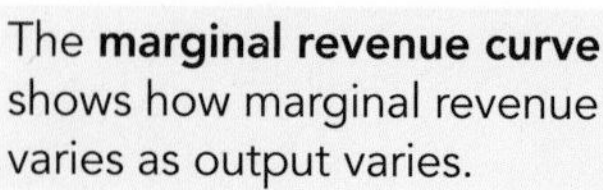
The **marginal revenue curve** shows how marginal revenue varies as output varies.

Does this mean that the firm's production decision can be entirely summed up as "produce up to the point where the marginal cost of production is equal to the marginal revenue"? Not quite. Before applying the principle of marginal analysis to determine how much to produce, a potential producer must, as a first step, answer an "either-or" question: Should I produce at all? If the answer to that question is yes, the producer then proceeds to the second step—a "how much" decision: maximizing profit by choosing the quantity of output at which the marginal cost is equal to the marginal revenue.

To understand why the first step in the production decision involves an "either-or" question, we need to ask how we determine whether it is profitable or unprofitable to produce at all.

When Is Production Profitable?

Recall from the previous Module that a firm's decision regarding whether or not to stay in a given business in the long run depends on its *economic profit*—a measure based on the opportunity cost of resources used in the business. To put it a slightly different way: in the calculation of economic profit, a firm's total cost incorporates the implicit cost—the benefits forgone in the next-best use of the firm's resources—as well as the explicit cost in the form of actual money outlays. In contrast, *accounting profit* is profit calculated using only the explicit costs incurred by the firm. This means that economic profit incorporates the opportunity cost of resources owned by the firm and used in the production of output, while accounting profit does not. As in the example of Babette's Cajun Café, a firm may make positive accounting profit while making zero or even negative economic profit. It's important to understand clearly that a firm's long-run decision to produce or not, to stay in business or to close down permanently, should be based on economic profit, not accounting profit.

We will assume, as we always do, that the cost numbers given in Tables 3.5-1 and 3.5-2 include all costs, implicit as well as explicit, and that the profit numbers in Table 3.5-1 are economic profit. What determines whether Jennifer and Jayden's farm earns a profit or generates a loss? The answer is the market price of tomatoes—specifically, *whether selling the firm's optimal quantity of output at the market price results in at least a normal profit.*

In the next Module, we look in detail at a firm's decision to produce or not, and at the decision of new firms to enter a market.

Module 3.5  Review

Check Your Understanding

1. Suppose a firm can sell as many units of output as it wants for a price of $15 per unit and faces total costs as indicated in the table below. Use the profit-maximizing rule to determine the profit-maximizing level of output for the firm.

Quantity	Total cost
0	$2
1	10
2	20
3	33
4	50
5	71

2. Use the data from Question 1 to graph the firm's marginal cost and marginal revenue curves and show the profit-maximizing level of output.

Tackle the AP® Test: Multiple-Choice Questions

Use the data in the table provided to answer Questions 1–3.

Quantity	Total revenue	Total cost
0	$0	$14
1	18	30
2	36	36
3	54	44
4	72	56
5	90	72
6	108	92
7	126	116

1. What is the marginal revenue of the third unit of output?
   a. $8
   b. $14
   c. $18
   d. $44
   e. $54
2. What is the marginal cost of the first unit of output?
   a. $0
   b. $14
   c. $16
   d. $18
   e. $30
3. At what level of output is profit maximized?
   a. 0
   b. 1
   c. 3
   d. 5
   e. 7
4. A firm should continue to produce in the long run if its
   a. total revenue is less than its total costs.
   b. total revenue is greater than its total explicit costs.
   c. accounting profit is greater than its economic profit.
   d. accounting profit is not negative.
   e. economic profit is at least zero.
5. A firm earns a normal profit when its
   a. accounting profit equals 0.
   b. economic profit is positive.
   c. total revenue equals its total costs.
   d. accounting profit equals its economic profit.
   e. economic profit equals its total explicit and implicit costs.
6. Adherence to the principle of marginal analysis entails continuing activities until the
   a. total benefit exceeds the marginal benefit.
   b. total benefit equals the total cost.
   c. total benefit exceeds the total cost.
   d. marginal benefit equals the marginal cost.
   e. marginal benefit exceeds the marginal cost.
7. To maximize profit, a firm should produce the quantity at which marginal revenue equals marginal cost unless, in the long run, the firm would
   a. earn zero economic profit.
   b. earn less than normal profit.
   c. receive a price equal to its marginal revenue.
   d. earn positive accounting profit.
   e. earn positive economic profit.

Tackle the AP® Test: Free-Response Questions

1. Use the data in the table provided to answer the following questions.

Quantity	Total revenue	Total cost
0	$0	$7
1	18	23
2	36	29
3	54	37
4	72	49
5	90	65
6	108	87
7	126	112

   a. What is the marginal revenue of the fourth unit?
   b. Calculate profit at a quantity of two. Explain how you calculated the profit.
   c. What is the profit-maximizing level of output? Explain how to use the profit-maximizing rule to determine the profit-maximizing level of output.

Rubric for FRQ 1 (5 points)

1 point: $18

1 point: $7

1 point: $36 – $29 or *TR* – *TC*

1 point: 5 units

1 point: The profit-maximizing rule states that profit is maximized when *MR* = *MC*. Here, *MR* never exactly equals *MC*, so in this case, the firm should produce the largest quantity at which *MR* exceeds *MC*. At a quantity of 5, *MC* = $16 and *MR* = $18. For the sixth unit, *MC* = $22 and *MR* = $18, and because *MC* > *MR*, the sixth unit would add more to total cost than it would to total revenue, so it should not be produced.

2. Use a graph to illustrate the typical shape of the two curves used to find a firm's profit-maximizing level of output on the basis of the profit-maximizing rule. Assume all units of output can be sold for $5. Indicate the profit-maximizing level of output with a "*Q**" on the appropriate axis. (You don't have enough information to provide a specific numerical answer.) **(3 points)**

Firms' Entry and Exit Decisions

MODULE 3.6

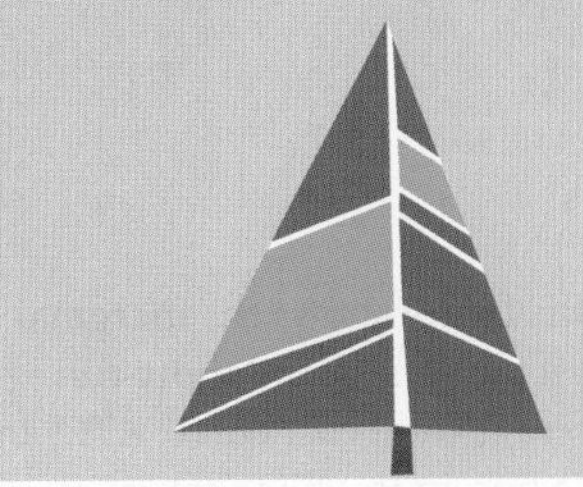

In this Module, you will learn to:

- Explain how a firm decides whether to produce or not in the short run and in the long run
- Calculate a price-taking firm's profit or loss and show this on a graph
- Summarize the criterion for new firms to enter a market

Recall the example of Jennifer and Jayden's organic tomato farm from Module 3.5. Suppose that many other organic tomato farmers also sell their output to the same grocery store chains as Jennifer and Jayden. Since organic tomatoes are a standardized product, consumers don't care which farmer produces the organic tomatoes they buy. And because so many farmers sell organic tomatoes, no individual farmer has a large market share, which means that no individual farmer can have a measurable effect on market prices. For these reasons, these farmers are considered *price-taking* producers, and the market for organic tomatoes meets the conditions of a *perfectly competitive* market. We will explore perfectly competitive markets in detail in the next Module. In this Module, we will focus on how firms decide to enter or exit such a market.

Tony Hertz/Alamy

Production and Profit

From the profit-maximization rule introduced in Module 3.5, we know that, if they produce any tomatoes at all, Jennifer and Jayden's farm will maximize its profit (or minimize its loss) by producing tomatoes up until the marginal revenue equals the marginal cost. This will be true for any firm in any market structure. The decision of whether to produce at all depends on the size of the firm's profit or loss, so we will begin with the question of whether a firm earns a profit, breaks even, or incurs a loss.

In **Table 3.6-1**, we calculate the short-run average variable cost and the short-run average total cost for Jennifer and Jayden's farm. These are short-run values because we are considering a period during which the quantity of at least one input is fixed and thus has a fixed cost. (We'll turn to the long run, when fixed costs can change, shortly.) **Figure 3.6-1** shows the average total cost values from Table 3.6-1 in the form of the short-run average total cost curve, *ATC*. The marginal cost curve, *MC*, was derived in the previous Module. As you can see, average total cost is minimized at point *C*,

Table 3.6-1 Short-Run Average Costs for Jennifer and Jayden's Farm

Quantity of tomatoes Q (bushels)	Variable cost VC	Total cost TC	Short-run average variable cost of bushel $AVC = VC/Q$	Short-run average total cost of bushel $ATC = TC/Q$
1	$16.00	$30.00	$16.00	$30.00
2	22.00	36.00	11.00	18.00
3	30.00	44.00	10.00	14.67
4	42.00	56.00	10.50	14.00
5	58.00	72.00	11.60	14.40
6	78.00	92.00	13.00	15.33
7	102.00	116.00	14.57	16.57

FIGURE 3.6-1 Costs and Production in the Short Run

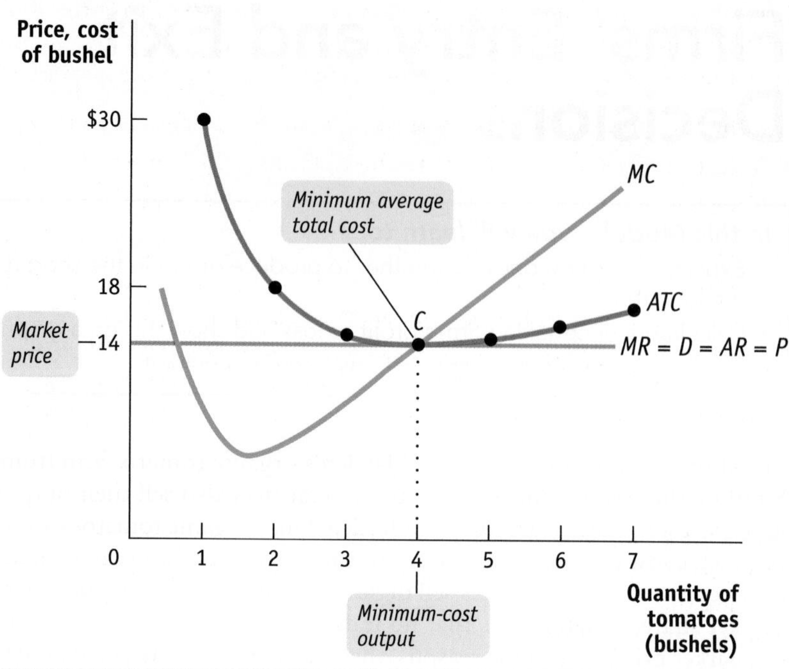

This figure shows the marginal cost curve, *MC*; the short-run average total cost curve, *ATC*; and the horizontal line that represents the marginal revenue, *MR*, the demand, *D*, the average revenue, *AR*, and the market price, *P*. The firm chooses the quantity of output at which *MR* = *MC*, 4 bushels of tomatoes. Four bushels is also the minimum-cost output, represented by point *C*. Because the price of $14 is equal to the firm's average total cost at the quantity produced, the firm breaks even.

AP® ECON TIP

Use the mnemonic device "MR. DARP" to remember all of the curves represented by the horizontal line at the market price for a perfectly competitive firm: *MR*, *D*, *AR*, and *P*.

The **average revenue** is the average amount of revenue received per unit of output. This can be found as the total revenue divided by the quantity of output. The average revenue equals the price if every unit sells for the same price.

AP® ECON TIP

A firm earns positive economic profit if its total revenue exceeds its total cost. If average revenue exceeds average cost, it is also true that total revenue exceeds total cost, so depending on which values are easiest to access, you can compare the averages or the totals to check for profits.

corresponding to an output of 4 bushels—the *minimum-cost output*—and an average total cost of $14 per bushel.

The horizontal line in Figure 3.6-1 with the height of the market price represents the firm's marginal revenue (*MR*), because each time Jennifer and Jayden sell another bushel of tomatoes, their total revenue increases by the price of $14. The horizontal line is also the firm's demand curve (*D*). This makes sense because a demand curve indicates how many units can be sold at each price, and each organic tomato farm in a perfectly competitive market is so small relative to the market that it can sell as many bushels as it wants at the market price of $14. The horizontal line is also the firm's **average revenue** (*AR*)—the average amount of revenue taken in per unit—because the price equals the average revenue whenever every unit is sold for the same price (*P*). That is, if Jennifer and Jayden sell every unit for $14, the average amount they take in per unit must be $14.

To satisfy the profit-maximization rule, the firm produces the quantity at which *MR* = *MC*: 4 bushels of tomatoes. Although that makes profit as large as possible, that maximized profit is zero, because $14 is received for each bushel and the average cost of producing each bushel is $14. We can verify that profit is zero by noting in Table 3.6-1 that the total cost of producing 4 units is $56, which equals the total revenue of selling 4 units for $14 each: 4 × $14 = $56. The graph shows that at any higher or lower quantity, the average total cost would exceed the average revenue of $14, so the firm would incur losses.

We can now speak more generally about the conditions for a firm making a profit, breaking even, or incurring a loss. We know that profit is total revenue minus total cost, $TR - TC$. This means:

- If the firm produces a quantity at which $TR > TC$, the firm is profitable.
- If the firm produces a quantity at which $TR = TC$, the firm breaks even.
- If the firm produces a quantity at which $TR < TC$, the firm incurs a loss.

We can also express this idea in terms of revenue and cost per unit of output. If we divide profit by the number of units of output, *Q*, we obtain the following equation for profit per unit of output:

$$\text{(3.6-1)} \quad \frac{\text{Profit}}{Q} = \frac{TR}{Q} - \frac{TC}{Q}$$

TR/Q is average revenue, which is the market price (*P*). *TC/Q* is average total cost. So a firm is profitable if the market price for its product is more than the average total cost of the quantity the firm produces; a firm experiences a loss if the market price is less than the average total cost of the quantity the firm produces. This means:

- If the firm produces a quantity at which $P > ATC$, the firm is profitable.
- If the firm produces a quantity at which $P = ATC$, the firm breaks even.
- If the firm produces a quantity at which $P < ATC$, the firm incurs a loss.

In summary, in the short run a firm will maximize profit by producing the quantity of output at which $MC = MR$. A perfectly competitive firm is a price-taker, so it can sell as many units of output as it would like at the market price. This means that for a perfectly competitive firm, it is always true that $MR = P$. The firm is profitable, or breaks even, as long as the market price is greater than, or equal to, the average total cost. Next, we develop the perfect competition model using graphs to analyze the firm's level of profit.

Graphing Profit and Loss

Figure 3.6-2 illustrates how the market price determines whether a firm is profitable. It also shows how profit is depicted graphically. Each panel shows the marginal cost curve, *MC*, and the short-run average total cost curve, *ATC*. Average total cost is minimized at point *C*. Panel (a) shows the case in which the market price of tomatoes is \$18 per bushel. Panel (b) shows the case of a lower, \$10 market price per bushel of tomatoes.

In panel (a), we see that at a price of \$18 per bushel the profit-maximizing quantity of output is 5 bushels, indicated by point *E*, where the marginal cost curve, *MC*, intersects the marginal revenue curve, *MR*, which for a price-taking firm is a horizontal line at the market price. At that quantity of output, average total cost is \$14.40 per bushel, indicated by point *Z*. Since the price per bushel exceeds the average total cost per bushel, Jennifer and Jayden's farm is profitable.

Jennifer and Jayden's total profit when the market price is \$18 is represented by the area of the shaded rectangle in panel (a). To see why, notice that total profit can be expressed in terms of profit per unit:

$$\textbf{(3.6-2)}\quad \text{Profit} = TR - TC = \left(\frac{TR}{Q} - \frac{TC}{Q}\right) \times Q$$

or, equivalently, because market price, *P*, is equal to *TR/Q* and *ATC* is equal to *TC/Q*,

$$\textbf{(3.6-3)}\quad \text{Profit} = (P - ATC) \times Q$$

The height of the shaded rectangle in panel (a) corresponds to the vertical distance between points *E* and *Z*. It is equal to $P - ATC = \$18.00 - \$14.40 = \$3.60$ per bushel. The shaded rectangle has a width equal to the quantity of output: $Q = 5$ bushels. So the area of the rectangle is equal to Jennifer and Jayden's profit: 5 bushels × \$3.60 profit per bushel = \$18.

Panel (b) illustrates the very different outlook for the farm with a relatively low market price of \$10 per bushel. In some cases, the price is so low that a firm should simply shut down; we'll see how firms make that determination later in this Module. When the best a firm can do is produce at a loss, that loss is minimized by following the profit-maximizing rule: produce until the marginal revenue (the price for a perfectly competitive firm) equals the marginal cost. So if Jennifer and Jayden produce at all, they should produce 3 units, because at that quantity the line representing the marginal revenue and price intersects the marginal cost curve at point *A*. At that output level, Jennifer and Jayden have an average total cost of \$14.67 per bushel, indicated by point *Y*. The average total cost of producing 3 bushels exceeds the \$10 market price, giving Jennifer and Jayden's farm a loss, but the smallest loss possible.

How much do they lose by producing when the market price is \$10? On average they lose $ATC - P = \$14.67 - \$10.00 = \$4.67$ per bushel, an amount corresponding to

AP® ECON TIP

Memorize the formula for profit because you won't be given a formula sheet for the AP® exam.

FIGURE 3.6-2 Profitability and the Market Price

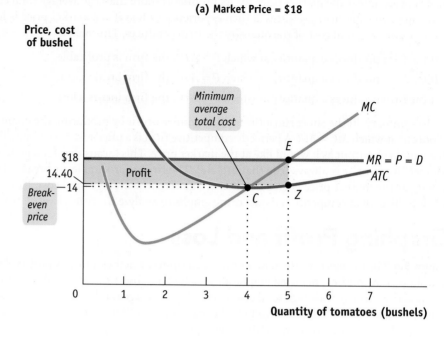

(a) Market Price = $18

In panel (a) the market price is $18. The farm is profitable because the market price exceeds the minimum average total cost of $14. The farm's profit-maximizing output of 5 bushels is found where marginal revenue equals marginal cost at point *E*. The average total cost of producing 5 bushels is $14.40, as shown by the height of the *ATC* curve at point *Z*. The vertical distance between point *E* and point *Z* indicates the farm's per-unit profit, $18.00 – $14.40 = $3.60. Total profit is given by the area of the shaded rectangle, 5 × $3.60 = $18.00. In panel (b) the market price is $10; the farm is unprofitable because the price is below the minimum average total cost of $14. If it continues to produce, the farm's optimal output choice is found where marginal revenue equals marginal cost at point *A*, 3 bushels. The vertical distance between point *A* and point *Y* indicates the farm's per-unit loss, $14.67 – $10.00 = $4.67. The shaded rectangle represents the farm's total loss, 3 × $4.67 = $14.00 (adjusted for rounding error).

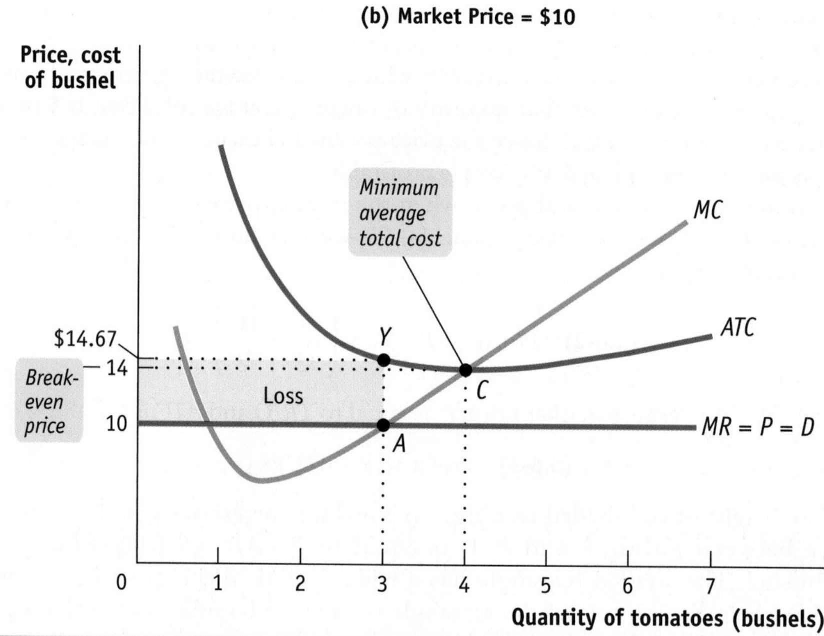

AP® ECON TIP

AP® exam questions may give you a scenario about profit, cost, or revenue at a specific output. Even if it is not required, drawing the firm's graph may help you visualize the answer more easily.

the vertical distance between points *A* and *Y*. Because they produce 3 bushels, the total value of the losses is $4.67 × 3 = $14.00 (adjusted for rounding error), an amount represented by the area of the shaded rectangle in panel (b).

How does a producer know whether its business will be profitable? It turns out that the crucial test lies in a comparison of the market price to the firm's *minimum average total cost*. On Jennifer and Jayden's farm, the average total cost reaches its minimum of $14 at an output of 4 bushels, indicated by point *C*. Whenever the market price exceeds the minimum average total cost, there are output levels for which the average total cost is less than the market price. In other words, the producer can find a level of output at which the firm makes a profit. So Jennifer and Jayden's farm will be profitable whenever the market price exceeds $14. And they will achieve the highest possible profit by producing the quantity at which the marginal cost equals the price (which is also the marginal revenue).

Conversely, if the market price is less than the minimum average total cost, there is no output level at which the price exceeds the average total cost. That means the firm will be unprofitable at any quantity of output. As we saw, at a price of $10 – an amount less than the minimum average total cost – Jennifer and Jayden did indeed lose money. By producing the quantity at which marginal cost equaled price, Jennifer and Jayden did the best they could, but the best they could do was a loss of $14. Any other quantity would have increased the size of their loss.

The minimum average total cost of a price-taking firm is called its **break-even price**, the price at which it earns zero economic profit (also known as *normal profit*). A firm will earn positive profit when the market price is above the break-even price, and it will suffer losses when the market price is below the break-even price. Jennifer and Jayden's break-even price of $14 is the price at point *C* in Figure 3.6-2.

The **break-even price** of a price-taking firm is the market price at which it earns zero economic profit, also known as normal profit.

The Short-Run Production Decision

You might be tempted to say that if a firm is unprofitable because the market price is below its minimum average total cost, it shouldn't produce any output. In the short run, however, the firm might actually be better off producing even if price falls below minimum average total cost. The reason, as we learned in Module 3.2, is that total cost includes *fixed cost* – cost that does not depend on the amount of output produced and can be altered only in the long run. In the short run, fixed cost must still be paid, regardless of whether a firm produces. For example, if Jennifer and Jayden have rented a tractor for the year, they have to pay the rent on the tractor regardless of whether they produce any tomatoes. *Since it cannot be changed in the short run, their fixed cost is irrelevant to their decision about whether to produce or shut down in the short run.* Although fixed cost should play no role in the decision about whether to produce in the short run, another type of production cost – variable cost – does matter. Part of the variable cost for Jennifer and Jayden is the wage cost of workers they must hire to help with planting and harvesting. Variable cost can be eliminated by *not* producing, which makes it a critical consideration when determining whether to produce in the short run.

TRIG/Shutterstock

Let's turn to **Figure 3.6-3**, which shows both the short-run average total cost curve, *ATC*, and the short-run average variable cost curve, *AVC*, drawn from the information in Table 3.6-1. Recall that the difference between the *ATC* and *AVC* curves – the vertical distance between them – represents average fixed cost, the fixed cost per unit of output, *FC/Q*. Because the marginal cost curve has a "swoosh" shape – falling at first before rising – the short-run average variable cost curve is U-shaped: the initial fall in marginal cost causes average variable cost to fall as well, and then the rise in marginal cost eventually pulls average variable cost up again. The short-run average variable cost curve reaches its minimum value of $10 at point *A*, at an output of 3 bushels.

The Shut-Down Price

We are now prepared to analyze the optimal production decision in the short run. We have two cases to consider:

- When the market price is *below* the minimum average variable cost
- When the market price is *greater than or equal to* the minimum average variable cost

When the market price is below the minimum average variable cost, the price the firm receives per unit will not cover its variable cost per unit. A firm in this situation should cease production immediately. Why? Because there is no level of output at which

FIGURE 3.6-3 The Short-Run Firm Supply Curve

When the market price equals or exceeds Jennifer and Jayden's *shut-down price* of \$10 – the minimum average variable cost indicated by point *A* – they will produce the quantity at which the marginal cost equals the price. So at any price equal to or above the minimum average *variable* cost, the firm's short-run supply curve is its marginal cost curve. When the market price falls below the minimum average variable cost, the firm ceases operation in the short run. For the range of prices that causes the firm to shut down, the firm's supply curve lies along the vertical axis.

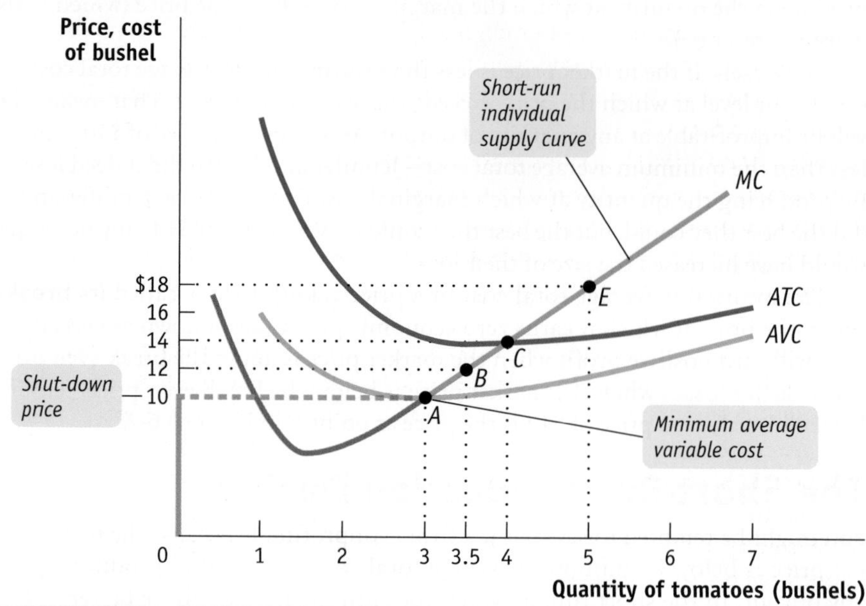

A firm will cease production in the short run if the market price falls below the **shut-down price**, which is equal to the minimum average variable cost.

the firm's total revenue covers its variable cost – the cost it can avoid by not operating. In this case the firm maximizes its profit by not producing at all – by, in effect, minimizing its loss. It will still incur a fixed cost in the short run, but it will no longer incur any variable cost. This means that the minimum average variable cost determines the **shut-down price**, the price at which the firm ceases production in the short run.

When the price is greater than the minimum average variable cost, however, the firm should produce in the short run. In this case, the firm maximizes profit – or minimizes loss – by choosing the output level at which its marginal cost is equal to the market price. For example, if the market price of tomatoes is \$18 per bushel, Jennifer and Jayden should produce at point *E* in Figure 3.6-3, corresponding to an output of 5 bushels. Note that point *C* in Figure 3.6-3 corresponds to the farm's break-even price of \$14 per bushel. Since *E* lies above *C*, Jennifer and Jayden's farm will be profitable; they will generate a per-bushel profit of \$18.00 – \$14.40 = \$3.60 when the market price is \$18.

What if the market price lies between the shut-down price and the break-even price – that is, between the minimum average *variable* cost and the minimum average *total* cost? This is the case for Jennifer and Jayden's farm if the market price is between \$10 and \$14 – say, \$12. At \$12, Jennifer and Jayden's farm is not profitable; since the market price is below the minimum average total cost, the farm is losing (on average) the difference between the price and the average total cost on every unit produced. Yet, even though the market price isn't covering Jennifer and Jayden's average total cost, that price is covering their average variable cost and some – but not all – of their average fixed cost. If a firm in this situation shuts down, it will incur no variable cost but will incur the *full* fixed cost. As a result, shutting down will generate an even greater loss than continuing to operate.

Whenever the price falls between the minimum average total cost and the minimum average variable cost, the firm is better off producing some output in the short run. The reason is that by producing, it can cover its variable cost and at least some of its fixed cost, even though it is incurring a loss. In this case, the firm maximizes profit – that is, minimizes loss – by choosing the quantity of output at which its marginal cost is equal to the market price. So if Jennifer and Jayden face a market price of \$12 per bushel, their profit-maximizing output is given by point *B* in Figure 3.6-3, 3.5 bushels.

A **sunk cost** is a cost that has already been incurred and is nonrecoverable. A sunk cost should be ignored in a decision about future actions.

The decision to produce when the firm is covering its variable cost but not all of its fixed cost is a decision to ignore a *sunk cost*. A **sunk cost** is a cost that has already been incurred and cannot be recouped, such as the cost of a rent payment already made on a farm; and because it cannot be changed, it should have no effect on a firm's current decision. In the short-run production decision, fixed cost is effectively a sunk cost – the money has been spent, and it cannot be recovered. This comparison also illustrates why variable cost does indeed matter in the short run: it can be avoided by not producing.

What happens if the market price is exactly equal to the shut-down price, the minimum average variable cost? In this instance, the firm is indifferent between producing 3 units or 0 units. As we'll see shortly, this is an important point when looking at the behavior of an industry as a whole. For the sake of clarity, we'll assume that the firm, although indifferent, does indeed produce output when the market price is equal to the shut-down price.

Putting everything together, we can now draw the **short-run firm supply curve** of Jennifer and Jayden's farm, the red line in Figure 3.6-3; it shows how the profit-maximizing quantity of output in the short run depends on the price. As you can see, the curve is drawn in two segments. The upward-sloping red segment starting at point *A* shows the short-run profit-maximizing quantity when the market price is equal to or above the shut-down price of $10 per bushel. As long as the market price is equal to or above the shut-down price, Jennifer and Jayden will produce the quantity of output at which the marginal cost is equal to the market price. So at market prices equal to or above the shut-down price, the firm's short-run supply curve corresponds to its marginal cost curve. But at any market price below the minimum average variable cost – in this case, $10 per bushel – the firm shuts down in the short run and output drops to zero. For that reason, the firm's supply curve lies along the vertical axis for prices below the shut-down price.

The **short-run firm supply curve** shows how an individual firm's profit-maximizing level of output depends on the market price, taking the fixed cost as given.

Do firms sometimes shut down temporarily without going out of business? Yes. In fact, in some industries temporary shut-downs are routine. The most common examples are industries in which demand is highly seasonal, like outdoor amusement parks in climates with cold winters. Such parks would have to offer very low prices to entice customers during the colder months – prices so low that the owners would not cover their variable cost (principally wages and electricity). The wiser choice economically is to shut down until warm weather brings enough customers who are willing to pay a higher price.

Canon2260/Alamy

Changing Fixed Cost

Although fixed cost cannot be altered in the short run, in the long run firms can acquire or get rid of machines, buildings, and so on. Module 3.3 showed how the level of fixed cost is a matter of choice in the long run, and a firm will choose the level of fixed cost that minimizes the average total cost for its desired output level. Now we will focus on an even bigger question facing a firm when choosing its fixed cost: whether to incur *any* fixed cost at all by continuing to operate.

In the long run, a firm can always eliminate its fixed cost by selling off its plant and equipment. If it does so, of course, it can't produce any output – it has exited the industry. In contrast, a new firm can take on some fixed cost by acquiring machines and other resources, which puts it in a position to produce – it can enter the industry. In most perfectly competitive industries the set of firms, although fixed in the short run, changes in the long run as some firms enter or exit the industry.

Consider Jennifer and Jayden's farm once again. In order to simplify our analysis, we will sidestep the issue of choosing among several possible levels of fixed cost. Instead, we will assume that if they operate at all, Jennifer and Jayden have only one possible choice of fixed cost: $14. Alternatively, they can choose a fixed cost of zero if they exit the industry. Changes in fixed cost cause short-run average total cost curves to differ from long-run total cost curves, so with this assumption, Jennifer and Jayden's short-run and long-run average total cost curves are one and the same.

Suppose that the market price of organic tomatoes is consistently less than the break-even price of $14 over an extended period of time. In that case, Jennifer and Jayden never fully cover their total cost: their business runs at a persistent loss. In the long run, then, they can do better by closing their business and leaving the industry. In other words, *in the long run* firms will exit an industry if the market price is consistently less than their break-even price—their minimum average total cost.

Conversely, suppose that the price of organic tomatoes is consistently above the break-even price of $14 for an extended period of time. Because their farm is profitable, Jennifer and Jayden will remain in the industry and continue producing. But the story doesn't end there. There are many potential organic tomato producers because the necessary inputs are easy to obtain. And the cost curves of those potential producers are likely to be similar to those of Jennifer and Jayden, since the technology used by other producers is likely to be very similar to that used by Jennifer and Jayden. If the price is high enough to generate profit for existing producers, it will also attract some of these potential producers into the industry. So *in the long run*, a price in excess of $14 should lead to entry: new producers will come into the organic tomato industry.

Summing Up: The Perfectly Competitive Firm's Conditions for Profitability and Production

In this Module, we've studied what's behind the supply curve for a perfectly competitive firm. A perfectly competitive firm is a price-taker and maximizes profit, or minimizes loss, by producing the quantity that equates marginal revenue, which is the market price, and marginal cost. There are two exceptions: If the market price is below the minimum average variable cost in the short run, the firm should shut down, and if the market price is below the minimum average total cost in the long run, the firm is better off exiting the industry. **Table 3.6-2** summarizes the perfectly competitive firm's profitability and production conditions. It also relates them to entry into and exit from the industry in the long run.

Table 3.6-2 **Summary of the Perfectly Competitive Firm's Profitability and Production Conditions**

Profitability condition (minimum *ATC* = break-even price)	**Result**
P > minimum *ATC*	Firm profitable. Additional firms enter the industry in the long run.
P = minimum *ATC*	Firm breaks even. No incentive for any firm to enter or exit the industry in the long run.
P < minimum *ATC*	Firm unprofitable. The firm and other firms in the industry exit in the long run.
Production condition (minimum *AVC* = shut-down price)	**Result**
P > minimum *AVC*	Firm produces in the short run. If *P* < minimum *ATC*, firm covers variable cost and some but not all of fixed cost. If *P* > minimum *ATC*, firm covers all variable cost and fixed cost.
P = minimum *AVC*	Firm indifferent between producing in the short run or not. Firm exactly covers variable cost.
P < minimum *AVC*	Firm shuts down in the short run. Does not cover variable cost.

Now that we understand how a perfectly competitive *firm* makes its decisions, we can go on to look at the supply curve for a perfectly competitive *market* and the long-run equilibrium in perfect competition. In the next Module, we'll take a closer look at how exit and entry affect a perfectly competitive market in the long run, including the distinction between the *short-run industry supply curve* and the *long-run industry supply curve*.

Module 3.6  Review

Check Your Understanding

1. Refer to the graph provided.
   a. At what level of output does the firm maximize profit? Explain.
   b. At the profit-maximizing quantity of output, is the firm profitable, does it just break even, or does it incur a loss? Explain.

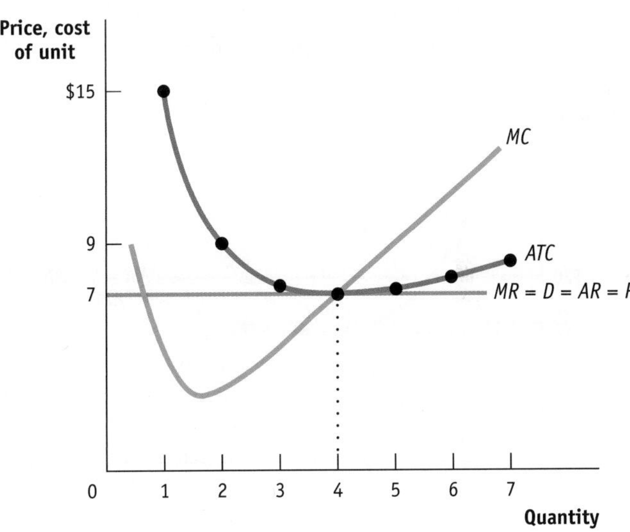

2. If a firm has a total cost of $500 at a quantity of 50 units, and it is at this quantity that average total cost is minimized for the firm, what is the lowest price that would allow the firm to break even (that is, earn a normal profit)? Explain.
3. Draw a short-run diagram showing a U-shaped average total cost curve, a U-shaped average variable cost curve, and a "swoosh"-shaped marginal cost curve. On your diagram, indicate the range of prices for which the following actions are optimal.
   a. The firm shuts down immediately.
   b. The firm operates in the short run despite sustaining a loss.
   c. The firm operates while making a profit.

Tackle the AP® Test: Multiple-Choice Questions

1. A perfectly competitive firm will maximize profit at the quantity at which the firm's marginal revenue equals
   a. price.
   b. average revenue.
   c. total cost.
   d. marginal cost.
   e. demand.
2. Which of the following is true for a perfectly competitive firm?
   a. The market demand curve is horizontal.
   b. The firm can increase its profit by charging a higher price than other firms.
   c. The firm charges a price that exceeds the marginal revenue.
   d. The firm's marginal revenue curve is also its demand curve.
   e. To maximize profit, the firm sets its price above its marginal cost.
3. A firm is profitable if
   a. $TR < TC$.
   b. $AR < ATC$.
   c. $MC < ATC$.
   d. $ATC < P$.
   e. $ATC > MC$.
4. If a firm has a total cost of $200, its profit-maximizing level of output is 10 units, and it is breaking even (that is, earning a normal profit), what is the market price?
   a. $200
   b. $100
   c. $20
   d. $10
   e. $2

5. What is the firm's profit if the price of its product is \$5 and it produces 500 units of output at a total cost of \$1,000?
   a. \$5,000
   b. \$2,500
   c. \$1,500
   d. –\$1,500
   e. –\$2,500

6. If a firm produces a quantity at which $P = ATC$, it will certainly
   a. incur a loss.
   b. break even.
   c. have a downward-sloping demand curve.
   d. maximize its profit.
   e. earn a profit, but it may or may not maximize its profit.

For Questions 7–9, refer to the graph provided, and assume that the firm produces the profit-maximizing quantity.

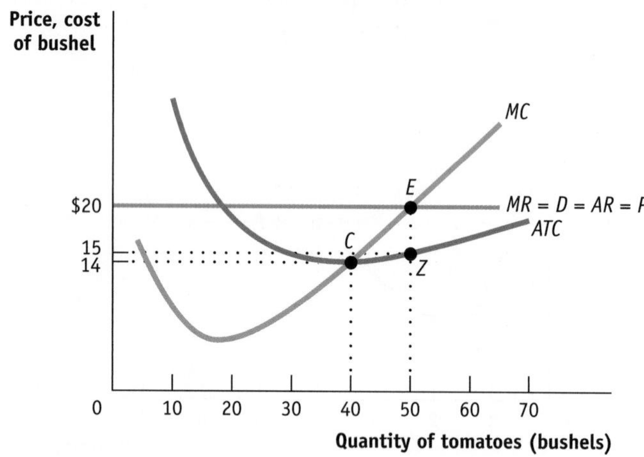

7. The firm's total revenue is equal to
   a. \$14.
   b. \$20.
   c. \$560.
   d. \$750.
   e. \$1,000.

8. The firm's total cost is equal to
   a. \$14.
   b. \$15.
   c. \$560.
   d. \$750.
   e. \$1,000.

9. The firm is earning a
   a. profit equal to \$5.
   b. profit equal to \$250.
   c. loss equal to \$15.
   d. loss equal to \$750.
   e. loss equal to \$250.

10. If the price is between the *AVC* and the *ATC*, by producing, the firm will certainly cover
    a. neither its fixed cost nor its variable cost.
    b. all of its fixed cost but only some of its variable cost.
    c. all of its variable cost but only some of its fixed cost.
    d. both its fixed cost and its variable cost.
    e. its total cost and its economic profit.

Tackle the AP® Test: Free-Response Questions

1. Draw a correctly labeled graph showing a profit-maximizing perfectly competitive firm producing at its minimum average total cost.

Rubric for FRQ 1 (6 points)

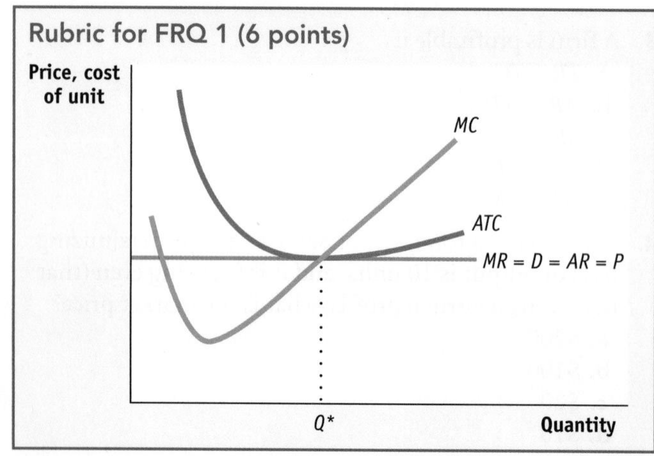

1 point: Vertical axis and horizontal axis labels are correct ("Price, cost of unit" on vertical axis; "Quantity" on horizontal axis).

1 point: The line representing marginal revenue, demand, average revenue, and price is horizontal and correctly labeled.

1 point: Marginal cost is "swoosh"-shaped (upward-sloping) and correctly labeled.

1 point: Average total cost is U-shaped and correctly labeled.

1 point: Quantity is found where $MC = MR$.

1 point: Average total cost reaches its minimum point at the profit-maximizing level of output.

2. Refer to the table provided. Price is equal to $14.

Short-Run Costs for Jennifer and Jayden's Farm

Quantity of tomatoes (bushels)	Variable cost	Total cost
0	$0	$14
1	16	30
2	22	36
3	30	44
4	42	56
5	58	72
6	78	92
7	102	116

a. Calculate the firm's marginal cost at each quantity.
b. Determine the firm's profit-maximizing level of output.
c. Calculate the firm's profit at the profit-maximizing level of output. **(3 points)**

3. Refer to the graph provided.

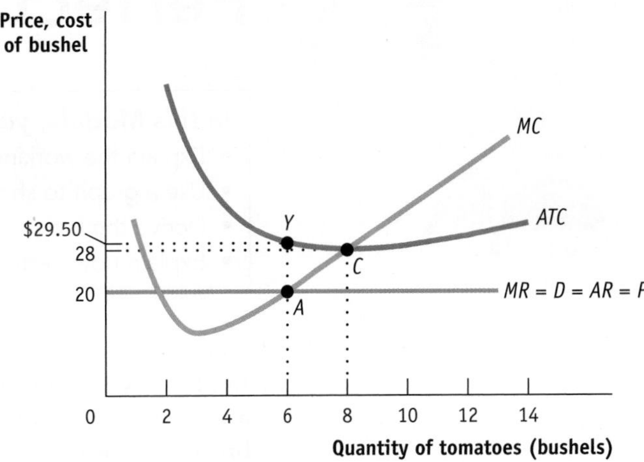

a. Assuming it is appropriate for the firm to produce in the short run, what is the firm's profit-maximizing level of output?
b. Calculate the firm's total revenue.
c. Calculate the firm's total cost.
d. Calculate the firm's profit or loss.
e. If *AVC* were $22 at the profit-maximizing level of output, would the firm produce in the short run? Explain why or why not. **(5 points)**

MODULE 3.7

Perfect Competition

In this Module, you will learn to:
- Explain the workings of a perfectly competitive market and define key terms
- Use a graph to show how profit leads to entry and a new market equilibrium
- Derive the long-run industry supply curve
- Explain how perfect competition results in efficiency in the long run

In Modules 3.5 and 3.6, we discussed the perfectly competitive firm's short-run situation – whether to produce or not, and if so, whether the firm earns a positive profit, breaks even with a normal profit, or takes a loss. In this Module, we become better acquainted with the characteristics of a perfectly competitive market and look at the transition from the short run to the long run in such a market. We will see that perfect competition leads to efficient market outcomes. In Unit 4, we will contrast these outcomes with those in imperfectly competitive markets.

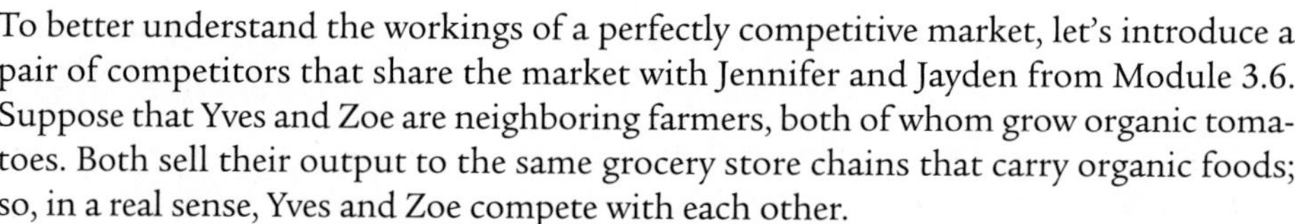

Defining Perfect Competition

Justin Sullivan/Getty Images

To better understand the workings of a perfectly competitive market, let's introduce a pair of competitors that share the market with Jennifer and Jayden from Module 3.6. Suppose that Yves and Zoe are neighboring farmers, both of whom grow organic tomatoes. Both sell their output to the same grocery store chains that carry organic foods; so, in a real sense, Yves and Zoe compete with each other.

Does this mean that Yves should try to stop Zoe from growing tomatoes, or that Yves and Zoe should form an agreement to restrict the supply and raise the price? Neither strategy would be effective because there are hundreds or thousands of organic tomato farmers, and Yves and Zoe are competing with all those other growers as well as with each other. Because so many farmers sell organic tomatoes, if any one of them produced more or fewer, there would be no measurable effect on market prices. And if Yves and Zoe tried to collude to raise the price of organic tomatoes, Jennifer and Jayden, among the many other competitors, would simply undercut their price and capture their sales.

When people talk about competing businesses, they often imagine a situation in which two or three rival firms are struggling for advantage. But economists know that when a business focuses on a few main competitors, either to run them out of the market or to work cooperatively to raise prices, it's actually a sign that competition is fairly limited. As the example of organic tomatoes suggests, when the number of competitors is large, it doesn't even make sense to identify rivals and engage in aggressive tactics because each firm is too small within the scope of the market to make a significant difference.

A **price-taking firm** is a firm whose actions have no effect on the market price of the good or service it sells.

A **price-taking consumer** is a consumer whose actions have no effect on the market price of the good or service purchased.

All of this means that Yves and Zoe, like Jennifer and Jayden and every other firm in a perfectly competitive market, are *price-takers*. Put formally, a **price-taking firm** is one whose actions cannot affect the market price of the good or service it sells. As a result, a price-taking firm takes the market price as given. There is a similar definition for consumers: a **price-taking consumer** is a consumer who cannot influence the market price of the good or service. That is, the market price is unaffected by how much or how little of the good the consumer buys. For example, individual car owners are price-takers in the car battery market, but some consumers do influence the market: When a major automaker shifts to making cars that run on electricity instead of gasoline, the price of electric car batteries may increase.

We can now define perfect competition very simply: In a **perfectly competitive market**, all market participants, both consumers and producers, are price-takers. That is, neither consumption decisions by individual consumers nor production decisions by individual producers affect the market price of the good. The terms *market* and *industry* are sometimes interchangeable, although a market brings together both consumers and producers whereas an industry is made up of producers. Depending on the context, it may be appropriate to discuss a market or an industry, so let's be clear that a **perfectly competitive industry** is an industry in which all firms are price-takers.

A **perfectly competitive market** is a market in which all consumers and producers are price-takers.

A **perfectly competitive industry** is an industry in which all firms are price-takers.

The supply and demand model is a model of a perfectly competitive market. That model depends fundamentally on the assumption that no individual buyer or seller of a good, such as coffee beans or organic tomatoes, can individually affect the price at which they can buy or sell the good. We have seen that for a firm, being a price-taker means that the demand curve is a horizontal line at the market price. If the firm charged more than the market price, buyers would go to any of the many alternative sellers of the same product. And it is unnecessary for the firm to charge a lower price because, as an insignificantly small part of the perfectly competitive market, the firm can sell all that it wants at the market price.

Instances in which consumers are able to affect the prices they pay are rare, so almost all consumers are indeed price-takers. However, many producers have a significant ability to affect the prices they receive, a use of what is called *market power*. The next Unit examines those markets that are not perfectly competitive. The model of perfect competition does represent many markets well. Under what circumstances will all participants be price-takers? As we'll discover next, there are four general conditions for a perfectly competitive market.

Conditions for Perfect Competition

The markets for major grains, such as wheat and corn, are perfectly competitive: individual wheat and corn farmers, as well as individual buyers of wheat and corn, take market prices as given. In contrast, the markets for some of the food items made from these grains – in particular, breakfast cereals – are by no means perfectly competitive. There is intense competition among cereal brands, but not *perfect* competition. To understand the difference between the market for wheat and the market for shredded wheat cereal is to understand the four conditions for perfect competition.

Steve Cavalier/Alamy

The market for wheat is perfectly competitive—many firms, each with a small market share, sell the same standardized product and take the market price as given.

Many Buyers and Sellers

For a market to be perfectly competitive, it must contain many firms, none of which have a large *market share*. A firm's **market share** is the fraction of the total industry output produced by that firm. The size of market shares constitutes a major difference between the grain industry and the breakfast cereal industry. There are thousands of wheat farmers, none of whom account for more than a tiny fraction of total wheat sales. The breakfast cereal industry, however, is dominated by four firms: Kellogg's, General Mills, Post, and Quaker. Kellogg's alone accounts for almost one-third of all cereal sales. Kellogg's executives know that if they try to sell more corn flakes, they are likely to drive down the market price of corn flakes because changes in their production will significantly affect the overall quantity supplied. Firms are price-takers only when they are numerous and relatively small.

A firm's **market share** is the fraction of the total industry output accounted for by that firm's output.

A Standardized Product

Second, an industry can be perfectly competitive only if consumers regard the products of all firms as equivalent. This clearly isn't true in the breakfast cereal market: consumers don't consider Cap'n Crunch to be a good substitute for Wheaties. As a result, the maker of Wheaties has some ability to increase its price without fear that it will lose all its customers to the maker of Cap'n Crunch. Contrast this with the case of

A good is a **standardized product,** also known as a **commodity,** when consumers regard the products of different firms as the same good.

a **standardized product**, sometimes known as a **commodity**, which is a product that consumers regard as the same good even when it comes from different firms. Because wheat is a standardized product, consumers regard the output of one wheat producer as a perfect substitute for that of another producer. This means that one farmer cannot increase the price for their wheat without losing all sales to other wheat farmers. So the second necessary condition for a perfectly competitive industry is that the industry output is a standardized product.

Free Entry and Exit

Module 3.6 explained how in a perfectly competitive industry in the long run, profit causes new firms to enter the industry and losses cause existing firms to exit the industry. Those transitions are made possible by the ease of entry and exit for firms. That is, no obstacles – such as government regulations or limited access to key resources – prevent new firms from entering the market. And no additional costs are associated with a company's decision to shut down and leave the industry. When there are no barriers to entry into or exit from an industry, we say that the industry has **free entry and exit**. Free entry and exit ensures that the number of firms in an industry can adjust to changing market conditions. And, in particular, it ensures that firms in an industry cannot act to keep other firms out.

An industry has **free entry and exit** when new firms can easily enter into the industry and existing firms can easily leave the industry.

Helen Sessions/Alamy

The market for breakfast cereal is competitive, but not perfectly competitive, because firms sell a differentiated product and may be able to charge a higher price than their competitors without losing all of their customers.

Full Information

The existence of many competing firms may not matter if market participants lack full information on the products and prices available. That would be the case if Yves and Zoe agreed to charge a higher price and the consumers are unaware that other firms, such as Jennifer and Jayden's, are offering a lower price. Even if consumers did know that Jennifer and Jayden have a lower price, consumers may end up paying the higher price if they don't know that the lower-priced organic tomatoes are identical to the higher-priced organic tomatoes. And if the competitors didn't have full information on what other competitors are charging, they may be unable to undercut high prices offered by other firms. In a perfectly competitive market, consumers and firms have all the relevant information about the products and prices available.

To sum up, there are four conditions for perfect competition. First, the industry must contain many firms, each having a small market share. Second, the industry must produce a standardized product. Third, perfectly competitive industries are characterized by free entry and exit in the long run. And fourth, buyers and sellers have full information about products and prices.

The Supply Curve for a Perfectly Competitive Industry

Module 3.6 explained that the short-run supply curve for a firm in a perfectly competitive industry is the firm's marginal cost curve above minimum average variable cost. The short-run supply curve for Jennifer and Jayden's farm was shown in Figure 3.6-3. For a perfectly competitive industry made up of many similar or identical firms, we can learn about the behavior of the industry by combining the supply curves for the firms to form the *industry supply curve*, which is the focus of the remainder of this Module. The **industry supply curve** represents the relationship between the price of a good and the total output of the industry as a whole. The industry supply curve is what we referred to in earlier Modules as the supply curve or the market supply curve. Here we take extra care to distinguish between the supply curve of an *individual firm* and the supply curve of the *industry as a whole*.

The **industry supply curve** (or market supply curve) shows the relationship between the price of a good and the total output of the industry as a whole.

As you might guess from the previous Module, the industry supply curve must be analyzed in somewhat different ways for the short run and the long run. Let's start with the short run.

The Short-Run Industry Supply Curve

Recall that in the short run, the number of firms in an industry is fixed. You may also remember from Module 2.2 that the industry or market supply curve is the horizontal sum of all of the individual firms' supply curves – you find it by summing the total output across all suppliers at every given price. We will do that exercise here under the assumption that all the firms are alike, which makes the derivation particularly simple. So let's assume there are 100 organic tomato farms, each with the same fixed and variable costs as Jennifer and Jayden's farm. Each of these 100 farms will have a short-run supply curve like the one in Figure 3.6-3 – shown here as panel (a) in **Figure 3.7-1**.

FIGURE 3.7-1 The Short-Run Supply Curve and Short-Run Market Equilibrium

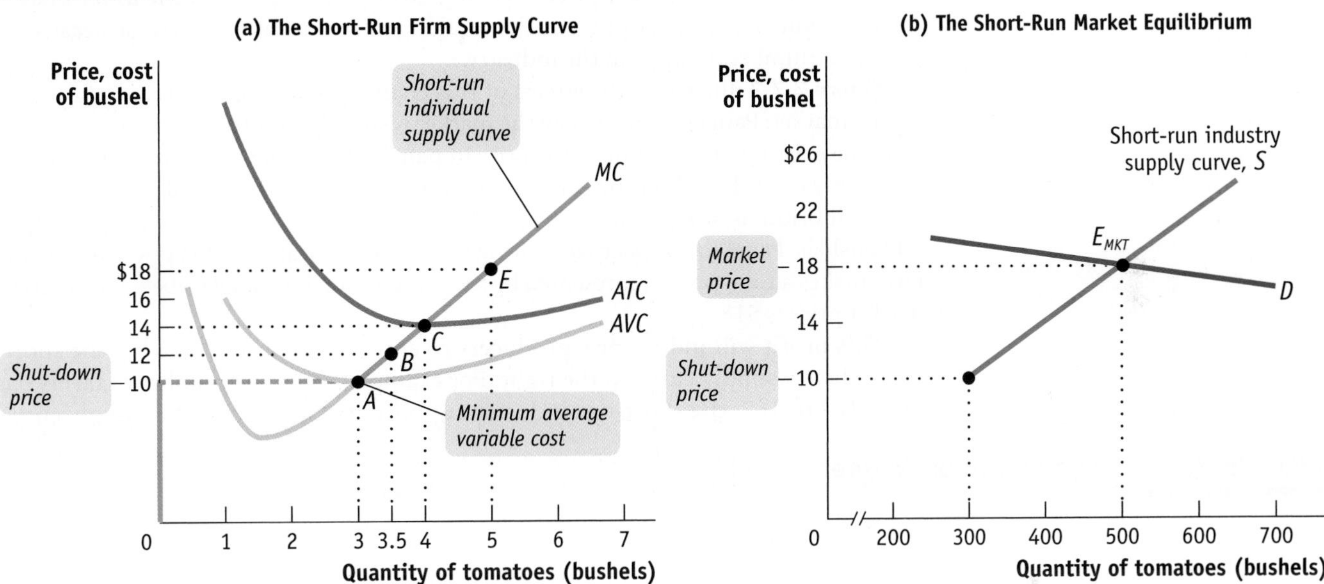

Figure 3.6-3, reproduced in panel (a), shows how each firm's short-run supply curve gets its shape. At any price equal to or above the minimum average *variable* cost, the firm's short-run supply curve is its marginal cost curve. When the market price falls below the minimum average variable cost, the firm ceases operation in the short run. (b) The short-run industry supply curve, *S*, is found by adding together the short-run firm supply curves of the 100 producers. Below the shut-down price of $10, no firm wants to produce in the short run. Above $10, the short-run industry supply curve slopes upward, as each firm increases output in response to higher prices. It intersects the demand curve, *D*, at point E_{MKT}, the point of short-run market equilibrium, corresponding to a market price of $18 and a quantity of 500 bushels.

At a price below $10, no farms will produce. At a price of more than $10, each farm will produce the quantity of output at which its marginal cost is equal to the market price. As you can see from panel (a) of Figure 3.7-1, this will lead each farm to produce 4 bushels if the price is $14 per bushel, 5 bushels if the price is $18, and so on. So if there are 100 organic tomato farms and the price of organic tomatoes is $18 per bushel, the industry as a whole will produce 500 bushels, corresponding to 100 farms × 5 bushels per farm. The result is the **short-run industry supply curve**, shown as *S* in panel (b) of Figure 3.7-1. This curve shows the quantity that producers in an industry will supply at each price, *taking the number of farms as given*.

The **short-run industry supply curve** shows how the quantity supplied by an industry depends on the market price, given a fixed number of firms.

The demand curve, labeled *D* in panel (b) Figure 3.7-1, crosses the short-run industry supply curve at E_{MKT}, corresponding to a price of $18 and a quantity of 500 bushels. Point E_{MKT} is a *short-run market equilibrium*: the quantity supplied equals the quantity demanded, taking the number of farms as given. The long run may look quite different because in the long run, farms may enter or exit the industry.

The Long-Run Industry Supply Curve

Suppose that in addition to the 100 farms currently in the organic tomato business, there are many other potential organic tomato farms. Suppose also that upon entering the industry, each of these potential farms would have the same cost curves as each of the existing farms, like the farm owned by Jennifer and Jayden.

What will lead additional farms to enter the industry? The existence of profit for the existing farms will. That is, if the market price is above the break-even price of $14 per bushel, the existing farms will earn profit and more farms will enter the industry. For example, at a price of $18 per bushel, new farms will enter the industry seeking a portion of the profit earned by existing farms.

What will happen as additional farms enter the industry? Clearly, the quantity supplied by the industry at any given price will increase, which means that the short-run industry supply curve will shift to the right. This shift will alter the market equilibrium and result in a lower market price. Existing farms will respond to the lower market price by reducing their output, but the total industry output will increase because of the larger number of farms in the industry.

Figure 3.7-2 illustrates the effects of this chain of events on an existing farm and on the market. Panel (a) shows how the market responds to entry, and panel (b) shows how one existing farm responds to entry. In panel (a), S_1 is the initial short-run industry supply curve based on the existence of 100 producers. The initial short-run market equilibrium is at E_{MKT}, with an equilibrium market price of $18 and a quantity of 500 bushels. Panel (b) shows that existing farms are profitable at this price: an existing farm makes a total profit represented by the green shaded rectangle labeled *A* when the market price is $18.

This profit will induce new producers to enter the industry, shifting the short-run industry supply curve to the right. For example, when the number of farms has increased to 167, the short-run industry supply curve is S_2. With this supply curve,

FIGURE 3.7-2 The Long-Run Market Equilibrium

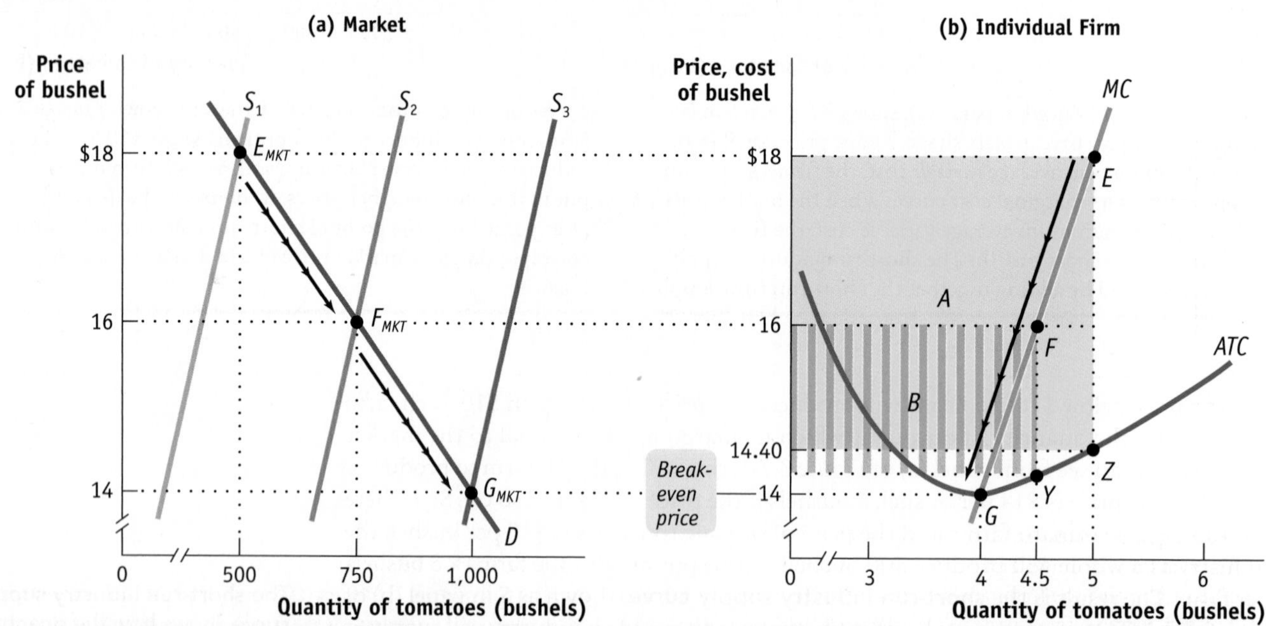

Point E_{MKT} of panel (a) shows the initial short-run market equilibrium. Each of the 100 existing producers makes a positive economic profit, illustrated in panel (b) by the green rectangle labeled *A*. Profit induces more firms to enter, shifting the short-run industry supply curve outward from S_1 to S_2 in panel (a). At the new short-run equilibrium point F_{MKT}, the market price has fallen and the industry output has risen. Existing firms reduce their output and each firm's profit falls to the area of the striped rectangle labeled *B* in panel (b). Entry continues to increase the supply and lower the price until, at point G_{MKT} in panel (a), the market price equals the break-even price and there is no incentive for entry or exit.

the short-run market equilibrium is F_{MKT} at a market price of $16 and a quantity of 750 bushels. For $16, each farm produces 4.5 bushels, so the industry output is $167 \times 4.5 = 750$ bushels (rounded). From panel (b) you can see how the entry of 67 new farms affects an existing farm: the lower price causes the existing farm to reduce its output, and its profit falls to the area represented by the striped rectangle labeled *B*.

Although diminished, the remaining profit of existing farms at F_{MKT} means that entry will continue and the number of farms will continue to rise. When the number of farms rises to 250, the short-run industry supply curve shifts out to S_3, and the market equilibrium is at G_{MKT}, with 1,000 bushels supplied and demanded and a market price of $14 per bushel.

Like E_{MKT} and F_{MKT}, G_{MKT} is a short-run equilibrium, but it is also something more. Because the price of $14 is each farm's break-even price, an existing producer makes zero economic profit—neither a profit nor a loss, earning only the opportunity cost of the resources used in production—when producing its profit-maximizing output of 4 bushels. At this price there is no incentive either for potential producers to enter or for existing producers to exit the industry. So G_{MKT} corresponds to a **long-run market equilibrium**—a situation in which the quantity supplied equals the quantity demanded, given that sufficient time has elapsed for producers to either enter or exit the industry. In a long-run market equilibrium, all existing and potential producers have fully adjusted to their optimal long-run choices; as a result, no producer has an incentive to enter or exit the industry.

For a better understanding of the difference between short-run and long-run equilibrium, consider the effect of an increase in demand on an industry with free entry that is initially in long-run equilibrium. Panel (b) in **Figure 3.7-3** shows how the market

Ozimages/Alamy

A market is in **long-run market equilibrium** when the quantity supplied equals the quantity demanded, given that sufficient time has elapsed for producers to enter or exit the industry.

FIGURE 3.7-3 The Effect of an Increase in Demand in the Short Run and the Long Run for a Constant-Cost Industry

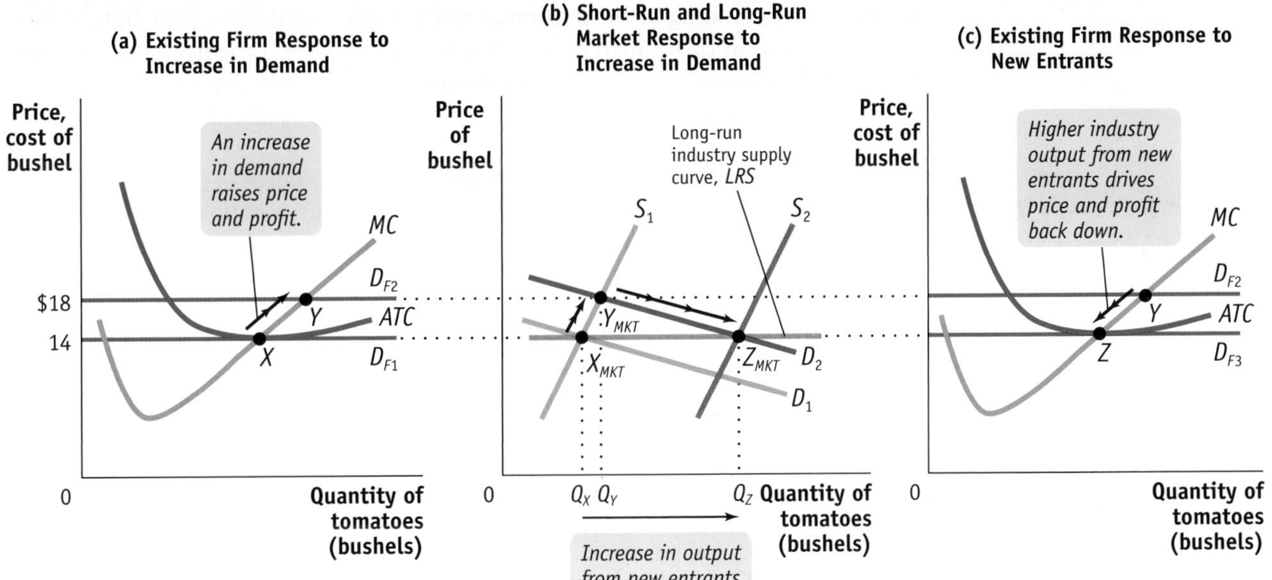

An existing firm makes zero economic profit, operating at point *X* in panel (a) at the minimum of average total cost. Demand increases as D_1 shifts rightward to D_2 in panel (b), raising the market price from $14 to $18. Existing firms increase their output, and industry output moves along the short-run industry supply curve S_1 to a short-run equilibrium at point Y_{MKT}. Correspondingly, the existing firm in panel (a) moves from point *X* to point *Y* as its demand rises from D_{F1} to D_{F2}. But at a price of $18, existing firms are profitable. As shown in panel (b), in the long run, new firms enter and the short-run industry supply curve shifts rightward. This continues until the supply curve reaches S_2 and the new equilibrium point is Z_{MKT}. Like X_{MKT}, Z_{MKT} is a both a short-run and a long-run equilibrium point because the existing firms earn zero economic profit and there is no incentive for any firms to enter or exit the industry. Panel (c) shows how an existing firm responds to the decrease in its demand to D_{F3} by moving from point *Y* to point *Z*, returning to its initial output level and zero economic profit. The horizontal *long-run industry supply curve* (*LRS*) passing through points X_{MKT} and Z_{MKT} in panel (b) indicates that in the long run, firms will produce any amount that consumers demand at the break-even price of $14.

AP® ECON TIP

When you are asked to draw side-by-side graphs for a representative firm and for the market in a perfectly competitive industry, draw dotted lines taking the equilibrium price from the market graph over to the firm graph to show your understanding that the firm is a price-taker.

adjusts; panels (a) and (c) show how a representative existing firm behaves during the process.

In panel (b) of Figure 3.7-3, D_1 is the initial demand curve and S_1 is the initial short-run industry supply curve. Their intersection at point X_{MKT} is both a short-run and a long-run market equilibrium because the equilibrium price of $14 leads to zero economic profit – and therefore neither entry nor exit. Point X_{MKT} corresponds to point X in panel (a), where an existing firm is operating at the minimum of its average total cost curve.

Now suppose that the demand curve shifts out for some reason to D_2. As shown in panel (b), in the short run, industry output moves along the short-run industry supply curve, S_1, to the new short-run market equilibrium at point Y_{MKT}, the intersection of S_1 and D_2. The market price rises to $18 per bushel, and industry output increases from Q_X to Q_Y. This corresponds to an existing firm's movement from point X to point Y in panel (a) as the firm increases its output in response to the rise in its demand curve (which also represents price and marginal revenue) from D_{F1} to D_{F2}.

We know that point Y_{MKT} is not a long-run equilibrium because $18 is higher than the minimum average total cost, so existing firms are making economic profit. This will lead additional firms to enter the industry. Over time, entry will cause the short-run industry supply curve to shift to the right. In the long run, the short-run industry supply curve will have shifted out to S_2, and the equilibrium will be at point Z_{MKT} – with the price falling back to $14 per bushel and industry output increasing yet again, from Q_Y to Q_Z. Like point X_{MKT} before the increase in demand, point Z_{MKT} is both a short-run and a long-run market equilibrium.

AP® ECON TIP

Approach changes that have long-run repercussions one small step at a time. First, show the initial change on your graph. Then, analyze the short-run effects of that change. Finally, focus on the adjustments that lead to long-run equilibrium.

Panel (c) illustrates the effect of entry on an existing firm with the movement from point Y to point Z along the firm's supply curve. The firm reduces its output in response to the fall in the market price, which lowers the firm's demand curve from D_{F2} in panel (a) to D_{F3} in panel (c). The firm ultimately arrives back at its original output quantity, corresponding to the minimum of its average total cost curve. In fact, every firm that is now in the industry – the initial set of firms and the new entrants – will operate at the minimum of the firm's average total cost curve, at point Z. This means that the entire increase in industry output, from Q_X to Q_Z, comes from production by new entrants.

The **long-run industry supply curve** shows how the quantity supplied responds to the price once firms have had time to enter or exit the industry.

In a **constant-cost industry**, the firms' cost curves are unaffected by changes in the size of the industry and the long-run industry supply curve is horizontal (perfectly elastic).

The line labeled *LRS* that passes through points X_{MKT} and Z_{MKT} in panel (b) is the **long-run industry supply curve**. It shows how the quantity supplied by an industry responds to the price, given that firms have had time to enter or exit the industry.

In our organic tomato market, the long-run industry supply curve is horizontal at $14. That means that in this industry, supply is *perfectly elastic* in the long run: given time to enter or exit, firms will supply any quantity that consumers demand at a price of $14. Perfectly elastic long-run industry supply is characteristic of a **constant-cost industry**. In a constant-cost industry, the firms' cost curves are unaffected by changes in the size of the industry, either because there is a perfectly elastic supply of inputs, or because the industry's demand for inputs is too small relative to the overall input market to influence the price of inputs. For example, the wooden pencil industry can expand without causing a significant increase in the price of wood.

Increasing-Cost Industry

In an **increasing-cost industry**, the firms' production costs increase with the size of the industry and the long-run industry supply curve is upward-sloping.

In an **increasing-cost industry**, even the long-run industry supply curve slopes upward. The usual reason is that producers must use a significant amount of an input that is in limited supply (that is, the input's supply is at least somewhat *inelastic*). As the industry expands, the price of that input is driven up. Consequently, the firms' production costs rise. An example is the cotton clothing industry, in which an expansion could drive up the price of cotton. **Figure 3.7-4** illustrates the short-run and long-run effects of an increase in demand in an increasing-cost industry. In panel (b), D_1 is the initial demand curve for cotton pants, and S_1 is the initial short-run industry supply curve. The market equilibrium at point X_{MKT} corresponds to point X in panel (a), where an individual firm is operating at the minimum of its average total cost curve.

FIGURE 3.7-4 The Effect of an Increase in Demand in the Short Run and the Long Run in an Increasing-Cost Industry

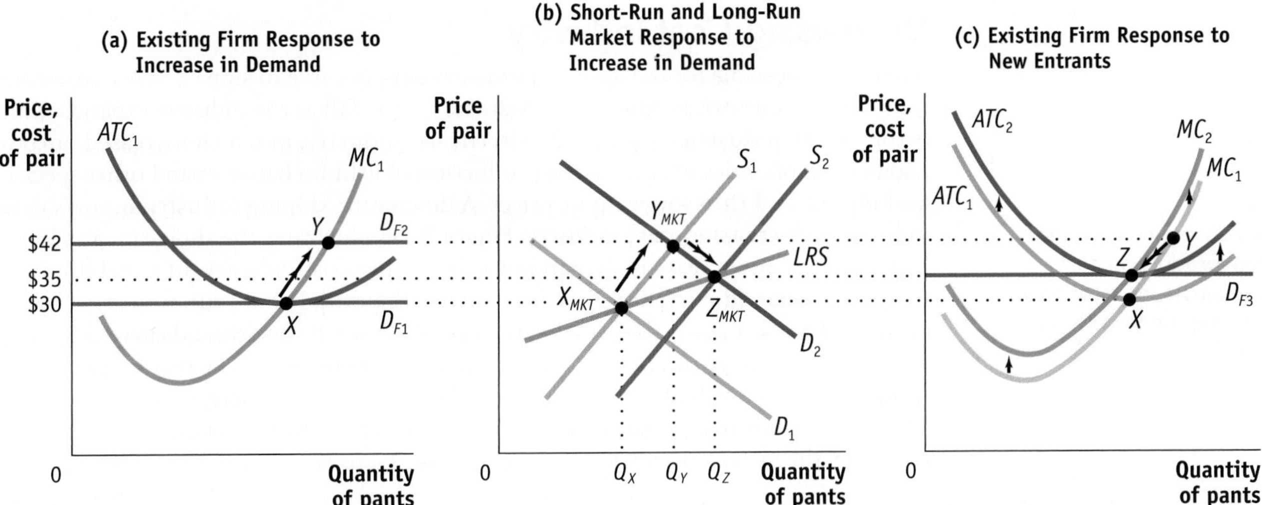

In an increasing-cost industry, an increase in demand leads to a higher price both in the short run *and* in the long run. Suppose demand increases from D_1 to D_2, as shown in panel (b). This raises the market price to \$42. Existing firms increase their output, and industry output expands along the short-run industry supply curve, S_1, to a short-run equilibrium at point Y_{MKT}. The increase in output from Q_X to Q_Y is the result of existing firms increasing their output, as shown for a representative firm by the move from point *X* to point *Y* in panel (a). Because the new price is above the minimum average total cost, economic profit attracts new entrants in the long run, shifting the short-run industry supply curve rightward and lowering the market price. Meanwhile, industry expansion drives up the cost of inputs and shifts the firms' cost curves upward, as shown in panel (c). This continues until the falling equilibrium price meets the rising minimum average total cost. As shown in panel (b), that occurs at equilibrium point Z_{MKT} with a price of \$35. In the long run, an existing firm moves from point *Y* to point *Z* in panel (c) and earns zero economic profit. The upward-sloping line passing through points X_{MKT} and Z_{MKT}, labeled *LRS*, is the long-run industry supply curve.

Now suppose the demand curve shifts out to D_2. As shown in panel (b), in the short run, industry output expands along the short-run industry supply curve, S_1, to the new short-run market equilibrium at point Y_{MKT}, the intersection of S_1 and D_2. The market price rises from \$30 to \$42 per pair and the industry output increases from Q_X to Q_Y as a result of higher output levels at existing firms. This change is shown for a representative firm in panel (a) by a movement from point *X* to point *Y* in response to the increase in the firm's demand curve from D_{F1} to D_{F2}.

At the new market price, existing firms earn economic profit, so additional firms enter the industry in the long run. Entry shifts the short-run industry supply curve to the right and lowers the price of pants. At the same time, increasing demand for cotton drives up the cost of this input. The resulting rise in input costs shifts the marginal and average total cost curves upward for firms. This process continues until the falling market price and the rising minimum average total cost meet somewhere in between the initial price of \$30 and the short-run price of \$42. In Figure 3.7-4, they meet at a price of \$35, after the short-run supply curve has shifted out to S_2 and the cost of making each pair of pants has risen by \$5.

When the market reaches long-run equilibrium at point Z_{MKT}, each firm faces a demand curve of D_{F3}, as shown in panel (c). Firms earn zero economic profit, and there is no incentive for additional entry. Assuming that the cost increase is the same for each unit of output, each of the original firms ends up making the same quantity of output as it did before the increase in demand. If the cost increase is not the same for each unit of output, the cost curves will not shift straight up as they did here, so the new profit-maximizing quantity of output could be more or less than before. For this increasing-cost industry, the long-run industry supply curve *LRS* slopes upward as it passes through points X_{MKT} and Z_{MKT} in panel (b).

A decrease in demand triggers the same process in reverse: the lower market price causes losses and, in the long run, the exit of firms. As firms exit, the market price rises. At the same time, the contraction of the industry lowers the cost of inputs and shifts the cost curves down until the falling minimum average total cost meets the rising market price.

Decreasing-Cost Industry

In a **decreasing-cost industry,** the firms' production costs decrease as the industry grows and the long-run supply curve is downward-sloping.

Finally, it is possible for the long-run industry supply curve to slope downward, a condition that occurs when the firms' production costs fall as the industry expands. This is the case in industries such as the electric car industry, in which increased output allows for economies of scale in the production of lithium batteries and other specialized inputs, and thus lower input prices. A downward-sloping industry supply curve indicates a **decreasing-cost industry. Figure 3.7-5** illustrates the short-run and long-run effects of an increase in demand in a decreasing-cost industry. In panel (b), D_1 is the initial demand curve for electric cars, S_1 is the initial short-run industry supply curve, and point X_{MKT} is the initial market equilibrium. If the demand curve shifts out to D_2, the new short-run market equilibrium is at point Y_{MKT}. The market price rises from \$40,000 to \$49,000 per electric car, and industry output increases from Q_X to Q_Y. This corresponds to an existing firm's movement from point X to point Y in panel (a), caused by the increase in its demand curve from D_{F1} to D_{F2}.

FIGURE 3.7-5 **The Effect of an Increase in Demand in the Short Run and the Long Run in a Decreasing-Cost Industry**

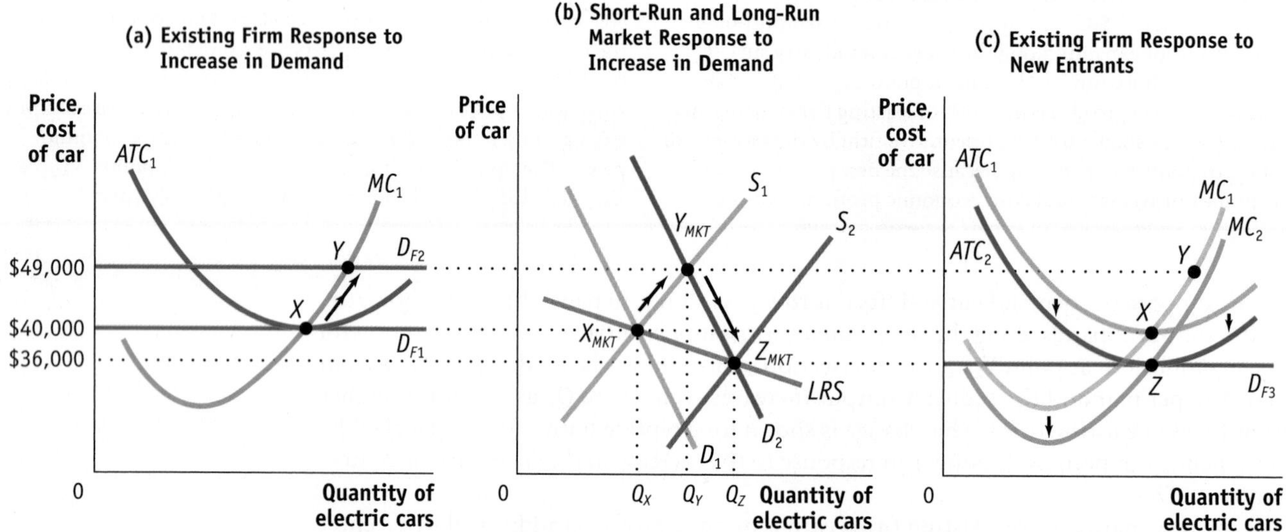

In a decreasing-cost industry, an increase in demand leads to a higher price in the short run and a lower price in the long run. Suppose demand increases from D_1 to D_2 as shown in panel (b). Existing firms increase their output in response to the higher price, and industry output expands along the short-run industry supply curve, S_1, to a short-run equilibrium at point Y_{MKT}. Economic profit attracts new entrants in the long run, shifting the short-run industry supply curve rightward and lowering the market price. Meanwhile, industry expansion lowers the cost of inputs and shifts the firms' cost curves downward, as shown in panel (c). This continues until the falling equilibrium price catches up to the falling minimum average total cost. As shown in panel (b), that occurs at equilibrium point Z_{MKT}. In the long run, an existing firm moves from Y to Z in panel (c) and earns zero economic profit. The downward-sloping line passing through points X_{MKT} and Z_{MKT}, labeled *LRS* in panel (b), is the long-run industry supply curve.

At the new market price, economic profit attracts additional firms. Entry shifts the short-run industry supply curve to the right and lowers the price of electric cars. At the same time, increasing demand for lithium batteries allows for economies of scale in battery production and lowers the cost of this input. The resulting decrease in input costs shifts the marginal and average total cost curves downward for firms. This process continues until the falling market price catches up to the falling minimum average total cost somewhere below the initial price of \$40,000. In Figure 3.7-5, that occurs at a price of \$36,000, after the short-run supply curve has shifted out to S_2 in panel (b).

At the long-run equilibrium point Z_{MKT}, each firm faces a demand curve of D_{F3}, as shown in panel (c). Firms earn zero economic profit, and there is no incentive for additional entry. Assuming that the cost decrease is the same for each car produced, each firm ends up making the same quantity of cars as it did before the increase in demand. For a decreasing-cost industry, the long-run industry supply curve *LRS* slopes downward as it passes through points X_{MKT} and Z_{MKT} in panel (b).

Regardless of whether the long-run industry supply curve is horizontal, upward-sloping, or downward-sloping, the long-run price elasticity of supply is *higher* than the short-run price elasticity whenever there is free entry and exit. As shown in **Figure 3.7-6**, the long-run industry supply curve is always flatter than the short-run industry supply curve. The reason is entry and exit: a price increase caused by an increase in demand attracts new firms, resulting in a rise in industry output and an eventual fall in price; a price drop caused by a decrease in demand causes some firms to exit, leading to a fall in industry output and an eventual increase in price.

FIGURE 3.7-6 **Comparing the Short-Run and Long-Run Industry Supply Curves**

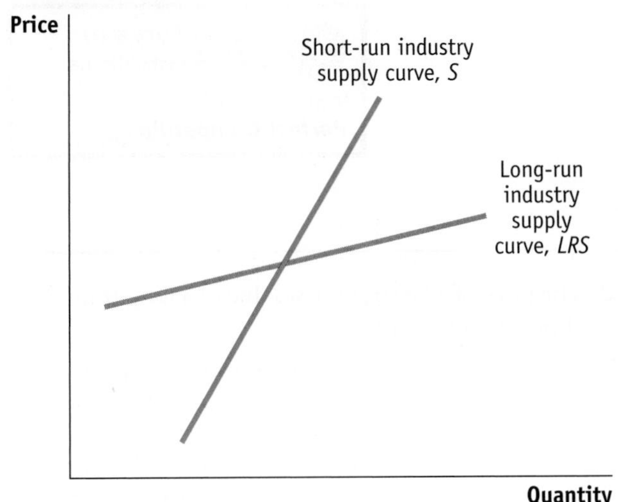

As a result of the entry and exit of firms in the long run, the long-run industry supply curve is always flatter—more elastic—than the short-run industry supply curve.

Efficiency in Long-Run Equilibrium

Our analysis leads us to three conclusions about efficiency in the long-run equilibrium of a perfectly competitive industry. These results will be important in our discussion of how monopoly gives rise to inefficiency in Unit 4.

First, when a perfectly competitive industry is in equilibrium, all firms produce the quantity of output that equates the marginal cost and the market price—that is, $P = MC$. This outcome leads to **allocative efficiency**, meaning that it yields the mix of goods and services that society most values, as discussed in Modules 1.3 and 2.8. This efficiency comes from the production of more of the good until the price consumers are willing to pay—an indication of the *marginal benefit* received from the good—equals the marginal cost of making it. Each unit beyond the quantity that equates price and marginal cost has a marginal cost that exceeds the marginal benefit, so additional units should not be made. And to stop before the quantity that equates price and marginal cost would be to miss out on opportunities for net gains from units that can be produced at a marginal cost that is below their value to consumers.

Allocative efficiency is achieved when the goods and services produced are those most valued by society.

Second, in a perfectly competitive industry with free entry and exit, each firm will earn zero economic profit in the long-run equilibrium. Each firm produces the quantity of output that minimizes its average total cost—corresponding to point *Z* in

Productive efficiency is achieved when firms minimize the average cost of producing their goods.

panel (c) of Figures 3.7-3, 3.7-4, and 3.7-5. As a result, a perfectly competitive industry achieves **productive efficiency** because the total cost of producing the industry's output is minimized.

Third, in the long-run market equilibrium of a perfectly competitive industry, the consumers who are willing to pay an amount greater than or equal to the sellers' marginal cost actually get the good. Economists call this *distributive efficiency*. No mutually beneficial transactions go unexploited because the market price matches the consumers who are willing to pay the most for the good with the sellers who have a cost of production that is less than or equal to the market price.

So the long-run equilibrium of a perfectly competitive industry delivers efficiency. There is allocative efficiency because $P = MC$; there is productive efficiency because costs are minimized and no resources are wasted; and there is distributive efficiency because the goods are distributed to the consumers who are willing to pay the most for them. Moreover, these conditions tend to persist over time as the situation changes: the force of competition makes producers responsive to changes in consumers' desires and to changes in technology.

Adventures in AP® Economics

Watch the video: ***Perfect Competition***

Module 3.7  Review

Check Your Understanding

1. Which of the following events will induce firms to enter an industry? Which will induce firms to exit? When will entry or exit cease? Explain your answers.
   a. A technological advance lowers the fixed cost of production of every firm in the industry.
   b. The wages paid to workers in the industry rise for an extended period of time.
   c. A permanent change in consumer tastes increases demand for the good.
   d. The price of a key input rises due to a long-term shortage of that input.
2. Assume that the egg industry is perfectly competitive and is in long-run equilibrium with a perfectly elastic long-run industry supply curve. Health concerns about cholesterol then lead to a decrease in demand. Construct a figure similar to Figure 3.7-3, showing the short-run behavior of the industry and how long-run equilibrium is reestablished.

Tackle the AP® Test: Multiple-Choice Questions

1. In the long run, a perfectly competitive firm will earn
   a. a negative market return.
   b. a positive profit.
   c. a loss.
   d. a normal profit.
   e. excess profit.
2. With perfect competition, productive efficiency is generally attained in
   a. the short run but not the long run.
   b. the long run but not the short run.
   c. both the short run and the long run.
   d. neither the short run nor the long run.
   e. specific firms only.
3. Compared to the short-run industry supply curve, the long-run industry supply curve will be more
   a. elastic.
   b. inelastic.
   c. steeply sloped.
   d. profitable.
   e. accurate.
4. Which of the following is generally true in a perfectly competitive industry?
   a. A firm's supply curve lies above its marginal cost curve.
   b. Firms have fixed costs in the long run.
   c. The short-run market equilibrium is efficient if firms earn a positive profit.
   d. Firms face barriers to entry into the industry.
   e. Firms maximize profit at the output level at which $P = MC$.

5. What will happen in a perfectly competitive industry in response to firms earning a positive economic profit?
   a. Firms will exit the industry.
   b. The short-run industry supply curve will shift to the right.
   c. The short-run industry supply curve will shift to the left.
   d. Firm output will increase.
   e. Market price will increase.

6. In a perfectly competitive, decreasing-cost industry, the long-run industry supply curve is
   a. vertical.
   b. upward-sloping.
   c. horizontal.
   d. downward-sloping.
   e. upward-sloping at low quantities and downward-sloping at high quantities.

7. In a perfectly competitive, constant-cost industry, an increase in demand leads to which of the following in the long run?
   a. an increase in price
   b. an increase in the output of firms that were operating when the demand increased
   c. a decrease in industry output
   d. an increase in industry output
   e. positive profit for firms

Tackle the AP® Test: Free-Response Questions

1. Draw a correctly labeled graph showing a perfectly competitive firm in long-run equilibrium.

Rubric for FRQ 1 (7 points)

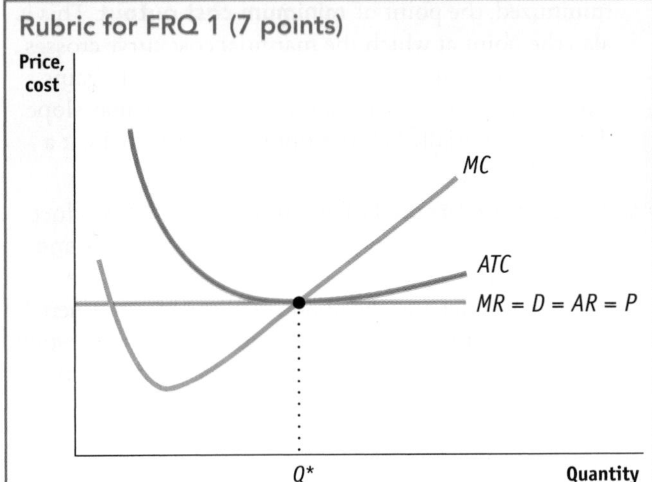

1 point: Axes are correctly labeled.

1 point: Demand curve is horizontal and labeled with some combination of "P," "MR," "AR," or "D."

1 point: Marginal cost curve is labeled and slopes upward.

1 point: Profit-maximizing quantity is labeled on horizontal axis where MC = MR.

1 point: Average total cost curve is labeled and U-shaped.

1 point: Average total cost is equal to price at the profit-maximizing output.

1 point: Marginal cost curve crosses the average total cost curve at the lowest point on the average total cost curve.

2. Suppose that paper is produced in a perfectly competitive, increasing-cost industry.
   a. Draw correctly labeled side-by-side graphs for a representative firm and for the paper market in long-run equilibrium.
      i. Label the market equilibrium price "P_{M1}" and the equilibrium quantity "Q_{M1}."
      ii. Label the firm's marginal cost "MC_1," its average total cost "ATC_1," its demand curve "D_{F1}," and its profit-maximizing price and quantity "P_{F1}" and "Q_{F1}," respectively.
   b. Now suppose that increased reliance on digital communications causes a decrease in the demand for paper. Show the following on the graphs you drew for part a:
      i. The new short-run market equilibrium price and quantity, labeled "P_{M2}" and "Q_{M2}."
      ii. The new short-run profit-maximizing price and quantity for the representative firm, labeled "P_{F2}" and "Q_{F2}."
   c. Now suppose the market and the representative firm have adjusted to a new long-run equilibrium.
      i. Label the new equilibrium market price and quantity "P_{M3}" and "Q_{M3}."
      ii. Explain how and why the representative firm's new average total cost curve differs from ATC_1.
      iii. Draw the long-run supply curve for the market and label it "LRS." **(8 points)**

UNIT 3

Review

Adventures in AP® Economics Videos

Mod 3.2: Production Costs
Mod 3.3: Returns to Scale
Mod 3.7: Perfect Competition

UNIT 3 Review Video

economics by example
Is Adam Smith Rolling Over in His Grave?

Module 3.1

1. The relationship between inputs and output is represented by a firm's **production function**. In the **short run**, the quantity of a **fixed input** cannot be varied, but the quantity of a **variable input**, by definition, can. In the **long run**, the quantities of all inputs can be varied. For a given amount of the fixed input, the **total product curve** shows how the quantity of output changes as the quantity of the variable input changes. The **marginal product** of an input is the increase in output that results from using one more unit of that input.
2. There are **diminishing returns to an input** when its marginal product declines as more of the input is used, holding the quantity of all other inputs fixed.

Module 3.2

3. **Total cost**, represented by the **total cost curve**, is equal to the sum of **fixed cost**, which does not depend on output, and **variable cost**, which does depend on output. Due to diminishing returns, **marginal cost**—the increase in total cost generated by producing one more unit of output—normally increases as output increases. The **marginal cost curve** shows the marginal cost for each unit.
4. **Average total cost** (also known as **average cost**) is the total cost divided by the quantity of output. Economists believe that **U-shaped average total cost curves** are typical because average total cost consists of two parts: **average fixed cost**, which falls when output increases (the spreading effect), and **average variable cost**, which rises with output (the diminishing returns effect).
5. When average total cost is U-shaped, the bottom of the U is the level of output at which average total cost is minimized, the point of **minimum-cost output**. This is also the point at which the marginal cost curve crosses the average total cost curve from below. Due to gains from specialization, the marginal cost curve may slope downward initially before sloping upward, giving it a "swoosh" shape.
6. The **average product** of an input is the total product divided by the quantity of the input, and the **average product curve** shows the relationship between the average product and the quantity of the input. When labor is the only variable input and the wage is constant, average variable cost falls when average product rises, and average variable cost rises when average product falls. Likewise, marginal cost rises when marginal product falls and vice versa.

Module 3.3

7. In the long run, a firm can change its fixed input and its level of fixed cost. By accepting higher fixed cost, a firm can lower its variable cost for any given output level, and vice versa. The **long-run average total cost curve** shows the relationship between output and average total cost when fixed cost has been chosen to minimize average total cost at each level of output. A firm moves along its short-run average total cost curve as it changes the quantity of output, and it returns to a point on both its short-run and long-run average total cost curves once it has adjusted fixed cost to its new output level. The **minimum efficient scale** is the smallest quantity at which a firm's long-run average total cost is minimized.
8. As output increases, there are **economies of scale** if long-run average total cost decreases and **diseconomies of scale** if long-run average total cost increases. As all inputs are increased by the same proportion, there are **increasing returns to scale** if output increases by a larger proportion than the inputs, **decreasing returns to scale** if output increases by a smaller proportion, and **constant returns to scale** if output increases by the same proportion.

Module 3.4

9. The cost of using a resource for a particular activity is the opportunity cost of that resource. Some opportunity costs are **explicit costs**; they involve a direct payment of money. Other opportunity costs, however, are **implicit costs**; they involve no outlay of money but represent the inflows of money that are forgone. Both explicit and implicit costs should be taken into account when making decisions. Firms use capital and their owners' time, so firms should base decisions on **economic profit**, which takes into account implicit costs such as the opportunity cost of the owners' time and the **implicit cost of capital**. **Accounting profit**, which firms calculate for the purposes of taxes and public reporting, is often considerably larger than economic profit because it includes only explicit costs and depreciation, not implicit costs. Finally, **normal profit** is a term used to describe an economic profit equal to zero—a profit just high enough to justify the use of resources in an activity.

Module 3.5

10. The **marginal revenue curve** shows the **marginal revenue** for each unit. A producer chooses output according to the **profit-maximizing rule**: produce the quantity at which marginal revenue equals marginal cost. More generally, the **principle of marginal analysis** suggests that every activity should continue until marginal benefit equals marginal cost. A **sunk cost** is a cost that has been incurred and cannot be recovered. A sunk cost should be ignored in decisions about future actions.

Module 3.6

11. A producer chooses output according to the profit-maximization rule: produce the quantity at which the price equals the marginal cost. However, a firm that produces the profit-maximizing quantity may not earn a positive economic profit.
12. A firm is profitable if its total revenue exceeds its total cost or, equivalently, if the average revenue exceeds the average total cost. A firm's **average revenue** is the average amount it takes in per unit of output, which equals the market price in a perfectly competitive market. The **break-even price** is the minimum average total cost. If the market price exceeds the break-even price, the firm is profitable. If the market price is less than the minimum average total cost, the firm is unprofitable. If the market price is equal to the minimum average total cost, the firm breaks even. When profitable, the firm's per-unit profit is $P - ATC$; when unprofitable, its per-unit loss is $ATC - P$.
13. A firm's fixed cost is irrelevant to its optimal short-run production decision. That decision depends on the firm's **shut-down price**—its minimum average variable cost—along with its marginal cost and the market price. When the market price is equal to or exceeds the shut-down price, the firm produces the quantity at which the marginal cost equals the market price. When the market price falls below the shut-down price, the firm ceases production in the short run. These decisions determine the shape of the **short-run firm supply curve**.
14. Fixed cost matters over time. If the market price is below the minimum average total cost for an extended period of time, firms will exit the industry in the long run. If the market price is above the minimum average total cost, existing firms are profitable and new firms will enter the industry in the long run.

Module 3.7

15. In a **perfectly competitive market**, all firms are **price-taking firms** and all consumers are **price-taking consumers**—no one's actions can influence the market price. Consumers are normally price-takers, but firms often are not. In a **perfectly competitive industry**, every firm in the industry is a price-taker.
16. There are four necessary conditions for a perfectly competitive market: there are many firms, none of which has a large **market share**, and the industry produces a **standardized product** or **commodity**—goods that consumers regard as equivalent. There is **free entry and exit** into and out of the industry, and buyers and sellers have full information about the available products and prices.
17. The **industry supply curve** depends on the time period (short run or long run). When the number of firms is fixed, the **short-run industry supply curve** applies. The short-run market equilibrium occurs where the short-run industry supply curve and the demand curve intersect.

18. With sufficient time for entry into and exit from an industry, the **long-run industry supply curve** applies. The **long-run market equilibrium** occurs at the intersection of the long-run industry supply curve and the demand curve. At this point, no producer has an incentive to enter or exit. The long-run industry supply curve is horizontal for a **constant-cost industry**. It may slope upward if the industry's demand represents a significant portion of the overall demand for an input, resulting in an **increasing-cost industry**. It may even slope downward, as in the case of a **decreasing-cost industry**. But the long-run industry supply curve is always more elastic than the short-run industry supply curve.

19. In the long-run market equilibrium of a competitive industry, profit maximization leads each firm to produce at the same marginal cost, which is equal to the market price. Free entry and exit means that each firm earns zero economic profit—producing the output corresponding to its minimum average total cost. So the total cost of production of an industry's output is minimized and **productive efficiency** is achieved. The outcome also achieves **allocative efficiency** because the price equals the marginal cost, and it achieves *distributive efficiency* because every consumer with a willingness to pay greater than or equal to the marginal cost gets the good.

Key Terms

Production function, p. 584
Fixed input, p. 584
Variable input, p. 584
Long run, p. 584
Short run, p. 584
Total product curve, p. 585
Marginal product, p. 585
Diminishing returns to an input, p. 586
Fixed cost (*FC*), p. 590
Variable cost (*VC*), p. 590
Total cost (*TC*), p. 590
Total cost curve, p. 591
Marginal cost, p. 592
Marginal cost curve, p. 593
Average total cost (*ATC*), p. 594
Average cost, p. 594
Average fixed cost (*AFC*), p. 595
Average variable cost (*AVC*), p. 595
Minimum-cost output, p. 597
Average product, p. 600
Average product curve, p. 600
Long-run average total cost curve (*LRATC*), p. 606
Economies of scale, p. 607
Increasing returns to scale, p. 607
Minimum efficient scale, p. 607
Diseconomies of scale, p. 607
Decreasing returns to scale, p. 608
Constant returns to scale, p. 608
Explicit cost, p. 611
Implicit cost, p. 611
Accounting profit, p. 612
Economic profit, p. 612
Implicit cost of capital, p. 613
Normal profit, p. 614
Principle of marginal analysis, p. 617
Marginal revenue, p. 617
Profit-maximizing rule, p. 617
Marginal revenue curve, p. 618
Average revenue, p. 622
Break-even price, p. 625
Shut-down price, p. 626
Sunk cost, p. 626
Short-run firm supply curve, p. 627
Price-taking firm, p. 632
Price-taking consumer, p. 632
Perfectly competitive market, p. 633
Perfectly competitive industry, p. 633
Market share, p. 633
Standardized product, p. 634
Commodity, p. 634
Free entry and exit, p. 634
Industry supply curve, p. 634
Short-run industry supply curve, p. 635
Long-run market equilibrium, p. 637
Long-run industry supply curve, p. 638
Constant-cost industry, p. 638
Increasing-cost industry, p. 638
Decreasing-cost industry, p. 640
Allocative efficiency, p. 641
Productive efficiency, p. 642

AP® Exam Practice Questions

Multiple-Choice Questions

1. Consider the data about the cost of each year of college in the table below:

Opportunity Cost of a Year of College

Explicit cost		Implicit cost	
Tuition	$17,000	Forgone salary	$32,000
Books and supplies	1,000		
Computer	1,500		
Total explicit cost	19,500	Total implicit cost	32,000
Total opportunity cost = Total explicit cost + Total implicit cost = $51,500			

A rational person would attend another year of college if the additional income expected plus the value of improved quality of life were worth at least
a. $17,000.
b. $19,500.
c. $32,000.
d. $51,500.
e. $83,500.

2. Accounting profit can
a. only be greater than economic profit.
b. only be less than economic profit.
c. be equal to or more than economic profit.
d. be equal to or less than economic profit.
e. only be equal to economic profit.

3. Which kind of profit is just enough to keep a firm operating in the long run?
  a. normal
  b. economic
  c. accounting
  d. implicit
  e. explicit

Refer to the cost data in the table below to answer Question 4.

Quantity of tomatoes Q (bushels)	Total cost *TC*	Marginal cost of bushel *MC* = $\Delta TC/\Delta Q$
0	$14	
1	30	$16
2	36	6
3	44	8
4	56	12
5	72	16
6	92	20
7	116	24

4. If this business can sell all it can produce at a market price of $16, the firm should produce how many units in order to maximize profits?
  a. 1
  b. 3
  c. 5
  d. 6
  e. 7

5. Assume a perfectly competitive firm is producing at a level of output where marginal revenue is greater than marginal cost. What should the firm do to maximize profits?
  a. continue to produce at that level
  b. increase output
  c. decrease output
  d. raise prices
  e. lower prices

6. When a firm is producing where marginal cost is equal to marginal revenue, the firm
  a. may be making profits or losses.
  b. will definitely be maximizing profits.
  c. should produce more to maximize profits.
  d. should produce less to maximize profits.
  e. will definitely be minimizing losses.

7. A fixed input
  a. never changes.
  b. is a long-run phenomenon.
  c. does not change with the output level in the short run.
  d. causes marginal cost to fall as it is increased.
  e. causes marginal cost to rise as it is increased.

8. If marginal product is positive and declining as more workers are hired, then total product is
  a. decreasing at an increasing rate.
  b. decreasing at a decreasing rate.
  c. increasing at an increasing rate.
  d. increasing at a decreasing rate.
  e. increasing at a constant rate.

9. Diminishing marginal returns always involve
  a. too much plant capacity.
  b. a rapid expansion of plant size.
  c. a slow expansion of plant size.
  d. a fixed input.
  e. inputs that are all variable.

10. If marginal cost is positive and rising as more output is produced, then total cost is
  a. decreasing at an increasing rate.
  b. decreasing at a decreasing rate.
  c. increasing at an increasing rate.
  d. increasing at a decreasing rate.
  e. increasing at a constant rate.

11. Marginal cost rises due to
  a. diminishing marginal returns.
  b. increasing marginal returns.
  c. constant returns to scale.
  d. increasing returns to scale.
  e. increasing average returns.

12. Which of the following statements describes the relationship between the marginal cost curve and the average cost curve?
  a. When marginal cost is rising, average cost must be rising.
  b. When average cost is falling, average cost must be falling.
  c. When marginal cost is above average cost, average cost must be rising.
  d. When marginal cost is below average cost, average cost must be rising.
  e. When marginal cost is above average cost, average cost must be falling.

13. In the short run, what happens to average fixed cost as output increases?
  a. It remains constant.
  b. It falls and then rises after a certain output level.
  c. It rises initially, and then falls continuously.
  d. It falls continuously.
  e. It rises continuously.

14. If at the current level of output of 200 units, average variable cost is $10 per unit and average total cost is $15 per unit, then
  a. total fixed cost is equal to $1,000.
  b. total fixed cost is equal to $2,000.
  c. total fixed cost is equal to $3,000.
  d. marginal cost is equal to $5.
  e. marginal cost is equal to $25.

15. If labor is the only variable input and the wage rate is constant, marginal cost reaches its minimum when
   a. marginal product reaches its maximum.
   b. average product reaches its maximum.
   c. marginal product reaches its minimum.
   d. average product reaches its minimum.
   e. average cost reaches its minimum.

16. The spreading effect causes the average total cost curve to
   a. rise, while the diminishing returns effect causes it to fall.
   b. rise, as does the diminishing returns effect.
   c. fall, while the diminishing returns effect causes it to rise.
   d. fall, as does the diminishing returns effect.
   e. remain constant until the beginning of the diminishing marginal returns effect.

17. If marginal cost is rising and lies above average variable cost, then average total cost
   a. may be rising or falling.
   b. will definitely be rising.
   c. will definitely be falling.
   d. will definitely be constant.
   e. None of the above are correct.

18. If the average product of labor is rising as more workers are hired, then
   a. the marginal product of labor must be rising.
   b. the marginal product of labor must be falling.
   c. the marginal product of labor must be higher than the average product of labor.
   d. the average total cost must be rising.
   e. the marginal cost must be falling.

19. Which of the following causes the long-run average cost curve to eventually slope upward?
   a. economies of scale
   b. economies of scope
   c. diseconomies of scale
   d. overcrowding of the fixed factors of production
   e. diminishing marginal returns

20. When a firm makes production decisions, sunk costs should be
   a. set equal to the variable cost.
   b. set equal to the marginal cost.
   c. set equal to the total cost.
   d. subtracted from the fixed cost to determine profit.
   e. ignored.

21. The profit-maximizing rule says that to earn as much profit as possible, a firm should produce the quantity of output that equates the
   a. marginal revenue and marginal cost.
   b. marginal cost and average total cost.
   c. average total cost and average revenue.
   d. marginal revenue and average total cost.
   e. marginal cost and fixed cost.

22. A firm should continue to produce in the short run as long as the price is at least equal to the
   a. *MR*.
   b. *MC*.
   c. minimum *ATC*.
   d. minimum *AVC*.
   e. *AFC*.

23. In a perfectly competitive industry, the short-run industry supply curve is
   a. horizontal.
   b. vertical.
   c. downward-sloping.
   d. less elastic than the long-run industry supply curve.
   e. more elastic than the long-run industry supply curve.

24. Diseconomies of scale can be caused by
   a. increasing returns to scale.
   b. overcrowding of the fixed factors of production.
   c. increasing average fixed cost.
   d. decreasing average fixed cost.
   e. communication problems.

25. At prices that motivate the firm to produce at all, the short-run supply curve for a perfect competitor corresponds to which curve?
   a. the *ATC* curve
   b. the *AVC* curve
   c. the *MC* curve
   d. the *AFC* curve
   e. the *MR* curve

26. If a perfectly competitive firm decides to operate at a loss in the short run, it will minimize that loss by producing the quantity at which
   a. the *ATC* is minimized.
   b. the *AVC* is minimized.
   c. the *MC* equals the price.
   d. the *ATC* equals the price.
   e. the *AVC* equals the price.

Free-Response Questions

1. Draw a correctly labeled graph showing a perfectly competitive firm operating at a price that would lead it to stay open in the short run, but to shut down in the long run. Label the loss-minimizing quantity Q^* and shade the area that represents the firm's loss. **(10 points)**

2. Suppose RunCo Shoes produces running shoes using robots and a fixed amount of labor to oversee and repair the robots. The table below indicates how the number of pairs of running shoes produced and the total cost depend on the quantity of robots acquired.

Robots	Total output (pairs)	Total cost ($)
0	0	40
1	2	90
2	5	140
3	10	190
4	15	240
5	19	290
6	22	340
7	24	390
8	25	440

   a. What is the marginal product of the third robot?

   b. How many robots does RunCo need to acquire before it begins to experience diminishing marginal returns? Explain using numbers from the table.

   c. Calculate the marginal cost of the 15th pair of running shoes. Show your work.

   d. Suppose RunCo can sell any quantity of running shoes to retail stores for $30 per pair:

      i. How many robots should this firm hire in order to maximize profits?

      ii. Calculate the profit at this level of output. Show your work. **(6 points)**

3. Suppose Roland's Roller Blades operates with a nonzero fixed cost, an upward-sloping marginal cost, and a constant marginal revenue.

   a. Draw a correctly labeled graph for this firm and label the following:

      i. marginal cost (*MC*)

      ii. marginal revenue (*MR*)

      iii. average total cost (*ATC*)

      iv. average variable cost (*AVC*)

   b. Label the profit-maximizing quantity of output Q_m.

   c. Suppose that $MC = 5$, $MR = 3$, $ATC = 10$, $AVC = 7$, and $Q_m = 20$. What is the fixed cost? Show your work. **(6 points)**

Imperfect Competition

AP® Economics Skills

1. Principles and Models (1.D)
2. Interpretation (2.C)
4. Graphing and Visuals (4.B, 4.C)

Some Carrots Are More Expensive Than Others

Having studied the behavior of perfectly competitive markets in Unit 3, we are ready to explore market structures with *imperfect competition*. A market's structure is determined by the number of firms in the industry, the type of product being sold, and the existence of barriers to entry. We can think about the four basic market structures as falling along a spectrum from perfect competition at one end to monopoly at the other, with monopolistic competition and oligopoly lying in between. To shed more light on the market structure spectrum, consider two very different markets: the market for carrots and the market for diamonds.

Carrots have long been a popular vegetable on the grocery store aisles, boasting color, crunch, and celebrity endorsements from cartoon rabbits. But when producers started packaging small chunks of carrot as "baby-cut carrots" in the late 1980s, they became the healthy finger food of choice. Demand has remained high ever since, but prices have not. Why? Because the carrot market resembles a perfectly competitive market, so the long-run outcome was as explained in Module 3.7: When rising demand pushed carrot prices upward, the resulting profit for carrot farmers worked like a carrot on a stick to lure new farmers into the market. Low barriers to entry allowed more and more farms to produce carrots until the price was too low to entice new carrot farmers. Today, thanks to market forces, carrot lovers can find store shelves filled with baby-cut carrots at reasonable prices.

In contrast, a *monopoly* has only one seller. For example, in the twentieth century, almost every diamond on the world market came from De Beers, a firm which still controls a quarter of the diamond market. Diamonds are valued not just for their beauty, but also for their rarity. Yet geologists will tell you that diamonds aren't all that rare. In fact, they are among the more common gem-quality stones. Diamonds *seem* rare because De Beers and other firms limit the quantity supplied to the market. De Beers's ownership of many of the world's diamond mines allowed them to control diamond supplies and hindered the ability of competitors to enter the market and increase the available quantity of diamonds.

In this Unit, we will study how markets like those for carrots and diamonds differ, and how these markets respond to market conditions. We will see how firms positioned at opposite ends of the spectrum of market power—from perfect competition to monopoly—make key decisions about output and prices. Then, we will complete our exploration of market structure with a closer look at oligopoly and monopolistic competition.

Wildroze/E+/Getty Images

MODULE 4.1

Introduction to Imperfect Competition

In this Module, you will learn to:

- Describe the principal types of imperfectly competitive markets—monopoly, oligopoly, and monopolistic competition
- Discuss the implications of a firm needing to lower its price to sell more units
- Explain why markets are inefficient when the price exceeds marginal cost

So far, we've learned a lot about one market structure: perfect competition. The reality is that nothing is perfect. Although the structure of many markets resembles perfect competition, there are plenty of cases in which competition is lacking. When the number of firms is small or the products sold by many firms are not alike, the conditions for perfect competition are not met and the market is **imperfectly competitive**. The implications of imperfect competition can include higher prices, lower production levels, lower quality, and inefficiency. In this Module, we begin to explore the principal types of imperfectly competitive markets. The Modules that follow take a deeper dive into each type of imperfect competition among sellers. Module 5.4 in the next Unit discusses the case of *monopsony* in which there is only one *buyer*.

A market that does not meet the requirements for perfect competition is **imperfectly competitive**.

Types of Market Structure

The real world holds a mind-boggling array of different markets. Patterns of firm behavior vary as widely as the markets themselves: in some markets, firms are extremely competitive; in others, they seem to coordinate their actions to limit competition; and some markets are monopolies in which there is no competition at all. A lack of competition gives producers **market power**, which is the ability to affect the prices they receive. To be clear, this is *not* the power to receive any price no matter how high; consumers always have limits on the highest amount they are willing and able to pay for any particular good.

Market power refers to a firm's ability to influence the price it charges for a good or service.

In order to develop principles and make predictions about market and firm behavior, economists have developed four primary models of market structure: *perfect competition*, *monopoly*, *oligopoly*, and *monopolistic competition*. This classification of market structure is based on two dimensions:

- the number of firms in the market (one, few, or many)
- whether the goods offered are identical or *differentiated*

Differentiated goods are goods that are different but considered at least somewhat substitutable by consumers (think Coca-Cola versus Pepsi).

Figure 4.1-1 provides a simple visual summary of the types of market structure classified according to these two dimensions. We present a more detailed summary at the end of the Module. In *perfect competition*, many firms each sell an identical product. In *monopoly*, a single firm sells a single, undifferentiated product. In *oligopoly*, a few firms – more than one but not a large number – sell products that may be either identical or differentiated. And in *monopolistic competition*, many firms each sell a differentiated product (think of producers of economics textbooks).

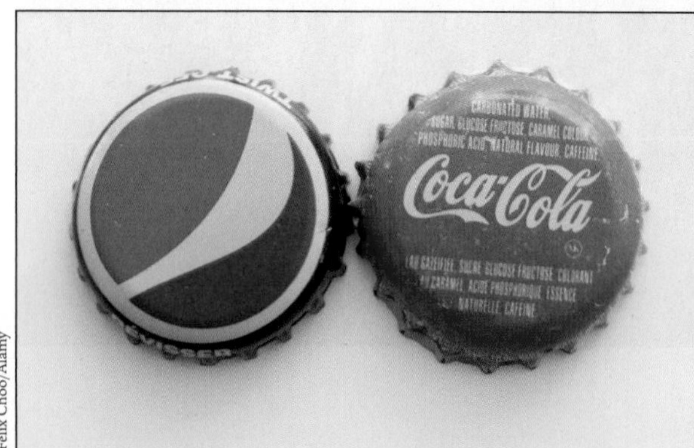

Felix Choo/Alamy

Pepsi and Coca-Cola are considered differentiated goods because they aren't the same, but one can serve as a substitute for the other.

FIGURE 4.1-1 Types of Market Structure

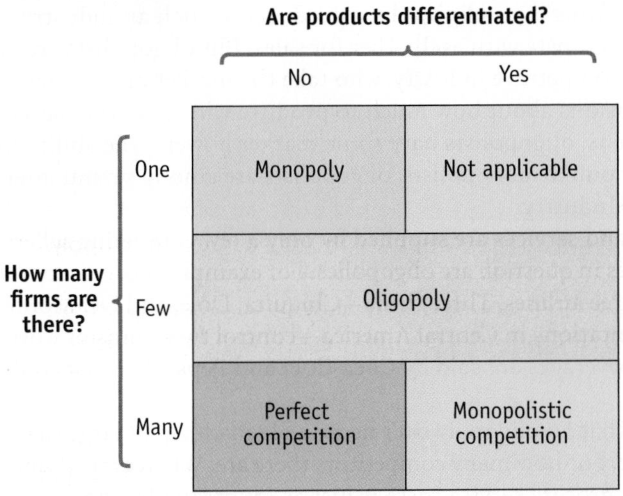

Are products differentiated?

How many firms are there?	No	Yes
One	Monopoly	Not applicable
Few	Oligopoly	
Many	Perfect competition	Monopolistic competition

The behavior of any given firm and the market it occupies are analyzed using one of four models of market structure—perfect competition, monopoly, oligopoly, or monopolistic competition. This system for categorizing market structure is based on two dimensions: (1) whether products are differentiated or identical, and (2) the number of firms in the industry—one, a few, or many.

Monopoly

The De Beers diamond monopoly based in South Africa was created in the 1880s by Cecil Rhodes, a British businessman. By 1880, mines in South Africa already dominated the world's supply of diamonds. However, there were many mining companies at the time, all competing with each other. During the 1880s, Rhodes bought the great majority of those mines and consolidated them into a single company, De Beers. By 1889, De Beers controlled almost all of the world's diamond production.

In other words, De Beers became a *monopolist*. But what does it mean to be a monopolist? And what do monopolists do?

Defining Monopoly

We have studied the supply and demand model of a perfectly competitive market made up of many firms, all of which produce the same good. *Monopoly* is the most extreme departure from perfect competition and the starkest example of market power. A **monopolist** is a firm that is the only producer of a good that has no close substitutes. An industry controlled by a monopolist—that is, an industry with one firm—is known as a **monopoly**. The next Module explains several types of barriers to entry by competing firms, including high fixed costs, legal barriers, and control of key resources (as in the case of De Beers's diamond supplies), that make it possible for one firm to be the only producer in a market.

A **monopolist** is a firm that is the only producer of a good that has no close substitutes. An industry with only one firm is known as a **monopoly**.

In practice, true monopolies are hard to find in the modern American economy, partly because of legal obstacles. A contemporary entrepreneur who tried to consolidate all the firms in an industry the way Rhodes did would soon end up in court, accused of breaking *antitrust* laws, which are intended to prevent monopolies from emerging. However, monopolies do play an important role in some sectors of the economy. There are many examples of local monopolies, including the only gas station in a small town and the only food-service provider at a school. Even at the national level, examples of near-monopolies include Amtrak in the passenger rail market, Luxottica in the sunglasses market, Microsoft in the market for word-processing software (among other types of software), and the makers of patented pharmaceutical drugs.

Oligopoly

An **oligopoly** is an industry with only a small number of firms. A producer in such an industry is known as an **oligopolist**.

An industry with only a few firms is an **oligopoly**; a producer in such an industry is an **oligopolist**. Oligopolists compete with each other for sales. But oligopolists aren't like producers in a perfectly competitive industry, who take the market price as given. Oligopolists know their decisions about how much to produce will affect the market price. That is, like monopolists, oligopolists have some market power—the ability to influence market prices. But unlike monopolists, oligopolists are among several interdependent firms in the same industry.

Many familiar goods and services are supplied by only a few competing sellers, which means the industries in question are oligopolies. For example, most air routes are served by only two or three airlines. Three firms—Chiquita, Dole, and Del Monte, which own huge banana plantations in Central America—control two-thirds of world banana exports. Most cola beverages are sold by Coca-Cola and Pepsi. This list could go on for many pages.

It's important to realize that an oligopoly isn't necessarily made up of large firms. What matters isn't size per se, but how many competitors there are. When a small town has only two grocery stores, grocery service there is just as much an oligopoly as air shuttle service between New York and Washington. Module 4.5 explains that, regardless of their size, the small number of competitors in an oligopoly makes it tempting—and often possible—for the firms to raise their profits by working together, or *colluding*, to limit direct competition and raise prices.

Why are oligopolies so prevalent? Essentially, an oligopoly is the result of the same factors that sometimes produce a monopoly, but in somewhat weaker form. An important source of oligopolies is the existence of economies of scale, which give bigger firms a cost advantage over smaller ones. When barriers to entry such as cost advantages are substantial, they can lead to a monopoly; when they are relatively limited, the result can be an industry with a small number of firms. For example, larger grocery stores typically have lower costs than smaller stores. But the advantages of large scale taper off once grocery stores are reasonably large, which is why two or three stores often survive in small towns.

Collage_Best/Getty Images

Two-thirds of the world's bananas are produced by three firms. An industry such as this with only a small number of firms is an oligopoly.

Is It an Oligopoly or Not?

In practice, it is not always easy to determine an industry's market structure just by looking at the number of firms. Many oligopolistic industries contain a number of small "niche" firms, which don't really compete with the major players. For example, the U.S. airline industry includes a number of regional airlines such as Nantucket Airlines, which flies propeller planes between Nantucket and Cape Cod. If you count these carriers, the U.S. airline industry contains nearly 100 firms, which doesn't sound like competition among a small group. But there are only a handful of national competitors like Delta, United, and American Airlines.

Concentration ratios measure the percentage of industry sales accounted for by the "X" largest firms, for example the four-firm concentration ratio or the eight-firm concentration ratio.

To get a better picture of market structure, economists often use *concentration ratios* to measure market power. **Concentration ratios** measure the percentage of industry sales accounted for by the "X" largest firms, where "X" can equal any number of firms. For example, the four-firm concentration ratio is the percentage of sales accounted for by the four largest firms, and the eight-firm concentration ratio is the percentage of industry sales accounted for by the eight largest firms. If the largest four firms accounted for 25%, 20%, 15%, and 10% of industry sales, then the four-firm concentration ratio would equal $25 + 20 + 15 + 10 = 70$. And if the next largest four firms in that industry accounted for 9%, 8%, 6%, and 2% of sales, the eight-firm concentration ratio would equal $70 + 9 + 8 + 6 + 2 = 95$.

The four- and eight-firm concentration ratios are the most commonly used. A higher concentration ratio signals that a market is more concentrated and therefore is more likely to be an oligopoly. For example, in 2022, the U.S. automobiles market had a four-firm concentration ratio of 55%, which is the sum of the market shares of

General Motors, Toyota, Ford, and Stellantis (formerly Fiat-Chrysler). The same year, the U.S. internet browser market had a four-firm concentration ratio of 96%, the sum of the market shares of Chrome, Safari, Edge, and Firefox. So the internet browser market is more concentrated than the automobile market. There is no particular market share that always indicates that an oligopoly exists, but both of these markets are considered oligopolies.

Monopolistic Competition

Leo manages the Wonderful Wok stand in the food court of a big shopping mall. He offers the only Chinese food in the mall, but there are more than a dozen alternative restaurants, from Bodacious Burgers to Pizza Paradise. When deciding what to charge for a meal, Leo knows that he must take those alternatives into account: even people who normally prefer stir-fry won't order a $15 lunch from Leo when they can get a burger, fries, and drink for $6.

But Leo also knows he won't lose all his business even if his lunches cost a bit more than the alternatives. Chinese food differs from burgers and pizza, and preferences vary among lunch customers. Some people love Chinese food, and they will buy from Leo even if they could have dined more cheaply on burgers. Some other people will choose burgers even if Chinese is a bit cheaper. In other words, Leo does have some market power: he has *some* ability to set his own price.

How would you describe Leo's situation? He definitely is not a price-taker, so he isn't in a situation of perfect competition. You wouldn't exactly call him a monopolist, either. Although he is the only seller of Chinese food in that food court, he faces competition from other food vendors. It would also be wrong to call him an oligopolist. Oligopoly, remember, involves competition among a small number of interdependent firms in an industry protected by some—albeit limited—barriers to entry. Also, the profits of firms in an oligopoly are highly interdependent, which gives firms an incentive to collude. But in Leo's case there are *lots* of vendors in the shopping mall, too many to make collusion practical. So the large food court where Leo manages the Wonderful Wok provides an example of our fourth market structure, *monopolistic competition*.

antony baxter/Alamy

A restaurant in a food court is not a perfect competitor, a monopolist, or even an oligopolist. The many firms serving differentiated products in an industry with free entry satisfy the recipe for monopolistic competition.

Defining Monopolistic Competition

Monopolistic competition is particularly common in service industries, such as the restaurant and gas station industries, but it also exists in some manufacturing industries such as the soap, coffee, and clothing industries. In a monopolistically competitive industry, each producer has some ability to set the price of their differentiated product. Exactly how high the price can go is limited by the competition the firm faces from other existing and potential firms that produce similar, but not identical, products.

Economists classify the market structure as **monopolistic competition** when three conditions are met. There must be:

- a large number of competing firms,
- differentiated products, and
- free entry into and exit from the industry in the long run.

Monopolistic competition is a market structure in which there are many competing firms in an industry, each firm sells a differentiated product, and there is free entry into and exit from the industry in the long run.

AP® ECON TIP

Don't confuse monopolistic competition and monopoly or perfect competition. Monopolistic competition has low barriers to entry, unlike a monopoly, and a differentiated product, unlike a perfectly competitive firm.

Large Numbers

In a monopolistically competitive industry, there are many firms. Such an industry does not look either like a monopoly, where the firm faces no competition, or like an oligopoly, where each firm has only a few rivals. Instead, each seller has many competitors. For example, there are many vendors in a big food court, many gas stations along a major highway, and many makers of hand soap.

Differentiated Products

Product differentiation is an attempt by a firm to convince buyers that its product is different from the products of other firms in the industry.

In a monopolistically competitive industry, firms engage in **product differentiation**, which means they try to make their product distinct from those of competing firms in the eyes of consumers. Such product differentiation can come in the form of different styles or types, different locations, or different levels of quality. At the same time, though, consumers see these competing products as close substitutes. If Leo's food court contained 15 vendors selling exactly the same kind and quality of food, there would be perfect competition: any seller who tried to charge a higher price would have no customers. But suppose that Wonderful Wok is the only Chinese food vendor, Bodacious Burgers is the only hamburger stand, and so on. The result of this differentiation is that each vendor has some ability to set their own price: each firm has some market power.

Free Entry and Exit in the Long Run

In monopolistically competitive industries, new firms, with their own distinct products, can enter the industry freely in the long run. For example, other food vendors would open outlets in the food court if they thought it would be profitable to do so. In addition, firms will exit the industry if they find they are not covering their costs in the long run.

Monopolistic competition, then, differs from the three market structures we have examined so far. It's not the same as perfect competition because firms have some power to set prices. It's not pure monopoly because firms face some competition. And it's not the same as oligopoly because there are many firms and free entry, which eliminates the potential for collusion that is so important in oligopoly. As we'll see in Modules 4.4 and 4.5, competition among the sellers of differentiated products is the key to understanding how monopolistic competition works.

Imperfect Competition and Efficiency

Module 3.7 explained how efficiency can result from perfect competition. Recall that firms in perfectly competitive markets are so small relative to the market that they can sell any number of units at the market price, and they choose the quantity at which the market price equals the marginal cost. That leads to allocative efficiency because firms produce every unit for which the price consumers would pay exceeds the cost of production. Unlike firms in perfectly competitive markets, firms in imperfectly competitive markets must lower their price to sell more units. As we'll see in the next Module, this fact leads the firms to charge a price that exceeds the marginal cost. The important result is that the firms do not produce the quantity at which $P = MC$, which is a condition for allocative efficiency. Instead, firms in imperfectly competitive markets typically produce less than the allocatively efficient quantity.

Barriers to entry, such as exclusive ownership of critical resources, cost advantages, and legal obstacles such as patents and copyrights (discussed further in Module 4.2), can perpetuate the inefficiency of monopolies and oligopolies. When the quantity of output in markets with those structures is inefficiently low, barriers to entry prevent competing firms from entering and expanding output as they do in perfectly competitive markets. The risk of sustained inefficiency makes imperfectly competitive market structures important to study and is a key reason for the adoption of antitrust legislation to promote competition.

Table 4.1-1 summarizes the characteristics of each market structure.

Now that we have introduced the four principal types of market structure, we can proceed in the remaining Modules in this Unit to model each type of imperfectly competitive market. These models will allow us to analyze particular markets and explain firm behavior, including the selection of prices and quantities.

Table 4.1-1 Market Structure

	Number of firms	Product differentiation	Control over price	Barriers to entry	Example
Perfect competition	Many	No	None	None	Agriculture
Monopolistic competition	Many	Yes	Within narrow limits	Few if any	Restaurants
Oligopoly	Few	Yes or No	Varies, depending on the degrees of mutual interdependence and collusion	Considerable	Airlines
Monopoly	One	No	Considerable, limited by consumers' willingness to pay	Prohibitive	Utilities

Module 4.1  Review

Check Your Understanding

1. In each of the following situations, what type of market structure do you think the industry represents?
   - **a.** There are three producers of aluminum in the world, a good sold in many places.
   - **b.** There are thousands of farms that produce indistinguishable soybeans, a commodity sold to thousands of buyers.
   - **c.** Many designers sell high-fashion clothes. Each designer has a distinctive style and a somewhat loyal clientele.
   - **d.** A small town in the middle of Alaska has one bicycle shop.

Tackle the AP® Test: Multiple-Choice Questions

1. Which of the following is true for a perfectly competitive industry?
   - **a.** There are many firms, each with a large market share.
   - **b.** The firms in the industry produce a standardized product.
   - **c.** There are barriers to entry.
   - **d.** There are barriers to exit.
   - **e.** There are a few firms, each with a small market share.
2. Which of the following is true for a monopoly?
   - **a.** It consists of only one firm.
   - **b.** A firm produces a product with many close substitutes.
   - **c.** The industry allows free entry and exit.
   - **d.** Firms are price-takers.
   - **e.** The monopolist can charge any price and consumers will pay it.
3. Which of the following is true for an oligopoly?
   - **a.** The firms typically experience diseconomies of scale.
   - **b.** There are many firms.
   - **c.** The firms have no market power.
   - **d.** There is a small number of interdependent firms.
   - **e.** It is impractical for the firms to collude.
4. Which of the following is true for a monopolistically competitive industry?
   - **a.** There are many firms, each with a small market share.
   - **b.** The firms in the industry produce a standardized product.
   - **c.** Firms are price-takers.
   - **d.** There are considerable barriers to entry.
   - **e.** There is a small number of independent firms.
5. Which of the following is an example of differentiated products?
   - **a.** Coca-Cola and Pepsi
   - **b.** automobiles and bicycles
   - **c.** trucks and gasoline
   - **d.** stocks and bonds
   - **e.** gold and silver
6. Which two market structures are normally characterized by free entry and exit in the long run?
   - **a.** perfect competition and monopoly
   - **b.** oligopoly and monopolistic competition
   - **c.** perfect competition and monopolistic competition
   - **d.** oligopoly and monopoly
   - **e.** monopolistic competition and monopoly

7. Which of the following is a common source of inefficiency in imperfectly competitive markets?
   a. too much similarity among the goods made by different firms
   b. too much competition
   c. a quantity of output that is too high
   d. a price that is too low
   e. a price that exceeds the marginal cost

Tackle the AP® Test: Free-Response Questions

1. For each of the following characteristics, indicate which market structure(s) exhibit that characteristic.
   a. many sellers
   b. price-takers
   c. barriers to entry
   d. differentiated product

Rubric for FRQ 1 (7 points)

a. **1 point:** perfect competition
   1 point: monopolistic competition
b. **1 point:** perfect competition
c. **1 point:** monopoly
   1 point: oligopoly
d. **1 point:** oligopoly
   1 point: monopolistic competition

2. Suppose the four largest producers of computer monitors in the country of Digiland have market shares of 35%, 30%, 15%, and 10%, respectively.
   a. What is the four-firm concentration ratio in Digiland?
   b. What is the structure of the computer monitor market in Digiland?
   c. What means of raising the price might be tempting for monitor producers in Digiland that would not be feasible in a perfectly competitive market? **(3 points)**

Monopoly

In this Module, you will learn to:

- Identify the types of barriers to entry that allow monopolies to exist
- Use a graph to show how a profit-maximizing monopolist chooses price and quantity
- Explain why monopolists charge a price that exceeds marginal cost
- Calculate consumer surplus, producer surplus, profit or loss, and deadweight loss for a monopoly

In this Module, we focus on monopoly, the market structure at the opposite end of the spectrum of competitiveness from perfect competition. A monopolist is the only producer in the market, so it faces the entire market demand curve. We will examine why that difference from a price-taking firm has large implications for the price charged, the quantity of output produced, and the net gains created by the market.

Why Do Monopolies Exist?

A monopolist earning economic profit will be noticed by potential entrepreneurs. Won't other firms crash the party and drive down the price and profit in the long run? If possible, yes, they will. For a profitable monopoly to persist, something must prevent other firms from going into the same business; that "something" is known as a **barrier to entry**. There are four principal types of barriers to entry: control of a scarce resource or input, economies of scale, technological superiority, and government-created barriers.

To sustain economic profit, a monopolist must be protected by a **barrier to entry**—something that prevents other firms from entering the industry.

Control of a Scarce Resource or Input

A monopolist that controls a resource or input crucial to an industry can prevent other producers from entering its market. By controlling a majority of the world's cobalt, producers in China dominate the market for batteries that contain cobalt, including the lithium-ion batteries used to power electric cars. And as discussed in the previous Module, Cecil Rhodes made De Beers into a monopolist by establishing control over the mines that produced the great bulk of the world's diamonds.

Natanael Natanael Alfredo Nemanita Ginting/Alamy

Facebook sustains dominance of the personal social networking market thanks to barriers to entry that include control of inputs (data), economies of scale, technological superiority, and copyrighted software.

Economies of Scale

Many Americans have natural gas piped into their homes for cooking and heating. Invariably, the local gas company is a monopolist. But why don't rival companies compete to provide gas?

In the early nineteenth century, when the gas industry was just starting up, companies did compete for local customers. But this competition didn't last long; soon local gas companies became monopolists in almost every town because of the large fixed cost of providing a town with gas lines. The cost of laying gas lines didn't depend on how much gas a company sold, so a firm with a larger volume of sales had a cost advantage: because it was able to spread the fixed cost over a larger volume, it had a lower average total cost than smaller firms.

The natural gas industry is one in which average total cost falls as output increases, resulting in economies of scale and encouraging firms to grow larger. In an industry characterized by economies of scale (described in Module 3.3), larger firms are more profitable and drive out smaller firms. For the same reason, established firms have a cost advantage over any potential entrant—a potent barrier to entry. So economies of scale can both give rise to and sustain a monopoly.

A **natural monopoly** exists when economies of scale provide a large cost advantage to a single firm that produces all of an industry's output.

A monopoly created and sustained by economies of scale is called a **natural monopoly**. The defining characteristic of a natural monopoly is that its minimum efficient scale is so large that the monopoly experiences economies of scale over the entire range of quantities that consumers might demand. Later in this Module, we will see how this looks on a graph. The source of this condition is large fixed costs: when large fixed costs are required to operate, a given quantity of output is produced at lower average total cost by one large firm than by two or more smaller firms.

The most visible natural monopolies in the modern economy are local utilities—water, gas, electricity, and, in some locations, internet service providers. As we'll see later, natural monopolies pose a special challenge to public policy.

Technological Superiority

A firm that maintains a consistent technological advantage over potential competitors can establish itself as a monopolist. For example, Apple dominated the smartphone market between 2007 and 2020. But technological superiority is typically not a barrier to entry over the longer term: over time, competitors invest in upgrading their technology to match the technology of the market leader. In fact, firms such as Samsung and Xiaomi have used very similar products to erode Apple's smartphone market share in recent years, and Samsung is now a contender for market leader.

We should note, however, that in certain high-tech industries, technological superiority is not a guarantee of success against competitors. Some high-tech industries are characterized by *network externalities*, a condition that arises when the value of a good to a consumer rises as the number of other people who also use the good rises. In these industries, the firm possessing the largest network—the largest number of consumers currently using its product—has an advantage over its competitors in attracting new customers, an advantage that may allow it to become a monopolist. Microsoft is often cited as an example of a company with a technologically inferior product—its computer operating system—that grew into a virtual monopolist through the phenomenon of network externalities.

Government-Created Barriers

In 2021, the pharmaceutical company BioMarin introduced Voxzogo, a drug for the treatment of a genetic condition affecting bone growth. Although other drug companies are capable of making Voxzogo, no other firms compete with BioMarin in the Voxzogo market. That's because the U.S. government has given BioMarin the sole legal right to produce the drug in the United States. The Voxzogo market is an example of a monopoly protected by government-created barriers.

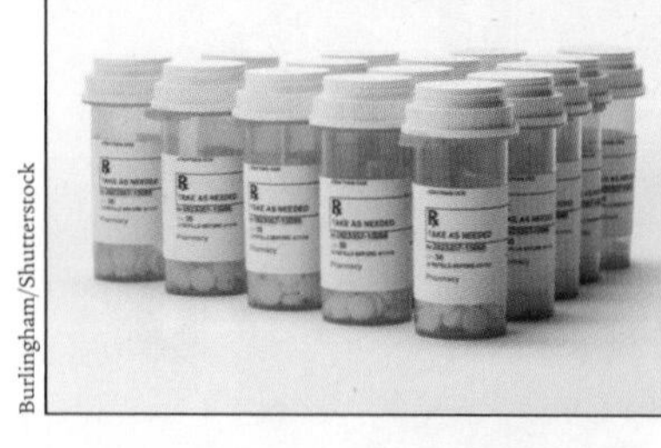

Burlingham/Shutterstock

A **patent** gives the owner a temporary monopoly in the use or sale of an invention.

A **copyright** gives the copyright holder for a literary or artistic work the sole right to profit from that work for a specified period of time.

The most important legally created monopolies today arise from *patents* and *copyrights*. A **patent** owner has the exclusive right to make, use, or sell an invention for a period of time that in most countries lasts between 16 and 20 years. Patents apply to new products, such as drugs or mechanical devices. Similarly, a **copyright** gives the copyright holder—typically the creator of a literary or artistic work—the sole right to profit from that work, usually for a period equal to the creator's lifetime plus 70 years.

The justification for patents and copyrights is a matter of incentives. Without patents, inventors would gain little reward from their efforts: as soon as a valuable invention was made public, others would copy it and sell products based on it. And if inventors could not expect to profit from their inventions, there would be no incentive to incur the costs of invention in the first place. The same is true for the creators of literary or artistic works. So the law allows a monopoly to exist temporarily by granting property rights that encourage invention and creation. Patents and copyrights are temporary because the law strikes a compromise. The higher price for the good that holds while the legal protection is in effect compensates inventors for the cost of invention. Then, after the legal protection lapses, the lower price that results from the entry of new competitors benefits consumers.

Because the lifetime of the temporary monopoly cannot be tailored to specific cases, this system is imperfect and leads to some missed opportunities. In some cases there can be significant welfare issues. For example, the violation of U.S. drug patents by pharmaceutical companies in less-developed countries has been a major source of controversy, pitting the needs of low-income patients who cannot afford to pay retail drug prices against the interests of drug manufacturers who have incurred high research costs to discover these drugs. To solve this problem, some U.S. drug companies and less-developed countries have negotiated deals in which the patents are honored but the U.S. companies sell their drugs at deeply discounted prices. (This is an example of *price discrimination*, which we'll learn more about in the next Module.)

The Monopolist's Demand Curve and Marginal Revenue

Recall the firm's profit-maximizing rule introduced in Module 3.5: a profit-maximizing firm produces the quantity of output at which the marginal cost of producing the last unit of output equals marginal revenue—the change in total revenue generated by the last unit of output. That is, $MR = MC$ at the profit-maximizing quantity of output. Although the profit-maximizing rule holds for *all* firms, decisions about prices and the quantity of output differ between monopolies and perfectly competitive industries due to differences in the demand curves that monopolists and perfectly competitive firms face.

We have learned that even though the *market* demand curve always slopes downward, each of the firms that make up a perfectly competitive industry faces a horizontal, *perfectly elastic* demand curve like D_C in panel (a) of **Figure 4.2-1**. Any attempt by an individual firm in a perfectly competitive industry to charge more than the going market price will cause the firm to lose all its sales. However, a firm can sell as much as

FIGURE 4.2-1 **Comparing the Demand Curves of a Perfectly Competitive Firm and a Monopolist**

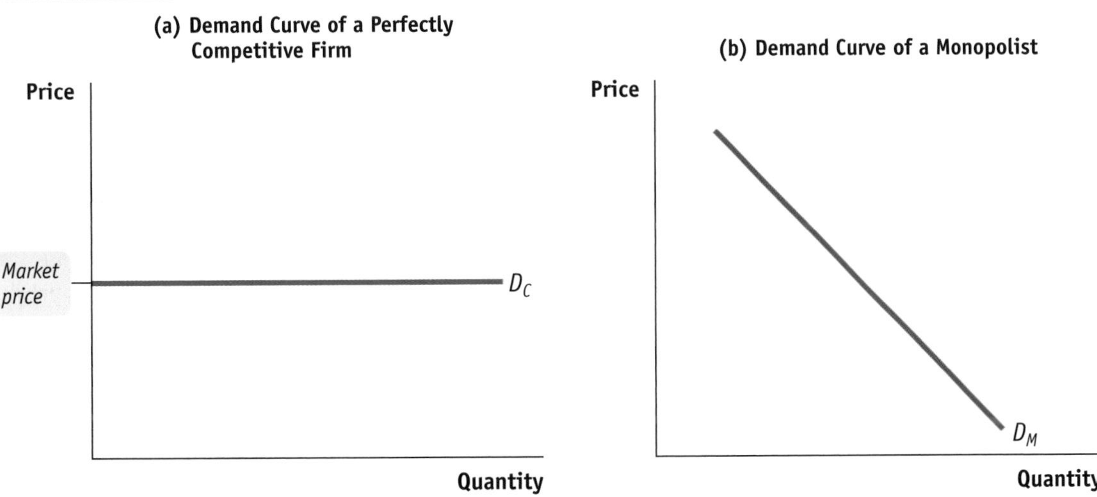

Because a firm in a perfectly competitive industry cannot affect the market price, it faces a horizontal demand curve like D_C in panel (a). A monopolist, on the other hand, can affect the price. Because it is the sole supplier in the industry, its demand curve is the entire market demand curve, which slopes downward like D_M in panel (b). To sell more output, it must lower the price.

it likes at the market price. We have seen that the marginal revenue of a perfectly competitive firm is, for that reason, simply the market price. As a result, the price-taking firm's profit-maximizing rule is to produce the output level at which the marginal cost of the last unit produced is equal to the market price.

By contrast, a monopolist is the sole supplier of its good. So its demand curve is simply the market demand curve, which slopes downward, like D_M in panel (b) of Figure 4.2-1. This downward slope creates a "wedge" between the price of the good and the marginal revenue of the good. **Table 4.2-1** shows how this wedge develops. The first two columns show a hypothetical demand schedule for De Beers diamonds. For the sake of simplicity, we assume that De Beers is a monopoly, all diamonds are exactly alike, and the number of diamonds sold is far smaller than is actually the case. For instance, at a price of $500 per diamond, we assume that only 10 diamonds are sold. The demand curve implied by this schedule is shown in panel (a) of **Figure 4.2-2**.

AP® ECON TIP

We have seen that in a perfectly competitive market, the height of the demand curve above each quantity also indicates the marginal revenue, average revenue, and price at that quantity. For a monopoly, the height of the demand curve is no longer the marginal revenue, but it still indicates the marginal revenue and the price that can be charged for that quantity.

Table 4.2-1 Demand, Total Revenue, and Marginal Revenue for the De Beers Diamond Monopoly

Price of diamond P	Quantity of diamonds demanded Q	Total revenue $TR = P \times Q$	Marginal revenue $MR = \Delta TR/\Delta Q$
$1,000	0	$0	
			$950
950	1	950	
			850
900	2	1,800	
			750
850	3	2,550	
			650
800	4	3,200	
			550
750	5	3,750	
			450
700	6	4,200	
			350
650	7	4,550	
			250
600	8	4,800	
			150
550	9	4,950	
			50
500	10	5,000	
			−50
450	11	4,950	
			−150
400	12	4,800	
			−250
350	13	4,550	
			−350
300	14	4,200	
			−450
250	15	3,750	
			−550
200	16	3,200	
			−650
150	17	2,550	
			−750
100	18	1,800	
			−850
50	19	950	
			−950
0	20	0	

FIGURE 4.2-2 A Monopolist's Demand, Total Revenue, and Marginal Revenue Curves

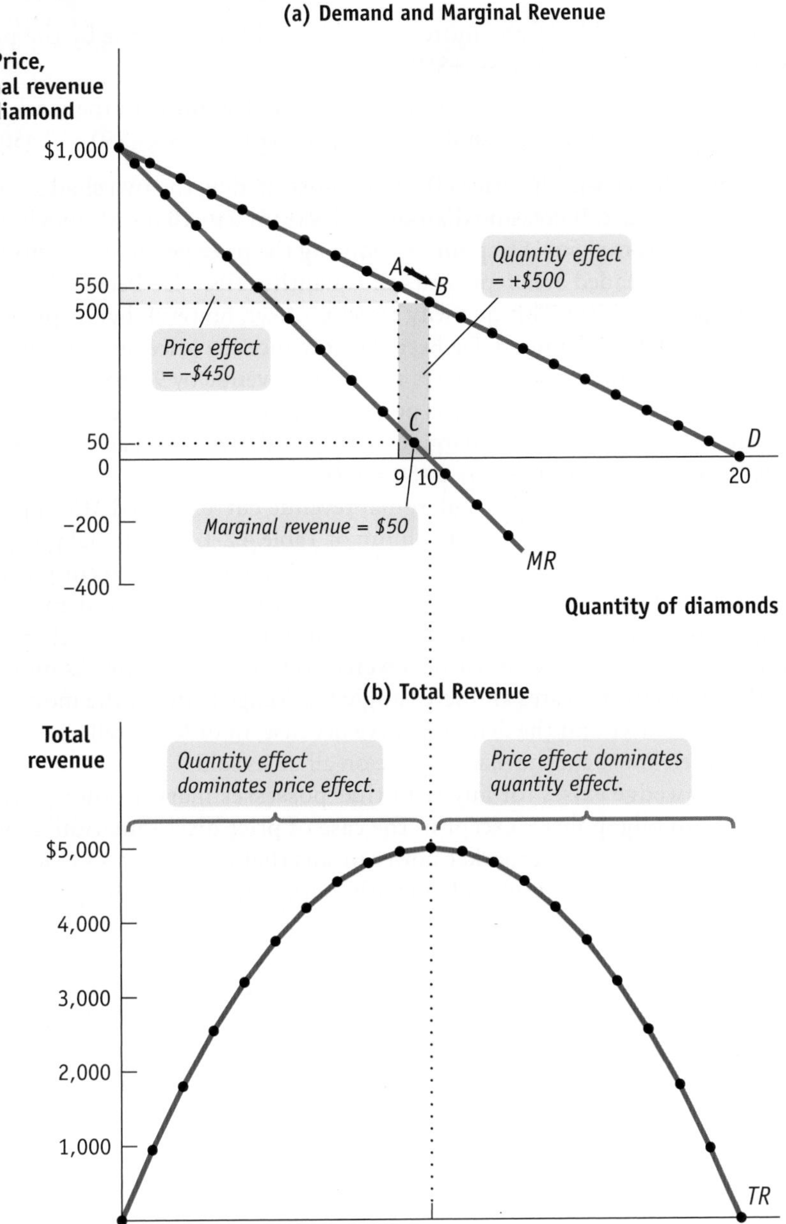

Panel (a) shows the monopolist's demand and marginal revenue curves for diamonds from Table 4.2-1. The marginal revenue curve lies below the demand curve. To see why, consider point *A* on the demand curve, where 9 diamonds are sold at $550 each, generating a total revenue of $4,950. To sell a 10th diamond, the price on all 10 diamonds must be cut to $500, as shown by point *B*. As a result, total revenue increases by the green area (the quantity effect: +$500) but decreases by the orange area (the price effect: −$450). So the marginal revenue from the 10th diamond is $500 − $450 = $50, which is much lower than its price of $500. Panel (b) shows the monopolist's total revenue curve for diamonds. Total revenue initially rises with an increase in output because the quantity effect dominates the price effect. Total revenue reaches its maximum at the level of output at which marginal revenue is zero. Total revenue then falls with an increase in output because the price effect dominates the quantity effect.

AnatolyM/iStock/Getty Images

The third column of Table 4.2-1 shows De Beers's total revenue from selling each quantity of diamonds—the price per diamond multiplied by the number of diamonds sold. The last column shows marginal revenue, the change in total revenue from producing and selling another diamond.

After selling the first diamond, the marginal revenue a monopolist receives from selling one more unit is less than the price at which that unit is sold. For example, if De Beers sells 10 diamonds, the price at which the 10th diamond is sold is $500. But the marginal revenue—the change in total revenue in going from 9 to 10 diamonds—is only $50.

Why is the marginal revenue from that 10th diamond less than the price? Because an increase in output by a monopolist has two opposing effects on revenue:

- *A quantity effect.* The sale of one more unit increases total revenue by the price at which the unit is sold (in this case, +$500).
- *A price effect.* In order to sell that last unit, the monopolist must cut the market price on *all* units sold. This decreases total revenue (in this case, by 9 × –$50 = –$450).

The quantity effect and the price effect are illustrated by the two shaded areas in panel (a) of Figure 4.2-2. Increasing diamond sales from 9 to 10 means moving down the demand curve from point *A* to point *B*, reducing the price per diamond from $550 to $500. The green-shaded area represents the quantity effect: De Beers sells the 10th diamond at a price of $500. This quantity effect is offset, however, by the price effect. In order to sell that 10th diamond, De Beers must reduce the price on all its diamonds from $550 to $500. This price cut lowers the firm's revenue by 9 × $50 = $450, represented by the orange-shaded area. So, as point *C* indicates, the total effect on revenue of selling one more diamond – the marginal revenue – derived from an increase in diamond sales from 9 to 10 is only $500 – $450 = $50.

Point *C* lies on the monopolist's marginal revenue curve, labeled *MR* in panel (a) of Figure 4.2-2 and taken from the last column of Table 4.2-1. The crucial point about the monopolist's marginal revenue curve is that, except where the two curves meet on the left side of the graph, the marginal revenue curve is always *below* the demand curve. The marginal revenue from the first unit is equal to the price because there are no other units on which the price must be lowered to sell the first one. As more units are sold, the price effect creates an increasingly tall wedge between the monopolist's marginal revenue curve and the demand curve because, in order to sell an additional diamond, De Beers must cut the market price on all units sold.

In fact, this wedge exists for any firm that possesses market power, such as a monopolist or an oligopolist – except in the case of price discrimination, as we will discuss in Module 4.3. Having market power means that the firm faces a downward-sloping demand curve. As a result, a firm with market power that charges every customer the same price will experience a price effect. So for such a firm, the marginal revenue curve lies below the demand curve.

AP® ECON TIP

The AP® exam sometimes asks questions about why a monopoly's marginal revenue is below its price. Be prepared to explain that the monopolist must lower its price on all units sold in order to sell more units.

Take a moment to compare the monopolist's marginal revenue curve with the marginal revenue curve for a perfectly competitive firm, which has no market power. For the perfectly competitive firm, there is no price effect from an increase in output: its marginal revenue curve is simply its horizontal demand curve. So for a perfectly competitive firm, the market price and the marginal revenue are always equal.

To understand how the quantity and price effects offset each other for a firm with market power, look at De Beers's total revenue curve in panel (b) of Figure 4.2-2. Notice that it is hill-shaped: as output rises from 0 to 10 diamonds, total revenue increases. This reflects the fact that *at low levels of output, the quantity effect is larger than the price effect:* as the monopolist sells more, it has to lower the price on only a few units, so the price effect is small. As output rises beyond 10 diamonds, total revenue actually falls. This reflects the fact that *at high levels of output, the price effect is larger than the quantity effect:* as the monopolist sells more, it now has to lower the price on many units of output, making the price effect very large. Correspondingly, the marginal revenue is negative at output levels that exceed 10 diamonds. For example, to sell the 12th diamond, the price must be cut to $400 on the 11 diamonds that would otherwise sell for $450 each. So the quantity effect of gaining $400 is smaller than the price effect of losing $550, making the marginal revenue of the 12th diamond $400 – $550 = –$150.

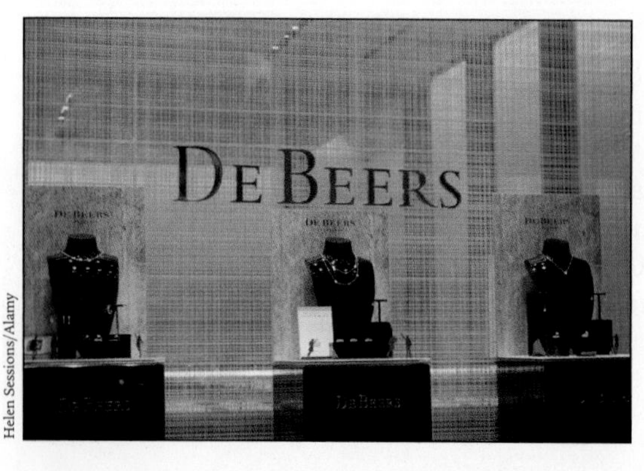

Helen Sessions/Alamy

Recall from Module 2.3 that the relationship between price changes and total revenue depends on the price elasticity of demand: a price cut increases total revenue along the section of the demand curve where the demand is elastic; a price cut has no effect on total revenue where the demand curve is unit elastic; and a price cut decreases total revenue where the demand is inelastic. So if you know how the price effect and the quantity effect change total revenue when the price changes, you know whether demand is elastic, unit elastic, or inelastic.

The Monopolist's Profit-Maximizing Output and Price

To complete the story of how a monopolist maximizes profit, we now bring in the monopolist's marginal cost. Let's assume that there is no fixed cost of production and that the marginal cost of producing an additional diamond is constant at $200, no matter how many diamonds De Beers produces. Since the only cost of producing each diamond is the $200 marginal cost, that marginal cost will always equal the average total cost, and the marginal cost curve and the average total cost curve coincide as a horizontal line with a height of $200, as shown in **Figure 4.2-3**.

FIGURE 4.2-3 **The Monopolist's Profit-Maximizing Output and Price**

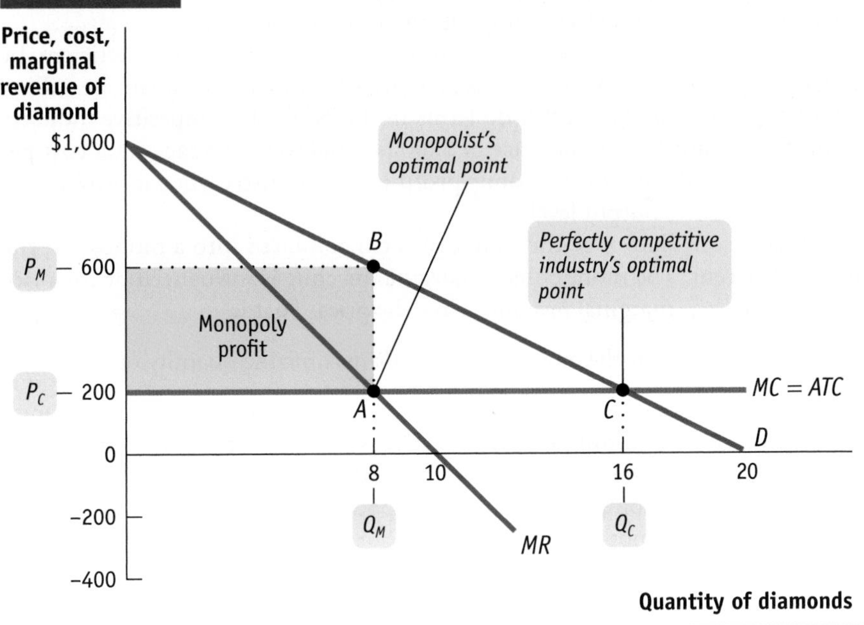

According to the profit-maximizing rule, the profit-maximizing quantity of output for the monopolist is where $MR = MC$, shown by point A at the intersection of the marginal cost and marginal revenue curves, at an output of 8 diamonds. The price De Beers can charge per diamond is found by going to the point on the demand curve directly above point A, shown by point B—a price of $600 per diamond. A perfectly competitive industry produces the output level at which $P = MC$, given by point C, where the demand and marginal cost curves cross. So a competitive industry produces 16 diamonds, sells at a price of $200, and makes zero profit.

To maximize profit, the monopolist compares the marginal cost with the marginal revenue. If the marginal revenue exceeds the marginal cost, De Beers increases profit by producing more; if the marginal revenue is less than the marginal cost, De Beers increases profit by producing less. So the monopolist maximizes its profit by using the profit-maximizing rule:

(4.2-1) $MR = MC$ at the monopolist's profit-maximizing quantity of output

The monopolist's optimal point is indicated by point A in Figure 4.2-3, where the marginal cost curve crosses the marginal revenue curve. The corresponding output level, 8 diamonds, is the monopolist's profit-maximizing quantity of output, Q_M. The price at which consumers demand 8 diamonds is $600, found by going straight up from point A to point B on the demand curve, so the monopolist's price, P_M, is $600. The average total cost of producing each diamond is $200, so the monopolist earns a profit of $\$600 - \$200 = \$400$ per diamond, and total profit is $8 \times \$400 = \$3{,}200$, as indicated by the shaded area.

AP® ECON TIP

Like a perfect competitor, a monopolist chooses the quantity at which $MR = MC$. The monopolist's price is found by going up from where $MR = MC$ to the demand curve, and then straight over to the price axis.

Monopoly Versus Perfect Competition

When Cecil Rhodes consolidated many independent diamond producers into De Beers, he converted a perfectly competitive industry into a monopoly. We can now use our analysis to see the effects of such a consolidation.

Let's look again at Figure 4.2-3 and ask how this same market would work if, instead of being a monopoly, the industry were perfectly competitive. We will continue to assume that there is no fixed cost and that the marginal cost is constant, so the average total cost and the marginal cost are equal.

If the diamond industry consists of many perfectly competitive firms, each of those producers takes the market price as given. Because they don't need to lower their price in order to sell more units, each producer's marginal revenue is equal to the market price. So each firm within the industry uses the price-taking firm's profit-maximizing rule:

(4.2-2) $P = MC$ at the perfectly competitive firm's profit-maximizing quantity of output

In Figure 4.2-3, this would correspond to producing at point *C*, where the price per diamond, P_C, is \$200, equal to the marginal cost of production. So the profit-maximizing output of an industry under perfect competition, Q_C, is 16 diamonds.

Recall that the perfectly competitive outcome of $P = MC$ is allocatively efficient: by producing up to point *C*, the firm provides every unit for which consumers are willing to pay at least the marginal cost. But do firms in the perfectly competitive industry earn any profit at point *C*? No: the price of \$200 is equal to the average total cost per diamond. As a result, there is no economic profit in this industry when it produces at the perfectly competitive output level.

We've already seen that once the industry is consolidated into a monopoly, the result is very different. The monopolist's marginal revenue is influenced by the price effect, which brings the marginal revenue below the price. That is,

(4.2-3) $P > MR = MC$ at the monopolist's profit-maximizing quantity of output

So the monopolist does not meet the $P = MC$ condition for allocative efficiency. As we've already seen, the monopolist produces less than the perfectly competitive industry—8 diamonds rather than 16. The price with a monopoly is \$600, compared to only \$200 with perfect competition. The monopolist earns a positive profit, but the competitive industry does not.

To summarize, compared to a competitive industry, a monopolist:

- produces a smaller quantity, $Q_M < Q_C$,
- charges a higher price, $P_M > P_C$, and
- earns a profit.

Monopoly: The General Picture

In Figure 4.2-3, we worked with specific numbers and assumed that the marginal cost was constant and that there was no fixed cost, which meant that the average total cost curve was a horizontal line. **Figure 4.2-4** shows a more general and realistic picture of monopoly in action. Here we return to the usual assumption that the marginal cost curve has a "swoosh" shape and the average total cost curve is U-shaped.

Applying the profit-maximizing rule, we see that the profit-maximizing level of output, identified as the quantity at which the marginal revenue curve and the marginal cost curve intersect (point *A*), is Q_M. The monopolist charges the highest price possible for this quantity, P_M, found at the height of the demand curve directly above Q_M (point *B*). At the profit-maximizing level of output, the monopolist's average total cost is ATC_M (point *C*).

FIGURE 4.2-4 The Monopolist's Profit

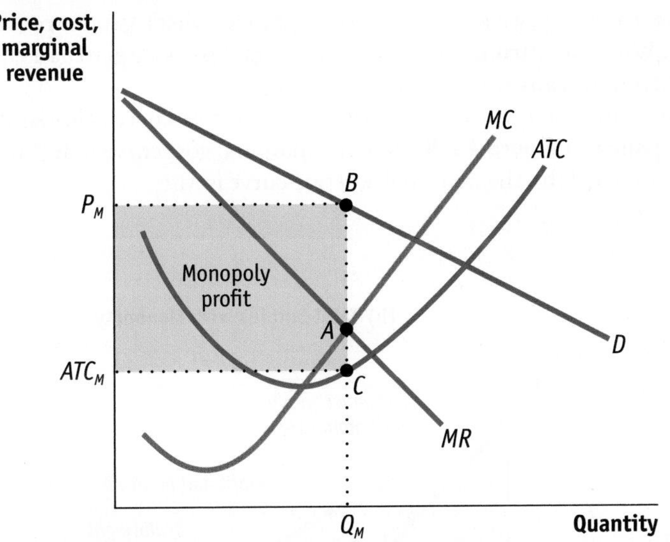

In this case, the marginal cost curve has a "swoosh" shape, and the average total cost curve is U-shaped. The monopolist maximizes profit by producing the level of output Q_M at which $MR = MC$, found directly below point A. It finds its monopoly price, P_M, from point B on the demand curve directly above point A. The average total cost of producing Q_M units is shown by the height of point C. Profit is given by the area of the shaded rectangle.

Recalling how we calculated profit in Equation 3.6-1, profit is equal to the difference between total revenue and total cost. So we have

$$\textbf{(4.2-4)}\quad \text{Profit} = TR - TC$$
$$= (P_M \times Q_M) - (ATC_M \times Q_M)$$
$$= (P_M - ATC_M) \times Q_M$$

Profit is equal to the area of the shaded rectangle in Figure 4.2-4, with a height of the profit per unit, which is $P_M - ATC_M$, and a width of Q_M.

In the previous Module, we learned that a perfectly competitive industry can have profit *in the short run but not in the long run.* In the short run, price can exceed average total cost, allowing a perfectly competitive firm to make a profit. But we also know that this cannot persist. In the long run, any profit in a perfectly competitive industry will be competed away as new firms enter the market. In contrast, while a monopoly can earn a profit or a loss in the short run, barriers to entry make it possible for a monopolist to make positive profit in the long run. This profit for the monopolist is associated with lost welfare for society.

The Welfare Effects of Monopoly

If you've ever played Hasbro's Monopoly game, you know that it's good to be a monopolist, but it's not so good to be a monopolist's customer. Players of the Monopoly game pay higher rents when they land on a monopoly. Likewise, in real life, customers generally pay higher prices when the seller is a monopolist. But buyers and sellers always have conflicting interests when it comes to prices. Are the problems under monopoly any different from those under perfect competition?

Simon Belcher/Alamy

The answer is yes, because monopoly is a source of inefficiency: the losses to consumers from monopoly behavior are larger than the gains to the monopolist. Because monopoly leads to net losses for the economy, governments often try either to prevent the emergence of monopolies or to limit their effects. Let's look more deeply into why monopoly leads to inefficiency. Then we will examine the policies governments adopt in efforts to prevent this inefficiency.

By holding output below the level at which the marginal cost equals the market price, a monopolist increases its profit but hurts consumers. To assess whether this is a net benefit or a net loss to society, we must compare the monopolist's gain in profit to the consumers' loss. What we learn is that the consumers' loss is larger than the monopolist's gain, so monopoly causes a net loss for society.

To see why, let's again consider a case in which the marginal cost curve is horizontal, as shown in the two panels of **Figure 4.2-5**. Here the marginal cost curve is MC, the demand curve is D, and, in panel (b), the marginal revenue curve is MR.

FIGURE 4.2-5 Monopoly Causes Inefficiency

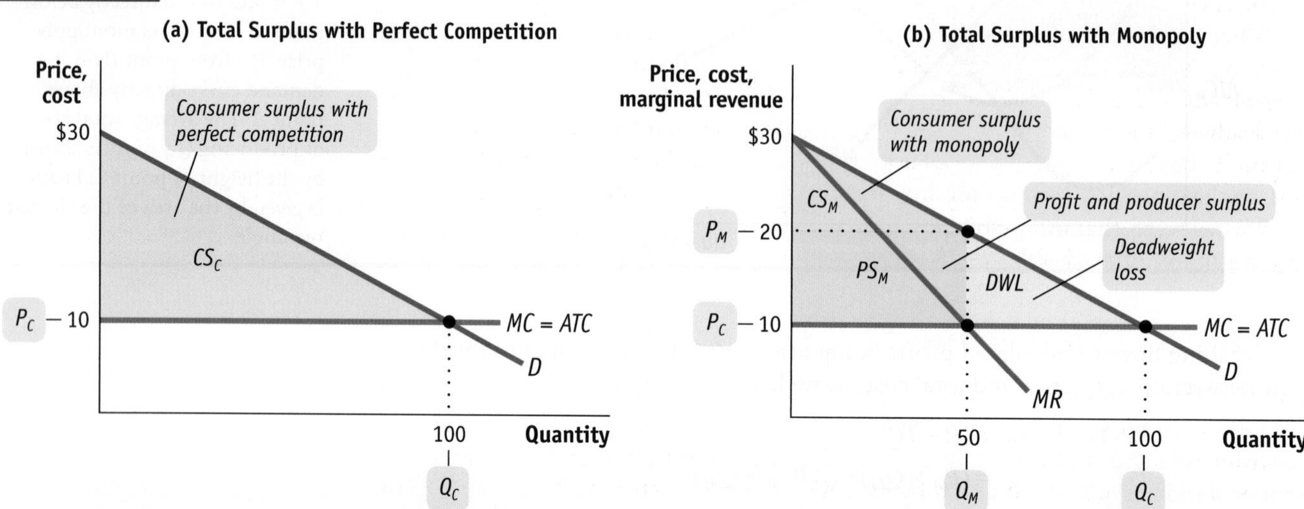

Panel (a) depicts a perfectly competitive industry: the output is Q_C and the market price is P_C. Since the price is exactly equal to the marginal cost of producing each unit, there is no producer surplus. So the consumer surplus is also the total surplus, represented by the blue-shaded area. Panel (b) depicts the industry under monopoly: the monopolist decreases output to Q_M and charges P_M. Consumer surplus (the blue area) has shrunk: a portion of it has been captured as producer surplus and profit (the green area), and a portion is the lost value of mutually beneficial transactions that do not occur because of monopoly behavior, which we know as deadweight loss (the yellow area). As a result, total surplus falls.

Panel (a) shows what happens if this industry is perfectly competitive. The equilibrium output, Q_C, is 100; the price of the good, P_C, is \$10, which is also the marginal cost and the average total cost because the marginal cost is the same for each unit and there is no fixed cost. Consumers pay firms exactly the marginal cost per unit of output, so there is no producer surplus in this equilibrium. The consumer surplus generated by the market is $\frac{1}{2} \times 100 \times \$20 = \$1{,}000$, represented by the area of the blue-shaded triangle labeled CS_C in panel (a). Since there is no producer surplus when the industry is perfectly competitive, CS_C also represents the total surplus.

Panel (b) shows the results if the market were instead a monopoly. The monopolist's level of output, Q_M, is 50, at which the marginal cost is equal to the marginal revenue. The monopolist's price, P_M, is \$20. The industry now earns profit—which is also the producer surplus in this case—equal to $(\$20 - \$10) \times 50 = \$500$, represented by the area of the green rectangle labeled PS_M. Note that this profit is part of what was consumer surplus in the perfectly competitive market, and the consumer surplus with the monopoly shrinks to $\frac{1}{2} \times 50 \times \$10 = \$250$, represented by the area of the blue triangle, CS_M.

By comparing panels (a) and (b), we see that in addition to the redistribution of surplus from consumers to the monopolist, another important change has occurred: the sum of producer surplus and consumer surplus—total surplus—is *smaller* under monopoly than under perfect competition. That is, the sum of CS_M and PS_M in panel (b), \$750, is less than the area CS_C in panel (a), \$1,000. In Module 2.8, we analyzed how taxes could cause *deadweight loss* for society. Here we show that a monopoly creates deadweight loss, which in this case is ½ × 50 × $10 = $250, as represented by the area of the yellow triangle, *DWL*. In other words, by capturing only $750 of the $1,000 surplus achieved with perfect competition, monopoly produces a $250 net loss for society.

This net loss arises because some mutually beneficial transactions do not occur. There are people for whom an additional unit of the good is worth more than the marginal cost of producing it but who don't consume it because they are not willing to pay the monopoly price, P_M. Indeed, by driving a wedge between the price and the marginal cost, a monopoly acts much like a tax on consumers, and produces the same kind of inefficiency.

When a sales tax or an excise tax is imposed on each unit of a good produced by a monopoly, even less of the good is sold, and the deadweight loss grows. However, a *lump-sum tax*—one that does not depend on the quantity sold—does not contribute to the deadweight loss unless it is so high that it causes the monopoly to close down. The reason is that a lump-sum tax does not affect the marginal cost or the marginal revenue, so the monopoly goes on producing the same profit-maximizing quantity.

We have seen that monopoly power detracts from the welfare of society as a whole and is a source of market failure. Is there anything government policy can do about it?

Dealing with a Natural Monopoly

Policy toward monopolies depends crucially on what type of monopoly is involved. If the industry is *not* a natural monopoly, the best policy is generally to prevent a monopoly from arising or to break it up if it already exists. Government policy used to prevent or eliminate monopolies is known as *antitrust policy*, which we will discuss in detail in Module 6.4. Here, let's focus on the problem of dealing with a natural monopoly, which is tricky because it isn't just a matter of prohibiting the monopoly.

Recall that a natural monopoly experiences economies of scale due to a large fixed cost. The average total cost would be high if the market were divided among many competing firms, but a single firm can bring the average total cost down by spreading the fixed cost across many units of output. For example, the fixed cost of building an oil pipeline is tremendous, but the average total cost becomes reasonable if the pipeline can carry billions of gallons of oil. If multiple pipelines each served a fraction of the same oil market, the average total cost of oil from each pipeline would be much higher.

Breaking up a monopoly that isn't natural will provide gains to consumers that outweigh the loss to the firm. Yet it's not so clear whether a natural monopoly should be broken up, because large firms have lower average total costs than small firms. For example, two small gas companies serving a single town would operate at a higher average total cost than one large gas company. However, even in the case of a natural monopoly, a profit-maximizing monopolist acts in a way that causes inefficiency—it charges consumers a price that is higher than the marginal cost and, by doing so, prevents some potentially beneficial transactions. Also, it can seem unfair that a firm that has managed to establish a monopoly position earns a large profit at the expense of consumers.

What can public policy do about this? There are two common answers.

Public Ownership

In many countries, the preferred answer to the problem of natural monopoly has been **public ownership**. Instead of allowing a private monopolist to control an industry, the government establishes a public agency to provide the good and protect consumers' interests.

With **public ownership** of a monopoly, the good is supplied by the government or by a firm owned by the government.

The advantage of public ownership, in principle, is that a publicly owned natural monopoly can set prices based on the criterion of efficiency rather than that of

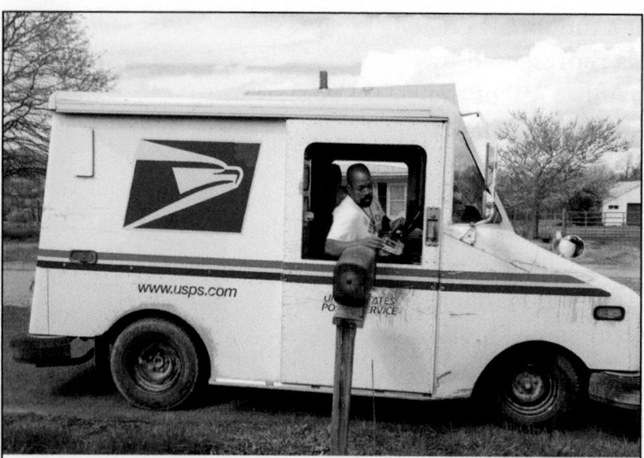

Pierre Rochon photography/Alamy

Public ownership of a natural monopoly, such as the United States Postal Service, can help to maintain efficient pricing for consumers.

profit maximization. In a perfectly competitive industry, profit-maximizing behavior *is* efficient because firms charge a price equal to the marginal cost; that is why there is no economic argument for public ownership of, say, wheat farms.

Experience suggests, however, that public ownership as a solution to the problem of natural monopoly often works badly in practice. One reason is that publicly owned firms are often less eager than private companies to keep costs down or offer high-quality products. Another reason is that publicly owned companies all too often end up serving political interests—providing contracts or jobs to people with the right connections rather than to the most qualified individuals.

Regulation

Price regulation limits the price that a monopolist is allowed to charge.

In the United States, the more common answer has been to leave the industry in private hands but subject it to regulation. In particular, most local utilities, such as electricity, water, natural gas, and so on, are covered by **price regulation** that limits the prices they can charge.

Figure 4.2-6 shows an example of price regulation of a natural monopoly—a simplified version of a local gas company. The company faces a demand curve, *D*, with an associated marginal revenue curve, *MR*. For simplicity, we assume that the firm's total cost consists of two parts: a fixed cost and a variable cost that is the same for every unit. So marginal cost is constant in this case, and the marginal cost curve (which here is also the average variable cost curve) is the horizontal line *MC*. The average total cost curve is the downward-sloping curve *ATC*; it slopes downward because the higher the output, the lower the average fixed cost (the fixed cost per unit of output). Because average total cost slopes downward over the range of output relevant for market demand, this is a natural monopoly.

FIGURE 4.2-6 Unregulated and Regulated Natural Monopoly

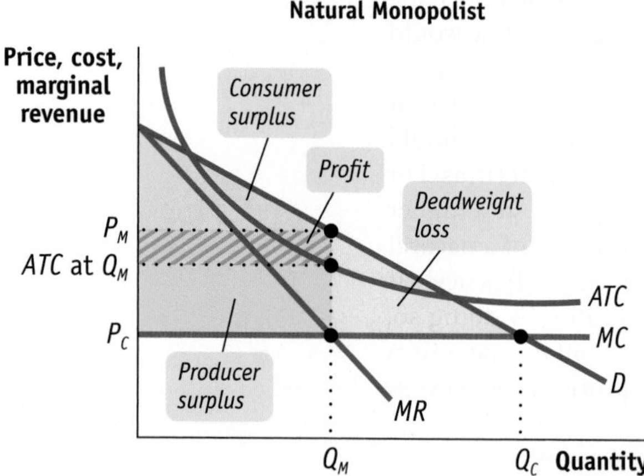

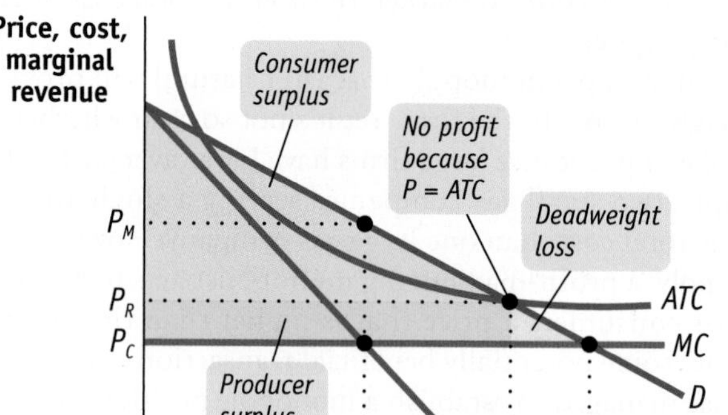

This figure shows the case of a natural monopolist. In panel (a), if the monopolist is allowed to charge P_M, it makes a profit, shown by the striped area; consumer surplus is shown by the blue area. The green area represents producer surplus and the yellow area represents deadweight loss. If the monopolist is regulated and must charge the lower price P_C equal to the marginal cost, at the quantity Q_C that will be demanded, the average total cost will exceed the price and the firm will incur losses. Panel (b) shows what happens when the monopolist must charge the price P_R equal to its average total cost where the *ATC* curve crosses the demand curve. Output expands to Q_R and consumer surplus is now the entire blue area. There is producer surplus, represented by the green area, but the monopolist makes zero profit because the price it receives equals its average total cost. The sum of the blue and green areas when the price is P_R represents the greatest total surplus possible without the monopoly incurring losses.

Panel (a) illustrates a case of natural monopoly without regulation. The unregulated natural monopolist chooses the monopoly output Q_M and charges the price P_M. Since the monopolist receives a price greater than its average total cost, it earns a profit, represented by the striped rectangle in panel (a). The blue triangle represents consumer surplus and the green rectangle represents producer surplus. Deadweight loss is shown by the yellow triangle.

Now suppose regulators pursued allocative efficiency by setting a price ceiling of P_C, so that price equaled marginal cost, as in a perfectly competitive industry in the long run. The monopolist would not be willing to produce at all in the long run, because at the quantity Q_C that would be demanded, the *ATC* would exceed the price and the firm would incur losses. The price ceiling must be set high enough to allow the firm to cover its average total cost.

Panel (b) shows a situation in which regulators have pushed the price down as far as possible, to the break-even level where the average total cost curve crosses the demand curve. The price the monopolist can charge is fixed at P_R by regulators, so the firm can sell any quantity between zero and Q_R for the same price, P_R. That makes the regulated price the marginal revenue for the monopoly, just like the market price is the marginal revenue for a perfectly competitive firm. With the marginal revenue being above the marginal cost until a quantity at Q_R (beyond which the firm would have to lower its price on all units to sell more), and with no losses at Q_R, the firm expands its output to Q_R.

This policy has appeal because with the price ceiling, the monopolist produces a larger quantity at a lower price. At any lower price, the firm loses money. The price P_R is the best regulated price: the monopolist is just willing to operate, and produces Q_R, the quantity demanded at that price.

The welfare effects of this regulation can be seen by comparing the shaded areas in the two panels of Figure 4.2-6. Consumer surplus is increased by the regulation, with the gains coming from two sources. First, profit is eliminated and added instead to consumer surplus. Second, the larger output and lower price lead to an overall welfare gain – an increase in total surplus. In fact, panel (b) illustrates the largest total surplus possible in this situation.

AP® ECON TIP

You may be asked to explain what happens to consumer surplus, producer surplus, and deadweight loss when a monopoly is regulated. Remember that a regulated price equal to the average total cost is the lowest price that would not cause the firm to take losses and eventually close.

Adventures in AP® Economics

Watch the video: *Monopoly*

Module 4.2  Review

Check Your Understanding

1. Use the accompanying total revenue schedule of Emerald, Inc., a monopoly producer of 10-carat emeralds, to derive the items listed in parts a–d. Then answer part e.

Quantity of emeralds demanded	Total revenue
1	$100
2	186
3	252
4	280
5	250

a. the demand schedule (*Hint:* the average revenue at each quantity indicates the price at which that quantity would be demanded.)
b. the marginal revenue schedule
c. the quantity effect component of marginal revenue at each output level
d. the price effect component of marginal revenue at each output level
e. What additional information is needed to determine Emerald, Inc.'s profit-maximizing output?

2. Replicate Figure 4.2-3 and use your graph to show what happens to the following items when the marginal cost of diamond production rises from $200 to $400. Use the information in Table 4.2-1 to identify specific numbers for prices and quantities on your graph.
   a. the marginal cost curve
   b. the profit-maximizing price and quantity
   c. the profit of the monopolist
   d. the quantity that would be produced if the diamond industry were perfectly competitive, and the associated profit

3. True or false? Explain your answer.
   a. Society's welfare is lower under monopoly because some consumer surplus is transformed into profit for the monopolist.
   b. A monopolist causes inefficiency because there are consumers who are willing to pay a price greater than or equal to marginal cost but less than the monopoly price.

Tackle the AP® Test: Multiple-Choice Questions

For Questions 1–4, refer to the graph provided and assume there is a profit-maximizing monopolist.

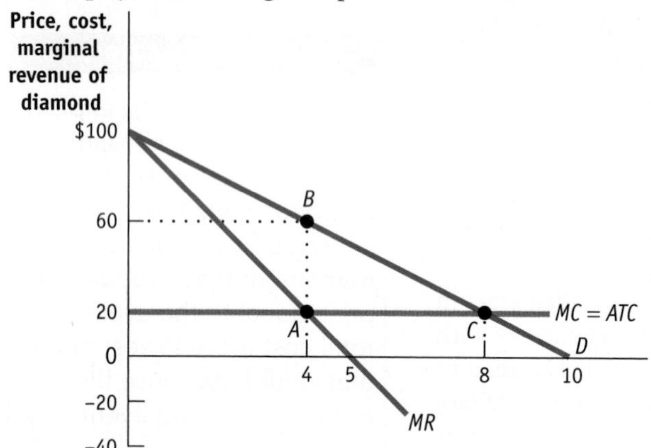

1. The consumer surplus in this market is
   a. 0.
   b. 40.
   c. 80.
   d. 160.
   e. 320.

2. The monopolist's total revenue equals
   a. $80.
   b. $160.
   c. $240.
   d. $300.
   e. $480.

3. The deadweight loss caused by the monopoly is
   a. $20.
   b. $80.
   c. $160.
   d. $240.
   e. $480.

4. The monopolist is earning a profit equal to
   a. $0.
   b. $40.
   c. $80.
   d. $160.
   e. $240.

5. How does a monopoly differ from a perfectly competitive industry with the same costs?
   a. The monopoly produces where *MR* = *MC*.
   b. The monopoly earns normal profit in the long run.
   c. The monopoly charges a lower price.
   d. The monopoly produces a smaller quantity.
   e. The monopoly can sell as many units as it wants at the equilibrium price.

6. Which of the following is always true of a natural monopoly?
   a. It experiences diseconomies of scale.
   b. *ATC* is lower if there is a single firm in the market.
   c. It occurs in a market that relies on natural resources for its production.
   d. There are decreasing returns to scale in the industry.
   e. The government should break up the monopoly to achieve efficiency.

7. A price cut will lead to an increase in total revenue if the
   a. marginal revenue is zero.
   b. quantity effect is larger than the price effect.
   c. quantity effect is zero.
   d. demand curve is inelastic.
   e. demand curve is unit-elastic.

8. Where the average total cost curve for a natural monopoly crosses the demand curve,
   a. the marginal cost curve is below the average total cost curve.
   b. the average total cost curve is rising.
   c. the marginal revenue curve is rising.
   d. the marginal revenue curve also crosses the demand curve.
   e. the marginal cost curve also crosses the demand curve.

9. Which of the following is most likely to be higher for a regulated natural monopoly than for an unregulated natural monopoly?
   a. product variety
   b. quantity
   c. price
   d. profit
   e. deadweight loss

10. In order to allow a natural monopoly to continue operations in the long run, the regulated price must be at least as high as the
   a. minimum point of the marginal cost curve.
   b. marginal cost where the marginal cost curve meets the demand curve.
   c. minimum point of the average total cost curve.
   d. minimum point of the average variable cost curve.
   e. average total cost where the average total cost curve meets the demand curve.

Tackle the AP® Test: Free-Response Questions

1. **a.** Draw a correctly labeled graph showing a monopoly incurring a loss in the short run. Assume that the marginal cost curve is swoosh-shaped.
   b. At the quantity at which $MR = MC$, how does the size of the quantity effect compare with the size of the price effect? Explain.

Rubric for FRQ 1 (9 points)

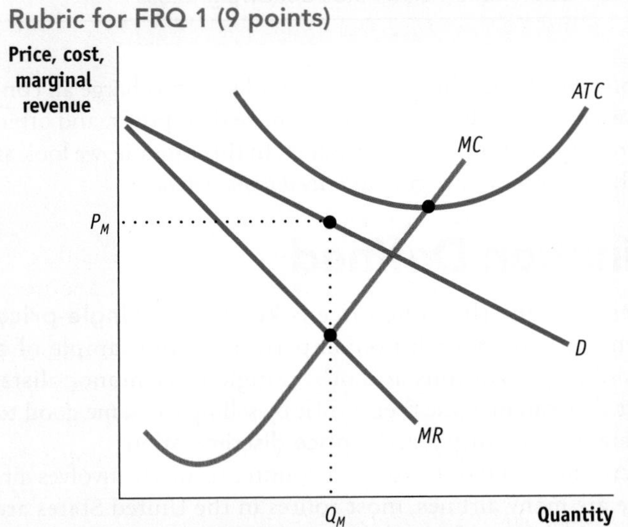

1 point: Axes are correctly labeled.

1 point: The demand curve is labeled and negatively sloped.

1 point: The marginal revenue curve is labeled, negatively sloped, and below the demand curve.

1 point: The profit-maximizing quantity is labeled on the horizontal axis where $MC = MR$.

1 point: Price is determined on the demand curve above the point where $MC = MR$.

1 point: The average total cost curve is labeled and U-shaped.

1 point: Average total cost is above price at the profit-maximizing output.

1 point: The marginal cost curve crosses the average total cost curve at the lowest point on the average total cost curve.

1 point: At that quantity, the quantity effect, which is positive, is larger than the price effect, which is negative. We know this because the *MR*—the sum of these effects—is positive.

2. Draw a correctly labeled graph showing a profit-making natural monopoly with the same marginal cost for each unit. On your graph, indicate each of the following:
   a. the monopoly's profit-maximizing output (Q_M)
   b. the monopoly's price (P_M)
   c. the monopoly's profit
   d. the regulated price that would maximize consumer surplus without creating losses for the firm (P_R) **(9 points)**

3. Draw a correctly labeled graph of a natural monopoly. Use your graph to identify each of the following:
   a. consumer surplus if the market were somehow able to operate as a perfectly competitive market
   b. consumer surplus with the monopoly
   c. monopoly profit
   d. deadweight loss with the monopoly **(8 points)**

MODULE 4.3 Price Discrimination

> ***In this Module, you will learn to:***
> - Define price discrimination
> - Explain why price discrimination allows monopolists to capture additional consumer surplus
> - Discuss how perfect price discrimination eliminates deadweight loss

Up to this point, we have considered only the case of monopolists who charge all consumers the same price. However, monopolists want to maximize their profit, and often they do so by charging different prices for the same product. In this Module, we look at how monopolists increase their profit by engaging in *price discrimination*.

Price Discrimination Defined

A **single-price monopolist** charges all consumers the same price.

Sellers engage in **price discrimination** when they charge different prices to different consumers for the same good.

A monopolist who charges everyone the same price is known as a **single-price monopolist**. A small-town gas station with no competitors is an example of a single-price monopolist. Unlike gas stations and other single-price monopolists, many monopolists find that they can increase their profit by selling the same good to different customers for different prices: they practice **price discrimination**.

An example of price discrimination that travelers encounter regularly involves airline tickets. Although there are many airlines, most routes in the United States are served by only a few carriers, which gives those carriers market power and the ability to influence prices. Any regular airline passenger quickly learns that the simple question "How much will it cost me to fly there?" rarely has a simple answer. If you are willing to buy a nonrefundable ticket a month in advance and stay over a Saturday night, the round trip may cost only $250. But if you have to go on a business trip tomorrow, which happens to be Tuesday, and want to come back on Wednesday, the same round trip might cost $650.

Caroline Purser/The Image Bank/Getty Images

You might object that airlines are not usually monopolies — that in most flight markets the airline industry is an oligopoly. In fact, price discrimination takes place under oligopoly and monopolistic competition as well as monopoly. But it doesn't happen under perfect competition. Once we've seen why monopolists sometimes price-discriminate, we'll be in a good position to understand why it happens in other imperfectly competitive markets, too.

The Logic of Price Discrimination

> **AP® ECON TIP**
>
> Unless a question on the exam indicates in some way that a monopolist is a price discriminator, such as by saying so or by saying that the firm charges different customers different prices, it is best to assume that the firm is a single-price monopolist.

To get a preliminary view of why price discrimination might be more profitable than charging all consumers the same price, imagine that Air Sunshine offers the only nonstop flights between Bismarck, North Dakota, and Ft. Lauderdale, Florida. Assume that there are no capacity problems — the airline can fly as many planes as the number of passengers warrants. Also assume that there is no fixed cost. The marginal cost to the airline of providing a seat is $200 no matter how many passengers it carries.

Further assume that the airline knows there are two kinds of potential passengers. First, there are business travelers, 2,000 of whom want to travel between the destinations each week. Second, there are leisure travelers, 2,000 of whom also want to travel each week.

Whether the potential passengers take the flight depends on the price. The business travelers, it turns out, really need to fly on particular dates; they will take the flight as long as the price is no more than $650. Since they are flying purely for business, we assume that cutting the price below $650 will not lead to any increase in business travel. The leisure travelers, however, have more options; if the price goes above $250, they will take the bus or vacation closer to home. The implied demand curve is shown in **Figure 4.3-1**.

FIGURE 4.3-1 Two Types of Airline Customers

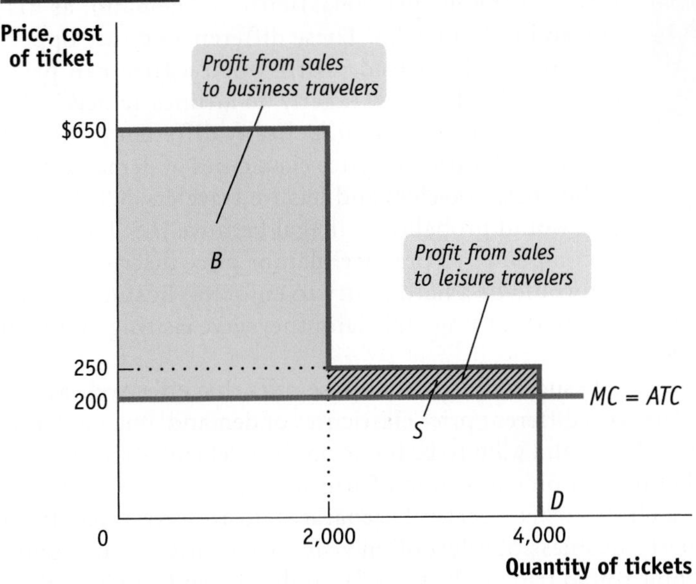

Air Sunshine has two types of customers: business travelers willing to pay at most $650 per ticket and leisure travelers willing to pay at most $250 per ticket. There are 2,000 of each kind of customer. Air Sunshine has a constant marginal cost of $200 per seat. If Air Sunshine could charge these two types of customers different prices, it would maximize its profit by charging business travelers $650 and leisure travelers $250 per ticket. This price discrimination would allow Air Sunshine to capture all of the consumer surplus as profit.

So what should the airline do? If it has to charge everyone the same price, its options are limited. It could charge $650; that way it would receive the highest price possible from the business travelers, but it would lose the more price-sensitive leisure travel market. Or it could charge only $250; that way it would get both types of travelers but make significantly less money from sales to business travelers.

We can quickly calculate the profit from each of these alternatives. If the airline charged $650, it would sell 2,000 tickets to the business travelers, earning a total revenue of 2,000 × $650 = $1.3 million and incurring costs of 2,000 × $200 = $400,000; so its profit would be $900,000, illustrated by the shaded area *B* in Figure 4.3-1. If the airline charged only $250, it would sell 4,000 tickets, receiving revenue of 4,000 × $250 = $1,000,000 and incurring costs of 4,000 × $200 = $800,000; so its profit would be $200,000. If the airline must charge everyone the same price, charging the higher price and forgoing sales to leisure travelers is clearly more profitable.

What the airline would really like to do, however, is charge the business travelers the full $650 but offer $250 tickets to the leisure travelers. That's a lot less than the price paid by business travelers, but it's still above the marginal cost; so if the airline could sell those extra 2,000 tickets to leisure travelers, it would make an additional ($250 − $200) × 2,000 = $100,000 in profit. That is, it would make a profit equal to the areas *B* plus *S* in Figure 4.3-1, $1,000,000.

It would be more realistic to suppose that there is some "give" in the demand of each group: at a price below $650, there would be some increase in business travel; and at a price above $250, some leisure travelers would still purchase tickets. Even so, price discrimination adds to profit. The important point is that the two groups of consumers differ in their *sensitivity to price*—that a high price has a larger effect in discouraging

Airlines benefit from prices that vary according to the flyer's price elasticity of demand.

purchases by leisure travelers than by business travelers. As long as different groups of customers respond differently to the price, a monopolist will find that it can capture more consumer surplus and increase its profit by charging them different prices.

Price Discrimination and Elasticity

Differences in sensitivity to price among consumers reflect different price elasticities of demand, as discussed in Module 2.3. These differences create opportunities for increased profit when a firm can price discriminate, but how exactly do airlines achieve this? In practice, airlines do not specify different prices for groups with different price elasticities of demand, such as business travelers and leisure travelers. Why? First, this would probably be illegal because U.S. law places some limits on the ability of companies to practice blatant price discrimination. Second, even if it were legal, it would be a hard policy to enforce – business travelers might be willing to wear casual clothing and claim they were visiting family in Ft. Lauderdale to save $400.

What the airlines do – quite successfully – is impose rules that effectively assign different fares to travelers with different price elasticities of demand. Business travelers usually travel on weekdays and want to be home on the weekend, so the round-trip fare is much higher if you don't stay over a Saturday night. The requirement of a weekend stay for a cheap ticket effectively separates business travelers from leisure travelers. Similarly, business travelers often visit several cities in succession rather than make a simple round trip, so the fares for multi-city and one-way travel are higher than fares for round-trip flights. Many business trips are scheduled on short notice, so fares are much higher if you book close to the date of travel. Fares are also lower if you forego amenities such as extra legroom, early boarding, free checked baggage, and advance seat selection – all of which price-sensitive customers can easily enough skip. And because customers must show their ID at check-in, airlines make sure there are no resales of tickets that would undermine their ability to price-discriminate. For example, those who buy low-priced tickets far in advance can't resell them to desperate last-minute flyers. Look at the rules that govern ticket pricing and you will see an ingenious implementation of profit-maximizing price discrimination.

> **AP® ECON TIP**
>
> Free-response questions involving various graphs may ask for calculations of areas that represent profit, surplus, or deadweight loss. Several Modules in this book, including Module 4.2, show how to find this area. Though we don't re-explain these calculations for every graph, in each case the area of a rectangle is *base* × *height* and the area of a *triangle is* (½) *base* × *height*.

Perfect Price Discrimination

In the example of business travelers and leisure travelers flying between Bismarck and Ft. Lauderdale illustrated in Figure 4.3-1, we saw that profit is maximized by charging each group its *willingness to pay* – that is, the maximum that each group is willing to pay. When business travelers pay their willingness to pay of $650 and leisure travelers pay their willingness to pay of $250, the airline earns its highest possible profit, represented by the combined areas of rectangle *B* and rectangle *S*.

You may have experienced a similar situation in which a seller with some degree of market power attempts to charge each buyer their willingness to pay. Venders at street markets sometimes size-up their customers and charge more when consumers appear willing and able to pay more. The same can be true for ticket scalpers, car dealers, taxi drivers, and sellers of various services for which there is no available price list, such as lawn care.

Consumers who pay a price equal to the most they are willing to pay do not get any consumer surplus. The entire surplus is captured by the seller in the form of profit. When a monopolist is able to capture the entire surplus by charging each customer their willingness to pay, we say that the monopolist achieves **perfect price discrimination.**

Perfect price discrimination takes place when a monopolist charges each consumer their willingness to pay—the maximum amount the consumer is willing to pay.

In general, the greater the number of different prices charged, the closer the monopolist is to perfect price discrimination. **Figure 4.3-2** shows a monopolist facing a downward-sloping demand curve. We assume the monopolist is able to charge different prices to different groups of consumers, with the consumers who are willing to pay the most being charged the most. In panel (a), the monopolist charges two different prices; in panel (b), the monopolist charges three different prices. It is apparent that the greater the number of prices the monopolist charges, the more money is extracted from consumers. With a very large number of different prices, the picture would look like panel (c), a case of perfect price discrimination. Here, every consumer pays the most they are willing to pay, and the entire consumer surplus is extracted as profit.

FIGURE 4.3-2 Price Discrimination

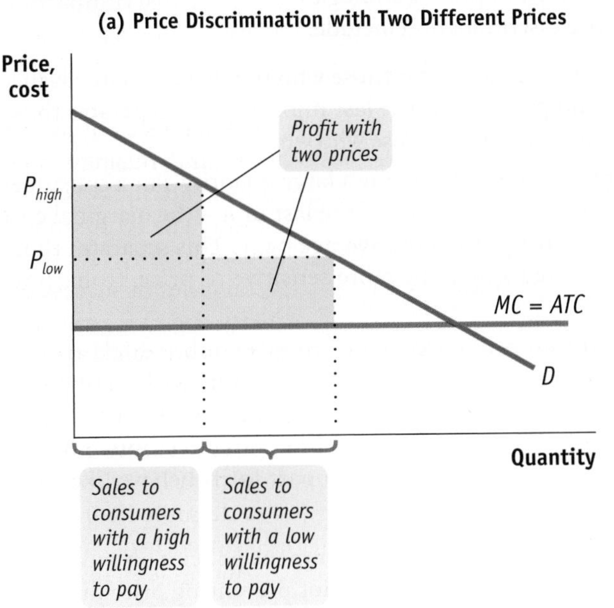

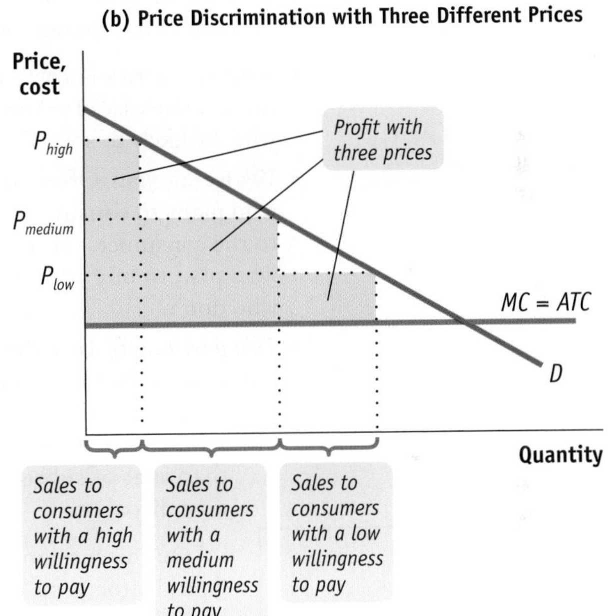

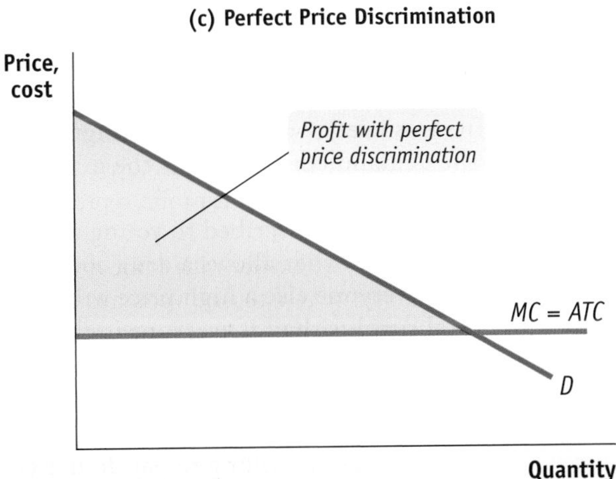

Panel (a) shows a monopolist that charges two different prices; its profit is shown by the shaded area. Panel (b) shows a monopolist that charges three different prices; its profit, too, is shown by the shaded area. It is able to capture more of the consumer surplus and to increase its profit. That is, by increasing the number of different prices charged, the monopolist captures more of the consumer surplus and makes a larger profit. Panel (c) shows the case of perfect price discrimination, where a monopolist charges each consumer that consumer's willingness to pay. The monopolist's profit is given by the shaded triangle, and there is no consumer surplus.

AP® ECON TIP

A perfectly price-discriminating monopolist produces the allocatively efficient quantity and there is no deadweight loss.

Both our airline example and the example in Figure 4.3-2 can be used to make another point: a monopolist who can engage in perfect price discrimination doesn't cause any allocative inefficiency! The reason is that the source of allocative inefficiency is eliminated: all potential consumers who are willing to purchase the good at a price equal to or above the marginal cost are able to do so. The perfectly price-discriminating monopolist manages to "scoop up" these consumers by offering some of them lower prices than others.

Perfect price discrimination is almost never possible in practice. At a fundamental level, firms' inability to achieve perfect price discrimination reveals a flaw in the use of prices as economic signals. When prices work as economic signals, they convey the information needed to ensure that all mutually beneficial transactions will indeed occur: the market price signals the seller's cost, and a consumer signals willingness to pay by purchasing the good whenever that willingness to pay is at least as high as the market price. The problem in reality, however, is that prices are often not perfect signals: a consumer's true willingness to pay can be disguised, as in the case of a business traveler who would claim to be a leisure traveler when buying a ticket in order to obtain a lower fare. When such disguises work, a monopolist cannot achieve perfect price discrimination. However, monopolists do try to move in the direction of perfect price discrimination through a variety of pricing strategies.

Common techniques for price discrimination include:

- *Advance purchase restrictions.* Prices are lower for those who purchase well in advance (or in some cases for those who purchase at the last minute). This separates those who are likely to shop for better prices from those who won't.
- *Volume discounts.* Often the price is lower if you buy a large quantity. For a consumer who plans to consume a lot of a good, the cost of the last unit – the marginal cost to the consumer – is considerably less than the average price. This separates those who plan to buy a lot, and so are likely to be more sensitive to price, from those who don't.
- *Two-part tariffs.* In a discount club like Costco or Sam's Club (which are not monopolists but monopolistic competitors), you pay an annual fee (the first part of the tariff) in addition to the price of the item(s) you purchase (the second part of the tariff). So the full price of the first item you buy is in effect much higher than that of subsequent items, making the two-part tariff behave like a volume discount.

Mark Mercer/Alamy

Costco and other discount clubs price discriminate by charging annual fees and providing volume discounts.

Our discussion also helps explain why government policies on monopoly typically focus on preventing deadweight loss, not preventing price discrimination, unless that discrimination causes serious issues of equity. Compared to the pricing practices of a single-price monopolist, price discrimination – even when it is not perfect – can increase the efficiency of the market. When a single, medium-level price is replaced by a high price and a low price, some consumers who were formerly priced out of the market will be able to purchase the good. Price discrimination increases efficiency because more of the units that provide net benefits to society – in that the willingness to pay (as indicated by the height of the demand curve) exceeds the marginal cost – are produced and sold.

Consider a drug that is disproportionately prescribed to young adults, who are often very sensitive to price. A policy that allows a drug company to charge young adults a low price and everyone else a high price will serve more consumers and create more total surplus than if everyone is charged the same price. But price discrimination that creates serious concerns about equity is likely to be prohibited – for example, an ambulance service that charges patients based on the severity of their emergency.

Module 4.3  Review

Check Your Understanding

1. True or false? Explain your answer.
   a. A single-price monopolist sells to some customers that would not find the product affordable if purchasing from a price-discriminating monopolist.
   b. A price-discriminating monopolist creates more inefficiency than a single-price monopolist because it captures more of the consumer surplus.
   c. Under price discrimination, a customer with highly elastic demand will pay a lower price than a customer with inelastic demand.

2. Which of the following are cases of price discrimination and which are not? In the cases of price discrimination, identify the consumers with a high price elasticity of demand and those with a low price elasticity of demand.
   a. Damaged merchandise is marked down.
   b. Hotels have senior citizen discounts.
   c. Food manufacturers place discount coupons for their merchandise in newspapers.
   d. Airline tickets cost more during the summer peak flying season.

Tackle the AP® Test: Multiple-Choice Questions

1. Which of the following characteristics is necessary in order for a firm to price-discriminate?
   a. free entry and exit
   b. differentiated product
   c. many sellers
   d. some control over price
   e. horizontal demand curve

2. Price discrimination
   a. is the opposite of volume discounts.
   b. is a practice limited to drug companies and the airline industry.
   c. can lead to increased efficiency in the market.
   d. rarely occurs in the real world.
   e. helps to increase the profit of perfect competitors.

3. With perfect price discrimination, consumer surplus
   a. is maximized.
   b. equals zero.
   c. is increased.
   d. cannot be determined.
   e. is the area below the demand curve and above the marginal cost curve.

4. Which of the following is a common practice of single-price monopolists?
   a. two-part tariffs
   b. advance purchase restrictions
   c. volume discounts
   d. differentiating customers based on their price elasticity of demand
   e. operating where marginal revenue equals marginal cost

5. A price-discriminating monopolist will charge a higher price to consumers with
   a. a more inelastic demand.
   b. a less inelastic demand.
   c. higher income.
   d. lower willingness to pay.
   e. less experience in the market.

6. In order to carry out perfect price discrimination, a firm must know each
   a. customer's income.
   b. competitor's marginal cost.
   c. customer's willingness to pay.
   d. competitor's advertising budget.
   e. customer's price elasticity of demand.

7. A perfectly price-discriminating monopolist
   a. creates the highest possible consumer surplus.
   b. earns no more than a normal profit.
   c. creates deadweight loss.
   d. achieves allocative efficiency.
   e. produces less output than a single-price monopolist.

Tackle the AP® Test: Free-Response Questions

1. Define price discrimination.
   a. Why do firms price-discriminate?
   b. In which market structures can firms price-discriminate? Explain why.
   c. Give an example of price discrimination.

Rubric for FRQ 1 (5 points)

1 point: Price discrimination is the practice of charging different prices to different customers for the same good.

1 point: Firms price-discriminate to increase their profit.

1 point: In order to price-discriminate, firms must be in the monopoly, oligopoly, or monopolistic competition market structure.

1 point: Because rather than being price-takers, firms in these market structures have some degree of market power, which gives them the ability to charge more than one price.

1 point: An example is different prices for movie tickets charged for people of different ages.

2. Draw a correctly labeled graph showing a monopoly with a horizontal average total cost curve practicing perfect price discrimination. On your graph, identify the monopoly's profit. What does consumer surplus equal in this case? Explain. **(6 points)**

Monopolistic Competition

MODULE 4.4

In this Module, you will learn to:

- Determine prices and profit in monopolistic competition, both in the short run and in the long run
- Explain how monopolistic competition can lead to inefficiency and excess capacity
- Discuss how advertising is used for product differentiation

The practice of *product differentiation* in the fast-food market occupies the minds of many marketing executives. Fast-food producers go to great lengths to convince us they have something special to offer beyond the ordinary burger: it is flame broiled or 100% beef or super-thick or lathered with special sauce! Or maybe they also offer chicken or fish or roast beef. The differentiation dance goes on in the pizza industry as well. Pizza Hut offers cheese in the crust. Papa John's claims "better ingredients." Domino's® has a "new recipe," and if you don't want thin crust, the alternative isn't "regular," it's "hand tossed"! The slogans and logos for fast-food restaurants often seem to differ more than the food itself. To understand monopolistic competition is to grasp the reason for the frenzy of fast-food marketing.

carlosgaw/E+/Getty Images

Understanding Monopolistic Competition

In Module 4.1, we learned that a monopolistically competitive industry consists of many producers, all competing for the same consumers but offering differentiated products. How does such an industry behave?

As the term *monopolistic competition* suggests, this market structure combines some features typical of monopoly with others typical of perfect competition. Because each firm offers something distinct, such as a special recipe for fried chicken or a convenient location for gasoline, it is in a way like a monopolist: it faces a downward-sloping demand curve and has some market power—the ability within limits to determine the price of its product. However, unlike a pure monopolist, a monopolistically competitive firm does face competition: the amount of its product it can sell depends on the prices and products offered by other firms in the industry.

AP® ECON TIP

In a monopolistically competitive industry, as in a perfectly competitive industry, there are many firms and low barriers to entry. However, the sale of differentiated products gives the monopolistically competitive firms some market power.

The same, of course, is true of an oligopoly. In a monopolistically competitive industry, however, there are *many* producers, as opposed to the small number that defines an oligopoly. The next Module explains that the "puzzle" of oligopoly is whether firms will collude or behave noncooperatively. This question does not arise in the case of monopolistically competitive industries. If all the gas stations or all the restaurants in a town could agree—explicitly or tacitly—to raise prices, it would be in their mutual interest to do so. But such collusion is virtually impossible when the number of firms is large and, by implication, there are no barriers to entry. So in situations of monopolistic competition, we can safely assume that firms behave noncooperatively and ignore the potential for collusion.

Monopolistic Competition in the Short Run

We introduced the distinction between short-run and long-run equilibrium when we studied perfect competition in Module 3.7. The short-run equilibrium of an industry is established by the firms already in existence. The long-run equilibrium, by contrast, is reached only after enough time has elapsed for firms to enter or exit the industry. To analyze monopolistic competition, we focus first on the short run and then on how an industry moves from the short run to the long run.

Panels (a) and (b) of **Figure 4.4-1** show two possible scenarios that a typical firm in a monopolistically competitive industry might face in the short run: profit and loss. It is also conceivable that in the short run, the firm will have just enough demand to break even, a case that is inevitable in the long run, as we will see a bit later in this Module. In all of these cases, the firm looks like any monopolist: it faces a downward-sloping demand curve, which implies a downward-sloping marginal revenue curve.

FIGURE 4.4-1 The Monopolistically Competitive Firm in the Short Run

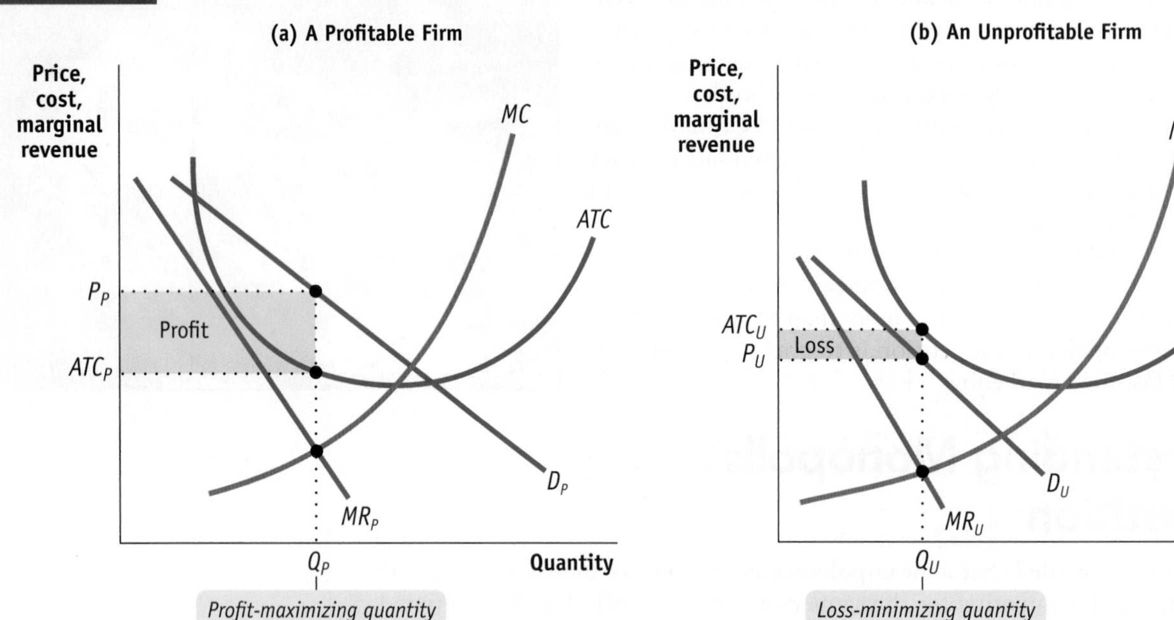

The firm in panel (a) can be profitable for some output quantities: the quantities for which its average total cost curve, *ATC*, lies below its demand curve, D_P. The profit-maximizing output quantity is Q_P, the output at which the marginal revenue, MR_P, is equal to the marginal cost, *MC*. The firm charges price P_P and earns a profit, represented by the area of the green-shaded rectangle. The firm in panel (b), however, is unprofitable because its average total cost curve lies above its demand curve, D_U, for every output quantity. The best that it can do if it produces at all is to produce the quantity Q_U and charge price P_U. This generates a loss, indicated by the area of the orange-shaded rectangle.

We assume that every firm has an upward-sloping marginal cost curve but that it also faces some fixed costs, so that its average total cost curve is U-shaped. This assumption doesn't matter in the short run; but, as we'll see shortly, it is crucial to understanding the long-run equilibrium.

AP® ECON TIP

You might see the term *negative profit* in an exam question. This simply means a loss.

In each case the firm, in order to maximize its profit or minimize its loss, sets marginal revenue equal to marginal cost. So how do these two figures differ? In panel (a), the firm is profitable; in panel (b), it is unprofitable. In panel (a), the firm faces the demand curve D_P and the marginal revenue curve MR_P. It produces the profit-maximizing output Q_P, the quantity at which the marginal revenue is equal to the marginal cost, and sells it at the price P_P. This price is above the average total cost at this output, ATC_P. The firm's profit is indicated by the area of the green-shaded rectangle.

In panel (b), the firm faces the demand curve D_U and the marginal revenue curve MR_U. It chooses the quantity Q_U at which the marginal revenue is equal to the marginal cost. However, in this case the price P_U is *below* the average total cost ATC_U; so at this quantity the firm loses money. Its loss is equal to the area of the orange-shaded rectangle. Since Q_U is the profit-maximizing quantity—which means, in this case, the loss-minimizing quantity—there is no way for a firm in this situation to make a profit. We can confirm this by noting that at every quantity of output, the average total cost curve in panel (b) lies above the demand curve D_U. Because $ATC > P$ at every quantity of output, this firm always suffers a loss.

As this comparison suggests, the key to whether a firm with market power is profitable or unprofitable in the short run lies in the relationship between its demand curve and its average total cost curve. In panel (a), the demand curve D_P crosses the average total cost curve, meaning that some of the demand curve lies above the average total cost curve. So there are some price-quantity combinations available at which price is higher than average total cost, indicating that the firm can choose a quantity at which it makes positive profit.

In panel (b), by contrast, the demand curve D_U does not cross the average total cost curve—it always lies below it. So the price corresponding to each quantity demanded is always less than the average total cost of producing that quantity. There is no quantity at which the firm can avoid losing money.

These figures, showing firms facing downward-sloping demand curves and their associated marginal revenue curves, look just like the ordinary monopoly graphs in Module 4.2. The "competition" aspect of monopolistic competition comes into play, however, when we move from the short run to the long run.

Monopolistic Competition in the Long Run

Obviously, an industry in which existing firms are losing money, like the one in panel (b) of Figure 4.4-1, is not in long-run equilibrium. When existing firms are losing money, some firms will *exit* the industry. The industry will not be in long-run equilibrium until the exit of some firms eliminates the persistent losses that firms had experienced.

JLFCapture/E+/Getty Images

In the long run, profit lures new firms to enter an industry.

It is less obvious that an industry in which existing firms are earning profits, like the one in panel (a) of Figure 4.4-1, is also not in long-run equilibrium. Given that there is *free entry* into the industry, persistent profits earned by the existing firms will lead to the entry of additional producers. The industry will not be in long-run equilibrium until the persistent profits have been eliminated by the entry of new producers.

How will entry or exit by other firms affect the profit of a typical existing firm? The differentiated products offered by firms in a monopolistically competitive industry are available to the same set of customers, so entry or exit by other firms will affect the demand curve facing every existing producer. If new gas stations open along a highway, each of the existing gas stations will no longer be able to sell as much gas as before at any given price. So, as illustrated in panel (a) of **Figure 4.4-2**, entry of additional producers into a monopolistically competitive industry will lead to a *leftward* shift of the demand curve and the marginal revenue curve facing a typical existing producer.

Conversely, suppose that some of the gas stations along the highway close. Then each of the remaining stations will be able to sell more gasoline at any given price. As illustrated in panel (b), the exit of firms from an industry leads to a *rightward* shift of the demand curve and marginal revenue curve facing a typical remaining producer.

The industry will be in long-run equilibrium when there is no profit or loss to motivate firms to entry or exit. This will occur only when every firm earns zero profit. So in the long run, firms just manage to cover their costs at their profit-maximizing output quantities.

We have seen that a firm facing a downward-sloping demand curve will earn positive profit if any part of that demand curve lies above its average total cost curve; it will incur a loss if its entire demand curve lies below its average total cost curve. To earn zero profit, the firm must be in a borderline position between these two cases; its demand curve must just touch its average total cost curve. That is, the demand curve must be just *tangent* to the average total cost curve at the firm's profit-maximizing output quantity—the output quantity at which marginal revenue equals marginal cost.

AP® ECON TIP

Like a monopolist, a monopolistically competitive firm faces a downward-sloping demand curve and a marginal revenue curve that is below the demand curve. Unlike a monopolist, a monopolistically competitive firm will necessarily earn zero economic profit in the long run.

FIGURE 4.4-2 Entry and Exit Shift Existing Firms' Demand Curves and Marginal Revenue Curves

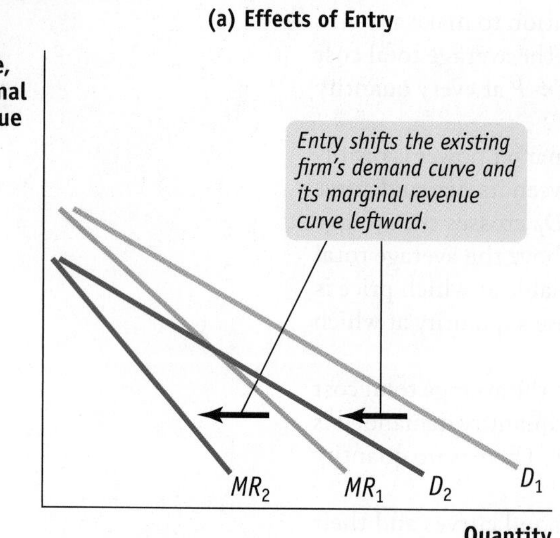

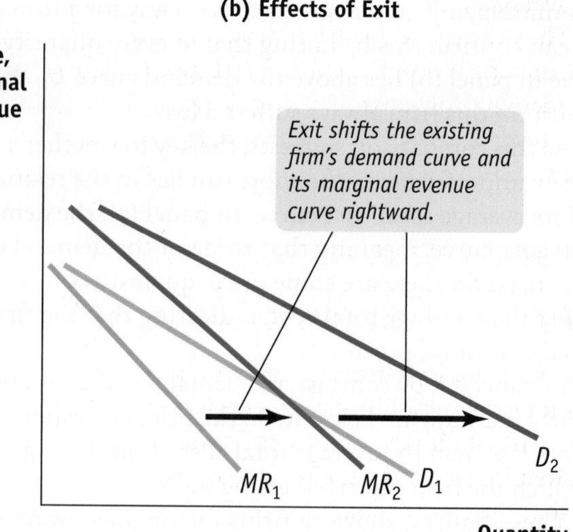

Entry will occur in the long run when existing firms are profitable. In panel (a), entry causes each existing firm's demand curve and marginal revenue curve to shift to the left. The firm receives a lower price for every unit it sells, and its profit falls. Entry will cease when firms make zero profit. Exit will occur in the long run when existing firms are unprofitable. In panel (b), exit from the industry shifts each remaining firm's demand curve and marginal revenue curve to the right. The firm receives a higher price for every unit it sells, and profit rises. Exit will cease when the remaining firms make zero profit.

If marginal revenue does not equal marginal cost, the firm operating at its profit-maximizing quantity will find itself making either a profit or a loss, as illustrated in the panels of Figure 4.4-1. But we also know that free entry and exit means that this cannot be a long-run equilibrium. Why? In the case of a profit, new firms will enter the industry, shifting the demand curve of every existing firm leftward until all profit is eliminated. In the case of a loss, some existing firms exit and so shift the demand curve of every remaining firm to the right until all losses are eliminated. All entry and exit ceases only when every existing firm makes zero profit at its profit-maximizing quantity of output.

Figure 4.4-3 shows a typical monopolistically competitive firm earning zero profit. The firm produces Q_{MC}, the output at which $MR_{MC} = MC$, and charges price P_{MC}. At

FIGURE 4.4-3 The Long-Run Equilibrium

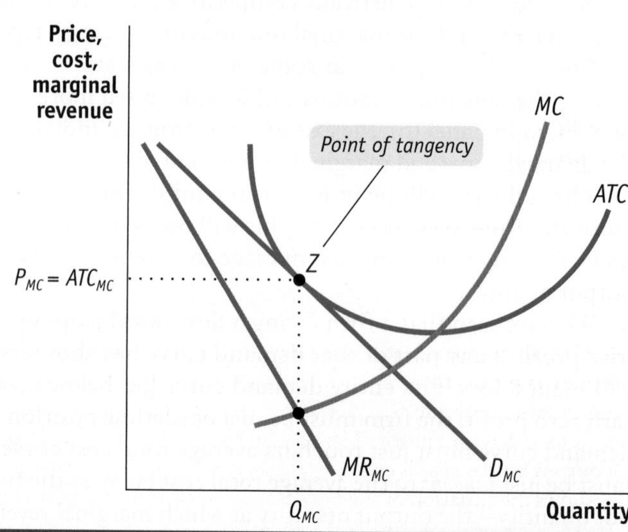

If existing firms are profitable, new firms will enter and shift each existing firm's demand curve leftward. If existing firms are unprofitable, each remaining firm's demand curve shifts rightward as some firms exit the industry. Entry and exit will cease when every existing firm earns zero profit at its profit-maximizing quantity. So, in long-run equilibrium, the demand curve of each firm is tangent to its average total cost curve at its profit-maximizing quantity: at the profit-maximizing quantity, Q_{MC}, the price, P_{MC}, equals the average total cost, ATC_{MC}.

this price and quantity, represented by point Z, the demand curve is just tangent to its average total cost curve. The firm earns zero profit because the price, P_{MC}, is equal to the average total cost, ATC_{MC}.

The normal long-run condition of a monopolistically competitive industry, then, is that each firm is in the situation shown in Figure 4.4-3. Each firm acts like a monopolist, facing a downward-sloping demand curve and setting marginal cost equal to marginal revenue so as to maximize profit. But this is just enough to achieve zero economic profit.

Monopolistic Competition Versus Perfect Competition

In some ways, long-run equilibrium in a monopolistically competitive industry resembles long-run equilibrium in a perfectly competitive industry. In both cases, there are many firms; in both cases, profits have been competed away; in both cases, the price received by every firm is equal to the average total cost of production. However, we will see that the two versions of long-run equilibrium are different in significant ways.

Price, Marginal Cost, and Average Total Cost

Figure 4.4-4 compares the long-run equilibrium of a typical firm in a perfectly competitive industry with that of a typical firm in a monopolistically competitive industry. Panel (a) shows a perfectly competitive firm facing a market price equal to its minimum average total cost; panel (b) reproduces Figure 4.4-3, which shows a monopolistically competitive firm in long-run equilibrium. Comparing the panels, we see two important differences.

FIGURE 4.4-4 Comparing Long-Run Equilibrium in Perfect Competition and Monopolistic Competition

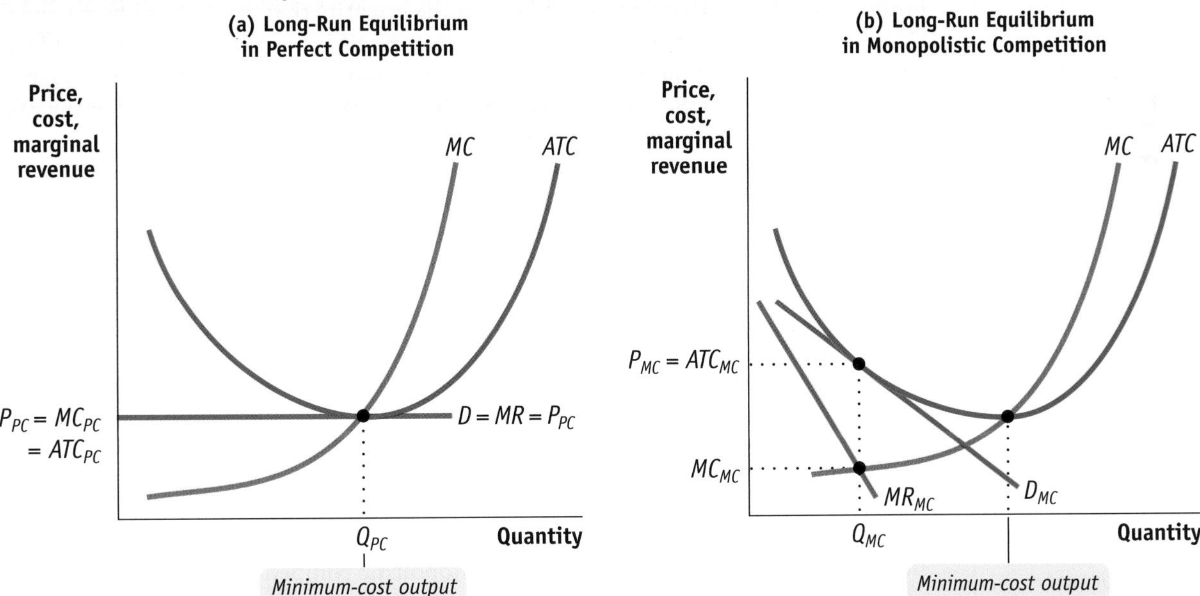

Panel (a) shows the situation of the typical firm in long-run equilibrium in a perfectly competitive industry. The firm operates at the minimum-cost output Q_{PC}, sells at the competitive market price P_{PC}, and makes zero profit. It is indifferent to selling another unit of output because P_{PC} is equal to its marginal cost, MC_{PC}. Panel (b) shows the situation of the typical firm in long-run equilibrium in a monopolistically competitive industry. At Q_{MC}, it makes zero profit because its price P_{MC} just equals average total cost, ATC_{MC}. At Q_{MC}, the firm would like to sell another unit at price P_{MC}, because P_{MC} exceeds marginal cost, MC_{MC}. But it is unwilling to lower the price to make more sales. It therefore produces less than the minimum-cost output level and has *excess capacity*.

First, in the case of the perfectly competitive firm shown in panel (a), the price, P_{PC}, received by the firm at the profit-maximizing quantity, Q_{PC}, is equal to the firm's marginal cost of production, MC_{PC}, at that quantity of output. By contrast, at the profit-maximizing quantity chosen by the monopolistically competitive firm in panel (b), Q_{MC}, the price, P_{MC}, is *higher* than the marginal cost of production, MC_{MC}.

This difference in whether the price equals or exceeds the marginal cost translates into a difference in the attitude of firms toward consumers. A wheat farmer who can sell as much wheat as that farmer wants at the going market price would not get particularly excited if you offered to buy some more wheat at the market price. Since the farmer has no desire to produce more at that price and can sell the wheat to someone else, you are not doing the farmer a favor.

But if you decide to fill up your tank at Josiah's gas station rather than at Katy's gas station, you are helping Josiah's business. Josiah is not willing to cut his price to get more customers—he's already made the best of that trade-off, and any lower price will add less to revenue than to cost. But if he can get a few more customers than he expected at the posted price, that's good news: an additional sale at the *posted* price increases his revenue more than it increases his cost because the posted price exceeds the marginal cost.

The fact that monopolistic competitors, unlike perfect competitors, want to sell more at the going price is crucial to understanding why they engage in activities like advertising that help increase sales.

The other difference between monopolistic competition and perfect competition that is visible in Figure 4.4-4 involves the position of each firm on its average total cost curve. In panel (a), the perfectly competitive firm produces at point Q_{PC}, at the bottom of the U-shaped *ATC* curve. That is, perfectly competitive firms produce the productively efficient quantity at which average total cost is minimized—the *minimum-cost output*. As a result, the total cost of industry output is also minimized.

Under monopolistic competition, in panel (b), the firm produces the quantity at which marginal revenue equals marginal cost, Q_{MC}. Note that Q_{MC} is in the range of output levels where the U-shaped *ATC* curve is *downward-sloping* and not yet at its minimum point. A firm that produces less than the quantity that would minimize average total cost can be described as having **excess capacity**. The typical vendor in a food court or a gas station along a road is not big enough to take maximum advantage of available cost savings. So the total cost of industry output is not minimized in the case of a monopolistically competitive industry.

Firms in a monopolistically competitive industry have **excess capacity**: they produce less than the output at which average total cost is minimized.

It is arguable that, because every monopolistic competitor has excess capacity, monopolistically competitive industries are inefficient. Yet the issue of efficiency under monopolistic competition turns out to be a subtle one that does not have a clear answer due to the tradeoffs involved.

Is Monopolistic Competition Inefficient?

A monopolistic competitor, like a monopolist, does not achieve allocative efficiency because it charges a price above marginal cost. As a result, some people cannot buy an egg roll at the Wonderful Wok restaurant despite being willing to pay at least as much for an egg roll as it costs to produce. In other words, in monopolistic competition, some mutually beneficial transactions go unexploited.

It can also be argued that monopolistic competition fails to achieve productive efficiency: that the excess capacity of every monopolistic competitor implies *wasteful duplication* because monopolistically competitive industries have too many firms. According to this argument, it would be better if there were only two or three vendors in a food court, not six or seven or more. If there were fewer vendors, they would each have lower average total costs and so could offer food more cheaply.

AP® ECON TIP

Like monopolists (and oligopolists, as discussed in Module 4.5), monopolistically competitive firms are allocatively inefficient both in the short run and in the long run because they charge a price that exceeds the marginal cost.

All things considered, there are pros and cons to having a relatively large number of firms. For example, it's true that if there were fewer gas stations along a highway, each gas station would sell more gasoline and so would have a lower cost per gallon. But there is a drawback: motorists would be inconvenienced because gas stations would be farther apart. The numerous firms and the diversity of products offered in a monopolistically competitive industry are beneficial to consumers. So the higher price consumers pay because of excess capacity is offset to some extent by the value they receive from having more locations and a wider variety of offerings.

Does a monopolistically competitive industry arrive at the socially optimal point in this trade-off? Probably not, but it is hard to say whether there are too many firms or too few! Most economists now believe that duplication of effort and excess capacity in monopolistically competitive industries are not large problems in practice.

Product Differentiation

In Module 4.1, we introduced product differentiation as an important tool that firms in imperfectly competitive industries use to distinguish themselves from competitors. Oligopolistic firms use product differentiation to increase their profits, and the small number of firms makes additional strategies based on *tacit collusion* available, as we will discuss in the next Module. Product differentiation is also crucial in monopolistically competitive industries because the large number of firms makes collusion virtually impossible, leaving product differentiation as the only way for firms to acquire some market power and maximize profits.

How do firms in the same industry—such as fast-food vendors, gas stations, or chocolate makers—set their products apart? Advertising and branding sometimes create perceptions of differences with little basis, but in general, firms differentiate their products by—surprise!—actually making them different. The key to product differentiation is that consumers have different preferences and are willing to pay somewhat more to satisfy those preferences. Each producer can carve out a market niche by producing something that caters to the particular preferences of some group of consumers better than the products of other firms. There are three important forms of product differentiation: differentiation by style or type, differentiation by location, and differentiation by quality.

AP® ECON TIP

Product differentiation allows monopolistic competitors and oligopolists to decrease competition, increase market power, and ultimately increase sales.

Differentiation by Style or Type

Let's return to the food court at the mall, where sellers offer different types of fast food: hamburgers, pizza, Chinese food, Mexican food, and so on. Each consumer arrives at the food court with some preference for one or another of these offerings. This preference may depend on the consumer's mood, diet, or meals eaten earlier that day. These preferences will not make consumers indifferent to price: if Wonderful Wok were to charge $15 for an egg roll, everybody would go to Bodacious Burgers or Pizza Paradise instead. But some people will choose a more expensive meal if that type of food is closer to their preference. So the products of the different vendors are substitutes, but they are not *perfect* substitutes—they are *imperfect substitutes.*

Vendors in a food court aren't the only sellers who differentiate their offerings by type. Clothing stores concentrate on women's or men's clothes, on business attire or sportswear, on trendy or classic styles, and so on. Book publishers provide another example of differentiation by type and style. Fantasy novels are differentiated from romances; and among fantasy works, we can differentiate among epics, sword and sorcery stories, and superhero fiction. And no two writers of epic stories are exactly alike: Robert Jordan and Ursula Le Guin each have their devoted fans, for example. In fact, product differentiation is characteristic of most consumer goods. As long as people differ in their tastes, producers find it possible and profitable to offer variety.

Patti McConville/Alamy

Product differentiation in the fantasy book market allows publishers to acquire some market power.

Differentiation by Location

Gas stations along a road offer differentiated products. True, the gas may be exactly the same. But the location of the stations is different, and location matters to consumers: it's more convenient to stop for gas near your home, near your workplace, or near wherever you are when the gas gauge gets low.

In fact, many monopolistically competitive industries supply goods differentiated by location. This is especially true in service industries, from dry cleaners to hairdressers, where customers often choose the seller who is closest rather than cheapest.

Differentiation by Quality

Do you have a craving for chocolate? How much are you willing to spend on it? You see, there's chocolate and then there's *chocolate*: although ordinary chocolate may not be very expensive, gourmet chocolate can cost several dollars per bite.

With chocolate, as with many goods, there is a range of possible qualities. You can get a usable bicycle for less than $100; you can get a much fancier bicycle for 10 times as much. It all depends on how much the additional quality matters to you and how much you will miss the other things you could have purchased with that money.

silvano audisio/Shutterstock

Some customers are willing to pay more for a high-performance bike, while others prefer to pay less for something less fancy. A diverse market satisfies many needs and desires.

Because consumers vary in what they are willing to pay for higher quality, producers can differentiate their products by quality—some offering lower-quality, inexpensive products and others offering higher-quality products at a higher price.

Product differentiation, then, can take several forms. Whatever form it takes, however, there are two important features of industries with differentiated products: *competition among sellers* and *value in diversity.*

Competition among sellers means that even though sellers of differentiated products are not offering identical goods, they are to some extent competing for a limited market. If more businesses enter the market, each will find that it sells a lower quantity at any given price. For example, if a new gas station opens along a road, each of the existing gas stations will sell a bit less.

Value in diversity refers to the gain to consumers from the proliferation of differentiated products. A food court with eight vendors makes consumers happier than one with only six vendors, even if the prices are the same, because some customers will get a meal that is closer to what they had in mind. A town with a convenience store every few blocks saves time for shoppers compared to a town where the convenience stores are inconveniently five miles apart. And when a product such as bicycles or chocolate is available in many different qualities, fewer people are forced to pay for more quality than they need, or to settle for lower quality than they want. Clearly, there are benefits to consumers from having a diversity of available products.

As we'll see next, competition among the sellers of differentiated products is the key to understanding how monopolistic competition works.

Controversies About Product Differentiation

So far we have assumed that products are differentiated in a way that corresponds to some real desires of consumers. There is real convenience in having a gas station in your neighborhood; Indian food and Mexican food are really different from each other.

In the real world, however, some instances of product differentiation can seem puzzling if you think about them. What is the real difference between Crest and Colgate toothpaste? Between Energizer and Duracell batteries? Or a Marriott and a Hilton hotel room? Most people would be hard-pressed to answer these questions. Yet the producers of these goods make considerable efforts to convince consumers that their products are different from and better than those of their competitors. No discussion of product differentiation is complete without spending at least a bit of time on the two related issues—and puzzles—of *advertising* and *brand names.*

The Role of Advertising

Wheat farmers don't advertise their product, but car dealers do. That's not because farmers are shy and car dealers are outgoing; it's because advertising is worthwhile only in industries in which firms have at least some market power. The purpose of advertisements is to persuade people to buy more of a seller's product at the going price. A perfectly competitive firm, which can sell as much as it likes at the going market price, has no incentive to spend money persuading consumers to buy more. Only a firm that has some market power, and which therefore charges a price that is above marginal cost, can gain from advertising. (Some industries that are very competitive, like the milk industry, do advertise—but these ads are sponsored by an association on behalf of the industry as a whole, not on behalf of a particular farm.)

AP® ECON TIP

Exam questions might ask which types of firms engage in advertising. Firms in perfectly competitive markets don't need to advertise because they can sell as much as they want at the market price. Monopolies sometimes advertise in order to increase demand for their products. Monopolistically competitive firms and oligopolists advertise to differentiate their products and boost demand.

Given the influence of advertising, it's easy to see why firms with market power would spend money on it. The big question about advertising is, *why* is it influential? A related question is whether advertising, from society's point of view, is a waste of resources.

Not all advertising poses a puzzle. Some advertising is a straightforward way for sellers to inform potential buyers about what they have to offer (or, occasionally, for buyers to use *want ads* to inform potential sellers about what they want). Nor is there much controversy about the economic usefulness of ads that provide information: the sleeping bag ad in the camping magazine that says "polyester fiber, warm down to 40 degrees" tells you things you need to know.

Michal Besser/Alamy

What can a giant pink bunny tell us about batteries? Nothing, but it might send a signal that these batteries are worth buying.

But what information is being conveyed when a famous actor, athlete, or rabbit declares that some company's batteries are better than those inside that pink mechanical rabbit? Surely nobody believes that the sports star is also a battery expert, or that they chose to represent the company they believe makes the best batteries as opposed to the company that offered the most pay. Yet companies believe, with good reason, that money spent on such promotions increases their sales—and that they would be in big trouble if they stopped advertising but their competitors continued to do so.

Why are consumers influenced by ads that do not really provide any information about the product? One answer is that consumers are not as rational as economists typically assume. Perhaps consumers' judgments, or even their tastes, can be influenced by things that economists think ought to be irrelevant, such as which company has hired the most charismatic celebrity to endorse its product. There is surely some truth to this. Consumer rationality is a useful working assumption; it is not an absolute truth.

However, another answer is that consumer response to advertising is not entirely irrational because ads can serve as indirect *signals* in a world in which consumers don't have good information about products. To take a common example, suppose you need some local service you don't use regularly, like repair service on a computer. You find a number of service providers listed online, some with a simple Facebook page and others with their own professionally made website. You know that those websites are expensive to design; still, it may be quite rational to contact one of the companies with a nice website. After all, the nice website probably means that the company is relatively large and successful—otherwise, the investment in professional website design wouldn't have been worthwhile.

The same principle may partly explain why ads feature celebrities. You don't really believe that the famous singer prefers that watch; but the fact that the watch manufacturer is willing and able to pay their fee tells you that it is a major company that is likely to stand behind its product. According to this reasoning, an expensive advertisement serves to establish the quality of a firm's products in the eyes of consumers.

The possibility that it is rational for consumers to respond to advertising also has some bearing on the question of whether advertising is a waste of resources. If ads work by manipulating only the weak-minded, the $296 billion U.S. businesses spent on advertising in 2021 was unproductive — except to the extent that ads sometimes provide entertainment. To the extent that advertising conveys important information, however, it is an economically productive activity after all.

Brand Names

A **brand name** is a name owned by a particular firm that distinguishes its products from those of other firms.

Most fast-food restaurants in the United States are members of major chains; the same is true of most motels and many, if not most, stores in shopping malls. Chain fast-food restaurants and motels are only part of a broader story about the role of **brand names**, which are names owned by particular companies that differentiate their products in the minds of consumers. In many cases, a company's brand name is the most important asset it possesses. Clearly, McDonald's is worth far more than the sum of the deep-fat fryers and hamburger grills the company owns. In fact, companies often go to considerable lengths to defend their brand names, suing anyone else who uses them without permission.

As with the associated practice of advertising, the social usefulness of brand names is a source of dispute. On the one hand, brand names often do create unjustified market power. Consumers often pay more for brand-name goods in the supermarket even though consumer experts assure us that the cheaper store brands are equally good. Similarly, many common medicines, like aspirin, are cheaper — with no loss of quality — in their generic form. On the other hand, for many products the brand name does convey information. A traveler arriving in a strange town can be sure of what awaits in a Holiday Inn or a McDonald's; a tired and hungry traveler may find this preferable to trying an independent hotel or restaurant that might be better — but might be worse.

Brand names also offer some assurance that the seller is engaged in repeated interaction with its customers and so has a reputation to protect. If a traveler eats a bad meal at a restaurant in a tourist trap and vows never to eat there again, the restaurant owner may not care, since the chance is small that the traveler would be a repeat customer even if the meal were satisfying. But if that traveler eats a bad meal at McDonald's and vows never to eat a McDonald's again, that matters to the company. This gives McDonald's an incentive to provide consistent quality, thereby assuring travelers that quality controls are in place.

Module 4.4  Review

Check Your Understanding

1. Suppose a monopolistically competitive industry composed of firms with U-shaped average total cost curves is in long-run equilibrium. For each of the following changes, explain how the industry is affected in the short run and how it adjusts to a new long-run equilibrium.
   a. a technological change that increases fixed cost for every firm in the industry
   b. a technological change that decreases marginal cost for every firm in the industry
2. Why is it impossible for firms in a monopolistically competitive industry to join together to form a monopoly that is capable of maintaining positive economic profit in the long run?
3. Indicate whether the following statements are true or false, and explain your answers.
   a. Like a firm in a perfectly competitive industry, a firm in a monopolistically competitive industry is willing to sell a good at any price that equals or exceeds marginal cost.
   b. Suppose there is a monopolistically competitive industry in long-run equilibrium that possesses excess capacity. All the firms in the industry would be better off if they merged into a single firm and produced a single product, but whether consumers would be made better off by this is uncertain.

Tackle the AP® Test: Multiple-Choice Questions

1. Which of the following is a characteristic of monopolistic competition?
   a. a standardized product
   b. many sellers
   c. substantial barriers to entry
   d. positive long-run profits
   e. a perfectly elastic demand curve

2. Which of the following necessarily exists for a monopolistic competitor in the short run?
   a. positive economic profit
   b. normal profit
   c. loss
   d. allocative efficiency
   e. competition

3. Which of the following necessarily exists for a monopolistic competitor in the long run?
   a. loss
   b. excess capacity
   c. positive economic profit
   d. productive efficiency
   e. allocative efficiency

4. Which of the following best describes a monopolistic competitor's demand curve?
   a. upward-sloping
   b. downward-sloping
   c. U-shaped
   d. horizontal
   e. vertical

5. Which of the following will necessarily eliminate profits in a monopolistically competitive industry in the long run?
   a. rising barriers to entry
   b. increasing production costs
   c. increasing advertising costs
   d. the entry of new firms
   e. the exit of firms

6. In addition to monopolies, firms in which of the following market structures will advertise?
   a. perfect competition only
   b. oligopoly only
   c. monopolistic competition only
   d. oligopoly and monopolistic competition only
   e. perfect competition, oligopoly, and monopolistic competition

7. Which of the following is certainly true?
   a. Travelers typically avoid restaurants with familiar brand names when they travel.
   b. Two gas stations selling the same product in different locations are an example of product differentiation.
   c. Firms in a perfectly competitive market have an incentive to advertise.
   d. Product differentiation is good for firms but bad for consumers.
   e. It is irrational for consumers to respond to advertising.

Tackle the AP® Test: Free-Response Questions

1. Draw a correctly labeled graph for a monopolistically competitive firm that is taking a loss in the short run. Shade the area that represents the firm's loss.

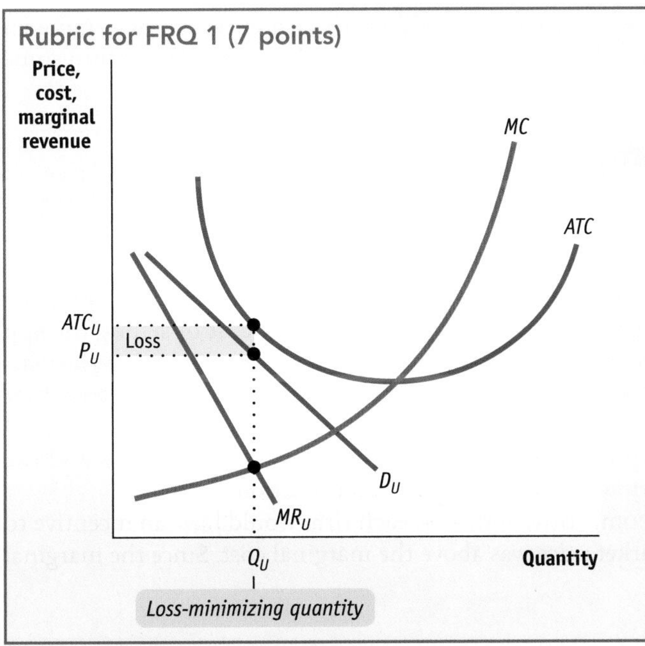

1 point: Correctly labeled axes

1 point: Downward-sloping demand curve

1 point: Marginal revenue curve below the demand curve

1 point: Loss-minimizing quantity below where $MC = MR$

1 point: Loss-minimizing price on demand curve above where $MC = MR$

1 point: U-shaped average total cost curve above the demand curve at every quantity

1 point: Correct loss area shaded

2. Draw a correctly labeled graph for a monopolistically competitive firm in long-run equilibrium. Label the distance along the quantity axis that represents excess capacity. **(6 points)**

3. Explain two ways in which product differentiation can be useful to consumers and two ways in which it can be detrimental to consumers. **(4 points)**

MODULE 4.5

Oligopoly and Game Theory

In this Module, you will learn to:
- Discuss how games are played among interdependent oligopolists
- Explain why oligopolists have an incentive to collude
- Analyze strategies for games using payoff matrices
- Determine dominant strategies and Nash equilibria in a variety of games
- Calculate the incentive needed to change a player's dominant strategy

In Module 4.1, we learned that an oligopoly is distinguished from a monopolistically competitive industry by having only a few firms. What number constitutes a "few"? There is no standard answer, so it is not always easy to determine an industry's market structure just by looking at the number of firms. Economists use various measures to gain a better picture of market structure, including concentration ratios as explained in Module 4.1. In this Module, we will see that the relationship between the firms is another good indication of market structure.

Firms are **interdependent** when the outcome (profit) of each firm depends on the actions of the other firms in the market.

Because an oligopoly has only a small number of firms in the industry, the behavior of each firm – their pricing, advertising, output levels, and so on – can affect the other firms. That is, an oligopoly is characterized by **interdependence**, a relationship in which the outcome (profit) of each firm depends on the actions of the other firms in the market. This is not true for monopolies because, by definition, a monopoly has no other firms to consider. On the other hand, perfectly competitive markets and monopolistically competitive markets contain so many firms that no one firm has a significant effect on the outcome of the others. The interdependence of oligopolists makes studying this market structure much more interesting because firms must observe and predict the behavior of other firms. Such a market is also more complicated. To understand the strategies of oligopolists, we must do more than find the point where the *MC* and *MR* curves intersect!

Understanding Oligopoly

How much will a firm produce? Up to this point, the answer has always been: a firm will produce the quantity that maximizes its profit. In an industry with one firm or many firms, we can assume that each firm will use its cost curves to determine its profit-maximizing output. When it comes to oligopoly, however, we run into some complexities.

A Duopoly Example

An oligopoly consisting of only two firms is a **duopoly**. Each firm is known as a **duopolist**.

Let's begin by looking at the simplest version of the oligopoly puzzle: an industry in which there are only two firms – a **duopoly** – and each is known as a **duopolist**.

Imagine that only two firms sell dictionary apps for smartphones and that the apps sold by the two firms are indistinguishable from each other. Once a company has incurred the fixed cost of creating an app, the marginal cost of selling the app to another customer is very low (to keep things simple, we will assume that the marginal cost is zero). In this case the companies are concerned only with the revenue they receive from sales.

Table 4.5-1 shows a hypothetical demand schedule for dictionary apps and the total revenue of the industry at each price–quantity combination.

If this were a perfectly competitive industry, each firm would have an incentive to sell more as long as the market price was above the marginal cost. Since the marginal

Table 4.5-1 Demand Schedule for Dictionary Apps

Price of app	Quantity of apps demanded (millions)	Total revenue (millions)
$12	0	$0
11	1	11
10	2	20
9	3	27
8	4	32
7	5	35
6	6	36
5	7	35
4	8	32
3	9	27
2	10	20
1	11	11
0	12	0

cost is zero, this would mean that at equilibrium, dictionary apps would be provided for free. Firms would sell more until the price equaled zero, yielding a total output of 12 million apps and zero revenue for both firms.

However, with only two firms in the industry, it would seem foolish to allow the price and revenue to plummet to zero. Like a monopolist, each firm sees that profits will be higher if the two firms charge a higher price, and therefore sell a smaller quantity, than they would in a perfectly competitive industry. What will the two firms do?

One possibility is that the two companies will engage in **collusion**—they will cooperate to raise their joint profits. The strongest form of collusion is a **cartel**, a group of firms with an agreement to work together to limit output and increase price, and therefore profit.

Firms engage in **collusion** when they cooperate to raise their joint profits. A **cartel** is a group of firms that agree to increase prices and reduce output in order to raise their joint profits.

The world's most famous cartel is the Organization of the Petroleum Exporting Countries (OPEC). As its name indicates, OPEC is actually a cartel made up of governments rather than firms. There's a reason for this: cartels among firms are illegal in the United States and many other jurisdictions, whereas organizations of governments can often evade restrictions on firm behavior. But let's ignore the law for a moment. Suppose the two firms selling dictionary apps were to form a cartel and that this cartel decided to act as if it were a monopolist, maximizing total industry profits. It's obvious from Table 4.5-1 that in order to maximize the combined profits of the firms, this cartel should set a price of $6 per app. At that price, they would sell 6 million apps, leading to revenue of $36 million, the maximum possible. Then the only question would be how many of those 6 million apps does each firm get to sell. A "fair" solution might be for each firm to sell 3 million apps and receive revenues of $18 million.

Even if the two firms agreed on such a deal, they might have a problem: each of the firms would have an incentive to break its word and sell more than the agreed-upon quantity at less than the agreed-upon price.

Anadolu Agency/Getty Images

OPEC representatives meet regularly to discuss the cartel's policies of cooperation.

Collusion and Competition

Suppose that the presidents of the two app sellers were to agree that each would charge $6 per app and sell 3 million apps over the next year. Both would understand that this plan maximizes their combined profits. And both would have an incentive to cheat.

To see why, consider what would happen if one firm honored its agreement to charge $6, but the other ignored its promise and lowered its price to $5 per app, the price at which 7 million apps are demanded. The industry's total revenue would fall from $36 million ($\$6 \times 6$ million apps) to $35 million ($\$5 \times 7$ million apps). However, the cheating firm would have the best price, attract all of the customers, and receive the entire $35 million in total revenue rather than half of $36 million. Since we are assuming a marginal cost of zero, this would mean a $17 million increase in profit over the $18 million the firm would have earned by charging $6. Then the other firm would see that by lowering its price to $4, it could sell 8 million apps and receive $32 million in revenue. As long as the price remained above the marginal cost, these firms would have an incentive to undercut each other's prices.

More generally, the incentive to cheat motivates firms in an oligopoly to lower their price and sell more than the quantity that maximizes their joint profits, rather than maintaining a higher price and limiting output as a true monopolist would.

In the oil industry, among others, some firms cheat on collusive agreements by producing more than the agreed-upon quantity, which has the effect of increasing the market quantity and decreasing the market price. Let's examine how this affects firm profits. We know that a profit-maximizing monopolist sets marginal cost (which in the dictionary app example is zero) equal to marginal revenue. But what is marginal revenue? Recall from Module 4.2 that producing an additional unit of a good has two effects:

1. A positive *quantity effect*: one more unit is sold, increasing total revenue by the price at which that unit is sold.
2. A negative *price effect*: in order to sell one more unit, the monopolist must cut the market price on *all* units sold.

The negative price effect is the reason marginal revenue for a monopolist is less than the market price. When considering the effect of increasing production, an oligopolist is concerned only with the price effect on its *own* units of output, not on those of its fellow oligopolists. In the apps example, both duopolists suffer a negative price effect if one firm decides to lower the price and sell additional apps. But each firm cares only about the portion of the negative price effect that falls on the apps it sells.

This tells us that an individual firm in an oligopolistic industry faces a smaller price effect from an additional unit of output than a monopolist; therefore, the marginal revenue for such a firm is higher. So it will seem to be profitable for any one firm in an oligopoly to increase output, even if that increase reduces the profits of the industry as a whole. The trouble for these oligopolists is that if everyone thinks that way, the result is that everyone earns a lower profit!

For the market structures we examined previously, we were able to analyze firm behavior by asking what a firm should do to maximize profits. But even if both duopolists are trying to maximize profits, what does this predict about their behavior? Will they engage in collusion, reaching and holding to an agreement that maximizes their combined profits? Or will they engage in **noncooperative behavior**, with each firm acting in its own self-interest, even though this has the effect of driving down everyone's profits? Both strategies can be carried out with a goal of profit maximization. Which strategy will actually describe their behavior?

When firms act in their own self-interest, ignoring the effects of their actions on each other's profits, they engage in **noncooperative behavior**.

If there were dozens or hundreds of firms, it would be safe to assume they would behave noncooperatively. Yet, when there are only a handful of firms in an industry, it's hard to determine whether collusion will actually occur. Now you see why oligopoly presents a puzzle: there are only a small number of players, making collusion a real possibility.

Since collusion is ultimately more profitable than noncooperative behavior, firms have an incentive to collude if they can. One way to do so is to formalize it—sign an agreement (maybe even make a legal contract) or establish some financial incentives for the companies to set their prices high—a practice known as *price fixing*. But in the United States and many other nations, firms can't do that—at least not legally.

AP® ECON TIP

To make sense of the discussions of cartels and related matters that might appear on the exam, remember that collusion is illegal in the United States but legal in some parts of the world.

A contract among firms to keep prices high would be unenforceable, and it could be a one-way ticket to jail. The same goes for an informal agreement. In fact, executives from rival firms rarely meet without lawyers present, who make sure that the conversation does not stray into inappropriate territory. Even hinting at how nice it would be if prices were higher can bring an unwelcome interview with the Justice Department or the Federal Trade Commission.

Allegations of price fixing are common in oligopolies. For example, in 2021, the United States Justice Department announced that several major broiler chicken producers had been indicted for price-fixing, including Pilgrim's Pride, which paid a fine of $107 million for its role in the conspiracy. And in the same year, three manufacturers of generic pharmaceutical drugs paid a total of $447 million to resolve alleged conspiracies to fix the prices of various drugs.

©Bryan Smith/Zuma Press

A contract among firms to keep prices high would be unenforceable, and could be a one-way ticket to jail.

Sometimes, oligopolistic firms just ignore the rules. More often, they develop strategies for making the best of the situation depending on what they know, or predict, about the other firms' behavior. As in the dictionary app example, some firms repeatedly undercut each other's prices—charging a bit less than the others to steal their customers—until the price reaches the level of the marginal cost, as under perfect competition.

Understandably, oligopolists would prefer to avoid direct price competition that leaves them earning zero economic profit. Modules 4.1 and 4.4 introduced price discrimination as a strategy for limiting competition that allows oligopolists to cultivate a loyal set of customers and to charge prices above the marginal cost. This violation of the $P = MC$ condition for allocative efficiency makes oligopoly an inefficient market structure.

We have seen that collusion is another approach to dodging the profit-suppressing effects of competition. Next, we examine efforts to collude that do not involve formal agreements.

Games Oligopolists Play

If you eat tuna salad, you most likely consume the product of StarKist or Bumble Bee, two of the largest firms in the U.S. tuna market. The tuna oligopoly includes other firms, but to keep things simple, we'll treat this market as a duopoly. Each firm in a duopoly realizes that its profit depends on what its competitor does, and that its competitor's profit depends on what it does. That is, the two firms are interdependent—each firm's decision significantly affects the profit of the other firm (or firms, in the case of more than two).

In effect, the two firms are playing a "game" in which the profit of each player depends not only on its own actions but on those of the other player or players. In order to better understand how oligopolists behave, economists and mathematicians developed **game theory**—the study of behavior among interdependent players. Game theory has many applications, not just to economics but also to military strategy, politics, and other social sciences.

Game theory is the study of behavior in situations of interdependence.

The Prisoner's Dilemma

Game theory deals with situations in which the reward to any particular player—the **payoff**—depends not only on their own actions but also on the actions of other players in the game. In the case of oligopolistic firms, the payoff for each player is simply the firm's profit.

The interdependence between the players can be represented with a **payoff matrix** as shown in **Figure 4.5-1**. A payoff matrix is a non-graphical type of model known as

A player's **payoff** in a game is that player's reward, such as an oligopolist's profit.

A **payoff matrix** shows how the payoff to each of the participants in a two-player game depends on the actions of both.

FIGURE 4.5-1 A Payoff Matrix

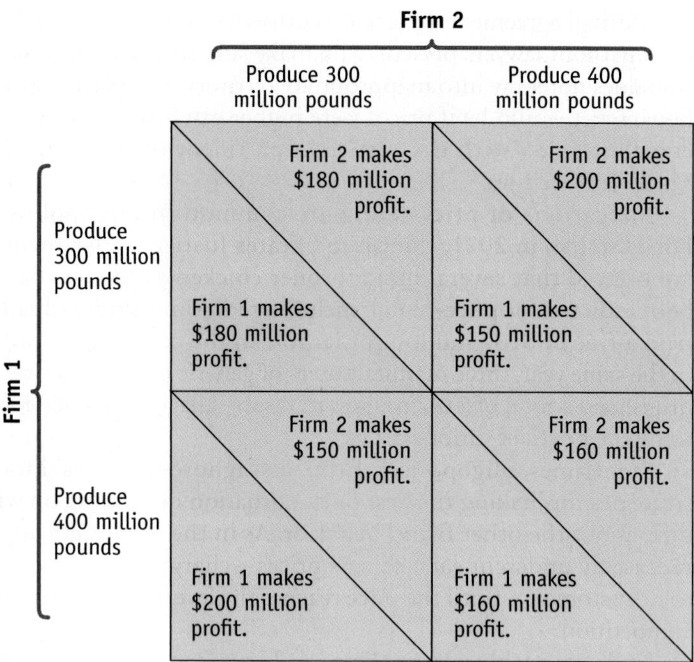

Two firms must decide how much tuna to produce. The profits of the two firms are *interdependent*: each firm's profit depends not only on its own decision, but also on the other's decision. Each row represents an action by Firm 1; each column represents an action by Firm 2. Both firms will be better off if they both choose the lower output, but it is in each firm's individual interest to choose the higher output.

a *normal form* model, which represents all of the possible strategies for each player and the corresponding payoffs. Each row corresponds to an action by one player; each column corresponds to an action by the other. For simplicity, let's assume that each firm can pick only one of two alternatives: produce 300 million pounds of tuna or produce 400 million pounds.

The matrix contains four boxes, each divided by a diagonal line. Each box shows the payoff to the two firms that results from a pair of choices; the number below the diagonal shows Firm 1's profits, the number above the diagonal shows Firm 2's profits.

These payoffs show that the combined profits of the two firms are maximized if they each produce 300 million pounds. However, either firm can increase its own profit by producing 400 million pounds if the other produces only 300 million pounds. But if both produce the larger quantity, both will have lower profits than if they had both produced the smaller quantity.

The **prisoner's dilemma** is a game based on two premises: (1) each player has an incentive to choose an action that benefits that player at the other player's expense; and (2) when both players follow that incentive, both are worse off than if they had acted cooperatively.

The particular situation shown here is a version of the famous case of interdependence known as the **prisoner's dilemma**, a type of game in which the payoff matrix implies the following:

- Regardless of what the other player does, each player has an incentive to take an action that benefits that player at the other player's expense.
- When both players follow that incentive, both are worse off than they would have been if neither had followed that incentive.

The original illustration of the prisoner's dilemma occurred in a fictional story about two accomplices in crime—let's call them Richard and Justin—who have been caught by the police. The police have enough evidence to put the suspects behind bars for 5 years. They also know that the pair have committed a more serious crime, one that carries a 20-year sentence; unfortunately, they don't have enough evidence to convict the young men on that more serious charge. To do so, they would need each of the suspects to implicate the other in the second crime.

So the police put the suspects in separate cells and say the following to each: "Here's the deal: if neither of you confesses, you know that we'll send both of you to jail for 5 years. If you confess and implicate your partner, and he doesn't do the same, we reduce your sentence from 5 years to 2. But if your partner confesses and you don't, you'll get the maximum of 20 years. If both of you confess, we'll give you both 15 years."

Figure 4.5-2 shows the payoffs for each suspect, depending on the decision to remain silent or to confess. (Usually higher payoffs are better than lower payoffs. This case is an exception: a higher number of years in prison is bad, not good!) Let's assume that the suspects have no way to communicate and that they have not sworn an oath to cooperate or anything of that sort. So each acts in his own self-interest. What will they do?

The answer is clear: both will confess. Look at it first from Richard's point of view: he is better off confessing, regardless of what Justin does. If Justin doesn't confess, Richard's confession reduces his own sentence from 5 years to 2. If Justin does confess, Richard's confession reduces his sentence from 20 to 15 years. Either way, it's clearly in Richard's interest to confess. And because he faces the same incentives, it's clearly in Justin's interest to confess, too.

Warner Bros./Photofest

In the movie *Murder by Numbers*, loosely based on a real 1924 murder case, the police know that high schoolers Richard and Justin were involved in a crime. Yet there is insufficient evidence to convict the suspects, so the police offer a lighter sentence in exchange for a confession from either one of them.

FIGURE 4.5-2 The Prisoner's Dilemma

Richard \ Justin	Don't confess	Confess
Don't confess	Justin gets 5-year sentence. / Richard gets 5-year sentence.	Justin gets 2-year sentence. / Richard gets 20-year sentence.
Confess	Justin gets 20-year sentence. / Richard gets 2-year sentence.	Justin gets 15-year sentence. / Richard gets 15-year sentence.

Each of two suspects, held in separate cells, is offered a deal by the police—a light sentence if he confesses and implicates his accomplice but his accomplice does not do the same. The sentence is heavy for a suspect if he does not confess but his accomplice does. It is in the joint interest of both suspects not to confess; it is in each one's individual interest to confess.

In this situation, confessing is what economists call a *dominant strategy*. An action is a **dominant strategy** when it is the player's best action regardless of the action taken by the other player. It's important to note that not all games have a dominant strategy—it depends on the structure of payoffs in the game. In the case of Richard and Justin, it is clearly in the interest of the police to structure the payoffs so that confessing is a dominant strategy for both suspects. As long as the two prisoners have no way to make an enforceable agreement that neither will confess (something they can't do if they can't communicate, and the police certainly won't allow them to do so because the police want to compel each one to confess), the dominant strategy exists as the best alternative.

An action is a **dominant strategy** when it is a player's best action regardless of the action taken by the other player.

If each prisoner acts rationally in his own interest, both will confess. Yet if neither of them confesses, both will receive a much lighter sentence! In a prisoner's dilemma, each player has a clear incentive to act in a way that hurts the other player—but when both make that choice, it leaves both of them worse off.

A **Nash equilibrium**, also known as a **noncooperative equilibrium**, is the result when each player in a game chooses the action that maximizes his or her payoff, given the actions of other players.

PLINIO LEPRI/AP Images

Mathematician and Nobel laureate John Forbes Nash Jr. proposed one of the key ideas in game theory.

When Richard and Justin both confess, they reach an *equilibrium* of the game. We have used the concept of equilibrium many times in this book; it is an outcome in which no individual or firm has an incentive to change his or her action. In game theory, this kind of equilibrium, in which each player takes the action that is best for him or her, given the actions taken by other players, is known as a **Nash equilibrium**, after the mathematician and Nobel laureate John Nash. (Nash's life was chronicled in the best-selling biography *A Beautiful Mind*, which was made into a movie.) Because the players in a Nash equilibrium do not take into account the effect of their actions on others, this is also known as a **noncooperative equilibrium**.

Now look back at Figure 4.5-1: the two firms face a prisoner's dilemma just like Richard and Justin did after their crimes. Each firm is better off producing the higher output, regardless of what the other firm does. Yet if both produce 400 million pounds, both are worse off than if they had followed an agreement to produce only 300 million pounds. In both cases, then, the pursuit of individual self-interest—the effort to maximize profit or to minimize jail time—has the perverse effect of hurting both players.

Prisoner's dilemmas appear in many situations. Examples include business competitors deciding whether to advertise high or low prices, athletes deciding whether to use illegal performance-enhancing drugs, and countries deciding whether to spend more or less on military hardware.

More Games

We can use payoff matrices to analyze any number of games played by individuals and firms. The equilibria of many of these games differ from what we've seen in the prisoner's dilemma. For example, in the prisoner's dilemma, the Nash equilibrium happens to be an equilibrium of two dominant strategies—a *dominant strategy equilibrium*—but Nash equilibria can exist when there is no dominant strategy at all. Also, a game can have multiple Nash equilibria.

Suppose two grocery store chains, Chain 1 and Chain 2, consider opening a store in either Ayville or Beeville. The chains do not want to operate in the same town because the resulting competition would lead to low prices. Neither chain has a dominant strategy because the best strategy for each depends on what the other is doing. However, Chain 1 opening a store in Ayville and Chain 2 opening a store in Beeville is a Nash equilibrium because each chain takes the action that is best given the action of the other. Chain 1 opening a store in Beeville and Chain 2 opening a store in Ayville is also a Nash equilibrium, because again, neither chain wants to change its behavior given what the other is doing. This game resembles those played by two people who are trying to avoid each other or two competing firms that don't want to advertise on the same website.

The following section explains tricks to identify dominant strategies and Nash equilibria using a payoff matrix. We'll use these methods to analyze several games with varying outcomes.

Approaches and Applications

Figure 4.5-3 provides a payoff matrix for the game of Chain 1 and Chain 2 trying to avoid opening a grocery store in the same town. The numbers in the matrix represent profits. In each case, the profit levels are influenced not only by the presence or absence of the other chain but also by the location of the town, because the distance of each town from the chains' distribution centers and other store locations differ. For example, the upper-left set of numbers indicates that if both chains go to Ayville, Chain 1 will receive \$2 million in profit and Chain 2 will receive \$4 million in profit. By comparing the profit levels, we can see that Chain 1 gets less profit in Ayville than Chain 2, and that both players would be happier if they were not in the same place. If, instead, Chain 1 goes to Ayville and Chain 2 goes to Beeville, Chain 1 will receive \$4 million while Chain 2 receives \$6 million, as indicated by the upper-right set of numbers.

FIGURE 4.5-3 A Game of Avoidance

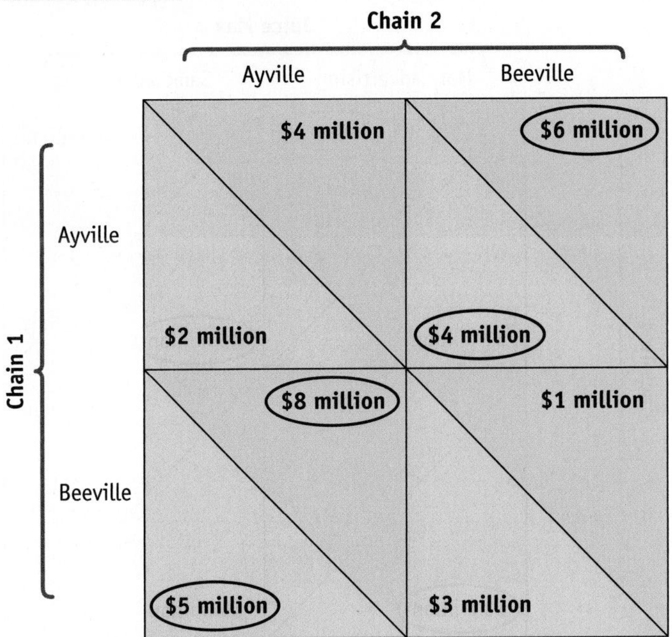

The game of two chains trying not to open grocery stores in the same town has no dominant strategies and two Nash equilibria.

Here's a trick for finding dominant strategies and Nash equilibria. Begin by supposing that Chain 2 goes to Ayville. In the "Ayville" column for Chain 2, we see that Chain 1 receives $2 million in profit by going to Ayville and $5 million in profit by going to Beeville. Circle the best outcome for Chain 1, which is the $5 million by going to Beeville. Then suppose that Chain 2 goes to Beeville. Circle the best outcome for Chain 1, which is to receive $4 million by going to Ayville.

Now look at things from Chain 2's point of view. If Chain 1 goes to Ayville, the options for Chain 2 are to receive $4 million by going to Ayville or $6 million by going to Beeville. Circle the best outcome for Chain 2: $6 million. Finally, suppose that Chain 1 goes to Beeville. Circle the best outcome for Chain 2 in that case, which is to receive $8 million by going to Ayville.

Chain 2 has a dominant strategy if there are two circles around his outcomes in the same column. In this game, Chain 2 does not have a dominant strategy because it has one circle in the "Ayville" column and one circle in the "Beeville" column. Chain 1 has a dominant strategy if there are two circles around its outcomes in the same row. Here, Chain 1 does not have a dominant strategy because it has only one circle in each row.

A combination of strategies is a Nash equilibrium if the box representing that combination contains two circles. In this game, there are two circles in the box representing Chain 1 going to Beeville and Chain 2 going to Ayville, so that is a Nash equilibrium. The two circles in the box representing Chain 1 going to Ayville and Chain 2 going to Beeville indicate a second Nash equilibrium. So the two Nash equilibria are: Chain 1 in Ayville and Chain 2 in Beeville, and Chain 2 in Ayville and Chain 1 in Beeville. Whichever chain can commit to being in a town first has the *first-mover advantage* of being able to ward off the other chain.

Sometimes firms face differing choices. For example, suppose that Juice Tree is deciding whether to raise its price on orange juice, while competitor Juice Max is deciding whether to spend more on advertising. **Figure 4.5-4** shows hypothetical profits for each firm, depending on the chosen strategies. For example, if Juice Tree raises its price and Juice Max doesn't advertise more, some of Juice Tree's customers will switch to Juice Max, increasing Juice Max's profit from $4 million to $6 million. In this case, Juice Tree's profit increases from $5 million to $6 million, indicating that the price effect of receiving more per unit is larger than the quantity effect of losing customers.

AP® ECON TIP

Learn how to interpret a payoff matrix. We've designed the matrices in this text to be easy to understand, but the matrices on the AP® exam may contain fewer words and won't be color-coded. The payoffs might simply be side by side, in which case the payoff on the left is for the player named on the left side of the matrix and the payoff on the right is for the player named above the matrix. For instance, the matrix in Figure 4.5-3 might appear like this:

		Chain 2	
		Ayville	Beeville
Chain 1	Ayville	$2, $4	$4, $6
	Beeville	$5, $8	$3, $1

FIGURE 4.5-4 Differing Choices

Players don't always face the same choices. In this game, Juice Tree is deciding whether to raise its price on orange juice, while competitor Juice Max is deciding whether to spend more on advertising. Juice Max has a dominant strategy of spending more on advertising, while Juice Tree has no dominant strategy. There is one Nash equilibrium of Juice Tree keeping the same price and Juice Max spending more on advertising.

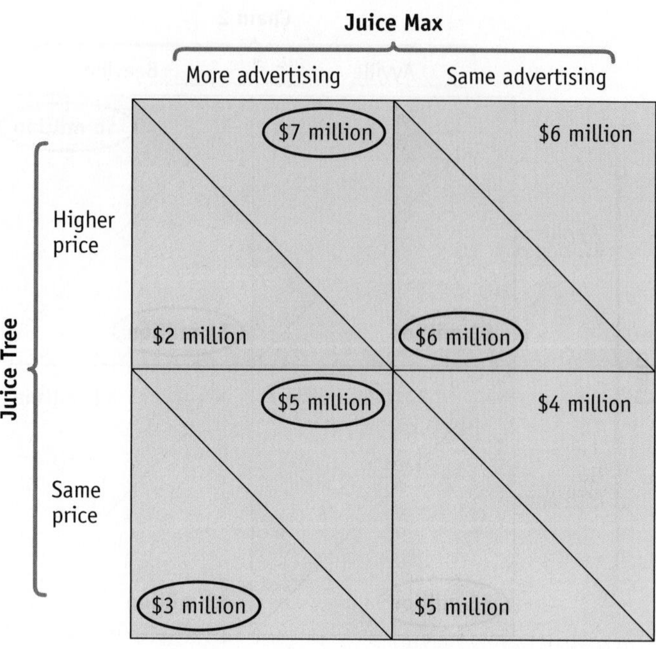

Top Photo Corporation/Alamy

The story changes if Juice Max advertises more: Juice Tree's profit decreases from $3 million to $2 million if it raises its price, because Juice Max is better able to draw attention to Juice Tree's higher prices and attract its customers.

Using the circle trick, we find one Nash equilibrium where Juice Tree keeps its price the same and Juice Max advertises more. The two circles around Juice Max's payoffs in the left column indicate that Juice Max has a dominant strategy of advertising more. Juice Tree does not have a dominant strategy because its best strategy depends on the strategy of Juice Max—Juice Tree is better off raising its price if Juice Max doesn't advertise more, and better off not raising its price if Juice Max does advertise more.

Spending more on advertising is a wise strategy for Juice Max, but in other situations the cost of more advertising can exceed the benefit. Suppose Ally and Mateo offer competing painting services, and each must decide whether to rent a billboard to attract customers. Panel (a) of **Figure 4.5-5** shows each painter's annual profits depending on the chosen strategies. Remember that oligopolists are not identical, so differing characteristics can result in differing payoffs for two firms in analogous situations. In this case, Mateo is relatively unknown among the potential customers and receives a net gain from billboard advertising regardless of Ally's decision. If Mateo does not rent a billboard, Ally receives a net gain of $5,000 from a billboard. But if Mateo does rent a billboard, he attracts so many new customers that Ally cannot gain enough to cover the cost of a billboard, and Ally loses $4,000 by renting one.

Applying the circle trick, the two circles around Mateo's payoffs in the left column indicate that Mateo has a dominant strategy of advertising. There are not two circles around Ally's payoffs in any one row, so she does not have a dominant strategy. The two circles in the box for Ally not getting a billboard and Mateo getting a billboard indicate that neither side would want to take a different action given what the other is doing, so that combination is a Nash equilibrium.

The situations we can explore with the payoff matrix are endless and include changes in prices, taxes, or related policies that affect oligopolists. For example, the

AP® ECON TIP

Using the circle trick, whenever there are two circles in the same box, a Nash equilibrium exists. Whenever there are two circles in a column (or row) for a player, a dominant strategy exists.

FIGURE 4.5-5 Differing Payoffs

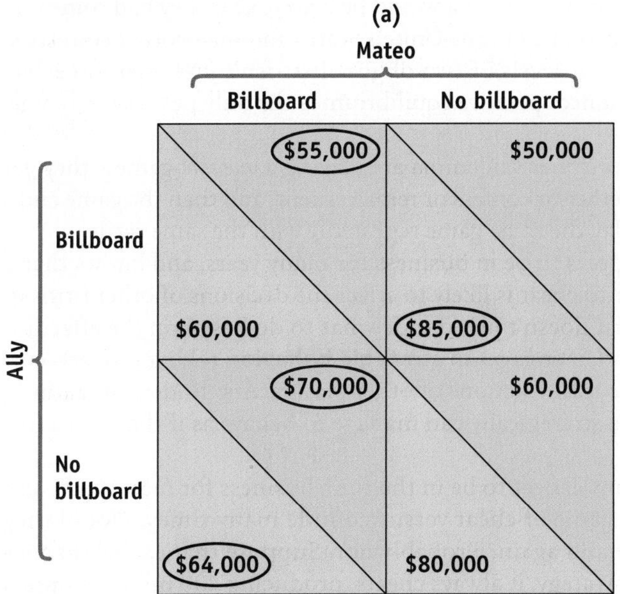

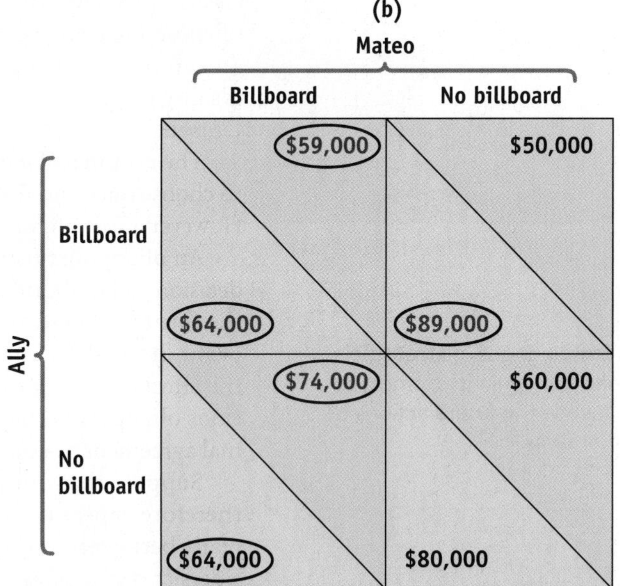

Even when facing the same choices, differences among oligopolists can cause them to receive different payoffs in analogous situations. In our example, Ally is a well-known painter in the area, but Mateo is a newcomer. Panel (a) shows a dominant strategy for Mateo to rent a billboard to make customers aware of his services, whereas Ally is better off not renting a billboard if Mateo rents one. The one Nash equilibrium in this case is for Mateo to rent a billboard and for Ally not to. Changes in prices, taxes, or related policies can change the payoffs of a game—if a change affects only one strategy, be careful to adjust only the payoffs for that strategy. Panel (b) shows the effect of a $4,000 decrease in the cost of renting a billboard, with the changes relative to panel (a) shown in bold green. The lower cost makes renting a billboard a weakly dominant strategy for Ally, meaning that the payoffs from that strategy are at least as good, and in some cases better, than the payoffs from the alternative strategy. The lower rental cost also creates an additional Nash equilibrium of both players renting a billboard.

company that rents billboards might want to adjust its prices in a way that would make billboard advertising a dominant strategy. Recall that Ally would currently want a billboard only if Mateo did not have one. By examining the payoff matrix, we can determine the drop in the annual rental price that would give Ally a sufficient incentive to rent a billboard regardless of whether Mateo rents one. Panel (a) of Figure 4.4-5 shows that if Mateo did rent a billboard, Ally's profit would be $64,000 without a billboard and $60,000 with a billboard. Her net loss from renting a billboard would be $4,000, so it would take a $4,000 price drop to eliminate that loss.

Panel (b) of Figure 4.5-5 shows how the payoff matrix is adjusted to reflect a $4,000 drop in the price of billboard rental. As shown with bold green numbers, the price drop increases each profit level associated with renting a billboard by $4,000. Notice that if Mateo rents a billboard, Ally receives a profit of $64,000 with or without a billboard. Which number do we circle when applying the circle trick to two identical choices? Both! This indicates that Ally is indifferent between the two strategies if Mateo has a billboard. If Mateo doesn't have a billboard, Ally earns more profit with a billboard. Because Ally is sometimes indifferent about having a billboard and sometimes she is better off with one, we describe having a billboard as a *weakly dominant strategy* for Ally. Having a billboard is again a dominant strategy for Mateo. And now there are two Nash equilibria: both having a billboard, and Ally having no billboard while Mateo does have a billboard.

If Ally and Mateo had to decide whether to rent billboards year after year, this would be considered a *repeated game*. Next, we examine how repeated games create new options for strategy and cooperation.

AP® ECON TIP

Game theory questions show up frequently on the AP® exam. To improve your performance on these questions, practice the circle trick and learn how to identify dominant strategies, Nash equilibria, and the payoff for each firm.

Tacit Collusion and the Prisoner's Dilemma

Clearly, the players in any prisoner's dilemma would be better off if they had some way of enforcing cooperative behavior. But in the United States and many other countries, an agreement setting the output levels of two oligopolists isn't just unenforceable, it's illegal. So it seems that a noncooperative equilibrium is the only possible outcome. Or is it?

The criminals facing the prisoner's dilemma are playing a *one-shot* game – they get to choose once and for all whether to confess or remain silent, and then the game ends. However, most oligopolists play the same game repeatedly with the same rivals.

A firm engages in **strategic behavior** when it attempts to influence the future actions of other firms.

An oligopolist usually expects to be in business for many years, and knows that a decision today about whether to cheat is likely to affect the decisions of other firms in the future. A smart oligopolist doesn't just decide what to do based on the effect on profit in the short run. Instead, it engages in **strategic behavior**, taking into account the effects of its action on the future actions of other players. And under some conditions oligopolists that behave strategically can manage to behave as if they had a formal agreement to collude.

Suppose that our two firms expect to be in the tuna business for many years and therefore expect to play the game of cheat versus collude many times. Would they really betray each other time and again? Probably not. Suppose that each firm considers two strategies. In one strategy, it always cheats, producing 400 million pounds of tuna each year, regardless of what the other firm does. In the other strategy, it starts out cooperating, producing only 300 million pounds in the first year, and watches to see what its rival does. If the other firm also keeps its production down, each firm will stay cooperative, producing 300 million pounds again for the next year. But if one firm produces 400 million pounds, the other firm will also produce 400 million pounds the following year. This latter strategy – start by behaving cooperatively, but thereafter do whatever the other player did in the previous period – is generally known as **tit for tat**.

A strategy of **tit for tat** involves playing cooperatively at first, then doing whatever the other player did in the previous period.

Playing "tit for tat" is a form of strategic behavior because it is intended to influence the future actions of other players. The tit-for-tat strategy offers a reward to the other player for cooperative behavior – if you behave cooperatively, so will I. It also provides a punishment for cheating – if you cheat, don't expect me to be nice in the future. For each of these strategies, the payoff to each firm would depend on which strategy the other chooses. Consider the following four possibilities, illustrated in **Figure 4.5-6**:

1. If both firms play "tit for tat," both firms will make a profit of $180 million each year.
2. If one firm plays "always cheat" but the other plays "tit for tat," the one that always cheats makes a profit of $200 million the first year but only $160 million per year thereafter.
3. If one firm plays "tit for tat" but the other plays "always cheat," the one that plays tit for tat makes a profit of only $150 million in the first year but $160 million per year thereafter.
4. If both firms play "always cheat," both firms will make a profit of $160 million each year.

Which strategy is better? In the first year, each firm does better playing "always cheat" and assuring itself either $200 million or $160 million, depending on whether the other plays "tit for tat" or "always cheat." But a strategy of "always cheat" gains the firm only $160 million per year for the second and all subsequent years, regardless of the other firm's actions. Over time, the total amount gained by playing "always cheat" is less than the amount gained by playing "tit for tat": for the second and all subsequent years, the firm would never get any less than $160 million and would get as much as $180 million if the other firm played "tit for tat" as well. Which strategy is

FIGURE 4.5-6 How Repeated Interaction Can Support Collusion

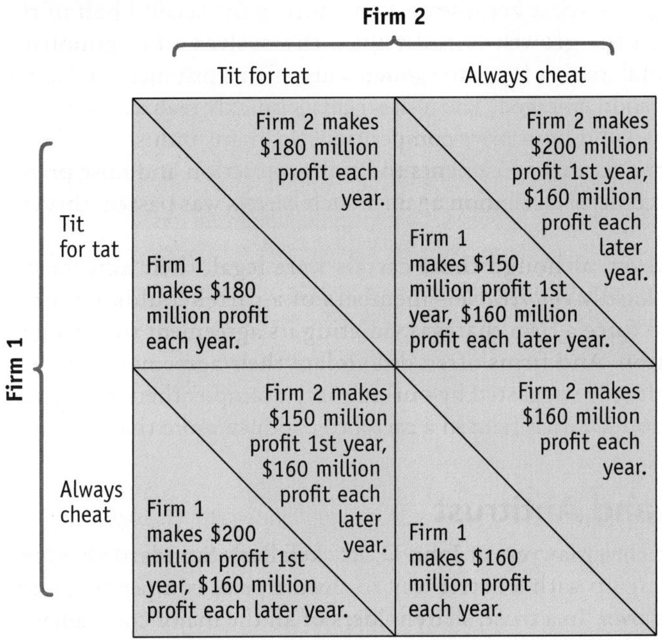

A strategy of tit for tat involves playing cooperatively at first, then following the other player's move. This rewards good behavior and punishes bad behavior. If the other player cheats, playing "tit for tat" will lead to only a short-term loss in comparison to playing "always cheat." But if the other player plays "tit for tat," also playing "tit for tat" leads to a long-term gain. So a firm that expects other firms to play "tit for tat" may well choose to do the same, leading to successful tacit collusion.

more profitable thus depends on two things: how many years each firm expects to play the game and what strategy its rival follows.

If the firm expects its tuna business to end before next year, it is effectively playing a one-shot game, so it might as well cheat and grab what it can. Even if the firm sees it as a repeated game because the rivalry will last many years, if for some reason the firm expects the other firm will always cheat, it should also always cheat. But if the firm expects to be in the business for a long time and thinks the other firm is likely to play "tit for tat," it will make more profit in the long run by playing "tit for tat," too.

The lesson is that when oligopolists expect to compete over an extended period of time, each firm has reason to cooperate with other firms in the industry. It makes sense for each firm to restrict its output in a way that raises the profit of the other firms, expecting them to return the favor. Although firms have no way of making an enforceable agreement to limit output and raise prices, they manage to act *as if* they had such an agreement. When this type of unspoken agreement comes about, we say that the firms are engaging in **tacit collusion**.

When firms limit production and raise prices in a way that raises each other's profits, even though they have not made a formal agreement, they are engaged in **tacit collusion**.

Business decisions in real life are nowhere near as simple as those in our tuna story; nonetheless, in most oligopolistic industries, most of the time, the sellers do appear to keep prices above their noncooperative level. Tacit collusion is so common in part because it can arise in many forms.

Consider the unwritten rules that helped the Big Three auto companies reach a tacit understanding on price back when most cars sold in the United States were produced by General Motors, Ford, and Chrysler. There was a tacit agreement that none of the three companies would undercut the prices of the other two. But then who would decide on the overall price of cars? The answer was normally General Motors: as the biggest of the three, it would announce its prices for the year first; and the other companies would adopt similar prices. This pattern of behavior, in which one company tacitly sets prices for the industry as a whole, is known as **price leadership**.

In **price leadership**, one firm sets its price first, and other firms then follow.

Price wars, which involve aggressive price competition, aren't as serious as military wars, but the principle is the same, and firms are keen on avoiding them. Interestingly, firms with a tacit agreement not to compete on price often engage in vigorous **nonprice competition**—adding new features to their products, spending large sums on ads that proclaim the inferiority of their rivals' offerings, developing their brand name, and so on.

Firms that have a tacit understanding not to compete on price often engage in intense **nonprice competition**, using advertising and other means to try to increase their sales.

Constraints on Collusion

In the United States, oligopoly first became an issue during the second half of the nineteenth century, when the growth of railroads—themselves an oligopolistic industry—created a national market for many goods. Large firms producing oil, steel, and many other products soon emerged. The industrialists quickly realized that profits would be higher if they could limit price competition. So, many industries formed cartels—that is, they signed formal agreements to limit production and raise prices. Until 1890, when the first federal legislation against such cartels was passed, this was perfectly legal.

However, although these cartels were legal, their agreements weren't legally *enforceable*—members of a cartel couldn't ask the courts to force a firm that was violating its agreement to reduce its production. And firms often did violate their agreements, for the reason already suggested by our duopoly example: there is always a temptation for each firm in a cartel to produce more than it is supposed to.

Hulton Archive/Getty Images

Carnegie, Morgan, and Rockefeller established trusts in the steel, electricity, and oil markets, among others, in the late nineteenth and early twentieth centuries.

Trust and Antitrust

In 1881, clever lawyers at John D. Rockefeller's Standard Oil Company came up with a better way to thwart price competition—the so-called *trust*. In a trust, shareholders of all the major companies in an industry placed their shares in the hands of a board of trustees who controlled the companies. This, in effect, merged the companies into a single firm that could then engage in monopoly pricing. In this way, the Standard Oil Trust established what was essentially a monopoly of the oil industry, and it was soon followed by trusts in sugar, whiskey, lead, cottonseed oil, and linseed oil.

Eventually, there was a public backlash, driven partly by concern about the economic effects of the trust movement and partly by fear that the owners of the trusts were simply becoming too powerful. The result was the Sherman Antitrust Act of 1890, which was intended both to prevent the creation of more monopolies and to break up existing ones. At first this law went largely unenforced, but the federal government became increasingly committed to making it difficult for oligopolistic industries either to become monopolies or to behave like them. Such efforts are known to this day as **antitrust policy**.

Antitrust policy involves efforts by the government to prevent oligopolistic industries from becoming or behaving like monopolies.

One of the most striking early actions of antitrust policy was the breakup of Standard Oil in 1911. Its components evolved into many of today's large oil companies—Standard Oil of New Jersey became Exxon, Standard Oil of New York became Mobil, and so on. In the 1980s, a long-running antitrust case led to the breakup of Bell Telephone, which once had a monopoly on both local and long-distance phone service in the United States. In 2000, a U.S. district judge ruled that Microsoft was a monopoly and should be split into two companies, but a federal appeals court overturned the decision. The Justice Department also reviews proposed mergers between companies in the same industry, such as AT&T and T-Mobile, and prohibits mergers that it believes will reduce competition.

Although antitrust policy is now effective against many forms of collusion, tacit collusion remains common. Even so, it is usually far from perfect. Several factors can prevent tacit collusion from pushing prices all the way up to their monopoly level.

Large Numbers

The more firms there are in an oligopoly, the less incentive any one firm has to behave cooperatively, taking into account the impact of its actions on the profits of the other firms. Larger numbers of firms in an industry also make the monitoring of price and output levels more difficult, and typically indicate low barriers to entry.

Complex Products and Pricing Schemes

Gilles Mingasson/Getty Images News/Getty Images

In our simplified tuna example, the two firms produce only one product. In reality, oligopolists often sell thousands or even tens of thousands of different products. A Walmart Supercenter sells over 100,000 items! Under these circumstances, just as when there are a large number of firms, keeping track of what other firms are producing and what prices they are charging is difficult. This makes it hard to determine whether a firm is cheating on the tacit agreement.

Differences in Interests

A tacit agreement for the tuna producers to split the market equally may be a natural outcome, probably acceptable to both firms. But firms can differ both in their perceptions about what is fair and in their real interests. For example, suppose that one firm in a duopoly is a long-established producer and the other a more recent entrant into the industry, as with painters Ally and Mateo. The long-established firm might feel it deserves to continue producing more than the newer firm, but the newer firm might feel it is entitled to 50% of the business.

Because tacit collusion is often hard to achieve, most oligopolies charge prices that are well below what the same industry would charge if it were controlled by a monopolist – or what they would charge if they were able to collude explicitly. In addition, sometimes tacit collusion breaks down and aggressive price competition amounts to a **price war**. Recent price wars in the hamburger, airline, and grocery industries caused prices to collapse to their noncooperative level, or even lower.

In the next Unit, we turn our focus from what comes out of firms to what goes into them – the factors of production with which goods and services are made.

AP® ECON TIP

If a question on the AP® exam mentions "mutual interdependence," be prepared to give an answer about oligopoly, because this market structure is characterized by interdependence among firms.

A **price war** occurs when tacit collusion breaks down and aggressive price competition causes prices to collapse.

Adventures in AP® Economics

Watch the video: ***Game Theory***

Module 4.5  Review

Check Your Understanding

1. Suppose world leaders Nikki and Margaret are engaged in an arms race and face the decision of whether to build a missile. Answer the following questions using the information in the payoff matrix below, which shows how each set of actions will affect the utility of the players (the numbers represent utils gained or lost).

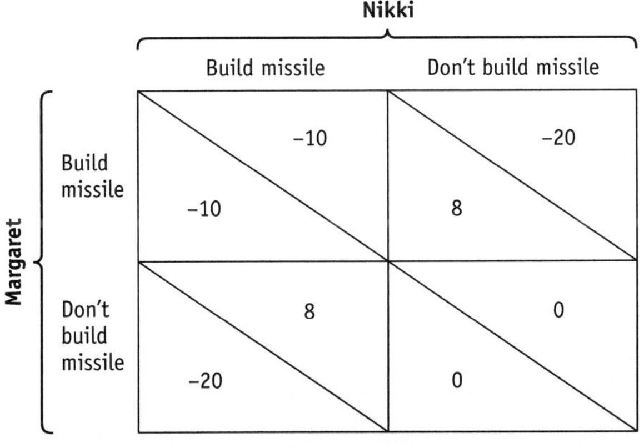

Margaret \ Nikki	Build missile	Don't build missile
Build missile	Nikki: −10; Margaret: −10	Nikki: −20; Margaret: 8
Don't build missile	Nikki: 8; Margaret: −20	Nikki: 0; Margaret: 0

   a. Identify any Nash equilibria that exist in this game, and explain why they do or do not exist.
   b. Which set of actions maximizes the total payoff for Nikki and Margaret?
   c. Why is it unlikely that they will choose the payoff-maximizing set of actions without some communication?

2. Consider a new version of the game in which two grocery store chains must decide whether to open a store in Ayville or Beeville (see Figure 4.5-3). In this version, Chain 1 and Chain 2 want to be in the same town, to provide shopping options that better compete with those in a big city. Based on the goal of being in the same place, describe any dominant strategies or Nash equilibria in this game.

Tackle the AP® Test: Multiple-Choice Questions

1. Within a group of firms, if the actions of the firms affect each other's profits, the firms are necessarily
   a. colluding.
   b. duopolists.
   c. in a cartel.
   d. monopolists.
   e. interdependent.

2. Oligopolists are tempted to produce more than the quantity that would maximize industry profits because when they increase output,
   a. the price effect is zero.
   b. the quantity effect is zero.
   c. the price effect equals the quantity effect.
   d. the price effect is larger than the quantity effect.
   e. the price effect is spread across multiple firms.

3. Each player has an incentive to choose an action that, when both players choose it, makes them both worse off than if neither had chosen it. This situation describes
   a. a dominant strategy.
   b. the prisoner's dilemma.
   c. interdependence.
   d. Nash equilibrium.
   e. game theory.

4. Which of the following is true of every Nash equilibrium?
   a. It is the only Nash equilibrium in the game.
   b. Neither player wants to independently change their strategy.
   c. It is also a dominant strategy equilibrium.
   d. Each player receives the same payoff.
   e. There is no better outcome in the payoff matrix for either player.

Use the following payoff matrix based on the story of Richard and Justin presented in the Module to answer Questions 5 and 6.

		Justin	
		Don't confess	Confess
Richard	Don't confess	5 years, 5 years	20 years, 2 years
	Confess	2 years, 20 years	15 years, 15 years

5. Suppose that Justin discovers Richard's action (confess or don't confess) before choosing his own action. Based on the payoff matrix provided, Justin will
   a. confess whether or not Richard confessed.
   b. not confess only if Richard confessed.
   c. not confess only if Richard didn't confess.
   d. not confess regardless of whether or not Richard confessed.
   e. confess only if Richard did not confess.

6. Which of the following is true on the basis of the payoff matrix provided?
   a. Justin has no dominant strategy, but Richard does.
   b. Richard has no dominant strategy, but Justin does.
   c. Both Richard and Justin have a dominant strategy.
   d. Neither Richard nor Justin has a dominant strategy.
   e. Justin has a dominant strategy only if Richard confesses.

7. If the bike shops in Cycle City do not have a formal agreement on pricing, but they increase their profits by adopting the prices of a price leader, these firms are necessarily participating in
   a. antitrust policy making.
   b. nonprice competition.
   c. a tit-for-tat strategy.
   d. tacit collusion.
   e. the formation of a trust.

8. When a firm considers how its behavior will affect the future actions of its competitors, it necessarily engages in
   a. price-fixing.
   b. strategic behavior.
   c. monopoly behavior.
   d. tit-for-tat behavior.
   e. a price war.

Tackle the AP® Test: Free-Response Questions

1. Refer to the table provided to answer the following questions. Assume that marginal cost is zero.

Demand Schedule

Price	Quantity	Price	Quantity
$24	0	10	7
22	1	8	8
20	2	6	9
18	3	4	10
16	4	2	11
14	5	0	12
12	6		

   a. If the market is perfectly competitive, what will the market equilibrium price and quantity be in the long run? Explain.
   b. If the market is a duopoly and the firms collude to maximize joint profits, what will market price and quantity be? Explain.
   c. If the market is a duopoly and the firms collude to maximize joint profits, what is each firm's total revenue if the firms split the market equally?

Rubric for FRQ 1 (7 points)

1 point: If the market is perfectly competitive, price will be zero.

1 point: If the market is perfectly competitive, quantity will be 12.

1 point: Price equals marginal cost in the long-run equilibrium of a perfectly competitive market, so price will be zero, at which price the quantity is 12.

1 point: If the market is a duopoly, price will be $12.

1 point: If the market is a duopoly, quantity will be 6.

1 point: In order to maximize joint profits, the two firms would act as a monopoly, setting marginal revenue equal to marginal cost and finding price on the demand curve above the profit-maximizing quantity. Marginal revenue passes through zero (going from 2 to –2) after the 6th unit, making 6 the profit-maximizing quantity. The most consumers would pay for 6 units is $12, so that is the profit-maximizing price.

1 point: Total revenue is $12 × 6 = $72. By dividing this equally, each firm receives $36.

2. Refer to the payoff matrix provided, which indicates the profits earned by two producers in various scenarios. You and your competitor must decide whether or not to market a new product.

		You: Market	You: Don't market
Your competitor	Market	$100, $100	$400, $0
	Don't market	$0, $400	$0, $0

   a. If you market the new product and your competitor does not, how much profit will you earn?
   b. If you market the new product, what should your competitor do?
   c. Do you have a dominant strategy? Explain.
   d. Does this situation have a Nash equilibrium? Explain. **(6 points)**

3. Like other firms, universities face temptations to collude in order to limit the effects of competition and avoid price wars. (In fact, the U.S. Department of Justice formally accused a group of universities of price-fixing in 1991.) Answer the following questions about behavior in the market for higher education.
   a. Describe one factor of the market for higher education that invites tacit collusion.
   b. Describe one factor of the market for higher education that works against tacit collusion.
   c. Explain one way in which universities could engage in illegal collusion.
   d. What are three ways in which universities engage in product differentiation?
   e. Explain how price leadership might work in the university setting.
   f. What forms of nonprice competition do you see universities engaged in? **(6 points)**

4. Suppose there are two firms in an oligopoly, Firm A and Firm B. If both firms charge a low price, each earns $2 million in profit. If both firms charge a high price, each earns $3 million in profit. If one firm charges a high price and one charges a low price, customers flock to the firm with the low price, and that firm earns $4 million in profit while the firm with the high price earns $1 million in profit.
   a. Draw a clearly labeled payoff matrix for this game and fill in each of the payoffs. Arrange the matrix so that Firm A is on the left, and make the upper-left set of strategies the low-price option for both firms.
   b. Identify the dominant strategy for each player, if one exists.
   c. Identify the Nash equilibria in this game, if any exist.
   d. Now suppose a tax on high-priced goods causes a $500,000 decrease in the payoffs received from charging a high price. Redraw the payoff matrix with adjustments for this change. **(5 points)**

UNIT 4

Review

 Adventures in AP® Economics Videos

Mod 4.2: Monopoly
Mod 4.5: Game Theory

UNIT 4 Review Video

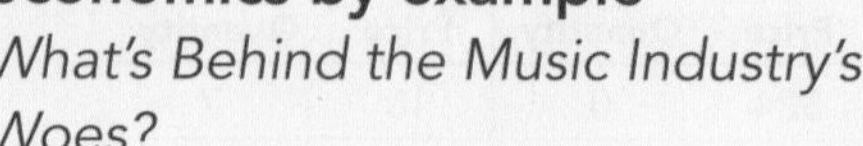

economics by example
What's Behind the Music Industry's Woes?

Module 4.1

1. There are four main types of market structure based on the number of firms in the industry and product differentiation: perfect competition, monopoly, oligopoly, and monopolistic competition. Markets that are not perfectly competitive are considered **imperfectly competitive**. Firms in imperfectly competitive markets can exercise **market power**, which is the ability to influence the prices they charge for their goods or services.
2. A **monopolist** is a producer who is the sole supplier of a good without close substitutes. An industry controlled by a monopolist is a **monopoly**.
3. To persist, a monopoly must be protected by a **barrier to entry**. This can take the form of control of a natural resource or input, increasing returns to scale that give rise to a **natural monopoly**, technological superiority, or government rules that prevent entry by other firms, such as **patents** or **copyrights**.
4. Many industries are **oligopolies**, in which there are only a few sellers, known as **oligopolists**. Oligopolies exist for more or less the same reasons that monopolies exist, but in weaker form.
5. **Monopolistic competition** is a market structure in which there are many competing firms, each producing a differentiated product, and there is free entry and exit in the long run. **Product differentiation** takes three main forms: by style or type, by location, and by quality. The extent of imperfect competition can be measured by the **concentration ratio**.

Module 4.2

6. The key difference between a monopoly and a perfectly competitive industry is that a single, perfectly competitive firm faces a horizontal demand curve, but a monopolist faces a downward-sloping demand curve. This gives the monopolist market power, the ability to raise the market price by reducing output.
7. The marginal revenue of a monopolist is composed of a quantity effect (the price received from the additional unit) and a price effect (the reduction in the price at which all units are sold). Because of the price effect, a monopolist's marginal revenue is always less than the market price, and the marginal revenue curve lies below the demand curve.
8. At the monopolist's profit-maximizing output level, the marginal cost equals the marginal revenue, which is less than the market price. At the perfectly competitive firm's profit-maximizing output level, the marginal cost equals the market price. So in comparison to perfectly competitive industries, monopolies produce less, charge higher prices, and can earn profit in both the short run and the long run.
9. A monopoly creates deadweight loss by charging a price above marginal cost: the loss in consumer surplus exceeds the monopolist's profit. This makes monopolies a source of market failure, and governments often make policies to prevent or end them.
10. A natural monopoly also causes deadweight loss. To limit such losses, governments sometimes impose **public ownership** and at other times impose **price regulation**. A price ceiling on a monopolist, as opposed to a perfectly competitive industry, need not cause shortages and can increase total surplus.

Module 4.3

11. Not all monopolists are **single-price monopolists**. Monopolists, as well as oligopolists and monopolistic competitors, often engage in **price discrimination** to make higher profit, using various techniques to differentiate consumers based on their sensitivity to price and then charging those with less elastic demand higher prices. A monopolist that achieves **perfect price discrimination** charges each consumer a price equal

to the consumer's willingness to pay and captures the total surplus in the market. Although perfect price discrimination creates no allocative inefficiency, it is practically impossible to implement.

Module 4.4

12. Monopolistic competition is a market structure in which there are many competing producers, each producing a differentiated product, and there is free entry and exit in the long run.
13. Short-run profits will attract the entry of new firms in the long run. This reduces the quantity each existing producer sells at any given price and shifts its demand curve to the left. Short-run losses will induce exit by some firms in the long run. This shifts the demand curve of each remaining firm to the right.
14. In the long run, the demand curve for each existing firm in a monopolistically competitive industry is tangent to its average total cost curve. There are zero profits in the industry and no entry or exit.
15. In long-run equilibrium, firms in a monopolistically competitive industry sell at a price greater than marginal cost. They also have **excess capacity** because they produce less than the minimum-cost output; as a result, they have higher costs than firms in a perfectly competitive industry. Whether or not monopolistic competition is inefficient is ambiguous because consumers value the product diversity that it creates.
16. Product differentiation takes three main forms: style or type, location, and quality. Firms will engage in advertising to increase demand for their products and enhance their market power. Advertising and **brand names** that provide useful information to consumers are valuable to society. Advertisements can be wasteful from a societal standpoint when their only purpose is to create market power.

Module 4.5

17. Many industries are oligopolies, characterized by a small number of **interdependent** sellers. The smallest type of oligopoly, a **duopoly**, has only two sellers, known as **duopolists**. Oligopolies exist for more or less the same reasons that monopolies exist, but in weaker form. They are characterized by imperfect competition: firms compete but possess market power.
18. Predicting the behavior of oligopolists poses something of a puzzle. The firms in an oligopoly could maximize their combined profits by acting as a **cartel**, setting output levels for each firm as if they were a single monopolist; to the extent that firms manage to do this, they engage in **collusion**. But each individual firm has an incentive to produce more than the agreed-upon quantity of output—to engage in **noncooperative behavior**. Informal collusion is likely to be easier to achieve in industries in which firms face capacity constraints.
19. The situation of interdependence, in which each firm's profit depends noticeably on what other firms do, is the subject of **game theory**. In the case of a game with two players, the **payoff** of each player depends on both its own actions and on the actions of the other; this interdependence can be shown in a **payoff matrix**. Depending on the structure of payoffs in the payoff matrix, a player may have a **dominant strategy**—an action that is always the best regardless of the other player's actions.
20. Some duopolists face a particular type of game known as a **prisoner's dilemma**; if each acts independently on its own interest, the resulting **Nash equilibrium** or **noncooperative equilibrium** will be bad for both.
21. Firms that expect to play a game repeatedly tend to engage in **strategic behavior**, trying to influence each other's future actions. A particular strategy that seems to work well in such situations is **tit for tat**, which often leads to **tacit collusion**.
22. In order to limit the ability of oligopolists to collude and act like monopolists, most governments pursue **antitrust policy** designed to make collusion more difficult. In practice, however, tacit collusion is widespread. Furthermore, a variety of factors make tacit collusion difficult: a large number of firms, complex products and pricing, differences in interests, and buyers with bargaining power. When tacit collusion breaks down, there can be a **price war**. Oligopolists try to avoid price wars in various ways, such as through product differentiation and through **price leadership**, in which one firm sets prices for the industry. Another approach is **nonprice competition**, such as advertising.

Key Terms

Imperfectly competitive, p. 652
Market power, p. 652
Monopolist, p. 653
Monopoly, p. 653
Oligopoly, p. 654
Oligopolist, p. 654
Concentration ratios, p. 654
Monopolistic competition, p. 655
Product differentiation, p. 656
Barrier to entry, p. 659
Natural monopoly, p. 660
Patent, p. 660
Copyright, p. 660
Public ownership, p. 669
Price regulation, p. 670
Single-price monopolist, p. 674
Price discrimination, p. 674
Perfect price discrimination, p. 677
Excess capacity, p. 686
Brand name, p. 690
Interdependent, p. 692
Duopoly, p. 692
Duopolist, p. 692
Collusion, p. 693
Cartel, p. 693
Noncooperative behavior, p. 694
Game theory, p. 695
Payoff, p. 695
Payoff matrix, p. 695
Prisoner's dilemma, p. 696
Dominant strategy, p. 697
Nash equilibrium, p. 698
Noncooperative equilibrium, p. 698
Strategic behavior, p. 702
Tit for tat, p. 702
Tacit collusion, p. 703
Price leadership, p. 703
Nonprice competition, p. 703
Antitrust policy, p. 704
Price war, p. 705

AP® Exam Practice Questions

Multiple-Choice Questions

1. The demand curve for a monopolist producing a normal good is downward-sloping because of
- **a.** the substitution effect being larger than the income effect.
- **b.** the income effect being larger than the substitution effect.
- **c.** diminishing marginal returns.
- **d.** price discrimination.
- **e.** diminishing marginal utility.

2. The marginal revenue curve for a monopolist lies below the demand curve because of
- **a.** the income effect.
- **b.** the quantity effect.
- **c.** price discrimination.
- **d.** the price effect.
- **e.** the substitution effect.

3. If a monopolist charges a price such that marginal revenue is greater than marginal cost, then the monopolist
- **a.** will earn profit.
- **b.** will earn losses.
- **c.** will break even.
- **d.** can improve its profit by reducing its price.
- **e.** can improve its profit by raising its price.

4. For a monopolist, when marginal revenue is positive,
- **a.** the quantity effect outweighs the price effect.
- **b.** the price effect outweighs the quantity effect.
- **c.** total revenue is rising at an increasing rate.
- **d.** total revenue is declining at an increasing rate.
- **e.** total revenue is declining at a declining rate.

5. Relative to a competitive industry with the same costs, a monopolist charges
- **a.** a higher price and produces more output.
- **b.** a lower price and produces more output.
- **c.** a higher price and produces less output.
- **d.** a lower price and produces less output.
- **e.** a higher price and produces the same level of output.

6. If a monopolist finds that demand is elastic at the level of output where marginal revenue is equal to marginal cost, the monopolist will
- **a.** maintain that level of output.
- **b.** increase output.
- **c.** decrease output.
- **d.** raise the price.
- **e.** lower the price.

7. A perfectly competitive industry will likely have
- **a.** more consumer surplus, more producer surplus, and more deadweight loss than a monopoly.
- **b.** more consumer surplus, less producer surplus, and less deadweight loss than a monopoly.
- **c.** less consumer surplus, more producer surplus, and more deadweight loss than a monopoly.
- **d.** more consumer surplus, less producer surplus, and more deadweight loss than a monopoly.
- **e.** less consumer surplus, more producer surplus, and less deadweight loss than a monopoly.

8. If a regulatory commission wants to ensure that a monopolist produces the largest quantity of output that is consistent with earning a normal profit, it will require the monopolist to charge a price equal to its
- **a.** marginal cost.
- **b.** average fixed cost.
- **c.** average variable cost.
- **d.** average total cost.
- **e.** total cost.

9. In order to practice price discrimination, a firm must have

a. market power.
b. customers of different ages.
c. customers with the same price elasticity of demand.
d. customers with different income levels.
e. customers in different locations.

10. Perfect price discrimination will result in

a. more output and more consumer surplus.
b. more output and less consumer surplus.
c. less output and more producer surplus.
d. less output and less consumer surplus.
e. less output and more consumer surplus.

11. Monopolistically competitive industries are characterized by

a. standardized products, many firms, and easy entry and exit.
b. standardized products, few firms, and easy entry and exit.
c. differentiated products, many firms, and easy entry and exit.
d. differentiated products, many firms, and high barriers to entry.
e. differentiated products, few firms, and high barriers to entry.

12. Government regulators should be concerned with __________ if firms in an industry have __________.

a. a prisoner's dilemma	found a Nash equilibrium
b. encouraging competition	started a price war
c. regulating profits	low barriers to entry
d. enforcing antitrust policy	acted as a cartel and not just in tacit collusion
e. increasing nonprice competition	differentiated their products

13. Which of the following is the most likely to lead to lower prices in an oligopoly?

a. the formation of a cartel
b. tacit collusion
c. low barriers to entry
d. price leadership
e. product differentiation

Use the information and following table to answer Questions 14 and 15.

Suppose that Firm A and Firm B are the only companies that make a common food preservative. The marginal cost of production is zero and the industry demand schedule for the preservative in a typical month is as follows:

Price (per pound)	Quantity demanded (millions of pounds)
$6	0
5	10
4	20
3	30
2	40
1	50
0	60

14. If the two companies agree to each produce half of the quantity that maximizes their combined profits and to share the revenue equally, what is the dollar amount (in millions) of revenue that each firm collects?

a. $100
b. $90
c. $50
d. $45
e. $40

15. Suppose Firm A continues to honor the production agreement from Question 18 while Firm B breaks it and produces more. Now what is the maximum dollar amount (in millions) that Firm B would collect?

a. $100
b. $90
c. $50
d. $45
e. $40

Suppose a breakfast cereal market consists of only two firms, Firm X and Firm Y. Each firm sets either high prices or low prices for one month at a time. Use the information on each firm's monthly profit in the following payoff matrix to answer Questions 16–19.

		Firm Y	
		Set high prices	Set low prices
Firm X	Set high prices	$500, $700	$100, $800
	Set low prices	$600, $400	$200, $300

16. Which of the following statements is true?

a. Firm X and Firm Y are engaged in a prisoner's dilemma.
b. At the noncooperative equilibrium, the total profits for both firms combined are equal to $1,200.
c. At the Nash equilibrium, the total profits for both firms combined are equal to $1,000.
d. At the noncooperative equilibrium, the total profits for both firms combined are equal to $900.
e. At the Nash equilibrium, the total profits for both firms combined are equal to $500.

17. Which of the following accurately describes the dominant strategies of Firm X and Firm Y?

	Dominant strategy for Firm X	*Dominant strategy for Firm Y*
a.	no dominant strategy	high prices
b.	high prices	no dominant strategy
c.	low prices	high prices
d.	low prices	low prices
e.	low prices	no dominant strategy

18. Suppose the same payoff matrix applies every month. For the current month, Firm X has set low prices and Firm Y has set high prices. If each firm follows a tit-for-tat strategy, then
   a. Firm X would set high prices next time, earn $500 for one month, and then $200 thereafter.
   b. Firm X would set low prices next time, earn $600 for one month, and then $200 thereafter.
   c. Firm X would set high prices next time, earn $100 for one month, and then $500 the following month.
   d. Firm X would set low prices next time, earn $200 for one month, and then $200 the following month.
   e. Firm X would set high prices next time, earn $100 for one month, and then $600 the following month.

19. Suppose all the profit payoffs for Firm X double, but they remain the same for Firm Y. Which of the following is a true statement?
   a. The noncooperative equilibrium would remain the same.
   b. The dominant strategy would change for Firm X but remain the same for Firm Y.
   c. There would be a second Nash equilibrium.
   d. Firm Y would be more likely to engage in a tit-for-tat strategy.
   e. Both firms would be more likely to engage in tacit collusion.

20. Which of the following works in favor of tacit collusion in an oligopolistic industry?
   a. The bargaining power of large buyers can keep prices low.
   b. Over time, firms realize it is in their best interest to collectively restrict output.
   c. Selling thousands of products makes it hard to keep track of competitors' output and prices.
   d. With a larger number of sellers, there is less incentive for any one firm to cooperate.
   e. The threat of enforcement of antitrust policy is always present.

21. Which of the following business tactics are ways that firms in an oligopolistic industry attempt to legally collude?
   a. engaging in nonprice competition
   b. using price leadership for signaling
   c. lowing prices in a trade war
   d. differentiating their products
   e. advertising

22. In a monopolistically competitive soda industry, assume the following facts: a typical firm produces 10,000 beverage cans in a month; the price per can is $1.00; average total cost is $0.50 at the current production level; and marginal cost is $0.25 at the current production level. What will happen to the equilibrium quantity and profits for a typical firm in the soda industry in the long run?

	Equilibrium quantity for a typical firm	*Profit for a typical firm*
a.	increase	decrease
b.	decrease	remain the same
c.	remain the same	increase
d.	decrease	decrease
e.	decrease	increase

23. Economists have argued that there may be inefficiencies in monopolistically competitive industries. Which of the following is a reason cited for this inefficiency?
   a. There is excess capacity at the chosen production level.
   b. The price is too low.
   c. There is zero profit in the long run.
   d. Price is set equal to marginal cost.
   e. Production occurs along the upward-sloping section of the average total cost curve.

Use the following graph of a typical firm in a monopolistically competitive industry to answer Questions 24–26.

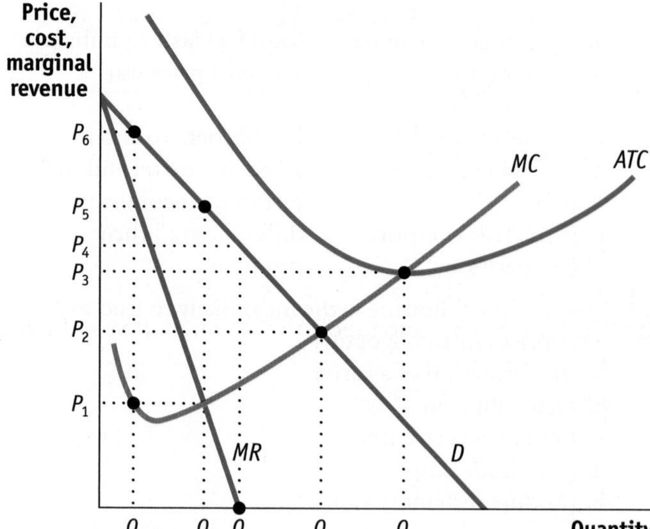

24. What price and quantity combination would we expect from a profit-maximizing firm in this monopolistically competitive industry?
   a. P_6, Q_1
   b. P_5, Q_2
   c. P_4, Q_3
   d. P_3, Q_5
   e. P_2, Q_4

25. Firms in this industry are experiencing ____________ and over time we would expect these earnings to ____________.

a.	economic losses	remain the same
b.	economic profits	increase
c.	economic losses	decrease
d.	economic profits	decrease
e.	economic losses	increase

26. Over time, what will happen to the number of firms in this industry and the output per firm?

	Number of firms	*Output per firm*
a.	decrease	increase
b.	increase	decrease
c.	decrease	decrease
d.	increase	increase
e.	decrease	remain the same

27. Which of the following is NOT an example of product differentiation?

a. a clothing store that advertises jean jackets that will make anyone cool
b. a grocery store that chooses to locate closer to customers than a competing grocer
c. a chef who chooses to put arugula and spinach on his hamburgers
d. a coffee house that offers drinks made from Fair Trade coffee beans
e. a farmer who doesn't advertise his watermelons because consumers already know that watermelon tastes better than other produce

28. Daddio Don and Fabulous Fred are hairstyling oligopolists. Daddio Don follows a tit-for-tat strategy and Fabulous Fred charged low prices in the previous period. What will Daddio Don do now?

a. go out of business
b. charge high prices
c. charge low prices
d. avoid all Nash equilibria
e. form a cartel

29. The long run in a monopolistically competitive industry is characterized by

a. productive efficiency.
b. allocative efficiency.
c. firms earning positive economic profits.
d. firms operating at the minimum of their average total cost curves.
e. firms with excess capacity.

30. In the short run, Marta's Zen Bakery earns profit in a monopolistically competitive industry. What will happen in this industry in the long run?

a. Marta's demand curve will shift to the left.
b. Marta's profit will increase.
c. Other firms will exit the industry.
d. Nonprice competition will become impossible.
e. Product differentiation will become impossible.

Use the payoff matrix provided to answer Questions 31 and 32. The values in the matrix represent the profits that WeSellLights and the Lighting Barn will earn depending on each firm's strategy to build or not build a new store. The first entry in each box represents the profit for WeSellLights; the second entry is the profit for the Lighting Barn.

		The Lighting Barn	
		Build	Don't build
WeSellLights	Build	\$25,000, \$25,000	\$100,000, \$0
	Don't build	\$0, \$100,000	\$0, \$0

31. If WeSellLights believes that the Lighting Barn will not build a new store, WeSellLights will

a. not build a new store and it will earn no profit.
b. not build a new store because not building is the dominant strategy.
c. build a new store and earn a \$25,000 profit.
d. build a new store and earn a \$100,000 profit.
e. be indifferent as to whether or not to build a new store.

32. Assume that WeSellLights offers the Lighting Barn \$30,000 not to build a new store. Given that new information, in which case will a Nash equilibrium occur?

a. If both companies build a new store.
b. If WeSellLights builds a new store and the Lighting Barn does not.
c. If WeSellLights does not build a new store and the Lighting Barn does.
d. If neither company builds a new store.
e. A Nash equilibrium does not exist.

Free-Response Questions

1. The Desert Oasis Water Company is a natural monopoly in the town of Dryville. The firm experiences a constant marginal cost and is currently operating at a loss.

a. Using a correctly labeled graph, illustrate the market for water in Dryville.
  i. Label the profit-maximizing quantity Q_1.
  ii. Label the profit-maximizing price P_1.
  iii. Shade the area that represents the firm's loss.
  iv. Label the allocatively efficient quantity Q_S.

b. In an effort to achieve the allocatively efficient quantity, the government of Dryville is considering a lump-sum subsidy (a fixed contribution of money) for the Desert Oasis Water Company. Assuming that the firm would continue to operate with or without the subsidy, what effect will this subsidy have on the firm's output level? Explain. **(7 points)**

2. Gary's Greenhouse is a single-price monopolist that sells tulips and earns a normal profit.
   a. Draw a correctly labeled graph for Gary's Greenhouse showing the following:
      i. the profit-maximizing price and quantity, labeled as P_m and Q_m
      ii. the area of total cost, shaded completely
   b. Label a point *A* to indicate the left end of the inelastic portion of the demand curve. **(7 points)**

3. The hot dog stand industry in Frankland is monopolistically competitive. A typical stand produces and sells 10,000 hot dogs during the summer season. For that stand, the price per hot dog is $3.00, the average total cost is $1.00 at the current production level, and the marginal cost is $0.50 at the current production level.
   a. Draw a correctly labeled graph of this typical hot dog stand under current market conditions, labeling the equilibrium quantity and the equilibrium price with the numbers provided.
   b. Calculate the economic profit or loss for the typical hot dog stand.
   c. On your graph from part a, shade in the area of the profit or loss.

   Now assume that the government imposes a $20,000 lump-sum license fee for the summer season.

   d. What happens to the price and quantity for the typical hot dog stand as a result of the license fee? Explain.
   e. Show the impact of the license fee on the graph from part a and provide a clear label for anything that changed.
   f. What will happen to the number of hot dog stands over the course of the season? Explain. **(10 points)**

4. The following diagram shows the pricing strategies and payoffs for the two bubble gum firms in town.

		Long Lasting Flavor Co.	
		Set high prices	Set low prices
Big Bubble Co.	Set high prices	$400, $250	$200, $350
	Set low prices	$500, $100	$150, $50

   a. Does Big Bubble Co. have a dominant strategy? Explain.
   b. Does Long Lasting Flavor Co. have a dominant strategy? Explain.
   c. Does this situation have any Nash equilibria? Explain. **(6 points)**

5. The drone industry is made up of a small number of interdependent firms.
   a. What market structure best describes this industry?
   b. Suppose drone makers try to collude by agreeing to restrict output and raise prices. Aside from issues of legality, what else would make it difficult for this form of collusion to succeed?
   c. Explain how price leadership could lead to relatively high prices in the drone industry.
   d. If one firm lowers its price this period, how would a competitor following the tit-for-tat strategy respond next period? **(4 points)**

Factor Markets

AP® Economics Skills

1. Principles and Models (1.A)
2. Interpretation (2.A, 2.C)
3. Manipulation (3.B)

From Whence Wages Arise

Module 1.1 discussed the costs of going to college. Those costs are substantial, but the benefits are even larger. In the modern economy, employers are willing to pay a premium for workers with more education. In fact, the size of that premium has increased a lot over the last few decades. Back in 1973, workers with advanced degrees, such as law degrees or MBAs, earned only 76% more than those who had only graduated from high school. By 2020, the premium for an advanced degree had risen to over 105%.

Who decided that the wages of workers with advanced degrees would rise so much compared with those of high school grads? No one, really—it was a market outcome. Wage rates are prices, the prices of different kinds of labor; and they are decided, like other prices, by supply and demand.

Still, there is a qualitative difference between the wage rate of high school grads and the price of, say, textbooks: the wage rate isn't the price of a *good*; it's the price of a *factor of production*. And although markets for factors of production are in many ways similar to those for goods, there are also some important differences.

In this Unit, we examine *factor markets*, the markets in which the factors of production, such as labor, land, and capital, are traded. Factor markets, like product markets, play a crucial role in the economy: they allocate resources to firms and help ensure that those resources are used efficiently.

Shakespeare wrote in *King Lear* that "all friends shall taste the wages of their virtue." This Unit concludes with a Module which qualifies Shakespeare's prediction with insights about the wages that workers "taste." How do actual wages compare with the lowest wages that workers would accept? How do they compare with the workers' contributions to a firm's revenue? And what controversies surround the markets for labor among other factors of production? Read on, or as Shakespeare wrote, "O, see, see!"

Thomas Barwick/DigitalVision/Getty Images

MODULE 5.1

Introduction to Factor Markets

In this Module, you will learn to:
- Define the key terms relating to factor markets
- Explain how prices are determined in perfectly competitive factor markets
- Calculate the marginal revenue product of a factor
- Determine the optimal quantity of a factor for a firm to purchase

The Economy's Factors of Production

AP® ECON TIP

The factors of production are sometimes referred to as *inputs* on the AP® exam.

A *factor of production* is any resource used to produce goods and services. The markets in which factors of production are bought and sold are called *factor markets*, and the prices in factor markets are known as *factor prices*. This Module takes a close look at what these factors of production are, where their prices come from, and how firms make their purchasing decisions.

The Factors of Production

Physical capital—often referred to simply as "capital"—consists of manufactured goods such as equipment, buildings, tools, and machines used to make other goods.

Human capital is the improvement in labor created by education and knowledge that is embodied in the workforce.

We have seen that economists divide factors of production into four categories. The first is *labor*, the work done by human beings. The second is *land*, which encompasses resources provided by nature. The third is *capital*, which can be divided into two categories: **physical capital** – often referred to simply as "capital" – consists of manufactured goods such as equipment, buildings, tools, and machines used to make other goods. In the modern economy, **human capital**, the improvement in labor created by education and knowledge, and embodied in the workforce, is at least equally significant. Technological progress has boosted the importance of human capital and made technical know-how essential to many jobs, thus helping to create a premium for workers with advanced degrees. The final factor of production, *entrepreneurship*, is a unique resource that is not purchased in an easily identifiable factor market like the other three. It refers to innovation and risk-taking activities that bring together resources for production.

Why Factor Prices Matter: The Allocation of Resources

The factor prices determined in factor markets play a vital role in the important process of allocating resources among firms.

Consider the example of labor shortages during the COVID-19 pandemic. Workers were needed to provide essential goods and services including food, health care, and freight transportation, even when safety concerns made workers reluctant to leave their homes. What brought the needed workers out? The factor market: the high demand for workers drove up wages. In the United States, several states provided extra pay for essential workers in both government and private-sector jobs, and employers such as Walmart and Amazon raised their wages to encourage more workers to stay on the job despite the risks. With the help of incentives in the factor markets, in most cases, food stores and hospitals were able to stay open and transportation systems continued to operate.

Like most firms, this solar farm uses inputs from each of the four classes of factors of production: land, labor, physical and human capital, and entrepreneurship.

In other words, the markets for various types of essential workers allocated their factor of production – labor – to where it was needed.

In this sense, factor markets are similar to goods markets, which allocate goods among consumers. But there are two features that make factor markets special. The first is that a factor, unlike a good, has a **derived demand**: demand for the factor is derived from demand for the product made by that factor. For example, the demand for butchers comes from the demand for meat. The second feature is that factor markets are where most people earn the largest shares of their income (government transfers in the form of social security checks being the next largest source of income in the economy).

The demand for a factor is a **derived demand**. It results from (that is, it is *derived* from) the demand for the output being produced.

Marginal Productivity and Factor Demand

Higher wages helped retailers attract workers during the pandemic.

Luis Alvarez/DigitalVision/Getty Images

All economic decisions are about comparing costs and benefits – and usually about comparing marginal costs and marginal benefits. This goes both for a consumer, deciding whether to buy more goods or services, and for a firm, deciding whether to hire an additional worker.

Although there are some important exceptions, most factor markets in the modern U.S. economy are perfectly competitive. This means that most buyers and sellers of factors are price-takers because they are too small relative to the market to influence the market price. And in a competitive labor market, it's clear how to define the marginal cost an employer pays for a worker: it is simply the worker's wage rate. But what is the marginal benefit of that worker? To answer that question, we return to the production function, which relates inputs to output. We begin by examining a firm that is a price-taker in the output market – that is, it operates in a perfectly competitive industry.

AP® ECON TIP

In factor markets, firms are the buyers of inputs and households are the sellers of inputs. The principles that guide the factor market are similar to those that guide the product market, making the factor market easier to understand.

Marginal Product of Labor

Figure 5.1-1 shows the production function for wheat on Mia and Liam's farm, as introduced in Module 3.1. Panel (a) uses the total product curve to show how total wheat production depends on the number of workers employed on the farm; panel (b) shows how the *marginal product of labor* (*MPL*), the increase in output from employing one more worker, depends on the number of workers employed. The table in Figure 5.1-1 shows the numbers behind the figure. Note that sometimes the marginal product (*MP*) is called the *marginal physical product* or *MPP*. These two terms are the same; the extra "*P*" just emphasizes that the term refers to the quantity of physical output being produced, not the monetary value of that output.

If workers are paid a daily wage of $200 each and Mia and Liam can sell an unlimited amount of wheat for $20 per bushel, how many workers should Mia and Liam employ to maximize profit?

Using the lessons in Unit 3, we could answer this question in several steps. First, we could use information from the production function to derive the firm's total cost and its marginal cost. Then we could apply the *profit-maximizing rule*: a firm's profit is maximized by producing the quantity of output at which the marginal cost is equal to the marginal revenue. Having determined the optimal quantity of output, we could go back to the production function to find the optimal number of workers – which is simply the number of workers needed to produce the optimal quantity of output.

FIGURE 5.1-1 The Production Function for Mia and Liam's Farm

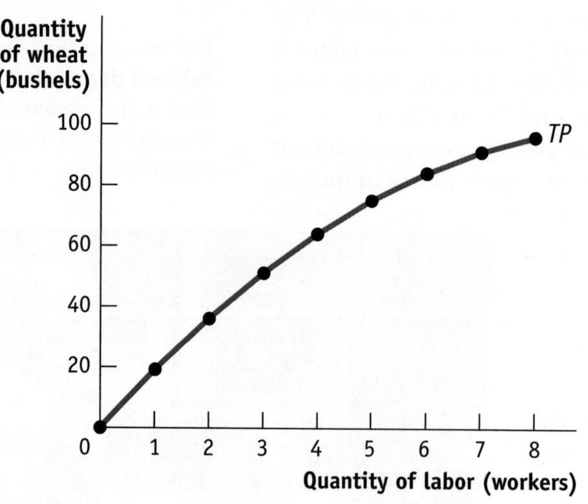

Quantity of labor L (workers)	Quantity of wheat Q (bushels)	Marginal product of labor $MPL = \Delta Q/\Delta L$ (bushels per worker)
0	0	
		19
1	19	
		17
2	36	
		15
3	51	
		13
4	64	
		11
5	75	
		9
6	84	
		7
7	91	
		5
8	96	

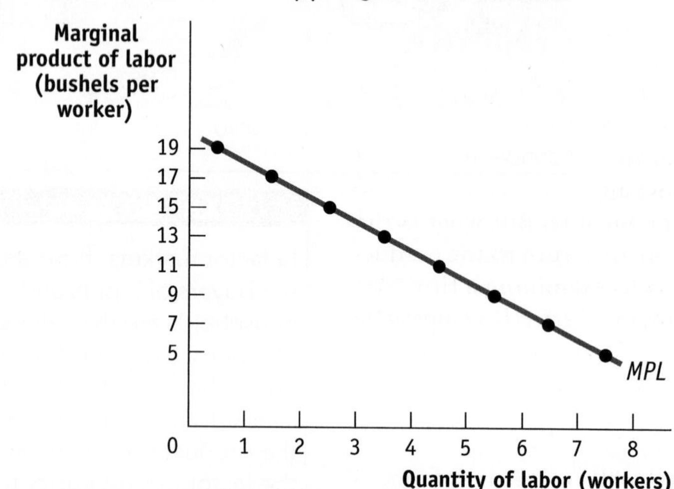

Panel (a) shows how the amount of wheat produced on Mia and Liam's farm (*TP*) depends on the number of workers employed. Panel (b) shows how the marginal product of labor (*MPL*) depends on the number of workers employed.

Marginal Revenue Product and Factor Demand

As you might have guessed, marginal analysis provides a more direct way to find the number of workers that maximizes a firm's profit. This different way of looking at the same question gives us more insight into the demand for factors as opposed to the supply of goods. To see how this alternative approach works, suppose that Mia and Liam are deciding whether to employ another worker. The increase in *cost* from employing another worker is the wage rate, *W*, at which the firm can hire any number of workers in a perfectly competitive labor market. The *benefit* to Mia and Liam from employing another worker is the additional revenue gained from the hire. To determine the change in revenue, we can multiply the additional output gained from another worker by the additional revenue gained from each additional unit of output. That is, we multiply the marginal product of labor, *MPL*, by the marginal revenue, *MR*. This amount—the additional revenue generated by employing one more unit of labor—is known as the **marginal revenue product** of labor (*MRPL*):

The **marginal revenue product** of a factor is the additional revenue generated by employing one more unit of that factor.

(5.1-1) Marginal revenue product of labor $(MRPL) = MPL \times MR$

An associated term specific to firms selling in perfectly competitive product markets is the *value of the marginal product of labor*, or *VMPL*. The *VMPL* is the marginal product of labor multiplied by the price. For a perfectly competitive firm, the *VMPL* is equivalent to the *MRPL* because, as we saw in Module 3.5, price and marginal revenue are the same for a competitive firm. The equivalence of *VMPL* and *MRPL* for such firms is clear from an examination of their formulas:

$$VMPL = MPL \times P = MPL \times MR = MRPL$$

So if you see a reference to the *VMPL* of a perfectly competitive firm, just treat it as the *MRPL*, because there is no difference. To avoid unnecessary complication, here we will use the *MRPL*, which is relevant to every type of firm.

So should Mia and Liam hire another worker? Yes, if the resulting increase in revenue exceeds the cost of the additional worker—that is, if $MRPL > W$. Otherwise, they should not.

The hiring decision is made using marginal analysis, by comparing the marginal benefit from hiring another worker (*MRPL*) with the marginal cost (*W*). And as with any decision that is made on the margin, the optimal choice is made by equating marginal benefit with marginal cost. So to maximize profit, Mia and Liam will employ workers until, for the last worker employed,

$$\textbf{(5.1-2)} \quad MRPL = W$$

What if they are never equal because the *MRPL* jumps from being above the wage for one worker to being below the wage for the next worker? Then hiring should continue until the *MRPL* of the next worker would fall *below* the wage.

This rule isn't limited to labor; it applies to any factor of production. The marginal revenue product of any factor is its marginal product times the marginal revenue received from the good it produces. And as a general rule, profit-maximizing firms that are price-takers in the factor market will keep adding more units of each factor of production until the marginal revenue product of the last unit employed is equal to the factor's price.

This rule is consistent with our previous analysis. We saw that a profit-maximizing firm chooses the level of output at which the marginal revenue of the good it produces equals the marginal cost of producing that good. It turns out that if the level of output is chosen so that marginal revenue equals marginal cost, then it is also true that with the amount of labor required to produce that output level, the marginal revenue product of labor will equal the wage rate.

Now let's look more closely at why firms should choose the level of employment that equates *MRPL* and *W*, and at how that decision helps us understand factor demand.

The table in **Figure 5.1-2** shows the marginal revenue product of labor on Mia and Liam's farm when the price of wheat (and thus the marginal revenue for this price-taker in the product market) is $20 per bushel. In Figure 5.1-2, the horizontal axis shows the number of workers employed; the vertical axis measures the marginal revenue product of labor and the wage rate. The curve shown is the **marginal revenue product curve** of labor. This curve, like the marginal product of labor curve, slopes downward because of diminishing returns to labor in production. That is, the marginal revenue product of each worker is less than that of the preceding worker because the marginal product of each worker is less than that of the preceding worker. For a firm that is not a price-taker in the product market, the curve also slopes downward because marginal revenue decreases as more units are sold, as discussed in Module 4.2.

We have just seen that to maximize profit, Mia and Liam hire workers until the wage rate is equal to the marginal revenue product of the last worker employed. Let's use the example to see how this principle really works.

Assume that Mia and Liam currently employ 3 workers and that these workers must be paid the market wage rate of $200 per day. Should they employ an additional worker? Looking at the table in Figure 5.1-2, we see that since Mia and Liam have 3 workers, the marginal revenue product of an additional worker is $260. So if they employ an additional worker, they will increase their revenue by $260 but increase their

AP® ECON TIP

If a question mentions the value of the marginal product of labor (*VMPL*) hired by a firm selling in a perfectly competitive market, treat it as the marginal revenue product of labor (*MRPL*). The two terms are equivalent for such firms.

The **marginal revenue product curve** of a factor shows how the marginal revenue product of that factor depends on the quantity of the factor employed.

FIGURE 5.1-2 The Marginal Revenue Product Curve

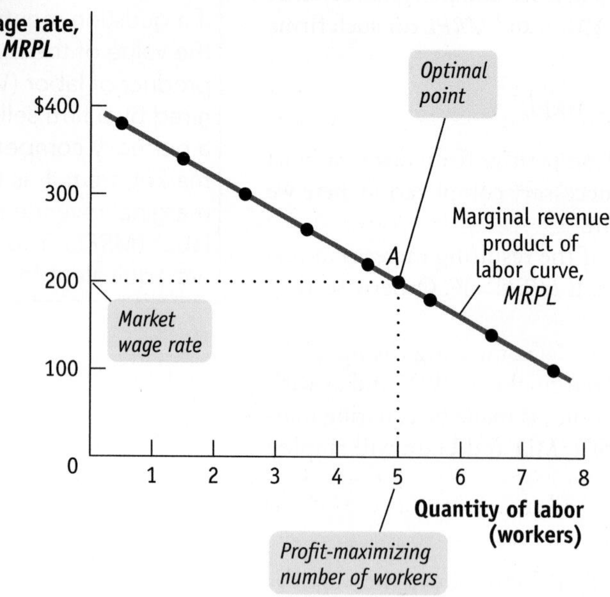

Quantity of labor L (workers)	Marginal product of labor MPL (bushels per worker)	Marginal revenue product of labor $MRPL = MPL \times MR$
0		
	19	$380
1		
	17	340
2		
	15	300
3		
	13	260
4		
	11	220
5		
	9	180
6		
	7	140
7		
	5	100
8		

This curve shows how the marginal revenue product of labor (*MRPL*) depends on the number of workers employed. It slopes downward because of diminishing returns to labor in production.

To maximize profit, Mia and Liam choose the level of employment (quantity of labor) at which the marginal revenue product of labor is equal to the market wage rate, at point *A*.

cost by only $200, yielding a $60 increase in profit. More generally, a firm purchasing from a perfectly competitive factor market can increase profit by employing one more unit of a factor as long as the marginal revenue product of that factor exceeds the factor price.

Alternatively, suppose that Mia and Liam employ 8 workers. By reducing the number of workers to 7, they can save $200 in wages. The marginal revenue product of the 8th worker is only $100. So, by reducing employment by one worker, they can increase profit by $200 – $100 = $100. In other words, a firm purchasing from a perfectly competitive factor market can increase profit by employing one less unit of a factor as long as the marginal revenue product of that factor is less than the factor price.

Using this reasoning, we can see from the table in Figure 5.1-2 that the profit-maximizing employment level is 5 workers, given a wage rate of $200. The marginal revenue product of the 5th worker is $220, so adding the 5th worker results in $220 of additional revenue ($20 of additional profit). But Mia and Liam should not hire more than 5 workers: the marginal revenue product of the 6th worker is only $180, $20 less than the cost of that worker. To maximize profit, Mia and Liam should employ workers up to but not beyond the point at which the marginal revenue product of the last worker employed is equal to the wage rate.

Glowimages/Getty Images

Firms keep hiring more workers until the marginal revenue product of labor equals the wage rate.

Look again at the marginal revenue product curve in Figure 5.1-2. To determine the profit-maximizing level of employment, we set the marginal revenue product of labor equal to the price of labor—a wage rate of $200 per worker. This means that the profit-maximizing level of employment is at point *A*, corresponding to an employment level of 5 workers. If the wage rate were higher than $200, we would simply move up the curve and decrease the number of workers employed; if the wage rate were lower than $200, we would move down the curve and increase the number of workers employed.

A small farm like Mia and Liam's, with no worker whose marginal revenue product happens to equal the wage rate, hires workers until the marginal revenue product of another worker would fall below the wage rate. For a larger farm with many employees, the marginal revenue product of labor falls only slightly when an additional worker is employed, so there will be some worker whose marginal revenue product almost exactly equals the wage rate. (In keeping with the Mia and Liam example, this means that some worker generates a marginal revenue product of approximately \$200.) In this case, as Equation 5.1-2 implies, the firm maximizes profit by choosing a level of employment at which the marginal revenue product of the last worker hired *equals* (to a very good approximation) the wage rate.

We will assume from now on that firms use this $W = MRPL$ rule to determine the profit-maximizing level of employment. This means that *the marginal revenue product of labor curve is the individual firm's labor demand curve.* Likewise, a firm's marginal revenue product curve for any factor of production is that firm's demand curve for that factor.

Because many firms are not price-takers, let's now consider the marginal revenue product for a firm in an imperfectly competitive market. Suppose John and Abigail own the only pizzeria in their town, and like all monopolists, they must lower their price in order to sell more pizzas. In this case, due to the *price effect* of charging a lower price on all units so that one more can be sold, the marginal revenue gained from each pizza is less than its price. **Table 5.1-1** shows the calculation of the marginal revenue product for each of John and Abigail's workers. For example, by hiring the 3rd worker, they are able to produce 18 additional pizzas. The marginal revenue received from these pizzas is \$9.43, so the marginal revenue product of the 3rd worker is $18 \times \$9.43 = \$169.74$.

Table 5.1-1 Marginal Revenue Product of Labor with Imperfect Competition in the Product Market

Quantity of labor *L*	Quantity of output *Q*	Marginal product of labor *MPL*	Product price *P*	Total revenue $TR = P \times Q$	Marginal revenue $MR = \Delta TR/\Delta Q$	Marginal revenue product of labor $MRPL = MPL \times MR$
0	0			\$0.00		
		20			\$10.00	\$200.00
1	20		\$10.00	200.00		
		19			9.61	182.59
2	39		9.81	382.59		
		18			9.43	169.74
3	57		9.69	552.33		
		16			8.96	143.36
4	73		9.53	695.69		
		13			8.67	112.71
5	86		9.40	808.40		

Demand in the Markets for Land and Capital

We have used a labor market example to explain why a firm's demand curve for a factor is its marginal revenue product curve for that factor. Other factor markets behave similarly but have some distinguishing characteristics. Before we end our discussion of factor market demand, let's consider demand in the markets for land and capital.

The reasoning firms use to decide how much labor to hire also applies to decisions about other factors of production. For example, suppose Mia and Liam are considering whether to rent an additional acre of land for the next year. They will compare the cost

Thomas Barwick/Getty Images

Even if a farmer owns her tractor, her opportunity cost of using it is the rental rate, because if she didn't use the tractor herself, she could rent it out to another farmer at that rate.

The **rental rate** of either land or capital is the cost, explicit or implicit, of using a unit of that asset for a given period of time.

of renting that acre with the additional revenue generated by farming an additional acre – the marginal revenue product of an acre of land. To maximize profit, Mia and Liam will rent more land up until the marginal revenue product of an acre of land is equal to the rental cost per acre. The same is true for capital: the decision of whether to rent an additional piece of equipment comes down to a comparison of the additional cost of the equipment with the additional revenue it generates.

What if Mia and Liam already own the land, or the firm already owns the equipment? As discussed in Module 3.4 in the context of Babette's Cajun Café, even if you own land or capital, there is an implicit cost – the opportunity cost – of using it for a given activity because it could otherwise be used for something else, such as renting it out to other firms. So a profit-maximizing firm employs additional units of land and capital until the cost of the last unit employed, explicit or implicit, is equal to the marginal revenue product of that unit. We call the cost of renting a unit of land or capital for a set period of time its **rental rate**. The rental rate is also the owner's opportunity cost of using the land or capital rather than renting it out.

As with labor, due to diminishing returns, the marginal revenue product curves for land and capital, and therefore the demand curves for those factors of production, slope downward.

We've seen the determinants of factor demand and how factor prices influence the quantity of each factor demanded by firms. Next, we complete our development of the factor market model by considering factor supply.

Factor Supply

As in our discussion of factor demand, we begin this discussion of factor supply with a look at decisions and outcomes in the labor market. Then we will consider the supply of land and capital, and equilibrium outcomes in those markets.

Labor Supply: A Matter of Work Versus Leisure

AP® ECON TIP

On the AP® exam you may see the price of land or capital referred to as the *rental rate*, which is the cost per period of renting the factor. This makes sense because users of the factor either rent it from someone else, or incur the opportunity cost of the rental rate by using the factor themselves rather than renting it out to someone else.

There are only 24 hours in a day, so to supply labor is to give up leisure. The resulting dilemma is among the reasons the labor market looks different from markets for goods and services. In the labor market, the roles of firms and households are the reverse of what they are in markets for goods and services. A good such as coffee is supplied by firms and demanded by households; labor, though, is demanded by firms and supplied by households. How do households decide how much labor to supply?

As a practical matter, most people have limited control over their work hours: sometimes a worker has little choice but to take a job for a set number of hours per week. However, there is often flexibility to choose among different careers and employment situations that involve varying numbers of work hours. There is a range of part-time and full-time jobs; some are strictly 9:00 A.M. to 5:00 P.M., others have much longer or shorter work hours. Some people work two jobs; others don't work at all. And self-employed people have many work-hour options.

To simplify our study of labor supply, we will imagine an individual who can choose to work as many or as few hours as desired. Why wouldn't such an individual work as many hours as possible? Because workers are human beings and have other uses for their time. An hour spent on the job is an hour not spent on other, presumably more pleasant, activities. So the decision about how much labor to supply involves making a decision about *time allocation* – how many hours to spend on different activities.

Leisure is time available for purposes other than earning money to buy marketed goods.

By working, people earn income they can use to buy goods. The more hours an individual works, the more goods that person can afford to buy. But this increased purchasing power comes at the expense of a reduction in **leisure**, the time spent not working. Leisure doesn't necessarily mean time wasted. It could be time spent with one's family, pursuing hobbies, exercising, and so on. And though purchased goods yield utility, so does leisure. Indeed, we can think of leisure itself as a normal good, which most people would like to consume more of as their incomes increase.

Time spent working is time not spent on leisure activities.

Anna Berkut/Alamy

How does a rational individual decide how much leisure to consume? By making a marginal comparison, of course. In analyzing consumer choice, we asked how a utility-maximizing consumer uses a marginal *dollar*. In analyzing labor supply, we ask how an individual uses a marginal *hour*.

Consider Fela, an individual who likes both leisure and the goods money can buy. Suppose that his wage rate is $20 per hour. In deciding how many hours he wants to work, he must compare the marginal utility of an additional hour of leisure with the additional utility he gets from $20 worth of goods. If $20 worth of goods adds more to his total utility than an additional hour of leisure, he can increase his total utility by giving up an hour of leisure to work an additional hour. If an extra hour of leisure adds more to his total utility than $20 worth of goods, he can increase his total utility by working one fewer hour to gain an hour of leisure.

At Fela's optimal level of labor supply, then, the marginal utility he receives from one hour of leisure is equal to the marginal utility he receives from the goods that his hourly wage can purchase. This is very similar to the *optimal consumption rule* we encountered in Module 1.6, except that it is a rule about time rather than money.

Our next step is to ask how Fela's decision about time allocation is affected when his wage rate changes.

Wages and Labor Supply

Suppose that Fela's wage rate increases from $20 to $30 per hour. How will he change his time allocation?

You could argue that Fela will work longer hours because his incentive to work has increased: by giving up an hour of leisure, he can now gain $30 instead of $20. But you could equally well argue that he will work less because he doesn't need to work as many hours to generate the income required to pay for the goods he wants.

As these opposing arguments suggest, the quantity of labor Fela supplies can either rise or fall when his wage rate rises. To understand why, let's recall the distinction between the *substitution effect* and the *income effect*, introduced in Module 2.1. We have seen that a price change affects consumer choice in two ways: by changing the opportunity cost of a good in terms of other goods (the substitution effect) and by making the consumer richer or poorer (the income effect).

Now think about how a rise in Fela's wage rate affects his demand for leisure. The opportunity cost of leisure – the amount of money he gives up by taking an hour off instead of working – rises. Other things equal, that substitution effect gives him an incentive to consume less leisure and work longer hours. Conversely, a higher wage rate makes Fela richer – and, other things equal, this income effect leads him to want to consume *more* leisure and supply less labor because leisure is a normal good.

So in the case of labor supply, the substitution effect and the income effect work in opposite directions. If the substitution effect is so powerful that it dominates the income effect, an increase in Fela's wage rate leads him to supply *more* hours of labor. If the income effect is so powerful that it dominates the substitution effect, an increase in the wage rate leads him to supply *fewer* hours of labor.

We see, then, that the **individual labor supply curve** – the relationship between the wage rate and the number of hours of labor supplied by an individual worker – does not necessarily slope upward at every wage rate.

The **individual labor supply curve** shows how the quantity of labor supplied by an individual depends on that individual's wage rate.

Figure 5.1-3 illustrates the two possibilities for the slope of the labor supply curve. If the substitution effect dominates the income effect, the individual labor supply curve slopes upward, as it does here up to a wage of $40. So an increase in the wage rate from $20 to $30 per hour leads to a *rise* in the number of hours worked from 40 to 50. However, if the income effect dominates the substitution effect, the quantity of labor

FIGURE 5.1-3 The Individual Labor Supply Curve

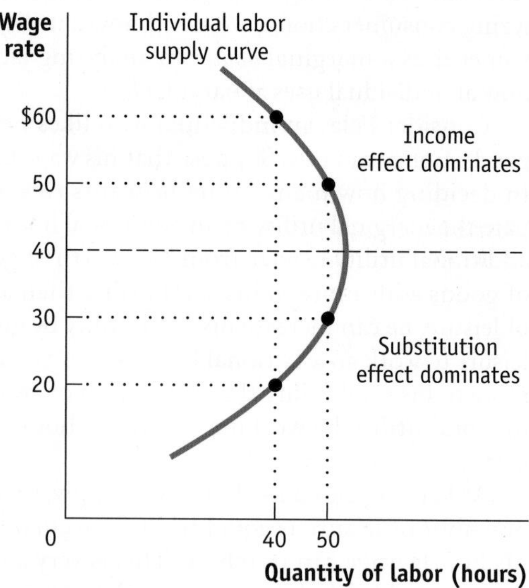

When the substitution effect of a wage increase dominates the income effect, the individual labor supply curve slopes upward, as it does in this graph up to a wage of $40 per hour. Here a rise in the wage rate from, for example, $20 to $30 per hour increases the number of hours worked from 40 to 50. But when the income effect of a wage increase dominates the substitution effect, the individual labor supply curve slopes downward. Here a rise in the wage rate from, say, $50 to $60 per hour reduces the number of hours worked from 50 to 40.

supplied goes down when the wage rate increases and the labor supply curve slopes downward. For instance, a rise in the wage rate from $50 to $60 leads to a *fall* in the number of hours worked from 50 to 40.

Economists refer to an individual labor supply curve that contains both upward-sloping and downward-sloping segments as a "backward-bending labor supply curve." At lower wage rates, the substitution effect dominates the income effect. At higher wage rates, the income effect eventually dominates the substitution effect.

Is a backward-bending labor supply curve a real possibility? Yes: many labor economists believe that income effects on the supply of labor may be somewhat stronger than substitution effects at high wage rates. You may know a doctor or dentist who works only four days a week, which supports this belief. The most compelling evidence comes from Americans' increasing consumption of leisure over the past century. At the end of the nineteenth century, wages adjusted for inflation were only about one-eighth what they are today; the typical work week was 70 hours, and very few workers retired at age 65. Today, the typical work week is less than 40 hours, and most people retire at age 65 or younger. So it seems that Americans have chosen to take advantage of higher wages in part by consuming more leisure.

Now that we have examined how income and substitution effects shape the individual labor supply curve, we can turn to the market labor supply curve. In any labor market, the market supply curve is the horizontal sum of the individual labor supply curves of all workers in that market. Although the individual labor supply curve can bend backward at very high wage rates, we will assume that the market labor supply curve has the more common upward-sloping shape. Next, we'll bring the market labor supply curve together with the market labor demand curve to see the source of the market wage that firms take as given.

Equilibrium in the Labor Market

We can use the supply and demand curves for labor to determine the equilibrium wage and employment level in the labor market. **Figure 5.1-4** illustrates the labor market as a whole. The *market labor demand curve*, like the market demand curve for a good, is the horizontal sum of all the individual labor demand curves of all the firms that hire labor. Recall that a firm's labor demand curve is the same as its marginal revenue product of labor curve.

FIGURE 5.1-4 Labor Market Equilibrium

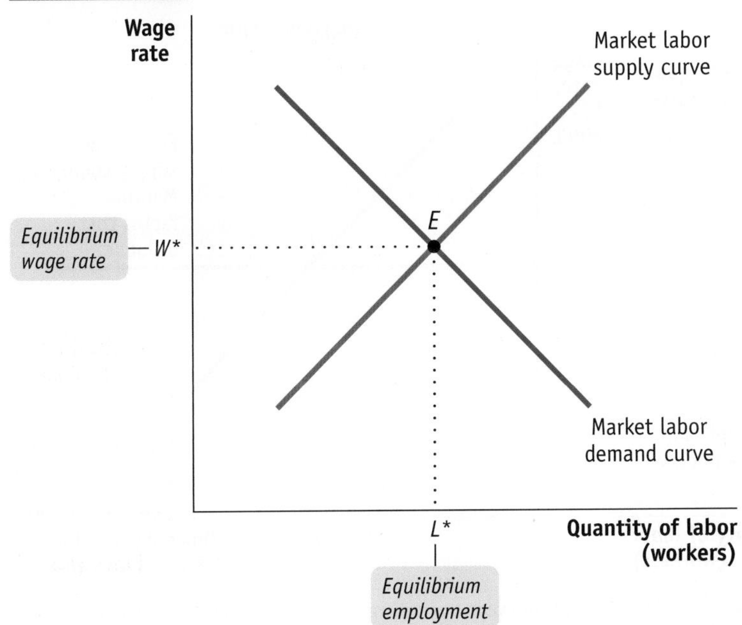

The market labor demand curve is the horizontal sum of the individual labor demand curves of all producers. Here, the equilibrium wage rate is W^*, the equilibrium employment level is L^*, and every producer hires labor up to the point at which $MRPL = W^*$. So labor is paid its equilibrium marginal revenue product, that is, the marginal revenue product of the last worker hired in the labor market as a whole.

The *equilibrium wage rate* is the wage rate at which the quantity of labor supplied is equal to the quantity of labor demanded. In Figure 5.1-4, this leads to an equilibrium wage rate of W^* and the corresponding equilibrium employment level of L^*. The equilibrium wage rate is also known as the *market wage rate.* Since every employer hires labor until $MRPL = W^*$, every worker in the market is paid the marginal revenue product of the last worker hired in the labor market.

AP® ECON TIP

The factor market graph is a supply and demand graph with different labels. For the AP® exam, you should be able to draw, label, and analyze changes in this graph just as you do for other supply and demand graphs.

Marginal Factor Cost and the Firm Labor Supply Curve

For firms hiring from perfectly competitive labor markets, the cost of each additional unit of labor is the wage. This makes sense because each firm is so small relative to the market that the firm's hiring decision does not affect the market; each firm can hire as much labor as it wants at the market wage. In Module 5.4, we'll see that the story is different in imperfectly competitive labor markets: the cost of hiring an additional unit of labor *exceeds* the wage. Regardless of market type, one term describes the cost relevant to decisions about the amount of every type of factor to purchase: the **marginal factor cost** (also called the **marginal resource cost**), which is the additional cost of employing one more unit of a factor of production.

Since the labor supply curve shows the relationship between the wage and the quantity of labor supplied, and each firm in a perfectly competitive labor market can hire as much labor as it wants at the market wage, each firm faces a labor supply curve that is horizontal at the market wage, as shown in **Figure 5.1-5**. That curve is a visual representation of the fact that, in a perfectly competitive labor market, the additional cost of hiring another worker—the marginal factor cost of labor—is always simply the market wage.

Firms will hire more of a factor of production until the marginal revenue product is equal to the marginal factor cost (*MFC*). This is similar to the profit-maximizing rule ($MR = MC$) for the product market, as discussed in Module 3.5. For example, the firm represented on the right side of Figure 5.1-5 will hire L units of labor, as indicated by the intersection of the marginal revenue product of labor curve (the firm's demand curve for labor) and the marginal factor cost curve (the firm's supply curve for labor).

Next, we'll examine the markets for two other factors of production.

The **marginal factor cost** (*MFC*, sometimes called the **marginal resource cost**, *MRC*) is the additional cost of employing an additional unit of a factor of production.

AP® ECON TIP

Remember: The marginal factor cost (*MFC*) is sometimes called the marginal resource cost (*MRC*). The two terms mean the same thing, and you could see either on the AP® exam.

FIGURE 5.1-5 Firm Labor Supply in a Perfectly Competitive Labor Market

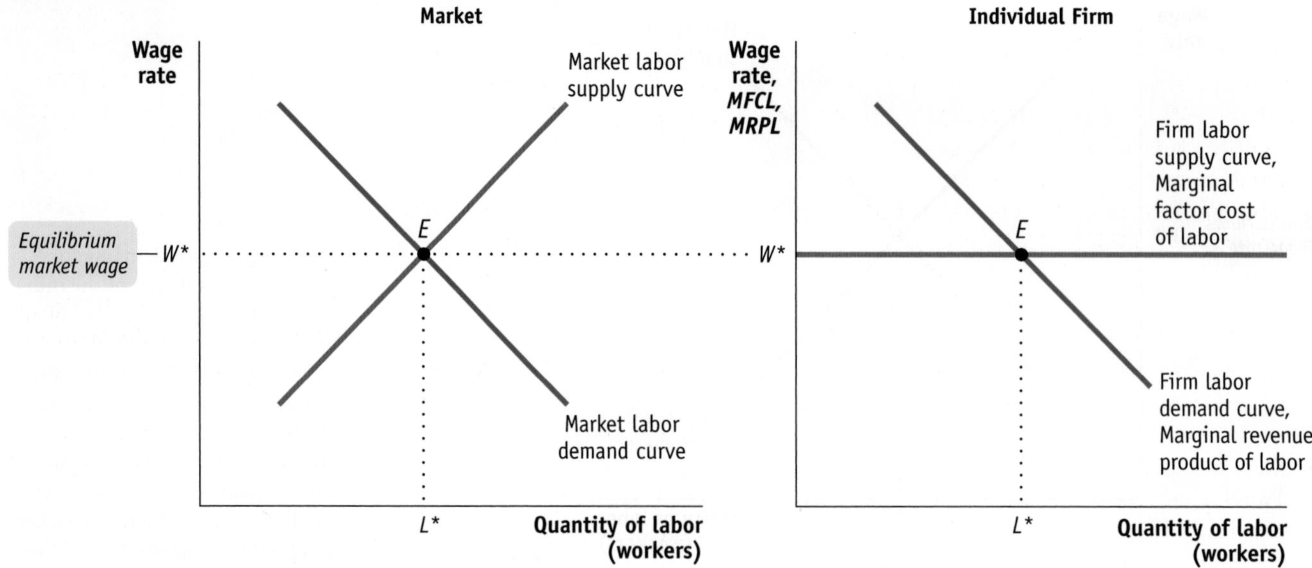

Each firm in a perfectly competitive labor market is so small relative to the market that it can hire all the labor it wants at the market equilibrium wage. As a result, each firm's marginal factor cost of labor (*MFCL*) is simply the market wage, and the individual firm labor supply curve is horizontal at that wage level. The firm will hire *L* units of labor, found at the intersection of the marginal revenue product of labor curve (the firm's demand curve for labor) and the marginal factor cost curve (the firm's supply curve for labor).

Supply and Equilibrium in the Markets for Land and Capital

The story for other factors resembles that for labor. **Figure 5.1-6** illustrates the markets for land and capital. The red curve in panel (a) is the supply curve for land. As we have drawn it, the supply curve for land is relatively steep and therefore relatively

FIGURE 5.1-6 Equilibria in the Land and Capital Markets

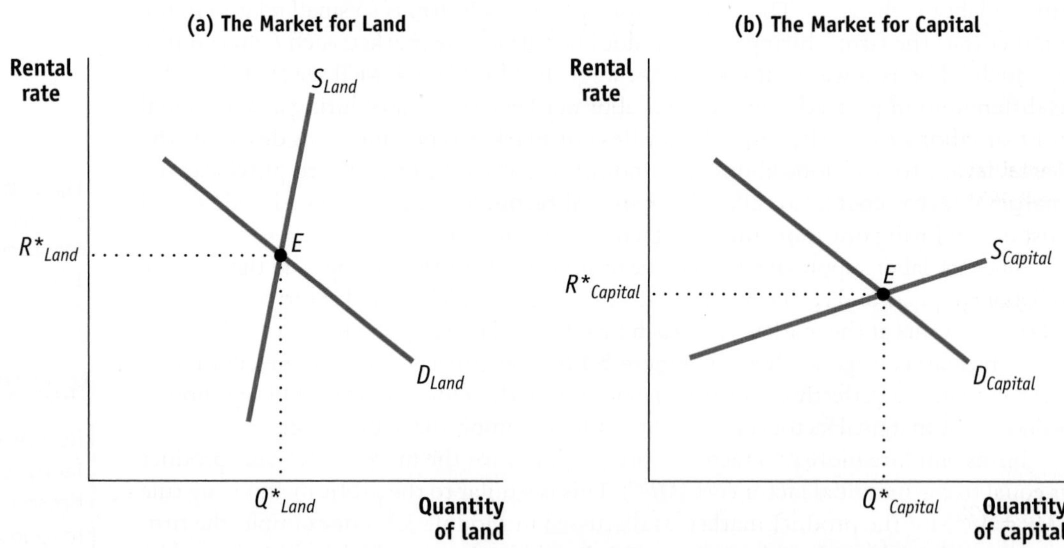

Panel (a) illustrates equilibrium in the market for land; panel (b) illustrates equilibrium in the market for capital. The supply curve for land is relatively steep, reflecting the high cost of increasing the quantity of productive land. The supply curve for capital, by contrast, is relatively flat because the supply of capital is relatively responsive to price changes.

inelastic. This reflects the fact that finding new supplies of land for production is typically difficult and expensive – for example, creating new farmland through expensive irrigation.

The red curve in panel (b) is the supply curve for capital. In contrast to the supply curve for land, the supply curve for capital is relatively flat and therefore relatively elastic. That's because the supply of capital is relatively responsive to price changes: capital is typically paid for with the savings of investors, and the amount of savings that investors make available is relatively responsive to the rental rate for capital.

The equilibrium rental rate and quantity in the land and capital markets are found at the intersection of the supply and demand curves in Figure 5.1-6. Panel (a) shows the equilibrium in the market for land. The market demand curve for land is found by summing (horizontally) all of the firm demand curves for land. The equilibrium rental rate for land is R^*_{Land}, and the equilibrium quantity of land employed in production is Q^*_{Land}. In a competitive land market, each unit of land will be paid the *equilibrium marginal revenue product* of land. The **equilibrium marginal revenue product** of a factor is the additional revenue generated by the last unit of that factor employed in the entire market for that factor.

Panel (b) shows the equilibrium in the market for capital. The equilibrium rental rate for capital is $R^*_{Capital}$, and the equilibrium quantity of capital employed is $Q^*_{Capital}$. In a competitive capital market, each unit of capital will be paid the equilibrium marginal revenue product of capital.

AP® ECON TIP

Read questions carefully to be clear on whether a firm is a price-taker in the factor market, the product market, or both. Only if a firm is a price-taker in the factor market does the factor price equal the marginal factor (resource) cost. And only if the firm is a price-taker in the product market does the price of the product equal the marginal revenue.

The **equilibrium marginal revenue product** of a factor is the additional revenue generated by the last unit of that factor employed in the factor market as a whole.

Economic Rent

When the payment for a factor of production is higher than it would need to be to employ that factor, the factor is earning **economic rent**, which is the excess of the payment over the minimum necessary payment.

Economic rent is the payment to a factor of production in excess of the minimum payment necessary to employ that factor.

Consider the 512 acres of flat land in Ouray, Colorado, which is ringed by mountains too steep to build or farm on. Because the land is in fixed supply, the supply curve is vertical, as shown in **Figure 5.1-7**, and the equilibrium monthly rental rate could be anywhere from zero up, depending on the level of demand. If the demand were D_1, the quantity supplied would exceed the quantity demanded even at a rental rate of $0, and the land would be available for $0. If the demand curve were D_2, the equilibrium rental rate would be $1,000 an acre. Since no payment is needed to make the land available, and economic rent is the excess of the payment over the minimum necessary payment, the entire payment of $1,000 × 512 × $512,000 would be economic rent. If the demand curve were D_3, the rental rate would be $4,000 per acre, and the economic rent would be $4,000 × 512 = $2,048,000.

FIGURE 5.1-7 Demand, the Rental Rate, and Economic Rent

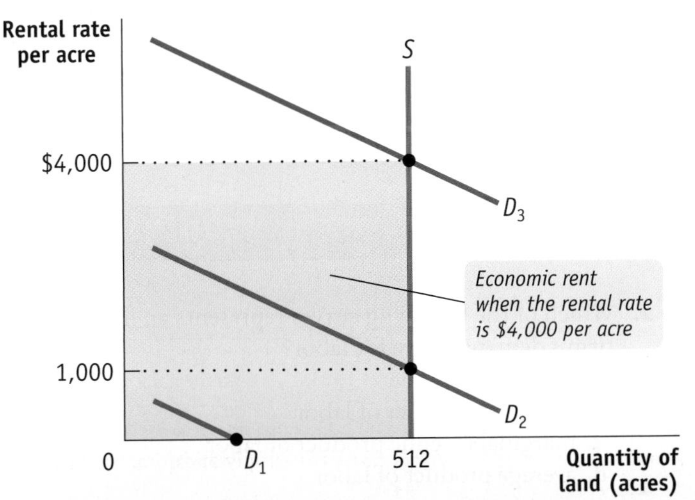

When the supply of a factor of production is fixed, the rental rate is determined by the level of demand. For example, if the demand curve for land were D_1, the annual rental rate would be zero. If the demand curve were D_2, the rental rate would be $1,000 per acre. And if the demand curve were D_3, the rental rate would be $4,000 per acre. The shaded area of the graph represents the economic rent of $4,000 × 512 = $2,048,000 that exists when the rental rate is $4,000 per acre.

Dave Anderson

When a factor of production, such as the land in this Colorado town, would be available regardless of its price, the entire payment for that factor is economic rent.

AP® ECON TIP

Economic rent is similar to producer surplus, except that economic rent applies to factor markets and producer surplus applies to product markets.

Likewise, any other payment for the land would be entirely economic rent because that payment would exceed the $0 necessary to make the land available.

The appropriate distribution of the economic rent from land is a source of debate. Socialists argue that land should be publicly owned so that its benefits can be shared broadly. Critics of this approach argue that markets provide incentives for resources to be allocated to their most productive uses, whereas publicly owned land might not be allocated with the same attention to opportunity costs.

With private land ownership, portions of the economic rent can be redistributed using a land tax, which creates no deadweight loss when land is in fixed supply. Recall from Module 2.8A that many types of taxes cause deadweight loss by reducing the equilibrium quantity and eliminating some mutually beneficial exchanges. When the quantity of land is fixed, a tax on land does not decrease the quantity of land that is bought and sold, so there is no deadweight loss. The entire burden of the tax is placed on landowners in the form of a loss of economic rent. Although a land tax is appealing from an efficiency standpoint, there is no consensus on the level of taxation that is fair to landowners.

Workers receive economic rent as well. If you earn $15 per hour, but you would be willing to work for as little as $11 per hour, you receive $4 of economic rent per hour. If you love your job so much that you would work for free, your income is pure economic rent.

In this Module, we have treated factor markets as if every unit of each factor were identical—that is, as if all land were identical, all labor were identical, and all capital were identical. But in reality, factors differ considerably with respect to productivity. For instance, land resources differ in their ability to produce crops, and workers have different skills and abilities. Rather than thinking of one land market for all land resources in an economy, and similarly one capital market and one labor market, we can instead think of different markets for different types of land, capital, and labor. For example, the market for computer programmers is different from the market for pastry chefs.

In the next Module, we will see how changes in labor supply and labor demand affect labor market outcomes.

Module 5.1  Review

Check Your Understanding

1. Explain in terms of the income and substitution effects how a decrease in the wage rate can induce a worker to increase the number of hours worked.

2. Explain the following statement: "When firms in different industries all compete for the same land, the marginal revenue product of the last unit of land rented will be equal across all firms, regardless of whether they are in different industries."

Tackle the AP® Test: Multiple-Choice Questions

1. Factor market demand is called a *derived* demand because it
   - **a.** derives its name from the Latin word *factorus.*
   - **b.** is derived from the market wage received by workers.
   - **c.** is derived from the productivity of workers.
   - **d.** is derived from the product market.
   - **e.** derives its shape from the price of the factor.

2. Which of the following curves represents an individual firm's demand curve for labor?
   - **a.** marginal revenue
   - **b.** marginal product of labor
   - **c.** marginal revenue product of labor
   - **d.** average product of labor
   - **e.** marginal factor cost

3. Which of the following is necessarily true if you work more when your wage rate increases?
   a. The income effect is large.
   b. The substitution effect is small.
   c. The income effect dominates the substitution effect.
   d. The substitution effect dominates the income effect.
   e. The income effect equals the substitution effect.
4. The implicit cost of capital that you own is
   a. the rental rate.
   b. greater than the rental rate.
   c. the original purchase price of the capital.
   d. greater than the original purchase price of the capital.
   e. zero because you already own it.
5. A very steep supply curve for land indicates that
   a. the supply of land is elastic.
   b. the quantity of land supplied is very responsive to price changes.
   c. it is very costly to increase the quantity of land supplied.
   d. an increase in the demand for land would have a relatively small effect on the price of land.
   e. a decrease in the demand for land would have a relatively large effect on the quantity of land supplied.
6. Which of the following is necessarily true for a firm in a perfectly competitive labor market?
   a. The labor supply curve is horizontal.
   b. The labor demand curve is horizontal.
   c. The marginal revenue product curve for labor is above the demand curve for labor.
   d. The firm has difficulty finding enough workers due to competition from other firms.
   e. The firm must increase its wage to hire more workers.
7. The entire payment for land that is in fixed supply constitutes
   a. a tax.
   b. a subsidy.
   c. deadweight loss.
   d. economic rent.
   e. price discrimination.
8. When a land tax is used to distribute the economic rent from land that is in fixed supply, the resulting deadweight loss is
   a. equal to the size of the tax.
   b. equal to the price paid for the land.
   c. larger than the size of the tax but smaller than the price paid for the land.
   d. negative.
   e. zero.

Tackle the AP® Test: Free-Response Questions

1. Refer to the table below. Assume that the rental rate for capital is $100 per unit and the price of the product is $10.

Quantity of capital (units)	Quantity of output
0	0
1	30
2	55
3	70
4	78
5	85
6	89

   a. What is the *MRP* of the 2nd unit of capital?
   b. Will the firm employ the 2nd unit of capital? Explain.
   c. How many units of capital will the firm hire? Explain.

Rubric for FRQ 1 (5 points)

1 point: *MRP* = 25 × $10 = $250

1 point: Yes, they will employ the second unit.

1 point: Because the *MRP* of $250 is greater than the rental rate of $100.

1 point: 3

1 point: Because the *MRP* exceeds the rental rate for the first 3 units.

2. Draw a correctly labeled graph for a land market in which land is in fixed supply. Label each of the following on your graph: the axes, the supply and demand curves for land, the equilibrium rental rate, and the equilibrium quantity of land employed. Shade and label the area that represents economic rent. **(5 points)**

MODULE 5.2

Changes in Factor Demand and Supply

In this Module, you will learn to:

- Identify changes that shift the demand curve or the supply curve for a factor
- Use a correctly labeled graph to show how changes in a factor market affect firm and market behavior

Factor markets change with the push and pull of *incentives* and *constraints*. Factor demand is driven by incentives to produce more output and constrained by the availability of technology and resources to support the productivity of factors. The suppliers of factors are similarly pushed by the incentives of higher input prices and pulled back by the constraints of resource availability, social norms, and limited opportunities.

In this Module, we'll examine how changes in incentives and the relaxation of constraints shift factor demand and supply curves and alter market outcomes.

Factor Demand Shifters

As with demand curves for goods, it is important to distinguish between movements along a factor demand curve and shifts of a factor demand curve. As we learned in Module 5.1, changes in the price of the factor itself—the wage rate for labor and the rental rate for land or capital—cause movements along the demand curve for that factor. What causes a factor's demand curve to shift? There are three main types of changes in the associated incentives or constraints:

- Changes in the price of the product the factor produces
- Changes in the supply of other factors
- Changes in technology

AP® ECON TIP

Although the factor demand curve looks and acts like other demand curves you have studied, the causes of a shift in demand are different.

Changes in the Price of the Product

Remember that factor demand is derived demand: The incentive to hire a factor of production comes from the revenue gained from selling the resulting output. A change in the price of the good or service produced with a factor changes the marginal revenue received from production and thus the marginal revenue product of the factor. For example, in the case of labor demand, if P changes, MR changes, and $MRPL = MPL \times MR$ will change at any given level of employment.

Figure 5.2-1 illustrates the effects of changes in the price of wheat on Mia and Liam's demand for labor. We'll assume the market equilibrium wage rate is \$200, so Mia and Liam face a labor supply curve that is horizontal at their marginal factor cost of \$200. Panel (a) shows the effect of an *increase* in the price of wheat. Note that in this example, the price increase is the same as the marginal revenue increase because $P = MR$ in a perfectly competitive market. This increase shifts the marginal revenue product of labor curve upward, because an increase in the product price raises the $MRPL$ at every level of employment. If the wage rate remains unchanged at \$200, then the point where $W = MRPL$ moves from point A to point B: the profit-maximizing level of employment rises from 5 to 8 workers.

Bim/E+/Getty Images

A rise in wheat prices increases the demand for labor on wheat farms.

FIGURE 5.2-1 Shifts of the Marginal Revenue Product Curve

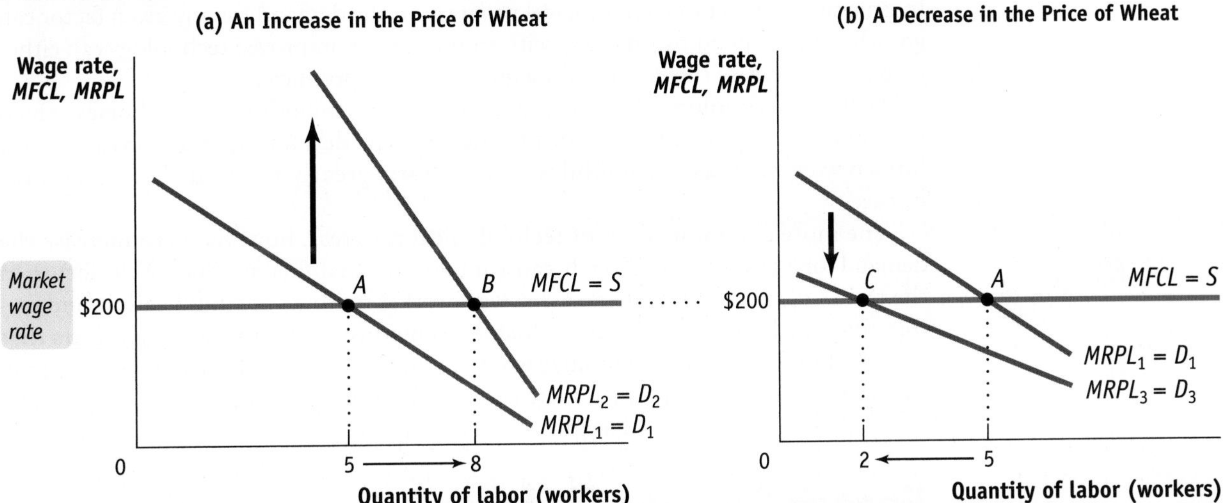

Panel (a) shows the effect of an increase in the price of wheat on Mia and Liam's demand for labor. The increase in price (and thus marginal revenue) shifts the marginal revenue product of labor curve upward from $MRPL_1 = D_1$ to $MRPL_2 = D_2$. If the firm's marginal factor cost – the market wage rate – remains at $200, the profit-maximizing quantity of labor rises from 5 workers at point *A* to 8 workers at point *B*. Panel (b) shows the effect of a decrease in the price of wheat. The marginal revenue product of labor curve shifts downward from $MRPL_1 = D_1$ to $MRPL_3 = D_2$. At the market wage rate of $200, the profit-maximizing quantity of labor falls from 5 workers to 2 workers, shown by the movement from point *A* to point *C*.

Panel (b) shows the effect of a *decrease* in the price of wheat. This shifts the marginal revenue product of labor curve downward. If the wage rate remains unchanged at $200, then the point where $W = MRPL$ moves from point *A* to point *C*: the profit-maximizing level of employment falls from 5 to 2 workers.

Note that a market-wide increase or decrease in the marginal revenue product of labor would affect the demand for labor enough to change the equilibrium market wage. But in this case, for simplicity, we'll assume that the change in the price of wheat is localized so that the market wage rate remains unchanged.

> **AP® ECON TIP**
>
> If the demand for labor increases, there is effectively a rightward shift of the labor demand curve (more labor is demanded at each wage) and an upward shift of the labor demand curve (firms are willing to pay more for each unit of labor). So depending on the context, you might see a labor demand increase described as a *rightward shift* or an *upward shift* of the labor demand curve. Likewise, a decrease in labor demand might be referred to as a shift of the labor demand curve *leftward* or *downward*.

Changes in the Supply of Other Factors

Goods and services are made using a combination of factors, and the productivity of each factor generally depends on the supplies of other factors. Suppose Mia and Liam clear a woodland on their property to make more land available to cultivate. Each worker now produces more wheat because each has more land to work with. The increase in productivity raises the marginal product of labor on the farm at any given level of employment. This change has the same effect as an increase in the price of wheat, as illustrated in panel (a) of Figure 5.2-1: the marginal revenue product of labor curve shifts upward, and at any given wage rate the profit-maximizing level of employment rises.

Similarly, suppose Mia and Liam decide to cultivate less land. Each worker produces less wheat because each has less land to work with. This lowers the marginal product of labor at any given employment level, and as a result, the marginal revenue product of labor curve shifts downward – as in panel (b) of Figure 5.2-1 – and the profit-maximizing level of employment falls.

Having more or less capital to work with would also shift the marginal revenue product of labor curve. For example, suppose Mia and Liam purchase more farming equipment such as tractors and hay rakes. Their workers will be more productive at every level of employment, so the marginal revenue product curve will shift upward.

Changes in Technology

In general, the effect of technological progress on the demand for any given factor can go either way, depending on the specific improvement: improved technology can either increase or decrease the demand for a given factor of production.

How can technological progress decrease factor demand? Consider horses, which were once an important factor of production. The development of substitutes for horsepower, such as automobiles and tractors, greatly reduced the demand for horses.

The more common effect of technological progress, however, is to increase the demand for a given factor, often because it raises the marginal product of the factor. In the case of labor, technology can assist with worker training, communication, and performance, making workers more valuable to employers. Despite persistent fears that new machines and other technology would reduce the demand for labor, over the long run, the U.S. economy has seen increases in both wages and employment, suggesting that technological progress has increased labor demand.

Factor Supply Shifters

The suppliers of factors of production have their own set of influences. A change in anything that alters the willingness to supply a factor *other than the price of that factor* causes a shift of the factor supply curve. We will again focus on examples in the labor market because they are common and relatable. There are four main types of changes that shift the labor supply curve:

- Changes in preferences and social norms
- Changes in the availability of labor
- Changes in opportunities
- Changes in wealth

Changes in Preferences and Social Norms

New preferences and social norms can lead workers to increase or decrease their willingness to work at any given wage. A striking example is the large increase in the number of employed women – particularly married women – in the United States over the past half century. Before 1978, most women did not work outside the home. In the decades that followed, changing preferences and cultural expectations brought large numbers of American women into the workforce. The catalysts of this change included the invention of labor-saving home appliances such as washing machines, the trend for more people to live in cities, and higher female education levels. Similar improvements in the labor force participation rate of women are observable in other countries experiencing social and technological changes.

Changes in Population

Changes in the population size generally lead to shifts of the labor supply curve. Population size is affected by birth rates, death rates, immigration (people entering a country to live permanently), and emigration (people leaving a country to live elsewhere permanently). A larger population tends to shift the labor supply curve rightward as more workers are available at any given wage; a smaller population tends to shift the labor supply curve leftward due to fewer available workers. The size of the U.S. labor force grows by approximately 0.5% per year, which is also the approximate population growth rate in this country. As a result, the labor supply curve in the United States is shifting to the right.

Changes in Opportunities

J. Conrad Williams, Jr./Newsday LLC/Getty Images

In recent decades, women have had increasing opportunities to choose among myriad careers.

At one time, teaching was about the only occupation considered suitable for well-educated women. However, as opportunities in other professions opened up to women starting in the 1960s, many women left teaching and chose other careers.

This generated a leftward shift of the supply curve for teachers, reflecting a fall in the willingness to work at any given wage and forcing school districts to pay more to maintain an adequate teaching staff. These events illustrate a general result: when superior alternatives arise for workers in another labor market, the supply curve in the original labor market shifts leftward as workers move to the new opportunities. Similarly, when opportunities diminish in one labor market – say, when there are fewer manufacturing jobs due to competition from competitors in other countries – the supply in alternative labor markets increases as workers move to those other markets.

Changes in Wealth

A person whose wealth increases will buy more normal goods, including leisure. So when a class of workers experiences a general increase in wealth – say, due to a stock market boom – the income effect from the wealth increase will shift the labor supply curve associated with those workers leftward as workers consume more leisure and work less. Note that *the income effect caused by a change in wealth shifts the labor supply curve*, but *the income effect from a wage rate increase is a movement along the labor supply curve* – as we discussed in the case of the individual labor supply curve in the previous Module.

Such an increase in the wealth levels of many families over recent decades has led to a shift of the summertime labor supply curve for teenagers. The Bureau of Labor Statistics reports that in 1980, 71% of Americans between the ages of 16 and 19 were in the summer workforce. Twenty years later, that number had fallen to 62%, and by 2019, it was 36%. (It was 31% in 2020, but the COVID-19 pandemic played a significant role in that change.) One explanation for the decline in the summer labor supply is that more students are using their summers to study. But an important factor in the decline is that, due to increasing household affluence, many teenagers no longer feel pressured to contribute to household finances by taking a summer job. That is, the income effect leads to a reduced labor supply.

Figure 5.2-2 shows how a decrease in the supply of labor for any reason affects the labor supply curves for a *perfectly* competitive labor market and an individual firm within that market. With less labor available, the market labor supply curve shifts to the left, indicating that fewer units of labor would be supplied at each wage rate. The movement of the equilibrium from E_1 to E_2 decreases the market equilibrium quantity of labor and increases the market equilibrium wage. As we've discussed, the firm's marginal factor cost in a perfectly competitive labor market is the market wage. The individual firm labor supply curve, which is horizontal at the level of the marginal factor cost, shifts upward to the height of the new equilibrium wage. At the higher wage, the firm decreases the quantity of labor hired from L_1 to L_2.

AP® ECON TIP

If the supply of labor increases, there is effectively a rightward shift of the labor supply curve (more labor is supplied at each wage) and a downward shift of the labor supply curve (workers are willing to accept a lower wage for each unit of labor). So depending on the context, you might see a labor supply increase described as a *rightward* shift or a *downward* shift of the labor supply curve. Likewise, a decrease in labor supply might be referred to as a shift of the labor supply curve *leftward* or *upward*.

Changes in the Supply of Other Factors of Production

As with the supply curve for labor, the supply curves for other factors of production shift as the factors become more or less available. For example, the supply of farmland could decrease as a result of a drought, or the supply of capital could increase as a result of a government policy to promote investment. In 2022, a shortage of semiconductor chips used in delivery trucks led to a situation analogous to that depicted in

FIGURE 5.2-2 A Decrease in Labor Supply in a Perfectly Competitive Market

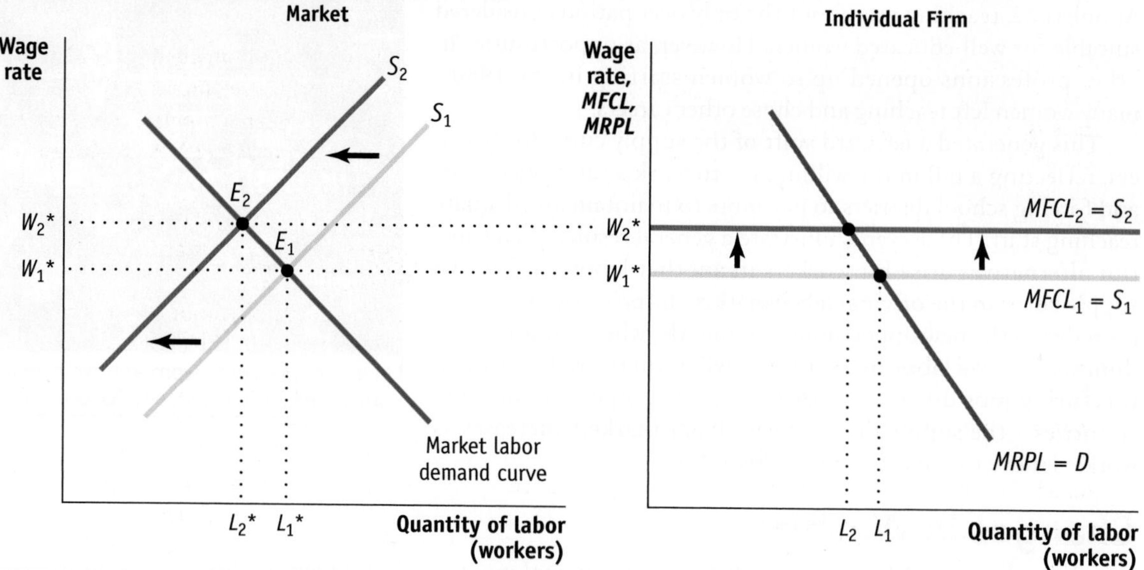

When the supply of labor in a perfectly competitive labor market decreases, the market labor supply curve shifts to the left. This change decreases the market equilibrium quantity of labor from L_1* to L_2* and increases the market equilibrium wage (from W_1* to W_2*). That wage is the marginal factor cost firms pay for each unit of labor. The individual firm labor supply curve on the right graph, which is horizontal at the level of the marginal factor cost, shifts upward from S_1 to S_2, taking the height of the new equilibrium wage. At the higher wage, the firm decreases the quantity of labor hired from L_1 to L_2.

Figure 5.2-2, except for capital instead of labor: the decrease in truck supply increased the equilibrium rental rate for trucks and decreased the equilibrium quantity in the market. Individual firms responded by renting or purchasing fewer trucks and seeking alternative means of transporting products and resources, such as trains.

In Modules 5.1 and 5.2, we have learned how firms determine the optimal amount of labor, land, or capital to hire in factor markets, as influenced by factor supply and demand. But often there are different combinations of factors that a firm can use to produce the same level of output. In the next Module, we look at how a firm chooses between alternative input combinations for producing a given level of output.

Adventures in AP® Economics

Watch the video: ***Factor Markets***

Module 5.2  Review

Check Your Understanding

1. Explain how each of the following events would affect the equilibrium rental rate and the equilibrium quantity in the land market.
   a. Developers improve the process of filling in coastal waters with rocks and soil to form large new areas of land.
   b. New fertilizers improve the productivity of each existing acre of farmland.
2. a. Suppose service industries, such as retail sales and banking, experience an increase in demand. These industries use relatively more labor than nonservice industries. Does the demand curve for labor shift to the right, shift to the left, or remain unchanged?
   b. Suppose diminishing fish populations off the coast of Maine lead to policies restricting the use of the most productive types of nets in that area. The result is a decrease in the number of fish caught per day by commercial fishers in Maine. The price of fish is unaffected due to growing supplies from elsewhere. Does the demand curve for fishers in Maine shift to the right, shift to the left, or remain unchanged?

Tackle the AP® Test: Multiple-Choice Questions

1. As a result of an increase in the supply of land, the demand curve for land
   a. shifts to the right.
   b. shifts to the left.
   c. shifts upward.
   d. shifts downward.
   e. does not shift.

2. Which of the following will shift a factor's demand curve to the right?
   a. a technological advance that replaces that factor
   b. a decrease in demand for the good being produced
   c. a decrease in that factor's marginal product
   d. an increase in the price of that factor
   e. an increase in the price of the good being produced

3. Which of the following will shift the supply curve for labor to the right?
   a. a decrease in the average retirement age
   b. a decrease in population
   c. an increase in wealth
   d. a decrease in the opportunity cost of leisure
   e. an increase in the percentage of women who participate in the labor market

4. An increase in the wage rate will
   a. shift the labor supply curve to the right.
   b. shift the labor supply curve to the left.
   c. cause an upward movement along the labor supply curve.
   d. cause a downward movement along the labor supply curve.
   e. have no effect on the quantity of labor supplied.

5. Which of the following are equal at the point where the labor supply curve intersects the labor demand curve for a firm hiring from a perfectly competitive labor market?
   a. the marginal factor cost and the marginal revenue product of labor
   b. the wage and the marginal product of labor
   c. the product price and the marginal revenue product of labor
   d. the marginal factor cost and the product price
   e. the wage and the product price

6. Suppose the market for office space is perfectly competitive and an increase in the number of people working from home causes a decrease in demand in the office space market. The supply curve for office space facing an individual firm is a/an ____________ line that would ____________ as a result of the change.

a.	upward-sloping	shift up
b.	upward-sloping	shift down
c.	horizontal line	shift up
d.	horizontal line	shift down
e.	horizontal line	not change

7. If Roland Bike Works makes more welding equipment available to the workers in its mountain bike factory, its *MRPL* curve will
   a. shift upward.
   b. shift downward.
   c. remain unchanged.
   d. shift to the left.
   e. become vertical.

Tackle the AP® Test: Free-Response Questions

1. Assume the demand curve for a firm's product is as shown below and that the firm can hire as many workers as it wants for a wage of $80 per day.

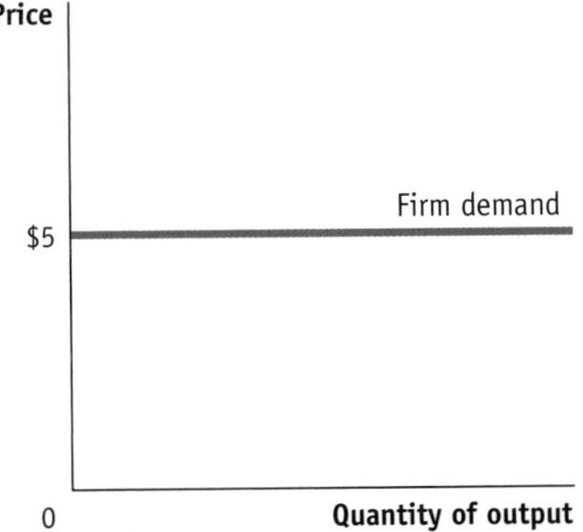

   a. What is the market structure of the factor market in which the firm hires labor? Explain.
   b. What is the market structure of the product market in which the firm sells its output? Explain.
   c. Define marginal factor cost. What is the marginal factor cost of labor for this firm?
   d. If the last worker hired produces an additional 20 units of output, what is the last worker's *MRPL*? Explain.

Rubric for FRQ 1 (8 points)

1 point: The firm hires labor in a perfectly competitive labor market.

1 point: The firm is a price-taker in the labor market. (It can hire all that it wants for $80 per day.)

1 point: The firm sells its output in a perfectly competitive product market.

1 point: The horizontal demand curve indicates that the firm is a price-taker in the product market (it can sell all the output it wants at the market price of $5).

1 point: The additional cost of hiring one more unit of a factor

1 point: $80

1 point: $100

1 point: *MRPL* = *MPL* × *MR*, *MPL* = 20, *MR* = $5, so *MRPL* = 20 × $5 = $100.

2. The table below shows the quantity of umbrellas that Umbrellarama can produce with various quantities of workers. Umbrellarama can sell all of the output it produces at a price of $15.

Quantity of labor (workers)	Quantity of umbrellas
0	0
1	300
2	550
3	700
4	800
5	850
6	890

a. What is the marginal revenue product of labor of the 3rd worker?

b. Draw a correctly labeled graph showing the firm's demand curve for labor.

c. What happens to the demand curve for labor if the price of umbrellas increases to $20? Show the result on your graph from part b.

d. Assume that a technological advance doubles the productivity of workers. Calculate the total quantity that will now be produced with each quantity of labor. **(7 points)**

3. Maggie's Pizzeria hires delivery drivers from a perfectly competitive labor market.

a. Draw correctly labeled side-by-side graphs of delivery driver supply and demand for Maggie's Pizzeria and for the entire delivery driver market.

b. On your graphs, show how an increase in the supply of delivery drivers would affect the equilibrium wage and the number of drivers hired, both by Maggie's Pizzeria and in the delivery driver market as a whole. **(8 points)**

4. Draw separate, correctly labeled graphs illustrating the effect of each of the following changes on the demand for labor. Adopt the usual *ceteris paribus* assumption that all else remains unchanged in each case.

a. The price of the product being produced decreases.

b. Worker productivity increases.

c. Firms invest in more capital to be used by workers. **(5 points)**

MODULE 5.3

Profit Maximization in Factor Markets

In this Module, you will learn to:
- Explain how firms determine the optimal input mix
- Apply the cost-minimization rule for employing inputs

In the past two Modules, we discussed the markets for factors of production—land, capital, and labor—and how firms determine the optimal quantity of each factor to employ. We have learned several key characteristics of perfectly competitive factor markets: We know that each firm faces a factor supply curve that is horizontal at the wage or rental rate established by the factor market equilibrium. We have identified that wage or rental rate as the *marginal factor (resource) cost*—the cost of purchasing one additional unit of the factor. And we have seen that a firm employs more of a factor until the marginal factor cost equals the marginal revenue product of the factor.

So far in this Unit, we have considered the employment decision for individual factors of production. But multiple factors are required for most types of production, and firms must decide what *combination* of these inputs to use to produce their output. In this Module, we will look at how firms in perfectly competitive labor markets make that decision. Note that even firms selling in imperfectly competitive product markets, such as monopolies and oligopolies, may purchase inputs from perfectly competitive factor markets. In the next Module, we examine how profit-maximizing behavior is somewhat different in imperfectly competitive factor markets.

Alternative Input Combinations

A firm can typically choose among a number of alternative combinations of inputs that will produce a given level of output. For example, on Mia and Liam's wheat farm, the decision might involve labor and capital. To produce their optimal quantity of wheat, they could choose to have a relatively *capital-intensive* operation by investing in several tractors and other mechanized farm equipment and hiring relatively little labor. Alternatively, they could have a more *labor-intensive* operation by hiring a lot of workers to do much of the planting and harvesting by hand. The same amount of wheat can be produced using many different combinations of capital and labor. Mia and Liam must determine which combination of inputs will maximize their profit.

To begin our study of the optimal combination of inputs, we'll look at the relationship between two inputs used for production. Depending on the situation, inputs can be either substitutes or complements.

Daniel Acker/Bloomberg/Getty Images

Additional capital can take the place of some labor, and vice versa.

Substitutes and Complements in Factor Markets

In Unit 2, we discussed substitutes and complements in the context of the supply and demand model for goods and services. Two goods are *substitutes* if a rise in the price of one good makes consumers more willing to buy the other good. For example, an increase in the price of oranges will cause some buyers to purchase tangerines instead. When buyers tend to consume two

©Ann Heath

Capital can often substitute for labor, as when vending machines substitute for human vendors.

goods together, the goods are known as *complements*. For example, cereal and milk are considered complements because many people consume them together. If the price of cereal increases, people will buy less cereal and therefore need less milk. The decision about how much of a good to buy is influenced by the prices of related goods.

The concepts of substitutes and complements also apply to a firm's purchase of inputs. And just as the price of related goods affects consumers' purchasing decisions, the price of other inputs can affect a firm's decision about how much of an input it will use. In some situations, capital and labor are substitutes. Mia and Liam can produce the same amount of wheat by substituting more tractors for fewer farm workers. Likewise, self-service kiosks can substitute for cashiers, and vending machines can substitute for sales clerks.

Capital and labor can also be complements when more of one increases the marginal product of the other. For example, a farm worker is more productive when Mia and Liam buy a tractor, and each tractor requires a worker to drive it. Office workers are more productive when they can use faster computers, and doctors are more productive when they have access to modern medical imaging equipment and sophisticated data entry software. In these cases, the quantity and quality of capital available affect the marginal product of labor, and thus the demand for labor. Given the relationship between inputs, how does a firm determine which of the possible combinations to use?

Determining the Optimal Input Mix

If several alternative input combinations can be used to produce the optimal level of output, a profit-maximizing firm will select the input combination with the lowest cost. This process is known as cost minimization.

Cost Minimization

How does a firm determine the combination of inputs that maximizes profit by minimizing costs? Let's consider this question using an example.

Imagine you manage a grocery store chain and you need to decide the right combination of self-checkout stations and cashiers at a new store. **Table 5.3-1** shows the alternative combinations of capital (self-checkout stations) and labor (cashiers) you can hire to check out customers shopping at the store. If the store puts in 20 self-checkout stations, you will need to hire 1 cashier to monitor every 5 stations for a total of 4 cashiers. However, trained cashiers are faster than customers at scanning goods, so the store could check out the same number of customers using 10 cashiers and only 10 self-checkout stations.

Table 5.3-1 Cashiers and Self-Checkout Stations

	Capital (self-checkout stations)	Labor (cashiers)
	Rental rate = $1,000/month	Wage rate = $1,600/month
a.	20	4
b.	10	10

If you can check out the same number of customers using either of these combinations of capital and labor, how do you decide which combination of inputs to use? By finding the input combination that costs the least – the cost-minimizing input combination.

Assume that the cost to rent, operate, and maintain a self-checkout station for a month is $1,000 and hiring a cashier costs $1,600 per month. The cost of each input combination from Table 5.3-1 is shown here.

a. Cost of capital	20 × $1,000 = $20,000
Cost of labor	4 × $1,600 = $ 6,400
TOTAL	$26,400
b. Cost of capital	10 × $1,000 = $10,000
Cost of labor	10 × $1,600 = $16,000
TOTAL	$26,000

Many stores have replaced some of their cashiers with self-checkout stations in efforts to reach the cost-maximizing combination of labor and capital.

Charles Stirling (Travel)/Alamy

Clearly, your grocery store chain would choose the lower-cost combination, combination b, and hire 10 cashiers and put 10 self-checkout stations in the new store.

When firms must choose among alternative combinations of inputs, they evaluate the cost of each combination and select the one that minimizes the cost of production. This can be done by calculating the total cost of each alternative combination of inputs, as shown in this example. However, because the number of possible combinations can be very large, it is more practical to use marginal analysis to find the cost-minimizing level of output—which brings us to the *cost-minimization rule*.

The Cost-Minimization Rule

We already know that the additional output that results from employing an additional unit of an input is the marginal product (*MP*) of that input. Firms want to get as much output as possible from each dollar spent on inputs. To do this, firms apply the **cost-minimization rule** by adjusting their combination of inputs until the marginal product per dollar is equal for all inputs, while maintaining their desired level of output. When the inputs are labor and capital, this amounts to equating the marginal product of labor (*MPL*) per dollar spent on wages to the marginal product of capital (*MPK*) per dollar spent to rent capital:

A firm determines the cost-minimizing combination of inputs using the **cost-minimization rule**: employ factors so that the marginal product per dollar spent on each factor is the same.

$$\textbf{(5.3-1)}\quad \frac{MPL}{\text{Wage}} = \frac{MPK}{\text{Rental rate}}$$

To understand why cost minimization occurs when the marginal product per dollar is equal for all inputs, let's start by looking at two counterexamples. Consider a situation in which the marginal product of labor per dollar spent on wages is greater than the marginal product of capital per dollar spent on capital rental. This situation is described by Equation 5.3-2:

$$\textbf{(5.3-2)}\quad \frac{MPL}{\text{Wage}} > \frac{MPK}{\text{Rental rate}}$$

Suppose the marginal product of labor is 20 units and the marginal product of capital is 100 units. If the wage is $10 and the rental rate for capital is $100, then the marginal product per dollar is 20/$10 = 2 units of output per dollar for labor and 100/$100 = 1 unit of output per dollar for capital. The firm is receiving 2 additional units of output for each dollar spent on labor and only 1 additional unit of output for each dollar spent on capital. In this case, the firm gets more additional output for its money by hiring labor, so it should hire more labor and rent less capital.

Figure 5.3-1 illustrates how the switch to more labor and less capital changes the marginal product of each factor. Because of diminishing returns, as the firm hires more labor, the marginal product of labor falls, as shown in panel (a). Panel (b) shows how the marginal product of capital rises as the firm rents less capital. Remember that the firm seeks to equate the marginal product *per dollar spent on each factor*, not simply the marginal product of each factor. But these changes in the marginal product of each factor also change the marginal product per dollar spent on each factor. The firm will continue to substitute labor for capital until the marginal product of labor per

AP® ECON TIP

Questions relating to the cost-minimization rule have appeared on many AP® exams. Remember, the goal is not to maximize the marginal product of an input or to equate the marginal products of the inputs. Instead, cost is minimized by equating the marginal product *per dollar spent* on each input.

FIGURE 5.3-1 Changes in Marginal Product When Some of One Factor Is Replaced by Another

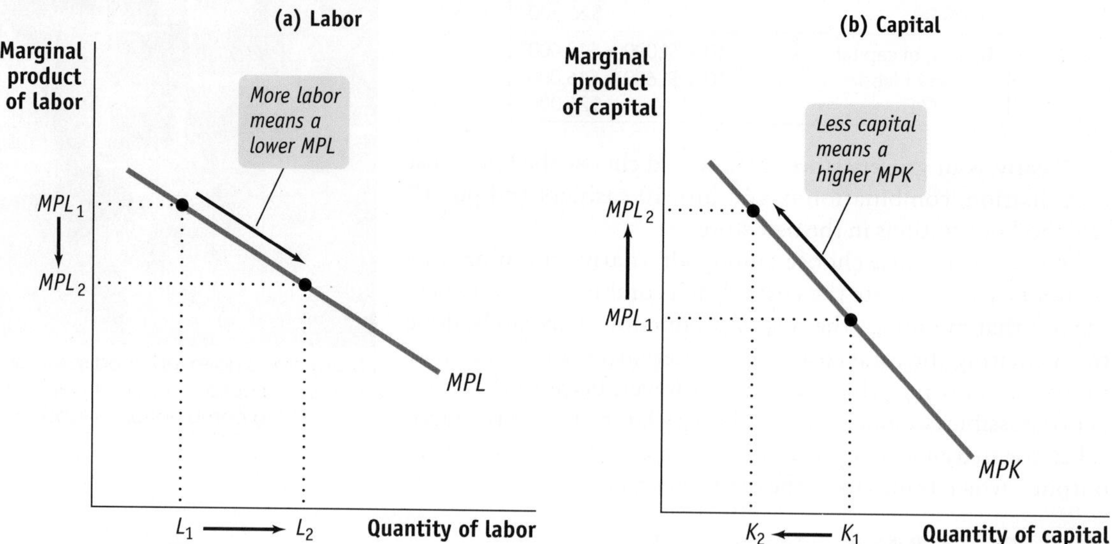

When a firm substitutes labor for capital, due to diminishing marginal returns, the marginal product of labor decreases, as shown in panel (a), and the marginal product of capital rises, as shown in panel (b). The firm minimizes costs by continuing to substitute labor for capital until the marginal product of labor *per dollar spent on labor* equals the marginal product of capital *per dollar spent on capital.*

dollar falls low enough to equal the rising marginal product of capital per dollar, as in Equation 5.3-1. For example, if the *MPL* drops to 15 and the *MPK* rises to 150, given the wage rate of \$10 and the rental rate of \$100, the *MPL* per dollar spent on labor will be $15/10 = 1.5$ and the *MPK* per dollar spent on capital will be $150/100 = 1.5$.

Next, consider a situation in which the marginal product of capital per dollar is greater than the marginal product of labor per dollar. This situation is described by Equation 5.3-3:

$$\textbf{(5.3-3)} \quad \frac{MPL}{\text{Wage}} < \frac{MPK}{\text{Rental rate}}$$

Let's again assume that the marginal product of labor for the last unit of labor hired is 20 units and the marginal product of capital for the last unit of capital rented is 100 units. If the wage is \$10 and the rental rate for capital is \$25, then the marginal product per dollar will be $20/\$10 = 2$ units of output per dollar for labor and $100/\$25 = 4$ units of output per dollar for capital. The firm is receiving four additional units of output for each dollar spent on capital and only two additional units of output for each dollar spent on labor. In this case, the firm gets more additional output for its money by renting capital, so it should rent more capital and hire less labor.

Because of diminishing returns, as the firm rents more capital, the marginal product of capital falls, and as it hires less labor, the marginal product of labor rises. The firm will continue to rent more capital and hire less labor until the falling marginal product of capital per dollar meets the rising marginal product of labor per dollar to satisfy the cost-minimization rule. That is, the firm will adjust its quantities of capital and labor until the marginal product per dollar spent on each input is equal.

The cost-minimization rule is analogous to the profit-maximization rule (introduced in Module 3.5), which states that consumers maximize their utility by choosing the combination of goods so that the marginal utility per dollar is equal for all goods.

Lou Linwei/Alamy

A firm will adjust the quantities of its inputs until the marginal product per dollar spent on each input is the same.

So far in this Unit, we have learned how buyers and sellers behave in a perfectly competitive factor market. Next, we'll see how behavior differs when the factor market lacks competition.

Module 5.3  Review

Check Your Understanding

1. A firm produces its output using only capital and labor. Labor costs $100 per worker per day and capital costs $200 per unit per day. If the marginal product of the last worker employed is 500 and the marginal product of the last unit of capital employed is 1,000, is the firm employing the cost-minimizing combination of inputs? Explain.

Tackle the AP® Test: Multiple-Choice Questions

1. An automobile factory can employ either assembly line workers or robotic arms to produce automobile engines. In this case, labor and capital are considered
   a. independent.
   b. complements.
   c. substitutes.
   d. supplements.
   e. human capital.
2. If an increase in the amount of capital employed by a firm leads to an increase in the marginal product of labor, labor and capital are considered
   a. independent.
   b. complements.
   c. substitutes.
   d. supplements.
   e. human capital.
3. If a firm is producing its desired level of output and the marginal product of labor per dollar is greater than the marginal product of capital per dollar, which of the following is necessarily true?
   a. The marginal product of labor is greater than the marginal product of capital.
   b. The wage rate for labor is less than the rental rate for capital.
   c. The firm should employ more labor and less capital.
   d. The firm should employ less labor and more capital.
   e. The firm should increase its desired level of output.
4. The cost-minimization rule states that costs are minimized when
   a. *MP* per dollar is equal for all factors.
   b. (*MP* × *P*) is equal for all factors.
   c. each factor's *MP* is the same.
   d. *MRP* is maximized.
   e. *MRC* is minimized.
5. The Orange Computer Company currently produces its desired level of output. Its marginal product of labor is 400, its marginal product of capital is 1,000, the wage rate is $20, and the rental rate of capital is $100. In this case, the firm should
   a. employ more capital and more labor.
   b. employ less labor and less capital.
   c. employ less labor and more capital.
   d. employ less capital and more labor.
   e. not change its employment of capital or labor.
6. The Grapefruit Computer Company currently produces its desired level of output. Its marginal product of labor is 10, its marginal product of capital is 50, the wage rate is $20, and the rental rate of capital is $100. In this case, the firm should
   a. employ more capital and more labor.
   b. employ less labor and less capital.
   c. employ less labor and more capital.
   d. employ less capital and more labor.
   e. not change its employment of capital or labor.
7. Which of the following is necessarily true if a firm is producing its desired level of output and its marginal product of labor exceeds its marginal product of capital?
   a. The firm should employ more labor and less capital.
   b. The firm should employ more capital and less labor.
   c. The firm should not change its employment of capital or labor.
   d. The firms should employ more of both capital and labor.
   e. More information is needed to determine the optimal combination of capital and labor.

Tackle the AP® Test: Free-Response Questions

1. Answer the following questions under the assumption that firms use only two inputs and seek to maximize profit.
   a. Would it be wise for a firm that does not have the cost-minimizing combination of inputs to employ more of the input with the highest marginal product and less of the input with the lowest marginal product? Explain.
   b. What is the cost-minimization rule?
   c. When a firm hires more labor and rents less capital, what happens to the marginal product of labor per dollar and the marginal product of capital per dollar? Explain.

Rubric for FRQ 1 (5 points)

1 point: No, it would not be wise.

1 point: The input with the highest marginal product might be much more expensive than the input with the lowest marginal product, making the marginal product per dollar higher for the input with the lowest marginal product. When that is the case, costs would be lower if the firm employed more of the input with the lowest marginal product (but the highest marginal product per dollar) and less of the input with the highest marginal product (but the lowest marginal product per dollar.)

1 point: The cost-minimization rule says that firms should adjust their combination of inputs to equalize the marginal product per dollar spent on each input.

1 point: The marginal product of labor per dollar decreases and the marginal product of capital per dollar increases.

1 point: Each factor has diminishing marginal returns. So when more labor is hired, the marginal product of labor (and thus the marginal product of labor per dollar) decreases. Likewise, when less capital is rented, the marginal product of capital (and thus the marginal product of capital per dollar) increases because the units of capital that are given up had a lower marginal product than those that remain.

2. Refer to the table below. Assume that the wage is $10 per day and the price of pencils is $1.

Quantity of labor (workers)	Quantity of pencils produced
0	0
1	40
2	90
3	120
4	140
5	150
6	160
7	166

   a. What is the *MPL* of the 4th worker?
   b. What is the *MPL* per dollar of the 5th worker?
   c. How many workers would the firm hire if it hired every worker for whom the marginal product per dollar is greater than or equal to 1 pencil per dollar?
   d. If the marginal product per dollar spent on labor is 1 pencil per dollar, the marginal product of the last unit of capital rented is 100 pencils per dollar, and the rental rate is $50 per day, is the firm minimizing its cost? Explain. **(5 points)**

Monopsony

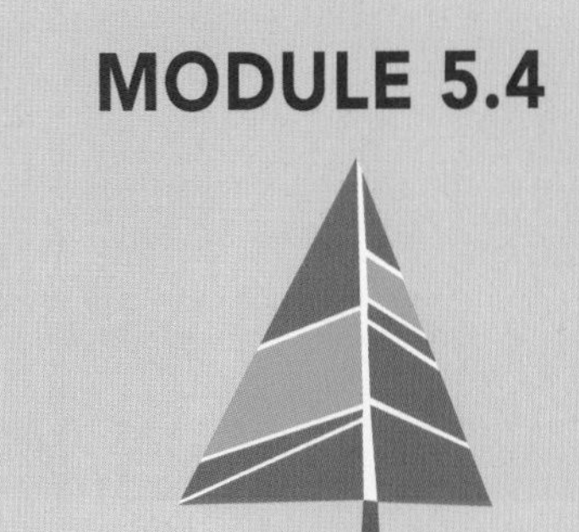

In this Module, you will learn to:

- Identify the characteristics of a monopsonistic market
- Use a graph to show how the marginal factor cost curve differs from the factor supply curve for a monopsony
- Explain how a monopsonist in the labor market chooses employment and wage levels to maximize profit
- Calculate the marginal factor cost in a monopsonistic market

Often there are so many buyers and sellers of the same factor of production that the factor market is best described as perfectly competitive, as has been our assumption so far in Unit 5. But there are also plenty of factor markets that are imperfectly competitive, such as labor markets in small towns with one main employer. In this Module, we examine the workings of an imperfectly competitive labor market.

When the Labor Market Is Not Perfectly Competitive

There are important differences when considering a factor market that is imperfectly competitive rather than being perfectly competitive. One major difference involves the marginal factor cost, which Module 5.1 defined as the additional cost of employing one more unit of a factor of production. We've seen that in a perfectly competitive labor market, each firm is too small for its hiring decisions to affect the market, so the firms are wage-takers and their marginal factor cost of labor curve is simply a horizontal line at the market wage.

A firm faces a very different labor supply curve in a labor market characterized by imperfect competition: the labor supply curve is upward-sloping, and the marginal factor cost is above the market wage. Unlike a perfect competitor that is small and cannot affect the market, a firm in an imperfectly competitive labor market is large enough to affect the market wage. For example, a labor market in which there is only one firm hiring labor is called a **monopsony**. A **monopsonist** is the single buyer of a factor.

A **monopsonist** is a single buyer in a factor market. A market in which there is a monopsonist is a **monopsony**.

Perhaps you've been to a small town where one firm, such as a meatpacking company or a lumber mill, is the only significant employer—that's an example of a monopsony. As the only buyer of labor, the firm faces the upward-sloping labor market supply curve. This means that if the firm wants to hire more workers, it has to offer a higher wage to attract them. The same higher wage goes to all workers, not just the workers hired last. Therefore, the additional cost of hiring an additional worker (the *MFCL*) is *higher* than the wage: it is the wage plus the raises paid to workers who would have been willing to work for less. **Table 5.4-1** shows a calculation of the *MFCL*.

The fact that a firm in an imperfectly competitive labor market must raise the wage to hire more workers means that, for every quantity of workers beyond one, the *MFCL* curve is *above* the labor supply curve, as shown in **Figure 5.4-1**. The explanation for this is similar to the explanation for why the monopolist's marginal revenue curve is below the demand curve: As explained in Module 4.2, to sell one more, the monopolist has to lower the price, so the additional revenue is the price minus the losses on the units that would otherwise sell at the higher price.

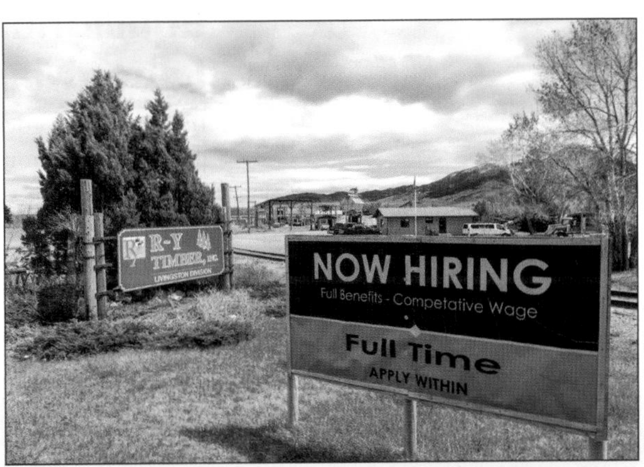

William Campbell/Getty Images

Table 5.4-1 Marginal Factor Cost of Labor with Imperfect Competition in the Labor Market

Quantity of labor *L*	Wage *W*	Total labor cost $= L \times W$	Marginal factor cost of labor *MFCL*
0	$0	$0	
			$6
1	6	6	
			8
2	7	14	
			10
3	8	24	
			12
4	9	36	
			14
5	10	50	

FIGURE 5.4-1 Supply of Labor and Marginal Factor Cost in an Imperfectly Competitive Market

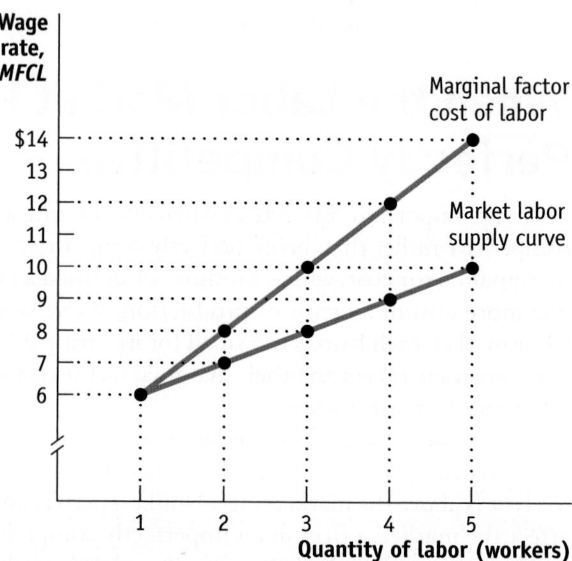

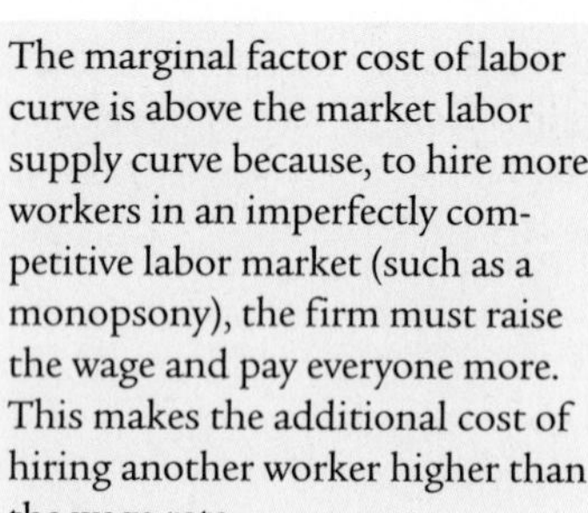

The marginal factor cost of labor curve is above the market labor supply curve because, to hire more workers in an imperfectly competitive labor market (such as a monopsony), the firm must raise the wage and pay everyone more. This makes the additional cost of hiring another worker higher than the wage rate.

In our imperfectly competitive labor market, to hire an additional worker, the monopsonist has to raise the wage, so the marginal factor cost is the wage plus the wage increase for those workers who could otherwise be hired at the lower wage.

Equilibrium in the Imperfectly Competitive Labor Market

In a perfectly competitive labor market, firms hire labor until the marginal revenue product of labor equals the marginal factor cost, which is the market wage. With imperfect competition in a factor market, a firm will hire additional workers until the marginal revenue product of labor equals the marginal factor cost of labor, which we have just seen is *not* the wage. So, as noted in Module 5.1, the term *marginal factor (resource) cost* is generally applicable to the analysis of hiring decisions in both perfectly competitive and imperfectly competitive labor markets. This allows us to generalize and say that every type of firm hires workers up to the point at which the marginal revenue product of labor equals the marginal factor cost of labor:

(5.4-1) Hire workers until $MRPL = MFCL$

Equilibrium in the labor market with imperfect competition is shown in **Figure 5.4-2**. An imperfectly competitive firm finds the optimal number of workers to hire, *L**, directly below the intersection of the marginal factor cost curve and the marginal revenue product curve. The firm then determines the wage necessary to hire that number of workers by starting at point *E* on the labor supply curve above the optimal number of workers and looking straight to the left to see the wage level at that point, *W**.

FIGURE 5.4-2 Equilibrium in an Imperfectly Competitive Labor Market

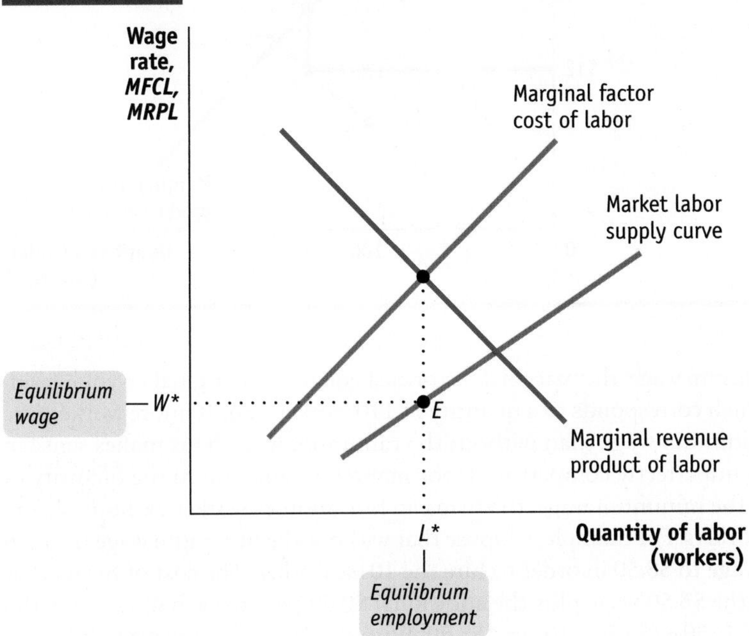

The firm hires the quantity of labor *L** found directly below the intersection of the marginal revenue product of labor curve and the marginal factor cost curve. The equilibrium wage, *W**, is found on the vertical axis at the height of the market supply curve at point *E*, directly above *L**.

Let's put together the information we just learned, again referring to Figure 5.4-2. In an imperfectly competitive labor market, the firm must offer a higher wage to hire more workers, so the marginal factor cost curve is above the labor supply curve. The equilibrium quantity of labor is found where the marginal revenue product equals the marginal factor cost, as represented by *L** on the graph. The firm will pay the wage required to hire *L** workers, which is found on the vertical axis at the height of the supply curve directly above *L**. That is, the labor supply curve shows that workers are willing to supply the quantity of labor *L** at a wage of *W**. The equilibrium wage in the market is thus *W**. Note that, unlike in a perfectly competitive labor market, the wage in the imperfectly competitive labor market is less than the marginal factor cost of labor, and even the last worker hired receives a wage that is below the marginal revenue product of labor.

In Module 2.8B, we learned that a minimum wage could cause unemployment in a perfectly competitive labor market. We can use the monopsony model in **Figure 5.4-3** to examine the effect of a minimum wage in an imperfectly competitive labor market. Without a minimum wage, the marginal revenue product equals the marginal factor cost at point *A*, which corresponds to a quantity of 100 workers. Point *B* shows that the firm must pay $8 per hour to attract 100 workers. With a minimum wage of $12 per hour, point C on the supply curve indicates that the firm can hire up to 110 workers without increasing the wage rate. This means that the marginal factor cost for each of the first 110 workers is $12. In order to hire more than 110 workers, the firm must raise the wage rate above $12—just as it did without a minimum wage—so the marginal factor cost returns to its pre-minimum wage level.

FIGURE 5.4-3 A Minimum Wage in an Imperfectly Competitive Labor Market

In the absence of a minimum wage, this monopsonist would find the point where *MRPL* = *MFCL* (point *A*), hire the corresponding 100 workers, and pay them the $8 wage found on the market labor supply curve for that quantity of workers (point *B*). With a $12 minimum wage, point *C* on the supply curve shows that up to 110 workers could be hired without raising the wage above $12, so the marginal factor cost for the first 110 workers is $12. For larger quantities of labor, the firm must raise its wage for all workers in order to hire any additional workers, just as it did without a minimum wage. That raises the marginal factor cost back up to the pre-minimum wage level. The firm will always hire workers until *MRPL* = *MFCL* (point *D*), which now occurs at a quantity of 110 workers.

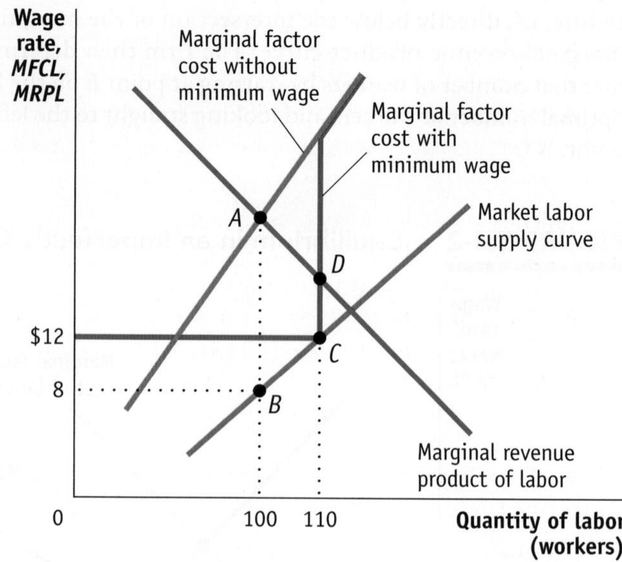

With the minimum wage, the marginal factor cost equals the marginal revenue product at point *D*, which corresponds to a quantity of 110 workers. So, 10 more workers are hired with the minimum wage than without the minimum wage. This makes sense in the context of an imperfectly competitive labor market because, up to the quantity of labor supplied at the minimum wage, the firm can hire another worker without raising the wage for all workers. For example, suppose that without the minimum wage the firm had to raise the wage to $8.50 in order to hire the 101st worker. The cost of hiring that worker would be the $8.50 wage plus the additional $0.50 paid to each of the first 100 workers; a total of $8.50 + ($0.50 × 100) = $58.50. With the $12 minimum wage, however, up to 110 workers can be hired without raising the wage any higher, so that 101st worker would cost only $12. Studies of real-world labor markets—most famously by economists David Card and Alan Krueger—support the prospect that minimum wages do not cause unemployment in imperfectly competitive labor markets.

Module 5.4  Review

Check Your Understanding

1. Explain why the marginal factor cost curve for a monopsonist is above the labor supply curve.

Tackle the AP® Test: Multiple-Choice Questions

1. Suppose a monopsonist is currently hiring 5 workers for $9 per hour, but to hire 6 workers, she would need to raise the wage to $10 per hour. What is the marginal factor cost?
   a. $5
   b. $9
   c. $10
   d. $12
   e. $15

2. In a monopsony, the equilibrium wage is
   a. above the marginal factor cost.
   b. below the marginal revenue product.
   c. equal to the marginal factor cost.
   d. equal to the marginal revenue product.
   e. equal to the price of the product being made.

3. If a minimum wage is imposed on an imperfectly competitive labor market,
   a. more workers will be employed.
   b. fewer workers will be employed.
   c. employment levels will not be affected.
   d. the unemployment rate will increase.
   e. the marginal factor cost for every unit of labor will increase.

4. Which of the following is true for a typical monopsony in the labor market?
   a. The demand curve for labor is horizontal.
   b. The supply curve for labor is horizontal.
   c. The marginal factor cost of labor curve is above the labor supply curve.
   d. The marginal revenue product of labor curve is below the labor demand curve.
   e. The marginal revenue product of labor curve is above the labor demand curve.

5. The quantity of labor demanded in an imperfectly competitive factor market is determined by the intersection of which two curves?
   a. marginal revenue and marginal factor cost
   b. marginal product and supply
   c. supply and marginal revenue product
   d. marginal revenue product and marginal factor cost
   e. marginal product and marginal factor cost

6. Suppose MediTaker has a patent on the medicine it makes and is one of many firms hiring the same type of labor. MediTaker is a __________ in the product market and a __________ in the labor market.

a.	perfect competitor	monopolist
b.	monopolist	perfect competitor
c.	monopsonist	perfect competitor
d.	perfect competitor	monopsonist
e.	monopolist	monopsonist

7. For a monopsonist with a minimum wage in place, the marginal factor cost of labor is
   a. vertical at the quantity of labor that would be hired in the absence of a minimum wage.
   b. horizontal until it meets the supply curve.
   c. downward-sloping to the left of the supply curve.
   d. downward-sloping to the right of the supply curve.
   e. steeper than it was without the minimum wage at all quantities of labor.

Tackle the AP® Test: Free-Response Questions

1. Draw the graph for a typical monopsonist and label the line and axes. Label the equilibrium wage W^* and the equilibrium quantity of labor L^*.
   a. Label as W_{min} the level of any wage that is below the intersection of the original *MFCL* and *MRPL* curves and above the intersection of the *MRPL* and market labor supply curves.
   b. Suppose the government establishes W_{min} as the minimum wage. Draw the resulting marginal factor cost of labor curve and label it *MFCL′*.
   c. Label as L' the quantity of labor that will be hired with the minimum wage in place.
   d. Label as N^* the highest minimum wage that would have no effect on this market.

Rubric for FRQ 1 (9 points)

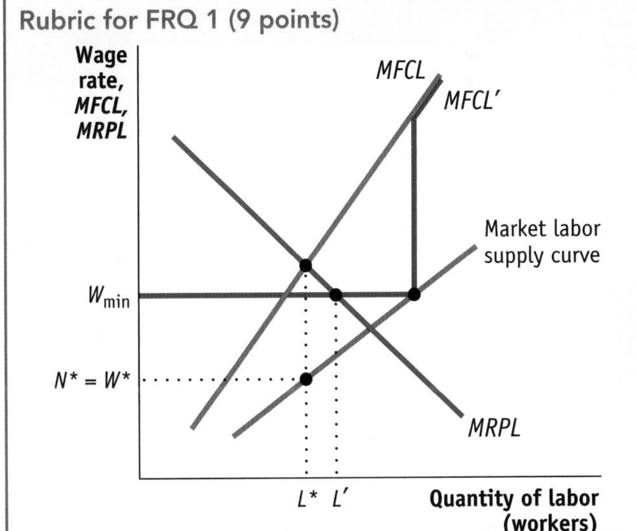

1 point: Axes on graph are correctly labeled.

1 point: The *MRPL* curve is labeled and downward-sloping.

1 point: The market labor supply curve is labeled and upward-sloping.

1 point: The *MFCL* curve is labeled, upward-sloping, and above the supply curve.

1 point: L^* is labeled on the horizontal axis below where $MFCL = MRPL$.

1 point: W^* is labeled on the vertical axis to the left of the point on the market labor supply curve that is above L^*.

1 point: W_{min} is labeled on the vertical axis between $MFCL = MRPL$ and $MRPL =$ market labor supply.

1 point: $MFCL'$ is labeled and drawn as a horizontal line until it reaches the market labor supply curve, and then it becomes vertical until it reaches $MFCL$, at which point it coincides with $MFCL$.

1 point: N^* is labeled at the level of W^*. (A minimum wage at the intersection of $MFCL$ and $MRPL$ would not affect the quantity of labor, but it would affect the wage.)

2. For each characteristic below, indicate whether the matching type of firm is a monopsonist in the labor market, a monopolist in the product market, a perfect competitor in the labor market, or a perfect competitor in the product market.
   a. Horizontal labor supply curve
   b. Upward-sloping labor supply curve
   c. Horizontal product demand curve
   d. Marginal factor cost of labor curve above the labor supply curve **(4 points)**

UNIT 5

Review

Adventures in AP® Economics Videos

Mod 5.2: Factor Markets

economics by example
Immigration: How Welcoming Should Lady Liberty Be?

UNIT 5 Review Video

Module 5.1

1. Just as there are markets for goods and services, there are markets for factors of production, including labor, land, and both **physical capital** and **human capital**.
2. A profit-maximizing firm hiring from a perfectly competitive factor market will keep employing more units of a factor until the factor's price is equal to the **marginal revenue product** – the marginal product of the factor multiplied by the marginal revenue of the output it produces. The **marginal revenue product curve** is therefore the firm's demand curve for a factor. Factor demand is often referred to as a **derived demand** because it is derived from the demand for the producer's output.
3. The market demand curve for labor is the horizontal sum of the individual demand curves of firms in that market.
4. When a perfectly competitive labor market is in equilibrium, the market wage is equal to the **equilibrium marginal revenue product of labor**, the additional revenue generated by the last worker hired in the labor market as a whole. The same principle applies to other factors of production: the **rental rate** of land or capital – the cost of renting a unit of labor or capital for a set period of time – is equal to the equilibrium marginal revenue product. The payment to a factor in excess of the minimum amount necessary to employ that factor is called **economic rent**.
5. Labor supply is the result of decisions about time allocation, with each worker facing a trade-off between **leisure** and work. An increase in the hourly wage rate tends to increase work hours via the substitution effect but decrease work hours via the income effect. If the net result is that a worker increases the quantity of labor supplied in response to a higher wage, the **individual labor supply curve** slopes upward. If the net result is that a worker decreases work hours, the individual labor supply curve – unlike supply curves for goods and services – slopes downward.
6. The market labor supply curve is the horizontal sum of the individual labor supply curves of all workers in that market.
7. When a firm is not a price-taker in a factor market due to imperfect competition, the firm will consider the marginal revenue product and the **marginal factor (resource) cost** when determining how much of a factor to employ. The marginal factor cost is equivalent to the wage (or the price of the factor) in a perfectly competitive market.

Module 5.2

8. The factor demand curve shifts for three main reasons: changes in output price, changes in the supply of other factors, and technological changes.
9. The supply curve for a factor shifts after any change that alters the willingness to supply the factor *except for a change in the price of the factor*. For labor, there are four main supply shifters: changes in preferences and social norms, changes in population, changes in opportunities, and changes in wealth.

Module 5.3

10. In many cases, inputs, such as capital and labor, are substitutes. Inputs can also be complements, which is the case when an increase in the quantity of one input increases the marginal product of the other. Firms will determine the optimal input combination using the **cost-minimization rule**: when a firm uses the cost-minimizing combination of capital and labor, the marginal product of labor divided by the wage rate is equal to the marginal product of capital divided by the rental rate.

Module 5.4

11. A **monopsonist** is the single buyer of a factor. A market in which there is a monopsonist is a **monopsony**. Like perfectly competitive firms in a factor market, monopsonists choose the quantity of a factor that equates the marginal factor cost and the marginal revenue product. However, unlike competitive firms, monopsonists face the entire upward-sloping factor supply curve and their marginal factor cost exceeds the wage rate.

Key Terms

Physical capital, p. 716
Human capital, p. 716
Derived demand, p. 717
Marginal revenue product, p. 718
Marginal revenue product curve, p. 719
Rental rate, p. 722
Leisure, p. 722
Individual labor supply curve, p. 723
Marginal factor (resource) cost, p. 725
Equilibrium marginal revenue product, p. 727
Economic rent, p. 727
Cost-minimization rule, p. 739
Monopsonist, p. 743
Monopsony, p. 743

AP® Exam Practice Questions

Multiple-Choice Questions

1. The four principal classes of factors of production are
   a. money, capital, land, and labor.
   b. money, capital, labor, and entrepreneurship.
   c. money, labor, land, and entrepreneurship.
   d. land, labor, capital, and entrepreneurship.
   e. land, labor, entrepreneurship, and money.

2. Because it results from the demand for automobiles, the demand for automobile workers is a/an
   a. derived demand.
   b. irrational demand.
   c. elastic demand.
   d. inelastic demand.
   e. unit elastic demand.

3. A firm will continue to employ more land until its marginal revenue product of land is
   a. zero.
   b. maximized.
   c. equal to the rental rate.
   d. equal to the wage rate.
   e. equal to the marginal revenue product of labor and capital.

4. For a perfectly competitive firm in both the product market and the factor market, the demand curve for labor slopes downward due to
   a. market power.
   b. economies of scale.
   c. diseconomies of scale.
   d. diminishing marginal returns.
   e. increasing marginal returns.

5. If marginal product is positive and falling as the firm hires more workers, then
   a. total product is rising at a decreasing rate.
   b. total product is falling at a decreasing rate.
   c. average product must be falling.
   d. the marginal revenue product of labor is increasing.
   e. the diminishing returns to labor are decreasing.

Use the following production data for a firm operating in both a perfectly competitive product market and a perfectly competitive factor market to answer Questions 6–8.

Number of workers	Total output/hour
1	10
2	22
3	30
4	36
5	40
6	43
7	45
8	46

6. Based on the production data above, at what level of employment does the firm begin to experience diminishing marginal returns?
   a. There are no diminishing marginal returns.
   b. 3 workers
   c. 4 workers
   d. 5 workers
   e. 6 workers

7. Assume the firm sells its product for $2 each and must pay each worker $8 per hour. What is the marginal revenue product of labor for the second worker?
   a. $10
   b. $22
   c. $24
   d. $60
   e. $176

8. Assume the firm sells its product for $2 each and must pay each worker $8 per hour. How many workers should the firm hire in order to maximize profit?
   a. 2 workers
   b. 3 workers
   c. 5 workers
   d. 6 workers
   e. 8 workers

9. Which of the following would shift the demand curve for labor to the right?
   a. a decrease in the wage rate
   b. an increase in the wage rate
   c. an increase in labor productivity
   d. a decrease in the final price of the product produced
   e. a decrease in the availability of physical capital per worker

10. Suppose a firm produces coffee mugs in a perfectly competitive output market. Which of the following would shift the firm's demand curve for labor to the left?
   a. an increase in the demand for mugs
   b. a decrease in the price of mugs
   c. a decrease in the availability of workers who make mugs
   d. improvements in technology that increase the marginal product of labor
   e. an increase in the availability of physical capital per worker

11. Suppose a firm hires labor in a perfectly competitive labor market. If the marginal revenue product is less than the wage, the firm should definitely
   a. shut down in the short run.
   b. shut down in the long run.
   c. hire more workers.
   d. hire fewer workers.
   e. not change the number of workers it hires.

12. Compared to the supply curve for capital, the supply curve for land is
   a. flatter, more elastic, and more responsive to factor prices.
   b. flatter, less elastic, and less responsive to factor prices.
   c. steeper, more elastic, and more responsive to factor prices.
   d. steeper, less elastic, and less responsive to factor prices.
   e. steeper, more elastic, and less responsive to factor prices.

13. The supply curve for labor slopes downward when
   a. the substitution effect outweighs the income effect.
   b. the income effect outweighs the substitution effect.
   c. the substitution effect equals the income effect.
   d. workers experience an overall decrease in wealth.
   e. wage rates are at very low levels.

14. The supply curve for labor may shift to the left due to
   a. an increase in wealth.
   b. an increase in the wage rate due to the income effect.
   c. a decrease in the wage rate due to the income effect.
   d. an increase in the wage rate due to the substitution effect.
   e. a decrease in the wage rate due to the substitution effect.

15. For a monopsony, the marginal factor cost of labor curve lies above the supply curve at every quantity of labor due to
   a. diminishing marginal returns.
   b. increasing marginal returns.
   c. different workers receiving different wage rates.
   d. all workers receiving the same wage rate.
   e. decreasing opportunity cost of leisure.

16. Compared to a competitive labor market, a firm with monopsony power in the labor market would pay a
   a. higher wage rate and hire more workers.
   b. higher wage rate and hire fewer workers.
   c. lower wage rate and hire more workers.
   d. lower wage rate and hire fewer workers.
   e. lower wage rate but hire the same amount of workers.

17. Assume an effective minimum wage is imposed on a monopsony labor market, and the minimum wage is set below the wage that would exist in a perfectly competitive market. Employment would
   a. decrease, and there would be unemployment.
   b. decrease, and there would be a shortage of workers.
   c. increase, but there would be a shortage of workers.
   d. increase, but there would be unemployment.
   e. increase, and there would be no shortages or surpluses of labor.

18. Assume a firm is operating as a monopolist in the product market and as a perfect competitor in the factor market. The firm's demand curve for labor will be
   a. horizontal due to the competitive labor market.
   b. horizontal due to the effects of market power.
   c. downward-sloping due to diminishing marginal returns and decreasing marginal revenue.
   d. downward-sloping due solely to diminishing marginal returns.
   e. downward-sloping due solely to decreasing marginal revenue.

19. If a former monopolist in the product market begins to face competition as firms enter the market, the firm's demand curve for labor would
   a. not change.
   b. become more elastic.
   c. become less elastic.
   d. show the effects of more rapidly diminishing marginal returns.
   e. show the effects of less rapidly diminishing marginal returns.

20. Suppose that a firm is currently producing its desired quantity of output and that the firm's marginal product of labor is 20, its marginal product of capital is 100, the wage rate for labor is $5, and the rent for capital is $25. All data are per hour. The firm should
   a. employ more labor and rent more capital.
   b. employ less labor and rent less capital.
   c. employ less labor and rent more capital.
   d. employ more labor and rent less capital.
   e. employ the current amount of labor and rent the current amount of capital.

21. In a perfectly competitive factor market, every unit of the factor of production is paid based on the
   a. increase in revenue generated by the last unit of the factor employed in the market.
   b. increase in output generated by the last unit of the factor employed in the market.
   c. average revenue generated by the factor of production employed in the market.
   d. average output generated by the factor of production employed in the market.
   e. average revenue generated by all factors of production employed in the market.

22. An individual firm in a competitive labor market has a demand curve for labor that is
   a. downward-sloping.
   b. upward-sloping.
   c. horizontal at the level of the product price.
   d. vertical.
   e. U-shaped.

23. Which of the following is an example of *physical* capital?
   a. manual labor
   b. welding equipment
   c. farmland
   d. lumber
   e. education

24. Stonehenge is a prehistoric stone monument that people pay to visit. Since the monument would be there whether or not people paid, the payment for visiting represents
   a. commodity money.
   b. physical capital.
   c. a price ceiling.
   d. a minimum wage.
   e. economic rent.

25. According to the cost-minimization rule, firms should equate
   a. the marginal product of each of their inputs.
   b. the price of each of their inputs.
   c. the marginal product per dollar spent on each input.
   d. the price of their input and the price of their output.
   e. the marginal factor cost and the marginal product of each of their inputs.

Free-Response Questions

1. Kyong and Courtney manage a factory in the toy airplane industry, which is perfectly competitive in both the product market and the factor market. They have compiled the following per-day data on worker productivity:

Number of workers	0	1	2	3	4	5	6
Marginal product	–	6	5	4	3	2	1

   a. The price of toy airplanes is $100, the wage per worker is $200, and the rent per machine is $400. Assume the firm always produces the profit-maximizing quantity of airplanes using the cost-minimizing combination of inputs. If the marginal product of capital is 4, how many workers do Kyong and Courtney hire?
   b. Draw a graph of Kyong and Courtney's supply and demand curves for labor using the data from part a above. Be sure to indicate the equilibrium wage rate and the number of workers hired. Label all curves and axes.
   c. Explain why the demand curve for labor slopes the way it does.
   d. On your factor market graph from part b, show the effect of a decrease in the supply of workers in the toy airplane industry. Add the subscript "new" to the label of anything that changes. **(7 points)**

2. The Pelican Perch Hotel hires workers in a perfectly competitive labor market.
   a. Draw side-by-side graphs for the hotel and the labor market and show the following:
      i. the equilibrium wage and quantity of workers in the market, labeled W_E and Q_{E1}, respectively
      ii. the labor supply curve for the hotel, labeled S_H
      iii. the quantity of workers hired by the hotel, labeled Q_1
   b. Suppose a minimum wage higher than W_E is imposed on the labor market. On your graph from part a, show the following:
      i. the new wage in the market, labeled W_{Min}
      ii. the quantity of workers hired in the market, labeled Q_{E2}
      iii. the quantity of workers hired by the hotel, labeled Q_2

   (7 points)

3. Colby Coal Inc. is a town's only employer of labor.
   a. Identify the market structure in which Colby Coal hires labor.
   b. Draw a correctly labeled graph of the labor market for Colby Coal and identify the following:
      i. the quantity of labor employed, labeled Q_M
      ii. the wage rate Colby Coal will pay, labeled W_M
   c. Suppose the government breaks up Colby Coal into many smaller firms, creating a perfectly competitive labor market. On your graph from part a, label the new equilibrium quantity of employment Q_C and the new wage rate W_C. **(7 points)**

Market Failure and the Role of Government

AP® Economics Skills

1. Principles and Models (1.A, 1.B)
2. Interpretation (2.A)
4. Graphing and Visuals (4.B, 4.C)

Incentives Matter, for Better or Worse

Rivers provide drinking water for neighboring communities, support wildlife, and can be beautiful places to swim, fish, and boat. They also receive industrial waste, sewage, and farm runoff containing chemical fertilizers, herbicides, and pesticides. Each year, millions of pounds of toxic chemicals enter the Mississippi River, causing problems for humans and wildlife alike. At the mouth of the Mississippi River lies a "dead zone" spread across thousands of square miles of the Gulf of Mexico. Nitrogen and phosphorus pollution in the dead zone unleashes algae blooms that deplete oxygen in the water and make it unviable for sea creatures.

The dead zone was larger than average in 2021, but some of the Mississippi River's worst pollutants—polychlorinated biphenyls, known as PCBs—are on the decline. For most of the last century, manufacturers used PCBs in everything from cables and caulking to paints and plastics. Levels of PCBs in waterways have slowly declined since 1979, when many industries phased out their use. But the industries didn't do this out of the goodness of their hearts; they did it in response to a ban on PCBs by the Environmental Protection Agency. Without such government intervention, manufacturers would have had few incentives to take the environmental effects of their actions into account.

Neglected pollution is one of several reasons why markets sometimes fail to deliver the optimal quantities of goods and services for society. In Unit 4, we learned that inefficiency can arise from market power, which allows monopolists and colluding oligopolists to charge prices that exceed the marginal cost and prevent mutually beneficial transactions from occurring. In this Unit, we will consider other reasons for inefficient market outcomes. In Module 6.2, we will see that inefficiency can arise from *externalities*, which create conflicts between the best interests of individuals, firms, and society as a whole. In Module 6.3, we will focus on how individuals can sometimes benefit from goods purchased by others, which leads to suboptimal purchases of those goods. In Modules 6.4 and 6.5, we will look at the role of government in addressing market power and income inequality, among other problems. The investigation of sources of inefficiency will deepen our understanding of the types of policy that can make society better off. But first, we'll set the stage in Module 6.1 with a discussion of what it means for a market to maximize society's net gains.

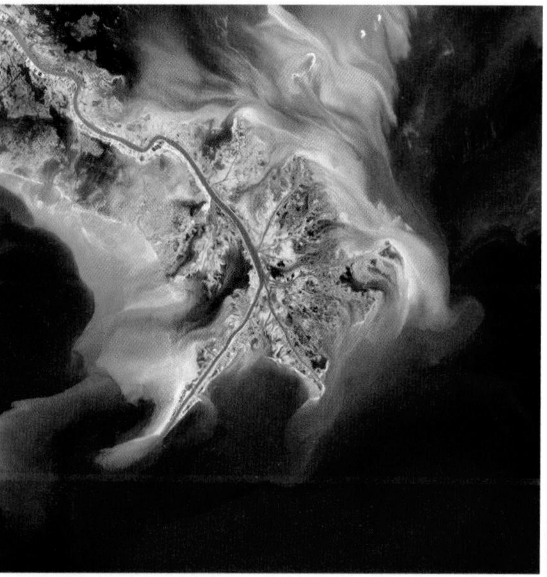

NASA/Science Source

MODULE 6.1

Market Outcomes and Social Efficiency

In this Module, you will learn to:

- Define social efficiency
- Identify market characteristics that lead to social efficiency or inefficiency
- Discuss approaches to inefficiency caused by asymmetric information
- Calculate the deadweight loss created by the production of a non-efficient quantity

Social Efficiency

Pollution is a bad thing. Yet most pollution is a side effect of activities that provide us with good things: our air is polluted by power plants generating the electricity that lights our cities, and our rivers are sullied by fertilizer runoff from farms that grow our food. Why shouldn't we accept a certain amount of pollution as the cost of a good life?

Actually, we do. Even highly committed environmentalists don't think we can or should completely eliminate pollution – *some* pollution comes as the unavoidable cost of producing the most basic goods and services, such as food, clothing, and health care. What environmentalists typically argue is that unless there is a strong and effective environmental policy, our society will generate *too much* pollution – too much of a bad thing. And the great majority of economists agree.

To see why, we need a framework that helps us think about how much pollution a society *should* have – that is, what quantity of pollution is *socially efficient*. We'll then be able to see why a market economy, left to itself, can achieve social efficiency in some cases, but not in the case of pollution among other things. We'll study the problem under the simplifying assumption that the amount of pollution emitted by a polluter is directly observable and controllable.

Costs and Benefits of Pollution

How much pollution should society allow? We learned in previous Units that "how much" decisions made by individuals or firms involve comparing the marginal benefit from an additional unit of something with the marginal cost of that additional unit. The same is true for society as a whole.

The **marginal social cost** of something is the additional cost imposed on society as a whole by one additional unit.

The **marginal social benefit** of something is the additional benefit to society as a whole from one additional unit.

The **marginal social cost** of something, be it a good, a service, a pollutant, or anything else, is the additional cost imposed on society as a whole by one additional unit. For example, each additional ton of sulfur dioxide released into the atmosphere by a coal-fired power plant increases the harm of this acidic pollution to waterways, plants, and human health.

The **marginal social benefit** of something is the additional benefit to society from one additional unit. So the marginal social benefit of pollution is the additional benefit to society from one more unit of pollution. This concept may seem counterintuitive – what's good about pollution? However, pollution avoidance requires the use of money and inputs that could be used for other purposes. For example, to reduce the quantity of sulfur dioxide they emit, power companies must either buy expensive low-sulfur coal or install special scrubbers to remove sulfur from their emissions. The more sulfur dioxide they are allowed to emit, the lower are these avoidance costs. If we calculated how much money the power industry would save if it were allowed to emit an additional ton of sulfur dioxide, that savings would be the marginal benefit to society of emitting that ton of sulfur dioxide.

Consider the "how much?" question for any activity—be it production or pollution or something else. The goal from a societal standpoint is to maximize the net gains from the activity that make up the *total surplus* (or *total economic surplus*), as discussed in Module 2.8A. If the marginal social benefit of the activity exceeds the marginal social cost, the net gain for society is not maximized because society's benefit from another unit would exceed its cost. That is, another unit would add to society's total surplus from the activity. If the marginal social benefit of another unit would fall below the marginal social cost, the activity should stop because another unit would introduce a net loss. The activity level is **socially efficient**, meaning that it maximizes society's total surplus, if the activity continues until the marginal social cost equals the marginal social benefit.

Oliver Strewe/The Image Bank/Getty Images

The effects of pollution.

At the socially efficient level of production, the quantity of output is described as the **socially optimal quantity** because it makes society as well off as possible, taking all costs and benefits into account. Using hypothetical numbers, **Figure 6.1-1** shows how we can determine the socially optimal quantity of pollution. The upward-sloping *marginal social cost curve*, labeled *MSC*, shows how the marginal cost to society of an additional ton of pollution emissions varies with the quantity of emissions. An upward slope is typical for the marginal social cost of pollutants because nature can often safely handle low levels of pollution but is increasingly harmed by additional units as pollution reaches high levels.

The **socially efficient** level of output maximizes the net gains for society by equating the marginal social cost and the marginal social benefit.

The **socially optimal quantity** is the quantity that makes society as well off as possible.

FIGURE 6.1-1 Why a Market Economy Produces Too Much Pollution

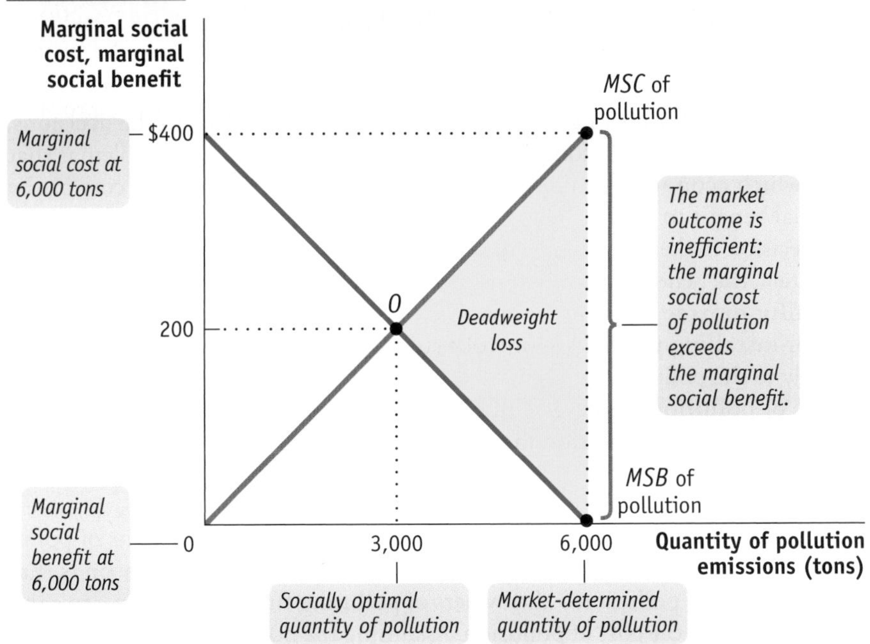

Pollution yields both costs and benefits. The socially optimal quantity of pollution is 3,000; at that quantity, the $200 marginal social benefit of pollution is equal to the marginal social cost. The market-determined quantity of pollution will be 6,000 tons, the quantity at which the marginal social benefit of pollution equals the price polluters pay for each unit of pollution they emit: $0. This is an inefficiently high quantity of pollution because the marginal social cost, $400, greatly exceeds the marginal social benefit, $0. The difference between the marginal social cost and the marginal social benefit for every unit produced in excess of 3,000 tons constitutes deadweight loss.

The *marginal social benefit curve*, labeled *MSB*, is downward-sloping because the first units of pollution can be used for the most beneficial purposes, such as heating hospitals and homes. Subsequent units of pollution enable less critical uses of energy and therefore provide smaller benefits. If pollution is reduced at the power plants, the

AP® ECON TIP

To find the socially optimal quantity of any good, service, or activity, determine where the marginal social cost curve intersects the marginal social benefit curve and go straight down from that point to the quantity axis.

first few units of pollution avoidance come from the lowest-cost avoidance methods; increasingly more expensive technology must be used to achieve further reductions. As a result, the marginal social benefit of being able to emit another ton of pollution is relatively high at low levels of pollution.

The socially optimal quantity of pollution in this example isn't zero. It's 3,000, the quantity corresponding to point *O*, where the marginal social benefit curve crosses the marginal social cost curve. At 3,000 tons, the marginal social benefit from an additional ton of emissions and its marginal social cost are equalized at $200. But will a market economy, left to itself, arrive at the socially optimal quantity?

When a Market Economy Is Socially Efficient

In Module 3.7, we learned that allocative efficiency is achieved by producing a good until the marginal benefit to consumers equals the marginal cost to producers. Allocative efficiency is the goal when decisions about the consumption and production of a good only affect buyers and sellers of the good (unlike, say, when pollution is involved, because pollution affects other people). Module 4.1 explained that monopolies, among other imperfectly competitive markets, produce less than the allocatively efficient quantity. In contrast, we learned that perfectly competitive markets achieve allocative efficiency by equating consumers' marginal benefit (indicated by the price they are willing to pay) with producers' marginal cost.

When the people making decisions about production and consumption feel all of the costs and benefits of their decisions, the market participants' marginal cost and marginal benefit are no different from society's marginal cost and marginal benefit. In that case, allocative efficiency (the equivalence of market participants' marginal cost and marginal benefit) implies social efficiency (the equivalence of society's marginal cost and marginal benefit). So in the absence of pollution and other side effects (discussed in the next Module), a perfectly competitive market achieves socially efficient outcomes by equating marginal social cost and marginal social benefit.

When a Market Economy Is Not Socially Efficient

When the decisions of buyers or sellers do affect people not involved in the decisions, the social efficiency of perfectly competitive markets breaks down. The problem is that side effects, which economists call *externalities*, cause the marginal social cost or the marginal social benefit to diverge from the marginal cost and marginal benefit considered by the decision makers involved. That is the case in our pollution example.

For polluters, the benefits of emissions take the form of monetary savings: by emitting more sulfur dioxide, a power company saves the cost of buying expensive, low-sulfur coal or installing pollution-control equipment. So the benefits of pollution accrue directly to the polluters.

The costs of pollution, however, fall on people who typically have no say in the decision about how much pollution takes place. For example, people who would like to fish or swim in rivers have no say in decisions about the efforts to reduce coal ash contamination from power plants upstream.

In a market economy without government intervention, only the benefits of pollution are taken into account in choosing the quantity of pollution. The reason is that those who benefit from pollution – the owners of polluting firms – don't have to compensate those who bear the cost of pollution. Assuming the polluter is not also the pollution victim, the entire cost of pollution is external, which gives polluters no incentive to limit the amount of emissions.

With polluters paying none of the cost of their pollution, emissions will continue as long as there is any benefit at all from another unit. So, in our example, the quantity of emissions won't be the socially optimal quantity – 3,000 tons. Instead, it will be 6,000 tons, the quantity at which the marginal social benefit of an additional ton of pollution is zero. This is problematic because the marginal social cost of that last ton is much larger than zero – it is $400, and every unit beyond the 3,000th creates a net loss for society. The resulting deadweight loss is $\frac{1}{2} \times \$400 \times (6{,}000 - 3{,}000) = \$600{,}000$.

More generally, the quantity of pollution in a market economy without government intervention will be higher than its socially optimal quantity. For example, before the Clean Air Act of 1970, power plants in the Midwest used the cheapest type of coal available, despite the fact that cheap coal generated excessive levels of pollution. And the production of any non-efficient quantity creates deadweight loss.

Asymmetric Information

Pollution isn't the only reason equilibrium outcomes can deviate from socially efficient outcomes. Another is **asymmetric information**, which exists when buyers and sellers, or any parties in a transaction, don't hold the same information. Shoppers don't always know the quality of products they could buy. Employers don't know everything about workers they could hire. And colleges don't know as much about prospective students as the students know about themselves. Decisions made without full information can lead to inefficient outcomes, such as purchases, sales, hires, or acceptances with benefits that fall short of their costs.

There is **asymmetric information** when the parties involved in a transaction, such as buyers and sellers, hold different information.

Economist George Akerlof pointed out problems with asymmetric information between buyers and sellers of used cars. Sellers know more about the quality of their used cars than potential buyers. Given the uncertainty about whether a car will be a "lemon" (bad), buyers might pay too much, and are reluctant to pay the full value of a "good" used car. This causes sellers of good used cars to have difficulty obtaining fair car prices, but sellers of lemons in disguise do not. The result is that owners of good used cars are more likely to hold on to their cars, and the used car market offers a lot of lemons.

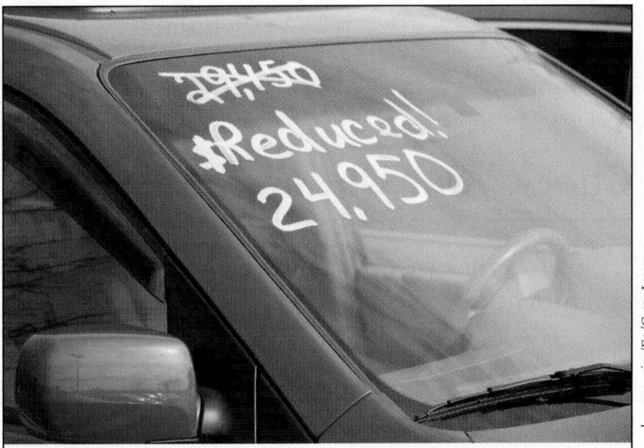

red_moon_rise/E+/Getty Images

Asymmetric information can make it dangerous to pay a lot for a used car.

Another problem stemming from asymmetric information is *adverse selection*. This occurs when some customers are more costly to serve than others, but sellers cannot distinguish between high-cost and low-cost customers. For instance, big eaters are more expensive to serve at all-you-can-eat restaurants, and people with health problems are more expensive to provide with health insurance. When there is asymmetric information about the type of customer someone is, the seller cannot adjust the price in proportion to the cost of service. This means that big eaters get a bargain at all-you-can-eat restaurants and people with unrevealed health problems get a better deal on health insurance. To receive deals like that, customers with one-sided knowledge of their appetite, health, or other relevant characteristics select purchases that place a disproportionate expense on others.

The related problem of *moral hazard* is the tendency for those with insurance against some type of loss to take fewer precautions to avoid that loss. You might be less careful about dropping your smartphone when you have insurance to cover the cost of screen repairs than when you do not. Insurance against fire, injury, and job loss can similarly lead customers to take risks they would not take if they bore the full cost of losses. Since insurance companies cannot monitor the behavior of their customers, asymmetric information leads to excessive levels of risk taking.

Several approaches can limit the inefficiencies of asymmetric information. When perfect information is unavailable, potential buyers and sellers can seek imperfect *signals* of the relevant information. For example, employers use college degrees and grades as signals of the quality of workers, and shoppers use name brands as signals of the quality of products. Buyers of used cars can have an independent mechanic examine the car and report problems the seller might already know about. Car buyers can also run a vehicle identification number (VIN) check on a website such as www.carfax.com to discover information on car repairs, the number of previous owners, and any major accidents in the vehicle's past. To limit adverse selection, health insurance companies typically require physical exams and may not cover preexisting illnesses. And to curtail moral hazard, insurers have customers share the cost of risk behavior. For example, customers may be responsible for a *copayment* that covers some of their own expenses, and the price for insurance – the insurance *premium* – is often based on the customer's history of losses.

The solutions to imperfect information are themselves imperfect and costly. You've probably seen amazing workers and products come from inferior colleges and brands (and vice versa!). Car and human checkups intended to level the informational playing field are costly and sometimes miss problems. Only a 100% copayment would bring insurance customers to feel the full costs of their behaviors, and that would eliminate the risk-sharing benefits of insurance. And experience-based premiums are as imperfect as the past is at foretelling the future. When solutions are unavailable or incomplete, asymmetric information can obscure true marginal benefits or marginal costs and prevent efficient decision making.

Modules 6.2 and 6.3 explain more obstacles to social efficiency, including externalities, imperfect competition, and *public goods* such as military protection that people can benefit from without paying for them. For more discussion of imperfect information, see Enrichment Module C.

Module 6.1  Review

Check Your Understanding

1. Identify the two measures that are equal when social efficiency is achieved.
2. Explain why perfectly competitive markets do not always produce the socially efficient quantity of output.

Tackle the AP® Test: Multiple-Choice Questions

1. The socially optimal level of pollution is
   a. less than that created by the market, but not zero.
   b. more than that created by the market.
   c. whatever the market creates.
   d. determined by firms.
   e. zero.
2. The socially efficient quantity of output can be expected from a ____________ market if the market participants ____________ bear all of the costs and benefits of their decisions.

a.	monopsonistic	do not
b.	perfectly competitive	do not
c.	imperfectly competitive	do not
d.	perfectly competitive	do
e.	imperfectly competitive	do

3. When the production level equates the marginal social cost and the marginal social benefit,
   a. there is deadweight loss.
   b. the quantity of output is socially optimal.
   c. net gains can be achieved by producing less output.
   d. net gains can be achieved by producing more output.
   e. total economic surplus would increase if more output were produced.
4. Suppose the output level exceeds the socially optimal output level. If one fewer unit is produced,
   a. deadweight loss will increase.
   b. the marginal social cost will increase.
   c. the marginal social benefit will increase.
   d. the total economic surplus will decrease.
   e. the deadweight loss will remain the same.
5. Asymmetric information exists whenever
   a. the output level is socially efficient.
   b. the output level is allocatively efficient.
   c. there is deadweight loss.
   d. parties involved in a transaction have full information.
   e. buyers and sellers hold different information.
6. One way to reduce the problem of adverse selection is to require
   a. people with large appetites to go to all-you-can-eat restaurants.
   b. people with insurance to take more risks.
   c. people who buy health insurance to receive a physical exam.
   d. firms to offer a greater selection of products.
   e. advertisers to make more thoughtful selection of ad content.

7. Which of the following is a problem caused by asymmetric information and not part of the solution?
   a. moral hazard
   b. copayments
   c. experience-based premiums
   d. signals
   e. brand names

Tackle the AP® Test: Free-Response Questions

1. Draw a correctly labeled graph showing the market-determined quantity of pollution.
   a. Explain why that quantity will be chosen in the absence of intervention.
   b. On the same graph, show the socially optimal level of pollution.
   c. Shade and label the area on the graph that represents deadweight loss.

Rubric for FRQ 1 (7 points)

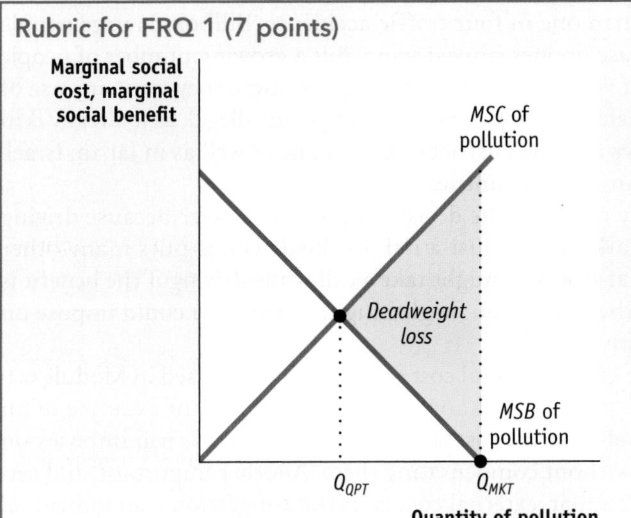

1 point: The vertical axis is labeled "Marginal social cost, marginal social benefit" or "Dollars per unit" and the horizontal axis is labeled "Quantity of pollution" or "Q."

1 point: The marginal social cost curve is labeled and upward-sloping.

1 point: The marginal social benefit curve is labeled and downward-sloping.

1 point: The market-determined level of pollution is shown on the horizontal axis where the marginal social benefit curve reaches the horizontal axis.

1 point: The proper deadweight loss area is shaded and labeled.

1 point: In the absence of intervention, the marginal cost to a polluter of polluting is zero. Thus, pollution will continue until the marginal social benefit (all of which goes to the polluter) equals the polluter's marginal cost of zero, which occurs at the horizontal intercept of the marginal social cost curve.

1 point: The socially optimal level of pollution is shown on the horizontal axis below the intersection of *MSC* and *MSB*.

2. a. Define the marginal social cost of pollution.
   b. Define the marginal social benefit of pollution and explain why polluting more can provide benefits to a firm even when it could produce the same quantity of output without polluting as much.
   c. Define the socially optimal level of pollution.
   (4 points)

MODULE 6.2

Externalities

In this Module, you will learn to:

- Define positive and negative externalities
- Distinguish between production and consumption externalities
- Use a graph to show the effect of an externality on the market for a good or service
- Differentiate private benefits and costs from social benefits and costs
- Explain private solutions to externality problems

External Costs and Benefits

Much of our behavior affects other people in ways we fail to consider. For example, the National Safety Council estimates that drivers who are texting or talking on cell phones account for more than one in four traffic accidents. Billboards urge people not to use phones while driving. But a growing number of people say that voluntary standards aren't enough; they want any use of hand-held cell phones while driving made illegal, as it already is in 27 states and the District of Columbia, as well as in Japan, Israel, and many other countries.

Sarah M. Golonka/Tetra images/Getty Images

The use of cell phones while driving endangers people not involved in the decision to use them.

Why not leave the decision up to the driver? Because driving while talking isn't just a risk to the driver; it puts many other people at risk. You might take a call while driving if the benefit is worth the risk to you, neglecting the costs you could impose on other drivers.

The environmental cost of pollution, discussed in Module 6.1, is perhaps the best-known and most important example of an **external cost**—a cost that an individual or a firm imposes on others without compensating them. Another important, and certainly familiar, external cost is traffic congestion—an individual who chooses to drive during rush hour increases congestion and so increases the travel time of other drivers.

There are also important examples of **external benefits**, benefits that individuals or firms confer on others without receiving compensation. For example, when you plant a tree in your yard, you provide the external benefit of beauty to passersby. External costs and external benefits are jointly known as **externalities.** External costs are called **negative externalities**, and external benefits are called **positive externalities**.

Externalities lead to inefficient market outcomes. Economists describe the problem of inefficiency in a market as **market failure**. We introduced one source of market failure, imperfect information, in Module 6.1. In this Module, we'll examine how externalities cause market failure. Other sources of market failure include *public goods* as discussed in Module 6.3 and market power as discussed in Unit 4 and in Modules 6.4 and 6.5.

An **external cost** is a cost that an individual or a firm imposes on others without compensating them.

An **external benefit** is a benefit that an individual or a firm confers on others without receiving compensation.

External costs and benefits are known as **externalities.**

External costs are **negative externalities**, and external benefits are **positive externalities**.

Market failure occurs when the outcome in a market is inefficient.

Production, Consumption, and Externalities

External costs aren't imposed out of malice. Pollution, traffic congestion, and other negative externalities are side effects of activities that are otherwise desirable, like electricity generation, manufacturing, or driving. It's also important to remember that not all externalities are negative. In fact, we encounter many positive externalities every day.

For example, a neighbor's bird-feeder has the external benefit of maintaining the local wild bird population for everyone's enjoyment. And a beautiful flower garden in front of a neighbor's house can be enjoyed by many passersby. We will study the effects of externalities using a variant of the supply and demand model, beginning with a look at positive externalities.

A flock of positive externalities.

Jeff Rzepka/500Px Plus/Getty Images

Private Versus Social Benefits

So far in this book, we have studied goods in the absence of external benefits, so the marginal benefits to the market participants have been no different from the marginal benefits to society. Sometimes what buyers and sellers do affects a larger swath of society. For example, when you get a flu shot, you help protect other people who might otherwise catch the flu from you. Similarly, beyond the buyers and sellers of doughnuts, a whole community can enjoy the indescribably wonderful smell of a bakery. And the education you are receiving right now benefits society in many ways: your wisdom will be shared with others, and your education will enable you to contribute more to society as a taxpayer, a voter, a role model, and a decision maker.

When a good or service creates positive externalities such as improved community health, nice smells, or shared wisdom, we call the marginal benefit to the consumer the **marginal private benefit**. Module 6.1 explained that the marginal benefit to society is called the *marginal social benefit*. The difference between the marginal private benefit (*MPB*) and the marginal social benefit (*MSB*) is the **marginal external benefit** (*MEB*) that indicates the increase in external benefits to society from one additional unit of the good:

The **marginal private benefit** of a good is the marginal benefit that accrues to consumers of a good, not including any external benefits.

The **marginal external benefit** of a good is the addition to external benefits created by one more unit of the good.

$$\textbf{(6.2-1)} \quad MSB = MPB + MEB$$

We can integrate external benefits into the model of supply and demand to examine the effects of positive externalities that come from consumption and production. A positive externality created by the consumption of a good or service is called a **positive consumption externality**. Flu shots and education are sources of positive consumption externalities. A positive externality arising from the production of a good or service is called a **positive production externality**. Sweet-smelling bakeries create positive production externalities, as does the production of a new convention center that creates more business for local stores, restaurants, and gas stations.

A positive externality created by the consumption of a good or service is called a **positive consumption externality**.

A positive externality arising from the production of a good or service is called a **positive production externality**.

The demand curve represents the marginal benefit that accrues to *consumers of the good*: the marginal private benefit. It does not incorporate additional benefits to society as a whole from consuming the good. When consumption creates external benefits, as shown in Equation 6.2-1, the marginal social benefit exceeds the consumers' marginal private benefit by the amount of the marginal external benefit.

Bakeries create appealing sights and smells that constitute positive production externalities for passers by.

Brasil2/E+/Getty Images

Consider the completion of a college degree, which has value both to the education recipient *and* to other members of society who benefit from the knowledge and productivity of the degree recipient. The marginal social benefit of each college degree is the sum of the benefit of that degree to the recipient (the marginal private benefit) and the benefit of that degree to other members of society (the marginal external benefit). We can use a graph to illustrate each of those types of benefit for each college degree. Panel (a) in **Figure 6.2-1** shows how the marginal external benefit of a college degree is added to the height of the marginal private benefit curve ($D = MPB$) to find the marginal social benefit curve, *MSB*. For, say, the 5th degree or the 100th degree, the height of the $D = MPB$ curve above that quantity indicates the private marginal benefit of that degree, the height of the *MSB* curve indicates the marginal social benefit of that degree, and the vertical distance between the *MPB* and *MSB* curves indicates its marginal external benefit.

Recall that in a competitive market, the market supply curve is the horizontal sum of the individual firms' supply curves, which are the same as their marginal cost curves. So the market supply curve, *S*, indicates the marginal cost to firms (which we'll identify

FIGURE 6.2-1 Positive Consumption and Production Externalities

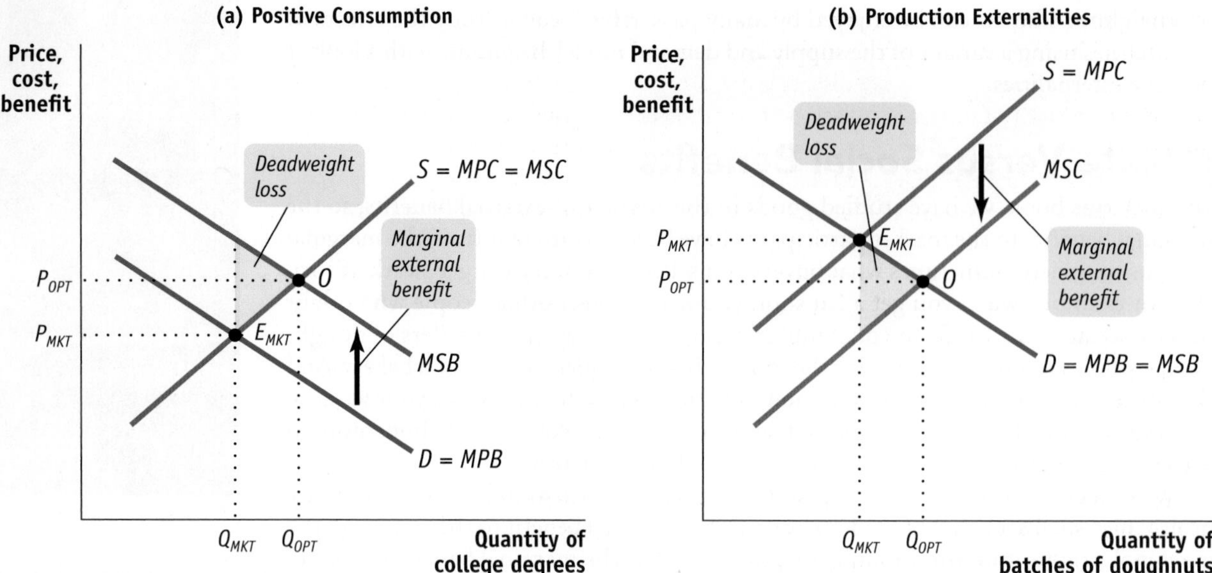

When consumption creates external benefits, the marginal social benefit (*MSB*) exceeds the marginal private benefit (*MPB*) by the amount of the marginal external benefit as shown in panel (a). The market quantity, Q_{MKT}, falls below the socially optimal quantity, Q_{OPT}, resulting in deadweight loss. When production creates external benefits, we model the situation differently to attribute the positive externality to the producers. Panel (b) shows how the marginal external benefit is subtracted from the producers' marginal private cost to determine the marginal social cost. Again, there is deadweight loss because the market quantity falls below the socially optimal quantity.

AP® ECON TIP

You might see different treatments of externalities on older exams, but starting in 2020, the AP® Microeconomics guidelines distinguished the graphs for consumption and production externalities as shown here.

shortly as the *marginal private cost, MPC*). You'll see that we draw the curve representing the marginal social cost, *MSC*, below or above the *MPC* curve in the case of a positive or negative production externality. But in the story for panel (a), there is no production externality, because we're assuming that teaching (as opposed to learning) does not create benefits or costs to people uninvolved in the education process. Because the supply curve coincides with the marginal private cost curve, and the marginal private cost curve is also the marginal social cost curve when there are no externalities, in this case, the *S*, *MPC*, and *MSC* curves are simply the same curve.

Guided by the marginal social benefit curve and the marginal social cost curve, we can find the socially optimal quantity of a good or activity that generates external benefits: it is the quantity Q_{OPT} that corresponds to point *O* at which the marginal social benefit equals the marginal social cost. The market quantity, Q_{MKT}, is determined by the equilibrium of supply and demand at point E_{MKT}, and is less than the socially optimal quantity, Q_{OPT}. In the context of education, this shortfall occurs because students don't internalize the benefits additional education would provide to society—they don't feel the gains other people receive from their educational pursuits. The result is deadweight loss, representing the missed opportunities for net gains from the units of education between Q_{MKT} and Q_{OPT}, all of which would provide a marginal social benefit in excess of the marginal social cost.

We identify the socially optimal price, P_{OPT}, as the price at which *MSC* = *MPB*. In the case of a positive consumption externality, P_{OPT} would be the equilibrium price *if* consumers felt the full marginal social benefit of their purchases. That would bring the demand curve (*D*) up to coincide with the *MSB* curve and lead to the quantity Q_{OPT}. In Module 6.4, we'll see how that can be accomplished with a subsidy for consumers equal to the marginal external benefit. Without intervention, a price of P_{OPT} would not bring about the socially optimal quantity because, although producers would supply Q_{OPT} for that price, consumers would buy less than Q_{OPT} at that price.

When production rather than consumption creates external benefits, we model the situation in a way that distinguishes a production externality from a consumption externality. In the case of a positive production externality, consumers do not create the external benefit, so we draw a single curve to represent *D*, *MPB*, and *MSB*. To attribute the external benefit to the producers, we subtract the marginal external benefit from the producers' marginal private cost to find the marginal social cost. This marginal social cost is essentially the net cost to society of another unit. Panel (b) in Figure 6.2-1 shows how the marginal external benefit of doughnut production—that delightful smell that wafts through the air—is subtracted from the marginal private cost to determine the marginal social cost.

You might be wondering how economists might estimate the marginal external benefit of a batch of doughnuts. One approach would be to survey passersby and ask them, "What is the most you would be willing to pay, if you had to, to enjoy the smells of another batch of doughnuts?" If the average passerby would pay 5 cents to enjoy that smell, and an average of 20 people pass by during the baking of each batch of doughnuts, then the marginal external benefit of a batch of doughnuts is $\$0.05 \times 20 = \$1.00$.

As always, the socially optimal price, P_{OPT}, is found at the intersection of *MSC* and *MSB*. For a positive production externality, P_{OPT} would be the equilibrium price if producers internalized the marginal external benefit of their decisions. A subsidy for producers equal to the value of the marginal external benefit would achieve that goal, as we will discuss further in Module 6.4. Again, there is deadweight loss because the market quantity falls below the socially optimal quantity.

Technology Spillover

The most important single source of external benefits in the modern economy is the creation of knowledge, which goes beyond formal education. In high-tech industries such as the semiconductor, software design, and bioengineering industries, innovations by one firm are quickly emulated by rival firms and put to use in the development of further advancements in related industries. This spreading of cutting-edge technological information among firms is known as *technology spillover*. Such spillovers often take place through face-to-face contact. For example, cafes, bars, and restaurants in California's Silicon Valley are famed for their technical chitchat. Workers know that the best way to keep up with the latest technological innovations is to hang around in the right places, have a drink, and gossip. Such informal contact helps to spread useful knowledge to other firms, which may also help to explain why so many high-tech firms are clustered close to one another.

Network Externalities

There is one type of externality that has no inherently favorable or adverse effect on society at large, but does affect other users of the associated good or service. Suppose you were the world's only user of a social media app such as TikTok. What would it be worth to you? The answer, of course, is nothing. TikTok derives its value from the fact that other people also use TikTok and you can view their posts or share your own. In general, the more people who use TikTok, the more valuable it is to you.

NurPhoto/Getty Images

The private benefit of network externalities, like TikTok and other social media platforms, depends on others using it.

A *network externality* exists when the value to an individual of a good or service depends on how many other people use the same good or service. Sometimes referred to as the "fax machine effect," the phenomenon of network externalities is so named because the classic examples involve networks of phones, computers, and transportation systems. When it comes to sharing digital information, it helps to have more users of the same software, hardware, and online networking services. In other contexts, it's better to have more users of the same stock exchanges, gauges of railroad line, and sizes of electrical plugs, among many examples. Congestion creates a form of negative network externality: it can make things worse for you when more people use the same highway, elevator, swimming pool, or computer network.

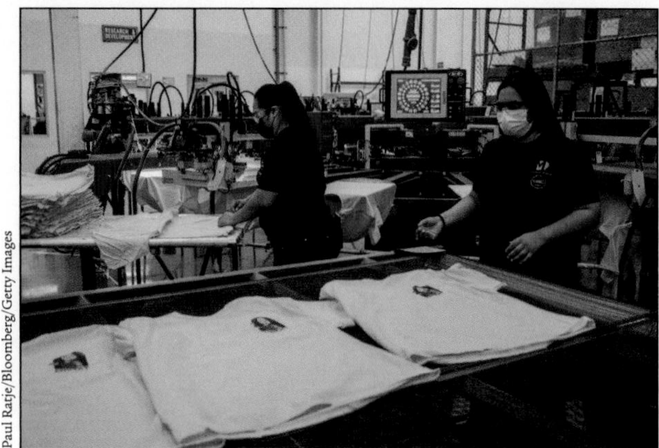
Paul Ratje/Bloomberg/Getty Images

The social cost of T-shirt production is felt beyond the factory.

Private Versus Social Costs

Now we'll examine the effects of negative externalities by considering a case in which the production of a good creates external costs—namely, the making of a cotton T-shirt. With organic cotton farms as an exception, cotton farms are typically chemical intensive. The application of chemical pesticides and herbicides wards off insects and weeds, but poses health and environmental risks. Cotton T-shirt production is also energy intensive due to the use of fossil fuels for farming, transportation, and manufacturing processes. From the point of view of society as a whole, then, the cost of T-shirt production includes both direct production costs (payments for factors of production and inputs) and the external health and environmental costs imposed as a by-product of production.

When a good such as T-shirts involves negative externalities, there is a difference between the marginal cost to the *firm*, which we distinguish as the **marginal private cost**, and the marginal cost to *society*, the *marginal social cost*. The difference between the marginal private cost (*MPC*) and the marginal social cost (*MSC*) is the **marginal external cost** (*MEC*)—the increase in external costs to society from an additional unit of the good:

The **marginal private cost** of a good is the marginal cost of producing that good, not including any external costs.

The **marginal external cost** of a good is the increase in external costs to society created by one more unit of the good.

A negative externality caused by the production of a good or service is called a **negative production externality**.

A negative externality created by the consumption of a good or service is called a **negative consumption externality**.

$$\textbf{(6.2-2)} \quad MSC = MPC + MEC$$

As with positive externalities, negative externalities can arise out of either production or consumption. When production causes a negative externality such as pollution, it is called a **negative production externality**. A negative externality brought about by the consumption of a good, such as the second-hand smoke created by cigarettes consumed in public, is called a **negative consumption externality**. T-shirts involve a negative production externality. And wearing a T-shirt could create a consumption externality if the T-shirt displayed something either appealing or offensive to other people. But we'll assume the T-shirts discussed here are too plain to affect others. We'll also assume that the T-shirt market is perfectly competitive.

Panel (a) of **Figure 6.2-2** shows the industry supply and marginal private cost curve of T-shirts, $S = MPC$, *shifted upward* by the amount of the marginal external cost to find the marginal social cost curve, *MSC*. In the absence of government intervention, the market equilibrium will be at point E_{MKT}, yielding an equilibrium quantity of Q_{MKT} and an equilibrium price of P_{MKT}.

We've seen that the ever-important socially optimal quantity of a good is the quantity at which *the marginal social benefit equals the marginal social cost*. In the T-shirt example in panel (a), this criterion is met at point *O*, where the *MSC* curve crosses the $D = MPB = MSB$ curve. Why does the demand curve, which represents the marginal benefit to consumers—the marginal private benefit—also represent the marginal social benefit curve in this case? Because for T-shirts, as for doughnuts in the previous example, there is no consumption externality. We draw the *MSB* curve above or below the *MPB* curve only in the case of a positive or negative consumption externality.

Unfortunately, the market equilibrium quantity Q_{MKT} in panel (a) is greater than Q_{OPT}, the socially optimal quantity of T-shirts. The yellow deadweight loss area represents society's net losses from producing Q_{MKT} rather than Q_{OPT}. Left to its own, the market produces too much of a good that generates an external cost in production, and the price to consumers of such a good is too low: P_{MKT} is less than P_{OPT}, at which $MSC = MSB$. For a negative production externality, P_{OPT} would be the equilibrium price if producers internalized the marginal external cost of their decisions. In Module 6.4, we'll see how the market can be prodded to produce the socially efficient quantity with taxes that bring private costs or benefits in line with social costs and benefits.

AP® ECON TIP

When a positive externality exists, the socially optimal quantity is higher than the market equilibrium quantity and the deadweight loss triangle points to the right. When a negative externality exists, the socially optimal quantity is lower than the market equilibrium quantity and the deadweight loss triangle points to the left.

Now let's consider a negative consumption externality. Excessive sugar consumption can lead to cavities and more severe health problems. Most health care costs are covered by private insurance or public programs such as Medicaid and Medicare,

FIGURE 6.2-2 Negative Production and Consumption Externalities

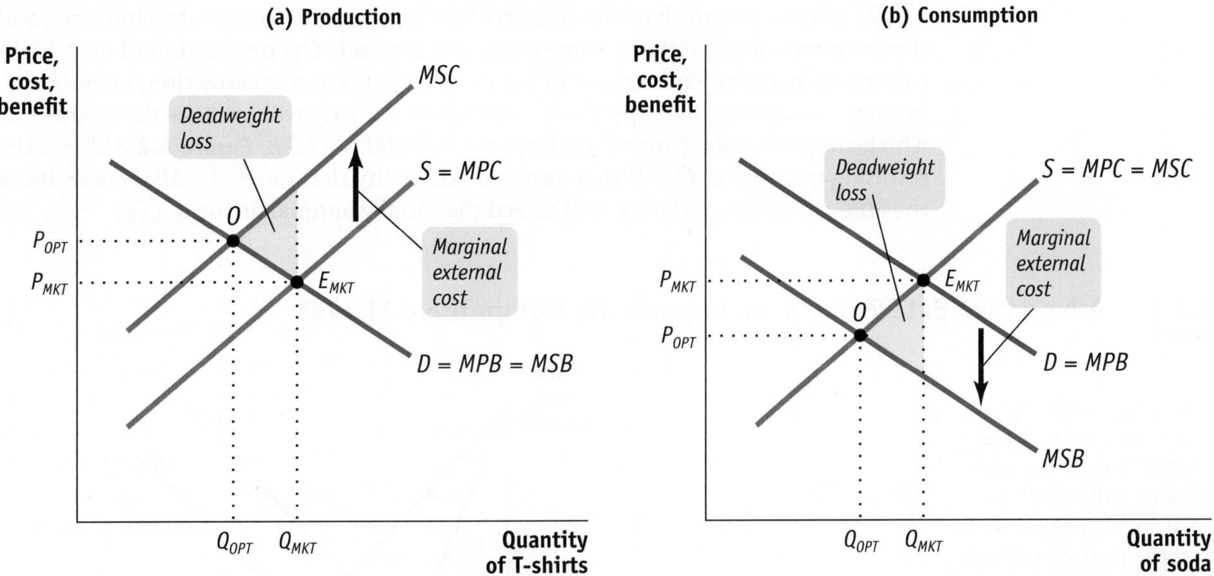

When production creates external costs, the marginal social cost exceeds the marginal private cost by the amount of the marginal external cost, as shown in panel (a). The market quantity, Q_{MKT}, exceeds the socially optimal quantity, Q_{OPT}, resulting in deadweight loss. When consumption creates external costs, we model the situation differently to attribute the negative externality to the consumers. Panel (b) shows how the marginal external cost is subtracted from the consumers' marginal private benefit to determine the marginal social benefit. Again, there is deadweight loss because the market quantity exceeds the socially optimal quantity.

making some of the costs of overconsuming sugar external costs—they are shared by other members of society through higher insurance premiums, lower earnings for insurers, or increases in various taxes used to fund public programs. To limit these external costs, several cities and the District of Columbia have imposed soda taxes intended to help decision makers internalize the effects of their consumption decisions. We can model the effect of soda's negative consumption externality.

When consumption creates the external cost, we model the situation in a way that distinguishes a consumption externality from a production externality. With no production externality (a simplifying assumption in this case), a single curve represents *S*, *MPC*, and *MSC*. To attribute the external cost to the consumers, we subtract the marginal external cost from the consumers' marginal private benefit to find the marginal social benefit, which in this case amounts to the net benefit to society of another unit. Panel (b) of Figure 6.2-2 shows how the marginal external cost of soda consumption is subtracted from the marginal private benefit to determine the marginal social benefit of soda.

The socially optimal price, P_{OPT}, is found at the intersection of *MSC* and *MSB*. For a negative consumption externality, P_{OPT} would be the equilibrium price if consumers internalized the marginal external cost of their decisions. A tax on soda equal to the value of the marginal external cost would achieve that goal, as discussed further in Module 6.4. As with each case of negative externalities, there is deadweight loss because the market quantity exceeds the socially optimal quantity.

External Costs and Imperfect Competition

We've just seen that a perfectly competitive market underproduces a good with a positive externality and overproduces a good with a negative externality. In contrast, the relationship between the socially optimal quantity and the quantity actually produced

AP® ECON TIP

You may be asked questions about a graph showing the effects of externalities on an imperfectly competitive market, but (as of this writing) the guidelines indicate you will not need to draw that graph.

is ambiguous for an imperfectly competitive industry. Let's examine why in the context of a negative production externality in the bathtub industry.

We will imagine the bathtub industry first as a perfectly competitive industry, and then as a monopoly with the same costs and demand. The production of each bathtub creates negative externalities in the processes of resource extraction, manufacturing, and transportation. A perfectly competitive industry will produce the quantity at which supply equals demand, and equivalently, $MPC = MPB$. **Figure 6.2-3** shows the resulting quantity as Q_C. With a negative externality that raises the MSC curve above the MPC curve, we see that Q_C will exceed the socially optimal quantity, Q_{OPT}.

FIGURE 6.2-3 A Negative Externality in an Imperfectly Competitive Market

A perfectly competitive industry will produce the quantity Q_C, found where $MPC = MPB$. If there is a negative externality, Q_C will exceed the socially optimal quantity, Q_{OPT}. When a monopoly creates negative externalities, the monopoly quantity, Q_M, might be above, below, or equal to the socially optimal quantity, Q_{OPT}, depending on the size of the marginal external cost. In this graph, the monopoly chooses an inefficiently low quantity, but if the marginal external cost were larger, thus placing the MSC curve further above the MPC curve, Q_M could equal or exceed Q_{OPT}.

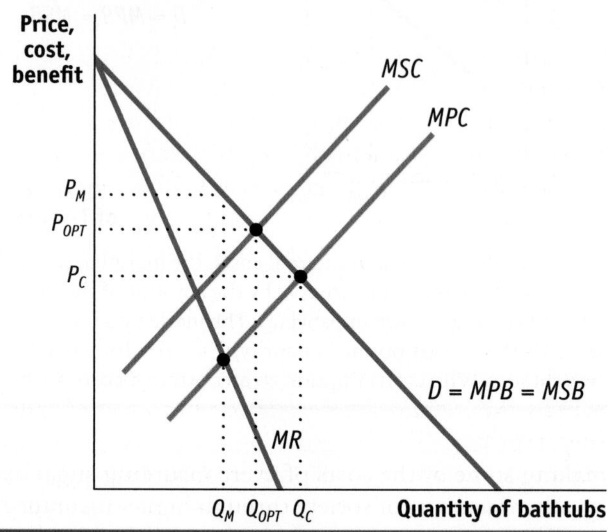

AP® ECON TIP

The AP® Microeconomics exam might use the term "rational agents" to describe market participants who make the appropriate decision to maximize their private gains, such as monopolists who maximize their profit.

Now suppose all the bathtub makers merge into a single seller. Recall that a monopolist such as this maximizes profit by choosing the quantity that equates its marginal revenue and its marginal private cost. When a monopoly creates negative externalities, the profit-maximizing quantity might be above, below, or equal to the socially optimal quantity, Q_{OPT}, depending on the size of the marginal external cost. In Figure 6.2-3, the monopolist's profit-maximizing quantity, Q_M, is actually below Q_{OPT}. If the marginal external cost were larger (as would be the case if bathtub production created more pollution), the MSC curve would be further above the MPC curve, and Q_M could equal or exceed Q_{OPT}. So if a monopoly produces a good with an associated negative externality, more information is needed to determine whether too much, too little, or the socially optimal quantity of the good will be produced.

Private Solutions to Externality Problems

According to the **Coase theorem**, payments between private parties can achieve an efficient solution to externality problems as long as **transaction costs**—the costs to individuals of making a deal—are sufficiently low.

When externalities are present, can the private sector achieve efficient outcomes without government intervention? In an influential 1960 article, economist and Nobel laureate Ronald Coase pointed out that in an ideal world, private negotiations could indeed resolve externality problems. According to the **Coase theorem**, payments between the parties involved can achieve an efficient solution to externality problems, provided that the legal and property rights of the parties are clearly defined and the costs of making a deal are sufficiently low. In some cases, it takes a lot of time, or even money, to bring the relevant parties together, negotiate a payment, and carry out the terms of the deal. The costs of making a deal are known as **transaction costs**.

To get a sense of Coase's argument, imagine two neighbors, Justin and Ada, who both like to barbecue in their backyards. Justin likes to blast music while barbecuing, but this annoys Ada, who can't stand loud music. Who prevails? You might think it depends on the legal rights involved in the case: if the law says that Justin has the right to play music at whatever volume he wants, Ada just has to suffer; if the law says that Justin needs Ada's consent to play loud music in his backyard, Justin can't blast his favorite bands while barbecuing.

But as Coase pointed out, the outcome need not be determined by legal rights, because Ada and Justin can make a private deal as long as the legal rights are clearly defined. Even if Justin has the right to play loud music, Ada could pay him not to. Even if Justin can't play loud music without an OK from Ada, he can offer to pay her to give that OK. These payments allow them to reach an efficient solution regardless of who has the legal upper hand.

Suppose playing loud music is worth $30 to Justin, and quiet is worth $50 to Ada. If Justin has the right to play loud music, Ada could pay Justin any amount between $30 and $50, say $40, not to. With this payment, both parties would be better off than if loud music were played—Justin would have $40 in cash rather than $30 worth of music, and Ada would pay $40 for $50 worth of quiet. If, instead, playing loud music is worth $80 to Justin and quiet is worth $50 to Ada, there is no amount that Ada would pay, and Justin would accept, to end the loud music. In both cases we have the efficient outcome: if the benefit of loud music to Justin exceeds its cost to Ada, the blasting will occur; if the benefit to Justin is less than the cost to Ada, the volume will be low.

The implication of Coase's analysis is that externalities need not lead to inefficiency because individuals have an incentive to make mutually beneficial deals—deals that lead them to take externalities into account when making decisions. When individuals *do* take externalities into account when making decisions, economists say that they **internalize the externalities.** If externalities are fully internalized, as when Justin must forgo a payment from Ada equal to the external cost he imposes on her in order to play music, the outcome is efficient even without government intervention.

When individuals take external costs or benefits into account, they **internalize the externalities.**

Why can't individuals always internalize externalities? Our loud music example implicitly assumes the transaction costs are low enough for Justin and Ada to be able to make a deal. In many situations involving externalities, however, transaction costs prevent individuals from making efficient deals. Examples of transaction costs include the following:

- *The costs of communication among the interested parties.* Such costs may be particularly high if many people are involved, or if the people involved don't know each other.
- *The costs of making legally binding agreements.* Such costs may be high if expensive legal services are required.
- *Costly delays involved in bargaining.* Even if there is a potentially beneficial deal, both sides may hold out in an effort to extract more favorable terms, leading to increased effort and forgone utility.

In some cases, transaction costs are low enough to allow individuals to resolve externality problems. For example, while filming *A League of Their Own* on location in a neighborhood ballpark, director Penny Marshall paid a man $100 to stop using his noisy chainsaw nearby. But in many other cases, transaction costs are too high to make it possible to deal with externalities through private action. For example, pollution from coal-fired power plants affects millions of people. It would be prohibitively expensive to strike a deal among all those people and the many power companies. When transaction costs prevent private deals from resolving externality problems, alternative approaches are needed.

Over the next few Modules, we will explore more solutions to externalities, among other sources of market failure. In Module 6.3, we discuss how the assignment of private property rights sometimes creates incentives for efficient behavior. In Module 6.4, we'll learn how taxes and subsidies can bridge the gap between the costs and benefits felt by market participants and those felt by society.

Module 6.2  Review

Adventures in AP® Economics

Watch the video: ***Externalities and Deadweight Loss***

Check Your Understanding

1. For each of the following cases, explain whether an external cost or an external benefit is created and indicate whether the market equilibrium quantity is larger than, smaller than, or equal to the socially optimal quantity.
   a. Trees planted in urban areas improve air quality and lower summer temperatures.
   b. Water-saving toilets reduce the need to pump water from rivers and aquifers. The water that is saved doesn't cost homeowners much, but does have a high value to other users of the water sources.
   c. Old computer monitors contain toxic materials that pollute the environment when improperly disposed of.

2. Wastewater runoff from large poultry farms adversely affects residents in neighboring homes. Explain the following:
   a. Why is this considered an externality problem?
   b. Will the market equilibrium quantity of poultry be efficient?
   c. How is the socially optimal outcome determined, and how does it compare with the no-intervention, no-deal outcome?

Tackle the AP® Test: Multiple-Choice Questions

1. When there are no consumption externalities, the demand curve is also which of the following curves?
   a. *MSB*
   b. *MEB*
   c. *MPC*
   d. *MSC*
   e. *S*

2. Which of the following is true in the case of a positive consumption externality?
   a. $MSC > MSB$
   b. $MPB > MSC$
   c. $MSB > MPB$
   d. $MPB > MSB$
   e. $MSC > MPC$

3. If external costs cause the socially optimal quantity to fall below the market quantity, the resulting deadweight loss is represented by the area between these two quantities that is
   a. above the *MPC* curve and below the *MSC* curve.
   b. above the *MSB* curve and below the *MPC* curve.
   c. above the *MSB* curve and below the *MSC* curve.
   d. above the *S* curve and below the *D* curve.
   e. above the *MPC* curve and below the *MSB* curve.

4. Which of the following is a source of negative externalities?
   a. loud conversations in a library
   b. smokestack scrubbers that reduce harmful emissions
   c. a beautiful view
   d. national defense
   e. a decision to purchase dressy but uncomfortable shoes

5. Unlike the model for a negative production externality, the model for a negative consumption externality shows the marginal external cost as the distance between which two curves?
   a. marginal private cost and marginal social cost
   b. marginal social cost and marginal social benefit
   c. marginal private benefit and marginal social benefit
   d. marginal private benefit and marginal private cost
   e. supply and demand

6. The Coase theorem asserts that, under the right circumstances, inefficiencies created by externalities can be dealt with through
   a. lawsuits.
   b. private deals.
   c. vigilante actions.
   d. government policies.
   e. mediation.

7. When a monopoly creates a negative production externality, relative to the socially optimal output level, the monopoly's output level will be
   a. higher.
   b. the same.
   c. lower.
   d. the same or higher.
   e. higher, the same, or lower.

Tackle the AP® Test: Free-Response Questions

1. The purchase of antivirus software by one person provides benefits to other people because they are less likely to receive a virus from the software purchaser.
   a. Draw a correctly labeled graph showing how the market will determine the quantity of antivirus software purchased and label that quantity Q_{MKT}.
   b. Characterize the associated externality as positive or negative and consumption or production.
   c. On the graph for part a:
      i. Draw (as needed) and label the marginal social cost and the marginal social benefit.
      ii. Label the socially optimal quantity of antivirus software Q_{OPT}.
      iii. Shade and label the area that represents deadweight loss.

Rubric for FRQ 1 (9 points)

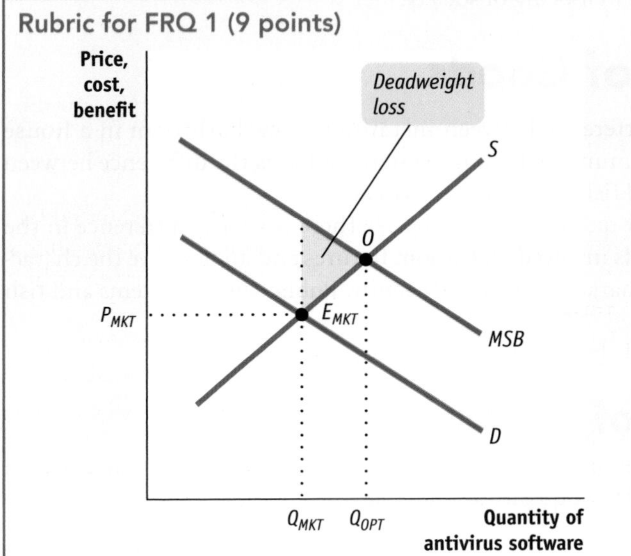

1 point: Vertical axis labeled "Price, cost, benefit" or "Dollars per unit," horizontal axis labeled "Quantity of antivirus software" or "Q"

1 point: Upward-sloping supply (or equivalently, marginal private cost) curve

1 point: Downward-sloping demand (or equivalently, marginal private benefit) curve

1 point: The market quantity of antivirus software is found at the intersection of supply and demand (or *MPC* and *MPB*) and shown on the horizontal axis.

1 point: The externality is characterized as being positive.

1 point: The externality is characterized as being a consumption externality.

1 point: Downward-sloping marginal social benefit curve drawn above demand curve

1 point: The optimal quantity of antivirus software is found at the intersection of supply (or equivalently, *MPC* or *MSC*) and marginal social benefit and shown on the horizontal axis.

1 point: The correct deadweight-loss area is shaded and labeled.

2. The production of plastic water bottles creates external costs as the result of drilling for the petroleum that is an input, plastic production, and transportation of the inputs and outputs. Draw a correctly labeled graph showing how the market will determine the quantity of water bottles produced. On the same graph, show the marginal external cost, the socially optimal quantity of water bottles, and the resulting deadweight loss.
(6 points)

MODULE 6.3

Public Goods

In this Module, you will learn to:

- Discuss what it means for public goods to be nonrival and nonexcludable
- Explain why markets fail to supply efficient quantities of public goods
- Describe the role of government in achieving the socially optimal quantity of public goods

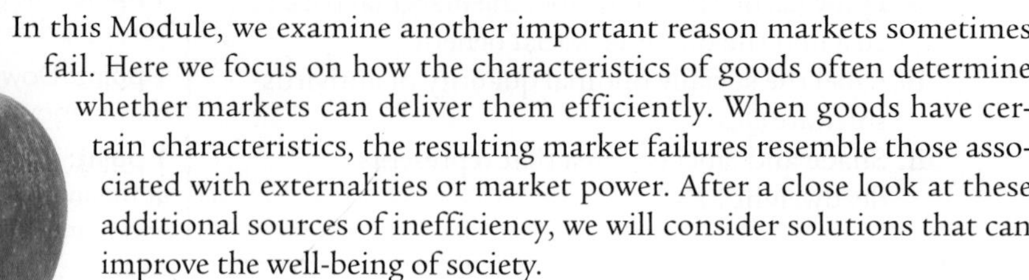

Nipaporn Panyacharoen/EyeEm/Getty Images

In this Module, we examine another important reason markets sometimes fail. Here we focus on how the characteristics of goods often determine whether markets can deliver them efficiently. When goods have certain characteristics, the resulting market failures resemble those associated with externalities or market power. After a close look at these additional sources of inefficiency, we will consider solutions that can improve the well-being of society.

Types of Goods

What is the difference between installing a new bathroom in a house and building a municipal sewage system? What is the difference between growing apples and fishing in the open ocean?

These are not trick questions. In each case there is a basic difference in the characteristics of the goods involved. Bathroom fixtures and apples have the characteristics necessary to allow markets to work efficiently. Public sewage systems and fish in the sea do not.

Let's look at these crucial characteristics and why they matter.

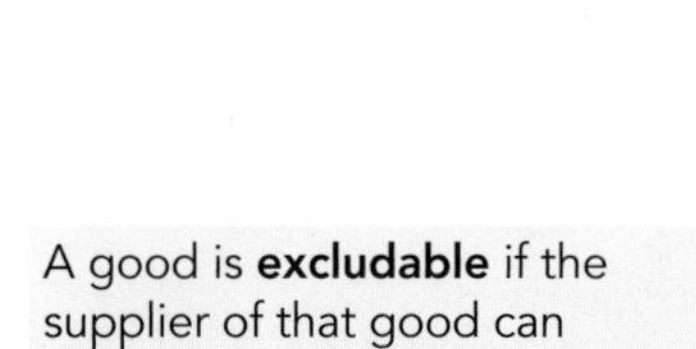

Characteristics of Goods

Goods like bathroom fixtures and apples have two characteristics that are essential if a good is to be provided in efficient quantities by a market economy.

- They are **excludable**: suppliers of the good can prevent people from consuming the good unless they pay for it.
- They are **rival in consumption**: the same unit of the good cannot be consumed by more than one person at the same time.

When a good is both excludable and rival in consumption, it is called a **private good**. Apples are an example of a private good. They are *excludable*: the farmer can sell a bushel to one consumer without having to provide apples to everyone in the community. And they are *rival in consumption*: if I eat an apple, that apple cannot be consumed by someone else.

Not all goods possess these two characteristics. Some goods are **nonexcludable**—the supplier cannot prevent consumption of the good by people who do not pay for it. Fire protection is one example: a fire department that puts out fires before they spread protects the whole city, not just people who have made contributions to the Firemen's Benevolent Association. An improved environment is another: pollution can't be ended for some users of a river while leaving the river foul for others.

Nor are all goods rival in consumption. Goods are **nonrival in consumption** if more than one person can consume the same unit of the good at the same time. Websites are nonrival in consumption because your decision to visit a site does not prevent other people from visiting the same site.

A good is **excludable** if the supplier of that good can prevent people from consuming the good unless they pay for it.

A good is **rival in consumption** if the same unit of the good cannot be consumed by more than one person at the same time.

A good that is both excludable and rival in consumption is a **private good**.

When a good is **nonexcludable**, the supplier cannot prevent consumption by people who do not pay for it.

A good is **nonrival in consumption** if more than one person can consume the same unit of the good at the same time.

Goods can be either excludable or nonexcludable, and either rival or nonrival in consumption, so there are four types of goods, illustrated by the matrix in **Figure 6.3-1**:

- *Private goods*, which are excludable and rival in consumption, like apples;
- *Public goods*, which are nonexcludable and nonrival in consumption, like a public sewer system;
- *Common resources*, which are nonexcludable but rival in consumption, like fish in the ocean; and
- *Artificially scarce goods*, which are excludable but nonrival in consumption, like songs from music-streaming services, such as Spotify.

FIGURE 6.3-1 Four Types of Goods

	Rival in consumption	Nonrival in consumption
Excludable	**Private goods** • Apples • Bathroom fixtures	**Artificially scarce goods** • Streaming music • Computer software
Non-excludable	**Common resources** • Fish in the ocean • Clean river water	**Public goods** • Public sanitation • National defense

There are four types of goods. The type of a good depends on (1) whether or not it is excludable—whether a producer can prevent someone from consuming it; and (2) whether or not it is rival in consumption—whether it is impossible for the same unit of a good to be consumed by more than one person at the same time.

Of course, there are many other characteristics that distinguish between types of goods—necessities versus luxuries, normal versus inferior, complements versus substitutes, and so on. Why focus on whether goods are excludable and rival in consumption? We explore this question next.

Why Markets Can Supply Only Private Goods Efficiently

As we learned in earlier Modules, markets can achieve efficient outcomes except in the case of market power, externalities, or other instances of market failure. One source of market failure is rooted in the nature of the good itself: markets cannot supply goods and services efficiently unless they are private goods—excludable and rival in consumption.

To see why excludability is crucial, suppose a farmer had only two choices: produce no apples, or provide a bushel of apples to every resident of the community who wants it, whether or not that resident pays for it. It seems unlikely that anyone would grow apples under those conditions.

Yet the operator of a public sewage system that anyone can dump sewage into faces pretty much the same problem as our hypothetical farmer. A sewage system makes the whole city cleaner and healthier—but that benefit accrues to all the city's residents, whether or not they pay the system operator. The general point is that if a good is nonexcludable, rational consumers won't be willing to pay for it. Instead, they will use the good for free at the expense of anyone who does pay, which is called the **free-rider problem**.

Goods that are nonexcludable suffer from the **free-rider problem**: individuals have no incentive to pay for their own consumption and instead will "free-ride" on anyone who does pay.

Examples of the free-rider problem are familiar from daily life. One free-rider problem you may have encountered arises when students are required to do a group project. There is often a tendency of some group members to shirk their responsibilities, relying on others in the group to get the work done. The shirkers in such cases *free-ride* on someone else's effort.

Because of the free-rider problem, the forces of self-interest alone do not lead to efficient production levels for nonexcludable goods, whether they are public goods or

ZephyrMedia/Shutterstock

When the benefits from a group project are nonexcludable, there is a temptation to free-ride on the efforts of others.

common resources. Even though consumers would benefit from increased production of a nonexcludable good, no individual is willing to pay for more, and so no producer is willing to supply more. The result is that nonexcludable goods suffer from *inefficiently low production* in a market economy. In fact, in the face of the free-rider problem, self-interest may not ensure that any amount of the good – let alone the efficient quantity – is produced.

Artificially scarce goods, which are excludable and nonrival in consumption, suffer from a different kind of inefficiency. As long as a good is excludable, it is possible to earn a profit by making it available only to those who pay. Therefore, producers are willing to supply an excludable good. Consider pay-per-view movies. The marginal cost of letting an additional viewer watch a pay-per-view movie is zero because it is nonrival in consumption. So the efficient price to the consumer is also zero – or, to put it another way, individuals should watch pay-per-view movies up to the point where their marginal benefit is zero. But if the movie provider actually charges viewers $4, viewers will consume the good only up to the point where their marginal benefit is $4. When consumers must pay a price greater than zero for a good that is nonrival in consumption, the price they pay is higher than the marginal cost of allowing them to consume that good, which is zero. So in a market economy, goods that are nonrival in consumption suffer from *inefficiently low consumption*.

Now we can see why private goods are the only goods that will be produced and consumed in efficient quantities in a competitive market. (That is, a private good will be produced and consumed in efficient quantities in a market free of market power, externalities, and other sources of market failure.) Because private goods are excludable, producers can charge for them and so have an incentive to produce them. And because they are also rival in consumption, it is efficient for consumers to pay a positive price – a price equal to the marginal cost of production. If one or both of these characteristics are lacking, a market economy will not provide the incentives to bring about efficient quantities of the good.

Yet there are crucial goods that don't meet these criteria – and in these cases, the government can offer assistance. Governments choose to produce some private goods that provide considerable positive externalities, such as educational services, and provide them for free to increase consumption. Next, we will look at another type of good that would be under-consumed in a private market.

Public Goods

A **public good** is both nonexcludable and nonrival in consumption.

A **public good** is the exact opposite of a private good: it is both nonexcludable and nonrival in consumption. A public sewage system is an example of a public good: if a river is kept clean by piping sewage elsewhere, no one who lives near the river can be excluded from the benefits of clean water, and your protection from sewage contamination does not prevent your neighbor from being protected as well.

Here are some other examples of public goods:

- *Disease prevention.* When a disease is stamped out, no one can be excluded from the benefit, and one person's health doesn't prevent others from being healthy.
- *National defense.* A strong military protects all citizens.
- *Scientific research.* New findings that particular substances are dangerous or healthy provide widespread benefits that are not excludable or rival.

Because these goods are nonexcludable, they suffer from the free-rider problem, so private firms would produce inefficiently low quantities of them. And because they are nonrival in consumption, it would be inefficient to charge people for consuming them. As a result, society must find nonmarket methods for providing these goods.

Providing Public Goods

Public goods are provided in a variety of ways. The government doesn't always get involved—in many cases, a non-governmental solution has been found for the free-rider problem. But these solutions are usually imperfect in some way.

Some public goods are supplied through voluntary contributions. For example, private donations help support public broadcasting and a considerable amount of scientific research. But private donations are insufficient to finance large programs of great importance, such as the Centers for Disease Control and Prevention and national defense.

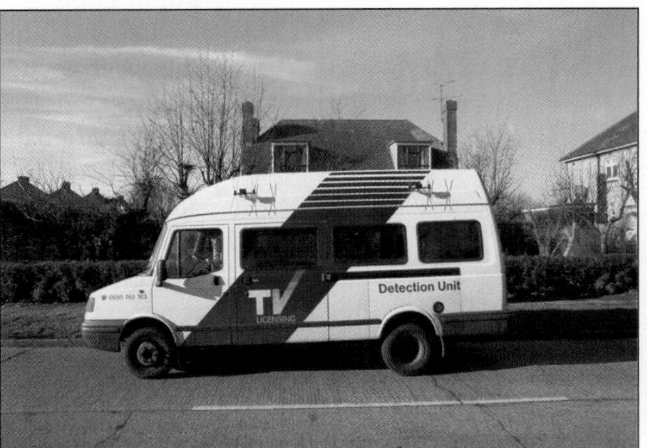

Sion Touhig/Sygma/Getty Images

On the prowl: a British TV detection van checks for unlicensed TV viewers to prevent broadcast television from becoming a public good.

Some public goods are supplied by self-interested individuals or firms because those who produce them are able to make money in indirect ways. A classic example is radio broadcasts, which in most cases are supported entirely by advertising. The downside of such indirect funding is that it skews the nature and quantity of the public goods that are supplied, while imposing additional costs on consumers. Radio stations broadcast the programs that yield the most advertising revenue, which are not necessarily the programs people most enjoy. And listeners must endure many commercials. The same is true for users of YouTube, Facebook, and other online resources that provide free access.

Some potentially public goods are deliberately made excludable and therefore subject to charge, like pay-per-view movies. In the United Kingdom, where most television programming is paid for by a yearly license fee assessed on every television owner (£159, or about $217, in 2022), television viewing is made excludable by the use of "television detection vans": vans that roam neighborhoods in an attempt to detect televisions in non-licensed households and fine them. However, as noted earlier, when suppliers charge a price greater than zero for a nonrival good, consumers will consume an inefficiently low quantity of that good.

In small communities, a high level of social encouragement or pressure can be brought to bear on people to contribute money or time to provide the efficient level of a public good. Volunteer fire departments, which depend both on the volunteered services of the firefighters themselves and on contributions from local residents, are a good example. But as communities grow larger and more anonymous, social pressure is increasingly difficult to apply, compelling larger towns and cities to tax residents and depend on salaried firefighters for fire protection services.

As this last example suggests, when other solutions fail, it is up to the government to provide public goods. Indeed, the most important public goods—national defense, the legal system, disease control, fire protection in large cities, and so on—are provided by the government and paid for by taxes. Economic theory tells us that the provision of public goods is one of the crucial roles of government.

How Much of a Public Good Should Be Provided?

In some cases, the provision of a public good is an "either–or" decision: a city can either have a sewage system or not. But in most cases, governments must decide not only whether to provide a public good but also *how much* of that public good to provide. For example, street cleaning is a public good—but how often should the streets be cleaned? Once a month? Twice a month? Every other day?

Imagine a city with only two residents, Tiana and Asher. Assume that the public good in question is street cleaning and that Tiana and Asher truthfully tell the government how much they value a unit of the public good, one unit being one street cleaning per month. Specifically, each of them tells the government his or her *willingness to pay* for another unit of the public good supplied—an amount that corresponds to that individual's *marginal private benefit* from another unit of the public good.

Using this information along with information on the cost of providing the good, the government can use marginal analysis to find the efficient level of providing the public good: the level at which the *marginal social benefit* of the public good is equal to the marginal social cost of producing it. Recall that the marginal social benefit of a good is the benefit that accrues to society as a whole from the consumption of one additional unit of the good.

AP® ECON TIP

Like private goods, public goods should be produced until the marginal social cost is equal to the marginal social benefit. Remember that for a public good, the marginal social benefit of each unit is found by adding up the marginal private benefit received by each person who benefits from that unit.

But what is the marginal social benefit of another unit of a public good—a unit that generates utility for any consumer that wants it, not just one consumer, because it is nonexcludable and nonrival in consumption? This question leads us to an important principle: *In the special case of a public good, the marginal social benefit of a unit of the good is equal to the sum of the marginal private benefits enjoyed by all consumers of that unit.* Or, to consider it from a slightly different angle, the marginal social benefit of a unit is equal to the sum of each consumer's willingness to pay for that unit, which is the most each consumer would pay if the good were somehow made excludable. Using this principle, the marginal social benefit of an additional street cleaning per month is equal to Tiana's marginal private benefit from that additional cleaning *plus* Asher's marginal private benefit.

Why does that sum equal the marginal social benefit? Because a public good is nonrival in consumption—Tiana's benefit from a cleaner street does not diminish Asher's benefit from that same clean street, and vice versa. Tiana and Asher can simultaneously "consume" the same unit of street cleaning, so the marginal social benefit is the *sum* of their marginal private benefits. And the efficient quantity of a public good is the quantity at which the marginal social benefit is equal to the marginal social cost of providing it.

Figure 6.3-2 illustrates the efficient provision of a public good, showing three marginal benefit curves. Panel (a) shows Tiana's marginal private benefit curve from street cleaning, MPB_T: she would be willing to pay $25 for the city to clean its streets once a month, an additional $18 to have it done a second time, and so on. Panel (b) shows Asher's marginal private benefit curve from street cleaning, MPB_A. Panel (c) shows the marginal social benefit curve from street cleaning, *MSB*: it is the vertical sum of Tiana's and Asher's marginal private benefit curves, MPB_T and MPB_A.

To maximize society's welfare, the government should increase the quantity of street cleanings until the marginal social benefit of an additional cleaning would fall below the marginal social cost. Suppose that the marginal social cost is $6 per cleaning. Then the city should clean its streets 5 times per month, because the marginal social benefit of each of the first 5 cleanings is more than $6, but going from 5 to 6 cleanings would yield a marginal social benefit of only $2, which is less than the marginal social cost.

Of course, if society really consisted of only two individuals, they would probably manage to strike a deal to provide the good. But imagine a city with a million residents, each of whose marginal private benefit from a good is only a tiny fraction of the marginal social benefit. It would be impossible for so many people to reach a voluntary agreement to pay for the efficient level of a good like street cleaning—the complexity of negotiations and enforcement along with the potential for free-riding would make it too difficult. But they could and would vote to tax themselves to pay for a citywide sanitation department.

One fundamental rationale for the existence of government is that it provides a way for citizens to tax themselves in order to provide public goods—particularly vital public goods like disease control, the legal system, and national defense.

Voting as a Public Good

As the economist Mancur Olson pointed out in his famous book *The Logic of Collective Action: Public Goods and the Theory of Groups*, voting is a public good, one that

FIGURE 6.3-2 A Public Good

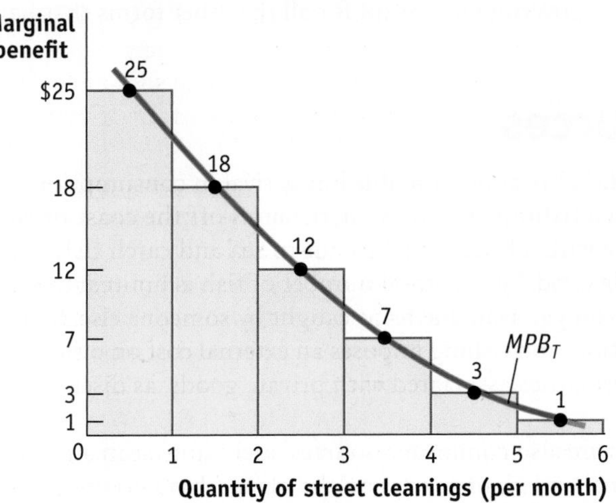

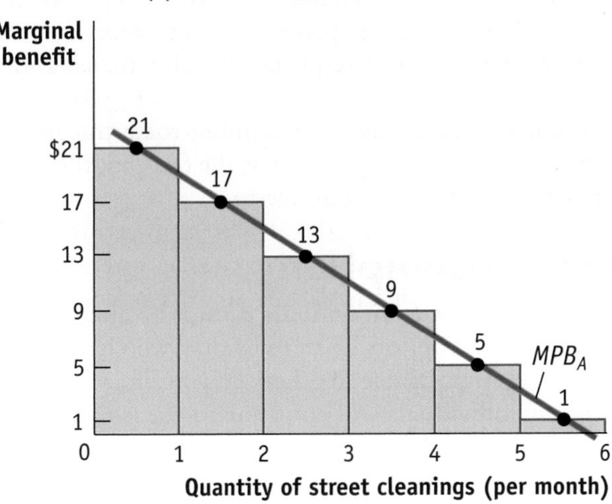

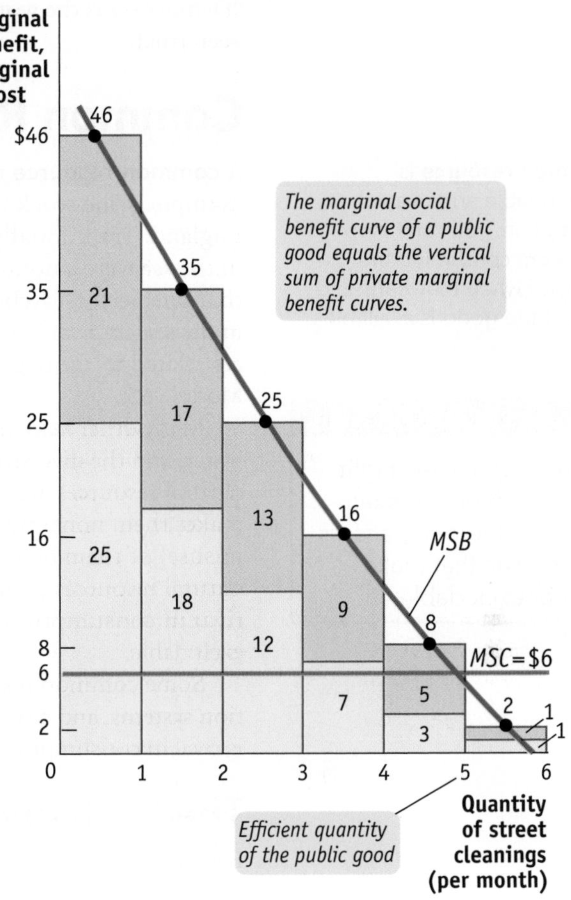

Panel (a) shows Tiana's marginal private benefit curve, MPB_T, and panel (b) shows Asher's marginal private benefit curve, MPB_A. Panel (c) shows the marginal social benefit of the public good, equal to the *sum* of the marginal private benefits to all consumers (in this case, Tiana and Asher). The marginal social benefit curve, *MSB*, is the vertical sum of the marginal private benefit curves MPB_T and MPB_A. At a constant marginal social cost of $6, there should be 5 street cleanings per month, because the marginal social benefit of going from 4 to 5 cleanings is $8 ($3 for Tiana plus $5 for Asher), but the marginal social benefit of going from 5 to 6 cleanings is only $2.

suffers from severe free-rider problems. It's a sad fact that many Americans who are eligible to vote don't bother to. As a result, their interests tend to be ignored by politicians. But what's even sadder is that this self-defeating behavior may be completely rational.

Imagine that you are one of a million people who would stand to gain the equivalent of $100 each if a plan to improve public schools is passed in a statewide referendum. And suppose that the opportunity cost of the time it would take you to vote is $10. Will you be sure to go to the polls and vote for the referendum? If you are rational, the answer is no! The reason is that it is very unlikely that your vote will decide the issue, and the benefits of the measure are nonexcludable: You benefit if the measure passes, even if you didn't bother to vote. If the measure doesn't pass, your vote would not have changed the outcome. Either way, by not voting—by free-riding on those who do vote—you save $10.

zentilia/Getty Images

Of course, many people do vote out of a sense of civic duty. But because political action is a public good, in general people devote too little effort to defending their own interests. Is this a reason to distrust democracy? Winston Churchill said it best: "Democracy is the worst form of government, except for all the other forms that have been tried."

Common Resources

A **common resource** is nonexcludable and rival in consumption: you can't stop others from consuming the good, and when they consume it, less of the good is available for you.

AP® ECON TIP

Common resources might be identified on the exam in terms of the *open access* characteristic that makes them nonexcludable.

A **common resource** is a good that is nonexcludable but is rival in consumption. An example is the stock of fish in a fishing area, like the fisheries off the coast of New England. Traditionally, anyone with a boat could go out to sea and catch fish – fish in the sea were a nonexcludable good. Yet the total number of fish is limited: the fish that one person catches are no longer available to be caught by someone else. So fish in the sea are rival in consumption, and fishing imposes an external cost on other fishers related to the negative externalities associated with private goods, as discussed in Module 6.2.

Many other *natural resources* are also common resources, including clean air, ocean water, and the diversity of animal and plant species on the planet (biodiversity). These natural resources are common resources because: (1) the public's open access to them makes them nonexcludable; and, (2) they are rival in consumption, in that the use (or misuse) of them by some people can reduce their availability to other people. Other natural resources, such as coal, oil, and diamonds, are private goods because they are rival in consumption and the enforcement of private property rights makes them excludable.

Some common resources are human-made goods, such as public roadways, irrigation systems, and city parks. For every type of common resource, the fact that the good is rival in consumption, and yet nonexcludable, poses a problem.

The Problem of Overconsumption

Because common resources are nonexcludable, individuals cannot be charged for their use. But the resources are rival in consumption, so an individual who uses a unit depletes the resource by making that unit unavailable to others. As a result, a common resource is subject to *overconsumption*: individuals will continue to use it until their marginal private benefit is equal to their marginal private cost, ignoring the cost that this action inflicts on society as a whole. This inefficient resource use is sometimes called the *tragedy of the commons*.

Fish are a classic example of an overconsumed common resource. Particularly in heavily fished waters, each fisher's catch imposes a cost on others by reducing the fish population and making it harder for others to catch fish. But fishers have no personal incentive to take this cost into account. As a result, from society's point of view, too many fish are caught. Traffic congestion is another example of overuse of a common resource. A major highway during rush hour can accommodate only a certain number of vehicles per hour. Each person who decides to drive to work alone, rather than carpool or work at home, causes many other people to have a longer commute, but there is no incentive for individual drivers to take these consequences into account.

In the case of a common resource, as in the earlier examples involving marginal external costs, the *marginal social cost* of your use of that resource is higher than your *marginal private cost*, the cost to you of using an additional unit of the good. **Figure 6.3-3** illustrates this point. It shows the demand curve for fish, which measures the marginal private benefit of fish (as well as the marginal social benefit because there are no external benefits from catching and consuming fish). The figure also shows the supply curve for fish, which measures the marginal private cost of production in the fishing industry. We know that the industry supply curve is the horizontal sum of each individual fisher's supply curve – equivalent to that fisher's marginal private cost curve.

FIGURE 6.3-3 A Common Resource

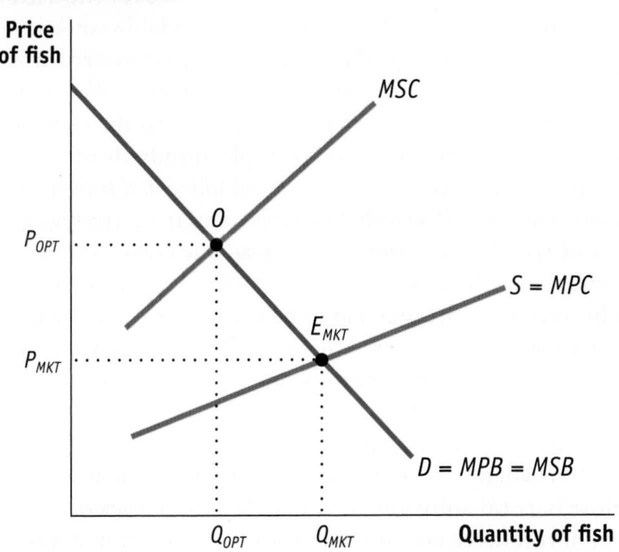

The supply curve, *S*, which shows the marginal private cost of production of the fishing industry, is composed of the individual supply curves of the individual fishers. But each fisher's marginal private cost does not include the cost that the fisher's actions impose on others: the depletion of the common resource. As a result, the marginal social cost curve, *MSC*, lies above the supply curve. In an unregulated market, participants respond to their private incentives, and the quantity of the common resource used, Q_{MKT}, at which $S = D$ exceeds the efficient quantity of use, Q_{OPT}, at which $MSC = MSB$.

The fishing industry supplies the quantity Q_{MKT} at which its marginal private cost equals the price. But the efficient quantity is Q_{OPT}, the quantity of fish that equates the marginal social benefit to the marginal social cost, not to the fishing industry's marginal private cost of production. Thus, the market outcome results in overconsumption of the common resource.

As we noted, there is a close parallel between the problem of managing a common resource and the problem posed by negative externalities. In the case of an activity that generates a negative externality, the marginal social cost of production is greater than the marginal private cost of production, the difference being the marginal external cost imposed on society. Here, the loss to society arising from a fisher's depletion of the common resource plays the same role as the external cost when there is a negative externality. In fact, many negative externalities (such as pollution) can be thought of as involving common resources (such as clean air).

The Efficient Use and Maintenance of a Common Resource

Because common resources essentially pose a negative externality problem, we can draw from the same set of solutions. To ensure efficient use of a common resource, society must find a way to get individual users of the resource to internalize the negative externality that arises from their actions.

There are three principal ways to induce people who use common resources to internalize the costs they impose on others:

- Tax or otherwise regulate the use of the common resource
- Create a system of tradable licenses for the right to use the common resource
- Make the common resource excludable and assign property rights to some individuals

These solutions overlap with the approaches to private goods with negative externalities discussed in Module 6.2 and coming up in Module 6.4. Just as governments use taxes to reduce the consumption of goods that cause negative externalities, they use alternative forms of taxes to reduce the use of common resources. For example, in London and elsewhere, there are "congestion charges" on those who drive during rush hour, in effect charging them for the use of highway space, a common resource. Likewise, visitors to national parks in the United States must pay an entry fee that is essentially a tax.

tacojim/Getty Images

If it weren't for fees and restrictions, some common resources, such as national parks, would be overrun.

A second way to correct the problem of overconsumption is to create a system of tradable licenses for the use of the common resource, much like the tradable emissions permit systems designed to address negative externalities, as discussed in the next Module. The policy maker issues the number of licenses that corresponds to the efficient level of use of the good. For example, hundreds of fisheries around the world have adopted *individual transferable quotas* that are effectively licenses to catch a certain quantity of fish. Making the licenses tradable ensures that the right to use the good is allocated efficiently: If the fisher who receives a license isn't the one who would benefit the most from it, the recipient can sell the license to the fisher with the most to gain from it. Those with the most to gain are willing to pay the most for the license, so they end up being able to use the good.

But when it comes to common resources, often the most natural solution is simply to assign *property rights.* At a fundamental level, common resources are subject to overconsumption because *nobody owns them*. The essence of ownership of a good – the *property right* over the good – is that you can limit who can and cannot use the good as well as how much of it can be used. When a good is nonexcludable, in a very real sense no one owns it because a property right cannot be enforced – and consequently, no one has an incentive to use it efficiently. So one way to correct the problem of overconsumption is to make the good excludable and assign property rights over it to someone. The good now has an owner who has an incentive to protect the value of the good – to use it efficiently rather than overuse it. This solution is applicable when currently nonexcludable goods can be made excludable, as with the privatization of land and even roads, but it cannot be applied to resources that are inherently nonexcludable, including the air and flowing water.

Artificially Scarce Goods

An **artificially scarce good** is a good that is excludable but nonrival in consumption.

An **artificially scarce good** is a good that is excludable but nonrival in consumption. As we've already seen, pay-per-view movies are a familiar example. The marginal cost to society of allowing an individual to watch a movie is zero because one person's viewing doesn't interfere with another person's viewing. Yet cable companies and movie-streaming services can prevent individuals from seeing a movie if they haven't paid. Goods like computer software and audio files, which are valued for the information they embody (and are sometimes called *information goods*), are also artificially scarce.

Markets will supply artificially scarce goods because their excludability allows firms to charge customers for them. However, since the efficient price is equal to the marginal cost of zero and the actual price is something higher than that, the good is "artificially scarce" and consumption is inefficiently low. The problem is that, unless the producer can somehow earn revenue from producing and selling the good, none will be produced, which is likely to be worse than a positive but inefficiently low quantity.

We have seen that, in the cases of public goods, common resources, and artificially scarce goods, a market economy will not provide adequate incentives for efficient levels of production and consumption. Fortunately for the sake of market efficiency, most goods are private goods. Food, clothing, shelter, and most other products are excludable and rival in consumption, so the types of market failure discussed in this Module are important exceptions rather than the norm.

Module 6.3  Review

Check Your Understanding

1. For each of the following goods, indicate whether it is excludable, whether it is rival in consumption, and what kind of good it is.
   a. a public space, such as a park
   b. a cheese burrito
   c. information from a website that requires a paid subscription to access
   d. publicly announced information about the path of an incoming hurricane
2. Which of the goods in Question 1 will be provided by a private producer without government intervention? Which will not be? Explain your answer.

Tackle the AP® Test: Multiple-Choice Questions

1. Which of the following types of goods are always nonrival in consumption?
   a. public goods
   b. private goods
   c. common resources
   d. inferior goods
   e. goods provided by the government
2. The free-rider problem occurs in the case of
   a. private goods.
   b. common resources.
   c. artificially scarce goods.
   d. motorcycles.
   e. all of the above.
3. Public goods are provided through which of the following means?
   a. the government only
   b. voluntary contributions only
   c. self-interested individuals and firms only
   d. the government and voluntary contributions only
   e. the government, voluntary contributions, and self-interested individuals and firms
4. Market provision of a public good will lead to
   a. the efficient quantity of the good and an inefficiently high price.
   b. the efficient quantity of the good and the efficient price.
   c. an inefficiently high quantity of the good and the efficient price.
   d. an inefficiently low quantity of the good and an inefficiently high price.
   e. an inefficiently high quantity of the good and an inefficiently low price.
5. The Pineland community has a public forest where citizens can harvest (cut down) as many trees as they desire for personal use. Which of the following would most likely worsen the overconsumption of this common resource?
   a. a tax on each tree harvested
   b. a government regulation that bans chainsaws in the forest
   c. tradable licenses for tree harvesting
   d. the assignment of property rights to the forest
   e. an increase in the price of firewood sold in stores
6. A common resource is
   a. excludable and nonrival in consumption.
   b. excludable and rival in consumption.
   c. nonexcludable and nonrival in consumption.
   d. nonexcludable and rival in consumption.
   e. a public good that is excludable.
7. The marginal social benefit curve for a public good is the
   a. horizontal sum of the marginal private benefit curves of all consumers.
   b. vertical sum of the marginal private benefit curves of all consumers.
   c. horizontal sum of the marginal external benefit curves of all consumers.
   d. vertical sum of the marginal external benefit curves of all consumers.
   e. demand curve of the consumer who values the public good the most.

Tackle the AP® Test: Free-Response Questions

1. Suppose Austin and Lin are the only soccer enthusiasts in a small town where any number of public soccer clinics could be put on by visiting experts for $80 each. There are no external costs involved. Austin's marginal private benefit curve for soccer clinics is horizontal at $60. Lin's marginal private benefit curve is a straight line starting at $100 on the vertical axis and ending at 10 clinics on the horizontal axis. Draw a correctly labeled graph for soccer clinics showing the marginal social cost, the marginal social benefit, and each resident's marginal private benefit. Label the quantity of clinics that Austin would purchase if he were the only resident as Q_{Austin}. Label the quantity of clinics that Lin would purchase if she were the only resident as Q_{Lin}. Label the optimal quantity of clinics for society as $Q_{Optimal}$.

Rubric for FRQ 1 (6 points)

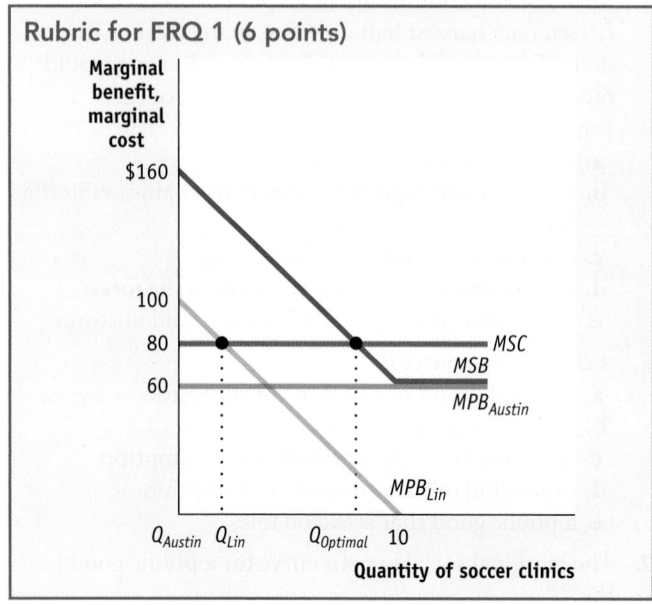

1 point: Correct axis labels ("Marginal benefit, marginal cost" or "Dollars per unit" on the vertical axis, "Quantity of soccer clinics" or "Q" on the horizontal axis)

1 point: *MSC* curve horizontal at a height of $80

1 point: *MSB* curve starts at a height of $160 where the quantity is zero, slopes downward to a height of $60 where the quantity is 10, and then coincides with MPB_{Austin}

1 point: Q_{Austin} labeled at a quantity of zero (because *MSC* exceeds MPB_{Austin} for every clinic)

1 point: Q_{Lin} found at the intersection of *MSC* and MPB_{Lin} and shown on the horizontal axis

1 point: $Q_{Optimal}$ found at the intersection of *MSC* and *MSB* and shown on the horizontal axis

2. Imagine that the city of Townville has 1,000 residents and, as a public good for the benefit of every member of the community, pays $100,000 per year to rent equipment to fight a serious problem with mosquitoes.
   a. Identify and explain the two characteristics shared by every public good.
   b. Suppose a new resident moves to Townville. What is the additional cost of providing the public good to the new community member? Explain. **(6 points)**

Government Policies

> ***In this Module, you will learn to:***
> - Define terms related to government intervention in imperfect markets
> - Use graphs to show how taxes and subsidies help decision makers internalize the effects of their behavior
> - Discuss how governments use antitrust policy to increase competition in markets
> - Explain how government intervention is used to prevent inefficiency in the case of natural monopoly

This Module begins with a look at how taxes and subsidies can correct externality problems in perfectly competitive markets. We then see how economic analysis has guided successful environmental policies, before ending with a discussion of government policies to limit market power.

Negative Externalities and Pigouvian Taxes

If you've ever been bothered by the unintended effects of other people's actions—perhaps in the form of traffic congestion, intrusively loud noises, or scenic views lost to development—you've been a victim of negative externalities, as introduced in Module 6.2. Negative externalities related to health and the environment can be so costly that governments take action against them. One common approach is to apply **Pigouvian taxes**, which are taxes designed to correct for the inefficiencies that result from external costs. As the name suggests, these taxes were first advocated by economist Arthur Pigou, who proposed them in the first half of the twentieth century. A Pigouvian tax is a type of *per-unit tax* because it is collected from consumers or producers as a set amount for each unit of the good purchased.

Taxes designed to correct for the inefficiencies of external costs are known as **Pigouvian taxes**.

Let's apply Mr. Pigou's tax solution to the problem of livestock production that leads to negative externalities, including manure runoff and the belching of methane, a greenhouse gas.

Figure 6.4-1 shows the marginal social cost curve for livestock, *MSC*, above the supply and private marginal cost curve, $S = MPC$, by the amount of the marginal external cost of livestock production. For simplicity, we assume that the marginal external cost is the same for each unit of livestock. The existence of a supply curve tips us off that this is modeled as a perfectly competitive market, because monopolists don't have supply curves. At Q_{MKT}, the marginal social cost of livestock, indicated on the price axis as P_{MSC}, exceeds the marginal social benefit of livestock, P_{MKT}. Likewise, for every unit between Q_{OPT} and Q_{MKT}, the marginal social cost exceeds the marginal social benefit, resulting in the deadweight loss shown by the yellow triangle.

Maxim Minaev/Shutterstock

An optimal Pigouvian tax on livestock production is equal to the marginal external cost at the socially optimal level of production, Q_{OPT}. The Pigouvian tax works by raising the price paid by consumers from P_{MKT} at the equilibrium of *S* and *D*, to P_{OPT} at the equilibrium of *MSC* and *MSB*. The same tax lowers the price received by producers, who keep only the non-tax part of what consumers pay: P_{OPT} minus the tax. The after-tax price to

FIGURE 6.4-1 A Pigouvian Tax

The negative production externality of the livestock industry places the marginal social cost curve for livestock, *MSC*, above the supply and marginal private cost curve, $S = MPC$, by the amount of the marginal external cost. Without government intervention, the market produces the quantity Q_{MKT}, which exceeds the socially optimal quantity, Q_{OPT}. The yellow deadweight loss area represents society's net losses from producing Q_{OPT} rather than Q_{MKT}. A Pigouvian tax on livestock production equal to its marginal external cost moves the production to Q_{OPT} by raising the price paid by consumers to P_{OPT} and lowering the price received by producers to P_{PRD}.

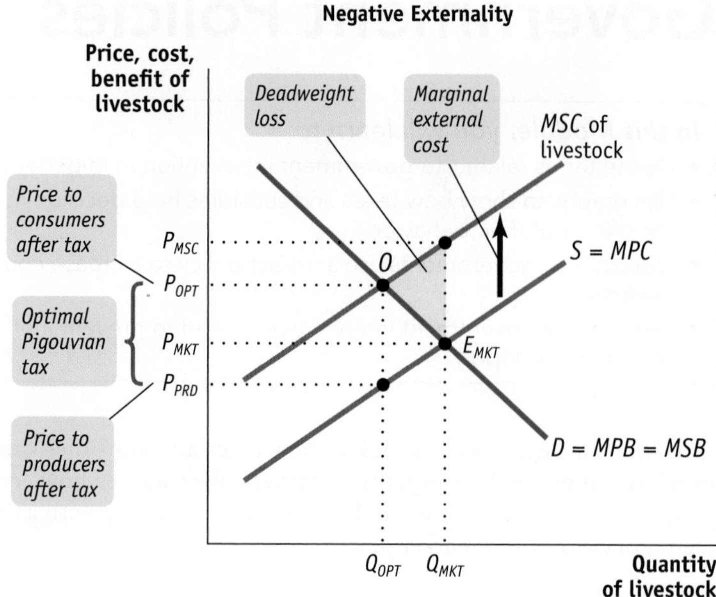

producers, P_{PRD}, is the price for which they will produce Q_{OPT} and no more. So with the optimal Pigouvian tax in place, consumers choose to buy Q_{OPT} and producers choose to sell Q_{OPT}.

Pigouvian taxes do present a challenge: in practice, government officials usually aren't sure at what level the tax should be set. If they set the tax too low, there will be too little improvement in the environment; if they set it too high, negative externalities will be reduced by more than is efficient. Economists have estimated the marginal external costs of many activities. But when the appropriate tax is unclear, another strategy is to change the nature of the risks by issuing tradable emissions permits, as explained later in this Module.

Positive Externalities and Pigouvian Subsidies

As with external costs, individuals and firms often have no incentive to consider the external benefits of their actions. Consider flu vaccines, which provide a positive externality in the form of less spreading of the flu by vaccine recipients. If you get vaccinated, you are less likely to catch the flu and pass it to people around you. Do you think about the benefits to other people when you decide whether to get a flu shot? It would be best if everyone did, but in the absence of government intervention, too few people choose to get vaccinated because people tend to ignore the external benefits their shot provides to others.

Figure 6.4-2 illustrates this point. Without government involvement, the market equilibrium will be at point E_{MKT}, with Q_{MKT} flu shots being bought and sold. At that quantity, the marginal social benefit of a flu shot, P_{MSB}, exceeds the marginal social cost, P_{MKT}, and the same is true for every shot between Q_{MKT} and Q_{OPT}. The yellow deadweight loss triangle represents the net loss to society from not having those shots.

How can the economy be induced to produce Q_{OPT}, the socially optimal level of flu shots? Pigou's idea about taxes guiding decision makers to socially optimal outcomes

FIGURE 6.4-2 A Pigouvian Subsidy

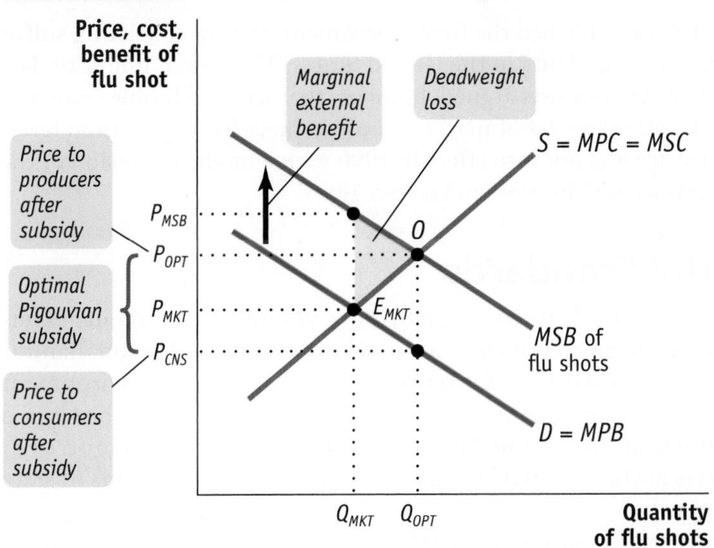

Consumption of flu shots generates external benefits, so the marginal social benefit curve, *MSB*, of flu shots, is above the demand and marginal private benefit curve, *D* = *MPB*, by the amount of the marginal external benefit. Without government action, the market produces Q_{MKT}. The market quantity is lower than the socially optimal quantity of consumption, Q_{OPT}, at which the marginal social benefit equals the marginal social cost (*MSC*). At Q_{MKT}, the marginal social benefit of another flu shot, P_{MSB}, is greater than the marginal private benefit to consumers of another flu shot, P_{MKT}. The yellow deadweight loss area represents the lost opportunities for net gains that could be achieved by producing Q_{OPT} rather than Q_{MKT}. A Pigouvian subsidy to consumers, equal to the marginal external benefit, moves consumption to Q_{OPT} by lowering the price paid by consumers to P_{CNS} and raising the price received by producers to P_{OPT}.

has a subsidy component: A **Pigouvian subsidy** is a payment designed to correct for the inefficiencies that result from external benefits. The goal is to eliminate the deadweight loss caused by an inefficiently low quantity of a good. The payment is a *per-unit subsidy* because it is a set amount paid to consumers or producers for each unit of the good purchased. The optimal Pigouvian subsidy, shown in Figure 6.4-2, is equal to the marginal external benefit of consuming another unit of flu shots at the socially optimal quantity. That is, if the marginal external benefit of each flu shot is the same, then the optimal Pigouvian subsidy is simply the amount of that marginal external benefit. But if the marginal external benefit of flu shots varies, the optimal Pigouvian subsidy is the amount of the marginal external benefit when the quantity is the socially optimal quantity.

A **Pigouvian subsidy** is a payment designed to correct for the inefficiencies of external benefits.

In this example, a Pigouvian subsidy is paid to consumers, and it works by lowering the price consumers pay to P_{CNS} and raising the price producers receive to P_{OPT}: consumers pay a price for a flu shot that is equal to the price producers receive *minus* the subsidy. At those prices, consumers want to purchase Q_{OPT} shots and producers want to sell Q_{OPT} shots. Many high schools, colleges, and communities offer subsidized flu shots in hopes of reaching the socially optimal level in a way that would make Pigou proud. Likewise, the U.S. government offered a 100% subsidy for COVID shots during the COVID pandemic, which made them free for recipients.

Note that so far in this Module, our examples have involved per-unit taxes and subsidies that depend on the quantity of livestock and flu shots, respectively. In contrast, a *lump-sum* subsidy or a *lump-sum* tax—one that is the same amount regardless of the chosen quantity, as discussed in Module 2.8A—will not have the same effects as a per-unit subsidy or tax. Lump-sum subsidies and taxes do not change marginal cost or marginal benefit, which are the determinants of quantity. They do affect fixed cost, so if it is large enough, a lump-sum subsidy could motivate a firm to enter an industry, and a lump-sum tax could drive a firm out of business.

Next, we will consider how taxes and permits can be used to address environmental externalities.

Your flu shot provides positive externalities to those whom you would otherwise make sick.

Environmental Policy

In 1970, the Clean Air Act established the first government policies restricting sulfur dioxide emissions from power plants in the United States. Thereafter, pollution levels declined significantly. Economists argued, however, that a more flexible system of rules that exploited the effectiveness of markets could achieve lower pollution levels at a lower cost. This theory was put into effect in 1990 with a modified version of the Clean Air Act. And guess what? The economists were right!

Environmental Standards

Because the economy, and life itself, depend on a viable environment, external costs that threaten the environment – air pollution, water pollution, habitat destruction, and so on – are worthy of attention. Protection of the environment has become a major focus of government in every advanced nation. In the United States, the Environmental Protection Agency (EPA) is the principal enforcer of environmental policies at the national level and is supported by the actions of state and local governments.

Environmental standards are rules that protect the environment by specifying limits for, or actions by, producers and consumers.

How does a country protect its environment? At present the main policy tools are **environmental standards**, which are rules that protect the environment by specifying limits for, or actions by, producers and consumers. A familiar example is the law requiring most vehicles to have catalytic converters, which reduce the emission of chemicals that can cause smog and lead to health problems. Other standards require communities to treat their sewage, factories to limit their pollution emissions, and homes to be painted with lead-free paint, among many other examples.

steinphoto/istockphoto

Environmental standards have helped to erase smog in many major U.S. cities, including Los Angeles.

Environmental standards came into widespread use in the 1960s and 1970s with considerable success. Since the United States passed the Clean Air Act in 1970, for example, the emission of air pollutants has fallen by more than a third, even though the population has grown by nearly two-thirds and the size of the economy has more than tripled.

Despite these successes, environmental standards are inflexible and often don't allow reductions in pollution to be achieved at the lowest possible cost. For example, two power plants might be required to reduce pollution by the same percentage, even if their costs of achieving that objective are very different. A more efficient policy would allow more pollution at the plant where it is more expensive to reduce pollution levels, and less pollution where it is more easily avoided.

How does economic theory suggest that pollution should be controlled? We'll examine two approaches: taxes and tradable permits. As we'll see, either approach can achieve the efficient outcome at the minimum feasible cost.

Emissions Taxes

One way to deal with pollution directly is to charge polluters an *emissions tax*, a per-unit tax that depends on the amount of pollution a firm produces. For example, rather than being required to use specific pollution reduction technology, power plants might be charged $200 for every ton of sulfur dioxide they emit.

Consider **Figure 6.4-3**, a graph introduced in Module 6.1. At the socially optimal quantity of pollution, 3,000, the marginal social benefit (*MSB*) and the marginal social cost (*MSC*) of an additional ton of emissions are both equal to $200. The familiar problem is that in the absence of government intervention, power companies have no incentive to limit pollution to 3,000; instead, they will push pollution up to the quantity 6,000, at which the marginal social benefit is zero.

FIGURE 6.4-3 A Tax on Pollution

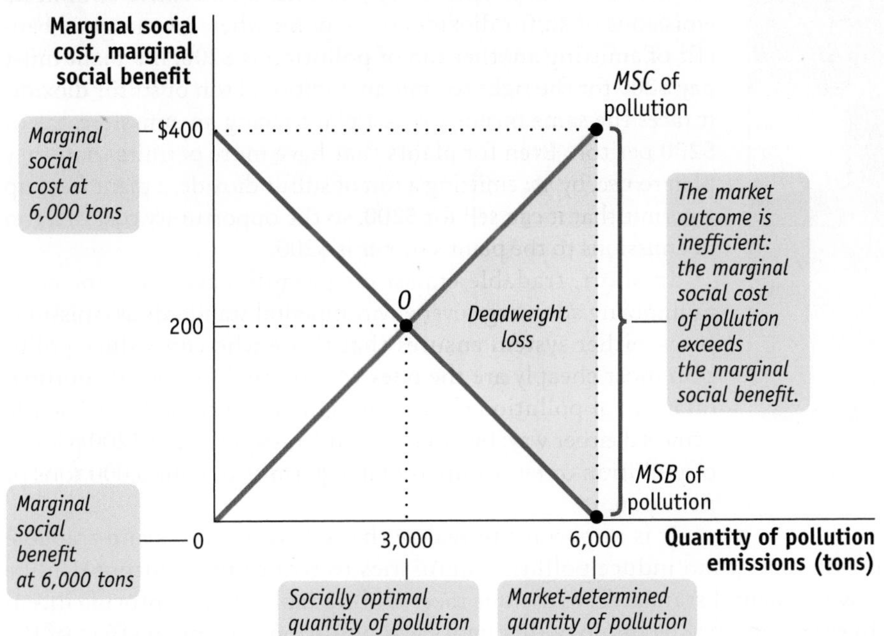

The socially optimal quantity of pollution is 3,000. At that quantity, the $200 marginal social benefit of pollution is equal to the marginal social cost. The market-determined quantity of pollution is 6,000 tons, the quantity at which the marginal social benefit of pollution equals the price polluters pay for each unit of pollution they emit: $0. Every unit beyond 3,000 creates a deadweight loss equal to the distance between the marginal social cost curve (*MSC*) and the marginal social benefit curve (*MSB*).

It's now easy to see how an emissions tax can solve the problem. The marginal social cost in this case is entirely external—it is equivalent to the marginal external cost because there is no marginal private cost. And unlike in the livestock story illustrated in Figure 6.4-1, the marginal external cost of the pollution modeled in Figure 6.4-3 rises as the quantity of pollution increases. To achieve social efficiency, the government could collect a Pigouvian tax equal to the $200 per-ton marginal external cost at the socially optimal quantity of emissions—3,000 tons. The $200 per-unit tax would raise polluters' marginal private cost of pollution from zero to the marginal social cost of $200 per ton, and polluters would emit only 3,000 tons because the tax would exceed the marginal benefit of additional emissions. This illustrates a general result: an emissions tax equal to the marginal external cost at the socially optimal quantity of pollution induces polluters to internalize the externality—to take into account the true cost to society of their actions.

The term *emissions tax* may convey the misleading impression that taxes are a solution to only one kind of external cost, pollution. In fact, taxes can bring decision makers to internalize the negative externalities of all sorts of actions, such as driving during rush hour, drinking too much alcohol, or raising livestock.

Tradable Emissions Permits

Tradable emissions permits are licenses to emit limited quantities of pollutants that can be bought and sold by polluters. They are usually issued to polluting firms according to some formula reflecting their history. For example, each power plant might be issued permits equal to 50% of its emissions before the system went into effect. The more important point, however, is that these permits are *tradable*. A system of tradable emissions permits, commonly known as a *cap and trade program*, creates a market in rights to pollute. Firms with differing costs of reducing pollution can use this market to engage in mutually beneficial transactions: those that find it easier to reduce pollution will sell some of their permits to those that find it more difficult. In the end, those with the lowest cost will reduce their pollution the most, and those with the highest cost will reduce their pollution the least.

AVTG/Getty Images

Emissions taxes and tradable emissions permits can guide power companies toward the efficient level of pollution.

Suppose the market price of a permit to emit one ton of sulfur dioxide is $200. Then every plant has an incentive to limit its emissions of sulfur dioxide to the point where its marginal benefit of emitting another ton of pollution is $200. If a plant must pay $200 for the right to emit an additional ton of sulfur dioxide, it faces the same incentives as a plant facing an emissions tax of $200 per ton. Even for plants that have more permits than they plan to use, by *not* emitting a ton of sulfur dioxide, a plant frees up a permit that it can sell for $200, so the opportunity cost of a ton of emissions to the plant's owner is $200.

In short, tradable emissions permits have the same cost-minimizing advantage over environmental standards as emissions taxes: either system ensures that those who can reduce pollution most cheaply are the ones who do so. The socially optimal quantity of pollution shown in Figure 6.4-3 could be efficiently achieved either way: by imposing an emissions tax of $200 per ton of pollution or by issuing tradable permits to emit 3,000 tons of pollution.

It is important to realize that emissions taxes and tradable permits do more than induce polluting industries to reduce their output. Unlike rigid environmental standards, emissions taxes and tradable permits provide incentives to create and use technology that emits less pollution. The main effect of the permit system for sulfur dioxide has been to change *how* electricity is produced rather than to reduce the nation's electricity output. For example, power companies have shifted to the use of alternative fuels such as low-sulfur coal and natural gas; they have also installed scrubbers that take much of the sulfur dioxide out of a power plant's emissions.

The main problem with tradable emissions permits is the flip-side of the problem with emissions taxes: because it is difficult to determine the optimal quantity of pollution, governments find themselves either issuing too many permits, or too few. And there must be vigilant monitoring of compliance if the system is to work.

Promoting Competition

Environmental policy involves limiting pollution and overconsumption, but government policy also targets monopolies, which typically produce too few units rather than too many. We begin this final section with an overview of public policy designed to lower prices and increase output by promoting competition. Then we will examine the case of natural monopolies, which require special treatment because, as we learned in Module 4.2, their ability to produce large quantities offers a tremendous cost savings.

Antitrust Policy

We have seen that, in general, equilibrium in a competitive market with no externalities is efficient. On the other hand, imperfectly competitive markets—for example, those with a monopoly or an oligopoly—typically create inefficient outcomes. Concern about the higher prices, lower quantities, and lower quality of goods that can result from imperfect competition has led to public policies to promote competition. In Unit 4, we touched on some of these policies, including antitrust laws and direct government regulation. Here, we will look more closely at the history and consequences of government intervention to promote competition and correct for market failure.

Module 4.5 told the story of imperfect competition becoming a problem in the United States during the second half of the nineteenth century, when industrialists formed trusts to facilitate monopoly pricing. By having shareholders place their shares in the hands of a board of trustees, major companies in effect merged into a single firm. That is, they created monopolies. Eventually, there was a public backlash, driven partly by concern about the economic effects of the trust movement and partly by fear that the owners of the trusts were simply becoming too powerful. The result was the Sherman Antitrust Act of 1890, which was intended both to prevent the creation of more monopolies and to break up existing ones. Following the Sherman Act, the government passed several other acts intended to clarify antitrust policy.

AP® ECON TIP

You may not need to know the names of antitrust policies, but governments' use of these policies to increase competition in markets is considered essential knowledge for the AP® exam.

The Sherman Antitrust Act of 1890

Credit card companies charge merchants "swipe fees" of roughly 1.5% to 3.5% of the purchase price for accepting payments with their card. When the American Express Company barred merchants from offering discounts to customers who use credit cards with lower swipe fees, and from educating consumers about how different companies charge different fees, merchants cried foul. In support of the merchants, the U.S. Department of Justice and many state attorneys general argued successfully that these rules hindered competition among credit card companies that could bring the fees down.

These plaintiffs received protection under the cornerstone of U.S. antitrust policy, the Sherman Antitrust Act. This act was the first of three major federal antitrust laws in the United States, followed by the Clayton Antitrust Act and the Federal Trade Commission Act, both passed in 1914. The Department of Justice, which has an Antitrust Division charged with enforcing antitrust laws, describes the goals of antitrust laws as protecting competition, ensuring lower prices, and promoting the development of new and better products. It emphasizes that firms in competitive markets attract consumers by cutting prices and increasing the quality of products or services. Competition and profit opportunities also stimulate businesses to find new and more efficient production methods.

Nattakorn_Maneerat/Shutterstock

Credit card companies that take steps to prevent competition may find themselves in violation of antitrust laws.

The Sherman Antitrust Act of 1890 has two important provisions, each of which outlaws a particular type of activity. The first provision makes it illegal to create a contract, combination, or conspiracy that unreasonably restrains interstate trade. The second provision outlaws the monopolization of any part of interstate commerce. In addition, under the law, the Department of Justice is empowered to bring civil claims and criminal prosecutions when the law is violated. The law provides little detail regarding what constitutes "restraining trade." And the law does not make it illegal to *be* a monopoly but to "monopolize," that is, to take illegal actions to become a monopoly. If you are the only firm in an industry because no other firm chooses to enter the market, you are not in violation of the Sherman Act.

The two provisions of the Sherman Act give very broad, general descriptions of the activities it makes illegal. The act does not provide details regarding specific actions or activities that it prohibits. The vague nature of the Sherman Act led to the subsequent passage of two additional major antitrust laws.

The Clayton Antitrust Act of 1914

The Clayton Antitrust Act of 1914 was intended to clarify the Sherman Act, which did not identify specific firm behaviors that were illegal. The Clayton Act outlaws four specific firm behaviors: price discrimination, anticompetitive practices, anticompetitive mergers and acquisitions, and interlocking directorates (two corporate boards of directors that share at least one director in common).

You are already familiar with the topic of price discrimination from our discussion of market structures in Module 4.3. The Clayton Act makes it illegal for a firm to charge different prices to different customers for the same product. Obviously, there are exceptions to this rule that allow the price discrimination we see in practice, for example, at movie theaters where children pay a different price than adults.

By prohibiting the anticompetitive practice of *exclusive dealing*, the Clayton Act makes it illegal for a firm to refuse to do business with you just because you also do business with its competitors. If a firm had the dominant product in a given market, exclusive dealing could allow it to gain monopoly power in other markets. For example, a company that sells an extremely popular classroom desk – the only one of its kind – could set a condition that schools that want to purchase the desk must also purchase all of their office supplies from the company. This would allow the company to expand its existing market power into the market for office supplies.

Sergey Peterman/Shutterstock

The Clayton Act prohibits *tying arrangements*, such as a requirement that you must buy your paper from the seller of your printer.

The Clayton Act also outlaws *tying arrangements* because, if it did not, a firm could expand its monopoly power for a dominant product by "tying" the purchase of one product to the purchase of a dominant product in another market. Tying arrangements occur when a firm stipulates that it will sell you a specific product, say a printer, only if you buy something else, such as printer paper, at the same time. In this case, tying the printer and paper together expands the firm's printer market power into the market for paper. In this way, as with exclusive dealing, tying arrangements can lessen competition by allowing a firm to expand its market power from one market into another.

Mergers and acquisitions happen fairly often in the U.S. economy; most are not illegal despite stipulations in the Clayton Act. The Justice Department regularly reviews proposed mergers between companies in the same industry and, under the Clayton Act, bars any that they determine would significantly reduce competition. But the Justice Department is not the only agency responsible for enforcing antitrust laws. Another of our major antitrust laws created and empowers the Federal Trade Commission to enforce antitrust laws.

The Federal Trade Commission Act of 1914

Passed in 1914, the Federal Trade Commission Act prohibits unfair methods of competition in interstate commerce and created the Federal Trade Commission (FTC) to enforce the Act. The FTC Act outlaws unfair competition, including "unfair or deceptive acts." The FTC Act also outlaws some of the same practices included in the Sherman and Clayton Acts. In addition, it specifically outlaws price fixing (including the setting of minimum resale prices), output restrictions, and actions that prevent the entry of new firms. The FTC's goal is to promote lower prices, higher output, and free entry – all characteristics of competitive markets (as opposed to monopolies and oligopolies).

Sandra Baker/Alamy

The Federal Trade Commission promotes fair practices, free entry by firms, and the virtues of competitive markets.

Dealing with Natural Monopoly

Antitrust laws are designed to promote competition by preventing business behaviors that concentrate market power. Breaking up a monopoly that isn't natural is clearly a good idea: the gains to consumers outweigh the loss to the firm. But what if a market is a natural monopoly? As you will recall from Module 4.2, a natural monopoly exists when economies of scale make it efficient to have only one firm in a market. For instance, the Board of Water and Light in Lansing, Michigan, completed a $500 million natural gas power plant in 2021. If many power plants competed for customers in the Lansing area, none would sell enough energy to warrant the cost of each plant. Here we see the *spreading effect* described in Module 3.2 in action – having just one plant allows the production level to be relatively high and the average fixed cost to be tolerably low.

How can public policy allow a natural monopoly to achieve low costs while also preventing the relatively high prices and low quantities that result when there is only one firm? The goal in these circumstances is to retain the advantage of lower average total cost that results from a single producer and still curb the inefficiency associated with a monopoly. In Module 4.2, we introduced two ways to do this – public ownership and price regulation. While there are a few examples of public ownership in the United States, such as Amtrak, a provider of passenger rail service, the more common approach has been to leave the industry in private hands but subject it to regulation.

Price Regulation

We've already seen evidence that price regulations must be applied carefully to avoid unintended consequences. Module 2.8B showed that in a perfectly competitive market, price ceilings cause shortages and price floors cause surpluses. Module 4.4 explained that monopolistically competitive firms, like perfectly competitive firms, earn zero economic profit in the long run, meaning that binding price ceilings in those markets can cause some firms to leave the industry. On the plus side, Module 5.4 showed how a price floor in a monopsony labor market could actually increase the quantity of workers hired. And Module 4.2 introduced a discussion of how appropriate price regulation can allow a natural monopoly to achieve economies of scale while limiting the price and increasing the quantity beyond what an unregulated monopoly would produce. This section expands on that discussion.

Most water, sewer, and power utilities are natural monopolies with regulated prices. By having only one firm produce in the market, society benefits from lower costs. That is, the average cost of production is lower due to economies of scale. But without price regulation, the natural monopoly would be tempted to restrict its output and raise its price. How, then, do regulators determine an appropriate price?

Since the purpose of regulation is to achieve efficiency in the market, a logical place to set the price is at the level at which the marginal cost curve intersects the demand curve. This is called **marginal cost pricing**. (Because we are no longer discussing situations with externalities, we will refer to a single marginal cost that is both the marginal social cost and the marginal private cost.) We have seen that the best allocation of resources for society – the allocatively efficient outcome – is generally achieved when firms charge a price equal to their marginal cost. So should regulators require marginal cost pricing in this case?

Marginal cost pricing occurs when regulators set a monopoly's price equal to its marginal cost to achieve efficiency.

Average cost pricing occurs when regulators set a monopoly's price equal to its average cost to prevent the firm from incurring a loss.

Figure 6.4-4 illustrates this situation. In the case of a natural monopoly, the firm is operating on the downward-sloping portion of its average total cost curve (it is experiencing economies of scale). When the average total cost is falling, the marginal cost must be below the average total cost, pulling it down. If the firm had to set its price equal to its marginal cost and sell Q_1 units (the quantity demanded when $P = MC$), the price would be below the average total cost and the firm would incur a loss: for each unit sold, the firm would lose the difference between the average total cost and the price. The firm would not continue to operate at a loss in the long run unless it received assistance, such as a lump-sum subsidy equal to the amount of the loss. The government could require the efficient price and subsidize the firm, resulting in an overall increase in efficiency for society. But firm subsidies funded from tax revenues are often politically unpopular. What other options do regulators have?

If regulators want to set the price so that the firm does not require a subsidy because it breaks even, they can set the price equal to the level of the average total cost at which the demand curve intersects the average total cost curve. This is called **average cost pricing**. As Figure 6.4-4 illustrates, average cost pricing results in output level Q_2 (the quantity demanded when $P = ATC$). The result, a lower quantity at a higher price than with marginal cost pricing, seems to fall short of the goals of antitrust regulation. But remember that there are always

Christy V. Henderson/Alamy

Allowing public utilities to operate as natural monopolies saves these firms money due to economies of scale. Regulating the prices that natural monopolies charge passes some of the savings on to consumers.

FIGURE 6.4-4 **Price Setting for a Regulated Monopoly**

This figure shows the marginal cost curve, *MC*, and the average total cost curve, *ATC*. When the price is set equal to the marginal cost (where the *MC* curve crosses the demand curve), the firm incurs a loss. When the price is set equal to the average total cost (where the *ATC* curve crosses the demand curve) the firm breaks even, but the quantity is below the allocatively efficient level.

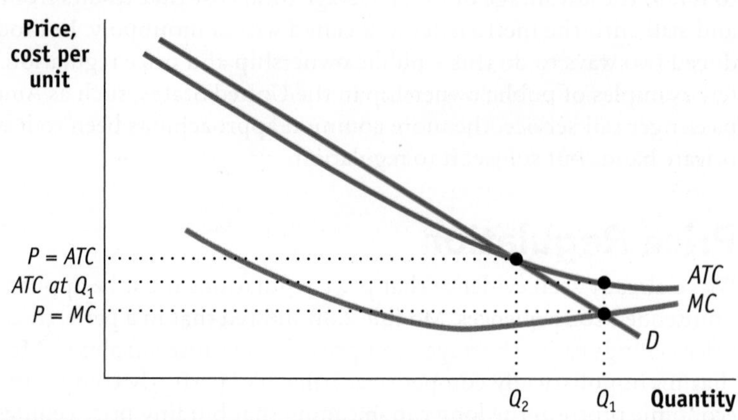

AP® ECON TIP

Understanding the different pricing options for a regulated natural monopoly is a key skill for the AP® exam. You may need to graph and explain marginal cost pricing and average cost pricing.

trade-offs, and it may be best to avoid subsidizing a loss even if it results in less than the allocatively efficient quantity.

Allowing a natural monopoly to exist permits the firm to produce at a lower average total cost than if multiple firms produced in the same market. And price regulation seeks to prevent the inefficiency that results when an unregulated monopoly limits its output and raises its price. This all looks terrific: consumers are better off, monopoly profits are avoided, and overall welfare increases. Unfortunately, things are rarely that easy in practice. The main problem is that regulators don't always have the information required to set the price exactly at the level at which the demand curve crosses the average total cost curve. Sometimes they set it too low, creating shortages; at other times they set it too high, increasing inefficiency. Also, regulated monopolies, like publicly owned firms, may be tempted to exaggerate their costs to regulators and to provide inferior quality to consumers.

Module 6.4  Review

Check Your Understanding

1. Which of the following business practices would be legal under antitrust law? Explain.
   - **a.** You have a patent for a superior electric car and therefore are the only person able to sell that type of electric car. You require buyers of your car to also purchase a service contract from you (even though other firms provide excellent service for your car).
   - **b.** You have invented a new type of coffee maker that is easy to use and makes incredible cappuccinos and espressos. In order to buy your coffee maker, you require purchasers to also buy all of their coffee-making supplies and accessories from you.
   - **c.** You own a car dealership and plan to buy the dealership across the street and merge the two companies. There are several other car dealerships in town.
2. Wind farms generate clean energy but have a high fixed cost. Explain why policy makers who don't want to pay subsidies would choose average cost pricing over marginal cost pricing in the market for wind energy.

Tackle the AP® Test: Multiple-Choice Questions

1. Suppose the use of each gallon of gasoline creates a negative consumption externality of $1, and at the current level of gasoline consumption, the marginal private benefit equals the marginal private cost. Which of the following is true?
   a. The current quantity is the socially optimal quantity.
   b. The current quantity is below the socially optimal quantity.
   c. The marginal social benefit exceeds the marginal social cost.
   d. A Pigouvian subsidy of $1 per gallon would achieve the socially optimal quantity.
   e. A Pigouvian tax of $1 per gallon would achieve the socially optimal quantity.

2. If the government wants to collect revenue from a business without affecting the business's level of output, it should impose a(n)
   a. Pigouvian tax.
   b. Pigouvian subsidy.
   c. lump-sum tax.
   d. lump-sum subsidy.
   e. emissions tax.

3. Which of the following is the most common policy approach to a natural monopoly?
   a. public ownership
   b. price regulation
   c. quantity regulation
   d. quality regulation
   e. a breakup of the monopoly into smaller firms

For Questions 4 and 5, refer to the graph below.

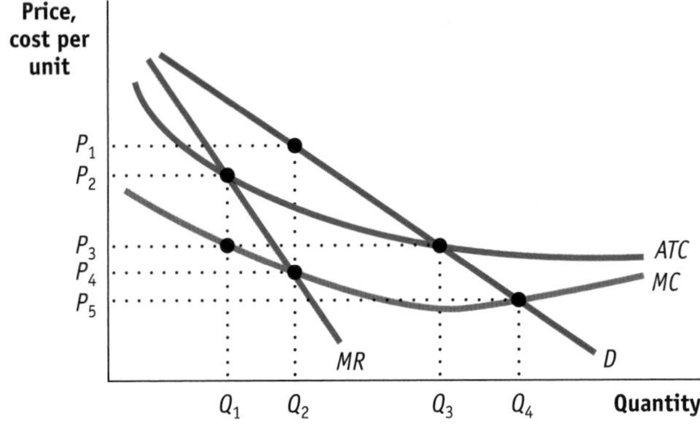

4. Without government intervention, a monopolist will produce __________ and charge __________.
   a. Q_3 P_3
   b. Q_2 P_4
   c. Q_2 P_1
   d. Q_1 P_3
   e. Q_1 P_2

5. The lowest regulated price the government could expect this monopolist to maintain in the long run is
   a. P_1.
   b. P_2.
   c. P_3.
   d. P_4.
   e. P_5.

6. If the regulated price of a natural monopoly is set where the marginal cost curve intersects the demand curve, the firm will certainly
   a. shut down in the long run.
   b. shut down in the short run.
   c. produce the quantity at which marginal revenue equals average total cost.
   d. increase its output.
   e. make a profit.

7. An optimal Pigouvian subsidy for a good is set equal to the good's
   a. external cost at the socially optimal quantity.
   b. marginal social benefit at the socially optimal quantity.
   c. marginal external cost at the socially optimal quantity.
   d. marginal external benefit at the socially optimal quantity.
   e. price at which $MSC = MSB$.

Tackle the AP® Test: Free-Response Questions

1. **a.** Draw a correctly labeled graph showing a natural monopoly. On your graph, label the price and quantity the monopoly will choose if unregulated as P_U and Q_U, respectively.

   b. On the same graph, shade in and label consumer surplus and the firm's profit in the absence of regulation.

   c. On the same graph, label the lowest price that regulators could expect the monopoly to maintain in the long run as P_R and the resulting quantity as Q_R.

   d. What happens to the size of consumer surplus when the firm is required to charge P_R rather than P_U? What happens to the firm's profit?

Rubric for FRQ 1 (10 points)

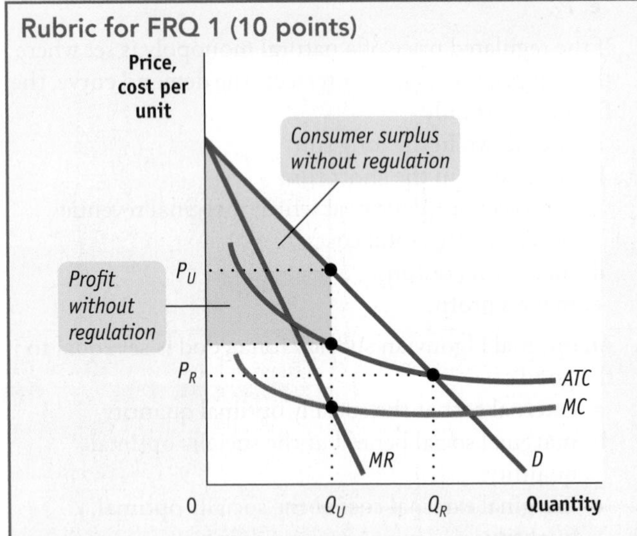

1 point: Correctly labeled axes ("Price, cost per unit" or "Dollars per unit" on the vertical axis, "Quantity" or "Q" on the horizontal axis)

1 point: Downward-sloping *ATC* curve

1 point: Downward-sloping *MC* curve below the *ATC* curve

1 point: Unregulated quantity Q_U shown on the horizontal axis where $MC = MR$

1 point: Unregulated price P_U found on a downward-sloping demand curve above Q_U and shown on the vertical axis

1 point: Correct profit rectangle

1 point: Consumer surplus triangle shown below the demand curve and above the price

1 point: Regulated price and quantity P_R and Q_R shown on the appropriate axes, corresponding to where the demand curve crosses the average total cost curve

1 point: Consumer surplus will increase.

1 point: Profit will decrease to zero.

2. List and explain three different public policy approaches to monopoly. **(6 points)**

Income and Wealth Inequality

MODULE 6.5

In this Module, you will learn to:
- Describe the causes and consequences of poverty
- Define measures of income and wealth inequality
- Discuss solutions to poverty and economic inequality

In Module 1.1, we distinguished between positive economics (the study of how the economy works) and normative economics (the study of how the economy should work). The descriptive *positive* side of economics offers information about the extent of poverty and *economic inequality*, a term that captures both income and wealth inequality. The prescriptive *normative* side presents more challenging questions about how to weigh equity in the distribution of income against associated losses in efficiency. For example, the redistribution of income from high-income households to low-income households reduces income inequality, but the taxes used to collect money for low-income households generally cause deadweight loss. How much income redistribution is appropriate? That is a subject of debate, and although there may not be a single "right" answer, the tools of economics do much to inform the debate. In this Module, we look at the problems of poverty and economic inequality with attention to the causes, consequences, and possible solutions.

Arnold Sachs/Archive Photos/Getty Images

President Johnson signing the War on Poverty bill in 1964.

The Problem of Poverty

Since the Great Depression, every U.S. president has promised to do his best to reduce poverty. In 1964, President Lyndon Johnson went so far as to declare a "war on poverty," creating a number of new programs to aid low-income households. Antipoverty programs account for a significant part of the U.S. *welfare state*—the system whereby the government takes responsibility for the welfare of its citizens—although social insurance programs, including Social Security and Medicare, are an even larger part.

What, exactly, do we mean by poverty? Since 1965, the U.S. government has provided an official **poverty threshold**, a minimum annual income that is considered adequate to purchase the necessities of life. Families whose incomes fall below the poverty threshold are officially considered poor. The official poverty threshold depends on the size and composition of a family. In 2022, the poverty threshold for an adult living alone was $13,590; for a household consisting of two adults and two children, it was $27,750.

The **poverty threshold** is the minimal annual income that is considered adequate to purchase the necessities of life.

Trends in Poverty

Contrary to popular misconceptions, although the official poverty threshold is adjusted each year to reflect changes in the cost of living, it has *not* been adjusted upward over time to reflect the long-term rise in the standard of living of the average American family. As a result, as the economy grows and becomes more prosperous, and as average incomes rise, you might expect the percentage of the population living below the poverty threshold to steadily decline.

Somewhat surprisingly, however, this hasn't happened. **Figure 6.5-1** shows the U.S. **poverty rate**—the percentage of the population living below the poverty threshold—from 1959 to 2020. As you can see, the poverty rate fell steeply during the

The **poverty rate** is the percentage of the population with incomes below the poverty threshold.

FIGURE 6.5-1 Trends in the U.S Poverty Rate, 1959–2020

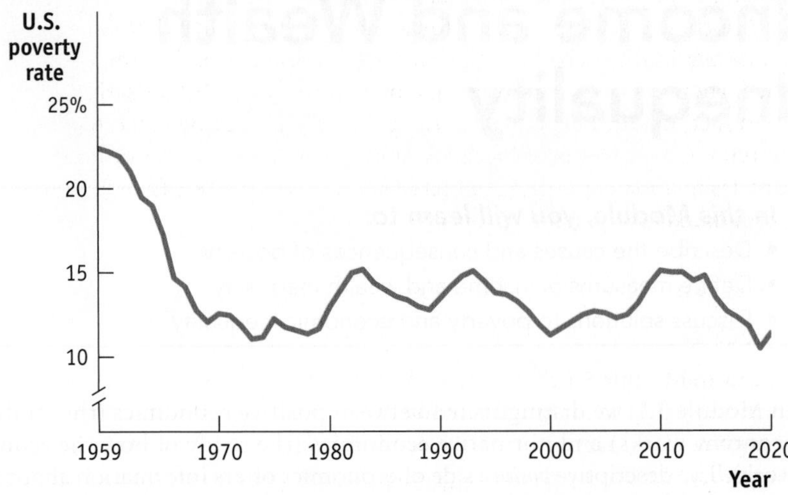

The poverty rate fell sharply in the 1960s but has not shown a clear trend since then.
Data Source: U.S. Census Bureau.

1960s. Since then, however, it has fluctuated up and down, with no clear trend. In fact, the poverty rate in 2020 was higher than it had been in 1973.

Who Experiences Poverty?

In 2020, about 37.2 million Americans were in poverty, or about one in nine persons. No particular stereotype is valid for a majority of America's low-income households, although poverty rates are disproportionately high among some groups. For example, about 23% of the poor in 2020 were African-American and about 19% were Hispanic. But there was also widespread poverty among non-Hispanic White people, who had a poverty rate of 8.2%.

There is a correlation between family makeup and poverty. Single-parent, female-headed families present had a very high poverty rate: 23.4%. And although married couples were much less likely to be poor – their poverty rate was only 4.7% – about 39% of families living below the poverty line were married couples.

What really stands out from the data, however, is the association between poverty and lack of adequate employment. Adults who work full time are very unlikely to live in poverty: only 1.6% of full-time workers were below the poverty line in 2020. Among adults who worked year-round, but less than full time, 11.3% were below the poverty threshold. Many industries, particularly in the retail and service sectors, now rely primarily on part-time workers. Part-time work typically lacks benefits such as health plans, paid vacation days, and retirement benefits, and it usually pays a lower hourly wage than comparable full-time work. As a result, many low-wage earners are members of what analysts call the *working poor*: workers whose income falls at or below the poverty threshold.

What Causes Economic Inequality?

Why are some people extremely rich while others have no financial wealth? In this section, we will explore several of the many reasons. Educational attainment clearly has a strong positive effect on income level – on average, those with more education earn higher incomes than those with less education. Some jobs pay higher wages due to the risky or uncomfortable working conditions, and some employers pay more to secure worker loyalty. Market power influences wages when workers or employers can band together to behave like a monopoly or a monopsony. Discrimination erects formidable barriers to advancement for many workers. And some workers choose to make trade-offs between income and leisure, earning less but having more time for family and other pursuits.

Another important reason for economic inequality that should not be overlooked is bad luck. Many families find themselves impoverished when a wage-earner loses a job or a family member falls seriously ill. In fact, medical expenses are the primary cause of personal bankruptcies. Other forms of bad luck among the major causes of bankruptcies include pay cuts, unexpected car repair expenses, divorce, and storm damage to personal property.

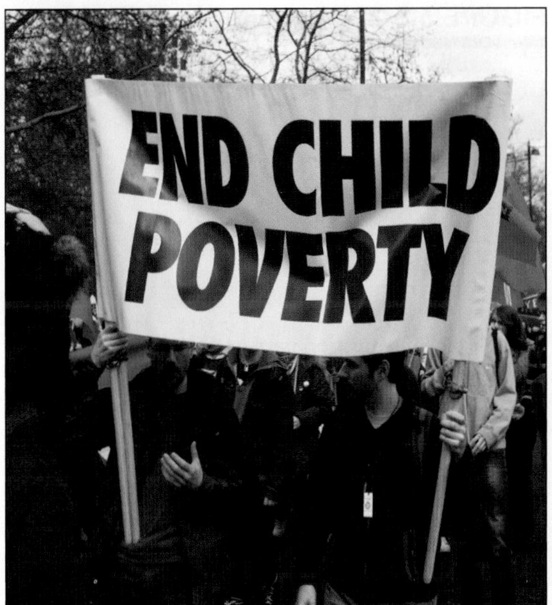

G Scammell/Alamy

One in five U.S. children live in poverty, the consequences of which can include poor health and lifelong learning disabilities.

Marginal Productivity and Wage Inequality

We saw in Module 5.1 that each worker in a perfectly competitive labor market is paid the marginal revenue product of the last worker hired. This gives marginal productivity relevance in the discussion of income inequality. According to the *marginal productivity theory of income distribution*, the division of income among the economy's factors of production is determined by each factor's marginal revenue product at the market equilibrium. A large part of the observed inequality in wages can be explained by considerations that are consistent with the marginal productivity theory of income distribution. In particular, there are three well-understood sources of wage differences across occupations and individuals.

Compensating differentials are wage differences across jobs that reflect the fact that some jobs are less pleasant or more dangerous than others.

The first is the existence of **compensating differentials**: across different types of jobs, wages are often higher or lower depending on how attractive or unattractive the job is. Workers in unpleasant or dangerous jobs receive a higher wage than workers in jobs that require the same skill, training, and effort but lack the unpleasant or dangerous qualities. For example, truckers who haul hazardous chemicals are paid more than truckers who haul bread. When work conditions are unfavorable, the relatively low supply of workers seeking such jobs will establish a higher equilibrium wage at a higher equilibrium marginal revenue product of labor.

A second reason for wage inequality that is clearly consistent with marginal productivity theory is differences in natural skill or aptitude that can be described as *talent*. People differ in their abilities: a more talented person, by producing a better product that commands a higher price, generates a higher marginal revenue product. And these differences in the marginal revenue product translate into differences in earning potential. We all know that this is true in sports: practice is important, but 99.99% (at least) of the population just doesn't have what it takes to control a soccer ball like Kylian Mbappé or swim like Katie Ledecky. The same is true, though less obvious, in other labor markets.

A third, very important reason for income inequality is differences in the quantity of *human capital*. Recall that human capital—education, training, and experience—is at least as important in the modern economy as physical capital in the form of buildings and machines. Different people hold quite different quantities of human capital, and a person with more human capital typically generates a higher marginal revenue product by producing more or better products. So differences in human capital account for substantial differences in wages. People with high levels of human capital, such as surgeons or engineers, generally receive high wages.

The most direct way to see the effect of human capital on wages is to look at the relationship between education levels and earnings. **Figure 6.5-2** shows earnings by education level for full-time workers 25 years or older in 2020. As you can see, higher education levels are generally associated with higher median earnings. For example, workers without a high school diploma had median earnings 21% less than those with a high school diploma and 53% less than those with a bachelor's degree.

FIGURE 6.5-2 Earnings by Education Level, 2020

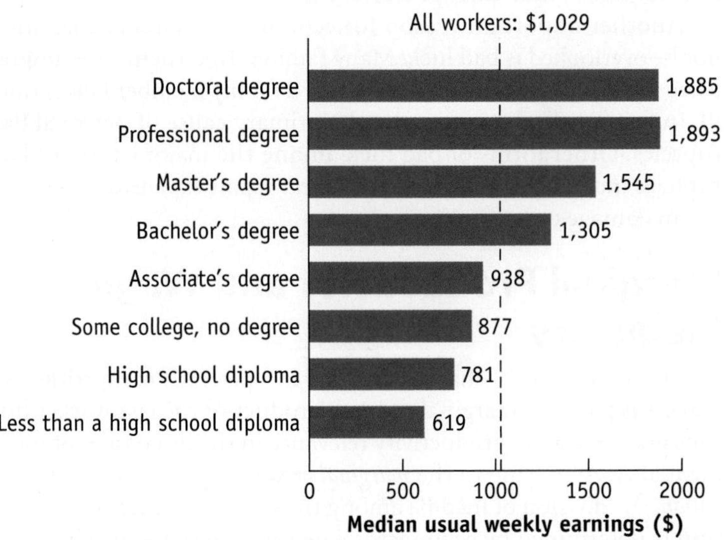

It is clear that education pays: those with a high school diploma earn more than those without one, and those with a college degree earn substantially more than those with only a high school diploma.
Data Source: Bureau of Labor Statistics.

Additional economic inequality can arise out of differences in *social capital*, which refers to the social networks and bonds created among friends and acquaintances. A worker's family, urban or rural location, and social skills all influence the development of social capital. The old saying that "it's not what you know but who you know" asserts that social capital is more important than human capital. Whether or not that's true, personal connections clearly lead to many jobs, as suggested by the popularity of social networking platforms such as LinkedIn.

Earnings differences arising from differences in human capital and social capital are not necessarily "fair." A society in which some children receive an inferior education because they live in underfunded school districts, and then go on to earn lower wages because of their differing educational opportunities, may have labor markets that are well described by marginal productivity theory. Even so, many people consider the resulting distribution of income unfair.

Beyond that, actual wage differentials cannot be entirely explained by compensating differentials, differences in talent, and differences in human capital. Market power, *efficiency wages*, and discrimination also play an important role. We will examine these forces next.

Market Power

The marginal productivity theory of income distribution is based on the assumption that factor markets are perfectly competitive. In such markets we can expect workers to be paid the marginal revenue product of the last worker hired, regardless of who the workers are. Exceptions occur in cases where there is market power on the buying side, as in a monopsony consisting of one employer of labor. Module 5.4 showed how workers in a monopsony receive less than the marginal revenue product of the last worker hired.

Unions are organizations of workers that try to raise wages and improve working conditions for their members by bargaining collectively.

Market power on the selling side of the employment story can also be a source of differences in wages among otherwise similar workers. **Unions**—organizations that try to raise wages and improve working conditions for their members—can empower workers. Labor unions, when successful, replace one-on-one wage deals between workers and employers with *collective bargaining*, in which the employer negotiates wages with union representatives. Without question, this leads to higher wages for those workers who are represented by unions. In 2021, the median weekly earnings of union members in the United States were $1,169, compared with $975 for workers not represented by unions—about a 20% difference.

AP® ECON TIP

Unions act like single sellers of labor. Through collective bargaining, they represent all the workers.

Just as workers can sometimes organize to demand higher wages than they would otherwise receive, employers can sometimes organize to pay *lower* wages than would result from competition. For example, health care workers – including doctors and nurses – sometimes argue that health maintenance organizations (HMOs) are engaged in a collective effort to hold down their wages.

Collective action, either by workers or by employers, is less common in the United States than it used to be. Several decades ago, approximately 30% of U.S. workers were union members. By 2021, union membership in the United States was relatively limited: 6.1% of the employees of private businesses were represented by unions. And the sheer size of the U.S. labor market and the ease with which most workers can move in search of higher-paying jobs probably mean that successful concerted efforts to hold wages below the unrestrained market equilibrium level are rare.

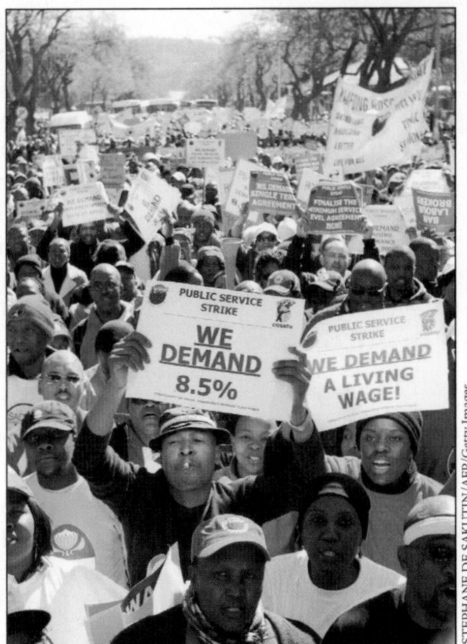

STEPHANE DE SAKUTIN/AFP/Getty Images

Union members rally to demand higher wages.

Efficiency Wages

Another source of wage inequality is **efficiency wages** – wages above the equilibrium level that employers pay to incentivize hard work and reduce worker turnover. Suppose a worker performs a job that is extremely important but difficult for the employer to monitor. This would be true, for example, for childcare providers. Then it often makes sense for the employer to pay more than the worker could earn in an alternative job – that is, more than the equilibrium wage. Why? Because earning a premium makes losing this job and having to take the alternative job quite costly for the worker. A worker who happens to be observed performing poorly and is therefore fired is now worse off for having to accept a lower-paying job. The threat of losing a job that pays a premium motivates the worker to perform well. Paying a premium also reduces worker turnover – the frequency with which an employee leaves a job voluntarily – and the associated costs of recruiting and training new workers. Although it may take no more effort and skill to be a childcare provider than to be an office worker, efficiency wages show why it often makes economic sense to pay a caregiver more than the equilibrium wage of an office worker.

Efficiency wages are wages that exceed the market equilibrium wage rate that employers use to motivate hard work and reduce worker turnover.

Henry Ford was an early adopter of efficiency wages. He paid workers $5 a day to build automobiles back in 1914, when the average daily wage for auto workers was less than $2.50. Efficiency wages allowed Ford to attract and retain the best workers and to keep them on task, even when worker performance was hard to track. For similar reasons, Adobe, Amazon, Capital One, ExxonMobil, Facebook, Google, and Microsoft are among dozens of companies that pay their student interns more than the median income for U.S. workers.

On the downside, by raising wages above the equilibrium wage, efficiency wages can attract more workers into the labor market and create unemployment. A similar surplus of labor can be caused by wages elevated by unions or minimum wage laws, as discussed in Module 2.8B.

bernardbodo/iStock/Getty Images

Some employers pay *efficiency wages*—wages above the equilibrium wage rate—to promote loyalty and motivate hard work, especially in jobs that are difficult to monitor.

Discrimination

It is an ugly fact that throughout history there has been discrimination against workers on the basis of race, ethnicity, gender, and other characteristics. People of color earn less and are less likely to be employed than White people with comparable levels of education. Studies find that African-American males suffer persistent discrimination by employers in favor of White people, African-American women, and Hispanic immigrants. Women earn lower incomes than men with similar qualifications. How does this fit into our economic models?

The main insight economic analysis offers is that discrimination is *not* a natural consequence of market competition. On the contrary, market forces tend to work against discrimination. To see why, consider the incentives that would exist if social convention dictated that women be paid, say, 30% less than men with equivalent qualifications and experience. A company whose management was itself unbiased would then be able to reduce its costs by hiring women rather than men—and such companies would have an advantage over other companies that hired men despite their higher cost. The result would be to create an excess demand for female workers, which would tend to drive up their wages.

But if market competition works against discrimination, how is it that so much discrimination has taken place? The answer is twofold. First, when labor markets don't work well, employers may have the ability to discriminate without hurting their profits. For example, market interferences (such as unions or minimum-wage laws) or market failures (such as efficiency wages) can lead to wages that are above their equilibrium levels. In these cases, there are more job applicants than there are jobs, leaving employers free to discriminate among applicants.

In research published in the *American Economic Review*, economists Marianne Bertrand and Sendhil Mullainathan documented discrimination in hiring by sending fictitious résumés to prospective employers on a random basis. Applicants with "White-sounding" names, such as Emily Walsh, were 50% more likely to be contacted than applicants with "African-American-sounding" names, such as Lakisha Washington. Also, applicants with White-sounding names and good credentials were much more likely to be contacted than those without such credentials. By contrast, potential employers seemed to ignore the credentials of applicants with African-American-sounding names.

Second, discrimination has sometimes been institutionalized in government policy. This institutionalization has made it easier to maintain discrimination despite market pressure. For example, until the mid-1950s, African-Americans were barred from attending "Whites-only" public schools and universities in many states and were forced to attend schools that tended to have more pupils per teacher and less funding than Whites-only schools. Although market competition generally works against *current* discrimination, it is not a remedy for the lingering repercussions of past discrimination on victims' income, education, and experience.

Wage Disparities in Practice

Wage rates in the United States cover a very wide range. In 2020, 1.1 million workers received wages at or below the federal minimum of $7.25 per hour. At the other extreme, the chief executives of several companies were paid more than $100 million for the year, which works out to $20,000 per hour even if they worked 100-hour weeks. Leaving out these extremes, there is still a tremendous range of wage rates. Are people really that different in their marginal productivities? Do workers really differ that much in their value to firms?

A particular source of concern is the existence of systematic wage differences across gender and ethnicity. **Figure 6.5-3** compares median weekly earnings in 2021 of workers 16 years or older classified by gender and ethnicity. As a group, White males had the highest earnings. Women (averaging across all ethnicities) earned only about 81% as much; African-American workers (male and female combined) only 71% as much; and Hispanic or Latino workers only 69% as much.

We are a nation founded on the belief that all men are created equal—and if the Constitution were rewritten today, we would say that *all people* are created equal. So why do the people receive such unequal pay? The pay differences may involve some differences in marginal productivity, but we also must allow for the possibility of other influences. Beyond the factors already discussed, differences in inheritances, geographic mobility, bargaining skills, tax structures (discussed in Module 2.8A), and access to financial markets for loans and investments can all feed into economic inequality.

FIGURE 6.5-3 Median Weekly Earnings by Gender and Ethnicity, 2021

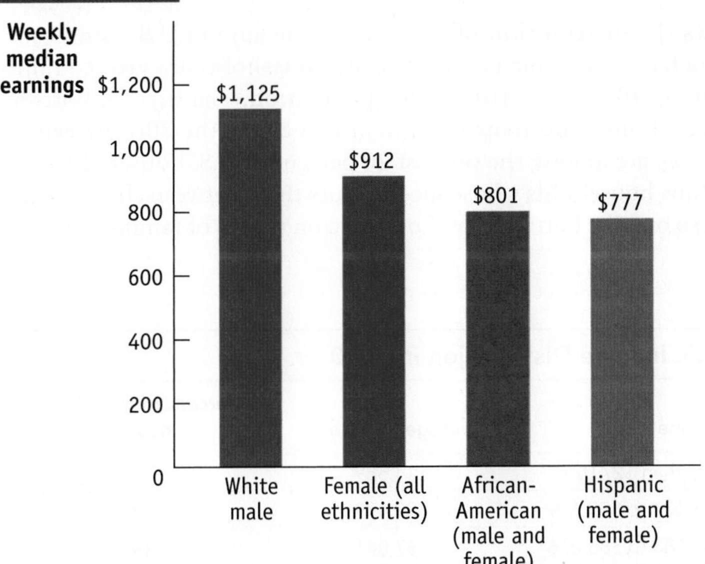

The U.S. labor market continues to show large differences across workers according to gender and ethnicity. Women are paid substantially less than men; African-American and Hispanic workers are paid substantially less than White male workers.
Data Source: Bureau of Labor Statistics.

Consequences of Poverty

The consequences of poverty are often severe, particularly for children. In 2020, 16% of children in the United States lived below the poverty threshold. Poverty is often associated with a lack of access to health care, which can lead to further health problems that erode the ability to attend school and work later in life. Recent medical studies have shown that children raised in severe poverty tend to suffer from lifelong learning disabilities. Affordable housing is also frequently a problem, leading poor families to move often, disrupting school and work schedules.

One of the most vexing problems facing any society is how to break what researchers call the *cycle of poverty*: children who grow up with disadvantaged socioeconomic backgrounds are far more likely to remain trapped in poverty as adults, even after we account for differences in ability. They are more likely to be unemployed or underemployed, to engage in crime, and to suffer chronic health problems. They are also unlikely to finish college.

Early childhood intervention has offered some hope of breaking the cycle. A study by the RAND Corporation found that high-quality early-childhood programs that focus on education and health care lead to significant social, intellectual, and financial advantages for kids who would otherwise be at risk of dropping out of high school and of engaging in criminal behavior. Children in programs like Head Start were less likely to engage in such destructive behaviors and more likely to end up with a job and to earn a high salary later in life.

A study by researchers at the University of Pittsburgh looked at early-childhood intervention programs from a dollars-and-cents perspective, finding that every $1 spent on early-childhood intervention programs provides between $4 and $7 worth of benefits to society. The observed external benefits to society of high-quality preschool education are so large that the Brookings Institution predicts that providing these programs to every American child would result in an increase in GDP by almost 2%, and would contribute over 3 million more jobs to the economy.

Economic Inequality

The United States is a rich country. In 2020, the average U.S. household had an income of $97,026, far exceeding the poverty threshold. How is it possible, then, that so many Americans still live in poverty? The answer is that income is unequally distributed, with many households earning much less than the average and others earning much more.

Table 6.5-1 shows the distribution of pre-tax income among U.S. families in 2020 – income before federal income taxes are paid. Households are grouped into *quintiles*, each containing 20% or one-fifth of the population. The first, or bottom, quintile contains households whose income puts them below the 20th percentile in income, meaning they are among the poorest 20 percent of U.S. households. The second quintile contains households whose income puts them between the 20th and 40th percentiles, and so on. The bottom row shows data on the 5% of families with the highest incomes.

Table 6.5-1 **U.S. Income Distribution in 2020**

Income group	Income range	Average income	Percent of total U.S. income
Bottom quintile	Less than $27,027	$14,589	3.0%
Second quintile	$27,027 to $52,179	39,479	8.1
Third quintile	$52,180 to $85,076	67,846	14.0
Fourth quintile	$85,077 to $141,110	109,732	22.6
Top quintile	More than $141,110	253,484	52.2
Top 5%	More than $273,739	446,030	23.0
Mean Income = $97,026		**Median Income = $67,521**	

Data Source: U.S. Census Bureau.

For each group, Table 6.5-1 shows three numbers. The second column shows the range of incomes that define the group. For example, in 2020, the bottom quintile consisted of households with annual incomes of less than $27,027; the next quintile of households with incomes between $27,027 and $52,179; and so on. The third column shows the average income in each group, ranging from $14,589 for the bottom fifth to $446,030 for the top 5%. The fourth column shows the percentage of total U.S. income received by each group.

Mean household income is the average income across all households.

Median household income is the income of the household lying in the middle of the income distribution.

At the bottom of Table 6.5-1 are two useful numbers for thinking about the incomes of American households. **Mean household income**, also called *average household income*, is the total income of all U.S. households divided by the number of households. **Median household income** is the income of a household in the exact middle of the income distribution – the level of income at which half of all households have lower income and half have higher income. It's very important to realize that these two numbers do not measure the same thing. Economists often illustrate the difference by asking people first to imagine a room containing several dozen more or less ordinary wage-earners, and then to think about what happens to the mean and median incomes of the people in the room if the CEO of a major corporation walks in. The mean income soars, because the CEO's multimillion-dollar income pulls up the average, but median income hardly rises at all because the person in the middle of the income distribution is still one of the ordinary wage-earners. This example helps explain why economists generally regard median income as a better guide to the economic status of typical American families than mean income: mean income is strongly affected by the incomes of a relatively small number of very-high-income Americans, who are not representative of the population as a whole; median income is not.

Patrick Pleul/picture alliance/Getty Images

When billionaire Elon Musk walks into a room filled with ordinary wage-earners, it has a large effect on the mean income and a small effect on the median income of people in the room.

What we learn from Table 6.5-1 is that income in the United States is quite unequally distributed. The average income of the poorest fifth of families is less than a quarter of the average income of families in the middle, and the richest fifth have an average income 3.7 times that of families in the middle. On average, the incomes of the richest fifth of the population are more than 17 times as high as those of the poorest fifth. Earlier in the last century, U.S. income inequality declined in the 1930s and 1940s, was stable for more than 30 years after World War II, but began rising again in the late 1970s. In fact, the distribution of income in the United States has become more unequal since 1980, rising to a level that has made it a significant political issue.

We can visualize income inequality with the *Lorenz curve* as shown in **Figure 6.5-4**. The **Lorenz curve** indicates the percentage of all income received by the poorest members of the population, starting from the poorest 0% who receive 0% of the income and ending with the poorest 100% who receive 100% of the income. If income were equally distributed—that is, if the poorest 20% of the population received 20% of the income, the poorest 40% of the population received 40% of the income, and so on—the Lorenz curve would coincide with the *line of equality*. However, from the data in Table 6.5-1, we know, for example, that the poorest 20% receive 3.0% of the income and the poorest 40% receive 3.0% + 8.1% = 11.1% of the income, so the Lorenz curve falls below the line of equality.

The **Lorenz curve** shows the percentage of all income received by the poorest members of the population, from the poorest 0% to the poorest 100%.

FIGURE 6.5-4 The Lorenz Curve

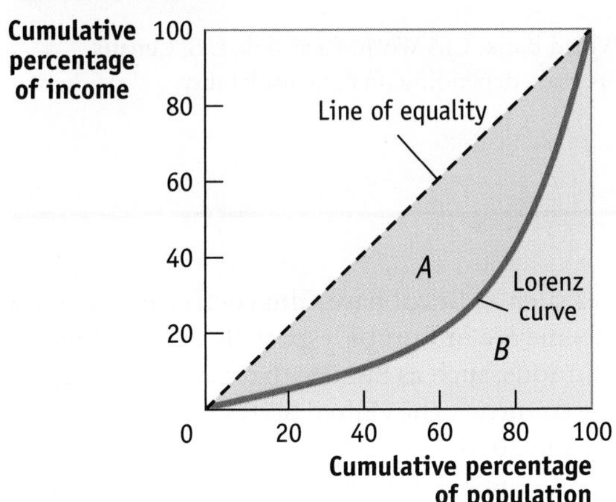

The Lorenz curve indicates the percentage of all income received by the poorest members of the population, starting from the poorest 0% who receive 0% of the income, and ending with the poorest 100% who receive 100% of the income. If everyone received the same income, the Lorenz curve would follow the line of equality. Income inequality causes the Lorenz curve to fall below the line of equality. The Gini coefficient, which summarizes a country's level of income inequality, is the ratio of area *A* to area *A* + *B*. The size of the Gini coefficient grows with the level of income inequality.

It's often convenient to have a single number that summarizes a country's level of income inequality. The **Gini coefficient**, the most widely used measure of inequality, is the ratio of area *A* in Figure 6.5-4, between the line of equality and the Lorenz curve, to area *A* + *B*, below the line of equality. So we have

The **Gini coefficient** is a number that summarizes a country's level of income inequality based on how unequally income is distributed.

$$\text{Gini coefficient} = \frac{A}{(A+B)}$$

A country with a perfectly equal distribution of income would have a Gini coefficient of 0, because the Lorenz curve would follow the line of equality, and area *A* would be zero. At the other extreme, the highest possible value for the Gini coefficient is 1—the level it would attain if all of a country's income went to just one person. In that case, area *A* would equal area *A* + *B*, because the Lorenz curve would lie along the horizontal axis until the richest person was included, at which point it would jump up to a height of 100%.

The Gini coefficient is useful for comparisons of income inequality across locations or time periods. For example, **Figure 6.5-5** assembles estimates of the Gini coefficient from the past decade for many of the world's countries. A few countries in Africa have Gini coefficients around 0.6. Elsewhere, the highest levels of income inequality are

FIGURE 6.5-5 Income Inequality Around the World

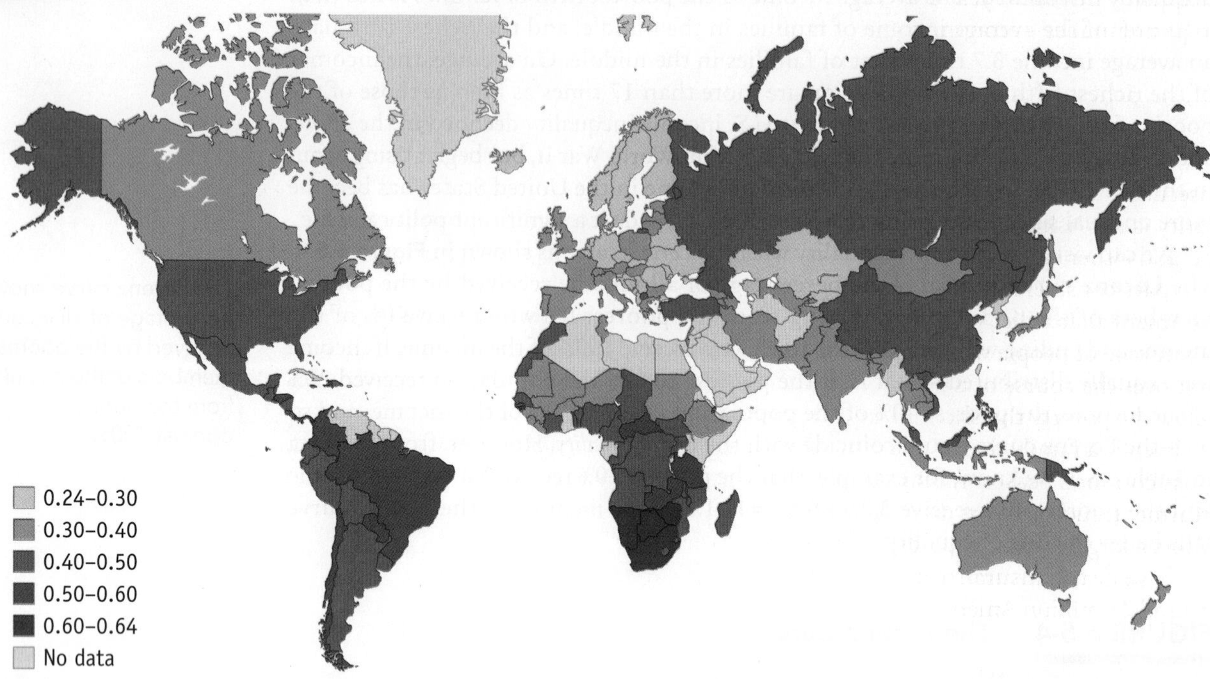

The highest levels of income inequality are found in Africa and Latin America. The most equal distributions of income are in Europe, especially in Scandinavia. Compared to other wealthy countries, the United States, with a Gini coefficient of 0.489 in 2020, has unusually high inequality.

Data Sources: World Bank, CIA World Factbook, U.S. Census Bureau, various years depending on data availability.

> **AP® ECON TIP**
>
> The College Board's *AP® Microeconomics Course and Exam Description* includes the Lorenz curve and the Gini coefficient among the "essential knowledge" for you to obtain, but says you will not need to draw the Lorenz curve or calculate Gini coefficients for the AP® exam. Instead, you should be prepared to interpret a Lorenz curve or Gini coefficient that is provided.

found in Latin America, where countries such as Brazil have Gini coefficients around 0.5. The most equal distributions of income are in Europe, especially in Scandinavia; countries with very equal income distributions, such as Sweden, have Gini coefficients around 0.25. Compared to other wealthy countries, the United States has high income inequality, with a Gini coefficient of 0.489 in 2020.

How serious an issue is income inequality? In a direct sense, high income inequality means that some people don't share in a nation's overall prosperity. As we've seen, rising inequality explains how it's possible that the U.S. poverty rate has failed to fall for the past several decades even though the country as a whole has become considerably richer. Also, extreme inequality, as found in Latin America, is often associated with political instability, because of tension between a wealthy minority and the rest of the population.

It's important to realize, however, that the data shown in Table 6.5-1 overstate the true degree of inequality in the United States among other countries, for several reasons. One is that the data represent a snapshot for a single year, whereas the incomes of many individual families fluctuate over time. That is, many of those near the bottom in any given year are having an unusually bad year, and many of those at the top are having an unusually good one. Over time, their incomes will revert to a more normal level. So a table showing average incomes within quintiles over a longer period, such as a decade, would not show as much inequality. Also, a family's income tends to vary over its life cycle: most people earn considerably less in their early working years than they will later in life, and then experience a considerable drop in income when they retire. Consequently, the numbers in Table 6.5-1, which combine young workers, mature workers, and retirees, show more inequality than would a table that compares families of similar ages.

Despite these qualifications, there is a considerable amount of genuine inequality in the United States. Moreover, the fact that families' incomes fluctuate from year to year isn't entirely good news. Measures of inequality in a given year *do* overstate true inequality. But those year-to-year fluctuations are part of a problem that worries even affluent families—economic insecurity.

Economic Insecurity

The rationale for the welfare state rests in part on the benefits of reducing economic insecurity, which afflicts even relatively well-off families. One source of economic insecurity is the risk of a sudden loss of income, as occurs when a family member loses a job and either spends an extended period without work or is forced to take a new job that pays considerably less. In a given year, according to recent estimates, about one in six American families will see their income cut in half. Related estimates show that the percentage of people who find themselves below the poverty threshold for at least one year over the course of a decade is several times higher than the percentage of people below the poverty threshold in any given year.

Even if a family doesn't face a loss in income, it can face a surge in expenses. The most common reason for such surges is a medical problem that requires expensive treatment, such as heart disease or cancer. Many Americans have health insurance that covers a large share of their expenses in such cases, but a substantial number either do not have health insurance or rely on insurance provided by the government. In 2021, around 31 million Americans were uninsured.

U.S. Antipoverty Programs

U.S. antipoverty programs include three large programs—Social Security, Medicare, and Medicaid—several other fairly big programs, including Temporary Assistance for Needy Families, the Supplemental Nutrition Assistance Program, and the Earned Income Tax Credit, and a number of smaller programs. **Table 6.5-2** shows one useful way to categorize these programs, along with the amount spent on each listed program in the most recent year available (2020 or 2021), not including program enhancements for the COVID pandemic.

Table 6.5-2 Major U.S. Welfare State Programs, 2020/2021

	Monetary transfers	In-kind
Means-tested	Temporary Assistance for Needy Families: $18 billion	Supplemental Nutrition Assistance Program: $113 billion
	Supplemental Security Income: $60 billion	Medicaid: $662 billion
	Earned Income Tax Credit: $73 billion	
Not means-tested	Social Security: $991 billion Unemployment insurance: $144 billion	Medicare: $776 billion

Data Source: Department of Labor, Bureau of Economic Analysis, Department of Health & Human Services, Congressional Joint Committee on Taxation.

First, the table distinguishes between programs that are **means-tested** and those that are not. In means-tested programs, benefits are available only to families or individuals whose income and/or wealth falls below some minimum. So means-tested programs are antipoverty programs designed to help only those with low incomes. By contrast, non-means-tested programs provide their benefits to everyone, although, as we'll see, in practice they tend to reduce income inequality by increasing the incomes of the lowest-income households by a larger proportion than the incomes of the wealthiest ones.

A **means-tested** program is available only to individuals or families whose incomes fall below a certain level.

Second, the table distinguishes between programs that provide monetary transfers that beneficiaries can spend as they choose and those that provide **in-kind benefits**,

An **in-kind benefit** is a benefit given in the form of goods or services.

which are given in the form of goods or services rather than money. As the numbers suggest, in-kind benefits are dominated by Medicare and Medicaid, which pay for health care.

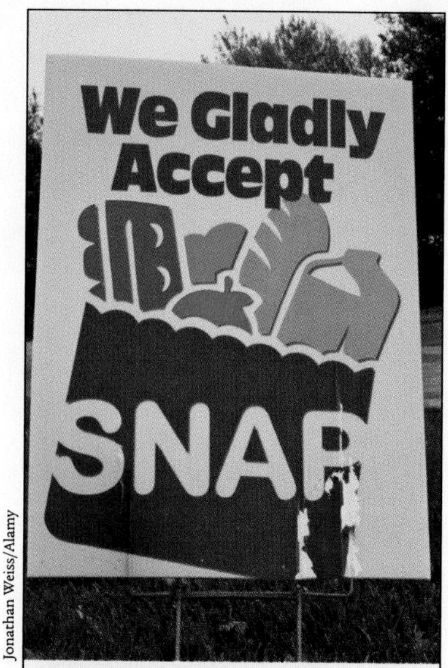

Jonathan Weiss/Alamy

The Supplemental Nutrition Assistance Program helps those with low incomes put food on the table. Purchases are made using an electronic benefits transfer card that works like a debit card but can be used only to purchase food.

A **negative income tax** is a program that supplements the income of low-income workers.

Means-Tested Programs

When people use the term *welfare*, they're often referring to monetary aid to low-income families. The main source of such monetary aid in the United States is Temporary Assistance for Needy Families, or TANF. This program does not aid everyone whose income falls below a certain minimum; it is available only to low-income families with children, and only for a limited period of time.

TANF was introduced in the 1990s to replace a highly controversial program known as Aid to Families with Dependent Children, or AFDC. The older program was widely accused of creating perverse incentives for low-income families, including encouraging family breakup. Partly as a result of the change in programs, the benefits of modern "welfare" are considerably less generous than those available a generation ago, once the data are adjusted for inflation. Also, TANF contains time limits, so welfare recipients – even single parents – cannot become dependent on it for long periods of time. As you can see from Table 6.5-2, TANF is a relatively small part of the modern U.S. welfare state.

Other means-tested programs, though more expensive, are less controversial. The Supplemental Security Income program aids disabled Americans who are unable to work and have no other source of income. The Supplemental Nutrition Assistance Program (SNAP, formerly known as the Food Stamp Program) helps low-income families and individuals to buy food staples.

Finally, economists use the term **negative income tax** for a program that supplements the earnings of low-income workers. For example, in the United States, the Earned Income Tax Credit (EITC) provides additional income to millions of workers. It has become more generous as traditional welfare has become less generous. As an incentive to work, only workers who earn income are eligible for the EITC. And as an incentive to work more, over a certain range of incomes, the more a worker earns, the higher the amount of EITC received. That is, the EITC acts as a negative income tax for low-wage workers. In 2021, married workers with three or more children earning less than $57,414 per year received EITC payments of up to $6,728. Payments were lower for workers with fewer children, and the earnings threshold was lower for single workers.

Social Security and Unemployment Insurance

Social Security, the largest program in the U.S. welfare state, is a non-means-tested program that guarantees retirement income to qualifying older Americans. It also provides benefits to workers who become disabled and "survivor benefits" to family members of workers who die. Social Security is supported by a dedicated tax on wages: the Social Security portion of the payroll tax pays for Social Security benefits. The benefits workers receive on retirement depend on their taxable earnings during their working years: the more you earn up to the maximum amount subject to Social Security taxes ($147,000 in 2022), the more you receive in retirement. However, benefits are not strictly proportional to earnings. High earners receive more benefits than low earners, but with a sliding scale that makes the program relatively generous for low earners.

Because most senior citizens don't receive pensions from their former employers, and most can't live off the income from their assets, Social Security benefits are a critical source of income. About half of Americans 65 and older rely on Social Security for at least half their income, and one in five of those 65 or older rely on Social Security for 90% or more of their income.

Unemployment insurance is a safety net for workers who lose their jobs. It provides them with around 40% of their previous salary until they find a new job or until 26 weeks have passed, whichever comes first. This period is sometimes extended when the economy is in a slump, as occurred during the COVID pandemic. Unemployment insurance is financed by a tax on employers.

The Debate over Income Redistribution

The goals of income redistribution seem laudable: to help the poor, protect everyone from financial risk, and ensure that people can afford essential health care. But there is an intense debate over how large the antipoverty programs should be, a debate that partly reflects differences in philosophy but also reflects concern about the possibly counterproductive effects of antipoverty programs. Disputes about the role of government in income redistribution are also one of the defining issues of modern politics.

Can economic analysis help resolve this political conflict? Only up to a point.

Some of the political controversy over the welfare state involves differences in opinion about how programs that reduce economic inequality affect incentives to work. If you believe that the disincentive effects of generous benefits and high taxes are very large, you're likely to look less favorably on welfare state programs than if you believe they're fairly small. Economic analysis can provide information on the influence of particular welfare and tax programs and has guided the redesign of such programs to improve work incentives.

To an important extent, however, differences of opinion on income redistribution reflect differences in values and philosophy. And those are differences economics can't resolve.

Adventures in AP® Economics

Watch the video: ***The Gini Coefficient and the Lorenz Curve***

Module 6.5 Review

Check Your Understanding

1. Recall that the poverty threshold is not adjusted to reflect changes in the standard of living. As a result, is the poverty threshold a relative or an absolute measure of poverty? That is, does it define poverty according to someone's wealth relative to others or according to some fixed measure that doesn't change over time? Explain.
2. Suppose that the incomes of members of an economy become more similar.
   a. Will the Lorenz curve move upward and to the right, upward and to the left, or downward and to the left?
   b. Will the area labeled *A* in Figure 6.5-4 become larger, become smaller, or remain the same?
   c. Will the area labeled *B* in Figure 6.5-4 become larger, become smaller, or remain the same?
   d. Will the Gini coefficient become larger, become smaller, or remain the same?

Tackle the AP® Test: Multiple-Choice Questions

1. If one person received all of the income in an economy, the Lorenz curve would
   a. rise steadily until the middle of the graph, and then fall.
   b. be upward-sloping.
   c. be downward-sloping.
   d. be vertical on the left side of the graph.
   e. lie along the horizontal axis except at the far right side of the graph.
2. If a country has a perfectly equal distribution of income, its Gini coefficient equals
   a. 0.
   b. 1.
   c. 10.
   d. 50.
   e. 100.
3. Compensating differentials mean that which of the following leads to higher wages for some jobs?
   a. danger
   b. discrimination
   c. government regulations
   d. market power
   e. a surplus of labor
4. Which of the following is a result of efficiency wages?
   a. compensating differentials
   b. greater worker loyalty
   c. shortages of labor
   d. discrimination
   e. a lack of motivation among workers

5. Which of the following statements regarding the marginal productivity theory of income distribution is correct?
   a. Each worker should earn a wage based on his or her marginal productivity.
   b. The wage rate should equal the rental rate for capital.
   c. Workers with higher marginal products always receive a higher wage than workers with lower marginal products.
   d. In perfectly competitive labor markets, each factor is paid the equilibrium marginal revenue product of that factor.
   e. The factor distribution of income is morally justified.

6. Which of the following statements about human capital is true?
   a. Human capital is another name for social capital.
   b. Human capital is found to have an insignificant influence on economic inequality.
   c. Experience is a source of human capital.
   d. There is general consensus that earnings differences arising from differences in human capital are fair.
   e. Human capital is the money humans hold in savings accounts.

7. Discrimination is
   a. a natural consequence of market competition.
   b. more likely when there is a surplus of labor in a market.
   c. absent from today's labor markets.
   d. never institutionalized into government policy.
   e. less likely when a minimum wage is in place.

Tackle the AP® Test: Free-Response Questions

1. There are 100 households in the economy of Equalor. Initially, 99 of them have an income of $10,000 each, and one household has an income of $1,010,000.
   a. What is the median income in this economy? What is the mean income?

   Through its antipoverty programs, the government of Equalor now redistributes income: it collects $990,000 from the richest household and distributes it equally among the remaining 99 households.

   b. What is the median income in this economy now? What is the mean income? Which indicator (mean or median household income) is a better indicator of the typical Equalorian household's income?

Rubric for FRQ 1 (5 points)

1 point: Median income = $10,000
1 point: Mean income = $20,000
1 point: Median income = $20,000
1 point: Mean income = $20,000
1 point: Median household income

2. Identify and explain the most likely reason for the wage differences among similar workers in each of the following situations.
   a. Test pilots for new jet aircraft earn higher wages than airline pilots.
   b. College graduates usually have higher earnings in their first year on the job than workers without college degrees have in their first year on the job.
   c. Experienced AP® teachers command higher salaries than new AP® teachers for teaching the same class.
   (6 points)

UNIT 6

Review

Adventures in AP® Economics Videos

Mod 6.2: Externalities and Deadweight Loss
Mod 6.5: The Gini Coefficient and the Lorenz Curve

UNIT 6 Review Video

economics by example
Why Not Split the Check?

Module 6.1

1. The **marginal social cost** of something is the additional cost of that unit, including every cost it imposes on society. The additional benefit to society of another unit is the **marginal social benefit**. The level of any activity, such as production or pollution, is **socially efficient** if the net gains for society are maximized by continuing the activity until the marginal social cost equals the marginal social benefit. The socially efficient output level is the best quantity of output for society, known as the **socially optimal quantity**. In the absence of government intervention, there is typically too much of things that affect people uninvolved in choosing the production levels. That is the case for pollution because polluters tend to consider only their benefit from polluting, not the costs imposed on others.
2. Markets can also fail to reach socially efficient outcomes due to **asymmetric information**, which exists when buyers and sellers don't hold the same information. The associated problem of *moral hazard* is the tendency for people with insurance to take fewer precautions. Another problem of asymmetric information is *adverse selection*, which occurs when firms such as insurance companies can't distinguish between high-cost customers and low-cost customers.

Module 6.2

3. The cost to society of pollution from a power plant is an example of an **external cost**; the benefit to neighbors of beautiful flowers planted in your yard is an example of an **external benefit**. External costs and benefits are jointly known as **externalities**, with external costs called **negative externalities** and external benefits called **positive externalities**. Externalities are among the sources of inefficiency in markets, which economists describe as **market failures**.
4. When the consumption of a good creates external benefits, the marginal social benefit of the good is equal to the **marginal private benefit** accruing to consumers plus its **marginal external benefit**. Without government intervention, the market produces too little of the good.
5. When there are external costs from production, the marginal social cost of a good exceeds its **marginal private cost** to producers, the difference being the **marginal external cost**. Without government action, the market produces too much of the good.
6. We model external costs and benefits differently depending on their source. A positive externality created by the consumption of a good or service is called a **positive consumption externality**. A positive externality arising from the production of a good or service is called a **positive production externality**. A negative externality brought about by the consumption of a good is called a **negative consumption externality**. When production causes a negative externality, it is called a **negative production externality**.
7. According to the **Coase theorem**, when externalities exist, bargaining will cause individuals to **internalize the externalities**, making government intervention unnecessary, as long as property rights are clearly defined and **transaction costs** – the costs of making a deal – are sufficiently low. However, in many cases transaction costs are too high to permit such deals.

Module 6.3

8. Goods may be classified according to whether or not they are **excludable**, meaning that people can be prevented from consuming them, and whether or not they are **rival in consumption**, meaning that one person's consumption of them affects another person's consumption of them.
9. Free markets can deliver efficient levels of production and consumption for **private goods**, which are both excludable and rival in consumption. When goods are **nonexcludable, nonrival in consumption**, or both, free markets cannot achieve efficient outcomes.

10. When goods are nonexcludable, there is a **free-rider problem**: consumers will not pay for the good, leading to inefficiently low production. When goods are nonrival in consumption, any positive price leads to inefficiently low consumption.

11. A **public good** is nonexcludable and nonrival in consumption. In most cases a public good must be supplied by the government. The marginal social benefit of a public good is equal to the sum of the marginal private benefits to each consumer. The efficient quantity of a public good is the quantity at which the marginal social benefit equals the marginal social cost of providing the good. As with a positive externality, the marginal social benefit is greater than any one individual's marginal private benefit, so no individual is willing to provide the efficient quantity.

12. One rationale for the presence of government is that it allows citizens to tax themselves in order to provide public goods. Governments use cost-benefit analysis to determine the efficient provision of a public good. Such analysis is difficult, however, because individuals have an incentive to overstate the good's value to them.

13. A **common resource** is rival in consumption but nonexcludable. It is subject to overconsumption, because an individual does not take into account the fact that their use depletes the amount available for others. This is similar to the problem with a negative externality: the marginal social cost of an individual's use of a common resource is always higher than his or her marginal private cost. Pigouvian taxes, the creation of a system of tradable licenses, and the assignment of property rights are possible solutions.

14. **Artificially scarce goods** are excludable but nonrival in consumption. Because no marginal cost arises from allowing another individual to consume the good, the efficient price is zero. A positive price compensates the producer for the cost of production but leads to inefficiently low consumption.

Module 6.4

15. Arthur Pigou proposed the general solution to externalities of imposing taxes or subsidies that cause buyers and sellers to internalize the effects of their decisions. The optimal **Pigouvian tax** on a good that causes negative externalities is equal to its marginal external cost. The optimal **Pigouvian subsidy** for a good that creates positive externalities is equal to the marginal external benefit. Pigouvian taxes and subsidies should lead to the socially optimal quantity of output in a well-functioning market.

16. Governments often deal with pollution by imposing **environmental standards**, an approach, economists argue, that is usually inefficient. Two efficient (cost-minimizing) methods for reducing pollution are emissions taxes and tradable emissions permits. These two methods also provide incentives for the creation and adoption of production technologies that cause less pollution.

17. The Sherman Act, the Clayton Act, and the Federal Trade Commission Act were the first major antitrust laws.

18. Antitrust laws and regulation are used to promote competition. When the industry in question is a natural monopoly, price regulation is used. **Marginal cost pricing** and **average cost pricing** are examples of price regulation used in the case of natural monopoly to allow efficiencies from large-scale production without allowing the deadweight loss that results from unregulated monopoly.

Module 6.5

19. Despite the fact that the **poverty threshold** is adjusted according to the cost of living but not according to the standard of living, and that the average income in the United States has risen substantially over the few decades, the **poverty rate**, the percentage of the population with an income below the poverty threshold, is no lower than it was 30 years ago. There are various causes of poverty: lack of education, the legacy of discrimination, and bad luck. The consequences of poverty are particularly harmful for children.

20. Large disparities in wages raise questions about the validity of the marginal productivity theory of income distribution. Many disparities can be explained by **compensating differentials** and by differences in talent, job experience, and human capital across workers. Market interference in the forms of **unions** and collective action by employers also creates wage disparities. Above-equilibrium wages known as **efficiency wages** result from employers' attempts to increase worker performance despite monitoring difficulties. Free markets tend to diminish discrimination, but discrimination remains a real source of wage disparity.

21. **Median household income**, the income of a family at the center of the income distribution, is a better indicator of the income of the typical household than **mean household income** because it is not distorted by the

inclusion of a small number of very wealthy households. The **Lorenz curve** indicates the percentage of all income received by the poorest members of the population, starting with the poorest 0% and ending with the poorest 100%. The **Gini coefficient**, a number that summarizes a country's level of income inequality, is used to compare income inequality across countries and across time.

22. **Means-tested** programs target aid to people whose income falls below a certain level. The major **in-kind benefits** programs are Medicare and Medicaid, which pay for medical care. Due to concerns about the effects on incentives to work and on family cohesion, aid to low-income families has become significantly less generous even as the **negative income tax** has become more generous. Social Security, the largest U.S. welfare program, has significantly reduced poverty among the elderly. Unemployment insurance is another key social insurance program.

Key Terms

Marginal social cost, p. 756
Marginal social benefit, p. 756
Socially efficient, p. 757
Socially optimal quantity, p. 757
Asymmetric information, p. 759
External cost, p. 762
External benefit, p. 762
Externalities, p. 762
Negative externalities, p. 762
Positive externalities, p. 762
Market failure, p. 762
Marginal private benefit, p. 763
Marginal external benefit, p. 763
Positive consumption externality, p. 763
Positive production externality, p. 763
Marginal private cost, p. 766
Marginal external cost, p. 766
Negative production externality, p. 766
Negative consumption externality, p. 766
Coase theorem, p. 768
Transaction costs, p. 768
Internalize the externalities, p. 769
Excludable, p. 772
Rival in consumption, p. 772
Private good, p. 772
Nonexcludable, p. 772
Nonrival in consumption, p. 772
Free-rider problem, p. 773
Public good, p. 774
Common resource, p. 778
Artificially scarce good, p. 780
Pigouvian taxes, p. 783
Pigouvian subsidy, p. 785
Environmental standards, p. 786
Marginal cost pricing, p. 791
Average cost pricing, p. 791
Poverty threshold, p. 795
Poverty rate, p. 795
Compensating differentials, p. 797
Unions, p. 798
Efficiency wages, p. 799
Mean household income, p. 802
Median household income, p. 802
Lorenz curve, p. 803
Gini coefficient, p. 803
Means-tested, p. 805
In-kind benefit, p. 805
Negative income tax, p. 806

AP® Exam Practice Questions

Multiple-Choice Questions

1. The poverty rate is
   a. the total number of people who earn less than $23,850 annually.
   b. the percentage of households that file for bankruptcy in a year.
   c. the percentage of the population that earns less than the poverty threshold.
   d. the percentage of the labor force that is unemployed at some point during a year.
   e. the percentage of the population that is in the lowest-income quintile.

2. Which of the following conditions contributes to the resolution of externality problems as suggested by the Coase theorem?
   a. It is awkward for the parties involved to approach each other about the problem.
   b. There is ambiguity about the legal rights of the parties involved.
   c. There are many parties involved.
   d. Transaction costs are high.
   e. The legal rights of the parties involved are clearly defined.

3. When the production of a good creates negative externalities, which of the following leads to the socially optimal quantity of output?
   a. a price ceiling set equal to the marginal external cost
   b. a price floor set equal to the marginal private cost
   c. a Pigouvian tax set equal to the marginal external cost
   d. a Pigouvian subsidy set equal to the marginal external cost
   e. average cost pricing

4. Which of the following policy changes would be the most likely to provide a gain in efficiency while achieving the same goal of reducing pollution?
   a. environmental standards instead of emissions taxes
   b. Pigouvian taxes instead of tradable emissions permits
   c. emissions taxes instead of Pigouvian taxes
   d. environmental standards instead of in-kind benefits
   e. tradable emissions permits instead of environmental standards

5. When the economy is producing the socially optimal amount of pollution, it is necessarily true that
   a. the marginal social benefit of pollution exceeds the marginal social cost.
   b. the marginal external cost of pollution equals the marginal external benefit.
   c. no pollution is being emitted.
   d. the marginal social benefit of pollution equals the marginal social cost.
   e. the marginal external cost of pollution is zero.

6. Market failure caused by a positive externality will involve
   a. deadweight loss.
   b. overconsumption.
   c. pollution.
   d. marginal external costs.
   e. taxation.

The graph below shows the marginal social cost, supply, and marginal social benefit in an industry that generates pollution. Use this graph to answer Questions 7 and 8.

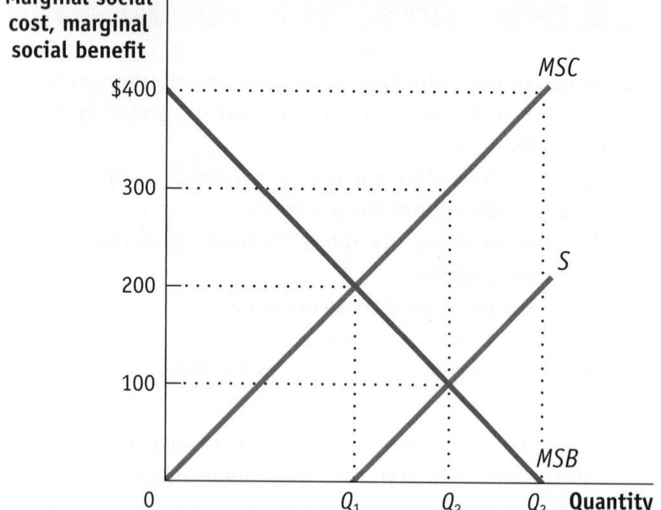

7. Suppose the industry is currently producing the quantity Q_2 and the price is \$100. If a Pigouvian tax equal to the marginal external cost is imposed, what will happen to society's total surplus and the deadweight loss in the industry?

	Total surplus	*Deadweight loss*
a.	decrease	stay the same
b.	increase	decrease
c.	increase	increase
d.	decrease	decrease
e.	increase	stay the same

8. The marginal social cost (*MSC*) and the marginal external cost (*MEC*) at the socially optimal equilibrium would be

	MSC	*MEC*
a.	\$200	\$200
b.	\$100	\$0
c.	\$200	\$100
d.	\$100	\$200
e.	\$200	\$0

9. When positive consumption externalities exist, the marginal external benefit is the difference between the
   a. marginal external cost and the marginal private benefit.
   b. marginal private benefit and the price.
   c. supply and the demand.
   d. marginal social benefit and the marginal private benefit.
   e. marginal social cost and the marginal private cost.

10. Which of the following curves is the same as the marginal social cost curve at every level of output in a perfectly competitive market with no externalities?
   a. marginal social benefit
   b. marginal external cost
   c. marginal external benefit
   d. marginal private benefit
   e. supply

11. Which of the following is accurate for goods provided by markets?
   a. Artificially scarce goods are likely to be produced in inefficiently large quantities.
   b. Common resources are likely to suffer from inefficiently low consumption levels.
   c. Private goods that are popular are likely to suffer from overconsumption problems.
   d. Public goods are likely to suffer from inefficiently low production.
   e. Artificially scarce goods are likely to suffer from the free-rider problem.

12. Which of the following is an example of market failure?
- **a.** Most people can't buy as many pairs of shoes as they would like.
- **b.** Most stores can't sell as much merchandise as they would like.
- **c.** Fishing in many waterways brings the quantity of fish below its socially optimal level.
- **d.** People typically pay more for a good than they would like to pay.
- **e.** Stores typically must charge a price that is less than they would like to charge.

13. Which of the following characteristics apply to private goods and common resources?

	Private goods	*Common resources*
a.	nonrival in consumption	nonexcludable
b.	rival in consumption	excludable
c.	nonexcludable	rival in consumption
d.	excludable	nonrival in consumption
e.	rival in consumption	nonexcludable

14. Based on economic analysis, why do so many people decide not to vote?
- **a.** The benefits of voting are nonexcludable.
- **b.** The costs of voting are nonrival.
- **c.** The benefits of voting are rival.
- **d.** The costs of voting are excludable.
- **e.** The benefits of voting outweigh the costs.

15. Which of the following statements regarding the passage of laws intended to promote competition in the marketplace is true?
- **a.** The Sherman Antitrust Act was intended to clarify the Clayton Act.
- **b.** The Clayton Antitrust Act made price discrimination illegal.
- **c.** The Federal Trade Commission Act made anticompetitive mergers illegal.
- **d.** The Sherman Antitrust Act outlawed price-fixing.
- **e.** The Clayton Antitrust Act made it legal for two boards of directors to share a director in common.

16. Which of the following statements regarding a natural monopoly is accurate?
- **a.** The FTC will try to break up the natural monopoly because it is inefficient.
- **b.** Marginal cost pricing would lead to an efficient outcome and monopoly profits.
- **c.** The cost of producing any given quantity of the good produced by the natural monopoly would increase if multiple firms produced it.
- **d.** Regulators require the natural monopoly to produce the quantity that equates marginal cost and marginal benefit.
- **e.** The information required for average cost pricing is readily available to regulators.

17. Which of the following welfare state programs provides means-tested, in-kind benefits?
- **a.** Temporary Assistance for Needy Families
- **b.** Medicaid
- **c.** the Earned Income Tax Credit
- **d.** Social Security
- **e.** Medicare

18. Which of the following is not a source of income inequality?
- **a.** compensating differentials
- **b.** discrimination
- **c.** market power
- **d.** progressive tax structures
- **e.** differences in human capital

19. A Gini coefficient of 0.5 would indicate
- **a.** that the richest 50% of the population receives all of the income.
- **b.** greater income inequality than a Gini coefficient of 0.4.
- **c.** that a country has perfect income equality.
- **d.** that a country has perfect income inequality.
- **e.** that the poorest 10% of the population receives half as much income as the richest 10% of the population.

20. An increase in which of the following practices would help to minimize wage inequality in labor markets?
- **a.** discrimination
- **b.** compensating differentials
- **c.** efficiency wages
- **d.** educational opportunities for the poor
- **e.** the wages paid to workers that produce a higher value of marginal product

21. Suppose the production of a smartphone imposes $10 worth of pollution costs on people unrelated to the sale or purchase of smartphones. This $10 is part of the smartphones'
- **a.** marginal private cost and marginal external cost.
- **b.** marginal private cost and marginal social cost.
- **c.** marginal external cost and marginal social cost.
- **d.** marginal social cost, but not marginal external cost.
- **e.** marginal external cost, but not marginal social cost.

22. If everyone in Equalville earns the same income, the Lorenz curve for Equalville is
- **a.** flat.
- **b.** circular.
- **c.** upward-sloping and then downward-sloping.
- **d.** straight and upward-sloping.
- **e.** curved and upward-sloping.

23. Markets for public goods generally experience problems with
a. overconsumption.
b. free riders.
c. consumers fighting over the use of products.
d. market power.
e. particularly high marginal external costs.

24. A Pigouvian subsidy is appropriate in a market with a significant
a. marginal external cost.
b. marginal external benefit.
c. difference between the marginal private cost and the marginal social cost.
d. difference between the equilibrium price and the marginal social cost.
e. Pigouvian tax.

25. Efficiency wages are wages that
a. are below the market equilibrium wage.
b. are above the market equilibrium wage.
c. never deviate from the market equilibrium wage.
d. result in lower levels of worker productivity.
e. necessitate greater amounts of worker supervision.

Free-Response Questions

1. Suppose there are 100 residents on the island of Sunshine. Whenever someone purchases a palm tree to plant on the island, everyone on the island receives the same benefits from the tree, which include beauty, shade, and erosion control. The table below shows the total social cost (which is also the total private cost) and the total private benefit received *per resident* depending on the quantity of palm trees purchased. Use this information to answer the questions that follow.

Quantity of palm trees	Total social cost (total private cost)	Total private benefit per resident
0	$0	$0
1	200	8
2	400	12
3	600	14
4	800	15

a. Does the purchase of palm trees create a negative consumption externality, a positive consumption externality, or no externality? Explain.
b. Draw a graph that depicts the marginal social cost and the marginal social benefit of palm trees.
c. What quantity of palm trees would be purchased if they were sold in a private market? Explain.
d. What is the socially optimal quantity of palm trees? Explain.
e. In this situation, are palm trees a private good, a public good, or a common resource?
f. What could be an appropriate governmental policy response to this situation? Explain. **(10 points)**

2. Suppose Dan and Ali are the only residents of Parkland. Their town can have up to 10 park benches, which are nonrival and nonexcludable. Dan would pay up to $900 for the first bench, $800 for the second bench, and $100 less for each additional bench, down to $0 for the tenth bench. Ali would pay up to $300 for each bench up to 10.
a. Are park benches in Parkland a private good, a public good, or a common resource? Explain.
b. Draw and label the individual demand curves for Dan and Ali.
c. Draw and label the social marginal benefit curve for benches in Parkland.
d. If benches cost $950 each, what is the socially optimal quantity of benches?
e. Why is it unlikely that a private bench market will sell the socially optimal quantity of benches?
f. What is a common solution for achieving the socially optimal quantity in situations like this? **(7 points)**

3. The country of Nina has a Gini coefficient of 0. The country of Pinta has a Gini coefficient of 1.
a. On a correctly labeled graph, draw the Lorenz curve for Nina. (You won't have to draw a Lorenz curve on the AP® exam, but try this one; it's simple and instructive.)
b. On your graph, draw any one point that lies on the Lorenz curve for Pinta and label it *X*.
c. The country of Santa Maria has a Gini coefficient of 0.5, and wants to enact tax legislation to move its Lorenz curve closer to that of Nina. Should Santa Maria adopt a tax that is regressive, progressive, or proportional? Explain. **(5 points)**

AP® Microeconomics Exam

Practice Test

Multiple-Choice Questions

1. The study of microeconomics includes measuring the
- **a.** profit of a corporation.
- **b.** national output level.
- **c.** size of the money supply.
- **d.** overall level of prices.
- **e.** number of people unemployed in the economy.

2. Economic models are
- **a.** exact replicas of the real world using the concept of *ceteris paribus*.
- **b.** exact replicas of the real world using the concept of *laissez-faire*.
- **c.** simplifications of the real world using the concept of *laissez-faire*.
- **d.** simplifications of the real world using the concept of *ceteris paribus*.
- **e.** simplifications of the real world using the concept of *caveat emptor*.

3. What does a straight production possibilities curve indicate?
- **a.** no specialization of resources and increasing opportunity costs
- **b.** no specialization of resources and decreasing opportunity costs
- **c.** no specialization of resources and constant opportunity costs
- **d.** specialization of resources and decreasing opportunity costs
- **e.** specialization of resources and constant opportunity costs

4. Due to shortcomings in pure forms of command and market economies, most counties today have
- **a.** traditional economies.
- **b.** socialist economies.
- **c.** barter economies.
- **d.** communist economies.
- **e.** mixed economies.

5. Optimal cost-benefit analysis does not factor in costs that are
- **a.** variable.
- **b.** marginal.
- **c.** sunk.
- **d.** explicit.
- **e.** implicit.

6. Which of the following would cause an increase in the quantity demanded of tea?
- **a.** an increase in the supply of coffee, a substitute
- **b.** a decrease in the price of coffee, a substitute
- **c.** a decrease in the price of tea
- **d.** a decrease in the supply of sugar, a complement
- **e.** an increase in the price of sugar, a complement

7. Which of the following would occur in the market for grapefruit if an increase in popularity caused the price of grapefruit to rise?
- **a.** a shift of the demand curve to the left
- **b.** a shift of the supply curve to the right
- **c.** a movement down along the supply curve
- **d.** a movement up along the supply curve
- **e.** a movement down along the demand curve

8. Assuming relatively elastic supply and demand curves, which of the following would occur if the market quantity were to fall below the equilibrium quantity due to a quota in a competitive market?
- **a.** a deadweight loss
- **b.** a market surplus
- **c.** a violation of the law of demand
- **d.** a less elastic demand
- **e.** the development of a horizontal demand curve

9. A new price ceiling set below the equilibrium price in a competitive market with relatively elastic supply and demand would result in which of the following?
- **a.** an increase in the quantity demanded and an increase in the quantity supplied
- **b.** an increase in the quantity demanded and no change in the quantity supplied
- **c.** an increase in the quantity demanded and a decrease in the quantity supplied
- **d.** a decrease in the quantity demanded and an increase in the quantity supplied
- **e.** a decrease in the quantity demanded and no change in the quantity supplied

10. Two goods are complements in consumption if the associated
- **a.** income elasticity of demand is positive.
- **b.** income elasticity of demand is negative.
- **c.** cross-price elasticity of demand is positive.
- **d.** cross-price elasticity of demand is negative.
- **e.** price elasticity of demand is greater than one.

Refer to the table provided to respond to Questions 11 and 12. The numbers in the table represent the numbers of solar panels or bicycles that can be produced by the countries of Alpha and Omega each day if they completely specialize in one good or the other using the same resources. Assume that each country faces constant opportunity costs.

	Quantity of solar panels	Quantity of bicycles
Alpha	12	24
Omega	5	15

11. What do the numbers in the table indicate about Omega?
- **a.** It has a comparative advantage in the production of bicycles.
- **b.** It has a comparative advantage in the production of solar panels.
- **c.** The opportunity cost of producing 1 solar panel is ⅓ of a bicycle.
- **d.** It should focus its effort on the production of solar panels only.
- **e.** Because Omega does not have an absolute advantage in producing either good, Omega cannot carry out mutually beneficial trade with Alpha.

12. If something changed in Omega that allowed it to make up to 15 solar panels or up to 45 bicycles,
- **a.** Omega's opportunity cost of producing 1 bicycle would be 3 solar panels.
- **b.** Omega would have the comparative advantage in the production of solar panels.
- **c.** Omega would not trade with Alpha, since Omega now has an absolute advantage in producing both goods.
- **d.** there would be no change in the good in which Omega should specialize in order to maximize the gains from trade.
- **e.** Omega would be willing to trade 4 bicycles for 1 solar panel.

13. Which of the following is true when marginal product is decreasing?
- **a.** Average product is necessarily decreasing.
- **b.** Average product is necessarily increasing.
- **c.** Average product could be increasing or decreasing.
- **d.** Total cost is increasing at a decreasing rate.
- **e.** Marginal cost is decreasing.

14. For what type of good does a decrease in income lead to an increase in demand?
- **a.** a normal good
- **b.** an inferior good
- **c.** a good with price-elastic demand
- **d.** a good with price-inelastic demand
- **e.** a good with price-unit-elastic demand

15. Which of the following curves always falls as output increases?
- **a.** the marginal cost curve
- **b.** the average variable cost curve
- **c.** the average total cost curve
- **d.** the average fixed cost curve
- **e.** the total fixed cost curve

16. If a firm's long-run average total cost falls as output rises, the firm is experiencing
- **a.** economies of scale.
- **b.** economies of scope.
- **c.** diseconomies of scale.
- **d.** increasing marginal returns.
- **e.** diminishing marginal returns.

17. If a firm experiencing decreasing returns to scale doubles all of its inputs, which of the following will occur?
- **a.** Output will decrease.
- **b.** Output will less than double.
- **c.** Output will more than double.
- **d.** Total cost will decrease.
- **e.** Fixed cost will decrease.

18. What is necessarily true about a perfectly competitive market?
- **a.** In the long run, economic profits are positive.
- **b.** In the short run, there are no fixed costs.
- **c.** Productive efficiency will be achieved in the short run.
- **d.** Allocative efficiency is not achieved in the short run.
- **e.** Productive efficiency will be achieved in the long run.

19. What is one way to distinguish implicit costs from explicit costs?
- **a.** Checks are written only for explicit costs.
- **b.** Checks are written only for implicit costs.
- **c.** All costs are implicit, but some are also explicit.
- **d.** All costs are explicit, but some are also implicit.
- **e.** All opportunity costs are implicit.

20. Having a minimum efficient scale that is relatively small contributes to the likelihood that a market will be
- **a.** perfectly competitive.
- **b.** a monopoly.
- **c.** an oligopoly.
- **d.** a monopsony.
- **e.** highly concentrated.

21. Which two market structures are characterized by free entry into and exit from the industry in the long run?
- **a.** monopolistic competition and monopoly
- **b.** monopolistic competition and perfect competition
- **c.** monopolistic competition and oligopoly
- **d.** oligopoly and perfect competition
- **e.** monopoly and perfect competition

22. If supply increases and the demand curve is downward-sloping, which of the following is necessarily true?
   a. consumer surplus increases
   b. consumer surplus decreases
   c. consumer surplus is unaffected
   d. producer surplus is unaffected
   e. producer surplus increases

23. Firms generally produce the quantity that equates marginal revenue with
   a. price, because that minimizes average total cost.
   b. average total cost, because that minimizes total cost.
   c. average variable cost, because that stabilizes costs.
   d. marginal cost, because that minimizes average total cost.
   e. marginal cost, because that maximizes profit or minimizes loss.

24. For a competitive firm, if marginal revenue exceeds marginal cost at the current level of output and the firm is currently earning economic losses, what could the firm certainly do?
   a. increase output to ensure economic profits
   b. decrease output to ensure economic profits
   c. increase output to reduce economic losses
   d. decrease output to reduce economic losses
   e. shut down to reduce economic losses

Use the following figure to answer Question 25.

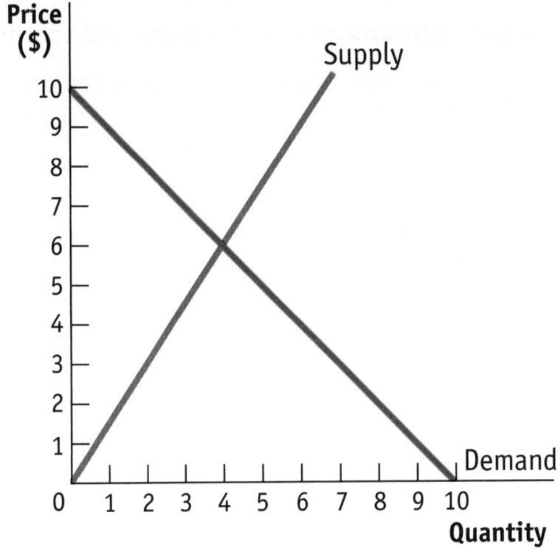

25. At the equilibrium price, producer surplus is
   a. $6.
   b. $8.
   c. $12.
   d. $16.
   e. $24.

26. The price below which a firm in a perfectly competitive industry will exit the market in the long run is determined by the minimum
   a. marginal cost.
   b. average total cost.
   c. total cost.
   d. total variable cost.
   e. average fixed cost.

27. To maximize utility, consumers should allocate their income to equate the
   a. marginal utility received from each good.
   b. marginal utility per dollar spent on each good.
   c. total utility received from each good.
   d. quantity purchased of each good.
   e. dollars spent on each good.

28. In a perfectly competitive industry, the long-run supply curve is flatter and more elastic than the short-run supply curve due to
   a. the availability of more substitutes.
   b. the availability of more complements.
   c. economies of scale.
   d. diseconomies of scale.
   e. easy exit and entry of firms.

29. Jennifer owns a hot dog vending business. Each month she spends $1,000 on fixed capital and $2,000 on buns, hot dogs, and supplies. Jennifer's monthly total revenue is $3,000. In order to start this business, Jennifer had to quit her teaching job, in which she earned $2,500 per month and had no work-related expenses. Jennifer earns
   a. an accounting profit of $5,500.
   b. an accounting profit of $3,000.
   c. a normal profit.
   d. an economic profit of $0.
   e. an economic profit of –$2,500.

30. When marginal revenue is positive and decreasing for a monopolist, what is happening to total revenue?
   a. It is increasing at an increasing rate.
   b. It is decreasing at the same rate as marginal revenue.
   c. It is decreasing faster than marginal revenue.
   d. It is increasing at a decreasing rate.
   e. It is decreasing slower than marginal revenue.

31. What type of tax would collect $1,000 from a person with a $10,000 income, $2,000 from a person with a $20,000 income, and $4,000 from a person with a $40,000 income?
   a. a progressive tax
   b. a proportional tax
   c. a regressive tax
   d. an excise tax
   e. a tax incidence

32. What would happen to the consumer surplus that was lost if a perfectly competitive market became a monopoly facing the same demand and costs?
   a. All of it would be gained by the monopolist.
   b. Some of it would be gained by the monopolist, and the rest would be part of the deadweight loss.
   c. It would all be part of the deadweight loss.
   d. It would be paid to the government in taxes.
   e. It would be transferred to the Federal Trade Commission.

33. A distinguishing characteristic of a natural monopoly, assuming it is capable of earning positive economic profit, is that
  a. profit is maximized at the output level that equates marginal revenue and marginal cost.
  b. profit is maximized at the output level that equates price and marginal cost.
  c. the average total cost curve crosses the demand curve twice in the economies of scale region.
  d. the average total cost curve crosses the demand curve in the diseconomies of scale region.
  e. the marginal cost curve crosses the average total cost curve at the minimum point of the average total cost curve.

34. Which of the following is true of a natural monopoly? If regulators
  a. set a price ceiling equal to marginal cost, firms will not be willing to produce in the long run unless they are subsidized.
  b. set a price ceiling equal to average total cost, there will be no deadweight loss.
  c. set a price ceiling above the average total cost, the firm will not be able to make a profit.
  d. choose not to set a price ceiling, the firm will be a price-taker and the market will determine the price.
  e. split the monopolist into several smaller firms, the average total cost will decrease.

35. Open-access forests are a common resource that tends to be overconsumed (logged excessively) because they are
  a. nonexcludable and nonrival.
  b. excludable and nonrival.
  c. public goods.
  d. nonexcludable and rival.
  e. excludable and rival.

36. Which of the following is a result of perfect price discrimination?
  a. a gain in producer surplus
  b. a gain in consumer surplus
  c. less output overall
  d. marginal revenue less than price
  e. marginal revenue greater than price

37. An oligopoly is a market with
  a. only one firm.
  b. fewer firms than in a monopolistically competitive market, and the existence of interdependent firms.
  c. more firms than in a perfectly competitive market, and the existence of interdependent firms.
  d. more firms than in a monopoly, and the existence of independent firms.
  e. more firms than in a monopolistically competitive market, and the existence of independent firms.

38. The numbers in the following payoff matrix indicate profits for firms Alpha and Beta.

		Beta's Price Policy	
		High	Low
Alpha's Price Policy	High	$20, $20	$10, $30
	Low	$30, $10	$15, $15

Which of the following is true?
  a. Charging a high price is a dominant strategy for Alpha.
  b. Charging a high price is a dominant strategy for Beta.
  c. Beta will charge a high price if Alpha charges a high price.
  d. Alpha will charge a high price if Beta charges a high price.
  e. Charging a low price is a dominant strategy for Alpha.

39. In the long run, a monopolistically competitive firm will earn
  a. positive or negative economic profit, depending on the situation.
  b. positive economic profit due to barriers to entry.
  c. normal profit.
  d. positive economic profit due to a differentiated product.
  e. positive economic profit due to price discrimination.

40. If a country had perfect income equality, its Lorenz curve would be
  a. U-shaped.
  b. L-shaped.
  c. V-shaped.
  d. a straight line.
  e. curved and downward-sloping.

41. The labor demand curve for a firm hiring in a perfectly competitive labor market is
  a. the firm's marginal revenue product curve.
  b. the firm's marginal product curve.
  c. horizontal.
  d. the firm's average product curve.
  e. the firm's marginal revenue curve.

42. Suppose Brenda's Boat Taxis rents capital in a perfectly competitive capital market. Brenda's Boat Taxis should rent more capital if which condition is true?
  a. The marginal revenue product of capital is equal to the rental rate.
  b. The average revenue product of capital is equal to the rental rate.
  c. The marginal revenue product of capital is less than the rental rate.
  d. The marginal revenue product of capital is greater than the rental rate.
  e. The average revenue product of capital is less than the rental rate.

Use the following per-day employment and output data for Lenny's Lattes to answer Questions 43 and 44.

Number of workers	Total number of lattes
0	0
1	10
2	30
3	60
4	100
5	125
6	140

43. If lattes sell in a perfectly competitive market for $4 each, what is the marginal revenue product of the third worker?
- **a.** $4
- **b.** $12
- **c.** $60
- **d.** $120
- **e.** $240

44. If lattes sell in a perfectly competitive market for $4 each and workers are paid $80 per day, how many workers should Lenny hire to maximize profit?
- **a.** 2
- **b.** 3
- **c.** 4
- **d.** 5
- **e.** 6

45. Which of the following is always horizontal?
- **a.** the demand curve facing a firm that sells its product in a perfectly competitive market
- **b.** the labor demand curve for a firm hiring in a perfectly competitive labor market
- **c.** the labor supply curve for a monopsony
- **d.** the demand curve for a monopoly
- **e.** the long-run industry supply curve in a goods market

46. If Keno's Cars is the only employer in a small town, that firm is a
- **a.** monopolist.
- **b.** monopolistic competitor.
- **c.** monopsonist.
- **d.** perfectly competitive firm.
- **e.** Keynesian.

47. The marginal factor cost curve of labor for a monopsonist is
- **a.** upward-sloping and above the supply curve at every quantity of labor beyond one.
- **b.** downward-sloping and above the supply curve at every quantity of labor beyond one.
- **c.** upward-sloping and below the supply curve at every quantity of labor beyond one.
- **d.** downward-sloping and below the supply curve at every quantity of labor beyond one.
- **e.** upward-sloping and coincident with the supply curve of labor.

48. A perfectly competitive firm's short-run supply curve
- **a.** does not exist.
- **b.** is perfectly elastic.
- **c.** is the same as the firm's marginal cost curve at every price.
- **d.** is that portion of the firm's marginal cost curve that lies above the *ATC* curve.
- **e.** is that portion of the firm's marginal cost curve that lies above the *AVC* curve.

49. For a market in an open economy with imports available at a constant world price, the imposition of a tariff will decrease the
- **a.** consumer surplus.
- **b.** producer surplus.
- **c.** deadweight loss.
- **d.** price paid in the domestic market.
- **e.** domestic supply.

50. To minimize the cost of producing a given quantity of output, a firm should
- **a.** equate the marginal product of capital per dollar spent on capital and the marginal product of labor per dollar spent on labor.
- **b.** equate the total amount spent on labor and the total amount spent on capital.
- **c.** make the marginal revenue product of capital per dollar spent on capital greater than the marginal revenue product of labor per dollar spent on labor.
- **d.** equate the marginal revenue product of capital and the marginal revenue product of labor.
- **e.** hire mostly the factor of production that has the lowest cost per unit of the factor.

51. Which of the following is likely to shift the labor demand curve but not the labor supply curve? A change in
- **a.** immigration rate.
- **b.** the education of citizens.
- **c.** the wealth held by households.
- **d.** the price of the product being made.
- **e.** social norms.

52. A market with external costs and no external benefits will do which of the following?
- **a.** produce too much output
- **b.** produce too little output
- **c.** have a price that is too high
- **d.** experience deadweight gains
- **e.** produce the socially optimal quantity

53. The deadweight loss caused by an excise tax
- **a.** consists of lost producer and consumer surplus.
- **b.** results in gains to consumers but losses to producers.
- **c.** results in gains to producers but losses to consumers.
- **d.** results from overproduction.
- **e.** results from externalities.

54. What is true if marginal social benefit exceeds marginal social costs at the market level of output?
   a. A negative externality exists, and the government could correct for it with a Pigouvian tax.
   b. A negative externality exists, and the government could correct for it with a Pigouvian subsidy.
   c. A positive externality exists, and the government could correct for it with a Pigouvian tax.
   d. A positive externality exists, and the government could correct for it with a Pigouvian subsidy.
   e. The market outcome is ideal, since there are positive marginal benefits.

55. What type of tax is the least likely to affect the profit-maximizing quantity of output for a firm?
   a. sales tax
   b. per-unit tax
   c. lump-sum tax
   d. excise tax
   e. Pigouvian tax

56. Company A and Company B are monopolistically competitive firms that make winter coats. If Company A adds fuzzy trim to its coats and Company B doesn't, then Company A is necessarily practicing
   a. price leadership.
   b. tit-for-tat strategy.
   c. product differentiation.
   d. tacit collusion.
   e. cartel behavior.

57. Income inequality decreases as the result of
   a. compensating wage differentials.
   b. progressive taxes.
   c. discrimination.
   d. differences in social capital.
   e. differences in human capital.

Use the graph provided to answer Questions 58 and 59.

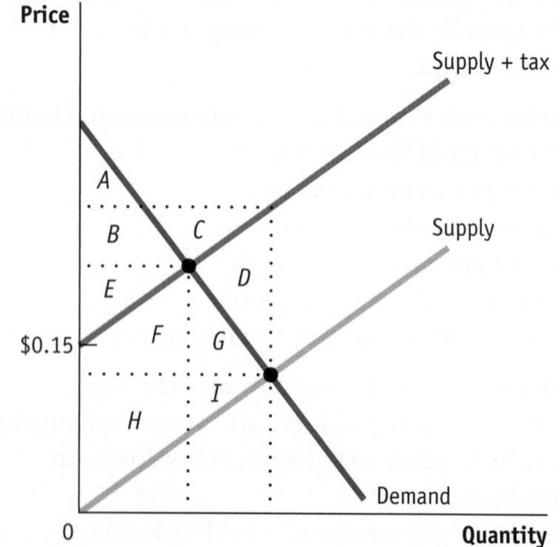

58. Suppose the peanut market is at equilibrium as shown in this graph. If an excise tax of $0.15 per unit is imposed on producers, the consumer surplus that would result after the imposition of the tax is represented by which area?
   a. *A, B, C, D, E, F, G*
   b. *A, B, C, D*
   c. *E, F, H*
   d. *A, B, E*
   e. *A, B*

59. What area represents the deadweight loss that would result from the imposition of the $0.15 per unit tax on producers?
   a. *A, B, E*
   b. *G, I*
   c. *C*
   d. *D*
   e. *F*

60. What is the term for a situation in which distorted incentives arise because an individual has private information about their own actions, but someone else bears the costs of a lack of care or effort?
   a. moral hazard
   b. adverse selection
   c. upper hand
   d. game theory
   e. prisoner's dilemma

Free-Response Questions

1. Patent Ted's Pharmaceutical Company is the only maker of a drug that cures laziness. The table below provides a portion of Patent Ted's demand schedule. Patent Ted's demand curve is linear.

Price	Quantity demanded
$101	0
100	1
51	50
50	51
1	100
0	101

   a. Draw Patent Ted's demand curve on a graph.
   b. Draw Patent Ted's marginal revenue curve on the graph for part a.
      i. What is the marginal revenue for the first unit?
      ii. What is the marginal revenue for the 51st unit?
   c. Label as *A* the point along the quantity axis at which the price elasticity of demand is 1.
   d. Each pill costs Patent Ted $10 to produce. Draw the company's marginal cost curve on the graph.
   e. On the graph, label the profit-maximizing price P^* and the profit-maximizing quantity Q^*.
   f. Suppose Patent Ted has no fixed cost. Completely shade in the area on the graph that represents profit.
   g. In a few years, the patent on these pills will expire and this market will become perfectly competitive. If there are no other changes related to the production or demand for these pills, what price will firms charge in the perfectly competitive market? Explain your answer. **(10 points)**

2. Suppose that Anya's Oregon Omelets uses both labor and capital such that the marginal product per hour of labor is 5 omelets and the marginal product per hour of capital is 15 omelets. The wage is $25 per hour, and the capital rents for $75 per hour.
   a. What should Anya do if she wants to minimize her cost at the current level of output? Explain.
   b. Now assume that the wage rate rises to $30 per hour while the marginal product of labor rises to 6 omelets and everything else remains the same. What should Anya do if she wants to minimize her cost? Explain.
   c. Using the data from part b and assuming Anya buys her labor in a perfectly competitive labor market, draw a correctly labeled graph of Anya's labor supply and labor demand. **(6 points)**

3. The country of MeTee has a perfectly competitive hot dog market with supply and demand curves as shown in the accompanying graph.

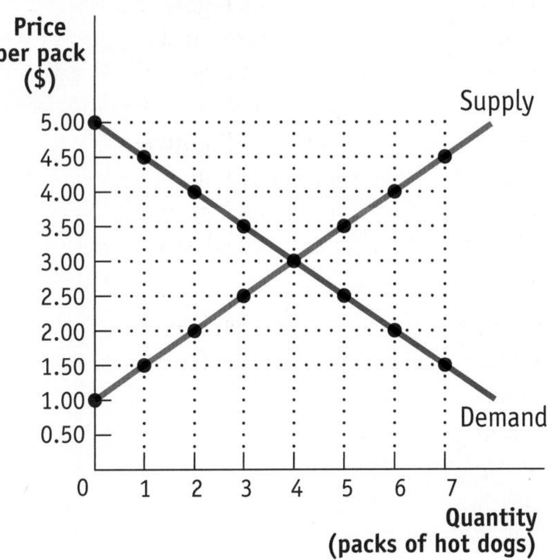

   a. If the government imposed a price ceiling of $3.50 per pack of hot dogs, would the quantity of hot dogs sold in the market increase, decrease, or stay the same? Explain your answer.
   b. Now suppose there is no price ceiling, but the government bans all hot dogs. Calculate the deadweight loss that results from this ban. Show your work.
   c. Now suppose that there is no price ceiling or ban, but that the government collects a $2.00 excise tax from consumers on each pack of hot dogs purchased. Indicate the values of each of the following:
      i. the consumer surplus
      ii. the total revenue received by sellers of hot dogs
      iii. the total tax revenue collected by the government of MeTee
   (6 points)

Micro Enrichment Modules

Hopefully this sampling of economics has kindled your interest in more than just the AP® exam content. Have you questioned the rationality of buyers or sellers? Enrichment Module C explains how economists deal with behavior that isn't so rational. If you've ever bought a used car, you know that even rational people sometimes don't have all the information they would like. Enrichment Module D explains how imperfect information affects markets and discusses related problems and remedies. In Enrichment Module E, you will learn how economists use indifference curves to illustrate preferences and model various aspects of consumer choice.

While these Modules cover material in greater depth than is expected for the current AP® exams, they provide interesting insights both for subsequent coursework and for sound economic decisions.

Behavioral Economics

In this Module, you will learn to:
- Identify barriers to rational decision making
- Discuss the role of psychology in consumer behavior
- Explain why assumptions of rationality are useful despite limits on the rationality of humans

Consumers and Rationality

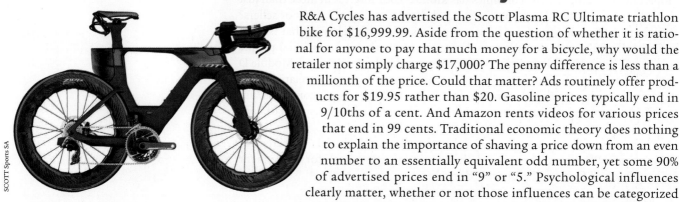

SCOTT Sports SA

R&A Cycles has advertised the Scott Plasma RC Ultimate triathlon bike for $16,999.99. Aside from the question of whether it is rational for anyone to pay that much money for a bicycle, why would the retailer not simply charge $17,000? The penny difference is less than a millionth of the price. Could that matter? Ads routinely offer products for $19.95 rather than $20. Gasoline prices typically end in 9/10ths of a cent. And Amazon rents videos for various prices that end in 99 cents. Traditional economic theory does nothing to explain the importance of shaving a price down from an even number to an essentially equivalent odd number, yet some 90% of advertised prices end in "9" or "5." Psychological influences clearly matter, whether or not those influences can be categorized as rational. A melding of psychology and economics, **behavioral economics** is the study of economic decision making as influenced by the limits of the human mind.

Behavioral economics is the study of economic decision making as influenced by the limits of the human mind.

Homo economicus ("economic man") is a fictional economic actor who makes self-interested, informed, rational judgments in pursuit of wealth and leisure.

Homo economicus

Economists have made great strides with models starring "economic man" or ***Homo economicus***, a fictional economic actor and amalgamation of all people, who makes self-interested, informed, rational judgments in pursuit of wealth and leisure. In neoclassical models, *Homo economicus* represents the typical member of society. *Homo economicus* is a reasonable depiction of the average economic decision maker in the many contexts in which variations in behaviors either average out across people or are unimportant. In those contexts, the neoclassical models form the basis for useful conclusions. For example, these models predict that people will buy more of a product when the price falls, work more when the wage rises, and prefer some money to none at all. In this Module, however, we'll explore challenges to the assumptions about *Homo economicus* and the implications of irrationality among economic actors.

Behavioral economics unveils *Homo economicus* and finds an individual who is sensitive, flawed, and biased in ways that can disrupt the efficient allocation of resources. Human decisions can go awry due to the scarcity of time, intelligence, and information. The importance of the psychological side of economic behavior is still controversial, but acceptance of the field of behavioral economics has grown considerably over the past four decades. Herbert Simon, Daniel Kahneman, and Richard Thaler won Nobel Prizes in economics in 1978, 2002, and 2017, respectively, for their research on behavioral economics. In addition, the *Journal of Behavioral Economics* was established in 1970. And a surge in popularity in the 1980s and 1990s led scholars at virtually every top economics department in North America to dive into the field of behavioral economics. Now it is your turn.

Homo misinformicus

There are differing schools of thought about the extent of information problems and behavioral anomalies. The work of neoclassical economists such as Milton Friedman, Arthur Pigou, and Gary Becker placed considerable reliance on *rational choice theory*, which holds that decision makers are able to compare all of their alternatives with full information about their choices. For example, based on this theory, one would predict that if R&A Cycles lowers the price of the Scott Plasma RC Ultimate bike from $16,999.99 down to $16,000.00, it will sell more bikes. The assumption is that consumers are aware of the product, its virtues, and the price change. However, unless you are a bicycle enthusiast, chances are that you did not know much about the Scott Plasma RC Ultimate before reading this Module.

In reality, information is imperfect, and consumers do not know every product's availability, quality, or price. The large amounts of money people pay for internet access, smartphones, and a college education exemplify the value placed on information. Yet the cost of perfect information is prohibitive — no one has the time or money to become all-knowing. The result is ill-informed behavior, such as people paying more than necessary for a Scott Plasma RC Ultimate because they are unaware of the deals that are available at particular bike shops.

Researchers in the field of behavioral economics study the rationality of market participants under realistic constraints on time, information, and intelligence. Because information takes time and sometimes money to obtain, it is appropriate to continue seeking information until the marginal benefit of doing so no longer exceeds the marginal cost. This is why rational people often act on incomplete information. For example, if you live in a large city, you wouldn't want to call every shoe store in town to check prices before buying a new pair of shoes. After you call a few stores, the likely savings from additional calls fall below the value of your time.

Many uses of information are not so rational. In defiance of rationality, individuals often respond to the way in which information is presented. For example, would a half-empty glass of soda pop sound as appealing to you as a half-full glass of soda pop? Psychologists Daniel Kahneman and Amos Tversky found that respondents who were presented with four identical outcomes with differing descriptions overwhelmingly preferred a disease-control program that would save 200 out of 600 people to a program that would allow 400 out of 600 people to die. In other words, it is perceived as better to have one-third of a population live than to have two-thirds of a population die.

Helen Sessions/Alamy

It takes time to acquire information about the prices and products available to consumers; at some point, the marginal cost of information gathering exceeds the marginal benefit. So shoppers typically buy shoes and other goods on the basis of incomplete information.

Descriptions also drive perceptions of products and policies. For example, Chocolate Fudge Brownie ice cream is one of Ben and Jerry's top sellers, whereas Bovinity Divinity and Dastardly Mash, though similarly chewy and chocolaty, were discontinued for lack of interest. Similarly, policies that environmentalists say would weaken current standards have gained steam due to appealing names such as the Clear Skies Initiative and the Healthy Forests Initiative. And, while the prospect of higher wages motivates employees to work harder, so does the prospect of loftier job titles, such as vice president or office manager.

Uninformed consumers may buy too much of products that have health risks, such as junk food; pay more for products or services than they are worth, such as counterfeit watches; or purchase products that are inferior in price or quality to those available elsewhere, such as full-priced triathlon bicycles. Uninformed managers face the same problems when purchasing from vendors. Incomplete information and irrational behavior stab at the heart of *Homo economicus*. With perfect information and rationality at the foundation of efficient decision making in many economic models, there is reason to be concerned about error, bias, and incomplete information.

Psychology and Economics

In *Blink: The Power of Thinking Without Thinking*, Malcolm Gladwell explains that by necessity or instinct, many decisions are made on the basis of first impressions. Snap judgments can lead to less-than-optimal choices when products – such as new cars – or people – such as potential employees, marital prospects, or presidential candidates – look better than they really are. Gladwell calls this the *Warren Harding Error* in reference to the 29th president of the United States, who looked winningly presidential to over 60% of the voters, but turned out to be a poor leader with a scandal-ridden administration. Harding reportedly said of himself, "I am not fit for this office and never should have been here." Clearly, Harding, and those who voted for him, made some mistakes due to limits on information and intelligence.

Universal History Archive/UIG/Getty Images

When decisions are made quickly, options can look better than they really are. Malcolm Gladwell calls this the *Warren Harding Error*, after the president who looked the part while campaigning, but once in office, even called himself unfit for the job.

Bounded Rationality

Dubious about models based on rationality and full information, Nobel laureate Herbert Simon explained that rationality is bounded by limitations in the ability of decision makers to formulate and solve complex problems. In *Models of My Life*, Simon argued that even Albert Einstein could not match the mental gymnastics ascribed to the fictional "economic man." Simon coined the phrase **bounded rationality** to describe the limits on optimal decision making that result from imperfect intelligence and the scarcity of time and information. Bounded rationality causes missteps, as when a price that ends in "99" makes a consumer perceive the amount as being lower than it really is.

Bounded rationality describes the limits on optimal decision making that result from imperfect intelligence and the scarcity of time and information.

Simon also studied the *judgmental heuristics* – rules of thumb – that people use to simplify decisions when constrained by time, information, or cognitive ability. Consumers and managers are like chess players: they cannot fully analyze every possible sequence of actions that will follow their move. Instead, they must rely on instincts, experience, advice, short-cuts, and guesswork. For example, rather than making pricing decisions by evaluating the consumer response and subsequent profit from every possible price point, many managers use the simple "keystone" technique of doubling the wholesale price of each good to establish the retail price.

Status quo bias causes people to stick with what they have despite equally attractive alternatives. In *Smart Choices: A Practical Guide to Making Better Decisions*, John Hammond, Ralph Keeney, and Howard Raiffa describe a natural experiment in which the state governments of New Jersey and Pennsylvania both adopted the same two options for automobile insurance, but each selected a different default plan. Under plan A, insurance premiums were lower, but drivers had a limited right to litigate after an accident. Under plan B, the premiums were higher, but litigation options were broader. In New Jersey, drivers received plan A unless they specified a preference for plan B; Pennsylvania drivers were assigned to plan B unless they opted for plan A. The result was that the majority of drivers in each state stuck with the status quo, meaning that they felt the best plan was the plan they were given in the first place.

Timothy Large/Alamy

Bounded rationality causes missteps, as when a price that ends in "99" makes a consumer perceive the amount as being lower than it really is.

Have you experienced status quo bias? Think about your family's choice of where to live and your favorite sports teams, politicians, and brand names. In some cases, the choice might be clear. In other cases, perhaps you've stuck with the status quo despite the existence of equally attractive alternatives. Herbert Simon felt that status quo bias and judgmental heuristics led to decisions that were satisfactory but not optimal, and described this type of decision making as *satisficing*.

Neoclassical theories rest on assumptions of rationality that are sometimes at odds with observed human behavior. For example, some theories of consumer choice are valid under the assumption that the largest amount an individual would be willing to pay for a good and the smallest amount he or she would accept in exchange for an identical good are the same. However, researchers have found *endowment effects*, meaning that people place a higher value on what they have than on what they don't have. In a famous example, Daniel Kahneman, Jack Knetsch, and Richard Thaler found that, after randomly selecting half the students in a class to receive coffee mugs, the largest amount that the average student without a mug was willing to pay to buy one was less than half as much as the smallest amount that the average student with a mug was willing to accept to give one up.

Behavioral economists use the concept of *loss aversion* to explain evidence that consumers consider sunk costs – those costs that have already been incurred and cannot be recovered – in their decision making. No matter how much money one has sunk into a project, it would be rational to abandon that project if the future benefits do not exceed the future costs. Yet some people choose to overeat in order to finish expensive meals, go to bad plays because they paid a lot for season tickets, or stick with a failing stock because they have invested so much money in it. Rather than ignoring the sunk cost as they always should, these people mistakenly let irrecoverable losses sway their decisions.

Excessive Optimism

Crime provides an important example of bounded rationality in the form of *excessive optimism* – some criminals are unrealistically confident that things will go their way. Neoclassical models treat crime as a rational activity, the price of which is the expected punishment. This implies that more severe punishments or higher rates of apprehension or conviction will deter crime. Yet a study by one of your authors, Dave Anderson, of the knowledge and mindset of criminals found that most criminals do not have the information required to perform cost-benefit analysis before committing their crimes. Specifically, 76% of the convicted criminals in the study either had no thought that they might be caught or had no idea of the punishment for their crime, or both. Among the violent offenders, 89% lacked the information needed for cost-benefit analysis. So in order to solve the crime problem, policy makers must go beyond the tenets of neoclassical economics and be open to solutions that address psychological problems and informational shortcomings.

Unfortunately, crime is just the tip of the iceberg of poor decisions caused by excessive optimism. Here are some additional examples:

- People underestimate the risks of common but unpublicized events such as work-related falls and motor vehicle accidents, and overestimate the risk of uncommon but dramatic, highly publicized events such as earthquakes, homicides, airplane crashes, and rare types of cancer. The result is inadequate safety precautions against the large risks and overinvestment in precautions against the small risks.
- More than half of all new businesses fail within five years, which may indicate excessive optimism among entrepreneurs. It is also possible that the potential benefits of a successful business outweigh the high risks of failure, but decision makers who underestimate the risks are prone to overinvest.
- The majority of Americans believe they are smarter than average and have better-than-average chances of winning the lottery, being professionally successful, and avoiding disease and automobile accidents. In the business world, most managers think they are more capable than the average manager.
- A common reason that many lawsuits go to trial is unrealistic optimism on the part of one side or both sides about the strength of their case. In a representative study, the average plaintiff's attorney expected a jury award 27% higher than the amount anticipated by the average defense attorney.

Phanuwat Nandee/Alamy

Distracted by excessive optimism? The improper use of information and poor understanding of risks and capabilities can lead to unfortunate resource allocation.

Even when good information is available, people may not use it wisely. Because people are capable of stubbornness, bias, and misjudgment to their own downfall, the improper use of information can lead to unfortunate and inefficient resource allocations.

Framing

It is standard procedure at several international hotel chains to place a card in the bathrooms of guest rooms with a message like this one:

> Save Our Planet. Every day millions of gallons of water are used to wash towels . . . A towel on the rack means "I will use again." Thank you for helping us conserve the Earth's vital resources.

If the hotels were really bent on saving Earth's resources, they would provide recycling bins, organic cotton sheets, and carpets made from recycled fibers. The pitch to avoid washing towels may have more to do with saving the financial resources of the hotels, but customer participation depends on how the appeal is framed.

Framing is the creation of context for a product or idea.

Context matters, and **framing** is the creation of context for a product or idea. Richard Thaler found that a typical consumer would pay no more than $1.50 for a good brand of beer from a grocery store, but would pay up to $2.65 for an identical beer from a fancy hotel, even if a friend was bringing the beer from either source to the consumer to drink at a beach. Brand managers spend millions of dollars to frame their brand names because, for example, consumers perceive apparel differently after seeing Olympic skier Mikaela Shiffrin wear it, and they perceive a hotel differently knowing that singer Bruno Mars stays there. Consumers pay more for a cup of coffee at Starbucks than at McDonald's, not because the Starbucks coffee itself is necessarily better (a *Consumer Reports* taste test suggests that McDonald's coffee is actually better), but because of the image and ambiance in which Starbucks coffee is framed.

The strategy of *odd* or *just-below* pricing—setting prices that end in an odd number or just below an even dollar amount—is about framing as well. In terms of damage to the pocketbook, there's little difference between paying $4.99 and paying $5.00. But the human mind finds it easier to accept a price of $4.99. Consumers subconsciously downplay the importance of the cents at the end of a price, and place more emphasis on the dollar amount at the beginning. Thus, $4.99 might seem close to $4.00, even though it is only a penny shy of $5.00. Also, prices ending in "99" or "95" convey the idea of a discount to bargain-hungry shoppers. Marketing professor Robert Schindler and management consultant Thomas Kibarian tested the influence of prices with odd-numbered endings by sending out three versions of a direct mail catalog for women's clothing. The catalogs were identical except for the prices, which ended with either 00, 99, or 88. The catalogs with prices ending in 99 generated 8% more sales volume and attracted more consumers than those with prices ending in the even numbers. Managers at upscale department stores such as Nordstrom are aware of the psychology of pricing as well, but they use the contrasting strategy of ending prices with even numbers, symbolic of their high-end brand image.

Ann Heath

At Nordstrom, prices ending in even numbers convey an upscale image.

Bounded Willpower

Bounded willpower is willpower constrained by limits on the determination needed to do difficult things.

It's rational to spend money, retire, or take vacations that decrease earnings, as long as the value of the resulting benefits exceeds the value of the money forgone. Yet sometimes people forgo money in irrational ways. **Bounded willpower**—willpower constrained by limits on the determination needed to do difficult things—can be the cause. The effects include spending too much money and earning too little money, but it isn't all about money. Bounded willpower can also explain decisions to do too little homework, procrastinate too much, overeat, or throw a career-ending temper tantrum in front of the boss.

In the analysis of behavior, it is important not to categorize everything that causes problems as irrational. Economists Gary Becker and Kevin Murphy pointed out that even the use of potentially addictive substances can be rational if the benefits outweigh the costs. They showed that people who care more about the present than the future are more prone to addiction because they discount future problems related to health, relationships, and finances when weighing them against ongoing desires for addictive substances. Becker and Murphy argue that when heavy drinkers and smokers say they want to quit but cannot, it may be a matter of the long-term benefits of quitting falling below the short-term costs of making that adjustment.

While some addictions may be rational, humans are subject to temptations and emotions that can lead them astray. Anger, jealousy, frustration, and embarrassment can overcome willpower and trigger irrational responses. Take, for example, the Wendy's customer who shot manager Renal Frage due to anger over not receiving enough packets of chili sauce. Similar examples appear frequently in the news.

Bounded Self-Interest

Neoclassical economic models rest on assumptions of self-interested behavior, which is seldom in short supply. But some behaviors exhibit elements of altruism uncharacteristic of *Homo economicus*. Billionaire businessman and investor Warren Buffett is apparently not *Homo economicus*, having pledged to give away 99% of his fortune to charity. Americans recycle tens of millions of tons of materials each year to the benefit of the environment and future generations. And the Bureau of Labor Statistics estimates that each year, more than a quarter of all Americans volunteer some of their time to help less fortunate individuals. Charitable efforts can be self-serving if they bring attention, gratitude, tax advantages, or other benefits to the donors. But to the extent that some decisions are made selflessly, **bounded self-interest** – self-interest that leaves room for concerns about the welfare of others – represents a third category of deviance from neoclassical economic models.

Bounded self-interest is self-interest that leaves room for concerns about the welfare of others.

Economists have examined the human struggle between self-interest and fairness with experiments involving *ultimatum games* and *dictator games*. In an ultimatum game, one person, whom we shall call *the divider*, has an amount of money, say $10, to divide between themself and another person, whom we shall call *the recipient*. After the divider makes the allocation, the recipient can either accept that division or reject it. If the allocation is rejected by the recipient, neither side gets anything. A rational, wealth-maximizing recipient will accept any positive share of the money, because some money is better than the alternative of no money. When working with such recipients, a rational, wealth-maximizing divider would allocate the smallest possible positive amount to the recipient: one cent. However, much experimentation has revealed strong interest in fair allocations, and punishment for those who make unfair allocations. Daniel Kahneman, Jack Knetsch, and Richard Thaler found that the typical recipient rejects anything less than a 23% share of the money to be divided, and that the average divider offers 45% of the money to the recipient. Related research has found fairness to be important even with changes in the culture of the participants, the amount of money at stake, and opportunities to learn from experience with the game.

In the dictator game, the recipient has no choice but to accept the divider's allocation. Thus, a rational, wealth-maximizing divider would give nothing to the recipient. Kahneman, Knetsch, and Thaler gave 161 students the option of dividing $20 evenly with an anonymous other student or giving the other student $2 while keeping $18. Even though the recipients had no say in the matter, 76% of the dividers gave half of the money to the recipient, again exhibiting substantial interest in fairness.

lendy16/Shutterstock

Would you divide $20 evenly between you and an anonymous recipient if you didn't have to?

Clearly, there is more to decision making than wealth maximization. Customers may pay more for a product that causes less harm to other people or the environment, as managers at Toyota discovered when their relatively expensive but environmentally friendly Prius hybrid flew out of showrooms faster than the company could make more. Attracting a new employee by offering a salary that eclipses the salary of existing employees can cause considerable strife due to those employees' interests in fairness, so employers should take the fairness of their salaries into consideration. And money can't separate most parents from their children: a recent Modern Family Index reveals that a majority of parents sacrifice financial gains in their careers to spend more time with their kids.

Evolving Models

Just as many anthropologists theorize that *Homo ergaster* evolved into modern men and women, in contemporary economic theory, the traditional model of *Homo economicus* is evolving into a modern conception of economic men and women. Behavioral economists have adapted earlier notions of economic man to capture decision making under the constraints on human rationality, willpower, and self-interest. Some strange behaviors can be traced to rational foundations, but others are sufficiently suspect to warrant policy that addresses the possibility of misinformation, mistakes, and psychosis.

We've seen that the information that neoclassical theory treats as fully and freely available is often incomplete and costly. We've also seen that market participants do not always put the information they have to its best use. The key question is whether problems with information justify an abandonment of neoclassical precepts, some revisions and expansions in rational choice theory, or none of the above. Most contemporary economists stake out a middle ground, leaning toward the neoclassical side. Despite their flaws, neoclassical models provide useful guidance and predictive power. Experiments demonstrate that people – not to mention rats, dolphins, and other decision makers broadly defined – generally respond to incentives in rational ways: they all tend to follow the money, cheese, or sardines. That being said, worthwhile improvements in theories and policy making can be achieved by acknowledging psychological influences beyond the desire for money and leisure. Consumers, managers, employees, and all other participants in an economy are more or less flawed, biased, emotional, benevolent, undisciplined, and uninformed, which helps to explain myriad behaviors that neoclassical models do not predict.

Enrichment Module C  Review

Check Your Understanding

1. Identify the cause of each of the following types of behavior:
   a. Nelson employs a worker whose family desperately needs the income, even though the worker's wage exceeds the revenue that worker brings into Nelson's firm.
   b. Roberto will pay more for the same steak in a restaurant with fancy tablecloths than in a restaurant without them.
   c. Alesia opens a new hardware store despite market research indicating insufficient consumer demand for the store's products.
   d. Karen knows she should stop eating chocolate, but she eats more anyway.
2. What do experiments with the ultimatum game reveal about the typical participant?

Multiple-Choice Review Questions

1. Behavioral economics is a combination of economics and which field?
   a. animal science
   b. government
   c. business
   d. psychology
   e. sociology
2. Who unquestionably represents a self-interested, informed, rational decision maker?
   a. *Homo misinformicus*
   b. *Homo economicus*
   c. *Homo ergaster*
   d. Malcolm Gladwell
   e. Warren Harding
3. A price that ends in "99" can be perceived as being significantly lower than a price that ends in "00" due to
   a. judgmental heuristics.
   b. bounded rationality.
   c. satisficing.
   d. loss aversion.
   e. bounded willpower.
4. Status quo bias causes people to
   a. try new things.
   b. favor what they have.
   c. prefer alternatives to the default option.
   d. always spend as little money as possible.
   e. overspend on items that will increase their social status.
5. Research suggests that criminals commit more than the rational number of crimes due to excessive
   a. optimism.
   b. pessimism.
   c. wealth.
   d. information.
   e. investments in stocks.
6. Suppose the Eat-It Truck Stop and the Royal Palace Restaurant serve food of the same quality. Which of the following is the most likely to allow the Royal Palace Restaurant to charge higher prices?
   a. bounded self-interest
   b. the dictator game
   c. framing
   d. sunk costs
   e. loss aversion
7. Bounded self-interest can most easily explain why
   a. people consider sunk costs.
   b. workers seek higher wages.
   c. consumers are more willing to buy goods if their prices end in "99."
   d. businesses carry out framing techniques.
   e. donors give anonymously to charity.

Discussion Starters

1. Which of your behaviors might be considered irrational? Do you consider sunk costs? Do emotions ever put you on an irrational path?
2. How gullible are you? Do you tend to believe what you hear from your friends and what you read on the internet? Have you ever learned that you were fooled by these or other information sources?
3. Do you sometimes exhibit altruism? In what instances have you forgone money for the benefit of others?
4. Would a product's effects on the environment influence your decision to buy it? Can you name the greenhouse gases that cause global warming? What sorts of costs weigh against the benefits of obtaining this information?
5. As a manager, would you set prices so that they ended in "99"? Why or why not? Does this approach ever work on you as a consumer?
6. What evidence have you seen of the failure or success of neoclassical models? Have you noticed changes in the price or quality of goods as the number of competitors changed? Does the quantity of a good demanded decrease as its price increases?

EM D

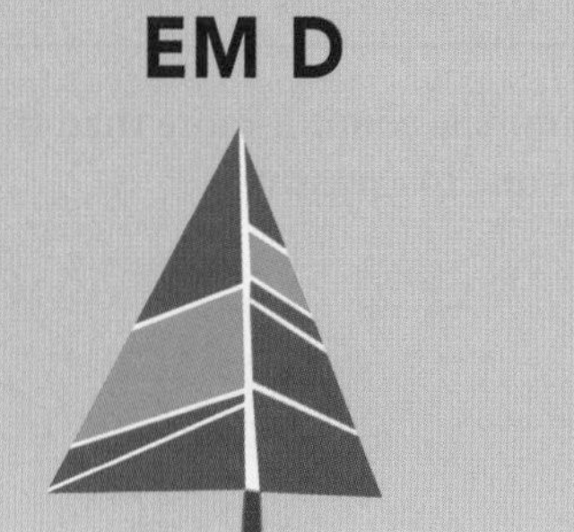

The Economics of Information

In this Module, you will learn to:

- Identify the special problems posed by information that some people have and other people do not
- Explain how information asymmetries can lead to the problem of adverse selection
- Discuss ways that firms can deal with imperfect information using screening and signaling
- Explain how information asymmetries can lead to the problem of moral hazard

Private Information: What You Don't Know Can Hurt You

Private information is information that some people have and others do not; it is also known as **asymmetric information**.

Markets can handle situations in which nobody knows what is going to happen. However, markets have much more trouble with situations in which *some people know things that other people don't know*—situations involving **private information** (also known as **asymmetric information**). As we will see, private information can distort economic decisions and sometimes prevent mutually beneficial economic transactions from taking place.

Why is some information private? The most important reason is that people generally know more about themselves than other people do. For example, you know whether or not you are a careful driver; but unless you have already been in several accidents, your auto insurance company does not have that information. You are more likely to have a better estimate than your health insurance company of whether or not you will need an expensive medical procedure. And if you are selling your used car, you are more likely to be aware of any problems with it than the buyer is.

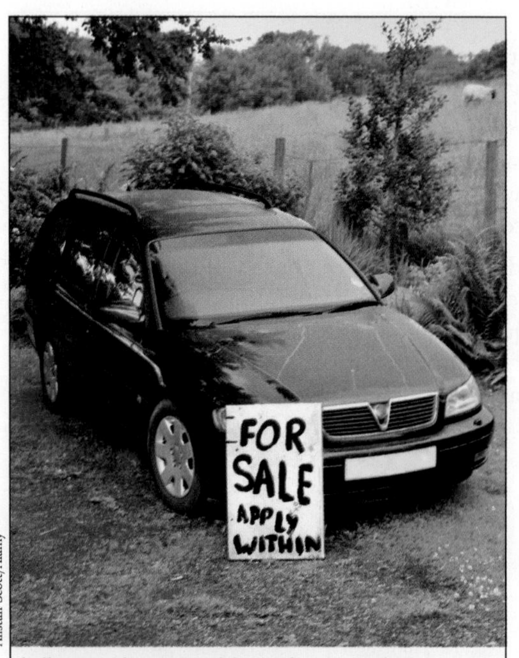

Alistair Scott/Alamy

Is the most you would pay for a used car influenced by the fact that the seller knows more about the car than you do?

But why should such differences in who knows what be a problem? It turns out that there are two distinct sources of trouble: *adverse selection*, which arises from having private information about the way things are, and *moral hazard*, which arises from having private information about what people do.

Adverse Selection: The Economics of Lemons

Suppose that someone offers to sell you an almost brand-new car—purchased just three months ago, with only 2,000 miles on the odometer and no dents or scratches. Will you be willing to pay almost as much for that car as you would pay for the same model purchased new from a car dealership?

Probably not, for one main reason: you cannot help but wonder why this car is being sold. Has the owner discovered that something is wrong with it—that it is a "lemon"? Having driven the car for a while, the owner knows more about it than you do—and people are more likely to sell cars that give them trouble.

You might think that the extra information held by sellers of used cars provides a distinct advantage to the sellers. But potential buyers know that potential sellers are likely to offer them lemons – they just don't know exactly which car is a lemon. Because potential buyers of a used car know that potential sellers are more likely to sell lemons than good cars, buyers will offer a lower price than they would if they had a guarantee of the car's quality. Worse yet, this poor opinion of used cars tends to be self-reinforcing, precisely because it depresses the prices that buyers offer. Used cars sell at a discount because buyers expect a disproportionate share of those cars to be lemons. Even a used car that is not a lemon would sell only at a large discount because buyers don't know whether it's a lemon or not. But potential sellers who have good cars are unwilling to sell them at a deep discount, except under exceptional circumstances. So it is relatively uncommon for good used cars to be offered for sale, and used cars that are offered for sale have a tendency to be lemons. (This is why people who have a compelling reason to sell a car, such as moving overseas, make a point of revealing that information to potential buyers – as if to say, "This car is not a lemon!")

Fabrizio Troiani/Alamy

The end result, then, is not only that used cars sell for low prices, but also that a large number of used cars have hidden problems. Equally important, many potentially beneficial transactions – sales of good used cars by people who would like to get rid of them to people who would like to buy them – end up being frustrated by the inability of potential sellers to convince potential buyers that their cars are worth the higher price demanded. So some mutually beneficial trades between those who want to sell used cars and those who want to buy them go unexploited.

Although economists sometimes refer to situations like this as the "lemons problem" (the issue was introduced in a famous 1970 paper by economist and Nobel laureate George Akerlof entitled "The Market for Lemons"), **adverse selection** is the more formal name for the problem of one person knowing more than other people about the way things are. Because potential sellers know more about the quality of what they are selling than potential buyers, they have an incentive to select the worst things to sell.

Adverse selection occurs when one person knows more about the way things are than other people do. Adverse selection exists, for example, when sellers offer items of particularly low (hidden) quality for sale, and when the people with the greatest need for insurance are those most likely to purchase it.

Adverse selection applies to more than just used cars. It is a problem for many parts of the economy – notably for insurance companies, and most notably for health insurance companies. Suppose that a health insurance company were to offer a standard policy to everyone with the same premium (the basic monthly fee for the policy). The premium would reflect the *average* risk of incurring a medical expense. But that would make the policy look very expensive to healthy people, who know that they are less likely than the average person to incur medical expenses. So healthy people would be less likely than less healthy people to buy the policy, leaving the health insurance company with exactly the customers it doesn't want: people with a higher-than-average risk of needing medical care, who would find the premium to be a good deal. In order to cover its expected losses from this less healthy customer pool, the health insurance company is compelled to raise premiums, driving away more of the remaining healthier customers, and so on. Because the insurance company can't determine who is healthy and who is not, it must charge everyone the same premium, thereby discouraging healthy people from purchasing policies and encouraging unhealthy people to buy policies.

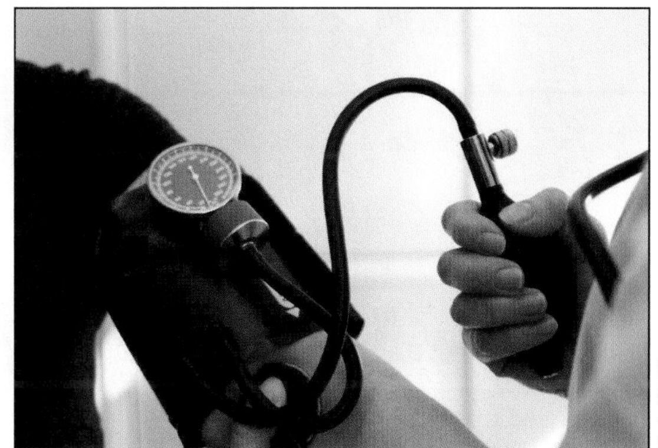
PhotoAlto/Alamy

The death spiral: Adverse selection can push healthy people out of the health insurance market, which raises the average cost of insuring a customer, resulting in higher premiums, causing more people to drop out, and so on.

Adverse selection can lead to an *adverse selection death spiral*: the relatively unhealthy customers drive up the insurance company's average cost per customer, which leads to higher premiums, which drive away the healthier remaining customers, which raises the company's average cost even higher, and so on. Eventually, only the least healthy customers are willing to pay the elevated premiums, which prevents the spreading of costs necessary for a viable insurance market, so the market for health insurance collapses. Because of the severe adverse selection problems, governments in many advanced countries assume the role of providing health insurance to their citizens. The U.S. government, through its various health insurance programs including Medicare, Medicaid, and the Children's Health Insurance Program, now disburses more than half the total payments for medical care in the United States.

Adverse selection can be reduced through **screening**: using observable information about people to make inferences about their private information.

In general, people or firms faced with the problem of adverse selection follow one of several well-established strategies for dealing with it. One strategy is **screening**: using observable information to make inferences about private information. If you apply to purchase health insurance, you'll find that the insurance company will demand documentation of your health status in an attempt to "screen out" less healthy applicants, whom they will refuse to insure or will insure only at very high premiums. Auto insurance also provides a very good example. An insurance company may not know whether you are a careful driver, but it has statistical data on the accident rates of people who resemble your profile – and it uses those data in setting premiums. A 19-year-old male who drives a sports car and has already had a fender-bender is likely to pay a very high premium. A 40-year-old female who drives a minivan and has never had an accident is likely to pay much less. In some cases, this may be quite unfair: some adolescent males are very careful drivers, and some mature women drive their minivans as if they were fighter jets. But nobody can deny that the insurance companies are right on average.

Adverse selection can be diminished by people **signaling** their private information through actions that credibly reveal what they know.

Another strategy is for people who are good prospects to somehow *signal* their private information. **Signaling** involves taking some action that wouldn't be worth taking unless they were indeed good prospects. Reputable used-car dealers often offer warranties – promises to repair any problems with the cars they sell that arise within a given amount of time. This isn't just a way of insuring their customers against possible expenses; it's a way of credibly showing that they are not selling lemons. As a result, more sales occur, and dealers can command higher prices for their used cars.

A long-term **reputation** allows an individual to assure others that they aren't concealing adverse private information.

Finally, in the face of adverse selection, it can be very valuable to establish a good **reputation**: a used-car dealership will often advertise how long it has been in business to show that it has continued to satisfy its customers. As a result, new customers will be willing to purchase cars and to pay more for that dealer's cars.

Moral Hazard

In the late 1970s, New York and other major cities experienced an epidemic of suspicious fires – fires that appeared to be deliberately set. Some of the fires were probably started by teenagers for amusement, others by gang members struggling over turf. But investigators eventually became aware of patterns in a number of the fires. Particular landlords who owned several buildings seemed to have an unusually large number of their buildings burn down. Although it was difficult to prove, police had few doubts that most of these fire-prone landlords were hiring professional arsonists to torch their own properties.

CrowdSpark/Alamy

Would you be more careful to avoid a fire if you didn't have fire insurance?

Why burn your own buildings? These buildings were typically in declining neighborhoods, where rising crime rates and middle-class flight had led to a decline in property values. But the insurance policies on the buildings were written to compensate owners based on historical property values, and so those policies would pay the owner of a destroyed building more than the building was worth in the current market. For a corrupt landlord who knew the right people, this presented a profitable opportunity.

The arson epidemic became less severe during the 1980s, partly because insurance companies began making it difficult to overinsure properties and partly because a boom in real estate values made many previously arson-threatened buildings worth more unburned.

The arson episodes make it clear that it is a bad idea for insurance companies to let customers insure buildings for more than their value—it gives the customers some destructive incentives. However, you might think that the incentive problem would go away as long as the insurance is no more than 100% of the value of what is being insured.

But, unfortunately, anything close to 100% insurance still distorts incentives—it induces policyholders to behave differently from how they would in the absence of insurance. The reason is that preventing fires requires effort and cost on the part of a building's owner. Fire alarms and sprinkler systems have to be kept in good repair, fire safety rules have to be strictly enforced, and so on. All of this takes time and money—time and money that the owner may not find worth spending if the insurance policy will provide close to full compensation for any losses.

Of course, the insurance company could specify in the policy that it won't pay if basic safety precautions have not been taken. But it isn't always easy to tell how careful a building's owner has been—the owner knows, but the insurance company does not.

The point is that the building's owner has private information about his or her own actions; the owner knows whether he or she has really taken all appropriate precautions. As a result, the insurance company is likely to face greater claims than if it were able to determine exactly how much effort a building owner exerts to prevent a loss. The problem of distorted incentives known as **moral hazard** arises when an individual has private information about his or her own actions but someone else bears the costs of a lack of care or effort.

Moral hazard arises when an individual knows more about his or her own actions than other people do. This leads to a distortion of incentives to take care or to exert effort when someone else bears the costs of the lack of care or effort.

To deal with moral hazard, it is necessary to give individuals with private information some personal stake in what happens, a stake that gives them a reason to exert effort even if others cannot verify that they have done so. Moral hazard is the reason salespeople in many stores receive a commission on sales: it's hard for managers to be sure how hard the salespeople are really working, and if they were paid only straight salary, they would not have an incentive to exert effort to make those sales. Similar logic explains why many stores and restaurants, even if they are part of national chains, are actually franchises, licensed outlets owned by the people who run them.

Insurance companies deal with moral hazard by requiring a **deductible**: they compensate for losses only above a certain amount, so that coverage is always less than 100%. The insurance on your car, for example, may pay for repairs only after the first $500 in loss. This means that a careless driver who gets into a fender-bender will end up paying $500 for repairs even if he is insured, which provides at least some incentive to be careful and reduces moral hazard.

A **deductible** is a sum specified in an insurance policy that the insured individuals must pay before being compensated for a claim; deductibles reduce moral hazard.

In addition to reducing moral hazard, deductibles provide a partial solution to the problem of adverse selection. Your insurance premium often drops substantially if you are willing to accept a large deductible. This is an attractive option to people who know they are low-risk customers; it is less attractive to people who know they are high-risk—and so are likely to have an accident and end up paying the deductible. By offering a menu of policies with different premiums and deductibles, insurance companies can screen their customers, inducing them to sort themselves out on the basis of their private information.

As the example of deductibles suggests, moral hazard limits the ability of the economy to allocate risks efficiently. You generally can't get full (100%) insurance on your home or car, even though you would like to buy full insurance, and you bear the risk of large deductibles, even though you would prefer not to.

Enrichment Module D  Review

Check Your Understanding

1. Your car insurance premiums are lower if you have had no moving violations for several years. Explain how this feature tends to decrease the potential inefficiency caused by adverse selection.
2. A feature of some home construction contracts is that when it costs more to construct a building than was originally estimated, the contractor must absorb the additional cost. Explain how this feature reduces the problem of moral hazard but also forces the contractor to bear more risk than the contractor would like.
3. True or false? Explain your answer, stating what concept discussed in this Module accounts for the feature.
   - **a.** People with higher deductibles on their auto insurance generally drive more carefully.
   - **b.** People with higher deductibles on their auto insurance pay lower premiums.

Multiple-Choice Review Questions

1. Which of the following is true about private information?
   - **a.** Everyone has access to it.
   - **b.** It has no value.
   - **c.** Adverse selection arises when people take fewer precautions because they are insured.
   - **d.** It can distort economic decisions.
   - **e.** Moral hazard arises when sellers have private information about the quality of goods.
2. Due to adverse selection,
   - **a.** mutually beneficial trades go unexploited.
   - **b.** people buy lemons rather than other fruit.
   - **c.** sick people buy less insurance.
   - **d.** private information is available to all.
   - **e.** public information is available to no one.
3. When colleges use grade point averages to make admissions decisions, they are employing which strategy?
   - **a.** signaling
   - **b.** screening
   - **c.** profit maximization
   - **d.** marginal analysis
   - **e.** adverse selection
4. Moral hazard is the result of
   - **a.** asymmetric information.
   - **b.** signaling.
   - **c.** toxic waste.
   - **d.** adverse selection.
   - **e.** public information.
5. A deductible is used by insurance companies to
   - **a.** allow customers to pay for insurance premiums using payroll deduction.
   - **b.** deal with moral hazard.
   - **c.** make public information private.
   - **d.** compensate policyholders fully for their losses.
   - **e.** avoid all payments to policyholders.
6. The used-car market has been described as the "market for lemons" because in that market,
   - **a.** information problems make the owners of flawed cars more likely to sell them than the owners of good cars.
   - **b.** moral hazard causes buyers of used cars to drive recklessly and damage the cars.
   - **c.** buyers often get a sour look on their faces when they hear the asking price for a car.
   - **d.** the documents used to transfer the title to a car are traditionally yellow, like a lemon.
   - **e.** used cars are often dented, like the skin of a lemon.
7. Which of the following would increase the problem of adverse selection in the health insurance industry?
   - **a.** higher insurance premiums
   - **b.** a legal requirement that everyone must buy health insurance
   - **c.** mandatory health screening for health insurance applicants
   - **d.** a taxpayer-funded system that provides health care to everyone at no cost except for the tax payment
   - **e.** lower insurance premiums for individuals whose good health is verified by a thorough physical examination

Free-Response Review Questions

1. Identify whether each of the following situations reflects moral hazard or adverse selection. Propose a potential solution to reduce the inefficiency that each situation creates.
   a. When you buy a second-hand car, you do not know whether it is a lemon (low quality) or a plum (high quality), but the seller knows.
   b. People with dental insurance might not brush their teeth as often, knowing that if they get cavities, the insurance will pay for the fillings.
   c. A company does not know whether individual workers on an assembly line are working hard or slacking off.
   d. When making a decision about hiring you, prospective employers do not know whether or not you are a productive worker.

Rubric for FRQ 1 (8 points)

1 point: Adverse selection

1 point: Sellers could offer a warranty with the car that pays for repair costs.

1 point: Moral hazard

1 point: Each insured person can be made to pay a co-payment of a certain dollar amount each time that person gets a filling.

1 point: Moral hazard

1 point: Pay the workers "piece rates," that is, pay them according to how much they have produced each day.

1 point: Adverse selection

1 point: Provide potential employers with references from previous employers.

2. Suppose individuals or corporations (for example, home-buyers or banks) believe that the government will "bail them out" in the event that their decisions lead to a financial collapse. This is an example of what problem created by asymmetric information? How does this situation lead to inefficiency? What is a possible remedy for the problem? **(3 points)**

Discussion Starters

1. In what situations have you experienced asymmetric information? What screening or signaling was involved?
2. Describe a situation in which you experienced moral hazard by taking fewer precautions when the cost of damage would be at least partially someone else's problem. For example, you might have done this when a product was under warranty, a car or home was being rented, or insurance would cover the cost of damage.
3. Describe a case in which you used a seller's reputation to deal with asymmetric information.

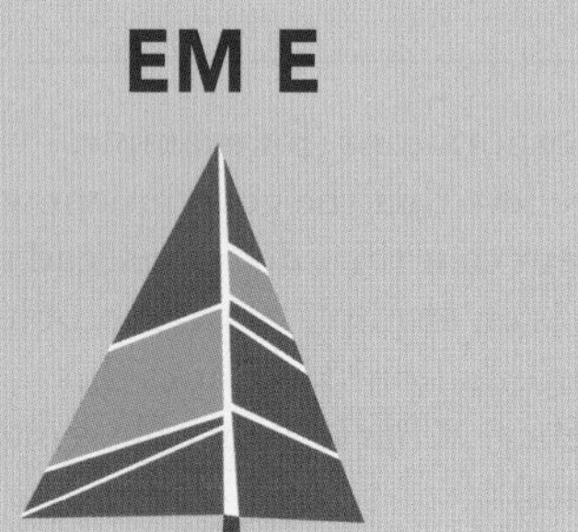

Indifference Curves and Consumer Choice

In this Module, you will learn to:

- Explain how economists use indifference curves to illustrate a person's preferences
- Discuss the importance of the marginal rate of substitution, the rate at which a consumer is just willing to substitute one good for another
- Use indifference curves and the budget line to find a consumer's optimal consumption bundle

Mapping the Utility Function

In Module 1.6, we introduced the concept of a utility function, which determines a consumer's total utility given that person's consumption bundle. Here, we will extend the analysis by learning how to express total utility as a function of the consumption of two goods. This will deepen our understanding of the trade-offs involved when choosing the optimal consumption bundle. We will also see how the optimal consumption bundle itself changes in response to changes in the prices of goods. We begin by examining a different way of representing a consumer's utility function, based on the concept of *indifference curves.*

Indifference Curves

Ingrid is a consumer who buys only two goods: housing, measured by the number of rooms in her house or apartment, and restaurant meals. How can we represent her utility function in a way that takes account of her consumption of both goods?

One way is to draw a three-dimensional picture, or "utility hill," as shown in **Figure E-1**. The distance along the horizontal axis measures the quantity of housing Ingrid consumes in terms of the number of rooms; the distance along the vertical axis measures the number of restaurant meals she consumes. The altitude or height

FIGURE E-1 Ingrid's Utility Function

The three-dimensional hill shows how Ingrid's total utility depends on her consumption of housing and restaurant meals. Point *A* corresponds to consumption of 3 rooms and 30 restaurant meals. That consumption bundle yields Ingrid 450 utils, corresponding to the height of the hill at point *A*. The lines running around the hill are contour lines, along which the height is constant. So point *B* and every other point along the same contour line as point *A* generate the same level of utility.

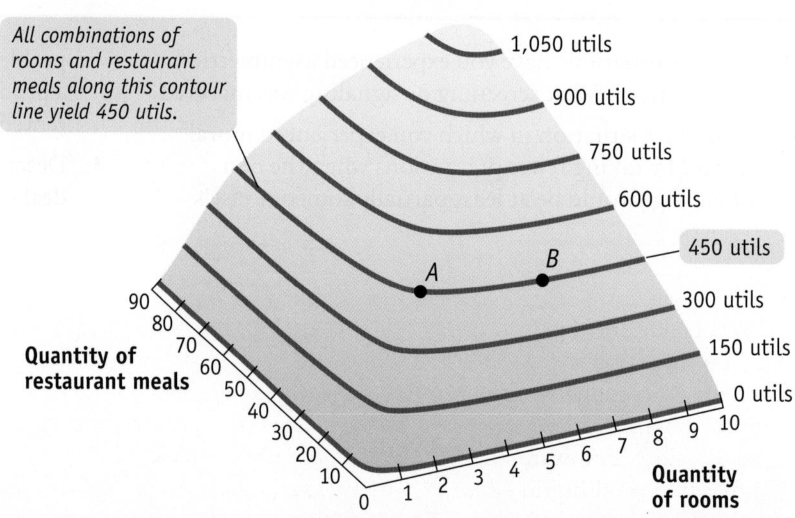

of the hill at each point is indicated by a contour line, along which the height of the hill is constant. For example, point *A*, which corresponds to a consumption bundle of 3 rooms and 30 restaurant meals, and point *B*, which corresponds to a bundle of 6 rooms and 15 restaurant meals, lie on the contour line labeled 450. So the total utility Ingrid receives from consuming either of these bundles is 450 utils.

A three-dimensional picture like Figure E-1 helps us think about the relationship between consumption bundles and total utility. But anyone who has ever used a topographical map to plan a hiking trip knows that it is possible to represent a three-dimensional surface in only two dimensions. A topographical map doesn't offer a three-dimensional view of the terrain; instead, it conveys information about altitude solely through the use of contour lines.

The same principle can be applied to the representation of a utility function. In **Figure E-2**, Ingrid's consumption of rooms is measured on the horizontal axis, and her consumption of restaurant meals is measured on the vertical axis. The curve here corresponds to the contour line in Figure E-1, drawn at a total utility of 450 utils. This curve shows all the consumption bundles that yield a total utility of 450 utils. As we've seen, one point on that contour line is *A*, a consumption bundle consisting of 3 rooms and 30 restaurant meals. Another point on that contour line is *B*, a consumption bundle consisting of 6 rooms but only 15 restaurant meals. Because *B* lies on the same contour line, it yields Ingrid the same total utility—450 utils—as *A*. We say that Ingrid is *indifferent* between *A* and *B*: because bundles *A* and *B* yield the same total utility level, Ingrid is equally well off with either bundle.

FIGURE E-2 An Indifference Curve

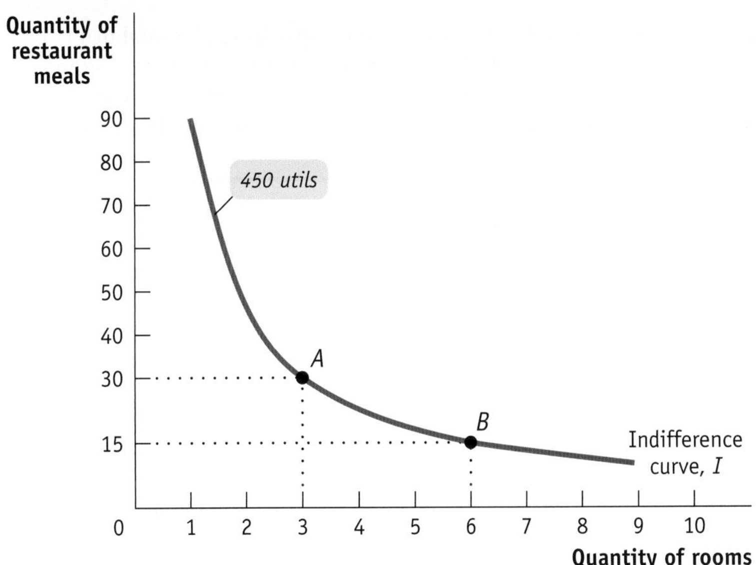

An indifference curve is a contour line along which total utility is constant. In this case, we show all the consumption bundles that yield Ingrid 450 utils. Consumption bundle *A*, consisting of 3 rooms and 30 restaurant meals, yields the same total utility as bundle *B*, consisting of 6 rooms and 15 restaurant meals. That is, Ingrid is indifferent between bundle *A* and bundle *B*.

A contour line representing consumption bundles that give a particular individual the same amount of total utility is known as an **indifference curve**. An individual is always indifferent between any two bundles that lie on the same indifference curve. For a given consumer, there is an indifference curve corresponding to each possible level of total utility. For example, the indifference curve in Figure E-2 shows consumption bundles that yield Ingrid 450 utils; different indifference curves would show consumption bundles that yield Ingrid 400 utils, 500 utils, and so on.

An **indifference curve** shows all the consumption bundles that yield the same amount of total utility for an individual.

A collection of indifference curves that represent a given consumer's entire utility function, with each indifference curve corresponding to a different level of total utility, is known as an **indifference curve map.** **Figure E-3** shows three indifference curves—I_1, I_2, and I_3—from Ingrid's indifference curve map, as well as several consumption bundles, *A*, *B*, *C*, and *D*. The accompanying table lists each bundle, its composition of rooms and restaurant meals, and the total utility it provides. Because bundles *A* and *B* generate the same number of utils, 450, they lie on the same indifference curve, I_2.

The entire utility function of an individual can be represented by an **indifference curve map**—a collection of indifference curves, each of which corresponds to a different total utility level.

FIGURE E-3 An Indifference Curve Map

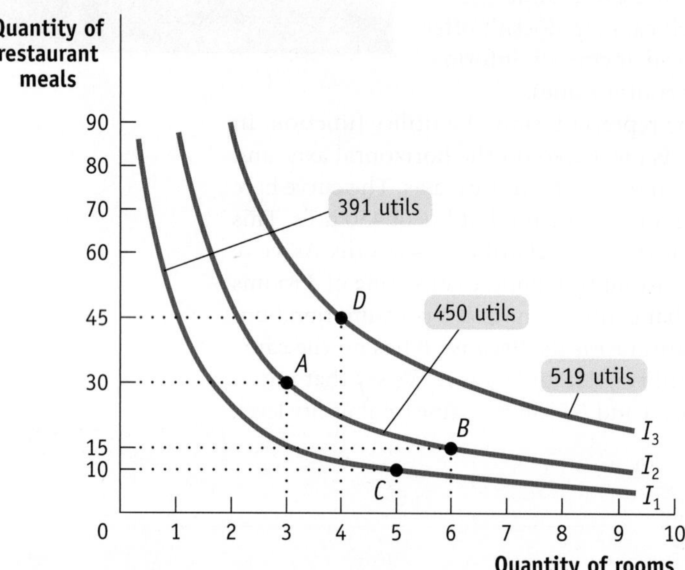

Consumption bundle	Quantity of rooms	Quantity of meals	Total utility (utils)
A	3	30	450
B	6	15	450
C	5	10	391
D	4	45	519

The utility function can be represented in greater detail by increasing the number of indifference curves drawn, each corresponding to a different level of total utility. In this figure, bundle *C* lies on an indifference curve corresponding to a total utility of 391 utils. As in Figure E-2, bundles *A* and *B* lie on an indifference curve corresponding to a total utility of 450 utils. Bundle *D* lies on an indifference curve corresponding to a total utility of 519 utils. Ingrid prefers any bundle on I_2 to any bundle on I_1, and she prefers any bundle on I_3 to any bundle on I_2.

Although Ingrid is indifferent between *A* and *B*, she is certainly not indifferent between *A* and *C*: as you can see from the table, *C* generates only 391 utils, fewer than *A* or *B*. So Ingrid prefers consumption bundles *A* and *B* to bundle *C*. This is evident from the graph because *C* is on indifference curve I_1, and I_1 lies below I_2. Bundle *D*, though, generates 519 utils, more than *A* and *B*. So bundle *D* is on indifference curve I_3, which lies above I_2. Clearly, Ingrid prefers *D* to either *A* or *B*. And, even more strongly, she prefers *D* to *C*.

As you will see shortly, the indifference curve map tells us all we need to know in order to find a consumer's optimal consumption bundle. That is, it's important that Ingrid has higher total utility along indifference curve I_2 than she does along I_1, but it doesn't matter how much higher her total utility is. In other words, we don't have to measure utils in order to understand how consumers make choices.

Consumer theory requires an ordinal measure of utility—one that ranks consumption bundles in terms of desirability—so that we can say bundle *X* is better than bundle *Y*. The theory does not, however, require cardinal utility, which actually assigns a specific number to the total utility yielded by each bundle.

Properties of Indifference Curves

No two individuals have the same indifference curve map because no two individuals have the same preferences. But economists believe that, regardless of the person, every indifference curve map has two general properties. These properties are explained below and illustrated in panels A1 and A2 of **Figure E-4**.

a. *Indifference curves never cross.* Suppose that we tried to draw an indifference curve map like the one depicted in panel A1, in which two indifference curves cross at *A*. What is the total utility at *A*? Is it 100 utils or 200 utils? Indifference curves cannot cross because each consumption bundle must correspond to one unique total utility level—not, as shown at *A*, two different total utility levels.

b. *The farther out an indifference curve lies—the farther it is from the origin—the higher the level of total utility it indicates.* The reason, illustrated in panel A2, is that we assume that more is better—we consider only the consumption bundles for which the consumer is not satiated. Bundle *B*, on the outer indifference curve, contains more of both goods than bundle *A* on the inner indifference curve. So *B*, because it generates a higher total utility level (200 utils), lies on a higher indifference curve than *A*.

Furthermore, economists believe that, for most goods, consumers' indifference curve maps also have two additional properties. They are explained here and illustrated in panels B1 and B2 of Figure E-4:

c. *Indifference curves slope downward.* Here, too, the reason is that more is better. Panel B1 shows four consumption bundles on the same indifference curve: *W*, *X*, *Y*, and *Z*.

FIGURE E-4 Properties of Indifference Curves

Properties of All Indifference Curves

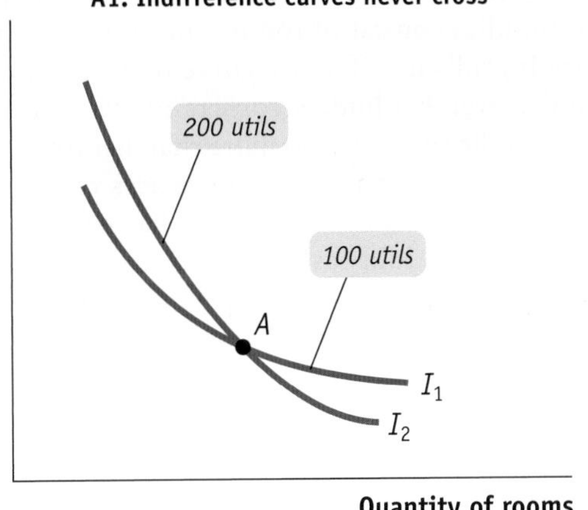

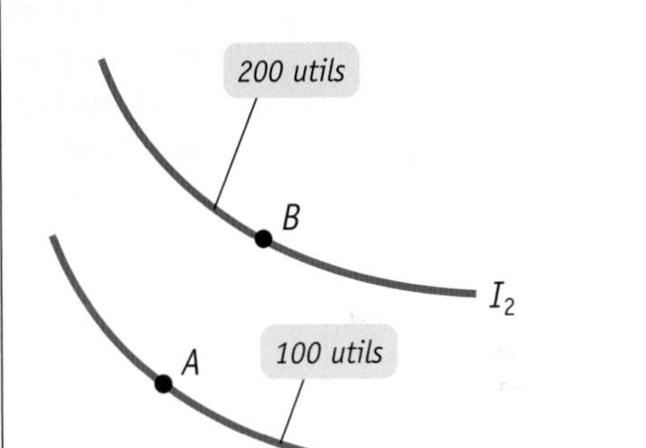

Additional Properties of Indifference Curves for Ordinary Goods

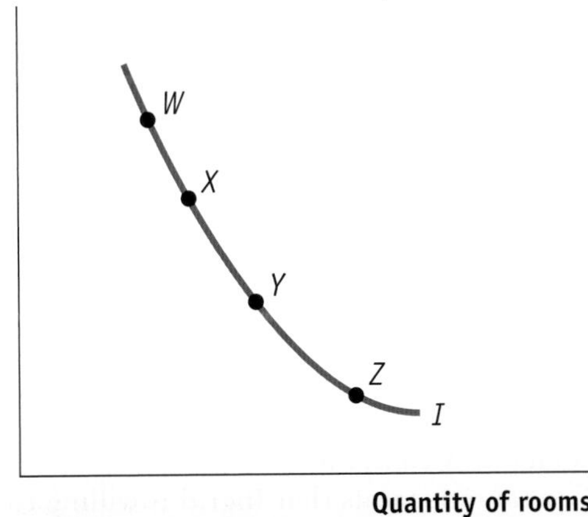

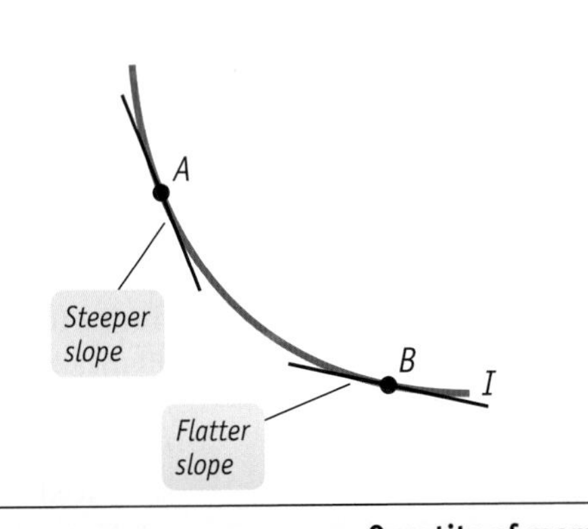

By definition, these consumption bundles yield the same level of total utility. But as you move along the curve to the right, from *W* to *Z*, the quantity of rooms consumed increases. The only way a person can consume more rooms without gaining utility is by giving up some restaurant meals. So the indifference curve must slope downward.

d. *Indifference curves have a convex shape.* Panel B2 shows that the slope of each indifference curve changes as you move down the curve to the right: the curve gets flatter. If you move up an indifference curve to the left, the curve gets steeper. So the indifference curve is steeper at *A* than it is at *B*. When this occurs, we say that an indifference curve has a *convex* shape—it is bowed-in toward the origin. This feature arises from diminishing marginal utility, a principle we discussed in Module 1.6. Recall that when a consumer has diminishing marginal utility, consumption of another unit of a good generates a smaller increase in total utility than the previous unit consumed. In the next section, we will examine in detail how diminishing marginal utility gives rise to convex-shaped indifference curves.

Goods that satisfy all four properties of indifference curve maps are called *ordinary goods.* The vast majority of goods in any consumer's utility function fall into this category. Next, we will define ordinary goods more precisely and see the key role that diminishing marginal utility plays for them.

Indifference Curves and Consumer Choice

In the previous section, we used indifference curves to represent the preferences of Ingrid, whose consumption bundles consist of rooms and restaurant meals. Our next step is to show how to use Ingrid's indifference curve map to find her utility-maximizing consumption bundle, given her budget constraint, which exists because she must choose a consumption bundle that costs no more than her total income.

It's important to understand how our analysis here relates to what we did in Module 1.6. We are not offering a new theory of consumer behavior in this Module—consumers are assumed to maximize total utility as before. In particular, we know that consumers will follow the *optimal consumption rule*: the optimal consumption bundle lies on the budget line, and the marginal utility per dollar is the same for every good in the bundle.

But, as we will see shortly, we can derive this optimal consumer behavior in a somewhat different way—a way that yields deeper insights into consumer choice.

The Marginal Rate of Substitution

The first element of our approach is a new concept, the *marginal rate of substitution*. We'll see that this concept is tied closely to the shape of the indifference curve, which gets flatter moving from left to right, as illustrated in **Figure E-5**.

We have just seen that for most goods, consumers' indifference curves are downward-sloping and convex. Figure E-5 shows such an indifference curve. The points labeled *V*, *W*, *X*, *Y*, and *Z* all lie on this indifference curve—that is, they represent consumption bundles that yield Ingrid the same level of total utility. The table accompanying Figure E-5 shows the components of each of the bundles. As we move along the indifference curve from *V* to *Z*, Ingrid's consumption of housing steadily increases from 2 rooms to 6 rooms, her consumption of restaurant meals steadily decreases from 30 meals to 10 meals, and her total utility is kept constant. As we move down the indifference curve, then, Ingrid is trading more of one good for less of the other, with the *terms* of that trade-off—the ratio of additional rooms consumed to restaurant meals sacrificed—chosen to keep her total utility constant.

Notice that the quantity of restaurant meals that Ingrid is willing to give up in return for an additional room changes along the indifference curve. As we move from

FIGURE E-5 The Changing Slope of an Indifference Curve

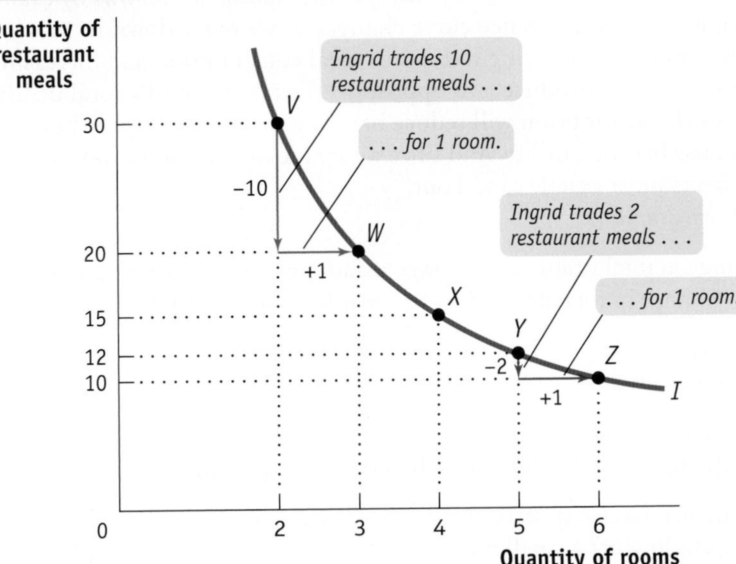

Consumption bundle	Quantity of rooms	Quantity of restaurant meals
V	2	30
W	3	20
X	4	15
Y	5	12
Z	6	10

This indifference curve is downward-sloping and convex, implying that restaurant meals and rooms are ordinary goods for Ingrid. As Ingrid moves down her indifference curve from *V* to *Z*, she gives up restaurant meals in exchange for a larger number of rooms. However, the terms of that trade-off change. As she moves from *V* to *W*, she is willing to give up 10 restaurant meals in return for 1 more room. As her consumption of rooms rises and her consumption of restaurant meals falls, she is willing to give up fewer restaurant meals in return for each additional room. The flattening of the slope as she moves from left to right arises from diminishing marginal utility.

V to *W*, housing consumption rises from 2 to 3 rooms and restaurant meal consumption falls from 30 to 20—a trade-off of 10 restaurant meals for 1 additional room. But as we move from *Y* to *Z*, housing consumption rises from 5 to 6 rooms and restaurant meal consumption falls from 12 to 10, a trade-off of only 2 restaurant meals for an additional room.

To put it in terms of slope, the slope of the indifference curve between *V* and *W* is −10: the change in restaurant meal consumption, −10, divided by the change in housing consumption, 1. Similarly, the slope of the indifference curve between *Y* and *Z* is −2. So the indifference curve gets flatter as we move down it to the right—that is, it has a convex shape, one of the four properties of an indifference curve for ordinary goods.

Why does the trade-off change in this way? Let's think about it intuitively and then work through it more carefully. When Ingrid moves down her indifference curve, whether from *V* to *W* or from *Y* to *Z*, she gains utility from her additional consumption of housing but loses an equal amount of utility from her reduced consumption of restaurant meals. But at each step, the initial position from which Ingrid begins is different. At *V*, Ingrid consumes only a small quantity of rooms; because of diminishing marginal utility, her marginal utility per room at that point is high. At *V*, then, an additional room adds a lot to Ingrid's total utility. But at *V* she already consumes a large quantity of restaurant meals, so her marginal utility of restaurant meals is low at that point. This means that it takes a large reduction in her quantity of restaurant meals consumed to offset the increased utility she gets from the extra room of housing.

Alexander Spataru/Moment/Getty Images

At *Y*, in contrast, Ingrid consumes a much larger quantity of rooms and a much smaller quantity of restaurant meals than at *V*. This means that an additional room adds fewer utils, and a restaurant meal forgone costs more utils, than at *V*. So Ingrid is willing to give up fewer restaurant meals in return for another room of housing at *Y* (where she gives up 2 meals for 1 room) than she is at *V* (where she gives up 10 meals for 1 room).

Now let's express the same idea — that the trade-off Ingrid is willing to make depends on where she is starting from — by using a little math. We do this by examining how the slope of the indifference curve changes as we move down it. Moving down the indifference curve — reducing restaurant meal consumption and increasing housing consumption — will produce two opposing effects on Ingrid's total utility: lower restaurant meal consumption will reduce her total utility, but higher housing consumption will raise her total utility. And since we are moving down the indifference curve, these two effects must exactly cancel out:

Along the indifference curve:

(E-1) (Change in total utility due to lower restaurant meal consumption) + (Change in total utility due to higher housing consumption) = 0

or, rearranging terms,

Along the indifference curve:

(E-2) −(Change in total utility due to lower restaurant meal consumption) = (Change in total utility due to higher housing consumption)

Let's now focus on what happens as we move only a short distance down the indifference curve, trading off a small increase in housing consumption in place of a small decrease in restaurant meal consumption. Following our notation from before, let's use MU_R and MU_M to represent the marginal utility of rooms and restaurant meals, respectively, and ΔQ_R and ΔQ_M to represent the changes in room and meal consumption, respectively. In general, the change in total utility caused by a small change in consumption of a good is equal to the change in consumption multiplied by the *marginal utility* of that good. This means that we can calculate the change in Ingrid's total utility generated by a change in her consumption bundle using the following equations:

(E-3) $$\text{Change in total utility due to a change in restaurant meal consumption} = MU_M \times \Delta Q_M$$

and

(E-4) $$\text{Change in total utility due to a change in housing consumption} = MU_R \times \Delta Q_R$$

So we can write Equation E-2 in symbols as:

Along the indifference curve:

(E-5) $$-MU_M \times \Delta Q_M = MU_R \times \Delta Q_R$$

Note that the left-hand side of Equation E-5 has a negative sign; it represents the loss in total utility from decreased restaurant meal consumption. This must equal the gain in total utility from increased room consumption, represented by the right-hand side of the equation.

What we want to know is how this translates into the slope of the indifference curve. To find the slope, we divide both sides of Equation E-5 by ΔQ_R, and again by $-MU_M$ in order to get the ΔQ_M, ΔQ_R terms on one side and the MU_R, MU_M terms on the other. This results in:

Along the indifference curve:

(E-6) $$\frac{\Delta Q_M}{\Delta Q_R} = -\frac{MU_R}{MU_M}$$

The left-hand side of Equation E-6 is the slope of the indifference curve; it is the rate at which Ingrid is willing to trade rooms (the good on the horizontal axis) for restaurant meals (the good on the vertical axis) without changing her total utility level.

The right-hand side of Equation E-6 is the negative of the ratio of the marginal utility of rooms to the marginal utility of restaurant meals—that is, the ratio of what she gains from one more room to what she gains from one more meal, with a negative sign in front.

Putting all this together, Equation E-6 shows that, along the indifference curve, the quantity of restaurant meals Ingrid is willing to give up in return for a room, $\frac{\Delta Q_M}{\Delta Q_R}$, is exactly equal to the negative of the ratio of the marginal utility of a room to that of a meal, $-\frac{MU_R}{MU_M}$. Only when this condition is met will her total utility level remain constant as she consumes more rooms and fewer restaurant meals.

Economists have a special name for the ratio of the marginal utilities found in the right-hand side of Equation E-6: the **marginal rate of substitution**, or ***MRS***, of rooms (the good on the horizontal axis) in place of restaurant meals (the good on the vertical axis). That's because as we slide down Ingrid's indifference curve, we are substituting more rooms for fewer restaurant meals in her consumption bundle. As we'll see shortly, the marginal rate of substitution plays an important role in finding the optimal consumption bundle.

The **marginal rate of substitution**, or *MRS*, of good *R* in place of good *M* is equal to $\frac{MU_R}{MU_M}$, the ratio of the marginal utility of *R* to the marginal utility of *M*.

Recall that indifference curves get flatter as you move down them to the right. The reason, as we've just discussed, is diminishing marginal utility: as Ingrid consumes more housing and fewer restaurant meals, her marginal utility from housing falls and her marginal utility from restaurant meals rises. So her marginal rate of substitution, which is equal to the negative of the slope of her indifference curve, falls as she moves down the indifference curve.

The flattening of indifference curves as you slide down them to the right—which reflects the same logic as the principle of diminishing marginal utility—is known as the principle of **diminishing marginal rate of substitution**. It says that the more of one good an individual consumes in proportion to a second good, the less of the second good they are willing to give up in exchange for another unit of the first good.

The principle of **diminishing marginal rate of substitution** states that the more of one good a person consumes in proportion to a second good, the less of the second good they are willing to substitute for another unit of the first good.

We can illustrate this point by referring to Figure E-5. At point *V*, a bundle with a low proportion of rooms to restaurant meals, Ingrid is willing to forgo 10 restaurant meals in return for 1 room. But at point *Y*, a bundle with a high proportion of rooms to restaurant meals, she is willing to forgo only 2 restaurant meals in return for 1 room.

From this example we see that, in Ingrid's utility function, rooms and restaurant meals possess the two additional properties that characterize ordinary goods. Ingrid requires additional rooms to compensate her for the loss of a meal, and vice versa; so her indifference curves for these two goods slope downward. And her indifference curves are convex: the slope of her indifference curve—*the negative of the marginal rate of substitution*—becomes flatter as we move down it. In fact, an indifference curve is convex only when it has a diminishing marginal rate of substitution. These two conditions are equivalent.

With this information, we can define *ordinary goods*, which account for the great majority of all goods. A pair of goods are **ordinary goods** in a consumer's utility function if they possess two properties: the consumer requires more of one good to compensate for less of the other, and the consumer experiences a diminishing marginal rate of substitution when substituting one good for the other.

Two goods are **ordinary goods** in a consumer's utility function when (1) the consumer requires additional units of one good to compensate for fewer units of the other, and (2) the consumer experiences a diminishing marginal rate of substitution when substituting one good for the other.

Next, we will see how to determine Ingrid's optimal consumption bundle using indifference curves.

The Tangency Condition

Now let's put some of Ingrid's indifference curves on the same diagram as her budget line to illustrate her optimal consumption choice. **Figure E-6** shows Ingrid's budget

FIGURE E-6 The Optimal Consumption Bundle

The budget line, BL, shows Ingrid's possible consumption bundles, given an income of \$2,400 per month, when rooms cost \$150 per month and restaurant meals cost \$30 each. I_1, I_2, and I_3 are indifference curves. Consumption bundles such as B and C are not optimal because Ingrid can move to a higher indifference curve. The optimal consumption bundle is A, where the budget line is just tangent to the highest indifference curve Ingrid can afford to reach. Higher indifference curves, represented by I_3, cannot be reached because they lie entirely above the budget line.

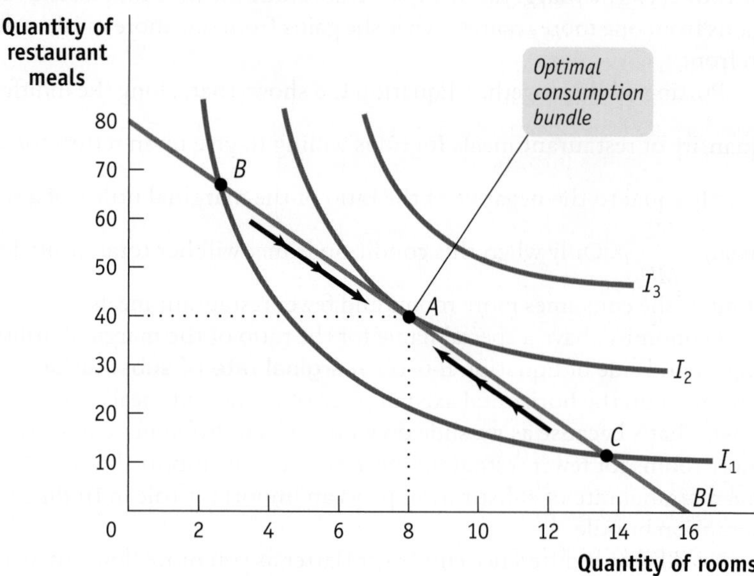

line, BL, when her income is \$2,400 per month, housing costs \$150 per room each month, and restaurant meals cost \$30 each. What is her optimal consumption bundle?

To answer this question, we consider three of Ingrid's indifference curves: I_1, I_2, and I_3. Of these curves, I_3 represents the highest total utility level, but Ingrid cannot afford to reach that level because she is constrained by her income: no consumption bundle on her budget line yields that much total utility. But she shouldn't settle for the total utility level generated by B or C, which both lie on I_1: there are other bundles on her budget line, such as A, that clearly yield more total utility than B or C.

In fact, A—a consumption bundle consisting of 8 rooms and 40 restaurant meals per month—is Ingrid's optimal consumption choice. The reason is that A lies on the highest indifference curve Ingrid can reach given her income.

The **tangency condition** between the indifference curve and the budget line holds when the indifference curve and the budget line just touch. This condition determines the optimal consumption bundle when the indifference curves have the typical convex shape.

At the optimal consumption bundle A, Ingrid's budget line *just touches* the relevant indifference curve—the budget line is *tangent* to the indifference curve. This **tangency condition** between the indifference curve and the budget line applies to the optimal consumption bundle when the indifference curves have the typical convex shape.

To see why, let's look more closely at how we know that a consumption bundle that *doesn't* satisfy the tangency condition can't be optimal. Reexamining Figure E-6, we can see that consumption bundles B and C are both affordable because they lie on the budget line. However, neither is optimal. Both of them lie on the indifference curve I_1, which cuts through the budget line at both points. But because I_1 cuts through the budget line, Ingrid can do better: she can move down the budget line from B or up the budget line from C, as indicated by the arrows. In each case, this allows her to get onto a higher indifference curve, I_2, which increases her total utility.

However, Ingrid cannot do any better than I_2: any other indifference curve either cuts through her budget line or doesn't touch it at all. And the bundle that allows her to achieve I_2, of course, is her optimal consumption bundle.

The Slope of the Budget Line

Figure E-6 shows us how to use a graph of the budget line and the indifference curves to find the optimal consumption bundle, the bundle at which the budget line and the indifference curve are tangent. But rather than rely on drawing graphs, we can determine the optimal consumption bundle by using a bit more math. As you can see from

Figure E-6, the budget line and the indifference curve have the same slope at the optimal consumption bundle, *A*. Why? Because two curves can be tangent to each other only if they have the same slope at the point where they meet. Otherwise, they would cross each other at that point. And we know that if a point is on an indifference curve that *crosses* the budget line (like I_1 in Figure E-6), it can't be on the indifference curve that contains the optimal consumption bundle (that is, I_2).

So we can use information about the slopes of the budget line and the indifference curve to find the optimal consumption bundle. To do that, we must first analyze the slope of the budget line, a fairly straightforward task. We know that Ingrid will get the highest possible utility by spending all of her income and consuming a bundle on her budget line. So we can represent Ingrid's budget line, made up of the consumption bundles available to her when she spends all of her income, with the equation:

$$\textbf{(E-7)} \quad (Q_R \times P_R) + (Q_M \times P_M) = N$$

where *N* stands for Ingrid's income. To find the slope of the budget line, we divide its vertical intercept (where the budget line hits the vertical axis) by its horizontal intercept (where it hits the horizontal axis) and then add a negative sign. The vertical intercept is the point at which Ingrid spends all her income on restaurant meals and none on housing (that is, $Q_R = 0$). In that case, the number of restaurant meals she consumes is:

$$\textbf{(E-8)} \quad Q_M = \frac{N}{P_M} = \frac{\$2{,}400}{(\$30 \text{ per meal})} = 80 \text{ meals}$$
$$= \text{Vertical intercept of budget line}$$

At the other extreme, Ingrid spends all her income on housing and none on restaurant meals (so that $Q_M = 0$). This means that at the horizontal intercept of the budget line, the number of rooms she consumes is:

$$\textbf{(E-9)} \quad Q_R = \frac{N}{P_R} = \frac{\$2{,}400}{(\$150 \text{ per room})} = 16 \text{ rooms}$$
$$= \text{Horizontal intercept of budget line}$$

Now we have the information needed to find the slope of the budget line. It is:

$$\textbf{(E-10)} \quad \text{Slope of budget line} = -\frac{\text{Vertical intercept}}{\text{Horizontal intercept}} = -\frac{\frac{N}{P_M}}{\frac{N}{P_R}} = -\frac{P_R}{P_M}$$

Notice the negative sign in Equation E-10; it's there because the budget line slopes downward. The $\frac{P_R}{P_M}$ quantity is known as the **relative price** of rooms in terms of restaurant meals, to distinguish it from an ordinary price in terms of dollars. Because buying one more room requires Ingrid to give up the quantity $\frac{P_R}{P_M}$ of restaurant meals, or 5 meals, we can interpret the relative price $\frac{P_R}{P_M}$ as the rate at which a room trades for restaurant meals in the market; it is the price—in terms of restaurant meals—Ingrid has to "pay" to get one more room.

The **relative price** of good *R* in terms of good *M* is equal to $\frac{P_R}{P_M}$, the rate at which *R* trades for *M* in the market.

Looking at this another way, the slope of the budget line—the negative of the relative price—tells us the opportunity cost of each good in terms of the other. The relative price illustrates the opportunity cost to an individual of consuming one more unit of one good in terms of how much of the other good in his or her consumption bundle must be forgone. This opportunity cost arises from the consumer's limited resources—the consumer's limited budget. It's useful to note that Equations E-8, E-9, and E-10 give us all the information we need about what happens to the budget line when relative price or income changes. From Equations E-8 and E-9 we can see that a change in income, N, leads to a parallel shift of the budget line: both the vertical and horizontal intercepts will shift. That is, how far out the budget line is from the origin depends on the consumer's income. If a consumer's income rises, the budget line moves outward. If the consumer's income shrinks, the budget line shifts inward. In each case, the slope of the budget line stays the same because the relative price of one good in terms of the other does not change.

In contrast, a change in the relative price, $\frac{P_R}{P_M}$, will lead to a change in the slope of the budget line. Next, we'll analyze in greater detail these changes in the budget line and examine how the optimal consumption bundle changes when either the relative price or income changes.

Prices and the Marginal Rate of Substitution

Now we're ready to bring together the slope of the budget line and the slope of the indifference curve to find the optimal consumption bundle. From Equation E-6, we know that the slope of the indifference curve at any point is equal to the negative of the marginal rate of substitution:

$$\textbf{(E-11)} \quad \text{Slope of indifference curve} = -\frac{MU_R}{MU_M}$$

The **relative price rule** says that at the optimal consumption bundle, the marginal rate of substitution between two goods is equal to their relative price.

As we've already noted, at the optimal consumption bundle, the slope of the budget line and the slope of the indifference curve are equal. We can write this formally by putting Equations E-10 and E-11 together, which gives us the **relative price rule** for finding the optimal consumption bundle:

$$\textbf{(E-12)} \quad \textit{At the optimal consumption bundle: } -\frac{MU_R}{MU_M} = -\frac{P_R}{P_M}$$

$$\text{or, } \textit{cancelling the negative signs, } \frac{MU_R}{MU_M} = \frac{P_R}{P_M}$$

That is, at the optimal consumption bundle, the marginal rate of substitution between any two goods is equal to the ratio of their prices. To put it in a more intuitive way, starting with Ingrid's optimal consumption bundle, the rate at which she would trade a room for more restaurant meals along her indifference curve, $\frac{MU_R}{MU_M}$, is equal to the rate at which rooms are traded for restaurant meals in the market, $\frac{P_R}{P_M}$.

What would happen if this equality did not hold? We can see this by examining **Figure E-7**. There, at point B, the slope of the indifference curve, $-\frac{MU_R}{MU_M}$, is greater in absolute value than the slope of the budget line, $-\frac{P_R}{P_M}$. This means that, at B, Ingrid values an additional room in place of meals *more* than it costs her to buy an additional room and forgo some meals. As a result, Ingrid would be better off moving down her budget line toward A, consuming more rooms and fewer restaurant meals—and because of that, B could not have been her optimal bundle! Likewise, at C, the slope of Ingrid's indifference curve is less in absolute value than the slope of the budget line. The implication is that, at C, Ingrid values additional meals in place of a room *more* than it costs her to buy additional meals and forgo a room. Again, Ingrid would be

FIGURE E-7 Understanding the Relative Price Rule

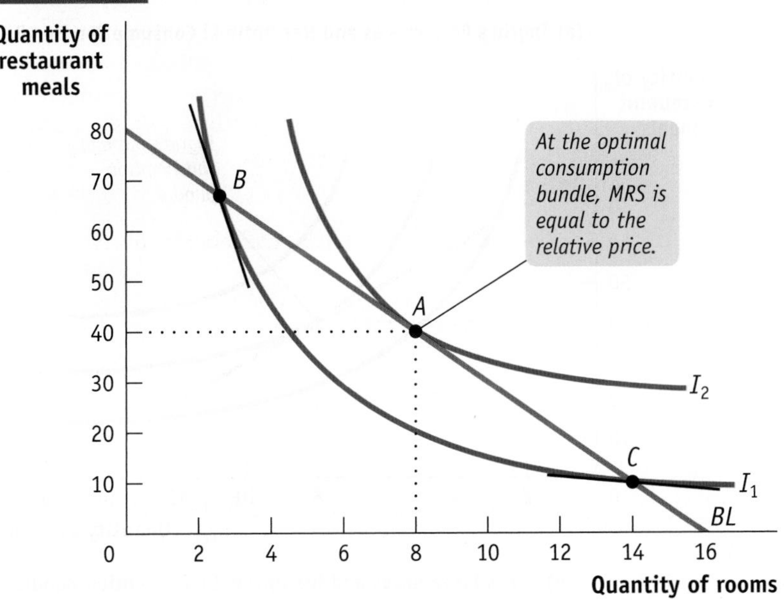

The *relative price* of rooms in terms of restaurant meals is equal to the negative of the slope of the budget line. The *marginal rate of substitution* of rooms for restaurant meals is equal to the negative of the slope of the indifference curve. The *relative price rule* says that at the optimal consumption bundle, the marginal rate of substitution must equal the relative price. This point can be demonstrated by considering what happens when the marginal rate of substitution is not equal to the relative price. At consumption bundle *B*, the marginal rate of substitution is larger than the relative price; Ingrid can increase her total utility by moving down her budget line, *BL*. At *C*, the marginal rate of substitution is smaller than the relative price, and Ingrid can increase her total utility by moving up the budget line. Only at *A*, where the relative price rule holds, is her total utility maximized, given her budget constraint.

better off moving along her budget line—consuming more restaurant meals and fewer rooms—until she reaches *A*, her optimal consumption bundle.

But suppose we transform the last term of Equation E-12 in the following way: divide both sides by P_R and multiply both sides by MU_M. Then the relative price rule becomes the optimal consumption rule:

$$\text{(E-13)} \quad \textit{Optimal consumption rule:} \ \frac{MU_R}{P_R} = \frac{MU_M}{P_M}$$

So using either the optimal consumption rule or the relative price rule, we find the same optimal consumption bundle.

Preferences and Choices

Now that we have seen how to represent the optimal consumption choice in an indifference curve diagram, we can turn briefly to the relationship between consumer preferences and consumer choices.

When we say that two consumers have different preferences, we mean that they have different utility functions. This in turn means that they will have indifference curve maps with different shapes. And those different maps will translate into different consumption choices, even among consumers with the same income and who face the same prices.

To see this, suppose that Ingrid's friend Lars also consumes only housing and restaurant meals. However, Lars has a stronger preference for restaurant meals and a weaker preference for housing. This difference in preferences is shown in **Figure E-8**, which shows *two* sets of indifference curves: panel (a) shows Ingrid's preferences, and panel (b) shows Lars's preferences. Note the difference in their shapes.

Suppose, as before, that rooms cost $150 per month and restaurant meals cost $30. Let's also assume that both Ingrid and Lars have incomes of $2,400 per month, giving them identical budget lines. Nonetheless, because they have different preferences, they will make different consumption choices, as shown in Figure E-8. Ingrid will choose 8 rooms and 40 restaurant meals, whereas Lars will choose 4 rooms and 60 restaurant meals.

FIGURE E-8 Differences in Preferences

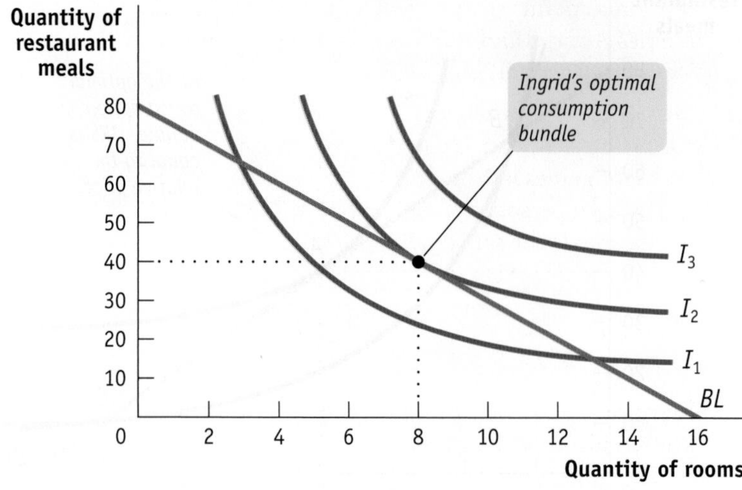

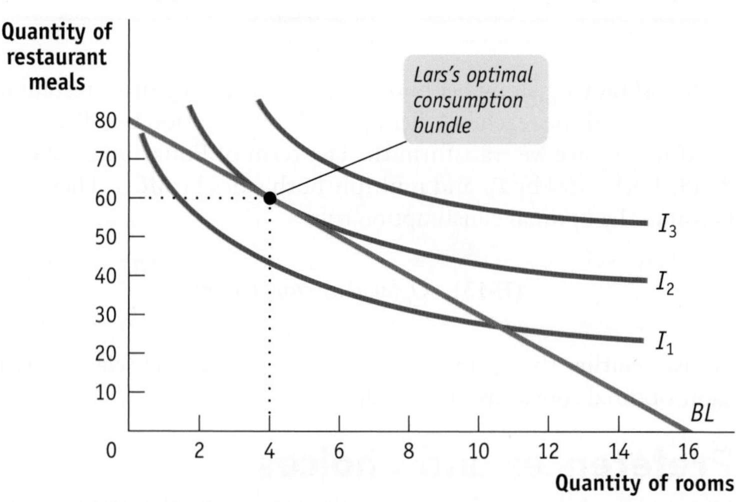

Ingrid and Lars have different preferences, reflected in the different shapes of their indifference curve maps. So they will choose different consumption bundles even when they have the same options. Each has an income of $2,400 per month and faces prices of $30 per meal and $150 per room. Panel (a) shows Ingrid's consumption choice: 8 rooms and 40 restaurant meals. Panel (b) shows Lars's choice: even though he has the same budget line, he consumes fewer rooms (4) and more restaurant meals (60).

Enrichment Module E  Review

Check Your Understanding

1. The accompanying table shows Samantha's preferences for consumption bundles composed of chocolate kisses and licorice drops.

Consumption bundle	Quantity of chocolate kisses	Quantity of licorice drops	Total utility (utils)
A	1	3	6
B	2	3	10
C	3	1	6
D	2	1	4

a. With chocolate kisses on the horizontal axis and licorice drops on the vertical axis, draw hypothetical indifference curves for Samantha and locate the bundles on the curves. Assume that both items are ordinary goods.

b. Suppose you don't know the number of utils provided by each bundle. Assuming that more is better, predict Samantha's ranking of each of the four bundles to the extent possible. Explain your answer.

2. On panel A1 of Figure E-4, draw a point *B* anywhere on the 200-util indifference curve and a point *C* anywhere on the 100-util indifference curve (but *not* at the same location as point *A*). By comparing the utils generated by bundles *A* and *B* and those generated by bundles *A* and *C*, explain why indifference curves cannot cross.

3. Lucinda and Kyle each consume 3 comic books and 6 video games. Lucinda's marginal rate of substitution of books for games is 2, and Kyle's is 5.
   a. For each person, find another consumption bundle that yields the same total utility as the current bundle. Who is less willing to trade games for books? In a diagram with books on the horizontal axis and games on the vertical axis, how would this be reflected in differences in the slopes of their indifference curves at their current consumption bundles?
   b. Find the relative price of books in terms of games at which Lucinda's current bundle is optimal. Is Kyle's bundle optimal given this relative price? If not, how should Kyle rearrange his consumption?

Multiple-Choice Review Questions

1. Which of the following is true along an individual's indifference curve for ordinary goods?
   a. The slope is constant.
   b. Total utility changes.
   c. The individual is indifferent between any two points.
   d. The slope is equal to the ratio of the prices of the consumption bundles.
   e. The individual doesn't care if utility is maximized.

2. Which of the following is/are true of indifference curves for ordinary goods?
   I. They cannot intersect.
   II. They have a negative slope.
   III. They are convex.
   a. I only
   b. II only
   c. III only
   d. I and II only
   e. I, II, and III

3. Moving from left to right along an indifference curve, which of the following increases?
   a. the marginal utility of the vertical axis good
   b. the marginal utility of the horizontal axis good
   c. the absolute value of the slope
   d. the marginal rate of substitution
   e. the demand for the vertical axis good

4. If the quantity of good *X* is measured on the horizontal axis and the quantity of good *Y* is measured on the vertical axis, the marginal rate of substitution is equal to
   a. $\frac{\Delta Q_X}{Q_Y}$.
   b. $\frac{MU_X}{MU_Y}$.
   c. $\frac{P_X}{P_Y}$.
   d. the ratio of the slope of the budget line and the slope of the indifference curve.
   e. 1, at the optimal level of consumption.

5. If the quantity of good *X* is again measured on the horizontal axis and the quantity of good *Y* is measured on the vertical axis, which of the following is true? The optimal consumption bundle is found where
   a. $\frac{MU_X}{MU_Y} = \frac{P_X}{P_Y}$.
   b. the slope of the indifference curve equals the slope of the budget line.
   c. the indifference curve is tangent to the budget line.
   d. $\frac{MU_X}{P_X} = \frac{MU_Y}{P_Y}$.
   e. All of the above are true.

Free-Response Review Questions

1. Each of the combinations of song and movie downloads shown in the table below give Kathleen an equal level of utility.

Quantity of songs	Quantity of movies
0	8
1	6
2	4
3	2
4	0

   a. Graph Kathleen's indifference curve.
   b. Economists believe that each individual indifference curve for ordinary goods exhibits what two properties?
   c. Does Kathleen's indifference curve exhibit the two properties from part b? Explain.

Rubric for FRQ 1 (8 points)

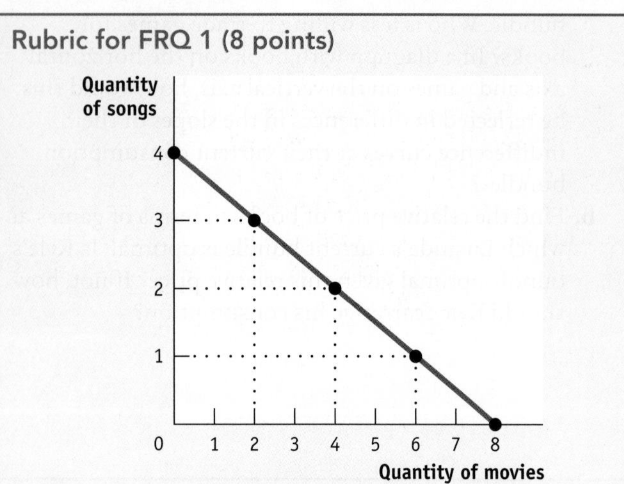

1 point: Axes labeled "Quantity of songs" and "Quantity of movies"

1 point: Correctly plotted indifference curve points

1 point: Negative slope

1 point: Convex shape

1 point: The indifference curve does have a negative slope.

1 point: As more movies are downloaded, there must be fewer song downloads to give Kathleen the same level of utility as before. This trade-off of more of one good for less of another gives the indifference curve a negative slope.

1 point: The indifference curve does not have a convex shape.

1 point: The indifference curve is a straight line with a constant slope, rather than being a convex line with a slope that decreases in absolute value from left to right.

2. Kathleen has $20 to spend on song and movie downloads each week. The price of a song download is $2 and the price of a movie download is $5.

a. Graph Kathleen's budget line.

b. Suppose all of Kathleen's indifference curves have the same shape and slope as the one in Question 1. How many song and movie downloads will Kathleen purchase to maximize her utility? Explain. **(4 points)**

Discussion Starters

1. What would it indicate about your preferences for two goods if your indifference curves were vertical? Can you think of examples of pairs of goods for which this is the case?
2. Suppose that on a Saturday afternoon you must divide your time between studying and playing sports, and both activities are free. Could you use a budget constraint and indifference curves to model this decision?
3. Consider the dilemma of how much money to spend now and how much to set aside for the future. Is this another trade-off that could be modeled with a budget constraint and indifference curves? What makes it possible to spend more now than you actually have? If you spend less than you have now, what can you do with your money so that the amount you have to spend in the future grows? What rate associated with these opportunities affects the slope of the budget constraint?

AP® Economics Skills Appendix

Graphs In Economics

In this Appendix, you will learn to:

- Recognize the importance of graphs in studying economics
- Describe the basic components of a graph
- Explain how graphs illustrate the relationship between variables
- Explain how to calculate the slope of a curve and discuss what the slope value means
- Describe how to calculate areas represented on graphs
- Explain how to interpret numerical graphs

Getting the Picture

Whether you're reading about economics in the *Wall Street Journal* or in your economics textbook, you will see many graphs. Visual presentations can make it much easier to understand verbal descriptions, numerical information, or ideas. In economics, graphs are the type of visual presentation used to facilitate understanding. To fully understand the ideas and information being discussed, you need to know how to interpret these visual aids. This Module explains how graphs are constructed and interpreted, and how they are used in economics.

Graphs, Variables, and Economic Models

One reason to attend college is that a bachelor's degree provides access to higher-paying jobs. Additional degrees, such as MBAs or law degrees, increase earnings even more. If you were to read an article about the relationship between educational attainment and income, you would probably see a graph showing the income levels for workers with different levels of education. This graph would depict the idea that, in general, having more education increases a person's income. This graph, like most graphs in economics, would depict the relationship between two economic variables. A **variable** is a measure that can take on more than one value, such as the number of years of education a person has, the price of a can of soda, or a household's income.

A **variable** is a measure that can take on more than one value.

As you learned in Unit 1, economic analysis relies heavily on *models*, simplified representations of real situations. Most economic models describe the relationship between two variables, simplified by holding constant other variables that may affect the relationship. For example, an economic model might describe the relationship between the price of a can of soda and the number of cans of soda that consumers will buy, assuming that everything else that affects consumers' purchases of soda stays constant. This type of model can be depicted mathematically, but illustrating the relationship in a graph makes it easier to understand. Next, we show how graphs that depict economic models are constructed and interpreted.

How Graphs Work

Most graphs in economics are built in a two-dimensional space defined by two perpendicular lines that show the values of two or more variables. These graphs help people visualize the relationship between the variables. A first step in understanding the use of such graphs is to see how the values of variables are indicated by the points on the graphs.

Two-Variable Graphs

Figure A.1 shows a typical two-variable graph. It illustrates the data in the accompanying table on outside temperature and the number of sodas a typical vendor can expect to sell at a baseball stadium during one game. The first column shows the values of outside temperature (the first variable) and the second column shows the values of the number of sodas sold (the second variable). Five combinations or pairs of the two variables are shown, denoted by points *A* through *E* in the third column.

FIGURE A.1 Plotting Points on a Two-Variable Graph

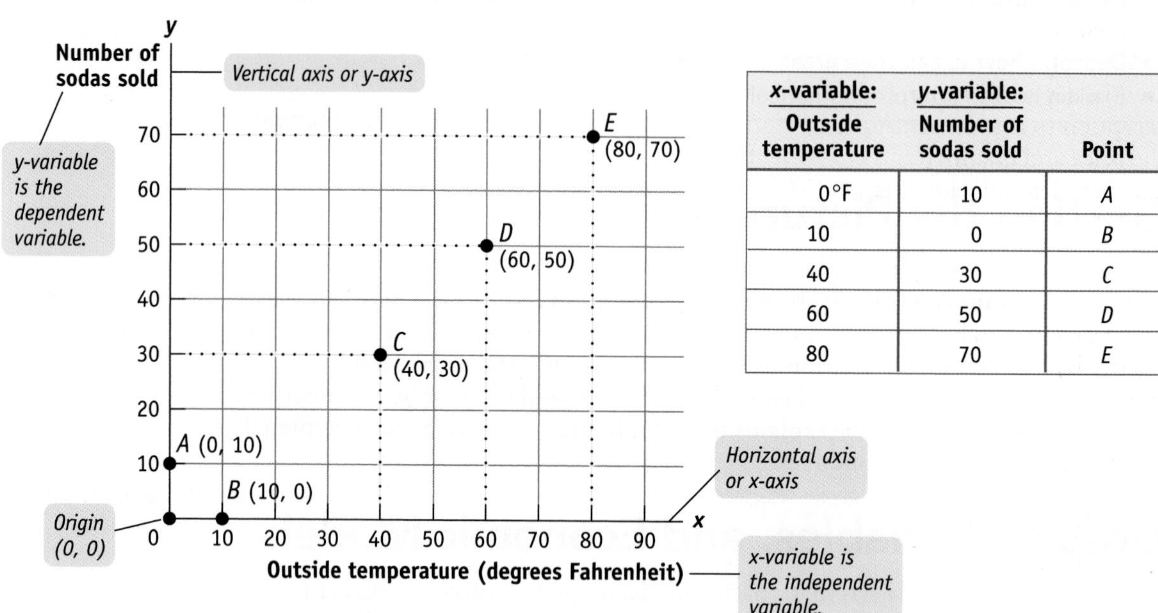

x-variable: Outside temperature	y-variable: Number of sodas sold	Point
0°F	10	*A*
10	0	*B*
40	30	*C*
60	50	*D*
80	70	*E*

The data from the table are plotted where outside temperature (the independent variable) is measured along the horizontal axis and number of sodas sold (the dependent variable) is measured along the vertical axis. Each of the five combinations of temperature and sodas sold is represented by a point: *A*, *B*, *C*, *D*, or *E*. Each point in the graph is identified by a pair of values. For example, point *C* corresponds to the pair (40, 30)—an outside temperature of 40°F (the value of the *x*-variable) and 30 sodas sold (the value of the *y*-variable).

The solid horizontal line that goes through the origin on a graph is called the **horizontal axis** or ***x*-axis**.

The solid vertical line that goes through the origin on a graph is called the **vertical axis** or ***y*-axis**.

The two axes meet at the **origin**.

Now let's turn to graphing the data in this table. In any two-variable graph, one variable is called the *x*-variable and the other is called the *y*-variable. Here we have made outside temperature the *x*-variable and number of sodas sold the *y*-variable. The solid horizontal line in the graph is called the **horizontal axis** or ***x*-axis**, and values of the *x*-variable—outside temperature—are measured along it. Similarly, the solid vertical line in the graph is called the **vertical axis** or ***y*-axis**, and values of the *y*-variable—number of sodas sold—are measured along it. At the **origin**, the point where the two axes meet, each variable is equal to zero. As you move rightward from the origin along the *x*-axis, values of the *x*-variable are positive and increasing. As you move up from the origin along the *y*-axis, values of the *y*-variable are positive and increasing.

You can plot each of the five points *A* through *E* on this graph by using a pair of numbers—the values that the *x*-variable and the *y*-variable take on for a given point. In Figure A.1, at point *C*, the *x*-variable takes on the value 40 and the *y*-variable takes on the value 30. You plot point *C* by drawing a line straight up from 40 on the *x*-axis and a horizontal line across from 30 on the *y*-axis. We write point *C* as (40, 30). We write the origin as (0, 0).

Looking at point *A* and point *B* in Figure A.1, you can see that when one of the variables for a point has a value of zero, it will lie on one of the axes. If the value of the *x*-variable is zero, the point will lie on the vertical axis, like point *A*. If the value of the *y*-variable is zero, the point will lie on the horizontal axis, like point *B*. (The location of point *B* was chosen to illustrate this fact and not because soda sales will really decrease when the temperature rises.)

Most graphs that depict relationships between two economic variables represent a **causal relationship**, a relationship in which the value of one variable directly influences or determines the value of the other variable. In a causal relationship, the determining variable is called the **independent variable**; the variable it determines is called the **dependent variable**. In our example of soda sales, the outside temperature is the independent variable. It directly influences the number of sodas that are sold, which is the dependent variable in this case.

A **causal relationship** is one in which the value of one variable directly influences or determines the value of the other variable.

In a causal relationship, the determining variable is called the **independent variable** and the determined variable is called the **dependent variable**.

By convention, we put the independent variable on the horizontal axis and the dependent variable on the vertical axis. Figure A.1 is constructed consistent with this convention: the independent variable (outside temperature) is on the horizontal axis, and the dependent variable (number of sodas sold) is on the vertical axis. An important exception to this convention is in graphs showing the economic relationship between the price and quantity of a product: although price is generally the independent variable that determines quantity, price is always measured on the vertical axis.

Curves on a Graph

Panel (a) of **Figure A.2** contains some of the same information as Figure A.1, with a line drawn through the points *B*, *C*, *D*, and *E*. Such a line on a graph is called a **curve**, regardless of whether it is a straight line or a curved line. If the curve that shows the

A line on a graph is called a **curve**, regardless of whether it is a straight line or a curved line.

FIGURE A.2 Drawing Curves

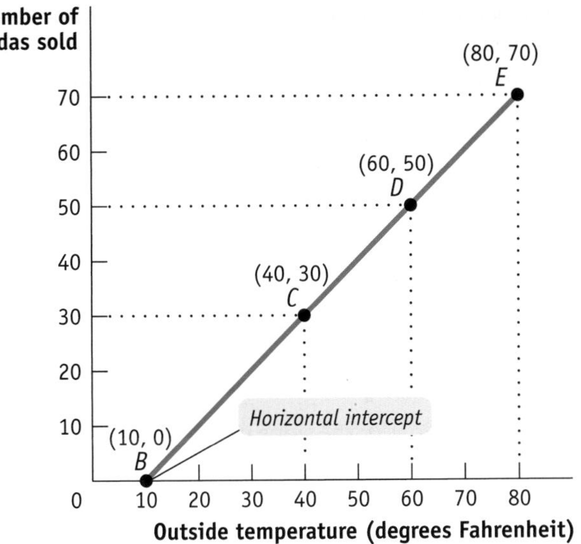

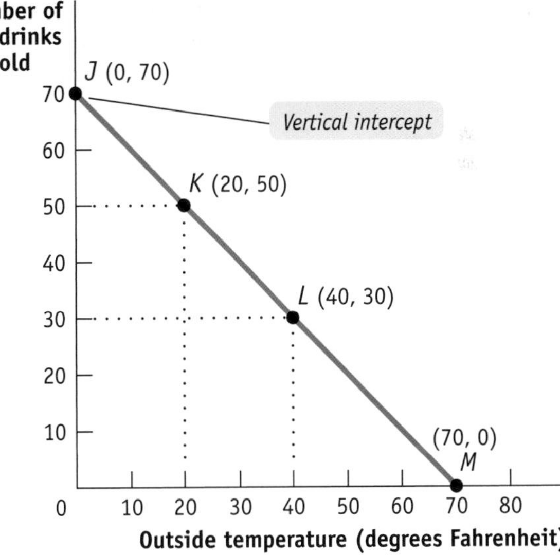

The curve in panel (a) illustrates the relationship between the two variables, outside temperature and number of sodas sold. The two variables have a positive linear relationship: positive because the curve has an upward tilt, and linear because it is a straight line. The curve implies that an increase in the *independent* variable (outside temperature) leads to an increase in the dependent variable (number of sodas sold). The curve in panel (b) is also a straight line, but it tilts downward. The two variables here, outside temperature and number of hot drinks sold, have a negative linear relationship: an increase in the *independent* variable (outside temperature) leads to a decrease in the dependent variable (number of hot drinks sold). The curve in panel (a) has a horizontal intercept at point *B*, where it hits the horizontal axis. The curve in panel (b) has a vertical intercept at point *J*, where it hits the vertical axis, and a horizontal intercept at point *M*, where it hits the horizontal axis.

If a curve that shows the relationship between two variables is a straight line, or linear, the variables have a **linear relationship**.

When a curve is not a straight line, it is nonlinear, and the variables have a **nonlinear relationship**.

When an increase in one variable is associated with an increase in the other variable, the variables are said to have a **positive relationship**.

When an increase in one variable is associated with a decrease in the other variable, the two variables are said to have a **negative relationship.**

relationship between two variables is a straight line, or linear, the variables have a **linear relationship**. When the curve is not a straight line, it is nonlinear, and the variables have a **nonlinear relationship**.

A point on a curve indicates the value of the *y*-variable for a specific value of the *x*-variable. For example, point *D* indicates that at a temperature of 60°F, a vendor can expect to sell 50 sodas. The shape and orientation of a curve reveal the general nature of the relationship between the two variables. The upward tilt of the curve in panel (a) of Figure A.2 suggests that vendors can expect to sell more sodas at higher outside temperatures.

When variables are related in this way—that is, when an increase in one variable is associated with an increase in the other variable—the variables are said to have a **positive relationship**. This relationship is illustrated by a curve that slopes upward from left to right. Because the relationship between outside temperature and number of sodas sold is also linear, as illustrated by the curve in panel (a) of Figure A.2, it is a positive linear relationship.

When an increase in one variable is associated with a decrease in the other variable, the two variables are said to have a **negative relationship**. Two variables that have such a relationship are the outside temperature and the number of hot drinks a vendor can expect to sell at a baseball stadium. This relationship is illustrated by a curve that slopes downward from left to right, like the curve in panel (b) of Figure A.2. Because this curve is also linear, the relationship it depicts is a negative linear relationship.

We've been looking at positive and negative relationships between variables that also have causal relationships. In some other cases the relationships shown on graphs can be misleading in terms of causality. For example, a graph displaying the size of a city's police force on the horizontal axis and the city's crime rate on the vertical axis might show a positive relationship, but this does not indicate that having more police causes the crime rate to rise. Instead, it may be that cities with higher crime rates employ more police, meaning that a higher crime rate is the cause for a larger police force. Another explanation could be that having more police leads to an increase in the number of existing crimes that are detected. Or perhaps big cities with large police forces have higher crime rates for reasons quite unrelated to policing. The important point is that a positive or negative relationship between two variables does not provide sufficient information to conclude that one variable causes the other to change.

The **horizontal intercept** indicates the value of the *x*-variable when the value of the *y*-variable is zero.

The **vertical intercept** indicates the value of the *y*-variable when the value of the *x*-variable is zero.

The **slope** of a curve is a measure of how steep the curve is; the slope indicates how sensitive the *y*-variable is to a change in the *x*-variable.

Return for a moment to the curve in panel (a) of Figure A.2, and you can see that it hits the horizontal axis at point *B*. This point, known as the **horizontal intercept**, shows the value of the *x*-variable when the value of the *y*-variable is zero: for example, when it is 10°F, no sodas are sold. In panel (b) of Figure A.2, the curve hits the vertical axis at point *J*. This point, called the **vertical intercept**, indicates the value of the *y*-variable when the value of the *x*-variable is zero: 70 hot drinks are sold when the temperature is 0°F.

A Key Concept: The Slope of a Curve 

The **slope** of a curve is a measure of how steep it is; the slope indicates how sensitive the *y*-variable is to a change in the *x*-variable. In our example of outside temperature and the number of cans of soda a vendor can expect to sell, the slope of the curve would indicate how many more cans of soda the vendor could expect to sell with each 1° increase in temperature. Interpreted this way, the slope gives meaningful information. Even without numbers for *x* and *y*, it is possible to arrive at important conclusions about the relationship between the two variables by examining the slope of a curve at various points.

The Slope of a Linear Curve

The slope, or steepness, of a linear curve is measured by dividing the "rise" between two points on the curve by the "run" between those same two points. The rise is the change in the value of the y-variable, and the run is the change in the value of the x-variable. Here is the formula:

$$\frac{\text{Change in } y}{\text{Change in } x} = \frac{\Delta y}{\Delta x} = \text{slope}$$

In the formula, the symbol Δ (the Greek uppercase delta) stands for "change in." When a variable increases, the change in that variable is positive; when a variable decreases, the change in that variable is negative.

The slope of a curve is positive when the rise (the change in the y-variable) has the same sign as the run (the change in the x-variable). That's because when two numbers have the same sign, the ratio of those two numbers is positive. The curve in panel (a) of Figure A.2 has a positive slope: along the curve, both the y-variable and the x-variable increase. The slope of a curve is negative when the rise and the run have different signs. That's because when two numbers have different signs, the ratio of those two numbers is negative. The curve in panel (b) of Figure A.2 has a negative slope: along the curve, an increase in the x-variable is associated with a decrease in the y-variable.

Figure A.3 illustrates how to calculate the slope of a linear curve. Let's focus first on panel (a). From point A to point B, the value of the y-variable changes from 25 to 20, and the value of the x-variable changes from 10 to 20. So the slope of the line between these two points is

$$\frac{\text{Change in } y}{\text{Change in } x} = \frac{\Delta y}{\Delta x} = \frac{-5}{10} = -\frac{1}{2} = -0.5$$

Because a straight line is equally steep at all points, the slope of a straight line is the same at all points. In other words, a straight line has a constant slope. You can check

FIGURE A.3 Calculating the Slope

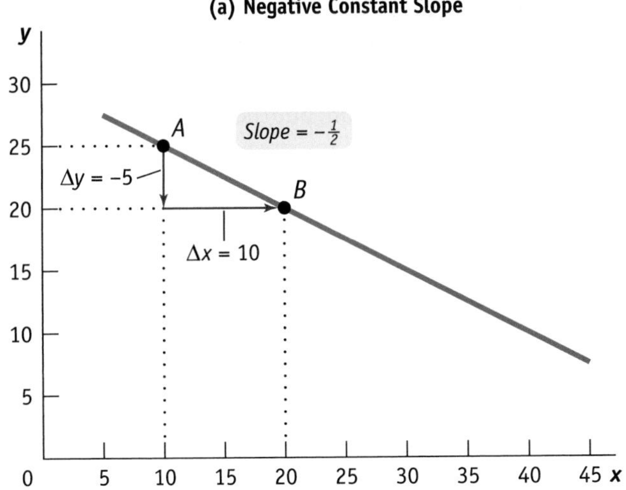

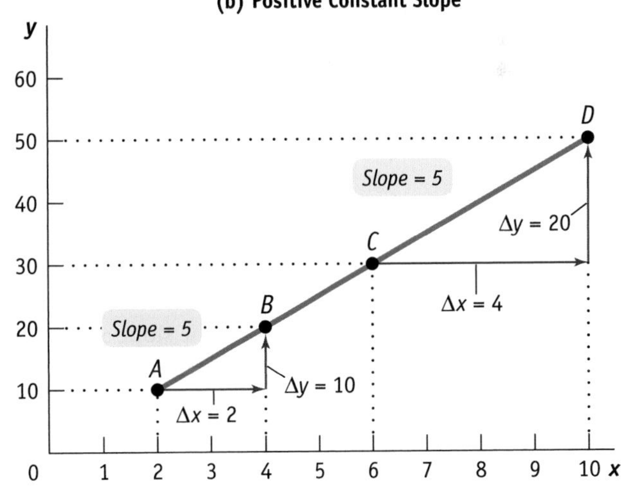

Panels (a) and (b) show two linear curves. Between points A and B on the curve in panel (a), the change in y (the rise) is −5 and the change in x (the run) is 10. So the slope from A to B is $\frac{\Delta y}{\Delta x} = \frac{-5}{10} = -\frac{1}{2} = -0.5$, where the negative sign indicates that the curve is downward-sloping. In panel (b), the curve has a slope from A to B of $\frac{\Delta y}{\Delta x} = \frac{10}{2} = 5$. The slope from C to D is $\frac{\Delta y}{\Delta x} = \frac{20}{4} = 5$. The slope is positive, indicating that the curve is upward-sloping. Furthermore, the slope between A and B is the same as the slope between C and D, making this a linear curve. The slope of a linear curve is constant: it is the same regardless of where it is calculated along the curve.

this by calculating the slope of the linear curve between points A and B and between points C and D in panel (b) of Figure A.3.

$$\frac{\Delta y}{\Delta x} = \frac{10}{2} = 5$$

$$\frac{\Delta y}{\Delta x} = \frac{20}{4} = 5$$

Horizontal and Vertical Curves and Their Slopes

When a curve is horizontal, the value of y along that curve never changes—it is constant. Everywhere along the curve, the change in y is zero. Now, zero divided by any number is zero. So regardless of the value of the change in x, the slope of a horizontal curve is always zero.

If a curve is vertical, the value of x along the curve never changes—it is constant. Everywhere along the curve, the change in x is zero. This means that the slope of a vertical line is a ratio with zero in the denominator. A ratio with zero in the denominator is an infinitely large number that is considered "undefined." So the slope of a vertical line is typically described as infinite or undefined.

A vertical or a horizontal curve has a special implication: it means that the x-variable and the y-variable are unrelated. Two variables are unrelated when a change in one variable (the independent variable) has no effect on the other variable (the dependent variable). If, as is usual, the y-variable is the dependent variable, the curve showing the relationship between the dependent variable and the unrelated independent variable is horizontal. For instance, suppose you eat lasagna once a week regardless of the number of hours you spend studying that week. Then the curve on a graph that shows lasagna meals per week on the vertical axis and study hours per week on the horizontal axis would be horizontal at the height of one. If the x-variable is the dependent variable and the independent variable is unrelated to the dependent variable, the curve is vertical.

The Slope of a Nonlinear Curve

A **nonlinear curve** is one along which the slope changes.

A **nonlinear curve** is one along which the slope changes. Panels (a), (b), (c), and (d) of **Figure A.4** show various nonlinear curves. Panels (a) and (b) show nonlinear curves whose slopes change as you follow the line's progression, but the slopes always remain positive. Although both curves tilt upward, the curve in panel (a) gets steeper as the line moves from left to right in contrast to the curve in panel (b), which gets flatter. A curve that is upward-sloping and gets steeper, as in panel (a), is said to have a *positive and increasing* slope. A curve that is upward-sloping but gets flatter, as in panel (b), is said to have a *positive and decreasing* slope.

When we calculate the slope along these nonlinear curves, we obtain different values for the slope at different points. How the slope changes along the curve determines the curve's shape. For example, in panel (a) of Figure A.4, the slope of the curve is a positive number that steadily increases as the line moves from left to right, whereas in panel (b), the slope is a positive number that steadily decreases.

The **absolute value** of a number is the value of that number without a minus sign, whether or not the number was negative to begin with.

The slopes of the curves in panels (c) and (d) are negative numbers. For simplicity, economists often prefer to express a negative number as its **absolute value**, which is the value of the negative number without the minus sign. In general, we denote the absolute value of a number by two parallel bars around the number; for example, the absolute value of -4 is written as $|-4| = 4$. In panel (c), the absolute value of the slope steadily increases as the line moves from left to right. The curve therefore has a *negative and increasing* slope. And in panel (d), the absolute value of the slope of the curve steadily decreases along the curve. This curve therefore has a *negative and decreasing* slope.

FIGURE A.4 Nonlinear Curves

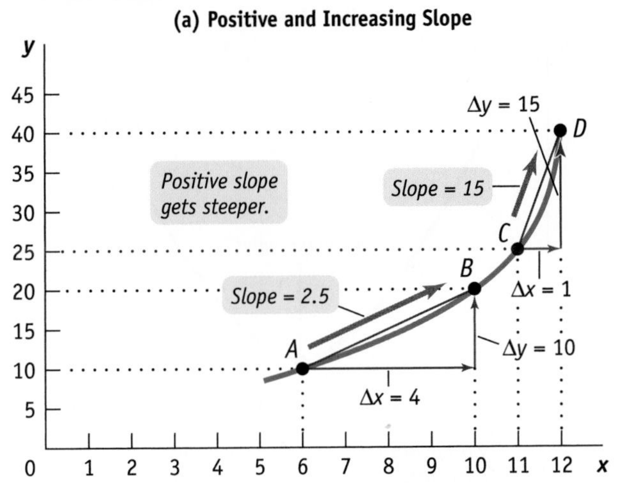

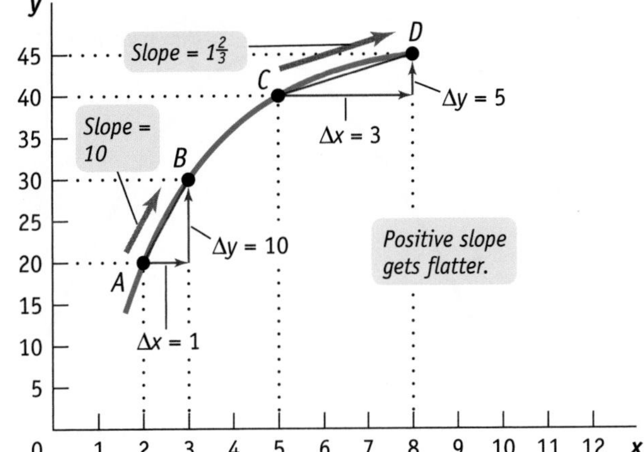

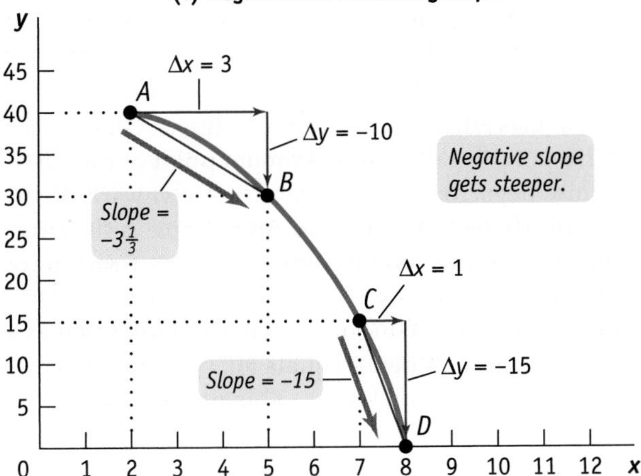

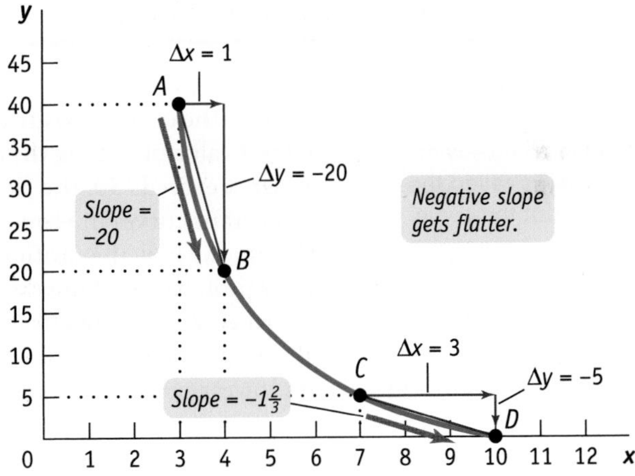

In panel (a), the slope of the curve from A to B is $\frac{\Delta y}{\Delta x} = \frac{10}{4} = 2.5$, and from C to D, it is $\frac{\Delta y}{\Delta x} = \frac{15}{1} = 15$. The slope is positive and increasing; it gets steeper as it moves to the right. In panel (b), the slope of the curve from A to B is $\frac{\Delta y}{\Delta x} = \frac{10}{1} = 10$, and from C to D, it is $\frac{\Delta y}{\Delta x} = \frac{5}{3} = 1\frac{2}{3}$. The slope is positive and decreasing; it gets flatter as it moves to the right. In panel (c), the slope from A to B is $\frac{\Delta y}{\Delta x} = \frac{-10}{3} = -3\frac{1}{3}$, and from C to D, it is $\frac{\Delta y}{\Delta x} = \frac{-15}{1} = -15$. The slope is negative and increasing; it gets steeper as it moves to the right. And in panel (d), the slope from A to B is $\frac{\Delta y}{\Delta x} = \frac{-20}{1} = -20$, and from C to D, it is $\frac{\Delta y}{\Delta x} = \frac{-5}{3} = -1\frac{2}{3}$. The slope is negative and decreasing; it gets flatter as it moves to the right. The slope in each case has been calculated by using the *arc method*—that is, by drawing a straight line connecting two points along a curve. The average slope between those two points is equal to the slope of the straight line between those two points.

Maximum and Minimum Points 

The slope of a nonlinear curve can change from positive to negative or vice versa. When the slope of a curve changes from positive to negative, it creates what is called a *maximum point* on the curve. When the slope of a curve changes from negative to positive, it creates a *minimum point*.

Panel (a) of **Figure A.5** illustrates a curve along which the slope changes from positive to negative as the line moves from left to right. When x is between 0 and 50, the

FIGURE A.5 Maximum and Minimum Points

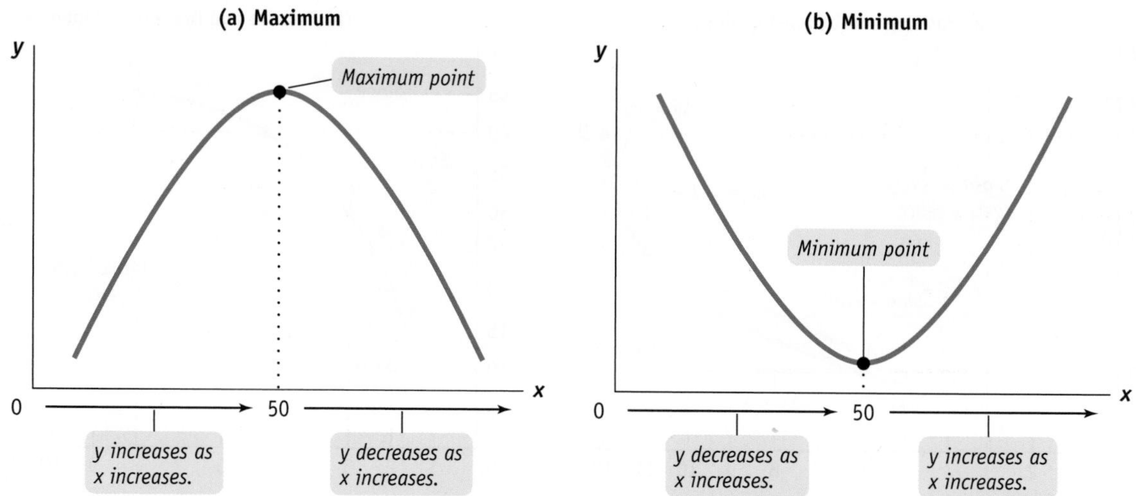

Panel (a) shows a curve with a maximum point, the point at which the slope changes from positive to negative. Panel (b) shows a curve with a minimum point, the point at which the slope changes from negative to positive.

The point along a curve with the largest value of y is called the **maximum point** of the curve.

The point along a curve with the smallest value of y is called the **minimum point** of the curve.

slope of the curve is positive. When x equals 50, the curve attains its highest point—the largest value of y along the curve. This point is called the **maximum point** of the curve. When x exceeds 50, the slope becomes negative as the curve turns downward. Many important curves in economics are hill-shaped like this one. An example is the curve that shows how the profit of a firm changes as it produces more output—firms maximize profit by reaching the top of the hill.

In contrast, the curve shown in panel (b) of Figure A.5 is U-shaped: it has a slope that changes from negative to positive. When x equals 50, the curve reaches its lowest point—the smallest value of y along the curve. This point is called the **minimum point** of the curve. Various important curves in economics, such as the curve that represents how a firm's cost per unit changes as output increases, are U-shaped like this one.

Calculating the Area Below or Above a Curve

Sometimes it is useful to be able to measure the size of the area below or above a curve. To keep things simple, we'll calculate only the area below or above a linear curve.

How large is the shaded area below the linear curve in panel (a) of **Figure A.6**? First, note that this area has the shape of a right triangle. A right triangle is a triangle in which two adjacent sides form a 90° angle. We will refer to one of these sides as the *height* of the triangle and the other side as the *base* of the triangle. For our purposes, it doesn't matter which of these two sides we refer to as the base and which as the height. Calculating the area of a right triangle is straightforward: *multiply the height of the triangle by the base of the triangle and divide the result by 2.* The height of the triangle in panel (a) of Figure A.6 is $10 - 4 = 6$ and the base of the triangle is $3 - 0 = 3$, so the area of that triangle is

$$\frac{6 \times 3}{2} = 9$$

How about the shaded area above the linear curve in panel (b) of Figure A.6? We can use the same formula to calculate the area of this right triangle. The height of

FIGURE A.6 Calculating the Area Below and Above a Linear Curve

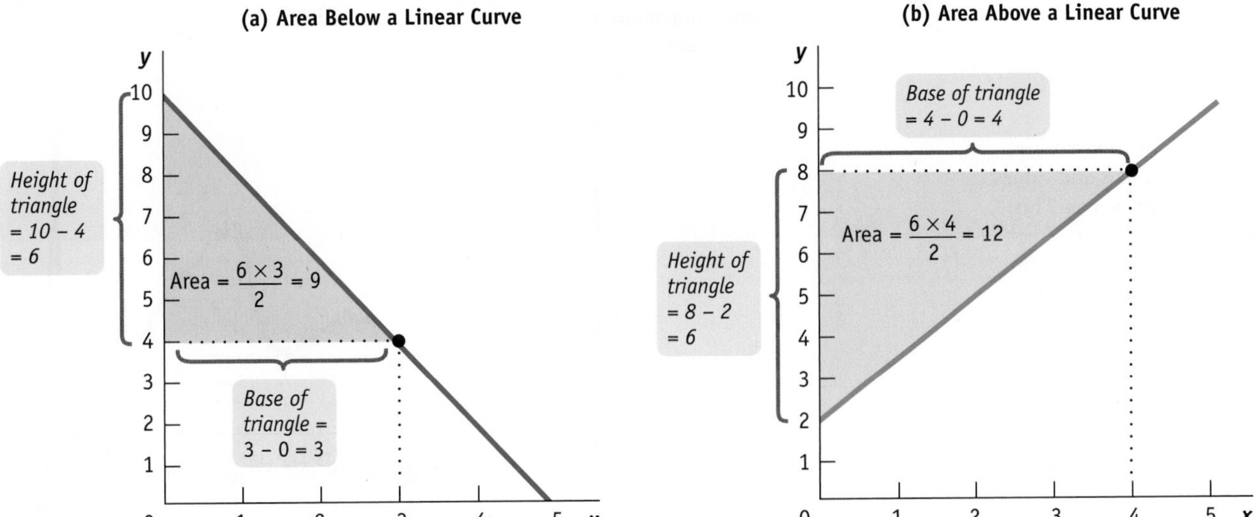

The area below or above a linear curve forms a right triangle. The area of a right triangle is calculated by multiplying the height of the triangle by the base of the triangle and dividing the result by 2. In panel (a), the area of the shaded triangle is 9. In panel (b), the area of the shaded triangle is 12.

the triangle is $8-2=6$ and the base of the triangle is $4-0=4$, so the area of that triangle is

$$\frac{6\times 4}{2}=12$$

Graphs That Depict Numerical Information

Graphs can also be used to summarize and display data without assuming some underlying causal relationship. Graphs that simply display numerical information are called *numerical graphs*. Here we will consider four types of numerical graphs: *time-series graphs*, *scatter diagrams*, *pie charts*, and *bar graphs*. These are widely used to display real empirical data about different economic variables, because they often help economists and policy makers identify patterns or trends in the economy.

Types of Numerical Graphs

You have probably seen graphs in newspapers that show what has happened over time to economic variables such as the unemployment rate or stock prices. A **time-series graph** has successive dates on the horizontal axis and the values of a variable that occurred on those dates on the vertical axis. For example, **Figure A.7** shows the unemployment rate in the United States from 1989 to 2021. A line connecting the points that correspond to the unemployment rate for each month during those years gives a clear idea of the overall trend in unemployment during that period.

A **time-series graph** has successive dates on the horizontal axis and the values of a variable that occurred on those dates on the vertical axis.

Figure A.8 is an example of a different kind of numerical graph. It represents information from a sample of 184 countries on average life expectancy and gross domestic product (GDP) per capita—a rough measure of a country's standard of living. Each point in the graph indicates an average resident's life expectancy and the log of GDP per capita for a given country. (Economists have found that the log of GDP rather than the simple level of GDP is more closely tied to average life expectancy.) The points

FIGURE A.7 Time-Series Graph

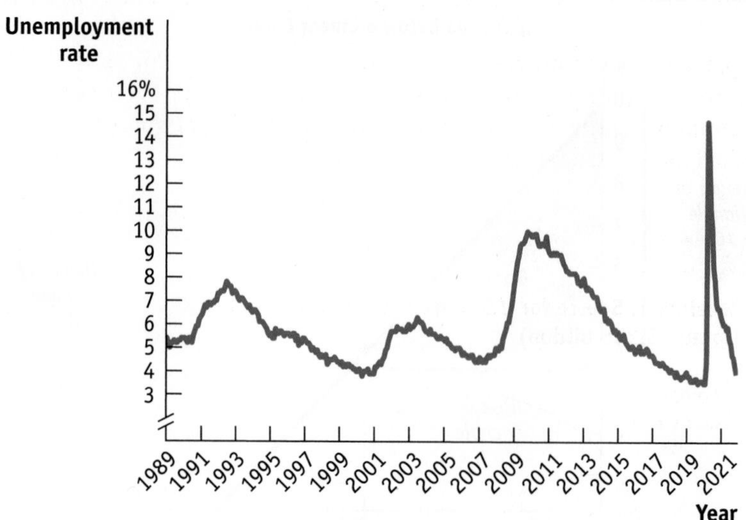

Time-series graphs show successive dates on the *x*-axis and values for a variable on the *y*-axis. This time-series graph shows the seasonally adjusted unemployment rate in the United States from 1989 to 2021. The two short diagonal lines toward the bottom of the *y*-axis are a *truncation sign*, indicating that a piece of the axis was cut out to save space.
Data Source: Bureau of Labor Statistics.

FIGURE A.8 Scatter Diagram

Standard of Living and Average Life Expectancy

Life expectancy at birth (years)

90 80 70 60 50 40 0

4 6 8 10 12 14

Log GNP (per capita)

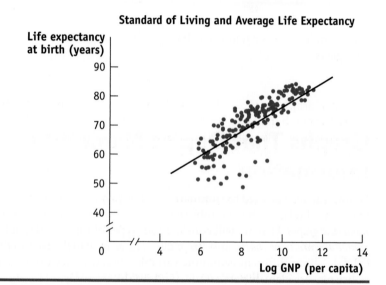

In a scatter diagram, each point represents the corresponding values of the *x*- and *y*-variables for a given observation. Here, each point indicates the observed average life expectancy and the log of GDP per capita of a given country for a sample of 184 countries. The upward-sloping fitted line here is the best approximation of the general relationship between the two variables.
Data Source: World Bank (2015).

lying in the upper right of the graph, which show combinations of high life expectancy and high log of GDP per capita, represent economically advanced countries such as the United States. Points lying in the bottom left of the graph, which show combinations of low life expectancy and low log of GDP per capita, represent economically less advanced countries such as Afghanistan and Sierra Leone. The pattern of points indicates that there is a positive relationship between life expectancy and log of GDP per capita: on the whole, people live longer in countries with a higher standard of living. This type of graph is called a **scatter diagram**, a diagram in which each point corresponds to an actual observation of the *x*-variable and the *y*-variable. In scatter diagrams, a curve is typically fitted to the scatter of points; that is, a curve is drawn that approximates as closely as possible the general relationship between the variables. As you can see, the fitted curve in Figure A.8 is upward-sloping, indicating the underlying positive relationship between the two variables. Scatter diagrams are often used to show how a general relationship can be inferred from a set of data.

Each point on a **scatter diagram** corresponds to an actual observation of the *x*-variable and the *y*-variable.

A **pie chart** shows the share of a total amount that is accounted for by various components, usually expressed in percentages. For example, **Figure A.9** is a pie chart that depicts the various sources of revenue for the U.S. government budget in 2017, expressed in percentages of the total revenue amount, \$3,316 billion. As you can see, payroll tax receipts (the revenues collected to fund Social Security, Medicare, and unemployment insurance) accounted for 35% of total government revenue, and individual income tax receipts accounted for 48%.

A **pie chart** shows the share of a total amount that is accounted for by various components, usually expressed in percentages.

FIGURE A.9 Pie Chart

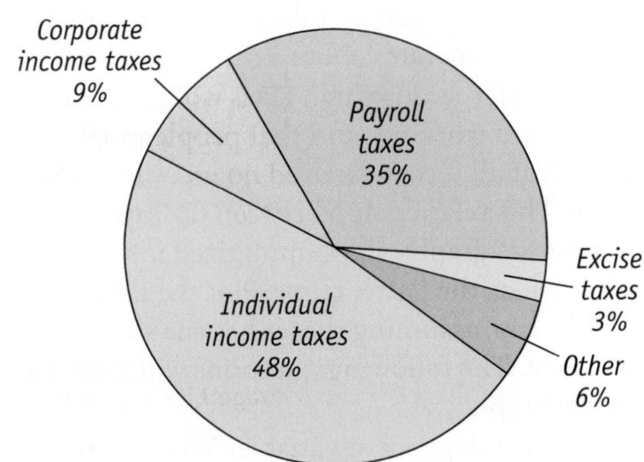

A pie chart shows the percentages of a total amount that can be attributed to various components. This pie chart shows the percentages of total federal revenues received from each source.
Data Source: Office of Management and Budget.

A **bar graph** uses bars of various heights or lengths to indicate values of a variable. In the bar graph in **Figure A.10**, the bars show the 2016 unemployment rates for workers with various levels of education. Exact values of the variable that is being measured may be written at the end of the bar, as in this figure. For instance, the unemployment rate for workers with a high school diploma but no college education was 5.2%. Even without the precise values, comparing the heights or lengths of the bars can give useful insight into the relative magnitudes of the different values of the variable.

A **bar graph** uses bars of various heights or lengths to indicate values of a variable.

FIGURE A.10 Bar Graph

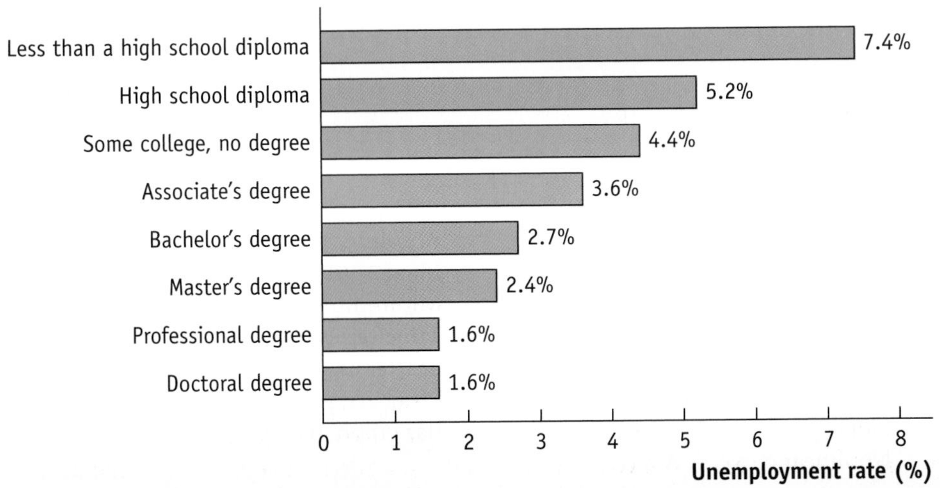

A bar graph measures a variable by using bars of various heights or lengths. This bar graph shows the unemployment rate for workers with various education levels.
Data Source: Bureau of Labor Statistics.

Skills Appendix Review

Adventures in AP® Economics

Watch the video: *Graphing Tricks & Tips*

Check Your Understanding

1. Study the four accompanying diagrams. Consider the following statements and indicate which diagram matches each statement. For each statement, tell which variable would appear on the horizontal axis and which on the vertical. In each of these statements, is the slope positive, negative, zero, or undefined?

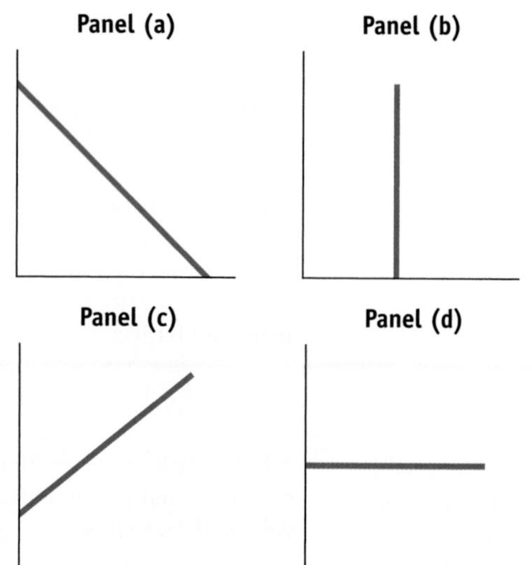

   a. If the price of movies increases, fewer consumers go to see movies.
   b. Workers with more experience typically have higher incomes than less experienced workers.
   c. Regardless of the temperature outside, Americans consume the same number of hot dogs per day.
   d. Consumers buy more frozen yogurt when the price of ice cream goes up.
   e. Research finds no relationship between the number of diet books purchased and the number of pounds lost by the average dieter.
   f. Regardless of its price, there is no change in the quantity of salt that Americans buy.

2. During the Reagan administration, economist Arthur Laffer argued in favor of lowering income tax rates in order to increase tax revenues. Like most economists, he believed that at tax rates above a certain level, tax revenue would fall (because high taxes would discourage some people from working) and that people would refuse to work at all if they received no income after paying taxes. This relationship between tax rates and tax revenue is graphically summarized in what is widely known as the Laffer curve. Plot the Laffer curve relationship, assuming that it has the shape of a nonlinear curve. The following questions will help you construct the graph.
   a. Which is the independent variable? Which is the dependent variable? On which axis do you therefore measure the income tax rate? On which axis do you measure income tax revenue?
   b. What would tax revenue be at a 0% income tax rate?
   c. The maximum possible income tax rate is 100%. What would tax revenue be at a 100% income tax rate?
   d. Estimates now show that the maximum point on the Laffer curve is (approximately) at a tax rate of 80%. For tax rates less than 80%, how would you describe the relationship between the tax rate and tax revenue, and how is this relationship reflected in the slope? For tax rates higher than 80%, how would you describe the relationship between the tax rate and tax revenue, and how is this relationship reflected in the slope?

Key Terms

FLH Financial Literacy Handbook

Part 1

Take It to the Bank

A bank account is a safe and convenient place to accumulate savings and to keep the money you need to pay bills and make everyday cash purchases. Keeping a large amount of cash at home or in your wallet isn't as safe because your money could be lost or stolen.

Overview of Banks

Banks can be small community institutions that have just one or a few locations, or they can be huge companies with thousands of branch locations all over the country. There are internet-only banks with no physical location to visit and only a website address. In addition to holding your money, banks also offer a variety of services to help you manage your money.

Banks stay in business by using the money you deposit to make a profit by offering loans to other customers or businesses. They lend to customers who want to borrow money for big purchases like cars or homes. They also lend to small and large businesses for making purchases like inventory and equipment.

When you take a loan from a bank, you're charged interest, which is an additional charge on top of the amount you borrow. To stay profitable, a bank must receive more money in interest from borrowers than it pays out in the form of loans to customers.

Despite the benefits banking institutions offer, about 5% of the population did not have a bank account as of 2020, and another 11% were considered "underbanked" and use no or few basic financial services. According to the Federal Reserve, these individuals typically have low income. Federal Reserve research shows that 84% of the unbanked have incomes below $25,000.

Individuals may not use banks for a variety of reasons, including the lack of a conveniently located branch office or the desire to avoid bank fees. However, some

FINANCE TIP
You can use the Electronic Deposit Insurance Estimator (EDIE) at fdic.gov/deposit to make sure your deposits in various bank accounts are fully covered by the FDIC.

potential customers do not take advantage of the services banks offer because they don't understand how banks work or how much nonbank alternatives cost. In this section, you'll learn why going without banking services is both expensive and inconvenient.

Types of Financial Institutions

When you're ready to open a bank account, there are three main types of institutions to choose from: savings and loan associations, commercial banks, and credit unions.

Savings and Loan Associations and Commercial Banks

Savings and loan associations (S&Ls) and commercial banks operate under federal and state regulations. They specialize in taking deposits for checking and savings accounts, making home loans (known as mortgages) and other personal and business loans, facilitating the flow of money into and out of accounts, and providing various financial services for individuals and businesses.

Have you ever wondered what would happen to your money if your bank went out of business or failed? Most banks insure your deposits through the FDIC up to the maximum amount allowed by law, which is currently $250,000 per depositor per account type for each insured bank.

FDIC insurance means that if your bank permanently closes for any reason, you won't lose your money. You'll know a bank is properly insured if it displays the FDIC logo at a local branch, on advertising materials, or online. To learn more, visit fdic.gov.

Credit Unions

Credit unions are nonprofit organizations owned by their customers, who are called members. Credit union members typically have something in common, like working for the same employer, working in the same profession, or living in the same geographic area. You must qualify to become a member of a credit union to be able to use its financial services, but qualification is usually a very easy process.

Credit unions offer many of the same services as commercial banks and S&Ls. Most also offer insurance for your deposits through the National Credit Union Administration (NCUA), which gives the same coverage (up to $250,000 per depositor) as the FDIC. Just look for the official NCUA sign at credit union branches and websites. To learn more, visit ncua.gov.

Fully Online Banks

If you're willing to do all of your banking electronically either through a computer or your phone, you may want to consider skipping the brick-and-mortar banks entirely and selecting a fully online bank. Benefits of fully online banks include higher interest rates paid on deposits since overhead costs are lower, and account fees in general are lower. Because there are no physical offices to go to, it may be difficult to complete cash transactions unless your online bank is part of a well-developed ATM network. You'll never see an actual person for customer service questions, but chat and telephone services can help you find the answers you need.

Why Keep Money in a Bank?

While it's possible to keep your money at home and manage your personal finances using a cash-only system, here are five reasons why it's better to use an insured bank or credit union:

1. **Safety**: Money you deposit in a bank account is safe from loss, theft, or destruction. Even the best hiding places for money can be found by a thief or be susceptible to a flood or fire.
2. **Insurance**: Deposits covered by FDIC or NCUA insurance are protected by a fund backed by the full faith and credit of the U.S. government. So if your bank closes

and can't return your money, the FDIC or NCUA will pay the insured portion of your deposits.

3. **Convenience**: Money in a bank account can be accessed in a variety of ways. You can make deposits by visiting a local branch or setting up electronic direct deposit. Many institutions have remote deposit services where you deposit a paper check by taking a picture of it with a mobile device or scanner and uploading it online. You can use online bill pay to send funds in the form of a paper check or electronic transfer.
4. **Low cost**: Different banks offer accounts with a variety of benefits, such as interest paid, debit cards, online banking, account alerts, bill pay, and overdraft protection. Many bank services are free to their customers, which makes using a bank to get cash or pay bills less expensive than alternatives, such as a check-cashing service. Some check cashers charge a fee that's a percentage of the check value, plus an additional flat fee. For instance, cashing a $1,000 check at a check-cashing service could cost 1.5%, or $15.
5. **Business relationship**: Building a relationship with a bank may give you the opportunity to qualify for premium banking services, loans, and credit cards that can improve your financial future.

FINANCE TIP

Did you know that funds deposited electronically into your bank account are available sooner than those deposited by a paper check?

Types of Bank Accounts

The two main types of bank accounts are deposit accounts and non-deposit accounts.

Deposit Accounts

Deposit accounts allow you to add money to or withdraw money from your account at any time. Examples of deposit accounts are checking, savings, and money market accounts.

Checking Account A checking account, also known as a payment account, is the most common type of bank account. It's a real workhorse that allows you to make purchases or pay bills using paper checks, a debit or check card, online bill pay, automatic transfer, or cash withdrawal from an automatic teller machine (ATM). The institution keeps a record of your deposits and withdrawals and sends you a monthly account statement. The best checking accounts offer no fees, no minimum balance requirement, free checks and debit cards, and online account access.

FINANCE TIP

***Rewards checking* accounts pay a relatively high rate of interest when you follow certain requirements, such as receiving e-statements, having at least one direct deposit per month, and using a debit card for a certain number of purchases each month.**

Savings Account A savings account is a safe place to keep money, and it earns you interest. It doesn't give you as much flexibility or access to your money as a checking account. While there's typically no limit on the number of deposits you can make into a savings account, federal rules prohibit you from making more than six withdrawals or transfers per month. Savings accounts typically don't come with paper checks, but they may offer a debit or ATM card that you can use a maximum of three times per month.

If your balance dips below a certain amount, you may be charged a monthly fee. The institution keeps a record of your transactions and sends you a monthly account statement.

Savings accounts are perfect for your short-term savings goals, like a down payment on a car or holiday gift-giving. Interest rates on savings accounts vary, so it's important to shop around locally or online for the highest offers. Interest rates on savings accounts are variable, which means they're subject to change and can decrease after you open an account. (You'll learn more about compounded interest in Part 2 of this handbook.)

FINANCE TIP

Use the power of the internet to shop for the best bank accounts. Sites like findabetterbank.com and bankrate.com gather up-to-date information about the best offers nationwide.

Money Market Account (MMA) A money market account has features of both a savings and a checking account. You can make up to six withdrawals or transfers per month, including payments by check, debit card, and online bill pay. You're paid relatively high interest rates, especially if you maintain a high minimum balance, such as $5,000 or more.

Money market accounts are a great choice when you start to accumulate more savings. Interest rates vary and are subject to change, so always do your research to find the best money market account offer.

There are also special types of deposit accounts, known as *time deposits*, in which you're restricted from withdrawing your money for a certain period of time.

Certificate of Deposit (CD) A certificate of deposit is a time deposit that requires you to give up the use of your money for a fixed term or period of time, such as 3 months, 12 months, or 5 years. In exchange for this restricted access, banks typically pay higher interest rates than for savings or money market accounts (where you can withdraw money on demand). In general, the longer the term of the CD, the higher the interest rate you receive.

For instance, a six-month CD might pay 1% interest, and a five-year CD might pay 3%. If you take money out of a CD before the end of the term, or maturity date, you generally have to pay a penalty. So before putting money in a CD, be sure that you won't need it until after the maturity date and that you understand all the charges and fees associated with early withdrawals.

Non-Deposit Accounts

Many banks offer non-deposit accounts that can be investments, such as stocks, bonds, or mutual funds. It's important to remember that non-deposit products are never insured by the FDIC or NCUA and may lose some or all of their value.

How Old Do You Have to Be to Open a Bank Account?

Many banks offer checking and savings accounts for young people. Some require you to open a joint account with a parent or guardian; however, some offer independent student accounts when you reach age 16.

The earlier you open up a bank account and start saving on a regular basis, the better. Having a checking and savings account established before you go to college will help you manage money and make necessary purchases. Money you earn from a job, get from a relative, or receive as a gift can be set aside for your future needs.

How to Maintain a Checking Account

It's important to maintain your checking account on a regular basis so you know exactly how much money you have at all times. You should reconcile each monthly statement's ending balance against your records so you never miss a transaction, such as an unexpected fee. Never write checks or make debit card purchases that exceed your balance.

Using ATM and Debit Cards

An ATM card allows you to use ATMs to make deposits, check your account balance, transfer funds between accounts, and make cash withdrawals 24 hours a day. You typically have to pay a fee for each ATM cash withdrawal at banks other than your own – unless your bank gives you free access to a network of ATMs or reimburses your ATM fees. Most credit unions belong to a network that will give you free access to ATM services across the country, but check with your bank to be sure about potential fees associated with ATM use.

A debit card, also known as a check card, looks like a credit card because it typically has a MasterCard or VISA logo. A debit card can be used just like an ATM or credit card or to make purchases where accepted by merchants. When you use a debit card, money is deducted immediately from your bank account and credited to the merchant's account. This reduces your available balance.

If you make a debit card purchase for more than your available balance, your transaction will be declined. However, if you enroll in overdraft protection, you authorize your bank to cover your transaction – but typically at the cost of a large service fee.

Peer-to-Peer Payment Apps

What do you do if you are out with friends and need to split a bill at a restaurant but have no cash? Or what if you owe your roommate $25 but forgot to stop at the ATM on the way home from work? To make these payments quickly and easily, you can use a peer-to-peer app (also called person-to-person), such as PayPal, Venmo, Zelle, or Apple Pay, that is linked to your bank account or bank card. By using these apps you are able to quickly make payments to friends and some businesses. Payment between friends is usually free from fees, but it may take a few days for the payment to make its way to your account.

Writing Checks

With the popularity of debit cards and online banking, people don't use paper checks as much anymore. However, if you need to write one, it's easy to fill in the blanks. Always write clearly using dark ink and never cross out a mistake—it's better to start over with a fresh check.

Reconciling Your Checking Account

Each month you'll receive a statement that shows activity in your account. The statement should include a reconciliation worksheet that you can follow. Reconciling or balancing your account is the process of making sure the information on the bank statement matches your records. Always keep track of your deposits, checks, debit card purchases, ATM withdrawals, and fees. Although you can use a paper check register, creating a spreadsheet online or using a program specifically to reconcile your account can quickly help you balance your account and find errors. Most financial software programs allow you to automatically download bank and credit card account transactions.

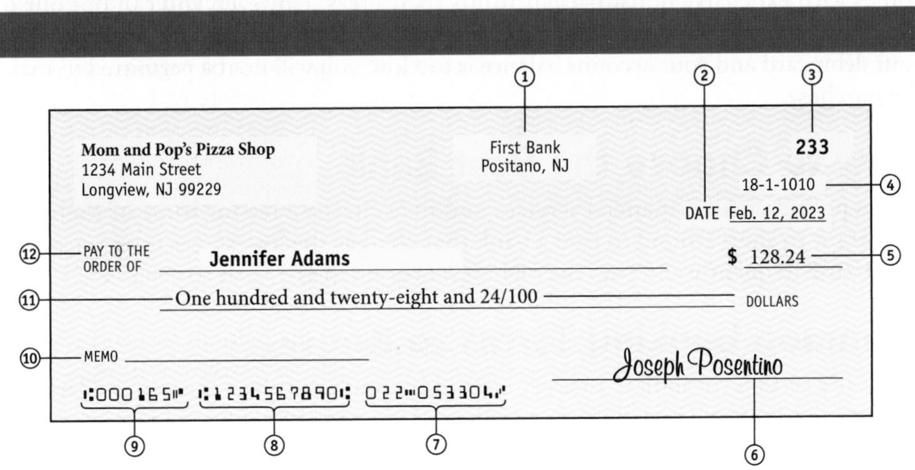

1. **Bank name**: This may be preprinted on each check.
2. **Date**: Enter the month, day, and year.
3. **Check number**: If your checks don't have preprinted numbers, label them with consecutive numbers.
4. **Bank ID numbers**: This may be preprinted on each check.
5. **Amount**: Enter the amount to pay in figures.
6. **Signature**: Sign your name exactly as you signed it on documents you completed when you opened the account.
7. **Check number**: This may be preprinted on each check.
8. **Account number**: This should be preprinted on each check.
9. **Bank routing number**: This should be preprinted on each check to identify your bank's unique routing number.
10. **Memo**: Write a quick note to remind yourself of the reason for the check.
11. **Amount**: Enter the amount to pay in words and draw a line over unused space so nothing can be added later.
12. **Payee**: Enter the person or company to pay.

✓ Tips for Secure Mobile Banking

Online and mobile banking isn't particularly risky, but it is important to be careful when making online transactions. Use these tips to avoid risk when you're making purchases or banking using a mobile device:

1. **Use a secured network** instead of public Wi-Fi so your personal information can't be exposed to criminals. The web address of a secured network begins with "https" instead of "http."
2. **Guard your mobile device** like you would your wallet, because it may contain information others can use to access your accounts if it were lost or stolen.
3. **Create strong passwords** for your devices (to turn them on or wake them from sleep mode) and for your online accounts. Most passwords are at least eight characters long and use a combination of letters, numbers, and symbols. Security experts also recommend that you change your important passwords frequently and never use the same password for more than one account. Some sites will offer the option of sending a text message with a code that can be used to access your accounts. Consider this feature for an additional level of security.
4. **Don't lend your mobile devices** or share your passwords with anyone you don't know or trust.
5. **Log off** from financial accounts and close the browser window or app when you finish using them.
6. **Only download trusted apps** from sources like your bank or other legitimate financial institutions.
7. **Delete text messages** from your bank once you've read them.
8. **Don't divulge personal information** such as your Social Security number or account number. A financial institution or authorized agency will *never* ask you for personal information over the internet or even on the phone.

Overdraft Protection

Having overdraft protection means your debit card purchases and ATM withdrawals will be processed, even if your bank account balance isn't high enough to cover them. You must give written permission for overdraft protection because using it typically comes with expensive nonsufficient funds (NSF) fees. However, you can opt out of overdraft protection and avoid the potential charges. This means that if you try to use your debit card and your account balance is too low, you will not be permitted to make the purchase.

How to Choose the Best Bank

Banks provide many financial services and may charge a fee for some of them. It's important to shop around to find a bank that charges the lowest fees for services you plan to use frequently and pays the highest rate of interest.

Common Banking Terms to Know

Banks use certain vocabulary that you should be familiar with so that you understand all you can about where your money is held. Here are several key banking terms to know:

account statement—a paper or electronic record of account activity, service charges, and fees, issued by the bank on a regular basis

bounced or **bad check**—slang for a check that is rejected due to insufficient funds in the account

check—a paper form that authorizes a bank to release funds from the payer's account to the payee

cleared or **canceled checks**—paper checks that have been processed and paid by a bank

deposit slip or **ticket**—a printed form you complete that lists cash and checks to be deposited into an account

direct deposit—an electronic payment method typically used by an employer or government agency

electronic payment or **transaction**—a deposit or charge to an account that happens without the use of a paper form

endorsement—the payee's signature on the back of a paper check that is required to deposit or to take cash out of an account

payee—the person or company to whom a check is made payable

payer—the person or company who writes a check or pays another party

peer-to-peer network—Apps that allow you to transfer money to another person through a linked bank account or a bank card.

reconciliation—the process of comparing a bank account statement to your records and resolving any differences until you determine an identical account balance

service charge or **maintenance charge**—a fee charged by a bank to maintain your account

Part 1 Review Questions

1. How do banks make money?
2. Describe the similarities and differences between commercial banks and credit unions. Why do you think someone would choose one over the other?
3. In your own words, describe why it's better to keep your money in a financial institution instead of holding large amounts of cash.
4. Give several reasons why someone would open more than one type of bank account.
5. Come up with at least five questions you should ask before deciding to put your money in a financial institution.
6. Why might you choose to pay a friend with an app like Venmo or Apple Pay instead of writing a check?

Project

Your aunt is going to give you $1,000 when you graduate from high school, but she wants you to use it to open a savings account. Select one commercial bank, one savings and loan association, and one credit union in your town and determine what is needed to open a savings account in each. How much money do they require to open an account? Do you need a cosigner if you're under 18? How much interest will they pay on your savings? Which of these three locations would you choose if you really had $1,000?

Part 2

Get Interested in Money Math

Whether you're shopping at the grocery store, choosing a car loan, or figuring out how much to invest for retirement, managing money comes down to the numbers. Making the best decisions for your personal finances always begins by doing some simple money math.

Pay Attention to Interest

When you borrow money by taking out a loan for college, a car, or any other expense, you'll be charged interest. Additionally, if you don't pay off a credit card balance in full by the statement due date, you'll also be charged interest on the balance owed. Lenders make money by charging interest to a borrower as a percentage of the amount of the loan or credit card balance due.

When you deposit money in a bank account that pays interest—for example, a savings account or CD—you become the lender and the bank is the borrower. The bank pays you interest for keeping money on deposit.

Interest is typically expressed as an annual percentage rate, or APR. To keep more of your money, it's wise to shop around and borrow at the lowest interest rates. Likewise, lend your money and deposit it in the bank that offers the highest possible interest rates, so you earn more.

How Simple and Compound Interest Work

But how does your money actually earn interest? There are two basic types of interest: simple interest and compound interest.

Simple Interest Simple interest is, well, pretty simple! That's because it's calculated on the original principal amount.

Say you borrow $100 from your friend John at a 5% annual rate of simple interest for a term of 3 years. Here's how the interest would be calculated for the loan:

Loan year	Principal amount (dollars)	APR (percent)	Annual interest earned (dollars) (Principle × APR)	Balance due (dollars)
1	$100	5%	$5	$105
2	100	5	5	110
3	100	5	5	115

Notice that the 5% APR is always calculated on the original principal amount of $100. At the end of the third year, you have to pay $100 plus $15 in interest. In other words, your $100 loan cost a total of $115.

Compound Interest Compound interest is more complex because it's calculated on the original principal amount and also on the accumulated interest of a deposit or loan. Compound interest allows you to earn interest on a growing principal balance, which allows you to accumulate interest at a much faster rate.

Say you get the same loan of $100 for 3 years from your friend John, but this time he charges you 5% interest that compounds annually. Here's how the interest would be calculated:

Loan year	Principal amount (dollars)	APR (percent)	Annual interest earned (dollars) (Principle × APR)	Balance due (dollars)
1	$100	5%	$5	$105
2	105	5	5.25	110.25
3	110.25	5	5.51	115.76

Notice that the 5% APR is calculated on an increasing principal balance. At the end of the third year you'd owe the original amount of $100 plus interest of $15.76. Your $100 loan cost $115.76 with annual compounding interest. This table also shows you how much you'd earn if you deposited $100 in the bank and earned a 5% annual return that compounds annually.

Interest can be compounded according to variety of schedules, such as annually, semiannually, monthly, or daily. **Table 2.1** shows how much you'd pay if John charged you 5% compounded semiannually, or every 6 months.

Table 2.1 Semiannual Compound Interest Calculation

Loan year	Principal amount (dollars)	Semiannual percentage rate (percent)	Annual interest earned (dollars)	Balance due (dollars)
1 (January)	$100	2.5%	$2.50	$102.50
1 (July)	102.50	2.5	2.56	105.06
2 (January)	105.06	2.5	2.63	107.69
2 (July)	107.69	2.5	2.69	110.38
3 (January)	110.38	2.5	2.76	113.14
3 (July)	113.14	2.5	2.83	115.97

At the end of the third year you'd owe the original loan amount of $100 plus $15.97 of interest—in other words, with semiannual compounding your $100 loan would cost $115.97. Likewise, this table shows how much you could earn from $100 in savings if compounded semiannually at a 5% annual rate of return.

Remember that the more frequent the compounding, the faster the interest grows. Annual percentage yield (APY) is the amount of interest you'll earn on an annual basis, including the effect of compounding. APY is expressed as a percentage and will be higher the more often your money compounds. Banks generally will show both APR and APY rates on investments and loans. APR reflects interest earned/paid without the benefits of compounding. It is generally associated with the cost of borrowing. APY is generally associated with deposit account, and the amount one can earn on savings.

FINANCE TIP
When comparing different bank accounts, always compare APY instead of APR to know which account pays more interest on an annual basis.

What Is the Rule of 72?

How long would it take you to double your money through savings and investments? It's easy to figure it out using a handy formula called the Rule of 72. If you divide 72 by the interest rate you earn, the answer is the number of years it will take for your initial savings amount to double in value.

For example, if you earn an average annual return of 1% on a bank savings account, dividing 1 into 72 tells you that your money will double in 72 years. But if you earn 6% on an investment, your money will take only 12 years to double ($72 \div 6 = 12$).

You can also estimate the interest rate you'd need to earn to double your money within a set number of years by dividing 72 by the number of years. For instance, if you put $500 in an account that you want to grow to $1,000 in 12 years, you'll need an interest rate of 6% ($72 \div 12 = 6$).

FINANCE TIP
Interest that you earn is considered income, and you may have to pay federal and state tax on it.

Understand Credit Cards

Using credit cards without fully understanding the relevant money math is a recipe for financial disaster. Credit cards start charging interest the day you make a purchase, take a cash advance, or transfer a balance from another account.

You're typically charged a daily rate that's equal to the APR divided by 365 (the 365 days in a year). Rates may be different for each transaction category and depending on your credit rating. For instance, your APR could be 11.99% for new purchases, 23.99% for cash advances, and 5% for balance transfers. Balances accumulate day after day until you pay them off in full.

You can make a monthly minimum payment and carry over the remaining balance from month to month. But that's not a wise way to manage credit cards because the interest starts racking up. Additionally, if you make a late payment, you're charged a late fee that gets added to your outstanding balance—and interest is calculated on that amount, too.

The bright spot in using a credit card wisely is that you're given a grace period for new purchases that allows you to avoid all interest charges—if you pay your balance in full by the billing statement due date. Note that there is generally no grace period for cash advances or balance transfers.

Credit cards are powerful financial tools that can enhance your life if you use them responsibly. But abusing them by making purchases that you can't afford to pay off in full each month can be devastating to your financial future. Your credit report history will also be harmed if you make late payments. You'll learn more about how to establish and maintain a good credit history in Part 5.

Calculate Credit Card Payoff

Question: If you buy a smart TV for $9,000 using a credit card that charges 23.99% APR, how long would it take to pay it off, if you make only minimum payments of 3% of your outstanding balance ($270 per month)? Answer: It would take over 4 years and 8 months to pay off the TV! So, if you're 17 years old right now, you'd be almost 22 years old before you finally pay off the TV. Due to the high rate of credit card interest, the total cost of the TV would actually be $14,973.91! That's an increase of more than 66% on the TV's original purchase price. Making only minimum payments can greatly raise the cost of purchase, which is why it's so important to pay off credit card balances in full every month.

FINANCE TIP
To determine how long it would take to pay off a credit card if you only made the minimum payments, do a web search for "credit card minimum payment calculator" and enter your balance, rate, and payment information.

Amortization

Gradually paying off a debt's principal and interest in regular installments over time is called *amortization*. Loans that amortize, such as a car loan or home mortgages, have fixed interest rates and charge equal monthly payments, though each payment is made up of a slightly different amount of principal and interest.

Take a look at **Table 2.2** to see how each payment is split up for the first six months on a three-year $20,000 car loan with an interest rate of 7%.

Table 2.2 Amortization Schedule

Payment month	Loan balance (dollars)	Monthly payment (dollars)	Interest portion of payment (dollars)	Principal portion of payment (dollars)
1	$20,000	$617.54	$116.67	$500.88
2	19,499.12	617.54	113.74	503.80
3	18,995.32	617.54	110.81	506.74
4	18,488.58	617.54	107.85	509.69
5	17,978.89	617.54	104.88	512.67
6	17,466.22	617.54	101.89	515.66

Notice that each month's beginning loan balance is reduced by the prior month's principal portion paid. The interest portion is slightly lower each month because it's calculated on an ever-decreasing principal balance.

How to Become a Millionaire

If you think that the only way to become a millionaire is to win the lottery, think again! Thanks to the power of compounding interest, it's easy – if you get an early start. **Table 2.3** shows you how.

Table 2.3 At What Age Could You Become a Millionaire?

Age to begin saving	Amount to save each month (dollars)	Average APR (percent)	Years to become a millionaire	Age you're a millionaire!
18	$250	7%	46	64
20	250	7	46	66
25	250	7	45	70
30	250	7	45	75
40	250	7	45	86

If you start saving and investing just $250 a month as soon as you get your first job, you could amass a million dollars by the time you're in your 60s. But if you wait until you're over 40 years old to get started and invest the same amount, you'd be close to 90 before becoming a millionaire because of the compounding interest and the number of years invested!

Millionaire Case Study

Samir and Alika are both 25 years old and work for the same company. They have the same financial goal: to retire at age 65 with one million dollars in savings. Samir starts contributing to his company's retirement plan right away, but Alika waits 10 years, until she's 35 years old, to begin investing. Here's what happens: Samir can reach his million-dollar goal by contributing $400 a month and earning an average 7% annual return. But since Alika gets a late start, she has to contribute much more than Samir. Alika must contribute $850 a month with the same 7% rate of return to reach her million-dollar goal by the time she's 65, as shown in **Figure 2.1**.

FIGURE 2.1 Saving to Be a Millionaire

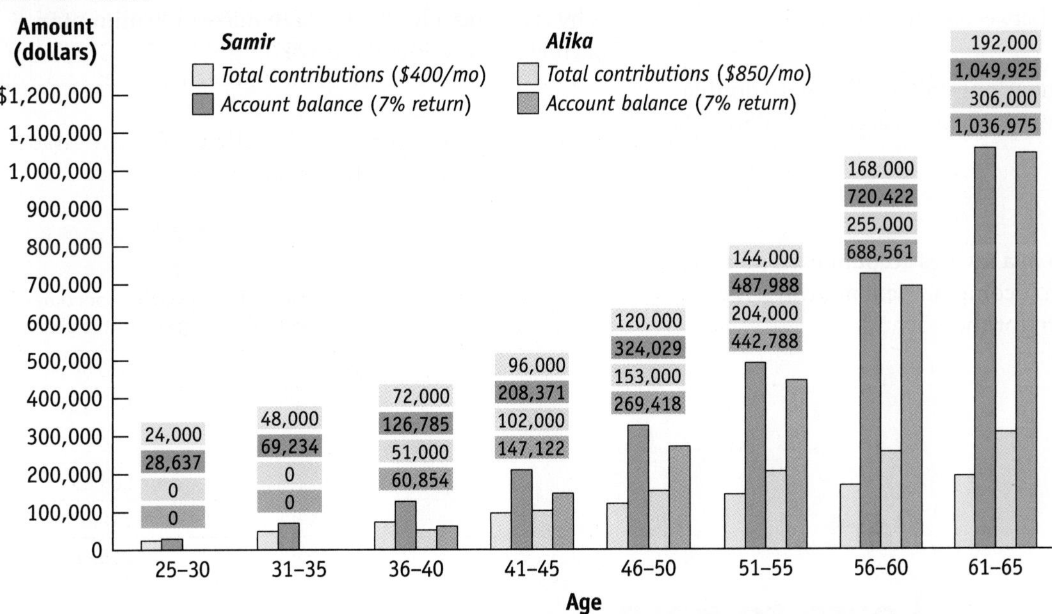

You'll notice that Samir had to invest only $192,000 over a 40-year period to amass over one million dollars. However, Alika had to invest $306,000, or 60% more than Samir, over a 30-year period to accumulate approximately the same amount.

The Power of Saving Early Case Study

Ava and Luis are both 25 years old, but they begin saving for retirement at different times. Ava begins saving $200 per month right away, but Luis decides to buy a new car instead. Luis ends up delaying his retirement savings for 10 years. After his 35th birthday, he finally gets started and saves $300 per month. They both earn an average annual return of 8%.

Here's what happens: When Luis reaches age 65, he has almost $450,000. But Ava has amassed close to $700,000. The benefit of choosing to invest earlier, rather than later, really pays off for Ava because she has $250,000 more than Luis to spend during retirement, as demonstrated in **Figure 2.2**.

FIGURE 2.2 Saving for Retirement

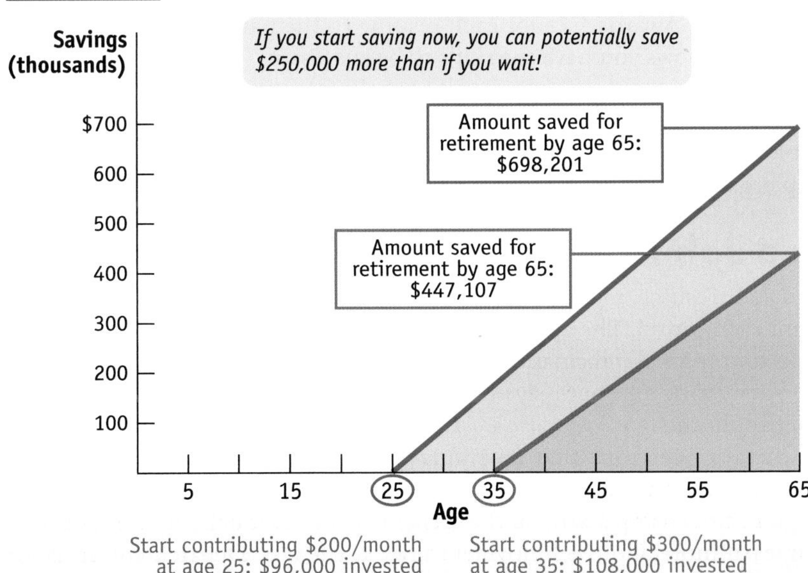

The sooner you start saving and investing, the more you will benefit from the power of compounding interest!

Part 2 Review Questions

1. What is the difference between simple and compound interest?
2. Using the Rule of 72, how long will it take you to double your savings if you have $3,200 in an account making 4% interest?
3. Why is it generally a bad idea to make only minimum payments on your credit card?

Project

Imagine you deposit $125 in a savings account each month. It pays 3% annually, which is compounded monthly. How much interest will you earn for the year?

Part 3

Learn to Earn

How can you earn enough money to cover your expenses and save for the future? It starts by having the education and skills to get a good job or to start your own business. Every work experience builds your level of knowledge, boosts your resume, helps you know what work you like best, and makes you more attractive to potential employers.

What Is a Resume?

A resume is a summary of your education, skills, and work experience – that you submit to a potential employer in person or online – that highlights many of your outstanding traits and experiences. It should be a one-page document that is succinct and well written.

Employers typically conduct a background check to verify data in your resume, so never include false information. Lying on a resume or job application can disqualify you for a job or cause an employer to fire you later on.

At the top of a resume, list your name, address, phone number, and e-mail address. The body should include sections titled "Objective," "Experience," "Skills," "Education," and "Honors or Awards." Tailor each resume to the particular job you apply for so the employer knows you have the skills to be successful.

If you have trouble creating a resume, ask for help from family, friends, or a professional resume writer, who can help you articulate the skills and experiences you have to offer a potential employer. You can also use free online resources such as careeronestop.org and myfuture.com.

What Is a Job Application?

In addition to your resume, many potential employers require you to complete a job or employment application. The application can be customized by the employer, but it typically asks for personal information, references, and specifics about the job you're applying for. Submitting an impressive resume and application will make you stand out from other applicants.

There are certain questions that an employer is not allowed to ask applicants under federal and some state and local laws. These may include topics such as your age, race, religion, citizenship status, and whether you are disabled, pregnant, or married. You can learn more about employment laws at the U.S. Department of Labor website at www.dol.gov.

Types of Income

The money you make falls into one of two basic categories: earned income and passive income.

Earned Income

Earned income is the income you receive by working for a company or someone who pays you, or from a business that you own and run. Earned income includes your hourly wages, salaries, tips, commissions, and bonuses. This is the most common way to make money. Of course, if you stop working, you stop earning. However, if you save and invest your earned income wisely, you can turn it into passive income.

Passive Income

Passive income is generated from assets you buy or create, such as financial investments, rental real estate, or something you have created, such as a book or a song. If you buy a house and rent it to someone else for more than your mortgage and other expenses, the profit is passive income. If you write and publish a book or a song that pays royalties, that is intellectual property that pays passive income. The benefit of passive income is that you get paid with little or no additional work on your part. That makes it possible to retire and still receive money to pay your everyday living expenses.

Although you must have income to meet your financial needs, an income doesn't give you lasting wealth unless you save or invest some amount of it on a regular basis. Even those with high incomes can live paycheck to paycheck and end up with no true wealth. Likewise, those with modest incomes can save small amounts of money over a long period of time and accumulate a nest egg for a healthy financial future.

Getting a Paycheck

It might surprise you to know that if you get a job earning $600 a week, you don't actually receive $600 a week. Although your gross income or pay will be $600, you'll have payroll taxes deducted from each paycheck before you receive it, which include federal, state, Medicare, and Social Security taxes. You may also have voluntary deductions for workplace benefits such as health insurance, life insurance, and contributions to a retirement account. The remaining amount that you'll have to spend after taxes and deductions is called your net income or net pay.

When you take a new job, one of the forms you must complete is the W-4. It tells your employer how much tax should be taken out, or withheld, from each of your paychecks. If too little tax is withheld during the year, you'll owe money to the government's Internal Revenue Service (IRS) on tax day (which is usually April 15 unless that date falls on a weekend or holiday). If too much tax is withheld, the IRS will pay a refund, but you will lose the use of your money until the refund payment arrives. So it is good to have your payroll withholding match the actual amount of tax you'll owe.

Significant events – such as marriage, divorce, the birth or adoption of a child, buying a home, or taking an additional job – will affect how much tax you owe. Additionally, earning income from savings accounts or investments affects the tax you owe. Any time your personal situation changes, you can file a new W-4 with your employer to make sure the right amount of tax is withheld so you don't have any surprises on tax day. You can learn more by visiting the IRS website at irs.gov and searching for Publication 505, Tax Withholding and Estimated Tax.

How Payroll Withholding Works

Employers are required to withhold four different types of tax from your paycheck:

1. **Federal income tax** is paid to the IRS for expenses such as salaries of elected officials, the military, welfare assistance programs, public education, and interest on the national debt.

2. **State income tax** is generally paid to your state's revenue department for expenses such as salaries of state employees and maintenance of state highways and parks. Depending on where you live, there may also be payroll deductions for county and city tax.
3. **Social Security tax** provides income for eligible taxpayers who are retired or disabled, or who survive a relative who was receiving benefits. The program's official name is OASDI, which stands for Old-Age, Survivors, and Disability Insurance. Employees pay 6.2% of their wages as Social Security tax and their employers match that payment amount.
4. **Medicare tax** provides hospital insurance benefits to eligible individuals who are over the age of 65 or have certain medical conditions. Social Security and Medicare taxes are collectively called the Federal Insurance Contributions Act (FICA) tax. Medicare tax is 1.45%, and like the Social Security tax, it is paid by both the employee and the employer.

FINANCE TIP

Employers are required to pay 50% of FICA on behalf of their employees. If you become your own boss, you must pay self-employment tax, which includes 100% of the Social Security and Medicare tax owed.

Filing an Income Tax Return

By April 15 of each year, you must complete and file, by mail or electronically, a federal tax return to the IRS for income from the prior year. Most states also require a state tax return at the same time. Whether you must file a tax return depends on your income, tax filing status, age, and whether or not you are a dependent. The filing requirements apply even if you don't owe any tax.

If you don't file taxes on time, you'll be charged a late payment penalty, plus interest on any amount owed. Willfully failing to file a return is a serious matter because it's against the law and may result in criminal prosecution.

If you are an unmarried dependent student, you must file a tax return if your earned or unearned income exceeds certain limits. You may also owe tax on certain scholarships and fellowships for education. Tax rules are subject to change each year, so be sure to visit irs.gov and review IRS Publication 501, Exemptions, Standard Deduction, and Filing Information, for income limits and up-to-date information.

In January and February of each year, you'll receive official forms from institutions that paid you, such as your employer, bank, or investment brokerage or firm. These forms provide the data you need to complete your taxes. Even if you don't receive these official tax documents, you must still declare all your income on a tax return. So be sure to request any missing information.

The IRS does not require a tax filing for individuals who earn under a certain minimum income threshold. However, you should file a tax return each year in case you are owed a refund – for instance, if you had income tax withheld from your pay, or you qualify for refundable tax benefits.

In addition to individuals and families, the IRS (and certain states) also taxes corporations, trusts, and estates.

How Much Income Tax Do You Pay?

The United States has a marginal or progressive tax system, which means that people with more earned income pay tax at a higher rate or percentage. A tax bracket is a range of income that's taxed at a certain rate. Currently, there are seven federal tax brackets that range from 10% up to 37%. So, someone with very little income may pay 10% while someone with high income could pay as much as 37% on their highest range of income for just federal income tax.

Every year the IRS adjusts many tax provisions as the cost of living goes up or down. It uses the Consumer Price Index (CPI) to calculate the prior year's inflation rate and adjusts income limits for tax brackets, tax deduction amounts, and tax credit values accordingly. All of these variables affect the net amount of tax you must pay.

FINANCE TIP

Use an online calculator at taxfoundation.org or taxact.com to find out how much federal tax you really pay (your effective tax rate) based on your income and tax filing status.

Here's a table showing the federal income tax brackets and rates for 2021 for some different types of taxpayers:

2021 Federal Income Tax Brackets and Rates

Tax rate	Single filers	Married joint filers	Head of household filers
10%	$0–$9,950	$0–$19,900	$0–$14,200
12%	$9,951–40,525	$19,901–81,050	$14,201–54,200
22%	$40,526–86,375	$81,051–172,750	$54,201–86,350
24%	$86,376–164,925	$172,751–329,850	$86,351–164,900
32%	$164,926–209,425	$329,851–418,850	$164,901–209,400
35%	$209,426–523,600	$418,851–628,300	$209,401–523,600
37%	$523,600 +	$628,300 +	$523,600 +

You'll notice that if you're single and earn $42,000, you're in the 22% tax *bracket* for 2021. However, the following table shows that your effective or net federal tax rate would be only 11.9%:

Net Federal Tax Rate for Single Filer Earning $42,000

Income tax bracket	Income taxed	Federal tax rate	Federal tax due
$0–$9,950	$9,950	10%	$995
$9,951–40,525	$30,575	12%	$3,669
$40,526–42,000	$1,475	22%	$324.50
Totals	$42,000		$4,988.50

As you can see, the effective tax rate = $4,988.50 ÷ $42,000 = 11.9%.

Although earning $42,000 means you're in the 22% tax bracket, your entire income is not taxed at this rate. A portion is taxed at 10%, another at 12%, and another at 22%, which generally makes your effective or net tax rate lower than your tax bracket rate.

There are four ways to file your federal and state tax returns:

1. *Free File* is tax preparation software provided free of charge at irs.gov for individuals with income below a certain amount. You're guided through a series of questions to calculate your tax liability, and your federal and state returns are filed electronically. While the federal returns are completed with no charge, some providers charge a fee for the preparation of state income tax returns.
2. *Fillable forms* are free online tax forms at irs.gov that you can complete and file electronically without the help of software, regardless of your income. State and local tax forms are not included.
3. *Tax software* can be purchased to help you prepare your federal and state returns and file them electronically.
4. *Tax preparers* are tax professionals who prepare your federal and state returns and file them electronically. Visit irs.gov for a list of authorized e-file providers or ask people you know to recommend a reputable tax accountant.

Not Every State Collects Income Tax In addition to federal taxes, you may have to pay state tax on your income. Each state has its own tax system. The following nine states don't collect any tax from income that residents earn: Alaska, Florida, Nevada, New Hampshire, South Dakota, Tennessee, Texas, Washington, and Wyoming.

Part 3 Review Questions

1. List several reasons that people work. What are some reasons people change jobs throughout their lifetime?
2. What are some "marketable skills" you possess? Think about skills you've developed and used in past jobs, volunteer opportunities, and even in school.
3. What are four different kinds of taxes withheld from your paycheck? What is the money ultimately used for?
4. Briefly describe how tax brackets work in the U.S. tax system.

Project

Research how the U.S. government spent last year's tax dollars. What percentages went to discretionary spending, mandatory spending, and interest on federal debt? What do discretionary and mandatory spending pay for?

Part 4

Save and Invest Money

Going to college. Buying a car. Starting a business. Retiring from work. Any financial goal or dream that you have can become a reality if you get in the habit of consistently setting aside small amounts of money over time. Starting this routine at a young age will really pay off and allow you to control your financial future.

Though we tend to use the terms *saving* and *investing* interchangeably, they're not the same. The difference has to do with financial risk. Investors walk a line between wanting to make money and not wanting to lose money. Saving money in a bank keeps it completely safe but pays a lower rate of return than some other investments. Investments that pay higher rates of return come with higher risk – the chance you could lose some or all of your money.

It's important to understand that, most often, high-return investments come with higher risk. And low-return investments or savings usually come with low risk.

Types of Savings Accounts

You will probably earn only a small amount of interest on savings. But the purpose of having savings is to keep your funds completely safe and accessible. Money you need to spend in the short term for planned purchases and emergencies should be kept in a federally insured savings account, so you can't lose it.

There are three basic types of savings accounts you can open at most banks and credit unions: a savings account, a money market account, and a certificate of deposit. Review Part 1 of this handbook for an explanation of these accounts and the protection offered by the Federal Deposit Insurance Corporation, or FDIC.

Investing Basics

Looking at the period from 1928 to 2021, we see that investing money in the stock market has historically rewarded investors with average returns of over 10%. Even from 2004 to 2013 – the decade that includes the Great Recession – investors earned approximately 9% on average.

So why would you put money in a bank savings account that might earn 0.1% to 1% instead? Because investing money always involves some amount of risk – the potential to lose money as well as the potential to make money.

Financial analysts make forecasts based on what happened in the past. But they include the disclaimer "Past performance does not guarantee future results." In other words, even the smartest analyst can't predict how much an investment will be worth in the future. Therefore, it's very important to invest with wisdom and caution.

The purpose of investing money is to increase your wealth over a long time period so you can achieve goals like paying for retirement or purchasing a home. Whether you should save or invest depends on your time horizon, which is the amount of time between now and when you'll actually need to spend the money. If you have a long time horizon — such as 10 years or more — investing makes sense. When you have a short time horizon — such as a year or less — many financial advisors recommend that you stick with an insured savings account.

What Is the Securities Investor Protection Corporation (SIPC)?

Investments, or securities, are not guaranteed by any federal agency such as the FDIC. There is no insurance against losing money in an investment. However, the Securities Investor Protection Corporation (SIPC) is a nongovernment entity that gives you limited protection in certain situations. They step in when an investment brokerage firm fails or when fraud is the cause of investor loss. The SIPC replaces missing securities up to $500,000 per customer. You can learn more at sipc.org.

Types of Investments

The earlier you start investing, the more money you'll have to pay for your financial dreams and goals. There are four basic types of financial securities and products that you can purchase for your investment portfolio. They are stocks, bonds, mutual funds, and exchange-traded funds.

Stocks

Stocks are issued by companies — such as Apple, Starbucks, and Disney — that want to raise money. When you buy shares of a stock, you purchase an ownership interest in a company, and your shares can go up or down in value over time. Stocks are bought and sold on exchanges, such as the New York Stock Exchange or the NASDAQ, and you can monitor their prices in real time online.

Stocks are one of the riskiest investments because the price per share can be volatile, swinging up or down in a short period of time. People can't be sure about which stocks will increase in value over the short or long term. However, historically, stocks have rewarded investors with higher returns than other major investment classes, such as cash or bonds.

Bonds

Bonds are loans you give to a corporation or government entity, known as the issuer, who wants to raise money for a specific project. Projects paid for by a bond include things such as building a factory or a school. Bonds pay a fixed interest rate over a set period of time. The time can range from weeks to 30 years. In general, interest is higher for longer-term bond terms and for bonds issued by companies with better credit.

Bonds are also called fixed-income investments because the return is guaranteed. In return for a higher degree of safety than stocks, you receive a relatively low rate of return. (Remember that lower-risk investments give you a lower return and higher-risk investments typically offer higher returns.) But these conservative investments still have some risk. For example, a bond issuer can default on repayment. Agencies such as Standard and Poor's (spglobal.com) do research and offer a rating system of bond safety.

Mutual Funds

Mutual funds are products that bundle combinations of investments, such as stocks, bonds, and other securities. They're operated by professional money managers who invest the fund's money according to stated objectives, such as achieving maximum growth or earning fixed income. Mutual fund shares are purchased directly from the fund company or from investment brokers and can go up or down in value over time.

> **FINANCE TIP**
> **You can reduce risk by diversification, which means owning a variety of investments in your portfolio.**

In general, mutual funds composed of stock have the greatest potential risk and reward; however, there's a wide range of risk within this category. Mutual funds composed of bonds also have a range of risk but are considered more conservative than stock funds.

Exchange-Traded Funds (ETFs)

Exchange-traded funds are products that bundle combinations of investments—just like mutual funds—but trade like a stock on an exchange throughout the day. These securities are growing in popularity due to their flexibility and low cost. The cost to operate an ETF is very low compared to many mutual funds.

Other Types of Investments

Other types of investments include real estate, precious metals (such as gold and silver), and businesses, just to name a few. They generally require greater expertise and skill to buy and sell than the four types of securities covered here. The drawback to these alternative investments is that they aren't as liquid, or sold as easily, as the mainstream investments described above.

What Is Financial Risk?

To be a successful investor, you need to understand the financial risks of different types of investments and gauge your own tolerance for risk. Many brokerage firms offer a questionnaire that can help you determine this.

What seems safe to one person may be deemed very risky by another. Your tolerance for risk is reflected in how you react when your investments decline in value. Someone who doesn't like risk is considered risk averse. A risk-averse person is willing to miss out on higher rates of return in exchange for financial safety. A more risk-tolerant person is willing to accept investment losses in exchange for potentially higher returns.

There is no right or wrong risk style that you should adopt. It just comes down to your personal feelings and preferences for how you want to manage your investments.

Ways to Invest

You have many choices when it comes to investing your money. The two most common are brokerage accounts and retirement accounts.

Brokerage Accounts

Brokerage accounts are available at local and online brokerage firms that are licensed to place investment orders, such as buying or selling shares of a stock, a mutual fund, or an ETF. You own the assets in a brokerage account and must pay tax each year on the earnings, which are called capital gains.

Retirement Accounts

Retirement accounts are special accounts you can open at a variety of institutions, such as local or online banks and brokerage firms, that allow you to save for retirement. One of the advantages is that they allow you to pay less tax because you can often defer income into a future time period.

There are different kinds of retirement accounts available for individuals, as part of an employee benefit package at work, and for the self-employed. Investment options include many of the instruments already mentioned, such as stocks, bonds, mutual funds, ETFs, or even bank CDs.

When you invest through a retirement account—as opposed to a regular brokerage account—you defer, or avoid paying, tax on your earnings. That means you save money on taxes and have more money for retirement! However, if you withdraw funds from a retirement account that weren't previously taxed, you are typically subject to an early withdrawal penalty, in addition to ordinary income tax.

The most commonly used retirement accounts include individual retirement arrangements, the 401(k) plan, and the 403(b) plan. In order to have enough money to live comfortably for decades during retirement, it's important to get in the habit of saving money in a retirement account.

Individual Retirement Arrangement (IRA) The IRA is a personal account available to anyone, regardless of age, who has taxable income. You can begin making contributions to an IRA as soon as you get your first job. However, you're in charge of it, not your employer. With a traditional IRA, you generally don't pay tax on contributions or earnings until after you retire and start taking withdrawals. In other words, taxes on the account are deferred until sometime in the future. With a Roth IRA, you pay tax on your contributions up front. However, you never pay tax on them again or on any amount of earnings. You get a huge tax benefit with a Roth because your entire account grows completely tax free.

401(k) Plan The 401(k) plan is a retirement account offered by many companies. You authorize a portion of your wages to be contributed to the plan before income tax is withheld from your paycheck. A 401(k) plan offers participants a set menu of investment choices. You can contribute amounts up to certain allowable limits each year. Many employers also offer a Roth 401(k) option that allows you to make after-tax contributions.

403(b) Plan The 403(b) plan is a retirement account offered by certain organizations such as schools, churches, and hospitals. It's similar to a 401(k) in most aspects and also limits contributions each year. This plan may also include a Roth option.

Retirement Accounts for Employees

There are two main types of retirement programs found in the workplace: defined benefit plans and defined contribution plans.

- A **defined benefit plan** is funded and managed by an employer and is commonly known as a pension. Employees don't pay into the plan, pick investments, or manage the money in any way. Defined benefit plans give retired workers a specific, defined benefit, such as $800 per month for the rest of their life. The benefit paid depends on various factors, such as age, length of employment, and salary history. These plans have become rare in the workplace because they're expensive to operate. However, some large companies, government agencies, and labor unions offer them.
- A **defined contribution plan** is established by an employer but requires that the employee manage it. This type of plan includes the 401(k) and 403(b) plans. The retirement benefit that an employee will receive depends on the amount that's invested and the performance of the chosen investments over the years. Defined contribution plans are more common because they're less risky for an employer to administer.

What Is Employer Matching?

If you could earn a guaranteed 100% return on your money, would you be interested? Many employers match a certain amount of the money you put in a workplace retirement plan. Say your employer matches 100% of your contributions to a 401(k) up to 3% of your salary. If you earn $30,000 a year and contribute $75 a month or $900 a year, that's a contribution of 3% of your salary. With matching, your employer would also contribute $900. So you'd invest $900 and automatically get $900 from your company—an immediate 100% return on your money!

How Much Will Social Security Pay in Retirement?

As a young person, it's not possible to know exactly how much you'll receive in Social Security retirement benefits. These benefits are calculated based on various factors, such as the current law, your future earnings, how long you pay payroll or self-employment taxes, the age you elect to start receiving benefits, and your military service.

However, according to the Social Security Administration, the benefit replaces only about 40% of your preretirement earnings, if you have average income. As of 2022, the average monthly benefit for a retired worker was $1,657. The maximum monthly benefit was $3,345; however, higher benefits may be possible if you choose to delay benefits until after you reach full retirement age.

Therefore, it's important not to count on Social Security retirement benefits as your sole source of income during retirement. The program was created as a supplement for personal savings, not as a substitute for having a retirement plan.

Investing for Education

Just as there are special accounts that allow you to invest for retirement and pay less tax, there are two education savings accounts, or ESAs, to be familiar with: 529 plans and Coverdells.

- A **529 plan** is a savings or investment vehicle that allows you to contribute money to pay for qualified expenses at a college, university, or vocational school. Since 2018, individuals can also spend up to $10,000 per year for eligible K–12 tuition. There are prepaid plans, where you prepay all or a portion of the future cost, and investment plans, where you choose specific investments. Contributions and earnings in a 529 plan grow tax free.
- A **Coverdell account** allows you to contribute money to pay for any level of education, from kindergarten through graduate school. It differs from a 529 plan in that it has more restrictions, such as how much can be contributed each year and the age of the student who will use the funds.

You can learn more about 529s and Coverdells at savingforcollege.com and finaid.org.

Part 4 Review Questions

1. What is the difference between *saving* and *investing*?
2. Briefly describe each of the four kinds of mainstream investments described in this Part.
3. Briefly describe the different kinds of retirement accounts. Why is it a good idea to invest in retirement accounts as soon as you start working?

Project

If you had $100,000 to save and invest for the future, what kinds of savings and investment options would you choose so that you diversify your money? What does it mean to "diversify" your savings plan?

Part 5

Give Yourself Some Credit

How is it possible to make a major purchase, like a home, if you don't have the cash? The answer is credit. If you're "creditworthy," you can be trusted to borrow money and pay it back over time.

What Is Credit?

Credit is the ability to borrow money that you promise to repay with interest. Credit is an important part of your financial life because it allows you to do the following:

- **Make a large purchase and pay for it over time.** If you don't have enough money saved up to buy a car, having credit allows you to get a loan and repay it over a set period of time.

- **Stay safe in an emergency situation.** If your car breaks down and you don't have enough to pay for the repair, having a credit card or line of credit allows you to get back on the road and repay the balance over time.
- **Avoid having to carry cash or paper checks.** When you're making a large purchase, like a computer or furniture, using a credit card is safer than carrying around a large amount of cash or paper checks that could be stolen.
- **Make online purchases and reservations.** When you need to buy something over the internet—such as books, clothes, or travel reservations—it's convenient to use a credit card.

If you don't have credit, the only way to get a loan or credit card is to have someone with good credit cosign an account. A cosigner might be a family member or friend who guarantees to take full responsibility for the debt if you don't repay it.

How do you become creditworthy, so that a potential creditor—such as a bank or credit card company—will allow you to borrow money? While each institution has different guidelines for evaluating a potential borrower, the following five criteria are generally used:

1. **Credit score**: How likely are you to make on-time payments based on your credit history? In this section you'll learn more about what a credit score is.
2. **Income**: Do you have a steady job and have enough income to repay a debt?
3. **Debt**: Do you have existing debts? If so, will you have enough money to pay your current debt and make payments on a new debt?
4. **Financial ratios**: How much debt do you have relative to your income?
5. **Collateral**: Will you secure a debt by pledging property (like a car or home) that a lender could sell if you don't make payments?

Understanding Credit Reports

Your credit history is maintained by three major nationwide credit reporting agencies: Equifax (equifax.com), Experian (experian.com), and TransUnion (transunion.com). These agencies receive information about you from your creditors and list it on your credit report. They are interested in things such as whether you make payments on time, your outstanding debt balances, and your available credit limits. Credit reporting agencies don't make credit decisions; they simply report information provided to them on your credit reports.

Each of your credit reports from the three agencies is slightly different, but they generally contain the following four types of information:

1. **Personal information** includes your name, current and previous addresses, Social Security number, birth date, and employer.
2. **Account information** lists your open accounts and your closed accounts for up to a certain period of time.
3. **Credit inquiries** include a list of companies and employers that have made inquiries about you because you applied for a credit account or job.
4. **Public information** is data that is available in the public records about you, including bankruptcies, foreclosures, liens for unpaid income taxes, and legal judgments.

The information in your credit report sticks with you for a long time. Credit accounts with negative information (for example, late payments) remain on your credit report for seven years from the date your payment became past due, even after you close the account or pay it off in full. Credit accounts with positive information remain on your credit report for 10 years after you close the account or pay it off in full.

Understanding Credit Scores

Just as your schoolwork determines your final grade in various classes, the information in your credit reports is used to calculate your credit scores. One of the most confusing things about credit scores is that there isn't just one. Your credit score depends on the particular scoring model that's used to calculate it. Companies can create their own scoring systems or use brand-name scores calculated by other firms, like the FICO (Fair Isaac Corporation) Score or the VantageScore.

Your credit score is different from the final grade you receive for a class because it isn't figured once and filed away. Your credit score is calculated fresh every time it is requested. Therefore, it's a snapshot of your credit behavior up to that moment in time.

Poor credit may indicate that you've mismanaged your finances by making late payments or maxing out credit accounts. However, having too little credit history can also be a reason for having a low credit score.

Having poor credit means you'll be viewed as a risky customer who may not repay a debt. You'll either be turned down for credit or charged an interest rate that's higher than the rate offered to a customer with good credit. Why? In exchange for taking a financial risk on a customer with poor credit, lenders protect themselves financially by charging higher interest rates, which means you have to make higher monthly payments.

How Much Can Poor Credit Cost You?

Dora has excellent credit and goes to her bank to apply for a $15,000 car loan. After a few days, the bank's lending representative calls her with good news – she's been approved! She can borrow $15,000 at 4% APR for a term of four years, which makes her monthly payment $338.69. The total amount of interest she'll pay on the loan principal is $1,256.92.

On the other hand, let's imagine Dora didn't have excellent credit and the bank charged her 12% APR instead of 4%. At this higher interest rate, her monthly payment would be $395.01. She'd pay a total of $3,960.36 in interest – or $2,703.44 more than if her credit was in good shape.

The larger a loan, the more poor credit costs you. **Table 5.1** shows different scenarios for a home mortgage of $150,000 paid over 30 years. Not having excellent credit means you could pay an additional $127,493.41 in interest – on top of the original loan amount of $150,000.

Table 5.1 The Cost of Poor Credit

Credit status	APR (percent)	Monthly payment (dollars)	Total interest paid (dollars)	Cost of having poor credit (dollars)
Excellent	3.75%	$694.67	$100,082.42	$0
Good	5.00	805.23	139,883.68	39,801.26
Average	7.50	1,048.82	227,575.83	127,493.41

Other Ways Having Poor Credit Hurts Your Finances

Did you know that having poor credit scores can cost you even if you don't want a loan or credit card? Here are five ways that having poor credit affects your personal finances:

1. **Paying high insurance premiums**: In most U.S. states, insurance companies are allowed to factor in your credit when setting car and home insurance rates. Having poor credit means you'll be quoted rates that could be double or triple the amount that someone with excellent credit would pay. That's because consumers with poor credit have been found, on average, to file more insurance claims.
2. **Paying high security deposits**: You may be asked to pay higher deposits for an apartment and for utilities such as power, gas, water, and phone accounts.

FINANCE TIP
To find out your credit score, you can visit the credit bureau websites mentioned earlier and purchase the information from them. You may also buy your FICO Score at myfico.com, or get several scores for free at creditkarma.com.

3. **Getting declined as a tenant**: You could be turned down for an apartment or house to rent because property managers prefer tenants who demonstrate good payment history.
4. **Getting turned down for government benefits**: You might not qualify for certain types of federal or state benefits that require a good credit history.
5. **Getting denied a job**: You might be turned down for a job by an employer who requires a credit check. Employers can't get your credit scores or see your entire credit report, but they can find out if you've had credit problems.

How to Establish Credit

The information in your credit report has a ripple effect throughout your entire financial life. How can you get started building good credit? Knowing how credit scores are calculated can help you improve them.

Each credit scoring model values the information in your credit report differently and uses a unique score range. The popular FICO Score uses a scale from 300 to 850 and values the following five factors:

1. **Payment history** (35%): making payments for bills and credit accounts on time
2. **Credit utilization** (30%): having lower amounts of debt relative to your available credit limits on credit cards and lines of credit
3. **Length of credit history** (15%): having credit accounts for a longer period of time
4. **Type of credit used** (10%): having a mix of credit types, including loans and credit cards
5. **Applications for credit** (10%): having fewer requests for new credit accounts

How to Build Your Credit

It may be difficult to get approved for a credit card before you've established a good credit history. However, everyone over age 18 can get a secured credit card, which can help you build credit for the first time—as long as it reports payment transactions to the credit agencies. With a secured credit card, you must make a refundable upfront deposit (as little as $200) that serves as your credit limit.

To build good credit, focus on actions within your control that have the biggest influence on typical scoring models. These include paying bills on time and not maxing out credit cards. But remember that it takes time to build good credit—it's a marathon, not a sprint.

How to Protect Your Credit

To protect the integrity of your credit, you should check your credit report on a regular basis. It's up to you to make sure that the information in your credit report is correct. Errors or fraudulent activity can hurt your credit scores without your knowing it.

Checking your credit reports is easy, and it never hurts your credit scores. You can purchase your credit report from any of the three credit agencies, but you're entitled to a free report from each once a year at annualcreditreport.com. You can report inaccuracies or put a stop to fraud by placing a credit alert or credit freeze on your credit reports. The Fair Credit Reporting Act (FCRA) is a federal law that regulates how your credit information can be used and your consumer credit rights. You can learn more on the Federal Trade Commission website at ftc.gov.

FINANCE TIP

To stay on top of your credit more than once a year, space out your requests and get a free report from a different credit agency every four months at annualcreditreport.com.

Part 5 Review Questions

1. Briefly describe the criteria a creditor uses to evaluate a potential borrower.
2. Why is it important to maintain an excellent credit score? Name ways that bad credit can hurt someone. How can good credit help you achieve some of your own financial goals?
3. Why do you think lenders have an interest in your credit history?
4. Do you think it's fair that consumers with good credit scores typically pay less for credit accounts, such as credit cards, loans, and certain insurance products? Why or why not?

Project

Imagine that your best friend just got approved for a credit card with a $500 available credit limit. He or she is excited to use a credit card for the first time and wants to go on a shopping spree. If you know that he or she doesn't have much money to pay off the credit card bill, what advice would you offer?

Part 6

Borrow Without Sorrow

It can be easy to get into financial trouble if you borrow money that you can't repay. Getting behind on bills – such as payments for a car loan, student loan, or credit card – results in large late fees and long-term damage to your credit history. Therefore, it's important to know how to use debt responsibly and to make wise choices that are best for your financial future.

What to Know About Debt

Before you apply for credit or take on any amount of debt, ask yourself some important questions:

- Do I really need this item?
- Can I wait until I save enough cash to pay for it?
- What's the total cost of the credit, including interest and fees?
- Can I afford the monthly payments?

There are many different kinds of debt, but they fall into two main categories: installment loans and revolving credit.

Installment Loan Basics

An installment loan is an agreement you make with a creditor to borrow a certain amount of money and repay it in equal monthly payments, or installments, for a set period of time. The length or term of the loan could be very short or in excess of 30 years, and the loan may be secured or unsecured.

Secured loans are backed by collateral, which is something of value that you pledge to the lender. For instance, a car you finance is collateral for the car loan. And a house is collateral for a home loan, which is also known as a mortgage. Collateral protects lenders because they can sell it to repay your debt if you don't make payments as agreed.

Unsecured loans are not backed by any collateral. They're often called personal or signature loans because you sign an agreement where you promise to repay the debt. For instance, credit card debt and student loans are both forms of unsecured loans.

When you take an installment loan, your monthly payment will depend on three factors:

1. **Principal amount**: The less you borrow, the lower your monthly payment will be.
2. **Interest rate**: The lower the rate, the lower your monthly payment will be.
3. **Loan term**: The longer the term, the lower your monthly payment will be; however, this generally results in paying more total interest.

Common Types of Installment Loans

Installment loans give consumers money to buy many different products and services, such as cars, homes, or a college education.

Consumer Loans

Consumer installment loans, also called personal or signature loans, are commonly used for small purchases, such as buying a computer or paying for unexpected expenses. You can apply for an unsecured consumer loan from local banks, credit unions, or online lenders.

Auto Loans

Installment loans to buy a new or used vehicle are available from local banks, credit unions, online lenders, and some car dealers. You may be required to make a down payment on the purchase price—especially if you don't have good credit.

For example, if you want to buy a used car that costs $10,000, the lender may require that you pay 20% or $2,000 up front in order to borrow the remaining balance of $8,000.

As previously mentioned, the car you buy becomes collateral for the loan. If you don't make payments as agreed, the lender can repossess, or take back, the vehicle to pay off the outstanding loan balance. The lender typically holds the title of the car until the loan is paid off in full.

The term or repayment period for a car loan is typically two to seven years. Choosing a longer loan term reduces the monthly payment but can significantly increase the amount of total interest you have to pay.

What's Being "Upside Down"? A new car depreciates, or loses its value, very quickly—especially in the first three years—depending on the make and model. For example, a $20,000 car might be worth only $15,000 after a year. But your outstanding loan balance could be over $16,000 after a year if you made a low or no down payment (depending on the loan terms).

When you owe more for a car than it's worth, you're "upside down" on the loan. If you want to trade or sell the car, you have to pay extra out of pocket to pay off the loan. Making a down payment helps you avoid this common financial problem of being upside down—and helps reduce your monthly loan payment. So, even if you have good credit, it's wise to make a down payment on a car loan.

FINANCE TIP
Use the car loan calculator at dinkytown.net to find out how changing the down payment, loan amount, interest rate, and term of a loan results in different monthly payments.

What's a Car Title? A car title is a document that shows who purchased a vehicle and lists information including the vehicle identification number (VIN), make, year of manufacture, purchase price, registered owner name and address, and legal owner if any money is owed. When a car is sold, the title must be transferred to the new owner.

What's Vehicle Leasing? Instead of owning a car, you can lease one for a set period of time. After the lease term (usually two, three, or four years) expires, you have to return the vehicle to the leasing company. Monthly lease payments may be less than a loan payment for the same vehicle and term. However, after you pay off a car loan, the vehicle belongs to you. You can sell it for cash or continue to drive it for many years without having to make a car payment. Therefore, purchasing a car is more cost effective when you keep it for the long term.

FINANCE TIP
The Kelley Blue Book at kbb.com is a guide that helps car buyers and sellers determine the market value of a new or used vehicle.

Student Loans

Student loans are funds you can use for education expenses, such as tuition, books, room and board, and other living expenses while you attend college. There are two main types of unsecured installment loans that may be available to you or your parents: federal student loans and private student loans.

Federal student loans are issued by the federal government, and most don't require a credit check for approval. Most students qualify for some type of federal loan, up to certain limits, depending on their income or their parents' financial qualifications. To apply, you must complete the Free Application for Federal Student Aid (FAFSA). You can submit it online at the U.S. Department of Education website at studentaid.gov.

Here are three types of federal student loans:

- **Stafford Loan** is the main federal loan for students. It can be subsidized by the federal government or unsubsidized. To receive a subsidized Stafford Loan, you must demonstrate financial need. The government pays, or subsidizes, the interest on the loan while you're in school.

  Unsubsidized Stafford Loans require you to pay all the interest; however, you can defer making payments until after graduation. All students, regardless of financial need, can get an unsubsidized Stafford Loan.
- **Perkins Loan** is a subsidized federal loan given to students who have the greatest financial need. The government pays the loan interest during school and for a nine-month grace period after graduating or withdrawing from school.
- **Parent Loan for Undergraduate Students (PLUS)** is an unsubsidized federal loan for parents of students. A credit check is made to verify that the parents have no adverse credit history.

FINANCE TIP
If you want to learn more about completing the FAFSA and paying for college, finaid.org is a leading resource for financial aid—including loans, scholarships, grants, and fellowships.

Private student loans originate from a private lender, such as an online institution, a local bank, or a credit union. Private education loans are generally used to bridge the gap between the cost of college and the amount you can borrow from the government.

Eligibility for a private loan depends on your or your parents' financial qualifications and credit scores. You submit an application directly to a private lender and don't have to complete any federal forms.

Private student loans typically have higher interest rates and less repayment flexibility than federal loans. Therefore, always apply for a federal student loan first.

Home Loans

You can get a home loan or mortgage from local banks, credit unions, or online lenders. Home loans can be used to

- buy real estate, such as a house or condominium,
- buy a parcel of vacant land,
- build a home, or
- borrow against the equity or value of a home you already own.

There are three main types of home loans:

1. A **purchase loan** is used to buy a home and is secured by the property. You must make a down payment that's typically 5% to 20% of the purchase price. The loan term is typically 30 years, but 15- and 20-year mortgages are also common.
2. An **equity loan** is secured by your home and can be used for any purpose. *Equity* is the current market value of your property less the amount of outstanding debt you owe. For instance, if your home is worth $200,000 and your mortgage balance is $140,000, you have $60,000 in equity.
3. A **refinance loan** replaces an existing home loan by paying it off and creating a brand new loan that has better terms, such as a lower interest rate. Refinancing at a lower interest rate may allow you to lower your monthly payments and save money.

What Is Foreclosure? Foreclosure is a legal process a home lender uses to collect the balance of an unpaid debt when a borrower defaults or stops making loan payments as agreed. The lender can take legal title to the property, evict the borrower(s), and sell the property to pay off the debt, according to state laws.

Revolving Credit Basics

Revolving credit is different from an installment loan (such as a car or student loan) because it doesn't have a fixed number of payments or a final due date. The account revolves, or stays open indefinitely, as long as the borrower makes minimum monthly payments. The lender approves a maximum loan amount, or credit limit, to use at any time. Credit cards, retail store credit cards, and home equity lines of credit (HELOCs) are common types of revolving credit.

Applying for a Credit Card

If you're under age 21, you must show that you have income or an eligible cosigner to qualify for a credit card. The law requires that you receive a Federal Truth in Lending Disclosure Statement from any company that offers you credit. Be sure to read it carefully so you understand the terms and can compare cards based on these features:

- annual percentage rate (APR) for purchases, promotions, cash advances, and balance transfers
- your credit limit
- potential fees and penalties
- how balances are calculated
- rewards or rebates for purchases
- additional protections (such as travel insurance or extended warranties)

Managing a Credit Card

A credit card gives you the ability to make purchases now and pay for them later. For example, if you have a credit card with a $1,000 credit limit, you can use it to buy products or services, or take cash advances, that total up to $1,000. However, you should never max out a credit card because that hurts your credit.

This flexibility makes credit cards powerful financial tools that can help you in an emergency situation. But credit cards can also devastate your finances if you get over your head in debt that you can't repay.

Because credit cards are so convenient for consumers and come with unsecured risk for lenders, card companies charge relatively high interest rates that can exceed 30%. Every time you make a credit card purchase, you're borrowing money that must be paid back. You'll also have to pay interest charges if you don't pay off your balance in full by the monthly statement due date. See Part 5 for more information on understanding and establishing credit.

Paying Off Your Credit Card

Credit cards issue an account statement each month that lists transactions from the previous month. The lowest amount you can pay—your "minimum payment"—varies depending on the card but may range from 2% to 4% of your outstanding balance. For instance, if you owe $500, your minimum payment could be 3%, or $15. The remaining balance of $485 will continue to accrue interest, in addition to any new transactions you make or late fees that may apply.

However, if you pay off your entire credit card balance by the due date on your statement each month, you can use a credit card without paying any interest charges or late fees. That's because no interest charges accrue during this "grace period."

✓ Tips to Reduce the Cost of Borrowing

The cost of borrowing money depends on several factors, such as current interest rates, your credit rating, the APR you're offered, loan fees, and how long it takes you to repay the debt. Here are 10 tips to reduce the cost of borrowing:

1. **Shop around for the lowest APR** for a loan or credit card before you accept an offer.
2. **Finance an item based on the total price** (including interest) that you can afford—not just on a monthly payment amount.
3. **Repay loans over a shorter term** so you pay less total interest over the life of a loan.
4. **Pay off credit card purchases in full each month** so you're never charged interest or late fees.
5. **Make payments on time** so you're never penalized with expensive late fees or an increased APR on a credit card.
6. **Build a good credit history** so you have high credit scores and will be offered low interest rates by lenders and credit card companies. Establishing credit was covered in Part 5 of this handbook.
7. **Make a bigger down payment** so you'll owe less and receive lower APR offers from auto and home lenders.
8. **Take out federal student loans** before accepting private education loans so you qualify for the most favorable interest rates and repayment terms.
9. **Claim tax benefits** that come with education loans, such as the student loan interest tax deduction, which may allow you to reduce the amount of tax you owe.
10. **Never take a payday loan**, which is a short-term unsecured advance against your next paycheck. The interest rate for one of these loans can be over 15% for just two weeks—which translates into a sky-high APR that can exceed 400%!

Part 6 Review Questions

1. What are the advantages and disadvantages of borrowing money?
2. What goals do you have that might require you to borrow money?
3. Briefly describe the different kinds of student loans. How can you be sure you don't borrow more than you can comfortably pay back, taking other lifetime financial burdens (such as buying a home or car, or having children) into consideration?
4. What are some important rules to remember when it comes to managing a credit card the right way?
5. Why should credit cards and loans never be viewed as "free money"?

Project

Compare interest rates associated with different types of borrowing. Look online or in local newspapers to determine interest rates for a 30-year home-purchase loan (mortgage), a new car loan, a credit card, and a check-cashing service. Which of these have the highest interest rates?

Part 7

Manage Your Money

Building wealth and creating financial security can be easy if you have a reliable income and manage your money wisely. Good money management starts with never spending more than you make each month. Your financial life will always be a balancing act between the short-term gratification of spending to fulfill your current wants versus the long-term benefit of saving. Striking the right balance will allow you to have enough money to fulfill your future wants and needs.

It's your job to have the willpower to resist unnecessary spending and get into the habit of saving for the future on a regular basis. If you use your financial resources responsibly, you'll be able to have a secure future and make your dreams a reality.

Setting Financial Goals

A financial goal is something you want to do with your money in a certain period of time. Goals can be short term, like buying a car this year or taking a vacation next summer.

Or goals can be long term, like accumulating a large nest egg for retirement. Retirement is one of the most important goals for everyone. Why? Because as you grow older, you may neither want nor be able to work. The hope is that we save enough money so it's possible to enjoy life and pursue other interests besides work when desired.

In Part 3 you learned that Social Security benefits are likely to provide you with a small amount of income after you retire. You'll need additional savings for everyday expenses, such as housing, food, and medical costs – otherwise, you won't have a comfortable lifestyle as you grow older.

Though you have many years to go, saving enough for retirement generally takes decades to achieve. That's why it's critical that you begin saving for the future as early as possible. Financial success doesn't happen overnight – so the earlier you start saving for retirement, the better.

What Is Social Security?

Social Security is a group of benefits paid to eligible taxpayers who are retired, who are disabled, or who survive a relative who was receiving benefits. The funds for Social Security come from taxes withheld from your paycheck. The amount you'll receive in retirement depends on how many years you work, how much payroll or self-employment tax you pay during your career, the age you elect to start receiving benefits, and the future financial health of the Social Security system. Visit ssa.gov for more information.

Creating a Budget

It's easy for everyday purchases like snacks, magazines, and music to get out of control if you're not watching them carefully. Keeping your expenses as low as possible can add up to huge savings over time. For instance, let's say bringing your lunch to work four days a week saves you $8 a day, or $32 a week. If you invested $32 a week for 40 years at a moderate rate of return, that savings would grow to over $330,000.

The best way to take control of your money is to create a budget, also known as a spending plan. A spending plan helps you understand how much money you have and where it goes, so you can prioritize expenses and set objectives to achieve your short- and long-term financial goals.

Managing money the right way is all about making choices and sacrifices – like whether to spend money on a night out with friends or save it to buy a car. You'll always have many needs and wants competing for your limited financial resources. You can apply an economic mindset to your financial planning too! It's up to you to choose your priorities and decide the best way to spend your money.

Four Steps to Preparing a Successful Budget

Knowing exactly how much you have to spend and where you spend it gives you power over your finances. You can keep track of your financial information on paper, using a computer spreadsheet or a mobile app, or by importing transactions from your bank or credit card accounts into a financial program, like Quicken.

Here are four easy steps to creating a successful spending plan:

- **Step #1 – Enter your net monthly income.**

To stay in control of your money and reach your financial goals, you must know how much money you have coming in each month. Recall that net income, or take-home pay, is the amount you have left after taxes and other voluntary workplace deductions. Enter this amount at the top of your spending plan because it's what you actually have to spend each month.

- **Step #2 – Enter your fixed and variable expenses.**

Many people don't achieve financial success because they spend money carelessly. It's critical that you keep a close watch on your spending so it never exceeds your net income. Enter all your expenses below your income.

Fixed expenses don't change from month to month and may include your rent, insurance, phone and internet bill, or loan payment. Variable expenses can change each month and can include discretionary spending, like dining out, using transportation services, or buying clothes.

Organize your expenses into major categories – such as rent, insurance, groceries, dining out, clothes, and entertainment – and enter the total amounts.

- **Step #3 – Compare your income and expenses.**

When you compare your total take-home pay to your total expenses, you may be pleased that you have money left over or disappointed that there's none to spare. Discretionary income is the amount of money you have left over each month after all your essential living expenses are paid.

You must spend less than you make in order to have enough discretionary income to save and invest for your future. Living paycheck to paycheck may satisfy immediate wants and needs, but it won't empower you to achieve long-term financial success.

- **Step #4 – Set priorities and make changes.**

The final step is to create new spending guidelines. Decide how much you want to allocate toward each of your short- and long-term financial goals and enter them as separate categories in your spending plan. You may need to reduce spending in other categories or find ways to earn extra income to cover all your expenses.

It's up to you to figure out the best way to balance your spending and saving so you enjoy life today and put away enough money for a safe and secure tomorrow.

What Does "Pay Yourself First" Mean?

"Pay yourself first" is a common saying in personal finance that means saving money should be your top priority. Putting your savings on autopilot is the best way to remove the temptation to spend it! A portion of each paycheck can be deposited automatically in a savings or retirement account before you receive the balance. That way you pay yourself before paying your living expenses or making discretionary purchases.

Paying Bills

Paying bills on time is one of the most important money management responsibilities. Late payments can result in expensive fees and damage to your credit. Thanks to online banking, it's never been easier to manage bills and pay them on time.

Most local and internet-only banks offer free bill pay, which allows you to pay any company or individual with the click of a button. If a company you want to pay accepts electronic payments, your funds will transfer electronically. If not, the bill pay service prints and mails a paper check on your behalf to any payee in the United States that has a mailing address.

E-bills and e-statements can be sent to your e-mail, bill pay center, or both. You can set up a bill to be paid automatically on a certain date and e-mail you when the transaction is complete. Or you can log on to your bill pay center and manually initiate a payment for up to one year into the future. You can set up reminder alerts for all your recurring bills so no payment due date ever falls through the cracks.

Tracking Your Wealth

A spending plan is the perfect way to track your income and expenses. But to monitor the big picture of your finances, you need to know your net worth. Your net worth can be summed up in this simple equation:

$$\text{net worth} = \text{assets} - \text{liabilities}$$

Assets are items you own that have real value, such as cash in the bank, vehicles, investments, real estate, personal belongings, and money owed to you. Liabilities are your debts and financial obligations to others, such as an auto loan, credit card debt, or money you borrowed from a friend.

If you have more assets than you owe in liabilities, your net worth will be a positive number. But if you owe more than you own, your net worth will be a negative number. The goal is to raise your net worth over time by increasing your assets or decreasing your liabilities, so you build wealth.

✓ Tips to Manage Money Like a Millionaire

One of the most surprising facts about wealthy people is that most of them weren't born that way. About 80% of the wealthiest people in the United States are first-generation millionaires. They accumulated wealth by working hard and saving and investing money. That means anyone who is disciplined with their money can achieve financial security. Here are 10 tips to manage your money like a millionaire:

1. **Live below your means.** Spending less than you make is a choice. Saving money, and not overspending, is how you build wealth.
2. **Know where your money goes.** If you don't have a spending plan to track your money, you won't know if you're making wise decisions. Getting ahead financially starts with taking control of your cash flow.
3. **Create an emergency fund.** Having money set aside for unexpected expenses is a safety net that you should never be without. That's how you'll make it through a financial rough patch, such as suddenly losing your job or having large unexpected expenses. Make a goal to accumulate at least six months' worth of your living expenses to keep on hand at all times.
4. **Focus on net worth instead of income.** No matter how much you earn, you can grow rich by slowly increasing your net worth over time. But even if you have a large income, you'll never grow rich if you don't get in the habit of setting aside money for the future.
5. **Have long-term financial goals.** Wealthy people know what they want to achieve and then work backward so they have a plan for what to do each year, month, week, or day to stay on track and meet their goals. Set objectives to achieve your goals.
6. **Begin saving for retirement early.** If you think you're too young to start saving for retirement, think again. Creating wealth for your future rarely happens overnight—unless you beat huge odds by having a winning lottery ticket or a big inheritance.
7. **Save and invest at least 15% of your income.** Make it a habit to save 15% to 20% of your income, starting with your first job, and adjust your lifestyle so you can easily live on the rest.
8. **Automate your savings and investments.** It's easier to save money that you never see. Participate in a workplace retirement account or have your paycheck split between a checking and savings account so your savings are on autopilot.
9. **View money as a tool.** Money is only as useful as what you do with it. So decide what's important to you and use money to achieve your needs and your dreams. Push away short-term gratification in favor of important, long-term goals like saving for retirement.
10. **Realize when you've made a money mistake.** Everyone makes mistakes with their money from time to time. If you overspend or make unwise decisions, stop and make the choice to get back on track right away.

Part 7 Review Questions

1. Do you think that writing down your goals and reviewing them on a regular basis could help increase your chances of accomplishing them? Why or why not?
2. What is the relationship between spending and the ability to build wealth?
3. Why does tracking how you spend money help you make better financial decisions?
4. What is the purpose of an emergency fund, and how much should be in it?

Project

Choose a savings goal that you'd like to achieve in one year. Create a savings plan and keep track of your progress over the next few months.

Part 8

Protect Yourself from Risk

Life is full of events that no one can predict. It's impossible to know if you'll get into a car accident, have your laptop stolen, or need to visit the emergency room for a broken bone. While you can't prevent these kinds of catastrophes, you can protect your personal finances by having enough of the right kinds of insurance.

Insurance is a special type of contract between you and an insurance company. The company agrees that when certain events – defined in an insurance policy – occur, they'll meet certain expenses or provide a payout. For example, with a car insurance policy, the insurer agrees to pay some amount of the cost to repair your car if you're in an accident. Health insurance pays a certain amount of your medical expenses if you need to go to the doctor.

Insurance eliminates or reduces the potential financial loss you could experience from an unforeseen event and protects the income and assets that you work hard for.

Types of Insurance

There are many different types of insurance products that can be purchased from an insurance company or a licensed insurance agent, either in person or online. The types you should have depend on your age and life circumstances. There are eight major types of insurance: health, disability, life, auto, homeowner's, renter's, long-term care, and umbrella.

Health Insurance

Without health insurance, you could get stuck with a huge bill if you have any kind of medical need, from a broken bone to a chronic illness. Even a quick trip to the emergency room can cost thousands of dollars.

The federal government, through the Affordable Care Act (ACA), provides access to health care insurance if you don't receive it through your employer. Guidelines for the program may change over time, depending on the actions of the government, but you may be eligible for a financial subsidy, which reduces the monthly cost of health insurance, depending on your income and family size. Annual open enrollment deadlines for this health insurance program vary based on your state of residency. You can learn more about the ACA and your eligibility to purchase insurance there at www.healthcare.gov.

Many employers offer group health insurance to their employees, or you can purchase an individual policy on your own. You can stay on your parents' health policy until you are 26 years old – unless you're offered insurance through your work.

Disability Insurance

A disability is a physical or mental condition that limits your ability to perform various types of activities. If you're unable to work due to a disability, accident, or illness, disability insurance replaces a portion of your income, typically 60%. Unless you have plenty of savings in an emergency fund, a disability could leave you unable to pay for everyday living expenses, such as housing or groceries. Remember that health insurance covers only a portion of your medical bills – not your everyday living expenses.

Many employers offer some type of disability coverage for employees, or, if you're self-employed, you can purchase an individual policy on your own. Professionals – such as surgeons, athletes, or dancers – who want to protect their financial health if their ability to do their jobs is compromised should always have disability coverage. Every disability policy is different, but there are two main types: short-term disability (STD) and long-term disability (LTD). A short-term policy usually pays you for a maximum of two years, while a long-term policy could provide benefits that last your entire life.

Life Insurance

Life insurance provides a lump-sum payment, known as a death benefit, to one or more named beneficiaries when the insured person dies. It's important to have life insurance when your death would cause a financial burden for those you leave behind—such as a spouse or child.

Many employers offer life insurance for employees, or you can purchase your own policy. There are two basic kinds of life insurance: term and permanent.

- **Term life insurance** provides less expensive coverage for a set period of time, such as 10 or 20 years, and pays the policy's death benefit amount to the beneficiary.
- **Permanent life insurance** provides lifetime coverage that pays a death benefit and accumulates a cash value that the beneficiary can withdraw later in life. This type of policy is much more expensive that a term life policy.

A good rule of thumb is to purchase life insurance with a benefit that's equal to 10 times your income. So if you make $50,000 a year, you might need coverage that would pay your beneficiary $500,000. However, factors such as your family size, debt, and assets, and the lifetime income needs of a surviving partner, spouse, or child are critical considerations.

Auto Insurance

Most U.S. states require you to have some amount of insurance for vehicles such as cars, trucks, motorcycles, and recreational vehicles. The required insurance types and minimum amounts vary depending on the state in which you live.

Auto insurance is a package of coverages that may include the following:

- **Collision** pays for damage to your vehicle caused by getting into an accident with another vehicle, even if you are at fault.
- **Comprehensive** pays for damage to your vehicle due to something other than a collision, such as fire, hail, or theft.
- **Property damage liability** pays for damage you cause to someone else's property, such as their vehicle or fence, or a city's stop sign.
- **Bodily injury liability** pays for injuries you cause to another person. It's important to have enough liability because if you're involved in a serious accident, you could be sued for a large sum of money.
- **Personal injury protection** pays for medical expenses of the driver and passengers of the policyholder's car regardless of who's at fault, in certain states.
- **Uninsured and underinsured motorist coverage** pays when you're in an accident with an at-fault driver who has insufficient or no insurance to pay for your loss.

The cost of auto insurance varies depending on many factors, such as your age, driving record, and credit history (in most states), the type and age of your vehicle, and the amount and type of coverage you choose. So remember to factor in the cost of insurance when choosing a new ride.

Homeowner's Insurance

When you have a home mortgage, the lender requires you to purchase and maintain insurance for the property. Basic homeowner's insurance pays for damage to your property or personal belongings caused by a covered event, such as a natural disaster or theft. Homeowner's insurance also includes liability coverage that protects you if someone gets hurt while on your property.

Renter's Insurance

When you rent an apartment or home, your landlord's insurance doesn't cover your personal belongings or liability. Renter's insurance pays for damage to your possessions (such as clothes, jewelry, electronics, furniture, artwork, household goods, and sporting equipment) if they're damaged by a covered event, such as a natural disaster, wind storm, theft, or faulty plumbing. It can also reimburse your living expenses if you're forced to move out temporarily while repairs are being made. And as with homeowner's insurance, the liability protection keeps you safe if someone is injured on the property and involves you in a lawsuit.

If you rent a home or apartment, you should never go without renter's insurance. According to the National Association of Insurance Commissioners (NAIC), the national average cost of a renter's policy in 2021 was only $219. So it's a very inexpensive way to protect your finances from an unforeseen crisis!

Long-Term Care Insurance

If you have a long-term illness or disability that keeps you from taking care of yourself, long-term care (LTC) insurance pays a certain amount of day-to-day care that isn't covered by other types of insurance. Remember that disability insurance replaces only a portion of your lost income if you're unable to work due to a disability. And health insurance pays for only a portion of your medical bills.

Individuals who require long-term care may need help with activities of daily living, such as dressing, bathing, eating, and walking. Long-term care insurance generally covers care provided in your home by a visiting professional or in an assisted living facility.

Umbrella Insurance

As you build wealth, you may find that you need additional liability insurance protection to cover the total value of your assets. An umbrella policy gives you broad coverage from losses above the limits of your existing policies.

For instance, say you have $100,000 of auto insurance liability and a $1 million umbrella policy. If you were in a car accident that caused serious injuries to another driver that exceeded $100,000, your umbrella policy would give you protection up to one million dollars.

What Is an Insurance Deductible?

Many types of insurance – such as health, auto, renter's, and homeowner's – require you to pay a certain amount of expenses before the policy covers your remaining costs. This out-of-pocket expense is called your deductible. For example, if you have a medical bill for $2,000 and your deductible is $500, then you must pay $500 before the policy will pay all or a portion of the remaining $1,500 in covered benefits.

Extended Product Warranties

If you've ever purchased a product like a computer or a TV, the salesperson probably gave you a sales pitch for an extended product warranty. These warranties give you additional protection if something breaks after the manufacturer's warranty expires. They can also cover issues that the manufacturer doesn't.

While the added protection of an extended product warranty can come in handy, the cost can be very high. Product warranties are typically very profitable for retailers, who train salespeople to sell them aggressively. If the benefit isn't worth the cost, never let a salesperson talk you into buying something you don't need.

Pay attention to the warranty coverage that is automatically included with the purchase of the item. Sometimes the item will include a year of manufacturers' warranty or even longer. Don't waste money duplicating manufacturer's warranties.

Check product reviews online if they're available to get a sense of the likelihood of product failure during the time of the initial coverage and determine if it's worth extending based on customer comments. Finally, many credit cards offer product warranty coverage when they are used to purchase the item. Determine your credit card coverage before spending money on more.

Identity Theft

Identity theft is a serious and growing crime. It happens when a criminal steals your personal information and uses it to commit fraud. A thief can use data – such as your name, date of birth, Social Security number, driver's license number, bank account number, or credit card number – to wreak havoc on your finances. An identity criminal can open new phone accounts, credit cards, or loans in your name, then go on a spending spree and leave you with a huge bill. Thieves have even filed fictitious tax returns and applied for driver's licenses in their victims' names.

Many insurance companies offer identity theft insurance to cover expenses that you may incur as a victim, such as lost wages, attorney fees, and certified mailing costs. You may have the option to add this protection to your homeowner's or renter's policy.

There are also companies that specialize in identity theft protection, credit monitoring, and identity restoration. These services may be sold through insurance agents, credit card companies, credit reporting agencies, or banks and credit unions. Be sure to read the fine print of these policies before signing up so you understand if do-it-yourself safeguards may be just as effective.

It's impossible to completely prevent identity theft; however, if you catch it early, you can stop it quickly and with less potential hassle and expense.

FINANCE TIP
Be cautious with the information you post online. Never give hints about possible passwords and resist the urge to share personal information in unsecured sites.

What to Do If You're the Victim of Identity Theft

Once your identity is jeopardized, getting it corrected can cost time and money. So be sure to keep an eye on your accounts and immediately take the following actions if you see any suspicious activity:

- **Step #1 – Place an initial fraud alert on your credit report** with one of the major credit reporting agencies (Equifax, Experian, TransUnion). They must inform the other two agencies on your behalf. This alert makes it more difficult for a thief to open additional accounts in your name because a business must take additional steps to contact you directly to verify your identity. An initial fraud alert lasts for 90 days; however, you can renew it for free as needed.
- **Step #2 – Request your credit reports** from each of the three major credit reporting agencies. Placing a fraud alert also gives you access to free copies of your credit reports. It's a good idea to request copies that reveal only the last four digits of your Social Security number.

  If you know which of your accounts have been compromised, contact those companies directly to discuss the fraudulent activity. Take notes about what actions are being taken and follow up in writing. Be sure to send all communication regarding an identity theft case by certified mail and ask for a return receipt. It's important to create a record that proves you have been diligent to resolve unauthorized charges on your account.
- **Step #3 – Submit an identity theft report** to the Federal Trade Commission (FTC) and then the local police. Having these formal reports will help you prove that you've been an identity theft victim to credit reporting agencies, businesses, and debt collectors. If a thief opened new accounts in your name and made large purchases, this could damage your credit history unless the creditor is willing to remove the account or the fraudulent charges from your report.

  Visit the FTC website at consumer.ftc.gov to submit an identity theft report or to learn more.

FINANCE TIP
Always protect the data on your phone, laptop, and other electronic devices by requiring passwords, facial recognition, or other forms of encryption of your information.

✓ Tips to Stay Safe from Identity Theft

Here are 10 tips to help you protect yourself and stay safe from identity theft:

1. **Never carry confidential information that you don't need.** Unless you plan to use them, remove your Social Security card, paper checks, and financial cards from your wallet and leave them at home so they can't be lost or stolen. The best place to keep important documents is in a secure place in your home, where you can access them quickly when needed but are safe from potential damage.
2. **Don't share your Social Security number.** There are only a few situations where you might need to provide it, such as for a new job, in tax-related matters, or when applying for credit or insurance. Never reveal your confidential information over the phone or internet to any person or company that you don't trust entirely.
3. **Keep a close watch over your debit and credit cards.** When you hand a financial card to a store clerk or restaurant server, watch to make sure that it isn't copied and get it back as soon as possible. Also, never loan your financial cards to anyone.
4. **Shred all documents with personal information.** Make confetti out of receipts, financial account statements, and unwanted credit card offers before putting them in the garbage. Identity thieves dumpster dive for paperwork and can even use the last few digits of a confidential number against you.
5. **Check your credit reports once a year.** If an identity thief opens an account in your name, it will show up on your credit reports. That's why it's important to review them on a periodic basis at annualcreditreport.com. Remember that you are entitled to a free credit report from each of the credit reporting agencies each year. It's best to spread those credit report requests out during the year so you can see a problem quickly if one develops.
6. **Resist clicking on links in e-mails or text messages.** Thieves can pose as a legitimate organization—such as the IRS, a bank, or PayPal—and send "phishing" e-mails with links to phony sites that ask for confidential information. Genuine companies never ask you for personal information over the phone or internet. Instead of clicking on a hyperlink, enter a website address directly into an internet browser.
7. **Use a secure internet connection.** Don't access a website where you enter confidential information using a public computer or an open Wi-Fi connection. Hackers can track what you're doing over an unsecured internet connection. Also, never send any personal information to a website unless the address begins with "https," which means that it's secure. You should also be careful to keep the antivirus and spyware software current on your computer.
8. **Create strong online usernames and passwords.** Each password for your financial accounts should be unique, with at least eight characters made up of uppercase and lowercase letters, numbers, and symbols. They should never include your Social Security number, name, address, or birth date.
9. **Opt for e-bills and e-statements when possible**. Criminals can change your mailing address so they receive your mail and have access to your personal information. Therefore, reducing the amount of paper documents you send and receive with confidential information is beneficial.
10. **Monitor your bank and credit card account activity.** Review your accounts online or view monthly statements to watch out for unauthorized transactions.

Can You Opt Out?

One way that businesses can make extra money is through the sale of your personal information to other companies, including credit card companies. It's very easy to find yourself receiving multiple credit card offers in the mail and through your e-mail account even when you haven't applied for a credit card in recent history. While some credit card application information may helpful when you're searching for a credit card, it can be problematic if it puts your personal information at risk. You can lower the risk of identity theft by choosing to opt out of receiving offers like these from a website called optoutprescreen.com. This website is a joint product of the three credit reporting agencies (Experian, Equifax, and TransUnion). Taking these steps will not completely eliminate the credit card applications from your e-mail or mailbox, but it will substantially lower their frequency for a period of five years.

Part 8 Review Questions

1. Why do you think most U.S. states require drivers to have some amount of auto insurance for liability? Do you agree with this requirement? Why or why not?
2. Why does your driving record affect your auto insurance rates?
3. Imagine your best friend has enrolled in a photography program at a fine arts school. He is required to purchase nearly $3,000 worth of photography equipment for his courses and will be keeping it all in his new apartment. What kind of insurance would you suggest he get, if any, and why?
4. Who should have renter's insurance, and why is it a good idea?
5. Why do you think mortgage lenders require homeowners to have a certain amount of homeowner's insurance?
6. Describe several precautions you or your family take to stay safe from identity theft.

Project

Research health insurance plans online, taking into account your specific situation and needs. Start by making a list of how you use health insurance (frequency of doctor visits, need for special dental or vision services, etc.) and decide what kind of insurance policy would fit your needs best. Is it one with a high deductible but low monthly premium? Or is it different? Once you have selected the right fit, list the details of the plan and explain why this plan was the best fit for you.

Glossary-Glosario

Italicized terms within definitions are key terms that are defined elsewhere in this glossary.

Los *términos en cursiva* dentro de las definiciones son términos clave que se definen en otras partes de este glosario.

English	Español
A	
absolute advantage the advantage held by an individual when producing a good or service if they can make produce more with a given amount of time and resources; contrasted with *comparative advantage*. (p. 21, 434)	**ventaja absoluta** ventaja que tiene un individio cuando produce un bien o servicio si logra producir más con una cantidad dada de tiempo y recursos; se contrasta con *ventaja comparativa*. (págs. 21, 434)
absolute value the value of a number without a minus sign, whether or not the number was negative to begin with. (p. A-6)	**valor absoluto** valor de una cifra sin el signo de menos, haya sido o no una cifra negativa inicialmente. (pág. A-6)
accounting profit a business's *total revenue* minus the *explicit cost* and *depreciation* (p. 612)	**utilidad contable** *ingresos totales* de un negocio menos los *costes explícitos* y la *depreciación* (pág. 612)
***AD–AS* model** model in which the *aggregate supply curve* and the *aggregate demand curve* are used together to analyze fluctuations in the *price level* and *real GDP*. (p. 150)	**modelo *AD-AS*** modelo en el que la *curva de oferta agregada* y la *curva de demanda agregada* se emplean juntas para analizar fluctuaciones en el *nivel de precios* y *PIB real*. (pág. 150)
administrative costs (of a tax) the resources used by the government to collect the tax, and by taxpayers to pay (or to evade) it, over and above the amount collected. (p. 548)	**costes administrativos** (de un impuesto) recursos que emplea el gobierno para recaudar el impuesto y que emplean los contribuyentes para pagarlo (o para evadirlo), por encima del importe recaudado. (pág. 548)
adverse selection when one person knows more about the way things are than other people do; for example, when sellers offer items of particularly low (hidden) quality for sale, and when the people with the greatest need for insurance are those most likely to purchase it. (p. 833)	**selección adversa** cuando una persona sabe más que otras personas acerca de cómo son las cosas; por ejemplo, cuando los vendedores ofrecen para la venta artículos de una calidad particularmente mala (oculta), y cuando las personas con la mayor necesidad de un seguro son aquéllas con la mayor probabilidad de comprarlo. (pág. 833)
aggregate demand curve shows the relationship between the *aggregate price level* and the quantity of *aggregate output* demanded by *households*, businesses, the government, and the rest of the world. (p. 124)	**curva de demanda agregada** permite apreciar la relación entre el *nivel de precios agregados* y la cantidad de *producción agregada* exigida por los *hogares*, los negocios, el gobierno y el resto del mundo. (pág. 124)
aggregate output the total quantity of final goods and services produced within an economy. (p. 101)	**producción agregada** la cantidad total de bienes y servicios de consumo que se producen en una economía. (pág. 101)
aggregate price level a measure of the overall level of prices in the *economy*. (p. 88)	**nivel de precios agregados** medida del nivel total de precios en la *economía*. (pág. 88)
aggregate production function a hypothetical function that shows how aggregate output depends on the stock of *physical capital* and the quantity and quality of labor resources, as well as the state of *technology*. (p. 306)	**función de producción agregada** función hipotética que nos permite apreciar cómo la producción agregada depende de las existencias de *capital físico* y la cantidad y calidad de recursos laborales, así como del estado de la *tecnología*. (pág. 306)
aggregate spending the total spending on domestically produced *final goods and services* in the *economy*; the sum of *consumer spending*, *investment spending*, *government purchases of goods and services*, and *exports* minus *imports*. (p. 68)	**gastos agregados** total de gastos en los *bienes y servicios finales* producidos internamente en la *economía*; suma de los *gastos de consumo*, los *gastos de inversión*, la compra por el gobierno de bienes y servicios, y las *exportaciones* menos las *importaciones*. (pág. 68)
aggregate supply curve shows the relationship between the *aggregate price level* and the quantity of *aggregate output* supplied in the *economy*. (p. 137)	**curva de oferta agregada** permite apreciar la relación entre el *nivel de precios agregados* y la cantidad de *producción agregada* ofertada en la *economía*. (pág. 137)
allocative efficiency achieved when the goods and services produced are those most valued by society. (p. 641)	**eficiencia en la distribución** se alcanza cuando los bienes y servicios que se producen son los más valorados por la sociedad. (pág. 641)
ample reserves describes an economy in which banks hold high levels of excess reserves and therefore changes in the supply of reserves does not change the interest rate significantly. (p. 239, 400)	**reservas abundantes** describe una economía en la que los bancos mantienen niveles altos de reservas adicionales y, por tanto, los cambios en el suministro de reservas no cambian la tasa de interés considerablemente. (págs. 239, 400)

antitrust policy involves efforts by the government to prevent *oligopolistic* industries from becoming or behaving like *monopolies.* (p. 704)	**política antimonopolio** implica esfuerzos de parte del gobierno para impedir que algunas industrias *oligopolísticas* se conviertan en *monopolios* o se comporten como tales. (pág. 704)
appreciate when a currency becomes more valuable in terms of other currencies. (p. 337)	**revalorización** ocurre cuando una moneda aumenta de valor en relación con otras divisas. (pág. 337)
arbitrage taking advantage of a price difference between two markets. (p. 405)	**arbitraje** sacar ventaja de la diferencia de los precios entre dos mercados. (pág. 405)
artificially scarce good a good that is *excludable* but *nonrival in consumption.* (p. 780)	**bien en escasez artificial** bien que es *excluible* pero que *no tiene rival en su consumo.* (pág. 780)
asymmetric information when the parties involved in a transaction, such as buyers and sellers, hold different information; also called *private information* (pp. 759, 832)	**información asimétrica** cuando las partes involucradas en una transacción, como los compradores y vendedores, manejan información distinta; también llamada *información privada* (págs. 759, 832)
automatic stabilizers government spending and taxation rules that cause *fiscal policy* to be automatically *expansionary* when the *economy* contracts and automatically *contractionary* when the economy expands. (p. 180)	**estabilizadores automáticos** reglas gubernamentales sobre gastos e impuestos que hacen que la *política fiscal* automáticamente se torne *expansiva* cuando la *economía* se contrae y automáticamente se torne *contractiva* cuando la economía se expande. (pág. 180)
average cost see *average total cost* (p. 594)	**coste promedio** véase *coste total promedio* (pág. 594)
average cost pricing occurs when regulators set a monopoly's price equal to its average cost to prevent the firm from incurring a loss. (p. 791)	**fijación del precio con base en el coste promedio** ocurre cuando los reguladores fijan el precio de un monopolio de manera que sea equivalente a su coste promedio a fin de impedir que la empresa genere una pérdida. (pág. 791)
average fixed cost (*AFC*) the *fixed cost* per unit of output. (p. 595)	**coste fijo promedio** *coste fijo* por unidad de producción. (pág. 595)
average product the total product divided by the quantity of an input. (p. 600)	**producto promedio** producto total dividido entre la cantidad de un insumo. (pág. 600)
average product curve shows the relationship between the *average product* and the quantity of an input. (p. 600)	**curva de producto promedio** permite apreciar la relación entre el *producto promedio* y la cantidad de un insumo. (pág. 600)
average revenue the average amount of revenue received per unit of output; it equals the price if every unit sells for the same price and can be found as the total revenue divided by the quantity of output. (p. 622)	**ingreso promedio** la cantidad media de ingresos que se recibe por unidad de producción; es igual al precio si cada unidad se vende al mismo precio y se puede hallar como el ingreso total dividido entre la cantidad de producción. (p. 622)
average total cost (*ATC*) *total cost* divided by quantity of output produced; also known as *average cost.* (p. 594)	**coste total promedio** *coste total* dividido entre la cantidad de producción producida; también denominado *coste promedio* (pág. 594)
average variable cost (*AVC*) the *variable cost* per unit of output. (p. 595)	**coste variable promedio** *coste variable* por unidad de producción. (pág. 595)

B

balance of payments (BOP) accounts a summary of a country's transactions with other countries. (p. 330)	**cuentas de balanza de pagos (BDP)** resumen de las transacciones que un país efectúa con otros países. (pág. 330)
balance of payments on goods and services the difference between the value of a country's *exports* and the value of its *imports* during a given period. (p. 332)	**balanza de pagos de bienes y servicios** diferencia entre el valor de las *exportaciones* de un país y el valor de sus *importaciones* en un período de tiempo dado. (pág. 332)
balance of payments on the current account see *current account (CA).* (p. 332)	**balanza de pagos de la cuenta corriente** ver *cuenta corriente. (CC)* (pág. 332)
balanced budget multiplier the factor by which a change in both spending and taxes changes *real GDP.* (p. 175)	**multiplicador del presupuesto equilibrado** factor mediante el cual un cambio tanto en los gastos como en los impuestos modifica el *PIB real.* (pág. 175)
bank a *financial intermediary* that provides *liquid* assets in the form of *bank deposits* to lenders and uses those funds to finance borrowers' *investment spending* on *illiquid* assets. (p. 197)	**banco** *intermediario financiero* que ofrece a los prestamistas activos *líquidos* en forma de *depósitos bancarios* y hace uso de dichos fondos para financiar los *gastos de inversión* que hacen los prestatarios para adquirir activos *ilíquidos.* (pág. 197)
bank deposit a claim on a *bank* that obliges the bank to give the depositor their cash. (p. 197)	**depósito bancario** compromiso de un *banco* que lo obliga a entregar a los depositarios su dinero. (pág. 197)
bank reserves the currency that *banks* hold in their vaults plus their deposits at the central bank. (p. 218)	**reservas bancarias** moneda corriente que los *bancos* mantienen en sus arcas más los depósitos que mantienen en el banco central. (pág. 218)

bar graph a graph that uses bars of various heights or lengths to indicate values of a variable. (p. A-11)	**gráfico de barras** gráfico que hace uso de barras de diferentes alturas o longitudes para indicar valores de una variable. (pág. A-11)
barrier to entry protects a *monopolist* (and allows it to persist and earn *economic profits*) by preventing other firms from entering the industry. (p. 659)	**barrera al ingreso** protege a un *monopolista* (y le permite persistir y obtener *utilidades económicas*) al impedir que otras empresas incursionen en la industria. (pág. 659)
base year year arbitrarily chosen for comparison when calculating a *price index*; the price level compares the price of the *market basket* of goods in a given year to its price in the base year. (p. 89)	**año base** año de referencia elegido arbitrariamente cuando se computa un *índice de precios*; el nivel de precios compara el precio de la *canasta familiar* de bienes en un año dado con su precio en el año base. (pág. 89)
behavioral economics the study of economic decision making as influenced by the limits of the human mind. (p. 824)	**economía conductual** estudio de la toma de decisiones económicas y la influencia que en el proceso ejerce la mente humana. (pág. 824)
black market a market in which goods or services are bought and sold illegally—either because it is illegal to sell them at all or because the prices charged are legally prohibited by a *price ceiling*. (p. 556)	**mercado negro** mercado en el que los bienes y servicios se compran y se venden ilegalmente, ya sea porque es totalmente ilícito venderlos o porque los precios que se cobran son prohibidos legalmente por un *techo de precios* establecido. (pág. 556)
bond an interest-bearing asset that represents a loan to a company or government (p. 195)	**bono** activo que devenga interés que representa un préstamo a una compañía o gobierno (p. 195)
bounded rationality describes the limits on optimal decision making that result from imperfect intelligence and the scarcity of time and information. (p. 826)	**racionalidad limitada** describe los límites en la toma de decisiones óptimas que se dan por inteligencia imperfecta y por falta de tiempo e información. (pág. 826)
bounded self-interest self-interest that leaves room for concerns about the welfare of others. (p. 829)	**interés propio limitado** interés propio que deja espacio para inquietudes relacionadas con el bienestar de los demás. (pág. 829)
bounded willpower willpower constrained by limits on the determination needed to do difficult things. (p. 828)	**voluntad limitada** voluntad restringida por límites en la determinación que se precisa para lograr cosas difíciles. (pág. 828)
brand name a name owned by a particular firm that distinguishes its products from those of other firms. (p. 690)	**nombre de marca** marca de propiedad de una empresa particular que distingue sus productos de los de otras empresas. (pág. 690)
break-even price the market price at which a price-taking firm earns zero (normal) profit. (p. 625)	**precio de equilibrio** precio de mercado en el que la empresa aceptadora de precios obtiene cero ganancias (normales). (pág. 625)
budget constraint limits the cost of a consumer's consumption bundle to no more than the consumer's income. (p. 450)	**restricción presupuestaria** limita el coste de lo que el consumidor compra a no más que los ingresos del consumidor. (pág. 450)
budget deficit the difference between tax revenue and government spending when government spending on goods, services, and transfer payments exceeds tax revenue. (p. 250)	**déficit presupuestario** diferencia entre los ingresos fiscales y los gastos del gobierno cuando los gastos del gobierno en bienes, servicios y prestaciones sociales son mayores que los ingresos fiscales. (pág. 250)
budget line (*BL*) shows the consumption bundles available to a consumer who spends all of their income. (p. 450)	**rubro del presupuesto (*RP*)** permite apreciar los grupos de consumo al alcance del consumidor que gasta la totalidad de sus ingresos. (pág. 450)
budget surplus the difference between tax revenue and government spending when tax revenue exceeds government spending on goods, services, and transfer payments. (p. 250, 287)	**superávit presupuestario** diferencia entre los ingresos fiscales y los gastos del gobierno cuando los ingresos del gobierno son mayores que los gastos del gobierno en bienes, servicios y prestaciones sociales. (págs. 250, 287)
business cycle the alternation between economic downturns, known as *recessions*, and economic upturns, known as *expansions*. (p. 106)	**ciclo de negocios** alternación entre desaceleraciones económicas, llamadas *recesiones*, y auges económicos, conocidos como *expansiones*. (pág. 106)

C

capital manufactured goods used to make other goods and services; also called *physical capital*. (p. 4, 413)	**capital** bienes fabricados que se emplean para hacer otros bienes y servicios; también denominado *capital físico*. (págs. 4, 413)
capital account measure of a country's transfers of assets not included in the *financial account*. (p. 332)	**cuenta de capital** medida de transferencia de activos de un país que no están incluidos en la *cuenta financiera*. (pág. 332)
capital and financial account (CFA) includes both the *financial accounts* and *capital accounts* and measures the status of a country as a net debtor or creditor to the rest of the world. (p. 332)	**cuenta de capital y financiera (CCF)** incluye tanto las *cuentas financieras* como las *cuentas de capital* y mide el estatus de un país en cuanto deudor o acreedor neto ante el resto del mundo. (pág. 332)

cartel a group of firms that agree to increase prices and reduce output in order to raise their joint profits. (p. 693)	**cartel** grupo de compañías que acuerdan aumentar los precios y reducir la producción con el fin de aumentar sus utilidades conjuntas. (pág. 693)
causal relationship a relationship between two *variables* in which the value taken by one variable directly influences or determines the value taken by the other variable. (p. A-3)	**relación causal** relación entre dos *variables* en la que el valor tomado por una variable influye directamente o determina el valor tomado por la otra variable. (pág. A-3)
central bank a government institution that issues currency, oversees and regulates the banking system, controls the *monetary base*, and implements *monetary policy*. (p. 211)	**banco central** una institución gubernamental que emite dinero, vigila y regula el sistema bancario, controla la *base monetaria* e implementa *políticas monetarias*. (pág. 211)
***ceteris paribus* assumption** see *other things equal assumption* (p. 11, 423)	**supuesto *ceteris paribus*** véase *supuesto de que todos los demás factores seguirán iguales* (págs. 11, 423)
change in demand a shift of the *demand curve*, which changes the *quantity demanded* at any given price. (p. 30, 469)	**cambio en la demanda** desplazamiento de la *curva de demanda*, el cual modifica la *cantidad demandada* a un precio dado cualquiera. (págs. 30, 469)
change in supply a shift of the *supply curve*, which indicates a change in the *quantity supplied* at any given price. (p. 39, 478)	**cambio en la oferta** desplazamiento de la *curva de oferta*, que indica un cambio en la *cantidad ofertada* a cualquier precio dado. (págs. 39, 478)
Coase theorem states that payment between private parties can achieve an efficient solution to externality problems as long as *transaction costs* are sufficiently low. (p. 768)	**teorema de Coase** explica que el pago entre particulares puede llegar a una solución de eficiencia siempre y cuando los *costes de transacción* sean lo suficientemente bajos. (pág. 768)
collusion when firms cooperate to raise their joint profits. (p. 693)	**colusión** cuando las empresas colaboran con el fin de aumentar sus utilidades conjuntas. (pág. 693)
command economy an *economy* in which the *factors of production* are publicly owned and a central authority makes production and consumption decisions. (p. 420)	**economía planificada** *economía* en la que los *factores de producción* son propiedad pública y una autoridad central toma las decisiones de producción y consumo. (pág. 420)
commodity see *standardized product* (p. 634)	**insumo** véase *producto normalizado* (pág. 634)
commodity money a good used as a *medium of exchange* that has intrinsic value in other uses. (p. 206)	**dinero mercancía** bien que se usa como *medio de intercambio* y que tiene un valor intrínseco en otros usos. (pág. 206)
commodity-backed money a *medium of exchange* with no intrinsic value, but whose ultimate value is guaranteed by a promise that it can be converted into valuable goods. (p. 206)	**dinero respaldado por materia prima** *medio de intercambio* que no tiene ningún valor intrínseco, pero cuyo valor definitivo está garantizado por la promesa de que se puede convertir en bienes de valor. (pág. 206)
common resource *nonexcludable* and *rival in consumption*; you can't stop others from consuming the good, and when they consume it, less of the good is available for you. (p. 778)	**recurso común** *no excluible* y *rival en su consumo*; uno no puede impedir que otros consuman el bien y cuando lo consumen, uno tiene alcance a una menor cantidad del bien. (pág. 778)
comparative advantage the advantage held by an individual if their *opportunity cost* of producing a good or service is lowest among the people who could produce that good or service; contrasted with *absolute advantage*. (p. 21, 434)	**ventaja comparativa** ventaja que tiene una persona si el *coste de oportunidad* para producir un bien o servicio es el menor entre quienes pueden produciir dicho bien o servicio; se contrasta con *ventaja absoluta*. (págs. 21, 434)
compensating differentials wage differences across jobs that reflect the fact that some jobs are less pleasant or more dangerous than others. (p. 797)	**diferenciales compensatorios** diferenciales salariales entre empleos que reflejan el hecho de que algunos empleos son menos agradables o más peligrosos que otros. (pág. 797)
complements two goods (often consumed together) for which a rise in the price of one of the goods leads to a decrease in the demand for the other good. (p. 33, 471)	**complementos** dos bienes (que a menudo se consumen juntos) para los cuales un aumento del precio de uno de los bienes lleva a una disminución en la demanda del otro bien. (págs. 33, 471)
complements in production describes two goods for which increased production of either good creates more of the other. (p. 41, 481)	**complementos en producción** describe cuando el aumento de la producción de uno de dos bienes genera una mayor producción del otro. (págs. 41, 481)
concentration ratios measure of the percentage of industry sales accounted for by the "X" largest firms; for example, the four-firm concentration ratio or the eight-firm concentration ratio. (p. 654)	**tasas de concentración** miden el porcentaje de las ventas de una industria que se le atribuyen a la cantidad equis de las empresas más grandes; por ejemplo, la tasa de concentración de cuatro empresas o la tasa de concentración de ocho empresas. (pág. 654)
constant returns to scale when output increases directly in proportion to an increase in all inputs. (p. 608)	**rendimientos constantes de escala** cuando la producción aumenta en proporcionalidad directa con un aumento en todos los insumos. (pág. 608)
constant-cost industry industry in which the firms' cost curves are unaffected by changes in the size of the industry and the long-run industry supply curve is horizontal. (p. 638)	**industria de costes constantes** en la que las curvas de costes de las empresas no se ven afectadas por los cambios de tamaño de la industria y la curva de suministros a largo plazo es horizontal. (pág. 638)

consumer price index (CPI) measures the cost of the *market basket* of a typical urban American family. (p. 90)	**índice de precios de consumo (IPC)** mide el coste de la *canasta familiar* de una familia estadounidense urbana típica. (pág. 90)
consumer spending *household* spending on goods and services. (p. 65)	**gastos de consumo** gastos del *hogar* en bienes y servicios. (pág. 65)
consumer surplus the difference between the amount paid for a good and the consumer's (or consumers') willingness to pay for the units purchased; can be used to refer to both *individual consumer surplus* and *total consumer surplus.* (p. 513)	**superávit del consumidor** la diferencia entre la cantidad pagada por un bien y la disposición del consumidor (o consumidores) de pagar por las unidades compradas; se refiere tanto al *superávit del consumidor individual* como al *superávit total del consumidor.* (pág. 513)
contractionary fiscal policy *fiscal policy* that reduces *aggregate demand* to close an inflationary gap; involves the government decreasing spending or transfer payments, or increasing taxes. (p. 170)	**política fiscal contractiva** *política fiscal* que reduce la *demanda agregada* para cerrar una brecha inflacionaria; supone que el gobierno disminuya el gasto o transfiera pagos, o aumente los impuestos. (pág. 170)
contractionary monetary policy *monetary policy* that reduces *aggregate demand.* (p. 238)	**política monetaria contractiva** *política monetaria* que reduce la *demanda agregada.* (pág. 238)
copyright gives the copyright holder for a literary or artistic work the sole right to profit from that work for a specified period of time. (p. 660)	**derechos de autor** dan al creador de una obra literaria o artística el derecho exclusivo a obtener utilidades de su obra durante un período de tiempo específico. (pág. 660)
cost the lowest price at which a seller is willing to sell a good. (p. 516)	**coste** el precio más bajo al cual un vendedor está dispuesto a vender un bien. (pág. 516)
cost-benefit analysis the process of comparing the costs and the benefits of an option. (p. 441)	**análisis de costos y beneficios** proceso de comparar los costos y los beneficios de una opción. (pág. 441)
cost-minimization rule employ factors so that the *marginal product* per dollar spent on each factor is the same; this rule is used by a firm to determine the cost-minimizing combination of inputs. (p. 739)	**regla de minimizar costes** emplear factores de manera que el *producto marginal* por dólar dedicado a cada factor sea equivalente; la empresa determina la combinación de insumos destinados a minimizar costes según esta regla. (pág. 739)
cost-push inflation *inflation* caused by a significant increase in the price of an *input* with economy-wide importance. (p. 158)	**inflación impulsada por costes** *inflación* causada por un aumento significativo en el precio de un *insumo* con importancia en toda la economía. (pág. 158)
counterparty the other party participating in a financial transaction. (p. 403)	**contraparte** la otra parte que participa en una transacción financiera (pág. 403)
cross-price elasticity of demand (between two goods) measures the effect of the change in one good's price on the quantity demanded of another good; is equal to the percentage change in the quantity demanded of one good divided by the percentage change in the other good's price. (p. 506)	**elasticidad de la demanda por cruce de precios** (entre dos productos) mide el efecto que el cambio en el precio de un bien tiene en la cantidad demandada de otro bien; es igual al cambio porcentual en la cantidad demandada de un bien dividida entre el cambio porcentual en el precio del otro bien. (pág. 506)
crowding out occurs when a government deficit drives up the *interest rate* and leads to reduced *investment spending.* (p. 255, 297)	**efecto expulsión** ocurre cuando el déficit gubernamental empuja la *tasa de interés* en sentido ascendente y lleva a la disminución en los *gastos de inversión.* (págs. 255, 297)
current account (CA) a country's balance of payments on goods and services plus net international transfer payments and factor income; also known as the *balance of payments on the current account* (p. 332)	**cuenta corriente (CC)** balanza de pagos de un país sobre los bienes y servicios más los pagos de transferencia neta internacional y el ingreso factorizado; también conocida como *balanza de pagos de la cuenta corriente.* (pág. 332)
curve any line on a graph, regardless of whether it is a straight line or a curved line. (p. A-3)	**curva** cualquier línea en un gráfico, sea una línea recta o una línea curva. (pág. A-3)
cyclical unemployment the deviation of the actual rate of *unemployment* from the *natural rate.* (p. 81)	**desempleo cíclico** desviación de la tasa de *desempleo* real a partir de su *tasa natural.* (pág. 81)

D

deadweight loss the net loss to society resulting from an inefficient quantity of output; when quantity is inefficiently low, that loss is the total surplus forgone on the transactions that would provide a net gain to society but did not occur. (p. 546)	**pérdida irrecuperable de eficiencia** pérdida neta de la sociedad que resulta de una cantidad poco eficiente de producción; cuando la cantidad es ineficientemente baja, dicha pérdida es el superávit total previsto en las transacciones que habrían ofrecido una ganancia neta a la sociedad. (pág. 546)
debt–GDP ratio the government's debt as a percentage of *GDP.* (p. 292)	**proporción de deuda a PIB** deuda gubernamental como porcentaje del *PIB.* (pág. 292)

decreasing returns to scale when output increases less than in proportion to an increase in all inputs. (p. 608)	**rendimientos decrecientes de escala** cuando la producción aumenta menos que en proporcionalidad con un aumento en todos los insumos. (pág. 608)
decreasing-cost industry industry in which the firms' production costs decrease as the industry grows and the long-run supply curve is downward-sloping. (p. 640)	**industria de costes decrecientes** industria en que los costes de producción de las empresas disminuyen a medida que crece la industria y la curva de suministros se inclina hacia abajo a largo plazo. (pág. 640)
deductible a sum specified in an insurance policy that the insured individuals must pay before being compensated for a claim; reduces *moral hazard*. (p. 835)	**deducible** suma que se detalla en una póliza de seguros que los asegurados han de pagar antes de que se les pague una reclamación; reduce el *riesgo moral*. (pág. 835)
deflation a falling overall price level. (p. 86)	**deflación** caída generalizada del nivel de precios. (pág. 86)
demand curve a graphical representation of the *demand schedule*; shows the relationship between *quantity demanded* and price. (p. 28, 468)	**curva de demanda** representación gráfica de la *tabla de demanda*; permite apreciar la relación entre la *cantidad demandada* y el precio. (págs. 28, 468)
demand price (of a given quantity) the price at which consumers will demand that quantity. (p. 561)	**precio de demanda** precio de una cantidad, llegado al cual los consumidores exigen dicha cantidad. (pág. 561)
demand schedule a table that shows how much of a good or service consumers will be willing and able to buy at different prices. (p. 28, 467)	**tabla de demanda** permite apreciar qué cantidad de un bien o servicio los consumidores están dispuestos a comprar y tienen la capacidad de comprar a diferentes precios. (págs. 28, 467)
demand shock an event that shifts the *aggregate demand curve*. (p. 156)	**crisis de demanda** evento que desplaza la *curva de demanda agregada*. (pág. 156)
demand-pull inflation *inflation* caused by an increase in *aggregate demand*. (p. 158)	**inflación arrastrada por la demanda** *inflación* causada por un aumento en la *demanda agregada*. (pág. 158)
dependent variable in a *causal relationship*, the variable that is determined by the *independent variable*. (p. A-3)	**variable dependiente** en una *relación causal*, la variable que es determinada por la *variable independiente*. (pág. A-3)
depreciate when a currency becomes less valuable in terms of other currencies. (p. 337)	**desvalorización** cuando una moneda se vuelve menos valiosa en términos de otras monedas. (pág. 337)
depreciation occurs when the value of a physical asset is reduced by wear, age, or obsolescence. (p. 310)	**depreciación** ocurre cuando el valor de un activo físico se ve reducido por desgaste, edad u obsolescencia. (pág. 310)
depression a very deep and prolonged economic downturn. (p. 107)	**depresión** desaceleración económica muy profunda y prolongada. (pág. 107)
derived demand demand for a factor that results from (that is, it is *derived* from) the demand for the output being produced. (p. 717)	**demanda derivada** la demanda por un factor que resulta de la demanda por la producción que se está produciendo. (pág. 717)
devaluation reduction in the value of a currency that is set under a *fixed exchange rate regime*. (p. 350)	**devaluación** reducción en el valor de una moneda que está fijada bajo un *régimen de cambio de divisas fijo*. (pág. 350)
diminishing marginal rate of substitution principle that states the more of one good a person consumes in proportion to a second good, the less of the second good that person is willing to substitute for another unit of the first good. (p. 845)	**tasa marginal de sustitución decreciente** principio que explica que cuanto más consuma una persona de un bien en proporción a otro bien, menos dispuesta estará dicha persona a reemplazar el segundo bien por otra unidad del primer bien. (pág. 845)
diminishing returns to an input when an increase in the quantity of that input, holding the levels of all other inputs fixed, leads to a decline in the marginal product of that input. (p. 586)	**rendimientos decrecientes de un insumo** cuando un incremento en la cantidad de un insumo (manteniendo fijo el nivel de todos los demás insumos) genera una disminución del producto marginal de dicho insumo. (pág. 586)
diminishing returns to physical capital exhibited by an *aggregate production function* when, holding the amount quantity and quality of labor and the state of *technology* fixed, each successive increase in the amount of *physical capital* leads to a smaller increase in *productivity*. (p. 306)	**rendimientos decrecientes del capital físico** en una *función de producción agregada* cuando, manteniendo la cantidad y la calidad de la fuerza laboral y el estado de la *tecnología*, cada aumento sucesivo en la cantidad de *capital físico* conduce a un aumento más pequeño en la *productividad*. (pág. 306)
discount rate the *interest rate* the *central bank* charges on *loans* to *banks*. (p. 240)	**tasa de descuento** *tasa de interés* que fija el *banco central* en *préstamos* que hace a *bancos*. (pág. 240)
discouraged workers nonworking people who are capable of working but have given up looking for a job due to the state of the job market. (p. 78)	**trabajadores desalentados** personas que no están empleadas y que tienen la capacidad de trabajar pero que han dejado de buscar empleo debido al estado del mercado laboral. (pág. 78)
discretionary fiscal policy *fiscal policy* that is the result of deliberate actions by policy makers rather than rules. (p. 180)	**política fiscal discrecional** *política fiscal* que es el resultado de acciones deliberadas de las autoridades en lugar de ser producto de las reglas. (pág. 180)

diseconomies of scale when *long-run average total cost* increases as output increases. (p. 607)	**deseconomías de escala** cuando el *coste total promedio a largo plazo* aumenta a medida que aumenta la producción. (pág. 607)
disequilibrium when the market price is above or below the price that equates the quantity demanded with the quantity supplied (p. 48, 524)	**desequilibrio** cuando el precio de mercado está por encima o por debajo del precio que equipara la cantidad en demanda con la cantidad en oferta (págs. 48, 524)
disinflation the process of bringing the *inflation rate* down. (p. 98)	**desinflación** proceso de bajar la *tasa de inflación*. (pág. 98)
disposable income income plus *government transfers* minus taxes; the total amount of *household* income available to spend on consumption. (p. 66)	**ingreso disponible** ingresos más *transferencias gubernamentales* menos los impuestos; cantidad total de ingresos que se puede utilizar en el *hogar* para el consumo. (pág. 66)
dominant strategy a player's best action regardless of the action taken by the other player. (p. 697)	**estrategia dominante** la mejor acción de un jugador independientemente de cualquier acción que tome el otro jugador. (pág. 697)
duopolist each of the two firms in a *duopoly*. (p. 692)	**duopolista** cada una de las dos empresas en un *duopolio*. (pág. 692)
duopoly an *oligopoly* consisting of only two firms. (p. 692)	**duopolio** *oligopolio* que consta de solamente dos empresas. (pág. 692)

E

economic growth an increase in the maximum amount of goods and services an *economy* can produce. (p. 15, 110, 428)	**crecimiento económico** aumento en la cantidad máxima de bienes y servicios que puede producir una *economía*. (págs. 15, 110, 428)
economic profit a business's *total revenue* minus the *opportunity cost* of its resources; usually less than the *accounting profit*. (p. 612)	**utilidad económica** *ingresos totales* de un negocio menos el *coste de oportunidad* de sus recursos; generalmente es menos que las *utilidades contables*. (pág. 612)
economic rent the payment to a factor of production in excess of the minimum payment necessary to employ that factor. (p. 727)	**renta económica** pago de un factor de producción en exceso del pago mínimo necesario para emplear dicho factor. (pág. 727)
economics the study of scarcity and choice. (p. 4, 412)	**economía** estudio de la escasez y de las opciones disponibles. (págs. 4, 412)
economies of scale when *long-run average total cost* declines as output increases. (p. 607)	**economías de escala** cuando el *coste total promedio a largo plazo* disminuye a medida que aumenta la producción. (pág. 607)
economy a system for coordinating a society's productive and consumptive activities. (p. 419)	**economía (sistema)** sistema para la coordinación de las actividades de producción y de consumo de una sociedad. (pág. 419)
efficiency wages wages that exceed the market equilibrium wage rate; employers use efficiency wages to motivate hard work and reduce worker turnover. (p. 799)	**salarios de eficiencia** salarios fijados por encima de la tasa de equilibrio salarial; los empleadores los utilizan como incentivo para lograr un mejor desempeño de los empleados. (pág. 799)
efficient describes a market or *economy* in which there is no way to make anyone better off without making at least one person worse off. (p. 12, 425)	**eficiente** describe un mercado o una *economía* en los que no es posible mejorar la condición de una persona sin empeorar la condición de otra. (págs. 12, 425)
elastic demand when the *price elasticity of demand* is greater than 1. (p. 492)	**demanda elástica** cuando la *elasticidad del precio de la demanda* es mayor que 1. (pág. 492)
employed people who are currently holding a job in the *economy*, either full time or part time. (p. 77)	**empleado** persona que a la fecha tiene empleo en la *economía*, ya sea con dedicación total o dedicación parcial. (pág. 77)
entrepreneurship the efforts of entrepreneurs in organizing *resources* for production, taking risks to create new enterprises, and innovating to develop new products and production processes. (p. 4, 413)	**espíritu emprendedor** los esfuerzos de los empresarios emprendedores para organizar *recursos* de producción y tomar riesgos a fin de crear empresas nuevas e innovar con miras a desarrollar nuevos productos o procesos de producción. (págs. 4, 413)
environmental standards rules that protect the environment by specifying limits for or actions by producers and consumers. (p. 786)	**normas ambientales** reglas que protegen el medio ambiente al fijar límites en lo que hacen tanto productores como consumidores. (pág. 786)
equilibrium an economic situation in which no individual would be better off doing something different; a *competitive market* is in equilibrium when the supply and demand curves intersect. (p. 46, 520)	**equilibrio** coyuntura económica en la que ninguna persona estaría en mejor condición si hiciera algo diferente; un *mercado competitivo* está en equilibrio cuando se intersecan las curvas de oferta y demanda. (págs. 46, 520)
equilibrium exchange rate the *exchange rate* at which the quantity of a currency demanded in the *foreign exchange market* is equal to the quantity supplied. (p. 344)	**tasa de cambio en equilibrio** *tasa de cambio* en la que la cantidad demandada de una divisa en el *mercado de divisas* es equivalente a la cantidad ofertada. (pág. 344)
equilibrium marginal revenue product the additional revenue generated by the last unit of a factor employed in the factor market as a whole. (p. 727)	**producto de ingreso marginal en equilibrio** ingresos adicionales generados por la última unidad de un factor empleado en el mercado de factores en su conjunto. (pág. 727)

equilibrium price in a competitive market, the price of a good at which the *quantity demanded* of that good equals the *quantity supplied* of that good; also known as the *market-clearing price.* (p. 46, 520)	**precio de equilibrio** en un mercado competitivo, precio de un bien al que la *cantidad demandada* de dicho bien es equivalente a la *cantidad ofertada* del mismo bien; también denominado *precio de compensación.* (págs. 46, 520)
equilibrium quantity the quantity of a good bought and sold at its *equilibrium price.* (p. 46, 520)	**cantidad de equilibrio** cantidad de un bien comprado y vendido a su *precio de equilibrio.* (págs. 46, 520)
excess capacity when firms in a *monopolistically competitive* industry produce less than the output at which *average total cost* is minimized. (p. 686)	**capacidad en exceso** cuando las empresas de una industria *competitiva monopolista* producen menos que la producción en la que el *coste promedio total* se minimiza. (pág. 686)
excess reserves a *bank's* reserves over and above its *required reserves.* (p. 224)	**reservas en exceso** las reservas de un *banco* en exceso de las reservas obligatorias. (pág. 224)
exchange rate effect (of a change in the *aggregate price level*) the change in *net exports* caused by a change in the value of the domestic currency, which leads to a change in the relative price of domestic and foreign goods and services (p. 126)	**efecto del tipo de cambio** (de un cambio en el *nivel de precios agregados*) cambio en las exportaciones netas causado por un cambio en el valor de la moneda nacional, el qual conduce a un cambio en el precio relativo de los bienes y servicios nacionales y extranjeros. (pág. 126)
exchange rates the prices at which currencies trade. (p. 336)	**tasas de cambio** precios a los cuales se intercambian divisas. (pág. 336)
excise tax a tax on sales of a particular good or service. (p. 540)	**impuesto de consumo** gravamen por la venta de un bien o servicio en particular. (pág. 540)
excludable a good is excludable if the supplier of that good can prevent people who do not pay from consuming it. (p. 772)	**excluible** un bien es excluible si el proveedor de dicho bien puede impedir que las personas que no pagan por el mismo lo puedan aprovechar. (pág. 772)
expansion a period of economic upturn in which output and employment are rising; also referred to as *recovery.* (p. 107)	**expansión** período de auge económico en el que la producción y el empleo están creciendo; también denominado *recuperación.* (pág. 107)
expansionary fiscal policy *fiscal policy* that increases *aggregate demand* to close a recessionary gap; involves the government increasing spending or transfer payments, or decreasing taxes. (p. 170)	**política fiscal expansiva** *política fiscal* mediante la cual se aumenta la *demanda agregada* para cerrar una brecha recesiva; implica que el gobierno aumente el gasto o transfiera pagos, o una disminución de los impuestos. (pág. 170)
expansionary monetary policy *monetary policy* that increases *aggregate demand.* (p. 238)	**política monetaria expansiva** *política monetaria* mediante la cual se aumenta la *demanda agregada.* (pág. 238)
expenditure approach an approach to calculating *GDP* by adding up *aggregate spending* on domestically produced *final goods and services* in the *economy* – the sum of *consumer spending, investment spending, government purchases of goods and services,* and *exports* minus *imports.* (p. 68)	**enfoque de gastos** enfoque para computar el *PIB* sumando los *gastos agregados* en *bienes y servicios finales* producidos internamente en la *economía.* Se trata de la suma de los *gastos de consumo*, los *gastos de inversión*, las compras de bienes y servicios por el gobierno, y las *exportaciones* menos las *importaciones.* (pág. 68)
expenditure multiplier equal to 1/(1 – *MPC*) or 1/*MPS*; the ratio of the total change in *real GDP* caused by an *autonomous change in aggregate spending* to the size of that autonomous change; indicates the total rise in *real GDP* that results from each $1 of an initial rise in spending. (p. 133)	**multiplicador de gastos** igual a 1/(1 – PMC) o 1/PMA; relación entre el cambio total en el *PIB real* ocasionado por *cambios autónomos en los gastos agregados* y las dimensiones de ese cambio autónomo; indica el aumento total en el *PIB real* que resulta de cada $1 de un aumento inicial en los gastos. (pág. 133)
explicit cost a cost that involves actually paying out money. (p. 611)	**coste explícito** coste que implica un desembolso de dinero. (pág. 611)
exports goods and services sold to other countries. (p. 67)	**exportaciones** bienes y servicios que se venden a otros países. (pág. 67)
external benefit a benefit that an individual or a firm confers on others without receiving compensation. (p. 762)	**beneficio externo** beneficio que una persona o empresa confiere a otros sin recibir ningún pago. (pág. 762)
external cost an uncompensated cost that an individual or a firm imposes on others. (p. 762)	**coste externo** coste no remunerado que una persona o empresa impone a otros. (pág. 762)
externalities *external costs* and *external benefits.* (p. 762)	**externalidades** *costes externo* y *beneficios externos.* (pág. 762)

F

factor of production see *resources.* (p. 4)	**factor de producción** ver *recursos.* (pág. 4)
factor markets where *resources*, especially *capital* and *labor*, are bought and sold. (p. 65)	**mercados de factores** mercados en los que los *recursos*, sobre todo el *capital* y la *mano de obra*, se compran y se venden. (pág. 65)

federal funds rate (in the United States) the *interest rate* that *banks* charge other banks for overnight *loans*, as determined in the *federal funds market*. (p. 239)	**tasa federal de fondos** (en los Estados Unidos) *tasa de interés* que los *bancos* cobran a otros bancos por concepto de *préstamos* pagaderos al día siguiente, tal como se determina en el *mercado federal de fondos*. (pág. 239)
fiat money a *medium of exchange* whose value derives entirely from its official status as a means of payment. (p. 207)	**dinero fiduciario** *medio de intercambio* cuyo valor se deriva totalmente de su estatus oficial como medio de pago. (pág. 207)
final goods and services goods and services sold to the final, or end, user. (p. 68)	**bienes y servicios finales** bienes y servicios vendidos al usuario final o definitivo. (pág. 68)
financial account the difference between a country's sales of assets to foreigners and its purchases of assets from foreigners during a given period. (p. 332)	**cuenta financiera** diferencia entre las ventas a extranjeros de los activos de un país y las compras efectuadas a extranjeros durante un período de tiempo dado. (pág. 332)
financial asset a nonphysical asset that entitles the buyer to future income from the seller. (p. 193)	**activo financiero** activo no físico que le da derecho al comprador a ingresos futuros provenientes de un vendedor. (pág. 193)
financial markets the markets that channel *private savings* into *investment spending* and *government borrowing*. (p. 66)	**mercados financieros** mercados que canalizan *ahorros privados* en *gastos de inversión y empréstitos gubernamentales*. (pág. 66)
financial risk uncertainty about future outcomes that involve financial losses and gains. (p. 194)	**riesgo financiero** incertidumbre acerca de los resultados futuros que implican pérdidas y ganancias financieras. (pág. 194)
firm any organization that produces goods and services for sale. (p. 6, 414)	**empresa** cualquier entidad que produce bienes y servicios para la venta. (págs. 6, 414)
fiscal policy the use of government purchases of goods and services, government transfers, or tax policy to stabilize the *economy*. (p. 168)	**política fiscal** uso de la compra de bienes y servicios por parte del gobierno, transferencias gubernamentales o políticas impositivas para estabilizar la *economía*. (pág. 168)
fixed cost (*FC*) a cost that does not depend on the quantity of output produced; the cost of the *fixed input*. (p. 590)	**coste fijo** coste que no depende de la cantidad de producción producida; coste del *insumo fijo*. (pág. 590)
fixed input an input whose quantity is fixed for a period of time and cannot be varied. (p. 584)	**insumo fijo** insumo cuya cantidad se fija por un período de tiempo y no se puede variar. (pág. 584)
foreign exchange market the market in which currencies are traded. (p. 336)	**mercado de divisas** mercado en el cual se compran y venden divisas extranjeras. (pág. 336)
fractional reserve banking system system in which only a fraction of bank deposits are backed by cash on hand and available for withdrawal (p. 218)	**sistema de banca de reserva fraccionaria** sistema en el que una fracción de los depósitos bancarios están respaldados por dinero en efectivo y disponible para ser retirado. (pág. 218)
framing the creation of context for a product or idea. (p. 828)	**marco conceptual** creación de un contexto para un producto o una idea. (pág. 828)
free entry and exit when new firms can easily enter into an industry and existing firms can easily leave that industry. (p. 634)	**entrada y salida libres** cuando las empresas nuevas pueden ingresar fácilmente en la industria y las empresas existentes pueden salirse fácilmente de ella. (pág. 634)
free-rider problem goods that are *nonexcludable* suffer from the free-rider problem: Individuals have no incentive to pay for their own consumption and instead will take a "free ride" on anyone who does pay. (p. 773)	**problema del polizón** los bienes que *no son excluibles* sufren del problema del polizón: Las personas no tienen ningún incentivo para pagar por lo que consumen y en lugar aprovechan para ser "polizones" de cualquiera que sí pague. (pág. 773)
frictional unemployment *unemployment* due to the time workers spend in job search. (p. 80)	**desempleo de fricción** *desempleo* atribuible al tiempo que los trabajadores dedican a la búsqueda de empleo. (pág. 80)
full-employment level of output the level of *real GDP* the economy can produce if all resources are fully employed. (p. 110, 146)	**nivel de producción de pleno empleo** el nivel del *PIB real* que la economía puede producir si se emplean todos los recursos disponibles. (págs. 110, 146)

G

game theory the study of behavior in situations of *interdependence*. (p. 695)	**teoría de juego** estudio de la conducta en situaciones de *interdependencia*. (pág. 695)
GDP see *gross domestic product*. (p. 67)	**PIB** véase *producto interno bruto*. (pág. 67)
GDP deflator (for a given year) 100 times the ratio of *nominal GDP* to *real GDP* in that year. (p. 103)	**deflactor del PIB** (para un año dado) 100 veces el cociente entre el *PIB nominal* y el *PIB real* en dicho año. (pág. 103)
GDP per capita *GDP* divided by the size of the population; equivalent to the average *GDP* per person. (p. 103)	**PIB per cápita** *PIB* divido entre el número de habitantes; es equivalente al *PIB* promedio por persona. (pág. 103)

Gini coefficient a number that summarizes a country's level of income inequality based on how unequally income is distributed. (p. 803)	**coeficiente Gini** cifra que resume el nivel de desigualdad en los ingresos de un país con base en la inequidad con la que se distribuyen los ingresos. (pág. 803)
government borrowing the amount of funds borrowed by the government in the *financial markets.* (p. 67)	**empréstito gubernamental** cantidad de fondos que el gobierno toma en préstamo en los *mercados financieros.* (pág. 67)
government debt the accumulation of past *budget deficits,* minus past *budget surpluses.* (p. 290)	**deuda gubernamental** acumulación de *déficits presupuestarios* del pasado menos los *superávits presupuestarios* del pasado. (pág. 290)
government spending total expenditures on goods and services by federal, state, and local governments (p. 65)	**gasto público** total de gastos por concepto de bienes y servicios de los gobiernos federal, estatales y locales. (pág. 65)
government transfers payments that the government makes to individuals without expecting a good or service in return. (p. 66)	**transferencias gubernamentales** pagos efectuados por el gobierno a personas sin esperar a cambio un bien o un servicio. (pág. 66)
gross domestic product (GDP) the total value of all *final goods and services* produced in the *economy* during a given year. (p. 67)	**producto interno bruto (PIB)** valor total de todos los *bienes y servicios finales* producidos en la *economía* durante un año dado. (pág. 67)

H

Homo economicus ("economic man") a fictional economic actor who makes self-interested, informed, rational judgments in pursuit of wealth and leisure. (p. 824)	***Homo economicus*** ("hombre económico") actor económico ficticio que toma decisiones informadas, racionales y de interés propio en su búsqueda de riqueza y ocio. (pág. 824)
horizontal axis see *x-axis* (p. A-2)	**eje horizontal** véase *eje x* (pág. A-2)
horizontal intercept indicates the value of the *x*-variable when the value of the *y*-variable is zero. (p. A-4)	**intersección horizontal** indica el valor de la variable *x* cuando el valor de la variable *y* es cero. (pág. A-4)
household a person or group of people who share their income. (p. 6, 414)	**hogar** persona o grupo de personas que comparten sus ingresos. (págs. 6, 414)
human capital the improvement in labor created by the education and knowledge that is embodied in the workforce. (p. 305, 716)	**capital humano** mejora en la mano de obra creada por la educación y los conocimientos de los integrantes de la fuerza laboral. (págs. 305, 716)

I

illiquid describes an asset if it cannot be quickly converted into cash without much loss of value. (p. 194)	**ilíquido** describe un activo si éste no se puede convertir rápidamente en dinero en efectivo sin perder mucho de su valor. (pág. 194)
imperfectly competitive describes a market that does not meet the requirements for perfect competition. (p. 652)	**competencia imperfecta** describe un mercado en el que no llena los requisitos de una competencia perfecta. (pág. 652)
implicit cost a cost that does not require an outlay of money; it is measured by the value, in dollar terms, of benefits that are foregone. (p. 611)	**coste implícito** coste que no precisa un desembolso de dinero; se mide según el valor, en términos de dólares, de los beneficios que son inevitables. (pág. 611)
implicit cost of capital the *opportunity cost* of the capital used by a business—the income the owner could have realized from that capital if it had been used in its next best alternative way. (p. 613)	**coste implícito del capital** *coste de oportunidad* del capital empleado por un negocio; ingresos que el propietario hubiera realizado de dicho capital si éste se hubiese utilizado en la siguiente mejor manera alternativa. (pág. 613)
import quota a limit on the quantity of a good that can be imported within a given period. (p. 352, 570)	**cuota de importaciones** límite de la cantidad de un bien que se puede importar dentro de un período de tiempo dado. (págs. 352, 570)
imports goods and services purchased from other countries. (p. 67)	**importaciones** bienes y servicios que se compran a otros países. (pág. 67)
incentive reward or punishment that motivates particular choices; in *supply-side policy,* incentives are motivation for household and business to work, save, and invest. (p. 321, 421)	**incentivo** premio o castigo que motiva a seleccionar una opción u otra; en las políticas fiscales del lado de la oferta, los incentivos son la motivación por la que los hogares y negocios trabajan, ahorran e invierten. (págs. 321, 421)
income approach an approach to calculating *GDP* by adding up the total factor income earned by households from firms in the economy, including rent, wages, interest, and profit. (p. 68)	**enfoque en ingresos** manera de computar el *PIB* mediante la suma total de los ingresos de factores ganados por los hogares de empresas en la economía, incluidos el arriendo, los salarios, los intereses y las utilidades. (pág. 68)

income effect (of a change in the price of a good) the change in the quantity of a good demanded that results from a change in the consumer's purchasing power when the price of the good changes. (p. 487)	**efecto de los ingresos** (de un cambio en el precio de un bien) el cambio en la cantidad de un bien que se demanda a raíz de un cambio en el poder adquisitivo del consumidor cuando cambia el precio del bien. (pág. 487)
income elasticity of demand the percentage change in the quantity of a good demanded when a consumer's income changes divided by the percentage change in the consumer's income; it measures how changes in income affect the demand for a good. (p. 507)	**elasticidad de la demanda según los ingresos** cambio porcentual en la cantidad de un bien demandado cuando los ingresos de un consumidor cambian dividido entre el cambio porcentual en los ingresos del consumidor; mide cómo los cambios en el ingreso afectan la demanda de un bien. (pág. 507)
income-elastic demand when the *income elasticity of demand* for a good is greater than 1. (p. 507)	**demanda elástica según los ingresos** cuando la *elasticidad de la demanda según los ingresos* por un bien es mayor que 1. (pág. 507)
income-inelastic demand when the *income elasticity of demand* for a good is positive but less than 1. (p. 507)	**demanda inelástica según los ingresos** cuando la *elasticidad de la demanda según los ingresos* por un bien es positiva pero menor que 1. (pág. 507)
increasing returns to scale when output increases more than in proportion to an increase in all inputs; for example, doubling all inputs would cause output to more than double. (p. 607)	**rendimientos crecientes de escala** cuando la producción aumenta más en proporción a un aumento en todos los insumos; por ejemplo, si se duplicaran todos los insumos, la producción aumentaría a más del doble. (pág. 607)
increasing-cost industry industry in which the firms' production costs increase with the size of the industry and the long-run industry supply curve is upward-sloping. (p. 638)	**industria de costes crecientes** industria en la que los costos de producción de las empresas aumentan a la par que el tamaño de la industria y la curva de oferta de la industria se inclina hacia arriba a largo plazo. (pág. 638)
independent variable in a *causal relationship*, the variable that determines the *dependent variable*. (p. A-3)	**variable independiente** en una *relación causal*, la variable que determina la *variable dependiente*. (pág. A-3)
indifference curve shows all the consumption bundles that yield the same amount of total *utility* for an individual. (p. 839)	**curva de indiferencia** permite apreciar todos los conjuntos de consumo que producen el mismo nivel total de *utilidad* para una persona. (pág. 839)
indifference curve map a collection of *indifference curves*, each of which corresponds to a different total *utility* level; represents an individual's entire *utility function*. (p. 840)	**mapa de la curva de indiferencia** colección de *curvas de indiferencia*, cada una de las cuales corresponde a un nivel total de utilidad diferente; representa la totalidad de la función de *utilidad* de una persona. (pág. 840)
individual choice decisions by individuals about what to do, which necessitate decisions about what not to do. (p. 412)	**opción individual** decisiones que toman las personas sobre qué hacer, las cuales necesariamente implican decisiones sobre qué no hacer. (pág. 412)
individual demand curve illustrates the relationship between *quantity demanded* and price for an individual consumer. (p. 474)	**curva de demanda individual** ilustra la relación entre la *cantidad demandada* y el precio para un consumidor individual. (pág. 474)
individual labor supply curve shows how the quantity of labor supplied by an individual depends on that individual's wage rate. (p. 723)	**curva de oferta de mano de obra individual** permite apreciar cómo la cantidad de mano de obra que proporciona una persona depende de la tasa salarial de dicha persona. (pág. 723)
individual supply curve illustrates the relationship between *quantity supplied* and price for an individual producer. (p. 482)	**curva de oferta individual** ilustra la relación entre la *cantidad ofertada* y el precio para un productor individual. (pág. 482)
industry supply curve shows the relationship between the price of a good and the total output of the industry as a whole; also known as *market supply curve*. (p. 634)	**curva de oferta de la industria** permite apreciar la relación entre el precio de un bien y la producción total de toda la industria; también denominado *curva de oferta del mercado*. (pág. 634)
inelastic demand when the *price elasticity of demand* is less than 1. (p. 492)	**demanda inelástica** cuando la *elasticidad del precio de demanda* es menor que 1. (pág. 492)
inferior good describes a good for which a rise in income decreases the demand for the good (p. 34, 473)	**bien inferior** describe cuando un aumento en los ingresos disminuye la demanda de un bien. (págs. 34, 473)
inflation a rising overall price level. (p. 86)	**inflación** aumento generalizado del nivel de precios. (pág. 86)
inflation rate the percentage increase in the overall level of prices per year. (p. 88)	**tasa de inflación** aumento porcentual en el nivel generalizado de precios por año. (pág. 88)
inflation targeting when the *central bank* sets an explicit target for the *inflation rate* and sets *monetary policy* in order to hit that target. (p. 237)	**inflación objetivo** ocurre cuando el *banco central* fija un objetivo explícito para la *tasa de inflación* y define la *política monetaria* de manera que se llegue a dicho objetivo. (pág. 237)
inflationary gap when *aggregate output* is above *potential output*. (p. 153)	**brecha inflacionaria** ocurre cuando la *producción agregada* está por encima del *potencial de producción*. (pág. 153)
infrastructure roads, power lines, ports, information networks, and other underpinnings for economic activity. (p. 316)	**infraestructura** vías públicas, tendidos eléctricos, puertos, redes de información y otros apuntalamientos de la actividad económica. (pág. 316)

in-kind benefit a benefit given in the form of goods or services. (p. 805)	**beneficio en especie** beneficio que se da en forma de bienes o servicios. (pág. 805)
input a good or service that is used to produce another good or service. (p. 41, 480)	**insumo** bien o servicio que se utiliza para producir otro bien o servicio. (págs. 41, 480)
interdependent when the outcome (profit) of each firm depends on the actions of the other firms in the market. (p. 692)	**interdependendiente** cuando el resultado (las utilidades) de cada empresa depende de lo que hagan las otras empresas en el mercado. (pág. 692)
interest on reserve balances (IORB) the amount the *central bank* pays in interest to *banks* for their balances held in reserve. (p. 243, 403)	**saldo del interés sobre la reserva (IORB)** cantidad que el *banco central* paga en interés a los *bancos* por sus saldos en la reserva. (págs. 243, 403)
interest rate the price, calculated as a percentage of the amount borrowed, charged by lenders to borrowers for the use of their savings. (p. 192)	**tasa de interés** precio, computado como un porcentaje de la cantidad tomada en préstamo, que los prestamistas cobran a los prestatarios por el uso de sus ahorros. (pág. 192)
interest rate effect (of a change in the *aggregate price level*) the change in investment and *consumer spending* caused by altered *interest rates* that result from changes in the demand for money. (p. 126)	**efecto de interés** (de un cambio en el *nivel de precios agregados*) cambio que ocurre en los gastos de inversión y de *consumo* a raíz de alteraciones en *las tasas de interés* como resultado de cambios en la demanda por dinero. (pág. 126)
intermediate goods and services goods and services bought from one firm by another firm to be used as inputs into the production of *final goods and services*. (p. 69)	**bienes y servicios intermedios** bienes y servicios comprados a una empresa por otra a fin de usarlos como insumos en la producción de *bienes y servicios finales*. (pág. 69)
internalize the externalities when individuals take *external costs* or *external benefits* into account. (p. 769)	**internalizar las externalidades** cuando las personas tienen en cuenta los *costes o beneficios externos*. (pág. 769)
inventories stocks of goods and raw materials held to facilitate business operations. (p. 67)	**inventarios** existencias de bienes y materia prima que se mantiene para facilitar las operaciones comerciales de un negocio. (pág. 67)
inventory investment the value of the change in *inventories* held in the *economy* during a given period. (p. 123)	**inversión en inventario** valor del cambio en los *inventarios* que se mantienen en la *economía* durante un período de tiempo dado. (pág. 123)
investment spending spending by firms on new productive *physical capital*, such as machinery and structures, and on changes in *inventories*. (p. 67)	**gastos de inversión** gastos de las empresas en *capital físico* nuevo y productivo, tal como maquinaria y estructuras, y en cambios en los *inventarios*. (pág. 67)
investment tax credit an amount that firms are allowed by law to deduct from their taxes based on their *investment spending*. (p. 254)	**crédito fiscal a la inversión** cantidad que las empresas están autorizadas por ley a deducir de sus impuestos con base a sus *gastos de inversión*. (pág. 254)

L

labor the effort of workers. (p. 4, 413)	**trabajo** esfuerzo de los trabajadores. (págs. 4, 413)
labor force the sum of the *employed* and the *unemployed*. (p. 77)	**fuerza laboral** suma de los *empleados* y los *desempleados*. (pág. 77)
labor force participation rate the percentage of the working age population (those aged 16 or older in the United States) that is in the *labor force*. (p. 77)	**tasa de participación de la fuerza laboral** porcentaje de la población en edad laboral (de los 16 años de edad en adelante en los Estados Unidos) que forma parte de la *fuerza laboral*. (pág. 77)
labor productivity output per worker; also known simply as *productivity*. (p. 304)	**productividad de la mano de obra** producción por trabajador; también denominado *productividad*. (pág. 304)
land all *resources* that come from nature, such as timber, wind, and petroleum. (p. 4, 413)	**terrenos** todos los *recursos* que provienen de la naturaleza, tales como la madera, el viento y el petróleo. (págs. 4, 413)
law of demand says that a higher price for a good or service, all other things being equal, leads people to demand a smaller quantity of that good or service. (p. 29, 468)	**ley de la demanda** establece que un precio más alto por un bien o servicio, si los demás factores son iguales, conduce a que las personas exijan una cantidad menor de dicho bien o servicio. (págs. 29, 468)
law of supply says that, other things being equal, the price and quantity supplied of a good are positively related. (p. 37, 477)	**ley de la oferta** establece que, si los demás factores son iguales, el precio y la cantidad ofertados de un bien están relacionados de manera positiva. (págs. 37, 477)
leisure the time available for purposes other than earning money to buy marketed goods. (p. 722)	**ocio** tiempo disponible para efectos que no sean ganar dinero que se usa par comprar bienes comercializados. (pág. 722)
liability a requirement to pay money in the future. (p. 193)	**obligación** requisito de pagar dinero en el futuro. (pág. 193)

license gives its owner the right to supply a good or service; a form of *quantity control*, as only those who are licensed can supply the good or service. (p. 560)	**licencia** da al licenciatario el derecho a suministrar un bien o servicio; forma de *control de cantidad*, ya que solamente aquellos que cuenten con la debida licencia pueden ofertar el bien o servicio. (pág. 560)
limited reserves describes an economy in which reserves are scarce and therefore relatively small changes in the supply of reserves shifts the money supply curve and changes the interest rate. (p. 239, 400)	**reservas limitadas** describe una economía en la que las reservas son escasas y, por tanto, la curva del suministro de dinero cambia con cambios relativamente pequeños del suministro y cambia la tasa de interés. (págs. 239, 400)
linear relationship the relationship between two *variables* when the *curve* that shows their relationship is a straight line, or linear. (p. A-4)	**relación lineal** relación entre dos *variables* cuando la *curva* que nos permite apreciar la relación es una línea recta o lineal. (pág. A-4)
liquid describes an asset if it can be quickly converted into cash without much loss of value. (p. 194)	**líquido** describe un activo si éste se puede convertir rápidamente en dinero en efectivo sin mucha pérdida de valor. (pág. 194)
loan a lending agreement between an individual lender and an individual borrower. (p. 195)	**préstamo** convenio para otorgar un crédito entre un prestamista individual y un prestatario individual. (pág. 195)
loanable funds market a hypothetical market that brings together those who want to lend money and those who want to borrow money. (p. 251)	**mercado de fondos prestables** mercado hipotético que une a aquellos deseosos de prestar dinero y a aquellos deseosos de recibir dinero en préstamo. (pág. 251)
the long run the time period in which all inputs or prices (including nominal wages) are fully flexible or can be varied. (p. 145, 584)	**largo plazo** período de tiempo en el que todos los insumos y precios (incluidos los salarios nominales) son completamente flexibles o pueden variar. (págs. 145, 584)
long-run aggregate supply (*LRAS*) curve shows the relationship between the *aggregate price level* and the quantity of *aggregate output* supplied that would exist if all prices, including *nominal wages*, were fully flexible. (p. 146)	**curva de oferta agregada a largo plazo** permite apreciar la relación entre el *nivel de precios agregados* y la cantidad de *producción agregada* ofertada que existiría si todos los precios, inclusive los *salarios nominales*, fueran totalmente flexibles. (pág. 146)
long-run average total cost curve (*LRATC*) shows the relationship between output and *average total cost* when *fixed cost* has been chosen to minimize average total cost for each level of output. (p. 606)	**curva de costes totales promedio a largo plazo** permite apreciar la relación entre producción y *coste total promedio* cuando se han seleccionado los *costes fijos* para minimizar el coste total promedio para cada nivel de producción. (pág. 606)
long-run industry supply curve shows how the quantity supplied responds to the price once firms have had time to enter or exit the industry. (p. 638)	**curva de oferta de la industria a largo plazo** permite apreciar cómo la cantidad ofertada responde al precio una vez que las empresas han tenido tiempo para ingresar o salir de la industria. (pág. 638)
long-run macroeconomic equilibrium when a short-run macroeconomic equilibrium is at the full-employment level of output (on the *LRAS* curves). (p. 151)	**equilibrio macroeconómico a largo plazo** cuando un equilibrio macroeconómico a corto plazo está al máximo nivel de empleo y producción (en las curvas de *LRAS*). (pág. 151)
long-run market equilibrium when the quantity supplied equals the quantity demanded, given that sufficient time has elapsed for producers to enter and exit the industry. (p. 637)	**equilibrio del mercado a largo plazo** cuando la cantidad ofertada equivale a la cantidad demandada, dado que ha transcurrido suficiente tiempo para que los productores entren y salgan de la industria. (pág. 637)
long-run Phillips curve (*LRPC*) shows the relationship between *unemployment* and *inflation* after expectations of inflation have had time to adjust to experience. (p. 276)	**curva de Phillips a largo plazo (*CPLP*)** permite apreciar la relación entre *desempleo* e *inflación* después de que se le haya dado a las expectativas de inflación tiempo suficiente para ajustarse a la experiencia. (pág. 276)
Lorenz curve shows the percentage of all income received by the poorest members of the population, from the poorest 0% to the poorest 100%. (p. 803)	**curva de Lorenz** permite apreciar el porcentaje de todos los ingresos percibidos por los integrantes más pobres de la población, desde el más pobre al 0% al más pobre al 100%. (pág. 803)
lump-sum tax a tax of a fixed amount paid by all taxpayers. (p. 548)	**impuesto de suma fija** impuesto de importe fijo que pagan todos los contribuyentes. (pág. 548)

M

M1 monetary aggregate that includes currency in circulation, checkable bank deposits, and other liquid deposits. (p. 207)	**M1** agregado monetario que incluye la moneda en circulación, los depósitos cobrables y otros depósitos líquidos. (pág. 207)
M2 monetary aggregate that includes *M1* plus less liquid "near monies" (financial assets that can be readily converted into cash). (p. 207)	**M2** agregado monetario que incluye a *M1* más "cuasimonedas" menos líquidas (activos financieros que se pueden convertir inmediatamente en dinero). (pág. 207)
macroeconomics the branch of *economics* that is concerned with the overall ups and downs of the *economy*. (p. 6, 415)	**macroeconomía** rama de la *economía (ciencia)* que trata de las subidas y bajadas generales de la *economía (sistema)*. (págs. 6, 415)

marginal analysis the study of the costs and benefits of doing a little bit more of an activity versus a little bit less. (p. 413)	**análisis marginal** estudio de los costes y beneficios de hacer un poco más de una actividad en contraste con un poco menos. (pág. 413)
marginal cost the cost of producing one more unit of output, which can be found as the increase in total cost when one more unit is made. (p. 592)	**costo marginal** costo de producir una unidad más de producción, que se puede hallar como el incremento del costo total cuando se hace una unidad más. (pág. 592)
marginal cost curve shows how the cost of producing one more unit depends on the quantity that has already been produced. (p. 593)	**curva de costes marginales** permite apreciar cómo el coste de producir una unidad más depende de la cantidad que ya se haya producido. (pág. 593)
marginal cost pricing occurs when regulators set a *monopoly's* price equal to its marginal cost to achieve efficiency. (p. 791)	**fijación de precio según los costes marginales** ocurre cuando los reguladores fijan el precio para un *monopolio* y dicho precio es equivalente a sus costes marginales; se hace con el fin de lograr la eficiencia. (pág. 791)
marginal external benefit the addition to *external benefits* created by one more unit of the good. (p. 763)	**beneficio externo marginal** incorporación de *beneficios externos* creados por una unidad más de un bien. (pág. 763)
marginal external cost the increase in *external costs* to society created by one more unit of the good. (p. 766)	**coste externo marginal** aumento en los *costes externos* para la sociedad creados por una unidad más del bien. (pág. 766)
marginal factor cost (*MFC*) the additional cost of employing an additional unit of a factor of production; also called the *marginal resource cost* (*MRC*). (p. 725)	**coste de los factores marginal (CFM)** coste adicional de emplear una unidad adicional de un factor de producción; también llamado *costo marginal de recursos* (*CMR*). (pág. 725)
marginal private benefit the marginal benefit that accrues to consumers of the good, not including any *external benefits.* (p. 763)	**beneficio privado marginal** beneficio marginal de un bien que corresponde a los consumidores, sin incluir ningún *beneficio externo.* (pág. 763)
marginal private cost the marginal cost of producing the good, not including any *external costs.* (p. 766)	**coste privado marginal** coste marginal de producir ese bien, sin incluir ningún *coste externo.* (pág. 766)
marginal product the additional quantity of output produced by using one more unit of an input. (p. 585)	**producto marginal** cantidad adicional de producción producida por el uso de una unidad más de un insumo. (pág. 585)
marginal propensity to consume (*MPC*) the increase in *consumer spending* when *disposable income* rises by $1. (p. 131)	**propensión marginal al consumo (*PMC*)** aumento en los *gastos del consumidor* cuando el *ingreso disponible* aumenta 1$. (pág. 131)
marginal propensity to save (*MPS*) the increase in household savings when *disposable income* rises by $1. (p. 131)	**propensión marginal al ahorro (*PMA*)** aumento de los ahorros del hogar cuando el *ingreso disponible* aumenta 1$. (pág. 131)
marginal rate of substitution (*MRS*) the ratio of the *marginal utility* of one good to the marginal utility of another; equal to MU_R/MU_M, for good *R* in place of good *M*. (p. 845)	**tasa marginal de sustitución (*TMS*)** relación entre la *utilidad marginal* de un bien y la utilidad marginal de otro; es equivalente a UM_R/UM_M, donde el bien *R* sustituye el bien *M*. (pág. 845)
marginal resource cost (*MRC*) see *marginal factor cost (MFC)*. (p. 725)	**costo marginal de recursos (*CMR*)** ver *coste de los factores marginal (CFM)*. (pág. 725)
marginal revenue the change in *total revenue* generated by an additional unit of output. (p. 617)	**ingreso marginal** cambio en el *ingreso total* generado por una unidad adicional de producción. (pág. 617)
marginal revenue curve shows how *marginal revenue* varies as output varies. (p. 618)	**curva de ingreso marginal** permite apreciar cómo los *ingresos marginales* varían en la medida en que varía la producción. (pág. 618)
marginal revenue product the additional revenue generated by employing one more unit of a factor. (p. 718)	**producto de ingreso marginal** ingresos adicionales generados al emplear una unidad más de un factor. (pág. 718)
marginal revenue product curve shows how the *marginal revenue product* of a factor depends on the quantity of that factor employed. (p. 719)	**curva del producto de ingreso marginal** permite apreciar cómo el *producto del ingreso marginal* de dicho factor depende de la cantidad del factor que se emplee. (pág. 719)
marginal social benefit the additional benefit to society as a whole from an additional unit. (p. 756)	**beneficio social marginal** beneficio adicional para toda la sociedad de una unidad adicional. (pág. 756)
marginal social cost the additional cost imposed on society as a whole by one additional unit. (p. 756)	**coste social marginal** coste adicional impuesto sobre toda la sociedad por una unidad adicional. (pág. 756)
marginal utility (of a good or service) the change in total *utility* generated by consuming one additional unit of a good or service. (p. 447)	**utilidad marginal** (de un bien o servicio) cambio en la *utilidad* total generado por el consumo de una unidad adicional de un bien o servicio. (pág. 447)
marginal utility curve shows how *marginal utility* depends on the quantity of a good or service consumed. (p. 448)	**curva de utilidad marginal** permite apreciar cómo la *utilidad marginal* depende de la cantidad de un bien o servicio que se ha consumido. (pág. 448)
market basket a hypothetical set of consumer purchases of goods and services. (p. 89)	**canasta familiar** conjunto hipotético de compras de bienes y servicios que hace el consumidor. (pág. 89)

market economy an *economy* in which the *factors of production* are privately owned and the decisions of individual producers and consumers largely determine what, how, and for whom to produce. (p. 420)	**economía de mercado** *economía* en la que los factores de producción son privados y las decisiones de los productores y consumidores individuales determinan en buena medida qué, cómo y para quién se produce. (pág. 420)
market failure when the outcome in a market is inefficient (p. 762)	**fallo de mercado** cuando el resultado en un mercado es ineficiente. (pág. 762)
market power refers to a firm's ability to influence the price it charges for a good or service. (p. 652)	**poder de mercado** se refiere a la capacidad de una empresa de influir en el precio que cobra por un bien o servicio. (pág. 652)
market share the fraction of the total industry output accounted for by a given firm's output. (p. 633)	**proporción del mercado** fracción de la producción total de la industria que está representada por la producción de una empresa. (pág. 633)
market supply curve see *industry supply curve* (p. 634)	**curva de oferta del mercado** véase *curva de oferta de la industria* (pág. 634)
market-clearing price see *equilibrium price* (p. 46, 520)	**precio de compensación** véase *precio de equilibrio* (págs. 46, 520)
maximum point the point along a *curve* with the largest value of *y*. (p. A-8)	**punto máximo** punto a lo largo de una *curva* con el valor más alto de *y*. (pág. A-8)
mean household income the average income across all *households*. (p. 802)	**media de ingresos del hogar** ingresos promedio teniendo en cuenta todos los *hogares*. (pág. 802)
means-tested program program available only to individuals or families whose incomes fall below a certain level. (p. 805)	**programa de selección según los medios** programa disponible solamente para personas o familias cuyos ingresos caen por debajo de cierto nivel. (pág. 805)
median household income the income of the *household* lying in the middle of the income distribution. (p. 802)	**ingresos medios de los hogares** ingresos del *hogar* que yacen en la mitad de la distribución de ingresos. (pág. 802)
medium of exchange an asset that individuals acquire for the purpose of trading for goods and services rather than for their own consumption. (p. 205)	**medio de intercambio** activo que las personas adquieren con el fin de intercambiarlo por bienes y servicios en lugar de consumirlo. (pág. 205)
microeconomics the branch of *economics* that studies how individuals, *households*, and firms make decisions and how those decisions interact. (p. 6, 414)	**microeconomía** rama de la *economía* en la que se estudia cómo las personas, los *hogares* y las empresas toman decisiones y cómo dichas decisiones interactúan. (págs. 6, 414)
minimum efficient scale the smallest quantity at which a firm's *long-run average total costs* is minimized. (p. 607)	**la escala mínima eficiente** la cantidad reducida en la que se minimizan los costos totales promedio a largo plazo de una empresa. (pág. 607)
minimum point the point along a *curve* with the smallest value of *y*. (p. A-8)	**punto mínimo** punto a lo largo de una *curva* con el valor más pequeño de *y*. (pág. A-8)
minimum wage a legal floor on the hourly wage rate paid for a worker's labor. (p. 557)	**salario mínimo** piso legal en la tasa salarial por hora que se paga por el trabajo de un trabajador. (pág. 557)
minimum-cost output the quantity of output at which *average total cost* is lowest; corresponds to the bottom of the *U-shaped average total cost curve*. (p. 597)	**producción al coste mínimo** cantidad de producción en la que el *coste total promedio* es más bajo; corresponde a la parte más baja de la *curva de costes totales promedio en forma de U*. (pág. 597)
mixed economy economy which combines elements of traditional, market, and command economies. (p. 420)	**economía mixta** economía que combina elementos de las economías tradicionales, de mercado y planificadas. (pág. 420)
model a simplified representation used to better understand a real-life situation. (p. 10, 423)	**modelo** representación simplificada que se usa para entender con más claridad una coyuntura de la vida real. (págs. 10, 423)
monetary aggregate an overall measure of the *money supply*. (p. 207)	**agregado monetario** medición general del *dinero en circulación*. (pág. 207)
monetary base the total amount of currency (cash) in circulation or kept on reserve by commercial banks; also known as M0 or MB. (p. 207)	**base monetaria** cantidad total de dinero en circulación o que mantienen en reserva los bancos comerciales; también conocido como M0 o MB. (pág. 207)
monetary policy lag the result from the time it takes to recognize a problem in the economy and the time it takes for a *monetary policy* action to take effect in the economy. (p. 247)	**retraso de política monetaria** resultado desde el momento en el que se reconoce un problema en la economía y el tiempo que se tarda una *política monetaria* en surtir efecto en la economía. (pág. 247)
money any asset that can easily be used to purchase goods and services. (p. 204)	**dinero** todo activo que se pueda utilizar fácilmente para comprar bienes y servicios. (pág. 204)
money demand curve (*MD*) shows the relationship between the quantity of money demanded and the *nominal interest rate*. (p. 230)	**curva de demanda de dinero** permite apreciar la relación entre la cantidad de dinero demandada y la *tasa de interés nominal*. (pág. 230)

money multiplier the ratio of the *money supply* to the *monetary base*; indicates the total number of dollars created in the banking system by each $1 addition to the *monetary base.* (p. 225)	**multiplicador monetario** relación entre el *dinero en circulación* y la *base monetaria*; indica el número total de dólares creados en el sistema bancario por cada adición de 1$ a la *base monetaria.* (pág. 225)
money supply the total value of *financial assets* in the *economy* that are considered *money.* (p. 204)	**dinero en circulación** valor total de los *activos financieros* en la *economía* que se consideran *dinero.* (pág. 204)
money supply curve (*MS*) shows the relationship between the quantity of money supplied and the *nominal interest rate*; it is independent of the *nominal interest rate.* (p. 232)	**curva del dinero en circulación (DC)** permite apreciar la relación entre la cantidad de dinero en circulación y la *tasa de interés nominal*; es independiente de la *tasa de interés nominal.* (pág. 232)
monopolist a firm that is the only producer of a good that has no close *substitutes.* (p. 653)	**monopolista** una empresa que es el único productor de un bien que no tiene *sustitutos* cercanos. (pág. 653)
monopolistic competition market structure in which there are many competing firms in an industry, each firm sells a differentiated product, and there is *free entry* into and exit from the industry in the *long run.* (p. 655)	**competencia monopolística** estructura de mercado en la que muchas empresas compiten en una industria, cada empresa vende un producto diferenciado y existe una *entrada y una salida libres* de la industria a *largo plazo.* (pág. 655)
monopoly an industry with only one firm; an industry controlled by a *monopolist.* (p. 653)	**monopolio** una industria con una sola empresa; una industria controlada por un *monopolista.* (pág. 653)
monopsonist a single buyer in a factor market. (p. 743)	**monopsonista** un comprador único en un mercado de factores. (pág. 743)
monopsony a market in which there is a *monopsonist.* (p. 743)	**monopsonio** mercado en el que hay un *monopsonista.* (pág. 743)
moral hazard a distortion of incentives when someone else bears the costs of a lack of care or effort; arises when an individual knows more about their own actions than other people do. (p. 835)	**riesgo moral** distorsión de incentivos cuando otra persona responde por los costes de la falta de atención o esfuerzo; surge cuando una persona tiene más información sobre sus propias acciones que otras. (pág. 835)
movement along the demand curve a change in the *quantity demanded* of a good that is the result of a change in that good's price. (p. 30, 469)	**movimiento a lo largo de la curva de demanda** cambio en la *cantidad demandada* de un bien. Es el resultado de un cambio en el precio de dicho bien. (págs. 30, 469)
movement along the supply curve a change in the *quantity supplied* of a good arising from a change in the good's price. (p. 39, 478)	**movimiento a lo largo de la curva de oferta** cambio en la *cantidad ofertada* de un bien. Es el resultado de un cambio en el precio de dicho bien. (págs. 39, 478)

N

Nash equilibrium the result when each player in a game chooses the action that maximizes their payoff, given the actions of other players; also called *noncooperative equilibrium.* (p. 698)	**equilibrio de Nash** resultado que se obtiene cuando cada jugador de un juego opta por la acción que maximiza sus ganancias, dadas las acciones de los demás jugadores; también denominado *equilibrio no cooperativo.* (pág. 698)
national accounts see *national income and product accounts* (p. 64)	**cuentas nacionales** véase *cuentas nacionales de rentas y productos* (pág. 64)
national income and product accounts keep track of the flows of money among different sectors of the *economy*; in the United States, calculated by the Bureau of Economic Analysis; also known as *national accounts* (p. 64)	**cuentas nacionales de rentas y productos** lleva el control de los movimientos de dinero entre los diversos sectores de la *economía*; en Estados Unidos las computa la Oficina de Análisis Económico; también denominado *cuentas nacionales.* (pág. 64)
national savings the sum of private savings and the *budget balance*; the total amount of savings generated within the *economy.* (p. 250)	**ahorros nacionales** suma de los ahorros privados y el *equilibrio presupuestario*; total de ahorros generados dentro de la *economía.* (pág. 250)
natural monopoly when *economies of scale* provide a large cost advantage to a single firm that produces all of an industry's output. (p. 660)	**monopolio natural** cuando las *economías de escala* ofrecen una ventaja grande en costes a una sola empresa que produce toda la producción de una industria. (pág. 660)
natural rate of unemployment the *unemployment rate* that arises from the effects of *frictional* plus *structural unemployment.* (p. 81)	**tasa natural de desempleo** *tasa de desempleo* que surge de los efectos del *desempleo de fricción* y del *desempleo estructural.* (pág. 81)
negative consumption externality a negative externality created by the consumption of a good or service. (p. 766)	**externalidad de consumo negativo** una externalidad negativa creada por el consumo de un bien o servicio. (pág. 766)
negative externalities *external costs.* (p. 762)	**externalidades negativas** *costes externos.* (pág. 762)
negative income tax a program that supplements the income of low-income workers. (p. 806)	**impuesto sobre la renta negativo** programa que complementa los ingresos de los trabajadores de bajos ingresos. (pág. 806)

negative production externality a negative externality caused by the production of a good or service. (p. 766)	**Externalidad de producción negativa** una externalidad negativa causada por la producción de un bien o servicio. (pág. 766)
negative relationship the relationship between two *variables* when an increase in one variable is associated with a decrease in the other variable. (p. A-4)	**relación negativa** relación entre dos *variables* en la que un aumento en una variable se asocia con una disminución en la otra variable. (pág. A-4)
net capital inflow equal to the total inflow of foreign funds minus the total outflow of domestic funds to other countries. (p. 250)	**flujo de capital neto** igual al flujo total de fondos extranjeros menos el flujo total de fondos nacionales a otros países. (pág. 250)
net exports the difference between the value of *exports* and the value of *imports*; $(X - M)$. (p. 69)	**exportaciones netas** diferencia entre el valor de las *exportaciones* y el valor de las *importaciones*; $(X - M)$. (pág. 69)
nominal GDP the total value of all *final goods and services* produced in the *economy* during a given year, calculated with the prices current in the year in which the *output* is produced. (p. 102)	**PIB nominal** valor total de todos los *bienes y servicios finales* producidos en la *economía* durante un año dado y computados con los precios vigentes en el año en que se produce la *producción*. (pág. 102)
nominal interest rate the interest rate actually paid for a *loan*. (p. 97, 199)	**tasa de interés nominal** tasa de interés que en efecto se paga por un *préstamo*. (págs. 97, 199)
nominal wage the dollar amount of the wage paid. (p. 138)	**salario nominal** cantidad en dólares que se paga por concepto salarial. (pág. 138)
noncooperative behavior when firms act in their own self-interest, ignoring the effects of their actions on each other's profits. (p. 694)	**conducta no cooperativa** cuando las empresas funcionan exclusivamente en su interés propio, haciendo caso omiso de los efectos que sus acciones podrían tener en las utilidades de los demás. (pág. 694)
noncooperative equilibrium see *Nash equilibrium*. (p. 698)	**equilibrio no cooperativo** véase *equilibrio de Nash*. (pág. 698)
nonexcludable when a good is nonexcludable, the supplier cannot prevent consumption by people who do not pay for it. (p. 772)	**no excluible** cuando un bien no es excluible el proveedor no puede impedir que lo consuman personas que no han pagado por él. (pág. 772)
nonlinear curve a *curve* along which the *slope* changes. (p. A-6)	**curva no lineal** *curva* a lo largo de la cual la *pendiente* cambia. (pág. A-6)
nonlinear relationship the relationship between two *variables* when the *curve* that shows their relationship is not a straight line, or is nonlinear. (p. A-4)	**relación no lineal** relación entre dos *variables* cuando la *curva* en la que se aprecia su relación no es rectilínea o no es lineal. (pág. A-4)
nonmarket transactions transactions that involve goods and services that are not bought and sold in a legal market. (p. 73)	**transacciones fuera del mercado** transacciones de bienes y servicios que no se compran y venden en un mercado legal. (pág. 73)
nonprice competition when firms that have a tacit understanding not to compete on price use advertising and other means to try to increase their sales. (p. 703)	**competencia no basada en el precio** cuando las empresas que tienen un acuerdo tácito de no competir por precio utilizan la publicidad u otros medios para tratar de aumentar sus ventas. (pág. 703)
nonrival in consumption a good is nonrival in consumption if more than one person can consume the same unit of the good at the same time. (p. 772)	**no rival en el consumo** un bien no es rival en el consumo si más de una persona puede consumir la misma unidad del bien al mismo tiempo. (pág. 772)
normal good describes a good for which a rise in income increases the demand for the good. (p. 34, 473)	**bien normal** describe un bien cuya demanda aumenta cuando hay un aumento en los ingresos. (págs. 34, 473)
normal profit an *economic profit* equal to zero; an economic profit just high enough to keep a firm engaged in its current activity. (p. 614)	**utilidades normales** *utilidades económicas* equivalentes a cero; utilidades económicas justo lo suficientemente altas para mantener a una empresa en marcha realizando su actividad actual. (pág. 614)

O

oligopolist a producer in an *oligopoly*. (p. 654)	**oligopolista** productor en un *oligopolio*. (pág. 654)
oligopoly an industry with only a small number of firms. (p. 654)	**oligopolio** industria con tan solo una cantidad pequeña de empresas. (pág. 654)
open market operation (OMO) a purchase or sale of *government debt* (e.g., a *bond*) by a *central bank*. (p. 215, 241)	**operación de mercado abierto** (OMA) compra o venta de la *deuda gubernamental* (por ejemplo, un *bono*) por el *banco central*. (págs. 215, 241)
opportunity cost the real cost of an item: the value of the next best alternative that you must give up in order to get that item. (p. 5, 414)	**coste de oportunidad** coste real de un artículo: valor de la siguiente mejor alternativa que se tiene que entregar para obtenerlo. (págs. 5, 414)

optimal consumption bundle the consumption bundle that maximizes the consumer's total *utility* given that consumer's *budget constraint.* (p. 451)	**conjunto de consumo óptimo** conjunto de consumo que maximiza la *utilidad* total para el consumidor dadas sus *restricciones presupuestarias.* (pág. 451)
optimal consumption rule says that in order to maximize *utility*, a consumer must equate the *marginal utility per dollar* spent on each good and service in the consumption bundle. (p. 456)	**regla de consumo óptimo** explica que a fin de maximizar la utilidad, el consumidor tiene que equilibrar la *utilidad marginal por dólar* dedicado a cada bien o servicio en el conjunto de consumo. (pág. 456)
ordinary goods in a consumer's *utility function*, goods for which (1) the consumer requires additional units of one good to compensate for fewer units of another, and vice versa; and (2) the consumer experiences a *diminishing marginal rate of substitution* when substituting one good for the other. (p. 845)	**bienes ordinarios** en la función de utilidad de un consumidor, bienes por los cuales (1) el consumidor requiere unidades adicionales de un bien para compensar las pocas unidades de otro, y viceversa; y (2) el consumidor experimenta una *tasa marginal de sustitución decreciente* cuando se sustituye un bien por otro. (pág. 845)
origin the point where the *(horizontal) x-axis* and *(vertical) y-axis* meet. (p. A-2)	**origen** punto en el cual se encuentran el *eje* x *(horizontal)* y el *eje* y *(vertical)*. (pág. A-2)
other things equal assumption in the development of a *model*, the assumption that all other relevant factors remain unchanged; also known as the *ceteris paribus assumption.* (p. 11, 423)	**supuesto de que todos los demás factores seguirán iguales** en la creación de un *modelo*, supuesto de que todos los demás factores pertinentes seguirán sin cambio; también denominado *supuesto ceteris paribus.* (págs. 11, 423)
output gap the percentage difference between actual *aggregate output* and *potential output.* (p. 110, 151)	**brecha de producción** diferencia porcentual entre la *producción agregada* real y el *potencial de producción.* (págs. 110, 151)
overnight interbank lending rate the interest rate that banks charge other banks for overnight loans. (p. 239)	**Tasa de préstamo nocturna interbancaria** tasa de interés que cobran los bancos a otros bancos por los préstamos nocturnos. (pág. 239)

P

patent gives the owner a temporary *monopoly* in the use or sale of an invention. (p. 660)	**patente** da al propietario un *monopolio* temporal en el uso o la venta de una invención. (pág. 660)
payoff the reward received by a player in a game, such as the profit earned by an *oligopolist.* (p. 695)	**pago** premio recibido por un jugador, tales como las utilidades obtenidas por un *oligopolista.* (pág. 695)
payoff matrix shows how the *payoff* to each of the participants in a two-player game depends on the actions of both. Such a matrix helps us analyze situations of *interdependence.* (p. 695)	**matriz de pago** permite apreciar cómo el *pago* a cada uno de los participantes en un juego de dos jugadores depende de las acciones de ambos. Tal matriz nos sirve para analizar coyunturas de *interdependencia.* (pág. 695)
peak (of a business cycle) the highest point of an expansion before the economy goes into a recession. (p. 107)	**pico** (de un ciclo comercial) punto máximo de una expansión antes de que la economía entre en recesión. (pág. 107)
perfect price discrimination when a *monopolist* charges each consumer their *willingness to pay*—the maximum that the consumer is willing to pay. (p. 677)	**discriminación de precios perfecta** cuando un *monopolista* cobra a cada consumidor en función de su *voluntad de pago*; el máximo que el consumidor paga por voluntad propia. (pág. 677)
perfectly competitive industry an industry in which firms are *price-takers.* (p. 633)	**industria perfectamente competitiva** industria en la que las empresas son *aceptadoras de precios.* (pág. 633)
perfectly competitive market a market in which all market participants are *price-takers.* (p. 633)	**mercado perfectamente competitivo** mercado en el que todos los participantes en el mercado son *aceptadores de precios.* (pág. 633)
perfectly elastic demand when any price increase will cause the *quantity demanded* to drop to zero; when demand is perfectly elastic, the *demand curve* is a horizontal line. (p. 492)	**demanda perfectamente elástica** cuando como resultado de cualquier aumento de precio la *cantidad demandada* cae a cero; cuando la demanda es perfectamente elástica la *curva de demanda* es una línea horizontal. (pág. 492)
perfectly elastic supply when the quantity supplied is zero below some price and approaches infinity above that price; a perfectly elastic *supply curve* is a horizontal line. (p. 502)	**oferta perfectamente elástica** cuando la cantidad ofertada es cero por debajo de cierto precio y se aproxima al infinito por encima de dicho precio; una *curva de oferta* perfectamente elástica es una línea horizontal. (pág. 502)
perfectly inelastic demand when the *quantity demanded* does not respond at all to changes in the price; when demand is perfectly inelastic, the *demand curve* is a vertical line. (p. 492)	**demanda perfectamente inelástica** cuando la *cantidad demandada* no parece responder a todos los cambios en el precio; cuando la demanda es perfectamente inelástica la *curva de demanda* es una línea vertical. (pág. 492)
perfectly inelastic supply when the price elasticity of supply is zero, so that changes in the price of the good have no effect on the quantity supplied; a perfectly inelastic *supply curve* is a vertical line. (p. 502)	**oferta perfectamente inelástica** cuando la elasticidad del precio de la oferta es cero, de manera que los cambios en el precio del bien no tienen ningún efecto en la cantidad ofertada; una *curva de oferta* perfectamente inelástica es una línea vertical. (pág. 502)

physical asset a tangible object that the owner has the right to use or dispose of the object as they wish. (p. 193)	**activo físico** un objeto tangible que el propietario tiene derecho de usar o del cual puede disponer como quiera. (pág. 193)
physical capital often referred to simply as *capital*—consists of manufactured (human-made) goods, such as equipment, buildings and machines, used to produce other goods and services. (p. 305, 716)	**capital físico** a menudo se le dice simplemente *capital*. Consta de bienes manufacturados (hechos por el hombre) tales como equipos, edificaciones y maquinaria, que se usan para producir otros bienes y servicios. (págs. 305, 716)
pie chart a chart that shows the share of a total amount that is accounted for by various components, usually expressed in percentages. (p. A-11)	**gráfico circular** cuadro en el que se aprecia la proporción un total que está representado por diversos componentes, generalmente expresados como porcentajes. (pág. A-11)
Pigouvian subsidy a payment designed to correct for the inefficiencies of *external benefits*. (p. 785)	**subsidio Pigouviano** pago diseñado para corregir las ineficiencias de *beneficios externos*. (pág. 785)
Pigouvian taxes taxes designed to correct for the inefficiencies of *external costs*. (p. 783)	**impuestos Pigouvianos** impuestos diseñados para corregir las ineficiencias de *costes externos*. (pág. 783)
planned investment spending the *investment spending* that businesses intend to undertake during a given period. (p. 122)	**gastos de inversión planificados** *gastos de inversión* que las empresas tienen la intención de emprender durante un período de tiempo dado. (pág. 122)
policy rate the *central bank*'s target range for an *overnight interbank lending rate*. (p. 239)	**interés oficial** rango de la *tasa nocturna de préstamo interbancario* del *banco central*. (pág. 239)
positive consumption externality positive externality created by the consumption of a good or service. (p. 763)	**externalidad positiva de consumo** externalidad positiva creada por el consumo de un bien o servicio. (pág. 763)
positive externalities *external benefits*. (p. 762)	**externalidades positivas** *beneficios externos*. (pág. 762)
positive production externality a positive externality arising from the production of a good or service. (p. 763)	**externalidad positiva de producción** una externalidad positiva que surge de la producción de un bien o servicio (pág. 763)
positive relationship the relationship between two *variables* when an increase in one variable is associated with an increase in the other variable. (p. A-4)	**relación positiva** relación entre dos *variables* cuando un aumento en una variable se asocia con un aumento en la otra variable. (pág. A-4)
potential output what an economy can produce when operating at maximum sustainable employment (that is, at the natural rate of unemployment); the level of *real GDP* the *economy* would produce if all prices, including *nominal wages*, were fully flexible—it represents the economy's maximum sustainable production capacity. (p. 110, 146)	**potencial de producción** lo que la economía puede producir cuando opera con el máximo empleo sustentable (es decir, a la tasa natural de desempleo); el nivel del *PIB real* que la *economía* produce si todos los precios, incluidos los *salarios nominales*, fueran completamente flexibles. Representa la máxima capacidad de producción sustentable de la economía. (págs. 110, 146)
poverty rate the percentage of the population with incomes below the *poverty threshold*. (p. 795)	**tasa de pobreza** porcentaje de la población con ingresos por debajo del *umbral de pobreza*. (pág. 795)
poverty threshold the minimum annual income that is considered adequate to purchase the necessities of life. (p. 795)	**umbral de pobreza** ingresos minimo anuales que se considera adecuado para comprar lo imprescindible para vivir. (pág. 795)
price ceiling a maximum price that sellers are allowed to charge for a good or service. (p. 553)	**techo de precios** precio máximo que a los vendedores se les permite cobrar por un bien o servicio. (pág. 553)
price controls legal restrictions on how high or low a market price may go; typically take the form of either a *price ceiling* or a *price floor*. (p. 553)	**controles de precios** restricciones legales de cuán alto o cuán bajo puede subir o bajar el precio de mercado; casi siempre se presenta en la forma de ya sea un *techo de precios* o bien de un *piso de precios*. (pág. 553)
price discrimination when firms charge different prices to different consumers for the same good. (p. 674)	**discriminación por precio** cuando los vendedores cobran precios diferentes a diferentes clientes por el mismo bien. (pág. 674)
price elasticity of demand the ratio of the percentage change in the *quantity demanded* to the percentage change in the price as we move along the *demand curve* (dropping the minus sign). (p. 488)	**elasticidad del precio de demanda** relación entre el cambio porcentual en la *cantidad demandada* y el cambio porcentual en el precio a medida que avanzamos en la *curva de demanda* (sin el signo de menos). (pág. 488)
price elasticity of supply a measure of the responsiveness of the quantity of a good supplied to changes in the price of that good; the ratio of the percentage change in the quantity supplied to the percentage change in the price as we move along the *supply curve*. (p. 500)	**elasticidad de precio de oferta** medida de la reacción de la cantidad de un bien ofertado a lo cambios en el precio de ese bien; relación entre el cambio porcentual en la cantidad ofertada y el cambio porcentual en el precio a medida que avanzamos en la *curva de oferta*. (pág. 500)
price floor a minimum price that buyers are required to pay for a good or service. (p. 553)	**piso de precios** precio mínimo que se les exige pagar a los compradores por un bien o servicio. (pág. 553)
price index measures the cost of purchasing a given *market basket* in a given year; the index value is always equal to 100 in the selected *base year*. (p. 89)	**índice de precios** mide el coste de comprar una *canasta familiar* dada en un año dado; el valor del índice es siempre igual a 100 en el *año base* escogido. (pág. 89)

price leadership one firm sets its price first, and other firms then follow. (p. 703)	**liderazgo en precios** una empresa fija el precio primero y luego las otras empresas la siguen. (pág. 703)
price regulation limits the price that a *monopolist* is allowed to charge. (p. 670)	**reglamentación de precios** limita el precio que se le permite cobrar a un *monopolista*. (pág. 670)
price stability when the overall price level is changing only slowly if at all. (p. 86)	**estabilidad de precios** cuando el nivel de precios en general apenas cambia lentamente o no cambia. (pág. 86)
price war when *tacit collusion* breaks down and aggressive price competition causes prices to collapse. (p. 705)	**guerra de precios** cuando se desploma una *colusión tácita* y la competencia de precios tenaz hace colapsar los precios. (pág. 705)
price-taking consumer a consumer whose actions have no effect on the market price of the good or service purchased. (p. 632)	**consumidor aceptador de precios** consumidor cuyas acciones no tienen ningún efecto en el precio de mercado del bien o servicio que se ha comprado. (pág. 632)
price-taking firm a firm whose actions have no effect on the market price of the good or service it sells. (p. 632)	**empresa aceptadora de precios** empresa cuyas acciones no tienen ningún efecto en el precio de mercado del bien o servicio que vende. (pág. 632)
principle of diminishing marginal utility states that each successive unit of a good or service consumed adds less to total *utility* than does the previous unit. (p. 449)	**principio de la utilidad marginal decreciente** explica que cada unidad sucesiva de un bien o servicio que se consume agrega menos a la *utilidad* total que la unidad anterior. (pág. 449)
principle of marginal analysis says that every activity should continue until marginal benefit equals marginal cost. (p. 617)	**principio del análisis marginal** explica que toda actividad debería proseguir hasta que el beneficio marginal sea equivalente al coste marginal. (pág. 617)
prisoner's dilemma a game based on two premises: (1) each player has an incentive to choose an action that benefits itself at the other player's expense; and (2) when both players follow this incentive, both are worse off than if they had acted cooperatively. (p. 696)	**dilema del prisionero** juego basado en dos premisas: (1) cada jugador tiene un incentivo para escoger una acción que lo beneficie a costas del otro jugador; y (2) cuando ambos jugadores actúan de tal manera a ambos les va peor que si hubieran actuado de manera cooperativa. (pág. 696)
private good a good that is both *excludable* and *rival in consumption*. (p. 772)	**bien privado** bien que es tanto *excluible* como *rival en el consumo*. (pág. 772)
private information see *asymmetric information*. (p. 759, 832)	**información privada o reservada** ver *información asimétrica*. (págs. 759, 832)
private savings *disposable income* minus *consumer spending*; household's disposable income that is not spent on consumption. (p. 66)	**ahorros privados** *ingresos disponibles* menos los *gastos de consumo*; ingresos disponibles de un hogar que no se utilizan para consumir. (pág. 66)
producer price index (PPI) measures the prices of goods and services purchased by producers. (p. 92)	**índice de precios del productor (IPP)** mide los precios de bienes y servicios que compran los productores. (pág. 92)
producer surplus the difference between the price received and the seller's (or sellers') cost; refers to both *individual* and *total producer surplus*. (p. 517)	**superávit del productor** diferencia entre el precio recibido y el costo del vendedor (o de los vendedores); se refiere tanto al *superávit del productor individual* como al *superávit total del productor*. (pág. 517)
product differentiation an attempt by a firm to convince buyers that its product is different from the products of other firms in the industry. (p. 656)	**diferenciación de productos** intento que hace la empresa de convencer a los compradores de que su producto es diferente a los productos de otras empresas en la industria. (pág. 656)
product markets where goods and services are bought and sold. (p. 64)	**mercados de productos** mercados en los cuales se compran y se venden bienes y servicios. (pág. 64)
production function the relationship between the quantity of inputs a firm uses and the quantity of output it produces. (p. 584)	**función de producción** relación entre la cantidad de insumos que emplea una empresa y la cantidad de producción que produce. (pág. 584)
production possibilities curve (*PPC*) illustrates the necessary *trade-offs* in an *economy* that produces only two goods; shows the maximum quantity of one good that can be produced for each possible quantity of the other good produced. (p. 11, 424)	**curva de posibilidades de producción (*CPP*)** ilustra las *compensaciones* necesarias que enfrenta una *economía* que produce solo dos bienes; permite apreciar la cantidad máxima de un bien que se puede producir por cada cantidad posible producida del otro bien. (págs. 11, 424)
productive efficiency achieved when firms minimize the average cost of producing their goods. (p. 642)	**eficiencia productiva** se logra cuando las empresas minimizan el costo medio de producir sus bienes. (pág. 642)
productivity see *labor productivity* (p. 304)	**productividad** véase *productividad de la mano de obra* (pág. 304)
profit-maximizing rule says that profit is maximized by producing the quantity of output at which the marginal revenue of the last unit produced is equal to its marginal cost. (p. 617)	**regla de maximización de las ganancias** establece que las ganancias se maximizan cuando se produce una cantidad de bienes en la que los ingresos marginales de la última unidad producida es igual a su costo marginal. (pág. 617)

progressive tax a tax that rises more than in proportion to income. (p. 539)	**impuesto progresivo** impuesto que aumenta más que en proporcionalidad directa con los ingresos. (pág. 539)
property rights establish ownership and grant individuals the right to trade goods and services with each other. (p. 421)	**derechos de propiedad** establece la propiedad y otorga a las personas el derecho a intercambiar bienes y servicios unas con otras. (pág. 421)
proportional tax a tax that rises in proportion to income. (p. 539)	**impuesto proporcional** impuesto que aumenta en proporcionalidad directa con los ingresos. (pág. 539)
protectionism the practice of limiting trade to protect domestic industries. (p. 352, 567)	**proteccionismo** práctica de limitar el comercio con el fin de proteger las industrias nacionales. (págs. 352, 567)
public good a good that is both *nonexcludable* and *nonrival in consumption*. (p. 774)	**bien público** bien que es tanto *ni excluible* ni *no rival en el consumo*. (pág. 774)
public ownership (of a *monopoly*) when a good is supplied by the government, or by a firm owned by the government, instead of by a *monopolist*. (p. 669)	**propiedad pública** (de un *monopolio*) cuando un bien es ofertado por el gobierno o por una empresa de propiedad del gobierno en lugar de por un *monopolista*. (pág. 669)
purchasing power parity (between two countries' currencies) the nominal *exchange rate* at which a given basket of goods and services would cost the same amount in each country. (p. 338)	**paridad en el poder adquisitivo** (entre las divisas de dos países) *tasa de cambio* nominal a la cual una canasta de bienes y servicios costaría la misma cantidad en cada uno de los países. (pág. 338)

Q

quantitative easing (QE) an *expansionary monetary policy* that involves *central banks* purchasing longer-term government bonds and other private financial assets. (p. 243, 401)	**expansión cuantitativa (EC)** una *política monetaria expansiva* que supone que los bancos centrales compren bonos gubernamentales a largo plazo y otros activos financieros privados. (págs. 243, 401)
quantity control an upper limit on the quantity of some good that can be bought or sold; also known as a *quota*. (p. 559)	**control de cantidad** límite superior de la cantidad que se puede comprar o vender de algún bien; también denominado *cuota*. (pág. 559)
quantity demanded the actual amount of a good or service consumers are willing and able to buy at some specific price; shown as a single point in the *demand schedule* or along a *demand curve*. (p. 28, 468)	**cantidad demandada** cantidad precisa de un bien o servicio que los consumidores están dispuestos (y tienen la capacidad) de comprar a un precio específico; se aprecia en un único punto en la *tabla de demanda* o a lo largo de una *curva de demanda*. (págs. 28, 468)
quantity supplied the actual amount of a good or service people are willing to sell at some specific price. (p. 37, 477)	**cantidad ofertada** cantidad precisa de un bien o servicio que las personas están dispuestas a vender a algún precio específico. (págs. 37, 477)
Quantity Theory of Money emphasizes the positive relationship between the price level and the *money supply*; relies on the velocity equation ($M \times V = P \times Y$). (p. 284)	**teoría cuantitativa del dinero** enfatiza la relación positiva entre el nivel de precios y el *dinero en circulación*; se basa en la ecuación de velocidad ($M \times V = P \times Y$). (pág. 284)
quota see *quantity control* (p. 559)	**cuota** véase *control de cantidad* (pág. 559)
quota rent the earnings that accrue to the license-holder from ownership of the right to sell the good; this is the difference between the demand and supply price at the quota amount and is equal to the market price of the *license* when the licenses are traded. (p. 562)	**alquiler de cuota** ganancias que acumula el licenciatario por ser propietario del derecho de vender el bien; es la diferencia entre el precio de demanda y el precio de oferta establecidos según la cuota y es igual al precio de mercado de la *licencia* cuando las licencias se comercializan. (pág. 562)

R

rational agents consumers, producers, and others who behave rationally and make optimal decisions. (p. 440)	**agentes racionales** consumidores, productores y otros individuos que se comportan racionalmente y toman decisiones óptimas. (pág. 440)
real exchange rates *exchange rates* adjusted for international differences in *aggregate price levels*. (p. 339)	**tasas de cambio reales** *tasas de cambio* ajustadas a las diferencias internacionales en los *niveles de precios agregados*. (pág. 339)
real GDP the total value of all *final goods and services* produced in the *economy* during a given year, calculated using the prices of a selected *base year* in order to remove the effects of price changes. (p. 102)	**PIB real** valor total de todos los *bienes y servicios finales* producidos en la *economía* durante un año dado, computado haciendo uso de los precios de un *año base* escogido a fin de eliminar los efectos de los cambios de precios. (pág. 102)
real income income divided by the price level to adjust for the effects of *inflation* or *deflation*. (p. 87)	**ingresos reales** ingresos divididos entre el nivel de precios a fin de ajustarse a los efectos de la *inflación* o *deflación*. (pág. 87)
real interest rate the *nominal interest rate* minus the rate of *inflation*; *nominal interest rate* adjusted for *inflation*. (p. 97, 199)	**tasa de interés real** *tasa de interés nominal* menos la tasa de *inflación*; *tasa de interés nominal* austada a la *inflación*. (págs. 97, 199)

real wage the wage rate divided by the price level to adjust for the effects of *inflation* or *deflation*. (p. 87)	**salario real** tasa salarial dividida entre el nivel de precios a fin de ajustarse a los efectos dela *inflación* o *deflación*. (pág. 87)
real wealth effect (of a change in the *aggregate price level*) the change in *consumer spending* caused by the altered purchasing power of consumers' assets. (p. 125)	**efecto de riqueza real** (de un cambio en el *nivel de precio agregado*) el cambio en los gastos de consumo causado por el cambio en el poder *adquisitivo de los consumidores*. (pág. 125)
recession a period of economic downturn when output and employment are falling. (p. 107)	**recesión** período de desaceleración económica cuando la producción y el empleo están en caída. (pág. 107)
recessionary gap when *aggregate output* is below *potential output*. (p. 153)	**brecha recesiva** cuando la *producción agregada* se encuentra por debajo del *potencial de producción*. (pág. 153)
regressive tax a tax that rises less than in proportion to income. (p. 539)	**impuesto regresivo** impuesto que aumenta menos en proporcionalidad con los ingresos. (pág. 539)
relative price the rate at which good *R* trades for good *M* in the market; equal to P_R/P_M (p. 847)	**precio relativo** precio al que el bien *R* se intercambia por el bien *M* en el mercado; es equivalente a P_R/P_M (pág. 847)
relative price rule states that, at the *optimal consumption bundle*, the *marginal rate of substitution* between two goods is equal to their *relative price*. (p. 848)	**regla del precio relativo** en el *conjunto de consumo óptimo* la *tasa marginal de sustitución* entre dos bienes es equivalente a sus precios relativos. (pág. 848)
rental rate the cost, explicit or implicit, of using a unit of an asset, either land or *capital*, for a given period of time. (p. 722)	**canon de alquiler** sea de terrenos o de *capital*, es el coste, explícito o implícito, de hacer uso de una unidad de dicho activo por un período de tiempo dado. (pág. 722)
reputation long-term credibility that allows an individual to assure others that they aren't concealing adverse *private information*. (p. 834)	**reputación** credibilidad a largo plazo que permite que una persona asegure a otras que no está ocultando ninguna *información reservada o privada* adversa. (pág. 834)
required reserve ratio the smallest fraction of deposits that the *central bank* requires *banks* to hold. (p. 220)	**tasa de reservas obligatorias** fracción más pequeña de los depósitos que el *banco central* autoriza que retengan los *bancos*. (pág. 220)
required reserves the reserves that *banks* must hold, as mandated by the *central bank* (p. 223)	**reservas requeridas** las reservas que los *bancos* deben retener por mandato del *banco central* (pág. 223)
reserve ratio the fraction of *bank deposits* that a *bank* holds as reserves. (p. 219)	**tasa de reserva** fracción de los *depósitos bancarios* que un *banco* retiene como reservas. (pág. 219)
reserve requirements rules set by the *central bank* that determine the *required reserve ratio* for *banks*. (p. 221)	**requisitos de reserva** reglas que fija el *banco central* en las que se determina la *tasa de reservas obligatorias* para los *bancos*. (pág. 221)
resource anything that can be used to produce something else; also called *factor of production*. (p. 4, 413)	**recurso** cualquier cosa que se pueda utilizar para producir otra cosa; también llamado *factor de producción*. (págs. 4, 413)
revaluation an increase in the value of a currency that is set under a *fixed exchange rate regime*. (p. 351)	**revaloración** aumento en el valor de una divisa que se encuentra bajo un régimen de cambio de divisas fijo. (pág. 351)
reverse repurchase agreements (RRAs) the sales of securities by the Federal Reserve to a counterparty with an agreement to repurchase the securities at a later date. (p. 404)	**acuerdo de recompra inversa (ARI)** venta de valores por parte de la Reserva Federal a una contraparte con el acuerdo de recomprar los valores más tarde. (pág. 404)
rival in consumption a good is rival in consumption if the same unit of the good cannot be consumed by more than one person at the same time. (p. 772)	**rival en el consumo** bien rival en el consumo si la misma unidad del bien no puede ser consumida por más de una persona a la vez. (pág. 772)

S

scarce when a *resource* is not available in sufficient quantities to satisfy all the various ways a society wants to use it. (p. 4, 413)	**escaso** cuando no se dispone de un *recurso* en cantidades suficientes para satisfacer las diversas necesidades en que la sociedad desea aprovecharlo. (págs. 4, 413)
scatter diagram a diagram in which each point corresponds to an actual observation of the *x*-variable and the *y*-variable. (p. A-10)	**diagrama de dispersión** diagrama en el que cada punto corresponde a una observación directa de la variable *x* y de la variable *y*. (pág. A-10)
screening using observable information about people to make inferences about their *private information*; a way to reduce *adverse selection*. (p. 834)	**selección** uso de información observable sobre las personas con el fin de inferir sobre su *información reservada o privada*; manera de reducir las *selecciones adversas*. (pág. 834)
the short run the time period in which many production costs, including nominal wages, are not fully flexible; time period in which at least one input is fixed. (p. 145, 584)	**a corto plazo** período de tiempo en el que muchos costos de producción, incluidos los salarios nominales, no son completamente flexibles; período de tiempo en el que al menos un insumo es fijo. (págs. 145, 584)

shortage when the quantity demanded of a good or service exceeds the *quantity supplied*; occurs when the price is below its *equilibrium* level; also known as *excess demand.* (p. 49, 525)	**escasez** cuando la cantidad demandada de un bien o servicio es mayor que la *cantidad ofertada*; sucede cuando el precio está por debajo de su nivel de *equilibrio*; también denominado *demanda excesiva.* (págs. 49, 525)
short-run aggregate supply (*SRAS*) curve shows the positive relationship between the *aggregate price level* and the quantity of *aggregate output* supplied that exists in the *short run*, the time period when many production costs can be taken as fixed. (p. 138)	**curva de oferta agregada a corto plazo** permite apreciar la relación entre el *nivel de precios agregados* y la cantidad de *producción agregada* ofertada que existe *a corto plazo*, el período de tiempo en el que muchos de los costes de producción se pueden adoptar como costes fijos. (pág. 138)
short-run equilibrium aggregate output the quantity of *aggregate output* produced in the short-run macroeconomic equilibrium; identified on the horizontal axis of an *AD-AS* graph. (p. 150)	**producción agregada de equilibrio a corto plazo** cantidad de *producción agregada* producida en el equilibrio macroeconómico a corto plazo; identificado en el eje horizontal de una gráfica *OA-DA*. (pág. 150)
short-run equilibrium aggregate price level the *aggregate price level* in the short-run macroeconomic equilibrium; identified on the vertical axis of an *AD-AS* graph. (p. 150)	**nivel de precios agregados de equilibrio a corto plazo** *nivel de precios agregados* en el equilibrio macroeconómico a corto plazo; identificado en el eje vertical de una gráfica *OA-DA*. (pág. 150)
short-run firm supply curve shows how an individual firm's profit-maximizing level of output depends on the market price, taking the *fixed cost* as given. (p. 627)	**curva de oferta individual a corto plazo** permite apreciar cómo el nivel de producción para maximizar las utilidades de una empresa individual depende del precio de mercado, tomando el *coste fijo* como un hecho dado. (pág. 627)
short-run industry supply curve shows how the quantity supplied by an industry depends on the market price, given a fixed number of firms. (p. 635)	**curva de oferta de la industria a corto plazo** permite apreciar cómo la cantidad ofertada por una industria depende del precio de mercado, dado un número fijo de empresas. (pág. 635)
short-run macroeconomic equilibrium where the quantity of aggregate output supplied is equal to the quantity of aggregate output demanded – that is, where the *AD* and *SRAS* curves intersect (p. 150)	**equilibrio macroeconómico a corto plazo** cuando la cantidad de la producción agregada suministrada es igual a la cantidad de la producción agregada demandada; es decir, cuando se intersecan las curvas *DA* y *OACP*. (pág. 150)
short-run Phillips curve (*SRPC*) represents the negative short-run relationship between the *unemployment rate* and the *inflation rate.* (p. 271)	**curva de Phillips a corto plazo** representa la relación negativa a corto plazo entre la *tasa de desempleo* y la *tasa de inflación.* (pág. 271)
shut-down price the market price at which a firm ceases production in the *short run*; equal to minimum *average variable cost.* (p. 626)	**precio de cierre definitivo** precio del mercado al cual una empresa deja de producir *a corto plazo*; es equivalente al *coste variable promedio* mínimo. (pág. 626)
signaling revealing *private information* through actions that establish credibility; a way to reduce *adverse selection.* (p. 834)	**señalización** revelar *información reservada o privada* mediante acciones que establecen credibilidad; manera de reducir la *selección adversa.* (pág. 834)
single-price monopolist firm that charges all consumers the same price. (p. 674)	**monopolista de precio único** empresa que cobra a todos los consumidores el mismo precio. (pág. 674)
slope a measure of how steep a *curve* is; indicates how sensitive the *y*-variable is to a change in the *x*-variable. (p. A-4)	**pendiente** medida de la profundidad de una *curva*; indica la sensibilidad de la variable *y* y cómo reacciona a cambios en la variable *x*. (pág. A-4)
socially efficient the level of output that maximizes the net gains for society by equating the marginal social cost and the marginal social benefit. (p. 757)	***socialmente eficiente*** nivel de producción que maximiza las ganancias netas de la sociedad al equiparar el costo social marginal con el beneficio social marginal. (pág. 757)
socially optimal quantity the quantity that society would choose, taking all costs and benefits into account. (p. 757)	**cantidad socialmente óptima** cantidad que la sociedad escogería si se tuvieran en cuenta todos los costes y beneficios de la contaminación. (pág. 757)
specialization situation in which each person specializes in the task that they are good at performing; key source of the gains from trade. (p. 19, 432)	**especialización** coyuntura en la que cada persona se especializa en la tarea que realiza bien; fuente clave de las ganancias del comercio. (págs. 19, 432)
stagflation the combination of *inflation* and stagnating (or falling) *aggregate output*. (p. 157)	**estanflación** combinación de *inflación* y estancamiento (o caída) de la *producción agregada*. (pág. 157)
standardized product describes a good produced by different firms, but that consumers regard as the same good; also known as a *commodity*. (p. 634)	**producto normalizado** describe un bien cuando los consumidores consideran que los productos de diferentes empresas son el mismo bien; también denominado *insumo*. (pág. 634)
sticky wages *nominal wages* that are slow to fall even in the face of high *unemployment* and slow to rise even in the face of *labor* shortages. (p. 138)	**salarios rígidos** *salarios nominales* que descienden lentamente incluso a la luz de *desempleo* alto y que suben lentamente incluso a la luz de escasez de *mano de obra*. (pág. 138)

stock type of equity that represents ownership of a company. (p. 196)	**existencias** tipo de acciones que representan propiedad de una compañía. (pág. 196)
store of value a means of holding purchasing power over time. (p. 205)	**valor refugio** manera de retener el poder adquisitivo a través del tiempo. (pág. 205)
strategic behavior when a firm attempts to influence the future behavior of other firms. (p. 702)	**conducta estratégica** cuando una empresa trata de influir en la conducta futura de otras empresas. (pág. 702)
structural unemployment *unemployment* that results when workers lack the skills required for the available jobs, or there are more people seeking jobs in a *labor market* than there are jobs available at the current wage rate. (p. 81)	**desempleo estructural** *desempleo* que se genera cuando los trabajadores carecen de las destrezas necesarias para los empleos disponibles o cuando hay más personas buscando empleo en un *mercado laboral* que empleos disponibles a la tasa salarial vigente. (pág. 81)
subsidy a government payment made to assist or incentivize producers or consumers. (p. 548)	**subsidio** pago gubernamental que se hace para ayudar o incentivar a productores y consumidores. (pág. 548)
substitutes two goods for which a rise in the price of one of the goods leads to an increase in the demand for the other good. (p. 33, 471)	**sustitutos** dos bienes para los cuales el aumento del precio de un bien conduce al aumento en la demanda del otro bien. (págs. 33, 471)
substitutes in production describes two goods for which producers can use the same inputs to make either. (p. 41, 481)	**sustituos** de producción describe dos bienes que pueden ser producidos con los mismos insumos. (págs. 41, 481)
substitution bias bias that occurs in the *consumer price index* because, over time, items with prices that have risen more receive too much weight (because households substitute away from them), while items with prices that have risen least are given too little weight (because households shift their spending toward them). (p. 92)	**sesgo de sustitución** sesgo que sucede en el *índice de precios de consumo* porque, a través del tiempo, artículos con mayores subidas de precio reciben demasiado peso (porque los hogares los sustituyen por otros), mientras que artículos con subidas de precio menores reciben demasiado poco peso (porque los hogares empiezan a utilizar sus ingresos para comprarlos). (pág. 92)
substitution effect (of a change in the price of a good) the change in the quantity of a good demanded as the consumer substitutes the good that has become relatively cheaper for the good that has become relatively more expensive. (p. 486)	**efecto de sustitución** (de un cambio en el precio de un bien) cambio en la cantidad de un bien que se demanda cuando el consumidor reemplaza el bien que se ha vuelto relativamente más costoso con el bien que se ha tornado relativamente menos costoso. (pág. 486)
sunk cost a cost that has already been incurred and is nonrecoverable; should be ignored in a decision about future actions. (p. 444, 626)	**coste hundido** coste que ya se ha pagado y que no se puede recuperar; debe pasarse por alto cuando se toma una decisión acerca de acciones futuras. (págs. 444, 626)
supply and demand model a *model* of how a *competitive market* works. (p. 27, 466)	**modelo de oferta y demanda** *modelo* de cómo funciona un *mercado competitivo*. (págs. 27, 466)
supply curve shows the relationship between the *quantity supplied* and the price. (p. 37, 477)	**curva de oferta** permite apreciar la relación entre la *cantidad ofertada* y el precio. (págs. 37, 477)
supply price (of a given quantity) the price at which producers will supply that quantity. (p. 561)	**precio de la oferta** (de una cantidad dada) precio en el que los productores ofertarán esa cantidad. (pág. 561)
supply schedule shows how much of a good or service producers would supply at different prices. (p. 37, 477)	**tabla de oferta** permite apreciar cuánto de un bien o servicio ofertarían los productores a precios diferentes. (págs. 37, 477)
supply shock an event that shifts the *short-run aggregate supply curve*. (p. 157)	**choque de oferta** evento que hace desplazar la *curva de la oferta agregada a corto plazo*. (pág. 157)
supply-side fiscal policies government policies that seek to promote economic growth by affecting *short-run* and *long-run aggregate supply*. (p. 320)	**políticas fiscales del lado de la oferta** políticas gubernamentales que buscan promover el crecimiento económico al afectar la *oferta agregada de corto y largo plazo*. (pág. 320)
surplus when the *quantity supplied* of a good or service exceeds the *quantity demanded*; occurs when the price is above its *equilibrium* level; also known as *excess supply*. (p. 49, 525)	**superávit** cuando la *cantidad ofertada* de un bien o servicio es mayor que la *cantidad demandada*; sucede cuando el precio está por encima de su nivel de *equilibrio*; también denominado *oferta excesiva*. (págs. 49, 525)

T

tacit collusion when firms limit production and raise prices in a way that raises each other's profits, even though they have not made any formal agreement. (p. 703)	**colusión tácita** cuando las empresas limitan su producción y aumentan sus precios de manera que aumenten las utilidades de unos y otros, pese a que no cuentan con un convenio formal. (pág. 703)
tangency condition on a graph of a consumer's *budget line* and available *indifference curves* of available *consumption bundles*, the point at which an indifference curve and the budget line just touch; this condition determines the *optimal consumption bundle* when the *indifference curves* have the typical convex shape. (p. 846)	**condición tangencial** en un gráfico del *rubro del presupuesto* del consumidor y las *curvas de indiferencia* disponibles de los *conjuntos de consumo* disponibles, el punto en el cual hay contacto entre la curva de indiferencia y el rubro del presupuesto; esta coyuntura determina el *conjunto de consumo óptimo* cuando las *curvas de indiferencia* tienen la forma convexa característica. (pág. 846)

tariffs taxes on *imports*. (p. 352, 568)	**aranceles** impuestos que se cobran por las importaciones. (págs. 352, 568)
tax incidence the distribution of the tax burden. (p. 542)	**incidencia tributaria** distribución de la carga impositiva. (pág. 542)
tax multiplier equal to $-MPC/(1 - MPC)$; the factor by which a change in tax collections changes *real GDP*. (p. 135)	**multiplicador impositivo** es igual a $-PMC/(1 - PMC)$; factor mediante el cual un cambio en las recaudaciones tributarias cambia el *PIB real*. (pág. 135)
tax revenue the total amount of funds the government receives from *taxes*. (p. 65)	**ingresos fiscales** total de ingresos de los fondos que el gobierno recibe mediante *impuestos*. (pág. 65)
taxes required payments to the government. (p. 65)	**impuestos** pagos que se exige pagar al gobierno. (pág. 65)
technology the technical means for producing goods and services. (pp. 16, 305, 429)	**tecnología** los medios técnicos para producir bienes y servicios. (págs. 16, 305, 429)
terms of trade indicate the rate at which one good can be exchanged for another. (p. 23, 435)	**términos del comercio** indican el ritmo al cual un bien se puede intercambiar con otro. (págs. 23, 435)
time-series graph a graph with successive dates on the *horizontal (x-) axis* and the values of a variable that occurred on those dates on the *vertical (y-) axis*. (p. A-9)	**gráfico de una serie temporal** gráfico con fechas sucesivas en el *eje horizontal (x)* y los valores de una variable que ocurrió en esas fechas en el *eje vertical (y)*. (pág. A-9)
tit for tat a strategy that involves playing cooperatively at first, then doing whatever the other player did in the previous period. (p. 702)	**toma y daca** estrategia que implica jugar de manera cooperativa al principio y luego hacer lo que el otro jugador hizo en el período anterior. (pág. 702)
total cost (*TC*) the sum of the *fixed cost* and the *variable cost* of producing a given quantity of output. (p. 590)	**coste total** suma de los *costes fijos* y el *coste variable* de producir una cantidad dada de producción. (pág. 590)
total cost curve shows how *total cost* depends on the quantity of output. (p. 591)	**curva de costes totales** permite apreciar cómo el *coste total* depende de la cantidad de producción. (pág. 591)
total product curve shows how the quantity of output depends on the quantity of the variable input, for a given quantity of the *fixed input*. (p. 585)	**curva del producto total** permite apreciar cómo la cantidad de producción depende de la cantidad del insumo variable para una cantidad dada del *insumo fijo*. (pág. 585)
total revenue the total value of sales of a good or service; equal to the price multiplied by the quantity sold. (p. 492)	**ingresos totales** valor total de las ventas de un bien o servicio; es igual al precio multiplicado por la cantidad vendida. (pág. 492)
total surplus the total net gain to consumers and producers from trading in a market; the sum of *consumer surplus* and *producer surplus*. (p. 535)	**superávit total** ganancia neta total de los consumidores y productores producto de intercambios en el mercado; suma de los *superávits de consumidores* y los *superávits de productores*. (pág. 535)
trade when, in a *market economy*, individuals provide goods and services to others and receive goods and services in return. (p. 19, 432)	**intercambio** cuando, en una *economía de mercado*, las personas ofertan bienes y servicios a otros y reciben bienes y servicios a cambio. (págs. 19, 432)
trade balance the difference between a country's *exports* and *imports* of goods; also referred to as a country's *net exports*. (p. 332)	**balanza comercial** diferencia entre las *exportaciones* e *importaciones* de bienes de un país (pág. 332)
trade-off when you give up something in order to have something else. (p. 4, 412)	**compensación** cuando se sacrifica algo con el objetivo de obtener otra cosa. (págs. 4, 412)
traditional economy economic system in which production and consumption decisions are based on precedent. (p. 419)	***economía tradicional*** sistema económico en el que las decisiones relacionadas con la producción y el consumo tiene como fundamento un precedente. (pág. 419)
transaction costs the costs to individuals of making a deal. (p. 768)	**costes de transacción** gastos que implica negociar y ejecutar una transacción. (págs. 768)
trough (of a business cycle) the lowest point of a recession before the economy starts to expand. (p. 107)	**depresión** (de un ciclo comercial) el punto más bajo de una recesión antes de que la economía empiece a crecer. (pág. 107)

U

underemployed workers who would like to work more hours or who are overqualified for their jobs. (p. 78)	**subempleados** trabajadores que quisieran trabajar más horas o que están sobrecualificados para los empleos que tienen. (pág. 78)
unemployed people who are actively looking for work but aren't currently *employed*. (p. 77)	**desempleados** personas que están buscando trabajo activamente pero que actualmente no tienen *empleo*. (pág. 77)
unemployment rate the percentage of the total number of people in the *labor force* who are *unemployed*. (p. 77)	**tasa de desempleo** porcentaje del número total de personas en la *fuerza laboral* que están *desempleadas*. (pág. 77)

unions organizations of workers that try to raise wages and improve working conditions for their members by bargaining collectively. (p. 798)	**sindicatos** organizaciones de trabajadores que aspiran a subir los salarios y mejorar las condiciones de trabajo para sus afiliados mediante negociaciones colectivas. (pág. 798)
unit of account a measure used to set prices and make economic calculations. (p. 206)	**unidad de cuenta** medición que se usa para fijar precios y realizar cómputos económicos. (pág. 206)
unit-elastic demand when the *price elasticity of demand* is exactly 1. (p. 492)	**demanda elástica unitaria** cuando la *elasticidad precio de la demanda* es exactamente. (pág. 492)
util a unit of *utility*. (p. 441)	**útil** unidad de *utilidad*. (pág. 441)
utility a measure of personal satisfaction. (p. 441)	**utilidad** medición de satisfacción personal. (pág. 441)

V

value added (by a producer) the value of a producer's sales minus the value of its purchases of inputs. (p. 69)	**valor agregado** (de un productor) valor de las ventas de un productor menos el valor de sus compras de insumos. (pág. 69)
value-added approach an approach to calculating *GDP* by surveying firms and adding up their contributions to the value of *final goods and services*. (p. 68)	**enfoque de valor agregado** enfoque para computar el *PIB* mediante una encuesta a empresas y la suma de sus aportes al valor de los *bienes y servicios finales*. (pág. 68)
variable a measure that can take on more than one value. (p. A-1)	**variable** medición que puede adoptar más de un valor. (pág. A-1)
variable cost (*VC*) a cost that depends on the quantity of output produced; the cost of the *variable input*. (p. 590)	**coste variable** coste que depende de la cantidad de producción; coste del *insumo variable*. (pág. 590)
variable input an input whose quantity the firm can vary at any time. (p. 584)	**insumo variable** insumo cuya cantidad la empresa puede variar en cualquier momento. (pág. 584)
velocity of money the ratio of *nominal GDP* to the *money supply*; a measure of the number of times the average dollar bill is spent per year. (p. 284)	**velocidad del dinero** relación entre el *PIB nominal* y el *dinero en circulación*; medición del número de veces que el billete promedio de un dólar se utiliza para pagar durante un año. (pág. 284)
vertical axis see *y-axis* (p. A-2)	**eje vertical** véase *eje y* (pág. A-2)
vertical intercept indicates the value of the *y*-variable when the value of the *x*-variable is zero. (p. A-4)	**intersección vertical** indica el valor de la variable *y* cuando el valor de la variable *x* es cero. (pág. A-4)

W

wealth the value of a *household*'s accumulated savings. (p. 121, 192)	**riqueza** valor de los ahorros acumulados en un *hogar*. (págs. 121, 192)
willingness to pay the maximum price at which a consumer would buy a good. (p. 512)	**voluntad de pago** el precio máximo que un consumidor pagaría para comprar un bien. (pág. 512)

X

x-axis the solid horizontal line on a graph that intersects with the *y-axis* at the *origin*; also called the *horizontal axis*. (p. A-2)	**eje x** la línea horizontal en un gráfico que se cruza con el *eje y* en el *origen*; también denominado *eje horizontal*. (pág. A-2)

Y

y-axis the solid vertical line on a graph that intersects with the *x-axis* at the *origin*; also called the *vertical axis*. (p. A-2)	**eje y** la línea vertical en un gráfico que se cruza con el *eje x* en el *origen*; también denominado *eje vertical*. (pág. A-2)

Z

zero-bound (for a *central bank*) point when the short-term interest rate has already been lowered to zero; at this point, further economic stimulus, if needed, requires the *central bank* to use nontraditional policy tools; represents a limit to expansionary monetary policy. (p. 243, 401)	**límite de cero** (de un *banco central*) punto en el que la tasa de interés a corto plazo ya se ha disminuido a cero; en este punto, si se necesita otro estímulo económico, el *banco central* debe aplicar políticas no tradicionales; representa el límite de una política monetaria expansiva. (págs. 243, 401)

Index

Note: **Boldface** type indicates key terms.